The Gospel of the Christ

The Gospel of the Christ

A Biblical Response to the Crossless Gospel Regarding the Contents of Saving Faith

Thomas L. Stegall

Grace Gospel Press
Milwaukee, Wisconsin

The Gospel of the Christ: A Biblical Response to the Crossless Gospel Regarding the Contents of Saving Faith

ISBN 978-0-9799637-4-2 (hardcover)
Library of Congress Control Number: 2008910584

Cover design by Cynthia Hart

The Greek fonts used to publish this work are available from www.linguistsoftware.com, +1-425-775-1130.

Grace Gospel Press
10328 W. Oklahoma Ave.
Milwaukee, WI 53227
U.S.A.
www.gracegospelpress.com

Printed in the United States of America

To Debbie, my truest co-laborer for Christ
and an heir together with me of the grace of life,
without whose support and sacrifice this
book would not have been written

ACKNOWLEDGMENTS

I would like to express my sincere appreciation for the many people that the Lord used to contribute to this book in one way or another. The faithful example of two pastors immediately comes to mind, namely my former pastor and now dear friend, Dennis Rokser, as well as his former pastor and mentor, the late Leonard Radtke. The heritage passed on to me by these faithful men of God has profoundly impacted not only my own ministry as a pastor but especially my personal convictions about the foundational importance of the gospel and God's grace for both eternal salvation and the Christian life. The Lord has used these servant-leaders to teach me to *"be strong in the grace that is in Christ Jesus"* (2 Tim. 2:1-2). I would also like to express my gratitude to others, such as Rick Gerhartz, Randy Zempel, and Dr. Robert Lightner who each read portions of the manuscript at various stages and offered valuable input and encouragement. Darrell Patterson created some of the graphics for the book and offered assistance early on in resolving many word processing problems. Katie Morrison joyfully served as a virtual, personal librarian by supplying me with a continuous stream of books and articles. Greg Cooper offered to design the website to advertise the book for the new Grace Gospel Press. Christian artist Laura Ibbotson graciously contributed an original painting for the cover of the condensed, reader-friendly version of this book that is forthcoming. Greg Schliesmann fulfilled the monumental task of typesetting the entire book and assisting in the compilation of the indexes. I am also appreciative to the entire congregation of saints at the Word of Grace Bible Church, along with other like-minded churches, for their faithful prayers and support. I am grateful to the Lord that so many members of His body have been willing to stand fast with me *"in one spirit, with one mind striving together for the faith of the gospel"* (Phil. 1:27).

But God forbid that I should glory, save in the cross of our Lord Jesus Christ, by whom the world is crucified unto me, and I unto the world.

Galatians 6:14 (KJV)

Down through the ages of history, Christianity has been subjected to a multitude of influences. There have been creative ideas, new programs, fascinating personalities, fresh approaches to theology, evangelism, missionary activity, and a myriad of other diverse developments in the ongoing mission of the church. It is probably undeniable that, with true spiritual discernment, these developments should be viewed with guarded favor, and given the opportunity to have their part in the cause of Christ.

However, that special and changeless message called "the gospel of the grace of God" must never be subject to creative ideas or diverse developments. The hope of eternal life, the central message of divine revelation, is based upon the finished work of Christ on Calvary's cross and the offer of divine mercy which issues therefrom. The death of the Son of the living God in space and time and the meaning of that sacrifice is what constitutes this glorious message called the gospel.

Should that message ever be changed, then the door to life is instantly closed and Christianity becomes a mere humanistic religion, fascinating perhaps, but valueless. The most valuable and sacred commodity, therefore, on the face of the earth is the truth of the gospel. This is a sacred message worth living for, worth sacrificing for, and worth gladly dying for. It is the only real value on earth today; it is the truth of all truths to which the church must be dedicated to propagate and protect.[1]

– Lance Latham

---

[1] Lance B. Latham, *The Two Gospels* (Streamwood, IL: Awana Clubs International, 1984), xv-xvi.

CONTENTS

PART III

CLARIFYING THE CHRIST OF SAVING FAITH

CONCLUSION

ABBREVIATIONS

AB	Anchor Bible
BAGD	Bauer, Walter. *A Greek-English Lexicon of the New Testament and Other Early Christian Literature.* Revised and augmented by F. Wilbur Gingrich and Frederick W. Danker. 2nd ed. Chicago: University of Chicago Press, 1979
BBR	*Bulletin for Biblical Research*
BDAG	Bauer, Walter. *A Greek-English Lexicon of the New Testament and Other Early Christian Literature.* Revised and edited by Frederick Danker. 3rd ed. Chicago: University of Chicago Press, 2000
BDB	Brown, F., S. Driver, and C. Briggs. *The Brown-Driver-Briggs Hebrew and English Lexicon.* Peabody, MA: Hendrickson Publishers, 1996
BDF	Blass, Friedrich, and Albert Debrunner. *A Greek Grammar of the New Testament and Other Early Christian Literature. Translated by Robert W. Funk.* Chicago: University of Chicago Press, 1961
BECNT	Baker Exegetical Commentary on the New Testament
BETL	*Bibliotheca Ephemeridum Theologicarum Lovaniensium*
BHS	Biblia Hebraica Stuttgartensia
Bib	*Biblica*
BJRL	*Bulletin of the John Rylands Library*
BKC	Bible Knowledge Commentary
BNTC	Black's New Testament Commentary
BR	*Bible Review*
BSac	*Bibliotheca Sacra*
CBQ	*Catholic Biblical Quarterly*
CGTC	Cambridge Greek Testament Commentary
CT	Critical Text
CTJ	*Conservative Theological Journal*
CTM	*Concordia Theological Monthly*
CTQ	*Concordia Theological Quarterly*
CTR	*Criswell Theological Review*
CTSJ	*Chafer Theological Seminary Journal*
DBSJ	*Detroit Baptist Seminary Journal*
EBC	Everyman's Bible Commentary
EDNT	*Exegetical Dictionary of the New Testament.* Edited by Horst Balz and Gerhard Schneider. 3 vols. Grand Rapids: Eerdmans, 1990-93
ETR	*Evangelical Theological Review*
EvQ	*Evangelical Quarterly*
ExpT	*Expository Times*

FN	*Filologia Neotestamentaria*
GFJ	*Grace Family Journal*
GNTMT	*Greek New Testament according to the Majority Text.* Edited by Zane C. Hodges and Arthur L. Farstad. Nashville: Thomas Nelson, 1982
GTJ	*Grace Theological Journal*
ICC	International Critical Commentary
IDB	*Interpreter's Dictionary of the Bible.* Edited by George A. Buttrick. 4 vols. Nashville: Abingdon Press, 1962
Int	*Interpretation*
ISBE	*International Standard Bible Encyclopedia.* Revised Edition. Edited by Geoffrey W. Bromiley. 4 vols. Grand Rapids: Eerdmans, 1980-88
ITQ	*Irish Theological Quarterly*
JBL	*Journal of Biblical Literature*
JETS	*Journal of the Evangelical Theological Society*
JOTGES	*Journal of the Grace Evangelical Society*
JSNT	*Journal for the Study of the New Testament*
JTS	*Journal of Theological Studies*
KJV	King James Version
L&N	Louw, Johannes P., and Eugene A. Nida. *Greek-English Lexicon of the New Testament: Based on Semantic Domains.* 2 vols. New York: United Bible Societies, 1988
LSJ	Liddell, Henry George, and Robert Scott, comps. *A Greek-English Lexicon.* Revised and augmented by Henry Stuart Jones and Roderick McKenzie. 9th ed. With a Revised Supplement 1996. Edited by P. G. W. Glare and A. A. Thompson. Oxford: Clarendon Press, 1940
LXX	*Septuaginta.* Edited by Alfred Rahlfs. Stuttgart: Deutsche Bibelgesellschaft, 1979
MGC	Moody Gospel Commentary
MSJ	*Master's Seminary Journal*
MT	Majority Text
NA[27]	*Novum Testamentum Graece.* Edited by Barbara and Kurt Aland, Johannes Karavidopoulos, Carlo M. Martini, and Bruce M. Metzger, 27th Revised Edition. Stuttgart: Deutsche Bibelgesellschaft, 1993
NASB	New American Standard Bible
Neot	*Neotestamentica*
NIBC	New International Biblical Commentary
NICNT	New International Commentary on the New Testament
NICOT	New International Commentary on the Old Testament
NIDNTT	*New International Dictionary of New Testament Theology.* Edited by Colin Brown. 4 vols. Grand Rapids: Zondervan Publishing House, 1975-78
NIDOTT	*New International Dictionary of Old Testament Theology and*

	Exegesis. Edited by Willem A. VanGemeren. 5 vols. Grand Rapids: Zondervan Publishing House, 1997
NIGTC	New International Greek Testament Commentary
NIV	New International Version
NKJV	New King James Version
NovT	*Novum Testamentum*
NT	New Testament
NTBT	*The New Testament in the Original Greek: Byzantine Textform*. Compiled and Arranged by Maurice A. Robinson & William G. Pierpont. Southborough, MA: Chilton Publishing, 2005
NTS	*New Testament Studies*
OT	Old Testament
PNTC	Pillar New Testament Commentary
RevExp	*Review & Expositor*
RTR	*Reformed Theological Review*
Sem	*Semeia*
SJT	*Scottish Journal of Theology*
ST	*Studia Theologica*
TB	*Tyndale Bulletin*
TDNT	*Theological Dictionary of the New Testament*. Edited by Gerhard Kittel and Gerhard Friedrich. Translated by Geoffrey W. Bromiley. Index compiled by Ronald E. Pitkin. 10 vols. Grand Rapids: Zondervan Publishing House, 1964-76
Them	*Themelios*
TLG	Thesaurus Linguae Graecae
TNTC	Tyndale New Testament Commentary
TR	Textus Receptus
TrinJ	*Trinity Journal*
TWOT	*Theological Wordbook of the Old Testament*. Edited by R. Laird Harris, Gleason L. Archer, Jr., and Bruce K. Waltke. 2 vols. Chicago: Moody Press, 1980
UBS^4	*The Greek New Testament*. Edited by Barbara Aland, Kurt Aland, Johannes Karvidopoulos, Carlo M. Martini, and Bruce M. Metzger. 4th rev. ed. Stuttgart: United Bible Societies, 1993
VC	*Vigiliae Christianae*
VE	*Vox Evangelica*
VT	*Vetus Testamentum*
WBC	Word Biblical Commentary
WTJ	*Westminster Theological Journal*
ZNW	*Zeitschrift für die neutestamentliche Wissenschaft*

FOREWORD

When I was 18 years old, I understood for the first time (through the witness of some friends) God's wonderful plan of salvation by grace. Though I was raised in a religious, God-fearing home, I was under the satanic deception (through my religion) that eternal salvation was a reward for good people and good works, instead of being a free gift for sinners paid for completely through the sacrifice of Christ and offered to me by God's love (Rom. 5:8; Eph. 2:8-9). While I believed the Bible to be the Word of God, I really had no clue what was written in it as I followed the traditions of men instead of the truth of God (Matt. 15:6-8). And though I believed several important facts about Jesus Christ and knew the stories of Christmas and Easter, my faith was in Christ PLUS, not in Christ alone PERIOD (John 3:16).

What made the difference in my thinking and opened my eyes to the truth of the Gospel of grace? It was the words of the Lord Jesus Christ upon the cross when He triumphantly declared, IT IS FINISHED! (John 19:30). For though I had believed that Christ's death was NECESSARY to go to Heaven, I finally understood that Christ's finished work was ENOUGH to be saved forever. He alone had died for all my sins past, present, and future and rose from the dead to give me eternal life freely and forever. My sins had been PAID IN FULL by Jesus Christ at Calvary and there was nothing left for me to do but to simply put my faith alone in the crucified and risen Savior, the Lord Jesus Christ (Acts 16:31). Then I finally possessed a KNOW-SO salvation instead of a HOPE-SO one (1 John 5:9-13). Finally I had a personal relationship with God by His grace through divine accomplishment instead of a religious system of meritorious performance through human achievement (Rom. 4:4-5). Now I could understand and fully agree with the words of the apostle Paul when he wrote, *"For the message of the cross is foolishness to those who are perishing, but to us who are being saved it is the power of God. . . . For since, in the wisdom of God, the world through wisdom did not know God, it pleased God through the foolishness of the message preached to save those who believe"* (1 Cor. 1:18, 21). It was an understanding of the work of the cross of Christ, not the elimination or downplaying of this that made the difference for me, like so many others.

Since the early days of my Christian life, I read in the Scriptures and heard preached from the pulpit both the crucial necessity of proclaiming accurately the message of the Gospel (Rom. 1:16) but also the critical importance of guarding its purity (1 Tim. 6:20-21) and contending for its contents (Jude 3). The words of Galatians 1:8-9 were burned like a hot iron into my conscience, *"But even if we, or an angel from heaven, preach any other gospel to you than what we have preached to you, let him be accursed. As we have said before, so now I say again, if anyone preaches any other gospel to you than what you have received, let him be accursed."* The Gospel must never be garbled or gutted but fearlessly guarded. Thus, even in a prison cell for preaching the Gospel, Paul penned that he was *"set for the defense of the Gospel"* (Phil. 1:17). What a contrast and source of conviction in our postmodern times that rejects moral absolute truth, and where even the evangelical church compromises the truth of the Gospel as it pragmatically practices the ends-justifies-the-means for the sake of attracting bodies into a building under the guise of church growth. May God be merciful to us.

Thus, the Gospel of grace is sacred ground. It is non-negotiable truth. It is the bottom-line that distinguishes Christianity from all the religions of the world. Remove the Gospel of grace from Christianity, and it becomes merely a system of meritorious salvation and ethical behavior without the power of God. So should it surprise us that Satan's attacks against the Gospel are endless like the waves of the sea beating upon the shore? Yet, what is so unfortunate about the necessity of this book is that the recent attack upon the Gospel is not from foes of the Free Grace movement but from its friends—those who have stood shoulder to shoulder in withstanding the false gospel of Lordship Salvation.

Dear reader, it is helpful to remember that controversy is not new to the Church. It's like what one old sage wrote, "The church is a lot like Noah's ark. If it wasn't for the judgment on the outside, you could never stand the smell on the inside." And though Satan seeks to use controversy to divide and conquer, God seeks to use it to refine our understanding of the Scriptures and to purify His Church. Thus, while I do not relish the controversy of the crossless gospel, it was foisted upon us and requires a biblical response and defense of the Gospel. Tom has done this admirably in this book by God's grace through *"speaking the truth in love."*

Therefore, I am grateful for this scripturally-sound, exegetically-based volume by my dear friend, Thomas Stegall. While this book is not light weight for the casual late-night reader, it is loaded with scriptural insights that emerge from the biblical text by recognizing its context, observing its content, and then comparing Scripture with Scripture in order to arrive at a biblical and balanced conclusion. In doing so, Tom has not been afraid to tackle a number of difficult passages and unscriptural defenses in targeting the faulty conclusions of the crossless adherents, while surfacing the correct interpretation of the Scriptures.

Frankly, I know of nothing in writing from the Free Grace perspective that interacts and intersects biblically like this book does regarding all of the following issues in one volume, such as . . .

- the false teaching of the crossless gospel
- the nature and content of saving faith
- the comparison of the evangelistic message of John as it relates to the Synoptic Gospels, Acts, and the Epistles

- the name of Jesus Christ referring to His person and work
- the reality of progressive revelation as it relates to the Gospel
- the distinction between the various forms of good news
- the problem passages in the Book of Acts
- the necessity of repentance for salvation
- the supposed wrath of God upon disobedient believers in Christ
- the issue of judicial forgiveness versus fellowship forgiveness
- the distinguishing of eternal and temporal salvation
- the relationship of various doctrines like the Virgin Birth to our redemption and the contents of the Gospel

May God be pleased to use His Word as set forth in this book to expound the truth of the Gospel and expose the error of the crossless gospel so *"that the truth of the gospel might continue with you"* (Gal. 2:5).

Dennis M. Rokser
December 26, 2008

PREFACE

The book you are reading concerns a question of the greatest eternal consequence: "What does God require a person to believe in order to receive eternal life?" While many books in the already flooded field of Christian literature deal with theology, and many even with the doctrine of salvation known as soteriology, this book focuses primarily on the question of the contents of saving faith. What must a person believe about Jesus Christ in order to go to heaven?

The answer to that question is so simple that even a child can know the truth about Christ, believe in Him, and be saved.[1] It is so simple that it can be answered in a single sentence. So I will offer my answer to that question, and the thesis of this book, right up front. A person must simply believe the gospel of Christ, which is the message that, as *"the Christ, the Son of God,"* Jesus is both God and man, and the One who died for all our sins and rose from the dead in order to provide salvation by grace through faith in Him (John 3:13-18; 5:24; 6:32-53; 8:24, 28; 20:30-31; Acts 16:30-31; 1 Cor. 1:17-21; 15:1-4; Eph. 2:8-9; 2 Thess. 1:6-10). While there are various ways to express the same truth, that's it, plain and simple. When people believe this, they receive eternal life.

But obviously this book is not written for children. Nor do children, or even adults, need to understand all the exegetical and theological complexities covered herein to be saved. The depth and scope of this book is necessary due to the doctrinal controversy in our day created by some well-meaning evangelical theologians who believe that the single-sentence answer provided above is unbiblical. They believe it is too complex, that the contents of saving faith must be simpler yet. They would deconstruct each portion of my answer, whittling it down phrase by phrase, word by word, denying that the lost even need to believe the gospel, or acknowledge that man is a sinner, or that Jesus Christ is God the Son, or that He died for man's sins and rose from the dead. In support of such an alarming conclusion, they have created whole new paradigms through which they are interpreting the Scriptures and in the process causing confusion and spiritual stumbling within the Body of Christ, especially in Free Grace circles.

It is my sincere prayer and heart's desire that God will use this book to not merely answer the errors of the crossless gospel, but more importantly, to provide a positive, constructive articulation of biblical truth

[1] Thomas L. Constable, "The Gospel Message," in *Walvoord: A Tribute*, ed. Donald K. Campbell (Chicago: Moody Press, 1982), 204; J. B. Hixson, *Getting the Gospel Wrong: The Evangelical Crisis No One Is Talking About* (n.p.: Xulon Press, 2008), 122; J. Gresham Machen, *Christianity and Liberalism* (Grand Rapids: Eerdmans, 1923), 118.

regarding the contents of saving faith. If this has been achieved by God's grace, then may He be pleased to use this book to bring clarity, resolution, and healing to the Body of Christ in the wake of the "crossless gospel." I have also chosen to keep the phrase "crossless gospel" in the subtitle and employ it consistently throughout this book, despite the misgivings of some Free Grace people. If you find this expression particularly objectionable, please be sure to read chapter 5 where I provide the rationale for why this phrase is fitting, though admittedly unpleasant.

Threefold Basis for the Contents of Saving Faith

As a reader, it will also be helpful for you to understand at the outset what the thesis of this book is based upon. The contents of saving faith articulated in this book have not been chosen arbitrarily. In the last few years, as I prayerfully and carefully studied each passage containing the various forms of the word "gospel," as well as studying the Johannine writings and many other individual, soteriologically significant passages, the consistency and coherence of God's Word became evident and overwhelming. The Lord has not been vague about what He requires us to believe in order to be born again. Nor has He hidden it from us. This is not a matter of the secret things belonging only to the Lord in contrast to the truths He has revealed (Deut. 29:29). He has provided abundant revelatory testimony to mankind in order to answer the question of what we must believe. He has provided a cord of at least three strands in testifying to the contents of saving faith.

First, the gospel itself is found to be equivalent with the contents of saving faith. While that may seem obvious to most evangelical Christians, it has enormous implications for the current crossless controversy. In terms of actual content, the gospel is not the broad, nebulous concept that crossless proponents have recently purported it to be. Rather, the gospel is specifically about the person and work of God's Son, as well as the provision of salvation and the sole condition of faith in Him. Though the term "gospel" most often stands alone in the New Testament without any other qualifying words or phrases, when it is modified, the most frequent modifier attached to it is the phrase "of Christ," as in "the gospel of Christ." However, the underlying Greek text is even more specific. It employs the article before "Christ" so that the phrase in Greek is literally, "the gospel of *the* Christ" (Rom. 1:16; 15:19, 29; 1 Cor. 9:12, 18; 2 Cor. 9:13; 10:14; Gal. 1:7; Phil. 1:27; 1 Thess. 3:2). This means that the gospel that lost sinners must believe for their deliverance from eternal condemnation is a particular message about a particular person. It is the particular message about Jesus being "the Christ." But this naturally raises the question, "What does it mean to be the Christ?"

Secondly, God has revealed the content of saving faith in Scripture through the meaning He has invested in the key titles, *"the Christ," "the Son of God,"* and *"the Son of Man."* It becomes clear that, in the evangelistic contexts of the Synoptic Gospels and the Book of Acts, these titles and terms convey the Lord's substitutionary death and bodily resurrection in addition to His deity and humanity. This is especially evident in the writings of the apostle John.[2] Thus, to believe in Jesus as *"the Christ, the Son of God"* (John 20:31) is equivalent to believing *"the gospel of the Christ."*

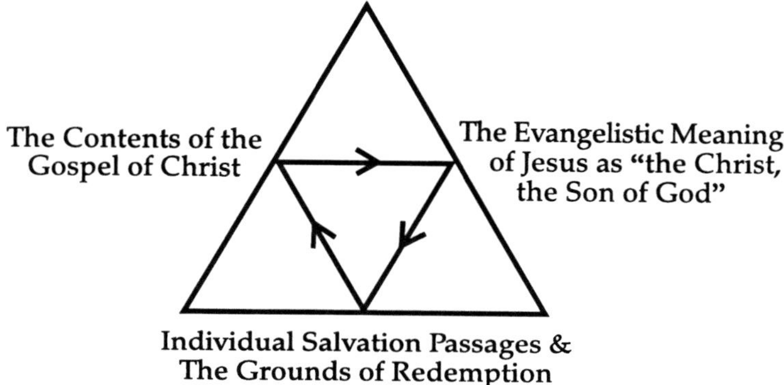
The Contents of the Gospel of Christ
The Evangelistic Meaning of Jesus as "the Christ, the Son of God"
Individual Salvation Passages & The Grounds of Redemption

Thirdly, the Word of God testifies that not every doctrine about Christ is part of the gospel or essential to believe for everlasting life. In the various individual passages of Scripture that require belief in some aspect of Christ's person or work, it is conspicuous that the doctrines about Christ that are essential to know and believe for eternal life happen to coincide with the very grounds of mankind's redemption. This again testifies to the Lord's deity, humanity, substitutionary death, and bodily resurrection, i.e., to His person, work, and provision.

All three of these lines of evidence function as virtual mirror reflections of one another in an amazing triangular testimony to the contents of saving faith. In some passages, the Lord requires the lost to believe the gospel in order to receive eternal salvation. In other passages, He conditions eternal life upon believing that Jesus is the Christ, the Son of God and Son of Man. These "gospel" versus "Christ"/"Son" passages do not represent two separate, disparate contents of saving faith; rather, they are alternate expressions for the same required content. The congruence of this testimony to the contents of saving faith cannot be a coincidence but is evidence of the divine design intended by the Spirit of God when He supernaturally inspired His Word. This means that the requirement to believe in Jesus' deity, humanity, substitutionary death, and bodily resurrection is not the result of imposing our own arbitrary, manmade evangelical orthodoxy upon the Scriptures. It is quite the opposite. God has placed this pattern in Scripture and it has been there all along for us to behold and believe. For this reason, the historic evangelical position

[2] If God graciously wills and permits, it is my intent to finish a separate volume already underway devoted entirely to the contents of saving faith from a Johannine perspective.

that belief in Christ's person and work is a divine requirement for salvation is affirmed by the resounding, diverse, and yet consistent testimony of God's Word rather than by human tradition or personal opinion.

Audience, Approach, and Assumptions

Though the content of saving faith is so simple that even a child can possess a rudimentary grasp of Christ's person and work and be saved, it is still a vast and sweeping subject in the Word of God. At times, this book will "zoom-in" to minutely exegete individual verses, while routinely "zooming-out" to recapture the bigger picture that these passages are painting. The use of technical language at points has been unavoidable in seeking to accurately interpret Scripture and to convey its truths with precision. At times, the riches of God's Word are lying right on the surface, waiting to be gathered up and put in our basket. At other times, they are found only through deep mining. In this respect, I have written for a target audience that will encompass not only fellow pastors and teachers, as well as highly trained theologians, but also any believer who is serious about studying God's Word with the heart and diligence of a Berean (Acts 17:11). With this diverse audience in mind, I have given the transliteration of Hebrew and Greek words as often as possible, except when providing an exact quotation from another source.

As a reader, you should also know up front what theological presuppositions I bring to this book on the contents of saving faith. I have written from a firm belief in the verbal, plenary inspiration and inerrancy of Scripture. In addition, I affirm without apology a normative premillennial, dispensational position. I am convinced that only a dispensational approach to Scripture yields a harmonious, non-contradictory doctrine of progressive revelation regarding the contents of saving faith. In addition, only a dispensational approach to Scripture allows the interpreter to properly distinguish the different forms of "good news" or gospels that exist in Scripture. If Augustine allegedly said, "Distinguish the ages and the Scriptures harmonize,"[3] we may also add, "Distinguish the ages and the *gospels* harmonize."

Though I have sought to accurately interpret God's Word to the best of my ability, and I am confident that my overall conclusions are correct, I am also conscious of my own fallibility. I am certain that others will find needed corrections and improvements to what I have written, and that is good. I know nothing yet as I ought to know it (1 Cor. 8:2; Gal. 6:3). But I trust that what I have written will generate Spirit-led discussion among God's people and a sincere searching of His Word with the intent to *"buy the truth and sell it not"* (Prov. 23:23).

---

[3] Lewis Sperry Chafer, *Dispensationalism*, Revised Edition (Dallas: Dallas Seminary Press, 1951), 11; *The Scofield Study Bible, King James Version*, ed. C. I. Scofield (Oxford: Oxford University Press, 1917), iii.

Motives in Writing

It is also fair that you know up front what my motives are in writing. I wish to say first of all that I have no animosity or hard feelings towards those leaders and teachers within the Free Grace movement who hold to a crossless gospel and who are referenced profusely throughout this book. Though I stand *against* their doctrine, I stand *for* them spiritually as fellow brothers in Christ, and I desire and pray for their repentance. In fact, I genuinely appreciate many of their valuable contributions made in Free Grace theology in the past, aside from their more recent doctrinal departures that are documented here.

But as a member of the Grace Evangelical Society for over 15 years, I became increasingly uneasy with both the number and magnitude of the doctrinal deviations taking place. Yet I remained largely a spectator, uninvolved until a few years ago. It was then that I began noticing how the problem of the crossless gospel and its doctrines was seeping down to the local church level and affecting many individual believers and even entire congregations around the country. More and more, I began to hear of grace-oriented brethren divided and confused over these new doctrines.

Along the way, I tried corresponding with certain Free Grace leaders who were teaching the new, crossless gospel. When it became clear that there was no repentance but instead a resolute determination to persist in their error, I formally resigned as a member of the Grace Evangelical Society. However, as one who still considers himself thoroughly "Free Grace" in doctrine and practice, I remain deeply concerned about the current doctrinal drift away from Scripture and about its damaging effects.

You should also know that I view this as a doctrinal matter, not a personal one; and for that reason, in this book I will not concern myself with the characters, personalities, or motives of the people quoted or cited. Those are internal matters of the heart, and I will leave them completely to the Lord who alone is able to fairly judge us all. Instead, I will examine only the *doctrine* of certain Free Grace men as it has been taught publicly in newsletters, journals, books, at conferences, and on websites. My intent is not to discredit these men personally, or their reputation or ministry, but only to compare their public teachings with the Scriptures and where needed to inform and warn Christian audiences of certain doctrinal errors.

This is especially true with respect to Zane C. Hodges (1932-2008) who unexpectedly went home to be with the Lord while this book was nearing completion. The fact that he is so frequently quoted or cited throughout the book is simply because he was the leading proponent of the views being assessed. I do not wish for one moment to deny or denigrate the lasting and profoundly positive impact he made upon the lives of so many Free Grace people over the years. For that I am truly grateful. But it would be willful negligence on my part to ignore his later doctrinal departures from the truth documented in this book simply out of respect for his memory. He was the most articulate and passionate promoter of today's crossless-content-of-saving-faith view, even to the very end of his life.[41] His grave errors regarding the gospel and various doctrines associated with it will continue to adversely affect scores of people for years to come; and so these departures from the truth must still be addressed and answered from Scripture.

Love and the Truth

With that said, some may still question my motives and approach. Some may consider it unloving or ungracious to openly critique the teachings of fellow believers in Christ, especially when they happen to be other brethren who have been part of the Free Grace movement. However, this would be a distorted and unbiblical view of both love and grace. According to 1 Corinthians 13:6, love *"rejoices in the truth."* There is no dichotomy between love and truth. True love would not want another brother or sister to be in error, especially on the gospel. Though I agree that the truth can be proclaimed without love (Phil. 1:15-18), in which case God must judge our hearts (1 Cor. 4:4-5), it is nevertheless true that speaking up and telling the truth is not inherently unloving. That is why we are to *"speak the truth in love"* (Eph. 4:15). And I trust that is what I have done in my writing.

While it is true that *unwarranted* correction is certainly contrary to grace, it is not inherently ungracious to correct another believer publicly if they have departed from the truth of the gospel and are leading others astray. In fact, we have a biblical obligation to do so. Is this not what Free Grace leaders have done with respect to the public teachings of those on the Lordship Salvation side? Has this been ungracious or unloving on our part? I would argue that it was necessary—and an act of love and grace. So it must be today with the members of our own household. If we will not confront error within our own ranks, then we have no right to expect the Lordship Salvation side of evangelicalism to listen to us. It is my earnest prayer that the Free Grace community will begin to take the error in our midst very seriously by biblically and lovingly correcting it.

Antioch Revisited

The example of Paul with Peter in Galatians 2:11-14 is very instructive at this point. Several spiritual lessons from this passage have application to the current situation. According to this passage, Peter was not being straightforward about the truth of the gospel (v. 14). He wasn't promoting

[4] Zane C. Hodges, "The Hydra's Other Head: Theological Legalism," *Grace in Focus* 23 (September/October 2008): 2-3.

another gospel through verbal or written teaching, as certain men in the Grace Evangelical Society are doing today. Rather, by his actions, he was speaking volumes against the truth of the gospel. By withdrawing from the Gentiles and keeping company only with the Jewish believers in the church at Antioch, he was denying the truth that we are all sinners who are equally justified by God in exactly the same way—through faith in Christ apart from works of law, whether we be Jews or Gentiles (Gal. 2:15-17). So Peter was publicly reproved, not only in Antioch, but before the entire Church to read on the pages of Scripture! How do you think that made Peter feel when he later read Paul's letter to the Galatians? There are some things in life far more important than hurt feelings—such as God's truth.

Notice what Galatians 2:14 also records: *"I said to Peter before them all."* This was *public* reproof. Peter was publicly reproved because he was a public leader among Christians whose actions led other Christians away from the gospel (v. 13). Public error demands public accountability. Should we hold today's Free Grace leaders to a lesser standard, especially when they have repeatedly, publicly published, preached, and promoted their erroneous views, while Peter was corrected merely for *conduct* unbecoming of the gospel?

Another important question we each need to ask ourselves is this: "Was Paul unloving or ungracious by reproving Peter in this way?" I wonder how many of us in the Free Grace community, if we had been in Antioch to observe this scene firsthand without the advantage of reading Galatians 2:11-14 beforehand—I wonder how many of us would have perceived Paul's actions to be unloving and ungracious. Yet who was actually being ungracious? Peter and the legalizers!

I can already hear another objection from a few fellow believers within the Free Grace community. Some will say, "But these Free Grace men who've departed from the gospel happen to be my personal friends and associates in ministry." I understand that. It is never pleasant to have to confront those closest to us, but this is the true test of loyalty to the Lord that reveals who we are really serving and seeking to please (Gal. 1:10). Does not Proverbs 27:5-6 say, *"Open rebuke is better than love carefully concealed. Faithful are the wounds of a friend, but the kisses of an enemy are deceitful"*?

Some may also object that these Free Grace teachers have done so much good for the cause of Christ that they should not be publicly critiqued because they are now worthy of our highest esteem. In fact, we could even call some of them "pillars." But wasn't Peter also reputed to be a pillar (Gal. 2:9)? And that is precisely why Paul wrote in Galatians 2:6, *"whatever they were, it makes no difference to me; God shows personal favoritism to no man."* We dare not think that we ourselves, or any other leaders within the Free Grace camp, are indefectible or beyond correction. Even Paul gave favorable commendation to those who were willing to eagerly hear and carefully examine his teaching under the searchlight of God's Word (Acts 17:11).

Unity and the Truth

Still others may object, "But if we openly correct our Free Grace leaders then we'll cause division when we ought to be maintaining unity." There is no question that the Lord wants unity among Christians (Eph. 4:3)—but not unity at the expense of truth! There is one thing the Lord hates worse than disunity; it is unity in error—a false unity. God puts a premium upon truth, saying through the apostle John, *"I have no greater joy than to hear that my children walk in truth"* (3 John 4).

Regarding unity among us in the Free Grace movement, do you realize that we actually had unity—until certain men changed the gospel and a number of other doctrines associated with it? They have actually created multiple divisions where these did not previously exist. This fact is in keeping with the principle of Romans 16:17, which says, *"Now I beseech you, brethren, mark those who cause divisions and offences contrary to the doctrine which you learned, and avoid them."* Contrary to popular ecumenical opinion, it is not those who wish to guard the truth and are even willing to separate over it if necessary *"who cause divisions."* Rather, it is those who teach *"contrary to the doctrines which you learned"* who cause the divisions and offences.

While some today may worry that by openly critiquing or even separating from others in the Free Grace movement we will cause division, the fact remains that there *already is* a very tragic division among us. Consider the example of Peter and Paul again. When Paul publicly corrected Peter, he was neither causing nor risking a division within the Church. A division already existed. The Scriptures say that before Paul reproved Peter, Peter *"withdrew and separated himself"* from the Gentiles along with *"the rest of the Jews also"* and *"even Barnabas"* (Gal. 2:12-13). Paul did not risk causing a division. He actually risked re-unification (if Peter would repent) or greater disunity (if Peter would not repent). Nevertheless, it was a risk Paul was willing to take in love.

Fortunately, by God's grace, Peter received the correction with humility as indicated by his responsiveness later to Paul (2 Peter 3:15). In fact, it is my understanding based upon a study of the chronology of Paul's life that the events recorded in Galatians 2:11-14, along with the writing of Galatians, occurred *before* the Jerusalem council. This council convened in A.D. 49 to resolve the doctrine of justification by faith alone (Acts 15). Why is this relevant? If Peter had not responded to Paul's correction in Antioch, we could be reading an entirely different account of things in Acts 15 and the rest of the New Testament. By Peter's apparent willingness to accept Paul's correction, a potentially enormous Church-split was avoided and Peter and Paul were able to present a unified voice at the Jerusalem council in Acts 15.

So why am I writing? Because I sincerely desire the Free Grace movement to avert such a tragedy and become united in the truth of the gospel once again. But the time to speak up is now, before it's too late, if it isn't already. And so I pray that God in His grace will use the following chapters to stir the hearts of believers to this very end. If what I've written helps in clearing up the confusion caused by the crossless gospel, and if it motivates other grace-oriented believers to faithfully stand up for the truth, and if it helps to restore the Lord Jesus Christ to His proper exalted place in our evangelism and ministry—then I will consider my prayers to have been answered.

A Resource on the Contents of Saving Faith

Besides writing to clarify the problem of the crossless gospel within the Free Grace camp, I am also writing to address a gaping void that currently exists throughout evangelical Christendom in articulating the contents of saving faith. While most evangelicals today would agree with the statement that a lost person receives eternal life by "believing in the person and work of Christ," there is sorely lacking any systematic attempt to explain this view from Scripture. A casual perusal of the shelves of any Christian bookstore, theological library, or even the indexes of most systematic theologies, quickly reveals the extent to which this topic has been sorely neglected. There is virtually nothing available in print that attempts a comprehensive treatment of this vital and practical evangelistic question.[5] With such a pressing need in mind for our generation, this book is offered to all sincere seekers of God's will and Word.

Finally, let me close this preface with a personal word to the skeptics, who may still doubt whether the new form of theology emanating from the Grace Evangelical Society is as aberrant as this book claims it to be. I ask only that you read the following chapters with an open mind and an open Bible, intent only upon believing God's truth. I realize that some people may respond emotionally to this issue, as this may hit close to home for some, but if so then remember the Lord's admonition to be *"swift to hear, slow to speak, and slow to wrath"* (James 1:19). So please, just *"consider what I say, and may the Lord give you understanding in all things"* (2 Tim. 2:7).

[5] There is, however, the welcome and recent appearance of Norman Geisler's massive, four volume Systematic Theology which has an entire chapter devoted to this question. Norman Geisler, *Systematic Theology* (Minneapolis: Bethany House, 2004), 3:524-51. In addition, see also J. B. Hixson's extensive chapter dealing with this subject in *Getting the Gospel Wrong*, 77-193.

Part I

Examining the Error of the Crossless Gospel

Chapter 1

The Tragedy of the Crossless Gospel

OVERVIEW

From within the Free Grace wing of evangelicalism, a new gospel has tragically emerged in recent years, one which does not require belief in Christ's deity, substitutionary death, or bodily resurrection in order to receive eternal life. The Grace position throughout its history has rightly rejected the error of Lordship Salvation, which adds meritorious conditions to the nature of saving faith. Today, however, the new "crossless" gospel errs in a different manner by subtracting from the contents of saving faith. The new gospel that is emanating from, and advocated by, the Grace Evangelical Society represents a radical departure from both Scripture and the historic Grace position. Grace-oriented Christians must address this plaguing problem in our midst by speaking the truth in love while affirming the biblical gospel of our salvation.

The world has never known anything like it. No human tongue or pen could ever devise its equal. Angels stand awed by it. Unseen spirits are at war over it. To mankind, groping in darkness, it offers the brightest ray of hope. It is low enough for a simple child to grasp it, yet profound enough to produce an eternity of reflection. It is powerful enough to penetrate the hardest human heart and overthrow death itself. It abases the proud and exalts the humble. It is pure truth amidst an ocean of lies and deceit. It is a message sent from heaven to earth. It is God's story, penned in red. The priceless ink used by the Author once coursed through His veins. The parchment He wrote upon was a Roman crucifix. Though the Author died composing His masterpiece, amazingly, His story ends in total triumph! O how marvelous is the gospel of Christ!

To me, an unworthy sinner saved by grace and redeemed by the blood of the Lamb, the gospel of my Savior is a sacred treasure. It was the power of God unto me for my own salvation many years ago, and it has not ceased to be the joy and rejoicing of my heart. It will be my song through the endless ages of eternity. I am convinced that its truth will never be extinguished because it is *God's* message.

The gospel itself is His story of triumph over human sin and death through the sufficient, sacrificial death and glorious resurrection of His Son, the Lord Jesus Christ. In itself, this glorious gospel of Christ is a cause for continual rejoicing and glory to God. But because the gospel is so magnificent and precious to God, the story of what has been done to it by man is a terrible tragedy indeed.

It is truly a tragedy when evangelical, fundamental, Bible-believing Christians are the ones who tamper with its precious contents. It is especially tragic when those among us who have been viewed as the vanguard of gospel purity are the very ones who are corrupting its sacred contents. This is precisely the tragedy that has occurred within the Free Grace wing of evangelicalism in recent years with the emergence of a "crossless" gospel. Though that in itself is tragic enough, I am afraid it gets much worse. Peculiar new doctrines have evolved as the supporting structure for the new "crossless" gospel. It is time for those of us in the Free Grace camp who love the gospel of our Lord Jesus Christ to speak up and confidently proclaim the truth.

You might be saying, "These are very serious claims. What do you mean the gospel has been corrupted?" There was once virtual unanimity among us who hold to the Free Grace position that in order for lost sinners to receive eternal life they ***must*** believe that Jesus Christ is God-incarnate who died for their sins and rose again to save them eternally.

However, today there are a number of fellow Free Grace brethren who no longer believe this once standard gospel. This *old* gospel is now considered "flawed."[1] It is something that certain Free Grace advocates now regard to be "adding to the gospel"[2] and something that makes them "shutter"[3] [sic] and feel "extremely uncomfortable."[4] To require belief in Christ's deity, death for sin, and resurrection in order to be saved is now openly derided as "theological legalism" on a level with Lordship Salvation, Roman Catholicism, the Jehovah's Witnesses, Mormonism, and Seventh Day Adventism.[5]

As one who considers himself an advocate of the utter "freeness" of salvation by grace through faith and who is opposed to the false teachings of Lordship Salvation, I am *deeply* disturbed by such sentiments and by the shocking statements now being made by leading representatives of the Free Grace position from the last few decades. The following is a brief sampling of what I'm talking about:

> *"I know that I trusted Christ for salvation before I realized that Jesus was the Son of God."* I was surprised because I had never heard anyone say this before. But I did not quarrel with that statement then, nor would I quarrel with it now.[6]

> John keeps the signs distinct from the message of life, so evangelicals must not confuse them either. John does not set forth the sign of the cross-and-resurrection as the message that one must believe in order to receive eternal life.[7]

> Neither explicitly nor implicitly does the Gospel of John teach that a person must understand the cross to be saved. It just does not teach this.[8]

> Let me say this: All forms of the gospel that require greater content to faith in Christ than the Gospel of John requires, are flawed. Evangelism based on such premises will also be flawed, because we will be tempted to test professions of faith in terms of doctrines we think must be believed.[9]

---

[1] Zane C. Hodges, "How to Lead People to Christ, Part 1: The Content of Our Message," *JOTGES* 13 (Autumn 2000): 8.

[2] Ibid., 7.

[3] Robert N. Wilkin, "Justification by Faith Alone is an Essential Part of the Gospel," *JOTGES* 18 (Autumn 2005): 14.

[4] Zane C. Hodges, "How to Lead People to Christ, Part 2: Our Invitation to Respond," *JOTGES* 14 (Spring 2001): 9.

[5] Zane C. Hodges, "The Hydra's Other Head: Theological Legalism," *Grace in Focus* 23 (September/October 2008): 2.

[6] Hodges, "How to Lead People to Christ, Part 1," 5.

[7] John Niemelä, "The Message of Life in the Gospel of John," *CTSJ* 7 (July-Sept. 2001): 18.

[8] Hodges, "How to Lead People to Christ, Part 1," 7.

[9] Ibid., 8.

> Jesus often never even brought up the issue of sin when He evangelized. Look at what He told Nicodemus in John 3. He never even mentioned sin there.[10]

> When you look at Genesis 3, how many times do you see sin there? None. But you find death—and life. Ok; sin plunged us into the problem of death, but let's stop focusing so much on the solution of the sin-problem when the fundamental truth is the person is left without life. They need to hear the message of life. That's the fundamental problem that man is left with. Sin has been taken care of so completely at the cross that sin has ceased to be the big issue. The big issue becomes: people are separated from God for eternity and Christ has made a promise to give those who believe in Him for life—to give them life. Let's get means separated from ends and let's focus on the big things as the big things.[11]

> The simple truth is that Jesus can be believed for eternal salvation apart from any detailed knowledge of what He did to provide it.[12]

> Without the name of Jesus there is no salvation for anyone anywhere in our world. But the flip side of the coin is this: Everyone who believes in that name for eternal salvation is saved, regardless of the blank spots or the flaws in their theology in other respects. Another way of saying the same thing is this: No one has ever trusted that name and been disappointed. In other words, God does not say to people, "You trusted my Son's name, but you didn't believe in His virgin birth, or His substitutionary atonement, or His bodily resurrection, so your faith is not valid." *We* say that, but God's Word does not.[13]

What is now being taught as the new, simplified version of the "good news" is that a lost person can receive eternal life by "faith alone in Christ alone," yet without needing to believe in or even know about Christ's person and work. According to the *new and improved* gospel, someone doesn't need to believe in Christ's deity, substitutionary death for sin, or bodily resurrection to be truly born again. As long as that person believes in the name of "Jesus," even without an understanding of who He is or what He's done, such a "believer" will receive eternal life and become justified by God's grace—just as long as he believes this "Jesus" can guarantee him eternal life.

---

[10] Bob Wilkin, "The Way of the Master," *Grace in Focus* 22 (July/August 2007): 4.

[11] John Niemelä, "What About Believers Who Have Never Known Christ's Promise of Life?" *Chafer Theological Seminary Conference*, Houston, TX, March 13, 2006.

[12] Hodges, "How to Lead People to Christ, Part 2," 12.

[13] Hodges, "How to Lead People to Christ, Part 1," 9.

Historical & Theological Context

Some historical and theological context is necessary to begin with in order to understand the reasons behind the rise of this new, unscriptural gospel. For those unfamiliar with the designations "Free Grace" and "Lordship Salvation," there has been a heated debate in recent decades among evangelical Christians over the sole condition and nature of faith in Christ for salvation. Those espousing what has come to be labeled as "Lordship Salvation" have claimed that though salvation is through faith alone, "genuine saving faith" will necessarily be accompanied by obedience, fruitfulness, faithfulness, and perseverance to the end of one's Christian life. To be eternally saved, they say, lost sinners must not only trust in Christ for their eternal salvation but also actively submit to His lordship and mastery until the end of their life. Anything less does not qualify as genuine, saving faith, they say.

On the other hand, "Free Grace" proponents, including this author, are those who reject Lordship Salvation as being unscriptural. The Grace position sees Lordship Salvation as inimical to the gratuitous nature of salvation and the sole condition of faith alone in Christ alone. The Lordship position ultimately requires works and service for Christ by all those who will be admitted to heaven. In practice if not in principle, Lordship Salvation ultimately makes believers' works for Christ determinative of their eternal destiny, rather than being solely dependent upon Christ's work. In the landmark book, *The Gospel According to Jesus*, leading Lordship Salvation proponent John MacArthur provides a classic example of the contradictory and inherently meritorious nature of Lordship soteriology. He states:

> Eternal life is indeed a free gift (Romans 6:23). Salvation cannot be earned with good deeds or purchased with money. It has already been bought by Christ, who paid the ransom with His blood. But that does not mean there is no cost in terms of salvation's impact on the sinner's life. This paradox may be difficult but it is nevertheless true: salvation is both free and costly. Eternal life brings immediate death to self. "Knowing this, that our old self was crucified with Him, that our body of sin might be done away with, that we should no longer be slaves to sin" (Romans 6:6). Thus in a sense we pay the ultimate price for salvation when our sinful self is nailed to a cross. It is a total abandonment of self-will, like the grain of wheat that falls to the ground and dies so that it can bear much fruit (cf. John 12:24). It is an exchange of all that we are for all that Christ is. And it denotes implicit obedience, full surrender to the lordship of Christ. Nothing less can qualify as saving faith.[14]

---

[14] John F. MacArthur, Jr., *The Gospel According to Jesus: What Does Jesus Mean When He Says, "Follow Me"?* (Grand Rapids: Zondervan, 1988), 140.

Lordship Salvation's "Crossplus" Gospel

When Lordship proponents claim, as MacArthur does here, that there is a sense in which "we pay the ultimate price for salvation when our sinful self is nailed to a cross," they are clearly adding to the finished work of Christ at Calvary. Make no mistake about it dear reader, the popular Lordship gospel of our day is not a cross*less* gospel; it is a cross*plus* gospel! Therefore, it is imperative that you the reader understand at the outset what I mean in this book by the expression "crossless gospel." I do not use this phrase in the manner that it is sometimes used by Lordship Salvationists themselves, namely to convey some stringent and toilsome path to achieving eternal life. This phrase is *not* used throughout this book to imply that unless we make the gospel more demanding by raising the entrance requirements to heaven, we will end up with a gospel to the lost that is cheapened, weakened, or watered down. When proponents of Lordship Salvation claim that saving faith is "a lifelong commitment" and that "it means taking up the cross daily,"[15] this is clearly adding *our* cross to *Christ's* cross as a condition for eternal life. The result is that the marvelous, infinite, matchless grace of God is nullified, and salvation becomes a meritorious work instead of a free gift. While the Lord does call all of us who are believers to daily carry our crosses as part of our walk of faith and obedient discipleship, doing so is not inherent to "saving faith"[16] and is not a requirement for eternal life.

---

[15] Ibid., 201-2.

[16] When the expression "saving faith" is used throughout this book, it is not referring to a special *quality* of faith, such as working faith, obedient faith, persevering faith, heart faith versus head faith, etc. Though many Lordship evangelicals speak of "saving faith" in these terms, nowhere in Scripture does God require a special *quality* or *kind* of faith to be eternally saved. James 2:14-26 is no exception to this. Despite his crossless gospel, John Niemelä's solid exegesis of James 2 in his three journal articles is simply irrefutable in my estimation. (See John Niemelä, "Faith Without Works: A Definition," *CTSJ* 6 [April-June 2000]: 2-18; "James 2:24: Retranslation Required, Part 1," *CTSJ* 7 [January-March 2001]: 13-24; "James 2:24: Retranslation Required, Part 2," *CTSJ* 7 [April-June 2001]: 2-15.) To my knowledge these articles have not yet been answered by a single critic of the Free Grace position. Biblically, salvation is a matter of having the right *content* and *object* of one's faith. Thus to have faith in one's works *plus* Jesus is to NOT have "saving faith" (Rom. 4:5). To have faith in Christ and His work alone is to have a faith that will save, hence a "saving faith." The real question with salvation is not, "What *kind* of faith do I have?" but "*Who* or *what* am I trusting to be saved?" Though the phrase "saving faith" can be easily misconstrued, it is used throughout this book because it is still standard theological nomenclature, even in Free Grace circles. See, for example, Robert N. Wilkin, *Saving Faith in Focus* (Irving, TX: Grace Evangelical Society, 2001). From a Reformed perspective that is at certain points agreeable with the Free Grace position, see Gordon H. Clark, *Faith and Saving Faith*, 2nd ed. (Jefferson, MD: Trinity Foundation, 1990). For two helpful resources specifically on the *nature* of saving faith from a solidly Free Grace perspective, see Fred Chay and John P. Correia, *The Faith that Saves: The Nature of Faith in the New Testament* (n.p.: Schoettle Publishing, 2008); Fred R. Lybrand, *Back to Faith: Reclaiming Gospel Clarity in an Age of Incongruence* (n.p.: Xulon Press, 2009).

The error of Lordship Salvation continues to be a plaguing problem in the evangelical world. In terms of its widespread and pervasive influence, it still poses a far greater threat today than even the crossless gospel. However, this fact does not absolve those of us within the Free Grace community of the responsibility to address the dreadful error that has arisen within our own ranks; and hence there is an urgent need for this book on the contents of saving faith.

It must be further clarified that though the Lordship Salvation position holds to a cross*plus* gospel by adding man's work to Christ's work, it does *not* advocate a cross*less* gospel. It does not remove the necessity to believe in Christ's finished work for eternal life. The crossless gospel is completely unique to the Free Grace side of the salvation controversy. I believe the reason for this is due to the characteristic concern among Free Grace proponents to guard against additions to the gospel. We are very conscientious about the innate, religious, human tendency to merit salvation by works and thus to nullify the gospel of God's grace. Though Lordship Salvationists would certainly dispute this claim, I am convinced that this concern is not nearly so pronounced among Lordship Salvationists. It is out of this genuine biblical desire among Free Grace people to guard the gospel from the addition of human works that an unbiblical and imbalanced zeal for minimization has arisen. This has led some contemporary Free Grace leaders to practically gut the saving gospel of its precious contents—the person and work of our Lord Jesus Christ.

Change within the Free Grace Movement

It is imperative that the world understands that the *new* crossless, resurrectionless, and deityless gospel of our day is not representative of the Free Grace community as a whole. The gospel currently being espoused by the Grace Evangelical Society has not always been the position of Free Grace Christians, and thankfully it is still not the doctrinal position of the majority in our movement. It is my contention that, with a prominent minority still associated with the G.E.S., there has been an intentional doctrinal shift in the last decade or two—a radical change for the worse. That some degree of change has occurred in the Free Grace camp can no longer be denied. It is even being openly touted by some as a sign of progress. For example, René López speaks of the evolving state of Free Grace theology. He cites approvingly the Executive Director of the Grace Evangelical Society, Bob Wilkin, saying:

> I must agree with Bob's conclusion: Free Grace theology is still being worked out. It has really taken shape in the last 25 years. *The Gospel Under Siege* by Zane Hodges came out in 1981 and it was a seminal work on Free Grace theology. Prior to that Free

> Grace theology was rather loosely defined. Even today, as we shall see, there is still work to be done to nail down all of the particulars.[17]

Free Grace theology certainly has "taken shape" in the last quarter century, but it is a shape that many in the movement no longer recognize as being true to Scripture or our own historical position. As a result, there presently exists a split among Free Grace Christians between those who uphold the necessity to believe in the person and work of Christ for eternal life and those who have aligned themselves with the Grace Evangelical Society and its new "crossless," or "promise-only," gospel.[18] However, there can no longer be any doubt that a significant doctrinal drift has occurred away from the gospel of Christ-crucified and risen as the saving message. Many Free Grace people over the last few years have conceded this unfortunate departure, though a few are still in a state of confusion or denial about it. But despite the reticence of some Free Grace people to recognize that sweeping changes have occurred, one prominent Free Grace leader openly admitted to this author that his doctrine did change. In 2005, he explicitly affirmed that his views on the gospel shifted sometime during the decade of the 1990s. In addition, the most prominent voice for the new G.E.S. gospel, the late Zane Hodges, openly acknowledged that his views changed over the years as well:

> In recent years I have become aware of a way of presenting the gospel invitation that troubles me. I believe I have heard it from my earliest years, and I admit it didn't really bother me for a long time. Now it does. I have heard people say this: "In order to be saved you must believe that Jesus died on the cross." In the context of our present discussion, I mean that this is their summary of the requirement of faith. It is not just one item, among others, to be believed. Whenever I hear that nowadays, I get extremely uncomfortable.[19]

Despite Hodges's personal displeasure over this cross-centered approach to evangelism, the apostle Paul writing under the inspiration of the Holy Spirit certainly had no such antipathy. He summarized his gospel presentation as centered in the cross-work of Jesus Christ. In the Epistle of 1 Corinthians, Paul repeatedly made the summary statement that his message *"to those who are perishing"* was *"the message of the cross"* (1 Cor. 1:17-18). And

---

[17] René A. López, "Basics of Free Grace Theology, Part 1," http://www.scriptureunlocked.com/papers/basicsfgprt1.pdf (accessed August 6, 2007), 2-3.

[18] This is exemplified by the contrasting doctrinal statements of the Grace Evangelical Society and the Free Grace Alliance. The G.E.S. statement does not require belief in Christ's redemptive work for eternal life, whereas affirmation #3 in the F.G.A. covenant explicitly states that the lost must become "persuaded that the finished work of Jesus Christ has delivered" them from condemnation and guarantees them eternal life.

[19] Hodges, "How to Lead People to Christ, Part 2," 9.

though he initially preached other gospel truths to the Corinthians besides the cross of Christ (1 Cor. 15:3-4), in recounting the message of his initial evangelization of them he did not hesitate to summarize it all by saying, *"And I brethren, when I came to you. . . . determined not to know anything among you except Jesus Christ and Him crucified"* (1 Cor. 2:1-2). This was also how he summarized his evangelistic message towards all Jews and Gentiles, not merely the Corinthians. He boldly declared, *"we preach Christ crucified, to the Jews a stumbling block, and to the Greeks foolishness"* (1 Cor. 1:23). It was through the *"foolishness"* of this *"message preached"*—this *"message of the cross"* (1:18)—that God would *"save those who believe"* (1 Cor. 1:21).

In Hodges's second article in the *Journal of the Grace Evangelical Society* in which he articulated the crossless-content-of-saving-faith position, he went on to explain even further:

> Now I know that the statement I am evaluating leaves a lot of things unspoken that are still implied by the speaker. Most of the time people who say you are saved by believing that Jesus died on the cross mean that He died for our sins. Indeed the phrase "for your sins" is often added. But even with that addition, there is still unspoken material that the person usually has in mind. They usually mean to say, for example, that this belief in Christ's death is all that is necessary for salvation. Thus they are normally proclaiming salvation by faith alone. Also unspoken, but usually implied, is the idea that Christ's work on the cross is sufficient to provide for our salvation. Thus they mean to say that we are trusting in the sufficiency of His work for salvation. Let me be honest. I don't like this way of presenting a gospel invitation.[20]

Hodges later concludes, *"I would like to see grace people abandon this form of invitation to faith."*[21] It is apparent from their numerous books, journal articles, newsletters, conference sessions, and on-line material on this subject that these spokesmen for the Grace Evangelical Society are absolutely convinced of their new version of the gospel as they actively seek to promote it. They would like the rest of us in the Free Grace movement to "abandon" our old approach to the gospel,[22] for in fact they now denounce

---

[20] Hodges, "How to Lead People to Christ, Part 2," 9-10.

[21] Ibid., 11.

[22] John Niemelä expresses a sentiment similar to Hodges. He explains that the Gospel of John nowhere requires the unregenerate to believe that Christ died for their sins and rose again in order to receive eternal life, but they must only believe in Jesus as the guarantor of eternal life, which he refers to as the "message of life." Niemelä then states, "Therefore, evangelicals should carefully examine what John treats as the content of this message of life. If what John says differs from what modern evangelicals preach, it is time to bring the modern message into conformity with the Gospel of John." Niemelä, "The Message of Life in the Gospel of John," 10. Clearly, the advocates of the new, crossless, G.E.S. gospel would like the rest of us in evangelicalism to conform our gospel to their crossless "message of life" which they claim to have recently discovered in the Gospel of John.

it in unmistakable terms as "theological legalism."[23] Personally, I would *not* like to see Free Grace people abandon this form of gospel invitation because the apostle Paul didn't!

Regrettably, Hodges himself even abandoned the form of gospel invitation that makes Christ's work on the cross and the requirement to believe in it the "core issue" for the sinner. Though he stated that this approach made him "extremely uncomfortable," it apparently didn't in years past. There occurred a definite shift in his theological perspective later in life. In his earlier book, *The Gospel Under Siege*, he concluded with a final evangelistic appeal to his readers. Notice carefully his emphasis on the sufficiency of Christ's work on the cross as the defining issue between the sinner and God. He once wrote:

> So what about you? Where do you look for peace and assurance of salvation? Are you asking, "Have I done enough to prove I am saved?" Or is the question instead, "Has Christ done enough on the cross to save me, whatever my faults and failures are or may become?" Does your entire hope for heaven rest on what *He has done* and *not at all* on what you can, have, or will, do? If your answer to this last question is yes, then—clearly!—you have believed the Gospel and you already know that your eternal destiny is secure. Let it be said plainly: any system of doctrine that forbids us to find complete peace by simply looking to God's Son, who was lifted up for us on the cross, can by no means claim to be the true Gospel. But if it is not, then it must be a false gospel and must stand under the anathema Paul pronounced in Galatians 1.[24]

This cross-centered approach to evangelism was once at the core of Hodges's message in *The Gospel Under Siege*. But two recent publications by Hodges reveal the drastic departure that occurred in his own perspective on the gospel. In the 32 page booklet, *Did Paul Preach Eternal Life? Should We?*, Hodges does not refer to Christ's death for our sins or His resurrection even once, yet he uses the term "gospel" over 25 times.[25] It is simply unfathom-

---

[23] Hodges, "The Hydra's Other Head: Theological Legalism," 2-3.

[24] Zane C. Hodges, *The Gospel Under Siege*, 2nd ed. (Dallas: Kerugma, 1992), 150 (italics original). Bob Wilkin also initially viewed the cross as essential to the content of saving faith. In the early years of G.E.S. as its Executive Director, he stated in respect to Matthew 7:21-23, "What would you say if you appeared before God and He said, 'Why should I let you into My kingdom?' Matthew 7:22 is the wrong answer. The right answer is, 'Lord, I am an unworthy sinner who has placed his complete trust upon what Jesus did for me upon the cross, and He promised that whoever believes in Him has eternal life' (Luke 18:13-14; John 3:16; Rom. 4:5; Eph. 2:8-9; Titus 3:5)." Bob Wilkin, *The G.E.S. News*, "Not Everyone Who Says 'Lord, Lord' Will Enter the Kingdom, Matthew 7:21-23," (December 1988).

[25] Zane C. Hodges, *Did Paul Preach Eternal Life? Should We?* (Mesquite, TX: Kerugma, 2007). The closest Hodges comes to mentioning Christ's work is the statement "dying on the cross (Matt. 27:40, 49)" on page 24. However, these verses merely record the taunts of the unbelieving Jews. When Hodges includes this phrase of the Jews, "dying on the cross,"

able that an evangelical theologian of Hodges's stature could compose a booklet articulating the gospel that both Jesus and Paul preached and yet never mention Christ's work on the cross or His resurrection!

In addition to this booklet, in a recent 12 page tract written by Hodges and Bob Bryant titled, *You Can be Eternally Secure*, Christ's death and resurrection are also never mentioned.[26] Some might wish to excuse this as a simple oversight, rationalizing that this tract was written to persuade those who are already regenerate of their eternal security in Christ. However, the publisher of the tract explicitly tells us that its intended use is for evangelism rather than the discipleship of believers. The Grace Evangelical Society offers the following advertisement of this tract:

> Written to be used in evangelism, this little booklet (12 pages) succinctly presents the message of everlasting life through faith alone in Christ alone. Those who read it will know that to receive everlasting life that cannot be lost, all they must do is believe in Jesus Christ for it. There is space on the back page to put your personal contact information so that when people believe, they can reach you for follow-up discipleship.[27]

Unfortunately, the desire expressed in the recent past by Hodges to "abandon" the cross as an *essential* part of the gospel to the lost has gained some traction among Free Grace proponents associated with the Grace Evangelical Society. His stated desire that other Grace people "abandon" the cross-centered focus of evangelism is now becoming a reality. In the last decade, the gospel presentations of certain Free Grace advocates have routinely downplayed the person and work of the Savior so as to emphasize the promise of eternal life aspect of the gospel. Belief in the person and work of Christ is no longer being required in today's new, crossless G.E.S. gospel. One example of this can be found in the book titled *Road to Reward* by Bob Wilkin. In the first two chapters of his book, Wilkin appropriately offers an evangelistic appeal to faith in Christ before delving deeply into the subject of rewards for Christians. However, there is a glaring and obvious omission in these two chapters: the death of Christ for our sins and His resurrection are *never* mentioned—only appeals to believe in Christ as the guarantor of eternal life. The cross of Christ and His glorious resurrection have dropped out completely in this "evangel-less" approach

---

he doesn't even state *who* died on the cross or *why* someone was "dying on the cross." In its context, Hodges only uses the phrase "dying on the cross" to invalidate the prevalent evangelical understanding of "salvation" as being primarily a spiritual deliverance versus a physical deliverance. Thus in its context, this statement is not even used as a direct reference to Christ's death. This is completely inexcusable and a direct reflection of how Hodges's theology shifted.

[26] Bob Bryant and Zane Hodges, *You Can Be Eternally Secure* (Irving, TX: Grace Evangelical Society, 2006).

[27] http://www.faithalone.org/bookstore/Eternally_Secure.html (accessed August 8, 2007).

to evangelism. Ironically, the first chapter is titled, "The Disaster of Poor Communication."

In a subsequent book by Wilkin, *Secure and Sure,* he states no less than 113 times throughout the book in almost mantra-like fashion that a person receives eternal life simply by believing in Jesus for it, or some varied form of the same expression. Yet *not once* in his entire book, despite 113 occasions to do so, does Wilkin state that by believing in Jesus for eternal life he means someone must believe that Jesus is God-incarnate who died for his sins and rose again. This is not an accidental oversight on his part; it is intentional and in keeping with the new, crossless gospel, which does not require belief in the Savior's person and work to be born again. Wilkin tells us candidly in one place that *"biblical faith in Jesus is not faith that He existed, nor faith in His deity, nor even faith that He died for our sins and rose again. In the Bible, to believe in Jesus is to be convinced that He who died and rose again guarantees eternal life to all who simply believe in Him."*[28] It may at first seem overly critical to see a distinction between saying a person must believe in Him "*who* died and rose again" versus saying he must believe *that* Christ died and rose again. Yet, such a distinction is enormously significant and precisely the problem at hand. For though Wilkin and certain Free Grace teachers do believe *personally* that Jesus Christ is God-incarnate who died for our sins and rose again, they do not believe *the lost* must accept these truths as part of believing in Him for eternal life.

Nor are they ambivalent or accepting of these so-called "extra" elements as a necessary part of the gospel to the lost. In their estimation, requiring a person to believe in Christ's deity, death for sin, and resurrection in order to receive eternal life is requiring *too much* theological content. In fact, I have even heard some crossless gospel advocates contend that to preach the gospel in this manner actually creates a stumbling block that may hinder the unsaved from believing in Christ as the guarantor of eternal life. They claim we are actually "adding to the gospel" in the same way the Lordship Salvationist adds extra-biblical conditions to "faith alone" in Christ alone.[29] Zane Hodges addressed this concern in one of his articles under the section heading, "ADDING TO THE GOSPEL," where he wrote:

> Most of us deplore efforts made by Lordship people to add provisos to the message of faith in Christ. According to them, true faith has not occurred if it is not accompanied by surrender or by a commitment to live for God. We rightly reject such ideas. But in our own circles, there is a tendency to add theological information to our message of faith.[30]

---

[28] Robert N. Wilkin, *Secure and Sure* (Irving, TX: Grace Evangelical Society, 2005), 28.

[29] Hodges, "The Hydra's Other Head: Theological Legalism," 2.

[30] Hodges, "How to Lead People to Christ, Part 1," 7-8.

What then follows is an argument against requiring belief in Christ's virgin birth before someone can be born again, along with a denial of the necessity to believe in Christ's death and resurrection in order to have eternal life. Let's put aside for a moment the red-herring of requiring belief in Christ's virgin birth, which we all agree is absolutely doctrinally true but is nowhere presented in the New Testament as part of the saving message that the lost must believe called "the gospel." It is simply egregious to claim that we are somehow "adding to the gospel" by preaching a gospel that necessitates belief in Christ's incarnation, death for sin, and resurrection.

It appears that the Grace Evangelical Society started out in the late 1980s nobly combating the extra-biblical *conditions* to "faith alone," but now they have turned their sights upon what they consider to be the extra-biblical *content* of that faith. Throughout the 80s and 90s the battle was waged over the sole condition and nature of faith for salvation. The emphasis was upon defending the "faith alone" portion of the slogan, "faith alone in Christ alone." But now, since at least 1999, the emphasis seems to have shifted towards clarifying what it means to have faith "in Christ alone." Many of us in the Free Grace movement were in solid agreement with the initial doctrine and direction of these men in addressing the extra-biblical requirements to faith, such as "commitment" to serve and "surrender," which Hodges previously mentioned. But now we must protest the major changes taking place to the gospel of our Lord Jesus Christ. Their aim was noble and true and biblical to begin with, but now they have gone too far.

Crossless gospel teachers have become like a person who is initially intent on becoming healthier through diet and exercise but somewhere along the line becomes manically obsessed with getting leaner. Initially he becomes healthier as he burns off unnecessary, excess fat; but then by obsessive diet and exercise he actually becomes *un*healthy as his body begins to metabolize muscle instead of fat. When the Grace Evangelical Society began, we were all in favor of stripping away the fat of Lordship Salvation "works" from the gospel of God's grace. But now the G.E.S. and others in the movement have gone to an unhealthy extreme, and they are consuming muscle off the bone—the precious contents of the gospel itself, namely our Lord's deity, humanity, substitutionary death, and resurrection from the dead. This is the terrible tragedy of the new, crossless gospel.

There will likely be three defining issues for the Free Grace movement in the next decade. These issues are so important that they will determine the entire course and effectiveness of our ministry for the Lord Jesus Christ and whether we will have God's blessing upon our movement and ministries. We must answer, first of all, the question of what exactly a person must believe about Jesus in order to truly believe in Him as *"the Christ, the Son of God"* for eternal life. Secondly, we must answer definitively the simple question of "What is the gospel?" And thirdly, we must answer biblically the once-obvious question, "Does a lost person have to believe the gospel to be born again?" These three fundamental questions are inextricably linked to one another and must be answered together. There is a desperate need right now for honest, soul-searching definition that is both biblical and unequivocal. If we can no longer agree among ourselves on the very definition of "the gospel" and whether or not the lost even need to believe it, then our movement will surely suffer a debilitating paralysis and we will become completely ineffective in advancing the truth of God's grace.

The years ahead will require us to define the *sine qua non*[31] of the gospel of grace, just as dispensationalism had to do a generation ago.[32] In the chapters ahead, I will seek to articulate from Scripture what I believe are the essential, defining elements of the gospel that must be believed for one to receive eternal salvation. For now, these may be summarized categorically according to Christ's person and work, along with the provision and condition for salvation.

Christ's Person: Jesus Christ is God ("Son of God" and "Lord") and human ("Son of man").

Christ's Work: Jesus Christ died for (*huper*, i.e., in a substitutionary sense) our sins and rose bodily from the dead.

Provision & Condition: Salvation is by God's grace, apart from works, through faith in Jesus Christ and His work alone.

These elements comprise the gospel of Christ as it has historically been understood from Scripture by Free Grace advocates. We have not changed, and the gospel itself certainly has not changed, but some leading proponents of Free Grace theology have changed and moved away from us.[33] Tragically, in recent years within the Free Grace camp there have been multiple "gospels" being preached and tolerated under the banner of "grace." This was exemplified at one Free Grace conference a few years ago where an attending pastor facetiously remarked, *"We ought to define what "the gospel" is. I think I've heard three or four of them since I've been here."*

The New Meaning of "the Gospel"

To many Free Grace teachers today, the term "gospel" is no longer permitted to have a technical usage in Scripture, where in various contexts it means the particular message or elements of truth about Christ that the

---

31 This is a Latin legal term meaning "without which it could not be," referring to an indispensable element or condition.

32 Charles Ryrie, *Dispensationalism* (Chicago: Moody Press, 1995), 38-41.

33 Fred R. Lybrand, "GES Gospel: Lybrand Open Letter," April 14, 2009, p. 14.

lost must know and believe for their eternal salvation. Instead, "the gospel" has become a broad, all-inclusive, catch phrase for "good news" of any kind. By claiming that "the gospel" is not a technical term in the New Testament, this has had the effect of flinging the door wide-open for the purpose of redefining the gospel. This has resulted in the truths of Christ's deity, humanity, sacrificial death, and resurrection being strained out of God's saving message of the gospel. For some Free Grace advocates, these truths are simply "facts surrounding the gospel" but not part of the gospel itself. For others, these truths comprise "the gospel" to the Christian that is necessary for practical sanctification but not the message that the lost must hear and receive by faith.

The result of this redefining process has been the emergence of a "mini" gospel that contains just the minimal, essential truth necessary to be believed for eternal life. This is often called "the saving message." This is in contrast to the "full gospel message,"[34] which includes Christ's substitutionary death and resurrection. The new, saving mini-gospel goes something like this, "The gift of eternal life is guaranteed to all who simply believe in Jesus for it." This is now considered by some to be a legitimate definition of "the gospel."

This distinction between a broad gospel (containing the cross and resurrection) and a narrower gospel (without the work of Christ) had already germinated among certain Free Grace leaders almost two decades ago. As early as 1990, Bob Wilkin stated:

> The term gospel may be used to describe the plan of salvation in its *fullest form*. We could in proclaiming the gospel mention Jesus' eternality, His leaving His heavenly throne, being born of a virgin, performing miracles which authenticated His message, living a sinless life, dying on the Cross, rising again, and our need to place our trust in Him alone. The term gospel may also be used to describe the plan of salvation in its *barest form*. It is possible to present *only the core truth of the gospel*: namely, that whoever believes in Jesus Christ has eternal life. That too is the gospel-albeit the *gospel in a nutshell*. If, for example, in sharing the gospel we were to fail to mention Jesus' virgin birth, we would not necessarily be failing to explain it clearly. We would, however, necessarily be sharing it less fully.[35]

---

[34] Hodges, "How to Lead People to Christ, Part 1," 11. Hodges actually used this phrase when he wrote, *"But more often than not, we have difficulty leading them to Christ, unless we lead them through the full gospel message."* In the context of this statement, Hodges says that the "full gospel message" includes Christ's payment for sin on the cross. But does this not imply that there exists a legitimate "gospel" which does not contain the cross, which is not the "full gospel message"?

[35] Robert N. Wilkin, *The Grace Evangelical Society News* (June 1990): 4 (italics added).

This distinction between a broader gospel to the saved and a narrower gospel to the lost also explains why Wilkin has taught more recently, *"You can believe many biblical concepts and still miss* ***the one truth that is saving—the truth of the gospel****. For example, you can attest to Jesus' deity, His virgin birth, and His bodily resurrection, and yet not believe Jesus' promise to give you eternal life freely if you just believe in Him for it. There is only one truth that will save: Jesus' guarantee that anyone who believes in Him for eternal life has it."*[36] This also explains why in 2005 the Grace Evangelical Society advertised the sale of coffee cups with "the gospel" supposedly printed on one side. That "gospel" turned out to be simply one verse, John 6:47, which says nothing about Christ's deity, death for sin, resurrection, or even His name.

It is very common to hear crossless proponents repeating biblical phraseology for the sole condition of salvation, saying that the unregenerate must "Believe in Jesus" or "Believe in Jesus Christ for eternal life." More often the error lies not in what they *are* saying but in what they are *not* saying or *will not* say. The subtle unscripturalness of the crossless position is often missed by many unsuspecting, uninformed Free Grace people who interpret such language as requiring belief in the same "Jesus" or "Christ" that they are thinking of. We think they are requiring belief in the One who is God-incarnate who died for our sins and rose again. We intuitively supply this information to the name "Jesus" or the title "Christ," but in fact that is *not* what crossless proponents would require to be supplied. More and more, when we in the Free Grace movement speak of "the gospel" and "believing in Jesus for eternal life," we are using the same vocabulary but we have completely different dictionaries.

For many within the Free Grace camp, there is now, at best, confusion regarding the meaning of "the gospel." At worst, there is deliberate redefinition. In either case, the gospel has certainly been changed. This can be seen quite easily in the sampling of quotes that follow from various crossless proponents:

> You see, as we noted previously, the facts surrounding the gospel message—such as the death and resurrection of Christ—are important facts for what they tell us about the reasons for trusting Christ. But believing these facts doesn't save anyone. People are only saved when they believe that Jesus gives them eternal life the moment they believe in Him for that.[37]

> Sometimes [the term] "gospel" is narrowly related to "what must I do to have eternal life?" but quite often it's the big picture and it's actually what's preached to the Christian. We're preaching the "good news" to the Christian.[38]

---

[36] Robert N. Wilkin, *Confident in Christ* (Irving, TX: Grace Evangelical Society, 1999), 10 (bold added).

[37] Hodges, "How to Lead People to Christ, Part 2," 12.

[38] Robert N. Wilkin, "The Three Tenses of Salvation Reconsidered," audiotape, Grace

> The good news in First Corinthians is the good news that Paul preached to the *believers,* not unbelievers, in the church in Corinth. The good news message he preached was Christ crucified. This was a sanctification message that a divided church needed to hear badly . . . The reason we don't find justification by faith alone anywhere in 1 Cor 15:3-11 is because this was *sanctification* good news.[39]

> When I hear people point to 1 Cor 15:3-11 and boldly proclaim that is the precise evangelistic message Paul preached, I shutter [sic]. How could we get it so wrong? Yes, Paul did tell unbelievers about Jesus' death and resurrection. But *that was not the sum total of his evangelistic message.* Nor is Paul's evangelistic message the point of 1 Cor 15:3-11.[40]

> In 1 Corinthians 15, when Paul defines the Gospel he had preached and the Corinthians had believed, he is telling the good news about sin, salvation and Christ's sacrifice. He added some elements in his gospel that we normally don't. But he could have added many more elements as well. In fact, the entire Bible is the Gospel, because it's all good news.[41]

> So what is the *gospel*? It can easily be proved from Scripture that *the gospel* is more than faith alone in Christ alone. Much more. The gospel "is not a consistent and clearly definable term which we can express in a brief formula." The gospel includes elements of the kingdom of God on earth. It includes facts about justification, sanctification, glorification, security in heaven, contentment on earth, and eternal reward. The gospel includes all of this.[42]

> Based on what has been learned, it is easy to see why many evangelistic presentations can become so convoluted and involved. If someone tries to share all that the NT includes in the *gospel* they must share the entire NT (and probably the OT as well).[43]

> Thus, the gospel encapsulates the message found in the entire book of Romans (i.e., justification, sanctification, glorification, and a future for Israel). Usually unrecognized, the term gospel

---

Evangelical Society, 2003.

[39] Wilkin, "Justification by Faith Alone," 13 (ellipsis added).

[40] Ibid., 14.

[41] Jeremy D. Myers, "Just the Gospel Facts P's" (www.tillhecomes.org, 2005; accessed June 5, 2007).

[42] Jeremy D. Myers, "The Gospel is More Than 'Faith Alone in Christ Alone'," *JOTGES* 19 (Autumn 2006): 50.

[43] Ibid., 51.

> also includes the unconditional promises to Israel that will be fulfilled in the future (10:15-16; 11:26-32).[44]

After reading these shocking statements as to what constitutes "the gospel" and the contents of faith required for salvation, can we question any longer whether a significant change has occurred? This was *not* the message being proclaimed when the Grace Evangelical Society was formed in the 1980s and it began responding to Lordship Salvation. A significant doctrinal shift has definitely occurred. According to the new Free Grace views being promulgated by the G.E.S. today, the gospel can be something as broad as the Epistle of Romans, or even the entire Bible, while at the same time it can be narrow enough to exclude the so-called "sanctification" truths of Christ's substitutionary death and resurrection. The result is that there can now exist a "mini-gospel" that is preached to the lost that doesn't contain Christ's substitutionary death and resurrection, and there can also exist a "full gospel" which considers these elements necessary only for the sanctification-salvation of the Christian. This is a radical departure—a paradigm shift—away from the one, true, saving gospel of Christ described in the Scriptures and historically preached by grace-oriented brethren.

Historical Grace Definitions of the Gospel

To see that a dramatic changing of the gospel has actually occurred within the Free Grace movement, note the contrast between the preceding descriptions of the gospel and the following statements from a few of the historic leaders of our doctrinal position.[45]

C. I. Scofield (and editors)

> In vv. 1-8 the apostle outlines the Gospel of God's grace. (1) It concerns a Person—the Christ of the Scriptures and history. (2) It concerns His death—"for our sins according to the Scriptures." And (3) it concerns His resurrection—likewise "according to the Scriptures." His burial is asserted as the evidence of His death; and that He was seen alive is declared as the proof of His resurrection. This is the Gospel that Paul preached; that the early Church accepted; and by which men are saved (vv. 1-2).[46]

Lewis Sperry Chafer & John Walvoord

> Jesus in His death was actually the substitute dying in the place of all men. Although "substitute" is not specifically a biblical

---

[44] René A. López, *Romans Unlocked: Power to Deliver* (Springfield, MO: 21st Century Press, 2005), 31-32.

[45] For further examples, see Appendix: "Other Free Grace Voices."

[46] *The Scofield Study Bible, New King James Version*, ed. C. I. Scofield, E. Schuyler English, et al. (Oxford: Oxford University Press, 2002), 1591-92.

word, the idea that Christ is the sinner's substitute is constantly affirmed in Scripture. By His substitutionary death the unmeasured, righteous judgments of God against a sinner were borne by Christ. The result of this substitution is itself as simple and definite as the transaction. The Savior has already borne the divine judgments against the sinner to the full satisfaction of God. In receiving the salvation which God offers, men are asked to believe this good news, recognizing that Christ died for their sins and thereby claiming Jesus Christ as their personal Savior.[47]

Charles Ryrie

Certainly, faith must have some content. There must be confidence about something or in someone. To believe in Christ for salvation means to have confidence that He can remove the guilt of sin and give eternal life. It means to believe that He can solve the problem of sin which is what keeps a person out of heaven. You can also believe Christ about a multitude of other things, but these are not involved in salvation. You can believe He is Israel's Messiah. . . . He was born without a human father being involved in the act of conception. . . . He will return to earth. . . . He is the Judge of all. . . . He is able to run your life. . . . But these are not the issues of salvation. That issue is whether or not you believe that His death paid for all your sin and that by believing in Him you can have forgiveness and eternal life. Faith has an intellectual facet to it. The essential facts are that Christ died for our sins and rose from the dead (1 Corinthians 15:3-4; Romans 4:25). In addition, faith involves assent or agreement with the truth of those facts. One can know the facts of the Gospel and either agree or disagree with them.[48]

Earl Radmacher

Sometimes people refer to the gospel as "the death, burial, and resurrection of Jesus Christ." However, the burial of Jesus is not part of the gospel as such. Rather, it is the proof of the death of Christ. . . . I am stressing this because a more balanced statement of the gospel needs to be made, not only by laypersons but also by pastors and theologians. In a seminary class I was making quite an impassioned presentation on the value of the death of Christ. A student (now a missions professor) interrupted by raising his hand and asking, "Don't you believe in the resurrection of Christ"? I responded, "Certainly I believe in the resurrection of Christ. Why would you ask such a question?" "Well," he said,

---

[47] Lewis Sperry Chafer and John F. Walvoord, *Major Bible Themes*, rev. ed. (Grand Rapids: Eerdmans, 1974), 60.

[48] Charles Ryrie, *So Great Salvation* (Wheaton, IL: Victor Books, 1989), 118-19 (ellipses added).

> "there seems to be such a neglect on the Resurrection in our books and teaching; whereas, when I turn to all the evangelistic messages in the Book of Acts, the emphasis is on the Resurrection. The death of Christ without the Resurrection would be no gospel at all. It would simply be a tragedy." How right he was![49]

When a comparison is made of the gospel that has traditionally been proclaimed among grace-oriented brethren versus the gospel being proclaimed by proponents of a crossless saving faith today, it becomes readily apparent to any unbiased observer that we are no longer preaching the same message. The new crossless, resurrectionless, deityless "saving message" of today's Grace Evangelical Society is *not* the gospel of Scripture or of the historic Grace position. There has been a radical departure from the truth in the last decade. This has tragically resulted in a fractured unity within the Grace camp over the most important doctrinal truth of our day—the gospel. But with such a seismic shift on the gospel, the most foundational truth of our faith, was there also not bound to be some ripple effect on other doctrines? Indeed, there has been as the next chapter will document.

---

[49] Earl D. Radmacher, *Salvation* (Nashville: Word Publishing, 2000), 47 (ellipsis added).

Chapter 2

What Other Doctrines Have Changed?

OVERVIEW

Along with the rise of the new crossless gospel, there has come a corresponding shift in several key auxiliary doctrines. The dispensational doctrine that the content of saving faith has changed with the progress of God's revelation is now rejected in favor of a view that teaches that there is a single, unchanging, transdispensational saving message of life. The doctrine of "salvation" is also shifting as now the idea of three tenses of salvation is being openly challenged. Forgiveness of sins is not a matter of eternal salvation but is wholly a sanctification truth for the Christian life. Likewise, repentance is no longer viewed as a requirement for eternal life, nor does it mean a change of mind but rather a turning from sins. When it comes to the doctrine of wrath, the new crossless view holds that there is no such thing as God's eternal wrath. It is only something temporal, which comes upon both believer and unbeliever alike due to disobedience. Even saving faith itself is being redefined as passive persuasion that Christ's promise is true rather than active "trust" in the work of Christ. Cumulatively, these doctrinal changes do not constitute a refinement of our theology but an abandonment of traditional Free Grace theology.

Having documented the fact that a major change to the gospel has occurred within our ranks, we must now begin to measure the fallout. I am convinced the magnitude of deviation from God's Word is much greater than most Grace people have realized. In conjunction with the crossless gospel, entirely new unscriptural doctrines have been spawned. A doctrinal domino effect is already well underway and does not show signs of abating. When we pause to consider the magnitude of the doctrinal deviation that has taken place, it becomes apparent that a distinctively new belief system, an entirely new theological creature, has emerged from within the Free Grace tradition. We dare not ignore it any longer.

The Doctrinal Domino Effect

When the gospel was redefined to exclude the necessity of believing in Christ's deity, substitutionary death, and resurrection for eternal life, it was inevitable that this would require adjusting several other major areas of doctrine. The Word of God is like a finely woven tapestry. Once such a critical thread as the gospel is pulled, the entire fabric begins to unravel. Right now, several foundational, auxiliary doctrines related to the gospel are being reformulated. These departures from sound doctrine are necessary to document at the outset of this book in order to understand the crossless gospel's perspective and rationale in subsequent chapters (especially chapters 15-17), since many key soteriological passages are being reinterpreted in novel, unfamiliar ways in order to support a crossless content of saving faith (Mark 16:16; Luke 24:46; Acts 2:36-38; 11:18; 17:30-31; Rom. 1:16; 2:4-5; 10:9-10; 1 Cor. 1:18; 15:3-4; 2 Thess. 1:6-10).

Before considering each of these doctrinal departures and biblical reinterpretations, an important qualification is in order. Some Free Grace brethren may hold to some or all of the following doctrinal reformulations without advocating a crossless gospel. It would be unfair and inaccurate to assume that simply because a person has embraced the new interpretations of progressive revelation, salvation, forgiveness, wrath, repentance, or faith that they will necessarily end up embracing the crossless gospel. On the other hand, these new doctrinal positions are a logical and hermeneutical necessity for those who do hold to a crossless gospel in order to maintain the consistency of their doctrinal system.

Progressive Revelation

The first area of doctrinal fallout to be considered that is associated with the crossless gospel is *progressive revelation*. When we consider the relationship between progressive revelation and the gospel, we are asking whether God has changed the requirements of what must be believed for eternal life over the course of time. The increase or progress of God's revelation over time is as indisputable as recognizing that there is a "New" Testament in addition to the "Old" Testament. But did God intend *not* to apply this progress or increase of His revelation to the gospel in any way? Crossless gospel advocates say, "No." They reason that if God now requires more to be believed for salvation than in ages past, then He has supposedly made salvation more difficult. Advocates of the new, crossless position seek to strengthen their claims by going back to conditions prior to Calvary in order to diminish the content of the gospel. But in the process, they end up gutting the gospel of its very contents, namely the Savior's sacrificial death, resurrection, and divine-human personhood.

It is also important to note that this new, aberrant form of the Free Grace gospel has moved away from the traditional, dispensational perspective on the doctrine of progressive revelation. Though the crossless gospel is advocated almost exclusively by men espousing dispensationalism, the crossless gospel position is actually at variance with the traditional, dispensational doctrine of progressive revelation as it relates to the question of what must be believed today for salvation. Thus Bob Wilkin argues:

> Logically what we must do to have eternal life cannot change. If the saving message changes, then so does the gospel. Dispensationalism has long said that men in every age are justified by faith in God, but as revelation progressed what they needed to believe about God changed as well. Well, if people before the time of Christ could be born again by some general faith in God, then logically so can anyone today who has not yet heard the name of Jesus. No one was ever born again by some general faith in God. The condition has always been faith that the Messiah gives eternal life to all who simply believe in Him.[1]

Dispensationalists have been consistent in the last century in their belief that with the progress of God's revelation over time, especially with such an epochal event as Christ's coming into the world, God has required more to be believed *after* Christ's coming than *before* His coming. The *condition* of eternal salvation has remained the same and has always been "faith alone," but the *content* of that faith has changed.

However, those who hold to the new crossless gospel maintain that the progress of revelation has *not* affected the contents of faith required for salvation. On this particular point, they actually agree with covenant theology against dispensationalism. However, they are even in conflict with

---

[1] Robert N. Wilkin, "Is Ignorance Eternal Bliss?" *JOTGES* 16 (Spring 2003): 13.

covenant theology on another vital point. Covenant theology teaches that the lost have always needed to believe in Christ's deity, substitutionary death, and resurrection for eternal life. They teach, along with crossless gospel proponents, that the contents of faith have not changed over time. But unlike crossless gospel proponents, covenant theology teaches that Old Testament saints had faith in the coming Redeemer as One who would be God and who would provide redemption from sin and even rise again.

So besides disagreeing with the Scriptures, most importantly, the new crossless theology is also at variance with the theological systems of both dispensationalism and covenant theology. They have, perhaps unwittingly, created an entirely new, third, theological position on the doctrine of progressive revelation and salvation. Their new doctrine of progressive revelation is at least the second doctrinal domino to fall in conjunction with changing the gospel.

Salvation

The new, crossless gospel has also led to at least a third domino tipping. The doctrine of *salvation* is now in a state of flux. There is currently a very strong aversion by some of the new gospel advocates toward using the terms "saved" and "salvation" interchangeably with terms such as "eternal life," "justification," or "regeneration." The reason for this appears to be theologically driven and not merely as the result of a fresh, diachronic study of the terms "save" and "salvation." It is now being claimed, for example, that the old gospel has too much emphasis upon the whole notion of "sin" with respect to evangelizing the lost, whereas the fundamental issue that the unregenerate need to be informed of is the matter of "life" or "eternal life."[2] However, there are several key evangelistic passages employing the word "saved" or "salvation" that oppose the crossless position by requiring Christ's deity, death for sin, and resurrection as the very contents of saving faith (Mark 16:15-16; Luke 24:45-47; Acts 16:30-31; Rom. 1:16; 10:9-10; 1 Cor. 1:18, 21; 15:1-4). Consequently, such passages must be systematically reinterpreted in order to protect the solvency of the crossless system of theology.

---

[2] John Niemelä, "Objects of Faith in John: A Matter of Person AND Content," Chafer Theological Seminary Conference, Houston, TX, March 2006. Niemelä also writes, "1 John 2:2 says that Christ is the propitiation for the sins of believers and for the sins of the whole world. However, it does not specify the content that one needs to believe in order to receive eternal life. Though the sin issue is important, John does not present it as the fundamental one facing the unbeliever." Niemelä, "The Message of Life," 160.

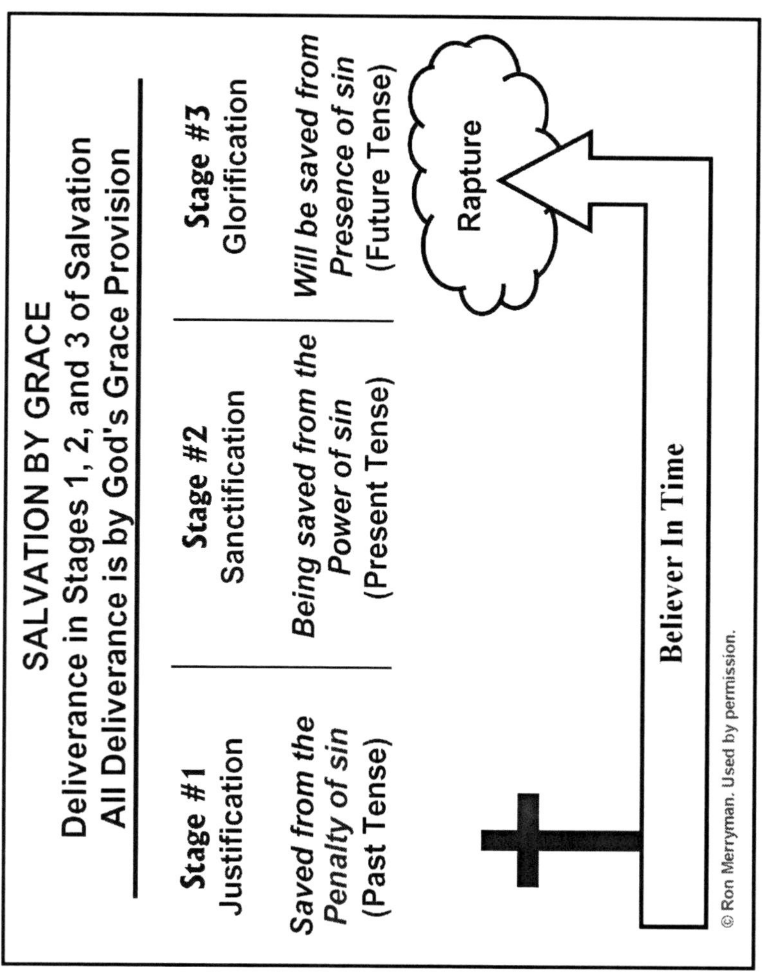

Now the terms "save" (Gr. *sōzō*) and "salvation" (Gr. *sōtēria*) are being understood by many crossless adherents to apply almost exclusively to a present process for Christians and non-Christians alike whereby we escape only the *temporal* wrath of God in this lifetime by our obedience and repentance.[3] This is reflected in the following statement from Bob Wilkin:

> Obviously Romans 3 and 4 has a section on justification, 3:21 to the end of chapter 4. But again, that's instructing believers, not really teaching how to evangelize. Romans is not designed to lead people to faith in Christ. Another big problem is the word

[3] Robert N. Wilkin, "The Three Tenses of Salvation Reconsidered," audiotape, Grace Evangelical Society, 2003.

> "salvation." The Greek word is *"sotēria."* Salvation in Romans is not deliverance from hell. . . . In the Book of Romans, salvation is to the believer, telling the believer how the believer can be saved from God's wrath here and now. God hates iniquity. And God judges those who suppress His truth, and that includes the believer. We find that in the Book of Romans in order to escape God's wrath, you must believe and you must confess Christ. You must be a confessing, honest Christian who is walking in the light in order to be one who escapes God's wrath. Believing in Jesus in Romans is not enough to escape the wrath of God in this life.[4]

Even the legitimacy of distinguishing "three tenses" of salvation is now being openly challenged. With respect to the "past tense" of salvation, Wilkin also claims:

> The point is, if a person was taught that when you look at the past tense of the word "save" in the New Testament, it means salvation from the penalty of sin, I can't find even one clear example of it, if they do exist. What I can find is many examples where it's referring to physical healing, physical deliverance . . . this sort of thing.[5]

One leading Free Grace figure personally told this author that he no longer knows what "second tense salvation" means. Having an advanced seminary degree and having formerly used this terminology himself, he was saying in essence that he now refuses to even recognize the usage of the expression "second tense salvation" as a biblically accurate description of the believer's practical growth in holiness and sanctification.

Forgiveness

In addition to these departures in the area of salvation, there is also a new soteriological twist being placed upon the doctrine of "forgiveness" by proponents of the crossless content of saving faith. This constitutes a fourth doctrinal domino falling. They are now claiming that the concept of "forgiveness" in Scripture is not properly soteriological but is strictly a matter of fellowship between God and one who is already regenerated as a child of God.[6] Biblically, they say, there is no such thing as a "forensic" or "judicial," once-for-all forgiveness, only "fellowship" forgiveness. This new doctrine appears directly attributable to Zane Hodges. Wilkin

---

[4] Robert N. Wilkin, *Why the Romans Road Ends in a Cul de Sac,* G.E.S. Grace Conference, March 1, 2006 (ellipsis added).

[5] Wilkin, *The Three Tenses of Salvation Reconsidered* (ellipsis added). While no one disputes the fact that the semantic range of the terms "save" and "salvation" in both the Hebrew OT and Greek NT include physical, temporal deliverance, and that this in fact is the most frequent contextual meaning of the term/s in the OT, this still does not negate the many occurrences of "save/salvation" referring to spiritual deliverance in all three tenses.

[6] Hodges, *The Gospel Under Siege,* 118; idem, *Harmony with God,* 70-75.

explains, "Around the turn of the century (2001), he came out with a book called *Harmony with God*. While ostensibly about repentance, it has a wonderful discussion of forgiveness. Here he breaks new ground of what forgiveness is. He sees repentance as a fellowship issue, not a relationship issue."[7] Two followers of Hodges's teaching on forgiveness, John Niemelä and Hank Hildebrandt, explained this new view while participating in a panel discussion sponsored by the Grace Evangelical Society on the role of the cross in evangelism. In the following transcription of that panel discussion, notice how forgiveness of sins has been relegated to being simply a second tense salvation issue:

John Niemelä: "What is needed in order for the person to be able to stand before God deals with judicial issues: justification, expiation, all those big sixty-four dollar words and so on and so forth. Forgiveness is not one of those terms. Forgiveness is a fellowship type of a concept, to be able to have free communication back and forth."

Hank Hildebrandt: "When Jesus died on the cross and secured—was a propitiation for the whole world—He freed God to be able to give eternal life. The righteous demands of God's justice were met, but this is not something that really needs to be transparent to the person who believes. They don't have to understand all this. What they need to understand is that God is in a position to be able to grant eternal life. Now of course when someone is granted eternal life they are also born into God's family; they become a member of the family. And so back to what John is saying here [in 1 John 1], the matter of fellowship. God wants to have fellowship with His children. And so when a person is born again, he receives the forgiveness of sins so that immediately when he is born into God's family he can have fellowship with his heavenly Father. When he sins, then he has to do the things that John talks about in 1 John 1 so that he can be restored to fellowship because fellowship is broken by sin. So the matter of sin and the matter of forgiveness as John [Niemelä] just said is a matter dealing with fellowship with the Father and really has nothing to do with our eternal destiny."[8]

Eternal Life

There is also another aspect of soteriology being affected by the new crossless gospel that represents more of an imbalance than another doctrinal domino falling. In addition to the strange soteriological departures regarding the terms "salvation" and "forgiveness," there is also now an imbalanced

[7] Bob Wilkin, "Zane Hodges: The New Testament Scholar Who Actually Studied the New Testament," *JOTGES* 21 (Autumn 2008): 8.

[8] John Niemelä and Hank Hildebrandt, "The Bible Answer Men," Grace Evangelical Society Seattle Regional Conference, September 29, 2007 (brackets inserted).

emphasis being placed upon the biblical truth of "eternal life." Since the new doctrinal system of the crossless gospel considers "eternal life" to be an indispensable element of saving faith, this has led some adherents to consider other soteriological terms and concepts to be insufficient for a lost person's regeneration. It is not enough that people be evangelized with the good news that God will "save" them or "forgive" them; they must have explicit knowledge of God's promise of "everlasting life."[9] This has led to egregious examples of eisegesis, as crossless advocates, driven by the need for doctrinal consistency, are reading their theology into biblical passages, finding the phrase or concept of "everlasting life" even where it does not occur in God's Word.[10] Apparently the entire branch of systematic theology known as "soteriology"—the doctrine of salvation (*sōtēria*)—has been mislabeled. Theologians should have designated it, "zoology," since "salvation" is really a mere sub-category of the more prominent doctrine of "life" (*zōē*) or eternal life.[11]

Where this whole new concept of "salvation" will end up is anybody's guess. It seems there is no such thing as "steady-state theology" with some Free Grace advocates these days. Even the most basic doctrines of Scripture, such as salvation, are now subject to change. But should it really come as any surprise that once the gospel changed, the most foundational doctrine of all, the doctrine of salvation was not far behind? For if the message to the lost has now been falsely dichotomized to be about Jesus guaranteeing *eternal life* rather than dying for our sins, and if *"salvation"* is now primarily about escaping God's judgment in our Christian lives due to sin, then *"salvation"* must now be dealing almost exclusively with the Christian's physical, earthly life, rather than *eternal life*. The shift on the gospel has affected the doctrines of salvation, forgiveness, and eternal life.

Wrath

This has also led logically, if not chronologically, to the tipping of a fifth domino, namely the doctrine of God's *wrath*. Since "salvation" is now regarded to be fundamentally a matter of Christians escaping God's physical, temporal judgment due to sin in our lives, and since this is the same type of temporal, physical, divine judgment *the unregenerate* are presently subject to, this must mean that Christians are also subject to the wrath of God in this lifetime for our sins and disobedience. But since the wrath of God now applies equally to the regenerate and unregenerate alike, and since Christians will not suffer in hell like the unregenerate, this must also mean that, logically, God's wrath is poured out only in the present, not the eternal future. Crossless gospel advocate, Zane Hodges, explained this

[9] Wilkin, *Secure and Sure*, 74-75.

[10] Hodges, *Did Paul Preach Eternal Life?* 10, 15.

[11] Ibid., 27-28.

new view of "wrath" and the primary underlying New Testament word for "wrath" (*orgē*), saying:

> There is not a single NT example of this word where it refers unambiguously to the experience of eternal punishment. Every NT instance of God's *orgē* can be understood as a reference to the temporal display of God's displeasure with human sin.[12]

The new crossless theology of God's wrath teaches that disobedient Christians are presently under the wrath of God and also that there is no such thing in the Bible as God's *eternal wrath* for the unsaved in hell. Apparently, Christians who have assumed such for centuries have all been wrong. But is this really true? What saith the Scriptures? There simply are no passages in the New Testament which teach that Christians, whether carnal or spiritual, are subjects of the direct outpouring of the wrath of God. In fact, not only are believers in Christ promised exemption from God's wrath due to Christ's propitiatory work and our unique, heavenly, Church-age position in Him (Rom. 5:9-10; 1 Thess. 1:10; 5:9), but it is unbelievers alone who are distinctively characterized as the ones who experience the direct judgment of God's wrath (John 3:36; Eph. 2:3; 5:6; Col. 3:6; 1 Thess. 2:16). And God's wrath upon the unsaved is eternal, not merely temporal (Rom. 2:5-9; 2 Thess. 1:6-9; Rev. 14:10-11). The doctrine of the wrath of God is at least the fifth doctrinal domino to fall in conjunction with the new, crossless view.

Repentance

Related to the new doctrine of God's wrath is the new doctrine of *repentance*. It was once the consistently held view among Free Grace advocates that the term itself simply, and always in its context, means "a change of mind." In eternal salvation contexts, it refers to that change of mind that is inherent to faith in Christ. Now repentance is regarded by many Free Grace people to be a remorseful turning from sin. This, they say, is something God expects even the unsaved to do, like the city of Nineveh, in order to avoid His wrath being poured out in temporal, physical judgment. This view also appears to have originated with Zane Hodges. Wilkin explains:

> In 1990, while he was on the board of my ministry, Grace Evangelical Society, he came out with his book *Absolutely Free! A Biblical Reply to Lordship Salvation*. It was a response to the Lordship Salvation position and especially to John MacArthur's 1988 book, *The Gospel According to Jesus*. At our winter board meeting that year the other GES board members begged him to drop the chapter on repentance. In that chapter he argued that repentance is not a condition of eternal life. They said it would ruin his book. He insisted on keeping that chapter in the book. Today many think that the view he advocated is the Free Grace view on repen-

[12] Zane C. Hodges, "The Message of Romans," *The Kerugma Message* 6 (February 1997): 1.

> tance. While it isn't yet the view, it is amazing how many people have come to adopt this position, myself included.[13]

What exactly is Hodges's new view of repentance? He succinctly summarized his position, stating:

> In this series on the doctrine of repentance, we have reached two fundamental conclusions. These are: (1) that repentance is not in any way a condition for eternal salvation; and (2) repentance is the decision to turn from sin to avoid, or bring to an end, God's temporal judgment. All the statements about repentance by the inspired writers of Scripture are consistent with these two basic principles, whether or not the repenting party or parties are saved or unsaved.[14]

While space does not permit a thorough scriptural reply to the new, crossless doctrine of repentance, it is sufficient for now to simply object that this is another unbiblical development. In the New Testament, the noun "repentance" (*metanoia*) and verb "repent" (*metanoeō*) simply speak of a "change of mind." Just as the word "gospel" in the New Testament always has the basic meaning of "good news" with the particular type of good news determined by the context, even so the words "repent" and "repentance" always mean "a change of the mind" with the particular object repented about determined by the context.[15]

---

[13] Wilkin, "Zane Hodges: The New Testament Scholar," 8. Indeed, it is amazing and regrettable that many Free Grace people have followed Hodges's unique teaching on repentance, especially Wilkin himself, who previously wrote an outstanding doctoral dissertation on repentance that was a major contribution to Free Grace theology. Robert N. Wilkin, "Repentance as a Condition for Salvation in the New Testament" (Th.D. dissertation, Dallas Theological Seminary, 1985).

[14] Zane C. Hodges, "Repentance and the Day of the Lord," *Grace in Focus* (September 1999): 1.

[15] In making this claim I am keenly aware of the root fallacy whereby the meaning of a word is determined simply on the basis of its etymology or philology rather than its current (synchronic) usage in a given context (see James Barr, "The Synchronic, the Diachronic and the Historical: A Triangular Relationship," in *Synchronic or Diachronic? A Debate on Method in Old Testament Exegesis*, ed. Johannes C. de Moor [Leiden: E. J. Brill, 1995], 1-14; D. A. Carson, *Exegetical Fallacies* [Grand Rapids: Baker Book House, 1984], 26-32; Moisés Silva, *Biblical Words and their Meaning: An Introduction to Lexical Semantics*, rev. ed. [Grand Rapids: Zondervan, 1994], 18-22). I am also well aware of the common practice of pouring into one particular occurrence of a word its entire, collective, semantic range, otherwise known as the illegitimate totality transfer. These problems have been well known in biblical studies for the last half century since James Barr's epochal book, *The Semantics of Biblical Languages*, changed the lexicological landscape. Though the semantic value of a biblical word is not determined on the basis of etymology, this does not mean that it *cannot* share its etymological meaning (as with *metanoia* and *euangelion*). My theological conclusions about repentance are based on a systematic, exegetical study of the various biblical terms and lexeme for repentance used in their individual contexts. When this process is followed, I am still convinced it yields the conclusion that repentance (at least in the case of *metanoia* and *metanoeō*) is always a change of mind, whether in respect to God, self, sin, salvation, or the Savior.

If the term "repent" means "a decision to turn from sin," as many crossless Free Grace people are now claiming, then this would be tautological in passages where the prepositional phrases "from sin" or "of sin" follow the command to repent (Acts 8:22; 2 Cor. 12:21; Heb. 6:1; Rev. 2:21-22; 9:20-21; 16:11). If the basic meaning of the word "repent" consistently means, "to turn from sin," then it would lead to the nonsensical redundancy, "(turn from sin) from sin." Therefore, a change of mind about the Lord Jesus Christ and the salvation He offers to undeserving sinners is inherent in the act of believing in Him (Luke 24:46-47; Acts 11:14-18; 20:21).[16]

Furthermore, repentance is not a work (Acts 26:20). It is also distinct from remorse for sin (2 Cor. 7:8-10; Heb. 12:17). Though some degree of remorseful turning from sin often accompanies repentance, it is not the same as repentance.

---

[16] In Hodges's book on repentance, there is no attempt to reconcile his theological conclusions about repentance with the syntactical significance of Acts 20:21 and the phrase, *"repentance toward and faith toward our Lord Jesus Christ."* At one point, after citing Acts 20:21, Hodges concludes that "repentance and faith are by no means synonymous. They are distinct issues" (see Zane C. Hodges, *Harmony With God: A Fresh Look at Repentance* [Dallas: Redención Viva, 2001], 86). However, in Acts 20:21, the expression *"repentance toward God and faith toward our Lord Jesus Christ"* contains a grammatical construction in which the terms "repentance" and "faith" are inseparably connected. The nouns *metanoian* ("repentance") and *pistin* ("faith") are both accusative, feminine, singular, joined by *kai* ("and") and preceded by one article in the same case, gender, and number (accusative, feminine, singular). It is literally, *"**the** repentance toward God and faith toward our Lord Jesus Christ."* There are other examples of similar grammatical constructions in the Greek NT that have great theological significance, such as Titus 2:13, which says, *"the great God and our Savior, Jesus Christ."* This is a very strong attestation of Christ's deity. Though the words "God" and "Savior" have distinctive emphases in terms of their meaning, they are inseparably connected to one another and refer to one and the same Person in terms of identity. As this pertains to Acts 20:21, *"repentance toward God"* does not have exactly the same shade of meaning as *"faith toward Jesus Christ,"* but the two terms (faith, repentance) cannot be conceptually or soteriologically separated from each other as Hodges proposes. A person cannot have faith in Christ without having had a change of mind (repentance) toward God, anymore than a person could have a Savior who is not God (Titus 2:13) or a predetermined plan of God that was not also foreknown by God (Acts 2:23), or a pastor given to a church by Christ who is not also a teacher (Eph. 4:11). Just as it is impossible for people to believe in Christ without also experiencing a change of mind regarding some aspect of divine revelation, even so it is impossible to believe in Christ without having repented. Repentance is inherent to believing though semantically distinguishable from it. It is like saying that in order to be saved, a person must *know* about Christ and *believe* in Him (John 6:69; 17:8; 1 Tim. 2:4). *Knowing* is inherent to *believing* and inseparable from it, just as repentance is to faith. Commenting on the grammatical significance of Acts 20:21, Greek grammarian Daniel Wallace states, "The evidence suggests that, in Luke's usage, saving faith *includes* repentance. In those texts which speak simply of faith, a 'theological shorthand' seems to be employed: Luke envisions repentance as the inceptive act of which the entirety may be called πίστις. Thus, for Luke, conversion is not a two-step process, but one step, faith-but the kind of faith that *includes* repentance. This, of course, fits well with the frequent idiom of first subset of second for impersonal TSKS constructions" (Daniel B. Wallace, *Greek Grammar Beyond the Basics: An Exegetical Syntax of the New Testament* [Grand Rapids: Zondervan, 1996], 289).

In addition, when repentance is properly understood, it is seen to be a clear scriptural condition for escaping God's eternal condemnation (Matt. 12:41; Luke 11:32; 16:30-31; 24:47; Acts 17:30-31; Rom. 2:4-5; 2 Peter 3:9). In some instances, this eternal judgment also commences with God's temporal judgment upon the lost at the moment of physical death.

The new, crossless doctrine of repentance is not only at variance with Scripture, it represents another entirely new theological position in the evangelical world. Crossless gospel advocates now claim that repentance is *not* a requirement for receiving eternal life, but *it is* a condition for escaping God's physical judgment upon disobedient Christians. The new *definition* of repentance as a remorseful decision to turn from sin agrees with the Lordship Salvation definition, but not with the traditional Free Grace definition. However, by claiming that repentance is not a *condition* for eternal salvation, they are no longer in agreement with either the historic Free Grace doctrine of repentance or the Lordship Salvation doctrine. They have once again carved out an entirely new, distinct, third theological position. So far we have seen that the shifting crossless gospel has required the dominos of progressive revelation, salvation, forgiveness, wrath, and repentance to fall; but there is at least one more doctrinal domino that is beginning to totter.

Faith

There may also be developing a new doctrine of faith. Admittedly, this is not as developed as the other doctrinal departures, but there already exists with some crossless adherents an alarming new antipathy toward the use of the term "trust" in the place of "faith." The crossless doctrine of faith claims that the terms for "believe" (*pisteuō*) and "faith" (*pistis*) in the New Testament primarily mean to be passively "persuaded" or "convinced" and that the meaning of active "trust" is secondary and rare, if it's even a permissible synonym at all. As with the terms "saved" and "salvation" not applying to eternal life, some crossless proponents have also developed a strong aversion toward commanding the lost to "trust" in the Lord Jesus Christ for eternal salvation. Initially this developed in response to the imbalance of other evangelical Christians who almost always substitute the term "trust" for the valid, scriptural term "believe" in their evangelism.[17] However, the pendulum has swung too far in the other direction, as some are now seeking to "purge" themselves of the use of "trust" in their

---

[17] This should not be confused with the classic Reformed understanding that faith contains the element of *fiducia*, understood by those espousing Reformed/Lordship Salvation theology to mean commitment or obedience, rather than simple reliance or dependence upon the person and work of Christ. It should be noted that the new G.E.S. doctrine of faith is not necessarily a response to this Reformed, Lordship position. It is a response to fellow Free Grace brethren who purportedly have over-emphasized the word "trust" and regard it to be preferable to the more frequent biblical translation of "believe." It is also a response to those who make the sole condition of faith in Christ for eternal life a matter of steps (i.e., first believe the facts about Christ then trust in Him).

preaching and teaching on faith. Once again, Bob Wilkin exemplifies this new position, explaining his own shift on "trust" as follows:

> And about ten years ago, I was visiting with a friend, and that friend was Zane Hodges. I was in his office and we were talking and I said something about people trusting in Jesus for eternal life. And he said, "Why did you say it that way?" I'm like, "What way? I said trusting in Jesus for eternal life." Right, why didn't you say "believing in Jesus for everlasting life"? I said, "Well, you know, it's the same thing, right, I mean you know, trusting." He said, but what does the Bible say? Well, I said, "Aaahh, believing, yeah it says believing in Him, yeah. I can't think of any verses where it says trusting in Him." He said, "I can't either." He said, "Well, why is it that you talk about trusting in Jesus instead of believing in Jesus?" I said, "Well, you know, it's the same thing." He said, "Well, if it's the same thing why don't you do what the Bible says?" So, about ten years ago, I changed. And I tried to purge myself from talking about "trusting in Jesus" and I tried to talk about "believing in Jesus."[18]

How this new doctrine has bearing upon the gospel is still not altogether clear, however it appears to be connected to the crossless gospel's teaching that eternal life is conditioned solely upon becoming convinced or persuaded of the *promise* of eternal life in Jesus, not by trusting or relying upon His *work* on our behalf. With the increased emphasis now upon the promise or guarantee of eternal life, there seems to be a corresponding de-emphasis on the work of Christ and the need to trust in, or rely upon, that finished work.

But once again, the crossless position simply exceeds the bounds of Scripture in its claims, for "trust" *is* a valid, biblical synonym for the noun "faith" and the verb "believe." While it is certainly true that the Greek words normally translated "faith" (*pistis*) or "believe" (*pisteuō; peithō*) all include the idea of being persuaded (Acts 28:24), they also include the idea of trust, reliance, or dependence. There is no contradiction between trust and persuasion, for they are both descriptive of biblical faith.[19] In some passages, "trust" is even the translation in many English Bibles (Matt. 27:43; Mark 10:24 [MT]; Luke 11:22; 16:11; 18:9; 2 Cor. 1:9; 1 Tim. 1:11; Heb. 2:13). There is no separate word for "trust" in Greek besides the words normally translated "believe" or "faith," or even at times, "hope" (*elpizō*). Trusting in Christ is inherent to believing in Him, just as repenting about Christ is inherent to faith in Him (Acts 20:21).

---

[18] Robert N. Wilkin, *Trusting in Christ is Not Quite the Same as Believing in Him*, Grace Evangelical Society Conference, March 1, 2006.

[19] George E. Meisinger, "Salvation by Faith Alone," in *The Fundamentals for the Twenty-First Century: Examining the Crucial Issues of the Christian Faith*, ed. Mal Couch (Grand Rapids: Kregel, 2000), 281-82.

Refinement or Abandonment?

There can be no question that things have changed in the Free Grace movement, but change is not inherently bad. The question is really whether these changes constitute a *refinement* of biblical doctrine or an *abandonment* of the truths which grace-oriented brethren of the past and present have believed and earnestly contended for. So, we must ask, are these recent changes in Free Grace theology a *development* in our understanding of the doctrines of God's Word, or are they a *departure*? This is the very debate currently taking place within dispensationalism regarding the recent aberrational teachings of progressive dispensationalism.[20] Is progressive dispensationalism still truly dispensationalism, or is it a third, separate, mediating position between dispensationalism and covenant theology? Do the "developments" claimed by progressives represent *refinement* of dispensationalism or *abandonment* in the direction of covenant theology?

Certainly there can be room for interpretational differences of opinion that can lead to doctrinal refinement rather than doctrinal departure. To illustrate the difference between doctrinal departure and doctrinal refinement, consider the example of how to interpret the phrase, *"born of water,"* in John 3:5. It says, *"Jesus answered, "Most assuredly, I say to you, unless one is born of water and the Spirit, he cannot enter the kingdom of God."*

This verse has been subject to various interpretations, some of which fall within the same acceptable, doctrinal framework, while other interpretations lead to the unscriptural and unacceptable doctrine of baptismal regeneration. Among those who rightly reject baptismal regeneration, the expression *"born of water and the Spirit"* has been interpreted at least three different ways. Some interpret it to mean, *"born of water, even (kai) the Spirit."* This is the ascensive use of the Greek conjunction *kai*, making water a metaphor of the Spirit. Others interpret "water" as metaphorical of the Word of God, in keeping with Ephesians 5:26. They understand John 3:5 to be saying, *"born of the washing of water by the Word and the Spirit."* Thirdly, "water" in this passage can be interpreted to simply mean *"water"*—the water expelled from a woman's womb in the physical birth process.[21]

All three interpretations are doctrinally acceptable in upholding salvation by grace. However, the third interpretation, in my estimation, is the most contextually and exegetically sound; and it represents a refinement of the non-baptismal regeneration position. However, to interpret "water" to be a reference to "water baptism" would be an interpretation that leads to a completely different doctrinal position. This would be a

---

[20] See Charles Ryrie, "Update on Dispensationalism," in *Issues in Dispensationalism*, ed. Wesley R. Willis and John R. Master (Chicago: Moody Press, 1994), 14-27; George Zeller, "Development or Departure?" in *Progressive Dispensationalism: An Analysis of the Movement and Defense of Traditional Dispensationalism*, ed. Ron J. Bigalke (Lanham, Maryland: University Press of America, 2005), 157-77.

[21] Ben Witherington III, "The Waters of Birth: John 3.5 and 1 John 5.6-8," *NTS* 35 (1989): 155-60.

departure. It is my contention that the manner in which some Free Grace proponents have reinterpreted whole series of Scripture passages has *not* led to the refinement of our over-all doctrinal position. It has led to different doctrines altogether.

Crossless advocates are not interpreting Scripture within the same doctrinal framework merely to bolster pre-existing Free Grace theology; they are now taking hermeneutical liberties to such an extent that they are developing entirely new doctrines. In the process, they are forcing the interpretation of whole series of passages in order to fit their new doctrinal conclusions. This wholesale realignment of Scripture has gone beyond refinement of our doctrinal position to the actual abandonment of a sizeable portion of it. It's like a car brought to an auto repair shop for an engine tune-up. The mechanic says he must replace a couple parts in your engine with some new ones. However, when you pick up your car, you discover that he has actually rebuilt a sizeable portion of your engine so that it is virtually a different engine.

It is my contention that the new, crossless theology has gone well beyond *refinement* of the truth to actual *abandonment* of certain truths. To see this, simply ask yourself whether whole doctrines are being either refined or abandoned. When it comes to the *contents of faith* required to be believed for eternal salvation, has there been a refinement of what Free Grace believers have held to be true or has there been an abandonment? There has clearly been an abandonment, as the deity, sacrificial death, and resurrection of Christ are now no longer necessary to be believed. Zane Hodges even expressed his desire that Christians *"abandon"* the form of evangelistic invitation that makes the cross-work of Christ the defining issue of what a sinner must believe for eternal life.

Secondly, when it comes to the very *definition of "the gospel"* preached to the lost, has there been a refinement or an abandonment? Again, to include the necessity to believe in the cross, resurrection, and deity of Christ is now considered to be "adding to the gospel." The gospel containing the cross, resurrection, and deity of Christ is now considered by crossless proponents to be a fuller gospel, necessary only for the sanctification of Christians. With the very definition of "the gospel" there has been an abandonment of a once universally held position within the Grace camp.

Thirdly, with respect to the doctrine of *salvation* applying almost exclusively to physical, temporal deliverance from judgment rather than eternal deliverance, has there been a refinement or an abandonment? There has been an abandonment of the usage of the term "salvation" by some when referring to either justification, sanctification, or glorification.

Fourthly, when it comes to the doctrine of *forgiveness*, has there been a refinement or an abandonment? There has been an abandonment, or a loss, of a once consistently held doctrine among Free Grace Christians. Crossless advocates no longer believe that Scripture ever uses the term "forgiveness" to refer to a forensic, legal, or once-for-all forgiveness from

God, but only a forgiveness for daily fellowship with God.

Fifthly, when it comes to the doctrine of the *wrath of God*, has there been a refinement or an abandonment? Again, there has been an abandonment, a subtraction, of the *eternal* aspect of God's wrath. One could even say there has also been an addition with this doctrine, in the sense that some are claiming that even Christians now are subject to the wrath of God, whereas before Christians were considered to be exempt from God's wrath. But from the standpoint of the Christian's spiritual blessings in Christ, this must actually be viewed as a subtraction, a loss, or an abandonment, since according to the crossless position we are no longer promised shelter from all of God's wrath, even though we are "in Christ."

Sixthly, with *repentance* being redefined to mean a turning from sin instead of a change of mind and with repentance also no longer being a requirement for eternal life, does this constitute a refinement or a definite abandonment? There has been an abandonment of a previously held doctrinal position, as both the definition of repentance and the condition of repentance have changed.

Lastly, regarding the doctrine of *faith*, we are currently facing the possibility of losing the term "trust" as a valid synonym for faith. While Scripture teaches that biblical faith involves both trust and persuasion, has there been a refinement of the doctrine of faith or a loss of vital truth, i.e., an abandonment? Previously, both Free Grace and Lordship proponents were consistently in agreement that "trust" was an essential element of "saving faith," but once again we could be facing the emergence of a third, entirely new doctrinal view of faith.

Over and over again the truths once held to be sacred and scriptural by those in the Free Grace camp are being abandoned for entirely new doctrines. And this has all occurred within only the last 15-20 years! Where will the Free Grace movement be in 50 years, assuming the Lord tarries, if we do not rectify these problems now? The time has long since passed to give these Free Grace leaders the benefit of the doubt. I never imagined when I joined the Grace Evangelical Society in its infancy that I would be hearing its leaders boldly denouncing as "theological legalism" an evangelistic message that requires belief in Christ's deity, substitutionary death, and resurrection. I never imagined I would be hearing them say that informing the lost of their need to believe these truths is actually "adding to the gospel" in the same way that Lordship Salvationists and cults add extra-biblical conditions to faith alone in Christ. Nor did I ever expect that these men would be replacing other well-established doctrines of Scripture with new doctrines of their own. Things have changed for the worse in G.E.S. theology; they are devolving rather than improving. The train of Grace has somehow gotten seriously off track with some in the Free Grace community. We must, therefore, find the necessary courage from the Lord to decisively and biblically begin repudiating this new false doctrine and its attendant deviations.

Chapter 3

Why the Crossless Gospel?

OVERVIEW

The new crossless gospel stems from at least four main convictions held by its supporters. First, they believe that John's many evangelistic passages found in his Gospel do not require belief in Christ's person and work to receive eternal life but only simple belief in the name of "Jesus." Second, they now interpret the expression "the Christ, the Son of God" in John 11:27 and 20:31 in a unique way to mean simply that Jesus is the guarantor of eternal life, not necessarily that He is God-incarnate who died for our sins and rose from the dead. Third, they believe that the message of guaranteed eternal life is what Scripture emphasizes as the evangelistic message for the lost instead of the message of the cross. Lastly, in a misguided effort to uphold the grace of God, they have come to the conviction that requiring belief in Christ's deity, humanity, death for sin, and resurrection for eternal life is requiring too much information. It is now considered to be "adding to the gospel."

By now, you might be asking, "How did such doctrines ever arise within Free Grace theology? And why would anyone come up with a crossless gospel anyway?" Well, there are reasons to be sure. Several of those reasons will be spelled out in this chapter in order to understand this new gospel from the perspective of its own supporters. Everyone has reasons for what they believe. Whether those reasons are biblical and valid is our only real concern. Of course, even heretical sects and cults claim support from Scripture for their beliefs, and the promoters of the new G.E.S. gospel are no exception. Their sincerity is unquestionable as they believe they are now simply following Scripture more faithfully. But we can, and must, call into question the scriptural soundness of their conclusions.

The Gospel of John

The new, crossless gospel cannot be comprehended without understanding how its supporters interpret the Gospel of John. Their unique hermeneutical approach to John's Gospel is a principal cause behind the emergence of the crossless gospel. Students of John's Gospel have always recognized that it is structured around a series of signs accomplished by the Lord Jesus that prove that He is the Christ, the Son of God. This is by divine design, as the purpose statement for the entire Gospel indicates in John 20:30-31. These verses state: *"And truly Jesus did many other signs in the presence of His disciples, which are not written in this book; but these are written that you may believe that Jesus is the Christ, the Son of God, and that believing you may have life in His name."*

From this passage, crossless gospel proponents claim that believing in Christ's death and resurrection (the last of John's recorded signs) is not essential for receiving eternal life. They deduce this from the fact that verse 31 speaks of "signs" (in the plural) that can lead a person to believe in Jesus as the Christ for his or her eternal life. They say that in his purpose statement at John 20:30-31, John was declaring that any one of these signs done during Christ's pre-cross ministry was sufficient to show that Jesus was the Christ.

Since the crossless doctrine of Jesus being "the Christ" means simply that He is the one who can guarantee eternal life but not necessarily that He died for our sins and rose again, they reason that if someone believes what any *one* of these signs indicates (that Jesus is "the Christ," the guarantor of eternal life), then such a person will receive eternal life. They allege that since the purpose statement of John's Gospel (20:30-31) was written *after* all these signs (including the crucifixion and resurrection) at the end of his Gospel, then people *today* are required to believe only that Jesus is the guarantor of eternal life in order to receive eternal life, not to believe that He is God-incarnate who died for our sins and rose again. In other words, they interpret this purpose statement of John to be teaching that what God required people to believe about Christ for eternal life *prior* to Calvary is exactly what He requires the world to believe about Christ now, *after* Calvary.

This conclusion has consequences for the entire doctrine of progressive revelation, which will be thoroughly examined in chapter 7. One proponent of this view, John Niemelä, has written at least three articles on the subject, with several more articles on John stated to be forthcoming.[1] He summarizes the new hermeneutical perspective on John's Gospel, saying:

> John keeps the signs distinct from the message of life, so evangelicals must not confuse them either. John does not set forth the sign of the cross-and-resurrection as the message that one must believe in order to receive eternal life. In other words, even after the cross-and-resurrection, John's message remains the same as in John 5:24 and 6:47. . . This message is consistent with the fact that Old Testament believers possessed eternal life, even though they died before the cross paid their penalty of sin. The gift of eternal life came to those people in Old Testament times that believed in the coming One who gives eternal life and would resurrect them in the future. Although as Hebrews 11 says, Abraham died without receiving (in his lifetime) what God had promised him. Even so, he believed the message of life. John shows that this remains the manner of salvation, even after Jesus' death and resurrection. Eternal life is a gift received the moment anyone believes that Jesus Christ has given him/her eternal life.[2]

Zane Hodges has also explained the role that their unique interpretation of John 20:30-31 plays in arriving at a crossless, resurrectionless gospel:

> This statement does not affirm the necessity of believing in our Lord's substitutionary atonement. If by the time of the writing of John's Gospel, it was actually necessary to believe this, then it would have been not only simple, but essential, to say so. Inasmuch as the key figures in John's narrative *did* believe in Jesus before they understood His atoning death and resurrection, it would have been even more essential for John to state that the

---

[1] John Niemelä, "The Message of Life in the Gospel of John," *CTSJ* 7 (July-Sept. 2001): 2-20; "The Cross in John's Gospel," *JOTGES* 16 (Spring 2003): 17-28; idem, "Objects of Faith in John: A Matter of Person AND Content," paper prepared for the Chafer Theological Seminary Bible Conference, Houston, TX, March 2006.

[2] John Niemelä, "The Message of Life in the Gospel of John," *CTSJ* 7 (July-Sept. 2001): 18 (ellipsis added).

> content of faith had changed. But of course he does not do this. The simple fact is that the whole Fourth Gospel is designed to show that its readers can get saved the same way as the people who got saved in John's narrative. To say anything other than this is to accept a fallacy. It is to mistakenly suppose that the Fourth Gospel presents the terms of salvation incompletely and inadequately. I sincerely hope no grace person would want to be stuck with a position like that. Let me repeat. Neither explicitly nor implicitly does the Gospel of John teach that a person must understand the cross to be saved. It just does not teach this. If we say that it does, we are reading something into the text and not reading something out of it![3]

Not only does the previous quote from Hodges reveal the new reasoning for how the Gospel of John should be interpreted, but it also demonstrates the level of conviction he possessed on this topic. It is a very bold claim to say that the entirety of evangelical Christianity, including the rest of the Free Grace camp who interpret John to be requiring belief in Christ's cross-work and resurrection for eternal life, are somehow guilty of an exegetical *"fallacy."* Without using the customary theological terms, he is claiming here that anyone who interprets John this way is guilty of eisegesis ("reading something into the text") instead of proper exegesis ("reading something out of it"). These contentions by Hodges cannot go unchallenged, and they will be addressed largely in chapters 15-17 which explain what it means for Jesus to be "the Christ."

The Christ, the Son of God

A second reason for the new crossless gospel comes from the unique meaning now being assigned to the phrase "the Christ, the Son of God" in John's Gospel. No longer does this phrase mean what it has traditionally been understood to mean. The phrase "the Son of God" has normally been interpreted to mean that Jesus is equal in deity with the Father, being God the "Son." For the lost to believe in Jesus as the "Son of God," as John 20:31 plainly requires, would seem to indicate that belief in Jesus' deity is essential for eternal life. But this is not their view.[4]

---

[3] Zane C. Hodges, "How to Lead People to Christ, Part 1: The Content of Our Message," *JOTGES* 13 (Autumn 2000): 6-7.

[4] Hodges states plainly that the phrase "Son of God" expresses "the deity of our Lord" and that He is a "divine person." Yet, strangely, Hodges does not require belief in Jesus as the "Son of God" for eternal life as John 3:16, 18; 11:27; 20:31, and many other passages require. He reasons, "In Jewish prophecy and theology the promised Christ was also the Son of God—that is, He was to be a divine person. Recall the words of Isaiah: "For unto us a Child is born, unto us a Son is given . . . and His name shall be called Wonderful, Counselor, Mighty God, Everlasting Father, Prince of Peace" (9:6-7). But in Samaritan theology, the Messiah was thought of as a prophet and the woman at the well is led to faith through our

Likewise, the phrase "the Christ" has traditionally been interpreted to mean that Jesus is the One who fulfills the Old Testament depictions of the Messiah who dies as a sacrifice for sin and rises from the dead to provide redemption for mankind. However, the crossless view of Hodges and others is that the combined phrase "the Christ, the Son of God" has a unique Johannine sense whereby it *only* means that Jesus is the guarantor of eternal life.

They arrive at their unique interpretation by noting that the exact phrase, "the Christ, the Son of God" (*ho Christos ho huios tou theou*), occurs only two times in the entire Gospel of John, once in John 11:27 and once in the purpose statement of John 20:30-31.[5] They reason that, therefore, John 11:27 must determine what John means in his purpose statement in 20:31 when he says, *"but these are written that you may believe that Jesus is the Christ, the Son of God, and that believing you may have life in His name."*

In John 11:26, Jesus says to Martha, *"whoever lives and believes in Me shall never die. Do you believe this?"* In response to Jesus' question about never dying (i.e. everlasting life), Martha does *not* respond directly in

---

Lord's prophetic ability to know her life. Her words, "Sir, I perceive that you are a prophet" (4:19) are a first step in the direction of recognizing Him as the Christ. There is no evidence that she or the other Samaritans understood the deity of our Lord. But they *did believe* that he was the Christ. And John tells us in his first epistle that "whoever believes that Jesus is the Christ is born of God" (5:1)! A full theology of His person is not necessary to salvation. If we believe that Jesus is the One who guarantees our eternal destiny, we have believed all we absolutely have to believe in order to be saved." Hodges, "How to Lead People to Christ, Part 1: The Content of our Message," 5.

[5] Curiously, proponents of the crossless gospel do not cite John 6:69 as a parallel passage to John 11:27 and 20:31 in order to further their unique definition of "the Christ, the Son of God," meaning simply the guarantor of eternal life. In John 6:68-69, Peter says, *"Lord, to whom shall we go? You have the words of eternal life. Also we have come to believe and know that You are the Christ, the Son of the living God."* Most proponents of the crossless gospel are also advocates of the Greek Majority Text as being the most faithful preservation of the original New Testament text. John 6:69 in the Greek Majority Text has virtually the identical expression as in John 11:27 and 20:31, *"the Christ, the Son of the living God"* (ὁ Χριστὸς ὁ υἱὸς τοῦ θεοῦ τοῦ ζῶντος). The only difference being the inclusion in John 6:69 of the adjectival phrase "the living" (τοῦ ζῶντος), which modifies "God." Among the many extant Greek manuscripts, there also exists at John 6:69 a slightly variant reading from the Majority Text which exactly matches John 11:27 and 20:31. At John 6:69, these manuscripts read: ὁ Χριστὸς ὁ υἱὸς τοῦ θεοῦ. This reading of 6:69 has some external manuscript support, being found in a few late uncial and minuscule manuscripts, along with the Syriac Sinaitic, Old Latin, Vulgate, and a few later versions. But it is doubtful as the original Greek text of 6:69 since it is absent from the early Greek papyri and uncials and even from most later minuscules. The only reading supported in Greek manuscripts prior to the 8th-9th century is the Critical Text reading found in the papyri ($\mathfrak{P}^{66,75}$) and uncials (א B C* D L W), which has *"the Holy One of God"* (ὁ ἅγιος τοῦ θεοῦ) or a slight variation, *"the Christ, the Holy One of God."* Regardless of whether the original text read, "the Christ, the Holy One of God" or "the Christ, the Son of (the living) God," both readings support the deity of Jesus. It is still curious why John 6:69 is not claimed by crossless gospel advocates in addition to John 11:27 as support for their unique interpretation of "the Christ" in John 20:31 as strictly meaning the guarantor of eternal life.

John 11:27 by saying, "Yes, Lord, I believe that all who believe in You shall never die." Rather, she *interprets* Jesus' promise of verse 26 by saying, *"Yes, Lord, I believe that You are the Christ, the Son of God, who is to come into the world."* In reference to John 11:27 in which Christ truly is presented as the guarantor of eternal life, Wilkin explains the crossless perspective saying, "The only other use of the phrase "the Christ, the Son of God" in John's Gospel is found in his purpose statement for the book (John 20:31), cited above. This suggests that biblical faith in Jesus as "the Christ, the Son of God," is the conviction that anyone who simply believes in Him is eternally secure."[6] Hodges also concurred claiming, "It is precisely the ability of Jesus to guarantee eternal life that makes Him the Christ in the Johannine sense of that term."[7]

It should be carefully distinguished at this point what they *are* claiming and what they are *not* claiming about Jesus being "the Christ." In arriving at their unique interpretation of the phrase, "the Christ, the Son of God," they are *not* denying that Jesus truly is deity as the "Son of God." Nor are they denying that He truly is "the Christ" who has fulfilled the Old Testament depictions of a Messiah who would die and rise again. They *are* orthodox in their personal beliefs about the deity of Jesus Christ and His vicarious death and bodily resurrection. Nor are they denying that Christ's deity, death for sin, and resurrection are absolutely necessary as the grounds upon which eternal life is even made possible. Nor are they denying that these truths are unnecessary for every Christian to believe for their practical sanctification and spiritual growth.

Specifically, what they *are* denying is that unbelievers must believe in the deity of Jesus and His death and resurrection in order to truly "believe in Him" and receive eternal life. They *are* claiming that to believe in Jesus as "the Christ" simply means to believe that He alone can guarantee eternal life on the sole condition of belief in Him. When someone believes that Jesus is the One who guarantees eternal life, they receive eternal life and are eternally secure from that point on—whether they ever know, understand, or believe in His deity, work on the cross, or resurrection from the dead.

This is a truly novel interpretation of the phrase, "the Christ, the Son of God." In fact, it is not even scriptural. While it is definitely true that Jesus is "the Christ, the Son of God" who can guarantee eternal life to all who believe in Him, it is simply *not* true that this is *all* the phrase means. The terms "Christ" and "Son of God" in John's Gospel and the rest of Scripture convey much more than the truth of Jesus being the guarantor of eternal life.

---

[6] Robert N. Wilkin, *Secure and Sure* (Irving, TX: Grace Evangelical Society, 2005), 33.

[7] Zane C. Hodges, "How to Lead People to Christ, Part 1: The Content of Our Message," 4. See also, Zane C. Hodges, "Assurance: Of the Essence of Saving Faith," *JOTGES* 10 (Spring 1997): 6-7.

Scripturally, the phrase "Son of God" means that Jesus is truly God. As God's Son, He shares the exact same nature as His Father.[8] So, one reason Jesus can be the guarantor of eternal life is precisely because He is God. Being God, He is able to insure our salvation because He is greater in power and dominion than any creature in the entire universe and greater than any circumstance that will ever arise in our lives, including sin. Additionally, as "the Christ," Jesus is also the guarantor of eternal life because of what He did to provide salvation by His finished work on the cross and His resurrection from the dead. However, restricting the meaning of "the Christ, the Son of God" to Jesus simply being the guarantor of eternal life has the practical effect of diminishing and even obscuring these cardinal doctrines that are essential to believe about Jesus in order to receive eternal life.

From the standpoint of the crossless gospel doctrine, one can readily see, however, the need to reduce the meaning of this important phrase. If it is admitted that the combination of the terms "Christ" and "Son of God" means that Jesus is God-incarnate who died for our sins and rose again, then John 20:31 must be teaching that belief in Jesus' deity and work is necessary for eternal life. Since crossless gospel proponents deny this, they must re-interpret the meaning of the entire expression "the Christ, the Son of God" to suit their theology. This is in fact what they are now doing. This is a transparent example of doctrinally-driven exegesis, of doctrine being imposed upon Scripture rather than derived from Scripture.

While it is certainly true that the phrase *"the Christ, the Son of God"* establishes that Jesus is the guarantor of eternal life, the crossless interpretation of this key phrase seriously errs by reducing it to that meaning *alone*. It also creates more exegetical problems than it solves. For example, why would John have a special "Johannine" definition of "the Christ, the Son of God" that is completely unique to his Gospel and distinct from all the other writers of Scripture? Also, why would John have a completely unique, distinctive meaning for the combined phrase "the Christ, the Son of God" that the two individual parts, "the Christ" and "the Son of God," do not have within his own Gospel? And is only one other identical reference in John's Gospel (11:27) really enough to establish such a precise, highly theological definition for the phrase used in 20:31? Would the average reader of John's Gospel, with his or her eternal destiny riding on the line, even make such a tenuous connection, a connection that has eluded

[8] Though the phrase "Son of God" is an emphatic declaration of the Lord Jesus' deity, a careful study of this phrase throughout Scripture reveals that it also encompasses His redemptive work. Similarly, though the phrase "Son of Man" clearly expresses the genuine humanity of the Lord, it also encompasses His deity and work of redemption. These two highly theological phrases are not strictly synonymous, but there is a significant degree of overlapping meaning between them. G. Michael Cocoris, *The Salvation Controversy* (Santa Monica, CA: Insights from the Word, 2008), 22.

even genuine believers for two millennia until the advent of the Grace Evangelical Society? And if the whole point of John's Gospel according to John 20:31 is to get people to believe that Jesus is "the Christ, the Son of God" in the sense that He is merely the guarantor of eternal life, then why would John wait until the 11th chapter to reveal this vital truth to his readers? Shouldn't he have done so in the first chapter where readers are likely to begin?[9] The unique interpretation of the key-phrase, "the Christ, the Son of God," that crossless gospel proponents have invented simply exceeds the limits of credulity.

Eternal Life

A third reason for the development of the new crossless gospel, and perhaps the primary reason, is the desire to see the message of assurance and certainty of eternal life included more explicitly in our gospel presentations. The proponents of today's new crossless gospel lament that often the bare facts of Christ's work on the cross and resurrection are presented to the lost along with an appeal to believe in Him, without any accompanying explanation that Christ also guarantees eternal life to all who simply believe in Him. Wilkin expresses this concern by saying,

> Sadly, the message of the cross and empty tomb has, in many churches, been divorced from the guarantee of everlasting life to all who merely believe in Jesus. So when you evangelize, make sure you call people to certainty. That is the promise of the good

---

[9] This point is underscored even further when the modern reader recognizes that the original, early readers of the Gospel of John would have read it in scroll form, rather than in codex (book) form. Even John Niemelä agrees on this particular point (John H. Niemelä, "The Infrequency of Twin Departures: An End to Synoptic Reversibility?" [Ph.D. dissertation, Dallas Theological Seminary, 2000], 401-39). Most codicologists and paleographers are convinced that the codex did not come into common use among Christians until the end of the 1st century to early 2nd century (Harry Y. Gamble, *Books and Readers in the Early Church: A History of Early Christian Texts* [New Haven: Yale University Press, 1995], 49-66). With the sheets (pages) of a codex falling open, this allowed for faster, random access in finding a particular passage, as opposed to the more tedious sequential access of the scroll. It has been estimated that the Gospel of Luke, the longest of the Gospels, would have required a scroll over 30 feet long (David Alan Black, *New Testament Textual Criticism: A Concise Guide* [Grand Rapids: Baker, 1994], 15; Bruce M. Metzger, *The Text of the New Testament: Its Transmission, Corruption, and Restoration*, 3rd Edition [New York: Oxford University Press, 1992], 5-6). Since the Gospel of John is approximately ¾ the length of Luke, we can estimate that the Gospel of John would have required a scroll approximately 22.5 feet long (A. Q. Morton and G. H. C. MacGregor, *The Structure of Luke and Acts* [New York: Harper & Row, 1964], 16). Accessing the vital meaning of "the Christ" in John 11:25-27 would therefore require unrolling the scroll approximately 11.5 feet; and without any chapter numbers and versification in the original manuscripts, the original reader would have had a much more difficult time locating John 11:27 to get the essential, saving definition of "the Christ." It is for this reason that all of the essential elements of the saving gospel (i.e., the contents of saving faith) are found in chapters 1-2 of John's Gospel where the reader is expected to begin.

> news. Tell them that the One who died and rose again guarantees everlasting life to all who simply believe in Him.[10]

Is there anyone in the Free Grace camp who can disagree with the fact that many Christians, professing and actual, talk about the cross and resurrection and yet there is a spiritual disconnect when it comes to the assurance of salvation that Christ's work provides? Certainly, and sadly, this is true! No one who believes in salvation by grace through faith alone in Christ alone would object to this, and the desire to see the absolute assurance of eternal life not only included in our evangelism, but emphasized, is commendable.

As it stands, there is no problem with a desire to include the certainty of eternal life in our gospel presentations; but there is a problem with the imbalanced emphasis now being made upon eternal life at the expense of Christ's person and work, and in some cases even creating a practical antithesis with Christ's person and work. In their teaching, people will not encounter an outright denial of Christ's person and work, but there certainly has been a noticeable de-emphasis upon these doctrinal truths in order to magnify the truth of eternal life and eternal security. Notice where one writer says we should put the *focus* of our evangelism:

> Let me say this: All forms of the gospel that require greater content to faith in Christ than the Gospel of John requires, are flawed. Evangelism based on such premises will also be flawed, because we will be tempted to test professions of faith in terms of doctrines we think must be believed. Instead we should be focusing on whether an individual believes that Jesus has given him eternal life.[11]

The "doctrines" he has in mind that we must not "focus" on, and that we must not test professions by, include Christ's deity, substitutionary death, and resurrection.

Where should our *focus* and *emphasis* be in evangelism—upon the person and work of Christ? Or, upon the provision of eternal life resulting from His person and work? Must it even be an either/or proposition? Why can't we focus upon both Christ's person and work *and* eternal life? If we are truly seeking to point people to Christ, to "believe in Him" for eternal life, then shouldn't we emphasize His person and work? Those who are now espousing the crossless gospel say the focus must be upon eternal life, not the "doctrines we think must be believed," such as Christ's deity, death for sin, and resurrection from the dead.

At this point it would be appropriate to ask whether this is the emphasis of the evangelism we find in the New Testament? When we pose this

---

[10] Robert N. Wilkin, *Secure and Sure* (Irving, TX: Grace Evangelical Society, 2005), 202.

[11] Hodges, "How to Lead People to Christ, Part 1," 8.

question, we find that eternal life *by itself* was certainly *not* the emphasis in the preaching and evangelism of the apostles as described in the Book of Acts, since the concept of eternal life is referred to only four times (Acts 5:20; 11:18; 13:46, 48).[12]

If a study is done of all the references in the New Testament to Christ's death and resurrection, compared to the number of references to the concept of eternal life, the unbiased reader will clearly see that the emphasis is upon Christ's substitutionary death. This is not to say that the message of eternal life and Christ's resurrection are unimportant. They are vital. In fact, they are also essential elements of the gospel that are emphasized throughout the New Testament.[13] It's just that Christ's death is referred to more than twice as often as eternal life and roughly three times as often as His resurrection. Therefore, it seems only fair that if these Free Grace men are going to maintain that eternal life must be our "focus" in evangelism, then the message of Christ's death and resurrection should get at least equal billing and not be de-emphasized as has been occurring in the last decade or so in some Free Grace circles.

A nearly exhaustive list is provided on the following pages of all the New Testament references to eternal life, Christ's death, and His resurrection. The listing is based on English translation (NKJV) for ease of reference, recognizing that some phrases are actually the same in Greek (e.g., *"eternal life"* = *"everlasting life"*; *"rose"* = *"arose"*). When a textual variant occurred (Col. 1:14; Rev. 22:19), it was automatically included for the sake of completeness.

Under the category of Christ's death, I chose *not* to include passages using the terms propitiation, reconciliation, redemption, imputation, etc., since these are technically the results or benefits of Christ's death rather than synonyms for His actual death. In this regard, it is debatable whether certain terms should be included under "Eternal Life" such as "regeneration" and "renewing"; but as a matter of principle I erred on the side of generosity by including them. All the book, chapter, and verse references are cited for the reader's benefit in order to be able to confirm the number totals for each category. Even if the reader rejects a few passages as not fitting the designated category, the numbers of such debatable passages

[12] Some proponents of the new gospel would not even include Acts 11:18, claiming it is a reference to *physical* life being preserved as one is delivered from God's wrath in the Christian's life. Zane C. Hodges, *Harmony with God* (Dallas: Redención Viva, 2001), 117-19.

[13] The phrase used throughout this book and even in the subtitle, "the Crossless Gospel," is admittedly only an abbreviation that doesn't capture the full scope of the new, aberrant gospel being propagated today. This phrase as it is used in this book should not be misconstrued as suggesting in any way that either the Lord's deity, humanity, or resurrection are dispensable elements of the gospel. They are not; they are as essential as the cross-work of Christ, just not referred to as frequently in the New Testament. It is also less cumbersome and awkward to say "the crossless gospel" versus "the deityless, crossless, and resurrectionless gospel."

are insignificant enough so as not to change the overall impression, or composite picture, of what Scripture itself truly emphasizes.

Eternal Life (146x)

"eternal life" – Matt. 19:16, 29; 25:46; Mark 10:17, 30; Luke 10:25; 18:18, 30; John 3:15; 4:36; 5:39; 6:54, 68; 10:28; 12:25; 17:2, 3; Acts 13:48; Rom. 2:7; 5:21; 6:23; 1 Tim. 6:12, 19; Titus 1:2; 3:7; 1 John 2:2, 25; 3:15; 5:11, 13, 20; Jude 1:21

"everlasting life" – John 3:16, 36; 4:14; 5:24; 6:27, 40, 47; 12:50; Acts 13:46; Rom. 6:22; 1 Tim. 1:16

"life" – Matt. 7:14; 18:8, 9; 19:17; Mark 9:43, 45; John 1:4; 3:36; 5:21, 24, 26 (2x), 29, 40; 6:30, 35, 48, 51, 53, 63 (2x); 8:12; 10:10; 11:25; 14:6; 20:31; Acts 5:20; 11:18; Rom. 5:17, 18; 2 Cor. 2:16; 3:6; 5:4; Gal. 3:21; Eph. 4:18; Phil. 2:16; 4:3; Col. 3:3, 4; 1 Tim. 4:8; 2 Tim. 1:1, 10; Heb. 7:3, 16; 1 John 1:1, 2; 5:11, 12 (2x); Rev. 3:5; 13:8; 17:8; 20:12, 15; 21:6, 27; 22:17, 19 (TR)

"live/s" – Luke 10:28; John 5:25; 6:51, 57, 58; 11:25; 14:19; Rom. 1:17; 10:5; Gal. 3:11, 12; 5:25; 1 Thess. 5:10; 2 Tim. 2:11; Heb. 7:25; 10:38; 1 John 4:9

"living" – John 4:10, 11; 6:51; 7:38; 1 Cor. 15:45; 1 Peter 1:3

"regeneration" – Titus 3:5

"renewing" – Titus 3:5

"begotten" – 1 Cor. 4:15; Philem. 1:10; 1 Peter 1:3

"born" – John 1:13; 3:3, 5, 6, 7, 8; Gal. 4:29; 1 Peter 2:23; 1 John 2:29; 3:9 (2x); 4:7; 5:1, 4, 18 (2x)

"brought forth" – James 1:18

Christ's Resurrection (113x)

"resurrection" – Matt. 27:53; John 11:25; Acts 1:22; 2:31; 4:2, 33; 17:18, 32; Rom. 1:4; 6:5; 1 Cor. 15:12, 13, 21; Phil. 3:10; 1 Peter 1:3; 3:21

"rise/ing" – Matt. 20:19; 27:63; Mark 8:31; 9:10, 31; 10:34; Luke 16:31; 18:33; 24:7, 46; John 20:9; Acts 17:3; 26:23

"risen" – Matt. 17:9; 27:64; 28:6, 7; Mark 9:9; 16:6, 14; Luke 24:6, 34; John 2:22; Rom. 8:34; 1 Cor. 15:13, 14, 16, 17, 20

"a/rose" – Mark 16:9; Acts 10:41; Rom. 14:9; 1 Cor. 15:4; 2 Cor. 5:15; 1 Thess. 4:14

"raise" – John 2:19, 20; Acts 2:30; 3:22; 7:37; 1 Cor. 15:15; 2 Cor. 4:14; Heb. 11:19

"raised" – Matt. 16:21; 17:23; 26:32; Mark 6:16; 14:28; Luke 9:22; John 21:14; Acts 2:24, 32; 3:15, 26; 4:10; 5:30; 10:40; 13:30, 33, 34, 37; Rom. 4:24, 25; 6:4, 9; 7:4; 8:11 (2x); 10:9; 1 Cor. 6:14; 15:12, 15; 2 Cor. 4:14; Gal. 1:1; Eph. 1:20; 2:6; Col. 2:12 (2x); 3:1; 1 Thess. 1:10; 2 Tim. 2:8; 1 Peter 1:21

"take again" – John 10:17, 18

"alive" – Mark 16:11; Luke 24:23; Acts 1:3; 25:19; Eph. 2:5; Col. 2:13; 1 Peter 3:18; Rev. 1:18

"from the dead" – Luke 16:30; Rom. 10:7; Col. 1:18; Heb. 13:20; Rev. 1:5

Christ's Death (312x)

"cross" – Matt. 27:32, 40, 42; Mark 15:21, 30, 32; Luke 23:26; John 19:17, 19, 25, 31; 1 Cor. 1:17, 18; Gal. 5:11; 6:12, 14; Eph. 2:16; Phil. 2:8; 3:18; Col. 1:20; 2:14; Heb. 12:2

"tree" (as synonym for cross) – Acts 5:30; 10:39; 13:29; Gal. 3:13; 1 Peter 2:24

"crucify" –Matt. 20:19; Mark 15:13, 14, 20; Luke 23:21 (2x); John 19:6 (3x), 10, 15 (2x); Heb. 6:6

"crucified" – Matt. 26:2; 27:22, 23, 26, 31, 35, 38, 44; 28:5; Mark 15:15, 24, 25, 32; 16:6; Luke 23:23, 33; 24:7, 20; John 19:16, 18, 20, 23, 32, 41; Acts 2:23, 36; 4:10; Rom. 6:6; 1 Cor. 1:13, 23; 2:2, 8; 2 Cor. 13:4; Gal. 2:20; 3:1; 5:24; 6:14; Rev. 11:18

"kill" – Matt. 17:23; 21:38; 26:4; Mark 9:31; 10:34; 12:7; Luke 18:33; 20:14; 22:2; John 5:16, 18; 7:1, 19, 20, 25; 8:22, 37, 40

"killed" – Matt. 16:21; 21:39; Mark 8:31; 9:31; 12:8; Luke 9:22; 20:15; Acts 3:15; 10:39; 1 Thess. 2:15

"blood" – Matt. 26:28; 27:4, 6, 8, 24, 25; Mark 14:24; Luke 22:20; John 6:53, 54, 55, 56; 19:34; Acts 1:19; 5:28; 20:28; Rom. 3:25; 5:9; 1 Cor. 10:16; 11:25, 27; Eph. 1:7; 2:13; Col. 1:14 (MT), 20; Heb. 9:12, 14; 10:19, 29; 12:24; 13:12, 20; 1 Peter 1:2, 19; 1 John 1:7; 5:6; Rev. 1:5; 5:9; 7:14; 12:11

"murder(ers)" – Acts 7:52

"lift/ed up" – John 3:14; 8:28; 12:32, 34

"gave" – John 3:16; Gal. 1:4; 2:20; Eph. 5:25; 1 Tim. 2:6; Titus 2:14

"give/s/en" – Matt. 20:28; Mark 10:45; Luke 22:19; John 6:51, 52; 10:11; Eph. 5:2

"lay/laid down" – John 10:15, 17, 18 (2x); 15:13; 1 John 3:16

"taken" – Acts 8:33

"offer/ed/ing" – Heb. 7:27; 8:3; 9:14, 25; 10:10, 14

"sacrifice/d" – 1 Cor. 5:7; Eph. 5:2; Heb. 9:26; 10:12

"redeem/ed" (the *act* of paying a price, not the *result*, i.e., "redemption") – Gal. 3:13; 4:5; Titus 2:14; 1 Peter 1:18; Rev. 5:9

"decease" – Luke 9:31

"deliver" – Matt. 20:19; 26:15; Mark 10:33

"delivered" – Matt. 26:2; 27:2, 26; Mark 15:1, 15; Luke 18:32; 23:25; 24:7, 20; John 18:30, 35, 36; 19:11, 16; Acts 2:23; 3:13; Rom. 4:25; 8:32

"destroy" – Matt. 12:14; 27:20; Mark 3:6; 11:18; Luke 19:47; John 2:19

"slain" – Rev. 5:6, 9, 12; 13:8

"suffer" – Matt. 16:21; 17:12; Mark 8:31; 9:12; Luke 9:22; 17:25; 22:15; 24:46; Acts 3:18; 17:3; 26:23; Heb. 9:26

"suffered" – Luke 24:26; Heb. 5:8; 13:12; 1 Peter 2:21, 23; 3:18; 4:1

"suffering/s" – Acts 1:3; Heb. 2:9-10; 1 Peter 1:11; 5:1

"die/s" – John 11:50, 51; 12:24 (2x), 33; 18:14, 32; 19:7; Rom. 5:7 (2x); 6:9

"died" – Acts 25:19; Rom. 5:6, 8; 6:2, 7, 8, 10 (2x); 7:6; 8:34; 14:9, 15; 1 Cor. 8:11; 15:3; 2 Cor. 5:14, 15 (2x); Gal. 2:19, 21; Col. 2:20; 3:3; 1 Thess. 4:14; 5:10; 2 Tim. 2:11; 1 Peter 2:24

"death" – Matt. 20:18; 26:59, 66; 27:1; Mark 10:33; 14:1, 55, 64; Luke 23:32; 24:20; John 11:53; 12:33; 18:32; Acts 2:23, 24; 13:28 (2x); Rom. 5:10; 6:3, 4, 5, 9, 10 (implied); 1 Cor. 11:26; Eph. 2:16; Phil. 2:8; 3:10; Col. 1:22; Heb. 2:9 (2x), 14; 9:15, 16; 1 Peter 3:18

Non-Essential Doctrines

The G.E.S. gospel and its aberrant doctrines are the result of (1) the new interpretative approach to the Gospel of John and its signs, (2) the new, redefined Johannine meaning of Jesus being "the Christ" and (3) a "focus" on eternal life in evangelism with a corresponding de-emphasis on the cross and resurrection. But there is also a fourth major reason for the emergence of the crossless gospel. It is the sincere but misguided desire to remove excess theological baggage from the gospel, which includes Christ's deity, cross-work, and resurrection as the necessary contents of saving faith.

It is not merely the imbalanced emphasis upon eternal life in everyday evangelism that is problematic; it is the sole requirement to believe in the message of eternal life without the person and work of Christ that is so unscriptural. Again, Wilkin explains that the issue that determines whether one is truly saved is whether or not that person has believed in the message of justification by faith alone (which he equates with the message of eternal life). The issue, Wilkin explains, is *not* whether that individual has believed in Christ's person and work:

> Justification *is* by faith alone. And Paul tells us justification by faith apart from works is the good news (Galatians 2:15-16). Thus the *only* valid litmus test for determining who is a false professor is whether or not a person believes in justification by faith alone.[14]

This is consistent with Wilkin's earlier definition of the gospel to the lost as being solely a matter of eternal life, not Christ's deity, cross-work, or resurrection. He states:

> You can believe many biblical concepts and still miss the one truth that is saving—the truth of the gospel. For example, you can attest to Jesus' deity, His virgin birth, and His bodily resurrection, and yet not believe Jesus' promise to give you eternal life freely if you just believe in Him for it. There is only one truth that will save: Jesus' guarantee that anyone who believes in Him for eternal life has it.[15]

It is apparent from the public teachings of those holding to this new gospel that, in their opinion, the rest of the Free Grace movement has not merely *underemphasized* the message of eternal life in its evangelism, but we have *wrongly added* extra-biblical content to saving faith. Zane Hodges shared the opinion of Wilkin expressed above, stating again:

[14] Wilkin, *Secure and Sure*, 85 (italics original).

[15] Robert N. Wilkin, *Confident in Christ* (Irving, TX: Grace Evangelical Society, 1999), 10.

> I have also just finished pointing out that the disciples who did believe in Jesus did not understand *the significance or necessity of His death and resurrection*, according to John 20:9. And this was true despite the fact that John the Baptist announced Him as "the Lamb of God who takes away the sin of the world" (1:29). If we require an understanding of *these truths* before faith in Christ can be valid, we are obviously requiring more than the Gospel of John does. Let me say this: All forms of the gospel that require greater content to faith in Christ than the Gospel of John requires, are flawed. Evangelism based on such premises will also be flawed, because we will be tempted to test professions of faith in terms of doctrines we think must be believed. Instead we should be focusing on whether an individual believes that Jesus has given him eternal life. Evangelism, therefore, is intended to bring men and women to the place where they believe that Jesus guarantees their eternal destiny. If a person does this and we insist on more than that, we will be guilty of seeking to invalidate the simple exercise of faith that really does bring salvation. Even in the grace movement, we are sorely tempted to make the gospel more complicated than God makes it. We can hardly bring ourselves to believe that a man who is largely ignorant of evangelical theology, yet genuinely trusts Christ for his eternal well-being, is truly saved. We have every reason to be embarrassed by this tendency on our part.[16]

Hodges expressed a similar sentiment in the same article under the heading "ADDING TO THE GOSPEL," where he wrote:

> Most of us deplore efforts made by Lordship people to add provisos to the message of faith in Christ. According to them, true faith has not occurred if it is not accompanied by surrender or by a commitment to live for God. We rightly reject such ideas. But in our own circles, there is a tendency to add theological information to our message of faith.[17]

---

[16] Hodges, "How to Lead People to Christ, Part 1," 8 (italics added).

[17] Ibid., 7. The heading, "ADDING TO THE GOSPEL," simply cannot be interpreted in its context to mean that *only* Lordship Salvationists and not Free Grace people are deemed by Hodges to be "adding to the gospel." This heading serves as a summary of Hodges's main point on the three pages which follow (ibid., 7-10). After referring to Lordship Salvation's excesses in the opening sentence under the heading and equating them to Free Grace excesses, Hodges then goes on to address *only* the Free Grace movement, which is his main point. Under the heading "ADDING TO THE GOSPEL," Hodges refers to the "gospel" (3x) "in the grace movement" (ibid., 8); and he states that "in our own circles, there is a tendency to add theological information to our message of faith" (ibid.). What then follows are the only examples given by Hodges of extra theological information wrongly added by grace people to the gospel: Christ's "virgin birth" (ibid., 7) and "the significance or necessity of His death and resurrection" (ibid., 8). Hodges then puts all three doctrines together in one statement, saying, "In other words, God does not say to people, "You trusted my Son's name, but you didn't believe in His virgin birth, or His substitutionary atonement, or His

If by adding too much "theological information" and "evangelical theology" to the gospel these men mean doctrines such as Christ's virgin birth, Davidic lineage, impeccability, bodily ascension, second coming, etc., then it is true that these are not part of the essential message to the lost that the Bible calls "the gospel," though they are all true. But can we honestly say that adding these doctrines to our gospel is a "tendency" within "the grace movement"? This seems to be a false charge. Personally, I have rarely, if ever, heard these doctrines presented as "the gospel" to the lost by Free Grace people. The problem seems to have been overstated by Hodges in an attempt to critique the principal and most frequent infraction he was concerned with in our evangelism, namely adding to "the gospel" belief in Christ's deity, cross-work, and resurrection for eternal life.

In itself, this is truly alarming; but what is equally alarming is the new attitude of condescension toward those who would wish to retain these vital truths as part of the gospel to the lost. When Hodges says, "we have every reason to be embarrassed by this tendency on our part," may we be fair and put the shoe on the other foot? Do we have an equal right to be "embarrassed" by the new "tendency" to gut the gospel of its essential contents? If crossless gospel proponents are free to say that we are "guilty" of this "tendency" within "the grace movement," are we prohibited from using the exact same language to say that they too are "guilty" of a "flawed" gospel?

Believers today must refuse to be subtly guilted into accepting this false characterization of "the grace movement." We must refuse to be shamed into submission to the crossless gospel. Paul said of the legalists in his day, *"of whom we did not yield submission even for an hour, that the truth of the gospel might continue with you"* (Gal. 2:5). If Paul withstood the false gospel of the legalists who added human works to Christ's work, so we too must not submit to the false gospel of the reductionists who have actually removed Christ's work itself as essential to believe for eternal life. We must resist this new "tendency" in order that the truth of the gospel might continue among us.

---

bodily resurrection, so your faith is not valid." *We* say that, but God's Word does not" (ibid., 9). It is in response to *these* doctrines that Hodges says, "All forms of the gospel that require greater content to faith in Christ than the Gospel of John requires, are flawed" (ibid., 8). The conclusion is unmistakable that in the article Hodges regards the requirement to believe in Christ's death and resurrection for eternal life as a "flawed" gospel. The "tendency to add theological information to our message of faith" which Hodges is so concerned about clearly includes the requirement to believe in the substitutionary atonement and bodily resurrection of Christ. It is this *"tendency* to add theological information to our message of faith" (ibid., 7; italics added) that he has in mind when he writes only one-half page later, "in *the grace movement,* we are sorely tempted to make the gospel more complicated than God makes it....We have every reason to be embarrassed by *this tendency on our part"* (ibid., 8, ellipsis & italics added). The conclusion seems obvious and inescapable to any objective reader that, to Hodges, requiring the lost to believe in Christ's substitutionary death and bodily resurrection is stated to be "ADDING TO THE GOSPEL."

Chapter 4

Is John 6:47 Really the Saving Message?

OVERVIEW

What essential information must the lost know and believe in order to receive eternal life? According to the new crossless gospel, all that must be known and believed is the name, "Jesus," the guarantee of eternal life associated with that name, and the sole condition of believing. These three basic elements are now considered to be the sine qua non or irreducible minimum of the contents of "saving faith." Those who are advocating this position believe these three elements are the common denominators found in several key evangelistic passages in the Gospel of John and Acts 16:31. John 6:47 is often cited as the model text of a single verse that clearly and concisely contains all three necessary elements. However, there are major logical, hermeneutical, and scriptural problems with this reductionist approach.

Thus far, four essential factors have been noted for the emergence of the new, aberrant form of the gospel within the Free Grace movement in recent years. To summarize and review, these include: (1) the new hermeneutical approach to the Gospel of John that views it as being the only evangelistic book in the Bible (2) the new meaning assigned to "the Christ" as being only the guarantor of eternal life (3) the desire to see the message of eternal life and assurance be the focus in evangelism (4) an over-zealous desire to purge the gospel to the lost of non-essential doctrinal content. These four factors have led to the redefinition and reduction of the saving gospel so that now the necessary good news to the lost is no longer the message that Christ died for their sins and rose again. Now it has been reduced to a simple guarantee, or promise, that all who believe in the name "Jesus" for eternal life will have it, regardless of how little they may know about the person who bears that name and regardless of the flaws in their theology.[1] However, according to Scripture, believing in the name of Jesus for eternal life involves definite knowledge of His person and work as chapter 6 will demonstrate. For a lost sinner's faith to be "saving," it must be in the right object. This requires a certain amount of divine revelation, or information, about the One bearing the name "Jesus."

But where do we find such essential information? And what exactly is essential? The proponents of today's "crossless" gospel believe that they have found the answer in John 6:47. This verse, they say, is the model text within the Gospel of John due to its conciseness and minimalistic content.

Message in a Bottle

In an attempt to get at this irreducible minimum in the required contents of saving faith, Zane Hodges proposed the now infamous illustration of a castaway stranded on a deserted island. He wrote:

> Let me begin with a strange scenario. Try to imagine an unsaved person marooned on a tiny, uninhabited island in the middle of the Pacific Ocean. He has never heard about Christianity in his life. One day a wave washes a fragment of paper up onto the beach. It is wet but still partly readable. On that paper are the words of John 6:43-47. But the only readable portions are: "Jesus therefore answered and said to them" (v43) and "Most assuredly, I say to you, he who believes in Me has everlasting life"

[1] Zane C. Hodges, "How to Lead People to Christ, Part 1: The Content of Our Message," *JOTGES* 13 (Autumn 2000): 9.

> (v47). Now suppose that our unsaved man somehow becomes convinced that this person called Jesus can guarantee his eternal future, since He promises everlasting life. In other words, he believes Jesus' words in John 6:47. Is he saved? I suspect that there are some grace people who would say that this man is not saved because he doesn't know enough. For example, he doesn't know that Jesus died for his sins on the cross and rose again the third day. Needless to say, there is a lot more he doesn't know either, such as the doctrine of the Trinity, the eternal Sonship of Jesus or the doctrine of the virgin birth. But why is he *not* saved if he believes the promise of Jesus' words?[2]

At first, this may seem like such an uncommon scenario that it is completely impractical and irrelevant for us to even speculate upon any correct answer. However, it is actually a helpful illustration that raises some extremely important spiritual questions. It gets right to the heart of the question of what it means to believe in Christ. In this sense, it cannot be compared to the fruitless theological speculations of scholastics in the Middle Ages who debated about how many angels could fit on the head of a pin. Hodges's scenario raises a legitimate question, and it demands an appropriate answer. If such a man is not saved with only John 6:43-47, then *why* is he not saved? And has he truly "believed in Christ"?

Hodges's scenario would also logically lead to the stranded islander asking the fundamental questions, "Who is Jesus?" and "Why should I believe in Him anyway?" Why would this castaway "believe in Jesus for eternal life" if he doesn't even know who He is or what He's done to provide him with eternal life? After all, in Hodges's scenario, it's not a matter of this man already being familiar with the Christian story of Jesus being God's Son who died on a cross for the sins of the world and rose from the dead, so that now he just needs to add the missing piece of the puzzle—the certainty of eternal life through belief in Him. No, we're told that this castaway is someone who has *"never heard of Christianity in his life."* We're also instructed to *"suppose that our unsaved man somehow becomes convinced that this person called Jesus can guarantee his eternal future."* This is an awfully big suppositional leap that cannot be lightly glossed over. Is it even possible for a lost soul to become convinced that Jesus can guarantee him eternal life if he has *"never heard of Christianity in his life"*?

Which Jesus?

What religious background would this man have that would predispose him in his interpretations of who this "Jesus" might be and whether "Jesus" could truly guarantee him eternal life? Multiple predispositions can be conceived for such a man, none of which lead to an adequate, sav-

[2] Ibid., 4.

ing knowledge of the truth (1 Tim. 2:3-6). For example, let's suppose for a moment that the man was an animist. What if he believes that this "Jesus" mentioned on this tattered page is simply the name of a spirit who speaks through rocks and animals saying, "Whoever believes in Me has eternal life"? In such a case, he would have no knowledge of this spirit even becoming incarnated as a man, to say nothing of a substitutionary death or resurrection as the grounds of eternal life. Would belief in such a spirit-Jesus save this animist?

Now let's suppose instead that the islander is a secular, humanistic, materialistic atheist. What if he not only doesn't believe that this "Jesus" is God, but that there is no God at all from whom mankind even needs salvation? What if he becomes persuaded that "Jesus" is the name of an extremely intelligent Russian scientist who discovered a materialistic medical solution for human mortality, so that all who believe in this "Dr. Jesus" will be guaranteed an endless physical existence? After all, we're told that he doesn't need to know who Jesus really is, what He's done, or for that matter what "eternal life" is either.[3]

Now, instead of the humanist atheist, let's suppose the castaway is a Buddhist who also doesn't believe in the notion of a transcendent, personal God, sin, or even an actual place called heaven. He believes in nirvana or becoming merged eternally with the astral plane or something along that order. What if this Buddhist becomes persuaded that this "Jesus," like his Buddha, is just a man who happened to receive enlightenment, but unlike his Buddha, this "Jesus" can guarantee this man nirvana (i.e., his "eternal future" or "eternal well-being")? Would this Buddhist be saved? If not, why not since he doesn't need to know who "Jesus" really is, what eternal life is, or even how it was provided for him?

Now consider a fourth possible scenario, that our stranded islander was part of the New Age movement and its angel cult before finding himself stranded on the deserted island. He was already acquainted with angels but not necessarily Christianity, so that he somehow comes to

---

[3] It is peculiar for Hodges to speak of this islander coming to believe that his "eternal future" is guaranteed (Hodges, "How to Lead People to Christ, Part 1," 4). Elsewhere Hodges used the phrase "eternal well-being" (ibid., 5, 8, 10). However, neither "eternal future" nor "eternal well-being" captures the real biblical significance of "eternal life." Eternal life in the Bible entails a reconciled relationship with God through His Son Jesus Christ. It is always something personal and relational between God and man (John 17:3). It is never something man-centered, implying mere unending human existence without the need to acknowledge the existence of a personal God or a need for peace in a relationship with Him. However, according to the crossless position, it is not absolutely necessary for a person to acknowledge that he is a sinner, or even that a personal God exists, in order to receive "eternal life." According to their position, though it is "illogical" for someone to deny being a sinner, or that God exists, and that this is not the "norm," it is still nevertheless conceivable for someone to believe in Jesus for eternal life without accepting these presuppositions to the gospel. See Robert N. Wilkin, "Should We Rethink the Idea of Degrees of Faith?" *JOTGES* 19 (Autumn 2006): 20-21.

believe that "Jesus" is simply the name of a powerful angel (like Michael the archangel in the Bible) who can somehow guarantee him eternal life.[4] Would the stranded islander be saved by his faith in a mighty archangel called "Jesus"?

Which "Jesus" must a person believe in for eternal life?

- the <u>Jehovah Witness</u> "Jesus," who is just "a god," even Michael the archangel in disguise?
- the <u>Mormon</u> "Jesus," who is just a god on par with other faithful Mormons who believe they'll also reach godhood?
- the <u>Muslim</u> (and so-called Samaritan) "Jesus," who never died on the cross or rose from the dead, and who is just a man, though a great prophet?
- the <u>Gnostic</u> "Jesus," who didn't really die & rise again, who is also not truly human?
- the <u>Hindu</u> "Jesus," who is just one god among many thousands if not millions of gods?
- the <u>Crossless Gospel</u> "Jesus," who can be virtually anyone or anything as long as the promise of John 6:47 is believed?
- the <u>Biblical</u> "Jesus," who is God the Son who became a man to die for our sins and rise from the dead!

In each of the preceding hypothetical and yet truly conceivable cases, the marooned islander fulfills all of the theological requirements spelled out thus far by proponents of the new, crossless gospel. As Hodges states, such a castaway *"somehow becomes convinced that this person called Jesus can guarantee his eternal future, since He promises eternal life,"* even though *"He has never heard about Christianity in his life."* In addition, regarding the name of "Jesus," we are informed by Hodges that *"Everyone who believes in that name for eternal salvation is saved, regardless of the blank spots or the flaws in their theology in other respects."*[5] Furthermore, the people in each of the preceding examples fulfill the terms and conditions set down by Hodges later in his same article where

[4] Amazingly, the cult of the Jehovah's Witnesses, who deny the deity of Christ, believe that the Lord Jesus is really Michael the archangel as described in the prophetic books of Daniel and Revelation (Dan. 10:13; 12:1; Rev. 12:7, 10, 12). See *Aid to Bible Understanding* (New York: Watchtower Bible and Tract Society, 1971), 1152.

[5] Hodges, "How to Lead People to Christ, Part 1," 9.

he wrote, *"No one has ever trusted in that name for his or her eternal well-being who has not been saved by doing so. And this is true no matter how little they might have known about the One whom that name represents."*[6]

So, regarding the four preceding hypothetical scenarios, are all of these people actually saved without believing the truth of who Jesus is or what He's done? To be consistent with his own theology, the answer of Hodges would have to be "Yes." In each case, the person becomes convinced or persuaded of a guarantee of eternal life associated with this one called "Jesus." But this is truly frightful theology. This is giving people a *false assurance* of their "eternal well-being"! This type of gospel will not lead the animist, atheist, Buddhist, or angel-worshipper to eternal life—it will lead them to hell.[7]

Scriptural Witnessing

In the process of arriving at their new reduced "gospel," the advocates of this view have adopted John 6:47 as their definitive, model text that contains the minimum content of necessary information. John 6:47 says, *"Most assuredly, I say to you, he who believes in Me has everlasting life"* (NKJV). However, selecting John 6:47 as the passage upon which to define the bare minimum gospel, and to pattern our evangelism after, leads to multiple scriptural problems.

Another reason for the emergence of the crossless gospel in our day is that many of its proponents believe this will enhance the witnessing process by making it more scriptural. As one leading proponent of this view stated to me, instead of subjecting the lost to "a course on Christology," which would likely result in the unsaved becoming confused or side-tracked by the matters of Christ's deity, sacrificial death, and resurrection, we should instead skip immediately to the one essential aspect of the gospel, namely Christ's promise of eternal life for all who simply believe in Him for it. Later, if necessary, we can go back and fill in the details of who Christ is and what He's accomplished for them. This same leader

[6] Ibid., 8.

[7] In fairness it should be noted that subsequent to this chapter appearing as an article (see Tom Stegall, "The Tragedy of the Crossless Gospel, Pt. 4," *Grace Family Journal* [Special Edition/September-October 2007]: 2-17), the *Journal of the Grace Evangelical Society* published an article by Hodges which seemed to qualify some of his previous written statements from his 2000-2001 articles (see Zane C. Hodges, "The Spirit of the Antichrist: Decoupling Jesus from the Christ," *JOTGES* 20 [Autumn 2007]: 37-46). In his 2007 article, Hodges states that the lost must believe in the "historical person" of Jesus in order to have eternal life. However, he never explains what "historical person" means, apart from the sole distinguishing characteristic that Jesus possesses "flesh and blood" based on 1 John 2:18, 22, and 4:3. Even with this concession, Hodges conspicuously fails to inform the reader that Jesus' "flesh and blood" means that the lost must believe in the Lord Jesus' humanity for eternal life. I have repeatedly heard some leading crossless proponents deny the necessity to believe in the humanity and deity of Christ. The new, G.E.S. gospel does not appear to be settled on the question of Christ's humanity in the contents of saving faith.

claimed that if we start with Christ's person and work, the poor unsaved soul may become confused with how God could possibly become incarnate and whether Christ rose bodily or just in some spiritual sense. He claimed this will result in that poor sinner never getting to the message of eternal life, which is the one truth that will save him. Along these lines, Bob Wilkin even suggests that we should start our evangelism with John 6:47 or "some variation that says that Jesus guarantees eternal life to all who simply believe in Him."[8] Sharing the deity of Christ, he says, "fails the test of giving the main parts of what you intend to say."[9] Nor does sharing Christ's death on the cross for sin "give the core of what you want to share."[10]

Single Evangelistic Verses

Advocates for the new view claim that the Gospel of John focuses on just believing in Jesus for eternal life, and therefore so should we. They also claim that since the Gospel of John repeatedly states this message of eternal life in many individual verses, then the witnessing process will be enhanced by simply showing the unsaved such individual verses. Since these verses contain all the essential truths of the saving message in a single verse, then there is no need, they say, to "combine" passages from other parts of the Bible that speak of Christ's deity, death for sin, and resurrection. Hodges has summarized this desire to supposedly be more scriptural in our evangelism:

> Just think for a minute of John 3:16; 5:24; 6:47; Acts 16:31, and so on, and not a one of these verses invites us to get saved by believing that Jesus died on the cross. Why is it that we like to verbalize our message in ways that the Bible does not do? What is wrong with biblical language? The associated question is this: what is wrong with *our language*? The simple fact of the matter is that the statement I am criticizing is technically incorrect. People are not saved by believing that Jesus died on the cross; they are saved by believing in Jesus for eternal life, or eternal salvation. If we say it the biblical way, we will be able to support our claim by direct biblical statements. But suppose a person I am witnessing to says, "Where does the Bible say we are saved by believing that Jesus died on the cross?" What am I going to do then? In that case I would be compelled to take him to a number of Scriptures and try to combine them to prove my point. But even then, I would not really have a statement from the Word of God that exactly verified the point I was making.[11]

---

[8] Bob Wilkin, "What's Your First Sentence in Evangelism?" *Grace in Focus* 23 (September/October 2008): 4.

[9] Ibid.

[10] Ibid.

[11] Zane C. Hodges, "How to Lead People to Christ, Part 2: Our Invitation to Respond,"

Certainly no one can argue with a desire to be more biblical in our witnessing endeavors. Yet Hodges's claims are again false and exaggerated in an attempt to substantiate the new reduced gospel. By claiming that John 3:16; 5:24; 6:47; and Acts 16:31 do not specifically tell the lost to believe that Christ died on the cross, Hodges essentially declares the surrounding contexts of these verses to be unnecessary in providing proper meaning to the content within each of these individual evangelistic verses.

John 3:16

This classic evangelistic verse is declaring more than the fact of Christ's incarnation; it proclaims the Savior's crucifixion as well. The very definition of how God *"**gave** His only begotten Son"* is illustrated and determined in the context just two verses earlier in John 3:14. There, Christ declares that He is going to be "lifted up" just as the bronze serpent was in Numbers 21. This is an obvious reference to the cross in its own immediate context, and the parallel passage later in John 12:32-33 confirms this interpretation. The capable and prolific Grace expositor, Thomas Constable, explains this point:

> The purpose of Jesus' uplifting, as was the purpose of the uplifting of the bronze serpent in the wilderness, was the salvation of those who believed. By comparing Himself to that serpent Jesus was teaching that whoever trusted in Him and His death would receive eternal life. This is the first reference to eternal life in this Gospel. . . . The eternal life people receive at new birth is the life of the eternal Word (1:4). It comes to them by believing in the person and saving work of Jesus.[12]

John 5:24

In the second passage cited by Hodges, John 5:24, the immediate context explains what Christ meant by *"he who hears My words and believes in Him who sent Me."* The One who *"sent"* the Lord Jesus was God the Father; and Christ's reference to *"My words,"* which an unsaved soul must believe, points to Christ's repeated explanations of His own equality with the Father in John 5:19-23 and 5:25-30. The whole objective of this discourse in John 5:17-30 is to illustrate the truth of verse 18, where Jesus *"said that God was His Father, making Himself equal with God."* What this means practically and evangelistically is that in order for the lost to fulfill the requirement to *"hear"* Christ's *"words"* and *"believe in Him who sent Me,"* they must know the words of Christ and the identity of the *"Him"* in verse 24. The preced-

---

JOTGES 14 (Spring 2001): 10 (italics original).

[12] Thomas L. Constable, *Expository Notes on John* (Garland, TX: Sonic Light, 2005), 60-61 (ellipsis added).

ing verses on Jesus' equality with the Father provide this vital information. The context of John 5:24 is critical in determining its meaning.

The words of John 5:24 cannot be taken in isolation but are dependent upon, and connected to, the words that precede it. This fact is underscored by observing that the Lord Jesus in John 5:24 begins the verse by saying, *"Most assuredly, I say to you."* The phrase *"Most assuredly"* (NKJV), is otherwise rendered in English translations by the words *"Truly, truly"* (NASB) and *"Verily, verily"* (KJV). In the Greek text, it is just the two words *"amēn amēn."* In English, the word "amen" is simply a transliteration of this Greek word *amēn*. When the Lord Jesus repeats this word twice in His speech, as He does in John 5:24, it is for emphasis, and it serves as an introduction to an important statement that is about to follow. This double occurrence of *amēn* in the Greek text is unique to the Gospel of John, and it occurs 25 times in this Gospel. A careful study of these 25 occurrences shows that this solemn declaration "never introduces a new saying unrelated to what precedes."[13]

This has significance for passages such as John 5:24 and 6:47, to which crossless gospel advocates often appeal as examples of self-contained evangelistic verses that have all the necessary content required for the unsaved to believe for eternal life. Yet John 5:24 and 6:47 were never intended to be taken in isolation from their preceding contexts. One Johannine scholar concludes regarding this point, saying, "The *'amen, amen, I say to you'* always has reference to something that has been said already, which is expanded or set in a new light."[14]

John 6:47

Crossless proponents also cite John 6:47 as an individually sufficient evangelistic verse containing all the content necessary for a lost soul to receive eternal life. This verse states, *"Most assuredly, I say to you, he who believes in Me has everlasting life."* However, when the Lord Jesus originally issued this wonderful evangelistic promise, it was not uttered in isolation from any surrounding context which might give it meaning. It is doubtful that the Lord Jesus envisioned the common evangelistic practice of today where this singular statement is extracted from its context and used as a silver bullet in witnessing. Instead, He intended His words in John 6:47 to be defined by their context. The proper meaning of John 6:47 can only be determined by its relationship to the rest of the Bread of Life Discourse. In the surrounding context of John 6:47, the Lord Jesus spoke metaphorically about Himself as the Bread from heaven. He stated this 5 times *prior* to verse 47 (6:27, 32, 33, 35, 41) and 8 times *after* it (6:48, 50, 51 [3x], 55, 58 [2x]).

---

[13] J. H. Bernard, *A Critical and Exegetical Commentary on the Gospel of St. John*, ICC (Edinburgh: T & T Clark, 1929), 1:67.

[14] Francis J. Moloney, *The Johannine Son of Man* (Rome: Libreria Ateneo Salesiano, 1976), 48.

According to the Lord's own discourse in John 6:26-58, to believe in Him in verse 47 means to believe in Him as the Bread of Life.

In this discourse, the Lord describes Himself as the object of faith (6:35, 41, 48, 51) using the expression, *"I am . . ."* (*egō eimi*).[15] He also states the condition for receiving eternal life by using the transitive verb *"believe"* (*pisteuō*) coupled with the preposition *"in"* (*eis*), saying he who *"believe/s in Him/Me"* (6:29, 35, 40, 47 [MT]). If the Lord Jesus describes Himself in the passage multiple times as the Bread of Life and then tells people to believe in Him, does it not stand to reason that He is defining Himself as the object of faith? Is He not telling people to believe in Him as the Bread of Life, whatever that metaphor may mean? What the Bread of Life discourse demonstrates is that it is not sufficient to take the *"he who believes in Me"* clause from John 6:47 and isolate it from its context so as to restrict the content of saving faith to Jesus being only the guarantor of eternal life but not the sacrificial Bread of Life. The Lord Jesus Himself purposely provided the content for saving faith. He Himself explained what He meant in John 6:47 when He said to believe *"in Me."* But what exactly is the content of this saving faith? What does it mean to believe in Him as the Bread of Life?

In the context of John 6:47, the Lord Jesus explains that *"the bread that I shall give is My flesh, which I shall give for the life of the world"* (John 6:51). This is an unmistakable reference to Christ's substitutionary death. Two verses later He warns, *"Most assuredly (amēn amēn), I say to you, unless you eat the flesh of the Son of Man and drink His blood, you have no life in you"* (John 6:53).[16] Does this not speak of the necessity for personal appropriation of Christ's sacrifice of His flesh and blood? But if the Bread which He gives in sacrifice for the life of the world is His own flesh and blood (6:51-53), then how can this be appropriated? Is it by believing in Him as someone or something less than the metaphorical Bread from Heaven given in sacrifice for the life of the world? The answer is already explicitly provided by the Lord Jesus earlier in the discourse.

Immediately after declaring in John 6:35, *"I am the bread of life,"* the Lord says it was *"he who believes in Me"* (*ho pisteuōn eis eme*) who *"shall never hunger"* and *"shall never thirst."* It is significant to note that the only other verse in all of John 6 where the exact expression *"he who believes in Me"*

---

[15] The expression, *egō eimi*, even with a predicate, is a declaration of Christ's deity.

[16] Crossless gospel advocates never quote John 6:53 as one of their individually sufficient evangelism passages; and yet they should by their own standards due to its parallelism and similarity with John 6:47. This is seen in at least three respects. First, John 6:47 begins with the solemn *amēn amēn* declaration (*"Most assuredly"*), as does John 6:53. Second, John 6:47 expresses the means of appropriating Christ (*"believes in Me"*), as does John 6:53 (*"eat My flesh and drink My blood"*); and eating/drinking is equated with believing by the Lord Himself in John 6:35. Thirdly, John 6:47 expresses the result of appropriating Christ positively (*"has eternal life"*), while John 6:53 states the same result negatively (*"unless you…you have no life in you"*).

(*ho pisteuōn eis eme*) occurs is in John 6:47. The Lord Jesus Himself establishes the meaning of believing *"in Me"* in verse 47. He defines Himself as the object of faith by the metaphor of Bread from heaven which would shortly be given in the sacrifice of His flesh and blood for the life of the world. There are no valid, contextual reasons for viewing the *"believes in Me"* phrase of John 6:47 as a crossless message of life.

Acts 16:31

Acts 16:31 is another single, sufficient evangelistic verse sometimes cited by those who promote a crossless "saving message." In Acts 16:31, we have the wonderful evangelistic promise, *"Believe on the Lord Jesus Christ, and you will be saved, you and your household."* This is the answer of Paul and Silas to the question in verse 30 where the Philippian jailor asks, *"Sirs, what must I do to be saved?"* Some who advocate a crossless gospel might be prone to conclude that the single verse of Acts 16:31 is sufficient to evangelize the lost, even without any explanation or qualification of its contents. They might even wrongly assume that since there is no explicit reference to Christ's death on the cross in verse 31, therefore Paul and Silas did not deem Christ's work as something absolutely necessary for the lost to believe for salvation.[17] However, these assumptions would be a serious mishandling of the Word of truth.

Acts 16:30-34

30 *And he brought them out and said, "Sirs, what must I do to be saved?"*
31 *So they said, "Believe on the Lord Jesus Christ, and you will be saved, you and your household."*
32 *Then they spoke the word of the Lord to him and to all who were in his house.*
33 *And he took them the same hour of the night and washed their stripes. And immediately he and all his family were baptized.*
34 *Now when he had brought them into his house, he set food before them; and he rejoiced, having believed in God with all his household.*

The reason the faith alone message is presented by Paul and Silas in the form that it is in verse 31 (*"Believe on the Lord Jesus Christ and you shall be saved"*) is only because they are answering the specific question of the Philippian jailor in verse 30 when he asks, *"Sirs, what must I do to be saved?"* Once they give the jailor the answer to his specific question right up front, then they

[17] The word "saved" in Acts 16:31 should still be interpreted contextually as a reference to *eternal* salvation, not a *physical, temporal* deliverance. Though some crossless gospel proponents have begun considering it as a reference to the salvation of the jailor's physical life, this was not the position of Zane Hodges, at least, who regarded it as a reference to eternal salvation. He stated, "Putting it simply, the salvation that is offered to the Philippian jailer is nothing less than the offer of eternal life." Zane C. Hodges, *Did Paul Preach Eternal Life? Should We?* (Mesquite, TX: Kerugma, 2007), 23.

go on to fill-in the details. Acts 16:32 tells us, *"Then they spoke the word of the Lord to him and to all who were in his house."* Because the Philippian jailor specifically asks what he must *"do to be saved"* in verse 30, they give him the one *condition* for salvation up front in verse 31, namely to *"believe."* They even give him the object of faith, *"the Lord Jesus Christ."* However, they do not immediately explain the *contents* of faith or who the Lord Jesus Christ is until verse 32. Had the jailor asked the question, *"**What** must I believe to be saved?"* in verse 30, Paul and Silas's answer in verse 31 would have been quite different. Acts 16:31 would have included an explanation of Christ crucified and risen.

It may also be the case that the Philippian jailor heard general truth about God, sin, and salvation in Christ prior to verse 30, as expressed through the prayers and singing of Paul and Silas while they were still in prison (Acts 16:25). This may be why the jailor even knew enough to ask how to be "saved" in verse 30. But regardless of how much the jailor knew prior to verse 30, it is clear that Paul and Silas proceeded to tell both him and his family about the Lord in verse 32. It should be carefully noted what Acts 16:32 does *not* say. It does *not* say that Paul and Silas proclaimed the word of the Lord only to the jailor's family, since presumably the jailor had already believed a crossless message in verse 31, and he was saved before his family. No, Acts 16:32 says that Paul and Silas *"spoke the word of the Lord **to him** and to all who were in his house."*

By this point in Acts 16:32, we still do not know if the Philippian jailor and his family believed, since this isn't indicated until verse 34. Even though the word *"believe"* in Acts 16:34 is a perfect tense, active voice participle, indicating that by the time of verse 34 the jailor's family had already believed, we still can't determine strictly from the grammar of the passage the exact time when they believed. We can safely assume, however, that this belief took place sometime after verse 32 (when they heard the word of the Lord) but prior to verse 33 (when they were all baptized as believers).

Judging from the order of events in Acts 16:32-34, we may reasonably conclude that the Philippian jailor and his family needed to know *who* "the Lord Jesus Christ" was and *what* He had done for them in order to fulfill the one condition to *"believe on the Lord Jesus Christ"* and *"be saved"* (Acts 16:31). Finally, in regards to the crossless gospel, we must also note that Paul and Silas tell the unsaved jailor to believe in *"the Lord Jesus Christ,"* not just some undefined, unspecified "Jesus." Even the *"Lord Jesus Christ"* is given some explanation according to verse 32. What we learn from this passage is that *what* the lost "must" believe (16:30) in order to be saved is more than just the name of a non-descript entity called "Jesus" and a bare promise of eternal life affixed to that name.

When we are proclaiming the gospel and using standard evangelistic passages such as Acts 16:31; John 3:16; 5:24; or 6:47, context is crucial. When we take people to passages in the Bible in our witnessing endeavors, we should not merely read a single evangelistic verse and ignore its immediate context. This is a characteristic practice of cults such as the Jehovah's Witnesses and Mormons, but it should have no place in the evangelistic approach of Bible-believing Christians.

How Many Verses?

Based on personal discussions with others in the Free Grace movement, it appears that more than a few have begun to embrace the new man-made hermeneutical requirement that all the essential truths needed to be believed for eternal salvation must be contained in a single reference. In correspondence with one prominent crossless gospel proponent, he objected, saying, *"Doesn't it bother you that you can't find all the things necessary to believe for eternal life in just one verse? Doesn't that bother you?"* I will explain in subsequent chapters that there definitely are single "passages" in the Bible that contain all the essential elements of the gospel.

But since the verse divisions of our Bible are man-made, not being created until the 16th century by Robert Estienne,[18] why is it necessary that all the elements of the gospel must be contained in a single verse? Does God state such an evangelistic requirement anywhere in His Word? Or is this a man-made, extra-biblical, and therefore legalistic requirement? And if crossless gospel advocates hedge at this point and admit (as some are doing already) that one "verse" is not required to state all that is essential to believe for eternal salvation, but one "passage" is, then the next logical question is what constitutes a "passage"?[19] How many verses are permissible to form a single "passage"? Two? If it's not one verse after all, and two verses are the necessary minimum, then why not three? And if three, then why not four? Why not a paragraph instead of a few verses? Why not a chapter instead of a paragraph? Who is to say what maximum, divine "word count" is necessary? God certainly doesn't state such. Since God in His Word did not inspire the verse divisions now found in our Bibles, nor even the chapter divisions, this reveals that He is far more concerned about actual content rather than space restrictions and versification.

The Practice of Combining Verses

Furthermore, crossless gospel advocates are not even consistent with their own principles on this point. For example, though Zane Hodges said that we should not have to "combine" passages "to prove" our points, that is exactly what he was required to do with John 6:47. By itself, this verse is not sufficient to tell us who to believe in for eternal life, for it simply says, *"Most*

---

[18] Normal L. Geisler & William E. Nix, *A General Introduction to the Bible, Revised and Expanded* (Chicago: Moody Press, 1986), 341. Estienne was more popularly known by his Latin name "Stephanus." His name in English was "Robert Stevens."

[19] Wilkin admits, "I feel it is vital that we can point to a single passage or even a single verse" (Bob Wilkin, "Four Free Grace Views Related to Two Issues: Assurance and the Five Essentials," *Grace in Focus* 24 [July/August 2009]: 2).

assuredly, I say to you, he who believes in Me has everlasting life." But without verse 43, which is the nearest reference to "Jesus," how can anyone know who "Me" is in verse 47? In Hodges's first article, he stated that John 6:43-47 is also necessary for the castaway to believe in Jesus for eternal life.[20] But in his second article, he narrowed it down to just John 6:47, saying:

> You see, as we noted previously, the facts surrounding the gospel message—such as the death and resurrection of Christ—are important facts for what they tell us about the reasons for trusting Christ. But believing these facts doesn't save anyone. People are only saved when they believe that Jesus gives them eternal life the moment they believe in Him for that. Let's return for a moment to that deserted island in the Pacific Ocean that I invented in my previous article. My hypothetical unsaved man has just read the words of Jesus in John 6:47, "Most assuredly, I say to you, he who believes in Me has eternal life." All this person needs to do is to believe that statement and eternal life is his.[21]

But even apart from isolating John 6:47 by itself, this whole attempt at minimization still has serious flaws. Even if we were to grant Hodges's initial point about the marooned islander receiving all of John 6:43-47 but with verses 44-46 washed out, how could the poor man be sure that the "Jesus" of verse 43 was still the same one speaking by the time he came to verse 47 where it says *"believes in Me"*? Perhaps in verses 44-46 someone besides Jesus began speaking and continued through verse 47? How could anyone know for sure without verses 44-46? If the stranded islander simply makes an educated guess, isn't he gambling his eternal destiny on a guess that it's the same person speaking in verse 47 as in verse 43?

To show the absurdity that the castaway could be saved with just John 6:43a and John 6:47 put together, imagine for a moment that instead of John 6:43-47 washing ashore, it is John 11:16-25. And just like Hodges's poor islander having a good portion of his text washed away, so this fragment is illegibly marred from John 11:16b-24, so that it reads as follows, *"Then Thomas, who is called the Twin, said. . . . to her, I am the resurrection and the life. He who believes in Me, though he may die, yet shall he live"* (John 11:16a, 25). Would God receive the sincere faith of the castaway and grant him eternal life if he just innocently assumed the guarantor of eternal life was named "Thomas" instead of "Jesus"? Would the man's faith be disqualified just because he had the name wrong? You see, context is crucial in determining the right content of our faith.

The crossless gospel advocates' claim of being more scriptural in witnessing logically breaks down at several other points as well. We have to ask the theological question, if God could cause John 6:47 to reach a poor

[20] Hodges, "How to Lead People to Christ, Part 1," 4.

[21] Hodges, "How to Lead People to Christ, Part 2," 12.

man stranded on a deserted island, then why couldn't He allow a few more verses or even the whole chapter to wash ashore, so the poor man would have absolutely no room to doubt who Jesus really is and who is really making the promise of verse 47? If God in His sovereignty, omnipotence, and love is able to give only two clear verses, why not a few more?

Secondly, depending on which text of John 6:47 the marooned man receives, this will determine his entire eternal destiny. If he receives a translation based upon the Greek Critical Text, the words *"in Me"* are absent, so that verse 47 simply reads, *"Most assuredly, I say to you, whoever believes has everlasting life."* If he receives this text, the object of faith is completely removed and he may be led to think he can have eternal life if he just "believes." He can receive eternal life just through the power of positive thinking! On a more practical level, could you witness on the streets of America with your New American Standard Bible in hand, which is based on the Critical Text, and just take people to John 6:47? Would this be sufficient for their salvation, without having to "combine" passages?

Thirdly, crossless gospel advocates are not consistent themselves about their claim to not "combine" Scripture passages to prove their point. Suppose that you guide an unsaved soul to John 20:31, an excellent verse for evangelism. Since the verse promises life to all who believe that Jesus is the Christ, the Son of God, the unsaved person at that point might naturally wonder what exactly believing in Jesus as *"the Christ and the Son of God"* means, especially since he sees that his eternal destiny is riding on this correct identification of Jesus. Where would crossless gospel teachers lead the unsaved man to define the object of faith? John 11:25-27! They have just "combined" verses to prove their point!

Fourthly, while crossless gospel advocates claim there are no single Bible verses or passages that instruct the unsaved to believe that Christ died on the cross for their eternal salvation, a claim that will be refuted in the chapters ahead, the fact remains that again they are not consistent with their own principles. Notice again Hodges's claim: *"The simple fact of the matter is that the statement I am criticizing is technically incorrect. People are not saved by believing that Jesus died on the cross; they are saved by believing in Jesus for eternal life, or eternal salvation. If we say it the biblical way, we will be able to support our claim by direct biblical statements."*[22] If we press this perspective to its logical conclusion, then frankly crossless gospel proponents shouldn't even be using their new, oft' repeated summary statement, *"Jesus guarantees eternal life to all who simply believe in Him for it."* Wilkin even seeks to encapsulate the gospel in one sentence, saying:

> When Jesus evangelized, as seen in passages like John 3:16; 5:24; 6:47; and 11:25-27, He routinely communicated three things. We, too, must share those three elements. They are:

---

[22] Ibid., 10.

> 1. believing
> 2. in Jesus
> 3. for eternal life
>
> I like to put it together in one sentence as follows: *Jesus* guarantees *everlasting life* to all who simply *believe* in Him.[23]

If we want to be technical at this point, we could ask where in the Bible can we even find the direct statement, *"Jesus guarantees everlasting life to all who simply believe in Him"*? There is no one verse that says exactly that. Similarly, the Grace Evangelical Society uses the scripturally accurate expression, *"Faith alone in Christ alone,"* as an apt Free Grace slogan. However, that "direct statement" is not even found in the Bible! So can we apply the same standard that Hodges used and ask at this point, *"Why is it that we like to verbalize our message in ways that the Bible does not do? What is wrong with biblical language? The associated question is this: what is wrong with our language"*?[24] While the slogan "Faith alone in Christ alone" is doctrinally correct and true, of course, it can only be deduced by combining verses to prove our point. Even when we use the theological phrase, saying, "Salvation is by grace alone," there is not one verse in the Bible containing that "direct statement" either, though it is still a vital biblical truth.

The New *Sine Qua Non*

In my introductory chapter, I proposed several essential elements of the saving gospel which constitute the contents of saving faith. These included Christ's deity, humanity, death for our sins, resurrection, and salvation by grace through faith alone. I stated that these essentials formed the *sine qua non* of the gospel, which will be developed in subsequent chapters. Crossless gospel advocates have developed their own list of three essentials based upon their John 6:47 version of the gospel. The public debate on this point is already well underway, since Bob Wilkin has proposed in a theological journal article three essential elements as the *"sine qua non* of the gospel."[25] Quoting Wilkin again from a book where he explains these elements under the heading, "THREE ESSENTIALS," Wilkin writes:

> When Jesus evangelized, as seen in passages like John 3:16; 5:24; 6:47; and 11:25-27, He routinely communicated three things. We, too, must share those three elements. They are:

---

[23] Robert N. Wilkin, *Secure and Sure* (Irving, TX: Grace Evangelical Society, 2005), 74-75 (italics original).

[24] Hodges, "How to Lead People to Christ, Part 2," 10 (italics original).

[25] Robert N. Wilkin, "Justification by Faith Alone is an Essential Part of the Gospel," *JOTGES* 18 (Autumn 2005): 12. See also, Jeremy D. Myers, "The Gospel is More Than 'Faith Alone in Christ Alone'," *JOTGES* 19 (Autumn 2006): 52.

> 1. believing
> 2. in Jesus
> 3. for eternal life
>
> I like to put it together in one sentence as follows: *Jesus* guarantees *everlasting life* to all who simply *believe* in Him. All who simply believe in Jesus are eternally secure. There are no hidden terms. That's it. If you don't mention Jesus, you haven't given enough information. How much detail you give on His substitutionary death (and His finished work) and resurrection depends on the time you have, the prior knowledge of the person you are talking with, and the flow of the conversation. However, to fail to mention Jesus is to drop the ball in evangelism. Additionally, you must mention what it is that He promises: *eternal life* to all who simply *believe* in Him. If you don't mention eternal life or the equivalent (salvation that can never be lost no matter what we do or don't do), you haven't given enough information. Jesus doesn't promise provisional salvation. No one is put on probation. God can't and won't take back eternal life once He gives it to us. Fail to make this clear and you haven't communicated the good news. And if you don't mention that this eternal life is given to all who merely believe in Jesus, you haven't given sufficient information.[26]

In this definitive statement on the necessary contents of saving faith, it must be carefully observed what Wilkin *does* say is required to believe versus what he *doesn't* say is required. He uses imperatival language to differentiate those elements he deems essential from those elements that are non-essential. Regarding the promise of ETERNAL LIFE, he says, *"you must mention"* what it is that Jesus promises; and if you don't, *"you haven't given enough information."* Also, if you fail to mention the sole condition of BELIEVING, *"you haven't given sufficient information."* Finally, if you don't mention JESUS, *"you haven't given enough information."* But when it comes to how much detail about *"Jesus"* you decide to share with the lost (such as His *"substitutionary death"* and *"resurrection"*), we're told it just *"depends."*

Nor does Wilkin believe that by mentioning "Jesus" you must explain His deity and humanity, for in a parallel journal article where he reiterates the same three essentials, he clarifies exactly what he means by the requirement to mention "Jesus." He says, *"If you don't mention the name of Jesus, you have not given enough information."*[27] This is his entire explanation of what it means to include "Jesus" in our gospel. In the theology of the new, reduced, crossless version of the gospel, the "name of Jesus" determines a person's eternal destiny, not a recognition and belief in Christ's

[26] Wilkin, *Secure and Sure*, 74-75 (italics original).

[27] Wilkin, "Justification by Faith Alone is an Essential Part of the Gospel," 12.

deity and humanity. Since Wilkin is unambiguous and doesn't hesitate to use imperatival language when describing those elements he deems truly essential, it is no accident therefore that he refrains from requiring belief in Christ's deity, substitutionary death, and resurrection as the *sine qua non* of the gospel. Clearly, it is *not essential* to believe in the person and work of Christ according to this new gospel.

The imbalanced emphasis and requirement to believe in the message of eternal life, without even knowing who Jesus is or what He did to provide that eternal life, has made a virtual *idol* out of the assurance of eternal life. For all practical purposes, aren't these men really saying that eternal life is given on the basis of whether you believe you have eternal life? If all that's missing is merely the name "Jesus," hasn't the identity of Jesus become virtually irrelevant? Some of their statements certainly give this impression. Regarding the focus of our evangelism not being on the person and work of Christ but on the promise of eternal life, Hodges has stated, *"Instead we should be focusing on whether an individual believes that Jesus has given him eternal life."*[28] And Niemelä echoes the same: *"Eternal life is a gift received the moment anyone believes that Jesus Christ has given him/her eternal life."*[29] Wilkin is the clearest of all on this point, saying:

> There aren't many evangelistic appeals. There is one. There aren't many ways to come to Jesus. There is but one way. Jesus guarantees eternal life to all who simply believe in Him. That is information we must never fail to communicate. When you tell people about Jesus' death and resurrection, don't stop there. Go on to tell them that all who simply believe in Him have everlasting life. He is able to fulfill that promise because of His death and resurrection. *But call people to believe the promise.* When we believe in Jesus, we believe in His promise of everlasting life to the believer. *The true object of saving faith is the faith-alone-in-Christ-alone message.*[30]

It seems the message of eternal life and personal assurance has become the end-all and be-all of evangelism, the new god of the crossless, resurrectionless, deityless gospel. Faith in the gift of eternal life itself has replaced faith in the Giver in whom is found everlasting life (John 14:6; 1 John 5:11-12, 20). In contemplating this tremendous tragedy, thoughtful Christians cannot help sympathizing with Mary Magdalene on Easter morning, *"They have taken away the Lord out of the tomb [i.e., out of the gospel], and we do not know where they have laid Him"* (John 20:2).

---

[28] Hodges, "How to Lead People to Christ, Part 1," 8.

[29] John Niemelä, "The Message of Life in the Gospel of John," *CTSJ* 7 (July-Sept. 2001): 18.

[30] Wilkin, "Justification by Faith Alone is an Essential Part of the Gospel," 14 (italics added).

Chapter 5

Is the New Gospel Truly "Crossless"?

OVERVIEW

While the phrase "crossless gospel" may not be pleasant, it is accurate and appropriate to use in identifying the message of eternal life that is being spread today that doesn't require belief in Christ's deity, death for sin, or resurrection from the dead. The crux of the controversy over the contents of saving faith is not merely about whether people preach the cross but whether God requires belief in Christ's work for eternal life. In this respect, it can be thoroughly documented that a segment of Free Grace evangelicals associated with the Grace Evangelical Society have indeed been teaching in recent years that the "gospel" is God's saving message and also that this saving message doesn't require belief in Christ's person and work. The result is a "gospel" that is "crossless." The use of the phrase "crossless gospel" is consistent with the manner in which Scripture itself speaks of false doctrine and its damaging effects; and it is in keeping with the way Free Grace people themselves have historically used the phrase "Lordship Salvation."

I recognize that labeling the evangelistic message of certain men within the Free Grace camp as a "crossless gospel" is a provocative statement. Some have already claimed it is a misrepresentation of their actual position, since virtually all who hold to this new view have an orthodox belief that Jesus Christ is truly God who became incarnate to die for all our sins and who rose gloriously from the dead. In addition, not only do they personally believe these cardinal doctrines to be true, they often preach these truths with the utmost conviction as being the absolutely necessary *basis* of our salvation. For that I am truly grateful; and I am definitely convinced that these are fellow, born again brothers and sisters in Christ. I have been very careful to this point specifically *not* to claim that they never preach Christ's person and work, or that they deny His deity, death for sin, and resurrection as the *essential grounds* upon which God provides the gift of salvation to mankind. What I have specifically objected to as unscriptural and alarming is their denial that these truths are essential for the unregenerate to know and believe for their eternal salvation. In this, they cannot claim I have misrepresented their position; for in fact, it is now well documented through their many published writings and recorded public teachings.

So how should we view their evangelistic message? First of all, we should admit that while they fervently deny that the lost *must* believe in Christ's deity, substitutionary death, and resurrection to receive the gift of eternal life, they also insist that these truths should still be proclaimed to the lost. John Niemelä calls these truths the *"greatest apologetic"* for the unbeliever becoming convinced of the promise of eternal life.[1] Hodges has even said, *"The preaching of the cross greatly facilitates the process of bringing men to faith in God's Son."*[2] Hodges added that *"we should"* preach the cross of Christ,[3] even saying that we *"emphatically"* should do so,[4] because it is *"so important,"*[5] and that it *"greatly facilitates"* and *"clarifies"* the message of eternal life,[6] even being a *"powerful argument"* for it.[7] Those who are espousing the new view of the gospel are NOT out telling people that

[1] John Niemelä, "Objects of Faith in John: A Matter of Person AND Content," Grace Evangelical Society Grace Conference, Dallas, TX, February 28, 2006.

[2] Zane C. Hodges, "How to Lead People to Christ, Part 1: The Content of Our Message," *JOTGES* 13 (Autumn 2000): 11.

[3] Ibid., 7.

[4] Ibid., 10.

[5] Ibid.

[6] Ibid., 11.

[7] Ibid., 12.

they *shouldn't* preach the cross! They are NOT saying, "Down with the cross-work of Jesus Christ! Let's stop preaching the gospel." On the contrary, they are saying we *should* preach the cross. In fact, at one point, Hodges even went so far as to pronounce that the preaching of the cross is *"essential"* in reaching the average unsaved American. He wrote:

> To be sure, trust in Christ *can occur* without a knowledge of the cross, but more often than not it doesn't. The message of the cross clarifies God's way of salvation. On a very **practical** level, when I am dealing with an unsaved person, I find that if I simply tell him he only needs to believe in Christ, this usually doesn't make sense to him. Why should it be so easy? Why are not works required? To the unregenerate American mind, it doesn't sound reasonable. So I find it not only useful, but indeed **essential**, to explain that the Lord Jesus Christ bought our way to heaven by paying for all our sins.[8]

After reading all that Hodges wrote previous to this statement, one is baffled as to how the preaching of the cross can seriously be considered *"essential."* After the Grace camp has been berated for its *"tendency"*[9] of *"adding to the gospel"*[10] in a manner similar to the *"lordship"*[11] camp who *"add provisos"*[12] to the condition for salvation—a *"tendency"* for which we are *"guilty"*[13] and should be *"embarrassed"*[14] since this is a *"flawed"*[15] gospel that conflicts with God's Word in the Gospel of John—after reading all that, we must seriously wonder how *"essential"* the preaching of the cross actually is! It is apparent that Hodges deemed it only *practically* necessary for reaching American audiences, not *scripturally* necessary before God Himself. In spite of all the positive statements from crossless gospel advocates about the unsurpassed value and potency of the cross in our evangelism, there is still something conspicuously absent in all their writings and teachings. It is the positive affirmation that *God Himself requires* the lost to believe in Christ's deity, humanity, substitutionary death, and resurrection. Not only are such affirmations lacking, but there are repeated, explicit denials that these truths are divinely required.

At this point, the objection might be raised, *"Well, if they're still preaching that Jesus Christ is the Son of God who died for our sins and rose again, then what's the problem? Aren't the unsaved still hearing the truth about Christ's person and work? Though I don't agree with their doctrinal idiosyncrasies here,*

---

[8] Ibid. (bold added; italics original).

[9] Ibid., 7-8.

[10] Ibid., 7.

[11] Ibid.

[12] Ibid.

[13] Ibid., 8.

[14] Ibid.

[15] Ibid.

what's the harm in tolerating this new view?" Several points must be made in response to this objection.

The Dilemma of Muslim Evangelism

First, the problem of the new, aberrant form of the gospel is *not* merely theoretical and harmless. Some proponents of this new gospel, when confronted with the possibility that their gospel allows a person to deny the deity of Christ and still receive eternal life, have averred that the problem is all just "hypothetical"[16] and inconsequential, since they also believe and proclaim Christ's deity, death for sin, resurrection, etc. However, this defense will not suffice for one moment.

Imagine that an advocate of crossless saving faith is evangelizing a Muslim with his abbreviated, John 6:47 version of the saving message. He tells the Muslim that Jesus can guarantee him everlasting life if he just believes in Him for it. Then the crossless gospel advocate dutifully proceeds to inform the Muslim that Jesus is also God's Son, who died on the cross for his sins and who rose from the dead. Then, at this juncture in the conversation, the crossless evangelist is met with an arresting question from the Muslim, who asserts the following:

> Well I don't believe that Jesus is God's Son, since the Qur'an repeatedly calls it a monstrous falsehood to believe that God has any equals. Jesus—blessed be his name—was a man and a great prophet; but my tradition also tells me in the Hadith that he is coming back again before judgment day. Perhaps that will be in my lifetime; so I can conceivably see and believe that he can guarantee me everlasting life somehow. However, I must also reject your claim that he died on the cross, since the Qur'an also rejects this in Sura 4:157. And therefore I must also deny that Jesus—peace be upon him—rose from the dead, since he never died, as Sura 4:158 states, *"they did not slay him for certain; God lifted him up to Him."* However, dear Christian, you said before that if I simply believe in him as the only one who can guarantee me eternal life, then I can receive eternal life on that basis, right? Well, I believe in Jesus—blessed be his name—as my guarantor of eternal life, though I reject your claim to his deity, and his death for my sins, and his resurrection.

Now what will the crossless gospel advocate say in response? Will he warn this Muslim that he has a false assurance and that he is still dead in his trespasses and sins until he believes in the Jesus of the Bible? But how can he warn him, since the Muslim is just consistently following the logic of the new crossless gospel? The same scenario could be replayed countless times simply by substituting members of other cults and world religions

[16] Brandon Wallace, "Free Grace Theology for Beginners," Grace Evangelical Society Conference, Dallas, TX, February 27, 2006.

in the place of the deceived Muslim. Clearly, this is not just a "hypothetical" problem with no eternal consequences.

Evangelizing the Way Jesus Did

Secondly, regarding the objection that the lost are still hearing the truth of Christ's person and work, crossless gospel proponents must acknowledge that there *has been* a noticeable de-emphasis in the last decade or so in their teaching when it comes to the subjects of Christ's deity, death on the cross for our sins, and resurrection. This is true, despite their repeated protests to the contrary, as was documented in chapter 1. This was the inevitable result of relegating belief in Christ's deity, death, and resurrection for eternal life from the status of being absolutely *necessary* to simply being *important*. It was the inevitable result of shifting their whole focus and emphasis from the person and work of Christ in the gospel to the provision of Christ—eternal life.

In the midst of the controversy over the contents of saving faith, it has been common to hear proponents of a crossless faith adamantly insist, "But we always make it a point to preach Christ's death and resurrection in our evangelism, even if it's not required by God. So, this whole debate is all a moot point!" While it is certainly true that the crux of this controversy is not over what is *presented* to the lost but what is divinely *required* by God according to His Word, we must still question their claim to consistently preach Christ crucified and risen. The logic of the doctrinal position undergirding their claim to always preach the death and resurrection is anything but consistent, which renders it suspect.

We are repeatedly told that we ought to evangelize the lost today simply by following the example of the Lord Jesus' evangelism in the Gospel of John. Specifically, we are told that "we should evangelize the way our Lord did. And we know how Jesus evangelized because the apostle John gave us an entire book, the fourth Gospel, which gives *the way of the Master* (John 20:30-31)."[17] But at the same time, advocates of a crossless saving faith also inform us that, in John's Gospel, "he has many nutshell statements on how to pass *from death to life*. What may surprise us is the **strange absence** of Christ's cross and resurrection from John's message-in-a-nutshell verses for unbelievers."[18] We are told that such verses include the classic evangelistic passages of John 3:16, 36; 4:5-26; 5:24; 6:47;

[17] Bob Wilkin, "The Way of the Master," *Grace in Focus* 22 (July/August 2007): 4. See also, Bob Wilkin, "Is the Evangelistic Message That Jesus Preached a Sufficient Evangelistic Message Today?" Grace Evangelical Society Conference, Fort Worth, TX, March 5, 2008; idem, "We Believe Jesus is Lord," *Grace in Focus* 23 (March/April 2008): 2.

[18] John Niemelä, "The Cross in John's Gospel," *JOTGES* 16 (Spring 2003): 17, 18, 27 (bold added). See also, John Niemelä, "The Message of Life in the Gospel of John," *CTSJ* 7 (July-September 2001): 2, 9, 18.

11:25-27; and 20:31.[19] Most of these are the words of Christ Himself in various evangelistic settings.

But if we are to evangelize the way Jesus did, and yet the cross and resurrection were supposedly "absent" in most instances of the Lord's own evangelism, why should crossless advocates bother to "always include" the cross and resurrection in their gospel preaching? Shouldn't they be evangelizing the way Jesus did by barely mentioning the cross and resurrection? And how can we even take their contention seriously when they insist that "the cross and resurrection have a vital role in John's Gospel and in our message to the unbeliever"[20] and that Christ's redeeming work is even the "greatest apologetic"[21] for the lost to believe in Jesus for eternal life? What we believe about the contents of faith required by God for salvation definitely has an impact upon the way we do evangelism, as our practice inevitably stems from our personal doctrinal convictions.

Apologetic Aid or Spiritual Alp?

The rationale that stands behind the crossless claim to always present the person and work of the Savior in evangelism is seen to be illogical on another count. Oftentimes crossless proponents express sentiments that appear to contradict their claim to value the preaching of the cross. In personal correspondence with one teacher of the crossless view I was reproved for suggesting that our evangelism is more effective when starting with a presentation of the person and work of the Savior, rather than the promise of eternal life, since His person and work form the very basis for possessing eternal life. After stipulating that a lost person must believe in the Savior's deity for eternal life, I was told that according to my evangelistic approach, the "poor soul" who heard my gospel would end up being "subjected to a course on Christology" before he could be saved. This claim was made despite the fact that John begins his Gospel with an unequivocal declaration of Christ's deity (John 1:1) and a prologue that is among the most highly Christological portions in the entire Word of God (John 1:1-18). But such sentiments clearly reveal the perspective of some crossless proponents that the doctrines of Christ's person and work are actually more of an *obstacle* than an *aid* to receiving eternal life.

This inconsistency in the crossless position is reflected in an article that appeared in the G.E.S. publication, *Grace in Focus*, which was written by a man who does mountain climbing as a hobby. In the article titled, "Alp upon Alp," the writer compared the experience of a lost person who is presented with the requirement to believe in Christ's person and work

---

[19] Niemelä, "The Cross in John's Gospel," 17-18; idem, "The Message of Life in the Gospel of John," 2, 9, 18; Wilkin, "Is the Evangelistic Message That Jesus Preached a Sufficient Evangelistic Message Today?"; idem, "The Way of the Master," 4.

[20] Niemelä, "The Cross in John's Gospel," 19.

[21] Niemelä, "Objects of Faith in John: A Matter of Person AND Content."

to the discouragement that a mountain climber faces at the prospect of having to scale a series of mountain peaks. He writes:

> I've many times experienced the heartache of *Alp upon Alp*. Just when I think I'm cresting the summit ridge and I've reached my goal, my heart sinks to see another difficult ridge (or two!) remaining to ascend before reaching the top. Tragically, thoughtless evangelism can also place Alps between people inquiring after Jesus Christ and the goal of eternal life. When someone draws near to Christ and wants to know what he must do to be saved, some presentations require agreement with long lists of Biblical truths along the way as a necessary precondition for attaining to that life. But these Alps, thrown up no doubt with good intentions, may instead have the effect of prohibiting all but the hardiest seeker from ever believing Jesus' promise.[22]

In spite of the continual refrain coming from crossless gospel proponents that they always present the cross and resurrection in their evangelism, sentiments such as the previous one stand directly opposed to that claim. Why should we present the person and work of Christ if it has a deflating and defeating effect upon the lost that actually discourages them from receiving the promise of eternal life? How can the cross-work of Christ really play a "vital role"[23] in evangelism and be the "greatest apologetic"[24] for believing that Christ guarantees eternal life when in fact it is viewed as an obstacle to obtaining that goal? With reasoning like this, it is not too surprising to discover that sometimes the importance of Christ's person and work are diminished by crossless proponents when they evangelize the lost. This is done so that the unbeliever, ostensibly, may accept more readily the promise of eternal life. Thus, the same writer goes on to propose a "promise-only" gospel in the place of the doctrinal "Alps" of Christ's deity, humanity, substitutionary death, and bodily resurrection that stand between the unbeliever and eternal life:

> Likewise, for eternal life, Christ need be known only as its Giver, no matter how that conviction arises, no matter how ignorant the believer may be of the underpinnings of the promise, and no matter even if he may hold to errors about Christ at the same time. The only Alp that stands before any person hungry for eternal life is the persuasion that Jesus' promise of it is true.
>
> In short, as we tell our inquiring friends at the Denver Rescue Mission, you're believing in the right Jesus if, whatever you may know—or not know—about Him, you're convinced He gives you eternal life when you believe Him for it. The more information

[22] Lon Gregg, "Alp upon Alp," *Grace in Focus* 24 (January/February 2009): 1.
[23] Niemelä, "The Cross in John's Gospel," 19.
[24] Niemelä, "Objects of Faith in John: A Matter of Person AND Content."

> the better, of course; the more we know, the easier it is to believe. But if we never rise to the level of full orthodoxy about the bodily resurrected, substitutionally offered, fully divine, fully and perfectly human, virginally conceived Son of God, thank God the simple promise of eternal salvation He made to us is true for the taking, now and forever![25]

Note carefully that this writer assures his unsaved inquirers that they have faith "in the right Jesus" even if they don't accept Christ's person and work. Does this not diminish the value of believing the gospel? How can we avoid the conclusion that in essence the crossless approach to evangelism amounts to telling the lost that the deity, humanity, death, and resurrection of Christ do not ultimately matter when it comes to believing in Jesus for eternal life? If this new teaching of a crossless gospel persists and gains a following, it will have devastating consequences upon the practical evangelization of lost souls as they are given the false assurance that they have "the right Jesus" even though they may believe in a Jesus who was not God the Son who became incarnate to die a substitutionary death for our sins and rise from the dead.

The radical and harmful effects of such a doctrine are demonstrated in the statements of one vocal internet promoter of a crossless, deityless saving faith, Antonio da Rosa. On his website, "Free Grace Theology," he affirms the salvation of Jehovah Witnesses and Mormons who believe the "promise-only gospel." In an article bearing the rather unvarnished title, "Believe Christ's Promise and You are Saved, No Matter What Misconceptions You Hold," Antonio da Rosa writes:

> Yet, I will not get into debates concerning things peripheral to the reception of eternal life. If a JW hears me speak of Christ's deity and asks me about it, I will say, "Let us agree to disagree about this subject." I will discuss with him Jesus' ability to impart eternal life by faith alone apart from works. This is where I want to zero in with the JW or the Mormon. They believe that salvation comes by faith AND works, and LOTS of works (not unsimilar to the Traditionalist religion). At the moment that a JW or a Mormon is convinced that Jesus Christ has given to them unrevokable eternal life when they believed on Him for it, I would consider such a one saved, REGARDLESS of their varied misconcetions and beliefs about Jesus. Both the Mormons and the JWs will say that Jesus IS "the son of God." Yet they will provide some other import other than monotheistic deity into it. For John, the "Son of God" and "the Christ" have the import "the one who promises (guarantees) eternal life to the believer in Him for it." I would never say you don't have to believe that Jesus is the Son of God. This has the import of the gospel proposition which makes it sal-

[25] Gregg, "Alp upon Alp," 4.

> vific! If someone asks me point blank, do I believe that one must believe that Jesus is God in order to go to heaven, I would say "NO!"[26]

Though it is certainly appropriate and necessary when witnessing to address the meritorious, works-based salvation that characterizes both the Jehovah Witnesses and the Mormons, this provides no biblical justification for giving members of each cult the false assurance that they possess eternal life. Furthermore, da Rosa provides another clear example where the truths of the Savior's person and work are not viewed as great apologetic aids to belief in Christ as the guarantor of eternal life. When a cultist hears da Rosa speaking of Christ's deity, instead of using the occasion and the subject of deity to apologetically underscore the truth that Christ can guarantee eternal life precisely because He is God, we are told that this is a "peripheral" issue that shouldn't be pressed but instead put on the backburner as we simply "agree to disagree" over it.

Preach the Maximum, Require the Minimum

It is inherently inconsistent for proponents of a crossless saving faith to claim that when it comes to evangelism "The more information the better, of course; and the more we know, the easier it is to believe."[27] We often hear proponents of the G.E.S. gospel defend their position by claiming that although they believe that the minimum content of saving faith consists of (1) the name "Jesus" (2) believing and (3) the promise of eternal life, they still preach the maximum of Christ's deity, humanity, substitutionary death, and bodily resurrection. But from a pragmatic standpoint, how will preaching the maximum make it "easier . . . to believe" and be "better" when at the same time these very truths are regarded as spiritual mountains or "Alps" that stand in the way of faith in Christ for eternal life? How will more information make it easier to be persuaded that Christ guarantees eternal life if the lost are potentially stumbled by each successive "peripheral" issue or mountain peak of truth about the Savior? When the cross of Christ is preached and the lost reject it in unbelief, and this is followed by a presentation of His resurrection that is also rejected in disbelief, and this is further followed by teaching on His deity with still more unbelief, won't the end result be that a person actually has *less confidence* in Christ as the guarantor of eternal life? Won't presenting these truths to the lost give them more to potentially reject and stumble over? According to the logic of the crossless position, it would be better to not even put a stumblingblock in the path of the unbeliever. Therefore, why not simply omit discussion of the Savior's person and work altogether?

---

[26] See the article titled, "Believe Christ's Promise and You are Saved, No Matter What Misconceptions You Hold," dated May 25, 2006 at http://free-grace.blogspot.com/ 2006_05_01_archive.html (accessed August 20, 2007).

[27] Gregg, "Alp upon Alp," 4.

Of course, the only reason for continuing to preach a known stumblingblock such as the message of the cross (1 Cor. 1:23) to an unbeliever is if this is a truth that *must be believed* for eternal life. If Paul removed all unnecessary, potential stumblingblocks from his own life in an all-out effort to see the lost get saved (1 Cor. 9:22; 10:33), and yet he continued preaching the cross knowing full-well that it was a major stumblingblock to the world (1 Cor. 1:17-23), then the only logical conclusion is that the cross is a *necessary stumblingblock* from the Lord's perspective. According to Scripture, it is the message of the cross that forms the universal dividing line between the perishing and the saved (1 Cor. 1:18). The soteriological line of demarcation is *not* the message of *eternal life regardless of the cross*—it is the message of the cross! However, according to the logic of the crossless gospel, there is no real impetus for continuing to preach a message that knowingly stumbles the lost. While the *practice* of crossless gospel proponents may be inconsistent with their *doctrine* as they practically "always" preach a known stumbling block to faith in Jesus for eternal life, it is likely that given the passage of time their practice will harmonize with the tenets of their doctrine and they will eventually evangelize only with a crossless saving message—the way Jesus supposedly did. Our *deeds* always follow close behind our *doctrine*.

The Doctrinal Domino Effect

Another reason why the preaching of a crossless gospel has significant consequences and is not just harmless and "hypothetical" is that it has led to a whole host of similar shifting doctrines. This was documented in chapter 2, but the impact of these related doctrines upon numerous salvation passages is seen especially in chapters 11-12 and 15-17. This tipping of multiple doctrinal dominos was the inevitable result of shifting on the most foundational doctrine of all—the gospel, which is nothing less than the saving message.

The New Level of Adamancy

Yet another reason why the preaching of a crossless gospel should not be viewed as merely a harmless aberration is because there is developing a very critical attitude toward other Free Grace Christians, past and present, who would wish to keep the person and work of Christ necessary as components of the gospel that the lost must believe for their eternal salvation. I personally observed this at one national conference. There, a well-known evangelist presented a passionate gospel presentation and salvation appeal that focused on Christ's cross-work and resurrection in 1 Corinthians 15:3-4. Afterwards, one crossless gospel proponent personally expressed to me his sore displeasure with this evangelist's deficient gospel presentation. Though the message emphasized the finished work of Christ in resolving man's sin-problem, along with the proper response of faith alone in

Christ, apparently this was viewed as both deficient and mis-focused by this crossless proponent. He informed me afterwards that the evangelist should have emphasized John's message of "eternal life" instead.

In addition, I have increasingly heard the normative, traditional Free Grace position referred to as "checklist" evangelism,[28] "theological legalism,"[29] "doctrinal legalism,"[30] and "scavenger hunt salvation without a list."[31] Why such heated rhetoric? Simply because the traditional Free Grace position insists upon the lost believing in Christ's deity, humanity, death for sin, and bodily resurrection in order to receive eternal life. This level of adamancy, hardened conviction, and crystallization of doctrine in opposition to the traditional Free Grace position is very disconcerting; and it is a likely harbinger of even further doctrinal departure from God's Word by those who have embraced the new crossless gospel.

A "Crossless" Gospel?

Finally, others might still raise another legitimate objection that needs clarification. They might insist, *"By your own admission these Free Grace advocates still often preach the cross, so how can you honestly claim that they've been preaching a crossless gospel?"* And the answer is quite simple: because they have!

---

[28] Zane C. Hodges, "The Hydra's Other Head: Theological Legalism," *Grace in Focus* 23 (September/October 2008): 2.

[29] Ibid. It is revealing that Hodges deliberately chose to identify the normative Free Grace gospel by the phrase "theological legalism." This shows the severity with which Hodges detested the inclusion of Christ's person and work in the contents of saving faith. According to Hodges's own testimony, he reserved the term "legalism" only for the direst theological conflict. It was literally his "nuclear" option. In response to the charges of some Lordship Salvation proponents that the Free Grace position is "antinomian," Hodges wrote: "Legalism is not a very nice word. No one wants to be accused of it anymore than one would want to be accused of despising motherhood or apple pie. In ecclesiastical circles, to call someone a legalist is to hurl an insult of the first magnitude. If someone says, 'You're a legalist,' the instinctive reply would be, 'Them's fighting words!'" Zane C. Hodges, "Legalism: The Real Thing," *JOTGES* 9 (Autumn 1996): 21. Later in the same article, Hodges went on to write: "So you see what I mean. If we could confine the designation antinomian to those who will not acknowledge any such thing as a Christian law, we would clarify the situation greatly. But don't hold your breath waiting for this to happen. Antinomian is too good a Christian 'cuss-word' to retreat easily to the fringes of theological debate in the way I am suggesting. It just happens to be a very convenient cudgel with which to bludgeon theological opponents whose attributes and theology offend us. I regret to say that Christian polemicists do not readily retire their most useful brickbats, anymore than the nuclear powers easily discard their nuclear arsenals. It's nice to have something with which to blow your opponents off the face of the map, and antinomianism serves very well for that purpose in some theological circles. So how about my own nuclear arsenal? What theological word is my big bomb? All right. I'm going to admit it. My own nuclear riposte is wrapped up in one word: legalism." (ibid., 25).

[30] Bob Wilkin, "Essential Truths About Our Savior," *Grace in Focus* 23 (November/December 2008): 2; idem, "Scavenger Hunt Salvation Without a List," *Grace in Focus* 23 (May/June 2008): 1.

[31] Ibid.

The conclusion that they have propagated a "gospel" that is "crossless" can be easily demonstrated from the answers to two simple questions:

1) First, have those who are propagating this new view of the gospel taught that a person *must* believe "the gospel" in order to be justified and born again?

2) Second, according to the new view, *must* a person believe that Jesus Christ died for his or her sins in order to be justified and born again?

If the answer to the first question is "Yes" and the answer to the second question is "No," then this is clearly a "gospel" that is "crossless." For decades, advocates of this new gospel have taught that a lost person must believe "the gospel" or the "good news" or "the gospel Jesus preached," etc. in order to receive eternal life. For example, Bob Wilkin has written, *"You can believe many biblical concepts and still miss* ***the one truth that is saving—the truth of the gospel.*** *For example, you can attest to Jesus' deity, His virgin birth, and His bodily resurrection, and yet not believe Jesus' promise to give you eternal life freely if you just believe in Him for it. There is only one truth that will save: Jesus' guarantee that anyone who believes in Him for eternal life has it."*[32] Advocates of this new view have repeatedly and publicly taught that a lost person must believe "the gospel" or the "good news" or "the gospel Jesus preached" in order to receive eternal life. So we must ask, "Have those who are propagating this new view of the gospel taught that a person *must* believe 'the gospel' in order to be justified and born again?" The answer is a definite "Yes!"

But what about the second question? According to the new view, *must* a person believe that Jesus Christ died for his or her sins in order to be justified and born again? Their answer to this question is an equally emphatic, "No!" For example, Hodges stated unequivocally, *"People are not saved by believing that Jesus* ***died on the cross****; they are saved by believing in Jesus for eternal life, or eternal salvation."*[33] And again, he wrote, *"The simple truth is that Jesus can be believed for eternal salvation apart from any detailed knowledge of what He did to provide it."*[34]

Could their position be any clearer? While they have repeatedly taught over the last two decades in their books, booklets, newsletters, journal articles, tracts, on the internet, in sermons, and in seminars all across the country that lost sinners must believe ***"the gospel"*** in order to receive eternal life, they have also taught that God does not require lost

---

[32] Robert N. Wilkin, *Confident in Christ* (Irving, TX: Grace Evangelical Society, 1999), 10 (bold added).

[33] Zane C. Hodges, "How to Lead People to Christ, Part 2: Our Invitation to Respond," *JOTGES* 14 (Spring 2001): 10 (bold added).

[34] Ibid., 12.

sinners to believe or even know that "*Jesus died on **the cross**.*" That, dear reader, is a "crossless gospel" no matter how you slice it!

For those who still remain in doubt that several key Free Grace teachers have been, in this last decade or so, propagating a "gospel" that is "crossless," the following pages will provide sufficient documentation through parallel statements in order to irrefutably demonstrate this point. In the succeeding parallel columns, the key words have been bolded to highlight this critical distinction. The left-hand column shows the necessity to believe the gospel, and the right-hand column shows the non-necessity to believe the message of the cross for eternal life. While some may protest that theological liberals who don't interpret the Bible literally are the only ones who preach a crossless gospel, the sad fact remains that a vocal minority of Free Grace advocates aligned with the Grace Evangelical Society have promoted a crossless gospel as well. This is the tragic irony of today's new, distorted version of the gospel of grace.

Gospel	Crossless
The Lord Jesus Christ made eternal life the very core and essence of His **gospel**. This is perfectly plain from many passages in the Gospel of John (see 3:15, 16; 4:14; 5:24; 6:27, 40, 54; 10:28; 17:2, 3). (Zane C. Hodges, *Did Paul Preach Eternal Life? Should We?* [Mesquite, TX: Kerugma, 2007], 9)	Neither explicitly nor implicitly does the Gospel of John teach that a person must **understand the cross to be saved**. It just does not teach this. (Zane C. Hodges, "How to Lead People to Christ, Part 1: The Content of Our Faith," *JOTGES* 13 [Autumn 2000]: 7)
While the message of what one must do to have eternal life is included in the ***gospel***, the term ***gospel*** is broader than that one message. (Robert N. Wilkin, review of *Christianity Is the Gospel of the Grace of God, Not the Gospel of the Kingdom*, by Robert C. Brock, *JOTGES* 17 [Spring 2004]: 90) The term **gospel** may be used to describe the plan of salvation in its fullest form. We could in proclaiming the **gospel** mention Jesus' eternality, His leaving His heavenly throne, being born of a virgin, performing miracles which authenticated His message, living a sinless life, dying on the Cross, rising again, and our need to place our trust	It is clear from the Gospel of John that it is possible to believe savingly in Christ **without understanding the reality of His resurrection.** A number of verses clearly show that when **Jesus died** the disciples—who were already believers as noted above—had not yet come to believe that He would **rise from the dead** (e.g., Luke 24:10-11; John 20:9). They thought that all hope was lost. Only after His post-resurrection appearances did they come to believe in His **resurrection**. As could also be said about the **death of Christ**, unless a person questions the relevancy of the many Johannine statements calling people to faith in **Christ before His death and**

in Him alone. The term **gospel** may also he used to describe the plan of salvation in its barest form. It is possible to present only the core truth of the **gospel**: namely, that whoever believes in Jesus Christ has eternal life. That too is the **gospel**-albeit the **gospel** in a nutshell. If, for example, in sharing the **gospel** we were to fail to mention Jesus' virgin birth, we would not necessarily be failing to explain it clearly. We would, however, necessarily be sharing it less fully. (Robert N. Wilkin, *The Grace Evangelical Society News* [June 1990]: 4)

resurrection had occurred and had been understood, they must admit that an **understanding of His resurrection** is not strictly necessary to saving faith. (Robert N. Wilkin, *The Grace Evangelical Society News* [June 1990]: 1)

No one would ever accuse Paul of minimizing the cross and resurrection, but the bottom line of his **gospel** was that Jesus saves from eternal condemnation all who simply believe in Him. John would express the same point in terms of receiving eternal life (John 3:16, 36; 5:24; 6:47; and 20:30-31). (John Niemelä, "The Cross in John's Gospel," *JOTGES* 30 [Spring 2003]: 27)

John keeps the signs distinct from the message of life, so evangelicals must not confuse them either. John does not set forth the sign of the **cross-and-resurrection** as the message that one must believe in order to receive eternal life. (John Niemelä, "The Message of Life in the Gospel of John," *CTSJ* 7 [July-Sept. 2001]: 18)

Paul told us that his **gospel** "came through the revelation of Jesus Christ" (Gal. 1:12). As far as Paul was concerned, this was the one and only **gospel** that God had given to men (see Gal. 1:6-9). He preached what Jesus preached. (Zane C. Hodges, *Did Paul Preach Eternal Life? Should We?* [Mesquite, TX: Kerugma, 2007], 30)

There is, was, and always will be only one **gospel**. The **gospel** of Adam, Moses, Abraham, and David is also the **gospel** according to Jesus, Peter, Paul, and the other apostles. (Robert N. Wilkin, "Salvation Before Calvary," *The Grace Evangelical Society News* [January 1998])

This statement [John 20:30-31] does not affirm the necessity of believing in our **Lord's substitutionary atonement.** If by the time of the writing of John's Gospel, it was actually necessary to believe this, then it would have been not only simple, but essential, to say so. Inasmuch as the key figures in John's narrative *did* believe in Jesus before they **understood His atoning death and resurrection**, it would have been even more essential for John to state that the content of faith had changed. But of course he does not do this. The simple fact is that the whole Fourth Gospel is designed to show that its readers can get saved the same way as the people who got saved in John's narrative. To say anything

If the **gospel** changed after Pentecost, then one could not be saved by believing the **gospel** which Jesus preached! (Ibid.)

To put it another way: the **gospel** Jesus preached is still the **gospel**! (Robert N. Wilkin, "Tough Questions About Saving Faith," *The Grace Evangelical Society News* [June 1990])

other than this is to accept a fallacy. (Zane C. Hodges, "How to Lead People to Christ, Part 1: The Content of Our Faith," *JOTGES* 13 [Autumn 2000]: 6-7 [brackets added for context])

The **gospel** that Paul subsequently proclaimed came directly from the Son of God. And the **gospel** that Jesus Himself preached centered on eternal life. It is therefore inherently illogical to think that Paul did not proclaim a **gospel** that was the same as the message Jesus Himself gave to men. (Zane C. Hodges, *Did Paul Preach Eternal Life? Should We?* [Mesquite, TX: Kerugma, 2007], 9)

Now suppose that our unsaved man somehow becomes convinced that this person called Jesus can guarantee his eternal future, since He promises everlasting life. In other words, he believes Jesus' words in John 6:47. Is he saved? I suspect that there are some grace people who would say that this man is not saved because he doesn't know enough. For example, he doesn't know that **Jesus died for his sins on the cross and rose again the third day**. (Zane C. Hodges, "How to Lead People to Christ, Part 1: The Content of Our Faith," *JOTGES* 13 [Autumn 2000]: 4)

It is this conviction that ought to arm us for the work of sharing the **gospel** with people. In the final analysis, therefore, salvation is the result of believing in Jesus to provide it. Salvation is not the result of assenting to a detailed creed. Salvation does not even require an I understanding of how it was provided for or made possible. (Zane C. Hodges, "How to Lead People to Christ, Part 1: The Content of Our Faith," *JOTGES* 13 [Autumn 2000]: 10)

In other words, God does not say to people, "You trusted my Son's name, but you didn't believe in His virgin birth, or **His substitutionary atonement, or His bodily resurrection**, so your faith is not valid." *We* say that, but God's Word does not. Suffice it to say, however, that Jesus never fails anyone who trusts Him for everlasting salvation. No one on earth will ever possess more than a rudimentary understanding of our Savior's **person and work**. (Zane C. Hodges, "How to Lead People to Christ, Part 1: The Content of Our Faith," *JOTGES* 13 [Autumn 2000]: 9-10)

However, few have a full understanding of substitutionary atonement until long after they came to faith in Jesus for eternal life. The point remains that millions do not understand or do not fully understand substitutionary atonement, yet they genuinely believe that Jesus died on the cross for their sins and that He bodily rose from the dead. Believing that Jesus died and rose again is great, but believing that does not mean that a person is regenerate. In other words, a person may believe that Jesus died and rose again and yet not believe the **gospel**!
(Bob Wilkin, "Justification by Faith Alone is an Essential Part of the Gospel," *JOTGES* 18 [Autumn 2005]: 6)

Just think for a minute of John 3:16; 5:24; 6:47; Acts 16:31, and so on, and not a one of these verses invites us to get saved by believing that **Jesus died on the cross**. Why is it that we like to verbalize our message in ways that the Bible does not do? What is wrong with biblical language? The associated question is this: what is wrong with *our language*? The simple fact of the matter is that the statement I am criticizing is technically incorrect. **People are not saved by believing that Jesus died on the cross**; they are saved by believing in Jesus for eternal life, or eternal salvation.
(Zane C. Hodges, "How to Lead People to Christ, Part 2: Our Invitation to Respond," *JOTGES* 14 [Spring 2001]: 10 [italics original])

What faith really is, in biblical language, is receiving the testimony of God. It is the *inward conviction* that what God says to us in the **gospel** is true. That—and that alone—is saving faith.
(Zane C. Hodges, *Absolutely Free: A Biblical Reply to Lordship Salvation* [Dallas: Redención Viva, 1989], 31)

Faith, then, is taking God at His Word. Saving faith is taking God at His Word in the **gospel**. It is nothing less than this. But it is also nothing more.
(Ibid., 32)

The error of theological legalism is extremely grave. It communicates to the unsaved person that he can only be saved *if his doctrine is correct*, rather than by simple faith in Christ. Moreover, it subverts the assurance of the saved person by making him wonder, "Did I believe *enough* doctrine to be truly saved?" Thus the effect of theological legalism is essentially the same as that of commitment legalism,

In offering eternal life, Jesus Himself never invited *anyone at all* to believe in:
(1) His eternal oneness with the Father and the Holy Spirit;
(2) His incarnation and virgin birth;
(3) His sinless and holy life;
(4) His **death on the cross for our sins**;
(5) His **bodily resurrection**;
(6) His ascension to the right hand of God;
(7) His intercessory work as our Great High Priest;
(8) His Second Coming.
Beyond question, all of these truths are of infinite importance. But **Jesus never conditioned eternal life on believing any of them**. Neither does the Fourth Gospel. Neither does the entire New Testament. In fact one could believe all eight of the truths listed above and not yet be born again. Believing *all these truths* is not the same as believing in Jesus for eternal life.
(Zane C. Hodges, "The Hydra's Other Head: Theological Legalism," *Grace in Focus* 23 [September/October 2008]: 3)

i.e., of Lordship salvation. Both claim to teach salvation by faith alone, but both actually subvert **the biblical gospel.** (Zane C. Hodges, "The Hydra's Other Head: Theological Legalism," *Grace in Focus* 23 [September/October 2008]: 3)

We have the real **good news**. We can say, "I know I have eternal life right now and that I will always have it no matter what. I know that I will spend eternity in God's kingdom. If you have a few minutes I can show you how you can be sure you have eternal life now and forever. Simple, believe Jesus' words in John 6:47, "Most assuredly, I say to you, he who believes in Me has everlasting life". (René A. López, "Basics of Free Grace Theology, Part 2," 9, http://www.scriptureunlocked.com/papers/basicsfgprt2.pdf [accessed August 6, 2007])

Both Free Grace understandings of repentance say that turning from sins may put an unbeliever in a position to hear **the gospel** and believe it and be born again. Cornelius in Acts 10 and Lydia in Acts 16 are examples of this. But that is not to say that turning from sins is a condition of eternal life. It is simply to acknowledge that it is a good thing for unbelievers to turn from their sins and when they do so they are more likely to go to church and hear **the saving message** and be born again. (Ibid., 3)

While Free Grace people believe in and proclaim **the cross and the resurrection**, all who simply just believe **He died and rose again** are wrong in thinking this guarantees eternal life. Why? Does anyone know how a person could believe **Jesus died and rose again** and yet not believe in Jesus for eternal life in the biblical sense? It is because a person must believe in justification by faith alone in order to have eternal life. It is not enough to believe that faith in Jesus is one of many conditions. One must believe that faith in Jesus is the only condition to receive eternal life. No strings attached. While believing in **the basis that accomplished our salvation, life, death and resurrection**, may supply the theological answer to how God can justify a guilty sinner, and may help one understand in order to influence one to believe in Christ (as Romans 3:21–4:25 shows), the only condition put forth to have eternal life is faith alone in Jesus (as John's Gospel clearly shows since the disciples had eternal life as early as chapter 1 yet denied the **resurrection**). (René A. López, "Basics of Free Grace Theology, Part 2," 1, http://www.scriptureunlocked.com/papers/basicsfgprt2.pdf [accessed August 6, 2007])

You can believe many biblical concepts and still miss **the one truth that is**

I like to put it together in one sentence as follows: *Jesus* guarantees

saving—the truth of the gospel. For example, you can attest to Jesus' deity, His virgin birth, and His bodily resurrection, and yet not believe Jesus' promise to give you eternal life freely if you just believe in Him for it. There is only one truth that will save: Jesus' guarantee that anyone who believes in Him for eternal life has it. (Robert N. Wilkin, *Confident in Christ* [Irving, TX: Grace Evangelical Society, 1999], 10)

Is the **gospel** what Paul says in Galatians? If so, we cannot proclaim the **gospel** clearly without preaching justification by faith alone. We don't need to use the word *justification*, but we must preach *the concept* or its equivalent if we wish to preach the **gospel** of Paul and Jesus. "He who believes in Me has everlasting life" (John 6:47) is justification by faith alone in different words. (Bob Wilkin, "Justification by Faith Alone is an Essential Part of the Gospel," *JOTGES* 18 [Autumn 2005]: 7)

everlasting life to all who simply *believe* in Him. All who simply believe in Jesus are eternally secure. There are no hidden terms. That's it. If you don't mention Jesus, you haven't given enough information. How much detail you give on His **substitutionary death (and His finished work) and resurrection depends** on the time you have, the prior knowledge of the person you are talking with, and the flow of the conversation. However, to fail to mention Jesus is to drop the ball in evangelism. Additionally, you must mention what it is that He promises: *eternal life* to all who simply *believe* in Him. If you don't mention eternal life or the equivalent (salvation that can never be lost no matter what we do or don't do), you haven't given enough information. . . . And if you don't mention that this eternal life is given to all who merely believe in Jesus, you haven't given sufficient information. (Robert N. Wilkin, *Secure and Sure* [Irving, TX: Grace Evangelical Society, 2005], 74-75 [italics original, ellipsis added])

Let me say it this way: whenever a person believes in Jesus, he knows for sure he has everlasting life that can never be lost, because it does not depend on the recipient to earn it or keep it but solely on Jesus who freely offers it to those who simply just believe in Him for it. Or, saying it the another way, if a person has never been sure that he has eternal life—that cannot be lost—simply by faith in Jesus, he has not yet been born again because he either does not understand **the gospel offer**, or has not yet believed in **the biblical gospel.** (René A. López, "Basics of Free Grace Theology, Part 2," 5, http://www.scriptreunlocked.com/papers/basicsfgprt2.

While confessing Jesus as Lord does refer to His **deity** (as vv 13 and 14:11 supports), the question remains, *"Does confession refer to justification-salvation?"* If confessing Jesus' **deity** is a prerequisite condition to obtaining justification how were the early disciples in the Old Testament and New Testament justified since they did not grasp His **deity** (Mark 4:41; John 14:7-9)? One would have to postulate an existing condition for justification *now* that was absent in a previous era. While information about the object of faith (Jesus) increases through new revelation (name, status, place of birth, **type of**

pdf [accessed August 6, 2007])

Paul continues to have Israel in mind as primarily those that have not **obeyed the gospel**. The Jews rejected this ***gospel*** that includes the command to believe in Christ (9:3, 30-33; John 12:37-41), and as seen above encompasses a broader scope of following Christ (cf. vv 1:2, 5, 15-16; 10:8-13). (René A. López, *Romans Unlocked* [Springfield, MO: 21st Century Press, 2005], 215-16 [italics original])

People are the present form of creation that now reveal God by witnessing on His behalf. No one can be saved through natural revelation (1:18-32). Hence one has to take the ***gospel*** to the ends of the world. (Ibid., 216 [italics original])

death and resurrection, etc...), the bare minimum of information and sole condition for justification does not change: the object of faith is God's promised Messiah (cf. 4:3) and the only condition for justification is to believe in Him alone (cf. 3:21-4:25).
(René A. López, *Romans Unlocked* [Springfield, MO: 21st Century Press, 2005], 212 [italics original])

And I really do think that you put your finger on a significant point, and that is, I think, that everyone whether they're young or old who is standing for a clear **gospel** and is fighting to make this thing as simple and clear as they can **to the unsaved world** is opposing Satan's program which is, according to 2 Corinthians 4, to blind the minds of **those that believe not**. Notice that Satan is the one who has to do the overtime here. If he just leaves everything alone, why, people would get saved all over the place because of the clarity and simplicity of the **gospel**. And I really do think that you put your finger on a significant point, and that is, I think, that everyone whether they're young or old who is standing for a clear **gospel** and is fighting to make this thing as simple and clear as they can **to the unsaved world** is opposing Satan's program

Question from Dr. Tony Evans:

Zane, whatever problem Lordship people had with you have just quadrupled after this presentation. I'm not sure that they will call a church council to discuss this [pause for laughter], but it would seem that one of the retorts that you would get to your thesis today is that since the Gospel of John included the whole life of Christ and since that life also included His **death and resurrection**—even spoken of, or at least alluded to earlier, **"God gave His only begotten Son"**— that it would seem like it would be argued that even in John's thinking, **the concept of the cross** was not just contributory so that it became support for this minimum level of faith, but that John may perhaps have viewed it as necessary to be understood. That's why those events were included in which is, according to 2 Corinthians 4, to blind the minds of **those that believe not**. Notice that Satan is the one who has to do the overtime here. If he just leaves everything alone, why, people would get saved all over the place because of the clarity and simplicity of the **gospel**. So, he's actively engaged in blinding people's minds; and those who are working against that blindness, I would assume all of them are in one way or another the objects of satanic opposition. We need to support each other. I know that Earl agrees with me on this. We older guys definitely need your support and prayer; but everyone who is out there preaching that **gospel**, way out on the mission field for example, or in a city where they're the only grace church, they need our prayers. (Zane C. Hodges, *Question and Answer Session*, following the message titled, "How to Lead People to Christ, Part 1," Grace Evangelical Society National Conference, 2000)

We have I think muddied the **gospel** waters considerably by telling people they can decide to believe. Nobody can decide to believe. They can be persuaded, and therefore that leaves a very significant area in which the Holy Spirit must operate. God who commanded light to shine out ofdarkness has shined into our heart to give the light of the knowledge of the glory of God in the face of Jesus Christ. God in the final analysis must persuade the heart; and therefore until a person has the divine illumination that amounts to persuasion they will remain **an unbeliever** and they can't decide differently. Now that's not the same as saying that man does not have the capacity to believe; he does. But he does not have the capacity **to believe the gospel** without the assistance and ministry of the Holy his Gospel. And therefore, if those events, the **death and resurrection**, are not included in the presentation, then the message that is to believed has not been fully communicated either. How would you respond to that?

Answer from Hodges:

Well I think, Tony, that I would say first of all that, yes, John obviously presents a lot of material that is supportive of his call to faith in Christ. But, also, against this is the fact that he makes it clear that **people did believe in Him without understanding these realities**. What I have said today is basically that the full gospel message is an effective and by far the best tool to bring people to faith in Christ. But if we are asking the theological question, "What is the **bare minimum** that a person could believe and still be born again?" then I think the Gospel of John would support the idea that the person who believes in Jesus for eternal life is the person who is saved. I admit the lordship people might have some problems with me, but all I can say is that I've got a few with them. (Zane C. Hodges, *Question and Answer Session*, following the message titled, "How to Lead People to Christ, Part 1," Grace Evangelical Society National Conference, 2000)

Spirit. I think we need to keep that balance. Otherwise, we will think, if I have led this person through the proper routine or the proper prayer or whatever technique I use that that does it. If he has decided to do what I told him to do then that does it. No, a man is not saved until he is persuaded that the **gospel message** is true. (Ibid., Part 2)

Should We Continue Using the Phrase "Crossless Gospel"?

In spite of the ample documentation demonstrating the accuracy of the phrase, "crossless gospel," some advocates of this view still insist it is an inappropriate and misleading description of their position. Though the phrase "crossless gospel" is certainly not needed in order to defend the biblical veracity of the "traditional" Free Grace gospel that is espoused in this book, a word of clarification about the legitimacy of its use is in order here due to the vehement protests of some crossless proponents that this phrase should be stricken from use.

It must be recognized that the leaders of the new gospel have not given their doctrine their own self-descriptive title or label. They prefer to continue bearing the mantle, "Free Grace," believing that their view represents the embodiment of the most biblically consistent and accurate doctrine of salvation among Free Grace people. Some vocal proponents of the crossless position, who are not necessarily the leading teachers and formulators of it, have begun using the designations, "Consistent Free Grace" and "Refined Free Grace" to distinguish their position. They are convinced that their position is more biblically consistent and thus a refinement rather than an abandonment of the Free Grace position. They prefer to call the position defended in this book the "Traditional Free Grace" view, portraying the current controversy as a choice between either biblical refinement or theological "tradition." Which sounds more appealing to you? Of course, we all want to be more biblically consistent and not follow *"the tradition of men"* (Col. 2:8).

But are such designations truly accurate and appropriate? Should Grace people begin using this kind of phraseology? Should the Free Grace community even use the expressions "crossless" or "crossless gospel" to designate this new form of the saving message? What designations or labels should we use, if any, now that a major doctrinal shift has taken place within our own theological camp?

Let's face it; few of us like the labels that are assigned by those who oppose our beliefs. We would much prefer to create our own designations in order to present our beliefs in the most favorable and acceptable light. But the real question with any label is not whether people like it, but whether it is accurate, appropriate, and able to be used honestly in the sight of God. I am convinced that the phrase "crossless gospel" meets each of these criteria. It is biblically accurate and can be applied with integrity to the current controversy, even while admitting the possibility that other theological labels may be used for the new, aberrant Free Grace position that may prove more fitting and may eventually replace the phrase "crossless gospel."

Is the Gospel Still the "Saving Message"?

Grace people on both sides of this issue may raise the objection that the phrase "crossless gospel" is no longer an accurate designation, since in the last two years, a significant new development has occurred within the crossless camp with respect to the term "gospel." It should be noted that the "crossless gospel" quotations provided on the preceding pages now need to be amended with a postscript such as this, since at least one major teacher of this view has changed his position on the meaning of the term "gospel." Approximately two years before the publication of this book, Bob Wilkin taught publicly for the first time that the lost do not have to believe "the gospel" to go to heaven. He stated:

> What if the word "gospel" doesn't *ever* mean the saving message? Now hang with me hear. I gave this same message, but I didn't say quite this, a little over a month ago in Omaha at a Regional we had there. And what I suggested is that the term "gospel" rarely, if ever, means, "What must I believe to have eternal life? What must I believe to be saved? What must I do to have, to go to heaven, to be sure I'll be in the kingdom?" But in the intervening time as I've been reflecting on it etcetera, I realized that we should go further than saying, "It's rare that this term refers to the saving message." I'm now of the opinion it *never* refers *specifically* to "What must I believe to have eternal life?"[35]

Wilkin now teaches that the gospel message of Christ's substitutionary death for sin and bodily resurrection is not the message that the lost must believe for their regeneration, rather it is only the message that the saved must believe for their on-going sanctification and spiritual growth. On the basis of this new position on the "gospel," some in the Free Grace community may feel that it would be more appropriate to drop the term "gospel" from the phrase "crossless gospel." They might object that the designation "crossless gospel" no longer accurately defines Wilkin's doctrine as *he himself*

---

[35] Bob Wilkin, "Gospel Means Good News," Grace Evangelical Society Southern California Regional Conference, August 24, 2007.

articulates it; and so to continue using it would unfairly mischaracterize Wilkin's own position. However, there are several reasons why such deference to the crossless position is inadvisable.

First, the crossless doctrine on this point is still developing, and it is not certain whether a significant percentage of those in the crossless camp will follow Wilkin in this distinctive. Based on precedent, however, it is likely that the majority of crossless proponents will follow suit; but this remains to be seen. The current crossless position is hardly monolithic on this particular point of doctrine. Even Zane Hodges used the term "gospel" as a synonym for the "saving message"[36] until recently. Just months prior to the publication of this book, Hodges wrote that requiring belief in Christ's death and resurrection is not only "theological legalism," it also subverts "the biblical gospel."[37] While Wilkin has openly changed positions on the meaning of the term "gospel," Zane Hodges continued using it as a reference to the content of saving faith. To date, only one other proponent of the crossless view, Jeremy Myers, has publicly articulated the same position as Wilkin.[38] It may be premature, therefore, to characterize the entire crossless position by the recent views of Wilkin and Myers on the term "gospel."

The Language of Accommodation or Correction?

Furthermore, whether Wilkin and Myers would accept it or not, from the Lord's perspective, the *Word of God* still uses the term "gospel" to refer to the "saving message" that the lost must believe in order to go to heaven. Simply because Wilkin and Myers no longer view the term "gospel" accurately does not mean that the rest of the Free Grace community must start using language that accommodates their doctrinal error. I have even noticed with some Free Grace people who are not crossless a new reluctance and apprehension to speak of "the gospel" as synonymous with, and equivalent to, the saving message. My fear is that some well-intentioned Grace people may be overly concerned about paying a courtesy to those in grave doctrinal error on the meaning of "the gospel," rather than showing a greater courtesy and respect to God who equates "the gospel" with the "saving message" in His Word (Rom. 1:16; 1 Cor. 1:17-21; 4:15; Eph. 1:13; 2 Thess. 1:8-10). By conceding to the wishes of those who no longer teach that "the gospel" is God's saving message, are we not subtly accommodating error

---

[36] In the context of explaining the nature of belief in Christ for eternal life, Hodges said, "I am convinced that some committed grace people are still a little scared by the simplicity of believing in Christ. They are eager to avoid the charge that we teach mere intellectual assent. It is hard for people like this to agree that faith and salvation occur when *the core message of the Gospel* is simply accepted as true." Zane C. Hodges, "The Spirit of the Antichrist: Decoupling Jesus from the Christ," *JOTGES* 20 (Autumn 2007): 39 (italics added).

[37] Hodges, "The Hyrda's Other Head: Theological Legalism," 3.

[38] Jeremy D. Myers, "The Gospel is More Than 'Faith Alone in Christ Alone'," *JOTGES* 19 (Autumn 2006): 33-56.

by adjusting our speech accordingly? Thus, any message that purports to be "saving," and yet is crossless, must still be regarded as a "crossless gospel" if we wish to continue speaking from a biblical standpoint.

If we concede to drop the term "gospel" from the phrase "crossless gospel," this will have the effect of legitimizing this false, unbiblical distinction between "the gospel" and "the saving message." Even if we concede to the wishes of Wilkin and others who share his doctrine by refraining from the use of the phrase "crossless gospel" while still personally and privately maintaining the correct, biblical view, will this not contribute towards the further establishment of unbiblical speech within the Free Grace community? Will this not establish an unbiblical precedent that others will be expected to follow as the distinct impression is given that it is actually wrong or somehow ungracious to portray the false doctrine held by some of our Grace brethren in a negative light?

Biblical Terminology for False Teaching

This leads to a third important consideration for the use of the phrase "crossless gospel." It is contrary to the biblical pattern to allow those who are in doctrinal error to dictate a more pleasant-sounding, appealing label for their views. This is why the Lord Jesus Himself did not consult with the Pharisees first in order to find a mutually agreeable, less offensive, moniker for their doctrine than the spiritually charged label of "leaven" (Matt. 16:12). Do you think the Pharisees viewed their own doctrine as "leaven"? Couldn't a less offensive label for their doctrine be chosen than one which every Israelite would have immediately associated with the presence of sin and evil? If the Bible itself repeatedly uses very unflattering language for doctrinal error, how can we refuse to do likewise or somehow consider it wrong to do so in the midst of this current gospel controversy?

Consider further the example of the apostle Paul. Was he required out of "grace" to check with Hymenaeus and Philetus before identifying their doctrine in 2 Timothy 2:17 as "gangrene" (*gangraina*)? Or was it actually the loving thing to do to warn other susceptible believers of the gravity of their false eschatological doctrines by employing such a potent and pejorative image as "gangrene"? To be sure, "crossless gospel" has an unpleasant ring to it; but false doctrine itself is unpleasant, and it *should* make us feel uncomfortable. Besides, the phrase "crossless gospel" is even milder than likening the new G.E.S. gospel to "gangrene," or calling it something like "the gangrenous gospel."

Now let's move from the false eschatological doctrine of Hymenaeus and Philetus to the realm of today's redefined Free Grace soteriology. Let's ask, which is the more serious error, to teach that the resurrection is past already or to teach that you don't even have to believe the gospel to go to heaven? Which has far greater eternal ramifications, to teach believers that the resurrection is past already and thus overthrow the faith of some who are already saved, or to teach that the lost don't even have to believe in a Christ who is God, who died for our sins and who is alive from the dead? If the apostle Paul deemed a false eschatology worthy of the repulsive analogy of "gangrene," can you imagine what he would say about today's reductionist saving message? At times, serious departure from the truth calls for an equally serious censure of that error, especially when people's eternal destinies are on the line. Webster's defines the noun "censure" to mean, "strong disapproval; condemnation." When used as a verb, it means, "to condemn as wrong."[39] There is no question that the phrase "crossless gospel" is meant to express "strong disapproval" of this new error and "to condemn [it] as wrong." Make no mistake about it; those who have chosen to use this phrase (including this author) have chosen to do so deliberately as an expression of reproof and rebuke, which is our biblical mandate (2 Tim. 4:2).

Again, when the apostle Paul wanted to warn the believers in Philippi about the dangerous teaching of the legalizers who added law-keeping to faith alone in Christ as the requirement for justification, he wrote to them to *"beware of the concision"* (Phil. 3:2, KJV) or *"mutilation"* (NKJV). Was this really a fair way to characterize the teaching of those who believed in law-keeping for justification? Was Paul mischaracterizing their doctrinal views by using such a powerful and pejorative expression? Though they obviously believed in more aspects of law-keeping than just circumcision, he still used the abbreviated expression "concision" or "mutilation." Was this depiction of the legalists' doctrine open to misinterpretation by those who heard it or read it? Possibly. But it was also a powerful deterrent. In the same way, the phrase "crossless gospel" is not intended to express all that its proponents believe; but it is still fitting. In addition, when Paul wrote to the Philippians, there was nothing wrong with circumcision in itself; but Paul chose to refer to the false teachers' views on circumcision in a negative, pejorative manner by characterizing them as a botched circumcision—a "mutilation" (*katatomēn*). Was this ungracious of the apostle Paul? Indeed, some today have mutilated the saving message by removing what they consider to be excess, unnecessary content, which is actually the heart and soul of the gospel—the person and work of Christ.

Some Grace people may object that the preceding biblical examples are not a fair and equal comparison to today's Free Grace teachers of a reductionist "message of life." Some may protest that today's teachers are regenerated men, whereas "the concision" of Paul's day were unbelievers. Therefore, such charged language is unfit for fellow brothers in Christ with whom we are in doctrinal disagreement. But is it really true that the legalists that Paul had in mind were all unbelievers? Certainly some were (Gal. 2:4). Perhaps even most were. But it would be hard to maintain that

---

[39] *Webster's New World Dictionary*, ed. Victoria Neufeldt (New York: Warner Books, 1990), 98.

all were unbelievers in light of Acts 15:5 and Paul's Epistle to the Galatians where he viewed the Galatians as regenerate (Gal. 4:6-7) but also as having fallen prey to the false gospel of the legalists (Gal. 1:6-7; 5:1-4). In conclusion, we must consider the case of Hymenaeus and Philetus one more time. These men were most likely genuine, but disobedient, believers.[40] In spite of the fact that they were fellow believers, Paul was still compelled to liken their doctrine to "gangrene."

The "Lordship Salvation" Label

Finally, the origin of the phrases "Free Grace" and "Lordship Salvation" is worth recollecting for a moment. Both designations resulted from the salvation controversy that peaked in American Evangelicalism in the 1980s. The Grace position coined the phrase "Lordship Salvation" for the opposing viewpoint, and like it or not, the label stuck. Initially, this designation was meant to convey the idea that something more was being added to the sole condition of faith in Christ for salvation. A commitment or submission to the Lordship of Christ over one's life was also being required by many evangelicals. Thus the phrase, "Lordship Salvation," was originally meant to convey a negative idea, conjuring up the impression in most people's minds of a works-oriented salvation that is contrary to God's grace. This was clearly how those on the Lordship side perceived it as well. That is why John MacArthur, the leading spokesman for the Lordship view, stated in 1988:

> I don't like the term "lordship salvation." It was coined by those who want to eliminate the idea of submission to Christ from the call to saving faith, and it implies that Jesus' lordship is a false addition to the gospel. As we shall see, however, "lordship salvation" is simply the biblical and historic doctrine of soteriology. I use the term in this volume only for the sake of argument.[41]

Clearly, MacArthur did not initially appreciate the designation and the negative associations it left in people's minds. Five years later, this was still smoldering in his thinking, as he reiterated the same point in his second book:

> I don't like the term *lordship salvation.* I reject the connotation intended by those who coined the phrase. It insinuates that a submissive heart is extraneous or supplementary to saving faith.

---

[40] Joseph C. Dillow, *The Reign of the Servant Kings: A Study of Eternal Security and the Final Significance of Man* (Miami Springs, FL: Schoettle Publishing, 1992), 334-36; Thomas L. Stegall, "Must Faith Endure for Salvation to be Sure? Part 9," *GFJ* (Fall 2003): 22-24; Bob Wilkin, "Saving Faith and Apostasy: Do Believers Ever Stop Believing?" *The G.E.S. News* (November 1991): 1.

[41] John F. MacArthur Jr., *The Gospel According to Jesus: What Does Jesus Mean When He Says, "Follow Me"?* (Grand Rapids: Zondervan, 1988), 28-29n20.

> Although I have reluctantly used the term to describe my views, it is a concession to popular usage. . . . Those who criticize lordship salvation like to level the charge that we teach a system of works-based righteousness. Nothing could be further from the truth. Although I labored to make this as plain as possible in *The Gospel According to Jesus*, some critics continue to hurl that allegation.[42]

Yet, in spite of the fact that MacArthur and many others voiced their objections to the "Lordship Salvation" label, and even felt it was a misrepresentation of their doctrinal position, those on the Grace side continued to use it based on their personal, biblical conviction that MacArthur and others really were advocating a works-gospel. That is why the crossless teachers of today's Free Grace movement have themselves routinely used the rather pejorative designation, "Lordship gospel," to summarize the message of MacArthur and others on the Lordship side.[43] There is not much difference between referring to the Lordship view as the "Lordship gospel" and referring to the crossless saving faith view as the "Crossless gospel."

The "No Lordship" Counter-claim

In spite of past precedent and practice, those aligned with the Grace Evangelical Society and its view of the gospel may still claim that it is unfair to label their teaching as "crossless." They may point out the fact that they each individually hold to faith in Christ's cross-work and that they often do include the preaching of the cross in their evangelism. They may even claim that they do require belief in Christ's cross-work in one respect, namely for sanctification and spiritual growth in the Christian life. So in light of these facts how can their view justly and rightly be called "crossless"? They may even try to draw a parallel to the way their view is being labeled "crossless" and the way Lordship Salvationists refer to the Free Grace position as the "no-lordship" view.[44] G.E.S. proponents may object that since Free Grace people *do* believe in the Lordship of Christ, it is unfair and inaccurate to refer to our view as the "no-lordship" view; and in just the same way, since they *do* believe in the cross-work of Christ and have a place for it, it is unfair and inaccurate to refer to their view as "crossless."

---

[42] John F. MacArthur, Jr., *Faith Works: The Gospel According to the Apostles* (Dallas: Word Publishing, 1993), 23 (ellipsis added).

[43] "Similarly, if the Lordship gospel is correct, then Free Grace theology is not" (Bob Wilkin, "Lordship Salvation for Dummies," *Grace in Focus* 21 [September-October 2006]: 2). "It follows from what I have just said that nobody ever got saved by believing the Lordship gospel. Of course some people *do* believe that gospel who are *already* saved. I am not talking about that. I just mean that on the terms of the Lordship gospel alone, no one can get saved, since this form of doctrine garbles the gospel so badly that assurance of salvation is not available. And if some people *do* find assurance in a Lordship gospel, that assurance is a delusion since it is not founded on biblical truth" (Zane C. Hodges, "Assurance: Of the Essence of Saving Faith," in *JOTGES* 10 [Spring 1997]: 4).

[44] Bob Wilkin, "We Believe Jesus Is Lord," *Grace in Focus* 23 (March/April 2008): 1-2.

So, is applying the phrase "crossless gospel" to the G.E.S. doctrine on the contents of saving faith really no different than the phrase "no-lordship" being applied unfairly to the Free Grace position?

There is at least one significant reason why this is *not* an equal or valid comparison. When Lordship Salvation proponents refer to the Free Grace position as the "no-lordship" view, they are specifically referring to the subject of *eternal salvation* or justification, not sanctification in the Christian life per se. They are referring to our view as the "no-lordship salvation" view. As this applies to the Free Grace movement historically, "no-lordship salvation" would *not* be an accurate or appropriate designation since Free Grace advocates have traditionally viewed belief in the *Lord* Jesus Christ as a requirement for eternal salvation or justification, just as Acts 16:30-31 and Romans 10:9-10 teach. While Lordship Salvationists have traditionally understood believing in Christ as "Lord" to include the inherent component of *submission of one's life* in service to Christ, Free Grace proponents have traditionally understood belief in Christ as "Lord" to mean belief in His *deity* due to His divine attribute and position of sovereignty.[45] In this respect, to claim that Free Grace people promote a "no-lordship salvation" is an inaccurate and misleading description of our position, since we have historically *required* belief in Jesus as "Lord" in the deistic sense specifically for justification and eternal salvation and not only for sanctification in the Christian life. However, the same can no longer be said of the Free Grace movement as a whole due to the advent of the new G.E.S. view of the gospel that doesn't even require belief in Christ's cross-work or His deity for eternal life.[46] For this reason, the charge of a "no-lordship" salvation has tragically become true and fitting right now for the G.E.S. faction of the Free Grace movement.

In light of these considerations, it would be neither inappropriate, nor contrary to historical precedent, to use the designation "crossless gospel" for the current theological controversy in the Free Grace camp. Yet, if we choose to do so, we must also be ready and willing to qualify what exactly we mean by the phrase. No label is perfect or immune from misinterpretation; and "crossless gospel" is no exception. Undoubtedly some

---

[45] Charles C. Bing, *Lordship Salvation: A Biblical Evaluation and Response*, GraceLife Edition (Burleson, TX: GraceLife Ministries, 1992), 104; Thomas R. Edgar, "What Is the Gospel?" in *Basic Theology: Applied*, ed. Wesley and Elaine Willis & John and Janet Master (Wheaton, IL: Victor Books, 1995), 158; J. B. Hixson, "Getting the Gospel Wrong: Case Studies in American Evangelical Soteriological Method in the Postmodern Era" (Ph.D. dissertation, Baptist Bible Seminary, 2007), 77-78; Robert P. Lightner, *Sin, the Savior, and Salvation: The Theology of Everlasting Life* (Nashville: Thomas Nelson, 1991), 204; Lou Martuneac, *In Defense of the Gospel: Biblical Answers to Lordship Salvation* (n.p.: Xulon Press, 2006), 170-75; Charles C. Ryrie, *So Great Salvation: What It Means to Believe In Jesus Christ* (Wheaton, IL: Victor Books, 1989), 69-70.

[46] Hodges, "How to Lead People to Christ, Part 1," 5; López, *Romans Unlocked*, 216; Niemelä, "Objects of Faith in John: A Matter of Person AND Content"; Wilkin, *Confident in Christ*, 10.

evangelicals who are uninformed of the current controversy will interpret the phrase to mean that some Free Grace people are no longer even preaching the cross. Though the cross has been a glaring omission or de-emphasis in the evangelism of some Free Grace leaders in recent years, this is not the primary implication of the phrase "crossless gospel."

Our use of the phrase is simply in keeping with the way in which 99% of evangelical Christendom understands the term "gospel." There is a consensus among evangelicals, whether Lordship or Free Grace, that the gospel is the message which people must believe in order *to become* a Christian and belong to Jesus Christ. Beyond that, opinions on the gospel diverge drastically. But it is highly doubtful that the rest of the evangelical world will pick up the nuance that certain crossless teachers are now putting on the term "gospel." Probably less than 1% of evangelicals interpret the word "gospel" in the manner that these crossless proponents are now using it, as being a Christian-life message that is only necessary to believe for sanctification and spiritual growth rather than for regeneration.

For these reasons, the phrase "crossless gospel" is still appropriate, even though some may dislike it or even despise it. Other Free Grace people who are opposed to the new crossless saving message prefer to use other labels, such as the "G.E.S. gospel" or the "Promise-only gospel." Both of these are also accurate and fitting designations for the new gospel since it is largely a creation of the Grace Evangelical Society with its requirement to believe only in the promise of eternal life and not the content of Christ's person and work. Believers should have the liberty to use whichever designation they believe is most appropriate, provided that it is accurate. In this regard, it must also be stated that the doctrinal position defended in this book is in no way dependent upon the use of a particular phrase. "Crossless gospel" is largely a literary and theological convention used throughout this book and the current controversy in order to abbreviate the new doctrinal error of our day. It is much easier to say "crossless gospel" than "the crossless content of saving faith." The latter expression is not nearly as recognizable to the average Christian and it often requires further elaboration. But regardless of which labels are used, it is virtually guaranteed that those on the so-called "Refined" side will not accept any label or descriptive phrase that we on the so-called "Traditional" side come up with unless it portrays their doctrine favorably, which is something we simply cannot do because we regard the crossless gospel to be utterly contrary to the Word of God.

Chapter 6

What Is the Significance of the Name of Jesus?

OVERVIEW

There is great confusion and misunderstanding today surrounding what it means to believe in Jesus' name. The crossless gospel position teaches that this expression represents the bare minimum of information required to receive eternal life. Advocates of the crossless position conclude that believing in His name is a lesser requirement than believing the gospel message of Christ's substitutionary death and resurrection. They believe that the Johannine phrase, "believe in His name," means merely knowing the name "Jesus" and believing the guarantee of eternal life associated with that name. They claim this is sufficient for someone to be born again regardless of how little else they might know about Christ. But according to Scripture, a person's "name" stands in the place of the person himself and encompasses the characteristics and deeds of that person that give him his unique identity. This truth is born out by the general use of "name" throughout Scripture, but especially as it relates to praying, being baptized, healing, and preaching in the "name" of Christ. To "believe in His name" means nothing less than believing in Christ's person and work as expressed in the gospel.

William Shakespeare's famous words have become proverbial. *"What's in a name? That which we call a rose by any other name would smell as sweet; so Romeo would, were he not Romeo call'd, retain that dear perfection which he owes without that title."*[1] Shakespeare may have been the greatest English poet and playwright, but he was certainly no sound, biblical theologian. His theology of the "name" just simply does not line up with Scripture. What's in a "name"? Everything! Lest we think otherwise, consider for a moment the name "Marion Morrison." Ring any bells? That's the name of the most famous Hollywood Western actor of all time—or at least that's his birth name. We all know him by his screen name. Apparently "Marion Morrison" didn't have quite the rugged flavor of "John Wayne." And did you know that the real name of the actor who played Moses and Judah Ben-Hur was just the rather plain and ordinary "John Carter." That doesn't quite carry the dignity and sophistication of "Charlton Heston."

Are names important? Do they have any real meaning or significance? The advertising world certainly thinks so. Why else are top marketing firms paid millions to create just the right name for a product? In the scientific realm, names are no less critical. Every discovery of nature is given a unique, identifying designation. Without them, scientists could not proceed in their fields. Names are certainly much more than just meaningless conventions. This is nowhere more true than in the biblical and theological realm.

What's in a Name?

Crossless gospel advocates support their reductionist approach to the saving gospel by appealing to the Johannine concept of believing in Jesus' name. At the core of their new gospel is a fundamental misunderstanding of what it means to believe in Jesus' "name." Regarding the scenario from the previous chapter of the islander marooned with only John 6:43-47 in a bottle, Zane Hodges went on to describe what it means to believe in Jesus' "name" and why such a man could truly be saved:

> No one has ever trusted in that name for his or her eternal well-being who has not been saved by doing so. And this is true no matter how little they might have known about the One whom that name represents. I think we need a renewed emphasis on the power of Jesus' name. As Peter declares in Acts 4:12, "Nor

[1] *Romeo and Juliet*, Act II, Scene 2.

> is there salvation in any other, for there is no other name under heaven given among men by which we must be saved." If there is one salient fact about the proclamation of the gospel in this present age, it is that God saves all those, but only those, who believe in this name for eternal salvation. Another way of saying this is that the name of Jesus is the one and only way to God. "No one comes to the Father, except through" Him (John 14:6). Naturally this eliminates the idea that a pagan person who has never heard the name of Jesus can be saved by believing in something like the light of creation. Therefore, that is why we must always have missionaries and witnesses to the saving power of Jesus' name. Without the name of Jesus there is no salvation for anyone anywhere in our world. But the flip side of the coin is this: Everyone who believes in that name for eternal salvation is saved, regardless of the blank spots or the flaws in their theology in other respects. Another way of saying the same thing is this: No one has ever trusted that name and been disappointed. In other words, God does not say to people, "You trusted my Son's name, but you didn't believe in His virgin birth, or His substitutionary atonement, or His bodily resurrection, so your faith is not valid." *We* say that, but God's Word does not. Suffice it to say, however, that Jesus never fails anyone who trusts Him for everlasting salvation. No one on earth will ever possess more than a rudimentary understanding of our Savior's person and work. But if I know I can believe on Him for salvation, and I do, He is too great to fail me. It is this conviction that ought to arm us for the work of sharing the gospel with people. In the final analysis, therefore, salvation is the result of believing in Jesus to provide it. Salvation is not the result of assenting to a detailed creed. Salvation does not even require an understanding of how it was provided for or made possible. All it requires is that the sinner understand the sufficiency of the name of Jesus to guarantee the eternal well-being of every believer. Thank God salvation is so wonderfully simple![2]

There are a whole host of scriptural problems with this new teaching on salvation through Jesus' name. In evangelicalism as a whole and particularly among Free Grace people, do we really need a *"renewed emphasis on the power of Jesus' name"* regardless of *"how little"* people might know *"about the One whom that name represents"*? When the concept of Jesus' name is studied in Scripture, it is very clear that there is no inherent "power" in the name "Jesus" by itself, as though it is some kind of religious rabbit's foot.

The Seven Sons of Sceva

This lesson about the name "Jesus" was learned rather poignantly by the

[2] Zane C. Hodges, "How to Lead People to Christ, Part 1: The Content of Our Message," *JOTGES* 13 (Autumn 2000): 8-10.

seven sons of Sceva (Acts 19:11-17). These unsaved Jewish exorcists called upon the name of "Jesus" to overthrow a demon; and after getting physically abused by the evil spirit they became the seven streaking spectacles of Sceva!

Crossless gospel proponents may object that the example of Sceva's sons is irrelevant to this discussion, since in the context of Acts 19 they did not believe in Jesus' name for eternal life but only for power to cast out a demon. While this is certainly true, it misses the larger point about faith and the name of "Jesus." It is evident that these exorcists had some faith in the power of Jesus' name. Of all the gods and names they could have chosen to call upon in their polytheistic milieu, especially as Jews, they chose to call upon the name of Paul's God. Why would they invoke the name of "Jesus" unless they believed He was greater in exorcism-power than all other names or gods whom they could have chosen? They obviously had some type of faith in the name of "Jesus" short of "saving faith."

In addition, we must ask another question in keeping with the crossless belief that God in His mercy saves those who simply believe in the name "Jesus" for eternal life *"apart from any detailed knowledge of"* Him and *"regardless of the blank spots or the flaws in their theology."* According to this new doctrine of Jesus' name, God is apparently willing to accept the faith of those who have no knowledge of His Son except the name "Jesus" and the promise of eternal life associated with that name. This is true, Hodges has said, even if their knowledge of Him is not merely deficient but false. According to the crossless doctrine, people can still be saved while maintaining false theological beliefs about Jesus' person and work in all other respects besides believing in Him as the guarantor of eternal life. But if God in His mercy is so willing to overlook all other gross errors about His Son and accept even deficient faith for the sake of granting eternal life, then why would He not at least honor the partial faith of Sceva's sons by mercifully casting out the demon at the invocation of Jesus' name? Obviously He requires more explicit knowledge of His Son combined with faith in such divinely revealed knowledge, rather than mere cognizance of the name "Jesus." The example of Sceva's sons shows that there is no power or life in the sheer arrangement of letters spelling "J-e-s-u-s." The dynamic is in the gospel of Christ, which is the power of God unto salvation for all who believe it (Rom. 1:16).

Missions and the Name "Jesus"

The new crossless doctrine of Jesus' name also has major ramifications for missions, even as Hodges himself has indicated. However, we must ask, do we really need *"missionaries and witnesses to the saving power of Jesus' name,"* or do we need missionaries and witnesses to the saving power of Jesus Himself, the One whom that name represents? The new crossless doctrine of Jesus' name sets up a false contrast between believing in Christ's name for eternal life versus believing in His person and work. In the Bible a person's "name" serves as a metonym for that person, standing in the place of that person's very attributes and characteristics. When the "name" of someone is used throughout Scripture, especially pertaining to deity, it is never a substitute for ignorance of that person, but quite the opposite. Believing in the name of Jesus is theological shorthand for believing in the essential identifying characteristics of His person and work.

On a practical level, any seasoned missionary will attest to the fact that merely proclaiming the name "Jesus" and telling lost souls to believe in that name for eternal life will spell disaster on the mission field. This approach will be the surest recipe for syncretism and false professions of faith in Jesus. People must understand the good news of the gospel of Christ in order to truly believe in His name for everlasting life.

In regards to preaching the name of "Jesus" to the lost as some sort of reduced, minimized "saving message," Hodges also claimed, *"If there is one salient fact about the proclamation of the gospel in this present age, it is that God saves all those, but only those, who believe in this name for eternal salvation."* However, if the importance of the name of Jesus is the *"one salient fact"* in our gospel proclamation for this age, then why is the emphasis of Scripture *not* upon believing in the "name" of Jesus? There are a grand total of five verses in the entire Bible that use the approximate expression, "believe in His name," to set forth the sole condition of saving faith in Jesus Christ (John 1:12; 2:23; 3:18; 1 John 3:23; 5:13). These five verses hardly constitute the *"one salient fact about the proclamation of the gospel in this present age."* Instead, the overwhelming emphasis of evangelism in the New Testament is upon believing in Christ's person and work as proclaimed in the gospel, which are the very truths that His name represents.

No Other Name Under Heaven (Acts 4:12)

Even Hodges's citation of Acts 4:12 and the theological conclusions he drew from it are a grave distortion of what the passage actually teaches in its original context. Hodges claimed that Acts 4:12 teaches that the name "Jesus" has power to save, *"no matter how little"* people might know about the One whom that name represents. He said, *"No one has ever trusted in that name for his or her eternal well-being who has not been saved by doing so. And this is true no matter how little they might have known about the One whom that name represents. I think we need a renewed emphasis on the power of Jesus' name. As Peter declares in Acts 4:12."* Yet, in Acts 4:12, Peter was *not* claiming that there is inherent saving power in the name "Jesus" by itself, apart from any knowledge of who He is or what He's done. To interpret this verse in such a manner is to completely ignore its context. In fact, the name "Jesus" isn't even found in Acts 4:12. In the context surrounding the verse, Peter and John are called by the Sadducees to account for having healed a man through the power of Jesus Christ.

Acts 4:7-12

7 *And when they had set them in the midst, they asked, "By what power or by what name have you done this?"*

8 *Then Peter, filled with the Holy Spirit, said to them, "Rulers of the people and elders of Israel:*

9 *"If we this day are judged for a good deed done to a helpless man, by what means he has been made well,*

10 *"let it be known to you all, and to all the people of Israel, that by the name of Jesus Christ of Nazareth, whom you crucified, whom God raised from the dead, by Him this man stands here before you whole.*

11 *"This is the 'stone which was rejected by you builders, which has become the chief cornerstone.'*

12 *"Nor is there salvation in any other, for there is no other name under heaven given among men by which we must be saved."*

It is clear from the context of this passage that accompanying the salvation exclusively associated with the "name" in verse 12, there is a previous description of who Jesus was and what He did. The name that exclusively has salvation associated with it in Acts 4:12 is specifically given in verse 10. And the name isn't even *"Jesus"* by itself, for that doesn't tell us enough about the person. In Acts 4:10, it says *"the name of Jesus Christ of Nazareth."* Here *"Jesus"* is also given the description of *"Christ."* In addition, Peter is referring specifically to Jesus Christ *"of Nazareth."* If that were not enough, Peter goes on to modify that appellation with the further description of Jesus according to His work. He is not merely *"Jesus Christ of Nazareth,"* He is *"Jesus Christ of Nazareth . . . whom you crucified"* (4:10). And not only that, He is *"Jesus Christ of Nazareth, whom you crucified . . . whom God raised from the dead"* (4:10). Then in Acts 4:11, before referring to the exclusiveness of that name by which we must be saved (4:12), Peter again specifically describes this crucified, risen Christ, saying: *"**This** is the stone which was rejected by you builders, which has become the chief cornerstone."* All of this precedes the reference to the great, exclusive "name" in Acts 4:12. The context of Acts 4:12 clearly reveals that the "fullness of the being and work of Jesus Christ may be seen in His name."[3] It is simply incorrect and a gross mishandling of God's Word to assure people that if they've believed merely in the name of "Jesus," they will receive eternal life *"no matter how little they might have known about the One whom that name represents."*[4]

The Name of "Jesus"

At this point it would be helpful, even necessary, to begin clarifying the truth about Jesus' name and what it means to "believe in His name." The

---

[3] Hans Bietenhard, "ὄνομα," *TDNT*, 5:272.

[4] Hodges, "How to Lead People to Christ, Part 1," 8.

significance of the name "Jesus" is not so much in the particular arrangement of the five letters that spell "J-e-s-u-s" as in the identity behind that name and what that name represents about the Lord. In this respect, the Lord's birth name is sacred. In modern Western culture, we normally name people based on only a few common factors, such as whether we find the sound of the name phonetically pleasing, whether it's currently popular, or simply in honor of a particular relative or friend. However, in ancient biblical cultures a person was often named, or even renamed, according to some distinguishable, prominent trait or attribute about that person. Jacob (heel catcher) and Esau (hairy) readily come to mind (Gen. 25:25-26).

So what does the name "Jesus" signify or represent about the One who bears it? A lot! For one thing, the name "Jesus" was not even chosen by Jesus' earthly parents. It literally came from heaven, as prescribed by an angel sent from God (Matt. 1:20-21). How many of us can say that about our names? In fact, the angel Gabriel was sent to Mary as well, so there would be no misunderstanding what her baby boy should be called (Luke 1:31). His name would be full of significance. Matthew 1:21 tells us the reason for the Messiah being named "Jesus," as the angel says to Joseph: *"And she will bring forth a Son, and you shall call His name Jesus, for He will save His people from their sins."* The name "Jesus" literally means "Yahweh saves"[5] or "Yahweh is salvation."[6] The name "Jesus" is simply the English translation of the Greek form of His name (*Ἰησοῦς/Iēsous*), and the Greek form is simply a form of the Old Testament name "Joshua" (*Yeshua*, or the older version *Yehoshua*). The name "Yeshua" actually combines the Hebrew name of God (*Yahweh*) with a Hebrew verb for "save" (*yasha*).[7]

It is common for many Christians today to speak in almost mystical terms about the name "Jesus." For instance, one contemporary Christian song, which was popular among Charismatics several years ago, goes, "Jesus, Jesus, Jesus, there's just something about that name. . . . Jesus, Jesus, Jesus, there's just something about that name." I often wondered, "Well, what is it about that name?!"[8] The name "Jesus" is not some magical incantation that has power in and of itself, which if repeated often enough (like a mantra) will bring even more power!

---

[5] Bruce K. Waltke, "Joshua," *ISBE*, 2:1133.

[6] *TWOT*, s.v. "הָוָה," by J. Barton Payne, 1:211.

[7] It should be clarified that in the passages where John speaks of believing *"in His name"* (John 1:12; 2:23; 3:18; 1 John 3:23; 5:13), this doesn't mean that lost people cannot be born again until they know that the proper name "Jesus" literally means "Yahweh saves." Many Christians learn this fact years later. The lost do not need an etymology lesson before they can be saved; they simply need to be evangelized with the gospel.

[8] Though the name of "Jesus" is repeated numerous times throughout the song, there is never a gospel explanation that He is God-incarnate who died for our sins and rose from the dead. The same could also be said for many hymns and traditional "gospel" songs. For instance, I've often wondered why the song "I Love to Tell the Story" never actually tells the gospel-story!

At the risk of sounding irreverent, I wonder if Christians today actually realize that our Lord's name was technically not even "Jesus"? That is merely the English transliteration of the original Greek form of His name, and the two names are pronounced differently in English and Greek. "Jesus" is not quite the same as "*Iēsous*" (i-ay-suse). And yet, to be even more technically correct, our Lord was probably not called by the Greek form of His name very often in comparison to the Aramaic form of His name, which was the spoken language of Jews in His time. Though it is still somewhat debated, it appears that His 1st century Hebrew or Aramaic name would have been "Yeshua" (pronounced Ye-shū-a). So if we want to be even more technically correct and precise, we could say that "Yeshua" is closer to His original name than any other, including "Jesus." Some Christians, especially Messianic Christians, even insist on calling Him "Yeshua" today in English speaking countries, rather than "Jesus."

The name "Jesus" or "Yeshua" was actually a very common Jewish name in our Lord's own day. There are at least two other men named "Jesus" in the New Testament besides the Lord Jesus (Acts 13:6; Col. 4:11). The first century Jewish historian Josephus mentions twenty different persons in his writings bearing the name "Jesus,"[9] ten of whom were 1st century contemporaries of the Lord Jesus.[10] And of course, the name "Jesus" is very common today in our Spanish-influenced Western society. Because the name "Jesus" by itself has been so widespread in both ancient and modern culture, the biblical concept of believing in His name must mean more than simply knowing the proper name "Jesus" by itself, without any corresponding knowledge of His deity, humanity, saving death, or resurrection.

To clarify even further, believing in His name does not mean having the proper spelling. The name "Jesus" is represented by a differently spelled name in hundreds of languages around the world other than English. Would some English speaking person's eternal destiny really be imperiled if he mistakenly believes that Christ's name is "Jesos" instead of "Jesus"? Would the poor soul really end up in hell even though he sincerely believes this "Jesos" is God-incarnate, who is the Christ, the Son of God, who died on the cross of Calvary 2,000 years ago for all his sins and rose from the dead to provide him with the free gift of eternal life if he

---

[9] Werner Foerster, "*Ἰησοῦς*," *TDNT*, 3:285; K. H. Rengstorf, "*Ἰησοῦς*," *NIDNTT*, 2:331.

[10] Christians should not have their faith shaken by reports that some unbelieving Hollywood film director and critic of Chistianity has "discovered" the bones of Jesus in a tomb in Israel. The name of "Jesus" was very common among Jews in Christ's day, being found inscribed on a number of ossuaries and tombs from that era (see Foerster, "*Ἰησοῦς*," 285). In fact, the name "Jesus" (*Yeshua*) was so common in early 1st century Israel that it has been estimated that among Jerusalem's roughly 80,000 member male population, approximately 7,000 residents would have born this name. An additional 11,000 or so would have been called "Joseph," resulting in approximately 1,000 males in Jerusalem (1 out of every 79) who were called "Jesus son of Joseph." René A. López, *The Jesus Family Tomb Examined: Did Jesus Rise Physically?* (Springfield, MO: 21st Century Press, 2008), 40.

would only believe in this "Jesos"?! To "believe in His name" surely must mean more than having the proper English spelling!

The point of all this is not to be pedantic, but to show that merely knowing the name "Jesus" is not sufficient to stake one's eternal destiny upon. Though the name "Jesus" is a valid identifier for the Savior, it is not sufficient by itself to provide an accurate identification. Other defining characteristics and attributes of the Lord Jesus are necessary in order to place one's faith in Him as the one, true, biblical "Jesus."

The Name vs. the Person

The crossless gospel position claims that a person who has simply believed in the name of "Jesus" for eternal life is saved, *"no matter how little they might have known about the One whom that name represents."*[11] Proponents of this view reason that if people don't know who Jesus is or what He's done for them, as long as they still put their trust in His name, Jesus Christ will still receive their sincere faith, since they have believed "the minimum." I have heard the illustration of "two boats" proposed as support for the crossless view. It has been argued that receiving eternal life by believing in Jesus' name is like a person who wants to get into a boat to cross a lake. It doesn't matter whether he believes the boat is made out of tinfoil or aluminum, because either way he still chooses to get in and he later discovers that the boat, being truly made of aluminum, is strong enough to buoy him up and deliver him to the yonder shore. The analogy, of course, is that whether a person believes Jesus is God or just a man doesn't ultimately matter because Jesus is still truly God and able to deliver any soul to heaven who believes in His name for eternal life. Advocates for the crossless view teach that whether a person believes Jesus is only a man or also God doesn't really matter, since in either case this person is still believing in the One called "Jesus," and Jesus will therefore receive the faith of such a "believer."

In order to illustrate the practical ramifications of this doctrine, consider the following statement from crossless gospel apologist, Antonio da Rosa, who hosts an internet site called "Free Grace Theology." He writes in an online article:

> When you believe in the name of Jesus, you believe on One who is God, who has died and rose again, who was born of a virgin, who did walk on water, who ascended into heaven bodily, etc. EVEN IF YOU ARE NOT AWARE, UNDERSTAND, OR BELIEVE THESE THINGS.[12]

---

[11] Hodges, "How to Lead People to Christ, Part 1," 8.

[12] Antonio da Rosa, "How Much Information is Really Needed?" (May 6, 2006), http://unashamedofgrace.blogspot.com/2006/05/how-much-information-is-really-needed.html (accessed August 20, 2007), capitalization original.

One doctoral student in theology from England agreed with da Rosa's statement and responded by posting his own comments to the article:

> Surely one believes in the same Jesus if one believes in the Jesus who lived in the first century, who was born of a virgin, who was a carpenter's son, who was baptized by John the Baptist, who was tempted by Satan, who had twelve apostles and who was crucified under Pontius Pilate and rose again from the dead. If I affirm those things do I not believe in the real Jesus, even if I was under the false notion that Jesus was an angel or a superman?[13]

These opinions are merely the bad fruit of Hodges's unbiblical teachings. His followers are now openly declaring on a popular level the obvious, practical implications of his doctrine. If people only need to believe that eternal life is guaranteed by believing in the name "Jesus," and this is true *"no matter how little they might know about the One whom that name represents,"* then why *couldn't* somebody be born again who believes that Jesus is just an angel or superman? But all of this is patently false. Having the correct name for someone is not equivalent to correctly identifying that person or even believing in that person.

For example, imagine that two people are talking to one another about me, the author, and they both claim to know me. Imagine the first person saying, *"Tom Stegall? Oh yes, I know Tom Stegall. He's the most devout Roman Catholic I've ever met. Did you know he even took his vows of poverty, celibacy, and obedience and became a priest? He's such a good person that if there's anyone who deserves to go to heaven, surely it's him."* Now imagine if the second person, who truly knows me, hears this false description of me. He would say, *"Oh no, that's not Tom Stegall. Let me tell you about the real Tom Stegall. He actually deserves to go to hell! He's a sinner saved by grace, happily married with children, and he pastors a Bible-believing, Protestant church."* In such a case, the person who truly knows me would not accept the first person's claim to know me. Nor, if I were physically present and overheard the first person's false description of me would I even accept his claim to know me! Though the first person might have my *name* correct, he certainly has another *person* in mind.

In just the same way, the Lord Jesus will not accept the faith of one who professes to "believe in Him" but who also believes Him to be an angel or superman! Such a person does not actually believe in "Jesus" because he does not believe the most fundamental identifying characteristics about the person of Jesus Christ, namely that He is God-incarnate who died for our sins and rose again.

The same principle of identification pertains in human courts of law, where cases of mistaken identity and stolen identity are heard every day.

---

[13] Ibid., Matthew Clarke, see under "comments." Clarke also propagates a crossless gospel and contributes to a group internet site with da Rosa and others called "Unashamed of Grace."

Imagine for a moment that a homeowner receives a rather large utility bill in the mail for a particularly hot summer month in which his air conditioner ran continuously. When the exorbitant bill arrives, his name is grossly misspelled by the electric company. If the homeowner refuses to pay the bill, claiming that the debtor is not properly identified on the bill and that it is all a case of mistaken identity, the electric company has legal recourse to correctly identify him as the debtor through other distinguishing attributes besides the man's name. Conversely, in cases of stolen identity in which large debts are accumulated under another person's name, the innocent party has the legal opportunity to prove that an entirely different *person* is responsible for the debts even though they were acquired under the use of his particular proper *name*.

Though a man can be identified by his proper name, and a proper name may be the most common way to distinguish someone, it is not the only way. A person is recognizable and distinguishable through a whole composite of features, including individual name, personal attributes and characteristics, nature, and the significant, defining events of his or her life. All of these contribute toward that person's unique identity, and the same applies to the Lord Jesus Christ.

The Biblical Concept of the Name

If the preceding generalizations about believing in Jesus' name are correct, the Bible should bear them out. On the other hand, if the crossless doctrine is correct, Scripture should demonstrate that believing in His name can occur *"no matter how little they might have known about the One whom that name represents,"*[14] and *"regardless of the blank spots or the flaws in their theology"* including disbelief in Christ's *"substitutionary atonement, or His bodily resurrection."*[15] In addition, if the crossless position is correct, then the Bible should be clear that *"Salvation does not even require an understanding of how it was provided for or made possible. All it requires is that the sinner understand the sufficiency of the name of Jesus to guarantee the eternal well-being of every believer."*[16] The crossless gospel position is clear that belief in the name "Jesus" can be nearly void of all content. The sole qualification is that this faith must entail the persuasion that "Jesus" can guarantee eternal life to all who believe. Apart from this, the other attributes and defining characteristics of Christ are not essential to know or accept when believing in His name for eternal life. But is this really what the Bible means when it commands the world to "believe in His name"?

The remainder of this chapter will demonstrate that the biblical concept of the "name" entails much more than this. When a systematic study

---

[14] Hodges, "How to Lead People to Christ, Part 1," 8.

[15] Ibid., 9.

[16] Ibid., 10.

of the "name" is done in Scripture, it yields completely different conclusions than those of the crossless position. The Bible could not be clearer that someone's "name" in Scripture stands in the place of the very person, as a metonym for that person. As such, the "name" encompasses the essential, defining, identifiable, and knowable characteristics of that person. That is why one Johannine scholar states that the name "is more than a label; it is the character of the person, or even the person himself."[17] Another believes the "name" of a person may indicate the very essence of the person.[18] Yet another commentator summarizes by saying:

> In the thought of the ancient world a name does not merely distinguish a person from other persons, but is closely related to the nature of its bearer. Particularly in the case of such powerful persons as deities, the name is regarded as part of the being of the divinity so named and of his character and powers.[19]

Is the general consensus of biblical scholarship correct, or are the conclusions of the crossless position right? Both cannot be correct since they are fundamentally opposed to one another. We shall see that according to the Bible, the "name" of someone stands in the place of that person as a substitute for his identifying attributes. The "name" is not the vacuous concept that the crossless position maintains, as a mere word divested of all identifying characteristics except one—being the guarantor of eternal life. When this doctrine is considered from various angles, whether human names, the divine name, or praying, baptizing, preaching, healing, and believing in Jesus' name, it will be evident that the characteristics or attributes of a person are always in view.

Human Names in the Bible

There are an abundance of examples from Scripture to illustrate the point that a person's name stands for a person's attributes or actions. For example, Adam called his wife "Eve," which means "life," because she was the mother of all living (Gen. 3:20). This was a term probably given in prospect of Eve's future role and function as the one giving birth essentially to the rest of the human race. Adam's name for his wife, therefore, was most appropriate.

In Genesis 17:5, God changes Abram's name (exalted father) to "Abraham" (father of a multitude). The Lord states His reason for the change: *"for I have made you a father of many nations."* This example shows that Abraham's name had an inherent meaning that matched a future

---

[17] D. A. Carson, *The Gospel According to John*, PNTC (Grand Rapids: Eerdmans, 1991), 125.

[18] J. H. Bernard, *A Critical and Exegetical Commentary on the Gospel According to St. John*, ICC (Edinburgh: T & T Clark, 1928), 1:17.

[19] O. S. Rankin, as quoted in *The Cross in the New Testament* by Leon Morris (Grand Rapids: Eerdmans, 1965), 117n24.

historical reality. Childless Abram would physically father many nations. Genesis 17:15-16 gives the maternal complement. There the Lord changes the name of Abraham's wife from Sarai to Sarah (princess) in view of the fact that she who was barren would, in effect, give birth to kings and nations. What each of these examples demonstrates is that a name often stands for a person's prominent traits, roles, and actions. A person's name stands for the most prominent distinguishing features about that individual.

In Genesis 32:28, after having wrestled with God all night, Jacob (heel-catcher) is renamed "Israel" (prince of God) by the Lord. This occasion marked a turning point in Jacob's spiritual life, in which he learned a valuable lesson about submitting to the will of God rather than scheming to accomplish his own devices. In addition, the change of name from Jacob to Israel signified a personal confirmation of God's promised blessings upon Jacob in fulfillment of the Abrahamic covenant. The name "Israel" was a suitable change in light of Jacob's actions and character, as well as his future function.

Jumping ahead in the Old Testament to the time of the Judges, we see in Ruth 1:20-21 the example of Naomi renaming herself "Mara," which means "bitter." Though this term has an inherent meaning by itself, Naomi also gives the reason for the name change saying, *"for the Almighty has dealt very bitterly with me. I went out full, and the Lord has brought me home again empty."* During Naomi's ten year sojourn in the land of Moab, her husband and both her sons died, before returning to Israel with her daughter-in-law Ruth, the Moabitess. Here is another example of a name standing for a prominent character trait about a person and even the key historical events that formed that negative trait.

Turning to the New Testament, we see a similar pattern with respect to the meaning of a person's name. In Mark 3:17, the two brothers James and John are called by the Lord, "the sons of thunder." This was most likely due to their fervent, arduous personalities and tendencies. This is best exemplified by their desire to call down "fire from heaven" to destroy some unreceptive Samaritans (Luke 9:54).

Similarly, Simon is given the name "Peter" or "Cephas" by the Lord, which means "rock" (Matt. 16:17-18; John 1:42). This certainly wasn't due to any stableness in Peter's character or primacy of authority over the other disciples, for during Christ's earthly life Peter was utterly impetuous, even dangerously so at times (Matt. 16:22-23). However, when the Lord graciously looked upon Simon coming to Him to be His disciple, with His omniscient gaze He saw in *Simon* the *Peter* (rock) that he would become as a result of the Lord's transforming power. Coupled with this, the Lord also foresaw the leadership role that Peter would have in preaching the gospel after His ascension during the formative years of the Church (Matt. 16:20; Acts 2-11). The name of "Peter" is another biblical example of how a person's character traits, role, and actions are all represented in a word. That word stands for those very features that are most prominent about that person.

One final example of a name representing a human person is that of Barnabas. Few people know this man's birth name, since his personality trait and actions became so prominent. Joseph the Levite became a believer in Jesus Christ and was later given the name "Barnabas" by the apostles, which means "Son of Encouragement" (Acts 4:36). His character and his actions so exemplified encouragement that this literally became his name.

In all of these biblical examples of human names, we see that a person's name not only served to identify the person, but it also signified the most prominent traits, actions, and roles of that person. This is not to imply that every name in ancient times had such significance, anymore than claiming that every person's name in our culture must have some deeper meaning. However, in the preceding examples where God gave people their names, or they were renamed or commemorated in some way, there is an obvious, unique significance in their names. In these special instances, as with the name "Jesus," we may conclude that a person's name signified vital information about the identity and character of that individual, as well as key historical events of that person's life. This is hardly consistent with the crossless notion that the name "Jesus" itself is *"sufficient"*[20] to be known by the lost, *"no matter how little they might have known"*[21] about the Person who bears it and *"regardless of the blank spots or the flaws in their"*[22] understanding of His person and work.

God's Name in the Bible

When it comes to the use of the "name" of the "LORD" in Scripture, we see that it also stands in the place of the person, conveying vital content about the Lord's character and actions. In Scripture, there is an extremely close association between God's name and His very person. That is why in some passages the divine "name" is substituted for the Lord Himself. Notice for example Psalm 20:1, where the name of God is used as a figure of speech for God Himself: *"May the LORD answer you in the day of trouble; may the name of the God of Jacob defend you."* This verse is a classic example of synonymous parallelism in Hebrew poetry, where the second half of the verse simply reiterates the truth of the first half of the verse. It is technically not the arrangement of letters that form the name of the God of Jacob itself that will do the defending; it is the God who bears that name who will defend. In this verse, "the name of the God of Jacob" is simply a figurative way of saying "the LORD."

---

[20] Hodges, "How to Lead People to Christ, Part 1," 10.

[21] Ibid., 8.

[22] Ibid., 9.

A similar example is found in Proverbs 18:10, which says, *"The name of the LORD is a strong tower; the righteous run to it and are safe."* Is this verse teaching that God's name by itself has some inherent power in which we are to trust? Does the Bible advocate the occultic notion that the correct arrangement of certain letters has some innate, magical power? Perish the thought! Proverbs 18:10 and passages like it are simply using *"the name of the LORD"* as another way of saying "the LORD Himself." This verse is also teaching that *"the name of the LORD"* is indicative of some characteristic or attribute about God Himself that makes Him trustworthy, which in this case indicates that He is like a high tower and able to protect those who put their trust in Him. The Bible uses figurative speech when telling people to put their trust in the "name" of God or in the Lord Himself (Isa. 50:10).

At this point, crossless gospel advocates may object that these Old Testament passages can be taken as proof that it is enough to simply believe in the name of God, and when someone does that, the Lord will act in accordance with His name, even if that person is ignorant of what God's name represents about Him. However, this would be an invalid deduction. The Bible also indicates that people trust in God's name based on what they have come to know about God through His mighty acts. His character and actions are connected with His name, so that His name is inseparable from His person and work. One source says of God and His name, "His historical dealings with men in the past (Exod. 3:6, 13, 15), present (Exod. 20:7), and future (Ezek. 25:17; 34:30 *et al.*) are inextricably bound up with his name."[23]

This truth can be easily observed in many passages from the Old Testament. Notice, for example, how the Gibeonites speak of the "name" of the Lord when seeking to preserve their lives:

Joshua 9:9-10

9 *So they said to him: "From a very far country your servants have come, because of the name of the LORD your God; for we have heard of His fame, and all that He did in Egypt,*

10 *and all that He did to the two kings of the Amorites who were beyond the Jordan—to Sihon king of Heshbon, and Og king of Bashan, who was at Ashtaroth."*

The Gibeonites associated *"the name of the Lord"* with *"all that He did in Egypt"* in redeeming the Israelites. This was in fact God's intention for His actions in Egypt, as the nations around Israel came to know of Him through His mighty work of redemption (Exod. 9:16; 15:13-16; Num. 14:15-16; Josh. 2:9-10). This same truth is also conveyed by the prophet Jeremiah.

Jeremiah 16:19-21

19 *O LORD, my strength and my fortress, my refuge in the day of affliction, the*

---

[23] Hans Bietenhard, "Name," *NIDNTT,* 2:650.

Gentiles shall come to You from the ends of the earth and say, "Surely our fathers have inherited lies, worthlessness and unprofitable things."
20 *Will a man make gods for himself, which are not gods?*
21 *"Therefore behold, I will this once cause them to know, I will cause them to know My hand and My might; and they shall know that My name is the LORD.*

According to the prophet Jeremiah, Israel and the Gentile nations would come to know that God's "name is the LORD" through the actions of His "hand" and His "might." The Scriptures are replete with similar passages and examples, but space does not permit a fuller treatment of this Old Testament theme. It is sufficient to underscore the principle that a person's name, especially God the Father's and the Lord Jesus', indicates the character of the person as well as the key, identifying historical events of that person's life. That is why one scholar summarizes by saying:

> "Name" and that which a person is are so close together in meaning that on occasion "name" by itself simply means "person(s)" (Acts 1:15; Rev. 3:4). Furthermore, because a person's name is so closely linked with the person himself, with *what he is* and *does*, it is not surprising to discover that "name" and "reputation" are again used synonymously.[24]

This is a consistent, transdispensational principle found throughout the Scriptures. The name of the LORD (Yahweh) was known throughout the ancient world due to His mighty, redemptive work of delivering Israel from bondage in Egypt. Likewise following Calvary, the "name" of the Lord Jesus stands not only for one aspect of His person, namely His deity, but also His work of redemption. He is the Redeemer not merely because of His divine character and nature but also because He paid the redemption price with His blood at Calvary and then conquered sin's wages, death itself, by rising from the grave.[25]

All of this has tremendous significance as it pertains to what it means to believe in the name of the Lord Jesus in this dispensation. The Lord warns His generation in the months leading up to His crucifixion, *"You will die in your sins; for if you do not believe that I AM, you will die in your sins"* (John 8:24). His death on Calvary and subsequent resurrection identify

---

[24] Gerald F. Hawthorne, "Name," *ISBE*, 3:482 (italics added).

[25] Regarding even works being part of the "name," it is surprising to hear one proponent of the G.E.S. gospel say, "Jews are in the business of using metonymy of effect and what is also called synecdoches. They use parts for wholes. They use basis at times for object, because Christ is no different from what He does, because He is what He does and He does what He is. A *'name'* referred to characteristics of what a person does in the Bible" (René Lopez, "The Use and Abuse of 1 Corinthians 15:1-11," Grace Evangelical Society Conference, Fort Worth, TX, March 31, 2009). What is most surprising is that this statement is made, in its context, while seeking to establish that the lost do not have to believe in Christ's death and resurrection for justification.

Him as the great "I AM," as the Lord goes on to say, *"When you lift up the Son of Man, then you will know that I AM"* (John 8:28). The mighty work of Christ's atoning sacrifice and glorious resurrection is now forever part of the fabric of His being as the risen Lamb of God. He will forever be known by His saving death and resurrection. If we are true to Scripture, we must not divorce either the person or work of Christ from His "name."

Praying in His Name

The principle of a person's name standing for the character, attributes, and actions of that person is observed again in the New Testament passages dealing specifically with prayer in Jesus' name. Six verses in the Gospel of John reveal that believers in this dispensation of Grace have an entirely new ground upon which to pray effectually (John 14:13-14; 15:16; 16:23-24, 26). On the eve of Christ's crucifixion, He reveals to His disciples that they can now pray in His name. He teaches, *"Most assuredly, I say to you, whatever you ask the Father in My name He will give you. Until now you have asked nothing in My name. Ask, and you will receive, that your joy may be full"* (John 16:23-24). There is a marked contrast between how the disciples had prayed *before* the cross ("until now") and how they were to pray *after* the cross ("in that day"). Before the cross, they did not pray in Christ's name; but after the cross, probably starting with Pentecost ("in that day"), they would be given the unprecedented privilege of praying in Jesus' name.

Praying in Jesus' name does not mean tacking on the right formula at the end of our prayers when we say "In Jesus' name." Though this practice is not wrong in itself, certainly the Lord meant more than this by this expression. Whatever praying in Jesus' name means (and opinions on the subject do vary), it must be related in some way to the finished work of Christ. The conclusion that it is related in some way to His atoning work is based on the timing of this disclosure to the disciples. Christ's announcement to His eleven disciples about this new, unprecedented basis for prayer coincided with His appointment at Calvary, which was less than 24 hours away. As this pertains to praying in Jesus' name and even the meaning of His name, John Walvoord concludes by saying, "Without dogmatic assumption, then, we can take the phrase *'in my name'* to refer to Christ largely as the Savior, Jesus. Prayer in the name of Jesus is, then, based first on His office as Savior."[26]

It is only reasonable that Christians are first to pray to God on the basis of the finished work of His Son. Commenting on the promise of John 16:23, one Johannine scholar writes, "The meaning is that the atoning death of Jesus will revolutionize the whole situation. On the basis of the Son's atoning work men will approach God and know the answers to

---

[26] John F. Walvoord, "Prayer in the Name of the Lord Jesus Christ," *BSac* 91 (October 1934): 465.

their prayers."[27] This is a reasonable interpretation because a Christian cannot pray with the confidence that his prayers are being answered unless he is first assured that he himself is fully accepted by God and that the work of Christ is sufficient on his behalf. Prayer to God in Jesus' name is first of all based on *what* Jesus has done and *who* He is. In this respect, our prayers rest upon the person and work of the Savior. Again, Walvoord explains this point, saying, "Prayer in the name of Jesus is the key to overcoming the hindrances to prayer. This is found first in the character of the "name," in that it rests on the work of Christ as Savior."[28] But as important as Christ's saving work is to praying in His name, doesn't it also convey more than this?

Prayer in Jesus' name also entails praying with an understanding of one's position in Christ and identification with Him. We see from the New Testament that the new basis for prayer also coincides with the Spirit's coming on the day of Pentecost (John 7:39; 14:16-17). From that point forward, all believers in Christ are baptized by the Holy Spirit into positional union with our spiritual Head, Jesus Christ. Thus every believer since Pentecost is positionally identified with Christ and can therefore pray on the basis of our new identification with Him. This means that when we as believers pray, God the Father hears our prayers and answers them as though His very own Son is petitioning Him. What an amazing privilege! And what amazing grace on God's part! So when we pray in Jesus' name, we are praying on the basis of both His work for us and our identification with Him. We are praying on the basis of His merits alone.[29] That is why one writer explains prayer in Jesus' name, saying, "This points to a new relationship established by Christ's work on the Cross, which the Pauline Epistles refer to as being *in Christ*."[30]

But all of this underscores again the problem with the crossless gospel's interpretation of Jesus' name. The Lord's name is not an empty label. It is full of significance about the Savior's person and work. While His name certainly indicates His role as the guarantor of eternal life, it cannot be divorced from His unique person and work. Just as praying in Jesus' name does not mean reciting an empty formula at the end of our prayers, neither does believing in His name mean the lost must only trust in a name, *"no matter how little they might have known"*[31] about the One who bears that name.

---

[27] Leon Morris, *Commentary on the Gospel of John*, NICNT (Grand Rapids: Eerdmans, 1971), 708.

[28] John F. Walvoord, "Prayer in the Name of the Lord Jesus Christ," 472.

[29] Craig S. Keener, *The Gospel of John: A Commentary* (Peabody, MA: Hendrickson, 2003), 2:948.

[30] Curtis Mitchell, "Praying 'In My Name'," *CTSJ* 4 (July 1998): 29.

[31] Hodges, "How to Lead People to Christ, Part 1," 8.

Baptism in His Name

Just as praying in Jesus' name is now a unique privilege in this Church age so is being baptized in the name of Jesus Christ. Water baptisms occurred in Israel prior to Pentecost, but it was only with the start of the Church age that people began to be baptized "in the name" of Jesus Christ. When it is kept in mind that the "name" of the Lord is often used as theological shorthand for the very person of Christ (Acts 3:16; 5:41; 8:12; 9:21; 15:14, 26; 19:17; 21:13; 22:16; 26:9), then it is easier to recognize that water baptism in "the name" of Christ symbolizes the believer's spiritual identification with the very person of the Lord Jesus. The use of "the name" occurs six times in the New Testament in conjunction with Christian water baptism (Matt. 28:19; Acts 2:38; 8:16; 10:48; 19:5; 1 Cor. 1:15), and each instance harmonizes well with a water baptism that pictures Spirit baptism into the person of Christ (Acts 1:5; 11:15).[32]

Water baptism for the Christian is simply a visible picture and public testimony to others of what God has already done spiritually for every believer in Christ. It signifies the real but non-visible baptism that takes place at the moment of initial faith and regeneration when the Holy Spirit places every believer in Christ into spiritual union with Christ. At the moment of initial faith and spiritual baptism into Christ, each believer is identified with Christ (1 Cor. 12:12-13; Gal. 3:27; Eph. 4:5). While it is true that water baptism pictures the believer's identification with the *person* of Christ, it also pictures the spiritual reality of our identification with Christ in His *death, burial,* and *resurrection* (Rom. 6:1-11; Gal. 2:19-20; 5:24; Col. 2:11-13, 20; 3:1-3). Every believer in Christ today who has been born again by God's grace can say on the authority of God's Word that he has *died* with Christ, been *buried* with Christ, and has *risen* with Christ, all through the baptizing ministry of the Holy Spirit. Water baptism simply pictures this reality. To be water baptized, therefore, in the "name" of the Lord Jesus is not just a baptismal formula to be recited while a believer is being immersed and raised up out of the water. It signifies the believer's spiritual identification with Christ in His person and work. It is a picture of the gospel! Once again, when the Scriptures speak of the "name" of Christ, they indicate more than just the bare word "Jesus."

Healing & Preaching in His Name

The early chapters of the Book of Acts record the apostles performing several miracles which accompany their evangelistic preaching (Acts 2:43; 3:6-8; 4:9, 16, 22, 30; 5:12, 15-16). Both their miracles and preaching are said to be done in the name of Jesus. But what does this mean? Was the name of Jesus simply the formula pronounced over people while the apostles

---

[32] Thomas L. Stegall, "Does Water Baptism Picture Spirit Baptism into Christ?" *GFJ* (Winter 2005): 12-18.

performed their miraculous healings, like the elocutions of a modern day faith-healer? Did they merely utter the phrase "in the name of Jesus," or was there some evangelistic content behind this name? And if there was content, was it merely the content of the crossless message that Jesus is the guarantor of eternal life, or did the "name" of Jesus encompass His substitutionary death and resurrection? The Book of Acts provides the answers to these critical questions.

In Acts 3:6, the apostle Peter speaks to a man who had been crippled for over forty years (Acts 4:22). Peter says to him, *"Silver and gold I do not have, but what I do have I give to you: In the name of Jesus Christ of Nazareth, rise up and walk."* The result is that the man's legs are immediately healed by the power of the Lord (Acts 3:12-13; 9:34), and he is able to walk and leap and praise God (Acts 3:8). When the people in the temple witness the miracle, they are amazed. Now with a captive audience, Peter uses the opportunity to present the gospel to the crowd as recorded in Acts 3:12b-16.

Acts 3:12b-16

12 *"Men of Israel, why do you marvel at this? Or why look so intently at us, as though by our own power or godliness we had made this man walk?*

13 *"The God of Abraham, Isaac, and Jacob, the God of our fathers, glorified His Servant Jesus, whom you delivered up and denied in the presence of Pilate, when he was determined to let Him go.*

14 *"But you denied the Holy One and the Just, and asked for a murderer to be granted to you,*

15 *"and killed the Prince of life, whom God raised from the dead, of which we are witnesses.*

16 *"And His name, through faith in His name, has made this man strong, whom you see and know. Yes, the faith which comes through Him has given him this perfect soundness in the presence of you all.*

Several elements of this passage are significant as they relate to the meaning of Jesus' "name." First, in Acts 3:6 when Peter commands the crippled man to rise up and walk, he commands the man in the name of "Jesus Christ of Nazareth." Peter does not command him merely in the name of "Jesus." The name of "Jesus" is not sufficient by itself to describe the Living One whose power actually heals this man. The title of "Christ" is added by Peter; and this significant term indicates the deity of Jesus as well as His sacrificial death and resurrection.[33] Secondly, and more significantly, the double reference to "His name" in Acts 3:16 is preceded by the essential elements of the gospel in verses 13-15.[34] It is for this reason that one author writes in regards to the "name" of Jesus Christ in this passage:

---

[33] This critical point will be addressed in chapters 15-17 on the meaning and use of the title "Christ."

[34] Each element of the gospel in this passage will also be explained in greater detail in chapter 17.

> This reference to the name absolutely is not presented without content. It is preceded by an encapsulated presentation of the gospel in the strongly *heilsgeschichtlich* manner usually favoured by Luke, and this gives a strong content to the name. It is as if to say 'You cannot have the name working *ex opere operato*; you must have the gospel with it' (cf. similarly 19:13, 20). It is precisely the Jesus who came, as God's fulfillment of the hopes of Israel, who was crucified, was raised and vindicated, whose name has done this. The healing by the name is thus "gospelised" (of course in Luke's simple sense), and gospelised still in terms of the name.[35]

We see from Acts 3:6-16 that Jesus' "name" is inextricably bound up with the gospel itself. The miraculous healing done in His name points to the Living One whose substitutionary death and resurrection from the dead make the miracle possible. This pattern then continues in Acts 4-5.

In Acts 4:7, the Sanhedrin calls Peter to account for the miraculous healing, saying, *"By what power or by what name have you done this?"* What follows is Peter's explanation, not just of Jesus as the "guarantor of eternal life," but of His death and resurrection. Peter says, *"let it be known to you all, and to all the people of Israel, that by the name of Jesus Christ of Nazareth, whom you crucified, whom God raised from the dead, by Him this man stands before you whole"* (Acts 4:10). It is in this "name" that there is "salvation" by which men "must be saved" (Acts 4:12).

---

[35] J. A. Ziesler, "The Name of Jesus in the Acts of the Apostles," *JSNT* 4 (1979): 32. The German term *heilsgeschichte* used here by Ziesler is sometimes used by theologians to refer to "salvation history" (e.g. Oscar Cullmann, *Christ and Time*). Though the term has sometimes been employed by liberal and neo-orthodox theologians (Rudolf Bultmann, *"Historie; Geschichte/geschichtlich; historisch,"* in *Handbook of Biblical Criticism*, ed. Richard N. Soulen [Atlanta: John Knox Press, 1981], 88-89) to distinguish between empirically verifiable events that are accepted as fact (*Historie*) versus that which merely has historical significance (*Geschichte*), *heilsgechichte* in and of itself does not necessarily imply any historical inaccuracy in the Bible. The term is also used by moderate theologians, and sometimes conservatives as well, simply to convey the theological concept that salvation is inextricably connected to God's saving actions in time-space history (such as Christ's incarnation, passion, and resurrection) and not just to the nature and character of God's being as it exists apart from such events. This need not necessarily lead to a "functional" Christology that would exclude the Bible's own very clear "ontological" Christology (see Millard J. Erickson, "The Metaphysical Problem," in *The Word Became Flesh: A Contemporary Incarnational Christology* [Grand Rapids: Baker, 1991] 215-41). The other phrase in Ziesler's quote above, *ex opere operato*, is a Latin expression meaning literally, "from the work of the work itself," or simply "from the act itself." This phrase was debated during the time of the Reformation. The Roman Catholic Council of Trent in the 16th century used it in its Canon VIII on the Sacraments, teaching that God's saving grace is conferred *ex opere operato* through the sacraments. The Reformers objected to this medieval, even pagan notion, that the sacraments were rites that "automatically" conferred grace by the work itself instead of through the personal faith of the participant. Thus, Ziesler's point is that the "name" of Jesus in Acts 3 did not have some inherent power in itself apart from Peter's preaching of the gospel. It had an affected meaning—affected by a description of Jesus as the Christ via the gospel message in the context, which was the message of Christ's saving deeds (*heilsgeschichte*).

The response of the Sanhedrin to Peter's testimony is to threaten the apostles and to command *"them not to speak at all nor teach in the name of Jesus"* (Acts 4:18). In view of this injunction against speaking "in the name of Jesus," Peter replies on behalf of the apostles, saying, *"we cannot but speak the things which we have seen and heard"* (Acts 4:20). Peter interprets speaking in Jesus' name as speaking of the things which the apostles had seen and heard. Of course, the things which they had seen and heard, to which they now witness, are the death and resurrection of Jesus the Christ and the forgiveness of sins that is now available to all through His name (Luke 24:46-49; Acts 1:8; 2:32, 36; 3:15).

The apostles continue to preach Christ crucified and risen, and the Sanhedrin has them arrested. But an angel opens the prison doors to let God's witnesses out to continue their gospel preaching (Acts 5:19). As a result of this, the apostles are detained again by the temple guards and brought before the Sanhedrin. This episode is recorded in Acts 5:27-32.

<u>Acts 5:27-32</u>

27 *And when they had brought them, they set them before the council. And the high priest asked them,*

28 *saying, "Did we not strictly command you not to teach in this name? And look, you have filled Jerusalem with your doctrine, and intend to bring this Man's blood on us!"*

29 *But Peter and the other apostles answered and said: "We ought to obey God rather than men.*

30 *"The God of our fathers raised up Jesus whom you murdered by hanging on a tree.*

31 *"Him God has exalted to His right hand to be Prince and Savior, to give repentance to Israel and forgiveness of sins.*

32 *"And we are His witnesses to these things, and so also is the Holy Spirit whom God has given to those who obey Him."*

At least two significant points can be drawn from this passage. First, the meaning of the "name" in Acts 5:28 is not just the proper noun "Jesus." It is equated in verse 28 with the "doctrine" of the apostles concerning Jesus Christ, as the Sanhedrin says, *"Did we not strictly command you not to teach in this name? And look, you have filled Jerusalem with your doctrine, and intend to bring this Man's blood on us!"* The Sanhedrin is clearly concerned not just about Jews mouthing the common 1st century name, "Jesus," in the streets of Jerusalem but with the content of Jesus' name—His person and work. That is why we also observe that Peter and the apostles proclaim the gospel of Christ's deity, substitutionary death, and bodily resurrection in the verses that follow (Acts 5:30-31).[36]

---

[36] Each of the elements of the gospel in Acts 5:30-32 will be clarified further in chapter 17 on the biblical meaning of "the Christ."

The apostles are then beaten for their witness and commanded again not to *"speak in the name of Jesus"* (Acts 5:40). However, we are told in the immediate context that the apostles *"did not cease teaching and preaching Jesus as the Christ"* (Acts 5:42). We see from this passage that speaking *"in the name of Jesus"* is equivalent to *"preaching and teaching Jesus as the Christ."* We may even say that the "name" of Christ is used as a virtual synonym at times for "the gospel."[37] The conclusion that we may draw from all of this is that there is no distinction between believing in the "name" of Jesus, believing "the gospel" of His death and resurrection, and believing in Him as "the Christ." Believing in the "name" of Jesus is not some lesser, minimal requirement for eternal life than believing "the gospel," for the gospel tells us who Jesus is as "the Christ."

Believing in Christ's "Name" & Believing the "Gospel"

In the Bible, the use of "name" indicates that it is much more than just an appellation by which people are addressed. It is more than a label or an arrangement of letters. The "name" stands for the attributes and actions of a person that make that individual unique and identifiable. It is a serious mishandling of the biblical truth about the "name" to suggest that the lost can be saved today simply by believing that eternal life is guaranteed through an individual called "Jesus," regardless of how little else they might know about Him. While it is certainly true that the concept of "His name" includes the characteristic of Christ being the guarantor of eternal life (John 1:12; 3:15-16, 18; 20:31; 5:11-13), it also includes His saving work. The "name" of Christ speaks of "the sum total of His person, death and resurrection" that "people must believe."[38] To *"believe in His name"* does not mean merely knowing the name "Jesus," or even just the word "Christ," plus the solitary truth of Him being the guarantor. To *"believe in His name"* means to believe the gospel.

This is why the apostle Paul says, *"I have fully preached the gospel of Christ. And so I have made it my aim to preach the gospel, not where Christ was named (onomazō), lest I should build on another man's foundation, but as it is written: 'To whom He was not announced, they shall see; and those who have not heard shall understand'."* (Romans 15:19c-21).

Since this biblical passage was written under the inspiration of the Spirit of God, through the human instrument of the apostle Paul, it clearly sets forth the divine perspective and mind of God on the matter of the "name." This passage establishes beyond any shadow of a doubt that, from God's perspective, there is no difference between Christ being *"named"* or *"announced"* versus the preaching of *"the gospel"* to unbeliev-

[37] Ulrich Becker, *"εὐαγγέλιον," NIDNTT*, ed. Colin Brown (Grand Rapids: Zondervan, 1986), 2:110.

[38] John R. W. Stott, *The Cross of Christ* (Downers Grove, IL: InterVarsity Press, 1986), 35.

ers who are without spiritual sight and understanding. The apostle Paul was *not* in the practice of bringing only a "sanctification message" called *"the gospel of Christ"* to people who had already been born again simply by believing that one named "Jesus" could guarantee them eternal life. According to the Word of God, it is only when people believe the gospel message of Christ's person and work for eternal salvation that they actually *"believe in His name."* It is simply unwarranted and unbiblical to dichotomize believing *"in His name"* and believing *"the gospel of Christ."*

Part II

Clarifying the Saving Gospel of Christ

Chapter 7

Has Progressive Revelation Changed the Gospel?

OVERVIEW

The G.E.S. position on the gospel teaches that the content of faith required for eternal life has never changed since the fall of Adam, despite the evident progress of God's revelation. According to their new doctrine, the monolithic message of life down through the ages has always been that eternal life is guaranteed to all who simply believe in the Messiah for it. However, Scripture does not teach that every Old Testament saint was regenerated through faith in the coming Messiah for eternal life. Though each of the elements of the gospel was revealed in the Old Testament (minus the name of "Jesus" as the Christ), they were never stated anywhere in the Old Testament to be "the gospel"; nor were they required to be believed for eternal life. The crossless gospel position looks to covenant theology to gain support for its conclusions, but the crossless doctrine is actually in conflict with both covenant theology and dispensational theology. Most importantly it contradicts the Word of God.

The doctrine of "progressive revelation" is integral to the whole question of what constitutes the content of saving faith today. What specifically did people in the *Old Testament* have to believe before they were justified in God's sight? What specifically do people *today* have to believe in order to receive justification? Has there been any change? Does God require the lost today to believe only what people in the Old Testament era believed? All theological parties admit to the obvious fact that God has given more divine revelation with each successive age of human history; but the critical question is whether God now requires more truth to be believed today for salvation than He did in the past? Or, is there some minimal amount of revelation that God required in the past that is still the minimum for today?

These are relevant questions in light of what some Free Grace proponents are now claiming. Those affiliated with the Grace Evangelical Society and its crossless content of saving faith are asserting that, in spite of the progress of revelation, people today are only required to believe that the Christ can guarantee them eternal life, just like people in the Old Testament. They say that since lost sinners before Calvary were not required to believe in Christ's deity, death, and resurrection, neither are people today. This chapter will address another major tenet on which the crossless gospel rests—its denial that the progress of God's revelation has affected the content of faith necessary for salvation in this dispensation.

It would be helpful before testing the biblical veracity of the crossless gospel's position on "progressive revelation" and the content of saving faith to first make a few clarifications regarding this doctrine. What do I mean by the phrase "progressive revelation"? Regarding "revelation," I am referring specifically to *special* revelation given by God to man through His prophets. In this respect, I do not mean general revelation about God as seen in the created universe or even within the conscience of man, as Romans 1:19-20 describes.[1] Before the completion of the canon of the New

[1] The "progress of revelation" should also be distinguished from the "progress of dogma," as it is sometimes called within evangelicalism. See, for example, James Orr, *The Progress of Dogma* (London: Hodder & Stoughton, 1901). The "progress of revelation" refers to the increase in actual revelation from God—the Bible itself; whereas the "progress of dogma" refers to an increased doctrinal understanding of God's previously given revelation in the form of inspired Scripture. In very broad, general terms, we could summarize the progress of dogma by noting that in the first few centuries of Church history, the scriptural doctrines of Christology and the Trinity were clarified, followed by soteriology during the Reformation, and eschatology in the last two centuries. This increase in doctrinal discernment is not the result of additional "revelation" from God, since revelation is fixed with the Bible. Instead, it represents "progress" in terms of discernment about the dogmas or doctrines

Testament, God specially revealed divine truths to mankind through His prophets, who communicated these truths to people either verbally or through writing. That which was written down became a part of the Bible. This process went on throughout the Old Testament era as well as the New. However, when the 27 books of the New Testament were completed by the end of the first century, God ceased giving any additional revelation. Throughout the Church age we have the deposit of God's special revelation contained in the treasure of sacred Scripture—the Bible. But all 66 books of God's special revelation were not given to mankind simultaneously. The amount of divine revelation given by God over time "progressed," as the books of Job and Moses (Genesis–Deuteronomy) came first, followed successively by the other books of the Old Testament, until all 39 books of the Old Testament were completed, forming the canon of Old Testament Scripture.

This "progressive" accumulation of God's special revelation in the 39 books of the Old Testament transpired over the course of approximately 1,600 years, from about 2,000 B.C. (Job)–400 B.C. (Malachi). After a period of roughly 400 "silent" years, there was a sudden *explosion* of divine revelation with the coming of Jesus Christ. Between approximately A.D. 30—95, God gave additional special revelation in the form of 27 new books to be added to the Bible. Whereas the 39 books of the Old Testament took roughly 1,600 years to complete, the special revelation of God's inspired Word suddenly increased from 39 books to 66 books within a span of just 65 years. What accounted for this seismic shift? The Lord Jesus Christ! Though truths about Christ had been revealed prior to His incarnation, the effect of His actual coming was so dynamic that it could only be adequately accounted for by adding 27 new books to the Bible. That surely constitutes "progress."

This increase in God's revelation is eloquently stated by the author of Hebrews in his introduction: *"God, who at various times and in various ways spoke in time past to the fathers by the prophets, 2 has in these last days spoken to us by His Son, whom He has appointed heir of all things, through whom also He made the worlds; 3 who being the brightness of His glory and the express image of His person, and upholding all things by the word of His power, when He had by Himself purged our sins, sat down at the right hand of the Majesty on high"* (Heb. 1:1-3). Though God *"spoke"* in the Old Testament about the coming Christ's deity, humanity, substitutionary death, and glorious resurrection, He certainly raised His voice to a whole new decibel level with the incarnational entrance of His only begotten Son into the world. The sheer volume of new revelation regarding His Son and the degree of clarity with which it is explicated in the New Testament has led to a new level of responsibility on the part of man.

---

already contained in God's Word.

All evangelicals agree with the basic premise that increased revelation from God constitutes increased responsibility before God. This agrees with the principle of the Lord Jesus that *"to whom much is given, from him much will be required"* (Luke 12:48). But this principle leads to several important questions, such as, to what extent does this progress in revelation and responsibility affect the gospel and the contents of saving faith? What is the relationship between the gospel and the quantum leap in divine revelation with Christ's coming? Is progressive revelation only a matter of increased responsibility regarding the believer's sanctification? In other words, does the progress in revelation about Christ's death and resurrection mean that the greater responsibility to believe these truths is only for those who are already saved, who have already believed the "minimum" about "the Christ" as the guarantor of eternal life? And if the required content of saving faith has changed *after* Calvary, does this mean "the gospel" itself has changed, as crossless gospel advocates say about the traditional dispensational view on this subject? In addition, how have the different doctrinal systems of interpretation answered these questions, such as covenant theology and dispensational theology? And are their answers truly biblical?

Finally, is the *new* G.E.S. gospel doctrinally aligned with either covenant theology or dispensational teaching on this matter of progressive revelation and salvation, or has a new, third theological position emerged with the advent of the crossless gospel? To these questions, some almost prefer to remain in a state of sanctified spiritual agnosticism, pleading "Well, no one can be certain about these things since scholars on both sides have debated this doctrine for centuries..." However, the Word of God *does have* concrete answers on this subject if we really want to know the truth. Before searching the Scriptures for answers, it will be helpful to acquaint ourselves with three doctrinal positions on this subject.

The Crossless Gospel & Progressive Revelation

The new, crossless doctrine acknowledges that there has been progress or increase in the amount of revelation from God regarding His Son, but this has not changed the minimal content of faith required by God for eternal life. This position states that the content of saving faith has remained the same throughout every age, namely to believe simply that the Christ or Messiah is the guarantor of eternal life. They claim that the additional truths of His deity, death for sin, and resurrection were not essential to believe throughout the Old Testament and Gospel era before Calvary, so neither are they required to believe for eternal life today. The rationale for their belief is based, in part, upon a recognition that the eleven disciples of Christ were born again *before* they believed in Jesus' atoning death and resurrection from the dead (John 13:10-11; 15:3 cf. Matt. 16:16-22; Mark 16:11-

14). Therefore, they say, it must be admitted that people can be born again in any age without having to believe those specific truths about Christ.

This view *does* acknowledge that the doctrinal truths of Christ's person and work constitute greater revelation from God about His Son in this age versus previous ages. As a result, they even acknowledge that with that increase in revelation has come a greater responsibility as well. But they also teach that this greater responsibility is only laid upon the regenerate, those who already possess eternal life. In other words, the truths of Christ's deity, death for sin, and resurrection are Christian life truths that are only divine requirements to believe for the Christian's sanctification. The Executive Director of the Grace Evangelical Society, Bob Wilkin, has been the most vocal and prolific proponent of this view. Though the G.E.S. does not have an official position on this subject in the organization's doctrinal statement or affirmations of belief, it is the one doctrinal perspective that has been actively promoted by the G.E.S. over the years and consequently has come to characterize the organization. For this reason, I will occasionally refer to this view as the "G.E.S. view." This position is explained by its proponents in the following quotes.

Bob Wilkin

> While God expects people to believe He exists, that belief has never been sufficient to obtain eternal life. Eternal life has always been by faith in the Messiah whom God sends. No OT person was ever saved apart from such faith. How do we know this? The apostle Paul uses Abraham as an example of all who believe in Christ for eternal salvation apart from works (Rom 4:1-5; Gal 3:6-14). Paul's example is invalid if Abraham wasn't believing in the coming Messiah and Him alone for eternal life.
>
> Similarly, Jesus rebuked his Jewish audience for not believing in Him, when their forefather, Abraham, had (John 8:37-58, see esp. v 56, "Abraham rejoiced to see My day"). "You search the Scriptures, for in them you think you have eternal life; and these are they which testify of Me" (John 5:39). Many Jews mistakenly thought that by careful observance of the commands of the OT they would merit eternal life. Yet eternal life was only by faith in the Messiah. They claimed to believe Moses, who wrote the Pentateuch, yet to them the Lord said, "If you believed Moses, you would believe Me; for he wrote about Me" (John 5:46).
>
> A common misconception prevails that the content of the gospel changed as God gave more revelation. This causes some to think that prior to Calvary people were saved by works, or by faith in God apart from faith in the coming Messiah. However, the essential content of the gospel has not changed at all. Eternal salvation has always been conditioned upon faith in the Mes-

siah. They looked ahead. We look back. We both believe in the Messiah for eternal life. (Of course, prior to Jesus' beginning His ministry people who believed in the Messiah did not know what His given name would be. After that point people had to believe specifically in Jesus, since the coming Messiah had now come and His name was known.)[2]

Logically what we must do to have eternal life cannot change. If the saving message changes, then so does the gospel. Dispensationalism has long said that men in every age are justified by faith in God, but as revelation progressed what they needed to believe about God changed as well. Well, if people before the time of Christ could be born again by some general faith in God, then logically so can anyone today who has not yet heard the name of Jesus. No one was ever born again by some general faith in God. The condition has always been faith that the Messiah gives eternal life to all who simply believe in Him.[3]

Bob Bryant

"Abraham believed God," but what did God tell him to believe? Some suggest that God didn't tell Abraham to believe in Christ. But Jesus said, "...Abraham rejoiced to see My day, and he saw it and was glad." (John 8:56). Two thousand years before Jesus came, Abraham looked ahead in time and believed in the coming Christ for eternal life. Therefore, he was saved by faith alone in Christ alone. Job made a similar statement, "I know that my Redeemer lives, and He shall stand at last on the earth. And after my skin is destroyed, this I know, that in my flesh I shall see God" (Job 19:25-26). Two thousand years before Jesus came, Job knew that his Redeemer was coming to this earth to pay the price for his sins. Job had a certain assurance that because of his Redeemer, he would live with God after his death. We also know that Moses: "...esteemed the reproach of Christ greater riches than the treasures in Egypt; for he looked to the reward" (Heb. 11:26). Living 1,500 years before Jesus came, he not only believed in Christ, he also understood God's truth concerning discipleship and rewards. Moses even wrote about Christ. As Jesus said to the Jews, "For if you believed Moses, you would believe Me; for he wrote about Me" (John 5:46). Abraham, Job, and Moses illustrate that before Jesus came, people were saved by believing in the Christ who was yet to come. Today, we are saved by believing in the same Christ who has come. They looked forward. We look back. But people have always been saved in the same way, by faith alone in Christ alone.[4]

---

[2] Robert N. Wilkin, "Salvation Before Calvary," *Grace in Focus* 13 (January/February 1998): 2.

[3] Robert N. Wilkin, "Is Ignorance Eternal Bliss?" *JOTGES* 16 (Spring 2003): 13.

[4] Bob Bryant, "How Were People Saved Before Jesus Came?" *JOTGES* 16 (Spring 2003):

Ralph Grant

> People before Calvary were saved by believing in the Messiah who was to come (Gen 15:6; John 5:46; 8:56; Rom 4:1-8). People after Calvary are saved by believing in the Messiah who has already come. Abraham, David, John the Baptist, the thief on the cross, and Cornelius and his household, were all saved by grace through faith in Christ, plus nothing.[5]

Zane Hodges

> Let it be said, then, that Saul—like ourselves—was saved by faith in the Messiah. No other conclusion is reasonable. [6]

John Niemelä

> This message is consistent with the fact that Old Testament believers possessed eternal life, even though they died before the cross paid their penalty of sin. The gift of eternal life came to those people in Old Testament times that believed in the coming One who gives eternal life and would resurrect them in the future. Although as Hebrews 11 says, Abraham died without receiving (in his lifetime) what God had promised him. Even so, he believed the message of life. John shows that this remains the manner of salvation, even after Jesus' death and resurrection.[7]

Before providing a *scriptural* assessment of the crossless gospel's doctrine of progressive revelation and the contents of saving faith, it will be helpful to compare first its doctrine on this subject with that of covenant theology and dispensationalism. This comparison will provide a basis for more meaningful scriptural interaction later in this chapter as each view is compared and contrasted with what the Scriptures actually teach. It should be kept in mind while comparing these three views that crossless gospel men are virtually all dispensationalists, and yet they are inconsistent with their own dispensational theology on this issue. In one respect, namely the continuity of the contents of saving faith, they even agree with covenant theology.

Covenant Theology & Progressive Revelation

The position of covenant theology on the effects of progressive revelation

---

64-65.

[5] Ralph Grant, "Doesn't God Save Everybody the Same Way?" *Grace in Focus* 13 (January/February 1998): 4.

[6] Zane C. Hodges, "Eternal Salvation in the Old Testament: The Salvation of Saul," in *The Grace Evangelical Society News* 9 (July/August 1994): 3.

[7] John Niemelä, "The Message of Life in the Gospel of John," *CTSJ* 7 (July-Sept. 2001): 18.

and the necessary content of faith for eternal life is distinct from both the crossless gospel position and that of normative dispensationalism. Covenant theology maintains that God established a "covenant of grace" with mankind as the one unchangeable plan of salvation that spans each biblical era or dispensation. As a result of believing in this one, "unifying" covenant, Christians who espouse covenant theology are most insistent that the contents of faith did *not* change after Calvary. While they maintain that salvation has been by God's grace through faith in every era, they also teach that God has always required faith in Christ and His redemptive work in order to receive eternal life.[8] In this respect, they differ with the crossless gospel view by requiring a greater amount of content for eternal salvation.

While covenant theologians acknowledge the principle of progressive revelation, they do not believe it has changed the contents of faith required by God for eternal life. Through the light of God's increased revelation about His Son, they say that the content of faith necessary to believe about Christ is now much clearer than in the Old Testament, where the essential truths of Christ's person and work were revealed and still necessary to believe, just more dimly lit. Some of the quotes by covenant theologians below emphasize covenant theology's position on the contents of faith required *before* Calvary, and some quotes reflect covenant theology's belief about the necessary content of faith *today*.

William E. Cox

> Let us look at the saints of the Old Testament. How were they saved? Was the plan under which they were saved any different from God's plan of salvation for today? Let us look, through the eyes of that great theologian, Paul, at Abraham's salvation. Paul took painstaking care in showing that Abraham's salvation was exactly like that being accepted by Gentiles of Paul's day. Paul contended that, indeed, all men of all time are saved in the exact same manner. Men of the Old Testament looked forward and

---

[8] One prolific contemporary evangelical theologian, Walter Kaiser, purportedly maintains a mediating position between dispensationalism and covenant theology (Walter C. Kaiser, Jr., "An Epangelical Response," in *Dispensationalism, Israel and the Church: The Search for Definition*, ed. Craig A. Blaising and Darrell L. Bock [Grand Rapids: Zondervan, 1992], 360-76); and yet his conclusions are decidedly more opposed to the dispensational scheme than the covenantal (see Walter C. Kaiser, Jr., "The Old Testament as the Plan of Salvation," in *Toward Rediscovering the Old Testament* [Grand Rapids: Zondervan, 1987], 121-22, 125-26; idem, "Salvation in the Old Testament: With Special Emphasis on the Object and Content of Personal Belief," *Jian Dao* 2 [1994]: 1-2, 5, 10-11). Kaiser's position agrees with covenant theology in seeing a unity in the content of saving faith in both testaments but differs somewhat over the exact content of that faith. For him, saving faith in the Old Testament is faith in the promised coming Seed without necessarily requisite knowledge of, and belief in, His future redeeming work. Not surprisingly, the Grace Evangelical Society appeals to Kaiser's position on Old Testament saving faith in order to support its own crossless content of saving faith for the present dispensation. See Editorial, "Abraham Believed in Christ," *Grace in Focus* 22 (March/April 2007): 4.

> accepted the propitiation through Christ on faith while those of the New Testament era accept the finished sacrifice.[9]

> Men today are saved by hearing and believing the kerygma (the good news of Christ's death, burial, and resurrection). Abraham was saved through faith in that same gospel. This was the same gospel which was preached by John the Baptist, by our Lord himself, and by all the apostles. This gospel was preached, in advance, to Abraham (Gal. 3:8) so that he might be the father of all the righteous (Rom. 4:11).[10]

James Montgomery Boice

> It should be evident . . . that a person was saved in the Old Testament period in the same way in which a person is saved today. That is, the person who lived before Christ's time was saved by grace through faith in a redeemer who was to come, just as today a person is saved by grace through faith in the redeemer who has already come. The Old Testament women and men looked forward to Christ. We look back.[11]

Based on Christ's comment in John 8:56 and the account of Isaac being offered up in Genesis 22, Boice concludes that Abraham understood that the coming redeemer would be resurrected, as Isaac's offering pictured, and even that Christ would be sacrificed for our salvation. In reference to the statement, *"The LORD will provide"* (Gen. 22:14), Boice writes:

> Now it could only mean that the same God who provided a ram in substitution for Isaac would one day provide his own Son as the perfect substitute and sacrifice for our salvation. Thus Abraham saw the coming of Jesus, including the meaning of his death and resurrection and rejoiced in that coming.[12]

W. G. T. Shedd

> The Old Testament saint cast himself upon the Divine mercy. Ps. 32:1-11; Ps. 51; Ps. 103:2, 3. And this mercy he expected through the promised "seed of the woman," the Messiah; and through an atonement typified by the Levitical sacrifices.[13]

---

[9] William E. Cox, *Amillennialism Today* (Phillipsburg, NJ: Presbyterian and Reformed Publishing Co., 1966), 30.

[10] Ibid., 30-31.

[11] James Montgomery Boice, *Foundations of the Christian Faith*, rev. ed. (Downers Grove, IL: InterVarsity Press, 1986), 256 (ellipsis added).

[12] Ibid., 262.

[13] William G. T. Shedd, *Dogmatic Theology* (Grand Rapids: Zondervan, Reprinted 1971), 2:366.

Charles Hodge

In the general contents of the Scriptures there are certain doctrines concerning Christ and his work, and certain promises of salvation made through Him to sinful men, which we are bound to receive and on which we are required to trust. The special object of faith, therefore, is Christ, and the promise of salvation through Him. And the special definite act of faith which secures our salvation is the act of receiving and resting on Him as He is offered to us in the Gospel.[14]

If He is our Redeemer, we must receive and trust Him as such. If He is a propitiation for sins, it is through faith in his blood that we are reconciled to God. The whole plan of salvation, as set forth in the Gospel, supposes that Christ in his person and work is the object of faith and the ground of confidence.[15]

It is no less clear that the Redeemer is the same under all dispensations. He who was predicted as the seed of the woman, as the seed of Abraham, the Son of David, the Branch, the Servant of the Lord, the Prince of Peace, is our Lord, Jesus Christ, the Son of God, God manifest in the flesh. He, therefore, from the beginning has been held up as the hope of the world, the SALVATOR HOMINUM.[16]

As the promise was made to those who lived before the advent which is now made to us in the gospel, as the same Redeemer was revealed to them who is presented as the object of faith to us, it of necessity follows that the condition, or terms of salvation, was the same then as now. It was not mere faith or trust in God, or simply piety, which was required, but faith in the promised Redeemer, or faith in the promise of redemption through the Messiah.[17]

Not only, therefore, from these explicit declarations that faith in the promised Redeemer was required from the beginning, but from the admitted fact that the Old Testament is full of the doctrine of redemption by the Messiah, it follows that those who received the religion of the Old Testament received that doctrine, and exercised faith in the promise of God concerning his Son.[18]

Louis Berkhof

There are certain doctrines concerning Christ and His work, and certain promises made in Him to sinful men, which the

---

[14] Charles Hodge, *Systematic Theology* (Grand Rapids: Eerdmans, Reprinted 1989), 3:96.

[15] Ibid., 3:98.

[16] Ibid., 2:370.

[17] Ibid., 2:372.

[18] Ibid.

> sinner must receive and which must lead him to put his trust in Christ.[19]

James Oliver Buswell

Buswell says in regards to the Old Testament saints ("elders") referred to in Hebrews 11:2, *"That is, by their faith in the coming Messiah and in salvation through the sacrifice which He would make, the elders 'received a good report'."*[20] Buswell goes on to mention the example of Abel's sacrifice in Hebrews 11:4, saying, *"Abel's faith was, in substance, faith in the atoning work of Christ, the promised Redeemer."*[21]

Dispensational Theology & Progressive Revelation

The position of dispensational theology is that due to the progress of God's revelation with respect to His Son Jesus Christ there has been a corresponding change in the contents of faith required for eternal life. As a result, lost humanity throughout this Church age must believe in Jesus Christ's person and work. The dispensational doctrine of progressive revelation acknowledges that prior to the cross it was *not* necessary to believe specifically in Christ's substitutionary death and bodily resurrection to have eternal life. Though these great truths about God's Son were always known to God the Father (1 Peter 1:20; Rev. 13:8), and they were progressively revealed as a matter of prophecy in the Old Testament (Luke 24:25-27; 1 Peter 1:10-11), this does not mean they were universally made known to mankind as the required content of saving faith.

The traditional dispensational view asserts that in every dispensation the *basis* or *grounds* of eternal salvation is always the work of Christ and the grace of God (Rom. 3:21-25; Heb. 10:1-14); the *requirement* for salvation is always faith alone in particular truth specially revealed by God (Hab. 2:4; Gal. 2:16); the *object* of faith is always properly God Himself (Gen. 15:6; Rom. 4:20, 24; 1 Peter 1:21); but the necessary *content* of that faith has changed with the progress of revelation (Gal. 3:23; 1 Cor. 15:1-4). This has been the position espoused by the vast majority of dispensationalists in the last century,[22] and it is expressed in the following quotes.

---

[19] Louis Berkhof, *Systematic Theology* (Grand Rapids: Eerdmans, Reprinted 1991), 506.

[20] James Oliver Buswell, *A Systematic Theology of the Christian Religion* (Grand Rapids: Zondervan, 1962), 2:185.

[21] Ibid.

[22] For representatives of the normative, traditional dispensational view, see Mal Couch, "Salvation in the Dispensation of the Church," in *An Introduction to Classical Evangelical Hermeneutics*, ed. Mal Couch (Grand Rapids: Kregel Publications, 2000), 192-98; John S. Feinberg, "Salvation in the Old Testament," in *Tradition & Testament: Essays in Honor of Charles Lee Feinberg*, ed. John S. and Paul D. Feinberg (Chicago: Moody Press, 1981), 39-77; Norman L. Geisler, Systematic Theology (Minneapolis: Bethany House, 2004), 3:530-49; S. Jeff Heslop, "Content, Object, & Message of Saving Faith," in *Dispensationalism Tomorrow & Beyond:*

Paul Enns

> God's revelation to man differs in different dispensations, but man's responsibility is to respond to God in faith according to the manner in which God has revealed Himself. Thus when God revealed Himself to Abraham and promised him a great posterity, Abraham believed God, and the Lord imputed righteousness to the patriarch (Gen. 15:6). Abraham would have known little about Christ, but he responded in faith to the revelation of God and was saved. Similarly, under the law God promised life through faith. Whereas the Israelite under the law knew about the importance of the blood sacrifice, his knowledge of a suffering Messiah was still limited—but he was saved by faith (Hab. 2:4). Dispensationalists thus emphasize that in every dispensation salvation is by God's grace through faith according to His revelation.[23]

Mal Couch

> To argue that the content of the gospel has remained constant is to completely deny progressive revelation. Dispensationalists assert that, although salvation has always been and always will be by faith, the amount of knowledge one had of the future death of Christ was limited, and thus the content of faith was different at different stages of God's progressive revelation.[24]

Dallas Theological Seminary

> We believe that the dispensations are not ways of salvation, nor different methods of administering the so-called Covenant of Grace. They are not in themselves dependent on covenant relationships but are rules of life with responsibility to God which test the submission of man to God's revealed will during a particular time. We believe that, if man does trust in his own efforts to gain the favor of God or salvation under any dispensational test, because of his inherent sin, his failure to satisfy fully the just

---

A Theological Collection in Honor of Charles C. Ryrie, ed. Christopher Cone (Fort Worth, TX: Tyndale Seminary Press, 2008), 233-51; Allen P. Ross, "The Biblical Method of Salvation: A Case for Discontinuity," in *Continuity and Discontinuity: Perspectives on the Relationship Between the Old and New Testaments*, John S. Feinberg, ed. (Wheaton, IL: Crossway Books, 1988), 161-78; Ramesh Richard, *The Population of Heaven: A Biblical Response to the Inclusivist Position on Who will be Saved* (Chicago: Moody Press, 1994), 115-43; Charles C. Ryrie, *Dispensationalism* (Chicago: Moody Press, 1995), 105-22; Thomas Schultz, "Saving Faith in the Old Testament" (Th.M. thesis, Dallas Theological Seminary, 1959); Henry C. Thiessen, *Introductory Lectures in Systematic Theology* (Grand Rapids: Eerdmans, 1949), 281; John F. Walvoord, *Jesus Christ Our Lord* (Chicago: Moody Press, 1969), 58-59.

[23] Paul Enns, *The Moody Handbook of Theology* (Chicago: Moody Press, 1989), 522.

[24] Mal Couch, gen. ed., *An Introduction to Classical Evangelical Hermeneutics* (Grand Rapids: Kregel Publications, 2000), 196.

requirements of God is inevitable and his condemnation is sure. We believe that according to the *"eternal purpose"* of God (Eph. 3:11), salvation in every dispensation is always *"by grace through faith"* alone and rests upon the basis of the shed blood of Christ. We believe that God has always been gracious, regardless of the ruling dispensation, but that believers have not at all times been under an administration or stewardship of grace as a rule of life, as is true in the present dispensation (Rom. 6:14; 1 Cor. 9:17-21; Eph. 1:10; 3:2-9; Col. 1:24-27). We believe that it has always been true that *"without faith it is impossible to please"* God (Heb. 11:6), and that the principle of faith was prevalent in the lives of all the Old Testament saints. However, we believe that it was historically impossible that they should have had as the conscious object of their faith the incarnate, crucified Son, the Lamb of God (John 1:29), and that it is evident they did not comprehend as we do that the sacrifices depicted the person and work of Christ, nor did they fully understand the redemptive significance of the prophecies or types concerning the sufferings of Christ (1 Peter 1:10-12). However, we do believe that their faith toward God was manifested in other ways, as is shown by the long record in Hebrews 11:1-40, and consequently that their faith was counted unto them for righteousness (Gen. 15:6; Rom. 4:3-8; Heb. 11:7).[25]

Lewis Sperry Chafer

Are there two ways by which one may be saved? In reply to this question it may be stated that salvation of whatever specific character is always the work of God in behalf of man and never a work of man in behalf of God. This is to assert that God never saved any one person or group of persons on any other ground than that righteous freedom to do so which the Cross of Christ secured. There is, therefore, but one way to be saved and that is by the power of God made possible through the sacrifice of Christ. The far lesser question as to the precise human terms upon which men may be saved is quite a different issue. This feature is of less import for the reason that man never contributes anything to his salvation whether he be one who keeps the Law or one who trusts Christ alone apart from human works. The colossal error which supplies any point to the contention of those who accuse others of believing that there are two ways by which the lost may be saved is just this, that neither works nor faith of themselves can ever save anyone. It is God's undertaking

[25] Dallas Theological Seminary Doctrinal Statement, Article V, "The Dispensations," paragraph four. Even though the principal architect of this doctrinal statement was the school's founder, Lewis Sperry Chafer (see Jeffrey J. Richards, *The Promise of Dawn: The Eschatology of Lewis Sperry Chafer* [Lanham, MD: University Press of America, 1991], 39), the section of it dealing with the content of faith for the Old Testament believer has represented the views of most dispensationalists within and outside of Dallas Seminary for the last eighty plus years.

and always on the ground, not of works or faith, but on the blood of Christ. That God has assigned different human requirements in various ages as the terms upon which He Himself saves on the ground of the death of Christ, is a truth of Scripture revelation and is recognized as true, by those who receive their doctrine from the Sacred Text rather than from manmade creeds. Nevertheless, when the various human requirements of the different ages are investigated it is found that they come alike in the end to the basic reality that faith is exercised in God. And that one basic element of trust in *God* doubtless answers that which in every case God must require.[26]

Second, God imputes righteousness to those in this age who believe, which righteousness is the foremost feature of salvation, on the one demand that they believe; but this belief is not centered in a son which each individual might generate, as in the case of Abraham, but in the Son whom God has given to a lost world, who died for the world and whom God has raised from the dead to be a Savior of those who do believe. In Romans 4:23, 24 it is written, "Now it was not written for his sake alone, that it was imputed to him; But for us also, to whom it shall be imputed, if we believe on him that raised up Jesus our Lord from the dead." From this it will be seen that, though the specific object of faith—Isaac in the case of Abraham and Jesus Christ in the case of those becoming Christians—varies, both have a promise of God on which to rest and both believe God.[27]

Charles Ryrie

This dispensationalist's answer to the question of the relation of grace and law is this: The basis of salvation in every age is the death of Christ; the *requirement* for salvation in every age is faith; the *object* of faith in every age is God; the *content* of faith changes in the various dispensations. It is this last point, of course, that distinguishes dispensationalism from covenant theology, but it is not a point to which the charge of teaching two ways of salvation can be attached. It simply recognizes the obvious fact of progressive revelation.[28]

In examining salvation under the Mosaic Law the principal question is simply, How much of what God was going to do in the future did the Old Testament believer comprehend? According to both Old and New Testament revelation it is impossible to say that he saw the same promise, the same Savior as we do today. Therefore, the dispensationalists' distinction between the

---

[26] Lewis Sperry Chafer, Editorial, *BSac* 102 (January-March 1945): 2-3.

[27] Ibid.

[28] Charles C. Ryrie, *Dispensationalism* (Chicago: Moody Press, 1995), 115.

content of his faith and the content of ours is valid. The basis of salvation is always the death of Christ; the means is always faith; the object is always God (though man's understanding of God before and after the Incarnation is obviously different); but the content of faith depends on the particular revelation God was pleased to give at a certain time. These are the distinctions the dispensationalist recognizes, and they are distinctions necessitated by plain interpretation of revelation as it was given. If by "ways" of salvation is meant different content of faith, then dispensationalism does teach various "ways" because the Scriptures reveal differing contents for faith in the progressive nature of God's revelation to mankind. But if by "ways" is meant more than one basis or means of salvation, then dispensationalism most emphatically does not teach more than one way, for salvation has been, is, and always will be based on the substitutionary death of Jesus Christ.[29]

Robert Lightner

The Bible knows of only one way of salvation. It makes no difference which period of time one refers to. The salvation of a sinner has always been and will always be by God's grace through faith. The basis upon which God forgives sin has always been the substitutionary death of Christ. People have not always known what we know about the Person and work of Christ simply because all that has been revealed in the New Testament was not made known to the men of God who wrote the Old Testament. Therefore, while God has always required personal faith as a condition of salvation, the complexity of that faith has not always been the same. Those who lived before Calvary knew very little about the finished work of Christ so vividly portrayed in the New Testament. Many of the Old Testament sacrifices and offerings were types of the Savior and of the final and complete work He would do. However, even though the people may not have known all that was involved when they believed God and His promises, He accounted their faith to them for righteousness because He accepted the work of His Son as already finished. The resurrection of Christ is proof of this acceptance. The only difference between other dispensations and this one, as it relates to salvation, is the complexity of faith, that which was believed by the sinner. Before the full revelation of Scripture was given, faith was placed in the person and promises of God made known up to that time (Rom. 4:3). Since God has made known to man the meaning of the death of His Son, faith is now placed in His person and work. Salvation in any age is a work of God on behalf of the believing sinner, apart from human works of any kind.[30]

---

[29] Ibid., 121.

[30] Robert P. Lightner, *Sin, the Savior, and Salvation* (Nashville: Thomas Nelson Publishers,

The opinions of Lightner, Ryrie, Chafer, Couch, and Enns fairly represent the views of the vast majority of dispensationalists on this subject.[31] There has been a high degree of uniformity in the last century among dispensationalists about the fact that there was a change in the content of saving faith from the Old Testament to the New Testament due to the progress of revelation and that explicit belief in the gospel of Christ is required today.[32]

Thus far this chapter has surveyed the three doctrinal systems of dispensationalism, covenant theology, and the crossless/G.E.S. view of saving faith. The positions of each system with respect to progressive rev-

---

1991), 161-62.

[31] As with any system of interpretation, there are exceptions. One dispensationalist of the past, Louis Talbot, agreed with covenant theology that Old Testament saints were saved by looking forward to the cross in faith just as we look back to it. See Louis T. Talbot, *Bible Questions Answered* (Grand Rapids: Eerdmans, 1938), 86-87, 245.

[32] One dispensationalist, S. Jeff Heslop, has recently proposed a significant change to the traditional dispensational understanding of this subject. Though Heslop agrees that people in the OT were not required to believe specifically in the coming Messiah for eternal life as people are today ("Content, Object, & Message of Saving Faith," 233-51), he maintains that there is a distinction between the "content" of saving faith and the "message" to be believed (ibid., 235-41). He argues that the "content" of faith in every age is actually God Himself (who is also the "object"), but it is a third key element, the "message," that changes from age to age. According to this view, a person can believe the message *about God* while still not believing *in the person of God* Himself (ibid., 236), and for this reason, believing in the message is insufficient for salvation in each era without faith in God Himself. Heslop attempts to support this view by the example of Paul with King Agrippa in Acts 26:27. There Paul appeals to Agrippa saying, *"King Agrippa, do you believe the Prophets? I know that you do."* Based on this passage, he reasons that though Agrippa believed the message of the prophets, he had not yet believed in the person of God (ibid., 237). But this seems to be pressing the passage too far. It is more likely that Paul was merely acknowledging that even Agrippa had a general respect for the OT and that he regarded Israel's prophets as God's spokesmen. This is similar to the average Roman Catholic today believing that the Bible contains God's truth even though they are largely ignorant of its actual contents. Heslop also seeks to support his distinction between the "message" and the "content" of saving faith by distinguishing between the phrases "believing that" (i.e., believing a proposition or mere information) and "believing in" God/Christ Himself (ibid., 241). But no such distinction can be legitimately maintained from Scripture. See Fred Chay and John P. Correia, *The Faith that Saves: The Nature of Faith in the New Testament* (n.p.: Schoettle Publishing, 2008), 40-79; Richard W. Christianson, "The Soteriological Significance of ΠΙΣΤΕΥΩ in the Gospel of John" (Th.M. thesis, Grace Theological Seminary, 1987), 86-87; J. Dean Hebron, "A Study of ΠΙΣΤΕΥΩ in the Gospel of John with Reference to the Content of Saving Faith" (Th.M. thesis, Capital Bible Seminary, 1980), 45. Even Reformed Johannine scholar, Leon Morris, acknowledges that there is no distinction (at least in John's Gospel) between believing *in* versus believing *that*. Leon Morris, *Jesus is the Christ: Studies in the Theology of John* (Grand Rapids: Eerdmans, 1989), 188-89. John speaks of saving faith as both "believe that" (*pisteuō* + *hoti*) and "believe in" (*pisteuō* + *eis/en*). To "believe that" (*pisteuō* + *hoti*) Jesus is the Christ, the Son of God (John 20:31) is soteriologically equivalent to believing "in" (*pisteuō* + *eis/en*) Him for eternal life (John 3:15-16). This means that when a person has believed the message of the gospel, they have also believed in Christ (Eph. 1:13). Though the gospel sets forth a proposition to be believed, it also sets forth a person. To believe in Christ and to believe the gospel of Christ are synonymous concepts in Scripture and should not be viewed as two separate, consecutive steps in receiving eternal life.

elation and the contents of saving faith are summarized in the following chart. It must be underscored at this point that though the crossless view claims support for its position from covenant theology, the only agreement between the two is over the fact that the contents of faith *have not changed.*[33] With respect to the actual *contents* of that faith, they are poles apart. The crossless gospel's doctrine on this subject is an entirely new, third theological position within evangelicalism, and to my knowledge, it has never been held collectively before by any group in Church history.

Doctrinal System of Interpretation	Belief in Person & Work of Christ Required for Eternal Life ***before*** Calvary	Belief in Person & Work of Christ Required for Eternal Life ***after*** Calvary
Covenant Theology	YES	YES
Dispensationalism	NO	YES
Crossless Gospel	NO	NO

What Saith the Scriptures?

The real test of any doctrine's truthfulness is not whether it lines up with certain evangelical theologies per se, but whether it agrees with God's Word. On this account, the crossless gospel is unbiblical on the matter of progressive revelation and the content of faith required for salvation. The same Old Testament passages and examples are cited by crossless gospel advocates and covenant theologians in support of their claims for continuity in the contents of faith. Though they refer to the same Scripture texts and Old Testament characters to support their positions, they may as well be interpreting a piece of modern art, for the conclusions they reach are polar opposites on the contents of saving faith. Covenant theologians see Old Testament saints believing for their eternal salvation, however dimly, specifically in a Christ who is the Son of God, who provides redemption through His own sacrificial death and resurrection from the dead. The

[33] In spite of the editor's qualification, the *Journal of the Grace Evangelical Society* used a covenant theologian's article in an attempt to advance the crossless gospel position on this subject. In the article, author Sydney Dyer concluded, "*The Bible teaches only one way of salvation. It is by the grace of God through faith in Christ. Believers before the birth of Christ heard the same gospel, looked to the same Savior, were members of the same Church, and enjoyed the same blessings of salvation as we who believe today.*" Sydney D. Dyer, "The Salvation of Believing Israelites Prior to the Incarnation of Christ," *JOTGES* 14 (Spring 2001): 55.

crossless position sees the same Old Testament saints believing merely in the Messiah as the guarantor of eternal life, without necessarily understanding how He will provide redemption or eternal life.

In either case, several key questions must be asked of each Old Testament example cited by those upholding covenant theology or by the crossless position. First, does Scripture actually say that these Old Testament saints placed their faith specifically in the coming "Christ" for their eternal life, or is this an assumption that is being imposed upon each passage and character? Second, if these Old Testament saints did believe specifically in the coming Christ, did they believe in Him redemptively? Even if they understood and believed certain revealed truths about the Christ, did they necessarily know He was the guarantor of eternal life and believe in Him as such? In other words, when they believed in the coming Christ were they really staking their eternal destinies upon Him? Finally, it must also be asked, even if certain key Old Testament people (most of whom were also prophets) understood and believed that Christ alone would provide eternal life, how pervasive was this knowledge? Did God require this of everyone in the Old Testament?

Abraham

Abraham is usually cited as an example of an Old Testament saint who believed in the coming Christ for his eternal life or justification. In Genesis 15:6, the classic Old Testament passage on imputed righteousness and justification, it says that Abraham *"believed in the LORD (Yahweh) and it was counted to him for righteousness."* Nowhere in the verse or the context does it actually state that he believed in the Messiah for his eternal life. Was Abraham justified because he placed his faith specifically in the Christ who would come and guarantee eternal life? No passage in all of Scripture says anything even approximating that. In fact, the "gospel" or "good news" that Abraham heard and believed was something quite different from what we preach to the lost today. In Galatians 3:6-9, it says, *"just as Abraham "believed God, and it was accounted to him for righteousness." 7 Therefore know that only those who are of faith are sons of Abraham. 8 And the Scripture, foreseeing that God would justify the Gentiles by faith, preached the gospel to Abraham beforehand, saying, "In you all the nations shall be blessed." 9 So then those who are of faith are blessed with believing Abraham."*

This inspired New Testament commentary on Abraham's faith does *NOT* say that God *"preached the gospel to Abraham beforehand, saying, 'Christ died for our sins, was buried, and rose again'"* (1 Cor. 15:3-4). Nor does it say that God preached the gospel to Abraham saying, *"a man is not justified by the works of the law but by faith in Jesus Christ"* (Gal. 2:16). For that matter, Galatians 3:8 does not even say technically that Abraham had "the gospel" preached unto him by God. The phrase in Galatians 3:8, *"preached the gospel beforehand,"* is a single verb in the Greek, *proeuangelizomai*. As a verb, it has no article, unlike the noun *euangelion* which normally has an article in the Greek New Testament and is most often translated, "the gospel." Therefore, Galatians 3:8 does *not* say that Abraham had "*the* gospel" of justification by faith in Christ preached to him. It literally says he had "*good news preached*" to him by God. But what specifically was this "good news"? According to the text, it was the good news that "*In you all the nations shall be blessed*" (Gal. 3:8; cf. Genesis 12:3).

If crossless gospel advocates wish to use this reference in Galatians 3:8 to support their doctrine (and they often resort to this passage), I doubt they would advocate evangelizing the lost today with the message that says, "*In you all the nations shall be blessed.*" The particular divine promise that Abraham believed was that through him all the families of the earth would be blessed. From God's perspective, He knew in His omniscient foreknowledge that this would be fulfilled through a particular "Seed," the Christ (Gal. 3:16). But there is simply nothing stated in Genesis, or Galatians, or anywhere else in Scripture to indicate that Abraham understood God's promise here to be a reference to a particular Man, the Messiah, who would provide eternal life to Abraham if he would believe in Him for it.

But some may still object that the "LORD" referred to in Genesis 15:6 is the Lord Jesus Christ when it says, "*And he believed in the LORD, and He accounted it to him for righteousness.*" Was Christ the specific object and content of Abram's faith in this classic passage? In the context, Abram believes God's promise that his heir will not come through Eliezer, the steward of his estate (15:2-3), but from his own body (15:4) and that his descendents would be innumerable like the stars of heaven (15:5). The construction that immediately begins Genesis 15:6 is *wᵉhe'ĕmīn* (וְהֶאֱמִן) and is translated "*And he believed.*" The *waw* prefix serves as a simple conjunction ("and," "then," "so") rather than a consecutive or conversive *waw*. While the consecutive *waw does* occur in verses 2-5, the grammatical construction of verse 6 should *not* be viewed as a consecutive *waw*. This likely indicates an intentional break at this point in the narrative sequence of Genesis 15:1-6.[34] The nonconsecutive *waw* of Genesis 15:6 may simply be intended to highlight Abram's response of faith in verse 6 or it may even serve as a summarizing statement of Abram's faith up to that point. This would mean that Abram's faith in the LORD did not begin at Genesis 15:6, nor was this the precise moment of his justification in God's sight.[35] But if this was not the hour when Abram first believed, then

---

[34] There is a classical past tense narrative sequence in verses 1-5 (the perfect-imperfect sequence or *qatal-wayyiqtol*), with the Qal perfect verbal form in verse 1, "and the word of the LORD *came* (*hāyâ*) to Abram," followed by imperfect + *waw* consecutives in verses 2, 3, and 5. However, verse 6 begins with the perfect + *waw* construction (*wᵉhe'ĕmīn*) rather than another imperfect + *waw* (*wayya'ămēn*; cf. Ex. 4:31; 14:31).

[35] John J. Davis, *Paradise to Prison: Studies in Genesis* (Grand Rapids: Baker Book House, 1975), 186; Victor P. Hamilton, *The Book of Genesis*, Chapters 1-17, NICOT (Grand Rapids: Eerdmans, 1990), 371, 423; Allen P. Ross, *Creation & Blessing: A Guide to the Study and Exposition of Genesis* (Grand Rapids: Baker Books, 1996), 309-10; John H. Sailhamer, *The*

why even record verse 6 at this juncture in Genesis? It is likely that Moses would have placed the account of verses 1-6 at this juncture in the narrative because he wanted the reader to know that God was about to ratify (Gen. 15:7-21) His previously promised covenant (Gen. 12:1-3) with someone who was definitely a believer and a righteous man in God's sight by faith.[36]

Those who advocate a crossless saving faith agree with the interpretation that Genesis 15:6 does not indicate Abram's initial, justifying faith before God but that it actually occurred previous to this occasion. This allows them to acknowledge that Genesis 15:1-5 does not contain the content of Abram's faith that was necessary for justification, since there is no clear reference to the Messiah in the passage. Instead, they teach that the required content of Abraham's faith is found earlier in God's promise to him in Genesis 12:3.[37] There God gives a promise of universal blessing.

Setting aside for a moment the matter of the *content* of faith, a strong case can be made for the *timing* of Abram's initial faith occurring prior to his entrance into Canaan land, even before his delay at Haran, while he was still in Ur of the Chaldees. Acts 7:2-3 fixes the occasion of God's revelation to Abram in Genesis 12:1-3 as that time when he still dwelt in Ur of the Chaldees, since Acts 7:2 says that God appeared and spoke to him *"in Mesopotamia, before he dwelt in Haran."* Hebrews 11:8 also commends Abram for *leaving* Ur by faith, which is the initial act of faith documented in Abraham's record of faith in Hebrews 11. In addition, we know that Abram walked by faith and offered sacrifices to God as an act of worship on the basis of his faith in Genesis 12, which is also noted and commended in Hebrews 11:9. This means Abram must have believed in the LORD and been justified prior to Genesis 15:6. Otherwise, if the faith that Abram demonstrated prior to Genesis 15 stemmed from an unregenerate, unjustified, condemned man, it seems difficult to maintain that God would commend the faith of an "unbeliever" in the "Hall of Fame of Faith" in Hebrews 11:8-9.

Pentateuch as Narrative: A Biblical-Theological Commentary (Grand Rapids: Zondervan, 1992), 151-52; W. H. Griffith Thomas, *Genesis: A Devotional Commentary* (Grand Rapids: Kregel Publications, 1988), 116-17.

[36] Ross, *Creation & Blessing*, 310; Sailhamer, *The Pentateuch as Narrative*, 152. However, in arguing against the dispensational position, Walter Kaiser maintains that the placement of this great justification-by-faith verse is deliberate in the narrative of Genesis in order to demonstrate that Abraham's justification was conditioned upon conscious faith in the promised Seed as the One who would be the coming Savior. He writes, "Scripture probably deliberately delayed its discussion of Abram's belief and justification so that it might make the strongest connection between the Savior (i.e., the One Seed) and Abram's justification in order that no one might disassociate justification from the Seed that was to come" (Kaiser, *Toward Rediscovering the Old Testament*, 128). While Kaiser claims that dispensationalists have ignored the context of Genesis 15:6, his own interpretation misses the *prospective* connection between verse 6 and the remainder of the chapter dealing with the ratification of the Abrahamic covenant.

[37] John Niemelä, "The Bible Answer Men," a panel discussion at the Grace Evangelical Society Seattle Regional Conference, September 29, 2007.

But shifting the *timing* of Abram's justifying faith from Genesis 15:6 to Genesis 12:3 does not solve the problem of the *content* of Abram's saving faith as crossless proponents would like us to believe.[38] They must find a clear-cut example of an Old Testament character believing specifically in the coming Messiah for eternal life. But if Genesis 15:6 is not it, then neither is Genesis 12:3. In verse 3, the LORD promises to Abram, *"And in you all the families of the earth shall be blessed."* While this certainly does establish the universal extent of God's blessing to Abram (and even "through" Abram), it does not contain an explicit reference to the Messiah. Nor does it indicate that the blessing would be justification in particular. Those truths unfolded only with the progress of revelation throughout the rest of the Old and New Testaments. In the absence of any reference to the Messiah in the passage itself, it is impossible to determine from Genesis 12:1-3 whether Abram at this point in his life personally understood this to be a reference to the coming Messiah who would guarantee his justification.

Even Paul's interpretation of *"the blessing of Abraham"* in Galatians 3:14 as universal justification, and the *"Seed"* in Galatians 3:16 being singular in reference to Christ, are retrospective and only tell us the divine historical perspective on the Abrahamic promises *after* the coming of Christ. Galatians 3:14 and 16 do not tell us how *Abraham himself* interpreted these promises. It is for this reason that in Galatians 3:6-9, when Paul recounts what Abraham personally believed, he never mentions "Christ" in particular—only "God."[39] If Abraham did believe in the coming Christ for his justification, it would have been not only easy for Paul to say so in Galatians 3, it would have been opportune. Yet Paul never mentions this. It is also conspicuous that Paul does not say in Galatians 3:8 that Abraham had "*the* good news" preached to him, but only that he had "good news" preached to him. It is therefore an unsupportable inference that crossless and covenant theologians make when they insist that Abraham had faith specifically in the coming Messiah for his justification. While it is true that one of Abraham's descendants would bring universal blessing by virtue of being *"the Savior of the world"* (John 4:42), and that this is the fulfillment of Genesis 12:3, we know this now only with biblical hindsight due to progressive revelation. That particular truth is not explicitly stated in Genesis 12:3. Shifting the moment of faith from Genesis 15:6 to 12:3 does *not* prove that the content of Abram's faith included belief specifically in the Messiah as the guarantor of eternal life.

---

[38] Ibid.

[39] Some have contended that since the object of saving faith in the OT was the LORD (Yahweh) Himself, and the NT expressly equates Jesus Christ with the LORD (Yahweh) of the OT, then this means that even saints in the OT had an implicit faith in Christ. However, as Grogan states, "This is not to say that it was a conscious faith in Christ. John viii.56 may suggest that in Abraham's case it was even consciously so, but we cannot be sure that this is the meaning of it." Geoffrey W. Grogan, "The Experience of Salvation in the Old and New Testaments," *VE* 5 (1967): 21

At this point, some people appeal to Christ's teaching in John 8:56 that *"Abraham rejoiced to see My day, and he saw it and was glad."* Again we must ask, what did Abraham foresee about Christ, and what was Abraham's response? It must be admitted by crossless gospel advocates that this passage does not even remotely say, *"Abraham rejoiced to see Me as the guarantor of eternal life, and he believed it and was born again."* Nor from a covenant theology standpoint does it say, *"Abraham rejoiced to see My substitutionary death and resurrection, and he believed it and was saved."*[40] There is simply nothing in Christ's words to necessitate the conclusion that Abraham's justification was dependent upon what he foresaw about Christ. For all we know, Abraham could have just as easily foreseen Christ's day *after* he was justified![41] Abraham was a man of tremendous faith, and having walked with the Lord by faith for many decades, it may be that the Lord revealed this specific truth to Abraham, His "friend" (2 Chron. 20:7; Isa. 41:8; James 2:23), only after he grew in his faith. But even if this passage did teach that Abraham personally believed the coming Christ could guarantee him eternal life, this still doesn't indicate that this was God's *universal requirement* for all other lost sinners in Abraham's day or throughout the rest of the Old Testament.[42]

Finally, regarding Abraham, it is also noteworthy that in the "Hall of Fame of Faith" in Hebrews 11, there are twelve verses of inspired New Testament commentary on the faith of Abraham (and Sarah)—more than any other Old Testament saint. And yet there is not a single reference to Abraham believing anything about the coming Messiah, to say nothing of believing in Him specifically as the guarantor of eternal life which the crossless position requires.

Nor will it suffice to excuse this glaring omission by claiming that Hebrews 11 is all about a walk of faith and not initial faith for justification. Though it is true that Hebrews 11 deals with rewards and sanctifying faith, rather than justifying faith, even the Christian's walk of faith is based upon belief in Jesus Christ for justification. That is why the New Testament epistles are saturated with gospel truth pertaining to Christ's person and work and yet they are addressed primarily to believers who are already justified. This means that in Hebrews 11, if the crossless or covenant views are correct, we should expect to see at least *some* reference to faith in Christ for eternal life as the basis of the Old Testament saint's walk of faith. Yet, the silence of Hebrews 11 on this point is deafening.

Job

We turn next to the example of another prominent Old Testament believer,

---

[40] Heslop, "Content, Object, & Message of Saving Faith," 239.

[41] Philip W. Grossman, "Jewish Anticipation of the Cross, Part 1," *BSac* 106 (April 1949): 243.

[42] Grogan, "The Experience of Salvation in the Old and New Testaments," 21.

Job. He makes an amazing declaration in Job 19:25-26, saying, *"For I know that my Redeemer lives, and He shall stand at last on the earth; 26 and after my skin is destroyed, this I know, that in my flesh I shall see God."* This passage is often cited by crossless and covenant theology adherents as proof of an Old Testament believer who had faith specifically in the coming Christ for eternal life. But does this passage necessarily teach that Job foresaw Christ as the One who would guarantee him eternal life? In the context of this passage, Job has been pleading with the Lord to have his day in court and demanding to know why he is suffering so unjustly. He has also been put on trial by Eliphaz, Bildad, and Zophar, who act more like inquisitors than his "friends" (19:21). Amidst the pain and suffering of his physical trial, coupled with the indictments of these three friends, Job expresses confidence in two facts: (1) that his "Redeemer" is currently living, and (2) that even if he died he would yet see God.

It is noted by virtually all commentators on Job that the Hebrew of verse 26 is particularly difficult to translate, allowing for a broad range of possibilities.[43] Hebrew scholars describe it as "bewildering,"[44] "notoriously difficult,"[45] "unusually difficult,"[46] and "so difficult" that "any convincing reconstruction" of this passage is "unlikely."[47] More optimistically, we can at least identify the translational and interpretative possibilities for Job 19:25-26. First, in Job 19:26, it can legitimately be translated either "*in* my flesh I shall see God" or "*from* my flesh I shall see God."[48] The latter possibility would mean that Job would still see God "away from" his flesh or "without" his flesh (ASV). Some interpret this to mean that Job would see God posthumously in his spirit, or even in a vision, and that this passage is not necessitating a physical resurrection, even though that meaning may still be implied.[49] Based on the ambiguity of the Hebrew text itself, it is difficult to be dogmatic about the precise interpretation of this verse.

But what about Job 19:25 and Job's reference to his "Redeemer"? Isn't this a clear expression of Job's belief in the coming Messiah for eternal salvation? Job was confident that his "Redeemer" was living and would take up his case. The Hebrew term for "last" (*aḥărôn*) functions adjectivally

---

[43] Walter L. Michel, "Confidence and Despair: Job 19, 25-27 in the Light of Northwest Semitic Studies," in *The Book of Job*, ed. W. A. M. Beuken, *BETL*, CXIV (Leuven, Belgium: Leuven University Press, 1994), 157-58.

[44] James E. Smith, *The Promised Messiah* (Nashville: Thomas Nelson, 1993), 215.

[45] Francis I. Andersen, *Job: An Introduction and Commentary* (Downers Grove, IL: InterVarsity Press, 1976), 193.

[46] H. H. Rowley, *Job*, New Century Bible Commentary (Grand Rapids: Eerdmans, 1980), 138.

[47] Ibid., 140.

[48] Elliott E. Johnson, *Expository Hermeneutics: An Introduction* (Grand Rapids: Zondervan, 1990), 36.

[49] The *NET Bible*, First Beta Edition (n.p.: Biblical Studies Press, 1996), 851n4.

rather than adverbially in the sentence.[50] This means that it is better translated, "as the last" (NIV), rather than, "at the last" (NKJV). This means that Job regarded his Redeemer to be the One who would have the "last word" in arising to vindicate him. God could certainly do this because He Himself is the beginning and the end, the first and the last (Isa. 44:6; 48:12; Rev. 1:17; 22:13). In this respect, *aḥārôn* can be interpreted as a divine epithet uttered by Job, "the Last" or "the Ultimate One."[51] However, we still know from other passages in both the Old and New Testaments that Job's vindication will ultimately occur "at the last day" and that this day is nothing less than the day of Job's resurrection and reward.[52] But even though this is true scripturally and theologically, it is not altogether clear from *this passage* that Job is thinking in eschatological terms about the distant future and bodily resurrection, though that interpretation is still possible.[53]

Likewise, when it comes to the Hebrew term for "redeemer" in Job 19:25, *gō'ēl*, this term carries a broad range of meaning, from intercessor, mediator, protector, and vindicator, to one who literally buys back as a "kinsman-redeemer," such as Boaz did for Ruth (Ruth 4:6). In the larger context of the book, however, the protagonist Job has been longing for someone to provide mediation for him and to plead his case (Job 9:33; 16:19-21). Again, we know that theologically and ultimately this will be fulfilled in the future Messiah, the Lord Jesus Christ, who is the only true Daysman or Mediator between God and mankind (1 Tim. 2:5). But it is not clear from the immediate context that Job himself is thinking explicitly about the Messiah.[54] He has only used the more general term "God" (*'ĕlōah*) in the surrounding context in 19:6, 21-22, and 26, but no one else more specifically. We know looking back with further revelation from the New Testament that the "Redeemer" is none other than the Lord Jesus Christ (Luke 2:38; Rom. 3:24; Gal. 3:13; Titus 2:14; Rev. 5:9). But did an Old Testament saint such as Job living 2,000 years before Christ nec-

---

[50] Rowley, *Job*, 138; Smith, *The Promised Messiah*, 216.

[51] Michel, "Confidence and Despair: Job 19, 25-27 in the Light of Northwest Semitic Studies," 169-70; Rowley, *Job*, 138.

[52] Theological liberals often deny that the Old Testament teaches bodily resurrection and an afterlife. They teach that these doctrines supposedly developed many centuries later and that the apostles and early Christians simply borrowed these concepts of the afterlife from paganism when they wrote the New Testament. But nothing could be further from the truth. Even in the Old Testament, bodily resurrection is clearly taught (Gen. 50:25 [implied]; Ex. 3:6; Ps. 16:9-10; Isa. 26:19; Dan. 12:2), even if it is not as fully developed as in the New Testament. Furthermore, to deny that bodily resurrection was taught in the Old Testament is to flatly contradict the explicit teaching of the Lord Jesus Himself on this subject (Matt. 22:32; Mark 12:26; Luke 20:37).

[53] Andersen, *Job*, 194.

[54] It is perhaps for this reason that Hengstenberg in his tome on the Messianic prophecies of the Old Testament completely omits any reference to this passage. See E. W. Hengstenberg, *Christology of the Old Testament* (Grand Rapids: Kregel, 1970).

essarily connect the term "redeemer" (*gō'ēl*) with the coming "Messiah" (*māshîaḥ*)? Had God even revealed such an association of terms yet at that point? While certainly the Lord Jesus is the fulfillment of the *type* of the kinsman-redeemer revealed in the Book of Ruth, it must be noted that the time period of the Judges in which the events of Ruth occurred was still roughly 700 years future from Job's vantage point.

In addition, it is worth pondering the fact that in the rest of the Old Testament, the term *gō'ēl* is nowhere else specifically revealed to be the Messiah or Son of God. If Job 19:25 is a definite reference to the future Messiah, then it is the *only* such instance of the term applied specifically to the Messiah in the entire Old Testament. Elsewhere *gō'ēl* is always associated simply with the LORD (Yahweh). See Ps. 19:14; 78:35; Isa. 41:14; 43:13; 44:6, 24; 47:4; 48:17; 49:7, 26; 54:5, 8; 59:20; 60:16; 63:16; Jer. 50:34. Thus, most commentators have taken the term in verse 25 to apply to God generally rather than a possible future Messiah.[55] Some even interpret Job's reference to *gō'ēl* here to be a metaphorical reference whereby Job's cry "is personified as witness, advocate, and spokesman," since Job in essence has to be his own defense attorney.[56] But this seems to be going too far. Though it is obvious to any objective reader of Scripture that the Lord Jesus Christ of the New Testament is the Yahweh of the Old Testament, the question is whether this would have been so obvious to someone such as Job living 2,000 years prior to the Incarnation.

By all accounts, Job 19:25-26 is a difficult passage to translate and interpret, as any honest exegete would have to admit. It is by no means a clear cut case of an Old Testament saint with faith explicitly in the future Messiah for eternal life. But even if Job did have the Messiah specifically in view, we are still left with the same plaguing questions. If Job equated the Redeemer specifically with the coming Christ and he believed this Messiah would guarantee him eternal life, was he necessarily *required* to do so for his justification and regeneration? Furthermore, does this passage indicate that God required the same for *everyone else* in the Old Testament? We are simply not told from the passage. To insist that Job 19:25-26 is setting forth a 4,000 year old universal, divine requirement for everyone to believe in the Messiah for eternal life is pouring one's theology into God's Word. It is going beyond the text of Holy Scripture.

Moses

In addition to Abraham and Job, Moses is often cited as an example of an Old Testament believer who trusted in the Messiah for his justification and eternal life. For example, Bob Bryant claims:

---

[55] Andersen, *Job*, 194; Michel, "Confidence and Despair: Job 19, 25-27 in the Light of Northwest Semitic Studies," 164n17; Rowley, *Job*, 138.

[56] David J. A. Clines, *Job 1-20*, WBC (Dallas: Word Books, 1989), 459-60.

> We also know that Moses: "...esteemed the reproach of Christ greater riches than the treasures in Egypt; for he looked to the reward" (Heb. 11:26). Living 1,500 years before Jesus came, he not only believed in Christ, he also understood God's truth concerning discipleship and rewards. Moses even wrote about Christ. As Jesus said to the Jews, "For if you believed Moses, you would believe Me; for he wrote about Me" (John 5:46). Abraham, Job, and Moses illustrate that before Jesus came, people were saved by believing in the Christ who was yet to come. Today, we are saved by believing in the same Christ who has come. They looked forward. We look back. But people have always been saved in the same way, by faith alone in Christ alone.[57]

Regarding the statement in Hebrews 11:26 that Moses *"esteemed the reproach of Christ greater riches than the treasures in Egypt; for he looked to the reward,"* it is questionable that this is even a justification-statement. There are several reasons for this objection. First, in this passage it needs to be distinguished what it actually *does say* versus what it *doesn't say*. It *does* say Moses rejected Egypt's riches for the sake of "reward" but it *doesn't* say he did this because he understood the difference between the free gift of eternal life *through faith in the Messiah* versus rewards that are merited by being a disciple of the Messiah. To interpret the reference to "rewards" as biblical support for the conclusion that Moses believed in the Messiah alone for eternal life is concluding more than the passage states.

Secondly, if Hebrews 11:26 is an explicit reference to an Old Testament saint's faith in the coming Messiah, then it is the *only* such reference in the entire "Hall of Fame of Faith" in Hebrews 11. You would think that if salvation has always been based on the same content of faith, Hebrews 11 would be fertile ground to prove this point. You would expect it to be loaded with references to pre-cross faith in the coming Messiah. To be sure, there are figures of Christ alluded to in the list, such as Abel's sacrifice (11:4), the ark of Noah (11:7) and the receiving back of Isaac (11:19), but there is not a single statement anywhere in the chapter that says these Old Testament saints had faith specifically in the coming Messiah for eternal life.

Thirdly, with respect to Moses' faith, the statement in Hebrews 11:26 *may not* necessarily mean that Moses consciously believed in the future Messiah at this point as the reason for rejecting the treasures of Egypt. That is not even hinted at in the Exodus narrative or elsewhere in the Old Testament. There are other possible interpretations of Hebrews 11:26 besides concluding that Moses' faith in the coming Messiah for eternal life was the reason for his rejecting the wealth and glory of Egypt. The statement in verse 26 that he *"esteemed the reproach of Christ"* may simply mean that Moses' sufferings were for the sake of the God of Israel, who

---

[57] Bryant, "How Were People Saved Before Jesus Came?" 65.

we as Christian readers know in hindsight came to be identified later as the Lord Jesus Christ, so that from the standpoint of the Christian reader we know that Moses' sufferings were ultimately for Christ's sake.[58] It could also mean simply that Moses esteemed the type of suffering that Christ would later exemplify (again from the standpoint of these Hebrew-Christian readers) as greater in value than the riches of Egypt.[59] The point is that there are exegetically valid interpretations of Hebrews 11:26 other than Bryant's,[60] and so it should not be viewed as a proof-text for all Old Testament saints having explicit faith in the coming Messiah for the gift of eternal life.

However a person may choose to interpret *"the reproach of Christ"* in Hebrews 11:26, it must be acknowledged that Moses did understand some basic truths about the coming Messiah. He wrote the Pentateuch (John 5:46) and it contains several explicit references to the Coming One (e.g. Gen. 3:15; 49:10; Num. 24:15-19; Deut. 18:15-19), to say nothing of its rich typology depicting Christ. There should be no objection to admitting that Moses even had "faith in the coming Messiah." For that matter, it can even be admitted that Hebrews 11:26 may indeed be teaching that Moses was consciously rejecting Egypt's riches with a view toward a reward connected to the coming Christ. But it must also be honestly acknowledged that it never says in Hebrews 11:26, nor anywhere in Scripture, that Moses or any other Old Testament saint *was required* to believe in the coming Christ in order to receive the gift of eternal life or justification. This is something that the New Testament clearly requires, but it is never required in the Old Testament. Moses was an extraordinary Old Testament saint, being uniquely privileged to speak with God face to face and to receive repeated, direct revelation from the Lord (Ex. 33:11; Num. 12:8; Deut. 34:10). This fact, coupled with the truth that Moses was *"very humble, more than all men who were on the face of the earth"* (Num. 12:3), should give us reason to pause when claiming him as an example of what *the typical* Old Testament sinner had to believe to be saved eternally.

David

Finally, David is often put forth as an example of an Old Testament saint who believed explicitly in the Messiah for his eternal life and justification. Bob Wilkin uses David to substantiate his view, even instructing other

---

[58] Arnold G. Fruchtenbaum, *Ariel's Bible Commentary: The Messianic Jewish Epistles* (Tustin, CA: Ariel Ministries, 2005), 163.

[59] William L. Lane, *Hebrews 9-13*, WBC (Nashville: Thomas Nelson, 1991), 373-74; Schultz, "Saving Faith in the Old Testament," 43; B. F. Westcott, *The Epistle to the Hebrews* (Grand Rapids: Eerdmans, n.d.), 372.

[60] For further possible interpretations, see Paul Ellingworth, *The Epistle to the Hebrews*, NIGTC (Grand Rapids: Eerdmans, 1993), 614; Fruchtenbaum, *Ariel's Bible Commentary: The Messianic Jewish Epistles*, 163.

grace people about how to promote the crossless position on the contents of faith in the Old Testament:

> *Explain OT salvation by means of clear NT texts.* Scripture accurately interprets itself. Thus the simplest way to explain OT salvation is to go to a passage like Rom 4:1-8. There Paul uses Abraham and David to show that OT people believed in the Messiah for eternal life. They knew salvation was a gift, not a debt. They knew it was by faith alone, apart from their works. When people question you about OT salvation, suggest to them one of three or four clear passages. In addition to Romans 4, I would suggest John 5:38-47, Gal 3:6-14, and Heb 10:1-18. Remind them that the Gospel of John contains Jesus' message to "OT people" on how they could have eternal life, and that that message is still in effect today.[61]

Perhaps I need a check-up with my spiritual ophthalmologist, because I just can't see anywhere in Romans 4:1-8 where Abraham and David "believed in the Messiah for eternal life." I can't see any references to the "Messiah" or even "eternal life" technically. I do see "God" mentioned three times (4:2, 3, 6) and "the Lord" mentioned once (4:8), but no references to the Lord Jesus Christ specifically. At best, someone may read Christ into Romans 4:5, which says, *"But to him who does not work but believes on Him who justifies the ungodly, his faith is accounted for righteousness."* The phrase, *"believes on Him,"* does not specify Christ as the object of faith. It is equally adaptable to a believer either before Calvary or after it. One could argue that in the context of Romans, from a post-cross perspective, these Roman believers understood the *"Him"* in 4:5 to be the Lord Jesus Christ. That would certainly be true, but it still would not tell us whether Abraham or David understood *"Him"* that way and whether they believed specifically "in the Messiah" for their justification. The whole point of Romans 4:1-16 is not continuity in the *contents* of saving faith but continuity in the *condition* for justification being by faith alone. Once again, it is certainly true that David understood several truths about Christ's person and work. He was a "prophet" who wrote several messianic Psalms (Acts 2:30-31). But in spite of such precious and profound revelation about Christ given to David, it remains a conspicuous fact that there is not a single verse in the entire Old Testament informing us either that David believed in Christ for his justification or that he was required to do so.

Justification Before Calvary

Having considered the examples of Abraham, Job, Moses, and David, we have yet to find any conclusive evidence that these great Old Testament saints were required to believe specifically in the Messiah as the guarantor of eternal life. But if this was true throughout the Old Testament, then

---

[61] Wilkin, "Salvation Before Calvary," 3.

what about the New Testament? And what about that transitional time period during the Lord's earthly life prior to His crucifixion and resurrection? It is not surprising to discover at least one passage in the Gospels (Luke 18:9-14) that harmonizes with the contents of saving faith observed thus far from the Old Testament.

Luke 18:9-14

9 *Also He spoke this parable to some who trusted in themselves that they were righteous, and despised others:*

10 *"Two men went up to the temple to pray, one a Pharisee and the other a tax collector.*

11 *"The Pharisee stood and prayed thus with himself, 'God, I thank You that I am not like other men—extortioners, unjust, adulterers, or even as this tax collector.*

12 *'I fast twice a week; I give tithes of all that I possess.'*

13 *"And the tax collector, standing afar off, would not so much as raise his eyes to heaven, but beat his breast, saying, 'God, be merciful to me a sinner!'*

14 *"I tell you, this man went down to his house justified rather than the other; for everyone who exalts himself will be humbled, and he who humbles himself will be exalted."*

In Luke 18:9-14, the Lord Jesus gave a parable to His pre-Calvary audience in order to explain in real-life, real-time terms what God required for justification. In this account, it was the tax collector rather than the Pharisee who received salvation, who *"went down to his house justified"* (18:14). But what was it that the lowly tax collector believed that led to his justification in God's sight?

The content of the tax collector's faith is reflected in his words, *"God be merciful toward me, a sinner."* Literally, he said, *"God, be propitiated (hilasthēti) toward me, the sinner."* Here this humble, unworthy sinner expresses his faith verbally through prayer in keeping with the principle that out of the abundance of the heart the mouth speaks (Matt. 12:33-37). And what content of faith do we find pouring forth from this tax collector's lips? He believed in the one God and even that He is righteous. This is implicit in the fact that he thought God needed to be propitiated. He believed that his acceptance as an unworthy sinner was conditioned upon the righteous God being propitiated. Salvation has never been conditioned upon casting oneself *merely* upon the mercy of God, as though God grants justification out of sheer leniency and beneficence. This tax collector, as with any soul coming to justification prior to Calvary, trusted that God would provide propitiation for sin. The tax collector approached God on this basis and was declared "just" or "justified."

Conspicuously absent, however, in this vivid lesson by the Lord Jesus is any reference to belief in "the Christ" or "the Messiah" for everlasting life. You would think that if faith in "the Christ" was essential for justification prior to Calvary, then the Messiah Himself as the Master teacher and evangelist would not be remiss to inform His unregenerate audience (Luke 18:15, 18) of this critical fact on this occasion.

The Appeal to Extra-Biblical Revelation

Having just surveyed the testimony of Scripture leading up to Christ's sacrificial death and bodily resurrection, we may reasonably conclude that prior to Calvary explicit belief in the coming Messiah is nowhere specifically required for eternal life. Even one crossless, G.E.S. proponent comes very close to conceding this point when he says: "It seems that nowhere in the historical books do we find a passage that explains the way of salvation";[62] "This passage in Job [Job 19:25-26] seems to be the only passage in the wisdom literature were we find the way of salvation";[63] "There seems to be no passage in the prophetic section that by itself explains the way of salvation."[64] But with such a dearth of scriptural support for their view, how do G.E.S. proponents attempt to establish their doctrinal position? They appeal to inference and unwritten revelation. In particular, they reason that the requirement to believe in the coming Messiah for eternal life must have come through verbal revelation. They teach that this "saving message" was preached directly to people in the Old Testament by the Lord and by speaking prophets, rather than writing prophets. Wilkin defends this view, declaring:

> The preincarnate Christ appeared to many people in the OT besides Adam and Eve, including Abraham, Moses, and the three men in the fiery furnace. He spoke with them and revealed things to them, surely including the saving message. There were many OT prophets and yet only a small number of them wrote their messages down. Many OT prophets preached the saving message. Surely there was never a generation that lacked a prophet to preach the saving message at least until the 400 silent years when the OT canon was complete and the need for prophets would have been greatly diminished. And even during those silent years God surely raised up men and women who shared the saving message which they had believed. What was the saving message in the OT? It was the same message as we have today.[65]

But can we really say that God "surely" worked this way when Scripture nowhere states what Wilkin claims? It strikes the unbiased reader as strange that if there really were "many OT prophets" proclaiming the saving message of faith explicitly in the Messiah for eternal life, then why didn't such

---

[62] Bryant, "How Were People Saved Before Jesus Came?" 66.

[63] Ibid., 67 (brackets added).

[64] Ibid.

[65] Bob Wilkin, "God Has Always Revealed the Saving Message," November 20, 2008, http://unashamedofgrace.blogspot.com/2008_11_01_archive.html (accessed November 30, 2008).

a message get recorded *anywhere* in the 39 books of the Old Testament? It is odd that only the speaking prophets proclaimed the saving message, but mysteriously none of the writing prophets did. In order to account for this predicament, adherents to the G.E.S. view sometimes appeal to the example of Enoch whose message isn't recorded in Genesis or the rest of the Old Testament but is found in the New Testament epistle of Jude. Wilkin explains, "Jude tells us that Enoch, in the seventh generation from Adam, prophecied [sic] about the Second Coming of Christ (Jude 14-15). Yet the OT nowhere tells us that."[66]

While it is true that the content of Enoch's preaching is nowhere recorded in the Old Testament but is found in Jude, the inference that Wilkin draws from this example is not valid for several reasons. First, this reference to the content of Enoch's message does not form a legitimate supporting parallel example to crossless, saving faith in the coming Messiah. The Lord's Second Coming with His saints in judgment was a truth already revealed elsewhere in the Old Testament (Deut. 33:2; Isa. 34:1-8; 63:1-6; Joel 3:11; Zech. 14:5). So this is not an instance where unique, verbal revelation is preserved in the New Testament which wasn't revealed in the Old Testament. Second, no one is disputing the fact that explicit Second Coming truth was known and believed in the Old Testament era. What is disputed is whether Old Testament saints knew and believed explicitly in the Messiah's *first coming* coupled with the fact that He is the guarantor of eternal life and justification. A passage recording this truth is needed, not one pertaining to judgment at the Lord's Second Coming. Lastly, the Enoch passage in Jude 14-15 tells us only what *one man*, Enoch, *proclaimed*. It falls far short of telling us what *everyone* in the Old Testament was *required* to believe for their eternal salvation. But in order to support such a universal Old Testament requirement, G.E.S. proponents resort to a methodology employed for centuries by the Roman Catholic Church.

Verbal Revelation and Roman Catholic Methodology

If there are no passages in either the Old or New Testaments that teach that explicit faith in the future Messiah was necessary for eternal life, then where can a person turn to support such a doctrine? There is always non-written, *verbal revelation*. Wilkin is not alone among G.E.S. proponents in utilizing this approach. For example, Bob Bryant states:

> In summary, for over 2,500 years before the OT was written, God verbally revealed the way of salvation Himself, and later verbally revealed the way of salvation through prophets such as Enoch. In turn, the gospel would then have been verbally proclaimed by believers who learned the way of salvation from the prophets.[67]

---

[66] Ibid.

[67] Bryant, "How Were People Saved Before Jesus Came?" 66.

> In summary, while the OT was being written, prophets verbally proclaimed the gospel, and believers, in turn, verbally proclaimed what they heard from the prophets. The OT writers recorded pieces of information about the way of salvation, but this was not their focus.[68]

> There seems to be no passage in the prophetic section that by itself explains the way of salvation. While we can find various pieces of information about the way of salvation from Moses to Malachi, these pieces are hard to find because it was not the purpose of the OT writers to focus on this truth. Their focus was on discipleship. The writers assume that the readers already know the way of salvation through verbal revelation given by the prophets.[69]

There is no mistaking these quotations. Since the crossless, G.E.S. position cannot support its position from Scripture, it must appeal to suppositional logic and evidence that lies outside the bounds of God's Word. This goes beyond merely using an argument from silence. It appeals to a body of truth, namely verbal revelation from God, which no longer exists and cannot even be verified. Do we know for certain that God appeared to people in Old Testament times and disclosed truth verbally, long before the Word of God was written? Yes. The mere fact of Theophanies and Christophanies indicates this. No one disputes this point. But how do we even know about these appearances and such verbal revelation from God? It is only through the *written* Word—the Old Testament itself—where such divine appearances and revelations to people are recorded. And yet it is rather curious that in *none* of these recorded episodes do we read of God delivering the crossless "saving message" where faith in the coming Messiah is required for eternal life. If Christ *"surely includ[ed] the saving message"*[70] in the Christophanies that are *not* recorded in the Old Testament, then shouldn't we expect to find the same message *somewhere* in the Christophanies that *are* recorded in the Old Testament? And why is this saving message not found anywhere in the Old Testament? We are told that it is because "the readers already know" this message, and the "purpose" of the Old Testament writers was "discipleship" rather than faith in the Messiah for eternal life.[71]

This approach to doctrine is an abandonment of the biblical and Protestant principle of *Sola Scriptura*. It is an appeal, in part, to extra-biblical revelation for their doctrine of salvation. It also bears a striking resemblance to the methodology that the Roman Catholic Church uses to support doctrines that it cannot find in the Bible either.

---

[68] Ibid., 68.

[69] Ibid., 67.

[70] Wilkin, "God Has Always Revealed the Saving Message."

[71] Bryant, "How Were People Saved Before Jesus Came?" 67.

According to Roman Catholic theology, the Word of God is not fully contained in the Bible, since revelation from God has come to man through both written revelation (Sacred Scripture) and verbal, oral, or non-written revelation (Sacred Tradition).[72] According to Rome, this divine revelation "is contained in written books and in traditions without writing—traditions which were received from the mouth of Christ Himself and from the apostles under dictation of the Holy Spirit and have come down to us, delivered, as it were, from hand to hand."[73] We are told that this inspired tradition is passed on through the contemplation and study of the saints, through spiritual experiences, and through the preaching of those who are specially anointed by the Holy Spirit (as approved by the Church).[74] The teaching of Wilkin and Bryant is similar to Catholicism in this respect: they teach that extra-biblical, verbal revelation in the Old Testament era first came directly from Christ by way of Christophany, and it was received by prophets who were specially anointed by the Holy Spirit, who in turn preached it to other people, who in turn passed it on to others also.

The danger inherent in resorting to such supposed divine revelation is that it can never be confirmed as truth that originated from God. How do we know that the prophets and people of the Old Testament possessed explicit faith in the coming Messiah for eternal life if Scripture never tells us? Rome has justified many unbiblical doctrines and practices on this basis, appealing to oral tradition and verbal revelation for things that the Scriptures know nothing of, such as its priesthood, prelates, and papacy. A chief example of the inherent danger in using verbal, non-written revelation to prove a doctrine occurred in 1950 when Pope Pius XII changed the terms of salvation. Popular Roman Catholic piety toward Mary had been evolving until the 20th century when Pius elevated belief in Mary's bodily assumption to the level of dogma—a truth that must be universally held by every Catholic for eternal salvation.[75] Yet, this dogma was completely lacking in any explicit scriptural support. It was built upon conjectures from Scripture, coupled with the deposit of revelation supposedly passed down from oral tradition dating all the way back to the apostles.

Acts 10:43

At this point, some may protest and say, "Yes, but doesn't the New Testament itself refer to the existence of non-writing prophets in Old Testament times who preached Christ as the explicit object of saving faith?" While it is

---

[72] Dogmatic Constitution on Divine Revelation, Vatican II, *Dei Verbum*, November 18, 1965, 2:9.

[73] *The Catholic Encyclopedia*, Revised and Updated Edition, ed. Robert C. Broderick (Nashville: Thomas Nelson, 1987), 525.

[74] Dogmatic Constitution on Divine Revelation, Vatican II, *Dei Verbum*, November 18, 1965, 2:8.

[75] Apostolic Constitution of Pius XII, *Munificentissimus Deus*, November 1, 1950.

clear that there were non-writing prophets from the time of Abel onward (Luke 11:47-51), there is no biblical evidence that they preached faith in the future Messiah as the requirement for justification. This applies even to Acts 10:43, where in the context Peter has been preaching the gospel of Christ to a group of Gentiles in the house of Cornelius, and he concludes his gospel presentation with an evangelistic appeal to believe, saying, *"To Him all the prophets witness that, through His name, whoever believes in Him will receive remission of sins."*

Sometimes this verse is used to support the G.E.S. position that non-writing prophets in the Old Testament also proclaimed eternal salvation through faith in the Messiah.[76] But there are several problems with such an interpretation. First, the word for "witness" in the Greek, *marturousin*, is a present tense verb. This means that there was some sense in which these "prophets" were still presently witnessing contemporaneously with Peter.[77] This could be referring either to New Testament prophets within the Church or to the written prophetic Word of Old Testament Scripture (2 Peter 1:20-21), but not to speaking prophets of prior dispensations.

While it is easy to see how the written Word could continue to "witness" in this capacity, since it is the fresh and present voice of the Holy Spirit to each generation, it is not so easy to see how non-written, verbal revelation that was passed down from the Old Testament era through speaking prophets could be presently witnessing in Peter's generation. Peter was not referring to authoritative, oral traditions of any kind, over which the early Church exercised custody as Rome teaches. There is not a shred of evidence that any inspired, extra-biblical, verbal tradition that was passed down from speaking prophets of past dispensations was recognized by the apostles and early Church. Therefore, the phrase *"all the prophets"* in Acts 10:43 should not be interpreted as a reference to the speaking prophets of the Old Testament era.[78]

---

[76] Bryant, "How Were People Saved Before Jesus Came?" 67; Hodges, "Eternal Salvation in the Old Testament," 3.

[77] The verb *marturousin* in Acts 10:43 is most likely a customary or iterative present. Buist M. Fanning, *Verbal Aspect in New Testament Greek* (New York: Oxford University Press, 1990), 205-7. This is *not* an instance of the historical present, as some people may attempt to reason that Peter is recasting here the past testimony of the speaking prophets in present tense terms for the sake of vividness and dramatic effect. But historical presents in Luke-Acts are quite rare compared to the other narrative literature of the New Testament (John, Matthew, and Mark). In fact, it appears that Luke even avoids using the historical present in many places (Fanning, 238-39; Nigel Turner, *Syntax*. Vol. 3 in *A Grammar of New Testament Greek*, J. H. Moulton [Edinburgh: T & T Clark, 1963], 60-61). There are a total of 13 historical presents in Acts (8:36; 10:11, 27, 31; 12:8; 19:35; 21:37; 22:2; 23:18; 25:5, 22, 24; 26:24), *marturousin* in Acts 10:43 not being one of them. For a complete listing of historical presents in the New Testament, see John C. Hawkins, *Hore Synopticae: Contributions to the Study of the Synoptic Problem* (Oxford: Clarendon Press, 1909), 143-49.

[78] The reference to the non-writing prophet Abel in Hebrews 11:4 is no exception to this point when it says that *"he being dead still speaks."* The only way in which his righteous testimony still speaks to mankind is through the Scriptures, which is the only source of

There is a second reason why the reference to "prophets" in Acts 10:43 does not mean the speaking prophets of prior dispensations. It is because Peter was in the act of preaching *the gospel* in Acts 10 (cf. Acts 15:7-11). The New Testament consistently teaches that the gospel is *"according to the Scriptures"* (Acts 26:22-23, 27; Rom. 1:2; 1 Cor. 15:3-4). This is true whether it is Paul or Peter preaching the gospel, for they both preached the same gospel (Acts 15:2-12; Gal. 2:1-6), though to different target audiences (Gal. 2:7-9). It is conspicuous to note that nowhere in Scripture does it say that the gospel is "according to verbal revelation," as if the gospel message was given to speaking prophets in each generation or was passed down orally from generation to generation rather than coming through Old Testament Scripture. Not only does the New Testament say that the gospel is *"according to the Scriptures,"* but the Old Testament Scriptures served a practical and evidentiary role in the evangelism of the early Church. This can be observed in the many Scripture quotations and allusions used by Peter in the early chapters of Acts, as well as the explicit statement that Paul *"reasoned with them from the Scriptures"* (Acts 17:2, 11; 18:28; 26:22-27; 28:23). Nowhere do we read that the apostles ever appealed to the lost to believe on the basis of revelation that was passed down verbally through the speaking prophets.

A third reason why the "prophets" in Acts 10:43 are not referring to the speaking prophets of antiquity is because every other occurrence of "prophet" or "prophets" in the Book of Acts is in reference to one of two types of prophets, either New Testament prophets of the Church (Acts 11:27; 13:1; 15:32; 21:10) or more commonly Old Testament writing prophets (Acts 2:16-21, 25-28; 3:21-23, 24; 7:42-43, 48-50; 8:28-33; 13:15, 27, 40-41; 15:15-17; 24:14; 26:22-23, 27; 28:23, 25-28).[79] This means that to interpret the phrase *"all the prophets"* in Acts 10:43 as a reference to speaking prophets of Old Testament times would break Luke's established pattern of usage. It would be an exceptional instance in the Book of Acts. This fact alone renders such an interpretation of Acts 10:43 suspect.

In addition, thinking of Lucan pattern, many individual Old Testament writing prophets are quoted or mentioned throughout Acts, including Moses, Samuel, David, Isaiah, Joel, Amos, and Habakkuk. Everywhere that "prophets" are referred to in Acts, coupled with a quotation from one of these prophets, the quotation is *never* from an *extra-biblical* source, such as Jude's epistle does when it refers to Enoch in Jude 14-15. The apostles and disciples in Acts *only quote* from Old Testament Scripture. With respect to this last observation we must ask, where is all the verbal revelation that Peter and the early Church received through the supposed "speaking" prophets of the Old Testament era?! Apparently, it either did not exist

---

information we have for everything that we know about him.

[79] Even when Abraham is referred to in Acts 3:25, it is connected with a quotation of God's promise to him as found in Genesis 12:3.

or it was deemed unreliable, having become tainted and corrupted as it passed through multiple generations of fallible human witnesses.

At this point, two clarifications are necessary. Some people may be wondering how these conclusions fit with the fact that Acts describes prophets who "spoke" their messages. Some might erroneously conclude that these were ancient "speaking" prophets in contrast to the writers of the 39 books of the Old Testament. However, there are several places in Acts that refer to prophets who "spoke" (*laleō*), and yet somewhere in the immediate context of each of these passages a portion of Old Testament Scripture is quoted! The way these prophets "spoke" was clearly through their *written* Scriptures. We see this in Acts 1:16; 2:16, 31; 3:21-22, 24; 13:40-41; 28:25-28 (cf. Luke 24:25-27). This also fits with Peter's classic statement on inspiration in 2 Peter 1:20-21, where he unmistakably refers to *writing* prophets even though he uses the term "spoke" (*laleō*). In 2 Peter 1:20-21, Peter states,"*20 knowing this first, that no prophecy of* ***Scripture*** *is of any private interpretation, 21 for prophecy never came by the will of man, but holy men of God* ***spoke*** *(laleō) as they were moved by the Holy Spirit.*"

One other clarification is necessary before seeking to positively identify who Peter was referring to by "prophets" in Acts 10:43. In two other passages written by Luke besides Acts 10:43, he refers to prophets who have prophesied *"since the world began"* (Luke 1:70; Acts 3:21). Some proponents of either the G.E.S. doctrine or covenant theology may be tempted to see in this statement a reference to non-writing, speaking prophets, like Abel and Enoch, who predated Moses' writing of the Pentateuch (or even the writing of Job).[80] They may be prone to connect the statement about *"all the prophets"* in Acts 10:43 with these two other Lucan references to prophets who prophesied *"since the world began"* and assume that *"all the prophets"* in Acts 10:43 is referring to both writing and speaking prophets of ancient times. In addition, if they assume that Peter in Acts 10:43 is teaching that forgiveness of sins was always conditioned upon faith explicitly in the coming Messiah, then they may attempt to combine these passages in Acts to prove that speaking prophets in past dispensations always taught salvation through faith in Christ.[81]

Such reasoning, however, would all be built upon a faulty foundation, for the phrase *"since the world began"* (*ap' aiōnos*) in some English translations of Luke 1:70 and Acts 3:21 contains neither the words "world" (*kosmos*) or "began" (*archomai*) in the Greek text. The prepositional phrase

---

[80] Bryant, "How Were People Saved Before Jesus Came?" 67.

[81] Not coincidentally, some proponents of covenant theology who are staunchly anti-dispensational use these same passages to make a similar argument. See Curtis I. Crenshaw and Grover E. Gunn, III, *Dispensationalism Today, Yesterday, and Tomorrow*, 3rd ed. (Memphis, TN: Footstool Publications, 1994), 280-82.

in Greek is more literally translated, "of old,"[82] "from of old,"[83] "of old time,"[84] "from early times,"[85] or "from ages long past."[86] It is for this reason that other English Bibles translate *ap' aiōnos* as "from of old" (ASV), "from ancient time" (NASB), and "long ago" (NIV). To say that the prophets referred to in Acts dated all the way from the beginning of the world would be a gratuitous assumption. Even in the immediate context of Acts 3:21 and Luke 1:70, the timeframe implied goes back to the writing prophets who are referred to in each passage, such as Moses (Acts 3:22), David, and Samuel (Luke 1:69).[87] These are the prophets "of old" (*ap' aiōnos*) referred to in Luke 1:70 and Acts 3:21, not ancient speaking prophets who never penned a jot or tittle of Scripture.

Having explained what the phrase *"all the prophets"* in Acts 10:43 does *not* mean, it is time now to consider what it *does* mean. It could refer either to the writers of Old Testament Scripture, to New Testament prophets of the Church, or to both. It was previously stated that the term "prophet" or "prophets" is most often used in Acts in reference to writers of Old Testament Scripture. In addition, it would be consistent with the evangelistic approach of Peter and Paul in Acts to base their message on the Old Testament Scriptures, since the gospel is *"according to the Scriptures"* (1 Cor. 15:3-4).

But if the prophets referred to in Acts 10:43 are indeed writers of Old Testament Scripture, then this raises another interpretative problem. In Acts 10:43, it states that *"all the prophets"* give witness that through Jesus' name remission of sins is granted to all who believe *"in Him"* (*eis auton*). Does this mean that every book of the Old Testament contains the exact same message that Peter is proclaiming to Cornelius and the Gentiles in Acts 10 and that these prophets specifically require faith "in Him"—in the Messiah?[88] While there are an abundance of passages in the Old

---

[82] Darrell L. Bock, *Luke 1:1-9:50*, BECNT (Grand Rapids: Baker Books, 1994), 181; LSJ, 45.

[83] J. H. Thayer, ed., *The New Thayer's Greek-English Lexicon* (Peabody, MA: Hendrickson, 1981), 19.

[84] R. J. Knowling, "The Acts of the Apostles," in *The Expositor's Greek Testament* (Grand Rapids: Eerdmans, Reprinted 1990), 2:117.

[85] Bock, *Luke 1:1-9:50*, 181; I. Howard Marshall, *Commentary on Luke*, NIGTC (Grand Rapids: Eerdmans, 1978), 91.

[86] BAGD, 27.

[87] Darrell L. Bock, *Acts*, BECNT (Grand Rapids: Baker Academic, 2008), 178; idem, *Luke 1:1-9:50*, 181.

[88] In Acts 10:43, *marturousin* ("witness") serves as the controlling verb of the sentence, with the infinitive *labein* ("receive") being an infinitive of indirect discourse (James L. Boyer, "The Classification of Infinitives: A Statistical Study," *GTJ* 6 [Spring 1985]: 8; A. T. Robertson, *A Grammar of the Greek New Testament in the Light of Historical Research* [Nashville: Broadman Press, 1934], 1036). This means that the content of the prophets' "witness" (*marturousin*) is stated through the indirect discourse. So what did these prophets prophesy specifically? Whoever these prophets were, they "all" prophesied *"that through His name, whoever believes in Him will receive remission of sins."*

Testament that deal explicitly with Christ in His first and second comings (Luke 24:27, 47; John 5:39, 46), and while it is true that even the smallest portion of the Old Testament must be correlated to Christ since He is the center of all divine revelation, honest exegesis compels the majority of dispensationalists to admit that there are no explicit statements in the Old Testament requiring faith specifically in the coming Christ for the remission of sins. It is even more difficult to maintain that "all" 39 books of the Old Testament contain this particular message. So what is the solution?

Some commentators, like Henry Alford, also believe that the phrase *"all the prophets"* refers to the writers of Old Testament Scripture. But Alford also insists that the word "all" (*pantes*) in verse 43 should not be taken too literally. He writes, "All the prophets, generically: not that *every one* positively asserted this, but that the whole bulk of prophetic testimony announced it. To press such expressions to literal exactness is mere trifling."[89] According to Alford, Peter's aim was merely "to show the unanimity of all the prophets."[90] So, one proposed solution is to view the phrase, *"all the prophets,"* as merely a general statement of solidarity among the writers of the Old Testament.

Another interpretation of the phrase *"all the prophets"* is to equate the Lord who forgives sins in the New Testament (Jesus Christ) with the LORD of the Old Testament (Jehovah/Yahweh) who does the same.[91] Commentator I. Howard Marshall explains this view:

> At first sight this is a strange statement. Prophecies of forgiveness by the Messiah are hard to find, and the allusion to "*all* the prophets" seems highly exaggerated (cf. Luke 24:47). The solution to the problem lies in two statements. First, in the Old Testament forgiveness is associated with the name of Yahweh, "the Lord." It is the prerogative of God; those who seek the Lord find that he will abundantly pardon them (Isa. 55:6 f.). Second, the effect of the resurrection is that Jesus is exalted and receives the title of Lord (Acts 2:36). The conclusion is obvious: by virtue of his exaltation Jesus has received the prerogative of God the Lord to dispense forgiveness of sins (cf. perhaps Stephen's prayer, Acts 7:60). What is asserted of God in "all the prophets" can now be asserted of the exalted Jesus.[92]

This interpretation certainly has merit. It agrees doctrinally with the whole of Scripture and it even has some contextual support. In the pas-

---

[89] Henry Alford, *The Greek Testament* (Chicago: Moody Press, 1958), 2:121.

[90] Ibid., 2:40.

[91] Everett F. Harrison, *Acts: The Expanding Church* (Chicago: Moody Press, 1975), 174-75.

[92] I Howard Marshall, "The Resurrection in the Acts of the Apostles," in *Apostolic History and the Gospel: Biblical and Historical Essays Presented to F. F. Bruce on his 60th Birthday*, ed. W. Ward Gasque and Ralph P. Martin (Grand Rapids: Eerdmans, 1970), 104. See also, Joel B. Green, "The Death of Jesus, God's Servant," in *Reimaging the Death of the Lukan Jesus*, ed. Dennis D. Sylva (Frankfurt am Main: Anton Hain, 1990), 8-10.

sage, Christ's sovereignty as Lord following His resurrection is prominent (10:36, 42). The equation of the Lordship of Christ with the Lordship of Yahweh in the Old Testament is also implicit in the passage (see further discussion in chapter 17). If Peter was referring to the writing prophets of Old Testament Scripture by the phrase *"all the prophets"* in verse 43, then this interpretation deserves serious consideration.

One final interpretation that may also be correct is the view that *"all the prophets"* refers to all the prophets of the New Testament era.[93] According to this view, Peter is simply saying that all of his contemporaries who have also been given truth directly from God are proclaiming exactly the same message that he is delivering to Cornelius and the Gentiles. This view has support at all levels—grammatically, contextually, lexically, and doctrinally.

First, the verb for *"witness" (martureō)* in verse 43 is in the present tense, indicating that in some respect these "prophets" were presently testifying about remission of sins through faith in Christ. This was also the specific message that the entire Church was commissioned to preach, starting with the apostles.

Second, interpreting the clause in Acts 10:43, *"all the prophets witness,"* as a reference to New Testament prophets also fits with the usage of the terms for "witness" and "testify" in the rest of Acts. In Acts 10:43, the root verb for "witness" is *martureō*. Every other time this word is found in Acts it *always* refers to a testimony that was contemporaneous to the 1st century Church from someone who was then living (Acts 6:3; 10:22, 43; 13:22; 14:3; 15:8; 16:2; 22:5, 12; 23:11; 26:5). It is *never* used in Acts of the witness of Old Testament Scripture (or of speaking prophets from the OT era). This is also true of the related verb *diamarturomai* ("to testify") used in the preceding verse, Acts 10:42. In Acts, this term *always* refers to a contemporary witness of someone then living, *never* to the testimony of Scripture or of non-writing prophets of the past (2:40; 8:25; 10:42; 18:5; 20:21, 23-24; 23:11; 28:23).

Third, within the immediate context, Peter specifically tells Cornelius that Christ appeared *"not to all the people but to witnesses (martusin) chosen before by God"* (10:41). Then he says that these select witnesses were commanded *"to preach to the people and to testify (diamarturomai)"* about Christ (10:42). This is the context for Peter's final declaration in 10:43 that *"To Him all the prophets witness (martureō)."* Through the use of the stem, *mart,* in the noun *martusin* and in the verbs *diamarturomai* and *martureō,* we see the flow of thought connecting the activity of the "prophets" in verse 43 with the gospel proclamation of the apostles in verses 41-42. Though Old Testament Scripture has been alluded to earlier in Peter's preaching in Acts 10:38-42, which could favor the interpretation of *writing* prophets in verse 43, the immediate context leading up to verse 43 also emphasizes select, contemporary witnesses or prophets.

---

[93] Schultz, "Saving Faith in the Old Testment," 51-52.

Not only is the idea of present day prophets supported from the immediate context of verses 41-43, but the intermediate context of chapter 10 also supports this interpretation. Earlier in the chapter, Peter had been given a divine vision or revelation about going to the Gentiles (10:9-17). Even Cornelius knew that God had spoken directly to Peter, saying that these Gentiles had gathered *"to hear all the things commanded you by God"* (10:33). In the larger context of this pericope, Peter is both an apostle ("a sent one") and a prophet (one who receives direct revelation from God).[94] In verse 43, Peter could simply be saying to Cornelius and the Gentiles that, just as the Lord had sent him to these Gentiles in order to believe the saving message that Peter was proclaiming, so they could rest assured that all the other prophets and witnesses besides Peter were proclaiming the same message. Peter's message was harmonious with that of the other apostles and therefore credible and trustworthy.

Finally, this interpretation also agrees with the use of the word "prophet" or "prophets" elsewhere in Acts, where it sometimes refers to New Testament prophets of the Church age (11:27; 13:1; 15:32; 21:10).[95] Two of these passages even indicate that some "prophets" are also specially appointed by God to proclaim the gospel, as both Paul (13:1) and Silas (15:32) were prophets who were sent out by God as missionaries. Though the gift of prophecy was certainly intended for the edification of the Church (1 Cor. 14), there is no reason to think that those who possessed this divine gift were limited in their ministry only to fellow members of the Church—only to the saved. The gifts of "apostles" and "evangelists" were also given to the Church for its edification (Eph. 4:11), along with "prophets," and yet the apostles and evangelists clearly ministered in a special capacity to the lost with the gospel. Why not the prophets too?

We can conclude that the phrase *"all the prophets"* in Acts 10:43 may be referring to either New Testament prophets or Old Testament writers of Scripture. Both views have scriptural support and are plausible. But the interpretation that sees the "prophets" as speaking prophets from

---

[94] Ellis writes, "Peter also, who is not called προφήτης, nevertheless has the marks of a prophet, for example, in the knowledge of men's hearts (Acts 5:3; 8:21 ff.; cf. Luke 7:39) and in the experience and proclamation of revelations in visions and dreams." E. Earle Ellis, "The Role of the Christian Prophet in Acts," in *Apostolic History and the Gospel: Biblical and Historical Essays Presented to F. F. Bruce on his 60th Birthday*, ed. W. Ward Gasque and Ralph P. Martin (Grand Rapids: Eerdmans, 1970), 55. Ellis also goes on to explain correctly that though an apostle does all the activities of a prophet, this does not mean that a prophet does all the activities of an apostle. The apostle's ministry was broader and more authoritative than that of the New Testament prophet (ibid., 65).

[95] One serious weakness of this view is that Acts 10:43 has the fuller expression, *"all the prophets"* (*pantōn tōn prophētōn*), not merely the term "prophets." This fuller expression is used by Luke once of a speaking prophet (Luke 11:50) and four times of the writers of Old Testament Scripture (Luke 13:28; 24:27; Acts 3:18, 24); but it is *never* used of New Testament prophets of the Church.

antiquity who passed down extra-biblical, verbal revelation is unsupportable from the Scriptures and must be rejected.

1 Peter 1:10-11

At least one other New Testament passage is sometimes used in an attempt to prove that Old Testament saints had faith explicitly in the coming Christ for eternal life. In 1 Peter 1:10-11, it says, *"10 Of this salvation the prophets have inquired and searched carefully, who prophesied of the grace that would come to you, 11 searching what, or what manner of time, the Spirit of Christ who was in them was indicating when He testified beforehand the sufferings of Christ and the glories that would follow."* No one disputes the fact that the sufferings of Christ were revealed to the prophets and written in the Old Testament, but there is nothing in this passage showing that saints in past dispensations had faith explicitly in Christ for their eternal salvation. 1 Peter 1:10-11 still does not answer several critical questions relating to the contents of saving faith. If the atoning work of the Messiah was so clearly revealed in the Old Testament (and it was), then why was it not also recorded anywhere in the Old Testament as the content of justifying faith? And even if the prophets themselves believed that the coming Christ was the guarantor of eternal life, then where does it say that *everyone* in the Old Testament era was *required* by God to believe the same?

Exegesis or Eisegesis?

At this point, an ounce of caution is worth a pound of presumption. We must be careful not to read our theology into God's Word but let it speak for itself. The late covenant theologian, James Montgomery Boice said that the Old Testament saints *"undoubtedly understood more than we often give them credit for."*[96] I have heard crossless gospel advocates claim the same.[97] While I have no problem admitting that the Old Testament saints and prophets had far greater faithfulness with the revelation God gave to them than I will ever have with the revelation of the entire Bible that God has given to me, the fact remains that no matter how faithful or insightful they were, they were still limited by the amount of revelation that God in His sovereignty had disclosed to them up to that point in their lives.

It is very telling when covenant and crossless men, in the absence of any Old Testament passages, must repeatedly resort to the New Testament

---

[96] Boice, *Foundations of the Christian Faith*, 261.

[97] For example, Wilkin states, "Old Testament saints knew a lot more than we give them credit. [sic] They certainly knew the saving message. They might not have known that the Christ's name is Jesus, though even that some OT saints, like Simeon and Anna, knew and maybe even some like Abraham and Moses knew His name. (After all, quite a few met Him face to face, which is something we haven't done yet.) But they knew that they had eternal life because they believed in Him for it." See Bob Wilkin, "God Has Always Revealed the Saving Message," article on the Unashamed of Grace website (unashamedofgrace.blogspot.com), November 20, 2008 (accessed November 30, 2008).

to try to prove what Old Testament saints "must have" or "surely" or "certainly" believed.[98] This practice exposes the desperateness of their predicament, since there simply are no passages in the Old Testament stating that pre-cross believers trusted specifically in the coming Christ for eternal life. Even if the New Testament told us explicitly somewhere in just one verse that believers in the Old Testament were required to believe in Christ for eternal life, that single verse would be sufficient.

Personally, I would prefer to believe in the continuity of the contents of saving faith and be able to put it succinctly, "We're saved by *looking back* to Christ and His work; while Old Testament saints were saved by *looking forward* to Christ and His work." Though that would be very simple and convenient, it would not be true to the text of God's Word. In order to be approved workmen who do not need to be ashamed (2 Tim. 2:15), we need to handle the Word of truth accurately regarding the relationship between the contents of faith and the progress of God's revelation.

Progressive Revelation & Belief in "Christ"

It is a conspicuous fact as one searches Old Testament passages referring to the Messiah or Christ, that it is never stated a single time from Genesis to Malachi that people must believe specifically in the Christ or Messiah for eternal life, justification, redemption, resurrection, or any similar salvation-related concept. Nor can this fact be dismissed simply due to a lack of revelation in the Old Testament about the coming Christ, for there is an abundance of truth relating to His first and second comings. This fact surely indicates that God never intended belief in Christ prior to His first coming to be a requirement for eternal life. However, this is not the case after the advent of the Savior, where we are struck by the sudden change and specificity required in the contents and object of faith, where it is stated explicitly in no uncertain terms to be the Lord Jesus Christ. This is illustrated in the following chart.

---

[98] As a blatant example of this, in Sydney Dyer's article in the *JOTGES*, he uses Jude 14-15 to tell us what Enoch must have believed about Christ, John 8:56 and Galatians 3:16 to tell us the content of Abraham's faith in Genesis, Hebrews 11:26 to tell us what Moses believed about Christ, and John 12:37-41 to tell us what Isaiah surely believed about Christ in Isaiah 6:1-18. See Dyer, "The Salvation of Believing Israelites Prior to the Incarnation of Christ," 45-48. Putting aside Dyer's eisegesis of these New Testament passages, this continual reading back into Old Testament passages causes the reader to wonder, if all these pre-cross believers had faith in Christ as claimed, then why this need to continually resort to the New Testament in an effort to make them believers in Christ?! The reader gets the uneasy sense that Scripture is being forced to fit the author's theology.

Old Testament	New Testament
"And he believed in ***the LORD****, and He accounted it to him for righteousness."* Genesis 15:6	*"Believe on* ***the Lord Jesus Christ****, and you will be saved"* Acts 16:31
"Behold the proud, His soul is not upright in him; but the just shall live ***by his faith****."* Habakkuk 2:4	*"knowing that a man is justified by the works of the law but* ***by faith in Jesus Christ****, even we have* ***believed in Christ Jesus****, that we might be justified* ***by faith in Christ*** *and not by the works of the law"* Galatians 2:16 *"But now the righteousness of God apart from the law is revealed, being witnessed by the Law and the Prophets, even the righteousness of God,* ***through faith in Jesus Christ****"* Romans 3:21-22 *"to demonstrate at the present time His righteousness, that He might be just and the justifier of the one who has* ***faith in Jesus****."* Romans 3:26

Progressive Revelation & Belief in "Jesus"

The progress of God's revelation is readily apparent in the contrast between Genesis 15:6 and Acts 16:31. If belief in "the Christ" was always required for eternal life, then why doesn't Genesis 15:6 say Abraham believed *"in the Christ"* or *"in the Lord Christ"* or even *"in the promised Seed"* or something similar? Not only is the object of faith never stated to be the Christ in the Old Testament, neither is belief in "Jesus" Christ required. The addition of the terms "Christ" and "Jesus" in the New Testament indicates that the increase or progress of God's revelation has affected the specific object of faith[99] and the contents of faith required for eternal life. With respect to the name of "Jesus," Bob Wilkin even acknowledges, perhaps inadvertently, that progressive revelation has affected his *sine qua non* of eternal salvation. He writes:

[99] You will notice that I did not say "the ultimate object of faith," which dispensationalists maintain has always been God.

> Logically what we must do to have eternal life cannot change. If the saving message changes, then so does the gospel. Dispensationalism has long said that men in every age are justified by faith in God, but as revelation progressed what they needed to believe about God changed as well. Well, if people before the time of Christ could be born again by some general faith in God, then logically so can anyone today who has not yet heard the name of Jesus. No one was ever born again by some general faith in God. The condition has always been faith that the Messiah gives eternal life to all who simply believe in Him. The only dispensational change is that after Jesus' baptism people had to believe that Jesus of Nazareth is the Messiah who gives eternal life to all who simply believe in Him. But the message is the same.[100]

Several things must be said in response to Wilkin's doctrine here. First, Wilkin protests that *"If the saving message changes, then so does the gospel."* He then admits that the *"only dispensational change is that after Jesus' baptism people had to believe that Jesus of Nazareth is the Messiah who gives eternal life to all who simply believe in Him,"* while still maintaining, *"But the message is the same."* If, as crossless gospel advocates claim, the inclusion of the name of "Jesus" is now so essential that it has become one of the three elements required in the *sine qua non* of saving faith,[101] but the name of "Jesus" wasn't required for eternal life before the Lord's public ministry began, then logically "the saving message" *has* changed and it is *not* "the same."

It seems Wilkin is forced to acknowledge that some degree of progressive revelation has affected the content of saving faith, since he admits that from the point of Christ's baptism, belief specifically in Jesus of Nazareth as the Christ has been required for eternal life. It is curious that Wilkin would pick the Lord's baptism as the great pivotal event in human history when the *sine qua non* of saving faith changed. Why not Christ's incarnation? Why not at the cross or resurrection? If any change at all in "the saving message" is admitted, then crossless gospel advocates really have no basis for objecting to the elements of Christ's deity, humanity, death, and resurrection being added for today as required content for eternal life.

The proponents of the G.E.S. position must also address at least two more major problems inherent in their newly developed doctrinal system. We may now legitimately ask why there is even a need today to believe specifically in "Jesus" as the Messiah for eternal life. Crossless proponents are fond of using Peter and the disciples as examples of people who believed that Jesus is the Messiah and who received eternal life even *before*

---

[100] Wilkin, "Is Ignorance Eternal Bliss?" 13.

[101] Robert N. Wilkin, "Justification by Faith Alone is an Essential Part of the Gospel," *JOTGES* 18 (Autumn 2005): 12; idem, *Secure and Sure* (Irving, TX: Grace Evangelical Society, 2005), 74-75.

they believed in His cross-work and resurrection. They often claim that if people like Peter and the disciples were saved without explicit knowledge of the cross, then it is also possible for people *today* to receive eternal life on the same basis.[102] But following the very same logic we could reason that if people were saved in the *Old Testament* without any knowledge of the historical person of "Jesus," and people have always been saved the same way since the "saving message" has always been the same, then doesn't this demonstrate that it is not even necessary to believe in "Jesus" today for eternal life? Why limit our comparative samples to the timeframe of the earthly life of Christ? Why not go back to the Old Testament itself, if indeed the content of saving faith never changes?

There is at least one more glaring inconsistency with the G.E.S. view that progressive revelation has not affected the saving message. If the only defining characteristic about Jesus that must be believed for eternal life is the fact that He is the guarantor of eternal life, and in that sense He is the Christ and the Savior, then doesn't God the Father, or Yahweh, meet this qualification? He was also known as the "Savior" throughout the Old Testament (Deut. 32:15; Isa. 45:15, 21). God the Father has also been the guarantor of justification and eternal life from the dawn of creation. So, does that mean that the Father can now also be considered *"the Christ in the Johannine sense of that term"*?[103] But, if eternal life is now conditioned solely upon believing that "Jesus" in particular is the guarantor of eternal life, then what unique features or attributes about Jesus Christ have necessitated this change to faith being explicitly in Him as the object of saving faith? If neither His incarnation, sacrificial death for our sins, nor bodily resurrection constitute the contents of saving faith today, then why must "Jesus" be the specific object of faith at all? Why isn't faith in Yahweh for eternal life still sufficient? If Jesus Christ has some unique, defining, and requisite attributes that have distinguished Him as the conscious and specific object of faith from the time of Pentecost forward, then what are these attributes or features? Advocates of the G.E.S. view are reticent to state what these features are lest they commit themselves to including Christ's incarnation, substitutionary death for our sins, and resurrection from the dead. In these, and many other respects, the crossless gospel position is seen to be not only unbiblical but also completely lacking in any logical coherence and plausibility.

Inclusivism & Dispensationalism

The G.E.S. view of progressive revelation and the contents of saving faith is

---

[102] René A. López, "Basics of Free Grace Theology, Part 2," p. 1, http://www.scriptureunlocked.com/papers/basicsfgprt2.pdf (accessed August 6, 2007); idem, *Romans Unlocked: Power to Deliver* (Springfield, MO: 21st Century Press, 2005), 212.

[103] Zane C. Hodges, "How to Lead People to Christ, Part 1: The Content of Our Message," 4; idem, "Assurance: Of the Essence of Saving Faith," *JOTGES* 10 (Spring 1997): 6-7.

also incorrect about the fact that dispensationalists believe Old Testament saints were saved by "some general faith in God."[104] From the larger context of his article, Bob Wilkin implies that this leads to the position of inclusivism.[105] Inclusivism is the view that people in this Church age who have never heard the gospel can be saved on the grounds of Christ's redemptive work but without a particular knowledge of, and belief in, the gospel of Christ. In such cases, inclusivists say that the sincere piety of the unevangelized counts as "implicit" faith in Christ, and such "believers" will be saved. However, dispensationalists maintain that even Old Testament saints could not be saved unless they responded in faith to particular truth, from a particular God, via special revelation. In this respect, even inclusivists themselves, such as Clark Pinnock, have not accurately represented the dispensational position.[106]

In the Old Testament, there are several seminal passages dealing with the vital subject of justification before God. In one of these passages, Habakkuk 2:4, we learn not only that justification is by faith but that it is a matter of humbling oneself before God. This is clearly implied in the passage, as the justified believer is contrasted with the proud unbeliever: *"Behold the proud, his soul is not upright in him; but the just shall live by his faith."* To be justified in the Old Testament, the lost had to humbly accept their need for justification, accepting God's evaluation of them, that they were not good (Ps. 14:1-3; Eccl. 7:20) but in fact were sinful and separated from God (Isa. 59:2), lacking righteousness before Him (Ps. 143:2), being unclean in His sight and unable to justify themselves (Job 9:2; 15:14-16; 25:4-6) because their righteous deeds were as filthy rags before Him (Isa. 64:6).

---

[104] Wilkin, "Is Ignorance Eternal Bliss?" 13.

[105] This charge is not new to Wilkin. Non-dispensational theologian, Walter Kaiser, makes the same point, claiming that the dispensational position "opened the door for others to argue in our day" for the inclusivist position. Walter C. Kaiser, Jr., "Salvation in the Old Testament: With Special Emphasis on the Object and Content of Personal Belief," *Jian Dao* 2 (1994): 1-2.

[106] Pinnock attempts to gain support for his inclusivist doctrine by erroneously claiming agreement with dispensationalism. He states: "Dispensationalists have rightly opposed the notion that believers in other epochs needed to believe in the coming Savior in order to be saved. These people trusted in God, even though the content of their theology differed from our own." Clark H. Pinnock, *A Wideness in God's Mercy: The Finality of Jesus Christ in a World of Religions* (Grand Rapids: Zondervan, 1992), 162. While dispensationalists do believe that the content of saving faith changed with Christ's incarnation, death, and resurrection, we maintain, unlike inclusivists, that the content of this faith was always specific, special revelation from God and that the object of faith was always the one, true God. By contrast, inclusivism allows the content of saving faith to be general revelation (i.e., creation, conscience). This permits inclusivism to teach that the conscious object of faith can be a very general notion of "God" as He (or "it") is found even in other world religions. See Clark H. Pinnock, "An Inclusivist View," in *Four Views on Salvation in a Pluralistic World*, ed. Dennis L. Okholm and Timothy R. Phillips (Grand Rapids: Zondervan, 1995), 116-18. This is in stark contrast to the conscious object of saving faith being the one, true God who now reveals the saving content about Himself only through the special revelation of Scripture.

When a sinner in the Old Testament came to believe God's estimate of himself, he could then readily accept the further divine revelation that the LORD Himself (Yahweh) would have to provide him with salvation (Jonah 2:9) by graciously (Isa. 55:1-3) covering him with His very own righteousness (Isa. 61:10). This is all quite reminiscent of Romans 3-4, minus the progressively revealed truth that Jesus Christ in particular would be the One to provide this justification by means of His propitiatory death and bodily resurrection (Rom. 3:24-25; 4:24-25).

Sinners in the Old Testament not only had to accept their spiritual condition, but they had to believe specifically in the one, true God for their justification, namely the LORD (Yahweh). In a world immersed in idolatry and polytheism, this would have been humanly impossible apart from God's gracious initiative of disclosing Himself to lost mankind. The lost sinner in ancient times would have been utterly incapable of discovering on his own the identity of the One in whom he had to believe for his justification. He needed special revelation from God in order to have revealed to him the proper Object for his faith. This is precisely why the classic Old Testament "sola fide" passage, Genesis 15:6, indicates that Abraham believed in a particular God—the LORD (Yahweh)—*"And he believed in the LORD, and He accounted it to him for righteousness."*

This is also the reason why the LORD issued the great Old Testament salvation-invitation of Isaiah 45:21-22, literally commanding all mankind (both Jew and Gentile) to look to Him for salvation: *"21 Who has declared this from ancient time? Who has told it from that time? Have not I, the LORD? And there is no other God besides Me, a just God and a Savior; there is none besides Me. 22 Look to Me, and be saved, all you ends of the earth! For I am God, and there is no other."* Even in Isaiah's day, the command went forth to the entire globe to believe in the God of Israel for salvation.[107] It was not deemed optional by the LORD in Old Testament times for all humankind to turn to Him in faith. It was imperative![108]

We see from the Old Testament itself that general faith in God was insufficient for a sinner's justification. "Saving faith" in the Old Testament, just as today, required particular and specific knowledge about man's unrighteous condition, the identity and righteous character of the one, true God, and the LORD's non-meritorious provision of forgiveness and imputed righteousness solely on the condition of faith in Him. Salvation has always been a matter of taking God at His Word. This is a far cry from inclusivism's doctrine that people can be saved today through faith in a generic "God" based only on the *general revelation* of conscience and

---

[107] In Isaiah 45:22, there is actually a double imperative issued by God. First, the command is given to *"look"* to Him (Qal stem imperative), followed by the command to *"be saved"* (Niphal stem imperative).

[108] C. F. Keil and F. Delitzsch, *Commentary on the Old Testament*, trans. James Martin (Edinburgh: T & T Clark, 1866-1891; reprint ed., Peabody, MA: Hendrickson, 1996), 7:450; Edward J. Young, *The Book of Isaiah* (Grand Rapids: Eerdmans, 1972), 3:215-16.

creation.[109] Thus, Bob Wilkin's attempt to equate dispensationalism's doctrine of progressive revelation with the theologically liberal doctrine of inclusivism is seen to be a *non sequitur*; it simply does not "logically" follow as he claims.[110]

Inclusivism & Crossless Saving Faith

While Wilkin implies that the traditional dispensational view of progressive revelation and the gospel opens the door to inclusivism, it is actually the G.E.S. gospel that bears a striking resemblance to it in one important respect. Both theological positions affirm the necessity of Christ's work as the grounds of redemption while at the same time denying the necessity for the lost sinner to know about His work and believe in it. Clark Pinnock, a leading spokesman for the inclusivist position, writes:

> One does not have to be conscious of the work of Christ done on one's behalf in order to benefit from that work. The issue God cares about is the direction of the heart, not the content of theology.[111]

The only significant difference between this statement and the crossless position is that the latter would substitute "belief in Jesus' promise of eternal life" for Pinnock's more ambiguous statement about "the direction of the heart." Apart from this qualification, they both follow the same rationale. Thus Zane Hodges can say:

> In the final analysis, therefore, salvation is the result of believing in Jesus to provide it. Salvation is not the result of assenting to a detailed creed. Salvation does not even require an understanding of how it was provided for or made possible. All it requires is

---

[109] It is difficult to conceive how faith in such a vague, non-descript, generic "god" could even provide someone with real certainty. Even in the Old Testament a person needed to be certain of Yahweh's identity and divine revelation, as one lexical source for Hebrew words states regarding faith: "This very important concept in biblical doctrine gives clear evidence of the biblical meaning of 'faith' in contradistinction to the many popular concepts of the term. At the heart of the meaning of the root is the idea of certainty. And this is borne out by the NT definition of faith found in Heb 11:1. The basic root idea is firmness or certainty. . . . In the Hiphil (causative), it basically means 'to cause to be certain, sure' or 'to be certain about,' 'to be assured.' In this sense the word in the Hiphil conjugation is the biblical word for 'to believe' and shows that biblical faith is an assurance, a certainty, in contrast with modern concepts of faith as something possible, hopefully true, but not certain." *TWOT*, s.v. "אָמַן," by Jack B. Scott, 1:51 (ellipsis added).

[110] If it did "logically" follow, then we should expect dispensationalists to be leading the charge of inclusivism, however I am not aware of a single traditional dispensationalist who teaches the inclusivist doctrine. For a rebuttal of inclusivism from a distinctively dispensational viewpoint, see Bruno R. Giamba, "The Essential Content of Saving Faith in Response to Inclusivism" (Th.M. thesis, Dallas Theological Seminary, 2004) and Ramesh Richard, *The Population of Heaven: A Biblical Response to the Inclusivist Position on Who will be Saved* (Chicago: Moody Press, 1994).

[111] Pinnock, *A Wideness in God's Mercy*, 158.

> that the sinner understand the sufficiency of the name of Jesus to guarantee the eternal well-being of every believer.[112]

Apart from the name of "Jesus" and the guarantee of "everlasting life," the crossless gospel is only two hairs' breadth away from the inclusivist position. In addition, though inclusivism and the crossless saving faith position both deny that a lost man *must* believe in Christ's work to be reborn, they are also quick to maintain that we *should* still preach Christ's death and resurrection. Hodges states:

> What is my point? That we should not preach the cross of Christ to men? Not at all. I will make it emphatically clear a little later on that I think we should. Instead, I am arguing that we need to focus on the core issue in bringing men and women to faith and eternal life. What is that core issue? Very simply it is this: We want people to believe that Jesus guarantees their eternal destiny. Of course, we would like them to believe a lot more than this, but this at least must be believed.[113]
>
> But this is precisely where the preaching of the cross becomes so important. Why should men trust Christ for eternal life? The gospel gives us the wonderful answer. . . . The preaching of the cross greatly facilitates the process of bringing men to faith in God's Son.[114]

After claiming that the lost do not need to know about Christ's work to be born again, inclusivists also sense the need to issue a qualification, and so Pinnock echoes Hodges, saying:

> This is not to imply the unimportance of making historical facts about Jesus known everywhere. It is essential to make them known in order to clarify God's saving purposes for humanity and to motivate individuals to make their commitment to God in Christ.[115]

While reading such quotes from both the crossless and inclusivist camps, it is difficult to imagine that these theologians are unaware of the radical nature of their mutual departures from the historic evangelical consensus that requires belief in the gospel message of Christ's death and resurrection. As a result, each position apparently senses the need to claim that Christ's redemptive work is "essential" in some respect. But such attempts ring hollow. In the end, each school of thought denies that the death and resurrection of Christ are "essential" to believe for the sinner's eternal salvation. No matter how much the crossless camp may wish to avoid the

---

[112] Zane C. Hodges, "How to Lead People to Christ, Part 1," *JOTGES* 13 (Autumn 2000): 10.

[113] Ibid., 7.

[114] Ibid., 10-11 (ellipsis added).

[115] Pinnock, *A Wideness in God's Mercy*, 159.

association with inclusivism, they cannot escape the fact that neither their position nor inclusivism requires faith in the Lord Jesus' person and work for eternal life.

Progressive Revelation & Belief in the "Gospel"

Having noted that the object of faith now requires more specificity with the addition of "Christ" and "Jesus," we are now prepared to examine the specific contents of faith in this dispensation and the question of whether progressive revelation has changed "the gospel" itself. At this juncture we must also ask several important questions, such as, where in the Old Testament is "the gospel" specifically mentioned? Is it even articulated there as "the gospel" per se? Does the Old Testament ever refer to the "gospel *of Christ*"? Does the Old Testament ever refer to belief in the coming Christ for eternal life as "the gospel"? And if any change has occurred in the contents of faith, does this mean that "the gospel" changed? And if so, how would this relate to Galatians 1:8-9 where a solemn, double anathema is pronounced upon those who alter the gospel? And how do New Testament statements that the "gospel" was found in the Old Testament (Rom. 1:1-4; 1 Cor. 15:3-4 cf. Acts 26:22-23) relate to progressive revelation and the contents of faith?

Crossless gospel advocates claim that "the gospel" of eternal salvation has never changed, and so the truths of Christ's person and work must not be added to "the gospel" for the lost in this Church age either. Wilkin specifically addresses this subject, stating:

> Grace Evangelical Society's motto summarizes an accurate explanation of OT and NT salvation. There is, was, and always will be only one gospel. The gospel of Adam, Moses, Abraham, and David is also the gospel according to Jesus, Peter, Paul, and the other apostles. It always has been and always will be by faith alone in Christ alone. When Jesus conducted His ministry, the Jewish people were still under the Law of Moses. Yet Jesus promised the immediate reception of eternal life to all who believed in Him (e.g., John 3:14-18; 4:10ff; 5:24; 6:47; 11:25-27). His promise did not wait to go into effect until the cross. And John was completely comfortable proclaiming Jesus' saving message to people in the Church Age (John 20:31). If the gospel changed after Pentecost, then one could not be saved by believing the gospel which Jesus preached![116]

Sydney Dyer, while holding to covenant theology, also defends the view that "the gospel" did not change after Calvary. In his article in the *Journal of the Grace Evangelical Society*, Dyer says:

---

[116] Wilkin, "Salvation Before Calvary," 2-3.

> The author of the book of Hebrews explains in 4:2 that "the gospel was preached to us as well as to them." The "them" in this verse refers to the generation of Israelites who departed from Egypt with Moses. They heard the gospel. Believers today, of course, enjoy that same gospel with greater clarity, fullness, and glory (2 Cor 3:10-11).[117]

When Hebrews 4:2 is cited in support for the "same gospel" being preached today as in past dispensations, it merely shows the desperate lengths to which some Christians go to support their error.[118] Hebrews 4:2 does not teach that the gospel of Christ was preached in the Old Testament. Here, Dyer bases his argument on an English translation (NKJV). The Greek text of Hebrews 4:2 has the verb form, *euangelizō*, without an article preceding it. Just as with Abraham in Galatians 3:8, this passage does not use the noun *euangelion* with the article, which is translated "the gospel" throughout the New Testament. Hebrews 4:2 simply says the Israelites in the wilderness generation had "good news preached" to them. This is also how the New American Standard Bible translates Hebrews 4:2. It is very misleading to maintain from this verse that the Israelites had "the gospel" of Christ preached to them just as we preach it to the lost today.

So what was "the gospel" in the Old Testament? How can we confirm or deny the position of Dyer, Wilkin, and others who maintain that in spite of the progress of revelation, "the gospel" of the Church age is the same as "the gospel" of the Old Testament? A simple check of word usage in the Old Testament is a good place to start. However, when we do so, we search in vain for the term "gospel" in the Old Testament in our English translations—and for good reason. We do find its virtual equivalent phrases "good news" or "good tidings" or "glad tidings" used several times; but when these passages are examined in their contexts, it becomes immediately apparent that they will not help the case of the crossless gospel either.

When a diachronic Old Testament word study is done, we see that fifteen times the Hebrew terms *bāśar* (בָּשַׂר) and *b*e*śōrâ* (בְּשֹׂרָה) have the sense of "good news" or "good/glad tidings" and are translated as such (2 Sam. 4:10; 18:27, 31; 1 Kings 1:42; 2 Kings 7:9; 1 Chron. 16:23; Ps. 40:9; 96:2; Isa. 40:9 (2x); 41:27; 52:7 (2x); 61:1; Nahum 1:15). A few of these passages may initially appear to lend support for the crossless gospel and should be clarified. In Psalm 40:9 it says, *"I have proclaimed the good news of righteousness in the great assembly,"* but the *"good news of righteousness"* says nothing about the Messiah or eternal life in its context. Similarly in Psalm 96:2 and 1 Chronicles 16:23, we are instructed to *"Sing to the LORD, bless His name; Proclaim the good news of His salvation from day to day."* Here

---

[117] Dyer, "The Salvation of Believing Israelites," 45-46.

[118] Jeremy D. Myers, "The Gospel is More Than 'Faith Alone in Christ Alone'," *JOTGES* 19 (Autumn 2006): 56.

again, there is nothing stated about the Messiah or eternal life, only the LORD's salvation in a general sense.

There are also two passages in Isaiah that are quoted in the New Testament and should be clarified. In Isaiah 52:7 it says, *"How beautiful upon the mountains are the feet of him who brings good news, who proclaims peace, who brings glad tidings of good things, who proclaims salvation, who says to Zion, 'Your God reigns!'"* Again, there is nothing in this verse about Christ the Messiah or even specifically, "eternal life." The message of *"salvation"* that is proclaimed in this verse is simply, *"Your God reigns!"* This is hardly the message that the Christ dies for sin and rises again and guarantees eternal salvation to all who believe specifically in Him. A portion of Isaiah 52:7 is quoted in Romans 10:15, which says in the NKJV (following the TR and MT in Greek), *"And how shall they preach unless they are sent? As it is written: "How beautiful are the feet of those who preach the gospel of peace, Who bring glad tidings of good things!"* It is significant to observe that Paul only quotes the initial portion of Isaiah 52:7 when applying it to the preaching of the "gospel of Christ" in the Church age. He omits the second half of the verse that defines Isaiah's message of *"salvation"* as *"Your God reigns!"* Clearly, Isaiah 52:7 is not referring to the same "gospel" that Paul refers to in Romans 10:15. Paul is only drawing a parallel to the *principle* of "beautiful feet," not to the *content* of "the gospel."

Finally, Isaiah 61:1 also refers to the "good tidings" saying, *"The Spirit of the Lord GOD is upon Me, because the LORD has anointed Me to preach good tidings to the poor; He has sent Me to heal the brokenhearted, to proclaim liberty to the captives, and the opening of the prison to those who are bound."* This is quoted by the Lord Jesus in Luke 4:18 as having been fulfilled by Him personally in His own earthly ministry prior to Calvary (Luke 4:21). Therefore, Isaiah 61:1 is also not referring to the "gospel of Christ" that we preach in this Church age. This leads to the conclusion that there are simply no references in the Old Testament to "the gospel" as we Christians know it.[119]

Even if we were to broaden our search for "the gospel" by considering the equivalent Greek words for "the gospel" (*euangelion*) and "preach the gospel/good news" (*euangelizō*) in the Greek version of the Old Testament, the Septuagint (LXX), we would still not find the "gospel of Christ." The noun form of "the gospel" (*euangelion*) is found in only six verses (2 Sam. 4:10; 18:20, 22, 25; 2 Sam. 18:27; 2 Kings 7:9) and none of these use the "good news" to refer to the Christ/Messiah, eternal life, or any synonymous salvation-related concept. The same conclusion is true of Septuagint ref-

[119] Regarding the magnificent revelation of Christ's coming substitutionary work in Isaiah 53, Thomas Schultz writes, "Even in chapter 53, as complete as it is, all that is found is a mere foreshadowing of the plan of salvation revealed fully by the New Testament authors. . . . if this was the message to be believed after Isaiah penned it, the Old Testament does not reveal such. Isaiah is nowhere seen to be proclaiming the message of belief in the suffering Messiah" (Schultz, "Saving Faith in the Old Testament," 50-51 [ellipsis added]). See also Heslop, "Content, Object, & Message of Saving Faith," 246.

erences to proclaiming the good news. In all twenty three occurrences of the verb *euangelizō*, there is not a single reference to proclaiming the good news of Christ, eternal life, etc. (1 Sam. 31:9; 2 Sam. 1:20; 4:10; 18:19, 20 (2x), 26, 31; 1 Kings 1:42; 1 Chron. 10:9; Ps. 39:10; 67:12; 95:2; Song Sol. 11:1; Isa. 40:9 (2x); 52:7 (2x); 60:6; 61:1; Jer. 20:15; Joel 3:5; Nahum 2:1).

When it comes to actual *word usage*, "the gospel" is simply not found in the Old Testament to be the "saving message." Even when it comes to contexts where the *concept* of the Messiah/Christ is referred to, rather than just the term, *māshîaḥ* (מָשִׁיחַ), there is no mention of "the gospel" anywhere in the contexts of those passages either. The conclusion is clear and unmistakable. The gospel of Christ as we know it today is not found as such anywhere in the Old Testament. But how does this fit with the explicit New Testament teaching that the gospel of Christ was *"promised before through His prophets in the Holy Scriptures"* (Rom. 1:2) and that Christ died for our sins and rose again *"according to the Scriptures"* (1 Cor. 15:3-4)?

All the essential elements of the gospel can be found in the Old Testament, including Christ's deity (Ps. 2:2, 7, 12; 45:6-7 cf. Heb.1:8-9; 110:1; Prov. 30:4; Isa. 7:13-14; 9:6-7; Jer. 23:5-6; Dan. 3:25; Micah 5:2; Zech. 14:3-5; Mal. 3:1b-3), humanity (Gen. 3:15; 49:10; 2 Sam. 7; Isa. 7:14; 11:1, 10; Micah 5:2), death for sin (Ps. 22; Isa. 53; Dan. 9:26; Zech. 12:10; 13:7), bodily resurrection (Ps. 16:9-10; Isa. 53:10b, 12 cf. John 2:22; 20:9; 1 Cor. 15:4), provision of salvation from sin (Isa. 53:11), and even the sole condition of faith (Gen. 15:6; Hab. 2:4). But though every element of the gospel of Christ is revealed in the Old Testament, there is not a single Old Testament passage referring to any of these elements individually or collectively as "the gospel." Nor is there a single passage in the Old Testament requiring belief in all of these elements together for a person's eternal salvation, or even any one element individually.

We can conclude, therefore, that though all the essential elements of the gospel were promised and predicted in the Old Testament (Rom. 1:2), and each element of the gospel is certainly contained in the Old Testament (1 Cor. 15:3-4; Acts 26:22-23), the essential elements of the gospel of Christ had not yet coalesced into one definitive message called "the gospel" as we see it in the New Testament. This is why we can say that the Old Testament *contained* gospel truths, while also maintaining that people in the Old Testament were *not required* to believe "the gospel" in order to have eternal life. In this respect "the gospel" technically did not "change," since each essential element coalesced for the very first time after Calvary into the one saving message necessary to believe called *"the gospel of Christ"* (Rom. 1:16; 15:19, 29; 1 Cor. 9:12, 18; 2 Cor. 9:13; 10:14; Gal. 1:7; Phil. 1:27; 1 Thess. 3:2).

In discussing the doctrine of progressive revelation and the gospel with one Free Grace leader, he concluded that those who hold to the traditional dispensational position, as espoused in this chapter, have created a "hybrid-gospel." He claimed we have done this by combining the gospel for eternal life in John 6:47, which Jesus preached, with the gospel for the Christian life which Paul preached to believers, as recorded in 1 Corinthians 15:3-4. Crossless gospel advocates may charge their dispensational brethren with teaching that "the gospel changed after Pentecost,"[120] but this would merely be creating a straw-man out of the traditional dispensational position. For, how could the gospel of Christ change after Pentecost when technically it didn't even exist yet in the Old Testament as one definitive message called "the gospel"?! Rhetorically though, the charge that dispensationalists have "changed" the gospel is very dramatic and effective. Immediately people think of the anathemas against altering the gospel in Galatians 1:8-9. Biblically, however, this is a baseless charge.

In Galatians 1:8-9, Paul writes, *"But even if we, or an angel from heaven, preach any other gospel to you than what we have preached to you, let him be accursed. As we have said before, so now I say again, if anyone preaches any other gospel to you than what you have received, let him be accursed."* In these two verses the standard against which all other gospels are judged is not *"The gospel of Adam, Moses, Abraham, and David . . . also the gospel according to Jesus."*[121] It is the gospel that Paul preached in Galatia. He declares the standard of comparison to be *"what **we** have preached to **you**"* (Gal. 1:8) and *"what **you** have received"* (Gal. 1:9). Paul does not go back to the Old Testament or even Jesus' earthly ministry for the standard gospel. He goes back to the gospel that he, as an apostle, preached to the Galatians in this Church age as recorded in Acts 13:23-48.[122] Thus, crossless gospel teachers are completely mistaken when they claim, *"If the gospel changed after Pentecost, then one could not be saved by believing the gospel which Jesus preached!"*[123] This statement confuses the message that *Jesus Himself preached* with the message *about* Christ's person and work now called *"the gospel of Christ."* This distinction will be explained in more detail in the next two chapters.

A Transitional Passage

While it is clear that the content of saving faith has not remained the same throughout all dispensations, to this point we have yet to consider whether Scripture even explicitly states that such a change occurred. The fact that such a change did occur is readily observable by a comparison of Old Testament salvation passages with New Testament salvation passages. But are there any verses that plainly state that a change occurred to the content of saving faith? I have heard crossless proponents challenge their traditional, dispensational Free Grace brethren at times, saying, "Show us one verse that says the content of saving faith has changed." They confidently

---

[120] Wilkin, "Salvation Before Calvary," 3.

[121] Ibid., 2. See also Cox, *Amillennialism Today*, 30-31.

[122] This passage is covered in detail in chapter 10.

[123] Wilkin, "Salvation Before Calvary," 3.

assume that no such passage exists. In actuality, the Lord has provided at least one reference in the Epistle of Galatians.

Galatians 3:21-26

21 *Is the law then against the promises of God? Certainly not! For if there had been a law given which could have given life, truly righteousness would have been by the law.*
22 *But the Scripture has confined all under sin, that* ***the promise by faith in Jesus Christ*** *might be given to those who believe.*
23 ***But before faith came****, we were kept under guard by the law, kept for* ***the faith which would afterward be revealed.***
24 *Therefore the law was our tutor to bring us to Christ, that we might be justified by faith.*
25 *But after faith has come, we are no longer under a tutor.*
26 *For you are all sons of God through faith in Christ Jesus.*

This passage not only indicates *the fact* that a change occurred in the contents of saving faith but it also indicates *the time* when this transition occurred. In the larger context of this passage, the apostle Paul has been establishing the relationship between "law" as a meritorious method of God's dealing versus "promise" as a gracious method of divine dealing. Paul previously taught in Galatians 3 that the unilateral covenant of promise established by God with Abraham was not abrogated when the Mosaic Law was introduced as a bilateral covenant with Israel at Mount Sinai 430 years later (Gal. 3:17). But if the two methods of God's dealing with man, "law" versus "promise" (i.e. works vs. grace), are in contrast to one another, then how do they work together to fulfill God's purposes? Is the Law of Moses against the promises of God (Gal. 3:21)? Not at all! The Law actually furthered God's program of promise, which Paul explains in verses 21-26.

The Law fulfilled the role of prison guard (3:22) and child trainer (3:24) by leading people to faith in Jesus Christ for justification. The Law works to show mankind that we are *"all under sin"* (v. 22; cf. Rom. 3:9) and in need of a Savior. It drives the lost sinner to Christ. When people realize their state of condemnation due to their sin and God's righteousness, they turn to Jesus Christ in faith for their justification. As a result, Galatians 3:22 says that the promise by faith in Jesus Christ is given to all those who believe in Christ. In the context, *"the promise by faith in Jesus Christ"* refers to the simultaneous soteriological blessings of regeneration (v. 21, "life") and justification (v. 24) with its imputed righteousness (v. 21, "righteousness" not being "by the law").

Verse 23 contains the critical reference to the change in the content of saving faith. It says literally, *"But before* ***the faith*** *came, we were kept under guard by the law, kept for the faith which would afterward be revealed."* When it says, *"But before the faith came"* (*pro tou de elthein tēn pistin*), it is referring to the particular arrival of a particular faith. It is "the coming" of "the faith." The question is, however, what "faith" is this referring to? Is this referring to justifying faith? And who is the explicit object of this faith? The article preceding "faith" in verse 23 (*tēn pistin*) is anaphoric, referring to the faith in the previous verse (v. 22), where Paul spoke of *"the promise by faith in Jesus Christ."* It is this particular *"faith in Jesus Christ"* that came, he says. Prior to the arrival of this particular faith in Jesus Christ, Paul says in verse 23 that people were *"kept under guard by the law"* for *"**the faith** which would afterward be revealed"* (*tēn mellousan pistin apokaluphthēnai*). The faith that would afterward be revealed was a particular faith (*tēn pistin*). It is for this reason that one English translation of verse 23 reads, *"But before **this faith** came"* (NIV). The article precedes "faith" again in verses 25-26 (*tēs pisteōs*), where Paul is continuing to describe the arrival of the same faith—faith in Jesus Christ for justification.[124]

All of these details are significant when it comes to establishing both the fact of a change to the content of saving faith and the timing of this change. Galatians 3:23 states that "the faith" in Jesus Christ was only "revealed" with the coming of Christ. It does not say that *particular truths about Christ* had never been revealed prior to that point, but only that "the faith" in Jesus Christ was not previously revealed. In the Old Testament, all the elements of the gospel of Christ were revealed, but they had not yet come together in one cohesive message to be believed for justification until the arrival of Christ. Then "the faith" in Jesus Christ was "revealed."

Some crossless proponents may concede that Paul is referring to a particular faith ("the faith") that was revealed with Christ's first coming but then claim that this refers only to "the Christian faith" as a body of doctrine that is not equivalent to believing the saving message. While it is generally recognized that in Scripture "the faith" can refer to the objective body of doctrinal truth constituting the Christian faith,[125] "the faith" can also refer to the personal faith of one who is genuinely saved. In fact, the two concepts of personal faith and objective truth should not be divorced from one another.[126] Here in Galatians 3:23, 25-26, there is nothing in the

---

[124] Some may wonder why verse 24 does not contain the article before "faith" when it says, *"Therefore the law was our tutor to bring us to Christ, that we might be justified by faith (hina ek pisteōs dikaiōthōmen)."* In verse 24, the anarthrous reference to "faith" (*pisteōs*) occurs only because Paul is summarizing the contrast made earlier in the chapter that justification is *"by faith"* (*ek pisteōs*; cf. 3:7-9), as exemplified by Abraham in a previous dispensation, rather than *"by works of law"* (*ex ergōn nomou*; cf. 3:10), as exemplified by those who sought justification by keeping the Mosaic Law. Earlier in Galatians 3, Paul was not addressing the issue of the *content* of saving faith but the *nature* of saving faith—that it is apart from works (Gal. 3:7-12). In chapter 3 he is saying, in essence, that there are only two approaches to being justified in God's sight. There is the "by faith" approach which is non-meritorious by nature and there is the "by law" approach which is meritorious. In Galatians 3:24, Paul concludes this contrast between law/works vs. faith/grace as distinct approaches to justification regardless of the dispensation and thus regardless of the content of such saving faith.

[125] Gordon H. Clark, *Faith and Saving Faith* (Jefferson, MD: Trinity Foundation, 1990), 32.

[126] It is a common theological fallacy that one who merely holds to "the faith" possesses something less than genuine, personal, saving faith. In the 243 occurrences of the noun "faith" (*pistis*) in the Greek New Testament (based on NA[27]), *pistis* occurs with the definite

context that indicates that Paul is referring to the body of Christian truth *in contrast* to individual saving faith in the gospel of Christ. In Galatians 3:23, "the faith" should be interpreted as referring to both the personal exercise of faith and objective doctrinal truth about Christ. When people believe the gospel of Christ, both the individual and doctrinal elements of "faith" are inherent. They exercise personal faith and there is objective, doctrinal content to their faith. This is the justifying faith spoken of in the context of Galatians 3:23. It is simply indisputable from the immediate context that this passage is addressing faith in Christ for justification (3:21c, 24) and regeneration (3:21b, 26), rather than for sanctification, which Paul addresses elsewhere in Galatians.

Furthermore, this passage indicates that this particular faith in Jesus Christ for justification was not even "revealed" until the Law ended, which occurred at Calvary with Christ's cry of *"It is finished"* (John 19:30) and the rending of the Temple veil (Matt. 27:51). The Law lasted from Mount Sinai to Calvary. Afterwards, the particular justifying faith in Jesus Christ took effect. This also explains why the gospel of the grace of God—the gospel of Christ—was not preached to the whole world for its salvation until Pentecost, which marked the beginning of the Church age and the commencement of the Great Commission.

N.T. Christianity or O.T. Judaism?

When the fact is denied that progressive revelation has affected the contents of saving faith, some rather bizarre and unscriptural conclusions naturally result. With respect to covenant theology, if saints in the Old Testament believed with dimmer light the same truths about Christ that we believe as Christians today, then logically this means that saints in the Old Testament were "Christians" too! This is actually what some covenant theologians claim. In his article in the *Journal of the Grace Evangelical Society*, Sydney Dyer writes, "Thus, when Gen 15:6 declares that Abraham believed God and He counted it to him for righteousness, the object of Abraham's faith was undoubtedly the Son of God, the preincarnate Christ. Is it not appropriate therefore to say that Abraham was a Christian?"[127] The answer is: "No, it is not appropriate!" If all Old Testament saints believed in the coming "Christ" for eternal life, we should expect the Old Testament to have at least one reference to such people being "Christians." But we find

---

article (i.e., "the faith") 129 times. Yet, *never once* does this phrase describe someone who is not a believer—someone with something less than genuine faith in God. In numerous passages the phrase "the faith" doesn't even appear to be in reference primarily to the objective body of Christian doctrine; rather it seems to refer primarily to the personal, subjective exercise of faith. See Matt. 23:23; Luke 18:8; Acts 3:16; 15:9; 16:5; Rom. 3:30; 4:14, 19-20; 10:17; 11:20; 12:6; 14:1; 1 Cor. 13:2; 2 Cor. 1:24; 4:13; Gal. 2:20; 3:14, 23, 25-26; Eph. 3:17; 6:16; Phil. 1:25; 3:9; Col. 2:12; 1 Thess. 1:3; 2 Thess. 3:2; Heb. 4:2; 6:12; 11:39; James 2:14, 17, 18, 20, 22, 24, 26; 1 Peter 5:9.

[127] Dyer, "The Salvation of Believing Israelites Prior to the Incarnation of Christ," 47.

none. There is a reason why people were *"first called Christians in Antioch"* (Acts 11:26) and why the term "Christian" is exclusive to the Church age (Acts 11:26; 26:28; 1 Peter 4:16).

On the other hand, regarding the G.E.S. perspective on the gospel, if people living in this Church age need only to believe the same gospel that Abraham and David believed, and that message has not "changed," then logically we've returned to an Old Testament form of Judaism. In 2005, I asked one crossless Free Grace leader if the content of saving faith was exactly the same for Abraham and Job as it was for Peter and John. His only answer was "Yes, precisely." This is extremely troubling. Peter and John believed that the Christ, the Messiah, *had come* in the person of Jesus; Abraham and Job believed in a Christ who *hadn't come* yet. If the content of faith for Peter and John was "precisely" the same as it was for Abraham and Job, then logically a person can still receive eternal life even if they do not believe Christ *has historically come*—just as long as they believe the Christ is the guarantor of eternal life *who will yet come.* With this line of reasoning, we have just returned to Old Testament Judaism! We have just turned Christianity on its head. This is all consistent with Bob Wilkin's view that genuine "believers" in Christ today may not even be "Christians." He says:

> It's not clear in the New Testament whether "Christian" equals believer or "Christian" equals baptized, believing disciples of Jesus. I'm inclined to believe it's the latter, that you can be born again and not be a "Christian." But don't tell anybody I said that, because it sounds kind of funny.[128]

Are you thoroughly confused? You should be. Now we have Old Testament believers who are actually "Christians" and Church age believers who are not "Christians"! In all fairness to the adherents of the crossless gospel position, some have acknowledged that there is one difference between the content of saving faith for an Old Testament saint and a Church age saint, and that difference is simply the identification of "the Christ" with the historical person of "Jesus of Nazareth."[129] However, since they simultaneously claim that this is the same saving message that has always been preached and believed for eternal life, the best we can say about their doctrine of progressive revelation and the gospel is that it is logically and biblically inconsistent.

---

[128] Robert N. Wilkin, "The Current State of Grace," Grace Evangelical Society Conference, Dallas, TX, February 27, 2006. This also explains why Zane Hodges could claim on the one hand, "The central fact of the Christian faith is the resurrection of the Lord Jesus Christ" (Zane C. Hodges, "The Women and the Empty Tomb," *BSac* 123 [October 1966]: 301), while later in life not even holding that belief in the central fact of Christianity is required for someone to be born again and enter God's family.

[129] Wilkin, "Is Ignorance Eternal Bliss?" 13.

Chapter 8

Is the Gospel a Broad, Non-Soteriological Message?

OVERVIEW

A survey in the New Testament of the Greek words for "gospel" (euangelion) and "preach the gospel" (euangelizō) reveals that there is not just one broad, all-encompassing form of "good news" as crossless gospel teachers are now claiming in an attempt to obscure the person and work of Christ as the saving message. There are several different "good news" messages that are entirely distinct from one another. Prominent among these are the gospel of the kingdom, the everlasting gospel, and the gospel of Christ or the gospel of the grace of God. Since there is not a single instance in the New Testament where either euangelion or euangelizō applies to the crossless saving message that "Jesus guarantees eternal life to all who simply believe in Him for it" without even having to believe in His person and work, some crossless advocates are no longer requiring belief in "the gospel" for justification. Instead, "the gospel" is conceived as being a theological umbrella term for virtually all of the Old and New Testaments. But no uses of euangelion and euangelizō will support this notion, not even in the possible four original Gospel titles, nor in Mark 1:1.

The importance of knowing, defending, and preaching an accurate gospel simply cannot be overstated. Regarding the gospel, it must be recognized above all else that it is a message that glorifies the Lord Jesus Christ (2 Cor. 4:4; 1 Tim. 1:11), the very Lord of Glory. The gospel redounds to His glory every time it is accurately preached to the saving of a soul (2 Cor. 4:15; Eph. 1:12-13). It is the very message God uses to rescue lost souls (Rom. 1:16). It is His spiritual life-preserver in an ocean of sinking humanity. It is humanity's only real life-line to God. As believers in Jesus Christ, redeemed by the blood of the Lamb, we are already citizens of heaven while on earth; and that means we presently stand on the shores of heaven serving as rescuers to the sea of lost and drowning humanity. How vitally important therefore that we cast out to them the one, true, saving gospel message about Jesus Christ!

The clear and accurate proclamation of this powerful message is to be our great occupation, our singular corporate enterprise throughout this Church age until the Lord returns (Mark 16:15; Luke 24:46-47; 2 Cor. 5:18-20). It is no wonder that Satan has painted a spiritual bulls-eye on the back of this one, vital truth of the Bible. With laser-like focus, he has honed his diabolical energies upon corrupting this sacred message and nullifying its saving effects (2 Cor. 4:3-4). Is the gospel of Christ really that important? What other single truth in the entire Word of God is guarded by a double-divine anathema upon those who would corrupt it (Gal. 1:8-9)?!

You would think in light of these facts that people professing the name of Christ would be more careful when discussing "the gospel." Yet we have seen "evangelical" Christians in our generation writing joint declarations with Roman Catholic leaders, including members of Rome's ruling magisterium, referring jointly to "the Gospel we declare" and that "we contend together" in order to "proclaim this Gospel."[1] The abysmal state of evangelical affairs is also seen by evangelical leaders entering into dialogue and conversation with Mormon leaders who unapologetically preach a false gospel, even co-authoring a book that speaks duplicitously about the gospel, using language such as "accepting the gospel covenant" by "making Jesus Lord of our lives."[2] Today we have the claims of Lordship Salvationists that "The gospel Jesus proclaimed was a call to discipleship, a call to follow Him in submissive obedience"[3] and that the

---

[1] *Evangelicals and Catholics Together: The Christian Mission in the Third Millennium*, Fifth Draft, February 28, 1994.

[2] Craig L. Blomberg and Stephen E. Robinson, *How Wide the Divide? A Mormon and an Evangelical in Conversation* (Downers Grove, IL: InterVarsity Press, 1997), 145.

[3] John F. MacArthur, Jr., *The Gospel According to Jesus* (Grand Rapids: Zondervan, 1988), 21.

Sermon on the Mount in Matthew 5-7 "is pure gospel"[4]—even though the term "gospel" never occurs in Matthew 5-7, nor any mention of Christ's substitutionary death or bodily resurrection.

Now on top of it all, we have certain members of the Free Grace movement who are opposed to Lordship Salvation telling us that the good news that the lost must believe is not to be found in classic gospel passages such as 1 Corinthians 15:1-4 but in verses from the Gospel of John which we are told support a crossless content of saving faith, such as John 5:24; 6:47; and 11:25-27. Some leading crossless teachers of our day have even gone so far as to deny that a person must believe "the gospel" to be born again. Now, we are told, the lost must only believe "the saving message," since "the gospel" is actually the entire New Testament and possibly even the entire Bible. What confusion!

Like a blinding fog that has rolled in from the sea of subjectivism, a Babelesque spiritual condition has enveloped the whole of evangelicalism today, affecting even the current Free Grace movement. In pondering this sad state of affairs, we must regrettably ask, "Does anyone even know what 'the gospel' is anymore?" The only way to rectify this tragic situation and right the Free Grace ship that has veered off course in recent years is to go back to the drawing board. We must carefully re-examine every occurrence of term "gospel" in the New Testament. These next two chapters will therefore provide a synopsis of scriptural teaching on this subject based on an exegetical, detailed study of all 132 occurrences of the term "gospel" in the New Testament.

Euangelion/Euangelizō

In our English Bibles, the words "gospel" and "preach the gospel" are translations of two words in the Greek New Testament, the noun *euangelion* (gospel or good news) and its verb form *euangelizō* (preach or proclaim good news). For the sake of reference, every occurrence of these terms is listed on the following page.

The Greek word *euangelion* occurs 76 times in 73 different verses, while *euangelizō* occurs 56 times in 53 verses according to the Greek Majority Text[5] or 55 times in 53 verses according to the Critical Text.[6] This includes one occurrence of the compound form, *proeuangelizomai,* in Galatians 3:8. Later, this chapter will also consider four more possible uses of *euangelion* in the titles of Matthew, Mark, Luke, and John.

---

[4] Ibid., 179.

[5] GNTMT

[6] NA[27]

Euangelion (76x)

Matt. 4:23
Matt. 9:35
Matt. 24:14
Matt. 26:13
Mark 1:1
Mark 1:14
Mark 1:15
Mark 8:35
Mark 10:29
Mark 13:10
Mark 14:9
Mark 16:15
Acts 15:7
Acts 20:24
Rom. 1:1
Rom. 1:9
Rom. 1:16
Rom. 2:16
Rom. 10:16
Rom. 11:28
Rom. 15:16
Rom. 15:19
Rom. 16:25
1 Cor. 4:15
1 Cor. 9:12
1 Cor. 9:14 (2x)
1 Cor. 9:18 (2x)
1 Cor. 9:23
1 Cor. 15:1
2 Cor. 2:12
2 Cor. 4:3
2 Cor. 4:4
2 Cor. 8:18
2 Cor. 9:13
2 Cor. 10:14
2 Cor. 11:4
2 Cor. 11:7
Gal. 1:6
Gal. 1:7
Gal. 1:11
Gal. 2:2
Gal. 2:5
Gal. 2:7
Gal. 2:14
Eph. 1:13
Eph. 3:6
Eph. 6:15
Eph. 6:19
Phil. 1:5
Phil. 1:7
Phil. 1:12
Phil. 1:16 [CT]
Phil. 1:17 [MT]
Phil. 1:27 (2x)
Phil. 2:22
Phil. 4:3
Phil. 4:15
Col. 1:5
Col. 1:23
1 Thess. 1:5
1 Thess. 2:2
1 Thess. 2:4
1 Thess. 2:8
1 Thess. 2:9
1 Thess. 3:2
2 Thess. 1:8
2 Thess. 2:14
1 Tim. 1:11
2 Tim. 1:8
2 Tim. 1:10
2 Tim. 2:8
Philem. 1:13
1 Peter 4:17
Rev. 14:6

Euangelizō (56x)

Matt. 11:5
Luke 1:19
Luke 2:10
Luke 3:18
Luke 4:18
Luke 4:43
Luke 7:22
Luke 8:1
Luke 9:6
Luke 16:16
Luke 20:1
Acts 5:42
Acts 8:4
Acts 8:12
Acts 8:25
Acts 8:35
Acts 8:40
Acts 10:36
Acts 11:20
Acts 13:32
Acts 14:7
Acts 14:15
Acts 14:21
Acts 15:35
Acts 16:10
Acts 17:18
Rom. 1:15
Rom. 10:15 (2x)
[MT]; 1x [CT])
Rom. 15:20
1 Cor. 1:17
1 Cor. 9:16 (2x)
1 Cor. 9:18
1 Cor. 15:1
1 Cor. 15:2
2 Cor. 10:16
2 Cor. 11:7
Gal. 1:8 (2x)
Gal. 1:9
Gal. 1:11
Gal. 1:16
Gal. 1:23
Gal. 3:8 (*proeuangel-izomai*)
Gal. 4:13
Eph. 2:17
Eph. 3:8
1 Thess. 3:6
Heb. 4:2
Heb. 4:6
1 Peter 1:12
1 Peter 1:25
1 Peter 4:6
Rev. 10:7
Rev. 14:6

The Crossless Doctrine of "the Gospel"

One difficulty in defining the new crossless theology of "the gospel" is that it is still evolving and not all of its adherents share the same doctrine or parlance. As was explained previously in chapter 5, a new view of the term "gospel" has emerged in recent years (2006-2007) within the crossless camp. Some, such as Bob Wilkin and Jeremy Myers, are now advocating the position that the term "gospel" is *never* used in the New Testament to refer solely to the "saving message" or the contents of saving faith. In this respect, they no longer speak of "the gospel" as being part and parcel with the message that must be believed for eternal life, preferring instead to speak of the "saving message" or the "message of life." Most advocates of a crossless saving faith, however, still follow the original view and speak freely about the "gospel" as being the semantic equivalent of "the saving message." Yet, even in doing so, they understand this type of "gospel" only in a narrow, restricted sense that doesn't require belief in Christ's deity, substitutionary death, or bodily resurrection for eternal life.

Both the older and newer views maintain that, in terms of New Testament usage, the word "gospel" can include the doctrinal truths of Christ's person and work, but these truths of "the gospel" are only necessary for Christians to believe for their sanctification. By contrast, they claim that the "saving message" that the lost must believe for their justification is the limited message of John 6:47 consisting only of the three part *sine qua non* of the name of "Jesus," "believing," and the guarantee of "everlasting life." In this respect, whether it is the older or newer crossless view, neither interprets "the gospel" in the New Testament to be a singular, fixed message of Christ's person and work that is equally necessary for the lost to believe for their justification and for the regenerate to continue believing for their on-going practical sanctification.

A Broad vs. Narrow Gospel

One example of this crossless doctrine of the term "gospel" can be observed in the teaching of Bob Wilkin, who taught a session at one national conference of the Grace Evangelical Society titled, *"The Three Tenses of Salvation Reconsidered."* In it, Wilkin promoted the older crossless view by teaching that "the gospel" in the New Testament is sometimes simply the requirement to believe in Jesus for eternal life and sometimes more broadly the good news of how Christ provides deliverance for the Christian, for one who is already a believer. Wilkin stated, *"Sometimes [the word] 'gospel' is narrowly related to 'what must I do to have eternal life?' But quite often it's the big picture and it's actually what is preached to the Christian. We're preaching the 'good news' to the Christian."*[7] While it is true that the believer must hold fast to the gospel of Christ, since it is the basis for all faith and practice in the Christian life and necessary for growth in grace (1 Cor. 15:1-2; Phil. 2:16; Col. 1:23-28), the need to believe the gospel message of Christ's person and saving work is in no way *limited* to the *Christian*. When Wilkin spoke about the gospel "narrowly" versus "the big picture," he was *not* claiming that the one, fixed gospel message contains the same essential elements for both the lost and the saved. He was *not* teaching that there is only one message with the same elements that has application to unbelievers for their justification and to believers as the foundation for their on-going growth and sanctification. Rather, he was teaching that there is a narrow "gospel" *without* Christ's deity, death for sin, and resurrection that is essential for the unbeliever, and there is also an expanded "gospel" that contains these additional elements, which is essential only for the growth of one who is already a believer.

---

[7] Robert N. Wilkin, "The Three Tenses of Salvation Reconsidered," Grace Evangelical Society, 2003 (brackets added).

This explains why in Wilkin's original crossless view he defined "the truth of the gospel" as simply faith in Jesus and His guarantee of eternal life, without believing necessarily in Christ's deity, humanity, death, and resurrection. He formerly taught, *"You can believe many biblical concepts and still miss* ***the one truth that is saving—the truth of the gospel****. For example, you can attest to Jesus' deity, His virgin birth, and His bodily resurrection, and yet not believe Jesus' promise to give you eternal life freely if you just believe in Him for it.* ***There is only one truth that will save****: Jesus' guarantee that anyone who believes in Him for eternal life has it."*[8] However, contrary to Wilkin's assertion that the saving "truth of the gospel" is merely the message that Jesus will guarantee eternal life to all who believe in Him without even believing in His deity or resurrection, the word "gospel" is *never* used in the New Testament with such a narrow, limited meaning.

The Newest Interpretation of "the Gospel"

Wilkin, Myers, and a few other crossless proponents have recently conceded this point about the absence of any passages where the term "gospel" refers strictly to their version of the saving message. That is why they have adopted the newer crossless view that makes an unbiblical distinction between "the gospel" and "the saving message." It is an observable and verifiable fact that in all 132 occurrences of the terms *euangelion* and *euangelizō* in the New Testament, there is *not a single instance* in which either term refers to the form of "good news" being propagated by crossless proponents as the *sine qua non* of saving faith—that Jesus guarantees eternal life to all who believe in Him for it, regardless of what theological misconceptions they may have about Him being the Son of God and Son of Man who died for sin and rose again. It is for this reason that Jeremy Myers distinguishes between the gospel and the saving message. He concludes:

> So the real question then is not "How much of the gospel do you have to believe?" but rather "What do you have to believe to receive everlasting life?" If we want to know what a person must believe to receive everlasting life, we should not asks [sic] the question, "What is the gospel?" but rather, "What is the message of life?" When asked that way, the answer becomes crystal clear. The Gospel of John, which does not contain the word *gospel*, tells us over and over what people must do to receive everlasting life: believe in Jesus for everlasting life (John 3:16; 5:24; 6:47; etc.) You do not have to believe the gospel to receive everlasting life, you only have to believe in Jesus for everlasting life.[9]

---

[8] Robert N. Wilkin, *Confident in Christ* (Irving, TX: Grace Evangelical Society, 1999), 10 (bold added).

[9] Jeremy D. Myers, "The Gospel is More Than 'Faith Alone in Christ Alone'," *JOTGES* 19 (Autumn 2006): 51.

Historically, Free Grace proponents have recognized that the New Testament employs the term "gospel" in a variety of ways. They have recognized various categories of usage for the term "gospel," such as the gospel of the kingdom, the everlasting gospel, and the gospel of the grace of God/gospel of Christ. Free Grace people have traditionally understood that only the gospel of Christ or the gospel of the grace of God is the saving message for today and that it is entirely distinct from the other forms of "good news" found in the New Testament. But the latest crossless view claims that Scripture never uses the term "gospel" as being part and parcel with the saving message. Rather, they teach that "the gospel" is a composite message of various forms of good news. Bob Wilkin promoted this new doctrine at one Grace Evangelical Society Regional conference, where he asked:

> What if the word "gospel" doesn't *ever* mean the saving message? Now hang with me hear. I gave this same message, but I didn't say quite this, a little over a month ago in Omaha at a Regional we had there. And what I suggested is that the term "gospel" rarely, if ever, means, "What must I believe to have eternal life? What must I believe to be saved? What must I do to have—to go to heaven—to be sure I'll be in the kingdom? But in the intervening time as I've been reflecting on it etcetera, I realized that we should go further than saying, "It's rare that this term refers to the saving message." I'm now of the opinion it *never* refers *specifically* to "What must I believe to have eternal life?" Now it can include that message, but it's always a good news message about Jesus except in a few rare cases like 1 Thessalonians 3:6 where it's a good news message about the Thessalonians hanging in the faith or Revelation 14:6 where it's a good news message that Jesus is coming to judge the wicked and overthrow the wicked. And there are verses like that, but for the most part, what if the good news in the New Testament is a good news message about Jesus and His kingdom and that He's redeemed a people for Himself through the cross? And the resurrection tells us that all who believe in Him are one day going to be glorified and given glorified bodies and that they will live forever with glorified bodies in His kingdom, and that He will overthrow wickedness, and He will rule and reign forever? What if the good news that Jesus and His apostles preached was a kingdom message? And what if we've turned it into a "Let's get born again message"? What if we've gotten it wrong? [10]

Several points must be made regarding the preceding quote by Wilkin. First, his statement demonstrates unequivocally that there has been a definite and significant doctrinal shift on the meaning of "the gospel" in

---

[10] Bob Wilkin, "Gospel Means Good News," Grace Evangelical Society Southern California Regional Conference, August 24, 2007.

the Grace Evangelical Society. Secondly, Wilkin's quote also clearly reveals that the "gospel" is no longer considered to be equivalent with the saving message but that the saving message is now subsumed into one larger New Testament gospel. This has been taught explicitly on other occasions as well. Thus Wilkin boldly claimed at another G.E.S. conference, "I do not find a single verse anywhere in the Bible where the terms gospel or evangelist refers [sic] specifically and only to the saving message. In fact, quite often when the term gospel is used it doesn't even include the saving message. . . . while the term *gospel* in Galatians surely includes the saving message, I now do not believe it is only that message."[11]

These revolutionary statements by Wilkin also demonstrate that the dispensational distinctions between the various forms of "good news" in the New Testament are now being eroded and melded together so that the gospel of the kingdom, the everlasting gospel, and the gospel of the grace of God form one conglomerate message of general good news about Jesus Christ. Myers explains the rationale behind this blending and merging of all forms of "good news" in the New Testament into one, large, homogenous "gospel." He writes:

> The problem, however, is that different authors in different contexts have different *good-news* truths that they emphasize. This means one of two things. Either there are numerous different *gospels* with each author having one or more *gospel*, or there is one large, diverse, multi-faceted, all-encompassing *gospel* for the entire NT (which essentially *is* the entire NT).[12]

The view of Wilkin appears slightly more nuanced than Myers' as he continues to maintain some degree of distinction between the various forms of good news while upholding a larger, all-encompassing concept of "the gospel." Thus, Wilkin does distinguish the gospel of the kingdom from the gospel of Christ,[13] while still speaking of "the good news" as "everything from creation to the New Earth."[14]

A Faulty Methodology

Having noted the most recent crossless claims for "the gospel," we must

---

[11] Bob Wilkin, "Gospel Means Good News," a paper presented at the Grace Evangelical Society conference, March 6, 2008, Fort Worth, TX, p. 6 (ellipsis added).

[12] Myers, "The Gospel is More Than 'Faith Alone in Christ Alone'," 35.

[13] "*The gospel of the kingdom*. This expression is found twice times [sic] in Matthew (4:23; 24:14) and once [sic] Mark (Mark 1:14). It refers to the good news that the kingdom of heaven is at hand. It is not the good news that all who believe in Jesus have everlasting life. It is good news that is related to Jesus, but we can't substitute the words 'the gospel of Jesus Christ' for 'the gospel of the kingdom,' for those are two different messages. The former is the message that the kingdom has drawn near for Israel. It is a Jewish message to Israel." Wilkin, "Gospel Means Good News," 3.

[14] Ibid., 8.

now consider their bases. How do crossless proponents support their views? They have at their disposal the same 132 occurrences of *euangelion* and *euangelizō* in the New Testament to study, and yet they arrive at drastically different conclusions than their traditional Free Grace brethren. They erroneously claim that if we total up all of the elements that are contained within each occurrence of the term "gospel" in the New Testament, then the list of items that comprise "the gospel" becomes so ridiculously large that we must settle on the simple contents of John 6:47 as the saving message. Former staff member of the Grace Evangelical Society, Jeremy Myers, even claims that totaling up all the items mentioned in the New Testament as part of "the gospel" would require the lost to believe in at least 50 different items before they could receive eternal life.[15] Since such an inflated content of saving faith would be completely unreasonable, the only tenable solution, we are told, is to recognize that the saving message must be entirely distinct from "the gospel." However, the methodology used to arrive at such an unfounded conclusion is badly flawed. One example of this faulty methodology is Myers's explanation of Luke 1:19 where the word "gospel" occurs. He states:

> With this understanding, the NT *gospel* contains elemental concepts that are common throughout the NT, some minor details that are listed only once, certain truths that must be shared in evangelistic endeavors, and various ideas that should be reserved for discipleship purposes.
>
> For example, there are gospel truths which are clearly not evangelistic. For example, in Luke 1:19, the angel Gabriel declares the *gospel* to Zechariah. Most translations say that the angel is declaring glad tidings, or declaring good news, but the Greek word is *euangelizō*, to declare the *gospel*. The content of the angel's gospel is that Zechariah's wife, Elizabeth, will be the mother of John, who would prepare the way for the Messiah.
>
> No evangelist, to my knowledge, has ever claimed that knowledge of and belief in Elizabeth as the promised mother of John the Baptist is a necessary truth of evangelism. Yet it is part of the NT gospel. This example shows us that deciding what to include in witnessing is not as easy as just including everything the NT says about the gospel. In fact, by this author's count, the NT includes *fifty* truths and facts in the gospel. Some of them are so vague and general, that essentially, the gospel includes everything in the NT, if not everything in the entire Bible.
>
> So to say that a person has to know and believe everything the NT calls *gospel* in order to receive everlasting life is to say that a

[15] Myers, "The Gospel is More Than 'Faith Alone in Christ Alone'," 40.

> person has to know and believe most, if not all of the Bible. If this is so, then few, if any, actually have everlasting life, and unless the entire NT has been taught and explained, nobody has ever shared the entire gospel with anybody else.[16]

If we were to accept Myers's methodology, we would be led to agree with his conclusion that it is absurd to require the lost to believe these aspects of "the gospel" for their eternal salvation. However, there are several exegetical errors that underlie Myers's attempt to trivialize an "expansive" gospel to the lost that necessitates belief in Christ's deity, humanity, death, and resurrection. For example, multiple times he interprets the Greek verb *euangelizō* ("to preach/proclaim good news") used in Luke 1:19 in the specific sense of "the gospel."[17]

The term *euangelizō* is not necessarily synonymous with "the gospel," since it is a verb describing the process or act of proclaiming good news—good news of any kind. The specific content of the "good news" being proclaimed must be determined by each individual context, not by the mere occurrence of the word *euangelizō*. The differing uses of *euangelizō* in the New Testament make it clear that there is not one, broad "gospel" to which every occurrence of *euangelizō* contributes. Myers and Wilkin are correct that the term "gospel" has a broad range of usage, sometimes even having a non-theological usage (1 Thess. 3:6). But this fact has long been recognized among Free Grace people. What is new and revolutionary, however, is the approach to "gospel" passages now being taken that tends to exaggerate the broad range of usage for *euangelion* in order to obscure the fact that in the majority of occurrences in the New Testament the term "gospel" actually refers to the one, specific saving message for this dispensation of Christ's person and work. Every occurrence of *euangelizō* should not automatically be assumed to be a reference to the *euangelion*.

Secondly, even if Luke 1:19 is describing "the gospel" as a noun in a particular sense instead of just "proclaiming good news," how would we know if this particular "gospel" in the context of Luke 1:19 is the same "gospel" referred to after Christ's death and resurrection in the Book of Acts and the Epistles? Instead of including every item in the New Testament that is associated with the words *euangelion* and *euangelizō* in one big message that we call "the gospel," why can't there exist *more than one* "good news" message in the New Testament with their meanings determined by each individual context where the term occurs? Myers does recognize this possibility, but he rejects it due to pragmatic, evangelistic reasons rather

---

16 Ibid., 40-41.

17 Even if *euangelizō* in Luke 1:19 meant "the gospel," it still could be interpreted in a narrow sense as referring to only one particular form of good news that is distinct from others in the New Testament, namely the good news of John the Baptist's miraculous birth. J. B. Hixson, *Getting the Gospel Wrong: The Evangelical Crisis No One Is Talking About* (n.p.: Xulon Press, 2008), 79.

than due to sound hermeneutical principles. After noting that some grace-oriented expositors of the past, such as C. I. Scofield, have distinguished the gospel of the kingdom, the gospel of the grace of God, and the everlasting gospel, Myers concludes:

> It is very possible that such definitions and distinctions between the various gospels (or good news messages) in Scripture are correct. However, the downside to such distinctions is that they lead to numerous different *gospels* in the NT, which is not only confusing, but can be misleading. If there are different *gospels*, or different versions of the *good news*, how can we know which one to use in evangelism? Should we use them all? Maybe some of them weren't even for evangelism, but were *good news* messages for the Jewish people, or for believers.
>
> But even if we could distinguish an evangelistic gospel from a discipleship gospel, the evangelistic gospel still seems to include large amounts of information. How much of it must be shared and believed in order for enough information to be imparted so that a person might receive everlasting life? If one only has five minutes to evangelize a person on their deathbed, which of these good news messages should be shared, and how much of it must be shared?
>
> In light of these, and other possible pitfalls, the multiple gospel view is not the best way to understand the NT data concerning the gospel.[18]

This is another transparent example of crossless doctrine driving exegesis of Scripture, rather than letting the text of God's Word speak for itself and submitting our doctrine and practice accordingly. Myers's statements are consistent with the *Zeitgeist* prevalent among today's new evangelicals that seeks to deconstruct the dispensational tenets of an earlier age. Wilkin and Myers attempt to collapse the various forms of "good news" in the New Testament into one multifaceted "gospel," just as covenant theology collapses the different dispensations under one overarching covenant of grace. By merging the gospel of the kingdom and the everlasting gospel (Rev. 14:6) with the gospel of Christ's death and resurrection, the new homogenous "gospel" of the Grace Evangelical Society sounds virtually indistinguishable from the position of non-dispensational, covenant theologians who see only one "gospel" in Scripture. For example, Cox claims that *"Abraham was saved through faith in that same gospel. This was the same gospel which was preached by John the Baptist, by our Lord himself, and by all the apostles."*[19] This

---

[18] Ibid., 39-40.

[19] William E. Cox, *Amillennialism Today* (Phillipsburg, NJ: Presbyterian and Reformed Publishing Co., 1966), 31. For another example, see Frank Stagg, "Gospel in Biblical Usage,"

amalgamation of the different gospels in Scripture represents another instance where the novel theology of the G.E.S. has departed from normative dispensationalism.

When every occurrence of *euangelion* and *euangelizō* in the New Testament is examined in light of its contextual usage, it must be acknowledged that there is not just one "gospel" referred to in the New Testament; there are several entirely different forms of "good news," each with distinctive contents. But to lump the contents of all of these "good news" messages into one "gospel" would be as illogical as pooling together every reference in the Greek New Testament to "baptism" (*baptisma* or *baptismos*), or "baptize" (*baptizō*), and then concluding that it is all part of the same "baptism." Depending on the context, however, Scripture could be describing any one of several entirely different baptisms, such as Holy Spirit baptism (1 Cor. 12:13), a baptism of suffering (Mark 10:38-39), a baptism with fire and judgment (Matt. 3:11), a baptism in water (Mark 1:8a), etc. Yet, the end result of such a flawed methodology would be a conclusion that is self-contradictory. For, how could there be a "baptism" that is simultaneously by fire and water? How can a person have a wet-dry baptism? Another contradiction stemming from Myers's faulty methodology is his inclusion of water baptism from Mark 16:15 within his 50 different items comprising the "multi-faceted, all-encompassing" New Testament gospel.[20] If water baptism is part of the New Testament "gospel" and yet the New Testament explicitly excludes baptism from the gospel (1 Cor. 1:14-17), then the new crossless doctrine of the "gospel" is self-contradictory.[21]

The same predicament arises when applying this method of interpretation to the person of "Herod" mentioned in the Gospels and Acts. In the forty occurrences of "Herod" in the New Testament, no second descriptive name or modifier is attached to "Herod" as in secular history, so that a naïve interpretation of Scripture would assume that there is only one "Herod" from the first recorded use of that name in Matthew 2:1 to the last use in Acts 13:1. Yet, "Herod" was not a personal name but a family name or surname. We know from a comparison of secular historical records with Scripture that there are actually six different Herods referred to in the New Testament (Herod the Great, Herod Archelaus, Herod Antipas, Herod Philip II or Philip the tetrarch, Herod Agrippa I,

---

RevExp 63.1 (1966): 5-13, where he combines every New Testament usage of the terms *euangelion* and *euangelizō* into one composite "Gospel."

[20] Myers, "The Gospel is More Than 'Faith Alone in Christ Alone'," 53.

[21] This is also the position of Wilkin, who states regarding the words *evangelism* and *evangelistic*, "In my opinion, the words actually have a broader meaning than that in the NT. They refer to sharing the entire good news about Jesus, including both sanctification and justification truth, both how to be born again and how to follow Christ via baptism and discipleship." Bob Wilkin, "Is Jesus' Evangelistic Message Sufficient Today?" a paper presented at the Grace Evangelical Society Conference, March 5, 2008, Fort Worth, TX, p. 2. See also Wilkin, "Gospel Means Good News," 5.

Herod Agrippa II). What is also significant with the 40 occurrences of "Herod" in the New Testament is that they are all spoken of in the singular. Even though there are six entirely different Herods in the New Testament, Scripture invariably speaks of "Herod," not "Herods." This is just like the term "gospel." The fact that the New Testament always uses the singular, "gospel," rather than the plural, "gospels,"[22] does *not* prove that there is only one all-encompassing gospel.[23] Just as it would be wrong to conclude that there is only one Herod in Scripture with many different features about him, or one baptism in Scripture expressed in several diverse, even contradictory ways, so it would be wrong to conclude that there is only one "gospel" in the New Testament with over fifty different components to it.

An Illegitimate Theological Construct

The problem of the "illegitimate totality transfer" has been well-known among biblical lexicologists since James Barr's accurate assessment of the faulty methodology employed for determining word meanings in the earlier volumes of Kittel's *Theological Dictionary of the New Testament.*[24] Free Grace proponents, such as Dillow, have also clearly demonstrated how Lordship Salvationists resort to this practice in order to invest "repentance" as a condition for eternal salvation with a distended, unbiblical, and meritorious meaning.[25] Though the new G.E.S. approach to determining the meaning of "the gospel" in Scripture is technically *not* an illegitimate totality transfer, it still ends up creating an illegitimate and unbiblical theological construct for the term "gospel," and thus it still suffers from semantic overload.

An illegitimate totality transfer is when any one occurrence of a word in Scripture is made to bear all the meanings possible for that word or its

---

[22] Ralph P. Martin, "Gospel," *ISBE*, 2:529. The plural forms of *euangelion* and *euangelizō* do occur on occasion in the LXX, particularly in 1 and 2 Samuel.

[23] Dispensationalists apply the same methodology in distinguishing between Christ's coming in the air to rapture His Church versus His coming to the earth in judgment to establish His kingdom. These two separate phases of Christ's second advent are readily discernable in the New Testament, and yet Scripture nowhere speaks in the plural of two second "comings." Rather, the distinction between Christ's coming *for* His Church and His return *with* the Church is duly noted by comparing all of the various passages on Christ's coming and noting the many evident contrasts that exist. The same principle and methodology applies to the Messiah's coming as it was revealed in the Old Testament. Nowhere did it state in explicit terms that there would be two "comings"; and yet a comparison of messianic passages demonstrates an evident contrast between a suffering Messiah and a reigning, glorious Messiah. From the standpoint of the discerning Old Testament saint, this contrast would have been explainable only by deducing that there would be two separate advents of the Messiah.

[24] James Barr, *The Semantics of Biblical Language* (London: Oxford University Press, 1961), 218, 222.

[25] Joseph C. Dillow, *The Reign of the Servant Kings: A Study of Eternal Security and the Final Significance of Man* (Miami Springs, FL: Schoettle Publishing, 1992), 29-37.

root.[26] In essence, it takes the sum of all individual meanings for a particular term or root and then reads that sum back into each occurrence of the particular term. To borrow Barr's example with the New Testament term, *ekklēsia* (normally translated "church"), this word can be used to express several diverse meanings depending on the context.[27] It may refer to a local assembly of believers in Christ (Acts 8:1; 13:1; 20:17), the universal Body of Christ (Matt. 16:18; Eph. 1:22), the nation of Israel gathered in the wilderness (Acts 7:38), or even a socio-political gathering of non-Christians (Acts 19:32, 39, 41). Yet, it would certainly be wrong to read into each occurrence of *ekklēsia* in the New Testament all four of these possible meanings.

The hermeneutical approach of Wilkin and Myers doesn't go quite that far. For example, in Myers's article, he is not claiming that in each instance of *euangelion* and *euangelizō* in the New Testament these terms bear the full range of the 50 plus items that he includes in "the gospel." Rather, the Wilkin-Myers methodology interprets the term "gospel" theologically rather than biblically. In other words, the term "gospel" is viewed as a theological construct or doctrinal formulation that combines all the various biblical and lexical meanings of "gospel." In so doing, they have created one diverse entity known as "the gospel" that contains all of their 50 plus elements, of which the "saving message" is just one facet.[28] It is not clear from Myers's article whether he is claiming that the New Testament itself ever uses the terms *euangelion* or *euangelizō* of this broad, singular entity. But it is an incontestable fact that when all 132 uses of *euangelion* and *euangelizō* are examined, there is not a single instance where either term means the "all-encompassing" form of good news containing the 50 plus elements listed by Myers. Perhaps that is why Myers, in his own list of every occurrence of these terms along with their corresponding content from each context, does not provide *even a single biblical reference* where either term means the entire "all-encompassing" gospel that he is arguing for. If indeed the Grace Evangelical Society is now using the term "gospel" only in a theological sense rather than in a strict biblical or lexical sense, then is this not a tacit admission that their "gospel" is not based on actual biblical usage of the terms *euangelion* and *euanglizō* but it is theologically contrived?

Obscuring the Saving Message

Proponents of the G.E.S. gospel have tried to make the "saving message"

[26] Moisés Silva, *Biblical Words and Their Meaning: An Introduction to Lexical Semantics*, rev. ed. (Grand Rapids: Zondervan, 1994), 25.

[27] Barr, *The Semantics of Biblical Language*, 218.

[28] Myers states, "Of course, as this study revealed, faith in Christ for everlasting life is an element of the gospel. . . . But there is a vast difference between saying that this truth is *part* of the gospel and saying that it *is* the gospel." Myers, "The Gospel is More Than," 51 (ellipsis added, italics original).

simpler and clearer by denying that "the gospel" is equivalent with the contents of saving faith. They have denied that the gospel *is* the saving message. But ironically, in the process, they have actually *confused* and *obscured* the saving message itself. This can be seen by tracing their logic on "the gospel." We are told by Myers that we shouldn't view one particular form of good news (i.e., the gospel of the grace of God/the gospel of Christ) as distinct from other forms of good news (i.e., the gospel of the kingdom, the everlasting gospel, etc.). Instead, we should view them all collectively, since this will enhance the clarity of our witness. We should do this because "the downside to such distinctions is that they lead to numerous different *gospels* in the NT, which is not only confusing, but can be misleading. If there are different *gospels*, or different versions of the *good news*, how can we know which one to use in evangelism?"[29] In addition, we are told that the gospel is not the saving message but that the saving message is part of the gospel. *Yet, we were just told not to look at the parts of the gospel to find the saving message* since this is confusing to people when it comes to evangelism. Apparently, we really shouldn't look to *any* biblical occurrences of the word "gospel" since "the gospel" has at least 50 different elements to it. In light of this, we are still stuck with Myers's dilemma, how can anyone know which of these are saving versus non-saving elements?

Wilkin and Myers believe that the dispensational view of unique, distinguishable gospels should be replaced in favor of their view of one homogenous gospel. But, we must ask, how will this clarify the contents of saving faith if "the saving message" is still contained within a broad, all-encompassing "gospel" that has over 50 different elements to it? If recognizing a few different forms of good news in the New Testament (kingdom, grace/Christ, everlasting) is confusing to people when it comes to identifying which one is the saving message, then how is finding the saving message within 50 plus elements any less confusing? The new G.E.S. perspective on "the gospel" doesn't solve anything for the reader of Scripture who is now forced to view all 132 uses of the term "gospel" homogenously. By merging a once well-recognized category of usage for the saving message (the gospel of Christ) with other forms of good news in the New Testament, this actually obscures the contents of saving faith.

Despite the new G.E.S. claim that the saving message is *not* the gospel but that it is contained *within* the broad, all-encompassing gospel, this new view ultimately instructs us *not* to look to the biblical occurrences of the word "gospel" for the saving message. This is the very reason why they appeal to the Gospel of John in order to find the saving message, since it does not contain a single occurrence of the word "gospel." This rationale is revealed in the teaching of Bob Wilkin who recently taught at a national G.E.S. conference that "The word *gospel* doesn't occur anywhere in the

[29] Ibid., 39.

text of the only evangelistic book in Scripture, the Gospel of John," and that "The object of faith in John's Gospel is always Jesus and His promise of everlasting life. The object of faith in John's Gospel is never something called *the gospel*."[30] Wilkin concluded that "This alone should cause us to reject the idea that the word *gospel* is a special word that means the message we must believe to have everlasting life."[31] Based on statements such as these, it would be more logically consistent for crossless advocates to abandon altogether their claim that the saving message is even part of "the gospel."

The Need for a Comprehensive Study of "the Gospel"

All of this inconsistency and redefinition on "the gospel" reveals the desperate need that exists today within the Free Grace camp for a comprehensive, biblical analysis of every occurrence of the noun and verb forms of "gospel." Even the relatively recent 2006 article by Jeremy Myers in the *Journal of the Grace Evangelical Society* is hardly sufficient in addressing the need to define the gospel based on a systematic study of all 132 occurrences of *euangelion* and *euangelizō*. Myers himself acknowledges that his article is only intended as a survey. He writes, "Needless to say, this sort of study for all 130 uses of *euangelion* and *euangelizō* is well beyond the scope of this article. Therefore, a more generic approach will be taken."[32]

When one stops and considers the magnitude of importance that the term "gospel" carries in Scripture, it is astonishing that it took 19 years before the *Journal of the Grace Evangelical Society* published an article by a living Free Grace advocate attempting to define the gospel based on an overview of New Testament usage. In the very first edition of *JOTGES* in 1988, it was affirmed that the purpose of G.E.S.'s existence was to educate people about the gospel. The initial editor, the late Art Farstad, wrote: "Grace Evangelical Society is neither a church nor a denomination. Rather, it is a parachurch organization designed to encourage and educate churches and individuals concerning the Gospel."[33] While two articles on the gospel appeared in *JOTGES* prior to Myers's article,[34] neither of these were intended as a comprehensive New Testament study of the terms *euangelion* and *euangelizō*. As such, neither article represented fresh exegetical investigation into the gospel since both came from "A Voice from the Past." And yet, ironically, both articles reached conclu-

---

[30] Wilkin, "Gospel Means Good News," 2.

[31] Ibid.

[32] Myers, "The Gospel is More Than 'Faith Alone in Christ Alone'," 41.

[33] Arthur L. Farstad, "An Introduction to Grace Evangelical Society and Its Journal," *JOTGES* 1 (Autumn 1988): 4.

[34] William R. Newell, "A Voice from the Past: Paul's Gospel," *JOTGES* 7 (Spring 1994): 45-50; H. A. Ironside, "A Voice from the Past: What is the Gospel?" *JOTGES* 11 (Spring 1998): 47-58.

sions about the gospel that were diametrically opposed to today's new G.E.S. perspective.

A comprehensive investigation of every occurrence of "gospel" is still very much in order in our day. Even Myers's recent article begins its first sentence by noting, "Surprisingly little work has been done on the definition and content of the *gospel* (*euangelion, euangelizō*) in the N.T."[35] It is this author's opinion that if such a systematic, exegetical examination of every "gospel" passage had been done in the late 80s, or even early 90s, the tragedy of today's crossless gospel could have been averted. While this book makes no pretense to provide such a comprehensive analysis (which would require a separate book in itself), the remainder of this chapter and the following will provide a general survey of the biblical usage of the terms *euangelion* and *euangelizō* from a normative dispensational and historic Free Grace perspective. In doing so, it will be observed that there are several entirely distinct gospels or forms of good news in the New Testament that should not be mixed or confused. It will also be observed that the message of Christ's person and work ("the gospel of Christ") is equivalent to the saving message today. But before examining the various categories of good news in the New Testament, the following section will provide a few pertinent observations about the general usage of *euangelizō* and *euangelion*.

Observations on *Euangelizō*

When the 56 occurrences of the verb *euangelizō* in the Greek New Testament are studied, several relevant facts emerge. First, as with the noun *euangelion*, the verb *euangelizō* can refer to different forms of "good news" being proclaimed depending on the context. For instance, *euangelizō* is used of good news being proclaimed to Zacharias that he will have a son who will be a great prophet, namely John the Baptist (Luke 1:13-19). The Lord Jesus' birth as the Savior is heralded by the angel as a joyful message of good news (Luke 2:10). There is also good news of the kingdom coming to Israel, which was a message proclaimed by both John the Baptist and the Lord Jesus (Matt. 11:5; Luke 4:18, 43; 7:22; 8:1; etc.).[36] The most frequent occurrence of *euangelizō* and the act of proclaiming good news regards the specific message that Jesus is the Christ, the Son of God who died for our sins and rose again (1 Cor. 15:1-4 cf. 2 Cor. 1:19). *Euangelizō* has this meaning 35 times in the New Testament (as documented in the next chapter). There is also a reference to the preaching of good news to the Israelites in the Old Testament who were of the wilderness generation but who refused to enter Canaan land by faith (Heb. 4:2, 6). There is good news announced to Paul by

---

[35] Myers, "The Gospel is More Than 'Faith Alone in Christ Alone'," 33.

[36] In two passages, the good news being proclaimed by John the Baptist (Luke 3:18) and the Lord Jesus (Luke 20:1) is unspecified.

Timothy of the Thessalonian congregations' continued faith and love after Paul had left Thessalonica (1 Thess. 3:6). There is good news proclaimed during the coming tribulation regarding God's impending righteous rule for the rest of eternity (Rev. 14:6). The term *euangelizō* is even used of the act of proclaiming a false form of the gospel that masquerades as "good news" (Gal. 1:9). It is transparently obvious that all of these uses of *euangelizō* do not represent one, monolithic "gospel" that we are to preach today or that the lost must believe for their eternal salvation. The term *euangelizō* is used of several different forms of good news in the New Testament.

Of the 56 occurrences of the word *euangelizō* in the New Testament, it is also used 4 times as an articular participle (Rom. 10:15; Gal. 1:11; 1 Peter 1:12, 25), and thus as a verbal part of speech rather than as a verb. In three of these cases, the articular participle functions adjectivally in the Greek sentence (Rom. 10:15; Gal. 1:11; 1 Peter 1:25) and once substantivally (1 Peter 1:12). In each instance, however, particular good news is being described rather than the proclaiming of good news in general. In addition, of the 56 occurrences of *euangelizō*, it is preceded in two places (Gal. 1:8; 1 Cor. 15:1) by the relative pronoun, *ho*, which functions as a descriptive modifier of particular good news in each context.

Although the four uses of *euangelizō* in articular participle form and the two cases of the relative pronoun do indicate a specific gospel message, the context of each passage must still determine the particular content of this good news. In some cases, the immediate context does not specify the contents in precise terms (1 Peter 1:12), in which case the contents must be deduced from the larger context. In other cases, the message is specified either by the immediate context (1 Cor. 15:1 cf. 1 Cor. 15:1-11) or by the intermediate context (Rom. 10:15 cf. Rom. 9:30-10:10) or by the intermediate context (Gal. 1:8, 11 cf. Gal. 1:1-4) in combination with the larger context of the entire epistle and the historical context (Acts 13; Galatians). The immediate context of 1 Peter 1:25 does not specify exactly what is included in the content of the gospel preached in that passage. It says, *"the word (to rhēma) which by the gospel was preached (to euangelisthen) to you (eis humas)."* In the context, the gospel or good news preached is stated to be part of the eternal and imperishable Word of God, and therefore the gospel or good news preached is also imperishable. But the content of this good news is not specified in the *immediate* context of verses 23-25, although a case could certainly be made that Christ's redeeming sacrifice and His resurrection are referred to in the *intermediate* context of verses 18-21.[37]

---

[37] Even though 1 Peter 1:18-19 does not use the word "gospel," this passage still bears indirect testimony in support of Christ's substitutionary death being essential to the contents of saving faith. Peter writes, *"knowing (eidotes) that you were not redeemed with corruptible things, like silver or gold, from your aimless conduct received by tradition from your fathers, but with the precious blood of Christ, as of a lamb without blemish and without spot."* The term "knowing" is the perfect, active, participle form of *oida*. In these verses, Peter assumes that his elect (1 Peter 1:2), regenerate (1 Peter 1:3) audience have all known about the sacrificial work of

What all of these details indicate is that even in its verb or verbal form, *euangelizō* can still refer to one specific, unalterable form of good news that is equivalent to the saving message. And this saving message is nothing less than the gospel of Christ. This particular form of good news will be clarified in the next chapter. Chapters 10-14 will also demonstrate in greater detail that this one, specific, unalterable "gospel of Christ" (Gal. 1:7-11) is no different from "the gospel" that Paul preached to the Corinthians (1 Cor. 1:17-2:2; 15:1-4).

With respect to the crossless gospel it must also be noted that the term *euangelizō* is *never used* in the New Testament to refer to the one specific message of eternal life as proclaimed by proponents of a crossless saving faith. The threefold *sine qua non* of the name of Jesus, believing, and eternal life is never stated anywhere in the New Testament to be "the gospel" (*euangelion*) or even "the preaching of good news" (*euangelizō*). Therefore, those who maintain that the redemptive work of Christ is not part of the required content of saving faith cannot justifiably use the term "gospel" to describe their saving message, which is a fact that some crossless proponents are now conceding.

By contrast, it must also be observed that *euangelizō* is used repeatedly in reference to Jesus as the Christ (Acts 5:42) in terms of His deity as sovereign Lord (Acts 10:36) and in terms of His crosswork (1 Cor. 1:17-21) and resurrection (Acts 17:18). It is even used for the combination of these elements—of the Lord Jesus' being the Christ who died for sin and rose again (1 Cor. 15:1-4). *Euangelizō* is also used in reference to proclaiming the good news of "peace" between the believing sinner and God (Eph. 2:17), which was provided by Christ's work on the cross (Eph. 2:15-16). All of these details are consistent with the conclusion that the preaching of the gospel includes Christ's person and work as the contents of saving faith in this dispensation.

Observations on *Euangelion*

When the 76 occurrences of the Greek noun *euangelion* are studied carefully, the same conclusions are reached as with the verb *euangelizō*. First, there does not exist even a single use of the term *euangelion* where its contents are stated to be the crossless gospel's three-part *sine qua non* that "*Jesus* guarantees *everlasting life* to all who simply *believe* in Him" for it.[38] This means that the saving message of the crossless position cannot be regarded as a genuinely *biblical* gospel.

Christ's death. If Peter subscribed to the crossless gospel position, his statement in verses 18-19 would be an unwarranted assumption. The only way that all believers could know about the redeeming work of the Lamb is if this is requisite to becoming a believer in Christ in the first place.

[38] Robert N. Wilkin, *Secure and Sure* (Irving, TX: Grace Evangelical Society, 2005), 74-75 (italics original).

Second, of the 76 occurrences of *euangelion* in the New Testament, all but 3 are preceded by the Greek article to specify a particular message of good news being preached and believed. This means that the writers of the New Testament had in mind a definitive message of good news when they penned each occurrence of *euangelion* in sacred Scripture. This also means that they assumed their first century readers knew the type of good news referred to by *euangelion* with the definite article. The phrase, "the gospel," could not possibly have been regarded as one expansive amalgamation of differing forms of good news that was ever-expanding as newer forms of "good news" were added with the writing of each successive book of the New Testament. How could anyone be sure that he or she had believed "the gospel" in a given year, such as A.D. 45, if "the gospel" was an entity that was continually evolving until at least A.D. 70?[39]

Though there are 3 anarthrous cases out of the 76 occurrences of *euangelion* in the New Testament, even these 3 instances are consistent with the specific nature of "the gospel." The first anarthrous use of *euangelion* occurs in Romans 1:1, where Paul says that he was *"separated to (the) gospel of God"* (*aphōrismenos eis euangelion theou*). The mere fact that *euangelion* is anarthrous here does not mean that an indefinite sense is intended, since the genitive *theou* is also anarthrous and yet it is clear from the passage that there is one, definite *theos* in mind (*not* "gospel of a God"). This provides a balanced construction, where semantically the monadic sense of *theou* also makes *euangelion* definite.[40] However, the anarthrous construction *euangelion theou* in Romans 1:1 is particularly arresting when compared to parallel passages using *"the gospel of God"* which, by contrast, all possess the article with *euangelion* (Mark 1:14 [CT]; Rom. 15:16; 2 Cor. 11:7; 1 Thess. 2:2, 8, 9; 1 Peter 4:17). The emphasis of the anarthrous construction, *"gospel of God,"* in Romans 1:1 then becomes the "God" aspect of the gospel, where Paul says in effect that he was set apart for *God's* gospel. In this case, the genitive *theou* becomes the "driving force" in the construction,[41] giving *euangelion* special emphasis or solemnity as *God's* gospel. Paul may have done this in Romans 1:1 to deliberately contrast his *euangelion* with the pagan *euangelia* ("gospels") of the 1st century which were associated with

---

[39] Bob Wilkin believes not only that the Gospel of John was written as early as A.D. 45 but also that the entire New Testament canon was complete by A.D. 70. See "The Bible Answer Men," a panel discussion at the Grace Evangelical Society Seattle Regional Conference, September 29, 2007.

[40] Thus, *euangelion theou* becomes semantically (though crudely) equivalent to saying, "the gospel of (the) God." This is an example of the corollary to the canon of Apollonius Dyscolus. See Nigel Turner, *Syntax*, Volume 3 of *A Grammar of New Testament Greek*, by J. H. Moulton, 4 vols. (Edinburgh: T & T Clark, 1963), 179-80; Daniel B. Wallace, *Greek Grammar Beyond the Basics: An Exegetical Syntax of the New Testament* (Grand Rapids: Zondervan, 1996), 250-53; Maximilian Zerwick, *Biblical Greek* (Rome: Editrice Pontificio Instituto Biblico, 1963), 59; Maximilian Zerwick and Mary Grosvenor, *A Grammatical Analysis of the Greek New Testament* (Rome: Editrice Pontificio Instituto Biblico, 1996), 457.

[41] Wallace, *Greek Grammar*, 251.

emperor worship, where good news was announced about an heir being born to a Roman emperor and of his accession to the throne.[42]

Paul may also be emphasizing in Romans 1:1 that this is not a gospel of his own devising or promotion but a gospel originating with God as its *source*, being a subjective genitive,[43] though some regard it is as being a plenary genitive functioning as both a subjective and objective genitive.[44] In this headline verse for the entire Epistle of Romans, there is no reason to regard *euangelion* in verse 1 as containing separate content from the gospel of Christ articulated elsewhere in the epistle. That is why in the immediately succeeding verses of Romans 1:2-4, the principal subject of this *"gospel of God"* is described as being God's Son, the Lord Jesus Christ. A little later in Romans 1, Paul goes on to describe the *"gospel of God"* as *"the gospel of His Son"* (Rom. 1:9) and *"the gospel of Christ"* (Rom. 1:16 [MT]). There are no grammatical, contextual, or linguistic factors in Romans 1 to indicate that these three occurrences of *euangelion* should be viewed as distinct from one another. This conclusion also harmonizes with Paul's only other use of *"the gospel of God"* in Romans 15:16, where in the immediate context, this expression is used interchangeably with *"the gospel of Christ"* (Rom. 15:19) that Paul preached to the Gentiles who had never heard the name of Christ before (Rom. 15:20).

Besides Romans 1:1, the only other anarthrous occurrences of *euangelion* are in Galatians 1:6 and Revelation 14:6. The Galatians 1:6 passage speaks of *"a different gospel,"* which is a false gospel according to the context, and thus it stands outside of our consideration of all divine forms of good news found in the New Testament. The remaining anarthrous passage, Revelation 14:6, refers to *"an everlasting gospel."* This is also referring to a specific and distinct form of good news from God, since it has a unique messenger, a unique message, and even a unique moment in which it is delivered. This lone reference to "an everlasting gospel" will be covered later in this chapter.

The fact that *euangelion* is nearly always referred to as a particular gospel through the use of the Greek article also corresponds with the fact that the word never occurs in the plural ("gospels") in the New Testament but always in the singular ("gospel"). As was explained earlier, this does not mean that there is only one homogenous, multifaceted "gospel" in the

---

[42] C. E. B. Cranfield, *A Critical and Exegetical Commentary on the Epistle to the Romans*, ICC (Edinburgh: T & T Clark, 1975), 1:55.

[43] Cranfield, *A Critical and Exegetical Commentary on the Epistle to the Romans*, 55n1; James D. G. Dunn, *Romans 1-8*, WBC (n.p.: Nelson Reference & Electronic, 1988), 10; Douglas J. Moo, *The Epistle to the Romans*, NICNT (Grand Rapids: Eerdmans, 1996), 43n18; Leon Morris, *The Epistle to the Romans*, PNTC (Grand Rapids: Eerdmans, 1988), 40; idem, "The Theme of Romans," in *Apostolic History and the Gospel*, ed. W. Ward Gasque and Ralph P. Martin (Grand Rapids: Eerdmans, 1970), 259; Turner, *Syntax*, 211.

[44] Ulrich Becker, *"εὐαγγέλιον," NIDNTT*, 2:111; Thomas R. Schreiner, *Romans*, BECNT (Grand Rapids: Baker Academic, 1998), 37; Wallace, *Greek Grammar*, 121.

New Testament, anymore than it means that there is only one "Herod" or one "coming" of Christ or one "salvation."[45] Rather, this fact most likely indicates that only one form of good news predominates in each respective dispensation. For instance, the gospel message of Christ's death and resurrection was not operative within God's dispensational program of Law for Israel, so that it was not instituted or preached concurrently with the gospel of the kingdom during the ministry of John the Baptist or early in the Lord's earthly ministry.[46] Conversely, the good news of the kingdom being at hand is not the message that the Church has been commissioned to proclaim simultaneous with the gospel of Christ. Even the everlasting gospel of Revelation 14:6 was not admixed with the gospel of the kingdom that was proclaimed during the pre-cross time period recorded in the Gospels, nor has it been subsequently combined with the gospel of Christ in the Church age according to Acts and the Epistles. The burden of the everlasting gospel is reserved for those living in that very specific period of time known as the tribulation, between the Church and the millennial kingdom.

Despite the particularity with which the term *euangelion* is used in the New Testament, the term is also modified by several descriptive words and phrases that clarify the particular gospel being referred to in each context. These additional words or phrases even clarify the character and content of each respective gospel. All of the different modifying words or phrases that occur with *euangelion* are provided below.

"gospel" (38x) – Most frequently *euangelion* occurs absolutely. Some of these 38 occurrences are references to the gospel of the kingdom in their contexts but most are in reference to the gospel of Christ. Matt. 26:13; Mark 1:15; 8:35; 10:29; 13:10; 14:9; 16:15; Acts 15:7; Rom. 10:16; 11:28; 1 Cor. 4:15; 9:14, 18 (2x [CT], 1x [MT]), 23; 15:1; 2 Cor. 4:3; 8:18; Gal. 1:11; 2:2, 5, 7, 14; Eph. 3:6; 6:19; Phil. 1:5, 7, 12, 16 [CT]/17 [MT]; 2:22; 4:3, 15; Col. 1:5, 23; 1 Thess. 2:4; 2 Tim. 1:8, 10; Philem. 1:13

---

[45] The Bible does not speak of "salvations," as the noun *sōtēria* invariably occurs in the singular in the New Testament ("salvation"), and yet it is evident from the various contexts in which the terms *sōtēria* and *sōzō* are used that there is more than one form of salvation or deliverance.

[46] The references to "the gospel" in relation to Mary of Bethany's anointing of Christ's body before His death (Matt. 26:13; Mark 14:9) will be discussed in chapter 15 under the section on Mark 16:15-16 and the Great Commission. The gospel in Matthew 26:13 and Mark 14:9 is not in reference to the gospel of the kingdom, as Ryrie states, "All of Matthew's references to the Gospel concern this good news about the kingdom except one, Matthew 26:13. There the Lord said that wherever the good news about His death was preached, Mary Magdalene's good deed of anointing Him in anticipation of that death would be known." Charles C. Ryrie, *So Great Salvation: What It Means to Believe in Jesus Christ* (Wheaton, IL: Victor Books, 1989), 38-39.

"gospel of God" (8x) – Mark 1:14 [CT]; Rom. 1:1; 15:16; 2 Cor. 11:7; 1 Thess. 2:2, 8, 9; 1 Peter 4:17

"gospel of Christ" (11x) – Rom. 1:16 [MT]; 15:19, 29 [MT]; 1 Cor. 9:12, 18 [MT]; 2 Cor. 2:12; 9:13; 10:14; Gal. 1:7; Phil. 1:27; 1 Thess. 3:2

"gospel of our Lord Jesus Christ" (1x) – 2 Thess. 1:8

"gospel of Jesus Christ, the Son of God" (1x) – Mark 1:1

"gospel of His Son" (1x) – Rom. 1:9

"my gospel" (3x) – Rom. 2:16; 16:25; 2 Tim. 2:8

"our gospel" (3x) – 2 Cor. 4:3; 1 Thess. 1:5; 2 Thess. 2:14

"gospel of the grace of God" (1x) – Acts 20:24

"gospel of peace" (2x) – Rom. 10:15 [MT]; Eph. 6:15

"gospel of your salvation" (1x) – Eph. 1:13

"gospel of the glory" (2x) – 2 Cor. 4:4; 1 Tim. 1:11

"gospel of the kingdom" (4x) – Matt. 4:23; 9:35; 24:14; Mark 1:14

"everlasting gospel" (1x) – Rev. 14:6

"a different gospel"/"any other gospel" (4x) – 2 Cor. 11:4; Gal. 1:6, 8-9

The Gospel of the Kingdom

In the New Testament, the Greek words *euangelion* and *euangelizō* are used approximately 14 times in reference to the gospel of the kingdom according to their contexts (Matt. 4:23; 9:35; 11:5; 24:14; Mark 1:14-15; 13:10; Luke 4:18, 43; 7:22; 8:1; 9:6; 16:16; Acts 10:36). This is the good news that God will set up a literal, physical, earthly kingdom in fulfillment of the promised Davidic Covenant (2 Sam. 7) and many other Old Testament promises to the nation of Israel. This good news of the kingdom was preached by John the Baptist and the Lord Jesus as being *"at hand"* (Matt. 3:2; 4:17, 23; Mark 1:14-15; Luke 3:18; 4:43; 10:9-11; etc.). During the earthly life of the Lord Jesus a legitimate, *bona fide* offer of the kingdom was made to Israel, and in this sense it was imminent or "at hand" during their lifetime. However, since the King of that kingdom was rejected by the nation, the kingdom offer was suspended in the sovereign counsels of God until after the Church age.

Of all the uses of *euangelion* and *euangelizō*, this form of good news is conspicuously never preached or required to be believed during the Church age. However, Matthew 24:14 and Mark 13:10 state that the gospel of the kingdom will be preached once again during the tribulation after the Church has been raptured. During those seven years of tribulation, the establishment of Christ's kingdom on earth will be considered so near and so certain from the viewpoint of prophetic anticipation that believers will begin proclaiming it again. While there does exist a present form of the kingdom of God in this Church age (Acts 20:25; Rom. 14:17; 1 Cor. 4:20; Col. 1:13; 4:11), this is not the same as the kingdom of heaven coming to earth (Matt. 6:10) in the form of the establishment of Christ's righteous rule and reign over the whole earth in the millennium. Good news concerning the coming kingdom is not synonymous with "the gospel of Christ" or "the gospel of the grace of God" that the Church is to preach today.[47]

It should also be qualified that although the gospel of the kingdom will be preached again in the tribulation, technically Matthew 24:14 and Mark 13:10 do not say it will be preached as being *"at hand"* (*eggus; eggizō*), as it was preached earlier by John the Baptist and the Lord Jesus. The difference is that in their day, the kingdom could have been established at any moment contingent upon Israel's repentance and acceptance of Christ, whereas in the tribulation, there will be seven years of predicted judgment which must occur before the establishment of Christ's kingdom can take place. Though the kingdom will be near and certain from the standpoint of those living within the tribulation, the establishment of the kingdom will not technically be *"at hand"* or imminent. This is in contrast to the doctrine of the rapture. Regarding the rapture of the Church and subsequent judgment of God upon the world, a correct understanding of imminency leads to the conclusion that the rapture could occur at any moment throughout this Church age since it is also said to be *"at hand"* (Rom. 13:12; Phil. 4:5; James 5:8; 1 Peter 4:7; Rev. 22:10).

At this point, one potential misunderstanding regarding the gospel of the kingdom must also be clarified. Some may object that in at least one passage, Acts 8:12, the verb *euangelizō* appears to equate the preaching of the kingdom with the preaching of Christ's name. It says, *"But when they believed Philip as he preached (euangelizō) the things concerning the kingdom of God and the name of Jesus Christ, both men and women were baptized."* If the "name" of the Lord stands for both His person and work, and it is used in Acts and the Epistles interchangeably with the saving message of the gospel of Christ, then some might object that the example of Philip's gospel preaching in Acts 8:12 contradicts this conclusion. They might claim that this verse shows that the good news of the kingdom is part of the gospel of Christ which we proclaim to the lost today.

Two points should be noted about the content of Philip's preaching to the Samaritans in Acts 8:12. First, this verse is not teaching that the truths

---

[47] Helmut Koester, "From the Kerygma-Gospel to Written Gospels," *NTS* 35 (1989): 368.

about "the kingdom" and "the name of Jesus Christ" are both part of one message called "the gospel." According to the grammatical construction of this verse, Philip preached good news about two separate subjects, "the kingdom" and "the name of Jesus Christ." The phrases "the kingdom" (*tēs basileias*) and "the name of Jesus Christ" (*tou onomatos Iēsou Christou*) are preceded by two separate articles of different cases in Greek, though they are joined by the coordinating conjunction *kai* ("and"). This means that they do not meet the grammatical qualifications for the syntactical TSKS construction where the two subjects, "kingdom" and "name," are to be regarded as equivalent or inseparably connected.[48] This means that preaching good news about "the kingdom" is not the same as preaching "the name of Jesus Christ."

Secondly, in Acts 8:12 we simply do not know what Philip's kingdom preaching to the Samaritans entailed. Quite possibly he explained to them how the promise of a literal, earthly, *Jewish* kingdom fit in relation to Christ's first coming and where they, as Samaritans, fit in relation to this kingdom program of God. This would have been similar to the Lord Jesus' instruction to the apostles in Acts 1:3-7 and Paul's instruction to the Jews in Acts 28:23, 31, which clearly went beyond the preaching of good news about Christ's saving death and resurrection. It is also possible that in Acts 8:12 Philip could have explained how they, as Samaritans, now had a place in the *present* form of God's kingdom (Acts 19:8; 20:25; Col. 1:13). Regardless, the singular reference to the kingdom as the object of *euangelizō* in Acts 8:12 should not be taken to mean that Philip was preaching the same message of *"the gospel of the kingdom"* (*to euangelion tēs basileias*) that John the Baptist and the Lord Jesus preached prior to Calvary (Matt. 4:23; 9:35; 24:14; Mark 1:14).

The Everlasting Gospel

In Revelation 14:6 there is a unique usage of the term *euangelion* where it refers to *"an everlasting gospel."* It says in Revelation 14:6-7, *"Then I saw another angel flying in the midst of heaven, having the everlasting gospel to preach to those who dwell on the earth—to every nation, tribe, tongue, and people—7 saying with a loud voice, "Fear God and give glory to Him, for the hour of His judgment has come; and worship Him who made heaven and earth, the sea and springs of water."* Some proponents of a crossless saving faith may wish to co-opt the reference to an *"everlasting gospel"* in Revelation 14:6 and use it to support their doctrine that the saving message is transdispensational, eternal, and never changes with the progress of revelation. However, to do so would be to completely ignore the context and uniqueness of the term "gospel" as it is used in Revelation 14:6. John Walvoord, the late 20th

[48] Wallace, *Greek Grammar*, 270-90.

century dean of dispensational, premillennial eschatology, noted in his commentary on this passage that the term "gospel" here is not in reference to the gospel of salvation. Commenting on the *"everlasting gospel"* in Revelation 14:6, he stated:

> Ordinarily, one would expect this to refer to the gospel of salvation. In verse 7, however, the content of the message is quite otherwise, for it is an announcement of the hour of judgment of God and the command to worship Him.
>
> Some expositors use the term "gospel" to include all the revelation God has given in Christ and hence conclude that there is only one gospel with various phases of truth belonging to this gospel. There are others who prefer to distinguish various messages in the Bible as gospel or "good news" even though they contain only one aspect of divine revelation, hence, the expression "gospel of grace," referring to the goodness of grace, or to the gospel of the kingdom, dealing with the good news that God at last is about to deal with the world in righteousness and establish His sovereignty over the world. This is an ageless gospel in the sense that God's righteousness is ageless. Throughout eternity God will continue to manifest Himself in grace toward the saints and in punishment toward the wicked. *To refer to the gospel of grace as an everlasting gospel is to ignore the context and usage of the term.*[49]

In Revelation 14:6, the noun *euangelion* occurs once, "having an everlasting gospel (*euangelion*)"; and the verb *euangelizō* occurs once in the aorist, infinitive form, "to preach (*euangelisai*)." This everlasting form of "good news" is actually perceived as *bad news* by unbelieving and disobedient earth-dwellers, but it is truly good news from the standpoint of heaven. And it is good news to surviving believers during the great tribulation that God is about to establish His righteous rule upon the earth. It is an *eternal or everlasting* form of good news, not necessarily because of the reference to the Creator-creature relationship mentioned in verse 7, but in the sense that, when *"the hour of His judgment has come"* (Rev. 14:7), the corresponding result will be the permanent establishment of God's righteous rule upon the earth. When *"the hour of His judgment has come,"* this will coincide with the coming of His kingdom and the long awaited, desired establishment of God's will prevailing on earth even as it does in heaven (Matt. 6:10). The effects will be permanent and irreversible from that time forward. Once the kingdom is established, it will never cease. It will be everlasting (Isa. 9:7; Dan. 2:44; 7:18; Luke 1:33). It is in this sense that the "everlasting gospel" is a message of good news (*euangelion*) that is proclaimed as good news (*euangelizō*). Earth's citizens will be expected to fear God, give Him

---

[49] John F. Walvoord, *The Revelation of Jesus Christ* (Chicago: Moody Press, 1966), 217 (italics added).

glory, and worship Him (Rev. 14:7) in light of the establishment of His sovereign, righteous rule that will shortly take place. Though God's commands to fear Him, glorify Him, and worship Him have always existed prior to the preaching of this gospel, the "everlasting" (*aiōnion*) aspect of this announcement must be contextually determined by the phrase, *"for the hour of His judgment has come"* (Rev. 14:7).

The prophet Daniel wrote specifically about this transitional moment in history. It will be an hour when Satan's rule over the world through the Antichrist in the tribulation will end and when Christ's rule, along with His saints, will be established for all eternity in an everlasting kingdom of righteousness. We see this transition prophesied in Daniel 7:25-27:

Daniel 7:25-27

25 *He shall speak pompous words against the Most High, shall persecute the saints of the Most High, and shall intend to change times and law. Then the saints shall be given into his hand for a time and times and half a time.*
26 *But the court shall be seated, and they shall take away his dominion, to consume and destroy it* ***forever.***
27 *Then the kingdom and dominion, and the greatness of the kingdoms under the whole heaven, shall be given to the people, the saints of the Most High. His kingdom is an* ***everlasting kingdom,*** *and all dominions shall serve and obey Him.*

Though the "everlasting gospel" is closely related to the message of the kingdom, it should not be confused with the gospel of the kingdom. It constitutes a distinctive form of "good news" within the plan of God for human history. This *"everlasting gospel"* in Revelation 14:6 is referred to only one time in all of Scripture. It is completely unique and distinct. It has a unique *message, messenger,* and *moment.* It has a unique messenger in the sense that it is not a message preached by mankind, nor even by all the angels, but by one particular angel (14:6, *"another angel,"* singular). This everlasting gospel also has a unique *moment* in which it will be preached. Chronologically within the tribulation, it falls within the latter half of the tribulation, technically known as the great tribulation. To be even more specific, this everlasting gospel is preached by the angelic herald (Rev. 14:6) sometime in conjunction with the sounding of the seventh trumpet judgment (Rev. 11:15) and the pouring out of the first bowl judgment (Rev. 15:1). With the sounding of the seventh trumpet, heavenly voices will utter a message very consistent with the angel's everlasting gospel, *"The kingdom of this world has become the kingdom of our Lord and of His Christ, and He shall reign forever and ever!"* (Rev. 11:15). Because of the unique message, messenger, and moment of this everlasting gospel, this form of "good news" should not be regarded as the gospel that the Church is to be preaching to the lost today. The champion of grace-teaching and famous dispensationalist of the past, C. I. Scofield, also noted that this gospel "is neither the Gospel of the kingdom, nor of grace.

Though its burden is judgment, not salvation, it is good news to Israel and to those who, during the tribulation, have been saved."[50]

Euangelion in the Gospel Titles

This leads to another possible category of usage for the term *euangelion* in the New Testament and one that is entirely distinct from the everlasting gospel, the gospel of the kingdom, or the gospel of the grace of God in Christ. It is the four occurrences of *euangelion* in the titles of Matthew, Mark, Luke, and John. The usage of *euangelion* in the titles of the four Gospels is rarely discussed because of the complexity and technical nature of the manuscript data and because of the cloud of skepticism surrounding the authenticity of these titles. Nevertheless, this subject will be covered here for the sake of completeness in this survey of every occurrence of *euangelion* and *euangelizō* in the New Testament.

There are four more potential uses of *euangelion* in the New Testament if we factor in the titles of the four canonical Gospels that appear in the Greek manuscripts as either superscriptions (titles at the beginning of each Gospel) or as subscriptions (titles at the end of each Gospel). Since the exhaustive listing earlier in this chapter of all 76 occurrences of *euangelion* in the Greek New Testament was based only on printed *editions* of the Majority and Critical Texts, rather than individual Greek *manuscripts*, there are possibly four more occurrences of *euangelion* if we factor in the Gospel titles found in the vast majority of early and late Greek manuscripts.

Before considering the exact form of these titles, along with the meaning and significance that they bear upon the question of the identification of "the gospel" and the contents of saving faith, the evidence for the authenticity of these titles must be weighed. Do the extant manuscripts support the conclusion that these titles are part of the original, inspired autographs? Or, should these titles be regarded as later scribal additions, as most textual critics currently regard them? The evidence for their authenticity is surprisingly strong and is provided below.

The External Evidence for Euangelion in the Gospel Titles

The longer title in Matthew, *EUANGELION KATA MATTHAION* is supported by one papyrus manuscript, $\mathfrak{P}^{4}$ (3rd) or $\mathfrak{P}^{62}$ (4th),[51] the early uncials W (4th-

[50] *The Scofield Reference Bible*, ed. C. I. Scofield (Oxford: Oxford University Press, 1909), 1343.

[51] There is some confusion regarding the classification of this papyrus fragment containing the title for Matthew's Gospel. The $\mathfrak{P}^{4/64/67}$ manuscripts are grouped together because they are thought by many to belong to the same scribal hand and were once part of the same codex. See *The Text of the Earliest New Testament Greek Manuscripts*, ed. Philip W. Comfort and David P. Barrett (Wheaton, IL: Tyndale House Publishers, 2001), 53-54; S. D. Charlesworth, "T. C. Skeat, $\mathfrak{P}^{64+67}$ and $\mathfrak{P}^{4}$, and the Problem of Fibre Orientation in Codicological

5th cent.),[52] C (5th), D (5th),[53] and many later uncials of the 6th-9th centuries with some minor variations among them. The inclusion of *euangelion* in Matthew's title is also supported by the mass of minuscules[54] (though with some additions among them[55]), including 33 ("the Queen of the minuscules") which is considered to reflect a very early exemplar and normally Alexandrian text-type. The omission of *euangelion* in Matthew's title is supported only by the uncials א (4th) and B (4th), which simply have the short form for a Gospel title, *kata matthaion,*[56] along with the single Syriac Curetonian manuscript.

The longer title in Mark, *EUANGELION KATA MAPKON* is supported by the early uncials W (4th-5th), A (5th), D (5th), and many later uncials of the 6th-9th centuries. It is also supported by the host of minuscules, again including 33, but also 2427, which the Alands rate as a "Category I" wit-

---

Reconstruction," *NTS* 53 (2007): 582-604; Peter M. Head, "Is P4, P64 and P67 the Oldest Manuscript of the Four Gospels? A Response to T. C. Skeat," *NTS* 51 (2005): 450-57; T. C. Skeat, "The Oldest Manuscript of the Four Gospels?" *NTS* 43 (1997): 1-34; Graham N. Stanton, "The Fourfold Gospel," *NTS* 43 (1997): 327-29, 333n54. The brief papyrus fragment containing the title to Matthew is thought by some papyrologists and textual scholars to have been the title page to the 𝔓4/64/67 group. Thus some sources designate this fragment containing Matthew's title as 𝔓4. But according to the Institute for New Testament Textual Research in Münster, Germany, the writing of this title more closely aligns with the scribal hand of 𝔓62 (4th). Thus, this fragment is variously assigned by different sources to either 𝔓4 or 𝔓62.

[52] Codex Freerianus (Washingtonensis) has a variant spelling for "Matthew," MAΘΘAION rather than MATΘAION (NA27, 1).

[53] Codex Bezae also contains the variant spelling for "Matthew," MAΘΘAION rather than MATΘAION. The manuscript is also lacking the title and opening verses to Matthew's Gospel (Frederick H. Scrivener, *Bezae Codex Cantabrigiensis* [Reprint; Eugene, OR: Wipf and Stock Publishers, n.d.], 1), but since it does contain the subscription *euangelion kata maththaion* (ibid. 95), as well as this longer form of superscription and subscription for each of the other Gospels (ibid. 95, 159, 262-63) with the exception of Mark's ending at Mark 16:15, it is highly probable that Bezae originally contained the longer title for Matthew as a superscription.

[54] I recognize that this is at best a generalized claim, since no one has yet to critically collate the readings of all 3,000 plus minuscule mss., including even Von Soden himself. Nevertheless, the citation from the apparatus of NA27 upon which the claim above is made is still based on a representative sampling of the mass of minuscules.

[55] The article *to* as well as the adjective *hagion* (*to hagion euangelion kata matthaion*) were added to the titles of the four Gospels in many later Greek uncial and minuscule manuscripts. Bruce M. Metzger, *Manuscripts of the Greek Bible: An Introduction to Greek Palaeography* (Oxford: Oxford University Press, 1981), 40; A. T. Robertson, *Word Pictures in the New Testament* (Grand Rapids: Baker Book House, n.d.), 1:xiv; Samuel P. Tregelles, *An Introduction to the Textual Criticism of the New Testament* (London: Longmans, Green, and Co., 1856), 410; B. F. Westcott, *The Gospel According to St. John* (Grand Rapids: Eerdmans, 1967), 1.

[56] Even the shorter titles of Matthew, Mark, Luke, and John in codices Sinaiticus and Vaticanus are considered by most textual critics today to be scribal additions by a later second hand (*sed secunda manu*). See the *variae lectiones minores* in NA27, 719, 721, 727, 732; David Trobisch, *The First Edition of the New Testament* (Oxford: Oxford University Press, 2000), 126n142. But some believe that the superscriptions and subscriptions of Sinaiticus were written by the same two scribes who completed its main text. See H. J. M. Milne and T. C. Skeat, *Scribes and Correctors of the Codex Sinaiticus* (London: British Museum, 1938), 18-29.

ness normally reflecting an Alexandrian text-type.[57] As with Matthew, *euangelion* in Mark's title is omitted only by the uncials א (4th) and B (4th) and a few minuscules.

The longer title in Luke, *EUANGELION KATA LOUKAN* is supported by one papyrus manuscript, $\mathfrak{P}^{75}$ (early 3rd cent.),[58] by the early uncials W (4th-5th), A (5th), D (5th), Ξ (6th), and many later uncials of the 7th-9th centuries, as well as most minuscules, again including 33. The shorter reading of *kata loukan* in Luke's title is supported only by the uncials א (4th), B (4th), and a few minuscules.

The longer title in John, *EUANGELION KATA IOANNĒN* is supported by two very early papyri, $\mathfrak{P}^{66}$ (circa A.D. 200) and $\mathfrak{P}^{75}$ (early 3rd cent.),[59] which normally correspond to an Alexandrian text-type. Besides the two papyrus manuscripts supporting *euangelion* in John's title,[60] the longer reading is also supported by early uncials W (4th-5th), A (5th),[61] C (5th), D (5th), and many later uncials of the 6th-9th centuries, as well as the host of minuscules, again including 33. *Euangelion* in John's title is omitted only by the uncials א (4th) and B (4th) and the single Syriac Curetonian manuscript.

When it comes to the patristic testimony for the titles of the four Gospels, the evidence for the inclusion of *euangelion* as the original reading is also seen to be early, uniform, and convincing. The inclusion of *euangelion* is supported by Irenaeus[62] (2nd), Justin Martyr[63] (2nd), the Muratorian

---

[57] Kurt Aland and Barbara Aland, *The Text of the New Testament: An Introduction to the Critical Editions and to the Theory and Practice of Modern Textual Criticism*, trans. Erroll F. Rhodes, 2nd Edition (Grand Rapids: Eerdmans, 1989), 137, 162.

[58] This reading in $\mathfrak{P}^{75}$ occurs as a subscription at the end of Luke and before the superscription of John. *The Text of the Earliest New Testament Greek Manuscripts*, ed. Philip W. Comfort and David P. Barrett (Wheaton, IL: Tyndale House Publishers, 2001), 567.

[59] $\mathfrak{P}^{75}$ shares the variant spelling of Codex Vaticanus in the title for "John." It reads *Iōanēn* rather than *Iōannēn*.

[60] Though John has two papyri attesting to *euangelion* in its title, and Matthew and Luke each have only one, it should be kept in mind that the more than 100 extant papyri are quite fragmentary and spotty. Each contains only a relatively small portion of the New Testament. Only the four papyri cited above contain the beginning or ending to any of the four Gospels, and thus the remaining papyri are simply unavailable as witnesses either for or against the inclusion of *euangelion* in the Gospel titles.

[61] Codex Alexandrinus has *euangelion kata Iōannēn* for the title as a subscription at the end of John (NA^{27}, 732).

[62] In his *Adversus haereses*, Irenaeus varies from the early Greek papyri and uncials by normally using the article, *tō kata Matthaion euangeliō* (3.11.7) and *to . . . kata Loukan euangelion* (3.12.12), though he does use *euangelion* anarthrously (3.1.1) saying that Matthew "published a writing of Gospel" (*graphēn exēnegken euangeliou*). For a fuller treatment of every occurrence of *euangelion* in *Adversus haereses*, see Annette Yoshiko Reed, "ΕΥΑΓΓΕΛΙΟΝ: Orality, Textuality, and the Christian Truth in Irenaeus' *Adversus Haereses*," *VC* 56 (2002): 11-46.

[63] Martin Hengel, *The Four Gospels and the One Gospel of Jesus Christ* (Harrisburg, PA: Trinity Press International, 2000), 248n247.

Fragment[64] (circa A.D. 200[65]), and Clement of Alexandria[66] (late 2nd to early 3rd). The short form for the Gospel titles (*kata matthaion*, etc.) has no patristic support.

Finally, the inclusion of *euangelion* in the titles of the four Gospels also finds general support among the language versions. The versions serve the same text-critical role for titles as they do for the rest of the New Testament text by helping to establish the age of a particular reading as well as its geographical diversity. As a general rule, the older and more diverse a particular reading is, the more likely it is to be original. It should also be kept in mind that though the versional witnesses substantially agree in including *euangelion* in the titles of the four Gospels, certain languages are limited as witnesses to the original Greek text since no two languages correspond with one another exactly. For instance, Latin cannot tell us whether the original title was *to euangelion kata matthaion* or simply *euangelion kata matthaion* since Latin lacks the definite article.[67] Even Coptic's use of the article does not precisely reflect its usage in Greek.[68] The presence or absence of the article with *euangelion* will become a factor later when considering the original form of the Gospel titles as well as their meaning and significance for the contents of saving faith.

Among the language versions that the Greek New Testament was translated into, three are regarded as primary witnesses to the original text: Coptic, Syriac, and Latin. The New Testament was translated into other languages following these three, and often not directly from the Greek text, and thus the testimony of these later language versions is not deemed to be as valuable. But regarding the testimony of the first principal language version, Coptic, one of its two dialectic versions, the Coptic Bohairic, has the longer, anarthrous form for all four Gospel titles, *euangelion kata maththaion, etc.*,[69] and it also contains *euangelion* within the lengthier and more embellished subscriptions to each Gospel.[70] The testimony of the Coptic Sahidic version also firmly supports the inclusion of *euangelion* in the titles but has a mixed testimony with respect to *euangelion* being anarthrous or articular.[71]

---

[64] Geoffrey Mark Hahneman, *The Muratorian Fragment and the Development of the Canon* (Oxford: Oxford University Press, 1992), 6; Graham N. Stanton, "The Fourfold Gospel," *NTS* 43 (1997): 323.

[65] Some scholars such as Hahneman reject this traditional dating and argue that the Muratorian Fragment dates as late as the 4th century (Hahneman, *The Muratorian Fragment*, 215-18).

[66] Clement's use of *euangelion* is preserved only in Eusebius, *Ecclesiastical History*, 6.14.5-7.

[67] Bruce M. Metzger, *The Early Versions of the New Testatment: Their Origin, Transmission, and Limitations* (Oxford: Oxford University Press, 1977), 366.

[68] Ibid., 148.

[69] George W. Horner, *The Coptic Version of the New Testament in the Northern Dialect, otherwise called Memphitic and Bohairic*, 4 vols. (Oxford: Clarendon Press, 1898-1905), 1:2, 282; 2:2, 332.

[70] Ibid., 1:278, 480; 2:328, 580.

[71] The titles in Coptic Sahidic are somewhat varied, with the superscription of

The Vulgate of Syriac, the Peshitta, represents hundreds of Syriac manuscripts of the New Testament that have been preserved. The Syriac Peshitta also contains the longer titles for the four Gospels, "Gospel Acccording to Matthew, Mark, etc.,"[72] and in many manuscripts the word "Gospel" in the titles is indefinite rather than articular.[73] The Old Syriac form, which likely predates the Peshitta, is represented by just two extant manuscripts, the Curetonian and Sinaitic manuscripts, which have a mixed testimony. In the Syriac Curetonian manuscript the beginnings of Mark and Luke have not been preserved, nor have any of the endings to the four Gospels. The portions that do exist for the titles of Matthew and John reflect the shorter reading as found in Codex Vaticanus and Codex Sinaiticus.[74] The Syriac Sinaitic manuscript is likewise badly damaged, but it has preserved the ending of Mark and the beginning of Luke. The longer reading containing the word "Gospel" is found in this manuscript in both Mark's subscription and Luke's superscription.[75]

The witness of the Latin language is based upon the Old Latin manuscripts and the Latin Vulgate, and these sources also generally support the inclusion of *euangelion* in the four Gospel titles. The Old Latin is technically not a single version but a collection of some 30 manuscripts in Latin from both European and North African ancestry that reveal the textual complexity of the New Testament in Latin prior to Jerome's Vulgate.[76] These Old Latin manuscripts have a mixed testimony, with some containing the Gospel titles in the short form and some in the longer form.[77] However, the vast majority of Latin Vulgate manuscripts do contain the reading *evangelium* in the titles.[78]

Matthew reading simply "Matthew" and the subscription, containing the articular *euangelion*, "The Gospel According to Matthew." George W. Horner, *The Coptic Version of the New Testament in the Southern Dialect, otherwise called Sahidic and Thebaic*, 7 vols. (Oxford: Clarendon Press, 1911-24), 1:1, 352. The titles to Mark read, "The Gospel According to Mark" for the superscription (ibid., 1:354) and "According to Mark" for the subscription (ibid., 1:648). Luke reads, "Gospel According to Luke" for the superscription (ibid., 2:1) and "The Gospel According to Luke" for the subscription (ibid., 2:478). John has "Gospel According to John" for the superscription (ibid., 3:1) and no subscription at all (ibid., 3:336).

[72] P. E. Pusey and G. H. Gwilliam, *Tetraeuangelium Sanctum: juxta simpliceum Syrorum versionem* (Oxford: Clarendon Press, 1901), 24, 198, 318, 482.

[73] B. F. Westcott, *The Gospel According to St. John* (Grand Rapids: Eerdmans, 1967), 1.

[74] Constantin Tischendorf, *Novum Testamentum Graece* (Leipzig: J. C. Hinrichs, 1872), 1:1, 739.

[75] R. L. Bensley, J. R. Harris, and F. C. Burkitt, *The Four Gospels in Syriac: Transcribed from the Sinaitic Palimpsest* (Piscataway, NJ: Georgias Press, 2005), 45-46.

[76] Philip Burton, *The Old Latin Gospels: A Study of their Texts and Language* (Oxford: Oxford University Press, 2000), 3-4.

[77] Tischendorf, *Novum Testamentum Graece*, 1:1, 214, 411, 739; John Wenham, *Redating Matthew, Mark, and Luke: A Fresh Assault on the Synoptic Problem* (Downers Grove, IL: InterVarsity Press, 1992), 134.

[78] Ibid., Tischendorf.

The Marks of Authenticity

When each category of witness to the original Gospel titles is heard, the evidence for the inclusion and authenticity of *euangelion* in the four titles is surprisingly strong. Whether it is the papyri, the uncials, the minuscules, the versions, or the writings of early Christendom, they overwhelmingly include *euangelion* in the Gospel titles, whether as a superscription or subscription. The reading of *euangelion* among the Gospel titles can even be said to possess an "original character,"[79] not only because it is pervasive among every category of witness for the first five centuries but also because of the remarkable degree of uniformity that exists among the papyri and uncials as the earliest Greek witnesses and the relatively high degree of consistency among the versions. This fact seems inexplicable if the titles are not original. Incredibly, however, some scholars view such early uniformity as an indication of inauthenticity! Metzger, for example, declares, "Since the writings of the four Evangelists have one and the same title (εὐαγγέλιον), this general title probably was added to the four by the same person."[80] Trobisch also expresses his doubts and suspicions. On the one hand, he admits that when "Examining the titles of the New Testament writings, one of the first observations is that they are transmitted with few variants."[81] On the other hand, he demurs, "The possibility that the titles were independently formulated this way by the authors of the Gospels may be safely ruled out. It would be too much of a coincidence for two independently working publishers to have decided on the same unusual genre designation, the same authorial source, and *kata* as the syntactical connector."[82] But is this really so improbable? Admittedly, from a strictly human perspective, the odds of all four Gospel writers using the exact same form of superscription seems unusually high. But the Gospels are unusual books in one respect. To deny the possibility that Matthew, Mark, Luke, and John could all arrive at the same titular form independently is to discount the unique quality of divine inspiration that each book possesses (2 Tim. 3:16) as well as the superintending ministry of the Holy Spirit that guided the process of production (2 Peter 1:20-21).

We must also ask, if the four Gospel titles are not original, then what can possibly account for the phenomenon of their remarkable age and uniformity? What is the alternative to supernatural unity? Trobisch theorizes that it must be the result of an extremely early redaction in Church history, whereby the entire New Testament was edited and assembled into

[79] Hengel, *The Four Gospels*, 54.

[80] Bruce M. Metzger, *The Canon of the New Testament: Its Origin, Development, and Significance* (Oxford: Oxford University Press, 1987), 302.

[81] David Trobisch, *The First Edition of the New Testament* (Oxford: Oxford University Press, 2000), 38.

[82] Ibid.

a "Canonical Edition." However, we are never presented with any traces of positive, verifiable evidence as to *who* performed this sweeping task, *where* it happened, or even *when* exactly it took place.[83] In modern Da Vinci Code fashion, we are led to believe this is a scandalous secret shrouded in the vagaries of antiquity. In fact, there exists no historical evidence for such a stupendous literary feat. Trobisch's bold thesis is based upon critical speculation and one supposition built on top of another.[84]

It is also worth considering for a moment the prospect that the Gospels possessed no titles at all in the original autographs, as Trobisch, Metzger, and many other contemporary textual critics believe. In such a case, how would we realistically account for the uniform inclusion of *euangelion kata matthaion, euangelion kata markon,* etc. among the earliest witnesses? Supposing that such a comprehensive redaction occurred in the latter 1st century or even early 2nd century, then we must reckon with the glaring fact that no centralized ecclesiastical hierarchy existed in the first few centuries that would have possessed the authority or ability to mandate conformity to the new standard form of Gospel title for all future copying of the canonical Gospels. In addition, the reality that the earliest language versions of Coptic, Syriac, and Latin possess a relatively small degree of variation among their titles, while still witnessing predominantly to the inclusion of *euangelion,* is a fact that cannot be reconciled with such a centralized process of editorial revision.

---

[83] If early redaction produced the first New Testament in the form of a standardized, "Canonical Edition" by the early 2nd century as Trobisch theorizes, then why would all of the early Church writers completely fail to mention this epochal event in all of their writings? One major weakness in Trobisch's thesis is the fact that the 4th century writer, Eusebius, whose *Ecclesiastical History* is cited frequently by Trobisch, contains no reference to any Canonical Edition that would presumably have been in existence for nearly two hundred years by that time. This fact is inexplicable if indeed a Canonical Edition predated the 4th century debates occurring in Eusebius's era over the extent of the New Testament canon.

[84] Trobisch's approach is not too dissimilar from the highly subjective practice of conjectural emendation whereby textual critics postulate that all existing manuscript evidence for a particular reading does not accurately preserve the original and therefore they have license to proceed in altering ("emending") the biblical text of their printed critical editions without any actual manuscript evidence. This highly subjective process ends up making the personal opinions of textual critics more authoritative than the entire body of preserved manuscripts. When textual critics claim that the four Gospels originally existed without titles, they are forming this conclusion on the basis of sheer conjecture rather than a single extant manuscript of the Gospels that exists without some form of a title. If we follow the methodology of Trobisch, Metzger, and many other textual critics and reject the authenticity of the Gospel titles which have solid Greek manuscript support as far back as the 2nd century, then how can we even be certain about the authenticity of any other portion of the New Testament text, which in many places is supported by manuscript evidence dating only to the 4th century? The problem is not a lack of sufficient and credible manuscript evidence but a highly subjective and suspect process used by some critics for determining the text of Scripture.

Second, though it was more common in the first two centuries for books to exist without titles than it is today,[85] when titleless books did exist, they were normally assigned a title whenever they were placed in a particular ancient library. This resulted in multiple titles being assigned to the same literary work by different copyists and libraries.[86] The existence of a widely varying title for a book in the ancient world was a sure indication of that title's inauthenticity.[87] Yet, there is a remarkable degree of uniformity for the Gospel titles among the various categories of witnesses in the first five centuries. How do we account for this fact if the original Gospel manuscripts completely lacked a title or even had just the short form (*kata matthaion, kata markon,* etc.)? Modern textual critics routinely provide "A" ratings for readings that have far less support than the longer Gospel titles possess.

Finally, the case of the Epistle to the Hebrews is also worth reflecting upon for a moment. The writer of this epistle is never revealed in Scripture and the authorship of Hebrews is still very much in dispute. This epistle remained anonymous, despite the itching temptation that most certainly existed among some early Christians to ascribe its authorship to a particular apostle, or his associate, in order to give it more canonical clout.[88] This is especially likely when considering that Hebrews was one of a handful of New Testament books whose canonical status was disputed in the first few centuries.[89] And yet to their credit, the early Christians retained its anonymity and refrained from assigning to it any title at all, leaving just the simple and unembellished, *pros ebraious* ("to Hebrews").[90] This raises a pertinent question with respect to the four Gospel titles. If the early Church exercised scribal restraint by not adding to the title of Hebrews, then why would it act in a contrary fashion with respect to the titles of the four Gospels? There appears to be no valid explanation for why these titles in their longer form (*euangelion kata matthaion*) are not original.

Interpreting the Evidence of Codices Sinaiticus & Vaticanus

Admittedly, the prevailing opinion among textual critics today is that the four Gospels were originally written without any titles and that even the earliest form of titles that did exist is the one printed in most editions of the Greek New Testament, namely the short form of *kata matthaion* ("According to Matthew"), *kata markon* ("According to Mark"), etc.[91] However, the opinion

---

[85] Johannes Munck, "*Evangelium Veritatis* and Greek Usage as to Book Titles," *ST* 17.2 (1963): 133-38. This was especially true for shorter works of poems and speeches (ibid., 134).

[86] Hengel, *The Four Gospels*, 48, 239n198.

[87] Munck, "*Evangelium Veritatis*," 136.

[88] Hengel, *The Four Gospels*, 52-53.

[89] Metzger, *The Canon of the New Testament*, 232-38.

[90] This title is supported by 𝔓^{46} (2nd), א (4th), A (5th), and B (4th).

[91] Bruce M. Metzger, *The Text of the New Testament*, 3rd ed. (New York: Oxford, 1992), 26;

that these titles were later additions, whether in their short form or in the form containing *euangelion*, does not stem from an even handed evaluation of the evidence. As we have seen, even the existence of titles in their short form does have some early support, being found in codices Sinaiticus and Vaticanus and some of the early versions. However, against this shorter reading stands the testimony of virtually all other Greek papyri, uncials, and minuscules, in addition to the patristic writings and the general testimony of the versions. Support for the longer form of the titles with *euangelion* is verifiably early, consistent, and pervasive. The reason that modern textual critics in their printed editions of the Greek New Testament elect to omit *euangelion* from the Gospel titles appears to be out of deference to the readings of just two early uncial parchment manuscripts, Codex Vaticanus and Codex Sinaiticus. These two manuscripts are given preferential weight as witnesses to the original text by most textual scholars. However, even the readings of these two esteemed codices are subject to interpretation.

First, it is possible that the existence of the short form of the Gospel titles in Sinaiticus and Vaticanus can be accounted for by the rise of the codex over the scroll. It is conceivable that the manuscripts containing the original four Gospel titles each included *euangelion* along with the name of their individual author (*euangelion kata mattaion, euangelion kata markon, etc.*) while they existed in scroll form through at least the 1st century. But with the rise of the codex in the second century,[92] it is possible that the four Gospels gradually came to be placed into a single large codex volume that scribes in the early Church then collectively titled, "*euangelion.*"[93] In such a case, the four individual uses of "*euangelion*" in the Gospel titles would be dropped and each Gospel title copied only in abbreviated form, *kata matthaion* ("According to Matthew"), *kata markon* ("According to Mark"), etc.[94] Comfort and Barrett refer to this possible process, stating:

> Later, fourth-century codices have the wording κατα μαθθαιον, κατα μαρκον, κατα λουκαν, κατα ιωαννην superscribed to each Gospel, thereby presuming a multipartite codex all under a single title, ευαγγελιον (Gospel), as in codex Vaticanus and codex Sinaiticus.[95]

Leon Vaganay and Bernard Amphoux, *An Introduction to New Testament Textual Criticism* (New York: Cambridge University Press, 1991), 9, 112.

[92] Metzger, *The Text of the New Testament*, 6.

[93] A single codex would have been capable of holding all four Gospels by the 2nd century, rather than just one of the four Gospels. See T. C. Skeat, "Irenaeus and the Four-Fold Gospel Canon," *NovT* 34.2 (1992): 199. This represents a modification of Skeat's earlier view in C. H. Roberts and T. C. Skeat, *The Birth of the Codex* (London: British Academy, 1983), 62-66.

[94] D. A. Carson, *The Gospel According to John* (Grand Rapids: Eerdmans, 1991), 23-24.

[95] *The Text of the Earliest New Testament Greek Manuscripts*, ed. Philip W. Comfort and David P. Barrett (Wheaton, IL: Tyndale House Publishers, 2001), 54. See also Hengel, *The Four Gospels*, 238n195; B. F. Westcott and F. J. A. Hort, *The New Testament in the Original Greek* (New York: Macmillan, 1896), 321-22; Theodor Zahn, *Introduction to the New Testament*, trans. from

Though this scenario is conceivable in providing an explanation as to why Vaticanus and Sinaiticus omit the longer title, it still doesn't do justice to the actual extant manuscript evidence. First, let us assume that the word *euangelion* was a later scibal addition and it first appeared early in the 2nd century as an overarching title to a multipartite codex containing the four Gospels, each with their respective shorter titles as in Vaticanus and Sinaiticus. In such a case, we should then expect to see at least *some* actual manuscript evidence for a codex with this form and structure, either in Vaticanus or Sinaiticus or in other Greek manuscripts. But there is *none*. Such a codex structure is merely assumed by modern textual critics. There has yet to be discovered a single multipartite codex of the Gospels with *euangelion* as the collective title preceding all four Gospels. Instead, the full title *euangelion kata matthaion, loukan*, etc. is affixed to each individual Gospel as it appears in the earliest Greek manuscripts, with the exception of Sinaiticus and Vaticanus. Therefore, in the face of actual existing Greek manuscript evidence to the contrary, the theory that *euangelion* was a later addition to the Greek manuscripts should be given up. Could it be possible that the reason why Vaticanus and partly Sinaiticus uniquely possess shorter titles is simply because their scribe/s had a penchant for abbreviation and/or omission?[96]

Second, the readings of Codex Sinaiticus, at least, are subject to interpretation. It is true that in Vaticanus the word *euangelion* does not exist in either the superscriptions of the four Gospels or their subscriptions. The titles of Vaticanus appear in both the superscriptions and subscriptions of all four Gospels in uncial script as follows: κατα μαθθαιον, κατα μαρκον, κατα λουκαν, and κατα ϊωανην.[97] However, the situation in Codex Sinaiticus is different. Though it also lacks *euangelion* in each superscription, reading only κατα μαθθαιον, κατα μαρκον, κατα λουκαν, and κατα ϊωαννην,[98] it does have the anarthrous *euangelion* in the subscriptions of Mark, Luke, and John, appearing in Sinaiticus as follows: ευαγγελιον κατα μαρκον, ευαγγελιον κατα λουκαν, and ευαγγελιον κατα ϊωαννην.[99] As for a subscription to the Gospel of Matthew in Sinaiticus,

---

3rd German edition (Edinburgh: T & T Clark, 1909), 2:388.

[96] Even Trobisch, who is no fan of the authenticity of the longer reading containing *euangelion*, theorizes regarding the shorter reading of Vaticanus, "The short form is not representative for the tradition; in my opinion, it should be interpreted as an editorial characteristic of the Codex Vaticanus and not of the original form." David Trobisch, *The First Edition of the New Testament* (Oxford: Oxford University Press, 2000), 126n142.

[97] Constantin Tischendorf, *Novum Testamentum Vaticanum* (Leipsig: Giesecke and Devrient, 1867), 1, 43, 69-70, 115, 148.

[98] Note the variant spelling for "John" between Vaticanus and Sinaiticus.

[99] Constantin Tischendorf, *Novum Testamentum Sinaiticum* (Leipsig: F. A. Brockhaus, 1863), 1, 18, 29, 47-48, 61.

it is not that it lacks the longer title, ΕΥΑΓΓΕΛΙΟΝ ΚΑΤΑ ΜΑΘΘΑΙΟΝ, it curiously has no subscription at all.[100]

Based on this testimony from Codex Sinaiticus, its manuscript evidence needs to be qualified as not necessarily excluding the word *euangelion* from the original titles of the four Gospels.[101] It would be easy to get the wrong impression from the apparatuses of critical Greek editions that the Gospel titles of Sinaiticus uniformly omit *euangelion* when in fact they do not. Despite the omission of *euangelion* in the superscriptions of Sinaiticus and the superscriptions and subscriptions of Vaticanus, there exists solid external manuscript evidence (worthy of serious reconsideration in my opinion) for the authenticity of the longer titles that include *euangelion*. Some prominent voices in New Testament scholarship do seem willing to finally concede this need for reevaluation,[102] while one prolific scholar, Martin Hengel, has been like a voice crying out in the wilderness for such a wholesale re-appraisal.[103]

The Majority Text and the Gospel Titles

Considering the uniformity of the Byzantine textual tradition for the inclusion of *euangelion* in the Gospel titles, it is astonishing that both current editions of the Majority Text (Robinson & Pierpont; Hodges & Farstad) share the same Gospel titles as do the editions of the Critical Text, which simply follow Vaticanus and the superscriptions of Sinaiticus in their readings of

---

[100] Ibid., 18. This may simply be a case of scribal oversight or error. Martin Hengel, *Studies in the Gospel of Mark*, trans. John Bowden (Philadelphia: Fortress Press, 1985), 164n11.

[101] It is possible that the existence of end-titles (subscriptions) in such high percentages among the Greek papyri, uncials, and versional manuscripts is directly attributable to the fact that these codices derived from early copies of the four Gospels in scroll form. With scrolls rather than codices, readers would often unroll their manuscript from the end of a book and work backwards towards its beginning. In such a case, the end of the book would need a title to inform the reader which book he or she had just opened (Eugene LaVerdiere, *The Beginning of the Gospel* [Collegeville, MN: Liturgical Press, 1999], 1:2n5; Emanuel Tov, "Scribal Practices and Physical Aspects of the Dead Sea Scrolls," in *The Bible as Book: The Manuscript Tradition*, ed. John L. Sharpe III and Kimberly Van Kampen [New Castle, DE: Oak Knoll Press, 1998], 25; E. G. Turner, *Greek Manuscripts of the Ancient World*, 2nd ed. [London: Institute of Classical Studies, 1987], 13-14). These end-titles of the four Gospels as they originally existed in scroll form apparently continued to get copied centuries later when the early Church shifted almost exclusively to the codex, and thus the subscriptions of the four Gospels were preserved in the early papyri and uncial codices and even in copies of the early versions.

[102] D. A. Carson and Douglas J. Moo, *An Introduction to the New Testament*, 2nd Edition (Grand Rapids: Zondervan, 2005), 140; John Wenham, *Redating Matthew, Mark, and Luke: A Fresh Assault on the Synoptic Problem* (Downers Grove, IL: InterVarsity Press, 1992), 133-35. Even the theologically liberal Harvard University professor, Helmut Koester, concedes that the view "that the canonical Gospels must have circulated from the very beginning under the name of specific authors may be correct." Helmut Koester, *Ancient Christian Gospels: Their History and Development* (Philadelphia: Trinity Press International, 1990), 27.

[103] See Martin Hengel, *The Four Gospels and the One Gospel of Jesus Christ* (Harrisburg, PA: Trinity Press International, 2000), 48-53; idem, *Studies in the Gospel of Mark*, 64-84, 163-83.

kata matthaion, kata markon, etc. The rationale for this decision is explained in the introduction to the Hodges & Farstad Majority Text:

> The titles of the books of the New Testament are those in general modern use. No effort was made to consult the textual tradition, either for these or for the subscriptions which so often appear in the manuscripts at the ends of books. It cannot be assumed that the superscriptions and subscriptions found in the Greek manuscripts have the same transmissional history as the manuscripts themselves. Their use could too easily be influenced by local tradition and practice in the period when the manuscripts were copied. Nevertheless they are worthy of special study for the light they may shed on the history of the text. But such a study lies beyond the scope of the present edition.[104]

But even if such an extensive study lies, understandably, beyond the scope of their edition, it is still curious why the readings of codices Sinaiticus and Vaticanus would suddenly be given preference over the unified voice of the entire Byzantine textual tradition, especially in an edition of the Greek text that purports to follow the majority of Greek manuscripts at all other points. The reading of *euangelion* in the Gospel titles consistently appears with a high degree of uniformity not just among the manuscripts of the Byzantine tradition but even among the papyri and uncials normally considered to possess an Alexandrian text-type. And yet even more surprising than the approach of the Hodges & Farstad Majority Text is the rationale of Robinson & Pierpont for their Majority Text where they follow the shorter Gospel titles of Sinaiticus and Vaticanus, just as in the editions of the Critical Text. They write:

> The New Testament book titles are not part of the inspired canonical text. Their wording varies dramatically among the different manuscripts and editions of the Greek New Testament. The book titles that appear in this edition represent a minimal consensus as found within the canonical tradition.[105]

While dramatic variation may have occurred in later centuries with some New Testament book titles such as Revelation, whose title at times became embarrassingly grandiose and adorned with praise for John,[106] the same simply cannot be said for the titles of the four Gospels. Their titles show a high degree of uniformity from their first appearance among all the various categories of witness; and these unified readings in the Gospel titles date back even farther than the witnesses for many other portions of the New Testament text that are accepted without reservation as original. And if the

---

[104] GNTMT, xliii.

[105] NTBT, xvi.

[106] Metzger, *The Text of the New Testament*, 205.

Robinson & Pierpont edition of the Byzantine/Majority Text is not based on "a minimal consensus" for all other portions of its text, then why switch methods just for the Gospel titles? It does not appear that the Gospel titles have been given their due in the world of New Testament textual criticism, even by Majority Text proponents.

The Form and Meaning of the Four Gospel Titles

We have now reached the point where we can address the critical question of the meaning and use of *euangelion* in the Gospel titles. If the titles to the four Gospels are indeed original, and they constitute four more biblical uses of *euangelion*, then what exactly does *euangelion* mean when it is used in titular form? Does *euangelion kata matthaion* simply mean "Matthew's Gospel," as if *euangelion* refers to a certain well-recognized type or genre of literature known as "Gospel"? Or, should these four uses of *euangelion* be interpreted as referring to *the* Gospel in the sense that Matthew, Mark, Luke, and John are part and parcel with a broad but singular message known as "the Gospel"? Or similarly, if the occurrence of *euangelion* in the titles does not mean that the whole books written by Matthew, Mark, Luke, and John are part and parcel with "the Gospel," then perhaps we should understand *euangelion kata matthaion, euangelion kata markon*, etc. as meaning that the books of Matthew, Mark, Luke, and John all contribute to one larger theological construct known as "the Gospel." If this interpretation is correct, then wouldn't this mean that the claims of certain crossless gospel proponents are biblically correct when they teach that "the Gospel" is a very broad message containing any truth related to Jesus Christ? Or, perhaps another possibility is correct, that these four uses of *euangelion* in the titles simply indicate a message or narrative that has the character of being "good news"? Could *euangelion kata matthaion* merely mean "a narrative that has the character or quality of good news as told by Matthew"? In order to answer these questions and determine the proper meaning of the four uses of *euangelion* in the titles of Matthew, Mark, Luke, and John, we must first address the exact form of these titles as they are found in the earliest manuscripts.

It must be observed that the earliest Greek text of the titles does *not* read literally, "The Gospel According to Matthew," "The Gospel According to Mark," etc. Though this is the translation of the titles found in virtually all English Bibles, it is not an accurate rendering of the Greek text of the titles that existed in the manuscripts of the first five or six centuries. It is conspicuous that in all of the early Greek manuscripts containing *euangelion* in their titles, whether as a superscription or subscription, *euangelion* is always anarthrous rather than articular.[107] Thus, there are no early

[107] Regarding the papyri, this is true whether it is $\mathfrak{P}^{4/62}$ for Matthew's title (S. D. Charlesworth, "T. C. Skeat, $\mathfrak{P}^{64+67}$ and $\mathfrak{P}^{4}$, and the Problem of Fibre Orientation in Codicological Reconstruction," *NTS* 53 [2007]: 596; *The Text of the Earliest New Testament Greek Manuscripts*,

occurrences of *to euangelion kata matthaion*, etc. This construction does not appear among the Greek manuscripts until the later uncials (7th-9th centuries) and minuscules.[108] The earliest appearance of *euangelion* with the article occurs outside of the biblical manuscripts in the 2nd century writings of Justin Martyr. Justin uses the articular *euangelion* once in the plural (*euangelia*) in reference to the collection of the four canonical "Gospels."[109] This is regarded to be the first indisputable, documented Christian usage of *euangelion* where it refers specifically to a literary work or works rather than a spoken message,[110] though the term may have been used this way among early Christians prior to Justin.[111] By the 2nd and early 3rd centuries, the meaning of the term "Gospel" appears to have become established within popular Christian usage as referring essentially to one of the biblical "Gospels" of Matthew, Mark, Luke, or John.[112]

The articular use of *euangelion* in the singular also appears early in the writings of Justin. It is used twice in the singular to refer to one larger entity known as "the Gospel" consisting of all four written Gospels.[113] Apparently, professing Christians began referring to the four written Gospels collectively with the singular, articular phrase, "the Gospel."[114]

---

ed. Philip W. Comfort and David P. Barrett [Wheaton, IL: Tyndale House Publishers, 2001], 53-54; T. C. Skeat, "The Oldest Manuscript of the Four Gospels?" *NTS* 43 [1997]: 18; Graham N. Stanton, "The Fourfold Gospel," *NTS* 43 [1997]: 333n54), 𝔓[75] for Luke, or 𝔓[66,75] for John. This is also true of the form found in the uncials of the 4th-6th centuries, as well as the subscriptions for Mark, Luke, and John in Codex Sinaiticus.

[108] On this point, Metzger states, "As time went on scribes would enlarge the title, first by individualizing each Gospel by using the article, 'The Gospel according to . . .,' and later by emphasizing the character of the book by the addition of the adjective 'holy' (τὸ ἅγιον εὐαγγέλιον κτλ.)." Metzger, *The Canon of the New Testament*, 303.

[109] In his *First Apology* (*Apol.* i. 66), Justin has *ha euangelia kaleitai* ("which are called gospels").

[110] Robert H. Gundry, "ΕΥΑΓΓΕΛΙΟΝ: How Soon a Book?" *JBL* 115 (1996): 325; Ralph P. Martin, "Gospel," *ISBE*, 2:530; Annette Yoshiko Reed, "ΕΥΑΓΓΕΛΙΟΝ: Orality, Textuality, and the Christian Truth in Irenaeus' *Adversus Haereses*," *VC* 56 (2002): 16.

[111] Gerhard Friedrich, "εὐαγγελίζομαί, εὐαγγέλιον, προευαγγελίζομαί, εὐαγγελιστής," *TDNT*, 2:721-35. Some have attempted to prove that *euangelion* was used to designate a written "Gospel" of some kind as early as the Didache which predates Justin. James A. Kelhoffer, "'How Soon a Book' Revisited: ΕΥΑΓΓΕΛΙΟΝ as a Reference to 'Gospel' Materials in the First Half of the Second Century," *ZNW* 95 (2004): 1-34.

[112] Irenaeus, *Against Heresies*, 3.11.8; cf. 3.1.1; Clement of Alexandria, *Stromateis*, 1.136.1. See Ulrich Becker, "εὐαγγέλιον," *NIDNTT*, 2:113; D. Moody Smith, "When Did the Gospels Become Scripture?" *JBL* 119.1 (2000): 5.

[113] In his *Dialogue with Trypho* (*Dial.* 10.2; 100.1), Justin uses the phrase, "in the Gospel" (*en tō euangeliō*) as a reference to the written Gospels as though they were a single entity, "the Gospel."

[114] This plural versus singular usage for "gospel" also occurs in the Muratorian Canon (2nd-4th). Luke is called "the third book of the Gospel" (*tertium euangelii librum*), while the Book of John is referred to as "the fourth of the Gospels" (*quartum euangeliorum*). See F. F. Bruce, "When Is a Gospel Not a Gospel?" *BJRL* 45.2 (March 1963): 319-20; Hahneman, *The Muratorian Fragment*, 6.

This may lend some credence to the theory for the origin for the short form of Gospel title, *kata matthaion, kata markon,* etc., where *euangelion* would have served as the title to a multipartite codex of the four Gospels. But this is speculative and cannot be confirmed since no such codex and title has been discovered. Regardless, the occurrence of the phrase "the gospel" in reference to all four Gospels may simply have been a handy convention that arose within popular Christian usage, much like referring to the five books of the Pentateuch singularly as "the Law."[115] Justin's use of *euangelion,* therefore, appears to vary from his earlier use of the term in his *First Apology* (*Apol.* i.66). Justin's two singular, articular uses of *euangelion* also appear to be the first historical references that provide any support for the G.E.S. doctrine that there is one broad theological construct known as "the Gospel" compromised of virtually the entire New Testament. However, it must be remembered that this meaning of "gospel" is derived from extra-biblical usage, not from the four anarthrous uses of *euangelion* in the biblical titles of Matthew, Mark, Luke, and John.

Since there are no articular uses of *euangelion* in the titles of the early Greek manuscripts of the Gospels, there appears to be no biblical basis for interpreting *euangelion kata matthaion, markon, etc.* to mean that there is one all-encompassing message about the life of Jesus Christ that is known as "the Gospel." Nor does the title *euangelion kata matthaion* refer to the book proper, as if to say, "Matthew's Book" or "Matthew's Gospel." Instead, each title containing the anarthrous expression, *euangelion kata matthaion* simply means, "good news as reported by Matthew." This means that the anarthrous *euangelion* in the title is not used as a definite noun to identify a particular message; rather it is used as a qualitative noun referring to the *character* or *quality* of the message contained within the book.[116] When the simple expression "Good News According to Matthew" is used for the title of a book, it is not attempting as yet to specify the exact content of the book that may be considered "good news," but instead it is only seeking to grab the reader's attention as any good headline would and draw the reader into the book to find out what is considered "good news." Thus, *euangelion kata matthaion* does not necessarily mean that the entire content of Matthew's narrative must be considered "good news" (for indeed it contains much bad news regarding judgment), but only that there is some "good news" contained within it that is sufficient enough to

[115] It is noteworthy that in the latter 6th century A.D., even Muhammed appears to have inherited this meaning of the term "Gospel." Consequently, the Qur'an perpetuates the misconception that there is only one "Gospel" (*injil*) in the Bible and that Jesus received this single book from Allah just like Moses received "the Law" at Mt. Sinai (Sura 5:47, 65; 7:157; 9:111; 48:29; 57:27). It is for this reason that some Muslims who have never read the Bible before are confused by the existence of four Gospels bearing the names of Matthew, Mark, Luke, and John when they begin reading the New Testament (Bassam M. Madany, *The Bible and Islam: Sharing God's Word with a Muslim* [Palos Heights, IL: Back to God Hour, 1981], xi).

[116] Wallace, *Greek Grammar,* 244-45.

characterize the message of the entire book as being qualitatively "good news" or *euangelion*.

Of course, simply because a noun is anarthrous in Greek does not necessarily mean that it cannot have a definite, articular sense. Wallace cites at least ten different constructions by which an anarthrous noun may still be definite and practically articular.[117] But *euangelion* in the four Gospel titles does not match any one of these constructions. Though some may view *euangelion* as an abstract noun, like the words "salvation," "truth," and "love" which occasionally have a definite sense, abstract nouns are normally qualitative in force rather than definite. So even if *euangelion* was an abstract noun, a definite sense would be its rare usage,[118] making it unlikely that all four titles use it this way.

Perhaps some would even attempt to identify the titular use of *euangelion* as a monadic noun which is also definite in force.[119] Monadic nouns do not require the article because they are the only entity of their kind. For example, "sun" and "moon" in Luke 21:25 are both anarthrous because there is only one "sun" and one "moon" in the lexicon of vernacular speech, and thus there is no need for the article before such a word. However, *euangelion* cannot be considered a monadic noun because it is not completely unique. As this chapter has already demonstrated, there are other *euangelia* referred to in Scripture that almost always have the article. In the midst of this crossless controversy, it is common to hear the protest that *euangelion* is linguistically not a "technical term"[120] because it does not always refer to one and the same thing (like the words "sun" or "moon" do). This fact is acknowledged by all parties,[121] as even the non-theological use of *euangelizō* in 1 Thessalonians 3:6 demonstrates that the words *euangelion* and *euangelizō* are not used of only one form of "good news" or "gospel" throughout the New Testament. But even though *euangelion* is not a technical or monadic term, this does not deny that it has a technical or specific *usage*. In any given context, *euangelion* refers to only one particular, individual message, whether it is the "gospel of the kingdom," the "gospel of Christ," etc.

As all of this relates to the meaning of *euangelion* in the four Gospel titles, the anarthrous construction in the earliest Greek manuscripts indicates that the quality or characteristic of "good news" is being emphasized rather than the specific identity or form of good news. The anarthrous *euangelion* should not be interpreted as having an articular force—as though the titles to Matthew, Mark, Luke, and John were announcing that each book consisted of the same monolithic message called "the Gospel." This interpretation would immediately conflict with the fact that not all

---

[117] Ibid., 245-54.

[118] Ibid., 244.

[119] Ibid., 248-49.

[120] Myers, "The Gospel is More Than 'Faith Alone in Christ Alone'," 50.

[121] Hixson, *Getting the Gospel Wrong: The Evangelical Crisis*, 78-79, 147-48n4.

four Gospels contain precisely the same content. Though the four Gospels are perfectly consistent and complementary to one another, and there is a significant amount of overlapping material among them, there are still substantial differences in the content chosen for each book. John, for instance, contains a very high percentage of unique material that is not found in the Synoptics. And only Matthew and Luke record the Savior's virgin birth, whereas Mark and John begin their accounts with the Lord Jesus having already matured to full manhood at the beginning His public ministry. For these reasons, it is fair to say that if the anarthrous *euangelion* in the Gospel titles actually has an articular force, meaning "the Gospel" (as in Justinian usage), then there would have been no need to add *kata matthaion, kata markon*, etc. to each title. All four books should have all been titled simply, "*Euangelion*"—"the Gospel."

The Question of Literary Genre

Even though *euangelion* in the Gospel titles does not mean "the Gospel" but rather the qualitative sense of "Good News as told by Matthew, Mark, etc.," some might still opt for a different anarthrous meaning, namely the indefinite sense, whereby *euangelion kata matthaion* means, "A Gospel According to Matthew." According to this interpretation, *euangelion* could be viewed as an indefinite noun[122] where Matthew's *euangelion* is just one member of a particular group of other *euangelia*.[123] If interpreted this way, the phrase *euangelion kata matthaion* would mean that Matthew's Gospel belongs to a particular literary genre that was recognizable in the 1st century as "Gospel" literature. This is the meaning that many Christians assume for the four titles since the word "Gospel" in modern English vernacular has come to mean essentially a book that details the life story of Jesus Christ. In this sense, the term "Gospel" has developed into its own literary genre, like "Gospel" music. But is this what the anarthrous construction of *euangelion* initially conveyed in the titles of Matthew, Mark, Luke, and John? Was *euangelion* originally intended to function as an indefinite noun? Some who advocate the G.E.S. gospel believe so.[124]

If the four books written by Matthew, Mark, Luke, and John were all part of a distinctly recognizable genre of 1st century literature known as "Gospel" literature, then the New Testament usage of *euangelion* ought to reflect this. But it is quite revealing that in all 132 occurrences of *euangelion* and *euangelizō* in the New Testament apart from the four titles themselves, neither *euangelion* nor *euangelizō* are *ever* used in reference to a book.

Even in places where we might expect a writer of Scripture to use *euangelion* with this meaning, he does not. For instance, Luke begins his Gospel by declaring in his prologue, "*Inasmuch as many have taken in hand*

---

[122] Wallace, *Greek Grammar*, 244.

[123] Ibid.

[124] Myers, "The Gospel is More Than 'Faith Alone in Christ Alone'," 36-37n9.

to set in order a narrative (diēgēsis) of those things which have been fulfilled among us, 2 just as those who from the beginning were eyewitnesses and ministers of the word delivered them to us, 3 it seemed good to me also, having had perfect understanding of all things from the very first, to write to you an orderly account (kathexēs sou grapsai), most excellent Theophilus, 4 that you may know the certainty of those things in which you were instructed." In verse 1, Luke acknowledges the existence of other narratives about Christ in the 1st century that were either written or spoken but were definitely not the other three canonical Gospels.[125] In doing so, Luke employs the term *diēgēsis,* rather than *euangelion,* for this kind of "narrative" (Luke 1:1).[126] And this occurs in the very context in which Luke states his purpose *"to write to you an orderly account (kathexēs sou grapsai)"* (Luke 1:3). It is significant to note that he does *not* say that he is writing "a Gospel" to Theophilus, even though this would have been the perfect occasion to use *euangelion* in this "bookish" sense of a written document. Matthew, Mark, Luke, and John were not consciously creating literary works of a distinctive genre known in the 1st century as "Gospel" books.[127] The use of the word *euangelion* among Christians specifically in reference to a book appears to have developed in the next century. For these and a variety of other reasons, many scholars do not view the four Gospels as fitting an ancient literary genre known as "Gospel" or as fitting any specific genre for that matter.[128]

New Testament scholarship has ebbed and flowed in the last one hundred years on this question of the genre of the four canonical Gospels. Many are now convinced that the Gospels are most closely aligned with ancient biography (*bios*) and that "Gospel" literature, if it truly forms its own literary type, should be viewed as a subgenre of biography. This view that sees the genre of "gospel" as separate from "biography" was the view held by liberal and conservative scholarship alike through most of the 20th century. To be sure, there have been theologically liberal tendencies or motives underlying the identification of the four Gospels as either "gospel" or "biography," which must be acknowledged and not falsely attributed to one view versus the other.

The position that views Matthew, Mark, Luke, and John as belonging to the genre of "gospel" emerged as a result of early form and redaction

---

[125] Tom Stegall, "The Tragedy of the Crossless Gospel, Pt. 7," *GFJ* (Summer 2008): 3-4.

[126] Ulrich Becker, "*εὐαγγέλιον*," *NIDNTT,* 2:113; Helmut Koester, "From the Kerygma-Gospel to Written Gospels," *NTS* 35 (1989): 367.

[127] Robert Guelich, "The Gospel Genre," in *Das Evangelium und die Evangelien: Vorträge vom Tübinger Symposium 1982,* ed. Peter Stuhlmacher (Tübingen: Mohr Siebeck, 1983), 183-217.

[128] Robert H. Gundry, "Recent Investigations into the Literary Genre 'Gospel'," in *New Dimensions in New Testament Study,* ed. Richard N. Longenecker and Merrill C. Tenney (Grand Rapids: Zondervan, 1974), 101-13; Donald Guthrie, *New Testament Introduction,* 4th edition (Downers Grove, IL: InterVarsity Press, 1990), 16-21.

criticism.[129] According to these fields of literary criticism, the canonical Gospels were regarded to be little more than collections of traditions about Jesus assembled by later communities of Christian disciples, not as the authoritative accounts of first-hand, apostolic eyewitnesses (Matthew, John) or their associates (Mark, Luke). On the other hand, among those who have maintained that the Gospels are part of the genre of "biography" rather than "gospel," there has been a critical, unbelieving tendency as well. Often the lines of comparison between strictly literary matters of structure and form have blended into comparisons and critiques of theological content. Some who see the Gospels as fitting the broad genre of "biography" have tended to explain inspired Scripture in purely rationalistic or naturalistic terms. Thus, they end up seeing the New Testament as the product of writers who were merely following the conventions of the literary style current in 1st century Greco-Roman society where the feats and achievements of its god and goddess heroines were simply fabricated. Unbelieving critics have viewed other portions of Scripture in a similar vein, starting with the flood account of Genesis, the Egyptian plagues and parting of the Red Sea in Exodus, the preservation of Jonah for three days in a great fish, and many other miracles recorded in the Bible. We are told in essence, "These miracles are no different from the myths and legends that were current in other parts of the world during the time that these epical accounts were written in the Bible," thus indicating that the Bible was adapted from paganism. But such an approach is a patent denial of the inspiration of Scripture. The divine inspiration of the four Gospels makes them entirely distinct as writings, regardless of any strictly literary features they may have in common with ancient literature.

The four Gospels are historically accurate narratives about the Lord Jesus' life, death, resurrection, and ascension, and they uniquely possess a divine quality, authority, and purpose (2 Tim. 3:15-17). In this respect, the four canonical Gospels must also be regarded as distinct from the apocryphal "Gospels" that mushroomed in the 2nd century, with titles such as the "Gospel of Thomas," the "Gospel of Truth," and the "Gospel of Peter." These so-called "Gospels" contain an assortment of fanciful, esoteric statements attributed to Jesus but they have no structured, organized, cohesive narration of the times, places, and events of Christ's life and ministry. They do not have the ring of authenticity or credibility about them. It is obvious that many of these so-called "Gospels" bearing the name of an apostle or early Church figure were written pseudonymously generations after the life of Christ. Thus, they could not have been written by an eyewitness of the actual words and works of Jesus Christ. The Gnostic and apocryphal "Gospels" lack all the attributes of authenticity and for this reason they cannot be lumped together in the same literary genre as

---

[129] Richard A. Burridge, *What Are the Gospels? A Comparison with Graeco-Roman Biography*, 2nd ed. (Grand Rapids: Eerdmans, 2004), 9-13.

the four canonical Gospels. Most importantly, the Gnostic "Gospels" do not contain content that makes them characteristically "good." They not only lack Christ's literal, atoning death and bodily resurrection, but many of them actually deny these two great works which form the heart of the saving message. If the Gnostic "Gospels" lack, and even deny, the principal content that makes them truly "good news" from God to man, then they are not worthy to bear the title "Gospel" and they should not be put in the same category with the four biblical Gospels.

It seems best, ultimately, to concede that the four biblical Gospels share several literary features common to the diverse genre of ancient biography, while at the same time acknowledging the vital differences that exist between them. Admittedly, all four Gospels, even John, share parallel features with the various subcategories of biography that existed in Greco-Roman literature.[130] For this reason, if they are viewed from a purely literary standpoint, they should be viewed as a subgenre in the diverse ancient genre of *bios* or biography.[131] Yet their distinctiveness as divinely inspired, authoritative, trustworthy documents that are characterized as being "good news" from God to man must not be overlooked since they are the only four books of their kind in the entire world—ancient or modern.

In the final analysis, we can conclude that when the Gospel titles read, *euangelion kata matthaion, euangelion kata markon*, etc., they do not mean "a Gospel" in the indefinite sense as if referring to a *book* belonging to a common *genre* of ancient literature known as "gospel." *Euangelion kata matthaion* does not mean, for instance, "Here is a book written by a man named Matthew that is a piece of Gospel literature." Nor does *euangelion* in the title mean "the Gospel," taking the anarthrous *euangelion* in the definite sense as a reference to *one specific gospel message*, as if to say, "This book is part and parcel with *the* message of Good News." This means that the anarthrous construction of *euangelion* in the four titles does not support the idea that the entire content of each book comprises a singular message known as "the gospel," which consequently does not support the G.E.S. doctrine of a broad, all-inclusive meaning for "the gospel." When *euangelion* is used anarthrously it does not mean that everything within each book forms "the gospel." Rather, it means that the four narratives are

---

[130] Charles H. Talbert, *What Is a Gospel? The Genre of the Canonical Gospels* (Philadelphia: Fortress Press, 1977), 134-35. Shuler is even more specific, arguing that the Gospels fit a specific subcategory of biography known as encomium which is characterized by laudatory praise for its principal subject (Philip L. Shuler, *A Genre for the Gospels: The Biographical Character of Matthew* [Philadelphia: Fortress Press, 1982], 58-106).

[131] David E. Aune, *The New Testament in Its Literary Environment* (Philadelphia: Westminster Press, 1987), 17-74; Richard A. Burridge, *What Are the Gospels? A Comparison with Graeco-Roman Biography*, 2nd ed. (Grand Rapids: Eerdmans, 2004), 105-232; Larry W. Hurtado, "Gospel (Genre)," in *Dictionary of Jesus and the Gospels*, ed. Joel B. Green, Scot McKnight, and I. Howard Marshall (Downers Grove, IL: InterVarsity Press, 1992), 276.

characterized as being "good news" because they contain within them, as a subset of the whole, at least two prominent yet distinct forms of good news—the gospel of the kingdom to Israel and the gospel of Christ's atoning death and bodily resurrection for the entire world.

Euangelion in Mark 1:1

Having considered to this point the gospel of the kingdom, the everlasting gospel, and the use of *euangelion* in the four Gospel titles, we must address one more unique occurrence of *euangelion* before focusing upon the gospel of Christ and the contents of saving faith in the next chapter. In the opening verse of the second Gospel, it says, *"The beginning of the gospel of Jesus Christ, the Son of God (archē tou euangeliou Iēsou Christou huiou tou Theou)."* Does this verse function as a title for all of Mark's narrative? Is this verse teaching that the entire contents contained in Mark should be considered "the gospel" (*tou euangeliou*)? If so, wouldn't this lend some validity to the G.E.S. position? Wouldn't it be quite unreasonable to expect the lost today to believe the entire contents of Mark's Gospel in order to be saved? Shouldn't we therefore admit that belief in "the gospel" is not necessary to receive eternal life? It is not surprising that some crossless gospel advocates turn to Mark 1:1 in order to support their broad, all-encompassing notion of "the gospel" and to deny the necessity of believing in Christ's saving death and resurrection for eternal life. Myers, for example, believes that Mark 1:1 refers to "The full story in Mark."[132] He concludes from this verse:

> So the entire Gospel of Mark is included in what the New Testament calls "the gospel" in a vague and general sense. So basically what you come down to is everything in the New Testament can be considered "gospel," if not everything in the entire Bible when you get some logical deductions in there. So if we say that a person has to believe the entire gospel we're saying a person has to know and believe most, if not all, of the Bible. And we're also saying that few of us, if any, have ever shared the entire gospel with anybody else, unless you're a pastor or somebody who has taught through the entire New Testament to somebody else or read through it with somebody else.[133]

But is Mark 1:1 really descriptive of the entire contents of Mark? Does this lone use of *euangelion* in Mark's introduction justify extrapolating "the gospel" to the entire New Testament and even to the entire Bible? If *euangelion* in Mark 1:1 isn't indicating a broad, all-encompassing "gospel," then what is it referring to? Mark 1:1 is generally regarded to be a "title"

---

[132] Myers, "The Gospel is More Than 'Faith Alone in Christ Alone'," 53.

[133] Jeremy Myers, *The Gospel is More Than "Faith Alone in Christ Alone,"* Grace Evangelical Society Conference, Dallas, TX, March 2, 2006.

or "headline"[134] for some portion of Mark, whether for the introduction in chapter 1 or for all 16 chapters. A few biblical scholars are convinced, however, that it is not a title in any sense.[135] While crossless interpreters may assume that Mark 1:1 is descriptive of "the full story in Mark," this conclusion is far from certain.

The meaning of Mark 1:1 and its relationship to the rest of the book bristles with hermeneutical questions and challenges.[136] In terms of syntax, Mark 1:1 is a phrase containing a subject without a predicate. Mark 1:2-3 constitute a subordinate clause that is not clearly attached to either verse 1 or verse 4. Also, Mark 1:4 associates John the Baptist with the Old Testament prophecies cited in verses 2-3, and yet verse 4 is grammatically unconnected to the previous verses. Besides grammatical and syntactical difficulties, this passage also contains serious lexical questions, such as identifying the proper meaning of *archē* and *euangelion* in verse 1. There is even a textual variant in Mark 1:1 for the phrase, "Son of God." As a result, there exists nothing even remotely close to a consensus among New Testament scholarship on the correct interpretation of Mark 1:1.[137] Wikgren sets forth six different positions on the meaning of Mark 1:1 and its relationship to the verses following it.[138] Cranfield has upped the count to ten.[139] While space will not permit a thorough interaction with each view, this section will address the two most prominent interpretations. The crux of the matter in Mark 1:1 boils down to whether the phrase, *"the beginning of the gospel of Jesus Christ, the Son of God,"* applies to the entirety of Mark's book or just some portion of it, perhaps even just the introductory section in chapter 1.[140] But regardless of which position is correct,

---

[134] Craig L. Blomberg, *Jesus and the Gospels: An Introduction and Survey* (Nashville: Broadman & Holman, 1997), 118.

[135] N. Clayton Croy, "Where the Gospel Text Begins: A Non-theological Interpretation of Mark 1:1," *NovT* 43 (2001): 114; R. T. France, *The Gospel of Mark: A Commentary on the Greek Text*, NIGTC (Grand Rapids: Eerdmans, 2002), 51; Mary Ann Tolbert, *Sowing the Gospel: Mark's World in Literary-Historical Perspective* (Minneapolis: Fortress Press, 1989), 241-46.

[136] Robert H. Gundry, *Mark: A Commentary on His Apology for the Cross* (Grand Rapids: Eerdmans, 1993), 29-30.

[137] Due to so many hermeneutical hurdles, one writer even goes so far as to propose that Mark 1:1 must not be part of the original sacred text—that it was a later scribal gloss added to Mark's Gospel in the second century (Croy, "Where the Gospel Text Begins," 119-27). Yet, students of God's Word should never view it as an option to excise portions of the Scripture that are difficult to understand (2 Peter 3:16) or that do not agree with us.

[138] Allen Wikgren, "ΑΡΧΗ ΤΟΥ ΕΥΑΓΓΕΛΙΟΥ," *JBL* 61 (1942): 11-12.

[139] C. E. B. Cranfield, *The Gospel According to Saint Mark*, CGTC (Cambridge: Cambridge University Press, 1959), 34-35.

[140] A few scholars are not convinced either way, saying that it may apply to Mark's prologue in chapter 1 or to all 16 chapters or possibly even to both. See Knox Chamblin, "*EUANGELION* in Mark: Willi Marxsen Revisited," *WTJ* 59 (1997): 33; Joel Marcus, *Mark 1-8: A New Translation with Introduction and Commentary*, AB (New York: Doubleday, 2000), 143; A. T. Robertson, *Word Pictures in the New Testament* (Grand Rapids: Baker Book House, n.d.), 1:252.

the new G.E.S. doctrine of "the gospel" does not necessarily follow from either the "entirety" view or the "portion" view.

View #1—Mark 1:1 Refers Narrowly to Mark's Introduction

It is often assumed that Mark 1:1 is a title for the whole Gospel of Mark; but it may come as a surprise to learn that there are many scholars and commentators who view Mark 1:1 as a heading only for the introductory section of chapter 1 rather than for the entire book.[141] Among those who hold to this view, opinions vary as to how far verse 1 extends, with ranges anywhere from verse 3 to verse 15. But more importantly we must ask, if the phrase in verse 1, *"The beginning of the gospel of Jesus Christ, the Son of God,"* connects only to some portion of Mark's introduction in chapter 1, then what does *"the beginning of the gospel"* mean if it is not a reference to "the full story in Mark"?

The meaning of the Greek word for "beginning" (*archē*) in this verse is pivotal. The word *archē* in many contexts can mean a chronological starting point and it is even used this way in Philippians 4:15 in combination with *euangelion* (*en archē tou euangeliou*) to refer to the moment when Paul first preached the gospel in Philippi. If *archē* in Mark 1:1 has such a strictly temporal, chronological meaning, then this verse could be interpreted as saying that *"the gospel of Jesus Christ"* contains everything from Mark 1:2 onwards. It would be saying essentially, "Here begins the gospel." However, *archē* can also mean "origin" or "principle" or "the first cause . . . source."[142]

Archē may have this meaning in Revelation 3:14 where the Lord Jesus is called *"the beginning (archē) of the creation of God."* Since there was never

---

[141] Collins, *Mark*, 131; Cranfield, *The Gospel According to Saint Mark*, 34-35; R. T. France, "The Beginning of Mark," *Reformed Theological Review* 49 (1990): 11-19; idem, *The Gospel of Mark*, 51; Hengel, *The Four Gospels*, 267n374; Ezra P. Gould, *The Gospel According to St. Mark*, ICC (New York: Charles Scribner's Sons, 1913), 1-2; Robert A. Guelich, "The Beginning of the Gospel," *Biblical Research* 27 (1982): 5-15; idem, *Mark 1-8:26*, WBC (Dallas: Word Books, 1989), 12; Gundry, *Mark*, 31; Helmut Koester, *Ancient Christian Gospels: Their History and Development* (Philadelphia: Trinity Press International, 1990), 13; idem, "From the Kerygma-Gospel to Written Gospels," *NTS* 35 (1989): 370; M.-J. Lagrange, *Évangile selon Saint Marc*, 4th ed. (Paris: J. Gabalda et Fils, 1929), 1; William L. Lane, *The Gospel According to Mark: The English Text with Introduction, Exposition and Notes* (Grand Rapids: Eerdmans, 1974), 42; A. E. J. Rawlinson, *The Gospel according to St. Mark*, Westminster Commentaries (London: Methuen, 1949), 250-52; C. H. Turner, "Text of Mark 1," *JTS* 28 (1926): 145; Nigel Turner, *Grammatical Insights into the New Testament* (Edinburgh: T & T Clark, 1965), 27-28.

[142] BDAG, 138; LSJ, 252. See also Cranfield, *The Gospel According to Saint Mark*, 34; James R. Edwards, *The Gospel according to Mark*, PNTC (Grand Rapids: Eerdmans, 2002), 23; Mark E. Glasswell, "The Beginning of the Gospel: A Study of St. Mark's Gospel with Regard to Its First Verse," in *New Testament Christianity for Africa and the World: Essays in Honour of Harry Sawyerr*, ed. Mark E. Glasswell and Edward W. Fasholé-Luke (London: SPCK, 1974), 37; Willi Marxsen, *Mark the Evangelist: Studies on the Redaction History of the Gospel*, trans. James Boyce, Donald Juel, William Poehlmann with Roy A. Harrisville (Nashville: Abingdon, 1969), 132.

a time when Christ did not exist (John 1:1-2) and He, in fact, is the Creator of all things (Col. 1:15-16), this cannot mean that Jesus Christ was the first created being who in turn became God's agent of creation for all other things. Such is the teaching of Arianism and the Jehovah's Witnesses. Instead, Revelation 3:14 may be teaching that Jesus Christ was the origin or source for all that came into existence. This would be consistent with Johannine teaching elsewhere (John 1:3). *Archē* in Revelation 3:14 could also be translated "ruler" with the sense that Jesus Christ is the supreme authority over all creation.[143] These two ideas may, in fact, even be inseparable since He is the supreme authority over all creation precisely because He is its Creator. In either case, Jesus Christ was the origin or source of the creation, but He was clearly not *part of* the creation. He stands outside of the creation. In the same way, "the *beginning (archē)* of the gospel" in Mark 1:1 does not necessarily mean "this is the beginning *part of* the gospel" but rather "this is the *origin* or *source* of the gospel."

According to this meaning of *archē*, the immediate context of Mark 1:1 would make it clear that *"the gospel of Jesus Christ"* contained within Mark's book had its origins, source, or basis in the Old Testament Prophets (Mark 1:2-3) and particularly the last of the prophets—John the Baptist (Mark 1:4-8). In this sense, the gospel grew out of, or resulted from, these sources of divine revelation. Thus, it may indeed be true that *archē* is *not* used in Mark 1:1 "in the sense of chronological starting-point but 'basis' or 'origin.'"[144] If this meaning is correct, then the phrase, *"the beginning of the gospel"* in Mark 1:1, does not mean, "Here begins all those events comprising the gospel," but simply, "this is where the gospel came from" or "this is how the gospel originated."

Some people may question how this interpretation relates to the long-time standard Greek lexicon, *Bauer, Arndt, Gingrich, and Danker*, which lists *archē* in Mark 1:1 as meaning "a beginning of a book."[145] If *"the beginning of the gospel"* in Mark 1:1 is an alternative way of saying, "a beginning of a book," then this could be misconstrued as indicating that the "gospel" in Mark 1:1 is equivalent to Mark's entire "book." But lexical entries are somewhat subjective and often in need of refinement, as Free Grace Christians know well.[146] With respect to *archē* in Mark 1:1, it is significant to note that in the updated edition of this same lexicon, the definition of *archē* as "a beginning of a book" has been slightly modified and replaced with, "the beginning, i.e. initial account, in a book."[147] This may be due to

---

[143] Michael J. Svigel, "Christ as Ἀρχή in Revelation 3:14," *BSac* 161 (April 2004): 215-31.

[144] Glasswell, "The Beginning of the Gospel," 37.

[145] BAGD, 111.

[146] Michael D. Makidon, "Soteriological Concerns with Bauer's Greek Lexicon," *JOTGES* 17 (Autumn 2004): 11-18; idem, "The Strengthening Constraint of *Gar* in 1 and 2 Timothy," (Th.M. thesis, Dallas Theological Seminary, 2003), 66.

[147] BDAG, 137.

the fact that the entire category of meaning for *archē* as a title of a book has been roundly rejected by several scholars in the last generation.[148] They demonstrate that when *archē* is used in extra-biblical sources, it introduces just the opening section of a piece of literature,[149] or more rarely, the start of a section further into the body of that literature.[150] But *archē* never functions as a title for the entire contents of a literary work.[151] This casts serious doubt upon *euangelion* in Mark 1:1 meaning "the full story in Mark."

Consistent with this usage of *archē* is the pattern of *kathōs* as it is used in Mark and the other Synoptic Gospels. Following Mark 1:1, the beginning of verse 2 goes on to say, *"As it is written"* (*kathōs gegraptai*). It has been observed that when *kathōs* is used with a quotation from Scripture, such as with the phrase *"it is written"* (*gegraptai*), the *kathōs* construction is always a subordinate clause referring back to the previous main clause, which in this case would be Mark 1:1.[152] This would indicate that verse 1 should not stand alone as a title and be punctuated with a period at the end of the verse as most translations have it.[153]

So, if *euangelion* in Mark's opening phrase, *"the beginning of the gospel,"* is not describing the entire contents of Mark or even Mark's book viewed as a piece of "Gospel" literature, then what "gospel" is it referring to? Later in Mark's introduction there is a double-usage of the term *euangelion* in Mark 1:14-15, which is a clear reference to the gospel of the kingdom in its context. Is the expression, "the gospel," in Mark 1:1 possibly referring to this gospel of the kingdom? *Euangelion* in Mark 1:1 might form an *inclusio* with 1:14-15.[154] But if this is the case, then we must ask along with Hooker, "but is it not just as likely that the two references to the gospel are meant to stand in parallel, marking the openings of two sections, rather

---

[148] Gerhard Arnold, "Mk 1.1 und die Eröffnungswendungen in griechischen und lateinischen Schriften," *ZNW* 68 (1977): 123-27; M. Eugene Boring, "Mark 1:1-15 and the Beginning of the Gospel," *Sem* 52 (1990): 52, 71n18; Guelich, "The Beginning of the Gospel," 8, 14nn31-33; Gundry, *Mark*, 31.

[149] Isocrates, *Address to Philip* 1; Philo *De Sobrietate* 1 §1; idem, *De Specialibus Legibus* 1 §1; Diodorus Siculus 11.1.1; Tacitus, *Historiae* 1.1.1 (Latin); Polybius 1.5.1, 4-5; Dionysius Halicarnassenis, *Antiquitates Romanae* 1.8.1, 4; Josephus, *Jewish Wars* 1.12 §30 with 1.6 §18.

[150] Aristoteles, *Poetica* 7.1-7.

[151] Sometimes it is objected that the use of *archē* in the Septuagint of Hosea 1:2 contradicts this point, which says, *"The beginning of the word of the Lord by Hosea."* However, in regards to the non-titular sense of *archē* in Hosea 1:2, Guelich writes, "This observation holds for Hos 1:2 LXX, commonly cited as a parallel for Mark's use of *archē* in 1:1. Hos 1:1 represents the heading for the whole work, and 1:2 LXX, if indeed a heading at all, is merely the heading for the opening section of 1:2-9." Guelich, "The Beginning of the Gospel," 14n33.

[152] J. K. Elliott, "ΚΑΘΩΣ and ΩΣΠΕΡ in the New Testament," *FN* 7.4 (1991): 55-56; Gundry, *Mark*, 30.

[153] Elliott, "ΚΑΘΩΣ and ΩΣΠΕΡ," 55-56.

[154] Leander E. Keck, "The Introduction to Mark's Gospel," *NTS* 12 (1966): 359-60; Helmut Koester, *Ancient Christian Gospels: Their History and Development* (Philadelphia: Trinity Press International, 1990), 13; idem, "From the Kerygma-Gospel to Written Gospels," *NTS* 35 (1989): 369-70.

than the beginning and ending of one?"[155] If the gospel of the kingdom is explicitly introduced in Mark 1:14-15 and this begins a separate section in Mark's book, then "the gospel" in Mark 1:1 can be viewed as distinct from the gospel of the kingdom that is preached by John the Baptist in verses 4-14 and by the Lord Himself in Mark 1:15ff.

It is quite possible that the phrase, *"the beginning of the gospel,"* in Mark 1:1 refers to the origins of the gospel that Mark is primarily occupied with in his book, namely the gospel of Christ's person and work in His death and resurrection (Mark 8:35; 10:29;[156] 14:9; 16:15). This would mean that although the phrase *"the beginning"* in verse 1 refers strictly to the introduction of Mark in chapter 1, the content of this "gospel" consists of Christ's person and saving work via His death and resurrection, which are the focal point of the rest of Mark's book.[157] This interpretation has another advantage. When the full phrase, *"the beginning of the gospel,"* in verse 1 is understood this way, as a reference to the origin, source, or basis for the gospel of salvation that unfolds later with Christ's death and resurrection, then there is no need to collapse the gospel of the kingdom (Mark 1:14-15) and the gospel of Christ into one overarching, all-encompassing "gospel" that is "the full story in Mark." To do so would effectively end up blurring and obscuring the lines of distinction between the gospel of the kingdom and the gospel of Christ, which is exactly what some dispensationally inconsistent Lordship Salvationists[158] and crossless gospel proponents are calling for.[159] Instead, it is better to maintain this distinction and interpret *"the beginning of the gospel"* in Mark 1:1 as expressing the fact that the gospel of Christ, which is the saving message today, had its origin or source or basis in the prophetic ministry of the Old Testament prophets and John the Baptist as described in Mark 1:2-15. This interpretation has real merit and must be acknowledged as a legitimate interpretative possibility by advocates of the crossless position.

---

[155] Morna D. Hooker, *Beginnings: Keys That Open the Gospels* (Harrisburg, PA: Trinity Press International, 1997), 8.

[156] Some may reason that the "gospel" in Mark 10:29 is a reference to the gospel of the kingdom since the Lord Jesus speaks in the past tense of the one "who has left" kindred and possessions for His sake and the gospel's. It is possible, however, that the Lord is speaking of a timeless truth or principle about sacrifice and reward for preaching good news, whether it is the gospel of the kingdom or the gospel of grace. Or, it may even be a proleptic statement about what His followers would do after His imminent death and resurrection. That is, individually, each disciple would be considered one "who has left" family, possessions, etc. for the cause of Christ and the spread of the gospel (16:15).

[157] Collins, *Mark,* 131; France, *The Gospel of Mark,* 51; Robert A. Guelich, "The Gospel Genre," in *Das Evangelium und die Evangelien: Vorträge vom Tübinger Symposium 1982,* ed. Peter Stuhlmacher (Tübingen: Mohr Siebeck, 1983), 204-7; idem, *Mark 1-8:26,* 12; Hengel, *The Four Gospels,* 91, 93, 267n374.

[158] John F. MacArthur Jr., *The Gospel According to Jesus: What Does Jesus Mean When He Says, "Follow Me"?* (Grand Rapids: Zondervan, 1988), 25, 89, 213-14; idem, *Kingdom Living Here and Now* (Chicago: Moody Press, 1980), 5-22.

[159] Myers, "The Gospel is More Than 'Faith Alone in Christ Alone'," 36-40.

View #2—Mark 1:1 Refers Broadly to Mark's Book or Message

The possibility must also be entertained that Mark 1:1 does function as a title, as many commentators maintain.[160] In such a case, the title would be viewed as summarizing Mark's entire book.[161] But even if this interpretation is correct, it would not necessarily lead to the doctrinal conclusions drawn from it by those promoting the crossless gospel. For example, if Mark 1:1 refers to the whole book, it is still possible to interpret Mark's entire book as constituting only "the beginning" of the gospel that was being propagated later by the Church in Acts and the Epistles. In this respect, the phrase, *"the beginning of the gospel,"* assumes a vantage point that is retrospective on the part of the one reading Mark, where it is learned what events transpired to form the gospel message that was presently being proclaimed by the time of Mark's composition a few decades after the cross and resurrection. Although this interpretation is a minority view within New Testament scholarship,[162] it must still be noted as one more possible interpretation of *euangelion* in Mark 1:1 that does not support the crossless position.

But if the G.E.S. interpretation of Mark 1:1 is correct and *euangelion* in this verse refers to "the full story in Mark," then this presupposes that

---

[160] Henry Alford, *The Greek Testament*, rev. Everett F. Harrison (Chicago: Moody Press, 1958), 1:309; Ulrich Becker, *"εὐαγγέλιον," NIDNTT*, 2:112; Boring, "Mark 1:1-15 and the Beginning of the Gospel," 43, 50-51; Donald W. Burdick, "Gospel of Mark," in *The Wycliffe Bible Commentary*, ed. Everett F. Harrison (Chicago: Moody Press, 1962), 989; John R. Donahue and Daniel J. Harrington, *The Gospel of Mark* (Collegeville, MN: Liturgical Press, 2002), 59-60; James R. Edwards, *The Gospel according to Mark*, PNTC (Grand Rapids: Eerdmans, 2002), 23, 26; John D. Grassmick, "Mark," in BKC (Wheaton, IL: Victor Books, 1983), 2:102; Walter Grundmann, *"χρίω," TDNT*, 9:537; D. Edmond Hiebert, *Mark: A Portrait of the Servant* (Chicago: Moody Press, 1974), 27; James A. Kelhoffer, "'How Soon a Book' Revisited: EUAGGELION as a Reference to 'Gospel' Materials in the First Half of the Second Century," *ZNW* 95 (2004): 29; Eugene LaVerdiere, *The Beginning of the Gospel: Introducing the Gospel According to Mark* (Collegeville, MN: Liturgical Press, 1999), 4; Ralph P. Martin, "Gospel," *ISBE*, 2:531; Willi Marxsen, *Mark the Evangelist: Studies on the Redaction History of the Gospel*, trans. James Boyce, Donald Juel, William Poehlmann with Roy A. Harrisville (Nashville: Abingdon, 1969), 131-32; Frank J. Matera, "The Prologue as the Interpretative Key to Mark's Gospel," *JSNT* 34 (1988): 6; John A. T. Robinson, *Redating the New Testament* (London: SCM Press, 1976), 115; Frank Stagg, "Gospel in Biblical Usage," *RevExp* 63.1 (1966): 7; John Wenham, *Redating Matthew, Mark, and Luke: A Fresh Assault on the Synoptic Problem* (Downers Grove, IL: InterVarsity Press, 1992), 133-35; Theodor Zahn, *Introduction to the New Testament*, trans. from 3rd German ed. (Edinburgh: T & T Clark, 1909), 2:456-61.

[161] C. C. Broyles, "Gospel (Good News)," in *Dictionary of Jesus and the Gospels*, ed. Joel B. Green, Scot McKnight, and I. Howard Marshall (Downers Grove, IL: InterVarsity Press, 1992), 285; A. B. Bruce, "The Synoptic Gospels," in *The Expositor's Greek Testament*, ed. W. Robertson Nicoll (Grand Rapids: Eerdmans, Reprinted 1990), 1:341; Alfred Plummer, *The Gospel According to St. Mark*, CGTC (Cambridge: Cambridge University Press, 1914), 51; Vincent Taylor, *The Gospel According to St. Mark: The Greek Text with Introduction, Notes, and Indexes* (New York: St. Martin's Press, 1966), 152.

[162] Leander E. Keck, "The Introduction to Mark's Gospel," *NTS* 12 (1966): 366-67; Frank J. Matera, "The Prologue as the Interpretative Key to Mark's Gospel," *JSNT* 34 (1988): 6; Rudolf Schnackenburg, "'Das Evangelium' im Verständnis des ältesten Evangelisten," in *Orientierung an Jesus*, ed. Paul Hoffmann (Freiburg: Herder, 1973), 321-23.

Mark 1:1 functions as a virtual title. So what evidence exists for Mark 1:1 being a title? Those who support the "title" view often note that in the rest of Mark's Gospel there are no other pericopes or narrative sections that are preceded by a construction similar to verse 1.[163] This would make it less likely that Mark 1:1 is the heading merely for the introductory section of chapter 1, whether it extends only to verse 3 or all the way to verse 15. A second reason for viewing Mark 1:1 as a title is the awkward syntax found in verses 1-4. If verse 1 was intended to be syntactically related to verses 2-3 or 2-4 as one continuous sentence with no period at the end of verse 1 and with verses 2-3 being parenthetical, then admittedly such a connection is not readily apparent based upon a casual reading of the text.

As sound as the reasons are in favor of viewing Mark 1:1 as a title for the whole book, there are also valid reasons to support the non-titular, introductory-section view, making it difficult to decide which interpretation is correct. The exegetical support for either view should make the proponents of the crossless position pause and not be overly dogmatic that the term *euangelion* in Mark 1:1 must refer to "the full story in Mark." Furthermore, even if *euangelion* does have a titular sense in Mark 1:1 and it refers to the entire contents of Mark's Gospel, then it must also be conceded that Mark 1:1 stands by itself as a completely distinct usage of *euangelion* in the entire New Testament. In this respect, Mark 1:1 would stand alone as a separate category of usage for *euangelion* in the same way that Revelation 14:6 is unparalleled. This would still be consistent with the fact that the vast majority of occurrences of *euangelion* and *euangelizō* in the New Testament refer to the specific saving message known as the gospel of Christ.

Inherent Problems with the "Full Story" Concept of Euangelion

Even if *euangelion* in Mark 1:1 is part of a title, then this creates an apparent interpretative problem. Assuming that the conclusions made previously are correct about the authenticity of the superscription *euangelion kata markon*, and assuming that Mark 1:1 is a title for the entirety of Mark's book, then this would appear to give the Gospel of Mark two titles. While this would be unusual, and therefore somewhat suspect, it would not be out of the realm of possibility. But if the superscription of Mark is original and Mark 1:1 is descriptive of Mark's content as a whole, then how do these two uses of *euangelion* relate to one another? Are they harmonious? Do they form a coherent thought?

One possible solution may be as follows: if the superscription to the whole book stated, "Good News according to Mark," then this would naturally have begged the question in the mind of the reader, "What *'good*

[163] Taylor, *The Gospel According to St. Mark*, 152; Zahn, *Introduction to the New Testament*, 2:458.

news' is this title referring to that is according to Mark?" This would have been answered distinctively and immediately by Mark in the opening verse of his book, *"The beginning of the good news of Jesus Christ, the Son of God."* Here *euangelion* would function as a possible continuation of thought from the superscription of Mark so that the sense of the superscription plus Mark 1:1 would be: *"Good News according to Mark—the beginning of that good news about Jesus Christ, the Son of God."*[164] According to this scenario, the term *euangelion* in Mark 1:1 would have an explanatory force whereby it describes and specifies the character and content of Mark's book—that it is good news particularly about one named Jesus who is the Christ, the Son of God. However, even according to this scenario, *euangelion* in Mark 1:1 can be viewed as a reference to the particular "saving message" of the gospel of Christ, since Christ's person and the saving work of His death and resurrection are the focus of Mark's book. Even if Mark 1:1 is titular in some sense, in addition to the superscription, this does not necessarily support the view that *euangelion* in Mark 1:1 encompasses every detail of Mark's book.

There is a second problem that exists if *euangelion* in Mark 1:1 is a title that refers to everything in Mark; and this problem relates directly to the broad, all-encompassing, G.E.S. notion of "the gospel" as a message covering the entire Bible all the way back to creation. Even if "the gospel" in Mark 1:1 means the whole contents of Mark's book, then wouldn't this also mean that "the gospel," as Mark defines it, starts only with the adult status of Jesus Christ? Mark and John in their Gospels omit any reference to Christ's virgin conception and birth, or His infancy and childhood. This leads us to ask, did "the gospel" only begin when Jesus Christ was an adult? What verse among all 132 uses of *euangelion* and *euangelizō* includes the story of the Savior's miraculous virgin conception and birth? *There are none*! This is true even in Luke 1:19, a passage cited earlier by Myers to support the broad concept of "the gospel." There, *euangelizō* occurs in the annunciation of John the Baptist's birth to his mother Elizabeth. But even this event occurred chronologically before the description of John's preaching and baptizing ministry in Mark 1, and thus it is not included in Mark's supposedly broad, all-encompassing "gospel." *The fact remains that there is not a single usage of either euangelion or euangelizō in the entire New Testament that supports the all-inclusive G.E.S. concept of "the gospel."*

The new, crossless view of *euangelion* in Mark 1:1 also leads to other serious theological problems. For instance, in Mark 8:29-30, the Lord Jesus has been largely rejected by the nation of Israel and He is now set on an irreversible course to Jerusalem in order to suffer, die, and rise again. He then commands His disciples from that time forward to *"tell no one"* that He is the Christ (Matt. 16:21). If this passage in Mark is every bit as much

---

164 While this explanation is theoretically possible, I am not aware of any comparable examples of such a construction occurring elsewhere in early, extra-biblical literature.

"the gospel" for us today as the gospel of the grace of God (Acts 20:24), then how do we apply this command to *"tell no one"* that He is the Christ in light of His Great Commission command to do just the opposite? If Mark 8:29-30 is every bit as much "the gospel" for us today as Mark 16:15, then which passage do we follow, since they give contrasting commands?

A Lordship Salvation "Gospel"

If all of Mark is "the gospel," then this also leads to doctrinal confusion in other ways. For example, in what sense can the unpardonable sin (Mark 3:22-30), eternal suffering in hell (Mark 8:42-50), and the horrors of the great tribulation (Mark 13) actually be considered "good news"? While the "bad news" may form the pre-evangelistic context for the gospel, it is not "good news" in any sense. In addition, if all of Mark is equated with "the gospel" for today and Christ called His disciples to abandon all and follow Him (Mark 8:34), then hasn't obedient discipleship become part of "the gospel" now too? Although Wilkin and Myers categorically reject the teachings of Lordship Salvation and deny that its "gospel" is necessary to believe for eternal life, they are nevertheless stuck in the conundrum that "the gospel" as they have defined it is logically consistent with John MacArthur's "gospel."

Leading Lordship Salvation proponent, John MacArthur states, *"The gospel Jesus proclaimed was a call to discipleship, a call to follow Him in submissive obedience."*[165] Compare this to what Bob Wilkin is currently teaching. He states that "the gospel" includes "the call to discipleship."[166] When referring to the terms *"evangelism"* and *"evangelistic,"* Wilkin states that, "They refer to sharing the entire good news about Jesus, including both sanctification and justification truth, both how to be born again and how to follow Christ via baptism and discipleship."[167] Amazingly, though coming from completely opposite ends of the soteriological-spectrum, proponents of the new G.E.S. "gospel" now share with MacArthur a significant amount of agreement on the very definition of "the gospel."

Nor is the new G.E.S. definition of the gospel unique to Wilkin, as Myers concurs with Wilkin, writing, "However, Mark and Luke also make frequent mention of the *gospel* when mixed multitudes, Gentiles, disciples or the whole world is in view (Mark 14:9). *Frequently, in these gospel offers, commitment, discipleship and cost are required of those who will respond.* But in these instances, it is not everlasting life that is offered, but great reward in the life to come (Mark 8:35; 10:29)."[168] Myers goes on to say, "Many say that the Lordship of Christ is essential to the gospel, which here is seen

---

[165] MacArthur, *The Gospel According to Jesus*, 21.

[166] Wilkin, "Gospel Means Good News," 5.

[167] Wilkin, "Is Jesus' Evangelistic Message Sufficient Today?" 2.

[168] Myers, "The Gospel is More Than 'Faith Alone in Christ Alone'," 43 (italics added).

to be true."[169] It is no wonder that Myers opens his article with the shocking and confusing admission, "Like Lordship/Perseverance authors, we equate the gospel with what a person must believe in order to receive everlasting life. *Our definition of the gospel does not differ from theirs*; we just have different ideas on what is essential to the gospel."[170]

While Lordship Salvationists maintain that believing the gospel is necessary for eternal life, whereas the G.E.S. view requires it only for sanctification, both hold to essentially the same definition of the gospel. Statements such as the preceding by Myers and Wilkin ought to ring like alarm-bells in the minds of all believers dedicated to the gospel of the grace of God. We must now ask what the Free Grace movement is coming to when the very organization that was once founded to oppose the false doctrines of Lordship Salvation is now openly confessing agreement with it on the "definition of the gospel." Has the G.E.S. come full circle? Not quite; but there is still much cause for concern.

There was once a time when Free Grace people universally recognized the distinction between the gospel of salvation for the unbeliever and the message of discipleship for the believer. In the very first edition of the *Journal of the Grace Evangelical Society* in 1988, it was affirmed that the purpose of G.E.S.'s existence was to educate people about the gospel. In that opening edition, the late Art Farstad wrote: "Grace Evangelical Society is neither a church nor a denomination. Rather, it is a parachurch organization designed to encourage and educate churches and individuals concerning *the Gospel and the related yet distinct issues of discipleship*. GES seeks not only to talk about the Gospel, but also to share it actively with those who do not yet know the grace of God."[171]

Sadly, the G.E.S. has abandoned this position. Due to their redefinition of the gospel, they have not held fast to biblical truth and are no longer distinguishing the gospel from discipleship. Discipleship has now become part of the gospel message instead of being a separate truth that is based upon the gospel. And what is the reason for this confusion? It stems directly from the new view that "the gospel" is *not* "the saving message" but instead is a much broader message that is only necessary to believe for the Christian's sanctification.

---

[169] Ibid., 45 (brackets added).

[170] Ibid., 33 (italics added).

[171] Arthur L. Farstad, "An Introduction to Grace Evangelical Society and Its Journal," *JOTGES* 1 (Autumn 1988): 4 (italics added).

Chapter 9

Is the Gospel of Christ the Saving Message?

OVERVIEW

Of the 132 times in the New Testament that the terms euangelion and euangelizō occur, the vast majority of these refer to the good news of Jesus being the Christ, otherwise known as "the gospel of the Christ." This is a specific and identifiable message that has not been arbitrarily manufactured by any man but divinely revealed and determined by God alone. Although the exact number of elements in this message is not a matter disclosed by divine revelation, the essential content of the gospel has been revealed. This content consists of Christ's person and finished work along with the provision and condition for salvation. This entails His deity, humanity, substitutionary death, bodily resurrection, and salvation by grace through faith in Him alone. This content is perfectly harmonious with, and even inseparable from, belief in the person of Christ as the object of saving faith. Free Grace Christians must be clear and unequivocal in using biblical language, as we confidently proclaim "the gospel of the Christ" as God's saving message to the lost.

The previous chapter demonstrated that the terms *euangelion* and *euangelizō* are not in themselves technical terms but are used in the New Testament for a variety of "good news" messages that are entirely distinct from one another. These forms of "good news" included the gospel of the kingdom, the everlasting gospel, a narrative having the character or quality of good news (based on the four Gospel titles), and finally the difficult and debated reference in Mark 1:1 which may simply be a reference to the origin of the gospel of Christ or a heading limited to some portion of Mark 1:1-15. The entirety of this chapter will be devoted to another distinct category of usage for the terms *euangelion* and *euangelizō*, namely the message about Jesus Christ known as the "gospel of Christ."

At issue here is the question of whether the gospel of Christ is a specific, definable, and knowable message that is equivalent to the contents of saving faith in this present dispensation. This chapter will demonstrate from Scripture that the gospel of Christ is not just a message that is *sufficient* for eternal salvation, it is also *necessary* (Rom. 2:16; 1 Cor. 1:17-21; 2 Cor. 4:3-4; Eph. 1:13; 2 Thess. 1:8-10; 1 Peter 4:17-18). This chapter will demonstrate that the gospel is "the saving message." It is a specific, identifiable message that is able to be distinguished from false forms of the good news (Gal. 1:6-9). This means that it was intended by God to be understood and accepted in its simplicity (2 Cor. 11:3-4). As a comprehensible and accessible message, the gospel of Christ has specific content that can be supported by an abundance of passages in God's Word. Contrary to crossless gospel claims, it is not a message that is arbitrarily determined by each individual interpreter but it has been revealed by God Himself (Gal. 1:10-12) and placed in the Bible in order to be preached and believed for the justification of all (Rom. 1:16). Unfortunately, however, there seems to exist among some Free Grace evangelicals a subtle form of agnosticism creeping in regarding the precise contents of this gospel.

Evangelical Agnosticism & Uncertainty

Some Free Grace evangelicals object to any attempt at identifying the essential revelation that God requires to be believed for regeneration. This may be due to the postmodern mindset that has enveloped the western world with its aversion to all absolutes and claims of certainty.[1] Free Grace

[1] Herein lies the value of a book such as J. B. Hixson's, *Getting the Gospel Wrong: The Evangelical Crisis No One Is Talking About* (n.p.: Xulon Press, 2008). This helpful work not only addresses the true gospel in contrast to the many false forms of it that have sprung up in contemporary evangelicalism, but it also lays the ax to a principal root cause—the absence of the absolute authority of God's Word as the final arbiter of truth in the hearts and minds

Christians in America are not exempt from the subtle undermining influence of this worldly philosophy. As a result, some in their cynicism may be thinking that it is futile to even attempt to answer a question that they suppose God's Word does not answer. In other cases, Free Grace Christians have grown weary of the battle between the two sides in the present debate and are increasingly numb or apathetic about whether there really are clear biblical answers. Regardless of the causes for the present uncertainty that some have, it is tragic that these Free Grace brethren are taking an essentially agnostic approach to this content-question as they now embrace the view that God never intended us to know the exact contents of the saving gospel. This line of thinking, however, is not merely unbiblical, but in many cases it is nothing less than a smug, false piety and willful unbelief that is displeasing to the Lord (Heb. 3:12; 11:6).

I have also heard the sentiment expressed that this entire line of inquiry is misguided from the start. Some Free Grace Christians have concluded that we should simply be encouraging people to believe as much of the Bible as possible, and leave the matter of "how much content is needed" up to God to resolve however, whenever, and if ever He sees fit. Following this prescription, we should not bother even attempting to deduce any specific *sine qua non* of saving faith from the Bible. While it is certainly true that we should encourage people to believe the whole counsel of God, for us to leave the question of saving content open-ended actually gives people the *wrong* impression. They are left with the mistaken notion that they must believe as much of the Bible as possible *in order to be saved*. And, of course, since believing as much of the Bible as possible is entirely too broad and subjective, personal assurance of eternal salvation ends up being sacrificed as people cannot know with certainty that they have believed what God requires.

Occasionally in the present debate, some Free Grace brethren have stated that if we simply "preach the maximum not the minimum" then this whole debate is rendered moot and we can safely rest assured that we have fulfilled our evangelistic responsibilities. But this does not move us any closer toward resolution, since "the maximum" and "the minimum" are still unknown quantities. How will we know if we are even falling between these two boundaries if we do not know what the boundaries are? Just as any football game cannot be played, or its outcome properly determined, without clearly delineated sidelines and end zones, neither can a soul be personally assured of heaven in the high stakes game of evangelism without a clearly defined gospel as our baseline. Moving the marker somewhere between "the maximum" and "the minimum" is simply too vague to be of any value. And what extreme boundaries these are! What is "the maximum" anyway, if not the entire Bible?![2] Is our evan-

---

of our relativistic, narcissistic, postmodern generation.

[2] Unfortunately, even Clark embraced this flawed perspective in his highly touted book

gelistic goal, as given to us by the Master Himself, to preach to the lost "the whole counsel of God" in order for them to receive eternal life?[3] If preaching "the maximum not the minimum" is the standard, then how will we ever know if we've preached enough? Or too little? It is for this reason, thankfully, that Scripture never speaks in terms of "maximum" and "minimum" but only tells the lost to believe "the gospel."

The solution to the present confusion over the contents of the gospel and saving faith is to return to God's Word in earnest expectation that He has provided us with definite answers to this question if we would only apply our hearts to understanding (Prov. 2:2; 22:17; 23:12). The belief that the elements of the gospel can be known is based on the nature and fact of divine revelation—that God has actually delighted in disclosing to us, via the Scriptures, the precious contents of the soul-saving message. Proverbs 22:20-21 says, *"Have I not written to you excellent things of counsels and knowledge, 21 that I may make you know the certainty of the words of truth, that you may answer words of truth to those who send to you?"* This principle of the perspicuity of Scripture is especially applicable in the area of evangelism and the contents of the gospel. If God went to such great lengths to make our eternal salvation possible by not sparing His own Son (Rom. 8:32), would He then fumble the ball by obscuring the necessary contents of faith in His Word? Are we honestly to believe that among the 132 instances where the Spirit of God placed the words *euangelion* and *euangelizō* in the Bible that the contents of saving faith are never specifically spelled out for us?!

It is amazing that we in the Free Grace movement, in our dealings with the doctrine of Lordship Salvation, have spent several decades diligently studying the Scriptures and writing articles, books, theses, and dissertations on the worthy subject of works and spiritual fruit in relationship to saving faith. We have approached the topic of the nature of saving faith with the presupposition that God has provided objective truth to guide us in what is a rather subjective area of our lives—fruit-bearing. We have proceeded to scrutinize the matter of the "amount" of works, the "nature" and "kind" of saving faith, along with "perseverance" in faith and good works, all in relationship to regeneration and assurance. But suddenly when the subject switches from the *nature* of saving faith to the *contents*

---

on the nature of saving faith. See Gordon H. Clark, *Faith and Saving Faith*, 2nd ed. (Jefferson, MD: Trinity Foundation, 1990), 109-10.

[3] Ibid. Clark suggested that "the maximum" may be the "multi-paragraph thirty-three chapters of the Westminster Confession" (ibid., 109), since Christ said regarding discipleship in the Galilean Great Commission of Matthew 28:20, "teaching them to observe *all things* that I have commanded you" (ibid., 110). Thus, Clark concluded, "a minister should not confine himself to topics popularly thought to be 'evangelistic,' but should preach the whole counsel of God, trusting that God will give someone the gift of faith through sermons on the Trinity, eschatology, or the doctrine of immediate imputation" (ibid., 110).

of saving faith, we become pensive and wonder whether God has spoken with as much precision and clarity in His Word.

Crossless Confusion and Ambiguity

Down through Church history, the allegorical method of interpreting Scripture has thrown a veil over God's Word, shrouding it in uncertainty. This approach to hermeneutics was a primary contributing factor in launching the Church into the Dark Ages. In our day, the modern crossless gospel and its false paradigms have begun causing confusion, uncertainty, and doubt about God's Word among Free Grace Christians by obscuring the biblical meaning of "the gospel." Within the collective consciousness of the Free Grace community, the gospel was once commonly understood to be the saving message of Christ's person and finished work. Even the seminal book by Zane Hodges titled, *The Gospel Under Siege*, reflected this once assumed meaning. Ironically, however, such a book title would not be chosen by crossless gospel proponents today. Instead, it would need to be called, *The Saving Message Under Siege*. In recent years there has been a sudden change with the advent of the Grace Evangelical Society's new teaching on "the gospel." The new doctrine states that "the gospel" is a broad, all-encompassing message that is not synonymous with the saving message. This new view of "the gospel" is reflected in a recent G.E.S. journal article where the author, Jeremy Myers, surveys the use of the term "gospel" in the New Testament. In the article, Myers makes the astonishing claim, *"You do not have to believe the gospel to receive everlasting life, you only have to believe in Jesus for everlasting life."*[4] He then qualifies this comment by saying that a lost person must still believe "part of the gospel" to be born again:

> Of course, as this study has revealed, faith in Christ for everlasting life is an element of the gospel, for what better news in Scripture is there that anyone who believes in Jesus has everlasting life? There is no better news. But there is a vast difference between saying that this truth is *part* of the gospel and saying that it *is* the gospel. Similarly, saying that one has to believe the gospel to be saved is like saying one has to believe the Bible to be saved. Such a statement is not wrong; it's just too vague.[5]

Even with this qualification, the conclusion that people can receive eternal life without believing the gospel is simply unsalvageable and hopelessly unbiblical. If, as Myers claims, it is technically "not wrong" to tell people "to believe the gospel" but "just too vague," then what shall we say of God's Word itself when in various passages it requires the lost to believe only

[4] Jeremy D. Myers, "The Gospel is More Than 'Faith Alone in Christ Alone'," *JOTGES* 19 (Autumn 2006): 51.

[5] Ibid.

"the gospel" (Mark 16:15-16; 1 Cor. 1:17; 4:15; 15:1)? Nor is it biblical to teach that people are regenerated by believing *"part of* the gospel." The Word of God consistently teaches that the dividing line between heaven and hell is whether a person has believed "the gospel" or not (2 Thess. 1:8-10). A person is never said to be saved by believing "part of" the gospel.[6] But, if we accept the G.E.S. premise that the "gospel" in the New Testament is a broad, all-encompassing term comprised of at least 50 different items and that a lost sinner only has to believe one of those items (*"believe in Jesus for everlasting life"*), then this leads to a rather bizarre conclusion. It would mean that a person must believe only *one-fiftieth* of the gospel to go to heaven! This undoubtedly falls under the category of "various and strange doctrines" (Heb. 13:9). The G.E.S. doctrine of "the gospel" is not the natural by-product of interpreting each occurrence of the terms *euangelion* and *euangelizō* in the New Testament according to a normal, grammatical, historical method of interpretation. Rather, it is the result of imposing the new crossless theology upon these "gospel" passages.

The Gospel Is a Specific Message

In contrast to the breadth and vagueness with which some Free Grace Christians are now speaking of "the gospel," the New Testament is quite specific about this message. On this point, New Testament scholar Gerhard Friedrich makes a very significant observation regarding the use of the term *euangelion* in the New Testament. He states, "Most of the NT εὐαγγέλιον passages are in Paul. . . . How firm a magnitude the concept is for him may be seen from the fact that in almost half of the passages he speaks of τὸ εὐαγγέλιον in the absolute. He does not need any noun or adj. to define it. The readers know what it is. Hence explanation is unnecessary."[7] What this observation indicates is that the gospel was a precise, concrete, recognizable message that was mutually understood by Paul and his first century Christian readers.[8] But this is inconsistent with the notion of "the gospel" in

---

[6] For further elaboration on this point, see the section in chapter 14 under the subheading, *Believing "Part of" the Gospel?*

[7] Gerhard Friedrich, "εὐαγγελίζομαί, εὐαγγέλιον, προευαγγελίζομαί, εὐαγγελιστής," *TDNT* (Grand Rapids: Eerdmans, 1964-76), 2:729 (ellipsis added). Unfortunately, after making this clarifying, exegetical observation, Friedrich immediately goes on to disclaim the clear inference of his own observation, saying, "Nevertheless, for us εὐαγγέλιον is not a consistent and clearly definable term which we can express in a brief formula" (2:729). While it's true that the gospel is not a brief formula, Friedrich's disavowal of the Bible's clarity, and even the clear implications of his own exegetical observation, reflects the liberal, higher-critical unbelief that pervades his entire entry in Kittel's *TDNT.* If, admittedly, τὸ εὐαγγέλιον was known as an absolute message by both Paul and his original readers, so that an explanation of its contents was normally not necessary, then why can't its meaning be understood absolutely by us as well? Why must it be lost on modern readers but not first century readers?

[8] Ulrich Becker, "εὐαγγέλιον," in *NIDNTT,* ed. Colin Brown (Grand Rapids: Zondervan, 1986), 2:110; Helmut Koester, "From the Kerygma-Gospel to Written Gospels," *NTS* 35 (1989): 362.

today's crossless theology. If the New Testament "gospel" includes upwards of 50 different elements and possibly even the contents of the entire Old and New Testaments, then how could Paul so frequently assume that his readers understood what he meant by "the gospel"?

It may even be added that the use of the definite article in 73 out of 76 occurrences of *euangelion* provides further support for the conclusion that "the gospel" is a specific, recognizable message. The consistent use of the article with *euangelion* goes beyond the category of being a "well-known article" but is instead the use of the article "par excellence."[9] Regarding this category of usage, Wallace states, "Often '**the** gospel' (*τὸ εὐαγγέλιον*) and '**the** Lord' (*ὁ κύριος*) employ articles par excellence. In other words, there was only *one* gospel and *one* Lord worth mentioning as far as the early Christians were concerned."[10]

And why should we be surprised that the Scriptures speak with such specificity regarding the gospel? Of God's "works" in general, we are told, *"The works of the LORD are great, studied by all who have pleasure in them"* (Ps. 111:2). A reverent, scientific study of God's work in creation reveals Him to be the God of infinite order, complexity, and detail. The same observation is true with respect to biblical prophecy. God has chosen to reveal His prophetic plan for the future in such minute detail that devout believers are able to create elaborate charts and diagrams depicting the precise chronology of future events. But if God is so concerned with detail and order concerning non-redemptive subjects such as creation and prophecy, why would He be less concerned about specificity when it comes to the gospel and the contents of saving faith? The "gospel" was never meant to be cryptically concealed from mankind, as though God intended evangelism to be a game of hide-and-go-seek with taunts such as, "You're getting warmer!" Rather, the "gospel" was intended to be fully proclaimed, published, understood, and believed by every member of the human race as a very special revelation from a loving, gracious, and all-powerful God *"who desires all men to be saved and to come to the knowledge of the truth"* (1 Tim. 2:4). But what is *"the* knowledge" of *"the* truth"?

The Gospel of Christ

The form of good news that most evangelical Christians immediately think of when using the word "gospel" is the gospel of Christ. This gospel refers specifically to the message of good news about Jesus Christ being God's incarnate Son who died as a vicarious sacrifice for our sins and rose bodily from the dead to provide eternal salvation to all who put their faith in Him and not in their own works or righteousness. This is also, by far, the most

---

[9] Daniel B. Wallace, *Greek Grammar Beyond the Basics: An Exegetical Syntax of the New Testament* (Grand Rapids: Zondervan, 1996), 222-23.

[10] Ibid., 223.

prevalent usage of the term "gospel" in the New Testament, occurring 100-102 times out of 132 total instances of *euangelion* and *euangelizō*.[11] The noun *euangelion* refers to this particular gospel 65-67 times in the New Testament: Matt. 26:13; Mark 1:1 [?]; 8:35; 10:29 [?]; 14:9; 16:15; Acts 15:7; 20:24; Rom. 1:1, 9, 16; 2:16; 10:16; 11:28; 15:16, 19; 16:25; 1 Cor. 4:15; 9:12, 14 (2x), 18 (2x), 23; 15:1; 2 Cor. 2:12; 4:3-4; 8:18; 9:13; 10:14; 11:7; Gal. 1:7, 11; 2:2, 5, 7, 14; Eph. 1:13; 3:6; 6:15, 19; Phil. 1:5, 7, 12, 16 [CT]/17 [MT], 27 (2x); 2:22; 4:3, 15; Col. 1:5, 23; 1 Thess. 1:5; 2:2, 4, 8, 9; 3:2; 2 Thess. 1:8; 2:14; 1 Tim. 1:11; 2 Tim. 1:8, 10; 2:8; Philem. 1:13; 1 Peter 4:17. The verb *euangelizō* also has this meaning 35 times (34x [CT]) in the New Testament: Acts 5:42; 8:4, 12, 25, 35, 40; 11:20; 13:32; 14:7, 15, 21; 15:35; 16:10; 17:18; Rom. 1:15; 10:15 (2x in [MT]; 1x [CT]); 15:20; 1 Cor. 1:17; 9:16 (2x), 18; 15:1, 2; 2 Cor. 10:16; 11:7; Gal. 1:8 (2nd ref.), 11, 16, 23; 4:13; Eph. 2:17; 1 Peter 1:12, 25; 4:6.[12] Several observations are in order regarding these 100-102 references to the gospel of Christ.

First, on a practical level, what these 100 uses of *euangelion* and *euangelizō* reveal is that though the gospel (*euangelion*) itself is definitely emphasized in the New Testament, so is the *preaching* of that gospel (*euangelizō*). Even though there are almost twice as many references to the gospel of Christ using the noun, *euangelion* (65-67x), as compared to the verb, *euangelizō* (35x), the many existing references to *euangelizō* indicates that God not only expects believers today to know the *euangelion* well, but also to be actively engaged in preaching (*euangelizō*) it to a lost and needy world for whom Christ died.[13]

Second, among these 100 instances where *euangelion* and *euangelizō* refers to the particular message of the gospel of Christ, the word "gospel" most often occurs in the absolute sense as simply, "the gospel," without

[11] The two debatable references of Mark 1:1 and 10:29 are addressed in chapter 8.

[12] The conclusion that these 100-102 occurrences of *euangelion* and *euangelizō* refer to the same gospel is based on the confluence of several factors. First, many of these passages in their immediate contexts share in common an explicit reference to Christ's death and/or resurrection. Second, even in the passages above where no such contextual clues exist and *euangelion* and *euangelizō* occur absolutely (i.e., "the gospel") without any qualifiers, it is still clear that only one gospel is being referred to based on other occurrences of *euangelion* and *euangelizō* within that same book and based on that book's flow of thought. For example, even though 1 Cor. 4:15; 9:14, 16, 18 are absolute ("the gospel"), they are bounded by clear references to the work of Christ in 1:17 and 15:1-4. Since Paul does not introduce any other "gospel" after 1:17 or inform the reader that he has switched to another form of good news, it is safe and reasonable to conclude that only one gospel is being referred to throughout the entire epistle. Thirdly, on a larger, collective scale, Peter and Paul never speak of any other type of "gospel" in their epistles or the Book of Acts, such as the "gospel of the kingdom" or "the everlasting gospel" (with the exception of Paul's generic, non-theological "good news" in 1 Thess. 3:6). There is therefore no reason to suspect that either apostle is switching topics to a different gospel without any notification to the reader. Fourthly, since Peter and Paul preached the same gospel (Acts 15:1-11; Gal. 2:2-9), their respective uses of *euangelion* and *euangelizō* must fall within the same category.

[13] Dennis M. Rokser, *Let's Preach the Gospel* (Duluth, MN: Duluth Bible Church, n.d.), 16-18.

any other qualifying words or phrases. But when "the gospel" is modified by other descriptive words or phrases, the most frequent modifier attached to it is the phrase "of Christ," as in *"the gospel of Christ."* This occurs 11 times in the New Testament (Rom. 1:16 [MT]; 15:19, 29 [MT]; 1 Cor. 9:12, 18 [MT]; 2 Cor. 9:13; 10:14; Gal. 1:7; Phil. 1:27; 1 Thess. 3:2). To be even more precise, the Greek text uses the article twice in each of these 11 passages, once before "gospel" and once before "Christ." This means that this form of good news is literally, *"the gospel of the Christ."*

This expression conveys the truth that the gospel of salvation that lost sinners must believe is the particular message about Jesus being "the Christ." As chapters 15-17 will demonstrate, to *"believe that Jesus is the Christ, the Son of God"* (John 20:31) is biblically and theologically equivalent to believing *"the gospel of the Christ."* This also means that when the gospel is properly interpreted from Scripture, it is seen to be equivalent to the "saving message." The contents of this gospel are the very contents of saving faith. This also means that *"the gospel of the Christ"* is not a broad, all-encompassing message of good news comprised of "everything from creation to the New Earth,"[14] as we are told today; but rather, it is a specific message with specific content.

Thirdly, it may also be significant that there is not a single reference to the "gospel of Jesus" in the New Testament as one might expect. There are only two passages where the name "Jesus" is included with the gospel, *"The beginning of the gospel of Jesus Christ, the Son of God"* (Mark 1:1) and *"the gospel of our Lord Jesus Christ"* (2 Thess. 1:8).[15] It is significant to note that in the only two references to the name "Jesus" being associated with "the gospel," it is joined by the title "Christ" in both passages, as well as by "Lord" and "Son of God." The name "Jesus" is never the sole modifier of the phrase, "the gospel." Why is this significant? Because it further substantiates the biblical meaning of Jesus being "the Christ." Though the

---

[14] Bob Wilkin, "Gospel Means Good News," unpublished paper presented at the Grace Evangelical Society National Conference, March 6, 2008, Fort Worth, TX, p. 8.

[15] The Critical Greek Text omits the word "Christ" in this verse, reading *"the gospel of our Lord Jesus."* However, there is solid manuscript evidence for the inclusion of "Christ." The inclusion of "Christ" in 2 Thessalonians 1:8 is supported by uncials ℵ (4th cent.), A (5th), D^P Lat. (6th), 0111 (7th), F (9th), G (9th), 0150, (9th), 0151 (9th), 044 (9th/10th), 056 (10th), 075 (10th), 0142 (10th); and by versions including the Old Latin mss., Latin Vulgate, Syriac Peshitta (4th), Gothic (5th), and patristically by Irenaeus (circa A.D. 180) and Chrysostom (circa A.D. 400). The Critical Text omission of "Christ" in 2 Thessalonians 1:8 is supported by uncials B (4th), D^P Gr. (6th), K (9th), L (9th), P (9th); and by versions including the Syriac Harklensis (early 7th), Coptic Bohairic (9th), Ethiopic (13th); and patristically by one ms. of Chrysostom (circa A.D. 400), Theodoret (5th). The Critical Text reading reflects the inordinate weight given to one ms. here, Codex Vaticanus. Regarding the testimony of the minuscules, NA[27] cites them as being somewhat equally divided (*permulti*), which may explain why the Robinson & Pierpont Majority Text omits "Christ" in its text and places it in the margin (NTBT, 457), while Hodges & Farstad have "Christ" in the text and their footnote indicates that it is the Majority reading (GNTMT, 620).

name "Jesus" is full of import, the title "Christ" tells us even more about the One bearing that name. To believe the "gospel of Christ" is to believe that Jesus is "the Christ"—God-incarnate who died for our sins and rose from the dead to graciously provide eternal salvation. This means that "believing in Jesus" in the crossless gospel sense is simply insufficient. The fact that the Bible never speaks of a "gospel of Jesus" undermines the crossless contention that the lone name of "Jesus" is adequate as an element of the *sine qua non* of the saving message.

Fourthly, it must also be clarified that the category of good news known as the "gospel of Christ" is not derived simply from the 11 occurrences in the New Testament of the exact phrase, "the gospel of the Christ." The Spirit of God saw fit to refer to this form of good news using a variety of expressions. This particular gospel is like a diamond held up to the light that radiates its brilliance through a spectral array of several different multicolored beams, but all emanating from the same precious jewel. In the same way, the variegated terminology of Scripture reveals different facets of this marvelous good news message from God. Thus, "the gospel of Christ" is also referred to in the New Testament with the following expressions: the *"gospel of God"* (7x); the *"gospel of our Lord Jesus Christ"* (1x); the *"gospel of Jesus Christ, the Son of God"* (1x); the *"gospel of His Son"* (1x); the *"gospel of the grace of God"* (1x); the *"gospel of peace"* (2x); the *"gospel of your salvation"* (1x); the *"gospel of the glory"* (2x); *"my gospel"* (3x); *"our gospel"* (3x); and when used absolutely, just *"the gospel"* (34-36x).

The Number of Elements in the Gospel

Anyone who has dialogued with those espousing the crossless position will eventually be confronted with the question of the number of essentials for the elements of the gospel or saving message. There seems to be an obsessive occupation with the need for a "list" by many adherents of the G.E.S. gospel.[16] In fact, some even refer derisively to the traditional Free Grace view of the gospel as "checklist evangelism."[17] The sentiment is even expressed by some disaffected parties in the present debate that since the Holy Spirit nowhere provided us with a specific enumeration of the gospel's contents in God's Word, then we should cease and desist from all attempts at finding such content. At this point, others default to the crossless position and conclude that we should just admit that the gospel is a broad, nebulous, non-technical message encompassing a vast array of

---

[16] Zane C. Hodges, "The Hydra's Other Head: Theological Legalism." *Grace in Focus* 23 (September/October 2008): 2-3; Ken Neff, "What Is the Free Grace Gospel?" *Grace in Focus* 24 (March/April 2009): 3-4; Bob Wilkin, "Scavenger Hunt Salvation Without a List," *Grace in Focus* 23 (May/June 2008): 1, 4; idem, "What Must I Do to Be Saved? The 4, 5, or 6 Essentials," Grace Evangelical Society Conference, Fort Worth, TX, April 1, 2009.

[17] Antonio da Rosa, "Checklist Evangelism and the Dangers of It," Grace Evangelical Society Southern California Regional Conference, August 25, 2007.

items. Myers's conclusion that all of the New Testament is "gospel" is a primary example of this. But what is the result of such thinking? It surely comes at a cost. It leads to a relativistic uncertainty about the saving message of the gospel. Myers demonstrates this by saying:

> Do you see where this leads? As soon as someone starts adding things to the list of what a person must believe in order to have everlasting life, there is no rational stopping place. It's all subjective to how much doctrine you want to throw into the mix. Some will have three essentials, another will have five, while someone else will have eight or ten.[18]

The logic inherent in this line of reasoning is seriously flawed. If "there is no rationale stopping place," as Myers claims, then we must also ask, "Is there a rationale starting place?" And if there is a rationale starting place, where is it? What is it? Once we turn the question around this way, we have already begun the process of identification and specification for the elements of the gospel. But if it's futile to arrive at "five" or even "three" essentials, then should we have only two? How about one? Better yet, why even start the whole subjective process? Isn't it better just to concede that we shouldn't even start it? In which case, logically we should have *no essentials*. Some people's insinuation that we shouldn't even attempt to identify the elements of the gospel ultimately leads to the relativistic, even fatalistic, notion that the specific elements of the gospel cannot be known. This ultimately leads to the conclusion that God hasn't been specific in His Word, so therefore we shouldn't be either. But if there are no identifiable, necessary elements of the gospel to believe for one's eternal salvation, then haven't we arrived at the very subjectivity that Myers and other crossless advocates seek to avoid in their quest for personal assurance of everlasting life? Ironically, in the process of seeking absolute assurance, they have come full circle and actually undermined the very basis for it by their relativistic approach to defining "the gospel."

But putting aside for a moment this major dilemma, we must still respond to the point raised by Myers and other crossless advocates. Why isn't there an inspired list in 1 Corinthians 15 or Romans or Galatians or Acts? Why do we not have some type of New Testament evangelistic "decalogue" to guide us? Maybe you've wondered as I have, even before the emergence of the crossless gospel, why God didn't just provide us with such a bulleted, enumerated list anywhere in His Word. If He had done so, He would have eliminated all this confusion and debate—or so we think. We must be careful at this point not to judge the Almighty by our finite, fallen, human standards of what He should have done, for His judgments are *"unsearchable"* and *"His ways past finding out"* (Rom. 11:33).

---

[18] Jeremy D. Myers, "The Gospel is More Than 'Faith Alone in Christ Alone'," *JOTGES* 19 (Autumn 2006): 49.

The fact remains that God in His infinite wisdom and sovereignty has chosen, for reasons undisclosed to us, not to provide a whole assortment of "lists" that we would have preferred to see in Scripture. Consider, for example, the number of ordinances left by the Lord Jesus for those professing the name of Christ to practice. Roman Catholics believe there are seven sacraments. Most conservative, Bible-believing Christians affirm that there are simply two ordinances: the Lord's Supper and Water Baptism. Other Protestants hold to three sacraments or ordinances by including either confirmation or foot washing. Yet God has not seen fit to enumerate in any passage of Scripture that only "two" ordinances are to be practiced.

Similarly, when it comes to the number of dispensations throughout human history, dispensationalists admit that God did not state anywhere in Scripture the exact number of them.[19] Some dispensationalists, such as this author, agree with the traditional Scofield interpretation that there are seven, even though others such as J. N. Darby held to five,[20] while others such as R. B. Thieme have held to six.[21] Still other dispensationalists will go only so far as to admit that three are the subject of extended revelation in the Word of God (Law, Grace, Kingdom) that must therefore be recognized by all dispensational believers.[22] All dispensationalists agree on these three as the bare minimum; but how can we even agree on these if God hasn't specifically stated anywhere in His Word that there are a minimum number of "three"?

Some doctrines have far greater ramifications than the preceding examples when the issue of "number" is denied. For example, regarding the Trinity, does the Bible ever explicitly state that there are "three" persons in the Godhead? Oh how every Trinitarian wishes it did, if only for the sake of dealing with the Jehovah's Witnesses! And yet how do we know that the number of persons in the Godhead is not "two" or "four" without such an inspired list or number? Do we even need such an enumeration in order to be certain that the Bible teaches that there is one God in three persons, the Father, Son, and Holy Spirit? Even without the number "three" stated anywhere in the Bible, belief in the Trinity is a valid deduction we make from Scripture based on the fact that the Father, Son, and Holy Spirit are all revealed to be distinct persons, and they are all individually called "God." Yet the Scriptures also teach that there is only "one" God.

---

[19] By the same token, covenant theologians are not agreed among themselves on the number of theological covenants in their system, whether 2 (the covenant of works and the covenant of grace) or 3 (the covenants of redemption, works, and grace).

[20] Larry V. Crutchfield, *The Origins of Dispensationalism: The Darby Factor* (Lanham, MD: University Press of America, 1992), 67-140, 211.

[21] Robert B. Thieme, Jr., *The Divine Outline of History: Dispensations and the Church*, ed. Wayne F. Hill (Houston: R. B. Thieme, Jr. Bible Ministries, 1989), 4-6.

[22] Dallas Theological Seminary doctrinal statement, Article V; Charles C. Ryrie, *Dispensationalism* (Chicago: Moody Press, 1995), 46-47.

Similarly, when it comes to the number of inspired books in the Bible, without such a list to inform us, how can we really be sure that the canon of Scripture is closed? What passage says specifically that God has capped-off the number of inspired books at "sixty-six"? How can we be sure there are not fifty-two or eighty-seven books? For that matter, where does it say that there must be thirty-nine books in the Old Testament and twenty-seven in the New Testament? In spite of the fact that there are no revealed numbers or lists, we can be certain of these sixty-six books through the internal testimony of Scripture that explains the nature and qualifications of inspiration and through the confluence of several other factors.[23] Though there are no explicit verses in Scripture giving us the precise list or number of inspired, canonical books, the Lord has still revealed His truth in a definitive fashion that can be known, believed, and proclaimed with certainty.

One final example will suffice to illustrate the point that God does not need to speak in the language of ordinals and cardinals in order for us to have certainty in identifying divinely revealed truths. Returning specifically to the subject of the gospel and salvation, we must ask, "How many human conditions are necessary in order to receive eternal life? How can we be certain that salvation is received through faith *alone*?" No passage of Scripture says specifically that there is "one" condition for eternal salvation or even that it is by faith "alone." Yet, the traditional Protestant doctrine of *sola fide* is a perfectly valid, proper deduction of the facts of divine revelation. *Sola fide* is based on the fact that Scripture repeatedly says salvation is through faith or believing, coupled with the fact that it is *"not by works"* (Titus 3:5) and that it is to *"him who does not work but believes"* (Rom. 4:5).

The point is this, even without a divinely revealed list or number, we are simply not consigned to float on a sea of subjectivity and relativism regarding the specific contents of the gospel, as implied by the crossless position. Furthermore, arguing against a precise number of elements is actually a moot point that won't help establish the G.E.S. gospel either since they contend for three elements as the *sine qua non* of saving faith.[24] But what verse of Scripture actually says there are "three" essentials? We cannot even insist on the number "five," since God does not appear to be concerned with an exact number but only with actual, biblical content. That essential content can be categorized, divided, and subdivided several different ways to aid the comprehension of those seeking to grasp

---

[23] F. F. Bruce, *The Canon of Scripture* (Downers Grove, IL: InterVarsity Press, 1988), 255-69; Norman L. Geisler and William E. Nix, *A General Introduction to the Bible*, rev. ed. (Chicago: Moody Press, 1986), 203-34.

[24] Myers, "The Gospel is More Than 'Faith Alone in Christ Alone'," 52; Robert N. Wilkin, "Justification by Faith Alone is an Essential Part of the Gospel," *JOTGES* 18 (Autumn 2005): 12; idem, *Secure and Sure* (Irving, TX: Grace Evangelical Society, 2005), 74-75.

God's truth. For example, some proponents of the "traditional" Free Grace position might arrive at a *sine qua non* of only "three" elements by stating that the lost must believe in (1) the person of Christ (2) the work of Christ (3) the sole condition of salvation through faith alone. Yet, this saving gospel message would be quite different from the crossless gospel's saving message consisting of its "three" essentials. The number of elements in the gospel is ultimately not the issue—content is. We may never know exactly why the Lord didn't provide us with a list for the contents of saving faith, but neither are we at a loss because of it when our desire is to believe what the Bible reveals.

The Contents of the Saving Gospel

The New Testament teaches that there is a specific form of "good news" that exists today known as "the gospel" that also constitutes the saving message. This "gospel" is by its nature recognizable and distinguishable from the other forms of good news in the New Testament. This means it is definable as to its contents—the very contents of saving faith. This belief has long been held by virtually all evangelical Christians. Accordingly, J. Gresham Machen states:

> When a man, we observed, accepts Christ, not in general but specifically "as He is offered to us in the gospel," such acceptance of Christ is saving faith. It may involve a smaller or greater amount of knowledge. The greater the amount of knowledge which it involves, the better for the soul; but even a smaller amount of knowledge may bring a true union with Christ. When Christ, as he is offered to us in the gospel of His redeeming work, is thus accepted in faith, the soul of that man who believes is saved.[25]

But if salvation is predicated upon accepting Christ by faith "as He is offered to us in the gospel," this naturally raises the question, "What is this gospel and its constituent parts?"

The Gospel's Content Is Not Arbitrary

The nearly constant refrain coming from crossless quarters the last few years states that the contents of saving faith as held by traditional Free Grace proponents is purely "subjective" and "arbitrary" and it has been determined merely by "cherry-picking"[26] various unrelated passages of Scripture. The

[25] J. Gresham Machen, *What Is Faith?* (Grand Rapids: Eerdmans, 1946), 161.

[26] Zane C. Hodges, "The Hydra's Other Head: Theological Legalism," *Grace in Focus* 23 (September/October 2008): 3; Myers, "The Gospel is More Than 'Faith Alone in Christ Alone'," 49; Ken Neff, "What Is the Free Grace Gospel?" *Grace in Focus* 24 (March/April 2009): 3-4; Bob Wilkin, "Another Look at 1 Corinthians 15:3-11," *Grace in Focus* 23 (January/February 2008): 1-2; idem, "Essential Truths About Our Savior," *Grace in Focus* 23 (November/December 2008): 1.

implication is that there is no rationale basis for evangelicalism's inclusion of the person and work of Christ in the contents of saving faith. But are the elements of Christ's deity, humanity, death for sin, resurrection, and salvation by grace through faith simply legalistic "extras" that have been added to the saving message by evangelical tradition? Despite such claims, there are at least three levels of interlocking biblical evidence that support these very elements as the necessary content of saving faith in this present dispensation. The testimony of Scripture is threefold on this point. It consists of the contents observed from each occurrence of the word "gospel" in the New Testament, the meaning conveyed in evangelistic contexts by the use of the word "Christ," and individual salvation passages that condition eternal life on believing only those specific Christological truths that form the grounds of mankind's salvation.

When every occurrence of *euangelion* and *euangelizō* are carefully studied, it is an inescapable fact that the Lord's deity, humanity, substitutionary death and bodily resurrection are specifically stated in Scripture to be components of "the gospel" that must be believed for eternal salvation. These elements are not randomly drawn from various passages to form one disjointed, conglomeration called "the gospel." On the contrary, there are several "gospel" passages that contain every element of this saving message. Acts 13:23-41 is manifestly "the gospel" that Paul preached to the Galatians, as the next chapter demonstrates, and it contains each of these elements as the necessary "gospel" that must be believed for one's justification and eternal life. The same may also be said of Peter's evangelistic sermon in Acts 3. In addition, the Petrine gospel is spelled out in Acts 10:34-43 according to Peter's own testimony (Acts 15:7-11), and this passage also contains each element of saving faith (see chapter 17). In addition, though crossless gospel proponents refuse to acknowledge it, 1 Corinthians 15:1-4 is still a definitive text on "the gospel" that either explicitly or implicitly contains the contents of saving faith (see chapters 13-14).

Besides the contents of "the gospel," there is a second means by which we may identify the elements of God's saving message. There is a perfect symmetry between the contents of the message evangelistically preached to the lost, known as "the gospel of the Christ," and the very meaning of Jesus as "the Christ, the Son of God." This means that believing "the gospel of the Christ" is simply another biblical expression for believing that Jesus is "the Christ, the Son of God" (John 20:31). This conclusion is born out by a detailed, exegetical study of John's meaning for the titles "Christ" and "Son of God" in comparison with every occurrence of *euangelion* and *euangelizō* in the New Testament.

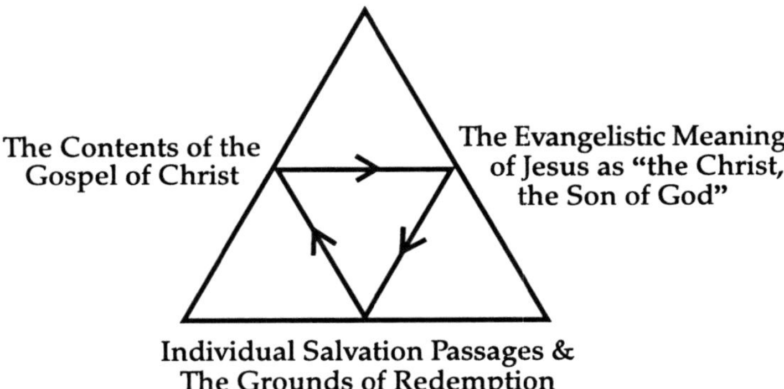
The Contents of the
Gospel of Christ
The Evangelistic Meaning
of Jesus as "the Christ,
the Son of God"
Individual Salvation Passages &
The Grounds of Redemption

Thirdly, the elements of saving faith can be observed from several individual passages of Scripture that limit requisite belief to those truths that form the grounds of mankind's redemption, namely Christ's deity, humanity, substitutionary death, and bodily resurrection (John 6:53; 8:24; Rom. 3:25; 10:9-10), in addition to salvation through faith apart from works (Luke 18:9-12; Eph. 2:8-9). Two significant points about these individual salvation verses must be addressed. First, the identification of these verses is no more "arbitrary" or "cherry-picking" than the methods employed by crossless proponents when they identify and isolate individual evangelistic verses within the Gospel of John—verses which also fit comfortably into the traditional Free Grace contents of saving faith (John 1:12; 3:16; 5:24; 6:47; 11:25-27; 20:31). Secondly, the assorted individual New Testament passages that require belief in some particular truth about Jesus Christ consistently correspond only with those aspects of the Savior's person and work (deity, humanity, death, and resurrection) that form the grounds of mankind's eternal salvation. This is beyond sheer coincidence. It is evidence of divine design.

Unfortunately, the new G.E.S. doctrine is inimical to the Bible's teaching that the grounds of our salvation constitute the very elements of saving faith in the present dispensation. For instance, Bob Wilkin teaches, "There is a difference Biblically between what we must believe to be born again and what the Savior had to be and do in order for us to be born again. The Bible distinguishes between these two."[27] He continues, "Never confuse what our Savior had to be and do to provide salvation with what we must do to obtain it."[28] But contrary to these claims, just the opposite is seen to be true from Scripture. The crossless view fails to properly distinguish

[27] Bob Wilkin, "Essential Truths About Our Savior," *Grace in Focus* 23 (November/December 2008): 1. See also, H. Graham Wilson, Jr., "The Importance of the Incarnation to Resurretion," paper presented at Grace Evangelical Society Conference, Fort Worth, TX, March 31, 2009, p. 15.

[28] Wilkin, "Essential Truths About Our Savior," 2.

between those messianic truths that were necessary for Christ to provide the grounds of mankind's redemption versus His non-redemptive qualifications as the Messiah. Conspicuously, and intentionally, it appears that God in His Word never requires belief in any one of Christ's non-redemptive messianic qualifications in order to grant eternal life. For example, nowhere does the Bible say that belief in Christ's virgin birth, or His tribal descent from Judah, or His ascension into heaven, or even His second coming to rule the world are necessary to believe for eternal life. Though these are essential traits of Jesus as the promised, authentic Messiah, and they should be embraced by every child of God, they are never stated as requirements for eternal salvation.[29] In addition, it should be recognized that while certain divine works apply the finished work of Christ to the believer, they are still distinct from the grounds of redemption. For example, our eternal security and preservation as children of God is assured by Christ's perpetual intercession for us in heaven (Rom. 8:34b; Heb. 7:25). Likewise, the baptizing and sealing work of the Holy Spirit are part of the total salvation package for every believer in this present dispensation (John 7:37-39; 1 Cor. 12:12-13; Eph. 1:13-14; 4:30). But neither of these divine activities constitute the grounds of our salvation, and consequently in the New Testament they are never required to be believed for eternal salvation.

But this raises an important theological question. Why would God require us to believe only those truths about Christ that provide the *grounds* of our eternal salvation rather than all other Christological and soteriological truths? The reason for this is nowhere stated specifically in Scripture, but the answer appears to be wrapped up in the mediatorial role of Jesus Christ (John 14:6; 1 Tim. 2:3-6). It is because the very redemptive grounds of Christ's deity, humanity, death, and resurrection form the only basis upon which God in His infinite holiness can accept unworthy sinners. God requires, therefore, all lost sinners to stake their own salvation upon the very same grounds that He has provided and that He presently offers to sinful mankind. If a sinner will not rest his or her own confidence upon this solitary grace provision of God, then there is no hope for such a person. There is no other way that God can save that guilty soul.[30] The condemned and unworthy sinner, in faith, must meet God on His terms through the person of Christ at Calvary and the Empty

[29] Norman Geisler, *Systematic Theology* (Minneapolis: Bethany House, 2004), 3:529; Charles C. Ryrie, *So Great Salvation: What It Means to Believe in Jesus Christ* (Wheaton, IL: Victor Books, 1989), 40.

[30] This truth was understood by the late Christian hymn writer, John W. Peterson, as reflected in his song, "There Was No Other Way." It states: "Before the stars were hung, or planets fashioned, before the clay was formed, to make a man, Christ was the Lamb of God, for sinners offered, this was redemption's one and only plan. There was no other way, a God of love could find, to reconcile the world and save a lost mankind; it took the death of His own Son upon a tree, there was no other way, but Calvary."

Tomb in order to be accepted by Him. Perhaps it is for this reason that the New Testament so frequently employs the Greek preposition, *epi* ("on, upon"), with *pisteuō* ("believe") and *metanoeō* ("repent") in many salvation passages (Luke 18:9; 24:25; 47; Acts 2:38; 3:16; 9:35, 42; 11:17, 21; 13:12; 16:31; 22:19; 26:18, 20; Rom. 4:5; 9:33; 10:11; 1 Tim. 1:16).[31] This construction illustrates the truth that God expects mankind to rest our salvation "upon" the one and only basis that is acceptable to Him—the person and work of His own Beloved Son.

There is a definite correspondence in Scripture between the grounds of our redemption, the elements of the gospel of Christ, and the meaning of Jesus being "the Christ" in John's Gospel and many other evangelistic passages in the Synoptic Gospels and Acts. This cord of three strands testifies harmoniously to the truth that the content of saving faith consists of Jesus Christ's deity, humanity, death for sin, resurrection, and God's gift of salvation solely by grace through faith in Him. This biblical symmetry between the three lines of evidence will now be demonstrated for each element in the contents of saving faith.

Jesus Christ's Deity

Though the word "deity" is never used in our English Bibles in reference to Jesus Christ, the truth of His equality with God the Father in essence and character is still a thoroughly biblical concept. Christ's deity is readily apparent by virtue of the fact that He is called "God" (*theos*) in several passages (John 1:1, 18; 20:28; Acts 20:28; Rom. 9:5; Titus 2:13; Heb. 1:8-9; 2 Peter 1:1; 1 John 5:20).[32] Even apart from the use of *theos* in reference to Christ, the evidence for His deity is extensive. It is communicated through a variety of descriptive terms and titles, such as "Son," "Lord," "Savior," and even "Christ," in addition to the narrative depictions of Him as the One who possesses all sovereignty and power over nature (Matt. 14:25-33; Mark 4:35-41; John 6:19), angels (Matt. 26:53; Luke 8:29-31), disease (Matt. 4:23; John 4:43-53), and even sin (1 Cor. 15:56-57) and death itself (Mark 5:21-43; Luke 8:40-56; John 11:43-44).[33]

As this relates to the contents of saving faith, the evangelistic use of the term "Christ" is vested with clear deistic meaning in the Gospels. This can be observed in an undisputed salvation passage such as John

---

[31] See also in chapter 16 how this explanation harmonizes with the correct interpretation of *epi* in Acts 2:38.

[32] Robert M. Bowman, Jr., and J. Ed Komoszewski, *Putting Jesus in His Place: The Case for the Deity of Christ* (Grand Rapids: Kregel Publications, 2007), 135-56; Murray J. Harris, *Jesus as God: The New Testament Use of Theos in Reference to Jesus* (Grand Rapids: Baker, 1992), 51-253.

[33] Henry M. Morris, *Miracles: Do They Still Exist? Why We Believe in Them* (Green Forest, AZ: Master Books, 2004), 110-12; J. Dwight Pentecost, *The Words and Works of Jesus Christ: A Study of the Life of Christ* (Grand Rapids: Zondervan, 1981), 163-64; Charles C. Ryrie, *The Miracles of Our Lord* (Neptune, NJ: Loizeaux Bros., 1984), 10; Tom Stegall, "The Tragedy of the Crossless Gospel, Pt. 8," *GFJ* (Fall 2008): 5.

5:24, where passing from death and condemnation into eternal life is conditioned upon hearing and believing Christ's "word" (*"he who hears My word and believes on Him who sent Me"*). In the context, Jesus refers to Himself repeatedly as the "Son" of the "Father" (John 5:18-27), clearly equating Himself with God (John 5:18). It is this "word" of equality with the Father that people must believe to be born again (John 5:24). Likewise, in the narrative development of John's Gospel, the testimony of Thomas forms the climactic confession of the entire book as to Jesus' real identity. In John 20:28, after beholding the crucified-risen Savior, Thomas exclaims, "My Lord and my God!" It is no coincidence that the evangelistic purpose statement for the entire book is placed immediately after this great confession in John 20:30-31. The meaning of Jesus as "the Christ, the Son of God" is directly affected and determined in the context by the preceding expression, "My Lord and My God." The revelation of "the Christ" as no one less than "God" is obviously John's evangelistic objective,[34] as the opening verses of the fourth Gospel immediately inform the reader that Jesus is the eternal God and creator (John 1:1-3) and source of all life (John 1:4). But John is hardly alone is ascribing deity to "the Christ." The Synoptic Gospels and Acts also teach the deity of Jesus as "the Christ." This will be demonstrated later in this book in chapters 15-17.

Christ's deity is also an element of "the gospel." Subsequent chapters will also show that the deity of Christ is an essential component of the saving message that is preached to the lost, where Scripture itself designates these messages as being examples of "gospel" preaching (Acts 10:36 cf. 15:7; Acts 13:33, 35 cf. Gal. 1:8; 4:13). In addition, certain individual occurrences of the term "gospel" establish that it is a message about the deity of Christ, such as Romans 1:9, which refers to *"the gospel of His Son."* Here, being called God's "Son" indicates the equality of Jesus with God His Father.[35]

Some crossless proponents object to such an equation, stating that this also necessitates belief in the Trinity as part of the contents of saving faith.[36] However, there are no passages in Scripture that specifically require knowledge of, or belief in, the Holy Spirit in order to be saved, only belief in God and/or His Son. While this logically means that a person must realize that there are at least two persons within the Godhead, God and His Son, this does not necessitate belief in the third member of the Trinity for eternal salvation.[37]

---

[34] Harris, *Jesus as God*, 124-25.

[35] Harris, *Jesus as God*, 317; Benjamin B. Warfield, *The Person and Work of Christ*, ed. Samuel G. Craig (Phillipsburg, NJ: Presbyterian & Reformed, 1950), 75-77.

[36] Bob Wilkin, "Four Free Grace Views Related to Two Issues: Assurance and the Five Essentials," *Grace in Focus* 24 (July/August 2009): 2.

[37] Contra Machen, who says, "no man can have faith in Christ without also having faith in God the Father and in the Holy Spirit. All three persons of the blessed Trinity are according to the New Testament active in redemption; and all three therefore may be the object

Some crossless proponents also object that if belief in Christ as "Son" equates to belief in His deity, then this must also require belief in the *eternal* Sonship of Christ. They reason that if a person professes to believe that Jesus is deity by virtue of being God's "Son," and such a person also believes that Jesus became the Son only at the incarnation, then that person cannot truly believe in the deity of Christ because it would mean that Jesus only became "God" at the time of the incarnation. They insist, therefore, that it is unreasonable to equate belief in Christ as "Son" with belief in His deity. But such a conclusion does not necessarily follow. As Zeller and Showers have shown in their sound treatment of the subject, though a denial of Christ's eternal Sonship *can* lead to a denial of His deity (and therein lies a legitimate cause for concern), it does not *necessarily* do so.[38] It may only mean that an individual is confused about the eternal *relationship* between the Father and Son within the Godhead while still believing that Christ eternally and ontologically existed as God (John 1:1) prior to the incarnation, at which time He would have ostensibly begun His functional relationship to the Father as "Son."

Besides the deity of Christ being contained in the gospel by the reference to *"the gospel of His Son"* (Rom. 1:9), it is also indicated by the expression, *"the gospel of our Lord Jesus Christ"* (2 Thess. 1:8). In this passage, the "Lord Jesus Christ" is more than the source for the gospel; He is its principal subject and object. If the gospel is a message about the "Lord" Jesus, then His deity is an element of that message. But does the word "Lord" really refer to Christ's deity? Pauline usage certainly confirms this to be the case, as Foerster explains, "Paul, then, does not make any distinction between θεός and κύριος as though κύριος were an intermediary god; there are no instances of any such usage in the world contemporary with primitive Christianity. . . . it is plain that κύριος is the One through whom God has come into the world to work and to save."[39] The fact that Paul puts *kurios* on the same level as *theos* unequivocally establishes that "Lord" is an appellation of genuine deity.[40] Theologian Robert Lightner, a strong proponent of grace theology, agrees with this conclusion, stating:

> When Scripture calls Jesus "Lord" it ascribes full and absolute deity to Him. He is sovereign. No one can have Christ as substi-

---

of faith when redemption is accepted by sinful men." J. Gresham Machen, *What Is Faith?* (Grand Rapids: Eerdmans, 1946), 87. While the Holy Spirit plays an active role in our salvation (Eph. 1:13-14; 4:30), He did not provide the grounds of our salvation, nor is He ever said to be the object of faith for eternal life.

[38] George W. Zeller and Renald E. Showers, *The Eternal Sonship of Christ* (Neptune, NJ: Loizeaux Brothers, 1993), 95.

[39] Werner Foerster, "κύριος," *TDNT*, 3:1091 (ellipsis added).

[40] Bowman and Komoszewski, *Putting Jesus in His Place*, 157-70; Harris, *Jesus as God*, 122-24. This is not to say that *kurios* always refers to deity in the NT, since there are instances where it is simply a respectful form of address such as "sir" (Matt. 21:30; 27:63; Luke 13:8; John 4:11, 15, 19; Rev. 7:14), but this is not Paul's usage.

> tute for his sin who does not accept Him as such. Unless He is God the Sovereign One, He could not have atoned for sin. Jesus Himself made this very plain when He told His fiercest religious critics, "If you do not believe that I am He, you will die in your sins" (John 8:24). But accepting Jesus for who He claimed to be—the Lord God who died as man's substitute—is not the same as promising Him complete surrender and dedication of one's entire life. The latter involves human effort or work and the former does not.[41]

In addition to Jesus' deity being an element of the "gospel" through the use of the terms "Son" and "Lord" as well as being expressed by the term "Christ" in evangelistic contexts, several individual passages of the New Testament condition salvation upon belief in Jesus' deity. This may be the case in Romans 10:9a, 10b where justifying faith acknowledges the deity of Christ, saying, *"Jesus is Lord."*[42] Also, when the jailor in Acts 16:31 is told to *"believe on the Lord Jesus Christ"* to be saved, the word "Lord" does not merely function as a portion of Jesus' proper name. It signifies His Lordship in terms of Him possessing the position and prerogatives of deity. Then, after hearing *"the word of the Lord"* from Paul and Silas (Acts 16:32), a summary statement of the jailor's faith follows in Acts 16:34 where it says he and his family *"believed in God."* Surely this does not mean that they merely became monotheists from that point forward. The phrase, *"believed in God,"* most likely indicates that they believed in "God" by virtue of believing in the "Lord" Jesus Christ whom they heard about in *"the word of the Lord"* (i.e., the gospel of Christ).

The deity of Christ is also seen to be an element of saving faith according to the individual passage of John 8:24. There, the Lord Jesus tells the unbelieving Jews of His day, *"Therefore, I said to you that you will die in*

---

[41] Robert P. Lightner, *Sin, the Savior, and Salvation: The Theology of Everlasting Life* (Nashville: Thomas Nelson, 1991), 204-5.

[42] There is disagreement among Free Grace Christians as to whether the confession of Jesus as the Lord/God is tied to justification by faith and Israel's eternal, national deliverance at the return of Christ (Charles C. Bing, *Lordship Salvation, Lordship Salvation: A Biblical Evaluation and Response,* GraceLife Edition [Burleson, TX: GraceLife Ministries, 1992], 108-13; Lewis Sperry Chafer, *Systematic Theology* [Dallas: Dallas Seminary Press, 1947-1948; reprint ed., Grand Rapids: Kregel Publications, 1993], 3:379-80; Lightner, *Sin, the Savior, and Salvation,* 168, 206-7; Charles C. Ryrie, *So Great Salvation: What It Means to Believe in Jesus Christ* [Wheaton, IL: Victor Books, 1989], 70-73) or whether it is to be a routine practice of the Christian life for daily sanctification and deliverance from the wrath of God upon carnal and disobedient Christians (Zane C. Hodges, *Absolutely Free: A Biblical Reply to Lordship Salvation* [Dallas: Redención Viva, 1989], 193-203; René A. Lopez, *Romans Unlocked: Power to Deliver* [Springfield, MO: 21st Century Press, 2005], 212-14; Bob Wilkin, "Why the Romans Road Ends in a Cul de Sac," Grace Evangelical Society Conference, Dallas, TX, March 1, 2006). However, this latter interpretation regarding a believer's practical sanctification held by most crossless proponents is entirely out of sync with the context of Romans 9-11 which deals with the justification and physical deliverance of national Israel, not with the Church's sanctification.

your sins; for if you do not believe that I am (egō eimi), you will die in your sins." Throughout the fourth Gospel the Lord's deity is highlighted by the use of the expression, "I am" (*egō eimi*). See especially the use of "I am" in John 8:58. In John 8:24, the Lord Jesus is clearly warning his audience that unless they come to believe that He is the "I am"—equal to Yahweh God—they will remain spiritually dead, unregenerate, and unforgiven in their trespasses and sins. In light of the clear testimony of John's Gospel on the meaning of Jesus as the "I am," it is not surprising to discover that Bob Wilkin, who does not affirm that the deity of Christ is essential to saving faith,[43] remains unconvinced that John 8:24 requires belief in Christ's deity as the basis for escaping *eternal* condemnation. He writes, "What does it mean to die in your sins (John 8:24) or in your sin, singular (John 8:21)? The Bible is not clear on this question. I think it means that unbelievers die with sinful desires."[44] Yet, it is clear from the theology of John that people either remain positionally and judicially in the sphere of sin and death or they enter the sphere of eternal life in Christ Jesus the moment they believe in Him (John 5:24-26; 20:31; 1 John 5:11-13, 20). John informs us in the last book of the Bible that God views all who are lost, who have never been washed in the blood of the Lamb, as being still positionally dead in their trespasses and sins (Rev. 21:8, 27; 22:15). In this respect, John's soteriology is in perfect accord with Paul's doctrine (Rom. 5:12; 1 Cor. 15:22; Eph. 2:1).

Jesus Christ's Humanity

In our day and age, few but the most hardened skeptics deny the existence of the historical man, Jesus of Nazareth. And though docetic Gnosticism has been lurking in the shadows of the professing Church for nearly two millennia, its historical denial of the corporeal Christ has not made any significant inroads since its heyday in the 2nd-3rd centuries. Consequently, Christians today rarely feel constrained to emphasize the truth of the Savior's humanity. In fact, it has become such an insignificant issue in the minds of most Christians (or even many non-Christians) that it is often not considered to be an element of the gospel or part of the contents of saving faith. In most cases, the emphasis of modern-day gospel presentations is largely upon the finished work of Christ, which is perfectly understandable and acceptable since this is where the challenge lies for most people in coming to faith in Christ for salvation. But even in such cases, the humanity of Christ as an historical person is still an assumed truth that is implied within any evangelistic presentation of Christ's substitutionary death and

---

[43] Robert N. Wilkin, *Confident in Christ* (Irving, TX: Grace Evangelical Society, 1999), 10; idem, "Essential Truths About Our Savior," *Grace in Focus* 23 (November/December 2008): 1-2.

[44] Robert N. Wilkin, *Secure and Sure: Grasping the Promises of God* (Irving, TX: Grace Evangelical Society, 2005), 92.

bodily resurrection. It should be recognized as well that even when a doctrine is *assumed* and *implied*, it is still truth that is *believed*. It is just not the emphasis of a person's belief. But what would the gospel be without the marvel of the incarnation? Without Christ's humanity, there would be no good news at all. Christ would have no ability to die (Heb. 2:14) or even for such a death to be vicarious for the rest of humanity. Nor would there be a bodily resurrection without a body prepared for Him through the incarnation (Heb. 10:5). The Savior's finished work and genuine humanity are simply inextricable from one another. The incarnation of Christ, therefore, is not merely a presupposition to the gospel, like the recognition of sin in the human race; it is an integral element of the gospel itself.

This is evidenced first by the fact that Christ is said to be the "Son of Man." While this phrase refers to Jesus as a "Man," it has definite deistic connotations as well (see chapter 15). "Son of Man" was the Lord Jesus' preferred self-descriptive title to identify Himself as a member of the human race and to reflect the redemptive mission and purpose of His incarnation.

The titles of "Christ," "Son of God," and "Son of Man" all set forth the Lord Jesus as being genuinely human and not a mere phantom. This is particularly true in John's writings (1 John 1:1-3; 4:2-3; 5:6; 2 John 7) and even in his Gospel (John 1:14) which is primarily evangelistic in purpose (John 20:30-31). While the deistic phrase "Son of God" is found in popular evangelistic passages like John 3:16 and John 20:31, it is often overlooked that other equally evangelistic passages in John use the phrase "Son of Man" (John 3:13-15; 6:53). These verses require belief "in Him" as the Object of faith; and in their immediate contexts, they define "Him" as the "Son of Man"—as One who is truly human.

Even the most popular evangelistic verse in the Bible, John 3:16, presents at least the incarnation of Christ when it says, *"For God so (houtōs gar) loved the world that (hōste) He gave (edōken) His only begotten Son."* In what sense was the Son given to the world? Since the immediate context presents both Christ's incarnation (John 3:13-14) and substitutionary death (John 3:14-15),[45] the intended manner[46] in which God "gave" (*didōmi*)

---

[45] Some say even the deity of Christ is implied by His omnipresence in verse 13 (David Alan Black, *New Testament Textual Criticism: A Concise Guide* [Grand Rapids: Baker, 1994], 49-55; idem, "The Text of John 3:13," *GTJ* 6 [Spring 1985]: 49-66; R. Larry Overstreet, "John 3:13 and the Omnipresence of Jesus Christ," *JBTM* 2 [Fall 2004]: 135-53) as well as His resurrection (G. Michael Cocoris, *The Salvation Controversy* [Santa Monica, CA: Insights from the Word, 2008], 22).

[46] Verse 16 is syntactically connected to the immediately preceding verses by the use of *houtōs gar . . . hōste* so that the emphasis of verse 16 is not so much upon the *degree* to which God loved the world (i.e., "God loved the world so much that...") but rather on the *manner* in which He loved the world (i.e., by giving His Son in sacrificial death as in 3:14). This interpretation accords with the theology of John expressed elsewhere (1 John 4:8-11) and it fits the grammatical patterns of *houtōs gar* and *hōste* elsewhere in the New Testament. See Robert H. Gundry and Russell W. Howell, "The Sense and Syntax of John 3:14-17 with

His Son must refer to both His humanity and His sacrificial death. He was given to humanity in order to die for humanity.[47] This corresponds with Christ's use of the verb *didōmi* twice in John 6:51 where the purpose for giving His flesh is also stated to be for the benefit of the "world." Then, two verses later in John 6:53, Christ issues the evangelistic challenge, saying, *"Most assuredly, I say to you, unless you eat the flesh of the Son of Man and drink His blood, you have no life in you."* The reference to eating is a metaphorical expression for personally appropriating Christ by faith (John 6:35).[48] Does John 6:53, therefore, not speak of the absolute necessity to believe in Jesus' humanity and substitutionary death in order to possess eternal life?[49]

The incarnation and substitutionary death of the Savior are so interconnected that it is often difficult to determine which truth is being referred to in a particular passage. For example, after speaking of belief in Jesus as "the Christ" in 1 John 5:1, verses 5-6 go on to speak of Christ as "the Son of God," which is the other half of John's appositional,[50] evangelistic purpose statement from John 20:31 (*"the Christ, the Son of God"*). 1 John 5:5-6 says, *"5 Who is he who overcomes the world, but he who believes that Jesus is the Son of God? 6 This is He who came by water and blood—Jesus Christ; not only by water, but by water and blood. And it is the Spirit who bears witness, because the Spirit is truth."* Coming by water may be a reference to a physical, flesh birth (John 3:5-7).[51] Or the entire expression of "water and blood" may only be in reference to the cross-work of Christ (John 19:30-35). It is likely that both senses are intended as the Lord's humanity is inseparably bound to His substitutionary sacrifice as our Savior.[52] But what these pas-

---

Special Reference to the Use of οὕτως . . . ὥστε in John 3:16," *NovT* 41 (1999): 24-39. The presence of the postpositive conjunction *gar* to start verse 16 indicates that John/Jesus is not introducing a separate, distinctive thought but is strengthening a thought from the previous verses. Stephen H. Levinsohn, *Discourse Features of New Testament Greek: A Coursebook on the Information Structure of New Testament Greek*, 2nd ed. (Dallas: SIL International, 2000), 91; Michael D. Makidon, "The Strengthening Constraint of *Gar* in 1 and 2 Timothy," (Th.M. thesis, Dallas Theological Seminary, 2003). This means that John 3:16 should not be wrested from its context and treated in isolation when interpreting it or building a doctrine upon it about the contents of saving faith.

[47] Roland Bergmeier, "ΤΕΤΕΛΕΣΤΑΙ Joh 19:30," *ZNW* 79 (1988): 289; Oscar Cullmann, *The Christology of the New Testament*, rev. ed., trans. Shirley C. Guthrie and Charles A. M. Hall (Philadelphia: Westminster Press, 1963), 70, 300.

[48] David Gibson, "Eating Is Believing? On Midrash and the Mixing of Metaphors in John 6," *Them* 27 (Spring 2002): 5-15.

[49] Charles C. Ryrie, *Biblical Theology of the New Testament* (Chicago: Moody Press, 1959), 340.

[50] In John 20:31, the phrase, "the Son of God," stands in epexegetical relationship to "the Christ." William Bonney, *Caused to Believe: The Doubting Thomas Story as the Climax of John's Christological Narrative* (Leiden: Brill, 2002), 27n63.

[51] Ben Witherington III, "The Waters of Birth: John 3.5 and 1 John 5.6-8," *NTS* 35 (1989): 155-60.

[52] Roland Bergmeier, "Die Bedeutung der Synoptiker für das johanneische Zeugnisthema.

sages also indicate is that "the Christ, the Son of God" in the Johannine sense is One who is both truly human and our sacrificial substitute.

Besides the Lord's humanity being inherent to the Johannine meaning of "the Christ," it is also an integral part of the "gospel." This is evident from the contents of Peter's "gospel" (Acts 10:41 cf. Acts 15:7-11) and Paul's "gospel" (Acts 13:38 cf. Gal. 1:6-9; 4:13).[53] In addition, Paul's great *"one Mediator . . . the Man Christ Jesus"* statement within 1 Timothy 2:3-7 should be compared with its parallel passage in 2 Timothy 1:10-11 where Paul is specifically referring to "the gospel." These parallel passages reveal not only that Christ's humanity is part of the gospel and part of the essential "knowledge of the truth" that God wills for every lost soul (1 Tim. 2:4), they also reveal that the contents of the gospel and the contents of saving faith are one and the same.

Besides being an element of "the gospel" and part of the evangelistic meaning of "the Christ," Jesus' humanity is also essential in providing the grounds of our eternal salvation (Gal. 4:4-5; Eph. 2:14-16; Heb. 2:9, 14, 17). Grace-oriented theologians of the past shared this conviction, such as Chafer, who stated, "Without the reality of the God-man, there is no sufficient ground for the truths of salvation, for sanctification, or for a lost world. This theanthropic Person is the hope of men of all ages and of the universe itself."[54] Consonant with Chafer, Walvoord wrote:

> In a similar way, the act of redemption in which Christ offered Himself a sacrifice for sin was an act of His whole person. It was traceable to both natures, not to the human nature alone nor to the divine. As Man Christ could die, but only as God could His death have infinite value sufficient to provide redemption for the sins of the whole world. Thus the human blood of Christ has eternal and infinite value because it was shed as part of the divine-human Person.[55]

Scripture plainly attests that the humanity of Christ is essential to the gospel, and the Johannine definition of "the Christ," and the grounds of our salvation. Scripture also testifies to the necessity of belief in Jesus Christ as the "Son of Man" in order to have divine life (John 3:13-15; 6:53). Therefore, both the deity and humanity of Christ are seen to be essential elements in the contents of saving faith.

Mit einem Anhang zum Perfekt-Gebrauch im vierten Evangelium," *NTS* 52 (2006): 475; F. F. Bruce, *The Gospel of John* (Grand Rapids: Eerdmans, 1983), 376-77; Robert L. Deffinbaugh, *That You Might Believe: A Study of the Gospel of John* (n.p.: Biblical Studies Press, 1998), 751; John A. T. Robinson, *Redating the New Testament* (London: SCM, 1976), 286; John Wilkinson, "The Incident of the Blood and Water in John 19.34," *SJT* 28 (1975): 172.

[53] See chapter 10 for the connection between Acts 13 and Galatians and also chapters 16-17 for the connection between Acts 10 and Acts 15 as Peter's gospel.

[54] Chafer, *Systematic Theology*, 1:350.

[55] John F. Walvoord, *Jesus Christ Our Lord* (Chicago: Moody Press, 1969), 120.

At this point, proponents of the G.E.S. gospel object that if belief in Christ's deity and humanity are required for eternal life,[56] then this means that a person must also understand the theological doctrine of the hypostatic union in order to be saved.[57] Since such a doctrine is very abstract and difficult to grasp, they reason that requiring belief in Christ's deity and humanity surely cannot be biblical. A few points must be made in response to this claim. First, the fifty-dollar theological phrase, "hypostatic union," never appears in the Bible; therefore knowledge of this particular phrase is certainly not necessary for salvation. Many, perhaps even most, Christians around the world have never even heard the expression; and for those who have, few know what it means. Secondly, while a person certainly does not need to be an expert in Chalcedonian theology in order to be saved, belief in the most elementary aspects of the hypostatic union essentially amounts to belief in the incarnation of Christ; and according to the Bible, at least this much is required to be believed (John 3:13-16).

In fact, even a child can possess an elementary grasp of the essential truths of the "hypostatic union" without necessarily understanding the deeper ontological and metaphysical complexities of Christ's two "natures"—unmixed and undiluted. A child is capable, for instance, of believing that Christ exists as one person who is both man and God. When my son was between the ages of 5-6, he asked me a profound theological question one day (as children often do!). He said, "Dad, how can Jesus be both God and a man at the same time?" After being taken aback for a moment, I replied, "I don't know son." After pausing for a moment, I asked him, "But do you believe that Jesus is God?" He answered, "Yes." I then asked him, "Do you also believe that He is a man?" Again he answered, "Yes." Then I asked him a third question, "Son, do you believe there are two Jesuses?" To that question, my boy burst into laughter and said, "No, dad, that's silly. There's only *one* Jesus!" With that, my 5-6 year old son just expressed the essence of the hypostatic union and the truth of the incarnation—that Christ is both God and man in one person. My son believed the truth of John 8:24 without ever hearing of the "hypostatic union" or the Council of Chalcedon.

---

[56] At times during the present controversy over the contents of saving faith, some leading exponents of the G.E.S. position appear to possibly concede that belief in the historical, human existence of Jesus is a requirement of saving faith. See Zane C. Hodges, "The Spirit of the Antichrist: Decoupling Jesus from the Christ," *JOTGES* 20 (Autumn 2007): 37-46; Robert N. Wilkin, "Is Ignorance Eternal Bliss?" *JOTGES* 16 (Spring 2003): 13. However, at other times, some have openly denied the necessity to believe in Christ's humanity. Due to the ambiguity of the G.E.S. position on this question, I have normally tried to portray their position as not requiring belief in only the three elements of Christ's deity, substitutionary death, and bodily resurrection.

[57] Bob Wilkin, "Four Free Grace Views Related to Two Issues: Assurance and the Five Essentials," *Grace in Focus* 24 (July/August 2009): 2.

Thankfully, the Lord Jesus did not say in John 8:24, "unless you *understand how* I can be the I am, you will die in your sins." Rather, He simply states, "unless you *believe that* I am, you will die in your sins." God never tells us that we must understand *how* Christ can be both God and man before we believe in His miraculous incarnation; He only tells us *that* we must believe it. In many respects, it is easier for a child to do this than an adult. Young children believe virtually anything an adult tells them. This is why it is fallacious for some crossless advocates to claim that the traditional Free Grace requirement to believe in the person and work of Christ amounts to requiring a "full theology of His person"[58] or a "full understanding"[59] of deep doctrinal truths such as the hypostatic union. No Free Grace person I've ever met has argued for a "full understanding" of any doctrine before God grants salvation. In fact, there isn't a theologian on the planet who can honestly claim to have a "full understanding" of any aspect of Christ's person and work. For that matter, it is fair to say that even among proponents of the G.E.S. gospel, there isn't a single person who can claim to have a "full understanding" of their version of the saving message either, whether it is the nature of believing or the concept of eternal life. Regarding the person of Christ and the requirement to believe in His deity and humanity, Dr. J. B. Hixson succinctly and aptly concludes by saying, "Yet, saving faith involves recognizing—however rudimentary this recognition may be—that Jesus *is God in the flesh*."[60]

Jesus Christ's Substitutionary Death

As with the deity and humanity of Christ, the substitutionary death of Christ is supported by the same three lines of harmonious witness to the contents of saving faith in the Word of God. The sacrificial death of the Savior is intrinsic to the evangelistic meaning of Jesus as "the Christ, the Son of God" (Luke 24:26, 46; Acts 3:18; 1 Cor. 2:2 cf. 2 Cor. 1:19; 1 John 5:1, 5-6). It is also an indisputable element of the gospel message (1 Cor. 1:17-18; 15:1-3; Acts 17:3-4 cf. 2 Thess. 1:8-10). Our eternal salvation is grounded upon Christ's death for us (Matt. 26:28; Mark 14:24; Acts 20:28; Rom. 3:25; 5:9-10; Eph. 1:7; Col. 1:20; Heb. 9:12-10:19; 1 Peter 1:18-19; Rev. 1:5; 5:9), and consequently certain individual passages explicitly require belief in this divine work of redemption (Acts 13:41; Rom. 3:25; John 6:53; 1 Tim. 2:4-6). The two key passages of 1 Corinthians 1 and Romans 3:25 merit special consideration.

---

[58] Zane C. Hodges, "How to Lead People to Christ, Part 1: The Content of Our Message," *JOTGES* 13 (Autumn 2000): 5.

[59] Bob Bryant, "The Search for the Saving Message Outside of the Gospel of John," Grace Evangelical Society Conference, Fort Worth, TX, March 6, 2008.

[60] J. B. Hixson, *Getting the Gospel Wrong: The Evangelical Crisis No One Is Talking About* (n.p.: Xulon Press, 2008), 86.

1 Corinthians 1:13-2:5

In seeking to answer the question of whether belief in Christ's cross-work is essential for eternal salvation we need look no further than 1 Corinthians 1. It is not an overstatement to say that the present crossless controversy could be settled if all parties would merely give this passage its due.[61] For, in it we see that the cross is plainly an element of the gospel and essential to saving faith. This can be observed by noting the interconnection between key terms and phrases in 1 Corinthians 1:13-2:5. As Paul reflects upon his initial evangelistic visit to Corinth, he mentions that the content/object of the Corinthians' faith was *"the power of God"* (1 Cor. 2:5). This is an unambiguous reference to Christ's cross-work since Paul had just previously referred to *"the message of the cross"* as *"the power of God"* (1 Cor. 1:18). This *"message of the cross"* in verse 18 is simply an alternative description for the message of *"the gospel"* referred to in the previous verse (1 Cor. 1:17). This means that the Corinthians had placed their faith in the gospel—the message of the cross—for their initial salvation. This logical connection is illustrated below:

the Corinthians' faith rested in	→	the power of God (2:5)
the power of God	=	the message of the cross (1:18)
the message of the cross	=	the gospel (1:17)
the Corinthians' faith rested in	→	the gospel

This interpretation is in keeping with Romans 1:16, where we are told that the gospel is the power of God unto salvation to all those who believe.[62] But this raises an important question about the correct tense of salvation that Paul is writing about in 1 Corinthians 1:17-2:5. When he states that the message of the cross is the power of God *"to us who are being saved"* (1 Cor. 1:18), is this referring to practical sanctification in the Christian life (2nd tense salvation)? Or, is it referring to justification (1st tense salvation)? Incredibly, but not surprisingly, the new position of the promise-only gospel interprets this section to be about the believer's present walk and future glorification with rewards. While teaching about not being "disapproved" (*adokimos*) as a Christian in 1 Corinthians 9:27, notice what Bob Wilkin states regarding salvation in 1 Corinthians:

---

[61] Fred R. Lybrand, "GES Gospel: Lybrand Open Letter," April 14, 2009, pp. 28-30.

[62] Admittedly, Romans 1:16 and 1 Corinthians 2:2 most likely have both justification and sanctification in view. It is certainly true that in 1 Cor. 2:2 Paul had the Lord Jesus' example of humility in mind whereby Christ left us an example to follow in submitting to the death of the cross. This kenotic mindset (Phil. 2:1-8) is certainly involved in our practical sanctification, and on this we can agree with Wilkin (Bob Wilkin, "What Was Paul's Message of Christ and Him Crucified? 1 Corinthians 2:2 Reconsidered," Grace Evangelical Society Conference, Fort Worth, TX, March 30, 2009). But this does not discount the fact that the cross was originally essential to believe for justification according to 1 Cor. 1:14-21.

> Well here the idea is his fleshly inclinations need to be destroyed so that he comes back into fellowship with God so that he will be healthy at the Bema. While that made sense to me, but then that got me to thinking 1 Corinthians 15:2 is probably talking about healthy at the Bema, and that got me to thinking 1 Corinthians 3:15, about "he'll be saved, yet so as through fire" is also talking about healthy at the Bema. And 1 Corinthians 1:18, about "the cross is foolishness to those who are perishing, but to us who are being saved it's the power of God." I took that as spiritually healthy. And if that's the case, then it would be possible to have a born again person who viewed the cross as foolishness, because if you had an unhealthy believer, they may no longer view the cross as the power of God. And indeed, that is a possibility.[63]

But is the reference to "us who are being saved" in 1 Corinthians 1:18, and all the "salvation" passages in 1 Corinthians, really about the future spiritual health/salvation of believers at the judgment seat of Christ? The clause, "to us who are being saved" (*tois sōzomenois hēmin*), contains a present tense, articular participle. If Paul in 1 Corinthians 1:18 wanted to more precisely describe a *future* deliverance, he would have used the *future participle* of *sōzō* so that the saving would be subsequent to the main verb in the sentence, "is" (*estin*), resulting in the sense, "but to us who will be saved, it is the power of God."[64] The ones who are being saved (*tois sōzomenois*) are descriptively set in contrast in verse 18 to "those who are perishing" (*tois apollumenois*). If "those who are perishing" refers to regenerate but carnal *believers* "perishing," then this would contradict other passages of Scripture, such as John 3:16 and 10:28, where believers are promised that we shall *never* "perish" (*apollumi*) along with the lost.[65]

---

[63] Bob Wilkin, "The Three Tenses of Salvation Aren't About Justification, Sanctification, and Glorification," Georgia Regional Grace Conference, Hampton, GA, September 23, 2006.

[64] In 1 Cor. 1:18, "the ones who are being saved" functions as a virtual descriptive noun, as articular participles frequently do. However, this does not completely negate the significance of the participle's tense. While tense may not be as significant with present and aorist participles, which are practically "timeless" (Nigel Turner, *Syntax*, Volume 3 of *A Grammar of New Testament Greek*, by J. H. Moulton, 4 vols. [Edinburgh: T & T Clark, 1963], 150-51; A. T. Robertson, *A Grammar of the Greek New Testament in the Light of Historical Research* [Nashville: Broadman Press, 1934], 1111), future participles do possess more significance as to the time of the action described (James L. Boyer, "The Classification of Participles: A Statistical Study," *GTJ* 5 [Fall 1984]: 166). Robertson states, "The future participle is always subsequent in time to the principal verb . . . not coincident and, of course, never antecedent. Hence the future participle comes nearer having a temporal notion than any of the tenses" (*A Grammar,* 1118, ellipsis added). This means that Paul had the grammatical option of the *future* articular participle available to employ in 1 Cor. 1:18, if he desired to be more definitive about a time of future salvation, just as he chose to do later in 1 Cor. 15:37 when specifying "that body that shall be" (*to sōma to genēsomenon*).

[65] Proponents of the crossless/promise-only position will no doubt object that a believer can still "perish" (*apollumi*) temporally and physically (Rom. 14:15; 1 Cor. 8:11; 10:9-10).

With respect to 1 Corinthians 1:18, this means that the expression, "but to us who are being saved" (*tois de sōzomenois hēmin*), is a categorical reference to those individuals from the world who are daily being born-again and joining the ranks of believers.[66] This phrase is collectively describing all those who have come to Christ by faith for salvation and whose eternal destinies have now irrevocably changed.[67] Conversely, "to those who are perishing" (*tois apollumenois*) in verse 18 is not a description of the daily way of life for a regenerated, carnal believer, as if such a Christian is in some abstract sense "perishing" along with the unregenerate. Rather, the whole world of unbelievers presently lies under God's wrath (John 3:36), under an eternal death-sentence (Eph. 2:1-3), and their entire course extending from the present into the eternal future is one of spiritual ruin or perishing (1 John 2:17) unless they come to faith in Christ and consequently join the class of those "who are being saved."[68] Though the participles for those who are "perishing" and those who are being "saved" are both present tense, this simply indicates a timeless condition,[69] or the extension of the present into the eternal future in the sense of two contrasting courses.[70] It certainly would encompass the postmortem condition of those who are lost (1 Cor. 15:18). It is not describing the individual sanctification process that is transpiring in the lives of believers now, as some contend.[71] The contrast between the "saved" and the "perishing" in verse 18 is between their saved versus unsaved status before God,[72] between their saved or ruined spiritual conditions. While this includes their present standing of either salvation or condemnation in God's sight, it also entails their future destiny. Since believers

---

Indeed, this is true since *apollumi* has this sense in the preponderance of its uses in the NT. But the promise of John 3:16 and 10:28 clearly pertains to the kind of *apollumi* that is true of unbelievers (i.e., eternal destruction), just as the context of 1 Corinthians 1 also indicates. For the eternal sense of *apollumi* according to Pauline usage, see Rom. 2:12; 1 Cor. 1:18-19; 15:18; 2 Cor. 2:15; 4:3; 2 Thess. 2:10.

[66] Robert G. Gromacki, *Called to Be Saints: An Exposition of 1 Corinthians* (Grand Rapids: Baker Book House, 1977), 18; Charles Hodge, *Commentary on the First Epistle to the Corinthians* (Grand Rapids: Eerdmans, reprinted 1994), 18-19.

[67] S. Lewis Johnson, "1 Corinthians," in *The Wycliffe Bible Commentary*, ed. Charles F. Pfeiffer and Everett F. Harrison (Chicago: Moody Press, 1962), 1232.

[68] Alford, *The Greek Testament* (Chicago: Moody Press, 1958), 2:479.

[69] G. G. Findlay, "1 Corinthians," in *The Expositor's Greek Testament* (Grand Rapids: Eerdmans, reprinted 1990): 767; Frederic Louis Godet, *Commentary on First Corinthians* (Grand Rapids: Kregel, 1977), 91; A. T. Robertson, *Word Pictures in the New Testament* (Grand Rapids: Baker Book House, n.d.), 4:77.

[70] H. A. Ironside, *Addresses on the First Epistle to the Corinthians* (Neptune, NJ: Loizeaux Brothers, 1938), 59-60.

[71] David K. Lowery, "1 Corinthians," in *BKC*, ed. John F. Walvoord and Roy B. Zuck (Wheaton, IL: Victor Books, 1983), 509; W. E. Vine, "1 Corinthians," in *The Collected Writings of W. E. Vine* (Nashville: Thomas Nelson Publishers, 1996), 2:11.

[72] Gordon D. Fee, *The First Epistle to the Corinthians*, NICNT (Grand Rapids: Eerdmans, 1987), 68-69.

will not "perish" in the future in the same sense as the lost, this passage must be distinguishing the course of the regenerate versus the unregenerate. Therefore, the distinction in verses 18-21 is not between *two classes of believers*, the carnal and the spiritual, but between *two classes of humanity*, the saved and the lost. Paul doesn't even introduce the distinction between two classes *of believers* until 1 Corinthians 2:14-3:4; and there he actually contrasts three types of people among humanity—the unbeliever who is a natural man, the believer who is spiritual, and the believer who is carnal.

The immediate context of 1 Corinthians 1:17-21 also clarifies the identity of those who are perishing. In verses 20-21, the contrast is between "those who believe" (v. 21) and "the world" (vv. 20-21). Even when believers are carnal, we are still viewed by God as distinct from the world (1 Cor. 5:12-6:2), since we have been positionally separated from it by our identification with Christ's cross-work (Gal. 6:14), even though we can be worldly at times in our thinking and practice (Rom. 12:2). The saved/believer versus unsaved/unbeliever distinction is also seen in the surrounding context of 1 Corinthians 1:22-24, where the two categories of "Jews" and "Greeks" (i.e., Gentiles[73]) are mentioned. Since these are the only two categories of humanity that exist outside of Christ's body, the Church, and there is neither Jew nor Gentile within Christ's Body (Rom. 1:16; 1 Cor. 11:32; 12:13; Gal. 3:28), this passage must be contrasting the regenerate/believer versus unregenerate/unbeliever.

Even later in the context in 1 Corinthians 1:30, where Christ is said to be the believer's wisdom, righteousness, redemption, and sanctification, the "sanctification" referred to is clearly the believer's permanent, positional sanctification, not practical sanctification. This is seen from the fact that sanctification (*hagiosmos*) is spoken of as a past, completed event in this epistle (1 Cor. 1:2; 6:11).[74] Believers are already saints (*hagios*), positionally holy, and set apart in Christ Jesus (1 Cor. 1:2; 3:17; 6:1-2; 14:33; 16:1, 15).

The evidence from 1 Corinthians 1 points decisively toward one conclusion. The type of salvation being described in 1 Corinthians 1:18 and 21 through the use of the word *sōzō* is clearly eternal salvation, not the ongoing sanctification of the believer with a view toward the future bema seat judgment. This passage could not be clearer in its meaning. Belief in the gospel of Christ-crucified is the dividing line between heaven and hell for all of humanity. Tragically, however, the new crossless redefinition of "the gospel" obscures this divinely drawn line of demarcation.

---

[73] The Critical Text reading of 1 Corinthians 1:23 actually has the broader "Gentiles" (*ethnesin*).

[74] 1 Cor. 7:14 is an exception, but there it is speaking of an unbeliever rather than a believer being sanctified or set apart practically, "For the unbelieving husband is sanctified by the wife, and the unbelieving wife is sanctified by the husband."

1 Corinthians 1 is clear that Christ's finished work upon the cross is a message that must not only be known by the lost, it must be comprehended and personally appropriated by faith lest people perish forever. The great American preacher of the last century, Harry Ironside, shared this conviction, as he once stated regarding the gospel:

> Someone says, "But I do not understand it." That is a terrible confession to make, for *"If our gospel be hid, it is hid to them that are lost."* If you do not understand this, if you do not see that there is no other way of salvation for you, save through the death of the Lord Jesus, then that just tells the sad story that you are among the lost. You are not merely in danger of being lost in the Day of Judgment; but you are lost *now*.[75]

So, if understanding and believing the message of the cross is essential to saving faith, what exactly does "the cross" refer to? What exactly is "the message of the cross"? If this message was foolishness to the Greeks and a stumblingblock to Jews, was it merely the negative *stigma* associated with Christianity and its cross that Jews and Gentiles had to overcome in order to be saved? Or, must a person understand the *significance* of the cross to be saved. Certainly, crucifixion was the most loathsome form of capital punishment in existence in the first century or ever since. The severity of the punishment it entailed and the base character of its victims usually elicited from society the highest degree of contempt and reprehension possible. To proclaim that the crucified Jesus was God in the flesh was therefore the most intolerable thought imaginable. A crucified Messiah was a scandal to the Jewish mind. It was a "contradiction in terms."[76]

A crucified Son of God was unfathomable to both Jewish and Gentile minds in the ancient world. This sentiment is represented from the Jewish perspective by Trypho, who disputed with the Christian, Justin Martyr. Trypho decried, "But we cannot understand . . . how you can set your hopes on a crucified man and expect good of him, although you do not observe God's commandments."[77] Later, he reportedly contested with Justin, "However, you must prove to us whether he had to be crucified and die such a shameful and dishonourable death, which is accursed by the law, since something like this is unthinkable to us."[78] The ancient Greek world, represented by Lucian, Origen, Celsus, and others, likewise taunted the notion of a "crucified" god.[79] An early Christian apologist, Minucius Felix, reports in his work, *Octavius* (9:3), some of the common,

---

[75] H. A. Ironside, "A Voice from the Past: What is the Gospel?" *JOTGES* 11 (Spring 1998): 55-56.

[76] Seyoon Kim, *The Origin of Paul's Gospel* (Tübingen: J. C. B. Mohr, 1981), 46-47.

[77] Justin, *Dialogue with Trypho*, 10.3.

[78] Ibid., 90.1.

[79] Martin Hengel, *The Son of God—The Origin of Christology and the History of the Jewish-Hellenistic Religion*, trans. John Bowden (Tübingen: J. C. B. Mohr, 1976), 91n152.

unfavorable Roman sentiments of his day toward Christians. Here is a sample of the contemptuous Roman perspective towards early Christians and their message of the cross:

> And anyone who says that the objects of their worship are a man who suffered the death penalty for his crime and the deadly wood of the cross, assigns them altars appropriate for incorrigibly wicked men, so that they actually worship what they deserve.[80]

Clearly, the unsaved mind could not fathom One who was truly God-incarnate dying such an ignominious death. Paul's message of the cross was inextricably linked to the Savior's deity. Without the deity of Christ, the cross loses its power. Yet, deity without the cross is powerless to save. Only the message of the Son of God, crucified, and risen from the dead, is the power of God unto salvation to all those who believe. Even the resurrection is implied[81] in 1 Corinthians 1:22-23 where Paul writes, *"The Jews seek after a sign, and the Greeks seek after wisdom; but we preach Christ crucified."* The resurrection of Christ was the greatest "sign" possible for any humble-minded Jew (Matt. 12:38-40; John 2:19-21), since it instantaneously validated the deity of Christ and the substitutionary, satisfactory nature of His death on the cross. The resurrection was also regarded as "foolishness" (1 Cor. 1:21, 23) by the Greeks (Acts 17:31-32; 1 Cor. 15:12). The finished work of Christ cannot be separated, therefore, from the person of Christ.

Nor is "the message of the cross" merely a message about wood, spikes, and Roman torture. It is a message about the sufficiency of Christ's work and God's grace. It is a message that debases man's pride while appealing to his heart to find in Christ-crucified the all-sufficient, saving grace of God. We see this in a parallel Pauline usage in Galatians 5:11 where Paul writes to the legalistically minded Galatian Christians who sought to add law to grace as a means of justification before God, *"And I, brethren, if I still preach circumcision, why do I still suffer persecution? Then the offense (skandalon) of the cross has ceased."* Paul knew that if he merely added one work to God's plan of salvation, such as circumcision (or in our day, baptism), he would effectively nullify the cross-work of Christ and the grace of God. This message of salvation by grace alone, through faith alone,

---

[80] Minucius Felix, "Octavius," in *The Fathers of the Church* (Washington, D.C.: Catholic University of America Press, 1977), 10:336.

[81] Often when either the death or resurrection of Christ appear alone in Scripture, there is still a certain implied reciprocity that exists. Hence, one writer concludes that "references to the death alone or to the resurrection alone are synecdochic. To speak of the one always brings into view the other; the significance of the one invariably entails the significance of the other. Paul's theology of the cross involves his theology of the resurrection and is simply unintelligible apart from it." Richard Gaffin, "Atonement in the Pauline Corpus," in *The Glory of the Atonement: Biblical, Historical & Practical Perspectives: Essays in Honor of Roger Nicole*, ed. Charles E. Hill and Frank A. James III (Downers Grove, IL: InterVarsity Press, 2004), 142.

in Christ and His finished work alone goes against the grain of man's pride whereby he thinks he can merit the righteousness of God. This *skandalon* of the cross, however, incurs persecution from prideful men who are offended at its preaching. Justification must be by grace through faith *alone*. The "message of the cross," therefore, challenges the heart of man to humble himself by admitting that he cannot save himself by his own merits before God; it must be by Christ's work and God's grace alone.

This leads us back to 1 Corinthians 1 and "the gospel," which is "the message of the cross." Proponents of today's crossless gospel frequently protest that they always include the cross in their evangelism of the lost. They claim it is a powerful apologetic, along with Christ's deity and resurrection, in persuading the lost that Jesus Christ guarantees eternal life to all who believe in Him for it.[82] They contend that the purpose of this "message of the cross" is only to draw people to the promise of eternal life, since believing in the cross itself is non-essential. However, if this is true, why would Paul insist on preaching the cross when he knew full-well that this message was *"to the Jews a stumbling block and to the Greeks foolishness"*? The only way to explain Paul's insistence on preaching a known stumblingblock to the lost is if it was *a necessary stumblingblock*.[83] Therefore, a person simply cannot be saved by believing anything less than "the gospel" (1 Cor. 1:17), which is "the message of the cross" (1 Cor. 1:18).[84]

Romans 3:25

Romans 3:25 presents another possible verse that supports Christ's substitutionary death as an essential element of justifying faith. It must be stressed that it is only a *possible* support because it is subject to two legitimately different translations/interpretations as illustrated below.

> *"whom God set forth as a propitiation by His blood, through faith, to demonstrate His righteousness, because in His forbearance God had passed over the sins that were previously committed"* (NKJV).

---

[82] Zane C. Hodges, "How to Lead People to Christ, Part 1: The Content of Our Message," *JOTGES* 13 (Autumn 2000): 11; René A. Lopez, "Basics of Free Grace Theology, Part 2," p. 1, http://www.scriptureunlocked.com/papers/basicsfgprt2.pdf (accessed August 6, 2007); John Niemelä, "Objects of Faith in John: A Matter of Person AND Content," Grace Evangelical Society Grace Conference, Dallas, TX, February 28, 2006.

[83] The same point pertains to Christ's evangelistic statement in John 6:53 about eating His flesh and drinking His blood, which greatly offends (v. 61, *skandalizō*) the Lord Jesus' audience (John 6:60-68). John 6:53 is not merely a more figurative way of expressing the crossless gospel's three part *sine qua non* of believing in Jesus for everlasting life. True, it is a promise of eternal life—but a promise of eternal life that is inseparable from believing in His incarnation and substitutionary death. The fact that Christ expressed this truth in terms that created such a scandal and offense to His original audience indicates that the incarnation and substitutionary death are a *necessary* stumblingblock and they are a *necessary* part of the contents of saving faith.

[84] Lybrand, "GES Gospel: Lybrand Open Letter," 16-17, 37.

> *"Whom God hath set forth to be a propitiation through faith in his blood, to declare his righteousness for the remission of sins that are past, through the forbearance of God"* (KJV).
>
> *"God presented him as a sacrifice of atonement, through faith in his blood. He did this to demonstrate his justice, because in his forbearance he had left the sins committed beforehand unpunished"* (NIV).

The syntax of Romans 3:25 allows for the prepositional phrase, *en tō autou haimati* ("in/by His blood") to be the object of faith, where the preposition *en* is interpreted with a locative sense, "faith in His blood" (KJV, NIV). This would make Christ's blood the explicit object of the sinner's justifying faith according to the context of Romans 3. This translation would more closely follow the word order of the Greek sentence (*hon proetheto ho theos hilastērion dia tēs pisteōs en tō autou haimati*). If this is the correct translation/interpretation, then of course this verse alone would refute a crossless content of saving faith.

However, it is just as grammatically and contextually possible that the prepositional phrase *en tō autou haimati* modifies the preceding word, *hilastērion* ("propitiation"), where *en* has more of an instrumental sense, "a propitiation by His blood" (NKJV, NASB).[85] Though a few older commentators subscribe to the "faith in His blood" view of the KJV and NIV,[86] the trend among modern scholars and commentators is toward the NKJV and NASB rendering for the primary reason that Paul nowhere else speaks of faith explicitly in Christ's "blood."[87] Not surprisingly, this was also the view of Zane Hodges.[88] However, the interpretation of another proponent of the G.E.S. gospel, René Lopez, is quite astonishing.[89] In his commen-

---

[85] If this latter interpretation is correct, "a propitiation in His blood, by faith...," then this passage would teach that Christ made satisfaction for sin only *at the cross* by His blood, not *in Hades*, as many positive-confessionist charismatics teach today.

[86] Robert Haldane, *An Exposition of the Epistle to the Romans* (Mac Dill, FL: MacDonald Publishing, n.d.), 150; Charles Hodge, *Commentary on the Epistle to the Romans* (Grand Rapids: Eerdmans, reprinted 1994), 94.

[87] Donald A. Carson, "Atonement in Romans 3:21-26," in *The Glory of the Atonement: Biblical, Historical & Practical Perspectives*, ed. Charles E. Hill and Frank A. James III (Downers Grove, IL: InterVarsity Press, 2004), 136; idem, "Why Trust a Cross? Reflections on Romans 3:21-26," *ERT* 28.4 (2004): 359; John D. K. Ekem, "A Dialogical Exegesis of Romans 3:25a," *JSNT* 30.1 (2007): 84; Daniel P. Leyrer, "Exegetical Brief: Romans 3:25: 'Through Faith in His Blood'," *WLQ* 104.3 (Summer 2007): 209.

[88] Zane C. Hodges, "Jesus Is the Propitiation for All, But Only the Mercy Seat for Believers: Romans 3:25 and 1 John 2:2," *Grace in Focus* 21 (July/August 2006): 3.

[89] Lopez's position does not appear to be consistent. On the one hand, he affirms that belief in Christ's deity, death, and resurrection are *not necessary* for eternal life (Lopez, *Romans Unlocked*, 212; idem, "Basics of Free Grace Theology, Part 2," 1). On the other hand, he states in his commentary at Romans 5:9-10, "When sinners believe God's reconciliation message of the cross of Christ (Rom 3:25; 2 Cor 5:20, 21), they personalize the universal scope of God's reconciliation. Hence, after God reconciled the world to Himself, the only

tary on Romans, he opts for the "faith in His blood" view of Romans 3:25, saying it is "the best and most natural reading" and that it "is appropriate to the context even if the construction is not found elsewhere."[90]

So which translation/interpretation is preferable? What are the merits of each view? The NKJV and NASB rendering, "a propitiation by His blood, through faith," has several points in its favor. First, as was mentioned already, if the alternate translation is correct, "through faith in His blood," this would be the only place where Scripture explicitly refers to faith in Christ's blood. Second, the NKJV and NASB translation has the advantage of agreeing with another "blood" passage within Romans. In Romans 5:9, Christ's "blood" is the basis of justification rather than the object of justifying faith,[91] and this holds true elsewhere in Paul's epistles (Eph. 1:7; 2:13; Col. 1:20).[92] Third, if the phrase, "through faith" in Romans 3:25 stands alone and faith is not explicitly "in His blood," this would be consistent with the two other surrounding passages that speak only of believing (Rom. 3:22) and of "faith in Jesus" (3:26).

But the translation, "a propitiation, through faith in His blood," also has several points in its favor. First, it does provide a word for word equivalency with the Greek text, but this is not a decisive factor due to the flexibility of Greek word order.

Second, Paul at times does use the *pistis en* ("faith in") construction when setting forth the object of faith (Gal. 3:26; Eph. 1:15; Col. 1:4; 1 Tim. 3:13; 2 Tim. 1:13; 3:15),[93] even if Christ's "blood" is never stated as the object.

Third, it would not be *un*biblical to take "in His blood" with "faith" ("through faith in His blood"), since there are other passages where "blood" must be personally appropriated by faith. This is true with respect to Christ's blood in John 6:53, *"Truly, truly, I say to you, unless you eat My flesh and drink My blood, you have no life in you."* This would also correspond with the typology of the Passover, where each Israelite household not only believed in God's promise of deliverance from His judgment but they trusted specifically in the means required by God, Lamb's blood (Exod. 12:12-13) and applied it to their doorposts. These Israelites not only clung to God's promise that fateful night, but they specifically did so by believing that the blood applied to their homes would be efficacious. There is no dichotomy between believing in the promise of eternal life (John 3:15) and believing in Christ's sacrificial death (John 3:14, 16).

---

barrier left between men and God is 'unbelief.' Therefore one has to hear and believe this message in order to be justified (2 Cor 5:20-21; Rom 3:25-26)." Lopez, *Romans Unlocked*, 111.

[90] Lopez, *Romans Unlocked*, 79.

[91] Carson, "Why Trust a Cross?" 359; Leyrer, "Exegetical Brief: Romans 3:25," 209.

[92] Douglas Moo, *The Epistle to the Romans*, NICNT (Grand Rapids: Eerdmans, 1996), 237.

[93] Hodge, *Commentary on the Epistle to the Romans*, 94; Moo, *The Epistle to the Romans*, 237n87.

Fourth, there is nothing that would prohibit the Lord from directing Paul to place a unique expression in Romans 3:25, "faith in His blood," since this passage is establishing the very point that Christ is now the mercy seat where sinners meet God in the person of His Son. Instead of bringing the blood of a bull and goat into the holy of holies to put on the mercy seat (Lev. 16:14-15), now we are only asked by God to have faith in the blood of Christ as the mercy seat where we find true atonement (Lev. 16:16; Heb. 9:12). There is nothing in the context of Romans 3:25 that would require that the *work* of propitiation be separated from the person of Christ as the *object* of faith, just as the G.E.S. gospel requires. Even though the surrounding verses speak only of "faith in/of Jesus Christ" (Rom. 3:22) and "faith in Jesus" (Rom. 3:26), the context itself strongly suggests that the person of Christ in whom people are to believe has become our propitiatory mercy seat (Rom. 3:25) and our redemption (3:22). The whole tenor of Romans 3:21-26 is antithetical to a crossless Christ as the object of justifying faith.

Corresponding to this, it should not be overlooked that Romans 3:25 begins by saying in reference to Jesus Christ, *"whom God set forth (proetheto) as a propitiation."* The word *proetheto* speaks of a public display[94] as opposed to a private disclosure in the holy of holies in the ancient tabernacle. Romans 3:25 is setting forth Jesus Christ's propitiatory death on the cross as the very truth that God is holding forth to the world as the object and content of justifying faith (John 3:14; 12:32; Gal. 3:1).

When the support for each interpretation/translation is weighed, we see that taking the prepositional phrase, "in His blood," with "faith" certainly cannot be discounted as a viable option. It is grammatically allowable and it "would be a quite legitimate combination."[95] For the crossless gospel, Romans 3:25 is a watershed. The G.E.S. view cannot allow the translation, "faith in His blood" to be correct; whereas the traditional Free Grace position neither stands nor falls upon either view.

The Cross and Blood

Having covered two salvation passages that mention Christ's cross and blood, some clarification is in order. Sometimes proponents of a crossless saving faith object that the logic of the traditional Free Grace gospel is inherently flawed. They claim that the traditional Free Grace view ought to require belief not only in the *fact* that Christ died for our sins but also in the *way* He died. Wilkin makes such an implication when stating, "Even if Jesus died for our sins by having His throat cut and bleeding to death, we wouldn't be able to have eternal life because His death had to include the

[94] BDAG, 889; J. H. Moulton and G. Milligan, *Vocabulary of the Greek Testament* (Peabody, MA: Hendrickson, reprint 1997), 554.

[95] William Sanday and Arthur C. Headlam, *A Critical and Exegetical Commentary on the Epistle to the Romans*, ICC (New York: Charles Scribner's Sons, n.d.), 89.

piercing of His hands and feet and His hanging on a tree/cross."[96] Do the unsaved really need to know not only that Christ died for their sins but also that the means of His death included being nailed to a cross? Would the price of our sin really not be paid if He was offered as a sacrifice through some other means besides Roman crucifixion?

To be sure, the death of Jesus Christ had to fulfill every detail of Old Testament prophecy and typology, including the piercing of His hands and feet (Ps. 22:16; Zech. 12:10), in order for Him to be the rightful Messiah. But the Bible nowhere states that the basis for our salvation is dependent upon the particular manner in which Christ died. For instance, would the sin of the world not be paid if His crucifixion had occurred from 8 a.m. to 2 p.m. rather than from 9 a.m. to 3 p.m.? Would the wages of sin not be paid if He died inside the temple on the altar of burnt offering rather than outside the walls of the temple? To insist on such details fails to distinguish between the *means* of our salvation and the *grounds* of it. The Bible does not require belief in the means by which Christ accomplished our salvation but only the grounds by which He did so, namely His sacrificial, atoning death. While every detail of Christ's death fulfilled the perfect plan of God, what was necessary and essential in order to provide the basis for our salvation was that He actually died for our sins, *"for the wages of sin is death"* (Rom. 6:23). The Bible does not say that the wages of sin is "death by Roman crucifixion, between the hours of 9 a.m. and 3 p.m., outside the walls of the temple" etc.

It is also imperative to recognize that when Scripture speaks of the "cross," "tree," and "blood" these terms are representative of Christ's literal, sacrificial, substitutionary death. The cross and blood of Christ have long been recognized among conservative evangelical Christians as figures of speech technically known as metalepsis or double metonymy.[97] They are "symbols of His death."[98] They stand in the place of His death and represent another form of expression for His death. Thus, when Paul writes in Galatians 6:14, *"But God forbid that I should glory, save in the cross of our Lord Jesus Christ"* (KJV), he is not promoting faith in the actual wooden instrument of the Savior's execution; rather he is expressing confidence in *what happened upon that cross.* To conclude otherwise would be idolatry—a point often missed by much of professing Christianity.[99]

---

[96] Bob Wilkin, "Essential Truths About Our Savior," *Grace in Focus* 23 (November/December 2008): 2.

[97] E. W. Bullinger, *Figures of Speech Used in the Bible* (Grand Rapids: Baker Book House, 1968), 609-12.

[98] Warfield, *The Person and Work of Christ*, 404.

[99] I recall as an unsaved, Roman Catholic seminarian, the annual Easter ritual. A large wooden cross would be brought into the chapel and placed before the altar. As each student went forward to receive communion, we were expected to kneel down before the wood and kiss it. Though I could not bring myself to actually kiss it (Job 31:27; Ps. 2:12), being under pain of conviction, I did kneel before it, still committing a partial act of idolatry (Ps. 95:6).

The same principle applies with respect to the phrase, "Calvary and the Empty Tomb." Many preachers and teachers in our day, including myself, occasionally use this phraseology with great fondness as an alternative expression for the essential content of Christ's death and resurrection. When we do so, we are not requiring people to know and believe that Christ's death occurred at a place called "Calvary" or for that matter that He was buried in a "tomb." The critical content that must be known and believed involves *what happened* at Calvary and *what happened* inside that tomb—He died for our sins and He rose from the dead.[100] The actual location of His crucifixion and resurrection did not provide the grounds of our redemption—what transpired at those locations did provide the basis for salvation. The cross and the empty tomb are now symbols of the finished work that accomplished our salvation, namely His substitutionary death and bodily resurrection.[101]

Even with respect to the "blood" of Christ spoken of so frequently throughout Scripture, this term also indicates the death of Christ but with the fuller connotations of His death being a vicarious, sacrificial, and atoning payment for sin. In this respect, Christ's blood was precious because it was Lamb's blood—sacrificial blood given in death to redeem the world (1 Peter 1:18-19). This blood, which contained the life of the Son of Man, was given up in death in order to pay the redemption price of man's sin. It is a fixed, immutable law that human sin requires *death* as its consequence in order to satisfy God's justice and righteousness.[102] Another fixed principle of Scripture is that life is in the blood (Gen. 9:4; Lev. 17:11). So long as man's circulatory system is working, he lives. When it stops, he dies. When the Lord Jesus voluntarily gave up His life in order to die (John 10:17-18), He died both physically and spiritually (Matt. 27:46). In order to die and pay the wages of sin, He gave up His whole body (Matt. 26:26; Heb. 10:5, 10, 12, 14), blood (Matt. 26:28; Heb. 10:29), soul (Isa. 53:10), and spirit (Luke 23:46) upon the cross. The shedding of blood in Scripture (lit. "pouring out" of blood), therefore, never indicates merely life-giving as modern liberal theologians teach, but the giving up of one's life *in death*.[103]

---

[100] Metonyms of place that represent an event that transpired or is still transpiring are a common feature of any language. In American English, we have several: "Wall Street" for the business world, "the White House" for the activities of the president, "Woodstock" for the rock festival of the 1960s, "Waterloo" when someone meets their downfall, like Napoleon.

[101] This answers, in part, Wilkin's implication that traditional Free Grace Christians who require belief in Christ's cross-work and resurrection are subject to the charge of preaching a "groundless gospel" for not also requiring belief in His burial. See Bob Wilkin, "Essential Truths About Our Savior," 2n5; idem, "A Review of J. B. Hixson's *Getting the Gospel Wrong: The Evangelical Crisis No One Is Talking About*," *JOTGES* 21 (Spring 2008): 18n42. This point is addressed more thoroughly in chapter 14.

[102] Leon Morris, *The Wages of Sin: An Examination of the New Testament Teaching on Death* (London: Tyndale Press, 1955).

[103] P. T. Forsyth, *The Cruciality of the Cross* (Carlisle, England: Paternoster Press, 1997), 85-

Since blood can be shed that does not result in death, and since Christ did not bleed to death, the atonement for sin was in the actual giving up of His life by dying, while His death was accompanied and signified by the pouring out of blood.[104]

Though this vital topic is worthy of a much fuller treatment, space permits only a few passages showing that blood, or shed blood, symbolizes death itself in the Bible.[105] In Acts 22:20, Paul recounts being present at the stoning of Stephen. He states, *"And when the blood of Your martyr Stephen was shed, I also was standing by consenting to his death, and guarding the clothes of those who were killing him."* Regarding this passage, Leon Morris comments, "for as that death was by stoning there is no emphasis on the literal outpouring of blood."[106] It may further be added that, although stoning may have induced bloodshed as jagged rocks lacerated the skin, death during stoning was not due to gradual hemorrhaging but due to the concussive blows the victim received.[107] Similarly in Revelation 6:9-11, the martyred souls under the altar in heaven cry out to God for justice, saying, *"How long, O Lord, holy and true, until You judge and avenge our blood on those who dwell on the earth?"* Morris says of this passage, "It makes nonsense of this passage to insist that there is any emphasis on a literal shedding of blood. The people in question are those 'that had been slain for the word of God, and for the testimony which they held' (Rev. vi. 9), quite irrespective of how they met their death."[108] While certainly some of these saints suffered actual bloodshed in the course of dying, even as their fellow saints later in the tribulation will (Rev. 13:10), it would be a gratuitous leap to insist that *every* tribulation saint depicted within the fifth seal of Revelation 6:9-11 will suffer some bloodshed in their deaths. Blood is obviously a figure here for death, perhaps even violent death as

---

104; Leon Morris, *The Apostolic Preaching of the Cross* (Grand Rapids: Eerdmans, 1956), 108-24; idem, "The Biblical Use of the Term 'Blood,'" *JTS* 3 (1952): 216-27; idem, *The Cross in the New Testament* (Grand Rapids: Eerdmans, 1965), 218-19; John R. W. Stott, *The Cross of Christ* (Downers Grove, IL: InterVarsity Press, 1986), 179-81, 202.

[104] In John 19:34, the blood (and water) that issued from the pierced side of the Lord Jesus' body gave testimony to the reality and fact of His sacrificial death only moments earlier, where in John 19:30 He cried out, *"It is finished"* and expired. This reference in John 19:34 is the first and last mention of blood from the time that Christ predicts His own death in John 6:51-56 until the end of John's Gospel.

[105] See also Gen. 9:4-6; 37:18-22; 42:22; Matt. 27:25; Acts 18:6; 20:26.

[106] Morris, *The Apostolic Preaching of the Cross*, 118.

[107] One conservative Bible teacher gives the biblically balanced perspective when he writes, "What is the significance of the shedding of blood? If Christ had been stoned to death (as the Jews desired to do to Him) would this have been considered as 'the shedding of blood'? The answer is 'yes' as we learn in Acts 22:20. In Christ's case we know that death by crucifixion was essential because the Scriptures must be fulfilled—John 12:32-34; 18:32; 19:36-37; Psalm 22; etc." George W. Zeller, http://www.middletownbiblechurch.org/romans/romans5.htm (accessed May 14, 2009).

[108] Morris, *The Apostolic Preaching of the Cross*, 118.

their lives will be taken from them. Finally, in Hebrews 9:14-15, the blood of Christ and His death are used interchangeably.[109] It says in Hebrews 9:14 that the "blood of Christ" was offered for our spiritual cleansing, while in the next verse this is described as having occurred "by means of death."

There is a near consensus among moderate to conservative biblical scholars on the fact that the term *blood* in the Bible is a figurative expression for *death*,[110] even sacrificial death.[111] Thus, Morris summarizes his extensive study on the subject by saying, "The OT evidence is that blood means death, in the sacrifices as elsewhere,"[112] and "References to blood are a vivid way of saying that we owe our salvation to the death of Christ."[113] Dillistone states, "the main sacrificial metaphor in Paul's writings is to be found in his references to 'blood.'"[114] Stibbs says, "'*By the blood of Jesus*' means, therefore, through the death of Jesus and its realized significance,"[115] and again, "So the term *'the blood of Christ'* is a metaphorical and symbolical way of referring to His earthly death in a human body upon a cross of shame, and to its innumerable and eternal consequences."[116] Behm echoes the same opinion, "Like the cross (*σταυρός*), the *'blood of Christ'* is simply another and even more graphic phrase for the death of Christ in its soteriological significance."[117] Motyer concurs, "Heb. 9:11-18 confirms in the NT the symbolism of blood as death and applies Lev. 17:11 to the sacrifice of the Lord Jesus Christ."[118] Zeller explains, "When the expression 'blood of Christ' is used in the epistles it refers to the precious CROSS-WORK of Jesus Christ, especially His SUBSTITUTIONARY DEATH on behalf of sinners. The shedding of His blood involves, among other things, the GIVING OF HIS LIFE (John 10:11)."[119] Even Spurgeon explains Hebrews 9:22 by saying, "'*Without the shedding of blood there is no remission*'; and the shed-

---

[109] Ibid., 121.

[110] Johannes Behm, "*αἷμα, αἱματεκχυσία*," *TDNT*, 1:172-77; Philip E. Hughes, "The Blood of Jesus and His Heavenly Priesthood in Hebrews, Part 1: The Significance of the Blood of Jesus," *BSac* 130 (April 1973): 109; Morris, *The Apostolic Preaching of the Cross*, 118, 121; Alan M. Stibbs, *The Meaning of the Word "Blood" in Scripture* (London: Tyndale Press, 1948), 17-22.

[111] Warfield, *The Person and Work of Christ*, 422.

[112] Leon Morris, "Blood," in *Evangelical Dictionary of Theology*, ed. Walter A. Elwell (Grand Rapids: Baker Book House, 1984), 163.

[113] Ibid.

[114] F. W. Dillistone, *The Significance of the Cross* (Philadelphia: Westminster Press, 1944), 88.

[115] Stibbs, *The Meaning of the Word "Blood" in Scripture*, 24 (italics added).

[116] Ibid., 19 (italics added).

[117] Johannes Behm, "*αἷμα, αἱματεκχυσία*," *TDNT*, 1:174 (italics added).

[118] J. A. Motyer, "Blood, Sacrificial Aspects of," in *Evangelical Dictionary of Theology*, ed. Walter A. Elwell (Grand Rapids: Baker Book House, 1984), 164.

[119] George W. Zeller, http://www.middletownbiblechurch.org/romans/romans5.htm (accessed May 14, 2009).

ding of blood intended is the death of Jesus, the Son of God."[120] Spurgeon elsewhere elaborates:

> But what does "the blood" mean in Scripture? It means not merely suffering, which might be well typified by blood, but it means suffering unto death, it means the taking of a life. To put it very briefly, a sin against God deserves death as its punishment, and what God said by the mouth of the prophet Ezekiel still standeth true, "The soul that sinneth, it shall die." The only way by which God could fulfill his threatening sentence, and yet forgive guilty men, was that Jesus Christ, his Son, came into the world, and offered his life instead of ours.[121]

Practically speaking, this means that to have *"faith in His blood"* as stated in Romans 3:25 is another way of expressing faith in Christ's vicarious death. If a man placed his faith in Christ's all-sufficient death for his sins but for some strange reason never heard that Christ shed His blood while dying, such a man would still have saving faith. The Lord has seen fit to use a multiplicity of metaphors,[122] images, and diverse terminology to depict the one truth of the Savior's death for our sins. These terms include "cross," "tree," "blood," "gave," "offered," "sacrificed," "redeemed," "suffered," "slain," etc. Yet, despite such rich diversity of expression, there is still a unity of content, as each of these terms point to the same substitutionary, atoning death of the Savior.[123] Diverse expression with unity of content also occurs with each of the other elements in the contents of saving faith. This is especially evident in the evangelistic speeches/sermons in Acts.[124]

Jesus Christ's Bodily Resurrection

In terms of evangelistic practice in North America, the emphasis of most gospel presentations is decidedly upon the cross-work of Christ rather than

---

[120] Charles H. Spurgeon, "The Blood of Sprinkling," in *The Metropolitan Tabernacle Pulpit* (Pasadena, TX: Pilgrim Publications, reprinted 1986), 32:123. The phrase in verse 22, "shedding of blood," is a tame translation. It is the translation of the single compound Greek word, *haimatekchusias,* which literally means "the pouring out of blood." It is a graphic expression for death, not just bleeding. Regarding this term, Gromacki writes, "The shedding of blood implies the death of the sacrificial substitute." Robert G. Gromacki, *Stand Bold in Grace: An Exposition of Hebrews* (The Woodlands, TX: Kress Christian Publications, 2002), 156. The use of this term in Hebrews may be an allusion to Christ's words at the Lord's Supper where He spoke of the cup as representing His blood that would be literally "poured out" (*ekchunnomenon*) in death the next day for the sins of the world (Matt. 26:28).

[121] Charles H. Spurgeon, "Blood Even on the Golden Altar," in *The Metropolitan Tabernacle Pulpit* (Pasadena, TX: Pilgrim Publications, reprinted, 1977), 40:325.

[122] Dillistone, *The Significance of the Cross,* 35-37; Frank A. James III, "The Atonement in Church History," in *The Glory of the Atonement: Biblical, Historical & Practical Perspectives: Essays in Honor of Roger Nicole,* ed. Charles E. Hill and Frank A. James III (Downers Grove, IL: InterVarsity Press, 2004), 215.

[123] Leon Morris, *The Cross in the New Testament* (Grand Rapids: Eerdmans, 1965), 364.

[124] See chapters 10, 16, 17 in this book.

His resurrection. This leads some born again Christians to ask years after their new birth, "Did I believe in Christ's resurrection at that time? I don't recall even hearing about it when I first heard the gospel and believed." One thing is sure—they most certainly did not believe in a *dead* Savior! In such cases, the resurrection, like Christ's humanity, is implied and assumed, if not even briefly included in a gospel presentation. The fact is that North American culture for the last few hundred years has been predominantly "Christian" in profession, and the biblical-historical facts of Christ's humanity, death on a cross, and even His resurrection from the dead have been widely known and familiar to most citizens. Consequently, these facts are often already assumed and believed by a lost person before a thorough explanation of Christ's cross-work is presented and believed. But this leads us to ask, is the resurrection really an element of the gospel that is essential to believe for justification?

As with the deity, humanity, and substitutionary death of Christ, the pattern holds true that the resurrection is also seen to be part of the triad of the gospel, the meaning of Jesus as the Christ, and the grounds of our salvation. Its inclusion as an element of the gospel is rarely a matter of dispute and is apparent from several verses (Acts 17:3 cf. 2 Thess. 1:8-10; Acts 17:18 [Gr., *euangelizō*]; 1 Cor. 15:1-4). Since believing the gospel of Christ is synonymous with believing that Jesus is the Christ (John 20:30-31), it is also not surprising to discover that certain passages define "the Christ" by the indispensable element of His resurrection from the dead (Luke 24:46; Acts 2:31, 36). If the resurrection is essential to Jesus being "the Christ" and believing that Jesus is "the Christ" is essential for eternal life (John 20:31), then we should expect to find individual passages requiring belief in Christ's resurrection for eternal salvation—and we do (Acts 17:3 cf. 2 Thess. 1:8-10; Rom. 10:9b-10a; 1 Thess. 4:14).

Likewise, just as it has been observed thus far for Christ's deity, humanity, and death that a real symmetry exists between the contents of the gospel, the meaning of the Christ, and the grounds of salvation, so the Lord's resurrection also forms an essential basis upon which our eternal salvation rests.[125] While Christ's death alone paid the penalty for sin, Christ's death without the resurrection was not sufficient to effect our justification. Both His death and His resurrection were essential for our justification and redemption (Rom. 4:25; 5:9-10).[126] There are at least two prominent passages that establish this truth.

---

[125] Norman L. Geisler, *The Battle for the Resurrection* (Nashville: Thomas Nelson, 1989), 33-34; Robert P. Lightner, *Sin, the Savior, and Salvation: The Theology of Everlasting Life* (Nashville: Thomas Nelson, 1991), 129.

[126] Michael F. Bird, "'Raised for Our Justification': A Fresh Look at Romans 4:25," *Colloquium* 35 (May 2003): 31-46; idem, *The Saving Righteousness of God: Studies on Paul, Justification and the New Perspective* (Carlisle, England: Paternoster Press, 2007), 40-59; I. Howard Marshall, *Aspects of the Atonement: Cross and Resurrection in the Reconciling of God and Humanity* (Carlisle, England: Paternoster Press, 2007), 80-86.

Romans 4:25

Romans 4:25 states that Christ *"was delivered up because of our offenses, and was raised because of our justification."* While it is obvious that Christ was delivered up to death for our sins, the meaning of the second clause is not so apparent. Some, like Tenney, interpret it to mean that the resurrection was necessary to "guarantee immunity from further sinning."[127] The resurrection, he says, provides power for sanctification and a pledge of glorification.[128] While there is an undeniable connection between the resurrection and the Spirit's power for sanctification (Rom. 6:3-13; 8:11; Eph. 1:18-20), and Christ's resurrection certainly guarantees our future glorification (1 Cor. 15:22-23, 51-57; 2 Cor. 4:14; 1 Thess. 4:14-18), it is doubtful that this is the meaning of Romans 4:25. In this passage, it says that Christ was raised up *"because of our justification"* not because of our sanctification or glorification.

More likely is the view that Christ's resurrection, coupled with His propitious death, provided the forensic basis for our own justification which is through faith in Christ. The parallelism of the two "because of" (*dia* + accusative) statements in Romans 4:25 should be maintained in any interpretation of this verse when it says that Christ was delivered to death because of our sins and that He was raised because of our justification.[129] While it is true that Christ's resurrection was the proof to mankind that God accepted the sacrifice of His Son as the payment for our sins, this verse appears to be saying more than that. Christ's resurrection was also necessary as the basis for our own justification.[130] Romans 4:25 is teaching that just as Christ showed solidarity with Adam's race by being condemned in our place at the cross, His resurrection also provided the basis for Him to be united to the host of a new, redeemed, justified humanity who are part of His body. The Savior's resurrection was the momentous turning point for the human race as God the Father terminated the forces of death acting upon the Last Adam and simultaneously justified (declared righteous) or vindicated His own Son (Rom. 1:4; 1 Tim. 3:16; 1 Peter 3:18)[131] from the condemnation of the cross,[132] thereby providing a basis for our

---

[127] Merrill C. Tenney, *The Reality of the Resurrection* (Chicago: Moody Press, 1972), 70.

[128] Ibid., 71-74.

[129] Leander E. Keck, *Romans* (Nashville: Abingdon Press, 2005), 132.

[130] Charles Hodge, *Commentary on the Epistle to the Romans* (Grand Rapids: Eerdmans, 1994), 129. One crossless gospel proponent has expressed his agreement with this point by stating that Christ's "resurrection is the basis of what gets us justified. . . . Without the resurrection we have no eternal life." René A. López, "The Use and Abuse of 1 Corinthians 15:1-11," Grace Evangelical Society Conference, Fort Worth, TX, March 31, 2009.

[131] George W. Zeller, "The Mystery of Godliness: Its Application to the Local Assembly (1 Timothy 3:14-16)," (M.Div. thesis, Grace Theological Seminary, 1975), 75-78.

[132] Richard B. Gaffin, Jr., *Resurrection and Redemption: A Study in Paul's Soteriology*, 2nd ed. (Phillipsburg, NJ: Presbyterian & Reformed Publishing, 1987), 119-24; Frederic L. Godet, *Commentary on Romans* (Grand Rapids: Kregel, reprinted 1977), 184-85; John Murray, *The*

own future justification by faith in the Righteous One.[133] The legal declaration that we are righteous in God's sight is based on our union with, or position in, Jesus Christ the Righteous/Justified One (1 John 2:1)—the One who is our righteousness (Isa. 45:24-25; Jer. 23:5-6; 1 Cor. 1:30; 2 Cor. 5:21; Phil. 3:9).[134] Regarding this truth, Chafer writes:

> Yet there is a sense in which it may be said too that, since imputed righteousness is the divine reason for that divine pronouncement which justification is and since imputed righteousness accrues to the believer on the sole basis of His union to the resurrected Christ, the believer's justification does rest perfectly on the resurrection of the Lord. It is therefore true that justification is made possible both by the death of Christ and by His resurrection, and so both are essential.[135]

Thus, our justification is truly based on Christ's resurrection. This interpretation of Romans 4:25 is also consistent with Paul's preaching of the gospel to the Galatians in Acts 13. There, after preaching about Christ being cursed for us on the "tree," he emphasizes how God raised up His Son from the dead at the resurrection. Immediately after this point, as if as a consequence of the resurrection, Paul preaches forgiveness of sins and justification "through Him" (*en toutō*) to everyone who believes (Acts 13:38-39).

1 Corinthians 15:17-18

A second key passage on Christ's resurrection forming the dual work on which our salvation rests is 1 Corinthians 15:17-18, where it says, *"And if Christ is not risen, your faith is vain; you are still in your sins! Then also those who have fallen asleep in Christ have perished."* Regarding this passage, Gaffin writes that "justifying faith is worthless, if Christ has not been raised (cf. v. 14), because a dead Christ is an unjustified Christ, and an unjustified Christ means an unjustified believer. Elsewhere the appeal for justifying faith (Rom. 10:9) and even justification itself (Rom. 8:34) is based primarily and directly on Christ's resurrection or on Christ as resurrected."[136] This interpretation is perfectly consistent with Romans 4:25 and 5:9-10, which

---

Epistle to the Romans, NICNT (Grand Rapids: Eerdmans, 1968), 154-57; Moo, *The Epistle to the Romans*, 288-90. Regarding Christ's justification, Vine adds a vital qualification, "But how was He justified? Not as we are. We are justified by grace as sinners. He was justified in vindication of His sinlessness. Righteousness is imputed to us; righteousness was inherent to Him." W. E. Vine, "The Twelve Mysteries of Scripture," in *The Collected Writings of W. E. Vine* (Nashville: Thomas Nelson Publishers, 1996), 4:181.

[133] Bruce A. Lowe, "Oh διά! How Is Romans 4:25 to be Understood?" *JTS* 57 (April 2006): 149-57.

[134] William R. Newell, *Romans Verse-By-Verse* (Grand Rapids: Kregel, reprinted 1994), 156-59.

[135] Chafer, *Systematic Theology*, 5:248-49.

[136] Gaffin, *Resurrection and Redemption*, 124.

show that both the death and resurrection of Christ form the necessary grounds for our justification and eternal salvation.

Reinterpretation and Redefinition

At this point it is worth pausing to reflect upon a startling fact regarding Scripture's testimony to the contents of saving faith in comparison to the crossless gospel's interpretation of Scripture. Having observed the many passages in God's Word that require belief in Christ's deity, humanity, death, and resurrection as elements of the gospel, it is alarming to consider the aggregate amount of reinterpretation that has occurred over a very short span of one or two decades. Many key passages testifying to the person and work of Christ in the gospel have been readjusted in order to accommodate the evolving system of the promise-only gospel. For example, we are told that John 8:24 no longer supports the deity of Christ as a requirement for eternal life. Even the key Christological terms of "the Christ" and "Son of God" do not necessarily indicate the Lord's deity. Regarding Christ's substitutionary death, Romans 3:25 is not teaching "faith in His blood" (according to Hodges) and 1 Corinthians 1:18-21 is really just a sanctification message to believers about rewards and salvation at the judgment seat of Christ (according to Wilkin). The cross and incarnation have been expunged from John 3:16, leaving only its promise of eternal life. Nor is John 6:53 requiring belief in Christ's incarnation and atoning death but is only a figurative expression for faith in Jesus as the guarantor of eternal life, the same truth taught in John 6:47, we are told. 1 Corinthians 15:1-4 is not requiring belief in Christ's death for sin and bodily resurrection, since this is also a sanctification passage. Romans 10:9-10 is also not requiring belief in the deity and resurrection of Christ for justification, since this passage is just showing Christians how to escape God's wrath. It is fair to say that in the last ten to twenty years there has been a wholesale doctrinal realignment underway within the Free Grace movement, particularly the Grace Evangelical Society, and it is all based on a shifting gospel and a radical change in the required contents of saving faith.

Salvation by Grace through Faith Alone

The provision of salvation and the condition to receive it are also part of the gospel of our salvation. The good news of *who* Jesus Christ is and *what* He has accomplished by His finished work cannot be separated from the good news that salvation is available to all based solely on God's grace and conditioned only on faith (Acts 16:31; Rom. 1:16-17; 3:23-28; 4:4-5; 1 Cor. 1:17-21; 15:1-2, 11, 14; Acts 13:38-48 cf. Gal. 1:8; 4:13; Acts 26:18 cf. Gal. 1:11-12). The person and work of Christ are inseparable from the provision and condition of salvation. Salvation by grace through faith alone is inexplicable apart from Christ's deity, humanity, death, and resurrection. When lost, condemned sinners learn that Jesus Christ became a man and died a substitutionary death for all their sins, they realize that salvation before God cannot be earned by their good works, but only by the work of God's Son on their behalf. The only appropriate response at that point is to simply receive this work by believing it. Likewise, when people understand that Jesus Christ is God-incarnate, who rose from the dead and conquered death itself—the very wages of sin—they know that He is uniquely qualified to grant eternal life. He alone, therefore, is the suitable Object of one's trust to meet the conscious need for eternal deliverance from sin's wages. Consequently, the person and work of Christ cannot be disconnected from the divine provision of salvation by grace and the non-meritorious response of faith alone.

This means that salvation by God's grace through faith alone is itself an element of the gospel. This can be observed from several passages that describe or define "the gospel" and which also include the condition of faith or believing as an integral part of that message (Acts 15:7-11; 20:21 cf. 20:24; Rom. 1:16-17; 1 Cor. 1:17 cf. 1:21; 15:1-2 11, 14; Acts 13:38-39 cf. Gal. 1:8; 4:13; Acts 26:18 cf. Gal. 1:11-12). It stands to reason that if salvation by grace through faith alone is part of the gospel, and if people must believe the gospel to be saved, then people must accept God's terms for salvation in order to be saved. And why wouldn't this be part of the gospel? It is good news to hear that salvation has been fully paid for by another and is now free to the recipient. It is good news that salvation can be received as simply as believing. Therefore, the response of faith alone is not merely the *response to* the gospel; it is also *part of* the gospel.[137] This also means that God not only *offers* salvation by faith but He *requires* that people receive it on that basis. But what is it about salvation that they must understand and believe?

Scripture uses several terms to describe the benefits or blessings that flow from the person and work of Christ and God's grace. Broadly, this element of the gospel is called "salvation" (Acts 4:12, 15:7, 11; Rom. 1:16; Eph. 1:13). Regarding "salvation," Tom Constable writes, "Basically this term means that the believer has been delivered from condemnation unto righteousness. There are several aspects of salvation expounded in Scripture that explain its richness and depth."[138] These aspects of divine deliverance are variously called in Scripture forgiveness, justification, sanctification, glorification, regeneration, reconciliation, redemption, eternal life, etc. The Bible uses great variety of expression for the element of salvation in the gospel. We see this in certain Scripture passages where this element of the gospel is explicitly referred to as "forgiveness" (Acts 10:43 cf. Acts

---

[137] Thomas R. Edgar, "What Is the Gospel?" in *Basic Theology Applied: A Practical Application of Basic Theology in Honor of Charles C. Ryrie and His Work*, edited by Wesley and Elaine Willis & John and Janet Masters (Wheaton, IL: Victor Books, 1995), 158.

[138] Thomas L. Constable, "The Gospel Message," in *Walvoord: A Tribute* (Chicago: Moody Press, 1982), 214.

15:7-11), "justification" (Acts 13:38-39 cf. Gal. 1:8; 4:13), "peace" with God (Eph. 2:15-17 cf. Rom. 5:1), the hope laid up for us in "heaven" (Col. 1:5), and "eternal life" (Acts 13:46, 48 cf. Gal. 1:8; 4:13). Though each of these various aspects of divine deliverance is part of the gospel and falls under the same broad umbrella of "salvation," this does not mean that the lost must know each term and its doctrinal significance before God will save them.[139] A person may only know and understand one of these terms at the point of initial faith and then grow thereafter in their appreciation and comprehension of this great multifaceted gift that was received at the moment of new birth. But people must at least apprehend the fact of their condemned conditioned before God due to sin and acknowledge their need for His gracious deliverance.

The Context of the Gospel

No study of the contents of the gospel would be complete without some discussion of its context. If the saving message of the gospel entails belief in Christ's substitutionary work on the cross, then this presupposes that people see their need for a Savior from sin and its wages. There is presently a paradigm shift underway among some Free Grace people not only regarding the content of the "saving message" but also regarding our emphases in evangelism—particularly with respect to man's sin-problem. The need to recognize personal sin before a holy God is now being downplayed as not "the fundamental issue" facing the unbeliever, because "sin has ceased to be the big issue."[140] Instead, we are told that the fundamental issue is merely life versus death. Thus, unbelievers only need to learn about God's promise of eternal life, not the reason that they need it or even what God has done to provide it through Christ's work. This problem is exemplified by how the crossless gospel treats evangelistic passages in John's Gospel. Wilkin writes:

> Jesus often never even brought up the issue of sin when He evangelized. Look at what He told Nicodemus in John 3. He never even mentioned sin there. Even in John 4 when He spoke with the woman at the well, while Jesus pointed out one area of sin in her life, He didn't call her to repent of it. Indeed, it is clear that the reason He pointed out that area of sin was to convince her that He was the Messiah (compare John 4:16-19, 25-26, 39).[141]

---

[139] George E. Meisinger, "The Gospel Paul Preached: A Church Age Model of Evangelistic Content," Chafer Theological Seminary Pastors Conference, Houston, TX, March 11, 2009.

[140] John Niemelä, "What About Believers Who Have Never Known Christ's Promise of Life?" Chafer Theological Seminary Conference, Houston, TX, March 13, 2006.

[141] Bob Wilkin, "The Way of the Master," *Grace in Focus* (July-August 2007). While it is true that repentance from sin, in the sense of turning from it, is not the condition for eternal life, the lost must still acknowledge that they are sinners in need of a Savior, which involves a change of mind—repentance.

This is a serious misinterpretation of John 3-4. In the case of Nicodemus, the subject of sin is certainly implied in John 3:14 by Jesus' reference to the lifting up of the brass serpent in the wilderness. Why did Moses need to put a serpent on a pole and lift it up, anyway? The answer is assumed and implied from the Old Testament account—it was due to the sin of certain Israelites who were snake-bitten (Num. 21:5-9). Likewise in John 4, the fact that the Samaritan woman became convinced that Jesus was the Messiah does not preclude the fact that she recognized her sin and need for the Savior. In neither John 3 nor John 4 did the Lord Jesus dismiss sin as no longer being "the big issue." Nor does John's Gospel as a whole. In terms of raw word count, "sin" occurs more frequently in John than in Matthew and Mark combined. In fact, the Gospel of John appears to emphasize man's sin-problem more than any of the other Gospels.[142]

But all of this underscores the fact that the *content* of the gospel needs a proper *context* if it is to be meaningful. Just as any single Bible verse can be taken "out of context" when read apart from the verses that surround it, so can the contents of the gospel. The good news of Christ's person and work, along with the gospel's provision of salvation and its sole condition of faith, all require some essential prior knowledge for it to be understood correctly. Consider, for example, the key gospel passage of 1 Corinthians 15:1-4. In this passage, why would the Corinthians even need to be "saved" (v. 2)? Why would a man named "Christ" even need to "die" (v. 3)? Furthermore, what are "sins" (v. 3)? And why does 1 Corinthians 15:3 say that this Christ died for "our sins"? After all, I'm not really a sinner, am I?

Without such basic prior knowledge, even the simplest salvation verses in the Bible cannot be properly apprehended. Even John 3:16 does not make sense without first believing that there is a "God" who gave His only Son. By the way, who is God's "Son" anyway?[143] In Acts 16:31, when Paul and Silas say, *"Believe on the Lord Jesus Christ and you shall be saved,"* does this not presuppose some understanding of being "saved"? "Saved" from what? Financial debt? A failing marriage? An abusive relationship? Drug addiction? In Acts 16:30, when the Philippian jailor asked Paul and Silas, *"Sirs, what must I do to be saved?"* how did the jailor even know he had a need to be "saved"?

With no biblical context, the gospel is meaningless . . .

---

[142] Morris, *The Cross in the New Testament*, 146.

[143] This poses a problem for those crossless proponents who simultaneously insist that the name "Jesus" is part of the threefold *sine qua non* of saving faith and who also insist that John 3:16, by itself, contains sufficient content for everlasting life.

. . . but with a biblical framework, the gospel has meaning.

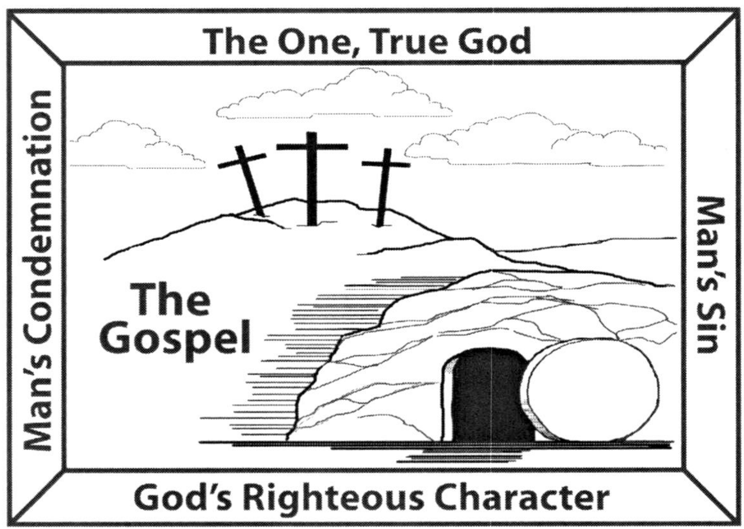

As we think of the necessary context for the gospel, we see from Scripture that without a basic understanding of God, sin, and judgment (John 16:9-11; 17:3), the gospel simply cannot be understood or believed.[144] Just as

[144] Constable, "The Gospel Message," 203-4, 210-11.

every text needs a context, and every building needs a foundation, and every window needs a frame, so the gospel needs a context, a foundation, or a framework.[145] Some prefer to call these the necessary presuppositions to the gospel.[146] Others prefer to simply say that the "good news" cannot be received apart from knowing the "bad news" of man's sin and God's judgment.[147] Regardless of what label or approach is used,[148] the idea is the same. Some context is required. We know that biblically this includes a basic understanding of God's character and identity, man's sin, and his lost, separated condition in view of God's righteousness and judgment. This is precisely what we see in the Book of Romans, where the apostle Paul begins by laying the foundation for the gospel. In Romans 1:18-3:20, he demonstrates that all people are sinners, unrighteous, and condemned before the ultimate standard of righteousness, God alone. Thus, while Romans 1:18-3:20 establishes the proper *context* for the gospel, this section of Romans is not a part of the *content* of the gospel of the grace of God,[149] which comes later in Romans 3:21-5:21.

The Contents vs. Object of Saving Faith

Having clarified the gospel's context and contents, some crossless proponents will surely protest that this is requiring belief in a list of doctrines rather

---

[145] See, for example, the framework approach of Charles Clough at Biblical Framework Ministries, http://www.cclough.com/about-framework.php (accessed May 9, 2009).

[146] Constable, "The Gospel Message," 203-4.

[147] Dennis M. Rokser, *Bad News for Good People and Good News for Bad People* (Duluth, MN: Duluth Bible Church, 2007).

[148] Some ministries, such as New Tribes Mission and GoodSeed International, emphasize the chronological approach to laying this foundation and providing a context for the gospel. This involves teaching in survey fashion the main biblical themes of God's identity and righteous character, man's sin and need for salvation, and the theme of a sacrificial substitute pointing to Jesus Christ as the coming Lamb of God. For New Tribes Mission, see Trevor McIlwain, *Firm Foundations: Creation to Christ*, 2nd ed. (Sanford, FL: New Tribes Mission, 2009). For GoodSeed International, see John R. Cross, *by this Name* (Olds, Alberta: GoodSeed International, 2007); idem, *The Lamb* (Olds, Alberta: GoodSeed International, 2004); idem, *The Stranger on the Road to Emmaus*, 3rd ed. (Olds, Alberta: GoodSeed International, 2003).

[149] The chronological approach to evangelism does not teach that the context for the gospel is part of the gospel itself. Regarding the new, broad G.E.S. view of "the gospel," Wilkin writes, "In one sense everything from creation to the New Earth is part of the good news. That is how many in New Tribes evangelize people who've never heard about Jesus. While I would suggest telling people each time that Jesus guarantees eternal life to all who simply believe in Him, and I wouldn't wait until the last scores of the message to tell the message of John 3:16, I do agree that it is all part of the good news" (Bob Wilkin, "Gospel Means Good News," a paper delivered at the Grace Evangelical Society Conference, Fort Worth, TX, March 6, 2008, p. 8). New Tribes Mission does not, however, teach that everything from creation to Christ is all part of one, big "gospel." They employ the chronological method in order to establish the necessary *context* for the gospel, along with prophetic foreviews of Christ, while recognizing that the actual *content* of the gospel itself is the message of salvation by grace through faith alone in the crucified, risen Christ.

than in the person of Jesus Himself. The criticism coming from crossless quarters in recent years against the traditional Free Grace position is that we have arbitrarily added our own set of orthodox doctrines to the contents of saving faith and that this amounts to "theological legalism."[150] Wilkin provides an example of this perspective and even explains why he objects to Christ's deity, substitutionary death, and bodily resurrection as part of the required content of saving faith. He states:

> Doctrinal legalists who profess to believe the Free Grace message claim that to be born again one must not only believe in Jesus, but he must also believe certain additional truths about His Person and work. Their position has a superficial logic. Here is how they reason:
>
> Major premise: We must believe *in the right Jesus* to be born again.
> Minor premise: The right Jesus is the One who is God and who died on the cross for our sins and who rose bodily from the dead.
> Conclusion: To be born again one must believe that Jesus is God, that He died on the cross for our sins, that He rose bodily from the dead, and that by faith in that Jesus and in those doctrines we have everlasting life.
>
> But the Lord Jesus never said that in order to be born again one must believe in His deity, His death, or His resurrection. The Lord Jesus simply called for faith in Himself.[151]

This line of thinking ends up creating a false antithesis between the object of saving faith ("Jesus") and the contents of saving faith ("additional truths about His person and work"). It fails to reckon with the fact that certain biblical truths define "Jesus" and what it means to have "faith in Himself." In fact, the promise-only position insists that the lost only have to believe that Jesus *guarantees* them eternal life, while not needing to know, understand, or believe the *basis* on which He provides that eternal life.[152] However, the truths of Christ's deity, humanity, death, and resurrection are not extraneous to His person or somehow dispensable; they are a matter of His essential identity, nature, and being.

Some extreme crossless advocates even go so far as to claim that saving faith doesn't require *any* content. For example, one speaker at a national conference of the Grace Evangelical Society stated, "However,

---

[150] Hodges, "The Hydra's Other Head: Theological Legalism," 2-3.

[151] Bob Wilkin, "Essential Truths About Our Savior," *Grace in Focus* 23 (November/December 2008): 2. See also, Bob Wilkin, "Four Free Grace Views Related to Two Issues: Assurance and the Five Essentials," *Grace in Focus* 24 (July/August 2009): 1-2.

[152] Lopez, "Basics of Free Grace Theology, Part 2," 1; idem, "The Use and Abuse of 1 Corinthians 15:1-11," Grace Evangelical Society Conference, Fort Worth, TX, March 31, 2009; H. Graham Wilson, Jr., "The Importance of the Incarnation to Resurrection," paper presented at Grace Evangelical Society Conference, Fort Worth, TX, March 31, 2009, p. 15.

the *'content of faith'* terminology is a misnomer. Faith has no content. Let me repeat. Faith has no content. Rather, it is only a persuasion, a reliance upon the object of faith."[153] In response to such an astonishing claim, it must be pointed out that even the G.E.S. version of the "saving message" has some required doctrinal content. It has three parts to its *sine qua non* of saving faith consisting of "Jesus," "eternal life," and "believing in Him for it."[154] And behind each of these elements is further doctrinal content. According to the G.E.S. notion of "Jesus" in its *sine qua non* of saving faith, the lost must believe specifically that He is the guarantor of eternal life, otherwise they have insufficient content and cannot be saved. Also according to the G.E.S. view, the lost person must understand that "eternal life" is nothing less than eternal security or else that person is not truly born again. Thirdly, the lost must also understand that "faith" means persuasion, not commitment, dedication, surrender, etc. It is an incontestable fact that everyone's version of the saving message contains specific content. It is just a matter of which content. In essence, the G.E.S. position boils down to believing in a promise without having to believe anything about the ontological make-up of Christ's person or anything about His historical redemptive work. But is it really sufficient to just believe that someone named "Jesus" can guarantee you eternal life?

The Uniqueness of Jesus Christ

The uniqueness of Jesus Christ makes Him the required object of saving faith today (Acts 4:12; 1 Tim. 2:5). There are only three categories of higher, intelligent beings in the universe—God, angels, and man. Jesus Christ is unique or distinct to all three categories in some way. He is not an angel in any sense, and thus He is completely distinct from that category. But He is God, sharing the same divine attributes as God the Father and God the Holy Spirit. Yet, within the triune Godhead, Jesus Christ is unique in the sense that He is the only person who also possesses a human nature. Conversely, among humanity, He is the only member of the human race who possesses a divine nature or equality of essence with the other two members of the Trinity. Jesus Christ is also unique among humanity with respect to His death. Though many men have died on behalf of their fellow human beings (e.g. soldiers, policemen, firemen), not one has ever died a propitious death for the sins of the entire race. Christ's death is completely unparalleled. Nor has any human being ever risen gloriously and incorruptibly from the dead. While others in the future will follow the Lord in resurrection, and He is the firstfruits of a great harvest, He alone is the "Last Adam" and the Federal

---

[153] Ken Neff, "What Is the Free-Grace Gospel?" Grace Evangelical Society Conference, Fort Worth, TX, March 31, 2009.

[154] Myers, "The Gospel is More Than 'Faith Alone in Christ Alone'," 52; Robert N. Wilkin, "Justification by Faith Alone is an Essential Part of the Gospel," 12; idem, *Secure and Sure*, 74-75.

Head of a new redeemed and glorified humanity (1 Cor. 15:20-23, 45). His own death and resurrection uniquely qualify Him for this distinction.

The unique features of Jesus Christ's person and work are the very reason that He is the necessary object of saving faith in this dispensation. His uniqueness also explains why it is insufficient to limit the only defining characteristic of saving faith to the fact that "Jesus" is the guarantor of eternal life. If being capable of guaranteeing eternal life is also an attribute shared by God the Father, and it is, then we must also ask why it is not possible today to be completely ignorant about Jesus but to believe in God the Father as the guarantor of eternal life and still receive the gift of regeneration. For that matter, if the only necessary characteristic about the object of faith is that He be the guarantor of eternal life, then couldn't a person believe that the Messiah never came to earth while simultaneously believing that Yahweh guarantees eternal life and such a person would still be born again? If the only defining attribute for the object of our faith is that He is the guarantor of eternal life, then there appears to be no basis for the necessity to believe in Jesus Christ in particular as the object of saving faith. However, it appears from Scripture that the very traits about Jesus Christ that make Him uniquely qualified to provide the grounds of salvation for all mankind coincide with the contents of saving faith, which also happen to be the contents of the gospel.

The Inseparability of Christ's Person & Work

At this point, another common objection must be addressed. Some say, if the Lord Jesus provided the grounds of man's redemption by His death and resurrection, and this *work* has become essential to the content of saving faith, then this conflicts with believing in the *person* of Christ. But are the two theological categories of "person" and "work" mutually exclusive and never the twain shall meet? Not according to Scripture. In several passages in the New Testament that describe the Lord Jesus following His resurrection, a perfect tense articular participle is used to connect the cross-work of Christ to His very person. The perfect tense describes action that is viewed as completed in the past with results abiding into the present. Thus, in these passages that describe Christ, He is not just the one who *was* crucified, but the one who was crucified and *remains* the crucified-One.

In Matthew 28:5, following the Lord's resurrection the angel does not just refer to Him as "Jesus" but describes Him as "Jesus who was crucified" (NKJV), or more literally, "Jesus the crucified" (*Iēsoun ton estaurōmenon*). A. T. Robertson comments on the significance of the use of the perfect tense articular participle here. He says that this indicates "a state of completion. This he will always be. So Paul will preach as essential to his gospel 'and this one crucified' (και τουτον εσταυρωμενον, 1 Co 2:2)."[155] In the same scene

[155] A. T. Robertson, *Word Pictures in the New Testament* (Grand Rapids: Baker Book House,

in the parallel account of Mark 16:6, the angel describes Christ again using the perfect articular participle, "Jesus of Nazareth who was crucified" (*ton estaurōmenon*), or more literally, "Jesus of Nazareth—the crucified."

There are also two notable references in 1 Corinthians that use the perfect participle to describe Christ. In 1 Corinthians 1:23, He is called "Christ crucified" (*Christon estaurōmenon*) and in 1 Corinthians 2:2, He is referred to as "Jesus Christ and Him crucified" (*Iēsoun Christon kai touton estaurōmenon*).[156] Similarly, Paul writes in Galatians 3:1, "*Jesus Christ was clearly portrayed among you as crucified.*" The phrase, "as crucified" (*estaurōmenon*), is once again the perfect tense participle.

Two more amazing passages occur in Revelation 5:6 and 5:12. In Revelation 5:6, John describes the scene in heaven by saying that there "stood a Lamb as though it had been slain" (*arnion hestēkos hōs esphagmenon*). Here, John sees Christ standing in heaven as the Lamb of God, alive, but paradoxically as one who was and remains slain. Imagine, a slain-living Lamb! Later in the same passage, in Revelation 5:12, the Lamb is worshipped by an innumerable host, who exclaim, "Worthy is the Lamb, who was slain" (*axion estin to arnion to esphagmenon*). Here, the perfect tense is used again for the word, "slay" (*sphazō*), so that Christ is literally the one who was and is slain, and yet He is alive forevermore.

Each of these examples contributes toward an extremely important theological point. It is the principle of inherence. The saving works of Jesus Christ's death and resurrection have become inseparably connected to the very fabric of His being and identity, so that even though we can continue to speak in the theological categories of "person" and "work," in reality Christ's work has become indissolubly united to His person so that He is forever identified by His redemptive, saving work. He cannot stop being the slain-living Lamb. He cannot go back to being an uncrucified Christ any more than He can go back to His pre-incarnate state and undo the miracle of the incarnation. The Savior's death and resurrection, just like His incarnation, marked an ontological change in Him in a way that none of the other 7 sign-miracles did that are recorded in John's Gospel. After Christ turned water into wine at Cana in John 2, He Himself did not turn into wine! After he multiplied the loaves and fishes in John 6, He did not become a loaf or a fish! It is only with the last and greatest of Christ's eight signs recorded in John's Gospel, the crucifixion-resurrection (John 2:19), that the sign and its referent merge as one. Thus, the evangelistic purpose statement of the book is placed immediately after Thomas's con-

n.d.), 1:241.

[156] It is possible that the emphasis on Christ's crucifixion in 1 Corinthians 1 and the resurrection at the end of the epistle in chapter 15 was intentional by Paul in order to form a large-scale literary *inclusio*. This would fit with the order of the cross first, resurrection second. See Gordon D. Fee, *Pauline Christology: An Exegetical-Theological Study* (Peabody, MA: Hendrickson, 2007), 533.

fession of faith, right after Thomas has beheld the eternal emblems of Christ's death in the hands and side of His resurrected body, and Thomas believes (John 20:30-31). This means that the person of Jesus Christ is forever God-incarnate, the living Lamb of God slain for the sins of the world. This is the object of saving faith today. This is the Christ of saving faith. Faith's object and content cannot be separated.

Sacrificial High Priesthood

At this point, some may wonder why the lost are not also required to believe in other aspects of the person of Christ, such as the fact that He is our heavenly High Priest and the Head of the Church. After all, they may reason that the Bible teaches that Jesus Christ has become a High Priest *forever* according to the order of Melchizedek (Heb. 7:15-17). If this has also become part of His being and identity, then why isn't this also requisite knowledge for saving faith? Wouldn't this also mean that the lost must not only know that He is the heavenly High Priest but specifically that He is a priest according to the order of Melchizedek? And wouldn't this also mean that the lost must be cognizant of the fact that Christ is presently conducting His intercessory ministry as a priest in heaven?

These are legitimate questions to ponder; but there are several reasons why belief in Christ's present priestly ministry and His being the Head of the Church are not part of the required content of saving faith. First, neither of these ministries provided the grounds or basis for mankind's salvation. Instead, Christ's role as Head of the Church and His present, priestly intercession are both based on the greater, foundational work of His dying for our sins[157] and rising from the dead.[158] Without His substitutionary death and bodily resurrection He could not fulfill His present role as High Priest or Head of the Church (Eph. 1:20-22). The Book of Hebrews makes it clear that it was only Christ's first great act as High Priest that provided the basis for our eternal salvation, namely that He offered His life in sacrifice for our sins (Heb. 2:17; 7:27; 9:12-15, 26; 10:12).[159] It is only this work that provided *propitiation* for sin,[160] not His on-going heavenly intercession. Even Reformed theology since the time of Calvin has viewed Christ's substitutionary death as the essential expression of all three of

---

[157] Lightner, *Sin, the Savior, and Salvation*, 82.

[158] Buist M. Fanning, "A Theology of Hebrews," in *A Biblical Theology of the New Testament*, ed. Roy B. Zuck and Darrell L. Bock (Chicago: Moody Press, 1994), 388, 92-93, 97; Alan M. Stibbs, *The Finished Work of Christ* (London: Tyndale Press, 1952), 33; John F. Walvoord, *Jesus Christ Our Lord* (Chicago: Moody Press, 1969), 241.

[159] Fanning, "A Theology of Hebrews," 393-96; James, "The Atonement in Church History," 212-14; John A. Witmer, "Jesus Christ: Knowing Jesus as Man and God," in *Understanding Christian Theology*, ed. Charles R. Swindoll and Roy B. Zuck (Nashville: Thomas Nelson, 2003), 367.

[160] Simon J. Kistemaker, "Atonement in Hebrews," in *The Glory of the Atonement: Biblical, Historical & Practical Perspectives: Essays in Honor of Roger Nicole*, ed. Charles E. Hill and Frank A. James III (Downers Grove, IL: InterVarsity Press, 2004), 163-67.

His offices as Prophet, Priest, and King.[161] In this sense, it is true that a person must have at least a rudimentary understanding that Christ provides mediation between sinful man and a holy God. But this does not require knowledge of His present position as High Priest or His being Head of the Church. Rather, it only requires that people know that He is the only way to the Father (John 14:6) as the one mediator between God and man via His redeeming death (1 Tim. 2:4-6). In addition, it is conspicuous that Christ's High Priesthood and His being the Head of the Church are never stated in Scripture to be part of "the gospel." Consequently, neither of these present functions is ever preached by the apostles to the lost in the evangelistic episodes recorded in Acts. For these reasons, Christ's present heavenly ministries as Head of the Church and High Priest are not the required contents of saving faith.[162] Grace-based evangelical theologian, Charles Ryrie, concurs with the opinion that knowledge of Christ's Melchizedekian priesthood is not required for salvation, but Christ's death and resurrection are necessary. He writes:

> Certainly, faith must have some content. There must be confidence *about* something or *in* someone. To believe in Christ for salvation means to have confidence that He can remove the guilt of sin and give eternal life. It means to believe that He can solve the problem of sin which is what keeps a person out of heaven.
>
> You can also believe Christ about a multitude of other things, but these are not involved in salvation. You can believe He is Israel's Messiah, and He is. You can believe He was born without a human father being involved in the act of conception, and that is true. You can believe that what He taught while on earth was good, noble, and true, and it was. You can believe He will return to earth, and He will. You can believe He is the Judge of all, and He is. You can believe He is a Prophet, and He is. You can believe He is a Priest. You can even believe that His priesthood is after the order of Melchizedek, and it is. You can believe He is able to run your life, and He surely is able to do that, and He wants to. But these are not the issues of salvation. The issue is whether or not you believe that His death paid for all of your sin and that by believing in Him you can have forgiveness and eternal life.
>
> Faith has an intellectual facet to it. The essential facts are that Christ died for our sins and rose from the dead (1 Corinthians 15:3-4; Romans 4:25). In addition, faith involves assent or agreement with the truth of those facts.[163]

---

[161] James, "The Atonement in Church History," 213.

[162] Norman Geisler, *Systematic Theology* (Minneapolis: Bethany House, 2004), 3:534.

[163] Ryrie, *So Great Salvation*, 118-19.

Gospel Content vs. Christ's Person

It is a false dichotomy to pit the person of Christ against the facts of the gospel, as though someone believing the message of the gospel believes only in "a set of facts" or "a list of doctrines" versus the "person" of Christ. The truth of the matter is that all faith is propositional and has content.[164] What determines whether a person's faith is saving or not is simply a matter of which propositions are believed—whether they are divinely revealed truths (i.e., the gospel) or something of human or satanic origin (i.e., false gospels). Both the incarnate Word (John 1:14, 18) and the word of the gospel (Gal. 1:11-12) are divine revelations to be believed. Therefore, when a person has believed the gospel of Christ, they have also believed in Christ for eternal life and vice versa. In this respect, the object of faith (i.e., Christ) and the contents of faith (i.e., the gospel) can be spoken of interchangeably. J. B. Hixson clarifies this point by saying "although there is a semantic distinction in identity between the *object* and *content* of faith, it is a distinction without separation. One cannot trust in a person (i.e., "object") without believing specific propositional truths made by or about that person (i.e., "content"). For example, if one trusts in Jesus as the *object* of his faith, but the specific *content* of his faith is that Jesus is the Easter Bunny, his faith will not result in eternal salvation."[165]

This conclusion is well supported by Scripture. There are dozens of passages in the New Testament that condition eternal salvation solely upon belief. Several of these simply have the verb "believe" used intransitively (Acts 13:39, 48; Gal. 3:22); that is, they do not have a stated object to receive the action of believing. In such cases, the object of faith is not specifically stated. However, many other "saving faith" passages do use "believe" transitively. In these, the object of belief is variously stated to be the *person* of Jesus, as in "the Lord Jesus Christ" (Acts 16:31), or "Christ" (Gal. 2:16), or even just "Him" (1 Tim. 1:16). Then there are passages that specifically require belief in some form of propositional truth or divine revelation in order to be saved, such as, "the word of the cross" (1 Cor. 1:18), "the message preached" (1 Cor. 1:21), "our testimony" (2 Thess. 1:10), "the testimony that God has given of His Son" (1 John 5:10), or even just "the truth" (2 Thess. 2:12). This biblical evidence leads to an important doctrinal conclusion. If the Word of God requires the lost to believe in both a person and a message to be eternally saved, then there must be no contradiction between believing in the person of Christ and believing the message of the gospel of Christ. J. Gresham Machen summarizes this point by saying, "a person cannot be trusted without acceptance of the

---

[164] Gordon H. Clark, *Faith and Saving Faith*, 2nd ed. (Jefferson, MD: Trinity Foundation, 1990), 105-7, 118; Machen, *What Is Faith?* 148-49.

[165] Hixson, *Getting the Gospel Wrong: Case Studies*, 45n.

facts about that person. . . . for it is just the message about Jesus, the message that sets forth his Cross and resurrection, that brings us into contact with Him. Without that message He would be forever remote—a great Person, but one with whom we could have no communion—but through that message He comes to be our Saviour."[166]

Preaching the Gospel of Christ

Finally, having established that the gospel of Christ is the "saving message" and that it contains the specific elements of Christ's deity, humanity, substitutionary death, bodily resurrection, and salvation by grace through faith alone, we must now address a few issues accompanying the practical preaching of the gospel relative to the crossless controversy. Specifically, do we as ambassadors for Christ need to present all of these elements every time we evangelize? Secondly, must we always explain these elements in the same sequence that they have been presented thus far in this book (i.e., person, work, provision and condition)?

How Much Information?

Regarding which elements we must preach to the lost in our evangelism, this depends largely upon the circumstances and the audience. Some crossless gospel leaders scoff at the notion of presenting all of the elements of the gospel every time we evangelize, claiming that the unsaved will be subjected to a 15 minute "monologue" or a "course on Christology," as one leading proponent objected to this author. Some have even suggested that since most Americans have been Christianized, they already believe in Christ's deity, humanity, death for sin, and resurrection. Therefore, the person and work of Christ can be, and even should be, bypassed for the last element, namely salvation by grace through faith alone.[167] While it is certainly true that the person and work of Christ do not need to be *repeated* to someone who already believes them, the crossless gospel position actually teaches that Christ's deity, death, and resurrection are not even *required* to be believed for new birth.

We should be able to admit that many individual evangelistic verses do not explicitly present every element of the gospel. For example, John 6:53 does not state Christ's deity. John 3:16 does not mention the resurrection. Likewise, though Romans 10:9-10 refers to Christ's resurrection, His substitutionary death is not contained in the passage. But does this mean that Romans 10:9-10 is teaching that belief in Christ's death for us isn't required for justification? Or, is John 3:16 teaching that belief in Christ's resurrection is not required for eternal life? Hardly! These elements of the

---

[166] Machen, *What Is Faith?* 151 (ellipsis added).

[167] Bob Wilkin, "What's Your First Sentence in Evangelism?" *Grace in Focus* 23.5 (September/October 2008): 1, 4.

gospel are all *required* to be believed for eternal life, though they do not all need to be *repeated* in every evangelistic encounter.

If someone affirms up front that they believe in Christ's deity, humanity, death for sin, and resurrection, it may be redundant and unnecessary to present these truths. However, I have found practically in my own evangelism that many who claim to already believe these truths of the gospel have only a specious understanding of them. Nor do they see these truths as necessarily connected to God's provision of salvation by grace through faith alone, and consequently they are not resting their eternal destiny upon Christ's person and finished work. While a man may claim to believe in Christ's death for his sins, his failure to recognize that eternal salvation is received through faith alone apart from works reveals his failure to grasp the significance and sufficiency of Christ's substitutionary death. So it is often wise to cover Christ's person and work anyway, prior to or in conjunction with the provision and condition of salvation.

Furthermore, unless the subject of Christ's person and work is at least broached, how will the evangelist ever know whether the person being witnessed to believes these truths or not, unless that other person preemptively offers such information? This information can be easily obtained in one-on-one and small group evangelism, where personal diagnostic questions can be asked. So, presenting each of the elements of the gospel need not entail a fifteen minute "monologue."

The approach of the Master evangelist is very instructive at this point. In John 4:1-29, the Lord Jesus witnessed to the Samaritan woman at Jacob's well. There the Lord engaged the woman in a very personal dialogue. He spoke to her exactly seven times, and she in turn spoke exactly seven times according to the passage (six times to the Lord, once to her fellow Samaritans). This approach is not only courteous when it comes to one-on-one and small group evangelism; it is more effective in determining what an individual really believes. However, this approach simply isn't possible when preaching the gospel before larger audiences. In such instances, it is wise to cover each point of the gospel, just as Peter did with those gathered in Cornelius' house (Acts 10:34-43) and as Paul did with the Jews and Gentiles in the synagogue at Antioch of Pisidia (Acts 13:23-41).

The Order of Presentation

Finally, with respect to the order in which the elements of the gospel are presented, must we always give them in the sequence of (1) Christ's person (2) His work (3) the provision of salvation and condition for it? Personally, I would never insist on this since it is nowhere prescribed in God's Word. Practically however, I would say that it is wise to at least present Christ's person and work *before* the provision of salvation and condition for it. This at least provides people with a reason to believe in Christ and to understand how eternal life can be guaranteed on the basis of His merits. Secondly, it is also more logical to explain who Christ is in His person *before* explaining what He's done by His work. When it comes to explaining the person of Christ, it makes little difference whether His deity or humanity are explained first. And with respect to His work, it seems more reasonable, of course, to explain Christ's death before His resurrection. But nowhere does Scripture mandate following such a precise sequence, so neither should we.

One leading advocate of the crossless gospel personally informed me that he used to present Christ's person and work first in his evangelism, followed by the last element on the sole condition of faith in Christ; but now he believes this is the incorrect approach to evangelism. Instead, we should present the faith alone message "right away" as the "first thing," he informed me.

Yet that approach is hardly consistent with 1 Corinthians 15:3-4, where the apostle Paul preached *"first of all"* (in terms of importance) the person of "Christ" and that He "died for our sins" and "rose again."[168] This was also the approach suggested by the Lord Himself in the Great Commission, where we see that "Christ" is presented first (Luke 24:46b), followed by His death and resurrection (Luke 24:46c). The single condition of repentance for the remission of sins comes last (Luke 24:47). Similarly, when Peter preached the gospel to those gathered in Cornelius' house, he first presented the person and work of Christ (Acts 10:34-42), followed lastly by the message of salvation through faith (Acts 10:43). This was also Paul's approach with the Galatians in Acts 13:23-41, where Christ's person and work are presented first (Acts 13:23-37), followed by the sole condition of faith/believing in (Acts 13:38-41). Ironically, this is even John's approach in his Gospel, where as the narrator, he inserts his personal, evangelistic invitation at John 20:30-31, only after Christ's work has been documented in chapters 19-20. So, it is most logical and helpful to present the provision and condition of salvation last, though this order is nowhere mandated by Scripture.

We may conclude that the normal order given to us in God's Word for presenting the elements of the gospel is certainly preferable to the crossless gospel approach, and much more logical too. It makes little sense to exhort people to believe in Christ when we haven't even defined *who* He is, *what* He's done, or *why* someone must believe in Him for eternal life!

Clarifying Free Grace Language

One final word is in order regarding the use of biblically accurate terminology for the gospel. In recent years, a palpable, disturbing new trend has developed within Free Grace circles directly accompanying the rise of the crossless gospel. Some of our brethren have become increasingly confused about the meaning of the gospel and whether it really is "the saving message" or whether it is a broader sanctification message containing at

[168] Rokser, *Let's Preach the Gospel*, 28.

least fifty different elements. This confusion has resulted in a noticeable hesitation to refer to the message that the lost must believe as simply "the gospel." In addition, a whole new nomenclature has developed. Among some crossless teachers, the term "gospel" has been dropped altogether and replaced with non-biblical substitutes such as "the saving message,"[169] "the saving proposition,"[170] and "the message of life."[171] Even those who have not necessarily embraced the crossless view have developed their own language of accommodation as they have shifted away from the once unanimous opinion that "the gospel" is synonymous with the contents of saving faith. Today we hear such fuzzy, unbiblical expressions as "the minimal gospel" versus "the normal gospel." We also hear of "the core"[172] of the gospel, "the essentials of the gospel," and even just "different formulations of the gospel." But can the gospel really be reformulated, like gasoline for our automobiles, and yet still be the power of God unto salvation? Are there "essentials" to the gospel, and by implication, therefore, non-essentials? And if there are elements of the gospel that make up the "core," then doesn't this imply that there are secondary elements surrounding the core that are non-essential? The use of such language betrays the whole spirit and intent of Galatians 1:6-9.

It is a conspicuous fact that the term *euangelion* in the New Testament is nearly always preceded by the article. In 73 out of 76 occurrences this is so. It is evident from a study of every occurrence of *euangelion* in its various contexts that "the gospel" of Christ is a singular, specific, definable, and intransmutable message that was known and understood by the first century readers of the New Testament. Consequently we do not read anywhere on the pages of Scripture about a "minimal gospel" or a "normal gospel" or anything approximating those concepts. We read only of "the gospel."[173] While "minimal gospel" may sound more palatable and congenial than "crossless gospel," it actually further perpetuates the current error by giving the false impression that the crossless, resurrectionless, and deityless gospel is still a legitimate "gospel" in some sense. However, according to Scripture, there is only "the gospel" in distinction to that which is not the gospel but a false form of it. There is only the one, true gospel versus that which is not another of the same kind (*allos*) but another of a completely different (*heteros*) kind (Gal. 1:6-7). The emphasis

---

[169] Wilkin repeatedly uses the phrase "saving message" while at the same time seeking to disprove that "the gospel" is the message that must be believed for justification, regeneration, eternal salvation, etc. See Bob Wilkin, "Another Look at 1 Corinthians 15:3-11," *Grace in Focus* 23 (January/February 2008): 1-2.

[170] Wilkin, "Justification by Faith Alone is an Essential Part of the Gospel," 14.

[171] John Niemelä, "The Message of Life in the Gospel of John," *CTSJ* 7 (July-September 2001): 2.

[172] Zane C. Hodges, *Did Paul Preach Eternal Life? Should We?* (Mesquite, TX: Kerugma, 2007), 9.

[173] Lybrand, "GES Gospel: Lybrand Open Letter," 16.

of Scripture is overwhelmingly upon that one form of good news about Christ that saves all who believe it—the gospel of the Christ. Therefore, Free Grace people should not shrink back from employing the term "gospel" frequently, but judiciously, as equivalent with the "saving message." But if we will not do this, then we can expect that divinely inspired terms and their meanings will continue to fall into disuse and become subject to redefinition and doctrinal error within the Free Grace movement.

Chapter 10

What Is the Gospel to the Galatians?

OVERVIEW

In Galatians 1:8-9, Paul declares that the one standard, unalterable gospel of salvation is the same gospel he initially preached to those living in the region of Galatia. A question of critical importance in determining the contents of the one, true gospel then becomes: "Where is Paul's Galatian gospel found?" If Paul was referring to the region of Northern Galatia, then we have no biblical record of the contents of the one, fixed, saving message of the gospel. However, it appears conclusive that Paul was referring to Southern Galatia, and his Galatian gospel is extensively recorded in Acts 13:23-48. In Acts 13, we see that the standard, unalterable gospel of Christ was the message that Jesus is the unique God-man who died for our sins and rose again to provide salvation by grace through faith in Him apart from our works. This was the message the Galatians had to receive and believe in order not to "perish" but to have "everlasting life." Interpreting Acts 13 to be the original Galatian gospel harmonizes perfectly with the gospel contained in Paul's Epistle to the Galatians, as well as his other epistles, for Paul received and preached only one gospel.

The Epistle of Galatians is another critical front in the battle over the truth of the gospel. It was one of the earliest epistles written in the New Testament, providing the Church of Jesus Christ with a trumpet call to stand boldly and firmly upon the gospel of the grace of God. Centuries later its blast of grace served as the reveille of the Reformation, along with other key New Testament books. During that contentious era, the grace-gospel of Galatians was fired often, like a cannon, to advance the biblical truth of justification by grace alone through faith alone in Christ alone.

Today the message of God's free grace in Galatians is just as vitally needed. Christendom is still thoroughly permeated with a proud works-righteousness that is antithetical to the Spirit's message in Galatians. On the other hand, this potent epistle is being claimed by certain Free Grace proponents today as another biblical witness for a crossless "saving message" or gospel. This new, aberrant form of the Free Grace position holds that the "gospel" of justification by faith contained in Galatians does not necessitate faith in the cross-work of Christ.

According to this new heretical gospel, the lost need only to believe in Jesus as the guarantor of justification in order to receive it. Proponents of this view rightly claim that the message in Galatians of justification by faith alone is virtually synonymous with the message in John's Gospel that eternal life is guaranteed to all who simply believe in Jesus for it. However, they also assert rather boldly that neither the Gospel of John nor Galatians require knowledge of Christ's finished work in order for justification and eternal life to be granted.

But, you may ask, "What do they do with the cross in Galatians?" Well, they have a place for it to be sure. They just relegate it to phase-two of salvation, practical sanctification, just as they do with 1 Corinthians 15:3-4. They maintain that the cross is only essential to know about and believe in for one's practical sanctification, not justification before God, though it is the grounds for both. One leading crossless gospel advocate even informed me that the word "gospel" in Galatians is not a technical term and therefore it is used in both a narrow and a broad sense. How convenient! Some claim that the message to the lost of justification by faith in Jesus without requisite knowledge of the cross is "the gospel" in a narrower sense; while the message that Christ's work on the cross provides power to overcome sin in your Christian life is "the gospel" in a broader sense.

We see again in their interpretation of Galatians that they have created a crossless gospel of salvation to the lost. Though they are opposing the works-righteousness blasted in Galatians, ironically and tragically in the process they, like the Galatians, have embraced a different gospel, a gospel that is not the gospel the apostle Paul originally preached to the Galatians, nor the gospel that the Galatians originally received.

In the opening verses of Galatians, Paul begins his epistle uncharacteristically without a single word of commendation for the believers of Galatia. He wastes no time with pleasantries but comes out swinging. In the first nine verses of this epistle, Paul uses the term "gospel" four times, letting us know that he is contending for the truth of "the gospel" itself. There is no mistaking the intent of this letter. The Galatian Christians had defected from the one, true gospel of Christ and they are now being severely censured for it. Galatians 1:8-9 contains one of the most solemn warnings in the entire Bible. And for what? Murder? Blasphemy? Immorality? Worldliness? As serious as those sins are, the wickedest transgression according to the Word of God is tampering with the gospel.

The whole tenor of Galatians thunders the truth that there is no "broader sense" of the gospel. There is no "narrower sense." There is only *one* sense. The gospel of Christ is not subject to innovation or improvement. To depart from its singular message is to invite the awful two-fold anathema of God declared in verses 8 and 9. The message of Galatians is clear: the gospel of Christ is not a playground for theologians; it is holy ground for us as servants of the Most High.

<u>Galatians 1:1-9</u>

1 *Paul, an apostle (not from men nor through man, but through Jesus Christ and God the Father who raised Him from the dead),*
2 *and all the brethren who are with me, To the churches of Galatia:*
3 *Grace to you and peace from God the Father and our Lord Jesus Christ,*
4 *who gave Himself for our sins, that He might deliver us from this present evil age, according to the will of our God and Father,*
5 *to whom be glory forever and ever. Amen.*
6 *I marvel that you are turning away so soon from Him who called you in the grace of Christ, to a different gospel,*
7 *which is not another; but there are some who trouble you and want to pervert the gospel of Christ.*
8 *But even if we, or an angel from heaven, preach any other gospel to you than what we have preached to you, let him be accursed.*
9 *As we have said before, so now I say again, if anyone preaches any other gospel to you than what you have received, let him be accursed.*

In reading the introductory verses of Galatians, we immediately observe the inextricable connection between Christ's resurrection (1:1) and His substitutionary death (1:4). These fraternal twin truths occur so frequently together in the New Testament[1] as part of the gospel that we should not

[1] Matt. 16:21; 17:22-23; 20:17-19; Mark 8:31; 9:31; 10:33-34; Luke 9:43-45; 18:31-33; 24:46; John

be surprised to be greeted by them at the beginning of Galatians. It is as though Paul is pouring the foundation of his epistle with these twin truths of the gospel before hammering away throughout the rest of Galatians at the other essential element of the gospel, namely salvation by grace through faith alone.

The first usage of the actual term "gospel" in Galatians is in verse 6 where there is a reference to a *"different gospel"* that the Galatians had embraced—a gospel of works. In contrast, verse 7 refers to the *"gospel of Christ."* The modifying phrase, *"of Christ,"* is in the genitive case in the Greek (*tou Christou*) and could be interpreted grammatically as a subjective genitive. This would indicate that the "gospel came from Christ." Since this idea is in the intermediate context (1:12), this could be the correct genitive sense intended here. However, it could also be understood as an objective genitive, having the meaning of "the gospel that is about Jesus Christ." This would be indicating that the gospel is all about a person, Jesus Christ. He is the object of the gospel.[2] The objective usage of the genitive would be consistent with the fact that the gospel truths of Christ's death and resurrection in verses 1-4 serve to identify the person of Christ (*"Jesus Christ and God the Father who raised* ***Him*** *from the dead"* and *"our Lord Jesus Christ,* ***who*** *gave* ***Himself*** *for our sins"*). This would also be consistent with the truth indicated by verse 6 that departing from the gospel of Christ is not merely a doctrinal departure in God's eyes; it is a personal departure from Him as well. Verse 6 indicates that to embrace a "different gospel" is to turn away ***"from Him*** *who called you in the grace of Christ."*

What this indicates is that the gospel is not merely a matter of justification by faith alone. It is first and foremost a message about a specific person and work—the Lord Jesus Christ and His death and resurrection. It is not merely "the gospel"; it is the gospel "of Christ." This is important to realize throughout the remainder of Galatians, as the subject of justification by grace through faith alone is covered. The problem in Galatia was the mixing of law with grace as a means of either justification or sanctification. In particular, circumcision seems to have been the work of choice that some Galatians were now regarding to be necessary for justification and/or sanctification (2:3, 12; 5:2-3, 6, 11; 6:12-15). Though the Galatians were not *explicitly* denying the facts of Christ's deity, humanity, death for sin, and resurrection, they were *practically* denying Christ's substitutionary death by virtue of adding just one work to faith alone as the

---

10:15-18; Acts 2:23-24; 4:10; 5:30; 10:39-40; 13:28-30; 17:3; 25:19; 26:23; Rom. 4:25; 5:9-10; 6:3-11; 8:34; 1 Cor. 15:3-4; 2 Cor. 4:10-11; Phil. 3:10-11; Col. 1:18-20; 3:1-4; 1 Thess. 4:14; 1 Peter 1:19-21; 3:18; etc.

[2] Since the genitive and ablative cases have the same form, it could also be categorized as an ablative of source. That which is produced by the subject (subjective genitive) owes its source (ablative of source) to that subject. So it could be either.

condition for salvation. This is why Christ's work on the cross is emphasized consistently throughout Galatians, in addition to the theme of God's grace (1:4; 2:20; 3:1, 13; 4:4-5; 5:11, 24; 6:12, 14).

In seeking to correct their defection, Paul points these Galatian believers back to the one, true gospel he had initially preached to them and the one they had initially received. In verse 8, he refers to that gospel that *"we have preached to you."* The expression *"we have preached"* (*euēngelisametha*) is the aorist tense, middle voice, indicative mood form of *euangelizō*. The aorist tense with the indicative mood would indicate specifically that gospel that Paul had preached to the Galatians *in the past*. This is further demonstrated by Paul's reference to the gospel that *"you have received"* in verse 9. This verb is the aorist, active, indicative of *paralambanō*, again indicating the particular gospel that these Galatian believers had received from Paul *in the past*. Why is this significant to note?

First, with respect to the crossless gospel, it is often claimed by its defenders that though Acts and the Epistles do contain a "gospel" that emphasizes Christ's cross and resurrection, these were written only to those who were already believers. Therefore Acts and the Epistles do not tell us the essential "message of life" for unbelievers today—the essential elements of the gospel necessary to believe in order to have eternal life. So, they say, we must stick with the Gospel of John and its supposed crossless "saving message." However, what they fail to realize about Galatians, as with 1 Corinthians 15:1-11, is that when these "believers" in Galatia and Corinth started defecting from their walk with the Lord in their Christian lives, Paul brought them right back to the gospel they *initially* heard for their justification. Why? Because the gospel is not only the power of God for justification-salvation, it is also the foundation for our sanctification-salvation. When believers shift on the gospel and the question of how to be eternally saved, their foundation for living the Christian life becomes crooked. This foundation must be fixed before one can build any further upon it. This is what Paul does in Galatians and 1 Corinthians 15. He articulates the gospel he first preached to them when they were unbelievers. So, Acts and the Epistles *do* contain the one, unchangeable message of "the gospel" to unbelievers, as well as the ramifications of the gospel to believers in Christ.

Secondly, what the Word of God is indicating with the use of the past tense in Galatians 1:8-9 is that there is one unalterable, timeless standard by which to measure all other "gospels." It is the gospel that Paul originally preached to the Galatians. If this is the standard set forth in the Word of God for preaching the gospel accurately, it behooves us to correctly identify this message. So where can we find this gospel that was preached to the Galatians *"at the first"* (Gal. 4:13)? The key to knowing the *contents* of Paul's original gospel to the Galatians is knowing *where* to find it.

Where is Paul's Gospel to the Galatians?

The advocates of the new aberrant form of the gospel seek to use Galatians in an attempt to redefine the saving message without the cross. This has resulted in a gospel of justification by faith alone that does not require faith in the cross-work of Christ. To support this crossless gospel, they have found a place in Galatians where justification by faith is referred to without any mention of the cross or resurrection. That place is Galatians 2:15-16. They believe these verses contain the essential evangelistic message that Paul preached to the Galatians and which defines for us the gospel we must preach to the lost today. They categorically reject any connection between Galatians and Acts 13, where Paul's evangelistic message to the churches of Southern Galatia is recorded. They *must* disclaim this connection since Acts 13 reveals that Paul proclaimed all the essential elements of the "gospel" in his evangelization of the Galatians. Keeping Paul's original gospel to the Galatians out of Acts 13 is truly a watershed issue for the crossless gospel position, though not for the classical Free Grace gospel since it can be supported elsewhere in Scripture. Their rationale for picking Galatians 2:15-16 as Paul's original gospel to the Galatians is explained below by Jeremy Myers. After reading Galatians 1:8-9, Myers asks:

> So what was the gospel message Paul preached to the Galatians? He doesn't define it here [in Galatians 1:8-9]. He just says, "You heard it. I preached it to you. Don't go to another one." What was the message he preached? How would you find it? Where would you go to see what message Paul preached? Well, there are several places you could go. You could try to go to Acts and see if you could find out what he preached there, but if you do that you'll find out Luke doesn't tell us what Paul preached when he was in Galatia. And you know some people are tempted to go to some of Paul's other writings, 1 Corinthians and Romans, to find out what this gospel he preached to the Galatians was, but you know, if Galatians tells us, if Paul tells us in Galatians what message he preached when he was in Galatia, let's just go with that, right—proper hermeneutics there. And in this very letter Paul thankfully does define for us the gospel he preached. He reminds them of the gospel he preached to them when he was there. So if he defines it in Galatians we don't really need to go anywhere else, at least not now. So, flip over to Galatians 2:14 where he does talk about the gospel again, and really he defines the gospel for us down in verse 16, so let's just skip there, where he says that this is the gospel he preached to the Gentiles, sinners of the Gentiles, that's verse 15, "knowing that a man is not justified by works of the law but by faith in Jesus Christ," then he goes on a little, but it appears that this is the gospel Paul preached when he was in Galatia, at least a summary of it. And inciden-

> tally that sounds like what I defined, or how I defined the gospel for years. See, "faith alone in Christ alone apart from works for eternal life." That's the gospel.[3]

Bob Wilkin also reiterates the same essential position, claiming:

> Paul in Galatians was defending his evangelistic gospel, his evangelistic good news. And that good news was justification by faith alone. Galatians 2:15-16, the thesis of the book, make this clear. A person is not justified by the works of the law but by faith in Jesus Christ. That is the good news Paul preached and the legalistic Judaizers opposed.[4]

The question must be asked at this point whether Galatians 2:15-16 truly reflects the version of the gospel Paul preached initially in Galatia? Wilkin and Myers give us no contextual or exegetical reasons for picking this passage, just the dogmatic assertion that this is "proper hermeneutics" and that here is where Paul "defines the gospel for us." There is one major problem with their position, however. In Galatians 2:15-16, Paul is not recounting the gospel message he originally preached to lost souls in *Galatia*; he's describing the contents of his rebuke of the apostle Peter while in *Antioch*! The audience in Galatians 2:15-16 is different; the setting is different; and the message is different since it only includes one element of the saving gospel.

<u>Galatians 2:15-21</u>

11 *Now when Peter had come to* ***Antioch****, I withstood him to his face, because he was to be blamed;*

12 *for before certain men came from James, he would eat with the Gentiles; but when they came, he withdrew and separated himself, fearing those who were of the circumcision.*

13 *And the rest of the Jews also played the hypocrite with him, so that even Barnabas was carried away with their hypocrisy.*

14 *But when I saw that they were not straightforward about the truth of the gospel,* ***I said to Peter*** *before them all, "If you, being a Jew, live in the manner of Gentiles and not as the Jews, why do you compel Gentiles to live as Jews?*

15 *"We who are Jews by nature, and not sinners of the Gentiles,*

---

[3] Jeremy Myers, *The Gospel is More Than "Faith Alone in Christ Alone,"* Grace Evangelical Society Conference, Dallas, TX, March 2, 2006 (brackets added from context). Myers makes essentially the same claim in a journal article based on his Grace Conference session. There he says, "So the initial goal is to discover what Paul preached when he was in Galatia. But thankfully, to find this information, we do not have to go to Matthew, Romans, 1 Corinthians or even Acts, since none of these tells us what Paul preached in Galatia. Instead, Paul reminds his initial audience (and so informs later readers) what he preached to the Galatians. After telling his readers that he is going to defend his gospel (1:8-9), he defines the gospel he preached (2:14-17). The gospel Paul preached in Galatia is that 'a man is not justified by the works of the law but by faith in Jesus Christ' (2:16)." Jeremy D. Myers, "The Gospel is More Than 'Faith Alone in Christ Alone'," *JOTGES* 19 (Autumn 2006): 44.

[4] Robert N. Wilkin, "Justification By Faith Alone is an Essential Part of the Gospel," *JOTGES* 18 (Autumn 2005): 11.

16 *"knowing that a man is not justified by the works of the law but by faith in Jesus Christ, even we have believed in Christ Jesus, that we might be justified by faith in Christ and not by the works of the law; for by the works of the law no flesh shall be justified.*
17 *"But if, while we seek to be justified by Christ, we ourselves also are found sinners, is Christ therefore a minister of sin? Certainly not!*
18 *"For if I build again those things which I destroyed, I make myself a transgressor.*
19 *"For I through the law died to the law that I might live to God.*
20 *"I have been crucified with Christ; it is no longer I who live, but Christ lives in me; and the life which I now live in the flesh I live by faith in the Son of God, who loved me and gave Himself for me.*
21 *"I do not set aside the grace of God; for if righteousness comes through the law, then Christ died in vain."*

Based on the context of Paul's statements in 2:15-16, it is clear that this was not Paul's gospel to the Galatians when he initially evangelized them. Galatians 2:15-16 is inseparable from Galatians 2:14, since it is the essence of Paul's public rebuke of Peter in an entirely different city and region, namely Antioch of Syria.

In the preceding quotation of Galatians 2:11-21 from the New King James Version, it must be observed that Paul's statement to Peter starting in 2:14b continues through the end of verse 21. This is indicated in the NKJV by the quotation marks supplied beginning at 2:14b, with the end-quote coming at the conclusion of verse 21. The New American Standard Bible and New International Version mark the passage the same way. Even the Hodges & Farstad Greek Majority Text marks it this way.[5]

Of course, these quotation marks are not part of the original inspired text, but the context is clear enough to most Bible scholars that Paul's message to Peter, begun in 2:14b, didn't conclude after only half a verse in 2:14c! Galatians 2:15-16 continues Paul's reproof of Peter, as is evidenced by the fact that in 2:15 Paul says, *"**We** who are **Jews** by nature and not sinners of the **Gentiles**."* The Galatians were predominantly Gentiles (Acts 13:42-50; Gal. 4:8); so Paul must not have been addressing them at this point. The other Jew to whom he was speaking in 2:15 was Peter, though Barnabas and the men from James were certainly within earshot since Paul rebuked Peter *"before them all"* (2:14). Paul continues to have himself, Peter, and the other Jewish Christians in mind by at least verse 17, where he twice uses the word "we" again. Contextually, Galatians 2:15-16 falls within Paul's address to Peter at Antioch.

Though justification by faith apart from works of the law (2:16) is an essential element of the gospel (Acts 13:38-39), and Peter's discriminatory

[5] GNTMT, 573.

behavior in Antioch of Syria was not consistent with this truth, it is clear from the context of Galatians 2:11-21 that 2:15-16 is *not* the record of Paul's gospel to the Galatians.

Another question that surfaces in the current gospel controversy is the extent of the gospel's contents in Galatians 2:14-21. Some proponents of the G.E.S. gospel have attempted to show that Galatians 2:14-21 supports a broad view of the gospel—that the gospel is a message about justification and sanctification. They reason that if Peter is rebuked for not being *"straightforward about the truth of the gospel"* in verse 14a, then everything in verses 14-21 must be "the gospel." In addition, they argue that the gospel must include content on Christian living because Peter was reproved for compelling the Gentiles "to live" as Jews under the law (v. 14c). Therefore, they claim that how we live must be part of "the gospel." But none of this disproves the view that the gospel is strictly a 1st tense salvation message, since Peter's example contradicted the gospel truth of justification by faith alone. By his refusal to eat with the Gentiles during times of corporate fellowship, Peter was communicating a non-verbal message to the Gentiles that they really did need to be circumcised in order to be justified. Peter's conduct was inconsistent with this gospel truth. Apparently, faith alone was not sufficient after all. It was for this reason that Paul begins his reproof of Peter in verses 15-16 with a threefold iteration of the truth of justification by faith apart from works of the law. There is a fourth reference to justification in verse 17, when it says, *"while we seek to be justified (dikaioō) by Christ."* Finally, there is a fifth reference to justification in verse 21, which concludes, *"for if righteousness (dikaiosunē) comes by the law, then Christ died in vain."* In verses 14-21, Paul begins and ends with justification. While verses 19-20 do refer to the believer's co-crucifixion with Christ and living by faith in light of our identification with Christ in His death, this only shows that the Christian life rests upon the gospel-truth of our Savior's death. Verses 19-20 establish the principle that sanctification truth is built upon justification truth and that the gospel is the foundation of all Christian living by grace. When the foundation is faulty, so will the edifice built upon it. Thus, Paul goes beyond the gospel itself in verses 14-21 to the practical effects of veering from the truth of the gospel.

Southern Galatia or Northern Galatia?

The key to resolving *what* gospel Paul initially preached to the Galatians is determined in large measure by *where* his gospel to the Galatians is recorded in the New Testament. As stated previously, the crossless gospel position simply *cannot* allow Acts 13 to be the record of Paul's gospel to the Galatians, for it is clear that there he preached both Christ's person and saving work to the Galatians as necessary to believe for justification and eternal life. The question is rather complex as to whether Paul wrote the

Epistle of Galatians to the same churches of Southern Galatia as recorded in Acts 13-14 or whether he wrote to churches in the region of Northern Galatia not technically recorded in the Book of Acts. In the last century, the South Galatian theory has gained the support of the vast majority of conservative scholars in America and Great Britain, while the North Galatian view is supported mainly by liberal scholars, particularly from France and Germany.[6] The location and identification of the audience of Paul's epistle is not in itself a measuring stick of doctrinal orthodoxy, but it does have significant bearing upon the crossless gospel issue and the question of the contents of the gospel Paul originally preached to the Galatians.

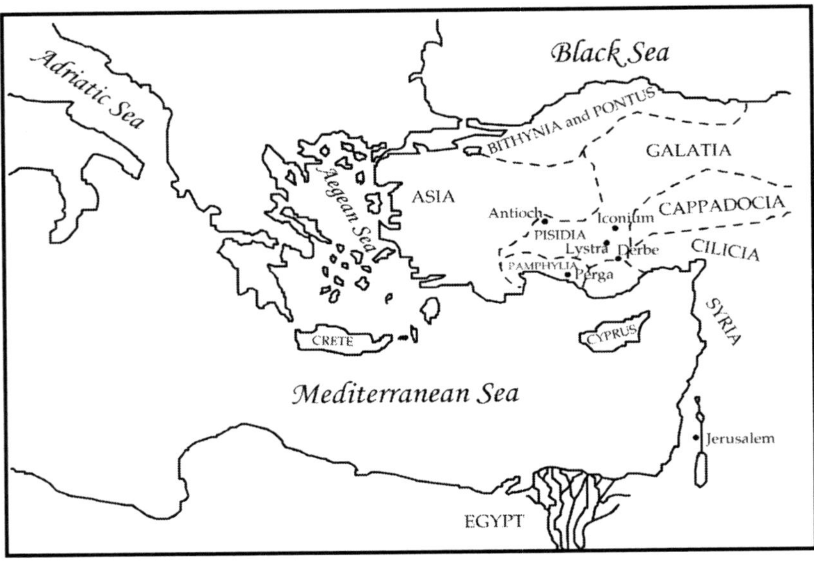

If the North Galatian theory is correct, presumably such churches would have been planted by Paul on his second missionary journey in Acts 16:6 and revisited on his third journey (Acts 18:23). In this case, Galatians would have been written in the early to mid 50s A.D. However, the conviction that Galatians was written to the churches of Southern Galatia, as recorded in Acts 13, comports far better with the facts revealed in Scripture. The biographical details of Paul's life mentioned in Galatians strangely fit only with Paul's life up to the point of A.D. 49, as expressed in the Book of Acts through the end of chapter 16. This is reflected in the following comparative chronology of Acts and Galatians for Paul's life. The major events of Paul's life after writing Galatians are also included for the sake of completeness.

---

[6] John B. Polhill, "Galatia Revisited, The Life Setting of the Epistle," *RevExp* 69 (Fall 1972): 448.

Comparative Chronology of Paul's Life in Galatians & Acts

1. *Paul's religious past prior to his new birth (Gal. 1:12-14; Acts 7:58-8:3; 22:1-5; 26:4-11)*

2. *Paul's regeneration through faith in Christ in approximately* A.D. 32-33 *(Gal. 1:15-16; Acts 9:1-8; 22:6-10; 26:12-18)*

3. *Paul briefly in Damascus following his new birth (Gal. 1:16-17a; Acts 9:8-21; 22:11-16; 26:19-20)*

4. *Paul in Arabia for 3 years, to approximately* A.D. *35 (Gal. 1:17b; Acts 9:22)*

5. *Paul returns to Damascus in approximately* A.D. *35 (Gal. 1:17c; Acts 9:23-25)*

6. *Paul goes to Jerusalem for 15 days to see Peter & James (Gal. 1:18-19; Acts 9:26-29)*

7. *Paul returns to his hometown of Tarsus in Cilicia, approx.* A.D. 35-45 *(Gal. 1:21; Acts 9:30)*

8. *Barnabas brings Paul from Tarsus to Antioch, approximately* A.D. 45 *(Acts 11:25-26)*

9. *Paul, Barnabas, Titus go to Jerusalem with famine relief, approximately* A.D. *46 (Gal. 2:1-10; Acts 11:27-30)*

10. *Paul and Barnabas go on 1st missionary journey, approximately* A.D. *47-48 (Acts 13-14)*

11. *Paul confronts Peter at Antioch, approximately* A.D. *48 (Gal. 2:11-14; Acts 14:26-28)*

12. *Paul writes letter of correction to Galatians, approximately* A.D. *49 (Gal. 1:6-7)*

13. *Paul, Barnabas go to Jerusalem for 1st Church council, approximately* A.D. *49 (Acts 15)*

14. *Paul's 2nd missionary journey, approximately* A.D. *49-52 (Acts 15:36 – 18:22)*

15. *Paul's 3rd missionary journey, approximately* A.D. *52-56 (Acts 18:23 – 21:17)*

16. *Paul's final visit and arrest in Jerusalem, approximately* A.D. *57-58 (Acts 21:18 – 23:11)*

17. *Paul's 2 years of imprisonment in Caesarea, approximately* A.D. *57/58 – 59/60 (Acts 23:12 – 26:32)*

18. Paul's journey to Rome as a prisoner, approximately A.D. 60 (Acts 27:1 – 28:16)

19. Paul's imprisonment in Rome, approximately A.D. 61–63 (Acts 28:17- 31)

20. Paul probably released around A.D. 62-63. Tradition declares he went to Spain (Rom. 15:24), and he probably wrote 1 Timothy and Titus during this time.

21. Paul re-imprisoned in Rome (and wrote 2 Timothy), then martyred in approximately A.D. 64-65 during the Neronian persecution following Nero's setting fire to Rome in A.D. 64

When the South Galatian view is embraced, the biographical details of Galatians harmonize well with the record of Acts.[7] This simply cannot be said of the North Galatian theory. It is conspicuous to note regarding the preceding chronology that suddenly after the writing of the Galatian epistle (see point #12), nothing in Galatians corresponds with Paul's life thereafter as contained in the Book of Acts. Why this sudden silence? This is one of the primary factors supporting the South Galatian view.

Secondly, if Paul wrote the Epistle of Galatians to churches in Northern Galatia, then it must be acknowledged that there is not a single reference anywhere in Scripture to Paul's church planting activities there. For that matter, there aren't any references in Scripture even to the existence of a single church in Northern Galatia. This glaring omission is difficult to dismiss when compared with the extensive detail provided to us in Acts 13-14. How much more fitting for the Holy Spirit to give us a fulsome revelation of Paul's church planting activities in Galatia as recorded in Acts 13-14! Paul's evangelism in the South Galatian city of Antioch of Pisidia, recorded in Acts 13:23-48, is the most extensive explanation anywhere in Scripture of the specific contents of his gospel preaching. Wouldn't it be only fitting for the Lord to provide this meticulous documentation and clarification of "the gospel" in conjunction with His issuing of the strongest warning in Scripture about corrupting the gospel (Gal. 1:8-9)? Though this inference is only conjecture and personal opinion, I believe it is beyond coincidence and it is entirely consistent with the Holy Spirit's work of superintending the composition of Scripture (2 Peter 1:21).

---

[7] Colin J. Hemer, "Acts and Galatians reconsidered," *Them* 2.3 (May 1977): 85-88; Robert G. Hoerber, "Galatians 2:1-10 and the Acts of the Apostles," *CTM* 31 (August 1960): 482-91; Joe Morgardo, "Paul in Jerusalem: A Comparison of His Visits in Acts and Galatians," *JETS* 37.1 (March 1994): 57-68; Stanley D. Toussaint, "The Chronological Problem of Galatians 2:1-10," *BSac* 120 (October 1963): 334-40. Some view Galatians 2:1-10 and Acts 11:27-30 as parallel passages explaining the same event but then claim that the Epistle of Galatians was written after the Jerusalem council in Acts 15 (Robert H. Stein, "The Relationship of Galatians 2:1-10 and Acts 15:1-35: Two Neglected Arguments," *JETS* 17 [Fall 1974]: 241-42) or possibly after the events of Acts 16:1-4 (Charles H. Talbert, "Again: Paul's Visits to Jerusalem," *NovT* 9 [January 1967]: 26-40).

Thirdly, if Galatians was written *after* the Jerusalem Council in A.D. 49 (Acts 15) to churches in Northern Galatia in the early to mid 50s, then why didn't Paul include any mention of this great historic event in the Epistle of Galatians, especially when it would have furthered his case for salvation by grace through faith alone—the very point of Galatians?!

It is with good reason, therefore, that the vast majority of New Testament scholars in the last century or so have accepted the South Galatian position as preferable.[8] Many additional reasons could be given in favor of this position; but the burden of proof lies heavily upon the advocates of the crossless gospel to explain why Acts 13 *cannot* be the record of Paul's original gospel to the Galatians referred to in Galatians 1:8-9.

Finally, before considering the question of *what* Paul's gospel to the Galatians consisted of, as found in Acts 13, we must linger a moment longer upon the *where* of Paul's gospel to the Galatians. If Paul's original gospel to the Galatians is to be found in Acts 13 as this chapter has proposed, then what is the correlation of Acts 13 and his evangelism in Antioch of Pisidia to Acts 14 and his evangelism to the other cities of Iconium, Lystra, and Derbe in Southern Galatia? Why should we look to Acts 13:23-48 for Paul's Galatian-gospel and not to Acts 14? The reason is simple: the content of Paul's gospel has already been recorded for us in Acts 13, before one reads Acts 14, and Luke does not deem it necessary to repeat this information.

In Acts 14, it is only mentioned that he *"preached the gospel"* to those Galatian cities. Paul's preaching in the city of Antioch of Pisidia in Acts 13 gets the most "press" in the annals of Paul and Barnabas' first missionary journey. Paul's preaching there (Acts 13:16) was greatly appreciated by the Gentiles but utterly rejected by the Jews (Acts 13:42-50). When they came to the next town of Iconium, their gospel is summarized simply as *"the word of His grace"* (Acts 14:3).[9] It also says that "a great multitude" believed this

---

[8] F. F. Bruce, *Commentary on Galatians*, NIGTC (Grand Rapids: Eerdmans, 1982), 3-18; D. A. Carson and Douglas J. Moo, *An Introduction to the New Testament*, 2nd ed. (Grand Rapids: Zondervan, 2005), 458-61; Ernest De Witt Burton, *A Critical and Exegetical Commentary on the Epistle to the Galatians*, ICC (Edinburgh: T & T Clark, reprinted 1988), xxi-xliv; Robert G. Gromacki, *New Testament Survey* (Grand Rapids: Baker Book House, 1974), 229-232; Donald Guthrie, *New Testament Introduction*, rev. ed. (Downers Grove, IL: InterVarsity Press, 1990), 465-81; Hemer, "Acts and Galatians reconsidered," 81-85; idem, *The Book of Acts in the Setting of Hellenistic History* (Winona Lake, IN: Eisenbrauns, 1990), 244-307; D. Edmond Hiebert, *An Introduction to the New Testament* (Winona Lake, IN: BMH Books, 1993), 2:74-75; Richard N. Longenecker, *Galatians*, WBC (Dallas: Word Publishers, 1990), lxi-c; William M. Ramsay, *The Church in the Roman Empire before A.D. 170* (New York: G. P. Putnam's Sons, 1919), 97-111; idem, *A Historical Commentary on St. Paul's Epistle to the Galatians* (New York: G. P. Putnam's Sons, 1900; reprint ed., Grand Rapids: Baker Book House, 1965), 1-234; Merrill C. Tenney, *New Testament Survey*, rev. ed. (Downers Grove, IL: InterVarsity Press, 1992), 267-70; Theodor Zahn, *Introduction to the New Testament*, trans. from 3rd German ed. (Edinburgh: T & T Clark, 1909), 1:164-193.

[9] The similar phrase, *"the word of the Lord,"* is often used interchangeably in Acts for the gospel (Acts 8:25; 13:48-49; 16:32; 19:10, 20).

message, consisting of both Jews and Gentiles (Acts 14:1). But the unbelieving Jews created opposition and Paul and Barnabas were driven from town again. When they came to Lystra, the next city of Southern Galatia, we are simply told that *"they were preaching the gospel there"* (Acts 14:7). The content of their gospel is not stated again. After further Jewish opposition there (Acts 14:19-20), they were forced on to the next town, Derbe, where again it says only that they *"preached the gospel to that city"* (Acts 14:21). We may conclude from this near complete absence of content for Paul's gospel in Acts 14 that after Luke recorded his gospel in Acts 13:23-48, no further explanation of it was needed. The standard Pauline "gospel" had been set for the reader of Acts.

Acts 13:14-48

14 *But when they departed from Perga, they came to Antioch in Pisidia, and went into the synagogue on the Sabbath day and sat down.*

15 *And after the reading of the Law and the Prophets, the rulers of the synagogue sent to them, saying, "Men and brethren, if you have any word of exhortation for the people, say on."*

16 *Then Paul stood up, and motioning with his hand said, "Men of Israel, and you who fear God, listen:*

17 *"The God of this people Israel chose our fathers, and exalted the people when they dwelt as strangers in the land of Egypt, and with an uplifted arm He brought them out of it.*

18 *"Now for a time of about forty years He put up with their ways in the wilderness.*

19 *"And when He had destroyed seven nations in the land of Canaan, He distributed their land to them by allotment.*

20 *"After that He gave them judges for about four hundred and fifty years, until Samuel the prophet.*

21 *"And afterward they asked for a king; so God gave them Saul the son of Kish, a man of the tribe of Benjamin, for forty years.*

22 *"And when He had removed him, He raised up for them David as king, to whom also He gave testimony and said, 'I have found David the son of Jesse, a man after My own heart, who will do all My will.'*

23 *"From this **man's seed**, according to the promise, God raised up for Israel a **Savior**—Jesus—*

24 *"after John had first preached, before His coming, the baptism of repentance to all the people of Israel.*

25 *"And as John was finishing his course, he said, 'Who do you think I am? I am not He. But behold, there comes One after me, the sandals of whose feet I am not worthy to loose.'*

26 *"Men and brethren, sons of the family of Abraham, and those among you who fear God, to you the word of this **salvation** has been sent.*

27 *"For those who dwell in Jerusalem, and their rulers, because they did not know Him, nor even the voices of the Prophets which are read every Sabbath, have fulfilled them in condemning Him.*

28 And though they found no cause for ***death*** *in Him, they asked Pilate that He should be* ***put to death.***
29 "Now when they had fulfilled all that was written concerning Him, they took Him down from ***the tree*** *and laid Him in a tomb.*
30 But God ***raised Him from the dead.***
31 "He was seen for many days by those who came up with Him from Galilee to Jerusalem, who are His witnesses to the people.
32 "And ***we declare to you glad tidings****—that promise which was made to the fathers.*
33 "God has fulfilled this for us their children, in that He has ***raised up*** *Jesus. As it is also written in the second Psalm: 'You are* ***My Son****, Today I have begotten You.'*
34 "And that He ***raised Him from the dead****, no more to return to corruption, He has spoken thus: 'I will give you the sure mercies of David.'*
35 "Therefore He also says in another Psalm: 'You will not allow ***Your Holy One*** *to see corruption.'*
36 "For David, after he had served his own generation by the will of God, fell asleep, was buried with his fathers, and saw corruption;
37 "but ***He whom God raised up saw*** *no corruption.*
38 "Therefore let it be known to you, brethren, that through this Man is preached to you the ***forgiveness of sins;***
39 "and by Him everyone who ***believes*** *is justified from all things from which you could* ***not be justified*** *by the law of Moses.*
40 "Beware therefore, lest what has been spoken in the prophets come upon you:
41 "Behold, you despisers, Marvel and perish! For I ***work*** *a* ***work*** *in your days, a* ***work*** *which you will by no means* ***believe****, though one were to declare it to you.' "*
42 So when the Jews went out of the synagogue, the Gentiles begged that these words might be preached to them the next Sabbath.
43 Now when the congregation had broken up, many of the Jews and devout proselytes followed Paul and Barnabas, who, speaking to them, persuaded them to continue in ***the grace of God.***
44 On the next Sabbath almost the whole city came together to hear the word of God.
45 But when the Jews saw the multitudes, they were filled with envy; and contradicting and blaspheming, they opposed the things spoken by Paul.
46 Then Paul and Barnabas grew bold and said, "It was necessary that the word of God should be spoken to you first; but since you reject it, and judge yourselves unworthy of ***everlasting life****, behold, we turn to the Gentiles.*
47 "For so the Lord has commanded us: 'I have set you as a light to the Gentiles, That you should be for ***salvation*** *to the ends of the earth.' "*
48 Now when the Gentiles heard this, they were glad and glorified the word of the Lord. And as many as had been appointed to ***eternal life believed.***

What was Paul's Gospel to the Galatians?

Now that the correct location of Paul's definitive gospel to the Galatians has been established, we must consider the actual contents of this gospel. In order to determine this, we must first observe where Paul begins and ends his gospel preaching. These parameters are critical to address at this point in order to show that we are not being arbitrary or "cherry picking" in determining the content of the gospel, as crossless advocates often claim about the normative Free Grace interpretation of gospel texts.[10]

In Acts 13:16-48, we see the apostle Paul preaching to a mixed multitude of Jews and Gentiles in the Galatian city of Antioch of Pisidia. In verses 16-22, Paul begins speaking and he lays a foundation for the good news by providing the historical connection between the elect nation of Israel (v. 17) and the Savior of the world who came from that nation—Jesus (v. 23). Though crossless gospel advocates often claim that even the Old Testament is "the gospel," Paul's preaching in Acts 13:16-22 should not be viewed as gospel-preaching but as *preparation* for the gospel starting with the announcement about the Savior in verse 23. The gospel is not about events such as the Exodus from Egypt (v. 17), the Conquest of Canaan (v. 19), or the time period of the Judges (v. 20). Nor is the good news of the gospel about individuals like Samuel, Saul, Kish, Benjamin, David, or Jesse (vv. 20-22). It is about "a Savior—Jesus." So, Paul actually *begins* preaching "the gospel" in verse 23 as he announces the good news that God has acted on the basis of His "promise" to Israel by raising up a Savior—Jesus.

It is imperative to understand, for the purpose of determining the content of the gospel, that from Acts 13:23 onward Paul is preaching "the gospel" of Christ. This observation is supported on the basis of two facts. First, the verb *euangelizō* occurs in Acts 13:32 and it is in the present tense, indicating that Paul considered himself to be presently in the act of preaching the good news. Since in the immediate context of verse 32 he had been proclaiming Jesus Christ as the Savior who died and rose in fulfillment of Old Testament Scripture, we may safely assume that Paul was preaching the particular form of "good news" known as the "gospel of Christ," in distinction to other types of good news such as the gospel of the kingdom. Secondly, in Acts 13:32, Paul connects the "promise" made to the fathers with the preaching of the gospel. He says, *"And we declare to you glad tidings (euangelizō)—that promise which was made to the fathers."* Since Paul connects the preaching of the "gospel" (*euangelizō*) and "the promise" in Acts 13:32 with the announcement in 13:23 that *"according to the promise, God raised up for Israel a Savior—Jesus,"* we may safely conclude

---

[10] Zane C. Hodges, "The Hydra's Other Head: Theological Legalism," *Grace in Focus* 23 (September/October 2008): 3; Bob Wilkin, "Another Look at 1 Corinthians 15:3-11," *Grace in Focus* 23 (January/February 2008): 1-2; idem, "Essential Truths About Our Savior," *Grace in Focus* 23 (November/December 2008): 1.

that Paul was preaching the good news about Jesus Christ as Savior starting at Acts 13:23.

It may also be significant that the Greek text does not contain the article before "promise" in verse 23. The text does not say, "according to *the* promise," but simply, "according to promise." The reference to "promise" does not seem to focus on one particular promise, such as the Messiah being of Davidic descent. While the fulfillment of this one particular promise about Christ is no doubt true (2 Sam. 7:12; Isa. 11:1; Jer. 23:5; Zech. 3:8),[11] the larger point of the passage seems to be on the general promise of Old Testament revelation that God would raise up a Savior, which He has now faithfully fulfilled in Jesus. The verb *agō* in verse 23 (*"raised up,"* NKJV, or *"brought to,"* NASB) recalls the general promise of Zechariah 3:8 (LXX) to *"bring forth"* (*agō*) the Servant of the Lord, where there is no emphasis on Davidic descent. In addition, it is grammatically ambiguous in verse 23 as to whether the phrase *"according to promise"* attaches to *"from this man's seed* (according to promise)" or whether it modifies *"God raised up for Israel a Savior* (according to promise)." Both are grammatically possible.[12]

The possibility must also be admitted that the phrase *"according to promise"* is not referring specifically to fulfillment of prophecy at this point but is referring to the gracious basis on which God provided a Savior for Israel in Jesus the Christ. The prepositional phrase, *"according to promise,"* also occurs in Galatians 3:29, where it is used in reference to Church age believers being Abraham's spiritual seed by virtue of being "in Christ." In Galatians 3:29, believers are also said to be "heirs," not of the land provisions of the Abrahamic Covenant (which are nowhere referred to in Galatians) but of the spiritual blessing of justification by faith in Jesus Christ (Gal. 3:10-14), that happens to be accompanied by the reception of the Holy Spirit in this dispensation (Gal. 3:14b). This heirship in Galatians 3:29 is literally, "according to promise," not "according to *the* promise." This means that Gentiles justified by faith in this dispensation of Grace are not heirs of a *particular* promise to Abraham, as though the Church fulfills some aspect of Israel's Abrahamic Covenant. But instead, we are heirs *on the basis* of a grace/promise method of divine dealing, in the same manner in which God dealt with Abraham, in contrast to a works/law method. This anarthrous expression, *"according to promise,"* is typically Pauline when setting forth a contrast between law and grace as two systems of divine dealing (Rom. 4:16; 6:14; 11:6; Gal. 3:11, 18, 29).[13] If this is the proper interpretation of the phrase "according to promise" in Acts 13:23,

---

[11] Max Wilcox, "The Promise of the 'Seed' in the New Testament and the Targumim," *JSNT* 5 (1979): 8-11.

[12] Daniel B. Wallace, *Greek Grammar Beyond the Basics: An Exegetical Syntax of the New Testament* (Grand Rapids: Zondervan, 1996), 199.

[13] Ron Merryman, *Galatians: God's Antidote to Legalism*, rev. ed. (Casa Grande, AZ: Merryman Ministries, 1999), 50-66.

then Paul would be teaching in this verse that God has provided a Savior for Israel on the basis of His grace.

This interpretation of *"according to promise"* fits the context and is well-supported in Paul's pre-evangelistic preaching in Acts 13:16-22 prior to his presentation of the gospel itself in Acts 13:23-48. In verses 16-22, Paul seems to be recalling for these Galatian Jews in the synagogue at Antioch that God has dealt graciously with Israel up to this point; and in this respect, He has dealt *"according to promise."* This interpretation can be observed in the terms Paul employs in verses 17-22, where he states that God: *"chose"* Israel (v. 17a; cf. Deut. 7:6-8); and He *"exalted"* them when He *"brought them out"* of Egypt (v. 17b; cf. Ex. 12:36-14:31; 19:4); and He *"put up with"* this people that no longer deserved to exist as a nation (v. 18; cf. Num. 14:11-20); and He *"destroyed"* the nations living in Canaan and *"distributed their land"* to Israel (v. 19; cf. Josh. 13-22); and He *"gave them"* judges to deliver them despite their cycle of sin (v. 20; cf. Judg. 2:10-16); and after *"they asked for a king"* in disobedience (1 Sam. 10:19) He *"gave them Saul"* (v. 21; cf. 1 Sam. 10:24); and after Saul's disobedience the Lord *"raised up for them"* the son of Jesse, king David, a man after God's own heart (v. 22), of whom they were not worthy as a nation (1 Sam. 16:1-13; 2 Kings 8:19). All of these divine dealings illustrate the manifold grace of God toward Israel. But the greatest grace of all was that God now provided for Israel and the Gentile nations *"a Savior—Jesus"* (v. 23). In this respect, God raised up for Israel a Savior *"according to promise"*—according to His grace/promise method of divine dealing.

All of these observations serve to illustrate not only the grace of God displayed through the nation of Israel but also the limits of Paul's gospel preaching in Antioch. Paul's gospel to the Galatians can be determined by distinguishing the section that serves as the *contextual framework* for the gospel (13:16-22) from the actual *content* of the gospel itself (13:23-41). Following Paul's initial evangelism in the synagogue, which ends in Acts 13:41, he continues to preach the good news on the following Sabbath (13:44), where the evangelization of Antioch of Pisidia ends with the Gentiles believing and receiving everlasting life (13:46, 48).

With these parameters in mind, the contents of "the gospel" that Paul preached to the Galatians and that they "received" (Gal. 1:8-9) will now be examined from Acts 13:23-48. Within these verses we see the Lord Jesus Christ set forth as the object of saving faith in terms of His person and work. All of the elements of the one, true, saving "gospel of Christ," are presented, including His deity, humanity, death for sin, bodily resurrection, and salvation by grace through faith. As each facet of the Lord's person and work in the gospel are examined in the following sections, it is vital to keep in mind that these elements of saving faith are not arbitrarily chosen. They are the common elements found in the rest of the New Testament where *euangelion* and *euangelizō* are used in salvation contexts. Not coincidentally, each of these elements is explicitly required as the content of saving faith elsewhere in individual passages in the New Testament.

If the "gospel of Christ" is a singular message that does not permit any variation or alteration upon pain of God's anathema, as Galatians 1:6-9 so clearly teaches, then it must be definable in terms of its contents. And if the gospel itself must be believed for eternal salvation (Acts 15:7-11; Eph. 1:13; 2 Thess. 1:8-10; 1 Peter 4:17), and the Lord's deity (John 8:24), humanity (John 6:51, 53; 1 Tim. 2:4-5; 1 John 5:5-6), death (John 6:51, 53; 1 Cor. 1:17-21), and resurrection (Rom. 10:9b-10a) are all individually required to be believed for justification before God and eternal life, then there must be no incongruity between the gospel of our salvation and each element of the Savior's person and work. This is not "theological legalism," whereby we are imposing our "orthodox" theology upon the content of saving faith, as some crossless proponents are now claiming that we are doing.[14] Rather, it is simply a matter of biblical and theological consistency.

It is not coincidental, but rather by divine design, that each of the individual elements of Christ's person and work that is required to be believed for eternal salvation is also contained in Paul's gospel to the Galatians in Acts 13. Yet, astonishingly, some crossless gospel proponents flatly deny that such elements even exist in this critical passage. Thus Bob Wilkin severely critiques the position of another Free Grace leader, J. B. Hixson, by issuing the following bold claim:

> But how can Acts 13 be used to support Hixson's essentials? There is no mention in Acts 13 that Christ died *on the cross*, or that He died *for our sins*. We don't learn that Jesus rose *on the third day*, or that *He rose bodily*. We do not find that the object of faith is the Person *and work* of Christ. Instead it is Jesus Himself who is the object of faith (v 39). Nor is the deity of Christ even mentioned. In fact, Jesus is called "this man" by Paul (v 38).[15]

But is this claim accurate? Are the key elements of Christ's person and work, such as His deity, substitutionary death for sin, and bodily resurrection, completely absent from Acts 13? And are the proponents of the normal, historical Free Grace position, such as Dr. Hixson, actually guilty of committing eisegesis with Acts 13? Or, are today's crossless gospel teachers merely being myopic? A careful examination of Acts 13 reveals that each of these essential elements of saving faith is indeed contained in this classic gospel text.

Jesus Christ's Deity

As we consider Acts 13:23-48 and the question of what it means to "believe in Jesus" for eternal life, we see that Paul clearly identifies this "Jesus."

---

[14] Hodges, "The Hydra's Other Head: Theological Legalism," 2.

[15] Bob Wilkin, "A Review of J. B. Hixson's *Getting the Gospel Wrong: The Evangelical Crisis No One is Talking About*," *JOTGES* 21 (Spring 2008): 25-26.

Since the lost must believe in the *person* of Jesus, we see the apostle Paul providing ample definition as to the identity of this Person. The Lord Jesus Christ is depicted through various titles and terms, with each in their own right conveying the Lord's status as truly God. When taken together, Paul left the definite impression upon the minds of his Jewish and God-fearing Gentile audience that Jesus was the unique, theanthropic Savior in whom they must believe.

"Son"

There are several references to the deity of Jesus Christ throughout this passage, even though Paul does not use the theological term, "deity." Both "Jesus" and "God" are referred to in 13:33, followed by a quotation from Psalm 2:7, where God the Father refers to Jesus as "My Son." The word "son" by itself does not inherently mean "deity" in either the Hebrew Old Testament (*bēn*) or the Greek New Testament (*huios*). However, based on usage in various contexts, "Son" certainly can, and often does, convey the meaning of unique, divine status as God the Son. It definitely has this meaning in Psalm 2:7, which Paul is quoting in Acts 13:33. In Psalm 2, the LORD's "Son" rules and judges the entire world. Then five verses later He is said to be worshipped, feared, and trusted by the entire world (Ps. 2:12). Such activities are solely attributable to deity in the Word of God.

Still, some may question this conclusion on the basis of the Father saying to the Son, *"Today I have begotten You."* The quotation of Psalm 2:7 in Acts 13:33, *"You are My Son, Today I have begotten You,"* is in no way a denial of the deity of Christ. It is not teaching that Jesus only became God's Son at the resurrection and that He wasn't always God's Son. By applying Psalm 2:7 to Christ's resurrection, Paul was not teaching that Jesus *became* the Son of God at the resurrection. He has always been God's Son throughout eternity (Ps. 2:12; Prov. 30:4; Dan. 3:25; Mark 12:6; John 1:18; 3:16-17; 16:28; Gal. 4:4; 1 John 4:9-10, 14-15). The term "begot" does not necessarily mean "created." It is better understood to mean "brought forth."[16] Christ was "brought forth" from the grave, as if from the womb of the earth, when the Father raised Him from the dead. Hence the phrase, *"You are My Son, Today I have begotten You,"* does not mean the Father begot or brought forth Jesus via resurrection in order *to become* His Son. Rather, because Jesus *was* God's Son (*"You are My Son..."*), for this reason the Father brought Him forth in resurrection (*"...Today I have begotten You"*). At the resurrection of Christ, the Father divinely decreed to the entire universe that Jesus Christ was His Son. As the Sovereign King over all creation, God the Father simply made it known forevermore that Jesus is who He always was—the one and only Son of God. If God the Father only made Jesus Christ His Son at the resurrection, this would contradict the

---

[16] Renald E. Showers, "The Meaning of Psalm 2:7," in *The Eternal Sonship of Christ* (Neptune, NJ: Loizeaux Bros., 1993), 56-64.

fact that the Father had always regarded Jesus as His Son and testified to this at Jesus' water baptism (Matt. 3:17; 17:5). Therefore, this reference to Jesus being declared God's "Son" at the resurrection in Acts 13:33 was nothing short of an attestation of His deity. This is consistent not only with its original usage in Psalm 2 but with how the term "Son" is used in John 5:18, Hebrews 1:5-6, and many other Christological passages.

"Holy One"

Besides the reference to Jesus as God's "Son" in Acts 13:33, a second reference to Jesus' deity in Paul's preaching occurs with the usage of the phrase "Holy One" (*hosios*) in Acts 13:35. This quotation from Psalm 16:10, *"Nor will You allow Your Holy One to see corruption,"* also establishes the deity of Christ. The "Holy One" referred to in Psalm 16 is not David but a particular descendant of David, the Messiah, as explained by Peter in Acts 2:29-31. This fact, by itself, does not prove that the phrase "Holy One" means deity, but other factors taken together point to such an intended meaning. First, the word *hosios* used in Acts 13:35 is elsewhere applied to God Himself in the Septuagint (Deut. 32:4; Ps. 145:17). Second, the broader concept of the "Holy One" in the Old Testament indicates deity, where the Hebrew term *qādôsh* is applied over 30 times as a title for God, such as in Isaiah 43:15, *"I am the LORD, your Holy One, the Creator of Israel, your King."* Thirdly, the actual Greek term *hosios* occurs only seven other times in the New Testament, where once it is used as a parallel to Acts 13:35 (Acts 2:27), three times as a simple adjective (Acts 13:34; 1 Tim. 2:8; Titus 1:8), and twice it is used explicitly in reference to the Lord God (Rev. 15:4; 16:5). *Hosios* also occurs once in Hebrews 7:26, where it indirectly affirms Christ's deity, since He is declared to be our High Priest, the One who is holy, sinless, higher than the heavens, and able to guarantee our eternal security (Heb. 7:25-26).

Finally, when the entire New Testament concept of "the Holy One" (*hohagios*) is taken into consideration, Christ's deity is again firmly attested.[17] It is legitimate to view both *hagios* and *hosios* together, since both have the same semantic domain[18] and are used in certain passages in the singular with the definite article to refer to the same Person, Jesus

---

[17] While Domeris argues that "Holy One" primarily speaks of agency and representation in the NT, he also concludes regarding Peter's confession of Christ as "the Holy One of God" in John 6:69 [CT], "Peter thus responds in verse 69 as the spokesman of the community, and of all true believers, in affirming his faith in the divine/human nature of Jesus. . . . He affirms the Johannine belief in the scandal of the incarnation—the paradox of a human agent who performs divine deeds and makes divine claims." William R. Domeris, "The Confession of Peter According to John 6:69," *TB* 44 (1993): 166-67 (ellipsis added). See also Joubert, who affirms not only the deity of Christ by the designation "Holy One" but also that as the "Holy One" Jesus is "the perfect Mediator between God and His people, He is the Suffering Servant of Yahweh Who vicariously gives His life for the life of the world." H. L. N. Joubert, "The Holy One of God (John 6:69)," *Neot* 2 (1968): 66.

[18] L&N, "pertaining to being holy in the sense of superior moral qualities and possessing certain essentially divine qualities in contrast to what is human" (1:745, §88.24).

Christ. In Mark 1:24 and Luke 4:34, the fallen angels fear *"the Holy One of God"* as having the authority to destroy them; and He is able to command them with the word of His mouth and they comply (Mark 1:27; Luke 4:36). This is *not* equivalent to a mighty angel having to *fight* and then *bind* Satan or his demons, as in the future tribulation (Jude 9; Rev. 12:7-9; 20:1-2). Whether or not the Jews from the synagogue at Antioch immediately understood Paul's use of the term *hosios* to be a reference to Jesus' deity, there is no question that Paul used the term in this sense. When combined with Paul's other descriptions of Jesus as God's "Son" and the "Savior," his usage of *hosios* in this context formed a strong composite witness of the Lord's deity.

"Savior"

Besides Jesus' deity being attested by the terms "Son" and "Holy One," it is further underscored in Acts 13:23 by Paul's reference to Him as Israel's "Savior" (*sōtēra*).[19] This title was used most frequently in Greek and Roman culture for its many pagan deities. It was also commonly used by the emperors who, though mere sinful men, accepted worship from their subjects as though they were gods. The term was also used sporadically of other statesmen and rulers, as well as doctors and philosophers.[20] However, these facts lend no credence to the teaching of some crossless gospel proponents that belief in Christ's deity is not essential for eternal life.[21] For crossless

---

[19] The reading of the Textus Receptus and Critical Text, "Savior" (σωτῆρα), is far better attested as the original than the Majority Text reading of "salvation" (σωτηρίαν), based on the external manuscript evidence. The reading of "Savior" (σωτῆρα) is supported uniformly by all the early uncials א (4th), A (5th), B (4th), C (5th), D (5th); by later uncials Ψ (9th), P (9th); by some minuscules; by the representatives of all three principal, early language versions: the Latin Vulgate, all the Syriac versions, both principal Coptic versions (Sahidic & Bohairic); and patristically by Athanasius (4th) and Theodoret (5th). The reading of "salvation" (σωτηρίαν) is supported by one late papyrus ms., 𝔓74 (7th); uncials E (6th), L (9th); the vast majority of minuscules; and the Ethiopic version (13th). The authenticity of the reading "salvation" (σωτηρίαν) is highly suspect, to say the least, based on its complete absence from the early Greek mss. coupled with the lack of any geographical distribution in the first millennium as seen among the versional witnesses, to say nothing of the silence of the early Church "fathers" for this reading. Regarding internal evidence, Henry Alford explains how the original reading in verse 23 might have changed: "The reading σωτηρίαν has probably arisen from the contracted way of writing Ἰησοῦν thus: σωτηραῖν; and then from ver. 26 σωτηρίαν was adopted." Henry Alford, *The Greek Testament* (Chicago: Moody Press, 1958), 2:147. Metzger also explains how this variant may have arisen as a paleographical oversight with the contraction of the nomina sacra of σωτῆρα and Ἰησοῦν. See Bruce M. Metzger, *A Textual Commentary on the Greek New Testament*, 2nd ed. (Stuttgart: United Bible Societies, 1994), 359.

[20] Craig R. Koester, "'The Savior of the World' (John 4:42)," *JBL* 109 (1990): 666-67; Werner Foerster and Georg Fohrer, "σῴζω, σωτηρία, σωτήρ, σωτήριος," *TDNT*, 7:1003-12; Johannes Schneider and Colin Brown, "σωτήρ," *NIDNTT*, 3:216-17.

[21] Zane C. Hodges, "How to Lead People to Christ, Part 1: The Content of our Message," *JOTGES* 13 (Autumn 2000): 5; John Niemelä, "Objects of Faith in John: A Matter of Person AND Content," Grace Evangelical Society Grace Conference, Dallas, TX, February 28, 2006.

advocates to pursue this line of argumentation for Acts 13:23 would be to place themselves in a dubious and unenviable position alongside the cults. They would be following the same distorted and deceitful interpretation as those who reject the Trinity and deity of Christ,[22] particularly the Jehovah's Witnesses, as they seek to divest the term "Savior" of its deistic import.[23] To be the "Savior" does not mean merely being a "mighty god" who is a god-like being that falls short of full deity, as if being the "Savior" merely meant being a mighty angel or an exalted human being.

According to biblical usage, the title "Savior" was truly an appellation for Jesus' deity in Acts 13:23. Paul employed this term in a manner consistent with both the Old Testament and New Testament doctrine of saviorhood.[24] The Hebrew verb for "save" (*yāsha*) occurs over two hundred times in the Old Testament; and when it is used substantively, it means "Savior."[25] This Hebrew term is often translated with the Greek noun, *sōtēr,* in the Septuagint. The vast majority of these uses are in reference to God,[26] but some are also in reference to men such as Moses (Ex. 2:17) and the Judges (Judg. 3:9, 15), who were viewed as instruments of physical deliverance with God as the ultimate source of that salvation. Advocates of the crossless, resurrectionless, and deityless content of saving faith should pause before considering these examples of human "saviors" or deliverers as somehow nullifying the divine status of Christ as "Savior" in Acts 13:23.

A diachronic study of the Hebrew word *yāsha* in the Old Testament yields an unusual pattern. Though this term is used of human deliverers as God's agents of physical salvation in the Historical books, this *suddenly changes* with the advent of the Prophetic books. From the time of the Writing Prophets, especially Isaiah and Hosea in the 8th century B.C., only the Lord God is referred to as the "Savior" in the inspired Word of God, with only two exceptions.[27] Though the reason for this startling pattern

---

[22] Patrick Navas, *Divine Truth or Human Tradition? A Reconsideration of the Roman Catholic-Protestant Doctrine of the Trinity in Light of the Hebrew and Christian Scriptures* (Bloomington, IN: AuthorHouse, 2006), 233-35.

[23] *Aid to Bible Understanding* (Brooklyn, New York: Watchtower Society, 1971), 1455; *The Greatest Man Who Ever Lived* (Brooklyn, New York: Watchtower Society, 1991), 3-4.

[24] Cullmann says that the term "Savior" in the New Testament is "an Old Testament title of honour for God transferred to Jesus" (Oscar Cullmann, *The Christology of the New Testament,* rev. ed., trans. Shirley C. Guthrie and Charles A. M. Hall [Philadelphia: Westminster Press, 1963], 238).

[25] E.g., 2 Sam. 22:3; Ps. 106:21; Isa. 19:20-21; 43:3, 10-11; 45:21-22; Hos. 13:4.

[26] Deut. 32:15; Judg. 12:3; Ps. 24:5; 27:1, 9; 62:2, 6; 65:5; 79: 9; 95:1; Isa. 12:2; 17:10; 45:15, 21; 62:11; Mic. 7:7; Hab. 3:18.

[27] The first exception is Nehemiah 9:27, where Nehemiah in the 5th century B.C. is simply referring retrospectively to the days of the Judges. The second reference is Obadiah 1:21, where it is prophesied that "saviors" (*môshi'im*) will overtake Edom and presumably reign under the Lord in the future millennial kingdom (Thomas J. Finley, *Joel, Amos, Obadiah,* Wycliffe Exegetical Commentary, ed. Kenneth L. Barker [Chicago: Moody Press, 1990], 378; Jeffrey Niehaus, "Obadiah" in *The Minor Prophets: An Exegetical & Expository Commentary,*

is nowhere specified in Scripture, it is noteworthy that this shift in usage coincides with the exclusive prophetic declarations revealed through Isaiah and Hosea. Through them, the Lord said, *"Before Me there was no God formed, nor shall there be after Me. I, even I, am the LORD, and besides Me there is no savior"* (Isa. 43:10-11); *"I am the LORD your God ever since the land of Egypt, and you shall know no God but Me; for there is no Savior besides Me"* (Hos. 13:4). These exclusive statements are combined with dozens of passages in the Prophetic books reminding Israel that idols and foreign gods cannot save—only the LORD. These facts seem to indicate that the prophets were calling Israel to shift their focus from men being "saviors" to God Himself being the true Savior. This thorough emphasis upon the LORD God as Savior effectively set the stage for the advent of Jesus Christ to be viewed as the exclusive *"Savior of the world"* (John 4:42). Israel was to think of a "savior" first in terms of God Himself and only secondarily, and rarely, of men.

The New Testament continues where the Writing Prophets left off, but actually goes further in reserving the term "Savior" *exclusively for God and God's Son with no exceptions*. That no man or god is ever called "savior" in the 27 books of the New Testament is particularly striking when compared to the backdrop against which the New Testament was written. The term *sōtēr* had wide currency in the polytheistic Greco-Roman world of the 1st century. Paul accurately reported that there were many gods and many lords in his day (1 Cor. 8:5-6), and history reports that many of these even bore the title "savior." Yet conspicuously, the New Testament applies this title *only* to God and His Son.

This is evident testimony to the deistic meaning intended by the apostle Paul when he employed the term in his Galatian evangelism in Acts 13:23. His Jewish and God-fearing Gentile audience would have first recognized the title as a claim for Jesus' deity. This is especially true when Paul combined "Savior" with other divine titles for Yahweh in his evangelism, such as "Holy One," just as Isaiah the prophet did before him, when God spoke through him saying, *"For I am the LORD your God, the Holy One of Israel, your Savior"* (Isa. 43:3). Though it is true that "Savior" was sometimes employed of mere humans, even in the Old Testament, this fact by itself does not negate the greater truth that "Savior" is *primarily* a term for deity. For some to argue against Jesus' deity in Acts 13 on the basis of secondary and secular usage would be similar to arguing that

---

ed. Thomas Edward McComiskey [Grand Rapids: Baker, 1993], 2:540-541n21). Other sources (Syriac Peshitta; LXX) render the Hebrew word here passively, as if it were *mûsha'im* instead, making this a reference to those who have been "saved" by God rather than the ones who do the saving, i.e., "saviors." The Nehemiah 9:27 reference looks back to the ancient past, while the *môshi'im* reference in Obadiah 1:21 looks to the distant future subsequent to the Church age. This means that no man living from the time of the Writing Prophets up to the millennial kingdom was ever properly designated a "savior" in the canonical Scriptures, except One—the Lord Jesus Christ.

the Hebrew terms *'ĕlōhîm* ("God") and *'ādôn* ("Lord") do not convey deity when applied to Christ simply because they are also used in Scripture of men.[28] However, as virtually all students of Scripture realize, God Himself is first and foremost "God" and "Lord," unless the context indicates clearly otherwise.

This leads us back to Paul's use of "Savior" in Acts 13:23. In what sense did he employ this title in the context of his gospel preaching to the Galatians? Did he use it of a human "savior" or "deliverer" like the Judges of Israel, or did he use it of God Himself? Two factors strongly suggest that he used "Savior" with a deistic meaning that exceeded a merely humanistic meaning. First, the functions of Jesus as Savior described in Acts 13 clearly depict exclusively divine prerogatives. It is through Christ that "forgiveness of sins" (Acts 13:38) is preached to Jews and Gentiles; and it is in/through Him that the world can "be justified" by believing (Acts 13:39). This was never claimed for any human "savior" or deliverer in Israel's past. In fact, for anyone other than God to claim this would be viewed as a usurpation of a solely divine prerogative (Mark 2:5-12; Luke 5:20-25; 7:47-49). Furthermore, the New Testament teaches that Jesus Christ not only *provides* forgiveness of sins by His saving work, but He actually *mediates* and applies this forgiveness![29] This is the clear teaching of Paul in Colossians 3:13 and of Peter in Acts 5:31. Peter even associates this forgiveness of sins with being Israel's "Savior" in Acts 5:31 when he testifies, *"Him God has exalted to His right hand to be Prince and Savior, to give repentance to Israel and forgiveness of sins."* No wonder Peter later testifies to Christ's deity as Savior, writing *"To those who have obtained like precious faith with us by the righteousness of our God and Savior Jesus Christ"* (2 Peter 1:1).

A second factor that should be considered regarding the interpretation of "Savior" in Acts 13:23 is Paul's usage of this term elsewhere in his writings. Does he *ever* use this title in a humanistic sense? It is apparent that he uses this term uniformly of God and God's Son (Eph. 5:23; Phil. 3:20; 1 Tim. 1:1, 2:3, 4:10; 2 Tim. 1:10; Titus 1:3, 4, 2:10, 13, 3:4, 6), but *never* of mere men. What is particularly revealing is the way Paul employs this term in Titus.[30] There he uses three couplets in three different chapters where "God" is described as our "Savior" (1:3; 2:10; 3:4) followed immediately in each context by a corresponding statement that "Jesus Christ" is our "Savior" (1:4; 2:13; 3:6). The apostle Paul could not be making a more

[28] In the Old Testament, the word *'ādôn* is used more frequently of a human lord or master than of God Himself, especially in the Historical books, but the references to God are also abundant and clear and seem to be the primary usage in the Prophetic books. The term *'ĕlōhîm* on the other hand is nearly a technical term for deity, applying almost exclusively to God Himself or other false deities, but it can also be applied to human beings (Psalm 82:6 is a notable case; cf. John 10:34).

[29] Robert M. Bowman, Jr., and J. Ed Komoszewski, *Putting Jesus in His Place: The Case for the Deity of Christ* (Grand Rapids: Kregel Publications, 2007), 211.

[30] Ibid., 210.

intentional declaration that Jesus is God by virtue of Him being the Savior. Christology scholar, Larry Hurtado, explains this very point regarding the application of the title "Savior" to Christ in the New Testament:

> In some cases God and Jesus are both referred to as "Savior" in such close proximity that we must infer a deliberate effort to link them through this appellative: e.g., Titus 2:11 (God) and 2:13 (Jesus), 3:4 (God) and 3:6 (Jesus). Both in the biblical/Jewish tradition and in the larger religious environment of the late first century as well, "Savior" was widely used as an epithet for divine beings, including the Roman emporer. Consequently the restricted application of the term to Jesus and God surely connotes a deliberate linkage of Jesus with divine attributes that would have been readily perceived by the intended reader.[31]

All of this leads to several plaguing problems for those who would seek to nullify the deistic meaning of "Savior" in Acts 13:23. For example, why would Paul use this title in this particular evangelistic episode with a sense contrary to how he uses it everywhere else in his inspired letters? And if Paul didn't use "Savior" with deistic connotations in Acts 13:23, then why would Paul use the term "Savior" in a manner distinct from Peter's usage and the rest of the New Testament? Wouldn't the crossless position be arguing for the exception against the rule in such a case? And if Acts 13:23 is the exception, then what factors in the context of Acts 13 *require* a merely humanistic meaning for the title, especially considering that Paul attributes divine prerogatives to Jesus in the same context (Acts 13:38-39)? And why would Paul employ a term that was primarily understood through Israel's prophets to be a term for Yahweh Himself? In addition, why would Paul combine this title for Jesus with other divine titles used in Scripture, such as "Son" and "Holy One"? Wouldn't Paul's initial Jewish and God-fearing Gentile audience have collectively understood these terms in their primary sense as ascriptions of deity? Would Paul be so careless as to run the risk of potential confusion if his audience misapplied to Jesus the deistic connotations of these titles and misinterpreted Paul to be requiring faith in the unique God-man for their salvation? The problems for those who would deny that Christ's deity is being preached in Acts 13 are truly insurmountable.

When the apostle Paul's collective testimony is weighed with respect to his use of the titles "Son" of God, "Holy One," and "Savior," it is no wonder that John the Baptist—the greatest man ever born prior to Jesus (Matt. 11:11)—testified that he was not even worthy to be Jesus' servant (*"there comes One after me, the sandals of whose feet I am not worthy to loose"*), a fact that Paul also cited in Acts 13:25 as support that the Lord Jesus is

---

[31] Larry W. Hurtado, *Lord Jesus Christ: Devotion to Jesus in Earliest Christianity* (Grand Rapids: Eerdmans, 2003), 515-16.

truly God. We may conclude that the deity of Christ was definitely an essential element of Paul's original gospel to the Galatians.

If Paul's Epistle to the Galatians reiterates and affirms his evangelistic message in Acts 13, we should not be surprised to discover, therefore, that the deity of Christ is also affirmed in this epistle. This is observed in a variety of ways. First, Jesus is simultaneously contrasted with mere men and put on a plane with "God the Father." As Paul declares the origin of his apostleship (1:1) and gospel (1:10-12), he states that he received his apostleship neither from men nor through man, but *"through Jesus Christ and God the Father"* (1:1). Likewise, he declares that he is not seeking "to please men" but "God" (1:10a), which, in the same verse, is synonymous with pleasing and serving "Christ" (1:10b). In this respect, Paul's literary approach in immediately introducing his readers to the deity of Christ in the opening verses of his letter is consonant with John's approach in beginning his evangelistic Gospel on the same note (John 1:1). This timeless, inspired approach to uplifting the deity of the Savior should not be so hastily dismissed in our evangelism today.[32]

The deity of Christ is also found in Galatians by Paul's statement that the spiritual blessings of grace, mercy, and peace come jointly *"from God the Father and our Lord Jesus Christ"* (1:3). Nowhere in the New Testament are human beings ever said to be the source of such spiritual blessings. This is also evidence that Jesus is equal in deity with God the Father.[33] Finally, Christ's deity is implicitly observed in Galatians by the fact that justification before God is by "faith in Jesus Christ" (Gal. 2:16) and in the case of Abraham by believing in "God" (Gal. 3:6). Throughout the entire Old Testament, justifying or saving faith was only permitted to be in God (Yahweh) Himself. Faith in any other object would have constituted sheer idolatry. Thus, when Galatians, the Gospel of John, and the rest of the New Testament require saving faith specifically in Jesus Christ, this is tantamount to a declaration of His deity.[34]

Jesus Christ's Humanity

The humanity of the Lord Jesus is also proclaimed at the outset of Paul's gospel presentation in Acts 13:23, where he declares that Jesus was *"from*

---

[32] By contrast, notice what one leading crossless gospel proponent claims about initiating evangelism with the subject of Christ's deity, "That approach might have drawn a listeners [sic] interest 50 years ago, but it doesn't do so well today. Most people have heard this a lot and are not interested in hearing more when this is the start." And what is his proposed alternative? We should start with "some variation" of John 6:47 (Bob Wilkin, "What's Your First Sentence in Evangelism?" *Grace in Focus* 23 [September/October 2008]: 4). Yet, there is a reason that the Holy Spirit inspired John 1:1 to come six chapters before John 6:47 in a highly evangelistic book.

[33] Bowman and Komoszewski, *Putting Jesus in His Place: The Case for the Deity of Christ*, 287; Murray J. Harris, *Jesus as God: The New Testament Use of Theos in Reference to Jesus* (Grand Rapids: Baker Books, 1992), 316.

[34] Ibid., Bowman and Komoszewski, 282; Ibid., Harris, 316.

this man's seed," in reference to David (13:22). The term "seed" (*spermatos*) establishes that the Lord Jesus was a biological descendant of David, not just a legal descendant as though He was merely adopted into the lineage of the promised Messiah. His humanity is also implicit throughout Paul's evangelism in Acts 13 through the references to Christ's death and resurrection, as only a man can truly experience death. It was for this very reason that the Lord Jesus became incarnate, as Hebrews 2:9 states, *"But we see Jesus, who was made a little lower than the angels, for the suffering of death crowned with glory and honor, that He, by the grace of God, might taste death for everyone."* Both the humanity and deity of Christ are also set forth by Paul in the Epistle of Galatians, as he explains in Galatians 4:4-5, *"But when the fullness of the time had come,* ***God*** *sent forth* ***His Son, born of a woman, born*** *under the law, 5 to redeem those who were under the law, that we might receive the adoption as sons."*[35] Not only are Christ's deity and humanity stated in the Epistle to the Galatians, but as we shall see, so are each of the other essential elements of the gospel. Though Christ's humanity is more assumed and implicit in Acts 13, it was still an essential element of Paul's gospel to the Galatians.

Jesus Christ's Substitutionary Death

The death of the Lord Jesus is also included in Paul's preaching in Acts 13:23-48 as a vital element of his gospel. The mere fact of Christ's death is stated several times in the passage. But what is also inferred in Acts 13, and confirmed in Galatians, is the substitutionary aspect of that death. This is evidenced by the fact that when Paul speaks of Christ's crucifixion, he conspicuously chooses not to use the normal word "cross" (*stauros*) in verse 29, but "tree" (*xulon*). Paul's Jewish audience, being acquainted with the Law, would have recognized the reference as an allusion to Deuteronomy 21:22-23,[36] which says, *"If a man has committed a sin deserving of death, and he*

---

[35] In reference to the phrase *"born of a woman"* in verse 4, Greek scholar A. T. Robertson wrote, "As all men are and so true humanity, 'coming from a woman.' There is, of course, no direct reference here to the Virgin Birth of Jesus, but his deity had just been affirmed by the words 'his Son' (τον υιον αυτου), so that both his deity and humanity are here stated as in Ro. 1:3." A. T. Robertson, *Word Pictures in the New Testament* (Grand Rapids: Baker Books, Reprinted n.d.), 4:301. See also Bowman and Komoszewski, *Putting Jesus in His Place: The Case for the Deity of Christ*, 88-89.

[36] Ardel Caneday, "'Redeemed from the Curse of the Law' The Use of Deut. 21:22-23 in Gal. 3:13," *TrinJ* 10 (Fall 1989): 206-7; Louis Diana, "The Essential Elements of the Gospel Message in the Evangelistic Speeches in Acts" (M.A.B.S. thesis, Multnomah Graduate School of Ministry, 1992), 51; Torleif Elgvin, "The Messiah Who Was Cursed on the Tree," *Them* 22 (April 1997): 14-21; I. Howard Marshall, "The Resurrection in the Acts of the Apostles," in *Apostolic History and the Gospel* (Grand Rapids: Eerdmans, 1970), 104-5; Frank J. Matera, "Responsibility for the Death of Jesus According to the Acts of the Apostles," *JSNT* 39 (1990): 85-86; Leon Morris, *The Cross in the New Testament* (Grand Rapids: Eerdmans, 1965), 142-43; C. Marvin Pate, *The Reverse of the Curse: Paul, Wisdom, and the Law* (Tübingen: Mohr Siebeck, 2000), 150-51; John R. W. Stott, *The Cross of Christ* (Downers Grove, IL: InterVarsity Press, 1986), 34; Max Wilcox, "'Upon the Tree'—Deut 21:22-23 in the New Testament," *JBL* 96 (1977): 92-94.

is put to death, and you hang him on a tree, 23 "his body shall not remain overnight on the tree, but you shall surely bury him that day, so that you do not defile the land which the LORD your God is giving you as an inheritance; for he who is hanged is accursed of God." When it is recognized that Paul claims that the Jewish authorities fulfilled the Scriptures by *"condemning Him"* (13:27) even though He was innocent and *"they found no cause for death in Him"* (13:28), and yet He was accursed of God by dying on a *"tree"* (13:29), it becomes readily apparent that He died not for His own sins, but for ours.

Regarding the significance of Jesus dying on a "tree" and how this might initially have been an obstacle to 1st century Jews accepting Jesus as the Christ, one New Testament scholar explains:

> The greatest problem that faced Jews who believed in Jesus as God's Messiah was the declaration of Deut 21:23: *"Anyone who is hung on a tree is under God's curse."* The statement originally had reference to the exposure of a criminal executed for a capital offense, whose lifeless body was to be hung on a tree for public ridicule. But it came to be understood among Jews as referring also to the impalement or crucifixion of a living person on a pole or cross (with, of course, the pole or cross viewed as parts of a tree). Paul reflects the general Jewish repugnance of the idea of a crucified Messiah when he speaks in Gal 5:11 and 1 Cor 1:23 of the "scandal" of Christ having been put to death by crucifixion. The earliest believers in Jesus, however, seem to have resolved this problem of a crucified Messiah by viewing God's curse of Christ on the cross as his sharing in humanity's curse—that is, as an "interchange" wherein Christ participated in our life and bore God's judgment on sin in order that we might participate in his life and death . . . and thereby receive righteousness before God.[37]

It is not a coincidence that Paul later reminded the Galatians of this very truth when he wrote, *"Christ has redeemed us from the curse of the law, having become a curse for us, for it is written, "Cursed is everyone who hangs on a tree"* (Galatians 3:13).[38] After Acts 13, the Galatians later lost sight of Christ's work on their behalf. This is why Paul reproved them and reminded them of what he had initially preached to them, saying, *"O foolish Galatians! Who has bewitched you that you should not obey the truth, before whose eyes Jesus Christ was clearly portrayed among you as crucified?"* (Gal. 3:1). They had taken their eyes off of Jesus Christ's finished work on their behalf and fixed their gaze upon their own works; and by doing so, they had turned aside to another gospel. The substitutionary death of Jesus was an essen-

[37] Richard N. Longenecker, "Christological Materials in the Early Christian Communities," in *Contours of Christology in the New Testament,* ed. Richard N. Longenecker (Grand Rapids: Eerdmans, 2005), 49-50 (ellipsis added).

[38] Caneday, "'Redeemed from the Curse of the Law' The Use of Deut. 21:22-23 in Gal. 3:13," 185-209; Stott, *The Cross of Christ,* 34.

tial element of Paul's gospel to the Galatians. In Acts 13, the redemptive work of Christ's crucifixion, along with His resurrection, was the "work" (3x, Acts 13:41) that provided salvation (13:26), forgiveness of sins (13:38), and justification (13:39) to the Galatians. This was the "work" they had to initially "believe" so that they would not "perish" (13:41) but have "everlasting life" (13:46, 48).

Jesus Christ's Bodily Resurrection

In Acts 13, the resurrection of Christ from the dead is directly referred to no less than three times (13:30, 34, 37). In terms of sheer space, the resurrection of Christ is emphasized more than any other one topic in Paul's gospel. This is probably why Paul reminds the Galatians of this essential truth at the very beginning of his epistle to them by referring to Christ as the One who not only *"gave Himself for our sins"* (Gal. 1:4) but was *"raised . . . from the dead"* (Gal. 1:1). This was the One (Acts 13:38)—this risen, living "Savior" (13:23)—whom the Galatians were expected to "believe" in for their justification (13:39). The resurrection, along with Christ's substitutionary death, was the "work" they had to "believe" so as not to "perish" (13:41). The resurrection of Jesus Christ from the dead was unquestionably an essential element of Paul's gospel to the Galatians.

Jesus Christ's Work in Acts 13:41

At this point, Acts 13:41 should be examined carefully and individually due to the considerable weight it bears upon the whole crossless gospel controversy. If the threefold occurrence of the term "work" in verse 41 is in reference to the work of Jesus Christ's death and resurrection, then the crossless gospel position is felled by the swing of this solitary verse. What did the apostle Paul mean when he concluded his preaching with a warning to the Galatians not to "despise" and disbelieve the "work" done "in your days"? Was this a reference to the "work" of Christ's substitutionary death and bodily resurrection in the sense that theologians use the term when referring to the "Person and Work" of Christ? Or, is this a reference to some other work? If so, what other work could it be? Similarly, what does the term "perish" mean in this context? Is it referring to a temporal, physical destruction or to everlasting destruction? The theological stakes could not be higher for verse 41.

In examining this verse in its context, we should note first that Paul cites verse 41 from the "prophets" (v. 40). Based on the Greek text of verse 41, we know that Paul was providing a near-complete quotation of Habakkuk 1:5 (LXX). In its original context, Habakkuk 1:5 was not a reference to God's redemptive work of raising up a Savior for Israel but to His work of *"raising up the Chaldeans"* (Hab. 1:6) as the instruments of His judgment upon His wayward, chosen people in the land of Judah. God literally fulfilled this prophecy with the Babylonian invasions of Judah and Jerusalem in 609, 605, and 586 B.C. Since Habakkuk 1:5 was literally and historically fulfilled centuries before Paul quoted this passage to the Galatians, we know that Paul was not actually claiming a second literal fulfillment of this verse for his 1st century Galatian audience. He was simply drawing an analogy from Habakkuk 1:5,[39] that just as the generation of Jews in the 7th century B.C. should have believed the divine "work" prophesied by Habakkuk of God's impending physical judgment upon their nation, so this generation of 1st century Jews living in Galatia must believe the work God had done in their days by raising up Jesus as their Savior, lest they perish eternally. Thus both key terms in the passage, "work" and "perish," must be determined by the way *Paul* used them, not the way *Habakkuk* originally used them. It is a well-established fact of sound hermeneutics that New Testament writers and speakers sometimes cited the Old Testament only for the purpose of borrowing a spiritual principle or application while not simultaneously intending or claiming a direct fulfillment of the Old Testament passage (Acts 2:16; 15:15; Rom. 2:23-24).[40]

It is evident from the context of Acts 13:41 that Paul meant to use the word "perish" (*aphanizō*) in the sense of *eternal* judgment (John 3:16) rather than mere *temporal, physical* death. Advocates of the crossless gospel position may be inclined to see only physical judgment in the term "perish," following the same hermeneutical tack they take when interpreting Acts 2:38-40. There they understand Peter to be warning the Jews in Jerusalem against God's coming destruction of that city due to its continued unbelief and rejection of Christ. The crossless gospel view maintains that it was this particular generation of Jews living in "Palestine" that had crucified its Messiah and bore special culpability before God who also had the unique responsibility to be baptized in order to receive God's forgiveness and avoid His temporal judgment upon them.[41] Regardless of whether or not Peter had such a restricted, temporal, physical judgment in view in Acts 2:38-40, we know that such a judgment did occur roughly four decades after Peter's evangelism on the day of Pentecost. In A.D. 70, the Roman army, under General Titus, slaughtered the citizens of Judea and razed the Jewish temple, just as the Lord Jesus had predicted (Luke 19:41-44).

However, it would be an extreme reach to employ this interpretation for the term "perish" in Acts 13:41. There the audience was a mixed mul-

---

[39] Darrell L. Bock, *Acts*, BECNT (Grand Rapids: Baker Academic, 2007), 460; Everett F. Harrison, *Acts: The Expanding Church* (Chicago: Moody Press, 1975), 214.

[40] Charles H. Dyer, "Biblical Meaning of 'Fulfillment'," in *Issues in Dispensationalism*, gen. ed. Wesley R. Willis and John R. Master (Chicago: Moody Press, 1994), 50-72; Thomas D. Ice, "Dispensational Hermeneutics," in *Issues in Dispensationalism*, gen. ed. Wesley R. Willis and John R. Master (Chicago: Moody Press, 1994), 39-41; Roy B. Zuck, *Basic Bible Interpretation* (Wheaton, IL: Victor Books, 1991), 261.

[41] Zane C. Hodges, *The Gospel Under Seige: Faith and Works in Tension*, 2nd ed. (Dallas: Kerugma, 1992), 119, 125, 178-80; idem, *Harmony with God: A Fresh Look at Repentance* (Dallas: Redención Viva, 2001), 89-107; Robert N. Wilkin, *Confident in Christ* (Irving, TX: Grace Evangelical Society, 1999), 195-96.

titude of Jews and God-fearing Gentiles, living in Southern Galatia, far beyond the environs of Judea, who had no such connection to the crucifixion of Christ in Jerusalem.[42] In addition, we have no historical record of any temporal, physical divine judgment on the Galatian Jews who rejected Paul's gospel preaching. Nor did Christ in the Gospels ever predict any such judgment or "perishing" for Galatian unbelievers as He did for Jerusalem's own unbelieving citizens.[43]

Lexical considerations will not further the crossless cause for Acts 13:41 either. The word "perish" (*aphanizō*) is certainly not a technical term in the New Testament, having the same semantic sense every time it is used. The term occurs only five times in the entire New Testament (Matt. 6:16, 19-20; Acts 13:41; James 4:14), and though the term is unquestionably used in reference to physical ruin or the cessation of physical life in other contexts, this meaning is not required in Acts 13. The meaning of a word is properly determined by its contextual usage; and in Acts 13 *aphanizō* is clearly used of permanent, spiritual destruction. This is evidenced from the fact that *aphanizō* is bounded by other key terms for eternal salvation that affect its meaning in Acts 13:41. Immediately *before* verse 41, the subject is the "forgiveness of sins" (v. 38) and being "justified" before God (v. 39). Immediately *after* Acts 13:41, the subject matter is "everlasting life" (vv. 46, 48). Physical, temporal death or judgment is not even hinted at anywhere in the context of Acts 13:41.

Even if crossless advocates claim that a physical, temporal destruction is intended for verse 41 since "eternal life" isn't even spoken of until the second Sabbath's preaching, then this also presents an insuperable problem for their position. Why would Paul expend so much effort in Acts 13:16-41 preaching a message intended to save them physically while waiting an entire week until Acts 13:46-48 to proclaim the way to eternal life? Why would Paul be more concerned about their physical well-being than their eternal destiny? There appears to be no valid exegetical basis or logical reason for holding to a temporal, physical sense of *aphanizō* in Acts 13:41. Instead, the context dictates that a spiritual, eternal judgment is in view.[44]

---

[42] Matera, "Responsibility for the Death of Jesus," 86-87.

[43] For a fuller examination of Hodges's views on temporal-physical judgment, wrath, repentance, and baptism for the forgiveness of sins for "Palestinian" Jews, see chapter 16 on the meaning of "the Christ" in Acts 2.

[44] Even Zane Hodges has stated that the issue in Acts 13:16-41 is eternal rather than temporal/physical. He wrote, "It would strain all credulity to suggest that nowhere in the synagogue speech did Paul actually mention eternal life." Zane C. Hodges, *Did Paul Preach Eternal Life? Should We?* (Dallas: Kerugma, 2007), 15. Also, in his book, *Harmony with God,* Hodges specifically highlighted the contrast between the eternal judgment in view in Acts 13 and the temporal, physical judgment facing unrepentant, unbaptized "Palestinian" Jews elsewhere in Acts. He stated that Paul's gospel preaching to the "Gentiles" and "Jewish audience outside of Palestine" in "the synagogue at Antioch of Pisidia" was concerned with the forgiveness of sins and justification (Acts 13:38-39), which he interpreted to mean "Harmony with God and a full clearance before the bar of His justice—that is, fellowship with

In addition to the word "perish," the second key term to consider in verse 41 is the term "work." It occurs three times in the verse for emphasis. What kind of "work" is in view? Is this necessarily a reference to Christ's death and resurrection? For starters, all parties can agree that it is *God's* work being referenced here, since it is the Lord who is speaking in Paul's quotation of Habakkuk 1:5, and He refers to Himself in the first person singular coupled with the personal pronoun for emphasis. He says, "For *I* work a work in your days" (*hoti ergon ergazomai egō*). Crossless gospel advocates may attempt to interpret this as the divine work of either regeneration or justification, which at least has some contextual representation. However, upon closer examination, we see from the context that this interpretation will not suffice.

The divine "work" that is specifically referred to in verse 41 is that which is modified by the two phrases, *"in your days"* and *"though one declare it to you."* What unique, extraordinary work of God was done in the days of Paul's Galatian audience? This most naturally points to the death and resurrection of Christ, since God's work of justification (Acts 13:38-39) and regeneration (Acts 13:44-48) was not unique to that generation because these were commonly done by God in all previous dispensations (Gen. 15:6; Ps. 32:1; John 3:3).

Some interpreters view the "work" here more broadly, as being the "fulfillment" of "God's promises to the ancestors" by implementing His "mission to the Gentiles," which, they say, is the larger purpose of the passage and the entire goal of Paul's preaching in verses 17-41.[45] According to this view, the "work" cannot refer to Christ's resurrection since such a work is too narrow for the context since Acts 13 marks a pivotal turning point in the Book of Acts where Paul's ministry shifts to the Gentiles (13:42-48).[46] However, in the immediate context of verse 41, Paul is still addressing both the "sons of Abraham" and those "who fear God" (Acts 13:26). He does not turn to the Gentiles until the Jews fulfill, in verses 44-48, the very unbelief that he warned them about in verse 41.

While it is true that Paul's synagogue sermon is framed by the larger theme of "fulfillment" and God's "promises to the ancestors," to relate and restrict this fulfillment to the Gentile mission, rather than to Christ's resurrection, completely misses the emphasis of Paul's preaching in verses 23-39. In Acts 13:17-22, God is plainly the agent actively at work in the history of the nation of Israel. But the history recounted in verses 17-22 transpired over 1,000 years prior to Acts 13, which hardly qualifies this divine activity as the "work" done *"in your days"* (13:41). In verses 23-39, the sovereign God continues to be the active agent who fulfills His promise to Israel in several specific ways. First, God fulfills His promise by

---

Him and security from eternal judgment." Hodges, *Harmony with God*, 106.

[45] David A. deSilva, "Paul's Sermon in Antioch of Pisidia," *BSac* 151 (January 1994): 47-48.

[46] Ibid., 47.

"raising up for Israel a Savior—Jesus" (13:23). Second, it is through Christ's crucifixion (13:27-29) that God's prophetic plan is twice said to be "fulfilled" (13:27, 29). Though it is the unbelieving Israelites and Romans who carry out the deed of crucifixion, the early Christians possessed a divine perspective and so confess to God that it is ultimately "Your hand" (Acts 4:27-28) that wrought Christ's death (Isa. 53:10; Acts 2:23; 3:18). Third, God is active in fulfilling His promise by raising up Jesus from the dead (13:30-37). It is especially evident that God is active in the resurrection of Christ by virtue of the active voice being employed five times (13:30, 33-35, 37). While it is true that justification and forgiveness are now mediated through Christ (13:38-39) and that these are also a divine work, it is clear that the "work" referred to by Paul in Acts 13:41 was nothing less than the Savior's substitutionary death and bodily resurrection. This was the work that was uniquely done "in [their] days" and that had just been "declare[d]" to them by Paul. According to verse 41, Paul's audience had to "believe" (*pisteuō*) this "work" lest they perish.

How appropriate that the apostle Paul, like the apostle Peter before him (Acts 2:40), closes his evangelism with a sobering word of warning against unbelief. How unlike the anemic, placating "evangelism" of our post-modern era that is so self-occupied and unconcerned with the eternal destinies of human souls! Paul's preaching here fits the pattern of Scripture, where not only is the sole condition for eternal salvation presented positively in terms of *believing* (Acts 13:39, 48) but also negatively in terms of *not believing* (Acts 13:41, 45-46). This pattern in Acts 13 is characteristically Pauline (Rom. 1:5; 10:16-17; 16:26; 2 Thess. 1:8-10); and it is also the Johannine pattern (John 1:11-12; 3:16, 18, 36; 1 John 5:10-13). This is exactly what we should expect if the sole condition of believing "the gospel" is equivalent in its essentials to believing that Jesus is *"the Christ, the Son of God."* How wonderfully consistent and harmonious is the inspired Word of God!

Salvation, Forgiveness, Justification, and Eternal Life

In Paul's gospel presentation to the Galatians in Acts 13, we see that the provision of "salvation" flowing from Christ's person and work is also an essential element of the gospel. The provision of "salvation" is stated twice as having come to both Jews and Gentiles (13:26, 47). This is also implied by the very fact that Jesus is called the "Savior" (13:23). The word "salvation" (*sōtēria*) is appropriately used as the umbrella term in Paul's preaching, since it has a broad semantic range that encompasses the variety of ways in which God provides deliverance for mankind. The other soteriological terms employed in this passage include "forgiveness of sins" (13:38), being "justified" (2x, 13:39), and "everlasting"/"eternal" life (13:46, 48). These latter three terms or phrases should be understood as subsets of the larger, inclusive concept of "salvation." In Acts 13, it is *"the word of this salvation"* (v. 26) that is emphasized at the outset of Paul's preaching and

Jesus is introduced by the term, "Savior" (*sōtēr*), in verse 23, not as merely the "guarantor of eternal life" in the limited crossless gospel sense.

In Paul's evangelism, we certainly don't see the "focus" on *eternal life* in particular that is demanded by today's crossless theology. Zane Hodges's approach to evangelism was completely incongruent with the apostle Paul's approach here in Southern Galatia. Hodges wrote, *"Let me say this: All forms of the gospel that require greater content to faith in Christ than the Gospel of John requires, are flawed. Evangelism based on such premises will also be flawed, because we will be tempted to test professions of faith in terms of doctrines we think must be believed. Instead we should be focusing on whether an individual believes that Jesus has given him eternal life."*[47] Was eternal life the "focus" of Paul's gospel? Was it presented by Paul as an element of the *sine qua non* of saving faith, as the crossless position requires?[48] In Acts 13, eternal life comes *last* in Paul's order of presentation, and it wasn't even part of his original recorded gospel presentation the week before (13:23-43). Luke only records it being included the following Sabbath in round two of Paul's Galatian gospel preaching (13:44-48).

The first mention of *"everlasting life"* occurs on the lips of Paul only after the Jews had heard and rejected *"the things spoken by Paul"* (v. 45). In verse 46, we have our first usage of eternal life where Paul and Barnabas say to them, *"It was necessary that the word of God should be spoken to you first; but since you reject it, and judge yourselves unworthy of everlasting life, behold, we turn to the Gentiles."* This was Paul's concluding warning to the Galatians. This passage does not tell us that *"everlasting life"* was necessarily even part of *"the things spoken by Paul"* (v. 45) that constituted *"the Word of God"* (v. 44) in his evangelistic message *"on the next Sabbath"* (v. 44). Though the Galatians clearly heard about *"everlasting life,"* it was only at the *conclusion* of Paul's evangelism on the second Sabbath and only *after* they had already rejected the gospel (*"the Word of God"*) in verse 44. Though we might speculate that the reference to *"everlasting life"* in verse 46 was probably not the first and only time Paul mentioned this truth to the Galatians, the text simply doesn't require such a deduction.

The second and only other reference to eternal life is in verse 48, and it is simply Luke's own commentary as a narrator that *"as many as had been appointed to eternal life believed."* This is not the recorded speech of Paul as part of his saving "message of life." There is nothing in the text of Acts 13 indicating that Paul specifically preached "eternal life" as part of his good news message to the lost on either the first Sabbath or the second. To insist that he did is sheer assumption.

Based on these facts, we must ask, was Paul's evangelistic message on the first Sabbath somehow deficient because he only mentioned "sal-

---

[47] Hodges, "How to Lead People to Christ, Part 1," 8.

[48] Wilkin, "Justification by Faith Alone is an Essential Part of the Gospel," 12; idem, *Secure and Sure* (Irving, TX: Grace Evangelical Society, 2005), 74-75.

vation," "justify," and "forgiveness of sins"? Tragically, there are some in the Free Grace movement who hold to the crossless saving faith position who have taught that a lost person must specifically hear about "eternal life." If the evangelist only informs a lost soul about "forgiveness of sins" or "salvation," then that lost person is not yet regenerated. While that soul may be prepared and disposed through the preaching of Christ's person and work to believe the crossless gospel's *sine qua non* of saving faith known as "the message of life," according to this view, they are still not born again. Yet, such aberrant theological conclusions simply cannot be sustained from Acts 13 or the rest of Scripture.

It is also difficult to conceive how believing in Jesus for "eternal life" was the "focus," "core," or "climactic moment" of Paul's evangelism in Acts 13, as proponents of a crossless saving faith have claimed. Commenting on Paul's evangelism in the synagogue at Antioch of Pisidia in Acts 13, Hodges also declared:

> It would strain all credulity to suggest that nowhere in the synagogue speech did Paul actually mention eternal life. Salvation and eternal life are unmistakably linked in Acts 13:46-48, just as they are in 1 Timothy 1:15-16. Clearly, in Acts, we have a skillful author at work. His condensation of Paul's speech does not contain the crucial term "eternal life" precisely because he wishes to reserve this pivotal phrase for the climactic section in Acts 13:42-52.[49]

Is this not pure eisegesis and a classic case of the theological tail wagging the hermeneutical dog? It is *not* a "strain" of "all credulity" to suggest that Paul might have never used the phrase "eternal life" while presenting the gospel to his original Galatian synagogue audience. After all, the Spirit-inspired text never states what Hodges has demanded of the passage. But clearly Hodges knew what was theologically at stake for the crossless gospel's *sine qua non* if, in the longest recorded example of continuous, uninterrupted preaching in Acts,[50] the apostle Paul *never* utters such a "pivotal phrase." While the traditional Free Grace interpretation of the gospel can accept the *prima facie* reading of the text of Acts 13:16-41, the crossless view cannot. Their doctrine necessitates that Paul not only mentioned "eternal life" somewhere in his synagogue sermon but also that he made it his "focus."

It is for this reason that Hodges rather creatively insisted that the second Sabbath's preaching was the "climactic" moment of Acts 13, since there we finally find the "pivotal" phrase used in verses 46 and 48. Yet it

---

[49] Hodges, *Did Paul Preach Eternal Life?* 15.

[50] Paul's total recorded preaching in Acts 13:16-41 (26 verses) is roughly the same length as Peter's recorded words in Acts 2:14-36, 38-40 (26 verses). However, this includes the two interruptions to Peter's preaching recorded in Acts 2:37 and 2:40. Otherwise, Peter's continuous preaching runs from 2:14-36 (23 verses).

strikes the objective, unbiased reader as rather odd that, if Paul's second round of preaching was indeed the "climactic" moment of Acts 13, the Holy Spirit would take only 5 verses (13:44-48) to describe such a pivotal, momentous occasion—as opposed to 27 verses (13:16-43) for the previous Sabbath. It is also peculiar if verses 42-52 are "climactic" that we are never told in verses 44-45 what the actual content of Paul's preaching was on the second Sabbath as we are for the first Sabbath in Acts 13:16-41. It appears that verse 41, which is the concluding "grand finale" of the first Sabbath's preaching, is the "climactic" moment of Acts 13, whereas verses 44-48 function as the dénouement. Far from forming the "climactic" moment of Acts 13, verses 44-48 form a transitional section, furthering the narrative of Acts by providing an explanation as to how the gospel advanced among the Gentiles.

The fact remains that we simply cannot know with certainty whether Paul ever originally uttered the phrase "eternal life" during that first Galatian gospel presentation in Acts 13:23-41 since the Scriptures are silent on the matter. Therefore, to insist that Paul must have done so is a transparently desperate argument from silence. However, we can assert, based on what *is revealed* in Acts 13, that "eternal life" itself was hardly the "focus" of Paul's gospel in Acts 13. "Eternal life" is mentioned the same number of times in Acts 13 as "salvation" and being "justified." As this relates to the Epistle of Galatians, we see that "eternal life" is also not the "focus" of the epistle; but justification is. The various forms of the cognate word group, "justify" (*dikaioō*), "just" (*dikaios*), and "righteousness" (*dikaiosunē*), occur a total of 13 times (Gal. 2:16, 17, 21; 3:6, 8, 11, 21, 24; 5:4, 5). Conversely, "life" or "eternal life" occurs only twice (Gal. 3:21; 6:8). Based on these facts, it appears that Paul would have flunked Evangelism 101 in today's school of crossless theology due to his "flawed"[51] gospel presentation that didn't put the "focus" where it needed to be.

Salvation by Grace through Faith Alone

Besides Paul's gospel containing the essential elements of Christ's person and work, his saving message was also about salvation by grace through faith apart from works. There is even a reference specifically to *"the grace of God"* in Acts 13:43. It is true that this passage technically does not say "salvation is by grace." Nor is the phrase *"the grace of God"* in verse 43 uttered from the lips of Paul. Instead, it is Luke's own narration. Yet, there are at least two reasons why we may still correctly infer that Paul's saving message contained the truth of salvation by God's grace alone through faith alone in Christ alone.

First, after Paul presented the gospel in Acts 13:23-41, according to Luke he and Barnabas urged the Galatians *"to continue in the grace of God"*

[51] Hodges, "How to Lead People to Christ, Part 1," 8.

(13:43). If Paul did not previously preach about *"the grace of God"* in some respect, then how could he urge them *"to continue"* in it? He was not introducing an entirely new concept to them at this point. Even though there is no record in verses 16-41 that Paul ever uttered the word "grace" in his original gospel presentation, it is clear from the context that the essence of Paul's gospel is being summarized by Luke in verse 43. There, the expression *"the grace of God"* is used as a figure of speech known as synechdoche, where one part ("grace") stands for, or represents, the whole (the gospel).[52] This is why *"the gospel of Christ"* (Gal. 1:7) is synonymous with *"the gospel of the grace of God"* (Acts 20:24). Though the gospel is substantially about the person and work of Christ, the Savior's person and redemptive work are also the very essence, expression, and embodiment of God's amazing "grace" toward unworthy mankind.

Thus in Acts 13:43, when Luke recounts Paul and Barnabas urging the Galatians *"to continue in the grace of God,"* it means that they were pleading with the Galatians to continue being receptive towards the message of grace—the gospel of Christ. The initial receptivity of these Galatians towards the gospel is illustrated in the two surrounding verses, where it says that they *"begged that these words might be preached to them the next Sabbath"* (v. 42) and that *"on the next Sabbath almost the whole city came together to hear the word of God"* (v. 44). This is how the Galatians initially *"continue[d] in the grace of God"* (v. 43).

Secondly, we may correctly infer that the concept of God's "grace" was originally preached to the Galatians by virtue of the fact that salvation (13:26) and justification (13:39) are said to be based on Christ's "work" (13:41), rather than our works, which are the result of trying to keep "the law of Moses" (13:39). When people understand the principle that due to the sufficiency of Christ's work they do not have to work for their salvation (Gal. 2:21), they recognize that salvation can therefore only be by God's grace (Rom. 11:6). By Paul and Barnabas urging the Galatians *"to continue in the grace of God"* (13:43), they were summarizing their gospel as being a message about God's grace. It is no coincidence, therefore, that later in the Epistle to the Galatians, the grace of God becomes a major theme that Paul assumed his readers were already familiar with but had fallen away from (Gal. 1:3, 6, 15; 2:9, 21; 5:4; 6:18).

Lastly, with respect to "salvation by grace through faith alone" being an essential element of the gospel, it should be recognized that the *response* of faith alone is also included in Paul's gospel to the Galatians. In Acts 13, the condition of faith alone, or simply believing, is stated twice in Paul's speaking (13:39, 41) and once in Luke's narration (13:48). No other condition for salvation besides believing is mentioned or alluded to anywhere in the passage. In keeping with the harmony that has been observed thus far

---

52 E. W. Bullinger, *Figures of Speech Used in the Bible* (Grand Rapids: Baker Book House, 1960), 625-29.

between Acts 13 and the Epistle to the Galatians with respect to Christ's person and work, it is not surprising to observe the same concurrence for faith being the sole condition of salvation. In Galatians, the terms "faith" (*pistis*) or "believe" (*pisteuō*) are prominent as well, occurring 25 times.

Evangelical and Bible-believing Christians often refer to faith as the proper *"response to* the gospel." While it is certainly correct to say this, it must also be recognized that the faith-alone condition is itself an *element of* the gospel. A portion of Paul's Galatian audience both *heard* that salvation was by faith alone and responded by *believing* that truth. Therefore, to truly believe the gospel, one must believe that salvation cannot be merited but comes only through faith. When the Galatians later forsook the gospel of grace (Gal. 1:6-9) they did not explicitly deny Christ's deity, humanity, death for sin, or resurrection. They simply added one work (i.e., circumcision) to faith as the requirement for justification. By so doing, they embraced "a different gospel." This is also seen in Galatians 2:3-5, where Paul explained that *"false brethren"* (2:4) were compelling Gentile Christians in his day to be *"circumcised"* (2:3), and yet he resisted the addition of circumcision to faith alone in order *"that the truth **of the gospel** might continue with you"* (2:5). Adding only one extra condition to faith alone for salvation would have completely altered the gospel. Therefore, salvation by grace through faith alone should also be considered an essential element of the gospel.

Conclusions on the Gospel in Acts 13

From what we have observed thus far in Acts 13, we may confidently conclude that not only is the gospel a message of salvation by grace through faith alone, it is also a message that defines the One in whom the lost are to believe. Jesus Christ's person and work are essential in the one, definitive, unalterable gospel to the Galatians. He is set forth as the unique God-man who died in our place and rose again, through whom salvation (forgiveness of sins, justification, eternal life) is given on the basis of grace through faith alone in Him. This is the One who is set forth as the Object of faith for the lost. This is the content of saving faith that is found in the original gospel to the Galatians. In addition, we have observed that each essential element of the gospel from Acts 13 is repeated later in the Epistle of Galatians. In this respect, we can certainly agree with Jeremy Myers and other crossless gospel defenders that *"Paul tells us in Galatians what message he preached when he was in Galatia,"*[53] even though we must vehemently disagree with their conclusions regarding the correct content and location of that gospel. While the proponents of today's deityless, crossless, and resurrectionless "saving message" frequently query their traditional Free Grace brethren for

---

[53] Myers, "The Gospel is More Than 'Faith Alone in Christ Alone'," 44.

just one definitive passage in all of Scripture that contains every essential element that the lost must believe,[54] they conveniently ignore Paul's gospel to the Galatians in Acts 13.[55]

Potential Objections

At this point, we may anticipate a potential objection being raised by those of the crossless persuasion. Regarding the content of Paul's gospel in Acts 13:23-48, they might assert that there are other details about Christ included in Paul's preaching that are not counted among the "essential elements" of the gospel. For instance, in Paul's preaching, he declared that the Lord Jesus was a descendant of "David" (13:22-23), that He was buried "in a tomb" (13:29), and that He was "seen" by "witnesses" from "Galilee" following His resurrection (13:31). Why are these details not part of the *sine qua non* of saving faith? In answer to this question, it should be noted that, conspicuously, not one of these items is later cited in Galatians where Paul defends his original, definitive gospel.

When it comes to the "witnesses" to Christ's resurrection cited by Paul in Acts 13:31, they are said to be from "Galilee" and no doubt consisted of the original apostolic band (1 Cor. 15:5). In the Epistle to the Galatians, however, Paul nowhere mentions these witnesses. Instead, he refers only to his own *"revelation of Jesus Christ"* in Galatians 1:12, which apart from knowing the historical background of Paul's life recorded after Galatians in Acts 9, 22, 26, and 1 Corinthians 15:8, a person could not conclusively interpret as his encounter with the risen Christ on the Damascus road. While Paul *may have* included his own personal testimony as a witness to the risen Lord when he evangelized the Galatians in Antioch of Pisidia, it is never recorded anywhere in Acts 13 that he did. And to insist that he did so would be another gratuitous hermeneutical leap.

The same point can be raised regarding the Lord's burial. While Paul did mention in his preaching that Christ's body was *"laid in a tomb"* (Acts 13:29), His burial is never mentioned in his Epistle to the Galatians. Its absence is particularly notable in those passages dealing with the believer's co-crucifixion and identification with Christ (Gal. 2:20; 3:27-28; 5:24; 6:14-15) where we might expect Paul to be more inclined to mention co-burial (cf. Rom. 6:4; Col. 2:12).

---

[54] Hodges, "The Hydra's Other Head: Theological Legalism," 3; Wilkin, "Another Look at 1 Corinthians 15:3-11," 2; idem, "Scavenger Hunt Salvation without a List," *Grace in Focus* 23 (May/June 2008): 1, 4.

[55] This is not an exaggerated claim. I personally presented Acts 13 to one leading proponent of crossless saving faith in 2005 after he demanded just "one verse" or "one passage" that contained all the essentials of Christ's person and work in addition to justification by grace through faith alone. Acts 13 was immediately rejected without explanation at the time, and to my knowledge, it has yet to be explained by any advocate of crossless saving faith.

All of this has relevance as it relates to the content of saving faith and determining which elements constitute the saving gospel. There are a few extreme Free Grace advocates who, in their overreaction to the crossless gospel, have concluded wrongly that Christ's burial and post-resurrection appearances to Peter and the twelve (1 Cor. 15:5) are also required content for saving faith. They say that it is not enough that lost sinners believe that Jesus Christ is God-incarnate who died for all their sins and rose from the dead and that salvation is by grace through faith alone. According to them, one can still believe all of these truths and go straight to hell. Yet, to this imbalanced position, we must ask, does Paul's Epistle to the Galatians contain the saving gospel or doesn't it? Are we honestly to believe that a lost soul could actually read and believe every word of Galatians and yet slip into hell for lack of knowledge about Christ's burial and post-resurrection appearances to Peter and the twelve?![56] Such a conclusion is so palpably in error that it hardly requires refutation. It is enough to note that the additional elements of Christ's burial in a tomb, His post-resurrection appearances to the apostles, and His lineal descent from David, are never explicitly stated anywhere else in Scripture to be the required contents of saving faith as are Christ's deity, humanity, death for sin, resurrection, and salvation by grace through faith alone.

These extra details in Acts 13 are similar to the additional details in 1 Corinthians 15:3-8, which offer proofs of the gospel but are technically not the gospel. For example, in Acts 13, the mention of Christ's burial "in a tomb" (13:29) gives proof to the fact that He really did die. The fact that Christ was "seen" by many "witnesses" following His resurrection (13:31) provides evidence that He really did rise from the dead. The fact that Jesus was from David's "seed" (13:22-23) bolsters the case for His genuine humanity and for Him being the promised Christ, particularly from the Jewish covenantal perspective, since it was prophesied in the Old Testament that the Messiah would not only be truly human (Isa. 7:14-16; 9:6-7) but also a lineal descendant of David (Isa. 11:1, 10). Presenting these additional facts would have had a corroborating effect for those "men of Israel" (13:13, 16) present in the synagogue that Jesus was the fulfillment of Old Testament messianic expectation. Although the details of Christ's burial, post-resurrection appearances, and genetic descent are important and they served an extremely valuable role in Paul's evangelism in Antioch of Pisidia, they do not in themselves form the ground or basis for mankind's redemption from sin, nor are they explicitly stated to be elements of "the gospel" anywhere else in Scripture.

---

[56] The same point could be raised regarding the Epistle of Romans. The burial of Christ is referred to only one time in the entire epistle in Romans 6:4. And even this lone reference occurs in the Christian life section of the epistle in chapters 6-8, rather than the justification section in chapters 3-5. However, the post-resurrection appearances of Christ (cf. 1 Cor. 15:5-8) are not referred to *even once* in Romans. So, are we honestly expected to believe that neither Romans nor Galatians contains the saving gospel?

We must also consider the fact that in Paul's closing appeal to his hearers in Acts 13:41, the subject concerning which he warns his audience not to reject through disbelief is the "work" (3x) of Christ. Yet, Christ's being born of a certain lineage, buried, and then seen by men were not redemptive "works" done by Christ, though they were all true of Christ.

It is also noteworthy that in Paul's evangelism in Acts 13, the scriptural, prophetic "promise" (13:23) that God is said to have "fulfilled" applies only to the Savior's death (13:27-29a) and resurrection (13:32-33). As was explained earlier in this chapter, the "work" that God actively performed in verses 23-39 that "fulfilled" His sovereign plan was nothing less than the substitutionary death and bodily resurrection of His Son. This is in marked contrast to the two verses in Acts 13 dealing with the burial and appearances where, conspicuously, no divine work is associated with either the burial or appearances. Paul does not apply the modifying terminology of promise and fulfillment to his statements about the Lord's burial (13:29b) and post-resurrection appearances (13:31) as he does for Christ's death (13:27-29a) and resurrection (13:32-33). This fits the pattern of 1 Corinthians 15:3-8, where only the phrases *"Christ died for our sins"* and *"He rose again"* are said to be *"according to the Scriptures."* Not coincidentally, the same pattern appears elsewhere in the New Testament (Luke 24:44-46; Acts 26:22-23). For these reasons the burial and post-resurrection appearances are not considered to be part of God's "work" that Paul's audience had to "believe" lest they "perish" (13:41). We can conclude that each of these additional details is subservient to,[57] and provides corroborating evidence for, the essentials of the gospel, but they are not in themselves elements of the saving gospel.

One final observation from Acts 13 should be pointed out with respect to the meaning of the "gospel of Christ" (Gal. 1:7), originally preached to the Galatians. Noticeably absent from Paul's gospel in Acts 13 is even a single occurrence of the term "Christ" (*Christos*); whereas the name "Jesus" is mentioned twice (13:23, 33). Did Paul, therefore, not preach the "gospel of Christ" by failing to mention that Jesus was the "Christ"? God forbid! He did preach Jesus as "the Christ" simply by virtue of preaching the gospel! When Paul proclaimed Jesus to be God's Son, who became a man and died for both Jews and Gentiles, and rose from the dead to offer salvation by grace through faith, he was proclaiming Jesus to be none other than the biblical "Christ." These elements of the gospel are the defining characteristics of "the Christ" as He was promised in the Old Testament. For this very reason Paul could even claim that the Galatians originally heard *"the gospel of Christ"* (Gal. 1:7).

---

[57] Stanley E. Porter, "The Messiah in Luke and Acts: Forgiveness for the Captives," in *The Messiah in the Old and New Testaments*, ed. Stanley E. Porter (Grand Rapids: Eerdmans, 2007), 163-64.

The fact that Paul originally preached to them *"the gospel of Christ"* is again in perfect harmony with the declaration by John that these things *"are written that you may believe that Jesus is the Christ, the Son of God, and that believing you may have life in His name"* (John 20:31). Paul preached exactly the same gospel as John, a message of belief in Jesus as the Christ, the Son of God, resulting in eternal life.

The Cross in Paul's Galatian Gospel

Now that the contents of Paul's gospel to the Galatians have been carefully examined, the place of Christ's cross-work in the gospel deserves special consideration. Advocates of the new crossless gospel are claiming that Galatians actually proves that the cross is not an essential element of the gospel to unbelievers. For example, Bob Wilkin states:

> The reason we don't find justification by faith alone anywhere in 1 Cor 15:3-11 is because this was *sanctification* good news. In Galatians the situation is the opposite. There Paul repeatedly speaks of justification by faith apart from works. Only rarely does he even mention the cross, and then it is in sanctification contexts. That is because in Galatians, Paul is defending his evangelism message.[58]

Here is yet another blatant example of crossless proponents promoting a version of the gospel to unbelievers that eliminates the need to believe in the cross of Christ. While the advocates of this new, aberrant version of the Free Grace gospel decry the label "crossless" being applied to their "saving message," how can we avoid such a conclusion from the preceding statement? If, as Wilkin claims, the cross is "only rarely" mentioned in the letter of Galatians and then only "in sanctification contexts," with the rest of Galatians being Paul's defense of his "evangelism message" to unbelievers, isn't this saying that the cross is a non-essential component of Paul's "evangelism message"?

Today's crossless gospel advocates seem to be turning a blind eye toward the many references to the cross in Scripture, not only in the Gospel of John, but also now in Galatians. Is it really true that, in Paul's Epistle to the Galatians, *"only rarely does he even mention the cross"*?! Christ's work on the cross is declared once in every chapter of Galatians, as the verses below reveal. Far from "rarely" mentioning the cross, it seems that the Spirit of God deliberately wanted the cross of Christ to be *emphasized* in this epistle.

---

[58] Wilkin, "Justification by Faith Alone is an Essential Part of the Gospel," 13 (italics original).

Galatians 1:3-4, *"Grace to you and peace from God the Father and our Lord Jesus Christ, 4* ***who gave Himself for our sins****, that He might deliver us from this present evil age, according to the will of our God and Father"*

Galatians 2:20-21, *"****I have been crucified with Christ****; it is no longer I who live, but Christ lives in me; and the life which I now live in the flesh I live by faith in the Son of God, who loved me and gave Himself for me. 21 "I do not set aside the grace of God; for if righteousness comes through the law, then* ***Christ died*** *in vain."*

Galatians 3:1, *"O foolish Galatians! Who has bewitched you that you should not obey the truth, before whose eyes* ***Jesus Christ*** *was clearly portrayed among you as* ***crucified****?"*

Galatians 3:13-14, *"****Christ has redeemed us*** *from the curse of the law, having become a curse for us (for it is written, "Cursed is everyone* ***who hangs on a tree****"), 14 that the blessing of Abraham might come upon the Gentiles in Christ Jesus, that we might receive the promise of the Spirit through faith."*

Galatians 4:4-5, *"But when the fullness of the time had come, God sent forth His Son, born of a woman, born under the law, 5* ***to redeem*** *those who were under the law, that we might receive the adoption as sons."*

Galatians 5:11, *"And I, brethren, if I still preach circumcision, why do I still suffer persecution? Then the* ***offense of the cross*** *has ceased."*

Galatians 5:24, *"And those who are* ***Christ's have crucified*** *the flesh with its passions and desires."*

Galatians 6:12-14, *"As many as desire to make a good showing in the flesh, these would compel you to be circumcised, only that they may not suffer persecution for* ***the cross of Christ****. 13 For not even those who are circumcised keep the law, but they desire to have you circumcised that they may boast in your flesh. 14 But God forbid that I should boast except in* ***the cross of our Lord Jesus Christ****, by whom the world has been* ***crucified*** *to me, and I to the world."*

Furthermore, it is simply not true, as Wilkin claims, that Christ's cross-work is relegated to *"sanctification contexts."* While our identification with Christ's work on the cross is the basis for sanctification in the Christian life and Galatians reflects this marvelous, liberating truth (2:19-21; 5:24;

6:14), there are at least six crucifixion passages where the concepts of justification, redemption, or eternal salvation are specifically in view (1:4; 3:1; 3:13; 4:5; 5:11; 6:12).

The crossless gospel position is also very clear that Paul's message to unbelievers of justification by faith alone is the gospel being referred to in Galatians (Gal. 2:15-16). It is this gospel in Galatians, they say, that does not necessitate faith in Christ's substitutionary death and resurrection, since these are merely necessary as sanctification truths or as "the gospel for Christians." But does this conclusion fit with the facts that we observe in Galatians?

In Galatians 6:12, Paul writes, *"As many as desire to make a good showing in the flesh, these would compel you to be* ***circumcised****, only that they may not suffer persecution for the* ***cross of Christ****."* Then in Galatians 5:11, Paul writes, *"And I, brethren, if I still preach* ***circumcision****, why do I still suffer persecution? Then the* ***offense of the cross*** *has ceased."* It is apparent from these two passages that adding just one work to God's grace, namely circumcision, amounted to a denial of the sufficiency of Christ's work on the cross. The addition of circumcision to Christ's work was a denial of **the gospel** itself according to Galatians 2:3-5. There Paul writes, *"Yet not even Titus who was with me, being a Greek, was compelled to be* ***circumcised****. 4 And this occurred because of false brethren secretly brought in (who came in by stealth to spy out our liberty which we have in Christ Jesus, that they might bring us into bondage), 5 to whom we did not yield submission even for an hour, that* ***the truth of the gospel*** *might continue with you."* The apostle Paul resisted the addition of circumcision to the message of Christ's work on the cross because it would have changed *the gospel.*

Nor was this addition by the false teachers an assault merely upon the more expansive so-called "sanctification" gospel of Christ's death and resurrection, because after all, it is acknowledged that *"in Galatians, Paul is defending his evangelism message."*[59] This would also fit with the context of Galatians 2:5, where in 2:2 and 2:7-9 Paul referred to the gospel he preached to the Gentiles. Most naturally, this refers to the initial message he preached in Gentile cities, which would be the message of how they could be justified. Paul did not go around telling unbelievers how they could be sanctified as Christians when they were still on their way to hell! The only logical and consistent conclusion is that the gospel in Galatians is the message of Christ's work on the cross, not merely of justification by faith alone (Gal. 2:15-16).

Ironically, while the Galatians two thousand years ago lost sight of Christ's cross-work in their attempt to add works to the sole condition of faith, today's crossless gospel leaders have taken their eyes off the cross while seeking to prevent works being added to faith. In Galatians 3:1,

---

[59] Wilkin, "Justification by Faith Alone is an Essential Part of the Gospel," 13.

Paul reproves the legalistic Galatians not just for shifting from a gospel of justification by faith alone to a gospel of *justification by works* but he also reproves them for getting their eyes off the cross-work of Christ. He says, *"O foolish Galatians, who has bewitched you that you should not obey the truth, before whose eyes Jesus Christ was clearly portrayed among you as crucified?"*

How was Jesus Christ originally set forth to unbelieving sinners in Galatia when Paul came to town preaching the gospel? He wasn't just presented as the guarantor of eternal life, but as the Savior who was *"crucified."* In Galatians 3:1, the phrase *"was publicly portrayed"* is one word in Greek, *prographō*. This verb is in the aorist tense and indicative mood, indicating a *past* tense portrayal of Christ as One who stands crucified.[60] Paul is referring to the message he preached to these Galatians *in the past* while they were unbelievers. This was the same message referred to in Galatians 1:8-9. What message had they now taken their eyes off of? Grace? Justification through faith alone? No, not merely these things, but the work of Christ on the cross from which God's grace and justification flows!

This is why the entire section in Galatians 3:1-14 that deals so heavily with justification begins with a riveting rebuke to get their focus back on the cross that Paul initially preached to them (3:1). Though Galatians 3:1-14 contains no less than 10 occurrences of the words for "faith" (*pistis*) or "believe" (*pisteuō*) as the sole condition for justification, the entire section begins with a call to look upon Christ-crucified again as the Object of faith (3:1) and it closes with a reminder of Christ-accursed for us on Calvary's tree (3:13).

The message of Galatians is clear: there can be no justification by grace through faith alone without knowing and believing in the crucified, risen Christ. All of this corresponds perfectly with the record in Acts 13 of Paul's missionary evangelism in Southern Galatia. The message he first preached to the lost Galatians (Acts 13:23-43) was exactly the same message underscored in the Epistle of Galatians, a message that they were turning away from, a message that some in the Free Grace movement have also tragically abandoned in our day.

---

[60] The word for "crucified" in Galatians 3:1, *estaurōmenos*, is a perfect tense participle, indicating One who was crucified and remains the Crucified One. This is who Jesus is today and forever—Christ-crucified (Matt. 28:5; Mark 16:6; 1 Cor. 1:23; 2:2; Rev. 5:6, 12).

Chapter 11

What Is the Gospel to the Thessalonians & Timothy?

OVERVIEW

The Thessalonian and Pastoral Epistles provide confirming evidence that the gospel is a specific message about Christ's person and work that must be believed for eternal salvation. 2 Thessalonians declares that the gospel is necessary to believe so that people would not "perish" (2:10), "be condemned" (2:12), and "be punished with everlasting destruction" (1:9). 1 Thessalonians 4:14, 5:9, and Acts 17:1-5 reveal that the content of this gospel includes Christ's substitutionary death and bodily resurrection. According to 1 Thessalonians 4:14, belief in Christ's death and resurrection is assumed for all Christians, not just belief in Jesus' promise of eternal life. In addition, 1 Timothy 2:3-7 expresses the contents of saving faith because it sets forth the requisite knowledge for all mankind to believe and be saved. The use of the term "gospel" in 1 Timothy 1:11 is not teaching that the law or its righteous standards are part of the gospel but rather that these are in agreement with the gospel. Likewise, 2 Timothy 2:8 does not teach that Christ's Davidic lineage is an element of the gospel but that it is truth which is consistent with the gospel.

Paul's epistles to the Thessalonians and Timothy are perfectly consistent with the rest of Scripture as to the content of the gospel and the necessity of the lost to believe it. These epistles establish once again that Paul's gospel was not a broad and nebulous entity that entailed upwards of fifty different elements. Nor do these epistles indicate that such vast content was only necessary for Christians to believe for their sanctification. Rather, these inspired letters demonstrate that Paul's gospel was specific and consistent with respect to its content and that it was equivalent to the saving message—the *sine qua non* of saving faith. This is true no matter which segment of Paul's Christian life and ministry is analyzed, for he was faithful to the one, true gospel that the Lord Jesus Christ had entrusted to him by finishing the race that was set before him and keeping the faith to the very end (Acts 20:24; 2 Tim. 4:7). The great apostle to the Gentiles consistently preached only one saving message throughout his entire evangelistic career. This can be seen first in his earlier ministry and letters to the Thessalonians, which occur historically within a few years of his ministry to the Galatians. Paul's faithfulness to one unchanging gospel can also be seen from the end of his earthly course as he wrote to Timothy shortly before his martyrdom. We start with his earlier message to the Thessalonians.

The Gospel of Christ to the Thessalonians

2 Thessalonians 1:6-10

6 *since it is a righteous thing with God to repay with tribulation those who trouble you,*

7 *and to give you who are troubled rest with us when the Lord Jesus is revealed from heaven with His mighty angels,*

8 *in flaming fire taking vengeance on those who do not know God, and on those* ***who do not obey the gospel of our Lord Jesus Christ.***

9 *These shall be punished with* ***everlasting destruction*** *from the presence of the Lord and from the glory of His power,*

10 *when He comes, in that Day, to be glorified in His saints and to be admired among all those who* ***believe,*** *because our testimony among you was* ***believed.***

Acts 17:1-4

1 *Now when they had passed through Amphipolis and Apollonia, they came to* ***Thessalonica,*** *where there was a synagogue of the Jews.*

2 *Then Paul, as his custom was, went in to them, and for three Sabbaths reasoned with them from the Scriptures,*

3 *explaining and demonstrating that* ***the Christ had to suffer and rise again from the dead,*** *and saying, "****This Jesus*** *whom I preach to you is* ***the Christ.****"*
4 *And some of them were* ***persuaded;*** *and a great multitude of the devout Greeks, and not a few of the leading women, joined Paul and Silas.*

The Contents of the Gospel to the Thessalonians

In 2 Thessalonians 1:8, there is a very significant occurrence of the term "gospel" (*euanglion*) as it pertains to the contents of saving faith. Though the contents of Paul's gospel are not detailed in 2 Thessalonians, they are summarized briefly in Acts 17, which marks the historical occasion and infallible record of Paul's evangelism in the city of Thessalonica. According to Acts 17:1-4, Paul and Silas preached the gospel in Thessalonica for three weeks. The essence of their evangelistic message to the unregenerate in Thessalonica is contained in one verse, Acts 17:3. There it states that Jesus was presented as *"the Christ"* who *"had to suffer and rise again from the dead."* Scripture itself bears witness that this was Paul and Silas's "gospel" (2 Thess. 1:8) that *"was believed"* by the Thessalonians (2 Thess. 1:10) and that resulted in them escaping *"everlasting destruction"* (2 Thess. 1:9). The connection of 2 Thessalonians 1:6-10 with Acts 17:1-4 firmly establishes that the Thessalonians did not believe in a crossless, resurrectionless "Christ" or a promise-only "gospel" for their eternal salvation. According to Acts 17:1-4 the Thessalonians did not merely receive the name "Jesus" coupled with a promise of eternal life in that name. Instead, they believed in a very specific Jesus. They believed in *"This Jesus"* (17:3) who was called *"the Christ"* (17:3) and who was described by the essential defining characteristics of the biblical Christ, namely that He *"had to suffer and rise again from the dead"* (17:3). It is for this reason that Paul later wrote to the Thessalonian Christians and assumed that they all believed in Christ's death and resurrection (1 Thess. 4:14).

The Gospel for Eternal Salvation

To date, those espousing the G.E.S. position have yet to provide any commentary on 2 Thessalonians as it relates to their view of the gospel and the contents of saving faith. As a result, we can only speculate on how they might attempt to harmonize this passage with their doctrine. Since they maintain that the gospel is only necessary for Christians to believe for practical sanctification and not for the lost to believe for their justification, they could teach that this passage is describing God's judgment *upon Christians,* rather than the unsaved. But such an interpretation would be fraught with contextual and theological problems. More likely, but still highly problematic, is the interpretative route of denying that this passage is describing hell as the consequence for not believing the gospel. G.E.S. proponents may reason that this passage is only about God's *physical judgment upon unbelievers* at the end of the future, seven-year tribulation.

But there are several reasons why 2 Thessalonians 1 cannot be describing this type of physical judgment only. Though physical judgment and death will occur at Christ's second coming, the passage describes more than this. It speaks of *"everlasting (aiōnion) destruction"* (v. 8), which must entail more than permanent physical consequences. When Christ returns to judge unbelieving earth-dwellers at the end of the tribulation, immediately upon their physical execution they will be irrevocably consigned to a spiritual condemnation that lasts throughout eternity. Thus, the "temporal" judgment of Christ's second coming will coincide with the commencement of their "eternal destruction." At the moment of physical execution at the end of the tribulation, these unbelievers will suffer destruction in Hades (Luke 16:19-31), followed by the Lake of Fire after the millennium (Rev. 20:11-15). Though Christ will cause the termination of the physical lives of all unbelievers at His second coming to the earth, by so doing He will simultaneously seal their eternal fate.[1] Therefore, the meaning of *"everlasting destruction"* in 2 Thessalonians 1:8 cannot be restricted to temporal, physical judgment alone. To do so would be shortsighted and theologically-driven.[2]

It must be further clarified that the term for "destruction" (*olethros*) in 2 Thessalonians 1:8 does not prove that this is only a physical judgment. *Olethros* is used by Paul in only three other places (1 Cor. 5:5; 1 Thess. 5:3; 1 Tim. 6:9), and admittedly physical destruction is involved in each. However, it must also be noted that none of these instances involve the adjective "everlasting" (*aiōnion*) joined to the word "destruction" as in 2 Thessalonians 1:9. Furthermore, with respect to 2 Thessalonians 1, if *olethros* only refers to physical, temporal destruction, then why would Paul emphasize only the *temporal* and *physical* consequences for those who reject the gospel when the far greater consequence is an *everlasting, spiritual* destruction? There is clearly more than a temporal consequence involved in this passage for those who reject the gospel in unbelief.

The Gospel to Unbelievers

Advocates of a crossless gospel today may also claim that this passage is

---

[1] William V. Crockett, "Wrath That Endures Forever," *JETS* 34 (June 1991): 196.

[2] Annihilationists notoriously engage in theologically-driven exegesis of this passage by denying the meaning and force of the phrase, *"everlasting destruction."* They interpret the *"destruction"* to be momentary with only the results being *"everlasting."* In this view, *"everlasting destruction"* means permanent physical and spiritual extinction. Accordingly, the *"destruction"* entails a complete cessation of existence at a moment in time. It does not continue everlastingly in any sort of post-mortem consciousness with torment and suffering. See Edward W. Fudge, *The Fire That Consumes: The Biblical Case for Conditional Immortality*, rev. ed. (Carlisle, England: Paternoster Press, 1994), 151-56. Though I am not aware of any proponent of the G.E.S. gospel who advocates annihilationism, this would not be a viable interpretative option of 2 Thessalonians 1:8 for any Christian to take since it violates the clear teaching of Scripture in other passages (Matt. 10:28; 25:41; Mark 9:42-48; Luke 12:4-5; 16:19-31; Rev. 14:10-11; 20:10).

simply teaching that *believers* will suffer the eternal consequences of lost rewards by not holding fast to the gospel through unbelief, unfaithfulness, or apostasy. The context, however, is clearly contrasting believers with unbelievers—the saved versus the lost. It is contrasting those who *"believed"* the *"testimony"* (1:10) of Paul and Silas's *"gospel"* (1:8) when they originally came to Thessalonica (Acts 17:1-4) versus those who did *"not obey (peithō) the gospel"* (1:8). Acts 17:4 describes the response of those who believed the gospel by saying that they were *"persuaded"* (NKJV).[3] The Greek term for *"persuaded"* in Acts 17:4 (*peithō*) conveys the same meaning as the term for *"obey"* in 2 Thessalonians 1:8 (*hupakouō*) . This means that to be persuaded *"that Jesus is the Christ"* (John 20:31) is to obey the gospel. And the way that the lost obey the gospel is simply by believing it (2 Thess. 1:10; Rom. 10:16-17; 1 Peter 4:17-18). Obeying the gospel, therefore, is not a secondary issue. It is not just for Christians to believe. The consequence for not obeying the gospel is explicitly declared in this passage to be *"everlasting destruction"* (1:9).

According to the context of 2 Thessalonians 1, the contrast in verses 6-10 is not between two categories of believers. It is not between those who initially believed but didn't persevere versus those who believed and continued in the faith to the very end. Nor is the contrast between the spiritual believer and the carnal believer. The aorist participle and aorist indicative forms for the two occurrences of *pisteuō* ("believe") in 2 Thessalonians 1:10 confirm that the past faith of the Thessalonians is in view. It was due to their initial faith that they will escape *"everlasting destruction,"* not because of their on-going faithfulness.

The phrase, *"those who do not know (eidosin) God,"* in 2 Thessalonians 1:8 must also be clarified. Is this a description of a carnal believer or an unregenerate unbeliever? Biblically, it is possible for believers not to be abiding in fellowship with the Lord and not knowing Him as we should (John 14:7-9; 1 John 2:3-4). But according to Pauline usage, the concept of "knowing God" most often contrasts unbelievers (especially Gentile unbelievers) with those who are already believers in Christ (Acts 17:23; 1 Cor. 1:21; Gal. 4:8-9; Eph. 4:17-18; 1 Thess. 4:5). While Paul at times speaks in terms of the believer's experiential knowledge of God (1 Cor. 15:34; Phil. 3:10), there are simply no other parallel Pauline passages where the saved and lost are both spoken of in the same context and simultaneously described as those who do not know God. This is another indication that Paul is contrasting believers with unbelievers in 2 Thessalonians 1:8-10. Also, grammatically in 2 Thessalonians 1:8, the Greek word for "know" (*eidosin*) in 2 Thessalonians 1:8 is a perfect tense participle. Paul is not describing those who once knew God but have fallen away in their rela-

---

[3] The Majority Text in Acts 17:5 also uses the term *apeithō* to describe the opposite response of those who rejected the gospel. In contrast to Acts 17:4, verse 5 states that many were not persuaded (*apeithō*) that Jesus is the Christ, and thus they were disobedient and unbelieving with respect to the gospel. Paul has such people in mind in 2 Thess. 1:6-10.

tionship with Him. Rather, he is describing those who literally "have not known God" in the past and still do not know God in the present. In other words, they have *never known God;* and therefore, they have never been known by God (Matt. 7:23; Gal. 4:9).

Finally, when 2 Thessalonians 1:8-10 is compared to its parallel passage in 2 Thessalonians 2:8-14, it becomes clear that the manner in which the unsaved have not known God is specifically by not believing the gospel. 2 Thessalonians 2:8 describes the destruction of the Antichrist when the Lord returns to the earth. The reason that many will *"perish"* with him (2:10) is specifically because they *"did not receive the love of the truth, that they might be saved"* (2:10). Instead, they will *"believe the lie"* (2:11) and *"not believe the truth"* (2:12). This is in contrast to the Thessalonians who will be raptured before the day of the Lord because of their *"belief in the truth"* (2:13). When the Lord called them through Paul and Silas's *"gospel"* (2:14), they obeyed by believing its message about Christ's death and resurrection (Acts 17:3-4; 1 Thess. 4:14). The conclusion seems inescapable when comparing 2 Thessalonians chapters 1 and 2. These two chapters deal with the same subject in their respective contexts, namely the return of the Lord in judgment. Each passage gives the explicit reason for either escaping Christ's judgment or for receiving it, namely belief or unbelief in the gospel of Christ. We may conclude, therefore, based on a comparison of Acts 17:1-4 with 2 Thessalonians 1:6-10 and 2:8-14 that "the gospel" is God's "saving message" to the lost. It is not merely a message that is *sufficient* to lead a lost person to Christ; it is *necessary* to believe to escape *"everlasting destruction."*

1 Thessalonians 4:14-18

13 *But I do not want you to be ignorant, brethren, concerning those who have fallen asleep, lest you sorrow as others who have no hope.*
14 *For* ***if we believe that Jesus died and rose again****, even so God will bring with Him those who sleep in Jesus.*
15 *For this we say to you by the word of the Lord, that we who are alive and remain until the coming of the Lord will by no means precede those who are asleep.*
16 *For the Lord Himself will descend from heaven with a shout, with the voice of an archangel, and with the trumpet of God. And the dead in Christ will rise first.*
17 *Then we who are alive and remain shall be caught up together with them in the clouds to meet the Lord in the air. And thus we shall always be with the Lord.*
18 *Therefore comfort one another with these words.*

1 Thessalonians 4:14 is another significant passage that corroborates the previous conclusions about Paul's gospel to the Thessalonians. In this verse, Paul assumes that all of the Thessalonian Christians had believed in Christ's death and resurrection. Though this passage does not use the term

"gospel," it is still quite relevant in addressing the problem of the crossless gospel. Why does Paul assume that all of the Thessalonians to whom he is writing have already believed in Christ's death and resurrection? The answer appears obvious. These elements of the gospel are essential to believe in order *to become* a child of God. They are not just necessary to believe some time *subsequent* to the new birth as part of the Christian's sanctification and walk with the Lord.

The Historical Fact or Significance of Christ's Death?

Before examining 1 Thessalonians 4:14 in relation to its prophetic context, another potential objection related to the cross must be addressed. Some may object on the basis of the reference to Christ's death in 1 Thessalonians 4:14 that Paul's gospel to the Thessalonians only includes the historical fact of Christ's death but not its spiritual significance. Did Paul preach to the Thessalonians the substitutionary atonement of Christ's death? Did they understand it and believe it? Or, did they just believe in the fact of His death? In recent decades, E. P. Sanders and James D. G. Dunn have proposed a radical "new perspective" on the Pauline doctrine of justification. In the process, they have wrongly concluded that the Thessalonians merely believed in the historical fact of Christ's death without understanding its atoning accomplishment. But the Thessalonian epistles *do set forth* the spiritual significance of Christ's death.[4]

The language and grammar of the Greek text of 1 Thessalonians 4:14 strongly suggest that Christ accomplished a *substitutionary atonement* by His death. The simple fact of Christ's death and resurrection is plainly revealed in verse 14a, *"For if we believe that Jesus died and rose again."* But verse 14b also implies the significance of Christ's death when it states, *"even so God will bring with Him those who sleep in Jesus"* (NKJV). The prepositional phrase, *"in Jesus" (dia tou Iēsou)*, must be given careful consideration. Some expositors have viewed this as an indirect reference to martyrdom, but this is unlikely for two reasons. First, neither epistle positively affirms that any of the Thessalonian believers had been martyred,[5] though persecution was taking place (1 Thess. 2:14-15; 2 Thess. 1:4-7). Secondly, if "those who sleep in Jesus" refers to martyrs for Christ, then the prepositional phrase, *dia tou Iēsou*, would more likely contain *dia* with the accusative case ("those who sleep for Jesus" or "on account of Jesus"), rather than *dia* with the genitive.[6] The clause of verse 14b may be translated more literally,

---

[4] Seyoon Kim, *Paul and the New Perspective: Second Thoughts on the Origin of Paul's Gospel* (Grand Rapids: Eerdmans, 2002), 86-88; W. E. Vine, "1 Thessalonians," in *The Collected Writings of W. E. Vine* (Nashville: Thomas Nelson Publishers, 1996), 3:79.

[5] Ernest Best, *A Commentary on the First and Second Epistles to the Thessalonians* (New York: Harper & Row, 1972), 189; F. F. Bruce, *1 & 2 Thessalonians*, WBC (Waco, TX: Word Books, 1982), 98.

[6] D. Edmond Hiebert, *1 & 2 Thessalonians*, rev. ed. (Chicago: Moody Press, 1992), 207.

"even so God will bring with Him those who sleep through Jesus." The prepositional phrase, *dia tou Iēsou* ("through the Jesus"), indicates that "Jesus is the means by which God achieves man's salvation."[7] Specifically, this is achieved "through what Jesus has done."[8] The *dia* + genitive construction is a familiar one for Pauline expressions of Christ's redemptive work (Rom. 3:24; 5:1, 9-10, 19, etc.). Hiebert insightfully explains how *"through Jesus"* points to the redemptive work of Christ, stating:

> The more probable meaning is that through the atoning work of Jesus, what was stark death for men without hope of the resurrection has become simply sleep. This glorious truth was first demonstrated in the death of Stephen, the first Christian martyr (Acts 7:59-60). Through His death and resurrection, Jesus has disarmed death and removed its sting for believers. "Through the Jesus" points to an effect wrought by "the Jesus" mentioned in the first part of the verse; His death and resurrection have changed the nature of death.[9]

1 Thessalonians 5:9-10

9 *For God did not appoint us to wrath, but to obtain salvation through our Lord Jesus Christ,*

10 *who died for us, that whether we wake or sleep, we should live together with Him.*

The interpretation of Christ's death in 1 Thessalonians 4:14 should also be understood in connection with the nearby reference to His death in 1 Thessalonians 5:9-10.[10] Both 4:14 and 5:9-10 occur in contexts dealing with the reassurance and comfort of believers in light of the Lord's coming. That comfort is grounded in both instances on the finality of Christ's accomplishment for us at His first coming. It is evident from 1 Thessalonians 5:9-10 that the Thessalonians believed not only the historical fact that Christ died, but specifically that He *"died for us"* (5:10) in order to deliver us from God's *"wrath"* (5:9). The reason that believers know today that we will escape the wrath of the coming day of the Lord is specifically because Christ *"died for us"* (5:10). It is not because we are either awake or asleep in our spiritual condition at the time of His coming (1 Thess. 5:6-10). It is only the assurance and certainty of Christ's work on our behalf that can bring true *"comfort"* to all believers (1 Thess. 4:18; 5:11), not our inconsistent, fluctuating daily walk.

---

[7] Best, *A Commentary on the First and Second Epistles to the Thessalonians*, 188.

[8] Leon Morris, *The First and Second Epistles to the Thessalonians* (Grand Rapids: Eerdmans, 1959), 140.

[9] Hiebert, *1 & 2 Thessalonians*, 207-208. For others who draw the same conclusion, see David A. Hubbard, "1 Thessalonians," in *The Wycliffe Bible Commentary* (Chicago: Moody Press, 1962), 1355; Charles C. Ryrie, *First and Second Thessalonians* (Chicago: Moody Press, 1959), 63; John F. Walvoord, *The Thessalonian Epistles* (Findlay, OH: Dunham, 1955), 60-61.

[10] Raymond F. Collins, *Studies on the First Letter to the Thessalonians* (Leuven: Leuven University Press, 1984), 226.

It should be noted further that 1 Thessalonians 5:9 may be referring to salvation from God's entire wrath, not just His tribulation wrath. It is a false antithesis to claim, as some commentators do,[11] that since the context of this passage is the future tribulation then eternal wrath cannot be in view. Though the day of the Lord is indisputably the context for 5:9-10, and 1 Thessalonians 1:10 does promise that Christ will deliver believers specifically from *"the wrath to come"* (*tēs orgēs tēs erchomenēs*), Paul's argument here is broader and should not be missed. In 1 Thessalonians 5:9, he is reasoning from a wider point to a narrower point. He is arguing in the direction of the general to the specific. The greater truth is that believers in Christ have been delivered from all divine wrath due to the work of Christ and our position in Him; and consequently, these Thessalonian believers could be assured that they would escape the particular divine wrath of the coming tribulation.[12]

In both preceding references to God's wrath (1 Thess. 1:10; 2:16), the articular construction occurs. It is deliverance from *"the wrath"* that is coming. But this is not the construction in 1 Thessalonians 5:9, where believers are assured that *"God did not appoint us to wrath"* (*ouk etheto hēmas ho theos eis orgēn*). There is no article of previous reference (an anaphoric article) in verse 9 that points back to *"the wrath to come"* in 1:10. While tribulation-wrath is encompassed within the exemption promised in 5:9, the anarthrous *orgēn* refers to wrath in general and thus to a wider deliverance. Some Free Grace people may take exception to this conclusion, especially if they have followed Hodges's teaching that there is no eternal wrath of God and that even believers in Christ may still be subject to God's temporal wrath in this lifetime due to unconfessed sin and carnality. But it appears from the New Testament that all believers are shielded from the direct outpouring of God's wrath because of our position in Christ and His propitiatory work on our behalf (Rom. 5:9-10). It is the unsaved who are characteristically called *"children of wrath"* in this dispensation (Eph. 2:3; 5:6; Col. 3:6), not the saved.

This conclusion is consistent with 1 Thessalonians 5:9. There, Paul is assuring the Thessalonians that they will escape the *particular* coming wrath of God in the tribulation because God has not appointed us to wrath *in general*. Paul reasons that, if we as children of God are "in Christ" and therefore children of the day and of the light (1 Thess. 5:5), then we should not live like those who are still positionally *"in darkness"* (1 Thess. 5:4). It is the unsaved who are positionally *"in darkness"* and *"children of wrath."* Our condition should be consistent with our position in Christ (1 Thess. 5:6-8). But regardless, even if we do not walk as chil-

---

[11] Zane C. Hodges, "The Rapture in 1 Thessalonians 5:1-11," in *Walvoord: a Tribute*, ed. Donald K. Campbell (Chicago: Moody Press, 1982), 75.

[12] Mal Couch, *The Hope of Christ's Return: Premillennial Commentary on 1 & 2 Thessalonians* (Chattanooga, TN: AMG Publishers, 2001), 141.

dren of light, we are promised deliverance from God's wrath due to our position, not our condition. Paul's point is that if God has already placed believers into Christ positionally, and we are saved from His wrath by virtue of our position in Christ, then why should believers fret over the particular wrath that is coming in the tribulation? The consummation of our "salvation" is guaranteed, with no dropouts slipping into the coming tribulation, because God has appointed us to salvation rather than wrath (1 Thess. 5:9); and this salvation is guaranteed by Christ's death for us (1 Thess. 5:10).

The Prophetic Context of 1 Thessalonians 4:13-18

All of this relates to Paul's statement in 1 Thessalonians 4:14, *"For if we believe that Jesus died and rose again, even so God will bring with Him those who sleep in Jesus."* What significance did the commonly held belief in Christ's death and resurrection have in relation to the events surrounding Christ's coming at the rapture? And how is this relevant to the contents of saving faith? This passage demonstrates that the common denominator in the content of every Thessanlonian's faith was belief in the work that Christ accomplished at His first coming. The two pillars of Christ's death and resurrection became the basis for assurance and comfort regarding the reunion of living believers with deceased believers at Christ's coming in the air for His Church. But in order to see this conclusion, 1 Thessalonians 4:14 must be understood in light of its prophetic context.

During Paul's three weeks of ministry in Thessalonica (Acts 17:2), besides preaching the gospel, he taught the Thessalonian believers a great deal of prophetic truth that he expected them to retain. This included Christ's coming for them at the rapture (2 Thess. 2:1), the subsequent tribulation and day of the Lord (2 Thess. 2:2), along with many details related to the Antichrist and his certain demise at Christ's return in judgment (2 Thess. 2:3-9). With so much prophetic truth under their belts, Paul admonishes them later, saying, *"Do you not remember that when I was still with you I told you these things?"* (2 Thess. 2:5).

These Thessalonian Christians already knew that Christ would return for them at the rapture, which is why the truth of the rapture is assumed throughout the first letter (1 Thess. 1:10; 2:19; 3:13; 5:23). However, concerning the question of believers who died and whose bodies had fallen asleep before Christ came back at the rapture, the Thessalonians were still in the dark. Thus, Paul writes to them stating that he doesn't want them to remain ignorant on this point (4:13). Though these young believers had been taught much prophetic truth during Paul's three-week residence in Thessalonica, apparently at this very early juncture in Church history they had received no instruction regarding the relationship of deceased saints to living saints at the time of the rapture. They lived with such an eager expectation of Christ's imminent return that this had not previously been a consideration. But subsequent to Paul's departure from the city, some believers apparently died, or they were facing the prospect of death, possibly due to persecution (1 Thess. 1:6; 2:2, 14; 3:3-4; 2 Thess. 1:4-6). This was the setting that precipitated Paul's response in 1 Thessalonians 4:13-18, where he proceeds to instruct them with new divine revelation in verses 14-18. He instructs them with *"the word of the Lord"* (4:15) regarding the relation of deceased believers to Christ's coming and our gathering together to Him at the rapture.

It is important to observe from this passage that the question in the minds of the Thessalonian congregation was not whether deceased believers would be resurrected. That was a settled fact.[13] Rather, the problem at hand was a matter of the *timing* and *circumstances* of their reunion with departed saints. The emphasis of verses 14-18 is clearly upon the question of *when* deceased believers will be raptured or resurrected *in relation to living saints.* This is indicated by the bolded portions of these verses as follows:

14 *For if we believe that Jesus died and rose again, even so* ***God will bring with Him those who sleep in Jesus.***
15 *For this we say to you by the word of the Lord, that we who are alive and remain until the coming of the Lord* ***will by no means precede those who are asleep.***
16 *For the Lord Himself will descend from heaven with a shout, with the voice of an archangel, and with the trumpet of God. And* ***the dead in Christ will rise first.***
17 ***Then*** *we who are alive and remain shall be caught up* ***together with them*** *in the clouds to meet the Lord in the air. And thus we shall always be with the Lord.*
18 *Therefore comfort one another with these words.*

There is no question here as to whether departed fellow saints will be resurrected. All believers in Christ will follow the pattern set by the risen Lord. If He died and rose again, as 1 Thessalonians 4:14 states, then it is guaranteed that we will also be raised following our death. But as true and biblical as this is, it does not appear to be the problem addressed in 1 Thessalonians 4:13-18. Nowhere in this passage, or the two epistles, do we see the Thessalonians sorrowing over the prospect that their departed loved ones might not even be resurrected if they missed the rapture. Surely they were originally told by Paul that all believers will be raised. That is eschatology 101. It is inconceivable that Paul would fail to instruct them on so fundamental a doctrine as resurrection while teaching them about virtually every other minute detail of end-time events, including the rap-

---

[13] Charles A. Wanamaker, *The Epistles to the Thessalonians*, NIGTC (Grand Rapids: Eerdmans, 1990), 169.

ture, the tribulation, the day of the Lord, the apostasy, the Antichrist, the Lord's second coming in judgment, etc.

The Thessalonian problem evidently had nothing to do with whether or not departed saints would be resurrected. The question was *when*? When would the Thessalonians be resurrected in relationship to other saints who had preceded them in death? There appear to be two plausible, similar answers as to why they were sorrowing, both of which relate to the *timing* of the resurrection for deceased believers, not the *fact* of resurrection itself. First, since the Thessalonians had undoubtedly been taught that believers will reign with Christ in glory in the kingdom following His coming, they might have been concerned that those who died before the rapture would miss this glorious reign by being resurrected *after the kingdom*.[14] A variation of this view sees the possibility that the Thessalonians were concerned that their loved ones would not be raised until *after the tribulation*.[15] But in either case, it appears that the Thessalonians were grieved at least over the prospect of a prolonged interval before reunification could take place with their fellow saints who would ostensibly miss the rapture due to dying before this great event. It was for this reason that Paul teaches in 1 Thessalonians 4:13-18 that both living and deceased saints will *all* be resurrected and caught up together with Christ at the rapture.

Common Belief in 1 Thessalonians 4:14

So how does all of this relate to the contents of the Thessalonians' faith as expressed in 1 Thess. 4:14, *"For if we believe that Jesus died and rose again, even so God will bring with Him those who sleep in Jesus"*? Specifically, why does Paul reference the death and resurrection of Christ in connection with His coming for the Church? Was it merely to remind the Thessalonians that they and their departed fellow-believers would follow the same pattern as Christ, that though they may die they would certainly rise again? It is true that the pattern of Christ's glorious resurrection following His death, as stated in 1 Thessalonians 4:14, provides believers with the certainty of our own future resurrection (1 Cor. 15:20-23; 2 Cor. 4:14). But as true as this is, Paul did not write 1 Thessalonians 4:13-18 to reassure the Thessalonian congregation that deceased believers will definitely be resurrected. The fact of resurrection itself was not at issue. In verse 14, the mention of Christ's death and resurrection and even sleeping "through Jesus" underscore a more fundamental point.

The finished work of Christ's first coming, namely His death and resurrection, provided the most solid foundation on which to assure the Thessalonians that He is coming again for the entire church, including

---

[14] Hiebert, *1 & 2 Thessalonians*, 208; Ryrie, *First and Second Thessalonians*, 61.

[15] Walvoord, *The Thessalonian Epistles*, 59; idem., *The Rapture Question*, rev. ed. (Grand Rapids: Zondervan, 1979), 200-1.

"the dead in Christ" (1 Thess. 4:16). Since the Thessalonians had been well taught on the fact of Christ's coming at the rapture, Paul *could have* made the basis for the Thessalonians' hope the rapture itself. In which case, he would have said something along this line in verse 14, *"For if we believe that Christ will return for us, even so God will bring with Him those who sleep in Jesus."* But he doesn't say this. Instead, he bases their hope of reunion with departed saints on even more fundamental grounds than Christ's promised return. Paul is teaching in verse 14 that just as the events of Christ's first coming (His substitutionary death and resurrection) were certain and factual, and all of the Thessalonians placed their faith in this work (4:14a), therefore they could also believe that their departed loved ones in Christ will not be left out at the rapture, for *"if we believe that Jesus died and rose again, even so God will bring with Him those who sleep in Jesus"* (4:14b). Christ's death and resurrection not only secure our justification (Rom. 4:24-25) and form the basis for our practical sanctification (Rom. 6:3-5), these two great works even guarantee our future glorification and reunion with other believers at His coming (Rom. 5:9-10; Col. 3:1-4).

It is for this reason that in 1 Thessalonians 4:14 Paul assumes every Christian has believed the gospel truths of Christ's death and resurrection. Belief in the redemptive work of His death and resurrection forms the dividing line between the saved and the lost.[16] It is "the testimony of the church as to its essential belief."[17] Paul could have appealed to many other doctrinal truths about Christ besides His death and resurrection in an attempt to provide the Thessalonians with assurance of their reunification with deceased believers. But he didn't. It is worth noting that the key clause in verse 14 expressing the content of the Thessalonians' faith, *"if we believe that Jesus died and rose again,"* finds no other comparable doctrinal parallel in the New Testament. Nowhere else in the New Testament does it say, for instance, *"For if we believe that Christ was born of a virgin"* or *"For if we believe that Christ will come again"* or even *"For if we believe that Jesus healed the sick, cast out demons, and raised the dead."* The common thread in the faith of all Christians is assumed to be the finished work of Christ, not His virgin birth, miraculous healings, second coming, or even a crossless promise of eternal life.

Paul assumed that all the Thessalonians believed *"that Jesus died and rose again."* The conditional statement *"if we believe"* does not imply any degree of doubt,[18] since it is in the first class condition in Greek, which is the condition of assumed reality. 1 Thessalonians 4:14 is the *only* passage in the entire New Testament where the exact formulaic construction, *"if we believe that"* (*ei pisteuomen hoti*), is used.[19] This is a content clause,

[16] Wanamaker, *The Epistles to the Thessalonians*, 168.

[17] Best, *A Commentary on the First and Second Epistles to the Thessalonians*, 187.

[18] Morris, *The First and Second Epistles to the Thessalonians*, 139.

[19] Even similar constructions containing a *pisteuō* + *hoti* (*"believe that"*) content clause

expressing essential content that was believed by all the Thessalonians. This establishes once again that there is no discrepancy between believing in the person of Christ versus believing truths about Him, since all faith requires some minimal knowledge or content.[20]

Jesus Christ's death and resurrection are so fundamental to the Christian faith that these essential truths are assumed to be known and believed by every child of God. The only way this can be true is if everyone must believe in Christ's death and resurrection in order *to become* a child of God. The fact that Paul assumed every Thessalonian saint knew and believed in the work of Christ corresponds perfectly with the record of Acts 17:2-4, *"Then Paul, as his custom was, went in to them, and for three Sabbaths reasoned with them from the Scriptures, explaining and demonstrating that the Christ had to* ***suffer*** *and* ***rise again from the dead****, and saying, '****This Jesus*** *whom I preach to you is* ***the Christ****.' And some of them were* ***persuaded****."*

The Gospel of Christ to Timothy

<u>1 Timothy 2:1-7</u>

1 *Therefore I exhort first of all that supplications, prayers, intercessions, and giving of thanks be made for all men,*
2 *for kings and all who are in authority, that we may lead a quiet and peaceable life in all godliness and reverence.*
3 *For this is good and acceptable in the sight of God our Savior,*
4 *who desires all men to be saved and to come to the knowledge of the truth.*
5 *For there is one God and one Mediator between God and men, the Man Christ Jesus,*
6 *who gave Himself a ransom for all, to be testified in due time,*
7 *for which I was appointed a preacher and an apostle—I am speaking the truth in Christ and not lying—a teacher of the Gentiles in faith and truth.*

A Gospel Passage

1 Timothy 2:3-7 is one of the most decisive passages in the New Testament for determining the contents of saving faith in the present dispensation. It contains an explicit reference to the cross-work of Christ that is essential to know and believe to be saved. Even though 1 Timothy 2:1-7 does not contain either *euangelion* or *euangelizō*, it is still a "gospel" passage, as demonstrated by the following chart. This confirms the fact that the gospel itself

---

are rare. This construction occurs in John 8:24, *"if you do not believe that I am,"* which indicates that belief in Christ's deity is essential for eternal life. Similarly, the content clause of Rom. 10:9, expresses belief in Christ's Lordship/deity and His resurrection. Conspicuously, there are no *pisteuō* + *hoti* content clauses in the NT that require belief in any extra-gospel doctrine.

[20] Best, *A Commentary on the First and Second Epistles to the Thessalonians*, 187; Collins, *Studies on the First Letter to the Thessalonians*, 226.

is the content of saving faith. It also shows that the gospel is not a broad, non-soteriological message that is only necessary for the Christian's sanctification, as the current G.E.S. doctrine maintains. The fact that 1 Timothy 2:3-7 is a "gospel" passage can be readily observed from a comparison of verses 6-7 with 2 Timothy 1:10-11.

1 Timothy 2:6-7	2 Timothy 1:10-11
v. 6 *"**the testimony** in due time,* v. 7 *to which I was appointed (eis ho etethēn) a preacher (kērux), and an apostle (apostolos) — I am speaking the truth in Christ and not lying—a teacher (didaskalos) of the Gentiles in faith and truth."*	v. 10 *"brought life and immortality to light through **the gospel**,* v. 11 *to which I was appointed (eis ho etethēn) a preacher (kērux), an apostle (apostolos), and a teacher (didaskalos) of the Gentiles."*

It is evident that Paul was appointed to be exactly the same thing in these two passages—a preacher, apostle, and teacher of the Gentiles. But both passages also highlight the fact that Paul was entrusted with a saving message. In 1 Timothy 2:6, it is called "the testimony" (*to marturion*). This is technically a noun in the Greek text, rather than an infinitive, "to be testified," as some English versions imply (KJV, NKJV). This "testimony" in 1 Timothy 2:6 is parallel to the "gospel" in 2 Timothy 1:10.[21] Since both passages are referring to the gospel, and since the clause in 1 Timothy 2:6, *"the testimony in due time,"* is appositional to the content preceding it[22] in verse 5 about Christ being the only mediator through His ransom sacrifice, then this must mean that 1 Timothy 2:5-6 is also expressing the testimony of the gospel. Furthermore, since 1 Timothy 2:3-7 is clearly expressing the content and knowledge that all people must come to for salvation, this means that the gospel is also essential for salvation. The gospel and the cross are seen to be the "saving message" after all!

But what is the content of this message? In verse 4, this message is simply called *"the knowledge of the truth."* This truth is clarified in verses 5-6, *"For there is one God and one Mediator between God and men, the Man Christ Jesus, 6 who gave Himself a ransom for all—(lit.) the testimony in due time."*

---

[21] Some may wonder whether *"testimony"* and *"gospel"* are really parallel by questioning whether the prepositional phrase in 2 Timothy 1:11, *"to which I was appointed"* (*eis ho etethēn*) points back to *"life and immortality"* in verse 10 or to *"the gospel."* There is no question that *"the gospel"* is the referent. The neuter, singular relative pronoun in verse 11, *"which"* (*ho*), agrees in gender and number only with *"the gospel"* (*tou euangeliou*) as its antecedent, rather than the feminine, singular nouns *"life"* (*zōēn*) and *"immortality"* (*aphtharsian*).

[22] A. T. Robertson, *Word Pictures in the New Testament* (Grand Rapids: Baker Book House, n.d.), 4:568.

The truth that all men must come to in order to be saved includes the fact that there is one God (John 17:3). While monotheism in itself is true and necessary for saving faith, it is not sufficient for salvation without the particular knowledge of God's Son. This passage spells out the need to know specifically about the *"one Mediator between God and men, the Man Christ Jesus"* (1 Tim. 2:5). This crucial clause contains several necessary truths. It demonstrates that lost people must understand that salvation is Godward. Salvation is not merely a gift given to all who believe in an undefined person named "Jesus" who can guarantee us an unending utopian existence without any recognition of God. In addition, the fact that Christ is called a "Mediator" affirms the need for mediation or reconciliation between two parties. The two parties in the passage are *"God and men."* Man cannot be saved without an acknowledgment of his separation from God. While "sin" is not explicitly referred to in the passage, it is implied by the mention of both Christ's mediatorship and His "ransom"/ redemption payment.

This passage also specifies particular truths about Jesus Christ that must be known and believed to be saved. Christ's humanity is explicitly declared by the statement, *"the Man Christ Jesus"* (*anthrōpos Christos Iēsous*). This is an anarthrous construction in the Greek text emphasizing the nature or character of Christ as a "man" (*anthrōpos*). In addition, the reference to Him as the sole "Mediator" (*mesitēs*) between God and men strongly infers His deity, as the ideal mediator is one who is capable of representing both parties to each other in the reconciliation process.[23] Being God, Christ can represent God to man; while being human, He can represent man to God. He is the unique, theanthropic Person. Thus, Scripture is unequivocal that Jesus Christ's deity (John 8:24) and humanity (John 6:51-54; 8:28) are both essential to know about, and believe, in order to receive eternal life.

Besides the person of Christ, 1 Timothy 2:1-7 also sets forth His mediating work. Specifically, it states in verse 6 that He *"gave Himself a ransom for all"* (*dous heauton antilutron huper pantōn*). The word for "gave" (*didōmi*) is a common one in the New Testament when referring to the sacrificial death of Christ (Matt. 20:28; Mark 10:45; John 3:16; 6:51; Eph. 5:25; Titus 2:14). The verse also speaks of a personal sacrifice by death, since it does not say that Christ gave "of Himself" or "from Himself" but rather that He gave "Himself." Christ did not give a portion of Himself with some in reserve. Rather, He gave His whole self. To give up one's self in this manner is an expression for sacrifice to the point of dying. This is underscored

[23] The term *mesitēs* is used only 6x in the NT (Gal. 3:19, 20; 1 Tim. 2:5; Heb. 8:6; 9:15; 12:24). In Gal. 3:19, it refers to Moses as the mediator of God's Law to Israel, who though only a man was "as God" when speaking to Aaron and the Israelites (Ex. 4:16; 20:18-21). Thus, he is regarded by some to be a type of Christ. See *The Scofield Study Bible, New King James Version*, ed. C. I. Scofield, E. Schuyler English, et al. (Oxford: Oxford University Press, 2002), 87.

further in verse 6 by the term describing Christ's sacrifice, "ransom" (*antilutron*). This term indicates "a price paid in exchange."[24] The root word, *lutron*, and its verb form, *lutroō*, are used elsewhere to speak of the paying of a price by a sinless, sacrificial substitute (1 Peter 1:18-19), and even to speak of redemption from *"every lawless deed"* (Titus 2:14). Even though sin is not explicitly referenced in 1 Timothy 2:6, clearly, the purpose for Christ paying the redemption price by giving (*didōmi*) Himself in death was *for our sins* (Gal. 1:4; Heb. 9:15). This is in keeping with the Romans 6:23 principle that the wages of sin is death. Christ paid these wages as our redemption/ransom price. The substitutionary nature of this payment for sin via death is heavily emphasized in the passage through the use of two important prepositions. The word *huper* is used to speak of substitution, *"for (huper) all,"* along with the preposition *anti* that is prefixed to the noun *lutron*. In some contexts in the New Testament, the preposition *huper* has a broader sense, "for our sakes" or "for our benefit," rather than the substitutionary sense, "in our place" or "instead of." However, in 1 Timothy 2:6, *huper* plainly conveys a substitutionary sacrifice since it is joined with the word for redemption (*lutron*) and the preposition *anti*, which is the more strictly substitutionary of the two prepositions.[25] Finally, the extent of this redemption/ransom payment is underscored in 1 Timothy 2:1-6 by the use of the word "all" (*pantōn, pantas*) three times in the passage (1 Tim. 2:1, 4, 6). God instructs believers to pray for "all men" (2:1) because He desires "all men" to know the truth and be saved (2:4) and because Christ has paid the redemption price "for all" (2:6).

The person and work of Christ proclaimed in this passage uniquely qualify Him to be the Mediator between God and men. As a man, Christ could fulfill the substitutionary (*huper, anti*) requirement of dying to pay the price for humanity's sin. As God-incarnate, His sacrifice could be universal in extent (*pantōn, pantas*) and truly redemptive in effect (*antilutron*). Since no other human being is God, and no other member of the Trinity is a human being, and no other human being's death has ever provided the rest of mankind with redemption, Jesus Christ alone is qualified to be the mediator between God and men (2:5). This is an essential element in the truth that God desires all men to know in order to be saved (2:4). A person must comprehend and believe that Jesus Christ is the only way to the Father (John 10:9; 14:6; Acts 4:12). A person cannot be saved who thinks that Jesus is just one of many effective alternative ways to salvation, as a

---

[24] Leon Morris, *The Apostolic Preaching of the Cross* (Grand Rapids: Eerdmans, 1956), 48n2.

[25] Rupert E. Davies, "Christ in Our Place—The Contribution of the Prepositions," *TB* 21 (1970): 90; A. T. Robertson, *A Grammar of the Greek New Testament in the Light of Historical Research* (Nashville: Broadman Press, 1934), 573, 631; Richard C. Trench, *Synonyms of the New Testament* (Grand Rapids: Eerdmans, 1973), 291; Bruce K. Waltke, "The Theological Significations of 'Αντί and 'Υπέρ in the New Testament" (Th.D. dissertation, Dallas Theological Seminary, 1958), 2:403.

Hindu might be inclined to believe. Rather, people must come to an exclusive knowledge and belief that Jesus Christ is the "one Mediator" between them and God by virtue of His redemption payment.

The "Saving Message"

Some who embrace the crossless gospel may reject these conclusions by claiming that the content of 1 Timothy 2:5-6 does not necessarily represent the saving *"knowledge of the truth"* spoken of in verse 4. It would be grammatically unwarranted, however, to disconnect verses 5-6 from verses 1-4. After stating in verse 4 that God *"desires all men be saved and to come to the knowledge of the truth,"* verse 5 begins with the explanatory conjunction "for" (*gar*), saying, *"For (gar) there is one God and one Mediator. . ."* It is important to recognize that while *gar* does serve as an explanatory conjunction here, and not merely as a simple connective, it actually goes beyond just marking out an explanation. It constrains the clause that follows it in verse 5 with the clause that precedes it in verse 4; and it thereby strengthens the assertion made in the previous clause of verse 4 about being saved and coming to the knowledge of the truth. Levinsohn writes regarding this explanatory, strengthening, and constraining function of the conjunction *gar*:

> Background material introduced by γάρ provides explanations or expositions of the previous assertion (see Winer 1882:566-67, Robertson n.d.: 1190, Harbeck 1970:12). The presence of γάρ constrains the material that it introduces to be interpreted as *strengthening* some aspect of the previous assertion, rather than as distinctive information.[26]

Levinsohn goes on to state that while this use is "relatively uncommon in the narrative sections of the Gospels and Acts," in non-narrative portions of the New Testament, *gar* is "used very frequently to strengthen some aspect of a previous assertion."[27] This usage has been demonstrated to hold true particularly in the Pastoral Epistles,[28] with 1 Timothy 2:5 being a "prime example" of *gar* strengthening a previous assertion and not merely serving as a simple connective.[29] This means that the content of verses 5-6 cannot be viewed as distinct and disconnected from the assertion made in verse 4 about the knowledge of the truth. The saving truth that all mankind must come to know is explained and even exemplified in verses 5-6.

Proponents of the promise-only gospel may also object that, while 1 Timothy 2:4-6 requires knowledge of Christ's person and work *"to be saved"* (v. 4), the salvation in view must be a broader temporal or sanctifi-

---

[26] Stephen H. Levinsohn, *Discourse Features of New Testament Greek: A Coursebook on the Information Structure of New Testament Greek*, 2nd ed. (Dallas: SIL International, 2000), 91.

[27] Ibid.

[28] Michael D. Makidon, "The Strengthening Constraint of *Gar* in 1 and 2 Timothy," (Th.M. thesis, Dallas Theological Seminary, 2003).

[29] Ibid., 66-67.

cation-salvation. But, this explanation will not suffice.[30] The term "save" (*sōzō*) is used in this epistle for both eternal life (1 Tim. 1:15-16) and practical sanctification (1 Tim. 2:15; 4:16). Therefore, word usage within this epistle is inconclusive. Instead, the immediate context of 2:4 must make the determination; and it points decisively to the salvation in mind being for the lost, or the unregenerate, rather than for the one who is already a believer. This is not a salvation for those who already have the truth and now just need to grow in it as Christians. It is specifically for those who must "*come to* the knowledge of the truth." In addition, the designation, "all men," points to those who are lost as the ones needing the salvation described in 1 Timothy 2:4. Just as Paul instructs Timothy to pray for "all men" in verse 1, including kings and governors, he continues without interruption in the context to speak of this same group of "all men" in verses 4 and 6. It is this group whom God desires "to be saved" (v. 4) and for whom Christ died (v. 6).

If crossless proponents were to argue that in verses 1-6 Paul is speaking of all different *kinds* of believers who need salvation (i.e., "king" believers, "governor" believers, etc.), this would be following the same bankrupt rationale that five-point Calvinists employ for this passage in seeking to defend their doctrine of limited atonement.[31] Whether it is the "all men" of this passage or the universal language of "the world" in other New Testament passages, these Calvinists consistently deny the plain meaning of Scripture that Christ paid the redemption price for the sins of the elect and the non-elect. He died for all men without exception, not just all men without distinction. He didn't merely die for all kinds of elect men, from elect kings to elect peasants; He died "for all." He is "*the Savior of all men, especially of those who believe*" (1 Tim. 4:10).

Which Theory of the Atonement?

Those who promote a crossless content of saving faith sometimes raise another objection based on the existence of varying atonement theories

---

[30] Yet, not even Zane Hodges took it only temporally. He viewed it as deliverance from "hell." Commenting on his view of temporal deliverance in 2 Peter 3:9, Hodges wrote, "God's wish, therefore, is that all should come to repentance. This statement should not be read as though it indicated God's desire that all men should be saved from hell, though that desire is expressed elsewhere in Scripture (1 Tim. 2:4-5; John 3:16-17; 2 Cor. 5:19-20). What is suggested here, however, is that if men would repent, the judgment of the Day of the Lord could be averted." Zane C. Hodges, "God Wishes None Should Perish 2 Peter 3:9," *Grace in Focus* 24 (July/August 2009): 4.

[31] Loraine Boettner, *The Reformed Doctrine of Predestination* (Phillipsburg, NJ: Presbyterian & Reformed Publishing, 1932), 295; Arthur C. Custance, *The Sovereignty of Grace* (Phillipsburg, NJ: Presbyterian & Reformed Publishing, 1979), 162; Curt Daniel, *The History and Theology of Calvinism* (Dallas: Scholarly Reprints, 1993), 375; George Smeaton, *The Doctrine of the Atonement According to the Apostles* (Peabody, MA: Hendrickson Publishers, 1988), 325; James R. White, *The Potter's Freedom: A Defense of the Reformation and a Rebuttal of Norman Geisler's Chosen But Free* (Amityville, NY: Calvary Press Publishing, 2000), 141-45.

throughout Church history. In essence, they argue that if 8-10 different, conflicting theories have existed for the atonement, then requiring the lost to believe in a substitutionary, satisfactory view of Christ's death is completely unreasonable and even legalistically adds an extra, man-made requirement for eternal life. But this objection is seen to be a ruse once it is realized that several of these theories have been held only in obscurity by very few individuals. The majority of these theories have never been prevalent within professing Christendom. In addition, some theories do not even require the death of Christ for sin *in any sense*, and so they can be immediately discounted as unbiblical and untenable. These would include Irenaeus's recapitulation theory, Peter Abelard's moral influence theory, Albert Schweitzer's accident theory, and the example view of Faustus Socinus and his modern day Unitarian followers. Even regarding the governmental theory of Grotius, Miley, and a segment of Arminians, it can be said that "According to this view God forgives sin without a payment for sin."[32] Under this theory, Christ's death merely makes it possible for man to redeem himself through moral reformation. Erickson summarizes the governmental atonement theory: "Christ's suffering, then, was not a vicarious bearing of our punishment, but a demonstration of God's hatred of sin, a demonstration intended to induce in us a horror of sin. As we turn from sin, we can be forgiven. Thus, even in the absence of punishment, justice and morality are maintained."[33] This leaves only three views worthy of serious consideration.

Sometimes appeal is made to the early popularity of the ransom-to-Satan theory. This view, which was introduced by Origen, became the majority opinion in the first millennium of professing Christendom. It holds that Christ's death was a ransom paid to Satan since he held humanity in bondage.[34] It is often assumed that any notion of the atonement as being substitutionary, or satisfactory toward God, did not even exist until Anselm in the 11th century. If this was the case, and if belief in Christ's cross-work is truly essential for eternal life, then how were people saved for 10 centuries? But this is a false depiction of Church history and its theology. While the ransom-to-Satan view did hold sway before Anselm, this does not mean that the substitutionary, satisfactory view was unknown or inaccessible to seekers until the 11th century. The recent book, *Pierced for Our Transgressions*, contains a section with evidence from the 2nd-7th centu-

---

[32] Paul Enns, *The Moody Handbook of Theology* (Chicago: Moody Press, 1989), 321.

[33] Millard J. Erickson, *Christian Theology*, 1 vol. edit. (Grand Rapids: Baker Book House, 1983-85), 790. This is not Erickson's own view but his description of the view of others.

[34] Origen was the first to openly deny that payment for sin was made to God, claiming instead that it was made to "the Evil One" (Origen, *Commentary on Matthew*, 16:8). Other patristic writers seemed to mix elements of atonement theories. Augustine, for example, clearly believed in a penal substitution view whereby Christ bore the "penalty" that God's righteousness demanded for our sins; and only as a consequence of this satisfaction is mankind freed from Satan's claims.

ries demonstrating that the satisfaction and penal substitution views were held long before Anselm in A.D. 1100.[35] In this book, the authors write, "The myth of the late development of penal substitution has persisted for quite long enough. It is time to lay it to rest for good."[36] Likewise, in a less than favorable review of the same book, Anglican bishop N. T. Wright agrees with the conclusion of the book on this historical point. He writes that the common notion that penal substitution "was invented by Anselm and developed by Calvin" is "an old canard."[37]

While it is true that Scripture never explicitly states to whom the ransom was paid, whether toward God, Satan, or sin,[38] the implication from Scripture is plain that God's righteousness and justice require satisfaction for sin. Satan does not possess these attributes and therefore needs no satisfaction. In Scripture, sin is always a Godward offense (Gen. 2:17-18; 3:8; Ps. 51:4; Isa. 59:2; Luke 18:13-14; Rom. 3:23). Even the law was introduced to pique personal conviction and awareness of sin *"before God"* (Rom. 3:19). While bondage to Satan is certainly a consequence of the fall, satisfaction towards God's justice is always the solution to the fall. Thus, even 1 Timothy 2:4-6 indicates that the issue of salvation and atonement is a matter between "God and men" (v. 5), not between God and Satan. Christ did not come to be a mediator between "Satan and men." The knowledge that God desires all men to come to for salvation (v. 4) entails a recognition that Christ's substitutionary death paid for our sins (*antilutron*, v. 6) and thereby made satisfaction and mediation toward God (v. 5). Charles Ryrie aptly concludes regarding the various atonement theories:

> While there may be truth in views that do not include penal substitution, it is important to remember that such truth, if there be some, cannot save eternally. Only the substitutionary death of Christ can provide that which God's justice demands and thereby become the basis for the gift of eternal life to those who believe.[39]

Ultimately, Scripture—not history or tradition—must be the arbiter of truth when it comes to determining which doctrine of the atonement is correct and necessary to believe for eternal life. As one studies the various atonement theories, it becomes apparent that few even attempt to establish their doctrine from explicit statements of Scripture. Most are built upon logic

---

[35] Steve Jeffery, Michael Ovey, and Andrew Sach, *Pierced for Our Transgressions: Rediscovering the Glory of Penal Substitution* (Wheaton, IL: Crossway Books, 2007), 161-83.

[36] Ibid., 163-64.

[37] N. T. Wright, "The Cross and the Caricatures: a response to Robert Jenson, Jeffrey John, and a new volume entitled *Pierced for Our Transgressions*." http://www.fulcrum-anglican.org.uk/news/2007/20070423wright.cfm?doc= 205 (accessed October 18, 2008).

[38] Charles C. Ryrie, *Basic Theology* (Wheaton, IL: Victor Books, 1986), 308.

[39] Ibid., 309.

and human reasoning with occasional inferences drawn from the Bible.[40] The assumption by some Free Grace people that belief in the cross-work of Christ must not be necessary for salvation since the biblical view of the atonement was unknown for 1,000 years is seen to be historically inaccurate and naïve. It is also terribly inconsistent with the biblical truth of *Sola Scriptura* (2 Tim. 3:15-17).

In addition, besides atonement theories, crossless gospel proponents could level the same accusation against the longstanding Free Grace requirement to believe that justification is by grace through faith alone. If the predominant view among professing Christians prior to the Reformation was that salvation was by faith + works, then couldn't we also make the claim today that belief in justification *sola fide* really isn't necessary for eternal life either? Of course, this would be a clear contradiction of God's Word (Rom. 4:5; Eph. 2:8-9). The current controversy over the contents of saving faith ultimately boils down to a personal willingness to submit in faith (Rom. 10:3) to the divine revelation of the Bible, not to our own human reasoning, philosophical speculation, religious tradition, or even Church history.

<u>1 Timothy 1:6-11</u>

6 *from which some, having strayed, have turned aside to idle talk,*
7 *desiring to be teachers of the law, understanding neither what they say nor the things which they affirm.*
8 *But we know that the law is good if one uses it lawfully,*
9 *knowing this: that the law is not made for a righteous person, but for the lawless and insubordinate, for the ungodly and for sinners, for the unholy and profane, for murderers of fathers and murderers of mothers, for manslayers,*
10 *for fornicators, for sodomites, for kidnappers, for liars, for perjurers, and if there is any other thing that is contrary to sound doctrine,*
11 *according to* ***the glorious gospel of the blessed God*** *which was committed to my trust*

1 Timothy 1:11 is another New Testament passage containing the term "gospel" that some proponents of the G.E.S. doctrine may use to support their broad, non-soteriological concept of "the gospel." In verse 11, some people may initially interpret it to be teaching that all the items identified in verses 8-10, including *"the law"* and *"sound doctrine,"* are part of the "gospel" that is committed to Paul's trust.[41] However, the phrase in verse 11, *"according to the glorious gospel,"* is not teaching that the law or

---

[40] Erickson, *Christian Theology*, 792.

[41] This is how some scholars (wrongly) interpret this passage. For example, one liberal scholar from the school of higher criticism concludes: "According to 1 Tim. 1:11 the Gospel contains teaching on the right use of the Law" (Gerhard Friedrich, "*εὐαγγελίζομαί, εὐαγγέλιον, προευαγγελίζομαί, εὐαγγελιστής*," *TDNT*, 2:733).

even sound doctrines themselves are part of the gospel. Those who would like to broaden the gospel so as to de-emphasize the necessity of the lost believing in the person and work of Christ will find no grounds for doing so in 1 Timothy 1:11.

There are two common, possible interpretations of verse 11, both of which are biblically accurate, but neither of which allows the gospel to be expanded as crossless gospel teachers would like. First, the phrase, *"according to the glorious gospel,"* may simply refer to what immediately precedes it in verse 10, namely *"sound doctrine."* By claiming that sound doctrine is *"according to the gospel,"* Paul would be saying that the gospel is the standard or benchmark against which all doctrine is measured. The gospel, therefore, is the foundation of all sound doctrine. This is one acceptable interpretation held many biblical expositors and commentators;[42] and it certainly harmonizes well with the rest of Scripture.

Secondly, the phrase, *"according to the gospel,"* could also be referring to the entire sentence in verses 8-11. This view is also held by many commentators.[43] According to this view, the teaching about the law in verses 8-10 is consistent with, or in accordance with, the gospel. Following this interpretation, 1 Timothy 1:8-11 is teaching that the law can only expose people to be unrighteous and sinners before God and that the works of the law cannot make anyone righteous. This aspect of sound doctrine is *"according to the glorious gospel"* since it is consistent with the gospel truth of justification by grace through faith apart from works (Acts 13:38-39; Rom. 2:12-16; Gal. 2:16). It is in agreement with, or in-line with, the gospel since people cannot believe the "good news" of salvation in Christ until they have accepted the "bad news" about themselves. The bad news revealed by the righteousness of the law in 1 Timothy 1:8-10 is that all are sinners separated from a holy God and cannot save themselves by their own righteousness, law-keeping, or good works. According to this interpretation, the "bad news" of man's sinful, lost condition in 1 Timothy 1:8-10 frames the *context* for the gospel, but it is not part of the gospel. With this interpretation, the "glorious gospel" referred to 1 Timothy 1:11 would still be the person and work of Christ and salvation by grace through faith alone.

---

[42] Gordon D. Fee, *1 and 2 Timothy, Titus*, NIBC (Peabody, MA: Hendrickson, 1984), 47; Robert G. Gromacki, *Stand True to the Charge: An Exposition of 1 Timothy* (Grand Rapids: Baker Book House, 1982), 30; George W. Knight, *The Pastoral Epistles: A Commentary on the Greek Text*, NIGTC (Grand Rapids: Eerdmans, 1992), 89-90; A. Duane Liftin, "1 Timothy," in BKC, ed. John F. Walvoord and Roy B. Zuck (Wheaton, IL: Victor Books, 1983), 2:732; William D. Mounce, *Pastoral Epistles*, WBC (Nashville, TN: Thomas Nelson, 2000), 42.

[43] Henry Alford, *The Greek Testament* (Chicago: Moody Press, 1958), 3:307; J. N. D. Kelly, *The Pastoral Epistles*, BNTC (Peabody, MA: Hendrickson, 1960), 51; Homer A. Kent, *The Pastoral Epistles*, rev. ed. (Winona Lake, IN: BMH Books, 1982), 84-85; Robert L. Thomas, *Exegetical Digest of First Timothy* (n.p.: Self-published, 1985), 27-28; W. E. Vine, "1 Timothy," in *The Collected Writings of W. E. Vine* (Nashville: Thomas Nelson, 1996), 3:148; Newport J. D. White, "First and Second Epistles to Timothy and the Epistle to Titus," in *The Expositor's Greek Testament*, ed. Robertson Nicoll (Grand Rapids: Eerdmans, reprinted 1990), 4:96.

This second interpretation of 1 Timothy 1:11 harmonizes well with all the other Pauline passages where the terms "according to" (*kata*) and "gospel" (*euangelion*) occur together (Rom. 2:16; 11:28; 16:25; 2 Tim. 2:8).

2 Timothy 2:8

8 *Remember that Jesus Christ, of the seed of David, was raised from the dead according to my gospel,*

Sometimes in an effort to support a crossless content of saving faith, 2 Timothy 2:8 is cited as evidence that Scripture has a very broad meaning for the word "gospel." Syntactically, it is true that the prepositional phrase, "according to my gospel," modifies the phrase immediately preceding it in the Greek text, "of the seed of David." It is assumed by some, therefore, that Christ's being a "physical descendant of David" is part of the "Content of the Gospel."[44] Proponents of the G.E.S. gospel reason that if Christ's Davidic lineage is truly an element of the gospel, and the gospel is necessary to believe for eternal life as traditional Free Grace people claim, then why don't we preach Davidic lineage as also being necessary? To omit it from the contents of saving faith is purely arbitrary, they claim. But this line of reasoning is based on a misinterpretation of yet another passage containing the word "gospel." To interpret 2 Timothy 2:8 accurately, the meaning of the phrase *"according to my gospel"* must be considered first.

"According to My Gospel"

What is the precise meaning of the prepositional phrase, *"according to my gospel"* (*kata to euangelion mou*)? Should this phrase be interpreted to mean, "this is my gospel" (NIV) or "such is my gospel" (NET)? Unfortunately, the dynamic equivalency method used for translating some English Bibles results in an overly interpretative and inaccurate rendering of this verse. The preposition *kata* ("according to") does not express equivalency (e.g., "this is," "such is"). Rather, it should be understood as meaning simply, "in accordance with," or "consistent with," or "in line with." This means that Jesus' Davidic lineage is in harmony or agreement with the gospel; but it is technically not part of the gospel.

To see this, it will be helpful to consider parallel Pauline usage. In the entire New Testament, the preposition *kata* is used with *euangelion* only 5x and only in Paul's writings (Rom. 2:16; 11:28; 16:25; 1 Tim. 1:11; 2 Tim. 2:8). One of these passages has been covered already (1 Tim. 1:11) and two are addressed in the next chapter (Rom. 2:16; 16:25). But none of these *kata* + *euangelion* constructions indicate that the gospel has a broad content that goes beyond the "saving message." In 1 Timothy 1:11, the gospel does not include the law, as we have seen, but it is consistent or harmonious with

[44] Jeremy D. Myers, "The Gospel Is More Than 'Faith Alone in Christ Alone,'" *JOTGES* 19 (Autumn 2006): 53-54, 56.

the law. In Romans 2:16, the good news of the gospel is not the bad news of final judgment but is harmonious or consistent with this fact, with the gospel even being the standard that is used for divine judgment (cf. 2 Thess. 1:8-10). In Romans 16:25, the gospel does not include the truth of the Christian's establishment in the faith, rather the gospel produces or results in sanctification if the Christian holds fast to it by faith.

Romans 11:28 is quite instructive for demonstrating that the phrase *"according to my gospel"* in 2 Timothy 2:8 does not mean "this is my gospel." In Romans 11:28, Paul writes regarding the unbelieving Israelites of his day, *"Concerning (kata) the gospel (to euangelion) they are enemies for your sake, but concerning (kata) the election they are beloved for the sake of the fathers."* This verse could be translated, *"According to the gospel they are enemies for your sake, but according to the election they are beloved for the sake of the fathers."* But interpreting the "according to" (*kata*) statements in this verse as expressions of equivalency ("this is," "such is") results in an absurd conclusion. It would mean that the content of the gospel actually includes the fact that the Jews are enemies for our sake since this is "according to the gospel." It is impossible to envision Paul traveling about, city to city, visiting synagogue after synagogue, and preaching the "good news" to Jews and Gentiles that the Jews are "enemies" of Christians! Perish the thought! Obviously, in Romans 11:28 the *kata* + *euangelion* construction simply means, "with respect to the gospel" or "in relation to the gospel." When the entire New Testament and Pauline Epistles are scoured, there are no *kata* + *euangelion* passages that set forth the contents of the gospel itself. Rather each of these five constructions shows how Paul's evangel is related to other extra-gospel content. It is more consistent with Pauline usage, therefore, to interpret Paul in 2 Timothy 2:8 to be stating that Christ's Davidic lineage is in agreement, or harmonious, with his gospel but not that it is part of the gospel.

Rewards and Kingdom Context

In addition to parallel Pauline usage, the context of 2 Timothy 2:8 supports this interpretation. In the immediate context of verse 8, Paul seeks to exhort Timothy to keep his eyes upon the victorious Christ who is destined to reign one day (2 Tim. 2:12) and who will reward faithful believers (2 Tim. 2:3-7, 12). The larger context of the epistle demonstrates that suffering is commensurate with preaching the gospel (2 Tim. 1:8-12; 2:9-10; 3:10-12; 4:5, 17-18). So how would Timothy be encouraged to press forward in the face of such certain opposition? The thought of Christ's risen and royal status would propel him. These two truths are found in 2 Timothy 2:8.

The main thought of verse 8 is reflected in the only verb in the verse, "remember" (*mnēmoneue*), which is a present tense, active voice, imperative mood command. Timothy is commanded to remember, or keep in mind, two important truths about Jesus Christ. First, he is to remember

Christ as having been raised from the dead. The perfect tense of *egeirō* for "raised" emphasizes that Jesus Christ stands perpetually risen from the dead. Second, Timothy is implored to keep in mind the Lord's lineage, specifically that He is a descendant of king David. Both Christological truths served Paul's larger point in the context. They were a reminder that amidst Timothy's suffering for the gospel, he is to remember the One who overcame suffering and death and who is certain to reign as king in His approaching kingdom (2 Tim. 4:1). In the setting of 2 Timothy, Paul himself was keeping his eyes upon this One, as his own suffering for the gospel was nearing its completion and his martyrdom was imminent and certain. The faithful apostle could almost see the lights of glory as he looked forward to his reward and coming reign with the Son of David (2 Tim. 4:6-8).

Knowing this context helps us to understand why Paul is emphasizing particular truths about the person of Jesus Christ in 2 Timothy 2:8 rather than providing a definition of the gospel. The truths of Christ's risen status, along with His Davidic lineage, provided special encouragement to Timothy. Some scholars think that Paul includes these two truths to represent two stages in the life of Christ, similar to Romans 1:3-4, where His earthly stage as the Son of David is followed by His post-crucifixion stage as the glorified Lord.[45] However, it is more likely that Paul is making a different point in 2 Timothy 2:8 since Christ's resurrection precedes His Davidic lineage in the Greek text of this passage. This is opposite from the order in Romans 1:3-4. It is better to interpret the two truths of Christ's resurrection and Davidic descent as representing only the Lord's post-crucifixion stage, which began with resurrection in anticipation of His millennial reign. In this respect, the phrase, *"from the seed of David"* is hardly "irrelevant in the context."[46] The two truths of Christ's resurrection and Davidic lineage were undoubtedly selected by Paul in order to demonstrate two means by which the Lord's sovereign, messianic status was vindicated.[47] Being of the seed of David meant that Jesus Christ was the fulfillment of God's covenant promises to David which will include a throne and kingdom that *"shall be established forever"* (2 Sam. 7:16). Christ's resurrection proved that He is truly the sovereign Lord who will possess His royal kingdom.[48] By keeping these truths in mind about the Christ he served, Timothy could endure the sufferings associated with the gospel just as Paul did. For this reason, 2 Timothy 2:8 should not be disassociated

[45] Martin Dibelius and Hans Conzelmann, *The Pastoral Epistles: A Commentary on the Pastoral Epistles*, Hermeneia (Philadelphia: Fortress Press, 1972), 108; A. T. Hanson, *The Pastoral Epistles*, New Century Bible Commentary (Grand Rapids: Eerdmans, 1982), 130-31.

[46] Kelly, *The Pastoral Epistles*, 177.

[47] I. Howard Marshall, *A Critical and Exegetical Commentary on the Pastoral Epistles*, ICC (Edinburgh: T & T Clark, 1999), 734-35.

[48] Walter Lock, *A Critical and Exegetical Commentary on the Pastoral Epistles*, ICC (New York: Charles Scribner's Sons, 1924), 95.

from 2 Timothy 2:11-13,[49] where the subject clearly involves rewards and co-reigning with Christ.[50] It is in this context that Paul adjoins, *"according to my gospel,"* to the phrase, *"out of the seed of David."* Just as rewards and co-regency with Christ are in accordance with the gospel, so also Christ's Davidic lineage is a truth that accords with the gospel, but it is technically not an element of the gospel.

Christ's Birth in Bethlehem and "the Gospel"

Besides 2 Timothy 2:8, some proponents of a broad, non-soteriological "gospel" point to Luke 2:10 for support. Myers, for instance, views the "Content of the Gospel" in Luke 2:10 as "Jesus [being] born in Bethlehem."[51] Neff also says, "Luke 2:10-11 could be used to support a position that His birthplace of Bethlehem is part of the gospel."[52] But what does Luke 2:10 actually teach? Does it really say that Christ's birth in Bethlehem is part of "the gospel"? It should be carefully observed what the angel says in this verse. He states, *"for behold, I bring you good tidings"* (*idou gar euangelizomai*). The Greek text uses the verb, *euangelizomai,* to describe the angel's activity. The angel literally says that he is "announcing good news" to the shepherds. There is no noun in the verse with the article (*to euangelion*) to indicate that the angel is technically proclaiming "the gospel." Crossless gospel proponents make the same erroneous assumption about "the gospel" in passages that simply describe "good news" being proclaimed (*euangelizō*) in previous dispensations (Gal. 3:8; Heb. 4:2).[53]

This announcement of the Savior's birth in Bethlehem, the city of David, should not be equated with "the gospel" of our salvation. Instead of the good news in Luke 2:10 contributing to one conglomeration called "the gospel," or even being part of the specific saving message, it is better to view this good news as an entirely distinct usage of "gospel" that is unique to this historical occasion.[54] In this respect, it is like the gospel of the kingdom (Matt. 4:23), or the everlasting gospel (Rev. 14:6), or the good news of the Thessalonians' faith and love (1 Thess. 3:6). Luke 2:10 is also similar to the use of the verb *euangelizō* in Luke 1:19 where the

---

[49] Gordon D. Fee, *Pauline Christology: An Exegetical-Theological Study* (Peabody, MA: Hendrickson, 2007), 453-54.

[50] Brad McCoy, "Secure Yet Scrutinized 2 Timothy 2:11-13," *JOTGES* 1 (Autumn 1988): 24.

[51] Myers, "The Gospel Is More Than 'Faith Alone in Christ Alone,'" 53 (brackets added).

[52] Ken Neff, "What Is the Free Grace Gospel?" *Grace in Focus* 24 (March/April 2009): 3.

[53] Sydney D. Dyer, "The Salvation of Believing Israelites Prior to the Incarnation of Christ," *JOTGES* 14 (Spring 2001): 45-46 (though Dyer does not advocate the G.E.S. gospel, Dyer's article is included by the editor, Bob Wilkin, to support the G.E.S. position). In addition, Myers writes, "Galatians 3:8 also includes in the gospel the fact that in Abraham, all people will be blessed (cf. Gen 12:1-3)." Myers, "The Gospel Is More Than 'Faith Alone in Christ Alone,'" 45n24.

[54] J. B. Hixson, *Getting the Gospel Wrong: The Evangelical Crisis No One Is Talking About* (n.p.: Xulon Press, 2008), 79.

angel Gabriel announces the birth of John the Baptist to Zacharias. John's birth was truly good news. Christ's birth in Luke 2:10 was even better news. But these separate historical episodes and uses of *euangelizō* are not pieces of one larger New Testament message called "the gospel." Nor are they elements of the particular soul-saving message for today known as "the gospel of the Christ." This conclusion is confirmed by the fact that, throughout the rest of the New Testament, Christ's birth in the city of David is *never preached* to the lost as part of the contents of saving faith.

The Seed of David and the Contents of Saving Faith

As important as Christ's Davidic descendancy is, there are at least four scriptural reasons why it is not an element of the gospel but is rather a supporting truth that accords with the gospel. First, when every reference to David is examined within the Book of Acts (Acts 1:16; 2:25, 29, 34; 4:25; 7:45; 13:22, 34, 36; 15:16), a striking pattern emerges. Christ's connection to David is only proclaimed in the presence of Jewish audiences. Christ's descent from David is not an essential feature of evangelism to the Gentiles. Though Paul in Acts 13 does proclaim the Davidic lineage of Christ, it should be kept in mind that he is in a Jewish synagogue (Acts 13:14-16), which happens to be attended by God-fearing Gentiles who likely possessed some familiarity with the Old Testament covenant promises to Israel (Acts 13:26). However, in all other preaching to the Gentiles recorded in Acts, the Lord's Davidic birth line is not mentioned once, while the other elements of the gospel are still proclaimed.[55] Unless God has a different gospel for the Jews than He does for the Gentiles, Christ's descendancy from David must not be a part of the contents of saving faith. While the proclamation of Jesus Christ's descendancy from David has inestimable apologetic and pre-evangelistic value in establishing that He is Israel's rightful Messiah (2 Sam. 7:16; Isa. 11:1; Jer. 23:5-6), awareness of this truth and belief in it are not essential to receive eternal life, even as other sound proponents of grace theology have stated.[56]

A second reason why Christ's Davidic descent is not an element of the gospel or the contents of saving faith is because of the testimony of John's Gospel. Though the fourth Gospel was written with a dual purpose in mind and is manifestly edifying to the Christian, it is primarily an evangelistic book according to its own purpose statement in John 20:30-31. Yet, within the entire Gospel of John, there is no clear affirmation that Jesus is a descendant of David. This is quite different from John's testimony in the Book of Revelation (Rev. 3:7; 5:5; 22:16). This is also in stark contrast to the Synoptic Gospels.[57] The names of "David" and "Bethlehem" occur

---

[55] See chapter 17.

[56] Hixson, *Getting the Gospel Wrong: The Evangelical Crisis*, 89; Ryrie, *So Great Salvation: What It Means to Believe in Jesus Christ*, 119.

[57] James M. Gibbs, "Purpose and Pattern in Matthew's Use of the Title 'Son of David',"

only one time in the entire Gospel of John in John 7:42. Even there, John records the confused and divided masses openly speculating about Jesus' genealogical lineage and birthplace; and yet he provides no confirming testimony either way for the reader. But this is not the case with the other elements of the gospel in John, where His deity, humanity, substitutionary death, and bodily resurrection are all avowed both implicitly and explicitly with unmistakable clarity.

A third reason why Christ's being *"of the seed of David"* is not an element in the contents of saving faith is because there are no individual verses requiring belief in this truth, as there are for Christ's deity, humanity, substitutionary death, and bodily resurrection. There are no verses, for instance, that state, "For if we believe that Jesus died and descended from David" (1 Thess. 4:14) or "Unless you believe that I am from the seed of David, you will die in your sins" (John 8:24). The complete lack of even a single verse prescribing belief in Christ's Davidic lineage is astonishing when considering that the name of "David" is found over 1,000 times in the Bible. This is more than the words "faith," "hope," and "love"—combined! And yet not once did the Spirit of God move the writers of Scripture to connect the blessed name of "David" to the content required to be believed for salvation.

A fourth and final reason why Christ's Davidic descent is not an element of saving faith is because it is nowhere stated in Scripture to form the grounds of salvation for mankind. Once again, this is very dissimilar to the Lord's deity, humanity, substitutionary death, and bodily resurrection which are amply attested throughout Scripture as the necessary grounds.[58] While the facts of Christ's birth in the lineage and city of David were absolutely essential to fulfill every letter of Bible prophecy and to uphold God's covenantal faithfulness to David and Israel, these facts do not provide the grounds or basis for our eternal redemption.

Regarding the Lord's humanity, millions of other human beings have also been Israelites, and tens of thousands have been descendants of Judah, and thousands have descended from David and even been born in Bethlehem. But this did not qualify any of them to be the Savior of mankind. Though it is true that Christ in His humanity will forever be a descendant of David (Rev. 5:5; 22:16), it is not this trait that He shares in common *with David* that brings redemption to mankind. It is what He shares in common *with all humanity*. It was only the fact that He is a son of Adam (Luke 3:38) as *"the Man, Christ Jesus"* (1 Tim. 2:5) that made it possible for Him to pay the redemption price *"for all"* (1 Tim. 2:6). While the fact of Christ's deity and incarnation distinguishes Him from the rest of humanity and made propitiation toward God possible, it was the fact of

---

NTS 10 (1963/64): 446-64; Jack D. Kingsbury, "The Title 'Son of David' in Matthew's Gospel," *JBL* 95 (1976): 591-602.

[58] See chapter 9.

His common humanity, not His narrow descent from David, that made His sacrifice efficacious toward the entire human race.

This conclusion harmonizes with the testimony of Scripture discovered elsewhere. The contents of saving faith correspond with the very grounds of our eternal salvation. This in turn reflects the content of the gospel that is required to be believed so as not to *"perish"* (2 Thess. 2:10) and suffer *"everlasting destruction"* (2 Thess. 1:9). If the Davidic lineage of Christ did not provide the basis for eternal life, then it is not part of the contents of saving faith or the gospel. Whether it is 1-2 Thessalonians or 1-2 Timothy, the testimony of the Lord as to the contents of the gospel is completely consistent.

Chapter 12

What Is the Gospel According to Romans?

OVERVIEW

The Epistle of Romans demonstrates that the gospel is synonymous with the saving message or the contents of saving faith. Though the gospel of Christ forms the basis for the Christian life, it is not a message about how to live the Christian life. Crossless gospel proponents teach that the gospel is a broad message about justification, sanctification, and even the entirety of Romans 1-16. But a detailed, contextual study of every occurrence of euangelion and euangelizō in Romans confirms the traditional Free Grace interpretation that the gospel is the narrower message of justification and eternal salvation. This is even true in passages that crossless gospel proponents claim as support for their broad concept of the gospel. Romans 1:3-4 is a description of Christ rather than a definition of the gospel. Romans 1:16-17 describes the progress of the gospel and the revealing of God's judicial righteousness each time a lost person believes the gospel and is justified. Romans 1:18 and 5:9-10 are not describing deliverance for the believer from God's wrath as part of sanctification. Romans 2:16 teaches that the gospel is God's standard by which He will eternally judge mankind. Romans 16:25-27 teaches that both the gospel and Christian life truth about Jesus Christ are able to establish believers. This interpretation harmonizes with the reference to "the mystery of the gospel" in Ephesians 6:19.

Romans is one of the most magnificent books in the entire Word of God. In terms of canonical order, it stands not only at the head of the Pauline Epistles but at the head of all New Testament epistles. It played a pre-eminent role during the Protestant Reformation in convincing many professing Christians of the biblical truth of justification by faith alone. Only eternity will tell the final tally of souls won to the Lord by its clear annunciation of the saving grace of God through faith in Jesus Christ. It is one of God's greatest gifts to mankind. If there is any book in the canon of Scripture that can bring clarity in the midst of the present controversy over the contents of saving faith, surely Romans is it.

And yet, not surprisingly, this epistle is being radically reinterpreted in our day by the advocates of crossless saving faith with respect to its teaching on the subjects of repentance, wrath, the meaning of salvation, and the meaning of the gospel. They are interpreting the gospel in Romans to be a very broad message about justification, sanctification, glorification, God's prophetic program for Israel, and possibly even the entire contents of its 16 chapters.[1] Lopez writes in this regard, "the gospel encapsulates the message found in the entire book of Romans (i.e., justification, sanctification, glorification, and a future for Israel). Usually unrecognized, the term *gospel* also includes the unconditional promises to Israel that will be fulfilled in the future (10:15-16; 11:26-32)."[2] Based on claims such as these, the plea is usually then made that since Romans and the rest of the New Testament clearly teach a broad gospel, it is unreasonable to insist that the lost must believe "the gospel" to gain eternal life. The only sensible alternative, we are told, is to admit that belief in the gospel is not a requirement to go to heaven after all. And just like that, the cross and resurrection are dispensed with as essential elements in "the saving message."

However, when all occurrences of *euangelion* (Rom. 1:1, 9, 16; 2:16; 10:16; 11:28; 15:16, 19; 16:25) and *euangelizō* (Rom. 1:15; 10:15 [2x/MT]; 15:20) in Romans are studied carefully in their respective contexts, it becomes clear that "the gospel" is a much narrower message. It is the message about how a guilty, condemned sinner can be freely justified in God's sight through faith alone in the Christ who died a propitious death for our sins and was raised for our justification. The gospel of Christ does

---

[1] Jeremy D. Myers, "The Gospel is More Than 'Faith Alone in Christ Alone'," *JOTGES* 19 (Autumn 2006): 35; Bob Wilkin, "Gospel Means Good News," unpublished paper presented at the Grace Evangelical Society National Conference, March 6, 2008, Fort Worth, TX, p. 8.

[2] René A. Lopez, *Romans Unlocked: Power to Deliver* (Springfield, Missouri: 21st Century Press, 2005), 31-32.

not include information about how to be sanctified and live the Christian life. Nor does it consist of Bible prophecy concerning God's dispensational dealings with the nation of Israel. Instead, the gospel of salvation in Romans 3-5 forms the *necessary basis* for living the Christian life (Rom. 6-8; 12-16) and for understanding God's plan for Israel (Rom. 9-11).

Thus, it must be clarified at the outset of this chapter, that while the gospel is definitely related to sanctification and God's dispensational program for Israel, it is still distinct from these subjects. Though holding fast to the gospel is necessary for edification in the Christian life, this does not mean that the gospel itself is a message about edification. To equate the two is to confuse the *elements* of the gospel with the *effects* of the gospel. In order to observe this critical distinction within each passage in Romans that uses the word "gospel," the context for the epistle must first be established.

The Context and Purpose of Romans

One key to correctly interpreting the "gospel" passages in Romans is to understand their relationship to the larger context of the book. To do this, one must understand Paul's purposes for writing and the various circumstances surrounding the composition of this epistle. Romans is not, first and foremost, a systematic treatise on Pauline theology. Rather, it is a letter. It is a letter to Christians living in a specific geographical locale for a specific historical purpose, even though the occasion of its writing did become an opportunity for Paul to expound upon several doctrines of the Christian faith.[3] It is also evident that Paul was selective in choosing his content. This explains why some doctrines are treated at length, such as Israel's place in the present and future dispensational plan of God (Rom. 9-11), while others are only alluded to vaguely,[4] such as the imminent return of Christ for His Church (Rom. 13:11-14), a theme emphasized in the other Pauline epistles.

The selective content of Romans certainly reflects the special circumstances and purposes for this letter. Paul wrote this epistle from Corinth in A.D. 56-58 while concluding his third missionary journey. From Corinth, he planned to sail to Jerusalem (Rom. 15:31), and from there to visit the saints in Rome. His expressed purposes in coming to Rome were to edify the believers of that city in their faith (Rom. 1:9-12) and then to be helped onward to Spain for a fourth missionary journey (Rom. 15:24, 28), since his divinely appointed task of preaching the gospel and establishing local churches in the east had come to completion (Rom. 15:23).

But what was the church in Rome like? Did they need edification? Did they agree on the gospel? Was there division in the church or were they united among themselves and able to support a large missionary expan-

---

[3] Moo, *The Epistle to the Romans*, 16.

[4] Thomas R. Schreiner, *Romans*, BECNT (Grand Rapids: Baker Academic, 1998), 16.

sion to the west spearheaded by the apostle Paul? And why should they support Paul anyway? It is not too difficult to envision a potential scenario in the Roman church where, following the expulsion of the Jews from that city in A.D. 49 under Emperor Claudius, many Jewish believers would have filtered back to their city over the next decade subsequent to the death of Claudius and the lifting of the ban. The churches in Rome by the late 50s would have been predominantly Gentile in composition, tendencies, and leadership. Based on this likely situation, some New Testament scholars have speculated that tensions between Jewish and Gentile believers existed.[5] And if such was the case, Paul would likely have been informed of this by his close friends and fellow Jewish believers from Rome, Aquila and Priscilla (Rom. 16:3).[6] It is further reasoned that this problem provided the impetus for Paul to write certain sections of Romans, such as chapters 9-11 and 14-15.[7] But such a rift among the churches of Rome is only speculation and is nowhere specified by Paul in the epistle. So it is better not to view this epistle as issuing pastoral correction as Paul does in his other letters—letters to churches he founded, unlike Romans.

With respect to Jewish-Gentile relations, it is likely that the complexion of the entire 1st century Church became predominantly Gentile by the late 50s, and by this time there was a growing need for divine revelation and scriptural clarification regarding the place of Israel in the plan of God in light of the new dispensation and the fact that the nation had largely rejected the gospel. But was this Paul's sole reason for writing Romans?

It is likely that Paul had multiple purposes in mind for writing and sending this letter.[8] In the epistle, he tells us why he plans to visit Rome, but not why he is writing; and yet, the historical occasion of his missionary plans and his reasons for writing should not be separated. He certainly used this letter to formally introduce himself and his doctrine to the believers in the empire's most prominent city, a city and a church that he had never visited before. It is also likely that the writing of Romans in anticipation of his visit was the opportune occasion for Paul to dispel rumors spread by his legalistic adversaries (Rom. 3:8) concerning his teaching on the subjects of law versus grace and Israel versus the Church.[9]

---

[5] Chip Anderson, "Romans 1:1-5 and the Occasion of the Letter: The Solution of the Two-Congregation Problem in Rome," *TrinJ* 14 (Spring 1993): 25-40; W. S. Campbell, "Why Did Paul Write Romans?" *ExpT* 85 (1974): 264-69; Robert Jewett, "Romans as an Ambassadorial Letter," *Int* 36 (January 1982): 5-20; A. J. M. Wedderburn, "The Purpose and Occasion of Romans Again," *ExpT* 90 (1979): 137-41.

[6] Douglas Moo, *The Epistle to the Romans*, NICNT (Grand Rapids: Eerdmans, 1996), 18; Schreiner, *Romans*, 21; Philip R. Williams, "Paul's Purpose in Writing Romans," *BSac* 128 (January 1971): 64.

[7] Schreiner, *Romans*, 13.

[8] C. E. B. Cranfield, *A Critical and Exegetical Commentary on the Epistle to the Romans*, ICC (Edinburgh: T & T Clark, 1975), 1:22-24; 2:814-23; Moo, *The Epistle to the Romans*, 20; Schreiner, *Romans*, 19.

[9] Moo, *The Epistle to the Romans*, 21.

By writing on these subjects, it is possible that Paul was presenting a "defense of the revelation of God's righteousness in the Gospel."[10] Such a letter from Paul would have re-assured the Romans about his worthiness to receive support for his plans to evangelize Spain[11] by setting forth a thorough exposition about the need for the gospel (Rom. 1-3), about the gospel itself (Rom. 3-5), about its implications for sanctification and spirituality by grace apart from the law (Rom. 6-8), about God's plans for Israel (Rom. 9-11), and about the Christian's relationship to government and other believers within the Church (Rom. 12-16). It appears based on the many parallels in content and structure between the introductory section of 1:1-17 and the closing section of 15:14-33 that such support was a principal reason for Paul writing this epistle.[12]

Paul was passionate and driven by the need to spread the gospel (Rom. 1:14; 1 Cor. 9:14-22; 2 Tim. 2:10). He was a gospel-man who had been commissioned directly by Christ to preach it (Acts 26:12-18; Gal. 1:12) and was separated unto it (Rom. 1:1). Romans, therefore, is an epistle about the gospel, though not all of Romans is the gospel. Romans is about the definition of the gospel (Rom. 3-5) as well as the implications of the gospel (Rom. 6-16). For this reason, Paul's purpose in writing must be viewed as being integrally connected to the gospel and to his relentless desire to spread this message along with its life-transforming implications and effects. The church in the city of Rome, the capital of the empire, was ideally situated geographically to play a strategic role in advancing the gospel further to the west. But would the Romans partner with Paul and support his evangelistic intentions? Certainly, as an initial step of faith on Paul's part, a personal apostolic letter would be necessary, followed by a personal visit (Rom. 1:10-15). Beyond this, we can only venture to guess what Paul's other reasons were for writing Romans.

The Gospel for Believers

We can be sure, however, that Paul was not writing to the Roman Christians because he had doubts about the genuineness of their faith. There is every indication throughout this epistle that he assumes its recipients were already justified believers in Jesus Christ. They are identified as "saints" (Rom. 1:7)

---

[10] Shawn Gillogly, "Romans 1:16-17: An Apologetic for the Gospel," a paper presented at the Evangelical Theological Society Southeastern Regional, March 16-17, 2001, p. 9.

[11] Wayne A. Brindle, "'To the Jew First': Rhetoric, Strategy, History, or Theology?" *BSac* 159 (April 2002): 221-22; James D. G. Dunn, *Romans 1-8*, WBC (Dallas: Word Books, 1988), lv-lvi; Moo, *The Epistle to the Romans*, 16-20; Anders Nygren, *Commentary on Romans*, trans. Carl C. Rasmussen (Philadelphia: Fortress Press, 1949), 4-5; Walter B. Russell, III, "An Alternative Suggestion for the Purpose of Romans," *BSac* 145 (April 1988): 182; Schreiner, *Romans*, 21-22.

[12] Paul S. Minear, *The Obedience of Faith: The Purposes of Paul in the Epistle to the Romans* (Naperville, IL: Alec R. Allenson, 1971), 37.

who have a "faith" in Christ that is commendable (Rom. 1:8), a "faith" that Paul expects to be personally encouraged by when he arrives for his visit (Rom. 1:12). It is conspicuous that in the chapters dealing with the context of the gospel (Rom. 1:18-3:20) and its content (Rom. 3:21-5:21), there is not a single command given to the Roman readers. They are never told to believe the gospel, because they are assumed to be believers already.

The first command of the epistle doesn't come until chapter 6, a whole 149 verses into the letter, and it occurs in the Christian life section of the epistle dealing with the subjects of sanctification and spirituality under grace. In Romans 6:11, the first imperative mood command is given to the readers, *"Likewise you also, reckon (logizesthe) yourselves to be dead indeed to sin, but alive to God in Christ Jesus our Lord."* This is a command that only a believer in Christ can obey—one who has already been justified. In order for a person to reckon upon the identification truth of his/her co-crucifixion and co-resurrection with Christ, that person would need to have prior belief in the truth of Christ's substitutionary death and bodily resurrection. The sanctification and spirituality section of Romans 6:1-8:13 presumes heavily that the cross and resurrection, along with justification by grace through faith alone, are a settled issue in the mind of the reader. But the fact that the gospel is assumed knowledge on the part of the Romans also demonstrates that the gospel is the common denominator among all true believers, not belief in a crossless, resurrectionless promise of eternal life.

This also leads to a crucial question. If Paul assumed the recipients of his letter had already believed the gospel, then why does he state in Romans 1:15 that he is ready to preach the gospel to them when he comes to Rome or when he writes this epistle? Does this mean that Paul's gospel must be broader than just the message of justification or eternal salvation—that it is actually a sanctification message and/or a prophetic message about Israel? This is the teaching of the crossless gospel position. Lopez writes in his commentary on Romans:

> But how can Paul preach the gospel to "saints" (1:7) whose "faith is spoken of throughout the world" (v 8)? This implies the *gospel* in Romans includes a much broader concept than merely justification (cf. v 1). In addition the *gospel* also furnishes power through Christ's resurrection for the believer to live victoriously now by the Spirit and be delivered from God's wrath brought by sin in the believer's life.[13]

Similarly, Wilkin comments regarding Paul's purpose statement in Romans 1:16-17:

[13] René A. Lopez, *Romans Unlocked: Power to Deliver* (Springfield, MO: 21st Century Press, 2005), 38.

> What is the power of God to salvation? The Gospel of Christ, right?! It is the power of God to salvation, that is deliverance, for everyone who believes, for the Jew first and also for the Greek. We often read this verse as though it says that the gospel is the power of God to eternal life to all who come to faith in Jesus. What it's saying is the good news is the power of God for deliverance from the wrath of God for every believer who is calling on the name of the Lord. This is a sanctification verse; this is not a justification verse.[14]

Putting aside for a moment the false paradigm of viewing Romans as an epistle about believers escaping the wrath of God, the statements of Wilkin and Lopez confuse the gospel's *effects* with its *contents*. There is no question that holding fast to the truth of the gospel is necessary and powerful to effect sanctification in the Christian's life (1 Cor. 15:2; Gal. 3:1-3; Col. 1:23, 28; Phil. 2:12, 16). But this does not make the gospel a message about how to live the Christian life or how to be sanctified. Rather, it simply means that the gospel is the solid foundation for a Spirit-filled and progressively sanctified Christian life. The reason that Paul could preach the gospel to fellow believers in Rome is because he recognized that the gospel—the message of assured justification and final salvation through Christ's finished work and God's amazing grace—is the bed-rock upon which the sanctification truths of the Christian life are built. One cannot reckon upon his co-crucifixion and co-resurrection with Christ (Rom. 6:11), and yield to God accordingly (Rom. 6:12-13) to be filled with the Spirit (Rom. 8:1-4), unless he is first assured that Christ truly did die in his place for all his sins and rose victoriously from the grave. One cannot know that sanctification is based on God's grace rather than the law (Rom. 6:14) unless he knows that he is already accepted in grace because of Christ's death (Rom. 7:4; 8:1-3). This helps us to understand the general flow of thought in Romans and why gospel truths are so pervasive throughout this epistle.

Though not all of Romans is the gospel, all of Romans is built upon the gospel. The magnificent superstructure of Romans is only possible due to its solid foundation of the gospel. Romans contains a lengthy section on the bad news of man's just condemnation (Rom. 1:18-3:20), followed by an equally extensive portion on the good news of justification by grace alone through faith alone in the crucified, risen Christ (Rom. 3:21-5:21).[15] Without this solid foundation, there would be no towering monument of truth to follow in Romans 6-16 on the Christian life, prophetic truths about Israel, and the functioning of the Church. The entire edifice would crumble to a heap without the gospel of Christ. To build high one must dig deep.

---

[14] Bob Wilkin, "Why the Romans Road Ends in a Cul de Sac," Grace Evangelical Society Grace Conference, Dallas, TX, March 1, 2006.

[15] Leander E. Keck, *Romans* (Nashville: Abingdon Press, 2005), 56.

Thus, when Paul seeks to "establish" the Roman Christians in their faith (Rom. 1:11; 16:25), he does not skimp on the gospel. Lewis Sperry Chafer understood this same principle. Though he is well-known as the great dispensational systematic theologian of the 1900s, what is not so well-known is that he formerly had an itinerant evangelistic ministry. Recognizing the immense role of the gospel, he stated that "in a well-balanced ministry, gospel preaching should account for no less than seventy-five percent of the pulpit testimony."[16] The gospel is absolutely essential both for the evangelization of the lost and for the sanctification of the saved. This perspective can be readily observed throughout Romans. When every occurrence of the terms *euangelion* and *euangelizō* are examined in their respective contexts, it becomes apparent that "the gospel" is not a broad message about sanctification and God's promises to Israel. Rather, it is the "saving message" about justification by grace through faith in Jesus Christ apart from any human works or merit. Each occurrence of the term "gospel" in Romans will now be addressed.

Romans 1:1-4

Romans 1:1-4

1 *Paul, a bondservant of Jesus Christ, called to be an apostle, separated to* ***the gospel of God***

2 *which He promised before through His prophets in the Holy Scriptures,*

3 *concerning His Son Jesus Christ our Lord, who was born of the seed of David according to the flesh,*

4 *and declared to be the Son of God with power according to the Spirit of holiness, by the resurrection from the dead.*

The term *euangelion* occurs in the very first verse of Romans. Advocates of the G.E.S. gospel sometimes claim that Romans 1:1 and the verses immediately following it support the concept of a broad, all-encompassing gospel that goes well beyond the saving message of justification by faith alone. Thus, Myers writes:

> So here we have several more elements in Paul's broad idea of *gospel*. It concerns Jesus Christ, who is Lord. Next, Jesus was born of the seed of David, according to the flesh. Many say that the Lordship of Christ is essential to the gospel, which here is seen to be true. But nobody says that His lineage from David is essential. Yet Paul includes both in his gospel. Third, we read that He was declared to be the Son of God. While this is either a reference to His deity, or to Him being the King of Israel, it primarily is a reference to the power and authority Jesus received *after* the

---

[16] Lewis Sperry Chafer, *Systematic Theology* (Dallas: Dallas Seminary Press, 1947-1948; reprinted, Grand Rapids: Kregel, 1993), 3:9.

resurrection. And nobody denies that the resurrection is central to the good news.[17]

Many evangelical commentators besides Myers and G.E.S. proponents simply assume that verses 3-4 comprise a "definition of the gospel."[18] However, Romans 1:3-4 is not a *definition* of the *gospel* but rather a *description* of *Jesus Christ*. Though it is true that the gospel concerns Jesus Christ, and the two are intimately related, this does not mean that every detail about Jesus Christ stated in the Bible comprises the gospel. And though we know from other passages of Scripture that some of the features stated about Christ in Romans 1:3-4 also happen to be elements of the gospel, this does not mean that everything about Christ in these verses is part of the gospel. There are several reasons why it is better to interpret Romans 1:3-4 as a description of Christ rather than a definition of the gospel.

First, the syntactical structure of the Greek sentence demonstrates that verses 3-4 are directly subordinate to the "Son" of verse 3a ("concerning His Son, who . . .") rather than "the gospel" of verse 1b. In typical Pauline style, verses 1-7 contain a single run-on sentence with several sub-points. The relevant portion of Romans 1:1-4 is provided below.

1 Paul,
- a bondservant of Jesus Christ,
- called *to be* an apostle,
- separated to the gospel of God
2 - which He promised before
- through His prophets in the Holy Scriptures,
3 - concerning His Son,
- who was born
- (*ek*) of the seed of David
- (*kata*) according to the flesh,
4 and
- (who was) declared to be the Son of God with power
- (*kata*) according to the Spirit of holiness,
- (*ek*) by the resurrection from the dead,
- Jesus Christ our Lord.[19]

The word order of the Greek sentence for verses 3-4 is significant, but unfortunately it is obscured in some English versions. The Greek word order is accurately reflected in the NASB and NIV but not in the KJV and NKJV. The phrases, *"concerning His Son"* at the beginning of verse 3 and

[17] Jeremy D. Myers, "The Gospel is More Than 'Faith Alone in Christ Alone,'" *JOTGES* 19 (Autumn 2006): 45-46.

[18] Daniel K. Davey, "The Intrinsic Nature of the Gospel," *DBSJ* 9 (2004): 147. See also, Anderson, "Romans 1:1-5 and the Occasion of the Letter," 31.

[19] The structure of this outline follows that of Gordon D. Fee, *Pauline Christology: An Exegetical-Theological Study* (Peabody, MA: Hendrickson, 2007), 241.

"Jesus Christ our Lord" at the end of verse 4 are appositional to one another.[20] In the Greek text, they form a bracketed enclosure, an *inclusio*, whereby Christ is being described by the content that falls between the two titles. The clauses in verses 3-4 that follow the phrase, "concerning His Son" (v. 3), are subordinated directly to the word "Son" (v. 3) rather than "gospel" (v. 1). This makes it evident that they properly constitute a description of Christ rather than a definition of the gospel (v. 1). This is also supported by a simple comparison of the pronouns used in verses 1-5. In verse 2, the neuter relative pronoun *ho* ("which") is used to refer back to the neuter *euangelion* ("gospel") in verse 1. However, this is in contrast to the masculine relative pronouns used in verses 3 and 5 to refer to Christ. Immediately after the highly Christological portion in Romans 1:3-4, Romans 1:5 begins with a masculine relative pronoun in the genitive case, *hou* ("who"/"whom"), *"Through Him/whom (dia hou) we have received grace and apostleship."* This corresponds with the person of Christ in the preceding verses of Romans 1:3-4, where He is described using masculine genitive nouns. The usage of *hou* at the beginning of verse 5 is another indication that the immediately preceding verses (vv. 3-4) are technically about the person of Christ ("who"/"whom") rather than the gospel ("which").

However, these observations do not mean that the role of the prepositional phrase at the beginning of verse 3, *"concerning His Son,"* should be downplayed or dismissed. It marks a significant transition from the mention of "the gospel" in verses 1-2 into a description of Christ in verses 3-4. In the process, it informs the reader that the gospel concerns God's Son. The gospel cannot be conceived of apart from Jesus Christ. This means that the gospel, which is so central to Romans, is founded and focused upon the person of Christ. All proper soteriology must stem from a sound Christology. For this reason, Jesus Christ is described and extolled immediately in this epistle. But simply because Christ is inseparable from the gospel does not mean that everything about Christ is part of the gospel, for there are some details given in verses 3-4 that are technically extra-gospel information.

A second reason for concluding that Romans 1:3-4 is a description of Christ rather than a definition of the gospel is the fact that verses 1-4 are part of Paul's salutation that is intended to introduce and describe people, not to give definitions of key theological concepts such as "the gospel." It should be noted that in each section of Paul's salutation, there is a brief description of the three parties involved: Paul (vv. 1-2, 5); Jesus Christ (vv. 3-4); and the Roman readers (vv. 6-7). In introducing himself as the writer, Paul emphasizes first and foremost his servant status (Rom. 1:1a) in contrast with Jesus Christ—the exalted Lord (Rom. 1:3-4). Though Paul also mentions his apostleship and being commissioned with the gospel, this

[20] Ibid.

should be viewed as the means by which he serves Christ as His bond-servant (*doulos*). This is why he writes a few verses later in 1:9, *"whom I serve with my spirit in the gospel of His Son."* While the Romans and Greeks prized their liberty as free citizens, Paul emphasized his low estate in contrast to Christ's position of absolute deity and honor.[21]

The objective of verses 1-4, therefore, is simply to introduce Paul, the writer of this letter, and Jesus Christ its principal object. In fact, it would be peculiar for Paul to begin defining the gospel in 1:1-4 before he has even finished his introductions and greeted his readers in 1:6-7. When meeting someone for the first time, it is generally considered to be bad manners to launch immediately into a monologue. Introductions are in order first. It is better to view Paul's reference to "the gospel" in 1:1 as a transitory reference that is set within the larger framework of his primary objective, which is introducing himself and the One whom he served. Verses 1-2 give Paul's perspective and description of himself; verses 3-4 give his perspective and description of Christ; and verses 6-7 conclude with his perspective and description of the Roman recipients. Though the gospel is given prominent mention in connection with Paul and Christ in this introductory context, there is no compelling reason to believe it is being defined yet.

A third reason why Romans 1:3-4 is a description of Christ rather than a definition of the gospel is because of what is *not* contained in these verses. While it is easy to see that Paul included the resurrection in verse 4, namely to highlight Christ's exalted status, there appears to be no plausible reason for omitting the other half of Christ's finished work. Glaring by its absence is any reference to the cross or Christ's substitutionary death. This is simply inexplicable if Paul is defining the gospel in these verses. Furthermore, other key elements of the gospel are missing, such as justification by faith, which is so central to Paul's theme throughout Romans. In addition, it would seem strange for Paul to provide a definition of the gospel in 1:3-4 when he hasn't even established yet man's need for Christ or the context of the gospel, which comes later in 1:18-3:20.

A fourth reason why verses 3-4 are technically not a definition of the gospel but a description of Jesus Christ is because of the emphases of these two verses. The contents of these verses appear to be deliberately chosen to contrast the servant status of Paul and the Roman Christians with Christ's exalted position as sovereign Lord through the crowning event of the resurrection. There is a two-stage progression in Christ's life depicted in verses 3-4, moving from his royal birth in verse 3 to His glorification and annunciation as the Son of God in verse 4.[22] Christ's human

---

[21] David J. MacLeod, "Eternal Son, Davidic Son, Messianic Son: An Exposition of Romans 1:1-7," *BSac* 162 (January 2005): 78.

[22] Anderson, "Romans 1:1-5 and the Occasion of the Letter," 31; Fee, *Pauline Christology*, 242-43.

and divine natures are not the primary point of verses 3-4, as though the messianic description "seed of David" and the title "Son of God" set forth only the twin-truths of His humanity and deity. It is preferable to view Paul here as "contrasting two stages in the historical process of Jesus' first coming: the incarnate and the glorified stages. Verse 3 speaks of His earthly stage of humiliation and weakness, and verse 4 speaks of His present state of exaltation and power. Verse 3 speaks of Christ's earthly life when Jesus appeared as the Davidic Messiah, and verse 4 speaks of His post-resurrection existence."[23] In light of this, Romans 1:3-4 should not be understood as defining the gospel but as providing an initial and general biographical description of Christ from His messianic birth to the annunciation of His unique Sonship status at the resurrection.

For these reasons, the references to Jesus' Davidic lineage and the Spirit of holiness should not be viewed as actual elements of the gospel but as broader descriptive features related to Christ. As stated in the previous chapter regarding 2 Timothy 2:8, the truth of Christ's Davidic lineage accords with the gospel, but it is not part of the gospel. If the phrase "seed of David" in Romans 1:3 is really an element of the gospel, then this is hard to reconcile with the fact that Jesus' Davidic ancestry is never mentioned again throughout the Epistle of Romans—an epistle dedicated to an exposition of the gospel and its manifold implications.[24]

However, this does not mean that the reference to Christ's Davidic lineage in verse 3 is incidental or unnecessary to the epistle.[25] On the contrary, it demonstrates that His earthly life and ministry are the fulfillment of Old Testament prophetic revelation, and in the process, it confirms His status as the rightful Messiah.[26] It may also be true that, since the Jew-Gentile theme is so prevalent throughout this epistle, Paul includes in his description of Christ those features that would encompass both groups by showing the universality of Christ—that He is both the Jewish Messiah (1:3) and universal Lord (1:4). If this is the case, it would also reveal that the dispensational Church age truth of Jewish-Gentile union in Christ ("the mystery of/from the gospel") is not an element of the gospel but is actually an important byproduct of the gospel.[27] It may be concluded regarding Romans 1:3-4 that although certain elements of the gospel are contained in these verses ("raised from the dead," "according to the flesh," "Son of God") this does not mean that these verses in their entirety constitute a definition of the gospel.

---

[23] MacLeod, "Eternal Son, Davidic Son, Messianic Son," 86. See also, James D. G. Dunn, "Jesus—Flesh and Spirit: An Exposition of Romans 1.3-4," *JTS* 24 (1973): 56-57.

[24] Leon Morris, *The Epistle to the Romans*, PNTC (Grand Rapids: Eerdmans, 1988), 43.

[25] Ibid.

[26] Cranfield, *Epistle to the Romans*, 1:58-59; Schreiner, *Romans*, 40-41.

[27] See the section on Romans 16:25-27 and Ephesians 6:19 at the end of this chapter.

Romans 1:16-18

Romans 1:9-18

9 *For God is my witness, whom I serve with my spirit in the* ***gospel of His Son,*** *that without ceasing I make mention of you always in my prayers,*

10 *making request if, by some means, now at last I may find a way in the will of God to come to you.*

11 *For I long to see you, that I may impart to you some spiritual gift, so that you may be established—*

12 *that is, that I may be encouraged together with you by the mutual faith both of you and me.*

13 *Now I do not want you to be unaware, brethren, that I often planned to come to you (but was hindered until now), that I might have some fruit among you also, just as among the other Gentiles.*

14 *I am a debtor both to Greeks and to barbarians, both to wise and to unwise.*

15 *So, as much as is in me, I am ready* ***to preach the gospel*** *to you who are in Rome also.*

16 *For I am not ashamed of* ***the gospel of Christ,*** *for it is the power of God to salvation for everyone who believes, for the Jew first and also for the Greek.*

17 *For in it the righteousness of God is revealed from faith to faith; as it is written, "The just shall live by faith."*

18 *For the wrath of God is revealed from heaven against all ungodliness and unrighteousness of men, who suppress the truth in unrighteousness.*

Verses 16-17 are rightly considered by most exegetes to be the key verses for the entire Epistle of Romans. How they are interpreted becomes the lens through which the rest of the book is viewed. Needless to say, the correct interpretation of these verses is absolutely critical to understanding the gospel and the contents of saving faith. Though many different interpretations of these verses have been suggested, this chapter will focus on just those two that are most relevant to the current controversy over the contents of saving faith. The interpretation espoused in this chapter as the correct view sees these verses as describing the progress of the gospel among Jews and Gentiles along with the revelation of God's imputed righteousness each time a lost person comes to faith in Christ and is justified. On the other hand, the view held by many crossless gospel proponents is that these verses are describing a broad concept of the gospel. That is, they are describing the progress from an individual believer's justification and imputed righteousness to his sanctification via God's power and infused righteousness. This position is spelled out below by two of its adherents, beginning with Ken Neff, who writes:

> Additionally in Rom 1:16-17, the result of Christ's work seems to indicate that the gospel refers both to justification (v 16 referring

> to chapters 3-5) and to sanctification (v 17 referring to chapters 6-8).[28]

Likewise, regarding Romans 1:17, René Lopez declares:

> Thus, the *righteousness of God* should not only be understood as a legal declaration, upon faith alone in Christ alone, but as also bestowing all believers with resurrection-power through the Spirit's indwelling that aids them to live righteously (6-8; 12:1-15:13; see BDAG, 249) and escape God's present wrath (1:18; 5:9-10; 10:9-14; 13:4-5).[29]
>
> Therefore, one may take **from faith to faith** to mean, "on the *basis* of faith *directed* by faith" to describe not only the forensic aspect of "the righteousness of God," but the life that stems from that righteousness on the basis of faith (cf. 6:12-13; 10:5-8). That is, God justifies the ungodly *on the basis* of faith from beginning, and continues to aid the believer in sanctification *directed* by faith, to the end (cf. 10:5-21). Hence faith becomes the sole means for justification and the life-blood for sanctification.[30]

Several major problems exist with the crossless gospel conclusion that Romans 1:16-17 is speaking of a progression from justification to sanctification. First, this interpretation does not handle the phrase in verse 17, *"from faith to faith,"* consistently. If the first reference to "faith" in the phrase indicates "the sole means for justification" as Lopez states, then logically why doesn't the second "faith" reference also indicate "the sole means of" sanctification? In both halves of the "faith to faith" phrase, "faith" stands alone without any modifiers and is therefore unqualified. Logically, this should lead to the view that even sanctification is by faith alone. Yet, according to the doctrine of sanctification held by most proponents of the G.E.S. gospel, sanctification is achieved by means of faith *plus* works.[31] For this interpretation of Romans 1:17 to fit the G.E.S. scheme of sanctification, the verse would need to say that the righteousness of God is revealed "from faith to faith *plus works*."

---

[28] Ken Neff, "What Is the Free Grace Gospel?" *Grace in Focus* 24 (March/April 2009): 3.

[29] Lopez, *Romans Unlocked*, 40-41.

[30] Ibid., 41.

[31] It is commonly, but erroneously, taught in Free Grace circles that our works energize our faith, rather than our good works issuing from an initial walk of dependence upon the Lord (John 15:4-5; Gal. 2:20; Col. 2:6; Titus 3:8; Heb. 11:6). Thus, Wilkin writes regarding James 2:24-26, "James is making the point that loving works directed to fellow believers in need give vitality and life to our faith. James doesn't say that faith—or true faith—makes our works good, as is commonly thought. . . . Faith is likened to the body, not the spirit. The energizing spirit of a Christian is his works, not his faith. His faith is the body that must be energized by the spirit which is works." Robert N. Wilkin, "Another View of Faith and Works in James 2," *JOTGES* 15 (Autumn 2002): 16 (ellipsis added).

Secondly, the crossless position confuses the *effects* of the gospel in Romans 1:16-17 with the *contents* of the gospel. We are repeatedly told that "the gospel" is a "sanctification" message. Yet, Romans 1:16 in itself does *not* technically say that the gospel is the message about (*peri*) salvation but that the gospel is the power of God unto (*eis*) salvation. This verse indicates that the gospel is for the purpose of, or results in, salvation. The "salvation" of verse 16 is best interpreted as referring to salvation in all three tenses.[32] The noun (*sōtēria*) and verb (*sōzō*) are used in the book for a complete salvation that encompasses our past-tense salvation that occurred at justification (Rom. 8:24) and our future tense salvation that will occur at glorification (Rom. 5:9-10; 13:11). When the message of God's justification provided through His free grace is believed, whether by a lost person or in an on-going sense by the child of God, it effects, or results in, either justification for the lost when initially believed or practical sanctification for the saint when persistently believed. The gospel is not *about* sanctification; but continuing to believe it will *result* in sanctification.

Salvation in Romans

At this point, some clarification and balance is needed regarding the broad concept of "salvation" or deliverance in the Book of Romans. With respect to the "salvation" in Romans 1:16 and the rest of Romans, the noun, *sōtēria*, occurs 5x in Romans 1:16; 10:1, 10; 11:11; 13:11. The verb, *sōzō*, occurs 8x in Romans 5:9-10; 8:24; 9:27; 10:9, 13; 11:14, 26. Several of these passages, such as Romans 1:16; 5:9-10; 10:9, 13 are interpreted by G.E.S. proponents as references to practical sanctification or temporal, physical deliverance from God's wrath upon the Christian due to disobedience.[33] Some even go so far as to claim that "salvation" in Romans cannot refer to justification or eternal deliverance because the words "salvation" and "saved" do not occur in the justification section of Romans 3-4.[34] However, if this is true, then the same standard must also be applied to the sanctification section of Romans 6:1-8:13, where neither *sōtēria* nor *sōzō* occur even once![35]

As a result, the latter portion of Romans 5 is often reinterpreted as a section about sanctification and temporal deliverance. Romans 5:9-10 is then viewed as filling the need for a "sanctification" passage that uses the term "saved" in the sanctification section of the epistle. This term is used in Romans 5:9 and 10, *"we shall be saved."* It should be noted that

[32] Johnson, "The Gospel That Paul Preached," 332.

[33] René A. Lopez, "An Exposition of 'Soteria' and 'Sozo' in the Epistle to the Romans" (Th.M. thesis, Dallas Theological Seminary, 2002), 32-49, 89-122; Bob Wilkin, "The Three Tenses of Salvation Aren't About Justification, Sanctification, and Glorification," Georgia Regional G.E.S. Conference, Hampton, GA, September 23, 2006.

[34] Bob Wilkin, "Why the Romans Road Ends in a Cul de Sac," G.E.S. Conference, Dallas, TX, March 1, 2006.

[35] For that matter, the terms *euangelion* or *euangelizō* also do not occur in Romans 6-8, which is quite peculiar if "the gospel" is a message about sanctification!

in Romans 5:9-10, the two occurrences of the verb *sōzō* are in the future, passive, indicative form (*sōthēsometha*), and thus they are an expression of certainty and hope, *"we shall be saved."* But these are not interpreted by crossless proponents as being indicative promises of future glorification (i.e., eternal security), but as merely "logical" or "relative" futures involving contingency, whereby the believer still needs to be "saved" from God's wrath through obedience in his or her Christian life.[36]

It is further claimed by some with respect to the twofold use of *sōthēsometha* in Romans 5:9-10 that the references to being justified (v. 9) and reconciled (v. 10) are set in contrast to the two indicative promises that *"we shall be saved."* Justification and reconciliation are thereby viewed as being excluded from the meaning of "salvation" in Romans.[37] But verses 9-10 do not *exclude* justification and reconciliation from salvation; rather, justification and reconciliation are assumed in the passage to be forms of salvation that are already past and complete. The two uses of *sōthēsometha* in verses 9-10 simply represent an *extension* and *continuation* of the past, settled salvation of justification and reconciliation. This future tense reference to salvation in Romans 5:9-10 is a "much more" (2x, *pollō mallon*) salvation, not a *mutually exclusive* salvation, since it builds on the past, settled salvation of justification and reconciliation.

With this radical redefinition of "salvation," some crossless proponents are now claiming that they "can't find even one clear example" in the New Testament where salvation refers to a past tense deliverance from the penalty of sin.[38] However, we should not let it escape our notice that, even in Romans, some future tense uses of *sōzō* refer to people being justified or reconciled in time. Though *sōzō* in Romans 10:1 may include Israel's national, physical deliverance at the return of Christ, the immediate context of Romans 9:30-10:4 indicates that justification and imputed righteousness are part of the salvation that Paul has in mind. In Romans 11:11, 14, the salvation referred to in the context is the reconciliation (Rom. 11:15) of the Gentiles to God that is transpiring at the present time in anticipation of Israel's future national repentance.

Outside of Romans, *sōzō* and *sōtēria* are also used for past tense justification/reconciliation. Luke 7:50 uses the perfect tense of *sōzō* to refer to the forgiveness of sins (Luke 7:48) that accompanies justification by faith. In Acts 13:26, *"the word of this salvation"* that is proclaimed to the Jews and Gentiles includes the promise of judicial forgiveness and justification by faith apart from works (Acts 13:38-39). Likewise, Titus 3:7 uses the aorist passive participle to speak of justification occurring simultaneously with the regeneration and aorist indicative of *sōzō* in 3:5-6. These examples

---

[36] Zane C. Hodges, "The Message of Romans," *The Kerugma Message* 5 (July 1996): 6.

[37] Wilkin, "Why the Romans Road Ends in a Cul de Sac."

[38] Bob Wilkin, "The Three Tenses of Salvation Reconsidered," audiotape EDW 211, Grace Evangelical Society, 2003.

demonstrate that there are no grounds for the sharp antithesis that has developed within the Free Grace movement in recent years between the terms "saved"/"salvation" and "justified"/"justification."

The Righteousness of God

Returning to the key passage of Romans 1:16-17, it is also dubious to claim that these verses are simultaneously addressing both imputed righteousness and infused righteousness. For advocates of the crossless position to teach that *"the righteousness of God"* in verse 17 goes beyond "forensic"[39] justification and is more than a "legal declaration"[40] is truly disconcerting. Though Lopez unmistakably affirms a Free Grace position by stating that "faith becomes the sole means for justification,"[41] nevertheless his interpretations of the phrases, the *"righteousness of God"* and *"from faith to faith,"* are shared by both Lordship and Roman Catholic interpreters. This fact in itself does not make his position wrong, since even Lordship and Catholic exegetes sometimes offer correct interpretations. But this should at least give us reason to pause, especially on so critical and highly consequential a passage as Romans 1:16-17. Catholicism has historically combined the concepts of justification and sanctification. When it comes to Romans 1:17, Catholic scholars have customarily interpreted the phrase, *"righteousness of God,"* to mean the process whereby one is made practically righteous and consequently declared by God to be actually righteous.[42] It is also true that, currently, some notable Protestant commentators are trending in the direction of the *"righteousness of God"* being both forensic and transformative,[43] a fact which Lopez is well aware of and mentions approvingly.[44] But despite the inclinations of certain Protestants today, the justification + sanctification view of "righteousness of God" in Romans 1:17 remains an alarming interpretative path for any Free Grace person to follow.

The phrase in Romans 1:17, the *"righteousness of God,"* has traditionally been interpreted by Protestants as a reference to the gift of God's imputed righteousness granted on the basis of faith. The expression *dikaiosunē theou* may be taken either objectively, as the gift of righteousness, or subjectively, as the righteousness that has its origin or source in God. In either case, it has normally been interpreted by Protestants

---

[39] Lopez, *Romans Unlocked*, 41.

[40] Ibid., 40-41.

[41] Ibid., 41.

[42] Patrick Boylan, *St. Paul's Epistle to the Romans* (Dublin: M. H. Gill & Son, 1947), 11-13; Joseph A. Fitzmyer, *Romans*, AB (New York: Doubleday, 1993), 116-24, 254, 258-63; idem, "Romans," in *The New Jerome Biblical Commentary*, ed. Raymond E. Brown, Joseph A. Fitzmyer, and Roland E. Murphy (Englewood Cliffs, NJ: Prentice Hall, 1990), 834-35; Robert A. Sungenis, *Not By Faith Alone: The Biblical Evidence for the Catholic Doctrine of Justification* (Santa Barbara, CA: Queenship Publishing, 1997), 53-55, 314-20.

[43] Schreiner, *Romans*, 63n8. See also, Dunn, *Romans 1-8*, 40-42.

[44] Lopez, "An Exposition of 'Soteria' and 'Sozo' in the Epistle to the Romans," 38-39n19.

as referring to a declarative, judicial righteousness accounted by God to the sinner on the sole condition of faith. It has not been understood as an ethical righteousness infused by God into that person's character or life. Luther had an epiphany regarding Romans 1:17 as he came to realize that this could only mean the judicial standing that one possesses in the sight of God. In his frequently quoted words, *"the righteousness of God"* meant "die Gerechtigkeit die vor Gott gilt." That is, "the righteousness that counts before God." It was just this interpretation—an interpretation of only one passage—that opened his eyes to the truth of justification by faith alone and in the process sparked the Protestant Reformation.[45] He testified regarding the impact of the interpretation of this one passage, saying:

> I greatly longed to understand Paul's Epistle to the Romans and nothing stood in the way but that one expression, "the justice of God," because I took it to mean that justice whereby God is just and deals justly in punishing the unjust. My situation was that, although an impeccable monk, I stood before God as a sinner troubled in conscience, and I had no confidence that my merit would assuage Him. Therefore I did not love a just and angry God, but rather hated and murmured against Him. Yet I clung to the dear Paul and had a great yearning to know what he meant.
>
> Night and day I pondered until I saw the connection between the justice of God and the statement that "the just shall live by his faith." Then I grasped that the justice of God is that righteousness by which through grace and sheer mercy God justifies us through faith. Thereupon I felt myself to be reborn and to have gone through open doors into paradise. The whole of Scripture took on a new meaning, and whereas before the "justice of God" had filled me with hate, now it became to me inexpressibly sweet in greater love. This passage of Paul became to me a gate to heaven. . . .[46]

It is doubtful, though, that Luther or any other struggling, seeking individual would ever come to see in Romans 1:16-17 the truth of justification *sola fide* by following today's crossless interpretation. To see in the phrase, *"the justice/righteousness of God,"* both concepts of imputed and infused righteousness simultaneously rolled into one ends up obscuring the type of righteousness intended by Paul in verse 17. When the phrase, "righteousness of God" (*dikaiosunē theou*), is used in the Pauline epistles, *it never refers*

---

[45] This is, of course, only a generalization. For a more nuanced perspective on Luther's "theological breakthrough" and its relation to the rest of the Reformation, see Alister E. McGrath, *Iustitia Dei: A History of the Christian Doctrine of Justification from 1500 to the Present* (Cambridge: Cambridge University Press, 1986), 8-10.

[46] Martin Luther as quoted in Ron Merryman, *Justification by Faith Alone & Its Historical Challenges*, revised edition (Colorado Springs, CO: Merryman Ministries, 2000), 65-66.

to the practical righteousness of sanctification but it always possesses a judicial sense (Rom. 3:5, 21, 22, 10:3 [2x]; 2 Cor. 5:21; Phil. 3:9). This is not to deny that the term "righteousness" (*dikaiosunē*) by itself is ever used in Romans to speak of sanctification, for it clearly does (Rom. 6:13, 16, 18-20). But the "righteousness" of Romans 1:17 is more precisely the "righteousness *of God*." It is the *iustitia dei* or *dikaiosunē theou;* and this can only refer to the act of God imputing His righteousness to the guilty sinner who believes in Christ or to the righteous status of the believing sinner as declared by God. Even when *dikaiosunē* is used in sanctification passages, it is never said to be a righteousness *from* God but a righteousness *to* God (Rom. 6:13) or *to* holiness/sanctification (Rom. 6:19). This is entirely distinct from the forensic righteousness described by Paul in other passages in Romans, and even Philippians 3:9, where the righteousness is alien to us and clearly not our "own" (cf. Rom. 10:3, *tēn idian dikaiosunēn*). In addition, the righteousness of God in Romans is a righteousness or justification that is reckoned or accounted (*logizomai*) to us, and therefore, it is judicial or forensic. This righteousness is imputed but not imparted.

For these reasons, and several more, many able commentators and expositors are in agreement that the "righteousness of God" in Romans 1:17 is speaking of justification rather than sanctification.[47] Some Protestant scholars, like Schreiner,[48] are vacillating over the question of whether justification is both forensic and transformative due to the fact that *dikaiosunē theou* may refer to both an activity of God and a status granted by God.[49] But even if the *"righteousness of God"* refers to an act of God, this would not necessarily support *dikaiosunē theou* being a reference to sanctification. Rather, *dikaiosunē theou* may simply refer to "an activity that is a

---

[47] Henry Alford, *The Greek Testament* (Chicago: Moody Press, 1958), 2:319; C. K. Barrett, *A Commentary on the Epistle to the Romans*, Black's New Testament Commentary (New York: Harper & Row, 1957), 31; Cranfield, *Epistle to the Romans*, 1:95; James Denney, "Romans," in *The Expositor's Greek Testament* (Grand Rapids: Eerdmans, reprinted 1990): 589-91; Frederic L. Godet, *Commentary on Romans* (Grand Rapids: Kregel Publications, 1977), 96; Robert Haldane, *An Exposition of the Epistle to the Romans* (Mac Dill, FL: MacDonald Publishing, n.d.); Charles Hodge, *Commentary on the Epistle to the Romans* (Grand Rapids: Eerdmans, 1994), 31; S. Lewis Johnson, "The Gospel That Paul Preached," *BSac* 128 (October 1971): 334; Alva J. McClain, *Romans: The Gospel of God's Grace* (Winona Lake, IN: BMH Books, 1973), 59; Douglas J. Moo, *The Epistle to the Romans*, NICNT (Grand Rapids: Eerdmans, 1996), 74-75; Leon Morris, *The Epistle to the Romans*, PNTC (Grand Rapids: Eerdmans, 1988), 100-3; H. C. G. Moule, *Studies in Romans* (Grand Rapids: Kregel Publications, 1977), 57; John Murray, *The Epistle to the Romans*, NICNT (Grand Rapids: Eerdmans, 1968), 1:30-31; William R. Newell, *Romans: Verse-By-Verse* (Grand Rapids: Kregel Publications, 1994), 24; Nygren, *Commentary on Romans*, 74-76; William Sanday and Arthur C. Headlam, *A Critical and Exegetical Commentary on the Epistle to the Romans*, ICC (New York: Charles Scribner's Sons, n.d.), 35-36.

[48] Schreiner, *Romans*, 66n11.

[49] Lopez appeals to this very point in order to advance his view that Romans 1:17 refers to both justification and sanctification. See Lopez, "An Exposition of 'Soteria' and 'Sozo' in the Epistle to the Romans," 32-38.

declaration of status."[50] When Moo, for instance, defines *dikaiosunē theou* as an "act by which God brings people into right relationship with himself,"[51] he correctly explains this to be a right relationship in terms of a "judicial status" that is "purely forensic," not an "infusing" of righteousness.[52] He rightly concludes regarding *dikaiosunē theou* in Romans 1:17, "In this sense, the noun 'righteousness' in this phrase can be understood to be the substantival equivalent of the verb 'justify.'"[53] The pivotal phrase in Romans 1:17, *"righteousness of God,"* is best interpreted, therefore, to mean justification rather than sanctification.

The Just Shall Live By Faith

But some may wonder how these conclusions fit with Paul's quotation of Habakkuk 2:4 in Romans 1:17. Why does he select this Old Testament passage? Is it used to prove that justification is through faith alone? Or, was it selected to show that justified people live their Christian lives by continual faith? When Paul quotes Habakkuk 2:4 as saying, *"For the just (ho de dikaios) shall live (zēsetai) by faith (ek pisteōs),"* is he using the two parts, "the just" and "shall live," respectively in reference to justification and sanctification? Some scholars take the phrase "by faith" (*ek pisteōs*) adverbially as qualifying "shall live" (*zēsetai*) rather than qualifying "the just" (*ho dikaios*). By doing so, the resulting sense of the Habakkuk quotation becomes "the one who is justified *shall live by faith*."[54] This interpretation could be used to support the conclusion that people who are already justified live the Christian life by continual faith.[55] On the other hand, the phrase "by faith" (*ek pisteōs*) has also been taken adjectivally with "the just" (*ho dikaios*) so that Romans 1:17 is viewed as a statement about how one is justified by faith.[56] In this case, the sense would be *"the one who is just/righteous by faith* shall live" or

---

[50] Moo, *The Epistle to the Romans*, 75.

[51] Ibid., 74.

[52] Ibid.

[53] Ibid., 75.

[54] Hans C. C. Cavallin, "Righteous Shall Live By Faith: A Decisive Argument for the Traditional Interpretation," *ST* 32.1 (1978): 33-43; R. M. Moody, "The Habakkuk Quotation in Romans 1:17," *ExpT* 92.7 (April 1981): 204-8; D. Moody Smith, "ΗΟ ΔΕ ΔΙΚΑΙΟΣ ΕΚ ΠΙΣΤΕΩΣ ΖΗΣΕΤΑΙ," in *Studies in the History and Text of the New Testament in Honor of K. W. Clark*, ed. B. L. Daniels and M. J. Suggs (Salt Lake City: University of Utah, 1967), 13-25; Wallis, "The Translation of Romans 1:17," 17-23.

[55] Myers, "The Gospel is More Than 'Faith Alone in Christ Alone,'" 54.

[56] Oddly, Lopez concludes that taking "by faith" with "the just" is preferable and "has better support contextually" (Lopez, *Romans Unlocked*, 41), even though this runs counter to his main theological conclusion about Romans 1:17 that "Paul means to emphasize 'life' since his definition of the gospel is not limited to justification" (ibid., 42). He even cites Nygren in support of taking "by faith" with "the just" rather than "shall live" (ibid., 41). Yet Nygren's extensive treatment establishes conclusively that Romans 1:17 is dealing with justification, not sanctification.

"the justified by faith one (*ho dikaios ek pisteōs*) shall live (*zēsetai*)."[57] The fact remains that the phrase, "by faith," can grammatically qualify either "the just" or "shall live." But even if it qualifies "shall live," this would not necessarily support the meaning of *sanctification* by faith. It may simply be teaching that all who are justified also find life (i.e., eternal life) when they believe. This conclusion is theologically supportable from other passages of Scripture, such as Titus 3:5-7, which teaches that justification and regeneration are simultaneous and inseparable soteriological blessings. This would also harmonize with the teaching of Romans itself based on statements such as *"the justification of life"* in Romans 5:18. For this reason, one Free Grace advocate, John Hart, writes, "That justification and eternal life are mutually inclusive terms is evident elsewhere in Romans (1:17; 5:17, 21; 6:23; 8:10)."[58]

However, to interpret the expression "shall live" (*zēsetai*) in Romans 1:17 to mean sanctification in the Christian life rather than justification coupled with regeneration leads to at least two theological problems. First, some conclude that Paul is quoting Habakkuk 2:4 to describe "living the resurrection-life of Christ (5-8; 12:1-15:13) that is able to deliver everyone from God's present wrath."[59] But this interpretation presents a dispensational dilemma. If this is the point of the quotation by Paul, then where in Habakkuk 2:4, or anywhere in the Old Testament for that matter, is it ever revealed that believers are to live the sanctified life by means of a co-crucifixion and co-resurrection with Christ, to say nothing of every believer being perpetually indwelt by the Holy Spirit who provides the power for present day sanctification? These are New Testament, Church age truths (John 14:16-17; Rom. 8:1-4; Col. 1:24-27; 3:1-4). Thus, Paul was not quoting Habakkuk 2:4 to explain how to live the Christian life.

Second, if *zēsetai* refers to sanctification, this can easily be misconstrued to teach Lordship Salvation. Since the future tense, indicative mood form of *zaō* is used in Romans 1:17, this could be taken as indicating that all who are justified will *necessarily* be practically and progressively sanctified, which is the theological point that some Lordship interpreters have drawn from the Habakkuk 2:4 quotation.[60] However, it appears best

---

[57] Cranfield, *The Epistle to the Romans,* 1:102; David S. Dockery, "Romans 1:16-17," *RevExp* 86.1 (Winter 1989): 87-89; Anders Nygren, *Commentary on Romans,* trans. Carl C. Rasmussen (Philadelphia: Fortress Press, 1949), 76-90; Moo, *The Epistle to the Romans,* 78; Grant R. Osborne, *Romans* (Downers Grove, IL: InterVarsity Press, 2004), 44; John R. W. Stott, *The Message of Romans,* BST (Downers Grove, IL: InterVarsity Press, 1994), 64-65.

[58] John F. Hart, "Why Confess Christ? The Use and Abuse of Romans 10:9-10," *JOTGES* 12 (Autumn 1999): 14n33.

[59] Lopez, *Romans Unlocked,* 42.

[60] Robert P. Martin, "'The Just Shall Live By Faith' Habakkuk 2:4 in Romans 1:16-17," *Reformed Baptist Theological Review* 3 (Fall 2006): 13-26; Wilber B. Wallis, "The Translation of Romans 1:17—A Basic Motif in Paulinism," *JETS* 16.1 (Winter 1973): 17-23; George J. Zemek, Jr., "Interpretative Challenges Relating to Habakkuk 2:4b," *GTJ* 1.1 (Spring 1980): 43-69.

to view Paul's use of Habakkuk 2:4 in Romans 1:17 as intended only to emphasize "faith" in contrast to "works" rather than making some theological point about the linear, productive nature of faith in the process of sanctification. Paul's point is simply to show that the righteous will live by "faith" and thus not by works.[61] He is only citing Habakkuk 2:4 analogously to show that the principle of justification by faith apart from works applies in the new dispensation—the gospel era—just as it did in the Old Testament. Thus, Johnson correctly captures Paul's authorial intent in Romans 1:17 when he writes, "His aim is to stress the means by which one becomes righteous (notice the phrases, 'every one that believeth,' 'from faith to faith,' in the preceding clauses), that is, faith, not works."[62]

It may also be true that Paul is citing Habakkuk 2:4 in order to develop the theme of God's righteousness which is predominant throughout the epistle. This would mean that Paul's point is broader than just providing a proof text for the truth of justification by faith. The theme of Romans must revolve around both the gospel and God's righteousness.[63] Thus, Romans should be viewed largely as an apologetic for, or vindication of, God's righteousness and the gospel that Paul proclaimed.[64] While the gospel is not the entire content of Romans, it is the foundation for all of Romans; and even chapters 6-16 develop the righteous effects and implications stemming from the gospel of justification by faith alone, which in turn demonstrate and vindicate God's righteousness.

From Faith to Faith

Another critical portion of Romans 1:17 that greatly affects one's perception of the gospel and its contents is the expression, "from faith to faith" (*ek pisteōs eis pistin*). If these combined prepositional phrases speak of only one individual's faith, there may be some basis for interpreting Romans 1:17 as a description of faith's progress from justifying faith to sanctifying faith. On the other hand, if this expression is not describing an individual's growth or progress in faith, then what is it referring to? Many different interpretations have been offered for this expression down through Church

---

[61] Johnson, "The Gospel That Paul Preached," 337-38; John W. Taylor, "From Faith to Faith: Romans 1.17 in the Light of Greek Idiom," *NTS* 50 (2004): 348.

[62] Johnson, "The Gospel That Paul Preached," 340n31.

[63] While Morris makes a strong case for the theme of Romans being simply "God" (Leon Morris, "The Theme of Romans," in *Apostolic History and the Gospel: Biblical Essays Presented to F. F. Bruce on his 60th Birthday*, ed. W. Ward Gasque and Ralph P. Martin [Grand Rapids: Eerdmans, 1970], 249-63), this is not adequate to address the particular attribute about God that is emphasized so heavily throughout the epistle—God's *righteousness*.

[64] Shawn Gillogly, "Romans 1:16-17: An Apologetic for the Gospel," a paper presented at the Evangelical Theological Society Southeastern Regional, March 16-17, 2001, pp. 1-10; Rikki E. Watts, "'For I am not ashamed of the gospel': Romans 1:16-17 and Habakkuk 2:4," in *Romans and the People of God* (Grand Rapids: Eerdmans, 1999), 3-4.

history, but since the literature on this subject is vast and complex,[65] these will be summarized in five main categories below.

1) Some in early Church history, such as Tertullian and Augustine, viewed this verse as describing the movement from faith in the law to faith in the gospel.[66] But nowhere does Paul use the word "faith" for confidence in the law. A related but peculiar view was held by Origen, who interpreted "from faith to faith" to mean that a person's righteousness depends on believing the prophets first and then believing the gospel.[67] But Gentiles who do not have the law or prophets are hardly required to know and believe the Old Testament before they can believe the gospel and be justified. Another interpretation held by some early Church expositors like Chrysostom,[68] and a few modern interpreters,[69] is that "faith to faith" is describing the progression from the faith of Old Testament believers to the faith of Church age believers. However, the immediate context of Romans 1:17 does not emphasize the faith of Old Testament saints, though there is some support for this view in Romans 4 with the mention of Abraham and David.

2) Another recent, popular interpretation views "from faith (*ek pisteōs*) to faith (*eis pistin*)" as indicating that man's faith stems from God's faithfulness.[70] This view interprets the first prepositional phrase (*ek pisteōs*) as a reference to God's (or Christ's) faithfulness, where the preposition *ek* and *pisteōs* (viewed as a subjective genitive) indicate that God is the source of man's faith, which is described in the second prepositional phrase (*eis pistin*). Thus, *ek pisteōs eis pistin* would be saying in effect, "out of God's/Christ's faithfulness unto man's faith."[71] There are at least three reasons why this interpretation is unlikely. First, it assigns the noun, *pistis*, two different meanings within the passage (i.e., "faithfulness" and "faith") when there is no compelling reason to do so from the passage. A change from *pistis* meaning "faithfulness" in the first instance but only "faith" in the second

---

[65] For a helpful, though somewhat dated, synopsis of these views with sources, see Cranfield, *Epistle to the Romans*, 1:92-99.

[66] Augustine, *The Spirit and the Letter*, 11.18; Tertullian, *Against Marcion*, 5.13.

[67] Origen, *Commentary on Romans*, 1.15.

[68] Chrysostom, *Homily on the Epistle to the Romans*, 2.

[69] Robert M. Calhoun, "John Chrysostom on ΕΚ ΠΙΣΤΕΩΣ ΕΙΣ ΠΙΣΤΙΝ in Rom. 1:17: A Reply to Charles L. Quarles," *NovT* 48.2 (2006): 131-46; Charles L. Quarles, "From Faith to Faith: A Fresh Examination of the Prepositional Series in Romans 1:17," *NovT* 45.1 (2003): 1-21; Herman C. Waetjen, "The Trust of Abraham and the Trust of Jesus Christ: Romans 1:17," *CTM* 30.6 (December 2003): 446-54.

[70] Dunn, *Romans 1-8*, 43-44; Douglas A. Campbell, "Romans 1:17—A *Crux Interpretum* for the ΠΙΣΤΙΣ ΧΡΙΣΤΟΥ Debate," *JBL* 113.2 (1994): 269.

[71] Douglas A. Campbell, "Romans 1:17—A *Crux Interpretum* for the ΠΙΣΤΙΣ ΧΡΙΣΤΟΥ Debate," *JBL* 113 (1994): 265-85; Morna D. Hooker, "ΠΙΣΤΙΣ ΧΡΙΣΤΟΥ," *NTS* 35 (1989): 321-42; Andrew J. Spallek, "St. Paul's Use of ΕΚ ΠΙΣΤΕΩΣ in Romans and Galatians: The Significance of Paul's Choice of Prepositions with ΠΙΣΤΙΣ as Object and Its Bearing Upon Justification by Faith" (S.T.M. thesis, Concordia Seminary, 1996), 93-118.

is too subtle and is not immediately apparent to the reader. Second, after Paul states in Romans 1:17 that the gospel reveals the righteousness of God "from faith to faith," he then quotes Habakkuk 2:4 to further substantiate his point; but there is nothing in the quotation, "the just shall live by faith," that corresponds to God's faithfulness. The expression refers to the faith of the justified one—a man's faith. Third, there are over 20x in Romans where the noun, *pistis*, can only refer to man's faith based on contextual factors,[72] whereas there is only one instance where it likely refers to God's faithfulness (Rom. 3:3). Though the theological truth of God's faithfulness is emphasized in various ways throughout Romans, the usage of *pistis* does not appear to be one of them.

3) Another major interpretation of the expression, "from faith to faith," regards it to be a reference to the growth or progression in an individual's faith from justification to sanctification.[73] In response to this interpretation, S. Lewis Johnson writes: "It is the opinion of some that the first phrase refers to saving faith and the second phrase to the life of faith. The interpretation is ingenious and expresses a biblical truth, namely, that one lives spiritually by the exercise of initial faith in Christ and continues to live by the continuous exercise of faith, but the context provides little support for the view."[74] It will be seen shortly that context does indeed play a decisive role in determining the correct meaning of this expression. In Romans 1:17, it is *not* likely that both references to "faith" in the expression, "from faith to faith," refer to only one *individual's* faith. In the context, there is an emphasis upon the universality of belief in the gospel among a *multitude* of people. The gospel is said to be for "all" (*panti*) people (1:16), whether Jew or Gentile (1:16), and to all nations (1:5).[75]

4) The most common interpretation of Romans 1:17 is to view "from faith to faith" as an intensified way of expressing "faith" itself. According to this view, justification is by faith—and faith alone! It is by faith and "nothing but faith"[76] or "entirely on the faith principle"[77] or "by faith from first to last" (NIV).[78] While this interpretation fits with the teaching of Scripture

---

[72] Brian Dodd, "Romans 1:17—A Crux Interpretum for the ΠΙΣΤΙΣ ΧΡΙΣΤΟΥ Debate?" *JBL* 114 (1995): 471n9.

[73] Lopez, *Romans Unlocked*, 41; Sanday and Headlam, *A Critical and Exegetical Commentary on the Epistle to the Romans*, 28; W. H. Griffith Thomas, *Commentary on Romans* (Grand Rapids: Kregel, 1974), 63.

[74] S. Lewis Johnson, "The Gospel That Paul Preached," *BSac* 128 (October 1971): 336.

[75] Brindle, "'To the Jew First': Rhetoric, Strategy, History, or Theology?" 224, 229-33; Quarles, "From Faith to Faith," 15; Taylor, "From Faith to Faith," 337.

[76] Moo, *The Epistle to the Romans*, 76; Davey, "The Intrinsic Nature of the Gospel," 156n51.

[77] H. A. Ironside, *Lectures on the Epistle to the Romans* (Neptune, NJ: Loizeaux Bros., 1928), 26.

[78] Alford, *The Greek Testament*, 2:320; Barrett, *Epistle to the Romans*, 31; James Montgomery Boice, *Romans, Volume 1, Justification by Faith, Romans 1-4* (Grand Rapids: Baker Book House, 1991), 117-18; Cranfield, *Epistle to the Romans*, 1:100; Denney, "Romans," 2:591; Godet,

elsewhere about the truth of justification *sola fide*, it must also be noted that some who subscribe to the "intensive" view believe it indicates the nature of saving faith. They believe it supports Lordship Salvation or the doctrine that a genuine saving faith will necessarily persevere to the end,[79] since justifying faith persists "from beginning to end." Thus, *"from faith to faith"* is not only speaking intensively of faith, it is describing the comprehensiveness of justifying faith—that it endures from justification to glorification. Even Roman Catholic scholars have interpreted the expression to mean "beginning and ending in faith"[80] or by faith "from start to finish."[81] This interpretation of verse 17 is even used to establish the Roman Catholic notion of keeping oneself in a state of grace by a continual, productive, living faith.[82] Hence, one Catholic apologist concludes regarding Romans 1:17, "The expression 'from faith to faith' implies a continuing life of faith, one that proceeds from one act of faith to the next throughout the person's life."[83] But the Lordship and Catholic perseverance views are readily seen to be false when it is observed that the two occurrences of "faith" in the expression, *"from faith to faith,"* do not refer to the faith of the same individual who progresses from justification to sanctification. Rather, the dual reference to "faith" refers to the faith of multiple individuals who are coming to Christ by faith and are thereby being justified.

5) The interpretation of the expression, *"from faith to faith"* that has the strongest support is the view that it refers to the spread of the gospel and the righteousness of God being revealed from one believer's faith to another believer's faith each time the gospel is believed.[84] Taylor summarizes this position well by saying that *"from faith to faith"* is "Paul's excited report of the success of the gospel and the growing number of believers, and in particular of the advance or growth of faith among the Gentiles. . . . (and) the increase in faith indicated by the idiom is not personal or individual

---

Commentary on Romans, 97; Haldane, *An Exposition of the Epistle to the Romans*, 49; Hodge, *Commentary on the Epistle to the Romans*, 32; Johnson, *Romans: The Freedom Letter*, 1:29; Morris, *The Epistle to the Romans*, 70; Newell, *Romans Verse-By-Verse*, 23; Nygren, *Commentary on Romans*, 78; Moo, *The Epistle to the Romans*, 76; Schreiner, *Romans*, 71-73; Osborne, *Romans*, 43; James M. Stifler, *The Epistle to the Romans* (Chicago: Moody Press, 1960), 29.

[79] Martin, "The Just Shall Live By Faith," 26.

[80] Maximilian Zerwick and Mary Grosvenor, *A Grammatical Analysis of the Greek New Testament* (Rome: Editrice Pontificio Instituto Biblico, 1996), 459.

[81] Joseph A. Fitzmyer, "Romans" in *The New Jerome Biblical Commentary*, ed. Raymond E. Brown, Joseph A. Fitzmyer, and Roland E. Murphy (Englewood Cliffs, NJ: Prentice Hall, 1990), 834.

[82] *Catechism of the Catholic Church*, English translation, Libreria Editrice Vaticana (Bloomingdale, OH: Apostolate for Family Consecration, 1994), 446.

[83] Sungenis, *Not By Faith Alone*, 54.

[84] Donald Grey Barnhouse, *Man's Ruin* (Grand Rapids: Eerdmans, 1952), 185; Murray, *The Epistle to the Romans*, 1:31-32; Sanday and Headlam, *A Critical and Exegetical Commentary on the Epistle to the Romans*, 28; John W. Taylor, "From Faith to Faith: Romans 1.17 in the Light of Greek Idiom," *NTS* 50 (2004): 337-48.

growth in faith but the mounting number of converts that Paul has seen in his ministry."[85] There are at least 12 exegetical reasons to support this view.

The Spread of the Gospel & Context

1) When it comes to proper hermeneutical method and seeking sound biblical conclusions, it is imperative to begin with the context of a verse or passage, especially its immediate context. In the verse immediately preceding the *"faith to faith"* declaration of verse 17, it says that the gospel *"is the power of God unto salvation to everyone that believes, to the Jew first and also to the Greek."* When the "faith to faith" statement of verse 17 is interpreted in light of the flow of thought from verse 16, the "faith to faith" expression most naturally expands, explains, and grows out of the statements in verse 16, *"to* (dative) *everyone who believes," "to/for* (dative) *the Jew first and also to/for* (dative) *the Greek."* The thought of the two verses taken together is that the righteousness of God is revealed from the faith of one person to the faith of another, such as a Jew believing first and then a Gentile believing. In other words, "faith to faith" means to *everyone* who believes, since all of humanity is either Jewish or Gentile when believing the gospel and becoming justified.

This conclusion is corroborated by the intermediate context. In Romans 1:5, Paul speaks of the *"obedience of faith among all nations."* Then in verse 8, he writes that the Romans' *"faith is spoken of throughout the whole world."* In both of these passages, there is an emphasis upon faith + all nations/whole world. Then in Romans 1:12-13, Paul speaks of *"the mutual faith"* (v. 12), *"both of you* (Gentiles in Rome) *and me* (a Jew)." Paul clearly has a Jew/Gentile universal inclusiveness in mind. This can also be seen in verses 13-15 where he wishes to have some fruit *"among **you** also, just as among the other **Gentiles**"* (v. 13). Then he speaks of going to the Gentiles with the gospel, to Greeks, to barbarians, to wise, to unwise, to you who are in Rome also (vv. 14-15). This would be an example of God's righteousness being revealed from the faith of one believer to the next. Thus, when it comes to verse 17, the "idiom of expansion of faith represented by ἐκ πίστεως εἰς πίστιν would then speak of the growth of faith, starting with Jews, and then among the Gentiles."[86]

This also leads to an important doctrinal consideration. If the gospel is to the Jew first and also to the Gentile (Rom. 1:16), and if Paul in verses 16-17 is teaching that the gospel refers to Christian life or sanctification truths for someone who is already a believer in Christ, then why would Paul use this Jew-Gentile terminology when in the Church age there is neither Jew nor Gentile in the Body of Christ (Gal. 3:28; Col. 3:11)?

---

[85] Taylor, "From Faith to Faith," 346 (ellipsis and parenthesis added).

[86] Ibid., 347.

Are Christian life truths "to the Jew" first and also "to the Greek" *in the Church*? According to the New Testament, there is neither Jew nor Gentile in Christ Jesus! This confirms that the substance of the gospel message concerns how the lost can be justified in God's sight. Nowhere in the New Testament do we read of Peter, Paul, John, or any early Christians preaching Christian life-sanctification truths to the unregenerate as part of evangelism.

The Spread of the Gospel & the Rest of Romans

2) Not only is the spread of the gospel view for the expression *"from faith to faith"* supported by the context of Romans 1:16-17, but it also finds abundant support from the rest of the epistle. In particular, this interpretation of the phrase, *"from faith to faith,"* is also seen in Romans 3:21-23, which is a parallel passage to Romans 1:16-17.[87] It says, *"21 But now the righteousness of God apart from the law is revealed, being witnessed by the Law and the Prophets, 22 even the righteousness of God, through faith in Jesus Christ, to all and on all who believe. For there is no difference; 23 for all have sinned and fall short of the glory of God."* There are several definite parallels between 3:21-23 and 1:16-17. First, the clause, *"righteousness of God is revealed,"* in Romans 3:21 is equivalent to the clause in Romans 1:17, *"for in it (gospel) the righteousness of God is revealed."* Second, when Paul writes in Romans 3:22-23, *"For there is no difference; for all have sinned,"* this is summarizing the previous section in Romans 3 where Paul had declared the universal condemnation of all people, saying, *"both Jews and Greeks that they are all under sin"* (3:9). This is found in the condemnation-justification section of Romans, not the sanctification section of Romans 6-8. This *"no difference"* language is also used by Peter to describe Jews and Gentiles being justified by faith in Acts 15:9, where he says, *"God...made no difference between us and them, purifying their hearts by faith."* Thirdly, the expression in Romans 3:22, *"to all and on all who believe,"* is seen to parallel the statements from Romans 1:16-17, *"to everyone who believes"* (1:16), *"to Jew first and also to Greek"* (1:16), and *"from faith to faith"* (1:17). The fact that such a direct parallel to 1:17 occurs within the justification section of Romans shows that verses 16-17 are about justification.

3) Another parallel passage to Romans 1:16-17 that occurs in the justification section of the epistle is Romans 3:29-30. There it says, *"29 Or is He the God of the Jews only? Is He not also the God of the Gentiles? Yes, of the Gentiles also, 30 since there is one God who will justify the circumcised by faith (ek pisteōs) and the uncircumcised through faith (dia pisteōs)."* These verses form two parallels to Romans 1:16-17, first with the Jew-Gentile language of 1:16, *"to the Jew first and also to the Greek,"* and second through a similar prepositional series as 1:17, *"from faith to faith"* (*ek pisteōs eis pistin*).

---

[87] Johnson, "The Gospel That Paul Preached," 337; Nygren, *Commentary on Romans*, 80.

4) Within the Epistle of Romans, it is conspicuous that the terms "Jew" and "Gentile"/"Greek" (Rom. 1:16) occur only in the sections dealing with condemnation-justification (Rom. 1-4; 9-11;[88] 15). Yet, they are not found once in the entire sanctification section of Romans 6-8. It is particularly striking that even in Romans 14 where Paul is addressing matters related to functioning within the Church, the Body of Christ, the issue of liberties is not framed in a "Jew" versus "Gentile" fashion but is spoken of in the language of "weak" versus "strong" brethren.

5) If the term *"gospel"* (Rom. 1:16) and the clause *"for in it the righteousness of God is revealed from faith to faith"* (Rom. 1:17) refer to both justification and sanctification by faith, then this presents a major problem regarding word distribution in Romans for the noun "faith" (*pistis*) and the verb "believe" (*pisteuō*).[89]

	Romans 1-5	Romans 6-8
pistis	28x	0x
pisteuō	11x	1x

If "faith" and "believe" in Romans 1:16-17 are referring to both justifying and sanctifying faith,[90] then we should expect a more balanced ratio than 39:1 for the condemnation-justification versus sanctification chapters of Romans. The only occurrence of *pisteuō* in Romans 6-8 is in 6:8, where it says, *"Now if we died with Christ, we believe that we shall also live with Him."* This could be referring to either justifying faith or sanctifying faith or both. The walk of Christians, whereby we reckon upon our co-crucifixion and co-resurrection with Christ, is predicated on an initial, justifying belief in Christ's death and resurrection, which is the assumed belief—the common denominator—of every regenerate person in this dispensation (1 Thess. 4:14). While it is certainly true that the Christian life is lived the very same way we received eternal life, namely by grace through faith, the fact remains that the Holy Spirit led Paul to use the terms "faith"/"believe" profusely throughout the chapters on justification but not in the chapters on sanctification. Romans does use the terms "faith" and "believe" later in the Church section in reference to the Christian life (Rom. 12:3, 6; 14:1-2, 22-23; 15:13); but in the primary sanctification section of Romans, chapters 6-8, the terms of emphasis are "reckon" (*logizomai*) and "present" or "yield" (*paristēmi*), not "faith" or "believe."

---

[88] Despite the recent tendency in Free Grace circles to interpret Romans 10 as an explanation of how to live a sanctified Christian life (through confession in order to avert the wrath of God), chapters 9-11 contextually deal with Israel, not the Church, and with the unrighteous, unjustified status of the Jews before God, not with the question of why the Jews aren't sanctified. It is apparent that they are not sanctified because they've never been justified.

[89] Nygren, *Commentary on Romans*, 86-87.

[90] Lopez, *Romans Unlocked*, 40-42.

6) Another reason why "faith to faith" in Romans 1:17 is referring to justification rather than sanctification is because of the manner in which its corresponding phrase, the "righteousness of God," is used by Paul, particularly in Romans. Lopez claims, "One may understand the expression *righteousness of God* in a broad sense as referring both to His judicial acceptance, granted 'to all and on all who believe' (3:22), and His delivering activity, given in resurrection-power (6:1-14) through the Spirit that enables the believer to live righteously (8:1-17)."[91] However, the phrase, *"righteousness of God"* (*dikaiosunē theou*), is not used by Paul to speak of sanctification. The phrase *dikaiosunē theou* (or its semantic equivalent, *dikaiosunē autou*) occurs 12x in the New Testament (Matt. 6:33; Rom. 1:17; 3:5, 21, 22, 25, 26; 10:3; 2 Cor. 5:21; Phil. 3:9; James 1:20; 2 Peter 1:1). The only instances in which this phrase may refer to practical, sanctifying righteousness are in Matthew 6:33 and James 1:20. In all other occurrences, it is uniformly used in a judicial sense of declaring to be righteous rather than becoming righteous in practice. Pauline usage is completely uniform. He never uses the expression in reference to the practical righteousness of sanctification. For this reason, in an extensive excursus on the *dikaioō* ("justify") word group (*dikaios; dikaiosunē*),[92] commentator Douglas Moo states specifically in reference to *dikaiosunē* ("righteousness") that "the idea of 'power' is not clearly present" in the word.[93] The fact that Paul uses *dikaiosunē theou/autou* 5 other times *in Romans itself* and consistently uses it in reference to the imputed righteousness of justification leads to the conclusion that in Romans 1:16-17 the "gospel" is a message about justification not sanctification.[94] It must be remembered that even though the gospel is the power of God *unto* salvation (even sanctification-salvation), this does not mean it is a message *about* sanctification.

7) If the preceding conclusions about the phrase, "righteousness of God," in Romans 1:17 are accurate, this should harmonize with the pattern of usage in Romans for the other key word in the clause of verse 17, "revealed" (*apokaluptō*). In Romans 1:17, it says, *"the righteousness of God is revealed from faith to faith."* The only other place in Romans where it says that the righteousness of God *"is revealed"* is in a justification verse, Romans 3:21. It is important to consider this additional term, "revealed," because Paul's point in Romans 1:17 is not merely about the righteousness of God being by faith, but how the righteousness of God *"is revealed"* from faith to faith, in contrast to how the wrath of God is presently being "revealed" in Romans 1:18. Though it is true that Romans also speaks of practical "righteousness" in

---

[91] Ibid., 40.

[92] Moo, *The Epistle to the Romans*, 79-90.

[93] Ibid., 89.

[94] Johnson, "The Gospel That Paul Preached," 334.

the life of a believer who is walking in yielded dependence upon the Lord (Rom. 6:13-20), this righteousness is not referred to in the same language as Romans 1:17, as the righteousness "of God" that is "revealed" when a person believes the gospel.

Even other terms in Romans that share the same semantic domain[95] as *apokaluptō* and *apokalupsis* occur only in justification contexts. The semantically related terms "manifest" (*phaneroō/phaneros*)[96] and "declare" (*endeixis*)[97] occur only in the condemnation-justification section of Romans (1:17, 18, 19; 2:5; 3:5, 21, 25, 26; 5:8).

8) The preceding observations also fit with the meaning and usage of the term "gospel" in Romans. Besides Romans 1:16-17, either *euangelion* or *euangelizō* occur only one other time in the condemnation-justification section of Romans 1-5. It is at Romans 2:16. There the context is dealing with how people are not justified, whether with the law or without it (2:11-15). By contrast, the term "gospel" conspicuously *never* occurs in Romans 6-8, where we would most expect it to be if sanctification and spirituality are part of the gospel.

Though the term "gospel" does occur a few times in the section dealing with national Israel in Romans 9-11 (10:15, 16; 11:28), it does so only in relation to the question of why many Israelites are not justified before God. These passages have absolutely nothing to do with the question of why Israelites are not becoming practically sanctified as Jewish-Christians.

Within this section, Romans 11:28 presents an illuminating usage of the term "gospel." It says, *"Concerning the gospel they are enemies for your sake, but concerning the election they are beloved for the sake of the fathers."* In the context of this verse, Paul is still addressing the larger question of God's righteousness and faithfulness to His previous covenant promises in light of the collective unbelief and unjustified status of his fellow Jews. Regarding Romans 9-11, some Free Grace proponents today are claiming that God's promises to Israel are part of the broad concept of the "gospel" in Romans. Thus, Lopez states, "Usually unrecognized, the term *gospel* also includes the unconditional promises to Israel that will be fulfilled in the future (10:15-16; 11:26-32)."[98] But Romans 11:28 teaches that God's promises to Israel are *not* part of the gospel. It establishes that the gospel and Israel's election based on God's unilateral promises to the patriarchs are separate concepts. Just as the terms "enemies" and "beloved" are set in contrast to one another in Romans 11:28, so the terms "gospel" and "election" are separate from one another as well. While the elect status of Israel is "good news" in its own right and consistent with the graciousness and righteousness of God, it is not part of "the gospel."

---

95 L&N, 339, §28.38.

96 Ibid., 338-39, §28.36.

97 Ibid., 341, §28.52.

98 Lopez, *Romans Unlocked*, 31-32.

Even later in Romans the term "gospel" does not have a broad, all-inclusive meaning. In Romans 15:16, 19-20, 29, Paul uses the term "gospel" in reference to his missionary journeys to the Gentiles, where he does not speak of preaching a gospel of sanctification to those who were already justified, but preaching to those who had never heard the name of Christ before (15:20-21). This indicates that the term "gospel" is only used of the message about how lost sinners can become justified. It is not a message explaining how saints in Christ can become more sanctified.

The Spread of the Gospel & Parallel Passages

9) The view that *"from faith to faith"* (Rom. 1:17) refers to the growing number of people who believe the gospel also finds support from outside the Epistle of Romans. 2 Corinthians 2:16 contains a parallel "from (*ek*) + to (*eis*)" construction. It says in reference to two categories of people, the "perishing" versus the "saved" (2 Cor. 2:15), that *"To the one we are the aroma of (ek) death to (eis) death, and to the other the aroma of (ek) life to (eis) life."* In this verse, there is a clear progression, but it is not the progress of one individual, as if Romans 1:17 is describing a progress from justifying faith to sanctifying faith. Rather, "those who are being saved" (*tois sōzomenois*) and "those who are perishing" (*tois apollumenois*) speaks of a plurality of both saved and lost people. As Paul preached and the gospel spread, so did the number of people receiving eternal life ("from life to life"). By contrast, when Paul preached and people rejected his message, he brought out, as an aroma, the eternal fate of these multitudes ("from death to death").

The *ek* + *eis* construction of 2 Corinthians 2:16 illustrates progression rather than emphasis. This is an important distinction since many Protestant commentators have claimed that the expression, *"from faith to faith,"* in Romans 1:17 is referring intensively and emphatically to "faith and only faith." While justification is by faith alone, and that is taught in Romans 1:16-17, the double prepositional expression, *"from faith to faith,"* is making a larger point. The linguistic construction, *ek* (noun) + *eis* (noun), was a common Greek idiom[99] of the Koine Period that did not indicate emphasis or intensiveness[100] but rather progression from one locale or state to the next.[101] This means that in 2 Corinthians 2:16, rather than attempting to define the preposition *ek* as source and *eis* as goal, a more fitting translation of the Greek idiom would be: "To some (we are) the aroma of the advance of death, but to others the aroma of the advance of life."[102] Thus, Quarles summarizes his extensive research into this construction by saying, "the ἐκ-εἰς prepositional series often expresses range, dura-

---

[99] Quarles, "From Faith to Faith," 5-11; Taylor, "From Faith to Faith," 341-44.

[100] BDAG, 298; L&N, 692.

[101] This conclusion is based on the extensive research of this construction by Quarles and Taylor using the *TLG* database.

[102] Taylor, "From Faith to Faith," 343.

tion, repetition, source and destination, previous state and new state or progression. It does not appear to function as an idiom of emphasis."[103]

10) Further support for the interpretation of Romans 1:16-17 as describing the spread of the gospel and justifying faith comes from the parallel reference in Galatians 3:11. This is the only other established Pauline usage of the phrase, *"the just shall live by faith"*;[104] and in its context, it is clearly dealing only with justification, not sanctification.[105]

11) Another close parallel passage to Romans 1:16-17 is Galatians 3:22, which also occurs in a decisively justification-regeneration context.[106] There it says, *"But the Scripture has confined all under sin, that the promise by faith (ek pisteōs) in Jesus Christ might be given to those who believe (tois pisteuousin)."* There appear to be two parallels between Galatians 3:22 and Romans 1:16-17. First, the phrase, "by faith" (*ek pisteōs*) corresponds with Romans 1:17, *"from faith (ek pisteōs) to faith."* Second, the participle of *pisteuō* in Galatians 3:22 (*pisteuousin*) is in the present tense, active voice, dative case, masculine, plural form. Whereas in the phrase in Romans 1:16, *"to everyone who believes"* (*tō pisteuonti*), the participle *pisteuonti* is in the exact same form but only singular. In Galatians 3:22, it might seem unnecessarily redundant for Paul to say, *"by faith . . . to those who believe."* But he appears to be emphasizing the point that not only does the salvation of God's imputed righteousness come *to us* by faith, but it also comes *to all* who believe.[107] That is, it comes *"to everyone that believes, to the Jew first and also to the Greek."* In this sense, justification is *"from faith to faith."*

12) Finally, the expression in Romans 1:17, "For in it the righteousness of God is revealed" (*dikaiosune gar theou en auto apokaluptetai*), is not a direct quotation from any one Old Testament passage, but it appears to be an allusion to several Old Testament texts that each indicate a progression of God's righteousness to the Gentile nations (LXX, Ps. 98:2/97:2; Isa. 51:4-8; 56:1, 3-8).[108] This fits with Romans 1:16-17 and its progression from *"the Jew first and also to the Greek"* (i.e., *"from faith to faith"*). This is even seen to be a theme throughout Romans, not only in Romans 3:21-28 as noted previously, but also in Romans 2:9-10; 9:24; 15:8-9, 19.[109]

The interpretation of Romans 1:17 that views "from faith to faith" as the spread of the gospel is supported at every level—contextually,

---

[103] Quarles, "From Faith to Faith," 13.

[104] The only other New Testament occurrence is in Heb. 10:38, where the Pauline authorship of Hebrews is highly questionable.

[105] Nygren, *Commentary on Romans*, 89; Spallek, "St. Paul's Use of ΕΚ ΠΙΣΤΕΩΣ in Romans and Galatians," 87-92.

[106] Murray, *The Epistle to the Romans*, 1:31-32.

[107] Ibid.

[108] Cranfield, *Epistle to the Romans*, 1:96; Taylor, "From Faith to Faith," 244-46.

[109] Taylor, "From Faith to Faith," 347.

elsewhere in the Book of Romans, and through parallel passages in the Old and New Testaments.

Romans 1:18

Romans 1:18 marks a significant shift in the Book of Romans. It begins a new section dealing with man's just condemnation in the sight of God (Rom. 1:18-3:20). But is this section dealing strictly with the condemnation and unjustified status of the lost, or is it also describing the need of believers to be delivered from the wrath of God as part of sanctification in the Christian life, as some crossless gospel proponents teach? However Romans 1:18 is to be interpreted, it cannot be separated from the immediately preceding verses of Romans 1:16-17. There are at least two reasons for this. First, Romans 1:18 begins with the postpositive particle "for" (*gar*), linking it to the preceding thought of verse 17.[110] Second, verses 17-18 are parallel to one another with respect to God's *righteousness* being "revealed" (*apokalupetai*) when the gospel is believed (v. 17) and God's *wrath* being "revealed" (*apokalupetai*) against all ungodliness and unrighteousness of men who suppress the truth in unrighteousness (v. 18). In both verses, the present tense, passive voice, indicative mood of *apokaluptō* is used respectively for God's righteousness and wrath.

Some proponents of the crossless view have deduced their broad concept of "the gospel" from the parallelism and connection between Romans 1:16-17 and Romans 1:18. They reason incorrectly that since verses 16-17 deal broadly with both justification and sanctification, and verses 17-18 form parallel thoughts to one another, then verse 18 must be teaching that *Christians* also need deliverance from God's wrath as part of their progressive sanctification. They conclude that since the present tense of *apokaluptō* is used in both verse 17 and verse 18 for "revealed," this must mean that both Christians and non-Christians need deliverance from God's wrath by repenting, or turning, from sin. They also wrongly conclude from Romans 1:18 and the verses following it in chapter 1 that there must be no eternal wrath of God, only temporal wrath. These deductions of the crossless position about the key introductory verses of Romans 1:16-18 constitute radically new paradigms that affect one's entire outlook on the Epistle of Romans. This new doctrine of wrath is also a logical and theological necessity for the crossless gospel. It is necessary in order to maintain the view that repentance is not a condition for eternal life, since certain passages in Romans taken at face value (e.g., Rom. 2:4-5, 8, 15-16) most certainly do require repentance as a condition for escaping God's eternal wrath.[111]

---

[110] C. E. B. Cranfield, "Romans 1.18," *SJT* 21 (1968): 330-32.

[111] Charles C. Bing, *Lordship Salvation: A Biblical Evaluation and Response*, GraceLife Edition (Burleson, TX: GraceLife Ministries, 1992), 88-89n124; G. Michael Cocoris, *Repentance: The Most Misunderstood Word in the Bible* (Santa Monica, CA: Self-published, 2003), 31-32; J. B.

Temporal vs. Eternal Wrath

One primary problem with the crossless position on Romans 1:18 is its limitation of God's wrath to the present. Simply because the present tense of *apokaluptō* is used in verses 17-18 does not limit the wrath of God to the present.[112] Just as *God's imputed, judicial righteousness* mentioned in verse 17 is both a present possession and an eternal, enduring reality for all who believe the gospel, so the *wrath of God* that abides upon unbelievers in verse 18 is a present reality that also extends into eternity.[113] This is the same truth conveyed in 1 Corinthians 1:18 by the use of the present participles for "being saved" (*sōzomenois*) and "perishing" (*apollumenois*). The fact that believers are presently "being saved" describes both a present salvation and a salvation that extends into eternity. Likewise, the fact that unbelievers are "perishing" means that they stand both currently condemned and destined for ruin in the eternal future. The same principle can also be seen in John 3:36a, where the everlasting life that believers in Christ possess is both a present and a future possession. Corresponding to this, the wrath of God in John 3:36b that abides upon unbelievers is parallel to the everlasting life referred to in the verse. This wrath is God's present and eternal disposition towards those who refuse to believe in His Son. God's wrath remains upon the unbeliever who never believes in Christ throughout this lifetime and into eternity.

The use of the present tense in Romans 1:18 for the wrath of God being "revealed" does not limit that wrath to the present earthly life in contrast to an eschatological or eternal wrath. To restrict our interpretative options to either the present or the eternal future is purely an "artificial" dichotomy that is "without basis in the text."[114] There is no need to make the interpretation of Romans 1:18 an either/or proposition. In reality, it is a case of both/and. The "wrath" of God that is "revealed" in Romans 1:18ff "transcends the antithesis between present and future."[115] It is clear that there is an eschatological wrath of God that is *eternal* according to Romans 2:5, 8, 15-16 and other passages such as 2 Thessalonians 1:8-10 and Revelation 14:10-11.

But other problems exist with the new view of wrath in the Free Grace camp. For instance, among proponents of the G.E.S. doctrine on wrath,

---

Hixson, *Getting the Gospel Wrong: The Evangelical Crisis No One Is Talking About* (n.p.: Xulon Press, 2008), 360. This was also Wilkin's original position on these verses. See Robert N. Wilkin, "Repentance as a Condition for Salvation in the New Testament" (Th.D. dissertation, Dallas Theological Seminary, 1985), 124-26.

[112] Keck, *Romans*, 58.

[113] Scott A. Ashmon, "The Wrath of God: A Biblical Overview," *Concordia Journal* 31 (2005): 356-57; R. V. G. Tasker, *The Biblical Doctrine of the Wrath of God* (London: Tyndale Press, 1951), 9.

[114] Nygren, *Commentary on Romans*, 99.

[115] Ibid., 100.

there is no consensus on when the wrath of God terminates, except that all agree it cannot be eternal. Hodges believed the wrath described in Romans is limited strictly to the present and does not even extend into the coming tribulation. Regarding God's wrath in Romans 2:5, Hodges states rather incredibly that Paul "is *not* talking about the eschatological future (i.e., the Tribulation, cf. 1 Thess. 5:9). He is talking about right here and now!"[116] On the other hand, Lopez believes "It will culminate at the tribulation."[117] Whereas Wilkin maintains "that God's wrath ends with the end of the millennium and He's never angry any more, because His wrath ceases. God's not a wrathful being that He wishes to have wrath for eternity."[118] Though God did not have wrath in eternity past when there was no sin,[119] since the advent of sin into the universe "Scripture definitely regards wrath as an attribute of God";[120] and there is no reason to believe His wrath is not a fixed disposition toward sin both now and eternally (Jer. 17:4; Mal. 1:4).[121] But in order for God to cease His fixed, wrathful, disposition toward sin, sin itself would need to cease to exist in His created universe; and the universe would have to revert to its original, impeccable, pre-temporal state. To accomplish this, He could choose to annihilate, instead of tormenting, all sinning creatures, namely the devil and his fallen angels along with all unregenerate, unbelieving humanity. But such a possibility is patently unbiblical (Matt. 25:41, 46; Rev. 14:10-11; 20:10).

Despite the claim that there can be no eternal wrath of God, each of the three proposed termination times faces problems. If God's wrath is strictly for the present prior to the tribulation, then are we to assume that all who have died up to the present have already received in their earthly lifetimes all the wrath they had "stored up" (Rom. 2:5; 1 Thess. 2:16; 2 Thess. 1:6)? What about the ungodly who die peacefully and in the lap of luxury like the rich man in Luke 16? What about the many proud, defiant, Christ-rejecting popes who lived and died as kings? Was Hitler's suicide in his underground bunker the full extent of wrath he had stored up? Even if God's wrath culminates at the end of the tribulation, as Lopez teaches, what about all the unregenerate who have died during the last 2,000 years of Church history prior to the tribulation? Have they also received the full extent of wrath that they had stored up by the time

---

[116] Zane C. Hodges, "The Moralistic Wrath-Dodger," *JOTGES* (Spring 2005), 20.

[117] Lopez, *Romans Unlocked*, 55. See also, Lopez, "Do Believers Experience the Wrath of God?" 59-60.

[118] Bob Wilkin, "Why the Romans Road Ends in a Cul de Sac," Grace Evangelical Society Conference, Dallas, TX, March 1, 2006.

[119] Ashmon, "The Wrath of God," 351.

[120] G. H. C. MacGregor, "The Concept of the Wrath of God in the New Testament," *NTS* 7 (1961): 103.

[121] Ashmon, "The Wrath of God," 357-58; Tasker, *The Biblical Doctrine of the Wrath of God*, 8-10.

of their deaths? In addition, if God's wrath ends with the tribulation, it is difficult to conceive how His wrath does not continue in the millennium when He rules with a rod of iron, and withholds rain and sends plagues upon those nations that refuse to worship Him (Zech. 14:16-19), and when His fire consumes the earth's armies arrayed against Him at the end of the 1,000 years (Rev. 20:7-9).

In addition, all three posssible timeframes suffer major logical inconsistencies when it comes to hades and hell. We are told that God's wrath cannot refer to hell or be eternal. We are also told that God's justice is only completely satisfied either in this lifetime, or at the end of the tribulation,[122] or at the end of the millennium.[123] Only at such times will His wrath be finally extinguished. But this raises serious problems regarding the lost who are suffering in hades today. Hades is the place of temporary punishment for the unsaved prior to the end of both the tribulation and millennium (Rev. 20:14). It is also a place of conscious torment in fire (Luke 16:24-28), just as the lake of fire will be (Rev. 21:8). But if God's wrath abides on unbelievers only during this earthly lifetime, why is the suffering of unbelievers in hades worse than any wrath they may have experienced while on earth? This is especially evident in the case of some like the rich man in Luke 16:19-31 *"who was clothed in purple and fine linen and fared sumptuously every day"* (v. 19) and received *"good things"* throughout his lifetime (v. 25). It seems terribly inequitable to think that he received only in this lifetime the entire wrath he had stored up.

Furthermore, it is inconsistent to claim that God's wrath cannot be experienced by unbelievers in hades today. Hades is only the temporary abode of the lost and it runs concurrent with the outpouring of God's wrath on earth until the ostensible consummation of His wrath at either the end of the tribulation or the end of the millennium. But if both hades and earth-history are temporary, concurrent, co-extensive, and preliminary to the final satisfying of God's justice and placating of His wrath, then why can't hades be the place of His wrath in the meantime, just like on earth, especially since hades is worse than any earthly suffering? Even if advocates of today's crossless doctrine of wrath end up conceding that hades is also the place of God's wrath, then this still presents a dilemma for their doctrine. If the conscious, fiery torment of hades consists of the same type of suffering that will characterize the future lake of fire, and hades is admitted to be a place of God's wrath, then why can't the lake of fire also be the place of God's *eternal* wrath? With such scriptural and logical inconsistencies, one wonders if the crossless position will ultimately lead some of its adherents to embrace the doctrine of annihilationism, with which it shares a logical and hermeneutical affinity.[124]

---

[122] Lopez, "Do Believers Experience the Wrath of God?" 50n18.

[123] Bob Wilkin, "Why the Romans Road Ends in a Cul de Sac."

[124] While those in the Free Grace movement who are advocating the new doctrine of

Christians Under Wrath

Besides the view that God's wrath is not eternal, another contention of the crossless position is that believers need routine deliverance from God's wrath due to sin in our lives. The assumption that carnal believers are subject to the wrath of God has become so paradigmatic for many Free Grace Christians that it is now being taught that Romans was written to instruct the believer about how to find deliverance from God's wrath in the Christian life.[125] Romans 1:18 is now interpreted as being descriptive of both sinning believers and unbelievers. Another passage that has suffered greatly at the hands of crossless gospel exegetes is Romans 5:9. This verse, along with Romans 5:10, has traditionally been interpreted by Free Grace evangelicals as a promise of the justified person's eternal security. But now it is viewed as a verse supporting the Christian's progressive sanctification and deliverance from divine wrath. Commenting on the future indicative of "save" in Romans 5:9, *"we shall be saved (sōthēsometha) from wrath through Him,"* Lopez explains the Christians-under-wrath view, saying:

> One should understand Paul's use of the future tense *sōthēsometha* as a logical future emphasizing something naturally expected to transpire upon the believer's obedience. (5) Hence the salvation theme has not recurred since 1:16, because Paul chooses to reserve the term to express deliverance from wrath resulting from Christians who "walk in newness of life" (6:4) experienced upon obedience (6:11-13; 8:1-13). That is why Paul does not use "save" (*sōzō*) and "salvation" (*sōtēria*) in the justification section (3:21-4:25). Unfortunately this has gone relatively unnoticed.[126]

But is Romans 5:9 really teaching the natural consequence of "obedience" in the Christian life? Is it really describing a subjective state of wrath that Christians might still need salvation from? There are at least four reasons why Free Grace people should reject this novel view and retain the traditional eternal security interpretation. First, this passage does not contain a single condition or obligation for the believer. It is a pure promise. It is *not*

---

temporal wrath still affirm the conscious, eternal torment of the unregenerate, in order to maintain the consistency of their position they are forced to interpret passages on the duration and extent of God's wrath and judgment in a manner similar to annihilationists. For example, the annihilationist, Edward Fudge, explains that God's wrath (*orgē*) and anger (*thumos*) in Romans 2, when coupled with "trouble" (*thlipsis*) and "distress" (*stenochōria*), are indicative of a judgment that does not persist for eternity but consummates at the end of time (Edward W. Fudge, *The Fire That Consumes: The Biblical Case for Conditional Immortality*, rev. ed. [Carlisle, England: Paternoster Press, 1994], 162-63). See also his similar treatment of 2 Thess. 1:6-10 (ibid., 151-56) and Rev. 14:10-11 (ibid., 185-90), where OT backgrounds and contexts dealing with temporal, finite judgment become superimposed upon NT contexts and end up nullifying the NT meaning in the process.

[125] Myers, "The Gospel is More Than 'Faith Alone in Christ Alone,'" 46.

[126] Lopez, *Romans Unlocked*, 109-10.

describing "something naturally expected to transpire upon the believer's obedience." This cannot be found anywhere in the verse or context. On the contrary, the immediately preceding context indicates that we will be delivered from wrath despite the fact that we were "still" (*eti*) without spiritual strength, ungodly (Rom. 5:6), and "still" (*eti*) sinners (Rom. 5:8). And according to Romans 5:9, our future deliverance is dependent upon Christ, not us. In verse 9, the promise that *"we shall be saved from wrath"* is said to be *"through Him"* and based upon the fact that we have been *"justified by His blood."* According to the verse itself, exemption from future divine wrath is entirely dependent upon Christ, not the Christian's faithful walk of obedience.

While Lopez and other proponents of the G.E.S. position might object that this deliverance is attributable first of all to Christ, since it is His resurrection power that enables the believer to escape sin and wrath when appropriated in our daily walk, in reality the burden of responsibility is still shouldered by the believer, not Christ. This can be seen in an article on wrath written by Lopez where he states, "As in the OT, the 'wrath of God' in the NT falls upon the unregenerate and on disobedient believers. Thus, God awaits one's choice—for the unregenerate to believe and for the believer to obey. Thus, to extinguish the wrath of God requires obedience for the regenerate; and for the unregenerate, faith."[127] But nothing could be further from the spirit and intent of Romans 5:9. To claim that the *obedience of the Christian* extinguishes the wrath of God, when Romans 5:9 says that we shall be saved from wrath *"through Him,"* is a hopeless contradiction.

In addition, this approach to the Christian life is not consistent with the believer's standing in grace. According to this relatively new view of spirituality within the Free Grace movement, God's wrath towards the believer is never really "extinguished"; it is just put on pause until the next time we sin, which may be only a matter of minutes or moments away since we sin in thought, word, and deed continually throughout each day. This means that God's wrath is continually re-ignited and extinguished multiple times each day throughout the entire course of our Christian lives. But is this a grace-approach to the Christian life? If a child lived in a home where the father's disposition was constantly determined on the basis of the child's obedience, what kind of nurturing environment would that be? What kind of growth would this induce in the child, if he thought he had to extinguish his father's wrath by the consistency of his obedience? This kind of spirituality will certainly not lead to growth in the grace and knowledge of our Lord and Savior Jesus Christ (2 Peter 3:18). Rather it will foster fear, uncertainty, and insecurity.

Tragically, this Christian-under-wrath doctrine is almost always coupled with the prospect of negative judgment at the bema following

---

[127] René A. Lopez, "Do Believers Experience the Wrath of God?" *JOTGES* 15 (Autumn 2002): 53.

the rapture of the Church. Thus, Dillow writes, "If God can bring condemnation upon believers in time as these illustrations prove, there is no necessary reason to believe He cannot condemn believers at the judgment seat of Christ."[128] If this theology is allowed to prevail in the daily thinking and perspective of the believer, it will not result in a truly Christ-centered Christian life. It will not focus the believer upon the finished work of Christ, on our identification with Him as the basis for a daily Spirit-filled walk, or on eagerly looking for Him as our Blessed Hope.

Returning again to Romans 5:9, we see a second problem with the sanctification and deliverance from divine wrath view of this verse by the way it interprets the future, indicative form of "save" (*sōzō*). The twofold occurrence of *sōthēsometha* ("we shall be saved") in Romans 5:9-10 is interpreted as being merely a "logical future," rather than a simple predictive future. The logical future would not necessarily indicate that an event or action will occur in the future but only that it is likely or expected to follow. In this respect, it may be used rhetorically to express an element of doubt or contingency. In response, it should be noted that the logical future is not a well-attested category of usage in Greek grammar.[129] But assuming that it is legitimate here in Romans 5:9-10, how would this affect the meaning of these verses? Treating the two future indicatives in verses 9-10 as logical futures would give these verses an indefinite sense that is contrary to the normal pattern of Pauline usage. Outside of the two verbs in Romans 5:9-10, the same inflected form of the future tense, passive voice, and indicative mood occurs in 20 other verses in Romans. Five of these are marked conditional sentences (Rom. 1:10; 2:26; 10:9; 11:23-24) with the future, passive, indicative verb occurring in the apodosis. But this is unlike either Romans 5:9 or 5:10, which are not conditional sentences. Of the remaining 15 occurrences (Rom. 2:12-13; 3:20; 5:19; 8:21; 9:7, 26-27, 33; 10:11, 13; 11:22, 26, 35; 14:4), only 1 has a possible indefinite, uncertain sense regarding future fulfillment (Rom. 14:4).[130]

Thus, to take *sōthēsometha* in either Romans 5:9 or 5:10 as implying some contingency or uncertainty about the future is an appeal to its rare,

---

[128] Joseph C. Dillow, *The Reign of the Servant Kings: A Study of Eternal Security and the Final Significance of Man* (Miami Springs, FL: Schoettle Publishing, 1992), 540.

[129] Though it is not unheard of for exegetes to refer to a future tense verb as a "logical future," it is noteworthy that none of the major NT Greek grammars lists the logical future as a recognized syntactical category. Even if exegetes mean the gnomic future, where a fact or action "may be rightfully expected under normal conditions" (H. E. Dana and Julius R. Mantey, *A Manual Grammar of the Greek New Testament* [New York: Macmillan Publishing, 1927], 193), this is "very rarely used" in the NT (Daniel B. Wallace, *Greek Grammar Beyond the Basics: An Exegetical Syntax of the New Testament* [Grand Rapids: Zondervan, 1996], 571); and Rom. 5:7; 7:3; Gal. 6:5; Eph. 5:31 "appear to be the only examples cited in the New Testament" (James A. Brooks and Carlton L. Winbery, *Syntax of New Testament Greek* [Lanham, MD: University Press of America, 1979], 98).

[130] This pattern and predominance also holds true with respect to the 51 active voice and 7 middle voice, future, indicatives in Romans.

and unlikely, usage. Furthermore, the logical future, as opposed to the simple predictive future, requires that some prior condition first be met as indicated somewhere in the context. When Lopez treats the *"we shall be saved"* statement of Romans 5:9 "as a logical future emphasizing something naturally expected to transpire upon the believer's obedience," this assumes that some human condition is contained in the context. But no "obedience" or condition can be found either explicitly or implicitly. This fact also makes it highly doubtful that *sōthēsometha* in Romans 5:9 is a logical future.

Third, the pattern of occurrences for the word "wrath" (*orgē*) in Romans does not fit with the interpretation of Romans 5:9 as a sanctification passage. The word "wrath" is not found once in the entire sanctification/Christian life section of Romans 6-8, where we would expect it to occur with greatest frequency if the interpretation of Lopez is correct. Conversely, however, the word *orgē* occurs with greatest frequency in the condemnation-justification section of Romans 1:18-4:25. In this section it occurs 6x (1:18; 2:5 [2x], 8; 3:5; 4:15), whereas later in the Church-related section of chapters 12-16 it occurs only 3x (Rom. 12:19; 13:4-5).[131] It is better, therefore, to interpret Romans 5:9 as a promise to all believers of certain,

---

[131] In the case of Rom. 12:19 where it says to give place to wrath, this speaks of believers deferring *to God* the right to exercise vengeance, not wrath coming *from God* upon believers. Rom. 13:4-5 is the only passage in Scripture that potentially indicates that Christians can in some sense receive God's wrath. However, while the context is explicit that governments are ordained by God (13:1-2) and that the one who performs capital punishment is in the position of being "God's minister" (13:4), some interpreters conclude that this passage does not clearly specify divine wrath (Alan F. Johnson, *Romans: The Freedom Letter* [Chicago: Moody Press, 1985], 2:110) and that the term "wrath" in 13:4-5 refers to man's wrath rather than God's (William L. Pettingill, *The Gospel of God: Simple Studies in Romans* [Findlay, Ohio: Fundamental Truth Publishers, n.d.], 211; Schreiner, *Romans*, 678-80, 85; W. E. Vine, "Romans" in *The Collected Writings of W. E. Vine* [Nashville: Thomas Nelson, 1996], 1:420). It would be difficult to conclude that the execution of Peter and Paul in Rome was God's wrath even though "God's minister" in such a case was the very Roman government referred to in Rom. 13:1-6. Likewise today, when a death-row inmate is put to death by lethal injection and it is later discovered through DNA analysis that he was innocent, did that man receive the wrath of God or man? Though government is in the position of being God's minister, this does not automatically mean that all wrath is divine. On the other hand, in light of the fact that "wrath" everywhere else in Romans refers to divine wrath rather than human wrath (Paul D. Feinberg, "The Christian and Civil Authorities," *MSJ* 10 [Spring 1999]: 93), and the immediate context of Rom. 13 strongly suggests that God's wrath is exercised through human governments, it seems best to interpret the "wrath" of 13:4-5 as indicating the general principle that divine wrath is mediated through human governments for capital offenses. However, it may also be significant that the believer's subjection and fear in the passage is not stated to be God-ward but is specifically directed towards the government (Rom. 13:1, 3-5, 7), while the believer's "conscience" is clearly God-ward (13:5). Therefore, it appears unwise to conclude from this single passage that all temporal consequences for sin are God's wrath upon the believer, or even that God's wrath is directly meted out to the believer as a result of general disobedience in the Christian life. Romans 13:1-7 does not substantiate the doctrine of the Christian's deliverance from divine wrath as a paradigm for Christian living or for the rest of Romans.

guaranteed deliverance from God's wrath—the wrath that comes solely upon the unjustified. The promise of the believer's eternal security at this juncture in Romans would also form the fitting basis upon which to introduce the sanctification truths of chapters 6-8 and for living the Christian life by grace through faith.

Finally, a fourth problem with the interpretation of Christians being under wrath in Romans 5:9 relates to the blessed hope of the Church. To teach that saints of the Church age must still be progressively saved from God's wrath ends up weakening a major supporting argument for the pre-tribulational rapture. Historically, dispensationalists have demonstrated from a comparison of biblical ecclesiology and eschatology that the nature of the Church and the nature of the coming tribulation are incompatible. Saints of the present era who comprise the Church have a unique position "in Christ." We are already citizens of heaven (Phil. 3:20), members of Christ's body (Rom. 12:4-5), and even His bride (2 Cor. 11:2; Eph. 5:25-32; Rev. 19:7-9). Because we are so intimately associated with Him, having been bought at the price of His own blood (Acts 20:28; 1 Cor. 6:19-20) and now having a position in the One who is our propitiation (1 John 2:2; 4:10),[132] we are shielded from God's wrath. "As forgiven men and women, we are outside the sphere in which God's wrath operates."[133] Dispensationalists have reasoned that, since the tribulation is characterized as the time of God's wrath (1 Thess. 1:10; Rev. 6:16-17), and Church age believers are promised categorical exemption from God's wrath (John 3:36; Rom. 5:9; 1 Thess. 5:9), we must therefore be kept from the particular hour of tribulation (Rev. 3:10).[134] Romans 5:9 has often been cited specifically in support of this conclusion.[135] But if, as we are told, "God's wrath

---

[132] This fact explains the example of Moses and passages such as Heb. 3:11 and 4:3, which are sometimes used to prove that believers in the age of grace need on-going deliverance from God's wrath (Lopez, "Do Believers Experience the Wrath of God?" 46-47, 52). These passages are simply describing God's dealings with the nation of Israel in the OT. Christ had not yet been provided as the propitiation for human sin, nor was Israel provided with the same exalted position in Christ that the believer in this dispensation is privileged to possess.

[133] Lawrence O. Richards, as quoted by G. Harry Leafe, "Wrath," in *Dictionary of Premillennial Theology: A Practical Guide to the People, Viewpoints, and History of Prophetic Studies*, ed. Mal Couch (Grand Rapids: Kregel, 1996), 425.

[134] E. Schuyler English, *The Rapture* (Neptune, NJ: Loizeaux Brothers, 1954), 56-62; Charles C. Ryrie, *Come Quickly, Lord Jesus: What You Need to Know About the Rapture* (Eugene, OR: Harvest House, 1996), 125-39; J. F. Strombeck, *First the Rapture: The Church's Blessed Hope* (Grand Rapids: Kregel, reprinted 1992), 93.

[135] Paul D. Feinberg, "The Case for the Pretribulation Rapture Position," in *The Rapture: Pre-, Mid-, or Post-Tribulational?* (Grand Rapids: Zondervan, 1984), 51-53; Renald E. Showers, *Maranatha: Our Lord, Come!* (Bellmawr, NJ: Friends of Israel, 1995), 194-95; Gerald B. Stanton, *Kept From the Hour: Biblical Evidence for the Pretribulational Return of Christ* (Miami Springs, FL: Schoettle Publishing, 1991), 44; John F. Walvoord, *The Rapture Question*, rev. ed. (Grand Rapids: Zondervan, 1979), 67.

falls equally on unbelievers as well as sinning believers"[136] today, then why should God keep Christians from His future wrath?[137]

Romans 2:16

Romans 2:12-16

12 *For as many as have sinned without law will also perish without law, and as many as have sinned in the law will be judged by the law*

13 *(for not the hearers of the law are just in the sight of God, but the doers of the law will be justified . . . .*

16 *in the day when God will judge the secrets of men by Jesus Christ, according to **my gospel.***

Romans 2:16 is sometimes enlisted as support for the notion of a broad gospel that goes beyond the saving message or the contents of saving faith. Myers, for instance, believes that Romans 2:16 is part of Paul's teaching on "How to live the justified life by faith."[138] Lopez explains that the bad news of God's future judgment is included in Paul's gospel. He writes regarding the prepositional phrase, *"according to my gospel,"* that "Paul's gospel includes the absolute certainty of final-judgment on sin (1 Cor. 4:5)."[139] Even the liberal scholar, Friedrich, concurs with Lopez that the "judgment" in Romans 2:16 "is part of the content of the Gospel."[140] But is this really what this verse is teaching?

There is nothing in Romans 2:16 or its context to indicate that Paul is saying in essence, "in the day when God will judge the secrets of men by Jesus Christ *which is my gospel*" or *"as my gospel declares"* (NIV). Instead, the details of the passage point to two possible interpretations of the *"according to my gospel"* phrase, both of which support the view that the gospel is limited to the saving message. First, the preposition *kata* ("according to") may simply mean "in accordance with," or "consistent with," so that Romans 2:16 is only indicating that the fact of coming judgment accords with, or is consistent with, the gospel that Paul preaches.[141] This interpretation recognizes that the bad news of God's judgment is consistent

---

136 Lopez, "Do Believers Experience the Wrath of God?" 48.

137 Although adherents of the G.E.S. position on wrath are virtually all pre-tribulational with respect to the rapture, the doctrine of Christians needing salvation from God's wrath actually shares the same rationale, or conceptual basis, as the partial rapture position. If disobedient believers receive the wrath of God now, why should they be exempt from God's wrath in the tribulation? According to both views, only obedient, worthy Christians escape God's wrath. The partial rapture view combined with the doctrine of believers being subject to God's wrath can be seen in the writings of Robert Govett, G. H. Lang, G. H. Pember, D. M. Panton, and modern proponents, J. D. Faust and Gary T. Whipple.

138 Myers, "The Gospel is More Than 'Faith Alone in Christ Alone,'" 54.

139 Lopez, *Romans Unlocked*, 62.

140 Gerhard Friedrich, "εὐαγγελίζομαί, εὐαγγέλιον, προευαγγελίζομαί, εὐαγγελιστής." *TDNT*, 2:730.

141 Nygren, *Commentary on Romans*, 147.

or harmonious with the gospel itself—the message of salvation through faith in Christ's person and work. The bad news of God's judgment forms the *context* for the actual *content* of the gospel, since people must see their need for salvation if they are going to believe in Christ as their Savior.

A second, and more likely interpretation, views verse 16 as teaching that "this judgment takes place through Christ Jesus according to the standard which is the gospel."[142] This interpretation maintains that acceptance or rejection of the gospel will be the decisive factor in determining where people will spend eternity. The context of Romans 2:16 is clearly dealing with final judgment and justification before God (*dikaioō*, v. 13), not with sanctification and the judgment seat of Christ to reward believers. Men will not be judged by God on the basis of their own personal opinions or religious traditions, but by the objective, unchangeable standard of the gospel that Paul and the other apostles preached.[143]

This view not only fits with a well-recognized category of usage for *kata*,[144] but it also harmonizes with Paul's usage and meaning elsewhere in this epistle (Rom. 4:4, 16; 10:2), and more importantly with the flow of thought in the context of chapter 2. In Romans 2:2, Paul teaches the general principle that the judgment of God is "according to truth" (*kata alētheian*) upon all who sin. This standard for judgment consists of the dual truth of the gospel (v. 16) and of man's worthiness/unworthiness (vv. 6-15). Paul says that God's wrath is being stored up in accordance with (*kata*) man's unrepentant heart (Rom. 2:5). God will judge mankind according (*kata*) to each man's work or by the standard of his works (2:6), whether he has persevered in doing good (2:7) or has unrighteously disobeyed/disbelieved (*apeitheō*) the truth (2:8). In the end, regardless of whether one is a Jew who possesses the Mosaic Law or is a Gentile who does not know the Law,

---

[142] H. A. W. Meyer, *Critical and Exegetical Handbook to the Epistle to the Romans* (Winona Lake, IN: Alpha Publications, reprinted 1979), 96. See also, Donald Grey Barnhouse, *God's Wrath* (Grand Rapids: Eerdmans, 1953), 109; Dunn, *Romans 1-8*, 106; Jeffrey S. Lamp, "Paul, the Law, Jews, and Gentiles: A Contextual and Exegetical Reading of Romans 2:12-16," *JETS* 42 (March 1999): 50; Pettingill, *The Gospel of God: Simple Studies in Romans*, 26; Stifler, *The Epistle to the Romans*, 43-44.

[143] The expression "my gospel" in Rom. 2:16 and 16:25 in no way indicates that the content of Paul's gospel differed from that of Peter, John, or any of the other apostles (1 Cor. 15:11), as hyper-dispensationalism teaches (Charles F. Baker, *A Dispensational Theology* [Grand Rapids: Grace Bible College Publications, 1971], 95, 327-28; idem, *Studies in Dispensational Relationships* [Grand Rapids: Grace Publications, 1989], 55-58; J. C. O'Hair, *Did Peter and Paul Preach Different Gospels? How Many Gospels in the Bible?* [Comstock Park, MI: Bible Doctrines Publications, 2001], 14-19; idem, *The Unsearchable Riches of Christ* [Chicago: Self-published, 1941], 99; Cornelius R. Stam, *Our Great Commission: What Is It?* [Germantown, WI: Berean Bible Society, 1984], 105-8; idem, *Things That Differ: The Fundamentals of Dispensationalism* [Chicago: Berean Bible Society, 1951], 68-82, 200-17). Paul's gospel was only *his* in the sense that he personally identified with it and because he had been specially separated unto it as God's apostle (Rom. 1:1), having received it directly from God without any human agency (Gal. 1:1, 12-18). But even so, it was still simply the gospel "of God" (Rom. 1:1) because it was God's gospel entrusted to Paul.

[144] BDAG, 512-13.

both will be judged in God's sight on the basis of whether they have kept the Law. Since no man can keep the Law by persevering in good (Rom. 3:9-20), the only hope for man is to believe the gospel (2:16) and not to rest or rely upon Law-keeping for justification (2:17).

This interpretation of Romans 2:16 is perfectly consistent with the fact that the New Testament elsewhere requires belief in the gospel to escape God's just condemnation (Mark 16:15-16; 1 Peter 4:17). This is particularly true of parallel Pauline teaching. 2 Thessalonians 1:8-10 and 2:12-14 reiterate the point of Romans 2 about God's standard of judgment being both *"according to truth"* (Rom. 2:2) and *"according to [Paul's] gospel"* (Rom. 2:16). These passages teach that eternal judgment is based on believing *"the truth"* (2 Thess. 2:12-13), which is another form of expression for believing *"the gospel"* (2 Thess. 1:8-10; 2:14).

Additionally, the fact that the standard of truth by which Jesus Christ will judge mankind (John 5:22; Acts 17:31; Rom. 2:16) is both the gospel and man's works does not present a contradiction. Revelation 20:11-15 states that at the Great White Throne people of all ages will be judged *"according to (kata) their works"* (Rev. 20:12-13). This judgment will be based on what is documented of their deeds in God's infallible record *"books."* When they are judged by this standard, their works will be found wholly inadequate to merit their salvation. Their names will not be found in the Lamb's book of life (Rev. 20:12, 15) because the unsaved invariably trust in their own works or human goodness to merit justification rather than the propitiation that God provides (Luke 18:9-12; Gal. 3:10-13), which in this dispensation is specifically stated in the gospel to be the work of Jesus Christ—the Lamb of God who takes away the sin of the world by His substitutionary death (John 1:29; Rev. 1:5; 5:6, 9; 7:14). Even unreached people groups today who have never heard of Jesus Christ and His gospel inherently rely on something or someone other than the Son of God. Consequently, they are justly condemned for their unbelief (John 3:18).[145] This is why the final judgment of the lost can be harmoniously *"according to their works"* (Rev. 20:12-13) and *"according to [Paul's] gospel"* (Rom. 2:16). Both standards of judgment are perfectly compatible. This interpretation of the term *"gospel"* in Romans 2:16 is consistent with the observations made thus far about *euangelion* in Romans and the rest of the New Testament. The gospel of Christ is equivalent to the saving message; and it is not a broad message that is only necessary for Christians to believe for their sanctification, as today's crossless gospel teaches.

---

[145] This answers the claim of some that Rom. 2:16 cannot be stating that the gospel is the universal standard of God's judgment since millions have never even heard it (Hodge, Commentary on the Epistle to the Romans, 57; McClain, Romans, 79). However, millions have also never even heard the name of "Jesus" and yet, according to Scripture, they are still condemned because they have not believed in Him (John 3:18), in addition to the fact that they are rejecting the light of conscience and creation which they already possess (John 3:19-21; Rom. 1:18-20).

Romans 16:25

Romans 16:25-27

25 *Now to Him who is able to establish you according to* ***my gospel*** *and the preaching of Jesus Christ, according to the revelation of the mystery kept secret since the world began*

26 *but now has been made manifest, and by the prophetic Scriptures has been made known to all nations, according to the commandment of the everlasting God, for obedience to the faith—*

27 *to God, alone wise, be glory through Jesus Christ forever. Amen.*

Romans 16:25 is the last verse in this epistle that uses the term "gospel" (*euangelion*); and here too, it will be observed that the "gospel" is *not* a broad, non-soteriological message. There are several reasons why *euangelion* should be viewed in verse 25 in a manner consistent with its usage throughout the rest of Romans as a reference to Paul's saving message of justification by faith alone in Christ alone. But in order to demonstrate this conclusion, it is necessary to wrestle with several hermeneutical challenges presented by the passage.

Aside from complex textual issues that go beyond the scope of this chapter,[146] the meaning of the preposition *kata* in verses 25-26 is of paramount importance. This is discussed below. The question must also be addressed whether the terms *"gospel"* (*euangelion*) and *"preaching"* (*kērugma*) refer to the same message or whether they are distinct messages. There is also the matter of determining to which statement in verse 25 the prepositional phrase, *"according to the revelation of the mystery,"* is syntactically related. Does it modify *"my gospel"* or *"the preaching of Jesus Christ"* or both? Then there is the meaning of the term *"mystery"* (*mustērion*). Does it speak of something previously revealed but unrealized until the pres-

[146] In the Majority Text, the doxology of Rom. 16:25-27 is located after Rom. 14:23 (GNTMT, 506, 511; NTBT, 374, 377) and the concluding blessing (*"the grace of our Lord Jesus Christ be with you"*) occurs twice—once in Rom. 16:20 and once again in Rom. 16:24. Whereas the Critical Text has the doxology in the traditional location of our English Bibles in Rom. 16:25-27, while containing the blessing only once at Rom. 16:20. For a detailed discussion of the problem, see Bruce M. Metzger, *A Textual Commentary on the Greek New Testament*, 2nd ed. (Stuttgart: United Bible Societies, 1994), 470-73 and 476-77. There are good reasons to believe that the doxology of Rom. 16:25-27 is original and belongs in its present location (T. Fahy, "Epistle to the Romans 16:25-27," *ITQ* 28 [1961]: 238-39; Larry W. Hurtado, "The Doxology at the End of Romans," in *New Testament Textual Criticism: Its Significance for Exegesis. Essays in Honor of Bruce M. Metzger*, ed. Eldon J. Epp and Gordon D. Fee [Grand Rapids: Eerdmans, 1981], 185-99; I. Howard Marshall, "Romans 16:25-27: An Apt Conclusion," in *Romans and the People of God* [Grand Rapids: Eerdmans, 1999], 170-84; Moo, *The Epistle to the Romans*, 936-41), despite the opinions of some radically eclectic textual critics (J. K. Elliott, "The Language and Style of the Concluding Doxology to the Epistle to the Romans," *ZNW* 72 [1981]: 124-30). It is doubtful that Paul would end so magnificent an epistle without this doxology but abruptly end it with the words of Rom. 16:23, *"and Quartus, a brother"* (Godet, *Commentary on Romans*, 502).

ent dispensation or does it refer to something previously unrevealed by God in past ages? Finally, the identity of the *"prophetic Scriptures"* (*graphōn prophētikōn*) in verse 26 must be addressed. Is this a reference to the Old Testament Scriptures, the New Testament Scriptures, or both? The answer to each of these questions will have a profound impact upon our view of this passage and particularly the meaning of the *"gospel"* in verse 25.

In this passage, it is clear that Paul desires the believers in Rome to be edified by this epistle. This is indicated in verse 25 by the verb, *"establish"* (*stērizō*), a term that has not been used in the epistle since the introduction (Rom. 1:11) where Paul expressed this as his purpose in coming to Rome. In the closing doxology of Romans 16:25, Paul states that this objective will be accomplished *"according to (kata) my gospel and the preaching of Jesus Christ, according to (kata) the revelation of the mystery."* However believers will be established is related to the meaning of the preposition *kata*. It appears that this edification takes place by two means—"by means of"[147] Paul's gospel and the preaching of Jesus Christ. Interpreting *kata* as possessing an instrumental sense here harmonizes with the introduction to Romans, where the gospel is seen to be one of the means by which existing believers are built up and established in their faith (Rom. 1:11-15). Interpreting *kata* in verse 25 with the instrumental sense, "by means of," also accords with Romans 2:16 where the gospel is the means by which the world is finally judged based on whether they believe it or not. This even fits with other Pauline passages, such as 1 Corinthians 15:1-4, as the next two chapters demonstrate.

Other interpreters view *kata* in the phrase, *"according to my gospel,"* as meaning that the building up or establishing takes place in accordance with the doctrinal norm or standard of the gospel.[148] According to this view, the establishing accords with, or fits with, the gospel in the sense that it is consistent with it.[149] The establishment of believers is in line with the gospel.[150]

A third interpretation of *kata* in verse 25 combines the two previous views and maintains that there is no significant difference between the gospel being the means by which believers are established and the gospel being the standard by which believers are established.[151] All three preceding interpretations of *kata* are doctrinally and exegetically sound and are valid interpretative possibilities, but the fourth one is not.

The fourth view interprets *kata* in the phrase, *"according to my gospel,"* to mean that the establishment of the Roman believers is part of the gospel

---

[147] Lopez, *Romans Unlocked*, 297.

[148] Godet, *Commentary on Romans*, 503.

[149] Hodge, *Commentary on the Epistle to the Romans*, 452; Murray, *Epistle to the Romans*, 2:241.

[150] Stifler, *Epistle to the Romans*, 252.

[151] Dunn, *Romans 9-16*, 914; Moo, *Epistle to the Romans*, 938.

itself. In this view of Romans 16:25, *kata* means that "God is able to establish you, just as my gospel teaches." This view sees the edification and establishment of believers as forming part of the content of the gospel. Friedrich espouses this view, stating, "More generally the content of the κατὰ τὸ εὐαγγέλιόν μου of R. 16:25 is that God can strengthen you in your life of faith."[152] This interpretation of *kata* would naturally support the G.E.S. notion of a broad gospel. But there are several exegetical reasons for rejecting this view, as the following section will show. Immediately problematic is the fact that the lexica do not support *kata* meaning "part of" or expressing the contents of something,[153] except in a distributive usage with respect to numbers, places, or time.[154]

Covenant Theology and Progressive Dispensationalism

The crossless position's broad notion of the "gospel" in Romans 16:25 also appears to be virtually indistinguishable from the position of covenant theology and progressive dispensationalism with respect to the "gospel" being a "mystery." Regarding the use of the terms "gospel" and "mystery" in Romans 16:25, René Lopez claims, "Because this gospel involves much more than justification, Paul can speak of it as a mystery that was kept secret since the world began."[155] He goes on to say that the mystery referred to in verse 25 was "mentioned in germ form through Old Testament prophetic Scriptures."[156] But this ends up confusing the meanings of both the "gospel" and a "mystery" in the New Testament.

The normative dispensational position[157] has long insisted that a mystery in the New Testament refers to a truth that was not previously realized or comprehended in past dispensations precisely because it had not been divinely revealed until the present dispensation of grace.[158] By contrast, covenant theology teaches that a mystery refers to something that was previously revealed in the Old Testament but was simply not realized until

---

[152] Friedrich, s.v. "εὐαγγελίζομαί," 2:730.

[153] BDAG, 511-13; LSJ, 882-84; J. H. Thayer, ed., *The New Thayer's Greek-English Lexicon of the New Testament* (Peabody, MA: Hendrickson Publishers, 1981), 326-29.

[154] BDAG, 512. See, for example, Mark 6:40, *"according to hundreds and according to fifties."*

[155] Lopez, *Romans Unlocked*, 297.

[156] Ibid., 298.

[157] Progressive dispensationalists and covenant theologians who seek to emphasize a great degree of change within dispensationalism in the last century reject the phrase, "normative dispensationalism," and prefer to call it dispensationalism in its "revised" form.

[158] Lewis Sperry Chafer, *The Kingdom in History and Prophecy* (Chicago: Moody Press, 1915), 97; Charles L. Feinberg, *Millennialism: The Two Major Views* (Winona Lake, IN: BMH Books, 1985), 153, 234; J. Dwight Pentecost, *Things to Come: A Study in Biblical Eschatology* (Findlay, OH: Dunham Publishing, 1958), 135; Charles C. Ryrie, *The Basis of the Premillennial Faith* (Neptune, NJ: Loizeaux Bros., 1953), 131; idem, *Dispensationalism* (Chicago: Moody Press, 1995), 204; idem, "The Mystery in Ephesians 3," *BSac* 123 (January 1966): 25; Jeremy M. Thomas, "The 'Mystery' of Progressive Dispensationalism," *CTJ* 9 (December 2005): 307.

the present age.[159] Thus, the mystery of the Church is eisegetically seen by covenant theologians throughout the Old Testament.[160] Progressive dispensationalists, who have departed from the normative dispensational position, have enjoyed a fair amount of rapprochement with covenant theologians in the last two decades. They also share essentially the same view of biblical mysteries as their covenantal colleagues. Thus, progressive dispensationalist, Robert Saucy, defends the view that the gospel is a mystery even though it was revealed in the Old Testament. After commenting on Romans 16:25-26, he reasons, "If the mystery of Christ and the divine plan of salvation has already been the subject of Old Testament prophecy, then in what sense can it be said to have been hidden and only now revealed by the New Testament apostles and prophets? . . . . A mystery may be hidden in the sense that its truth has not yet been realized."[161] Saucy's interpretation of the gospel and mystery in Romans 16:25 is the same as the one traditionally held by reformed, covenant theologians.[162] It is disconcerting, therefore, to read a dispensational, Free Grace exegete such as Lopez claiming that the gospel is a broad message, and that in this respect it was an Old Testament mystery.

While it appears that most crossless gospel proponents today do not agree with either covenant theology or progressive dispensationalism, and some are even vocally opposed to progressive dispensationalism's move toward covenant theology,[163] the G.E.S. gospel position is faced with a real dilemma regarding Romans 16:25. It is undeniable that the gospel was revealed in the Old Testament, for Romans itself teaches that *"the gospel of God"* was *"promised before through His prophets in the Holy Scriptures"* (Rom. 1:1-2; cf. 1 Cor. 15:3-4). In light of this, the crossless, G.E.S. position is left with only a few interpretative options, each of which involves its own set of problems. First, it could agree with normative dispensational-

---

[159] Oswald T. Allis, *Prophecy & the Church* (Phillipsburg, NJ: Presbyterian and Reformed Publishing, 1947), 90; J. Oliver Buswell, *A Systematic Theology of the Christian Religion* (Grand Rapids: Zondervan, 1962), 2:446-50; Curtis I. Crenshaw and Grover E. Gunn, *Dispensationalism Today, Yesterday, and Tomorrow* (Memphis, TN: Footstool Publications, 1985), 174-75; Leon Morris, *The Cross in the New Testament* (Grand Rapids: Eerdmans, 1965), 212-13; Murray, *Epistle to the Romans*, 2:241.

[160] See, for example, Buswell, *Systematic Theology*, 2:448.

[161] Robert L. Saucy, *The Case for Progressive Dispensationalism: The Interface Between Dispensational & Non-Dispensational Theology* (Grand Rapids: Zondervan, 1993), 150 (ellipsis added).

[162] Allis, *Prophecy and the Church*, 94-97; Daniel P. Fuller, *Gospel & Law: Contrast or Continuum? The Hermeneutics of Dispensationalism and Covenant Theology* (Pasadena, CA: Fuller Seminary Press, reprinted 1991), 170; John H. Gerstner, *Wrongly Dividing the Word of Truth: A Critique of Dispensationalism* (Brentwood, TN: Wolgemuth & Hyatt, 1991), 199.

[163] Zane C. Hodges, "A Dispensational Understanding of Acts 2," in *Issues in Dispensationalism*, ed. Wesley R. Willis and John R. Master (Chicago: Moody, 1994), 167-80; Stephen R. Lewis, "The New Covenant," in *Progressive Dispensationalism: An Analysis of the Movement and Defense of Traditional Dispensationalism*, ed. Ron J. Bigalke, Jr. (Lanham, MD: University Press of America, 2005), 135-43.

ism that a mystery is something that was completely unrevealed in the Old Testament. But to do so they would need to abandon their claim that the gospel in Romans 16:25 is a mystery that was partially revealed in the Old Testament and that it is a broad message about sanctification and spirituality under grace (Rom. 6-8) and about God's present and future dispensational plan for Israel in relation to the Gentiles and the Church (Rom. 9-11), since these are nowhere revealed in the Old Testament. They would be back to an acknowledgement that the gospel is limited to justification and eternal salvation, which clearly was revealed in the Old Testament. Secondly, the crossless camp could take the view that the sanctification truths of their allegedly "broad gospel" were revealed in the Old Testament but just not realized until the Church age. But by doing so they would be adopting the semi-spiritualizing, inconsistent hermeneutics of progressive dispensationalism and covenant theology since such Church-age truths about living under grace are not found in the Old Testament. Taking this tack amounts to a virtual admission that they have abandoned a consistently dispensational approach to interpreting Scripture. Lastly, they could still maintain that the gospel is a broad message in Romans 16:25 and that it is a mystery by claiming that only part of the gospel was revealed in the Old Testament. That is, the gospel is a mystery in the sense that the justification "part of" the gospel was revealed in the Old Testament while the sanctification and prophetic "parts of" the gospel were not revealed until the New Testament era. The problem with this, of course, is that the Bible nowhere teaches that the gospel is only *partially* "according to the Scriptures" (1 Cor. 15:3-4) or that *part of* the "gospel of God" was "promised before through His prophets in the Holy Scriptures" (Rom. 1:1-2).

Syntactical Structure

Besides the preceding biblical and theological inconsistencies, the crossless position on Romans 16:25 is also faced with a syntactical problem. It is demonstrable that the phrase in verse 25, *"according to the revelation of the mystery,"* should be viewed as subordinate to, and qualifying, only the statement, *"the preaching of Jesus Christ,"* rather than the first phrase, *"according to my gospel."* This means that Romans 16:25 is not teaching that the gospel is a mystery. This can be observed in the following diagrammatical outline of the passage that reflects the underlying syntactical structure of the Greek text.

v25 Now
to Him
- who is able to establish you
- according to my gospel
and
- (according to) the preaching of Jesus Christ
- according to (the) revelation of (the) mystery
- kept secret since the world began
v26 but now
- (it) has been made manifest,
and
- (it) has been made known
- by the prophetic Scriptures
- according to the commandment of the everlasting God,
- for obedience to the faith
- to all nations[164]
v27 to God
- alone wise
- be glory
- through Jesus Christ
- forever.
Amen.

Other exegetes, such as Marshall,[165] interpret the syntactical relationships differently, viewing the phrase, *"according to the revelation of the mystery,"* as being parallel to the two previous main thoughts. This results in three means by which Christians are established.

To Him who is able
- to establish you
- according to my gospel
and
- (according to) the preaching of Jesus Christ,
- according to the revelation of mystery
- kept secret since the world began
- but now is made manifest
- through the prophetic scriptures[166]

---

[164] Cranfield takes "to all nations" as subordinate to, and connected with, the "obedience of faith" phrase rather than to "it has been made known" (Cranfield, *Epistle to the Romans,* 2:812n2). This would also appear to parallel Rom. 1:5, aside from the difference in prepositions, "to" (*eis*) in Rom. 16:25 versus "among" (*en*) in Rom. 1:5.

[165] I. Howard Marshall, "Romans 16:25-27: An Apt Conclusion," in *Romans and the People of God* (Grand Rapids: Eerdmans, 1999), 173.

[166] Ibid.

However, it is preferable to view the critical phrase in verse 25, *"according to the revelation of the mystery,"* as subordinate and as modifying only the immediately preceding phrase, *"according to the preaching of Jesus Christ."*[167] If the phrase, *"according to the revelation of the mystery,"* is to be interpreted as a third means by which believers are established, parallel to *"my gospel"* and *"the preaching of Jesus Christ,"* then there would most likely be a second coordinating conjunction, "and" (*kai*), adjoining *"the preaching of Jesus Christ"* and *"according to the revelation of the mystery."*[168] Therefore, it is better to view the phrase *"according to the revelation of the mystery"* as a subordinate clause and not coordinate with the preceding two clauses.[169]

- according to my gospel
  and
- (according to) the preaching of Jesus Christ
    - according to the revelation of the mystery

If the third phrase in Romans 16:25, *"according to the revelation of the mystery,"* modified not only *"the preaching of Jesus Christ"* but also the first phrase, *"according to my gospel,"* it would have to extend over the conjunction, *kai*, posing a very unnatural and awkward syntax. But if *"according to the revelation of the mystery"* did modify *"according to my gospel,"* as shown below, it would be the only such instance of its kind in the entire New Testament where a subordinate *kata* phrase modifies two or more balanced statements preceding it that are separated by *kai*.

- according to my gospel and (according to) the preaching of Jesus Christ
    - according to the revelation of mystery

What this shows about Romans 16:25 is that, if the phrase *"according to the revelation of the mystery"* modifies both preceding phrases, then it constitutes a completely anomalous syntactical construction in the New Testament; and therefore, it is highly unlikely. The syntactical structure of Romans 16:25 does not indicate that the "gospel" is a "mystery."

The Gospel and the Kērugma

Though commentators often assume that "my gospel" and "the preaching of Jesus Christ" are synonymous in verse 25,[170] it is better to see some dis-

---

[167] Cranfield, *Epistle to the Romans*, 2:810.

[168] Godet, *Commentary on Romans*, 503-4.

[169] Cranfield, *Epistle to the Romans*, 2:810; Moo, *Epistle to the Romans*, 939; Murray, *Epistle to the Romans*, 2:241; Sanday and Headlam, *Epistle to the Romans*, 434.

[170] Daniel Jong-Sang Chae, *Paul as Apostle to the Gentiles: His Apostolic Self-Awareness and its Influence on the Soteriological Argument in Romans* (Carlisle, England: Paternoster Press, 1997), 298; Hodge, *Commentary on the Epistle to the Romans*, 452; Marshall, "Romans 16:25-27," 173; Moo, *Epistle to the Romans*, 938n13; Murray, *Epistle to the Romans*, 2:241. Moo claims that the

tinction between them, even though it is doctrinally true that preaching the gospel amounts to preaching Christ. Such a distinction in verse 25 is supported by the fact that these two clauses do *not* form a TSKS construction (article-substantive-*kai*-substantive),[171] sometimes referred to as a Granville Sharp construction. There is not *one* article preceding both substantive nouns, "gospel" (*euangelion*) and "preaching" (*kērugma*), but *two* articles (*to euangelion mou kai to kērugma Iēsou Christou*). This indicates that the two nouns are *not* regarded by Paul as equivalent in verse 25. Had Paul wanted to express equivalency between the gospel and the preaching of Christ, he would only have needed to omit the second article before "preaching," since both nouns already have the same case, gender, and number (accusative, neuter, singular). Grammatically, verse 25 does not indicate that the gospel and the preaching of Christ are equivalent.

This distinction between Paul's "gospel" and his "preaching of Jesus Christ" according to mystery-revelation can also be seen by noting the terminology employed in verse 25. The two words, "gospel" (*euangelion*) and "preaching" (*kērugma*), though having some semantic overlap, are still lexically and semantically distinct. *Kērugma* is used only 8x in the New Testament (Matt. 12:41; Luke 11:32; Rom. 16:25; 1 Cor. 1:21; 2:4; 15:14; 2 Tim. 4:17; Titus 1:3), though its verb form is used quite frequently. It is not a technical term standing synonymously for the gospel;[172] but at times it is used synonymously for the gospel (1 Cor. 1:21; 2:4; 15:14; Titus 1:3).[173] *Kērugma* does not refer strictly to the gospel in 2 Timothy 4:17, where Paul says, *"so that the message (kērugma) might be preached fully through me and that all the Gentiles might hear."* The reference to "the Gentiles" hearing the message recalls not only Paul's gospel (Gal. 2:7) but also the dispensation of the mystery that is for the Gentiles and that is built upon the gospel. This mystery truth that is for the Gentiles is distinct from the gospel, but built upon the gospel, and it is recorded in the parallel passages of Colossians 1:23-28 (cf. "gospel" 1:23) and Ephesians 3:1-11 (cf. "gospel" 3:6).

The Gospel and the Mystery of the Gospel

In Romans 16:25, the "gospel" and the "preaching of Jesus Christ" that is according to mystery-revelation are also seen to be distinct in terms of content. This can be demonstrated from a comparison of verse 25 with the contents and structure of Romans as a whole. But before doing so, it will

---

kai separating "my gospel" and "the preaching of Jesus Christ" is explicative (ibid.), with the sense, "my gospel, namely the preaching of Jesus Christ." But there are no grammatical or syntactical factors that compel us to view *kai* as having an ascensive force here rather than being a simple connective separating two similar but distinctive thoughts.

[171] Wallace, *Greek Grammar*, 270-90.

[172] William Baird, "What Is the Kerygma? A Study of 1 Cor. 15:3-8 and Gal. 1:11-17," *JBL* 76 (1957): 184; Lothar Coenen, "*κηρύσσω*," *NIDNTT*, 3:54-55.

[173] Baird, "What Is the Kerygma?" 184.

be helpful first to observe how the differing content of Paul's gospel and his broader *kērugma* is supported by parallel Pauline passages outside of Romans that also contain the words "gospel" and "mystery." Regarding the distinction in Romans 16:25 between the "gospel" and the "preaching" of mystery truth concerning Christ, the dispensational expositor of the past, Harry Ironside, insightfully stated:

> To Paul was committed a two-fold ministry—that of the gospel (as linked with a glorified Christ) and that of the Church—the mystery hid in God from before the creation of the world but now revealed by the Spirit. See this double ministry as set forth in Col. 1:23-29 and Eph. 3:1-12.[174]

The difference in Romans 16:25 between Paul's *"gospel"* and his *"preaching of Jesus Christ according to the revelation of the mystery"* can be discerned from the two parallel passages referred to by Ironside.

Colossians 1:23-29

23 *if indeed you continue in the faith, grounded and steadfast, and are not moved away from the hope of **the gospel** which you heard, which was preached to every creature under heaven, of which I, Paul, became a minister.*
24 *I now rejoice in my sufferings for you, and fill up in my flesh what is lacking in the afflictions of Christ, for the sake of His body, which is the church,*
25 *of which I became a minister according to the stewardship from God which was given to me for you, to fulfill the word of God,*
26 ***the mystery** which has been hidden from ages and from generations, but now has been revealed to His saints.*
27 *To them God willed to make known what are the riches of the glory of **this mystery** among the Gentiles: which is Christ in you, the hope of glory.*
28 *Him we preach, warning every man and teaching every man in all wisdom, that we may present every man perfect in Christ Jesus.*
29 *To this end I also labor, striving according to His working which works in me mightily.*

Here "the preaching of Jesus Christ" that accords with mystery-revelation (Col. 1:24-29) is clearly something *beyond* the "gospel" (Col. 1:23). In Colossians 1:28, Paul states, *"Him we preach,"* in reference to Jesus Christ. This preaching about Christ is in the context of the new mystery truth that has been revealed, which specifically states that Christ indwells every believer. This is one example of *"the preaching of Jesus Christ (that is) according to the revelation of the mystery"* (Rom. 16:25). If the indwelling of Christ constitutes unique, Church age truth that was revealed to Paul and the other apostles and prophets, and this is what Paul refers to in Romans 16:25 by "the preaching of Jesus Christ," then we should also expect to find this truth revealed earlier in the Epistle of Romans. And we do.

---

[174] Ironside, *Lectures on the Epistle to the Romans*, 174.

The sanctification and spirituality section of Romans 6-8 reveals not only the fact of the believer's position in, and identification with, Jesus Christ (Rom. 6:3-13; 8:1), but also the truth of Christ being in the believer. The indwelling of Christ referred to as a "mystery" in Colossians 1:26-27 is also explicitly taught in Romans 8:9-10, where Paul writes, *"But you are not in the flesh but in the Spirit, if indeed the Spirit of God dwells in you. Now if anyone does not have the Spirit of Christ, he is not His. 10 And if Christ is in you, the body is dead because of sin, but the Spirit is life because of righteousness."* The indwelling, abiding presence of Christ (John 15:4-5; Gal. 2:20) and the Holy Spirit in every Church age saint spoken of in Romans 8:9-10 and Colossians 1:27 is certainly one truth that was unrevealed and unknown in previous dispensations but is now revealed and made known in the present dispensation. Regarding this mystery-truth, one dispensational writer concludes:

> The "mystery" of the Christian life is that Christ empowers and works in and through believers as they live by faith and obedience. All of this was kept hidden in the O. T. Thus, it may be concluded that the best definition of the NT mystery is that Jesus Christ is now exalted both as Lord of all and also as the believer's only Life.[175]

Similarly, the fact of all believers, Jew or Gentile, being united equally in the body of Christ is also a Church age truth that is *"according to the revelation of the mystery."* Paul refers to this in Ephesians 3:1-11, which is a second passage that parallels Romans 16:25. But before examining Ephesians 3 and considering another aspect of Paul's preaching that accords with mystery-revelation, one more significant point must be made regarding Romans 16:25. Literally, this verse does not refer to only *one* specific mystery truth as our English translations imply by the double use of the definite article, "according to *the* revelation of *the* mystery." In the Greek text, the article is not found before either "revelation" (*apokalupsin*) or "mystery" (*mustēriou*), so that Romans 16:25 says that God is able to establish believers not only through Paul's gospel but through the preaching of Jesus Christ that is *"according to revelation of mystery"* (*kata apokalupsin mustēriou*). The absence of the article before each term means that in this anarthrous construction the *character* or *quality* of Paul's "preaching of Jesus Christ" is being emphasized rather than the *identity* of one particular mystery or revelation. Romans 16:25 states that the preaching of Jesus Christ accords with that which has the character or quality of mystery-revelation, namely previously unrevealed truth that was now divinely revealed and made known through Paul's preaching. This means that the Christological-sanctification truths of both Colossians 1:27 (Christ in us) and Ephesians 3:6 (us in

---

[175] Galen W. Wiley, "A Study of 'Mystery' in the New Testament," *GTJ* 6.2 (1985): 356.

Christ) fall within the purview of Paul's statement in Romans 16:25, *"the preaching of Jesus Christ according to revelation of mystery."*

Ephesians 3:1-11

1 *For this reason I, Paul, the prisoner of Christ Jesus for you Gentiles—*
2 *if indeed you have heard of the dispensation of the grace of God which was given to me for you,*
3 *how that by revelation He made known to me* ***the mystery*** *(as I have briefly written already,*
4 *by which, when you read, you may understand my knowledge in* ***the mystery of Christ****),*
5 *which in other ages was not made known to the sons of men, as it has now been revealed by the Spirit to His holy apostles and prophets:*
6 *that the Gentiles should be fellow heirs, of the same body, and partakers of His promise in Christ* ***through the gospel,***
7 *of which I became a minister according to the gift of the grace of God given to me by the effective working of His power.*
8 *To me, who am less than the least of all the saints, this grace was given, that I should preach among the Gentiles the unsearchable riches of Christ,*
9 *and to make all see what is the dispensation of* ***the mystery,*** *which from the beginning of the ages has been hidden in God who created all things through Jesus Christ;*
10 *to the intent that now the manifold wisdom of God might be made known by the church to the principalities and powers in the heavenly places,*
11 *according to the eternal purpose which He accomplished in Christ Jesus our Lord*

Ephesians 3:1-11 is a critical passage in setting forth both the meaning and nature of the term "mystery" in the New Testament as well as establishing that there is a distinction between Paul's gospel and his mystery-preaching. The interpretation of this passage also has major repercussions for dispensationalism and covenant theology, since it proves that the mystery spoken of here (Jews and Gentiles being one body in Christ—the Church) was not revealed until the time of the apostles and New Testament prophets in the early Church. In Ephesians 3:5, the adverbial conjunction, "as" (*hōs*), is not comparative or relative as covenant theologians claim,[176] as if Paul is saying that the mystery in Ephesians 3 is a matter of degrees of revelation—lesser in the Old Testament but greater in the New Testament. Rather, "as" (*hōs*) is contrastive.[177] The truth of Jew and Gentile unity in the one body of the Messiah was a truth that was previously unrevealed in the Old Testament

[176] Buswell, *Systematic Theology*, 2:449; Crenshaw and Gunn, *Dispensationalism Today, Yesterday, and Tomorrow*, 175; Charles Hodge, *Commentary on the Epistle to the Ephesians* (Grand Rapids: Eerdmans, reprinted 1994), 163; Murray, *Epistle to the Romans*, 2:242.

[177] Godet, *Commentary on Romans*, 504; Harold W. Hoehner, *Ephesians: An Exegetical Commentary* (Grand Rapids: Baker, 2002), 439-40; Ryrie, "The Mystery in Ephesians 3," 28-29.

and completely unable to be known by men. It was "hidden in God" (Eph. 3:9) and not even the angels knew about it (Eph. 3:10).[178] For Paul and the apostles, preaching this newly revealed truth in the early Church was like telling "a man born blind that the sun does not shine in the night as it does in daytime. It does not shine at all by night."[179]

Even if covenant theologians and progressive dispensationalists reject the interpretation of the adverbial conjunction, *hōs*, being contrastive versus comparative or relative, they must still concede that *hōs* does not even occur in the parallel passage of Colossians 1:26. For this reason, Paul is setting up a pure contrast in Colossians 1:26 when he says, *"the mystery which has been hidden from ages and from generations, but now (nun) has been revealed to His saints."* It is not surprising to discover that Colossians 1:26 is seldom discussed by covenant theologians, because it clearly contradicts their interpretation of the "mystery" in Ephesians 3.[180]

In addition, the presence of the adverb, *nun* ("now"), in Ephesians 3:5 "indicates that Paul is contrasting the verbal revelation known to past generations with the verbal revelation made known to his present generation. This is consistent with Paul's usage of *nun* in two other mystery passages (i.e. Rom 16:25-26 and Col 1:26)."[181] The consistent use of the adverb, *nun*, with *mustērion*, in all three parallel Pauline passages (Rom. 16:26; Eph. 3:5; Col. 1:26) points to new revelation, not just a new realization of previous revelation. This demonstrates that if the gospel was revealed in the Old Testament, it cannot be a mystery. The gospel and the mystery must be distinct.

Finally, it must be carefully noted from Ephesians 3 that the "mystery" of believing Jews and Gentiles having an equal standing in the body of Christ is only true as believers are positionally connected to Christ via the baptism by the Holy Spirit (1 Cor. 12:12-13). This is why Ephesians 3:6 says that even Gentile believers are *"partakers of His promise in Christ."*

The *"promise in Christ"* is a reference to *"the Holy Spirit of promise"* (Eph. 1:13), since the Holy Spirit is referred to twice in the immediately preceding section in Ephesians 2 on Jew-Gentile unity (Eph. 2:18, 22). This conclusion also harmonizes with Paul's statement in Galatians 3:14, where he says that as a result of Christ's propitious work on the cross (Gal. 3:13), *"the blessing of Abraham might come upon the Gentiles in Christ Jesus, that we might receive the promise of the Spirit through faith."* The Spirit of promise in these Pauline passages refers to the Holy Spirit who baptized believers into the spiritual body of Christ, the Church, starting on the day of Pentecost. This is why the Holy Spirit is called *"the Promise of the Father"* in

---

[178] Stifler, *Epistle to the Romans*, 255.

[179] Ibid., 254.

[180] Ryrie, "The Mystery in Ephesians 3," 29.

[181] Thomas, "The 'Mystery' of Progressive Dispensationalism," 307.

Acts 1:4, whom these early believers would receive *"not many days"* (Acts 1:5) later at Pentecost (Acts 2:4, 38).

This helps clarify the distinction in Romans 16:25 between Paul's *"gospel"* and his *"preaching of Jesus Christ according to the revelation of the mystery."* In Colossians 1:26, the "mystery" is subsequent to, and distinct from, the "gospel" that is referred to in the previous section of Colossians 1:20-23. Likewise, in Ephesians 3:6, the mystery is distinct from the gospel itself. The mystery is said to be *"through the gospel"* (*dia tou euangeliou*), not equivalent to it or part of it. The mystery cannot be simultaneously "the gospel" and "through the gospel." This means that the mystery in Ephesians 3:6 is built upon the gospel and results from it. According to Ephesians 3:6, this mystery consists of Gentiles being fellow heirs with the Jews, and of the same body, and partakers of His promise in Christ. But this is only true *"through the gospel."* That is, Gentiles and Jews have this co-equal standing in Christ only as a result of hearing and believing *"the gospel of salvation."* The Holy Spirit's uniting work is accomplished at the moment of initial faith and salvation, just as Paul wrote earlier in Ephesians 1:13, *"In Him you also trusted, after you heard the word of truth, the gospel of your salvation; in whom also, having believed, you were sealed with the Holy Spirit of promise."*

<u>Ephesians 6:18-20</u>

18 *praying always with all prayer and supplication in the Spirit, being watchful to this end with all perseverance and supplication for all the saints—*

19 *and for me, that utterance may be given to me, that I may open my mouth boldly to make known* ***the mystery of the gospel,***

20 *for which I am an ambassador in chains; that in it I may speak boldly, as I ought to speak.*

Some interpreters see Ephesians 6:19 as teaching that the gospel itself is a mystery based on Paul's unique expression, *"the mystery of the gospel."* Since covenant theologians maintain that a biblical mystery is something previously unrealized, not unrevealed, they view the gospel in this verse as being the mystery that was already revealed in the Old Testament.[182] Similarly, the non-dispensational theologian,[183] George E. Ladd, writes, "The gospel itself is 'mystery' (Eph. 6:19), i.e., a secret purpose of God now made known to men."[184] Progressive dispensationalists and non-dispensationalists

---

[182] Allis, *Prophecy & the Church*, 90; Buswell, *Systematic Theology*, 2:449; Hodge, *Commentary on the Epistle to the Ephesians*, 394; Morris, *The Cross in the New Testament*, 212-13; Murray, *Epistle to the Romans*, 2:241.

[183] Ladd, like Walter Kaiser, prefers to view himself as a proponent of neither dispensational theology nor covenant theology. Ladd prefers to label his theological persuasion "kingdom theology" (see George Eldon Ladd, *The Gospel of the Kingdom: Scriptural Studies in the Kingdom of God* [Grand Rapids: Eerdmans, 1959]). His mediating position between the two major schools results in a position closest to progressive dispensationalism.

[184] George Eldon Ladd, "Revelation and Tradition in Paul," in *Apostolic History and the*

alike erroneously interpret Ephesians 6:19 to be saying that the mystery is the gospel. Progressive dispensationalists, such as Robert Saucy, use this verse specifically to support the notion that a mystery is something that was previously revealed in the Old Testament but just not realized until the present dispensation.[185] The prolific author and non-dispensationalist, Walter Kaiser, is exuberant about the progressive dispensational interpretation of this verse. He writes, "Surely there is progress on this classical standoff when Robert Saucy acknowledges that the 'gospel of God' for which Paul was set apart was 'promised beforehand through his prophets in the Holy Scriptures' (Rom. 1:1-2) and is certainly the same message that Paul later called 'the mystery of the gospel!' in Ephesians 6:19. What a wonderful breakthrough!"[186]

Consistent with this, leading crossless gospel proponent, Bob Wilkin, also sees in Ephesians 6:19 support for a broad, non-soteriological "gospel." On the one hand, he agrees with covenant theology and progressive dispensationalism that "the mystery of the gospel" in Ephesians 6:19 means that the gospel itself is the mystery. On the other hand, Wilkin appears to uphold the traditional dispensational definition of a mystery as being something unrevealed in the Old Testament. He writes, "*The mystery of the gospel* (Eph 6:19). The gospel is clearly in the OT. So what is this mystery? Is this not the mystery of the church, Jews and Gentiles together in one body? Indeed, it is. That is the good news Paul has in mind here."[187] But this is self-contradictory. If "the gospel" was in the Old Testament by Wilkin's own admission, and yet the unity between Jewish and Gentile believers was not revealed anywhere in the Old Testament, then doesn't it make better sense to conclude that the union of Jew and Gentile in Christ is *not* part of "the gospel" but is a separate mystery-truth and spiritual blessing that *results from* the gospel (Eph. 1:13; 3:6)? It is much more consistent to maintain the traditional dispensational view of a biblical mystery and the gospel. Since a mystery was something previously unrevealed in the Old Testament, and yet the fact of Gentile salvation was plainly revealed, the "mystery" in Ephesians 6:19 must be referring to something beyond the gospel—beyond justification and redemption truth.[188]

Gospel: Biblical and Historical Essays Presented to F. F. Bruce on His 60th Birthday, ed. W. Ward Gasque and Ralph P. Martin (Grand Rapids: Eerdmans, 1970), 223-24.

[185] Robert L. Saucy, *The Case for Progressive Dispensationalism: The Interface Between Dispensational & Non-Dispensational Theology* (Grand Rapids: Zondervan, 1993), 149; idem, "The Church as the Mystery of God," in *Dispensationalism, Israel and the Church: The Search for Definition*, ed. Craig A. Blaising and Darrell L. Bock (Grand Rapids: Zondervan, 1992), 141, 143, 148, 151.

[186] Walter C. Kaiser, Jr., "An Epangelical Response," in *Dispensationalism, Israel and the Church: The Search for Definition*, ed. Craig A. Blaising and Darrell L. Bock (Grand Rapids: Zondervan, 1992), 372-73.

[187] Bob Wilkin, "Gospel Means Good News," unpublished paper presented at the Grace Evangelical Society National Conference, March 6, 2008, Fort Worth, TX, p. 3.

[188] Ryrie, "The Mystery in Ephesians 3," 27.

Identifying the Genitive in Ephesians 6:19

Covenant theology, progressive dispensationalism, and the crossless gospel all share in common the view that the expression in Ephesians 6:19, *"the mystery of the gospel"* (*to mustērion tou euangeliou*), means that the gospel is a mystery. Without necessarily labeling it as such, each of these theologies assumes that the genitive case in *tou euangeliou* is an appositional or epexegetical genitive. While this category of usage is grammatically possible for this verse, it does not fit with a holistic perspective of Ephesians. Prior to Ephesians 6:19, Paul distinguished the *"mystery"* from the *"gospel"* by stating that the mystery is *"through the gospel"* (Eph. 3:6); and to become a partaker *"of His promise in Christ"* (Eph. 3:6), one must first believe the gospel (Eph. 1:13). Thus, it is better from both a grammatical and larger epistolary perspective to see the genitive in 6:19 as expressing separation or result, rather than equality or identity. According to this view, Paul is not saying that *"the mystery is the gospel"* but that the mystery *stems from*, or is *produced by*, the gospel.

Such meaning and usage is not at all foreign to the genitive case. In fact, in some contexts, when the genitive is pressed too far to mean equivalency, it results in some rather strained and nonsensical statements. For example, in Romans 4:13, Paul speaks of *"the righteousness of faith."* Clearly he does not mean "the righteousness *that is* faith." Rather, he means "the righteousness *that results* from faith." In Romans 15:4, we read of *"the patience and comfort of the Scriptures."* Once again, Paul is not saying that patience and comfort *are the Scriptures*, but only that patience and comfort *result from* the Scriptures. Similarly, in Galatians 5:22 Paul says that *"the fruit of the Spirit is love, joy, peace, etc."* Is he saying here that the fruit *is* the Spirit? Or, is he simply saying that the fruit *results from* the Spirit? Obviously, it's the latter. With respect to Ephesians 6:19, it is best, therefore, not to view the genitive of "the gospel" (*tou euangeliou*) as appositional with "the mystery" but as the means by which the mystery is produced. While *tou euangliou* may be a genitive of separation or genitive of source,[189] it is more likely a genitive of production or product.[190]

However, some respected dispensational exegetes of Ephesians, such as Harris and Hoehner, take it as an appositional genitive. Harris, for example, notes 14 possible cases of the appositional genitive in Ephesians (1:14; 2:12, 14, 15, 20; 3:7; 4:3, 14; 6:14, 15, 16, 17 [2x], 19).[191] But he only considers three possible categories of genitive—partitive, comparative, and appositional.[192] He does not cite a fourth possible use labeled by Greek

[189] Wallace, *Greek Grammar*, 107-10.

[190] Ibid., 104-7.

[191] W. Hall Harris, III, "The Ascent and Descent of Christ in Ephesians 4:9-10," *BSac* 151 (April 1994): 204.

[192] Ibid., 203.

grammarian Daniel Wallace as the genitive of production or genitive of product. The late Harold Hoehner likewise viewed the appositional genitive as the most likely category for *euangeliou* in Ephesians 6:19. In his highly acclaimed commentary on Ephesians, he wrote, "The genitive is difficult to label though probably not subjective genitive ('the gospel proclaiming the mystery'), but it could be objective genitive ('the mystery about the gospel'), genitive of content ('mystery is contained in the gospel'), or, more likely, an epexegetical genitive ('the mystery, namely, the gospel')."[193] Later, however, Hoehner seemed to distinguish the mystery from the gospel by stating, "In the present context Paul is speaking not about the gospel per se, but the mystery of the gospel, which is the union of believing Jews and Gentiles into one body."[194]

This confusion can be cleared up rather quickly by considering the possibility of the genitive of production.[195] According to Wallace, this usage is similar to a subjective genitive or genitive of source but the emphasis is upon both source and involvement in production. Wallace explains, "It is also similar to a genitive of source, but tends to involve a more active role on the part of the genitive. Thus, 'angel from heaven' (source) simply indicates the source or origin from which the angel came. But 'peace of God' suggests both source and involvement on the part of God."[196] He goes on to cite two examples of the genitive of production, both from Ephesians.[197] In Ephesians 4:3, *"the unity of the Spirit"* does not mean that "unity" is equivalent to "Spirit" but that "the unity" is produced by "the Spirit." Likewise, Ephesians 5:9 speaks of "the fruit of the light [CT]/Spirit [MT]," where "the fruit" is not "the light/Spirit" but it is produced by the light/Spirit.[198] As this applies to Ephesians 6:19, it indicates that the gospel is the means of producing the mystery of Jew-Gentile union in Christ. This interpretation accords perfectly with the teaching of Ephesians elsewhere that "the mystery" is distinct from "the gospel" and even that it is "through/by (*dia*) the gospel" (Eph. 3:6).

Both Ephesians 3:4 and Colossians 4:3 contain the clause, *"the mystery of Christ,"* which appears similar to *"the mystery of the gospel"* in Ephesians 6:19. Since it can be demonstrated that *"the mystery of Christ"* in Ephesians 3:4 is not the gospel but stems from the gospel (Eph. 3:6), then the same is likely true in Colossians 4:3. The expression, *"the mystery of Christ,"* is

---

[193] Harold W. Hoehner, *Ephesians: An Exegetical Commentary* (Grand Rapids: Baker, 2002), 862-63.

[194] Ibid., 863.

[195] Wallace, *Greek Grammar*, 104-6.

[196] Ibid., 105.

[197] Ibid.

[198] Ephesians 2:3 may also be an example of the genitive of production when it speaks of *"the lusts of our flesh, fulfilling the desires of the flesh and of the mind."* Though it could be a genitive of source and comes close to a subjective genitive, the flesh and mind are still very much involved in the production of "the lusts."

a similar construction to Ephesians 6:19 but it is not a genitive of production. The content of *"the mystery of Christ"* is defined earlier in Colossians 1:26-27,[199] where the content is the mystery-revelation of *"Christ in you, the hope of glory,"* rather than the gospel itself (Col. 1:20-23). This mystery of Christ's indwelling of all believers is said to be part of *"the word of God"* (Col. 1:25), which is broader than the gospel. In this respect, Paul preached the person of Christ as sufficient for the Christian life. In the context of Christian living and maturity, not evangelism, Paul declared, *"Him we preach"* (Col. 1:28a). Why did Paul preach Jesus Christ? So *"that we may present every man perfect (teleion) in Christ Jesus"* (Col. 1:28b). Though the Christian-life truth of Christ's indwelling is built upon the foundation of the gospel, it must be properly distinguished from the gospel.

Romans 16:25 & Preaching Mystery-Revelation about Christ

If the parallel passages of Colossians 1 and Ephesians 3 set forth *"the preaching of Jesus Christ (lit.) according to revelation of mystery"* (Rom. 16:25),[200] and this was able to "establish" the Roman Christians, then we should expect to see throughout the Epistle of Romans the revelation of certain mystery-truth. And we do. In Romans 6:3-4, Paul explained the co-crucifixion, co-burial, and co-resurrection of all believers with Christ. But this was never taught in the Old Testament. Likewise, nowhere in the Old Testament do we read that believers are no longer under law but under grace (Rom. 6:14). And where in the Old Testament does it say that all saints are dead to the Law by virtue of their spiritual death and resurrection with Christ, in order that we might now serve according to the Spirit and not according to the Law (Rom. 7:4-6)? If a man preached these truths in Jerusalem in 750 B.C., stones would surely be thrown and he would not have lived to see another day!

Furthermore, where in the Old Testament does it say that the Holy Spirit indwells every child of God (Rom. 8:9) or even that Christ, the Messiah, indwells every believer (Rom. 8:10)? Where in the Old Testament does it predict that blindness in part will occur until the fullness of the Gentiles has come in,[201] as Romans 11:25 reveals?[202] And where in the Law, the Prophets, or the Writings does it say that believers have individual liberty of conscience in the areas of diet and holy days (Rom. 14)? Finally, while the Old Testament predicted that the Gentiles would hear of Christ and be saved, where does it say that one believer can expect another believer to assist him in his mission to preach the gospel to the

---

[199] Wiley, "A Study of 'Mystery' in the New Testament," 357.

[200] Stifler, *Epistle to the Romans,* 253.

[201] Ibid., 255.

[202] The mystery was not that Israel would be judicially blinded, which was a fact revealed prior to the Church age (Isa. 6:9-10; John 12:40-41), but that this would occur *"until the fullness of the Gentiles has come in"* (Rom. 11:25).

Gentiles (Rom. 15:24), as if all believers in the Old Testament were given a "Great Commission"? All of this constitutes *"the preaching of Jesus Christ (lit.) according to revelation of mystery."* It is by this truth contained largely in Romans 6-16, in addition to the "gospel" in Romans 1-5, that God is able to establish all believers (Rom. 16:25).

Distribution of Old Testament Quotations in Romans

The conclusions made thus far about Romans 16:25 and the "gospel" are further supported by noting the pattern of distribution for Old Testament quotations throughout the Book of Romans. If, indeed, the elements of Paul's "gospel" were previously revealed to Old Testament prophets (Rom. 1:1-2), and Romans 1-5 concerns the "gospel" truth of justification by faith alone in Christ alone in distinction to "the preaching of Jesus Christ" as new mystery-revelation for the Church, then this distinction should be reflected in *the pattern of distribution of Old Testament quotations* throughout Romans. In chapters 1-5 dealing with justification, the Old Testament is cited for support at least 16 times, along with several allusions to Old Testament characters such as David, Abraham, and Sarah. But by contrast, the Old Testament is quoted in Romans 6-8 only 2 times (Rom. 7:7; 8:36); and neither of these teach the Christian's sanctification and spirituality by grace. Romans 8:36 concerns the believer's eternal security, not practical sanctification; while Romans 7:7 is a citation from the ten commandments to convict Paul of his covetousness. This shows that Paul never quotes the Old Testament in Romans 6-8 in order to substantiate his doctrine of sanctification and spirituality under grace for the Church age believer.

The reason for this noticeable difference in the pattern of Old Testament quotations between chapters 1-5 and chapters 6-8 is obvious. The "preaching of Jesus Christ" according to mystery-revelation deals only with truths not revealed in the Old Testament. Such revelation occurred only through New Testament apostles and prophets (Eph. 3:5) and their "prophetic Scriptures" (16:26). On the other hand, "the Law and the Prophets" (Rom. 3:21) testified to the gospel-truth of justification by faith alone in Christ alone in Romans 1-5, because this truth was previously revealed in the Old Testament. But the truths that are distinctive to this Church age were not revealed until the newly completed "prophetic Scriptures," of which the Letter to the Romans is a part.

Identifying the "Prophetic Scriptures" in Romans 16:26

Crossless gospel advocate, René Lopez, states that the mystery truth referred to in Roman 16:25 was "mentioned in germ form through Old Testament prophetic Scriptures."[203] This interpretation is shared by proponents of covenant theology and progressive dispensationalism. They interpret

[203] Lopez, *Romans Unlocked*, 298.

the phrase "prophetic Scriptures" in Romans 16:26 to be a reference to the Old Testament in order to support their belief that a "mystery" in the New Testament can be something already revealed by God in previous dispensations but simply not realized or understood until the coming of Christ and the beginning of the Church age.[204]

For this reason, progressive dispensationalist, Darrell Bock, argues that Romans 16:26 cannot be a reference to the writings of New Testament prophets because Paul has made constant recourse throughout this epistle only to the Old Testament and never to other New Testament writings.[205] But Bock's objection simply does not pass muster when we consider that only a small percentage of the New Testament's 29 books even existed at the time Romans was written (James, Gal., 1-2 Thess., 1-2 Cor., and possibly Matthew). In addition, Bock's expectation is not a reasonable standard for any New Testament book. Though it is not impossible for a New Testament writer to quote another NT book since Paul later quotes Luke 10:7 in 1 Timothy 5:18, it must be acknowledged that this is the *only* case in the entire New Testament of self-quotation. Thus, the odds of such intratestamental quotation occurring even in other New Testament books besides Romans is exceptionally low.

Another reason frequently put forth for the "prophetic Scriptures" being a reference to the Old Testament is the parallelism between Paul's closing doxology and his introduction where he explicitly refers to the Old Testament writing prophets in Romans 1:2.[206] But why should a reference to Old Testament prophetic writings in the introduction to Romans require a reference to Old Testament writings at its conclusion? In fact, the opposite argument could be advanced that it is more likely that Paul would refer to New Testament prophetic writings in the doxology in keeping with the evident pattern of progression throughout Romans. Within Romans, there is progress from the Law and Prophets to new mystery revelation. Secondly, there is a progression of truth in Romans from the Jews to the Gentiles. If this interpretation is correct, then Romans itself, along with only a handful of other New Testament books were viewed by Paul as forming an incipient corpus of inspired, prophetic writings that were on a par with the Old Testament.

---

[204] Craig A. Blaising and Darrell L. Bock, "Dispensationalism, Israel and the Church: Assessment and Dialogue," in *Dispensationalism, Israel and the Church: The Search for Definition*, ed. Craig A. Blaising and Darrell L. Bock (Grand Rapids: Zondervan, 1992), 393n8; Darrell L. Bock, "Hermeneutics of Progressive Dispensationalism," in *Three Central Issues in Contemporary Dispensationalism: A Comparison of Traditional and Progressive Views*, ed. Herbert W. Bateman IV (Grand Rapids: Kregel, 1999), 117n28 (see also p. 81 in objection to Elliott E. Johnson); Robert L. Saucy, "The Church as the Mystery of God," in *Dispensationalism, Israel and the Church: The Search for Definition*, ed. Craig A. Blaising and Darrell L. Bock (Grand Rapids: Zondervan, 1992), 148-49, 152.

[205] Bock, "Hermeneutics of Progressive Dispensationalism," 117n28. See also, Alan F. Johnson, *Romans: The Freedom Letter*, EBC (Chicago: Moody Press, 1985), 2:137.

[206] Johnson, *Romans: The Freedom Letter*, 2:137.

But aside from the preceding rebuttals of the interpretation that sees the "prophetic Scriptures" as the Old Testament in Romans 16:26, there are several positive reasons based on the passage itself that support the traditional dispensational interpretation[207] that this is a reference to New Testament Scripture. Regrettably, these reasons have not been given their due by non-dispensational scholars.

First, when Paul refers elsewhere to the Old Testament Scriptures, he simply uses the term "Scriptures" (*graphōn*) without any qualification (Rom. 4:3; 9:17; 10:11; 11:2; 15:4), except in Romans 1:2 where he says "Holy Scriptures." It is peculiar for any New Testament writer, and unparalleled for Paul, to refer to the Old Testament Scriptures with the adjective "prophetic" (*prophētikōn*).[208] Elsewhere, he uses the noun "prophets"[209] with the definite article[210] (*tōn prophētōn*, cf. Rom. 1:2; 3:21; 11:3) to show that these were the "well known"[211] prophets of the Old Testament Scriptures. If Paul was describing Old Testament Scripture, its character as "prophetic" would already have been established and there would not have been a need to identify these Scriptures as "prophetic." However, if he was referring to newer writings that were not as well recognized as being part of inspired Scripture, he would be more prone to provide the qualifying description of them as "prophetic" in nature.[212]

Second, it is completely unique for any New Testament writer to state, as Paul does in Romans 16:25-26, that the *"revelation of the mystery"* was made known *"by prophetic Scriptures."* Of the 50 times that the term "Scriptures" (*graphōn*) is used in the New Testament, this is the only time it is coupled with the term "revelation" in the context in order to show that the revelation in view comes through Scripture.[213] This again appears to

---

[207] Ironside, *Lectures on the Epistle to the Romans*, 175; McClain, *Romans: The Gospel of God's Grace*, 252; Robert L. Thomas, *Evangelical Hermeneutics: The New Versus the Old* (Grand Rapids: Kregel, 2002), 364; idem, "The Hermeneutics of Progressive Dispensationalism," in *Progressive Dispensationalism: An Analysis of the Movement and Defense of Traditional Dispensationalism*, ed. Ron J. Bigalke, Jr. (Lanham, MD: University Press of America, 2005), 10; W. H. Griffith Thomas, *Commentary on Romans* (Grand Rapids: Kregel Publications, 1974), 439; George Zeller, "Development or Departure?" in *Progressive Dispensationalism: An Analysis of the Movement and Defense of Traditional Dispensationalism*, ed. Ron J. Bigalke, Jr. (Lanham, MD: University Press of America, 2005), 163-64.

[208] The adjective *prophētikōn* occurs only one other time in the New Testament in 2 Peter 1:19. In this passage, the "prophetic word" may be applying in principle to all inspired Scripture of both Testaments (cf. 2 Peter 3:16).

[209] Stifler, *Epistle to the Romans*, 254.

[210] Godet, *Commentary on Romans*, 505.

[211] Wallace, *Greek Grammar*, 222-23.

[212] Godet, *Commentary on Romans*, 505. Additionally, it may be observed that later when Paul refers to Luke 10:7 in 1 Tim. 5:18, he does not need to use the adjective *prophētikōn* because the quotation from Luke is linked with the quotation from Deut. 25:4, and thereby Luke is also put on the level of inspired "Scripture" (1 Tim. 5:18).

[213] Keck, *Romans*, 383.

indicate that Paul was authenticating the New Testament writings as being divine "revelation."

Third, if the phrase, "prophetic Scriptures," in Romans 16:26 refers to the Old Testament, then it is strange and even contradictory for Paul to say that the mystery revelation was kept secret until the Church age and only then (*nun*) was it "made known" through the Old Testament.[214] The whole purpose of the Old Testament Scripture's existence prior to the coming of Christ was to reveal truth, not conceal it. Divine revelation, after all, is for the purpose of revealing God's truth to man, not hiding it.

Fourthly, in Ephesians 3, Paul is clearly referring to New Testament *"apostles and prophets"* (Eph. 3:5) through whom the mystery-revelation came. It is vital to note that this revelation was not merely spoken, but written, as Paul mentions in Ephesians 3:3, *"the mystery (as I have briefly written already),"* referring back to what he had just written in Ephesians 2 about the Jew-Gentile union in Christ. If Paul in Ephesians could refer back to previous writing within the same epistle that dealt with mystery-truth, then why couldn't he be doing the same at the end of Romans?[215] In addition, since Ephesians 3 is plainly a written revelation of New Testament Scripture about mystery truth, and it has many parallels to Romans 16:25-27, this supports the likelihood that Romans 16:26 is referring to New Testament *"prophetic Scriptures."* The many parallels in language between Ephesians 3 and Romans 16 must be accounted for and cannot be ignored, as virtually all non-dispensational commentators do. See, for example, *euangelion* (Rom. 16:25; Eph. 3:6); *prophētikōn/prophētais* (Rom. 16:26; Eph. 3:5); *apokalupsis* (Rom. 16:25; Eph. 3:5); *nun* (Rom. 16:26; Eph. 3:5); *gnōrizō* (Rom. 16:26; Eph. 3:5); *ta ethnē* (Rom. 16:26; Eph. 3:6, 8); *mustērion* (Rom. 16:25; Eph. 3:3-4); *aiōn* (Rom. 16:25; Eph. 3:9); and *sophia* (Rom. 16:27; Eph. 3:10). There are even conceptual parallels, such as *sigaō* ("kept secret") in Romans 16:25 and *apokruptō* ("hidden") in Ephesians 3:9. To ignore this symmetry between the two passages requires almost willful blindness on the part of some non-dispensational interpreters.[216] The dispensational opinion that the *"prophetic Scriptures"* referred to in Romans 16:26 are New Testament Scriptures is based on sound, exegetical evidence. This adds further support for the conclusion that *"the preaching of Jesus Christ"* according to mystery-revelation in Romans 16:25 is distinct from Paul's *"gospel,"* and that the "gospel" in this verse is not a broad, non-soteriological message.

---

[214] Stifler, *Epistle to the Romans*, 254.

[215] Stifler, *Epistle to the Romans*, 255.

[216] It is astonishing for some commentators, such as Cranfield, to dismiss out of hand the New Testament Scripture interpretation and to declare, "The suggestion that the prophetic writings referred to are Christian, not OT, we regard as a counsel of desperation." Cranfield, *Epistle to the Romans*, 2:811n6.

Everlasting Destruction and the Entirety of Romans

In concluding this chapter, it is worth considering the theological implications if the "gospel" in Romans 16:25 is indeed a reference to the entire Epistle of Romans or at least to the sanctification and Christian life portions of it. If this is true, then the door is opened up for a rather bizarre and even harsh possibility for Christians. Imagine if some Christians who are delighted to be justified solely and freely by God's grace are then deceived into thinking that they must live their Christian lives by law-keeping. This should not be too difficult to conceive, for it seems that among the small percentage of professing Christians today who actually understand the freeness of justification by grace, an equally small percentage of that group grasps the fact that sanctification is also all of God's grace (though it results in Christ-honoring works). But imagine for a moment that among those who believe that we are justified freely by grace but sanctified by law that they come to learn from today's promise-only teachers that the term "gospel" in Romans 16:25 encompasses all of Romans, including the sanctification by grace section in Romans 6-8. If this teaching on the "gospel" is true, then logically such legalistic Christians have not "obeyed the gospel." They have, in such a scenario, embraced a false "gospel" by not adhering to the sanctification message of Romans.

But what comes next is truly bizarre and tragic; and yet it is a distinct possibility. If the term "gospel" in Scripture does not refer to the "saving message" of justification and regeneration but is also a sanctification message, as G.E.S. proponents currently teach, then how will the deceived, legalistic Christian interpret passages such as Mark 16:15-16; 2 Thessalonians 1:8-10; and 1 Peter 4:17-18 in conjunction with Romans 16:25? It is not too difficult to imagine that eternal condemnation passages could soon be applied to justified Christians who are not living according to the allegedly broad "gospel" of Romans. Imagine such justified but legalistic Christians reading 2 Thessalonians 1:8-9 in this manner: *"In flaming fire, God will take vengeance upon those who do not know God, and on all who do not obey the gospel (i.e., ALL OF ROMANS 1-16 or some sanctification section within it)—these shall be punished with everlasting destruction away from the presence of the Lord and from the glory of His power."* Is this what we are coming to in the Free Grace movement? God spare us from such an end.

In actuality, we never find the term "gospel" used in Romans or the rest of the New Testament to speak of the sanctification truths of the Christian life. In the Book of Acts, we *never* read of Peter, Paul, and the other evangelists explaining Christian life mystery-truths to the unsaved. Why? Because these are *not* the gospel. When Romans 16:25-26 is carefully studied in relation to every other occurrence of the term "gospel" in the New Testament, it becomes clear that the "gospel" is not the broad, all-inclusive, virtually indefinable entity that advocates of the new G.E.S. doctrine are currently making it out to be. When all occurrences of *euangelion* (Rom. 1:1, 9, 16; 2:16; 10:16; 11:28; 15:16, 19; 16:25) and *euangelizō* (Rom. 1:15; 10:15; 15:20) are studied in Romans contextually, lexically, grammatically, and syntactically, they point to the fact that the content of the "gospel" entails justification truth, not sanctification elements. The "gospel" is the good news of Jesus Christ's person and work, issuing in eternal salvation received solely by God's grace through faith in Christ-crucified for our sins and risen from the dead. The Epistle of Romans teaches that this singular message is necessary for the lost to believe for their justification and for the saved to continue believing as the basis for our practical sanctification.

Chapter 13

What Is the Gospel According to 1 Corinthians 15:1-2?

OVERVIEW

Despite the denials of crossless gospel proponents, 1 Corinthians 15:1-11 is still one of the most definitive texts in the entire Bible for determining the contents of the gospel that must be believed for eternal life. Because this is such a defining passage on the gospel, having major doctrinal ramifications not only for Free Grace theology but also intersecting with the soteriologies of Calvinism and Arminianism, this chapter provides a thorough, exegetical evaluation of the five most common interpretations of verses 1-2. This is followed by an evaluation of crossless gospel interpretations of these verses, contrasted with the correct interpretation of 1 Corinthians 15:1-2. A careful study of this passage reveals that Paul's evangelistic message of Christ crucified for sin and risen from the dead in verses 3-4 was the very message that the Corinthians initially believed for their regeneration and justification; and persevering in that same gospel was necessary for their practical sanctification as well.

The same scenario plays out countless times each day around the world. In the course of conversation with an unsaved person, an evangelistically minded Christian assumes he knows the Scriptures well enough to give a lost sinner "the gospel." And so with confidence in the Lord and love toward the lost, the believer in Christ beseeches the unsaved soul, declaring, *"To be saved, you must believe what it says in 1 Corinthians 15:1-4 regarding the gospel—that Christ died for your sins and rose from the dead. You MUST believe that in order to receive salvation."* Thus another soul is evangelized—or so we think.

For centuries, the consensus opinion among evangelical Christians has been that 1 Corinthians 15:1-11 contains the essential content that a lost person must believe in order to receive eternal salvation. But what was once considered an obvious and appropriate passage to define the contents of saving faith must now be stricken from our use in evangelism, or so we are told. A certain segment of the Free Grace community that is aligned with the Grace Evangelical Society now maintains that this key passage should not be used for evangelizing the lost! They believe that the message of Christ crucified for our sins and risen from the dead in 1 Corinthians 15:3-4 is only necessary for those who have *already* become Christians, not for the lost.

One teacher of this new crossless view, René Lopez, boldly declares regarding 1 Corinthians 15, "This is normally used as a passage for evangelism which I think is totally unwarranted. And we'll see hopefully today, after we cover what we'll cover that you'll be convinced that this is not, and you should not, use this evangelistically or to teach people how to have eternal life."[1] Lopez then informs us that this is really just a sanctification passage, "In conclusion, please do not use 1 Corinthians 15:1-11 as evangelism. It's used for sanctification."[2] To use these verses in evangelism to teach the lost how to have eternal life is now considered to be an "Abuse" of this passage! Based on shocking statements such as these, there can no longer be any doubt about the fact that 1 Corinthians 15:1-11 represents yet another example of a classic gospel text that has suffered at the hands of those promoting a crossless gospel today. It has been commandeered and redefined in order to arrive at a "saving message" that omits the cross and resurrection. It has become yet another exegetical casualty in the tragic saga of the crossless gospel.

---

[1] René A. Lopez, "The Use and Abuse of 1 Corinthians 15:1-11," Grace Evangelical Society Conference, Fort Worth, TX, March 31, 2009.

[2] Ibid.

The promise-only position of the G.E.S. on 1 Corinthians 15:1-11 teaches that though Christ's death for our sins and bodily resurrection are declared to be part of the gospel in verses 3-4, they are not required to be believed by the lost for their eternal salvation. However, they also acknowledge that Christ's death and resurrection were necessary as real historical events in order to provide the grounds of our eternal salvation. The crossless gospel position maintains that if Christ had not truly risen from the dead then the faith of the Corinthians would be effectively nullified or "in vain," and thus non-saving.

Some proponents of a crossless-saving-faith, such as John Niemelä, go so far as to interpret the message of Christ's substitutionary death and bodily resurrection in verses 3-4 as forming a completely distinct "gospel" message than the narrower "gospel" of salvation by faith alone in verses 1-2.[3] In such a case, the "gospel" of verses 1-2 is viewed as the crossless, resurrectionless message of life for the lost, while verses 3-11 are thought to contain the broader gospel that is only necessary to be believed by Christians for our sanctification. A slightly different interpretation is taught by Wilkin, who more accurately sees only one gospel spoken of throughout the entire passage but still erroneously concludes that the gospel is only necessary for sanctification. He states:

> Look at 1 Corinthians 15:2, and don't throw anything because I have a unique spin on this one, which shouldn't surprise you since I have a unique spin on most verses in the Bible . . . Now lots of people like to do 1 Corinthians 15:3-8 or 3-11. Why is it they start at verse 3? Oh, because there's a problem verse in verse 2. And so they just skip the first two verses and go to verse 3, because they can get to the discussion of the gospel they want but avoid the part of the discussion of the gospel they don't want. Well in 15:1-2, Paul says "Moreover brethren . . . I declare to you the gospel." The word gospel means good news. So I would suggest what he's saying here is not necessarily the message he preached to the unbeliever about what they must do to have everlasting life, but this is a good news message which I believe in this context relates to sanctification, and he's saying that what he's about to talk about is a sanctification message.[4]

Wilkin later explains that since Paul's gospel in 1 Corinthians 15 is a sanctification message rather than a justification message, it contains many different truths from the New Testament. He writes:

> Paul is talking here about his *gospel*, his good news message (15:1). Paul's gospel message included more than simply what we must

[3] John H. Niemelä, "The Cross in John's Gospel," *JOTGES* 16 (Spring 2003): 26-27.

[4] Robert N. Wilkin, "The Three Tenses of Salvation Aren't About Justification, Sanctification, and Glorification," Grace Evangelical Society Georgia Regional Conference, Hampton, GA, September 23, 2006.

> believe to be born again (1 Cor. 4:15). It also included fulfilled prophecies, the Rapture, Jesus' soon return, future judgment at the Bema (believers) and Great White Throne (unbelievers), Paul's own apostleship, the church, and Jesus' ultimate victory over wickedness and His establishment of righteousness on earth (see Rom. 2:16; 15:16, 29; 16:25; 1 Cor. 9:14; 2 Cor. 11:7-8; Phil. 1:5; 2:22; 4:3, 15; Col. 1:23; 1 Thess. 3:2; 2 Thess. 2:13-14; 1 Tim. 1:11; 2 Tim. 1:8, 10; 2:8-13). Paul's gospel was a message that he regularly proclaimed to believers for their sanctification (see Rom. 1:15; Gal. 2:14-21, noting especially v. 20).[5]

At this point, we must stop and ask, "Is the reference to the 'gospel' in 1 Corinthians 15:1 merely for sanctification? Or, is it a regeneration message? Or, is it essential to believe for both justification and sanctification?" How a person interprets 1 Corinthians 15:1-11 has broad, sweeping implications for the whole doctrine of soteriology. The proper interpretation of this passage has bearing upon a number of key questions related to the gospel, evangelism, and salvation. For instance, are all the elements of the gospel, the *sine qua non,* contained here? If we use 1 Corinthians 15 in our evangelism, is it complete and sufficient in itself to lead a soul to Christ, or are there some qualifications that we must make when using it? Did Paul intend this passage to be an explanation of what the Corinthians originally believed for their eternal salvation, or was this passage intended to set forth what the Corinthians had to believe for their sanctification? And what about holding fast to the gospel? Does this passage teach that Christians must persevere in their faith to make it to heaven as both Arminianism and Calvinism[6] teach?

<u>1 Corinthians 15:1-11</u>

1 *Moreover, brethren, I declare to you the* ***gospel*** *which I preached to you, which also you* ***received*** *and in which you stand,*
2 *by which also you are* ***saved,*** *if you hold fast that word which I preached to you—unless you* ***believed*** *in vain.*
3 *For I delivered to you first of all that which I also received: that* ***Christ died for our sins*** *according to the Scriptures,*
4 *and that He was buried, and that* ***He rose again*** *the third day according to the Scriptures,*

[5] Robert N. Wilkin, "Another Look at 1 Corinthians 15:3-11," *Grace in Focus* 23 (January/February 2008): 2.

[6] When the term "Calvinist" is used throughout this chapter, it refers particularly to Dortian Calvinism or Dort's fifth point on the doctrine of the perseverance of the saints. The traditional interpretation of this doctrine held by most Calvinists today follows the view of perseverance formalized at the Dutch Synod of Dordrecht (Dort) in A.D. 1619. Thus, the term "Calvinist" in this chapter does not refer to all who classify themselves as Calvinists since some Free Grace brethren believe in the Calvinist view of unconditional election while simultaneously rejecting the traditional, Calvinist doctrine that necessitates perseverance in faith and good works for final salvation.

5 *and that He was seen by Cephas, then by the twelve.*
6 *After that He was seen by over five hundred brethren at once, of whom the greater part remain to the present, but some have fallen asleep.*
7 *After that He was seen by James, then by all the apostles.*
8 *Then last of all He was seen by me also, as by one born out of due time.*
9 *For I am the least of the apostles, who am not worthy to be called an apostle, because I persecuted the church of God.*
10 *But by the **grace of God** I am what I am, and His **grace** toward me was not in vain; but I labored more abundantly than they all, yet not I, but the **grace of God** which was with me.*
11 *Therefore, whether it was I or they, so we preach and so you **believed**.*

The Provision of the Gospel: Salvation (15:1-2)

In the order of the elements of the gospel, the provision of salvation solely on the condition of faith would normally and logically come last. However, when Paul instructed the Corinthian saints in verses 1-11, he implicitly referred to this element of the gospel first, before the central verses on Christ's person and work in verses 3-4. In 1 Corinthians 15:1-2, Paul begins, *"Moreover, brethren, I declare to you the gospel which I preached to you, which also you received and in which you stand, 2 by which also you are **saved**, if you hold fast that word which I preached to you— unless you believed in vain."*

Great confusion and discord surrounds the meaning of the term *"saved"* in verse 2. Does this refer to the temporal, practical sanctification of the Christian life? Or, does it refer to the justification and eternal salvation of every believer? Or, does it refer primarily to practical sanctification, with one's eternal salvation or justification assumed and implied? Though the interpretation of *"saved"* in verse 2 has resulted in a wide divergence of opinion, the correct interpretation of this verse is absolutely critical and foundational to the whole discussion of the gospel and the question of whether or not Christ's cross-work and resurrection are indispensable elements of our saving message to the lost. Therefore, considerable space and careful attention will now be devoted to examining five different interpretative positions on the meaning of the word *"saved"* in 1 Corinthians 15:2, along with the crossless gospel position, followed by the sixth interpretation which is the correct view.

Interpretation #1: New Believers Are Continually Being Added

One interpretation of the term *"saved"* in verse 2 is the view that citizens of Corinth were daily hearing the gospel, believing it, being eternally saved, and being added to the Church. This interpretation sees the word *"saved"* as referring to justification or eternal salvation, not necessarily temporal sanctification in the life of a Christian. It also notes, correctly, that the Greek term for *"saved"* (*sōzō*) is in the present tense and could be translated, *"you are **being** saved."* S. Lewis Johnson mentions this interpretative position as being one exegetical possibility based on the present tense of "saved" in verse 2. He writes:

> **Ye are saved** (Gr., present tense) may refer to continual salvation from the power of sin in the lives of believers, or it may refer to the day-by-day salvation of the inhabitants of Corinth as they received the message and formed part of the church of Jesus Christ.[7]

While this view is doctrinally correct and the present tense of *sōzō* can be grammatically interpreted this way, to do so would create a logical contradiction within the passage that would mitigate the likelihood of it being correct. In verses 1-2, Paul says, *"Moreover, brethren, I declare to* ***you*** *the gospel which I preached to* ***you****, which also* ***you*** *received and in which* ***you*** *stand, 2 by which also* ***you*** *are (being) saved, if* ***you*** *hold fast that word which I preached to* ***you****—unless* ***you*** *believed in vain."*

In the passage, the group addressed with the phrase, *"by which also you are (being) saved"* is the same group identified as "you" seven other times throughout the passage. This singular group is identified as those who had heard, *"received,"* and *"believed"* the evangelistic message Paul personally *"preached"* to them *in the past*. This was not referring primarily to new, daily converts in Corinth who were getting saved subsequent to Paul's departure from the city. The ones who are now said to be *"(being) saved,"* provided they *"hold fast"* to the original message, are those whom Paul had previously led to the Lord. To interpret the passage otherwise would present an internal contradiction, whereby Paul would be saying in essence, *"by which also you new, daily converts are being saved, if you hold fast that word which I preached to you in the past."* This contradiction is probably the most serious strike against this view.

Sometimes 1 Corinthians 1:17-21 is enlisted to support this "continual addition of new believers" view since it also contains the word *"saved."* There *sōzō* is used twice, once as a present tense participle (1:18) and once as an infinitive (1:21) with the present tense participle of *"believe"* (*pisteuō*). It says, *"For Christ did not send me to baptize, but to preach the gospel, not with wisdom of words, lest the cross of Christ should be made of no effect. 18 For the message of the cross is foolishness to those who are perishing,* ***but to us who are being saved*** (*tois de sōzomenois hēmin*) *it is the power of God. 19 For it is written: "I will destroy the wisdom of the wise, And bring to nothing the understanding of the prudent." 20 Where is the wise? Where is the scribe? Where is the disputer of this age? Has not God made foolish the wisdom of this world? 21 For since, in the wisdom of God, the world through wisdom did not know God, it*

---

[7] S. Lewis Johnson, "1 Corinthians," in *The Wycliffe Bible Commentary*, ed. Charles F. Pfeiffer and Everett F. Harrison (Chicago: Moody Press, 1962), 1255. Gromacki also mentions this possible interpretation held by some (see Robert G. Gromacki, *Called to Be Saints: An Exposition of 1 Corinthians* [Grand Rapids: Baker Book House, 1977], 182n).

pleased God through the foolishness of the message preached **to save those who believe** (*sōsai tous pisteuontas*)."

Should 1 Corinthians 1:17-21 be considered a direct, parallel, supporting passage for the meaning of *sōzō* in 1 Corinthians 15:2? I do not believe so. There is a clear difference between these two passages with respect to the specific salvation being discussed in each immediate context. In 1 Corinthians 1:17-21, Paul includes himself (v. 18) with the use of the first person plural pronoun *"us"* (*hēmin*), linking himself with others who are *"being saved"* in verse 18. Paul and other believers in Christ stand in contrast in this passage to the *"world"* (v. 20) and *"those who are perishing"* (v. 18). This clear distinction between the ones who are being *"saved"* through faith in Christ and the *"perishing"* world of unbelievers is simply not found in the context of 1 Corinthians 15:1-2, as it is in 1 Corinthians 1:17-21.

In 1 Corinthians 15:1-2 Paul is not drawing a distinction between the salvation of believers versus the ruin of unbelievers. He is discussing the on-going salvation of those who had previously heard his gospel preaching, and who had received it by believing it. Paul identified these Corinthian Christians with the second person plural *"you"* eight times in the context. This is quite dissimilar to 1 Corinthians 1:17-21 where Paul is not discussing the on-going salvation of these Corinthian believers, but the salvation of those from the *"world"* of the *"perishing."* For these reasons, even though interpretation #1 handles the grammar of the present tense of *sōzō* correctly in 1 Corinthians 15:2, and it is doctrinally sound, it still suffers logical and contextual inconsistencies that render it doubtful. A better alternative should be sought.

Interpretation #2: Eternal Salvation Can Possibly Be Lost

Another interpretative option, which is certainly no improvement upon view #1, is the interpretation that holds that eternal salvation is in view in 1 Corinthians 15:2 but that it can actually be lost, since it is conditioned on persevering in the truth of the gospel. This is the classic Arminian position; and this passage is typically cited for support by those who reject the biblical doctrine of eternal security for every child of God.[8] One Arminian writer, Marshall, believes that the regenerate can lose eternal life. He writes, commenting on the phrase, *"if you are holding fast the word,"* in 1 Corinthians 15:2:

> Salvation depends upon continuing to hold fast to the apostolic message, and to give up belief in one essential item of it, viz.

[8] Daniel D. Corner, *The Believer's Conditional Security: Eternal Security Refuted* (Washington, PA: Evangelical Outreach, 2000), 240-42; Guy Duty, *If Ye Continue: A Study of the Conditional Aspects of Salvation* (Minneapolis: Bethany House, 1966), 113; David Pawson, *Once Saved, Always Saved? A Study in Perseverance and Inheritance* (London: Hodder & Stoughton, 1996), 57-58; Robert Shank, *Life in the Son* (Springfield, MO: Westcott Publishers, 1961), 239, 299.

> the resurrection, as some of them apparently had done, was to give up hope of final salvation. Paul's principal point here is that attainment of salvation depends upon continuance in the apostolic faith.[9]

This interpretation is riddled with problems and is most certainly incorrect. The first major problem with this view is that contextually, Paul is not primarily discussing "final salvation." Paul is not questioning whether the Corinthian Christians would make it to heavenly glory one day. While 1 Corinthians 15:2 does use the verb *"saved,"* it is in the present tense in the Greek, indicating a deliverance that was in the present from Paul's perspective. Had Paul been speaking of a final, future deliverance, contingent or not, he most likely would have used the future tense of *sōzō*, just as he did elsewhere in 1 Corinthians 3:15.[10] Contrary to Marshall's claims, Paul's point here was *not* the "attainment" of "final salvation" contingent upon their perseverance. Rather, Paul was concerned that these Corinthian believers would experience a present deliverance from the Lord, though it was dependent upon their holding fast to the gospel message. More will be said on this present salvation under interpretation #6.

A second major problem with interpretation #2 is that it contradicts what Paul had written previously to the Corinthians in assuring them of their eternal security in Christ. For example, in 1 Corinthians 1:8, Paul promised that the Lord *"will also confirm you to the end, that you may be blameless in the day of our Lord Jesus Christ."* Here Paul is not stating a wish for these Corinthian Christians; he is stating a fact. The Greek verb for "will confirm" (*bebaioō*) is in the future tense, indicative mood, indicating what God Himself will certainly do in the future—He will confirm them blameless *to the end*.

Another passage in 1 Corinthians that teaches eternal security for every saint is in 3:15, where Paul states, *"If anyone's work is burned, he will suffer loss; but he himself will be saved, yet so as through fire."* The context of this verse is dealing with future reward for having faithfully served the Lord. The works of the saved will be evaluated (put through the fire-test) to see if they were genuinely "good works" or just the products of fleshly religious service. Those works that pass through the fire are those for which the child of God will be rewarded. Those which are burned up will represent an opportunity lost for all eternity to glorify the Lord and earn a reward in the process. Yet even if the Christian's work is consumed, the passage promises that *"he himself will be saved."* This will be true even

---

[9] I. Howard Marshall, *Kept by the Power of God: A Study of Perseverance and Falling Away* (Minneapolis: Bethany House, 1969), 118.

[10] The two future occurrences of *sōzō* in 7:16 are most likely not in reference to a future time in glory (glorification) but a future time within the believer's earthly lifetime, when his or her spouse would be saved in the sense of justification. Paul also uses the aorist subjunctive of *sōzō* 3x in 1 Corinthians, in 5:5 (with a future sense in the context), 9:22, and 10:33.

for those who were persistently *"carnal"* and whose walk was externally indistinguishable from that of the unsaved (1 Cor. 3:1-4). This carnality of the Corinthians is the very context that precipitated the whole discussion of works and rewardable service for Christ in 1 Corinthians 3:10-15. Like 1 Corinthians 1:8, this promise in 3:15 is also not stating a wish by Paul, but declaring a fact. The Greek verb for *"will be saved"* (*sōzō*) is in the future tense, passive voice, and indicative mood. It is again indicating what God will do in the future, not what He might do. He will save even those whose earthly life goes up in smoke!

Yet another passage in 1 Corinthians that teaches every saint's eternal security is 11:30-32. There Paul says, *"For this reason many are weak and sick among you, and many sleep. 31 For if we would judge ourselves, we would not be judged. 32 But when we are judged, we are chastened by the Lord, that we may not be condemned with the world."* In the context, some Corinthians were not exercising proper self-judgment but were persisting in the flagrant sin of selfishness (11:20-22). Some were even getting drunk at church (11:21), and some were dishonoring the Lord's Supper (11:27-30). As a result, there were degrees of God's chastening upon His wayward children. Some were weak, some sick, and some even slept—a New Testament metaphor for the physical death of the believer in Christ. In other words, some were chastened to the point of the Lord simply ending their earthly life prematurely. Yet when they were chastened by the Lord to the maximal point of death, they were still not going to be *"condemned with the world."* While this passage shows the seriousness of God in dealing with sin in the life of His children, as well as the extent to which He will go to teach us (v. 32, *paideuometha*) to walk in the paths of righteousness, 1 Corinthians 11:30-32 also reveals the security of salvation since these Corinthians were still God's children, though disobedient and under maximum divine discipline.

It must be clarified with respect to 1 Corinthians 11:32 that this verse is not expressing any uncertainty as to outcome, as though Paul is saying to the Corinthian Christians, "You might or might not still be condemned with the world depending on how you respond to God's chastening." Some Free Grace Christians interpret it this way, such as Dillow who writes, "Failure to respond to discipline can result in a believer being condemned with the world (1 Cor. 11:32-33)."[11] Dillow applies this to future, penal condemnation that will be meted out to disobedient, carnal Christians at the Bema. He goes on to say, "If God can bring condemnation upon believers in time as these illustrations prove, there is no necessary reason to believe He cannot condemn believers at the judgment seat of Christ."[12]

However, the *hina* + subjunctive clause in 1 Corinthians 11:32, *"that (hina) we may not be condemned with the world,"* should be interpreted at least

---

[11] Joseph C. Dillow, *The Reign of the Servant Kings: A Study of Eternal Security and the Final Significance of Man* (Miami Springs, FL: Schoettle Publishing, 1992), 539.

[12] Ibid., 540.

ecbatically as expressing result,[13] just as the NIV has it, *"so that we will not be condemned with the world."*[14] This is a well-established lexical category of usage, even with the sense of certainty of result from the divine perspective.[15] The particle *hina* with the subjunctive certainly has an additional telic sense in verse 32, expressing both divine purpose and certain outcome. Although some older grammarians denied that *hina* clauses ever denote result in the New Testament,[16] this is now considered to be an overstatement. Wallace writes that this category of usage "indicates *both the intention and its sure accomplishment*" and "what God purposes is what happens and, consequently, ἵνα is used to express both the divine purpose and the result."[17] This means that 1 Corinthians 11:32 is not a negative warning, saying that we "might be condemned with the world." Rather, it is a positive declaration of God's purpose and certain result, *"that we might **not** be condemned with the world."* Paul's whole point in 1 Corinthians 11:28-32 is to show that even though we may be judged by the Lord, even severely to the point of physical death due to lack of self-judgment, it is God's purpose and certain outcome that we *not* be condemned (Rom. 8:1).

Sometimes the translation of the *hina* + subjunctive clause creates a misimpression in the mind of the modern reader. The idiomatic English expression, "in order that we might/may/should" often gives the initial impression that some human contingency is present, when in fact the outcome or result is never in doubt from the divine perspective. In this respect, John 3:16 should be viewed as a promise, not a statement of probability. It says, *"that whoever believes in Him should not perish"* (*hina pas ho pisteuōn eis auton mē apolētai all' echē zōēn aiōnion*). The subjunctive in this verse is "all but required" grammatically, but semantically John 3:16 does not mean that believers might still perish.[18] Rather it is a promise that *we will not* perish.[19]

One final passage establishing the eternal security of every believer within this epistle is 1 Corinthians 12:12-13, which states, *"For as the body is one and has many members, but all the members of that one body, being many,*

---

[13] BDF, 198, §391 (5); A. T. Robertson, *A Grammar of the Greek New Testament in the Light of Historical Research* (Nashville: Broadman Press, 1934), 997-99; Nigel Turner, *Prolegomena*, Volume 1 of *A Grammar of New Testament Greek*, by J. H. Moulton, 4 vols. (Edinburgh: T & T Clark, 1908), 206-9; idem, *Syntax*, Volume 3 of *A Grammar of New Testament Greek*, by J. H. Moulton, 4 vols. (Edinburgh: T & T Clark, 1963), 102.

[14] Gordon D. Fee, *The First Epistle to the Corinthians*, NICNT (Grand Rapids: Eerdmans, 1987), 566.

[15] BDAG, 477.

[16] Ernest De Witt Burton, *Syntax of the Moods and Tenses in New Testament Greek* (Chicago: University of Chicago Press, 1900; Reprint, Grand Rapids: Kregel, 1976), 94-95, §222-23.

[17] Daniel B. Wallace, *Greek Grammar Beyond the Basics: An Exegetical Syntax of the New Testament* (Grand Rapids: Zondervan, 1996), 473.

[18] Ibid., 474.

[19] For similar soteriologically significant examples of the *hina* + subjunctive mood clause expressing a definite result, see John 6:39-40; 10:10; 20:31; Gal. 2:16; 1 Tim. 1:16.

are one body, so also is Christ. 13 For by one Spirit we were all baptized into one body—whether Jews or Greeks, whether slaves or free—and have all been made to drink into one Spirit." These verses teach that all believers in Christ, without exception, have been placed into Christ's body by the Holy Spirit and are not only positionally *"in the Spirit"* (Rom. 8:9) but have the Spirit in them. Regarding the baptism or placing into Christ spoken of in verse 13, it is permanent, since nowhere in Scripture is our baptism by the Spirit into Christ ever said to be reversible. Secondly, the Holy Spirit's indwelling of every believer is also permanent according to the testimony of the rest of the New Testament (John 14:16-17; Rom. 8:23; 2 Cor. 1:22; Eph. 1:13-14; 4:30).

If interpretation #2 were correct, it would contradict the Epistle of 1 Corinthians itself.[20] Furthermore, it would contradict numerous other passages throughout the Bible that teach the eternal security of the believer (John 10:28-29; Rom. 5:9-10; 8:28-30, 35-39; Heb. 7:25; 10:12-14; 13:5; 1 Peter 1:3-5; etc.). Since all of Scripture is the inspired, inerrant Word of God, it cannot contradict itself. Therefore, any apparent contradiction must be the result of a wrong interpretation, such as interpretation #2. For these reasons, the possible loss of eternal salvation view cannot be correct and another interpretation should be sought.

Interpretation #3: Not Continuing in the Gospel Shows Non-Saving Faith

A third interpretative possibility views the term "saved" in 1 Corinthians 15:2 as referring to eternal salvation, not sanctification, just like the previous interpretation. However, instead of this salvation being *lost* by a failure to persevere in the faith (Arminianism), in view #3 Christians *prove* the

[20] There are several passages within 1 Corinthians that Arminians often cite in order to support the notion that a child of God can lose salvation if he or she does not stay faithful. These include 5:5; 6:9-11; 9:24-27; and 10:12. In 1 Cor. 5:5, Paul simply states the certain outcome or result of this persistently immoral brother being put out of the church. Paul knew that though his flesh needed to be destroyed under the instrumentation of Satan, the outcome would still certainly result in the wayward brother's spirit being saved at the imminent appearing of Christ. 1 Cor. 5:5 is parallel to 11:32 in this regard, where the *hina* clause expresses an outcome that is certain and never in doubt (i.e., his spirit *will be saved* in the day of the Lord Jesus, even if his flesh suffers "destruction" [*olethros*, not *paideuō*] in the meantime). There is nothing of contingency here, only certainty. 1 Cor. 6:9-11 is also not teaching that Christians can lose their salvation if they do not persist in righteous conduct. It is a passage teaching that the Corinthians had a positional righteousness in Christ, contrary to the unsaved world. It is not teaching that a walk of practical righteousness is a prerequisite for entering the kingdom of God. 1 Cor. 9:24-27 is dealing with rewards (*"crown," "prize"*) for perseverance in the faith, not the free gift of eternal life, which cannot be gained by running the race of the Christian life and disciplining our body. For further exposition of this passage, see Tom Stegall, "Must Faith Endure for Salvation to be Sure? Pt. 5," *GFJ* (November-December 2002): 22-27. Finally, 1 Cor. 10:12 is a warning regarding the Christian life, not eternal salvation, as interpretation #6 in this chapter will explain. None of these supposed proof texts for Arminianism teach the potential loss of eternal life, nor do they overturn the testimony of 1 Cor. 1:8; 3:15; 11:30-32; 12:12-13; and the rest of Scripture as to the eternal security of every regenerate person in Christ.

genuineness of their faith and salvation by necessarily persevering in faith and good works until the end of their lives. A failure to persevere shows that a person was never truly regenerated in the first place and never had a "saving," working kind of faith.[21] This interpretation of *"saved"* in 1 Corinthians 15:2 is based upon the traditional, Reformed doctrine of the "perseverance of the saints," the fifth point in the Five Points of Calvinism. This interpretation of 1 Corinthians 15:2 is found in Charles Hodge's commentary on this passage, where he writes:

> Their salvation, however, is conditioned on their perseverance. If they do not persevere, they will not only fail of the consummation of the work of salvation, but it becomes manifest that they never were justified or renewed. . . . Here it is evident that the condition of salvation is not retaining in the memory, but persevering in the faith. 'The gospel saves you,' says the apostle, 'if you hold fast the gospel which I preached unto you.'[22]

A more contemporary expression of this Calvinistic, Lordship Salvation view is found in John MacArthur's commentary on 1 Corinthians, where he writes regarding 15:2:

> Paul's qualifying phrase—**if you hold fast the word which I preached to you, unless you believed in vain**—does not teach that true believers are in danger of losing their salvation, but it is a warning against non-saving faith. So a clearer rendering would be, ". . . if you hold fast what I preached to you, unless your faith is worthless or unless you believed without effect." The Corinthians' holding fast to what Paul had preached (see 11:2) was the result of and an evidence of their genuine salvation, just as their salvation and new life were an evidence of the power of Christ's resurrection. It must be recognized, however, that some lacked the true saving faith, and thus did not continue to obey the Word of God.[23]

Interpretation #3 is at least as weak as the previous Arminian interpretation, view #2, for several reasons. First and foremost, the apostle Paul knew that those to whom he was writing in Corinth were genuine believers. This fact can be readily observed from Paul's descriptions of these Corinthians throughout this epistle. They were referred to by Paul twenty times throughout this epistle as his *"brethren"* (1 Cor. 1:10, 11, 26; 2:1; 3:1; 4:6; 7:24, 29; 10:1; 11:2, 33; 12:1; 14:6, 20, 26, 39; 15:1, 50, 58; 16:15). The term *"brethren"* spoke of a kinship in Christ. It went beyond mere ethnic brotherhood as the term is occasionally used in the New Testament (Rom. 9:3), since Paul

---

[21] Leon Morris, *1 Corinthians*, TNTC (Grand Rapids: Eerdmans, 2000), 201.

[22] Charles Hodge, *Commentary on the First Epistle to the Corinthians* (Grand Rapids: Eerdmans, 1950), 311 (ellipsis added).

[23] John F. MacArthur, *1 Corinthians*, MacArthur New Testament Commentary (Chicago: Moody Press, 1984), 399.

was ethnically Jewish and the Corinthians were largely Gentile (1 Cor. 12:2). In addition, nowhere in 1 Corinthians 15 does the apostle Paul even infer that the Corinthians might be *"false brethren"* (*pseudadelphous*), a term that he does not hesitate to employ elsewhere when seeking to distinguish genuine brothers in Christ from mere professors of Christ (Gal. 2:4).

Paul also knew that he was writing to those who possessed genuine faith in Christ and eternal salvation based on the fact that these Corinthians were regarded by Paul as *"called"* (1:2, 9, 26) and *"chosen"* (1:27-28). They were said to be *"in Christ"* (1:30), even *"baptized"* into Christ by the Holy Spirit (12:12-13), and therefore they were *"sanctified in Christ"* and *"saints"* (1:2). These Corinthians were also considered to be temples of the Holy Spirit individually (6:19) and His temple corporately (3:16). They were spiritually deficient in *"no gift"* of the Spirit (1:7). They were stated to be *"Christ's"* own possession (3:23), and they did not even belong to themselves anymore (6:19-20). They were instructed by Paul to expect instantaneous transformation at the rapture when Christ would come again (15:51-52 cf. 11:26). They were told by Paul that they would *"judge the world"* one day (6:2), even angels (6:3), as part of reigning with Christ (4:8; 15:25). And far from speculating as to whether these Corinthians were truly "justified" or "renewed" as Hodge claimed, Paul declares quite clearly that they were already *"begotten"* or regenerated (4:15), already *"washed,"* already *"sanctified"* (positionally in Christ, 1:2; but not practically, 3:1-4), and already *"justified"* in Christ (6:11).[24]

Secondly, with respect to the Corinthians' *faith* in particular, nowhere in this epistle does Paul issue "a warning against non-saving faith," as MacArthur claims that Paul is doing in 1 Corinthians 15:2. Far from questioning whether these Corinthians had originally, truly believed in Christ for their eternal salvation, Paul repeatedly, explicitly indicates that they had believed. Consider the following reasons for this conclusion:

- The Corinthians were consistently contrasted with *"unbelievers"* throughout this epistle (6:6; 7:13-14; 10:27; 14:22 cf. 14:1).

- They were even commanded by Paul to *"stand fast in the faith"* (16:13), something that would be impossible for someone without faith to do. If Paul doubted whether these Corinthians had ever exercised faith in Christ for salvation, so much so that he even issued "a warning against non-saving faith," then why would he command them to stand fast in a faith that they didn't even possess?!

- If Paul was questioning in 1 Corinthians 15:2 whether these Corinthians truly, originally believed in Christ as interpretation #3 affirms, then

[24] Each of these four verbs in 1 Corinthians 4:15 and 6:11 is in the aorist tense and indicative mood in Greek, indicating that these things had already become true of the Corinthians sometime in their past.

> this would create a glaring contradiction within this epistle, even within the immediate context of 1 Corinthians 15:2. The Calvinistic, Lordship Salvation interpretation ignores the fact that right in the passage Paul states that they had already believed! 1 Corinthians 15:11 says, *"Therefore, whether it was I or they, so we preach and so you believed."* The fact that Paul regarded the Corinthians as having already believed is also seen earlier in this epistle in 3:5, where Paul wrote, *"Who then is Paul, and who is Apollos, but ministers through whom you believed."* In both 1 Corinthians 3:5 and 15:11, the verb for *"believed"* in Greek is the aorist tense, indicative mood of *pisteuō*. This again indicates the fact that Paul regarded the Corinthians as having already believed sometime prior to his writing this epistle.

Far from issuing "a warning against non-saving faith" in 1 Corinthians 15:2, no more definite and complete depiction could be presented of a people that had genuinely believed in Christ for eternal salvation than that which is presented in 1 Corinthians.

A third main reason why interpretation #3 cannot be correct is because it misconstrues the meaning of *"unless you believed in vain"* in 1 Corinthians 15:2. By believing *"in vain"* (*eikē*), Paul does not mean to imply "that some lacked true saving faith" and that this "is a warning against non-saving faith" as MacArthur asserts. For the Corinthians to have believed *"in vain"* does not mean that they didn't genuinely believe in the first place, or that they didn't have the right *kind* of faith—an obedient, persevering, working kind of faith, a "true saving faith." Rather, believing *"in vain"* meant that their faith might yet fall far short of its God-intended purpose or goal of a productive, fruitful Christian life that would bring greater glory to God. Paul was not questioning whether they had genuinely believed in the past, but whether their past faith would fall incomplete and come to a deficient end. For this reason, the clause, *"unless you believed in vain,"* should be understood as, *"unless you believed to no purpose,"*[25] or *"to no avail,"*[26] or even *"without success or effect."*[27] It must be recognized that the phrase *"in vain"* throughout the New Testament consistently does *not* call into question the authenticity of the action (when used adverbially) or thing (when used adjectivally) that it modifies.[28] Consider the following passages:

- *"for he does not bear the sword in vain (eikē)"* (Rom. 13:4). In the context, was Paul questioning whether the government truly and genuinely

---

[25] A. T. Robertson, *Word Pictures in the New Testament* (Grand Rapids: Baker Book House, n.d.), 4:186. See also, BDAG, 281.

[26] BAGD, 222.

[27] J. H. Thayer, ed., *The New Thayer's Greek-English Lexicon* (Peabody, MA: Hendrickson, 1981), 176.

[28] This is true whether *"in vain"* is *eikē* in the Greek (1 Cor. 15:2), or other terms used synonymously, such as *kenoō/kenos* or *dōrean*.

bore the sword via capital punishment? No. That fact was beyond dispute. He was simply teaching that the government does not bear the sword "to no purpose." He was reminding the Roman Christians that the government practice of capital punishment fulfilled its intended end of discouraging evil conduct and maintaining civil order.

- *"His grace toward me was not in vain (kenos); but I labored more abundantly"* (1 Cor. 15:10). Was Paul questioning whether God really and genuinely extended His grace toward him? Or, was Paul simply teaching that the grace of God that he genuinely received wasn't for naught ("without success" or "to no avail"), since it resulted in his labor for the Lord?

- *"your labor is not in vain (kenos) in the Lord"* (1 Cor. 15:58). Was Paul questioning whether the Corinthians actually labored for the Lord? Was the authenticity of their labor in question? Did they *really* labor for the Lord? Or was he simply teaching that their labor as Christians, done "in the Lord," was not "without success" and was not "to no avail"?

- *"We then, as workers together with Him also plead with you not to receive the grace of God in vain (kenos)"* (2 Cor. 6:1). Here again, Paul is not questioning whether these Corinthians had in their past genuinely and actually received the grace of God, or would yet so receive it in their future, but whether they would do so without fulfilling the divinely intended purpose of that grace. Commentator Ralph Martin states regarding this verse, *"But we concur with Hughes (217) that it is doubtful in 6:1 that Paul is considering either counterfeit faith or the concept of perseverance."*[29]

- *"lest our boasting of you should be in vain (kenoō)"* (2 Cor. 9:3). Was Paul saying that he hadn't really, truly, and genuinely boasted of the Corinthians' previous willingness to give toward the poor saints

---

[29] Ralph P. Martin, *2 Corinthians*, WBC (Dallas: Word Publishing, 1986), 166. See also, Philip E. Hughes, *The Second Epistle to the Corinthians*, NICNT (Grand Rapids: Eerdmans, 1962), 217-19. Both commentators argue from the context that 6:1 is a plea for the Corinthians to let the grace of God transform their lives, resulting in greater reward at the judgment seat of Christ (2 Cor. 5:10). Martin says, "Therefore, it appears that the meaning behind Paul's understanding of receiving the grace of God in vain is. . . . to fail to grow and mature in the Christian life, as evidenced by a life under the control of the one who died for believers" (ibid., 167). Hughes states, "For them to receive the grace of God in vain meant that their practice did not measure up to their profession as Christians, that their lives were so inconsistent as to constitute a denial of the logical implications of the gospel, namely, and in particular, that Christ died for them so that they might no longer live to themselves but to His glory (5:15). This is a matter of which Paul had written more fully and graphically in his earlier letter: as recipients of the grace of God they were securely placed upon Jesus Christ, the only foundation, but they were in danger of building on that foundation with wood, hay, and stubble—a structure which would be made manifest and destroyed in the day of the Lord, though they themselves will be saved (1 Cor. 3:10-15). It is in this sense that the grace of God may be received in vain" (ibid., 218-19).

in Jerusalem (2 Cor. 9:2)? Was a special kind of boasting needed here? Or was Paul simply saying that his boasting about them to the Macedonians (2 Cor. 9:2) would be "to no purpose," or "to no avail," if they didn't follow through with their initial intent to give?

- *"lest by any means I might run, or had run, in vain (kenos)"* (Gal. 2:2). If there was not unity on the gospel between Paul and the "pillars" in Jerusalem, would Paul's previous running in the gospel ministry not have been genuine and authentic? Was Paul wondering if he had the right kind of running? Or was he simply saying that if they were not united on the gospel after all, their disunity would divide Jewish and Gentile believers and his running would not yield the divinely intended result or purpose? If such were the case, Paul's running would be "without success" and "to no avail."

- *"if righteousness comes through the law, then Christ died in vain (dōrean)"*[30] (Gal. 2:21). Was Paul questioning whether Christ's death was genuine here? Did He truly die? Did He have the right kind of death? Or would Christ's death have been "to no purpose" and not fulfill its divinely intended purpose if people could get to heaven through some other means, such as keeping the law?

- *"Have you suffered so many things in vain (eikē)—if indeed it was in vain (eikē)?"* (Gal. 3:4). Was Paul questioning here whether the Galatian Christians had truly, actually, and genuinely suffered in the past, following their conversion? No (Acts 14:21-22)! Was he questioning whether they had the right kind of suffering? No, he was simply saying that the Galatians' previous suffering for Christ would be *"in vain"* if they did not continue in the grace of God by now giving in to the legalists, the very ones who persecuted them in the first place (Acts 13-14). This would be bypassing the persecution associated with Christ's cross (Gal. 4:29; 5:11; 6:12-14). When Paul writes, in Gal. 3:4, *"if indeed it was in vain,"* the phrase *"it was"* isn't in the Greek text and is supplied by the translators. There is no past tense indicated here; and thus some translations render the verse with a present tense connotation, *"if it be indeed in vain"* (ASV) or *"if it be yet in vain"* (KJV). Whether the *"if indeed"* phrase in Galatians 3:4 is interpreted with a past tense or a present tense is ultimately inconsequential, since Paul was simply sounding a note of optimism that the situation in Galatia was not yet hopeless from his perspective, though the situation was still tenuous (Gal. 4:11).

---

[30] Though the term *dōrean* is translated *"in vain"* here in this unique instance, it falls within the same semantic domain as *eikē* (see L&N, §89.20 "for no reason" [1:780], §89.63-64 "for no purpose" [1:786]).

- *"lest I have labored for you in vain (eikē)"* (Gal. 4:11). Again, by using the modifying expression, *"in vain,"* was Paul questioning whether he had genuinely labored for these Galatians in the past? Did he have the right kind of labor? We see yet again that his genuine labors for the Lord would be "without success" and "to no avail" if these Galatians capitulated to the pressure from the legalists. Here again, as with the Corinthians, by possibly laboring *"in vain"* for the Galatians, Paul was not calling into question the authenticity of their eternal salvation, for he regarded them as children of God (Gal. 3:26-28; 4:6-7, 9).

- *"so that I may rejoice in the day of Christ that I have not run in vain (kenos) or labored in vain (kenos)"* (Phil. 2:16). Again, Paul is not doubting whether he really, truly, and genuinely had run and labored for the Lord with the Philippian Christians. But his running and laboring would not reach its divinely-intended goal or purpose if the Philippians did not continue to *"work out"* their own salvation (Phil. 2:12), via practical sanctification, until the Lord returned (2:16). That Paul was again not questioning the genuineness of their new birth by his statement that he possibly labored *"in vain"* can be easily seen from the fact that he regarded them as being fellow recipients of the grace of God (1:7), citizens of heaven (3:20), and as having their names written in the Book of Life (4:3).

- *"our coming to you was not in vain (kenos)"* (1 Thess. 2:1). Here, *"in vain"* modifies *"coming."* Did Paul really, genuinely come to the Thessalonians? Was Paul saying it took a special kind of coming to these Thessalonians in order for him to have truly come to them in the first place? No, his coming to them was not *"in vain"* only in the sense that the Thessalonians responded with a continual faith and obedience to the Word of God (1 Thess. 2:13-14), and thus, God's desired objective in having Paul come to them was fulfilled.

- *"and our labor might be in vain (kenos)"* (1 Thess. 3:5). Again, Paul's labor for the Thessalonian Christians was genuine. It would only have been *"in vain"* if these Thessalonians did not press on to maturity in the Lord.

- *"Or do you think that the Scripture says in vain (kenos), 'The Spirit who dwells in us yearns jealously'?"* (James 4:5). In this final example of the *"in vain"* principle in the New Testament, we see yet again that the authenticity and genuineness of the activity is not called into question simply by the use of the phrase *"in vain."* Rather, it merely indicates that there was truly a purpose for which the Old Testament Scriptures say, *"The Spirit who dwells in us yearns jealously"*—that purpose being the Holy Spirit's desire for believers to have a relationship with the Lord and not with the world (James 4:4).

In every occurrence in the New Testament of the Greek terms translated *"in vain"* (*eikē, kenos/kenoō,* or *dōrean*), there is not a single instance in which they call into question the genuineness or reality of the original action or thing modified. Thus, it is extremely unlikely in Paul's statement in Corinthians 15:2 (*"unless you believed in vain"*) that he is doubting the authenticity of the initial faith of the Corinthians, as interpretation #3 maintains.

A fourth reason why interpretation #3 cannot be correct is because it misses the force of the present tense of *"saved"* (*sōzō*) in 1 Corinthians 15:2, *"by which also you are (being) saved."* In verse 2, Paul is not even addressing the question of whether the Corinthians would attain the "consummation of the work of salvation," by holding fast to the gospel, as Hodge taught. Interpretation #3 misapplies the warning to *"hold fast"* in 15:2 not only to initial salvation (justification) but also to final salvation (glorification), just like interpretation #2 (the Arminian view). In 1 Corinthians 15:2, Paul was not questioning the Corinthians' past salvation or justification (6:11); nor was he doubting their future salvation or glorification (3:15; 15:51). Rather, he was questioning their present salvation or practical sanctification in their Christian lives. This fact will be explained further under interpretation #6.

A fifth and final reason why interpretation #3 cannot be correct is because, doctrinally, all genuine believers in Christ do *not* persevere to the end of their lives in faith and good works. Even the epistle under consideration, 1 Corinthians, establishes this truth. As already demonstrated under interpretation #2, passages such as 1 Corinthians 9:24-27 teach that we must diligently and intentionally strive to finish the race of the Christian life because it is not guaranteed to happen. If Paul believed in the Calvinist, Lordship Salvation doctrine of the guaranteed perseverance of the saints, then according to 1 Corinthians 9:24-27 he was clearly operating under false pretenses in his own Christian life! Furthermore, some persistently carnal Corinthians had been chastened by God to the point of physical death according to 1 Corinthians 11:30-32, and yet they were not condemned with the world but were genuinely born again and justified as the rest of the epistle clearly indicates. If interpretation #3 is correct, it would not only create internal contradictions within 1 Corinthians, it would also contradict the doctrine of Scripture as a whole which teaches that a genuine child of God may not necessarily continue in faith and good works and yet still possess the gift of eternal life.[31]

Interpretation #4: Some Never Understood the Gospel in the First Place

Interpretation #4 is similar to interpretation #3, yet distinct from it. This view also maintains that some in the Corinthian congregation were never

[31] For further support for the biblical doctrine of the preservation of the saints in contrast to the Calvinist doctrine of the perseverance of the saints, see Tom Stegall, "Must Faith Endure for Salvation to be Sure?" Parts 1-9, *GFJ* (March/April 2002—Fall 2003).

truly regenerated and eternally saved in the first place. But the reason for this conclusion is slightly different than in interpretation #3. It concludes that some of the Corinthians whom Paul was addressing were never originally saved because they never believed in the gospel truth of Christ's resurrection from the very beginning. Calvinist Robert Gromacki explains this fourth interpretation in his commentary on 1 Corinthians:

> The conditional clause (introduced by "if") served as a warning to the false teachers and to their converts (cf. 15:12). Failure to "keep" (*katechete*) the total essence and effects of the gospel message would indicate that some of the professing Christians were not really saved in the first place. A saving faith is a persevering orthodox faith. The issue here is not faulty, immoral living, but incorrect doctrine. A "vain" belief (*eikēi*, "in vain") is a belief in a crucified, nonresurrected Christ, or a belief in a crucified, resurrected Christ who would not raise their physical bodies. Either heresy, revealed later in life, would show that a person did not properly understand the full implications of the gospel message when he made his original profession (cf. 1 John 2:18-19).[32]

In Gromacki's exposition, we see both the similarity and dissimilarity between interpretations #3 and #4. Under interpretation #3, Calvinists Charles Hodge and John MacArthur allowed the possibility that unregenerate people could start out believing in the truth of the gospel, but thereafter not continue in it, thereby proving the spuriousness of their faith. On the other hand, Gromacki's interpretation #4 sees some of the Corinthians as having never been born again because they never had the gospel message straight from the start. At no time did they ever believe in a resurrected Christ. In view #3, some Corinthians were regarded as having never been saved because they did not *persevere in the truth* of the gospel; while in view #4, some Corinthians believed only *partial truth* and never got the gospel straight from the start.

Does interpretation #4 have any merit? It is certainly a doctrinal improvement upon interpretations #2 and #3, since it is true that people often never become regenerated with eternal life in Christ because the content of their faith has never been accurate. Many have always believed in *"another Jesus"* (2 Cor. 11:4) and have therefore always been lost, even though they have professed faith in Christ for many years. Aside from the

---

[32] Gromacki, *Called to Be Saints*, 182. Some commentators believe the phrase *"in vain"* (*eikē*) would be better translated as "without coherent consideration." In other words, they claim that the Corinthians believed with only a superficial or confused appropriation of the gospel, while not necessarily concluding with Gromacki that they were therefore not originally saved (see David E. Garland, *1 Corinthians*, BECNT [Grand Rapids: Baker, 2003], 683; Anthony C. Thiselton, *The First Epistle to the Corinthians*, NIGTC [Grand Rapids: Eerdmans, 2000], 1182, 1186; BDAG, 281, where *eikē* in 1 Corinthians 15:2 is said to mean, "being without careful thought" or "without due consideration," but the meaning of "to no purpose" is also considered probable).

Calvinistic perseverance perspective reflected in Gromacki's statement that a "saving faith is a persevering, orthodox faith" and his citation of 1 John 2:18-19 for support, interpretation #4 is doctrinally true to Scripture. This view can actually be held with or without a belief in the necessity of perseverance for final salvation. Though this view is doctrinally permissible, it has at least four exegetical weaknesses that render it doubtful.

First, like interpretation #2 and #3, interpretation #4 fails to adequately account for why Paul used the present tense of *"saved"* (*sōzō*) in 15:2. As has been demonstrated, Paul was not questioning the past-tense salvation (regeneration and justification) of these Corinthians or their future-tense salvation (glorification). There is no evidence in 1 Corinthians itself that Paul doubted the eternal salvation of some of the Corinthians; but on the contrary, the epistle consistently points to the genuineness of their salvation.

Secondly, if Paul was questioning whether some of these Corinthians were originally, eternally saved based on whether they originally believed in Christ's resurrection, this interpretation would fail to account for the use of the present tense form of the verb *katechō* (*"hold fast"*) in verse 2. There Paul writes, *"by which you are (being) saved if* ***you (are) hold(ing) fast*** *that word which I preached to you."* The question in Paul's mind was whether they would continue to hold fast to the gospel throughout their present, earthly, Christian lives and not just in the immediate present.[33] If Paul was questioning their original, eternal salvation and what they originally believed about Christ, he would have used a past tense form of the verb *katechō*, such as the aorist or even the perfect tense. Interpretation #4 would require Paul to say in verse 2, *"by which you are saved if* ***you held fast*** *that word which I preached to you"* or *"by which you are saved if* ***you have held fast*** *that word which I preached to you."*

Thirdly, interpretation #4, at least as expressed by Gromacki, has an inaccurate view of the conditional clause, *"if you hold fast that word which I*

[33] The present tenses of both *sōzō* and *katechō* in 1 Corinthians 15:2 should most likely be understood as *iterative presents*. The *instantaneous* or *aoristic present* is far too momentary and punctiliar to depict the saving and holding fast that Paul is describing. Paul is speaking of their sanctification-salvation in terms of the general present. It is to occur not just at a specific *point* in time, but at *points* in present time. The *customary* or *habitual present* is also doubtful here, since its temporal force is much too broad (as certainly is the *gnomic present*). Though it is true that Paul is primarily focusing on sanctification-salvation in 1 Corinthians 15:2, which is a process, it is still a salvation occurring at the approximate time of Paul's writing to the Corinthians and is not to be taken as a general maxim regarding their future. The *progressive* or *descriptive present* is also doubtful here, since it implies a sanctification process that is too continuous and uninterrupted to suit the spiritual condition of the Corinthians. As a regular pattern, they were not walking according to the Spirit but according to the flesh (3:1-4), which would not result in a continuous, uninterrupted practical sanctification. However, there certainly must have been moments in which they were not fleshly or carnal, but filled with the Spirit (Eph. 5:18), and thus they could still be described as being in the present process of salvation (15:2). This leaves the *iterative* as the most logical category of present tense usage here.

preached to you." Gromacki stated that "The conditional clause (introduced by "if") served as a warning to the false teachers and their converts." This passage might be viewed as "a warning" about false faith to some of the Corinthians if it contained a third class conditional clause, which is the condition of possibility (i.e., some of the Corinthians might or might not *"hold fast"* to the gospel). However, in 1 Corinthians 15:2, the first class condition is used in Greek. This is the condition of assumed reality for the sake of argument. Here, Paul assumed that they would continue to *"hold fast"* to the gospel; and thus the phrase *"if you hold fast"* should be viewed primarily as an expression of optimism on Paul's part, not "a warning."

It should also be clarified at this point that, though Paul optimistically assumed that they were holding fast to the gospel and would continue to do so, his statement should not be taken as a guarantee that they would persevere. The first class condition is often misconstrued to mean "since."[34] In 1 Corinthians 15:2, Paul is NOT saying, *"**Since** you will continue to hold fast that word which I preached to you."* He is not guaranteeing that they will necessarily persevere in the faith, as a Calvinist might be inclined to think here. There are 36 instances in the New Testament where the first class condition *cannot* be translated or interpreted to mean "since."[35] A blatant example of this occurs later in 1 Corinthians 15. In verse 13 it says, *"But **if** there is no resurrection of the dead, then Christ is not risen."* Paul obviously was not affirming the truth of the no-resurrection position by saying, *"**Since** there is no resurrection of the dead, then Christ is not risen."*

A fourth and final reason why interpretation #4 is unlikely is because of the unnatural division it creates within 1 Corinthians 15:1-12 and because of the erroneous assumption it makes in identifying those in verse 12 as unbelievers. It divides the people identified as *"you"* in verses 1-3 and 11 into the saved group and the *"you"* of verse 12 into the unsaved group. Regarding this, Gromacki writes, "The conditional clause (introduced by "if") served as a warning to the false teachers and to their converts (cf. 15:12)." Gromacki goes on to indicate that the people mentioned in Paul's statement in verse 12 (*"how say **some among you** that there is no resurrection of the dead"*) were never believers in the first place since they never understood the truth of Christ's resurrection in the gospel. Contextually however, the *"you"* of verse 12 is not identifying a subset of unbelievers among the Corinthians but a group from among those in verses 1-3 and verse 11 identified as those who had believed. This can be observed in the structure of the verses in the following outline:

---

[34] Donald A. Carson, *Exegetical Fallacies* (Grand Rapids: Baker Book House, 1984), 80-81.

[35] Wallace, *Greek Grammar*, 690.

- "which also **you** received" (v. 1)

- "and in which **you** stand" (v. 1)

- "by which also **you** are (being) saved" (v. 2)

- "unless **you** believed in vain" (v. 2)

- "so we preach and so **you** believed" (v. 11)

  - "how say some among **you**" (v. 12)

Contextually, the ones *"among"* the Corinthians who were claiming that there was no resurrection of the dead (v. 12) were from among those who had originally received the gospel and believed it. According to the passage, the *"some among you"* of verse 12 were a subset of the *"you"* who had earlier believed the gospel and were saved. Even if this subset of Corinthian believers had not only recently begun denying the general resurrection of humanity, but had always denied it, they still could have believed that Christ personally rose from the dead. This would mean that they would have still been saved originally, as illogical and contradictory as their beliefs may have been. Nowhere in 1 Corinthians 15 does it indicate that there were some among the Corinthians who were explicitly denying the resurrection of Christ in particular, though their logic was now dangerously heading in that direction, as Paul reveals to them in verses 12-19. Likewise, nowhere in the passage is there a group identified as those who had never understood or believed the one, true, saving gospel, as interpretation #4 maintains. Based on these exegetical problems, interpretation #4 cannot be correct, and a better alternative should be sought.

Interpretation #5: Hypothetically Believers Are Lost if Christ Never Rose

The fifth major interpretation of 1 Corinthians 15:2 holds that the faith of the Corinthians would be *"in vain"* or meaningless if Christ never historically rose from the dead. If the Corinthians believed in Christ for their eternal life, and yet Christ never actually rose from the dead, then their faith in Him for eternal life would be completely futile, since the very grounds of their salvation would be eviscerated. This interpretation of 1 Corinthians 15:2 must be considered carefully since it has been embraced by crossless-gospel proponents to further their interpretation of 1 Corinthians 15:1-11.[36]

---

[36] For instance, Bob Wilkin states regarding 1 Corinthians 15:2, "Now the last part, *'unless you believed in vain'* ties in with the purpose of 1 Corinthians 15 which is the great resurrection chapter, right? If there is no resurrection we're of all men most to be pitied. Obviously all of Christianity hinges on the resurrection of Jesus Christ. If that didn't occur, then Christianity is worthless. But his point is, if we didn't believe in vain, that is if Jesus really

It must be clarified, however, that interpretation #5 does not necessarily lead to a crossless gospel and thus it is held by many non-crossless gospel commentators.[37] Interpretation #5 is also sometimes characterized by the use of the term "irony" in explaining it.[38] One commentator who espouses this "irony" view, Gordon Fee, explains this interpretation saying:

> On the other hand, the final clause in B′ (*unless you received it in vain*) is surely irony, and is intended to anticipate the argument in vv. 14-19. If they do not hold fast to the gospel, that is, if their current position as to "no resurrection" is correct, then Christ did not rise, which in turn means that they did indeed believe in vain. If they are right, everything is a lie, and they cease to exist as believers altogether.[39]

This view does have some solid points to commend it. First, it is a doctrinally sound interpretation in its overall conclusion. Second, it does have some contextual support, since the *"in vain"* concept is found later in 1 Corinthians 15 in the section dealing with the grounds of salvation being removed if Christ theoretically never rose from the dead (vv. 12-19). In 1 Corinthians 15:14, Paul declares, *"And if Christ is not risen, then our preaching is empty and your faith is also empty."* Similarly, verse 17 states, *"And if Christ is not risen, your faith is futile; you are still in your sins!"* However, in spite of these positive points in its favor, interpretation #5 does have several problems that render it unlikely as the meaning intended by the Lord.

First, this view requires some assumptions in handling the *"in vain"* phrase in verse 2, *"by which also you are (being) saved, if you hold fast that word which I preached to you—unless you believed* ***in vain****."* Interpretation #5 sees "irony" in verse 2. Some among the Corinthians were insisting that there is "no resurrection" (v. 12), which as Paul argues in 1 Corinthians

---

did rise from the dead, then we are being saved if we hold fast to the good news that Paul preached to them." Robert N. Wilkin, "The Three Tenses of Salvation Aren't About Justification, Sanctification, and Glorification," Grace Evangelical Society Georgia Regional Conference, Hampton, GA, September 23, 2006. Wilkin seems to be basing his crossless interpretation upon the "no resurrection"/irony view, the view long-held by Hodges. See Zane C. Hodges, *The Gospel Under Siege: Faith and Works in Tension*, 2nd ed. (Dallas: Kerugma, 1992), 91-92. See also René A. López, "The Use and Abuse of 1 Corinthians 15:1-11," Grace Evangelical Society Conference, Fort Worth, TX, March 31, 2009.

[37] This interpretation has had an historic lineage, being held by several early Church "fathers" and the Reformers, Luther and Calvin. More modern proponents include: Henry Alford, *The Greek Testament* (Chicago: Moody Press, 1958), 2:602; Fee, *The First Epistle to the Corinthians*, 721; Frederic Louis Godet, *Commentary on First Corinthians* (Grand Rapids: Kregel, 1977), 756; Johnson, "1 Corinthians," 1255 (even though Johnson mentions other views of this passage, this seems to be his preferred view); William MacDonald, *Believer's Bible Commentary, New Testament* (Nashville: Thomas Nelson Publishers, 1990), 619-20; W. E. Vine, "1 Corinthians," in *The Collected Writings of W. E. Vine* (Nashville: Thomas Nelson Publishers, 1996), 2:105.

[38] Fee, *The First Epistle to the Corinthians*, 721; Thiselton, *The First Epistle to the Corinthians*, 1186.

[39] Fee, *The First Epistle to the Corinthians*, 721 (parenthesis added).

15, logically necessitates that Christ Himself never rose from the dead. If the Corinthians did *not* hold fast to Paul's gospel by their illogical insistence on "no resurrection," then this would also logically mean that there is *no* salvation possible for them. However, one problem with this "irony" interpretation is that it assumes the inverse of what the passage actually says. It must turn the positive statements in the inspired text into negative statements in order to derive its conclusion. Paul actually said, *"by which also you are saved* (positive statement), *if you hold fast* (positive statement)." Paul did not say, *"you will **not** be saved* (negative statement) . . . *if you do **not** hold fast* (negative statement)."

Secondly, the "irony" view also does not adequately account for Paul's use of the first class conditional clause in verse 2, *"if you hold fast . . . unless you believed in vain."*[40] In this conditional statement, Paul was not asking the Corinthians to entertain the theoretical possibility that there might not even be salvation for mankind if Christ did not truly rise from the dead. Rather, by using the first class condition, Paul was making a positive declaration that the gospel would continue to save them in the sense of sanctification, if they held fast to it—and he optimistically assumed they would. The first class condition is the condition of assumed reality for the sake of argument. By saying, *"if you hold fast,"* Paul was assuming that they would continue holding fast to the gospel in spite of the subset of resurrection-deniers among them (v. 12).

Sometimes proponents of this "irony" interpretation also erroneously conclude from the use of the first class condition in 1 Corinthians 15:2 that Paul was assuming for the sake of argument that Christ did *not rise* from the dead. Support for this conclusion is usually garnered from the fact that the first class condition also occurs seven times later in the same chapter in verses 12-19. However, an important distinction must be noted. In verses 1-11, Paul was actually assuming the *reality* of Christ's resurrection. He was seeking to prove Christ's resurrection in verses 3-8. This is the *immediate* context of verse 2. This must be distinguished from the later, *intermediate* context of verses 12-19, where Paul assumes the *unreality* of Christ's resurrection for the sake of his argument. This critical, contextual distinction must be kept in mind.

A third difficulty that interpretation #5 faces is its failure to account for the reference to Christ's substitutionary death in verse 3, if "irony" is truly intended by the *"in vain"* phrase at the end of verse 2. Immediately following the supposed "irony" statement of verse 2, the very next point that Paul recalls for the Corinthians is the substitutionary death of Christ for their sins. Verses 2-5 read as follows:

---

[40] In 1 Corinthians 15:2, the protasis ("if you hold fast") is *ei* with *katechō* in the indicative mood (*ei katechete*). This is followed by *ektos ei mē eikē episteusate* ("unless you believed in vain") in the apodosis.

2 *by which also you are (being) saved, if you hold fast that word which I preached to you—**unless you believed in vain.***
3 ***For I delivered to you first of all that which I also received: that Christ died for our sins** according to the Scriptures,*
4 *and that He was buried, and that He rose again the third day according to the Scriptures,*
5 *and that He was seen by Cephas, then by the twelve*

If, in verse 2, Paul was truly anticipating the implications of the "no resurrection" position of verses 12-19, then the mention of Christ's substitutionary death in verse 3 is superfluous to his point, and even out of place in a section dealing with the resurrection. Nor did Paul merely mention the fact of Christ's death in verse 3 in order to set up his next logical point on Christ's resurrection in verse 4, for he mentions the *substitutionary* death of Christ *"for our sins."* In light of this reference, we must ask, what possible relevance does verse 3 have to any supposed "irony" related to the resurrection?

A fourth problem with the "irony" interpretation is that it is probably too subtle to have been the original intended meaning. The only way one can catch the irony of verse 2 (if irony is truly present) is to know in advance what verses 12-19 are about. In order to catch any irony in verse 2, the reader must read verses 12-19 back into verse 2. In other words, this is an interpretation that can only be recognized in hindsight (or with foresight, depending on how you look at it). While this is rhetorically feasible, we must ask, did Paul intend to be so subtle? Would the Corinthians have likely caught such subtlety upon their initial reading of verse 2? This seems doubtful. Furthermore, we must ask whether all of verses 12-19 were intended to rest upon the single phrase at the end of verse 2, *"unless you believed in vain."* This seems to be too much freight for any one phrase of one verse to bear!

A fifth reason why the irony view, interpretation #5, is unlikely is because it logically requires that eternal salvation (justification & glorification) be the type of salvation referred to by *sōzō* (*"saved"*) in 1 Corinthians 15:2, rather than a present, temporal salvation (practical sanctification). The present tense of *sōzō* in verse 2 accords far better with a present salvation than with either a past salvation (justification & regeneration) or future salvation (glorification). By drawing the supposed "irony" of verse 2 from verses 12-19, interpretation #5 effectively makes the type of salvation referred to in verse 2 the same type of salvation referred to in verses 12-19. Eternal salvation is in view in verses 12-19 based on the references to being *"still in your sins"* (v. 17) and to the hypothetical possibility that deceased Christians have "perished" (v. 18). In verse 17, by saying to the Corinthians that "you are still in your sins" if Christ did not rise from the grave, Paul was addressing either regeneration (Eph. 2:1, 5) or the forensic forgiveness that occurs at justification (Rom. 4:6-8). In either case, both regeneration and justification occur simultaneously at the moment a person first believes and receives eternal salvation. Thus, 1 Corinthians 15:17 is referring to a salvation that is past. In verse 18, by stating that deceased Christians have *"perished"* if Christ did not rise from the dead, Paul was referring to a salvation that is yet future, beyond *"this life"* according to verse 19. It seems unlikely, however, that Paul intended the present salvation of verse 2 to be the same as the past salvation of verse 17 or the future salvation of verse 18, which interpretation #5 logically necessitates.

A sixth exegetical problem that the "irony" interpretation faces is that it does not adequately account for the use of the present tense of *sōzō* and *katechō* coupled with the aorist tense of *pisteuō* in verse 2. As will be explained next under interpretation #6, Paul's primary concern in verse 2 was the sanctification-salvation of these Corinthians, which was contingent upon their continuance in the truth of the gospel. Paul's concern at this point was not for their justification or their glorification.

However, consistent with the "irony" view, it is grammatically possible that Paul could be saying to the Corinthians in verse 2, *"by which also* ***you are being saved*** (present tense of *sōzō*—practically sanctified), *if* ***you are holding fast*** (present tense of *katechō*) *that word which I preached to you, unless* **you believed** (aorist tense of *pisteuō*—as at justification) *in vain* (i.e., since according to your view Christ logically never rose from the dead and there is therefore no salvation at all, whether past, present, or future)." But even this possible understanding for the "irony" view seems doubtful. If this is what Paul meant, then why not simply keep all three tenses for *sōzō*, *katechō*, and *pisteuō* the same in verse 2? Why not use the aorist tense throughout to consistently portray a past tense, saying for instance, *"by which* ***you were saved****, if* ***you held fast*** *what I preached to you, unless* ***you believed*** *in vain"*? Or, if Paul is merely implying that their faith is groundless if Christ didn't truly rise from the dead, then why not have all three verbs be present tenses, *"by which also* ***you are saved****, if* ***you hold fast*** *that word which I preached to you, unless* ***you believe*** *in vain"*? This would indicate that the faith they presently possess is "in vain" if Christ never rose from the dead in the past and remains in the grave.

A more adequate explanation that accounts for the shift from the two present tenses of *sōzō* and *katechō* to the aorist tense of *pisteuō* is that Paul was simply addressing their present salvation, which was contingent upon their holding fast to that gospel which they initially believed in the past. This understanding is much simpler and more likely, as interpretation #6 will soon explain.

A seventh and final reason why the "irony" view is doubtful is that its interpretation of the phrase *"in vain"* is not well supported by parallel Pauline usage. Paul's other uses of *"in vain"* in his epistles favor the likelihood that a present, temporal sanctification-salvation is being referred to in 1 Corinthians 15:2, rather than justification-salvation or glorification-resurrection-salvation. By saying, "unless you believed in vain (*eikē*)" in verse 2, Paul was simply saying that the Corinthians' initial, justifying faith would be *"in vain"* if they did not continue to fulfill God's will for them as Christians—to be presently sanctified and fruitful for Him, not merely be justified and glorified. The prevailing Pauline sense of the phrase *"in vain"* in the New Testament is that of Christians possibly failing to be faithful to the Lord, to grow in His grace, and to be fruitful in fulfilling His will in the Christian life. It is significant to note that outside of 1 Corinthians 15:14, there are no other parallel Pauline uses of either *eikē* or *kenos/kenoō* where the context establishes that *"in vain"* refers to eternal salvation rather than some present aspect of the Christian life (see 1 Cor. 15:10, 58; 2 Cor. 6:1; 9:3; Gal. 2:2; 3:4; 4:11; Phil. 2:16; 1 Thess. 2:1; 3:5).

The 1 Thessalonians 3:5 reference deserves special consideration since it is the only other Pauline passage where the phrase *"in vain"* is used contextually of *faith* in particular, thus forming a very close parallel to 1 Corinthians 15:2.

1 Thessalonians 3:1-10

1 *Therefore, when we could no longer endure it, we thought it good to be left in Athens alone,*
2 *and sent Timothy, our brother and minister of God, and our fellow laborer in the gospel of Christ, to establish you and encourage you concerning your* ***faith,***
3 *that no one should be shaken by these afflictions; for you yourselves know that we are appointed to this.*
4 *For, in fact, we told you before when we were with you that we would suffer tribulation, just as it happened, and you know.*
5 *For this reason, when I could no longer endure it, I sent to know your* ***faith,*** *lest by some means the tempter had tempted you, and our labor might be* ***in vain.***
6 *But now that Timothy has come to us from you, and brought us good news of your* ***faith*** *and love, and that you always have good remembrance of us, greatly desiring to see us, as we also to see you—*
7 *therefore, brethren, in all our affliction and distress we were comforted concerning you by your* ***faith.***
8 *For now we live, if you* ***stand fast*** *in the Lord.*
9 *For what thanks can we render to God for you, for all the joy with which we rejoice for your sake before our God,*
10 *night and day praying exceedingly that we may see your face and* ***perfect what is lacking in your faith****?*

While it is true that *"in vain"* in 1 Thessalonians 3:5 technically modifies *"labor,"* whereas in 1 Corinthians 15:2 it modifies *"believed,"* the context of 1 Thessalonians 3 makes it crystal clear that Paul would have regarded his labors as being *"in vain"* if the Thessalonians did not continue in their *"faith"* (5x). The use of *"in vain"* in 1 Thessalonians 3 and in many other passages strongly supports the understanding of a present tense sanctification-salvation in 1 Corinthians 15:2, rather than the past tense justification or future tense glorification view of the "irony" interpretation. For these seven reasons, it is extremely doubtful that interpretation #5—the "irony" view—is the interpretation intended by the Lord.

The Crossless, Resurrectionless Gospel Interpretation

The crossless gospel interpretation of 1 Corinthians 15:2 appears to be essentially the "irony" view, interpretation #5, with the meaning of *"the gospel"* altered in verse 1 in order to avoid the requirement for the lost to believe in Christ's substitutionary death and resurrection in verses 3-4. With respect to the meaning of *"saved"* and believing *"in vain"* in 1 Corinthians 15:2, crossless gospel proponent John Niemelä maintains that the faith of the Corinthians would only be *"in vain"* if Christ hypothetically never rose from the dead. By holding to the "irony" view, Niemelä can make the substitutionary death and resurrection of Christ in verses 3-4 essential only as the *grounds* of salvation, not as the *contents* of faith for eternal life. According to Niemelä, Christ's death and resurrection are the essential means by which God provides the free gift of eternal life to mankind. If Christ never historically rose from the dead, however, then even the promise of eternal life based on the sole condition of faith in Jesus would be "a false message." He explains his view, stating:

> The word translated *in vain* is a dative. The dative is the normal case for the direct object of *pisteuō* (e.g., *to believe in something vain*). Others take this as an adverbial dative (e.g., *to believe in a vain way*). In response, the direct object view fits normal grammatical usage. In addition, 1 Cor 15:14 shows that Paul's focus is on the truthfulness of Christ's resurrection: *And if Christ is not risen, then our preaching is empty and your faith is also empty.* In this light, vv. 1-2 teach that believing the gospel message saved the Corinthians, unless what they believed were a false message from Paul.[41]

[41] John H. Niemelä, "The Cross in John's Gospel," *JOTGES* 16 (Spring 2003): 27n. Whether or not *eikē* should be viewed as a dative direct object of *pisteuō* is a moot point and does not establish the "irony" view in any way. Instead of translating *eikē* in 1 Corinthians 15:2 with a locative sense, *"unless you believed* ***in something vain,****"* the dative case could just as easily be understood to mean: *"unless you believed* ***to no avail****"* or *"unless you believed* ***for nothing.****"* This latter sense would be perfectly consistent with the normal use of *"in vain"* (whether *eikē* or *kenos/kenoō*) discussed previously under interpretation #3. With respect to Niemelä's second point about the truthfulness of Christ's resurrection in Paul's evangelism message, he elaborated more fully on this at a Grace Evangelical Society conference (John Niemelä, *Objects of Faith in John: A Matter of Person AND Content,* Grace Evangelical Society Conference, Dallas, TX, February 28, 2006). There he explained that in 1 Corinthians 15:2, the question isn't whether the Corinthians believed *vainly* (i.e., believed in a vain way) but whether they believed in a *proposition* that was vain, namely, that if Christ did not truly rise from the dead, then a non-resurrected Savior would be insufficient to provide eternal salvation to everyone who believes in Him for it. Thus when Niemelä writes, *"vv. 1-2 teach that believing the gospel message saved the Corinthians, unless what they believed were a false message from Paul,"* he apparently does not mean that the Corinthians had to believe in a resurrected Christ in

In articulating a crossless gospel position on 1 Corinthians 15, Niemelä subtly writes so as to make the message of Christ's substitutionary death and bodily resurrection in verses 3-4 good news only for Christians, not necessarily for unbelievers. He says:

> Evangelicals often make believing the cross and resurrection their bottom-line for unbelievers to gain eternal life. We often define the gospel in terms of Christ's crucifixion, burial, and resurrection, seeking to echo 1 Cor 15:3-8. . . . Is the mere fact that God's Son died a horrible death on the cross good news for us? Is the fact that He was raised good news for us? These facts become good news for us for only one reason: They affect the destiny of believers. God uses the crucifixion and resurrection to enable believers to escape the Lake of Fire and to be with Him forever. We cannot limit our definition of the gospel to vv. 3-8, because what precedes these verses is what makes His death and resurrection good news for Christians.
>
> Therefore, let us not miss an important feature of vv. 1-2 where Paul demonstrates that what happened to Christ is indeed good news to us. He declares:
>
>> Moreover, brethren, I declare to you *the gospel* which I preached to you, which also you received and in which you stand, *by which also you are saved*, if you hold fast that word which I preached to you—unless you believed in [something] vain.
>
> We must always remember that vv. 1-2 show why this is good news for believers: *the gospel...by which also you are saved*. Specifically, Paul says that the gospel gives salvation to the believer. In other words, God gives life to everyone who believes in Jesus for that free gift. The gospel is not merely that Christ was crucified and resurrected. First Corinthians 15:1-8 is good news for us precisely because Christ saves believers through His death and resurrection.
>
> When Paul spoke with the Philippian jailer in Acts 16:31, he told him simply: *Believe on the Lord Jesus Christ and you will be saved*. No one would ever accuse Paul of minimizing the cross and resurrection, but the bottom line of his gospel was that Jesus saves from eternal condemnation all who simply believe in Him. John would express the same point in terms of receiving eternal life (John 3:16, 36; 5:24; 6:47; and 20:30-31).[42]

---

order to receive eternal life. Rather, he means that the supposed crossless gospel message that the Corinthians believed ("Jesus guarantees eternal life to all who simply believe in Him for it") would be *"a false message"* since Christ wouldn't be able to fulfill His promise to guarantee eternal life to all who believe in Him, if He never actually rose from the dead.

[42] John H. Niemelä, "The Cross in John's Gospel," *JOTGES* 16 (Spring 2003): 26-27 (ellipses added).

Niemelä carefully writes so as to avoid the conclusion that the message of Christ's death and resurrection in verses 3-4 is specifically the gospel that unbelievers must believe for their eternal salvation. He defines *"the gospel"* of 1 Corinthians 15:1 and the accompanying promise of being *"saved"* in 1 Corinthians 15:2 to be the message that *"God gives life to everyone who believes in Jesus for that free gift."* Later, he defines the gospel again without the cross and resurrection, stating:

> The word translated *hold fast* is *katechō* ("to grasp"). Here, it is equivalent to *believe.* Grasping the truth that Jesus Christ gives me eternal life and removes my death sentence is to believe it. In effect, Paul says that his Gospel saves people, if they believe (grasp) it.[43]

According to Niemelä, the *"Gospel"* that *"saves people, if they believe (grasp) it"* is equivalent to *"Grasping the truth that Jesus Christ gives me eternal life and removes my death sentence."* Once again, Niemelä is careful not to commit to the position that Christ gives people eternal life and removes their death sentence specifically by faith in Christ's substitutionary death and resurrection from the dead. For him, the *"gospel"* (v. 1) that *"saves"* people (v. 2) is apparently only the promise of eternal life without any requisite cognizance of, or belief in, Christ's work.

So what do crossless gospel proponents do with Christ's substitutionary death and resurrection in 1 Corinthians 15:3-4, since they must be accounted for somehow? In the case of John Niemelä, his interpretation of 1 Corinthians 15:2 leads to an apparent bifurcation of the gospel. To the *unbeliever,* the good news or gospel is the message that by simply believing in Jesus He will give eternal life or salvation. This is the message Niemelä says Paul is communicating in 1 Corinthians 15:1-2. But to the *believer,* the good news becomes broader, so as to include the message of the cross and resurrection as the grounds of our eternal salvation, a message that the believer needs for his or her sanctification as a Christian. Thus, the one, unchangeable gospel of 1 Corinthians 15:1-4 has now been divided into two separate messages of "good news."

In actuality, the gospel is a singular, cohesive message from the Lord Jesus Christ that applies both to the lost for their justification and to the saved as the basis for our on-going sanctification. But this fact of the gospel's singularity has been effectively side-stepped by the crossless gospel's handling of 1 Corinthians 15:1-4 in an effort to maintain a crossless, resurrectionless version of the "good news" toward unbelievers. Though we can certainly agree with Niemelä's main point that the gospel in 1 Corinthians 15:1-2 includes the truth of salvation by faith alone, we must categorically reject his attempt to divide the contents of 1 Corinthians 15:1-2 from the same gospel message found in verses 3-4.

---

[43] Ibid., 26-27n8.

By following the "irony" interpretation of 1 Corinthians 15:2, this has effectively allowed other crossless gospel advocates to make even bolder, less ambiguous claims regarding Christ's substitutionary death and resurrection from the dead in 1 Corinthians 15:3-4. It is now being pronounced with unmistakable clarity that the work of Christ in verses 3-4 is not gospel-truth for the eternal salvation of the lost, but only sanctification-truth for the believer. One example of this comes from Bob Wilkin, who has written:

> The good news in First Corinthians is the good news that Paul preached to the *believers,* not unbelievers, in the church in Corinth. The good news message he preached was Christ crucified. This was a sanctification message that a divided church needed to hear badly. . . . The reason we don't find justification by faith alone anywhere in 1 Cor 15:3-11 is because this was *sanctification* good news.[44]

This bifurcation of the gospel in 1 Corinthians 15:1-4 is reiterated in the teaching of Bob Bryant, who fielded an audience question at a Grace Evangelical Society conference in response to his topic of eternal security being an essential part of the gospel:

> *Audience Question*: Why is eternal life/eternal security not mentioned in 1 Corinthians 15:3-4?
>
> *Bryant's Answer*: Because Paul is writing to Christians to emphasize something about the big picture of the gospel, not trying to recap what someone must do to have eternal life. The gospel is a broad word in the New Testament. It can refer specifically to what someone must believe to have eternal life; it can refer to general truth about the good news—and part of that general truth is that Jesus died and rose again. So, I don't think Paul is trying to define what we tell people to believe for eternal life there at all.[45]

Jeremy Myers agrees with Wilkin and Bryant on 1 Corinthians 15:1-4, stating:

> The only other option is that the word *saved* is not referring to being saved from eternal condemnation, but refers to some other form of deliverance. This is the best option, since the term *saved* in 1 Corinthians generally refers to being healthy or blameless at the Judgment Seat of Christ (cf. 1:18, 21; 3:15; 5:5).

[44] Robert N. Wilkin, "Justification by Faith Alone is an Essential Part of the Gospel," *JOTGES* 18 (Autumn 2005): 13 (ellipsis added, italics original).

[45] Bob Bryant, *Eternal Security: Do You Have to Believe It?* Grace Evangelical Society Conference, Dallas, TX, February 28, 2006.

> So if the gospel Paul is about to define is a message for believers, to prepare them for the Bema, then this passage is not about the essential elements that must be believed in order to receive everlasting life. Rather, it contains essential discipleship truths which affect our sanctification.[46]

The crossless gospel position makes the fundamentally flawed assumption that 1 Corinthians 15:3-4 is not even a declaration of Paul's original evangelistic message to the Corinthians when they were yet unsaved. As such, they claim that verses 3-4 do not contain information that we *must* tell the lost to believe in today for eternal life. While claiming that Christ's cross-work and resurrection in verses 3-4 are only "sanctification" truths that are essential for believers, Bob Wilkin goes on to state that these truths were not even part of Paul's essential evangelistic message. He goes on to write:

> When I hear people point to 1 Cor 15:3-11 and boldly proclaim that is the precise evangelistic message Paul preached, I shutter [sic]. How could we get it so wrong? Yes, Paul did tell unbelievers about Jesus' death and resurrection. But *that was not the sum total of his evangelistic message*. Nor is Paul's evangelistic message the point of 1 Cor 15:3-11.[47]

Was "Paul's evangelistic message" the point of 1 Corinthians 15:1-11? It most certainly was! Putting aside for a moment Wilkin's implied claim that all the elements of the gospel are *not* contained in 1 Corinthians 15:1-11 (which will be addressed in the next chapter), Paul's whole point in this section of Scripture was to remind the Corinthians of the *"gospel"* message with which he originally *"evangelized"* them (v. 1). It was this same "evangelistic message" that they were now to *"hold fast"* to for their sanctification-salvation (v. 2).

---

[46] Jeremy D. Myers, "The Gospel is More Than 'Faith Alone in Christ Alone'," *JOTGES* 19 (Autumn 2006): 47.

[47] Robert N. Wilkin, "Justification by Faith Alone is an Essential Part of the Gospel," *JOTGES* 18 (Autumn 2005): 14 (italics original). On the same page, Wilkin adds, "May we never fail to tell people the saving proposition: Jesus, the One who died and rose again, *guarantees eternal life to all who simply believe in Him.* There aren't many evangelistic appeals. There is one. There aren't many ways to come to Jesus. There is but one way. Jesus guarantees eternal life to all who simply believe in Him. That is information we must never fail to communicate. When you tell people about Jesus' death and resurrection, don't stop there. Go on to tell them that all who simply believe in Him have everlasting life. He is able to fulfill that promise because of His death and resurrection. But call people to believe the promise. When we believe in Jesus, we believe in His promise of everlasting life to the believer. The true object of saving faith is the faith-alone-in-Christ-alone message." Here Wilkin declares again that the one essential truth that the lost must believe is only Christ's promise of eternal life. Christ's cross-work and resurrection are again intentionally left out as information that *"we must never fail to communicate"* to the lost. Instead, they are stated to be only the reason why Christ *"is able to fulfill"* His promise of eternal life to those who believe in Him. This apparently explains why, on the one hand, Wilkin can admit that the Corinthians originally heard Christ died for their sins and rose again, while on the other hand claiming that these truths did not constitute *"Paul's evangelistic message"* to the Corinthians in verses 3-11.

In verse 1, Paul literally says, *"I make known to you, brethren, the gospel (to euangelion) which I evangelized (ho euēngelisamēn) you (with), which also you received (parelabete)."* The fact that Paul is making his "evangelistic message" the point here in 1 Corinthians 15:1-4 is apparent from the twofold use of the term *"gospel"* in verse 1. Once it is used as a noun, *"I make known to you, brethren, the gospel (to euangelion)"*; and once it is used as a verb in the aorist tense, indicative mood, indicating a past event, *"which I preached (ho euēngelisamēn) to you."* The Greek verb *euangelizō* is, of course, where we get our English word, "evangelize." Paul is simply reminding them of the message with which he originally *"evangelized"* them. Furthermore, verse 1 goes on to indicate that this gospel was not only the message with which Paul originally evangelized them, but it was also the message originally *"received"* (*parelabete*) by them. The Greek verb *"received"* here is also in the aorist tense and indicative mood, indicating a past event, namely that occasion when they first heard the gospel of their salvation and believed it.

It is this very same "evangelistic message" that is being articulated by Paul in verses 3-4 as to its contents. Verse 3 begins, *"For (gar) I delivered (paredōka) to you first of all that which I also received (parelabon): that Christ died for our sins."* The fact that Paul in verses 3-4 is now declaring the contents of his "evangelistic message" from verse 1 is clear from the use of *"For"* (*gar*) at the beginning of verse 3, which effectively serves to connect verse 3 back to verse 1. In addition, the aorist tense, indicative mood verb, *"I delivered"* (*paredōka*), indicates a past event. This corresponds to the aorist tense, indicative mood verbs in verse 1, *"I preached"* (*euēngelisamēn*) and *"you received"* (*parelabete*). The syntax of verses 1-4 allows for no break between verses 1-2 and verses 3-4. It is simply undeniable that Paul has in mind in verses 1-4 his original "evangelistic message." He was reminding the Corinthians of the "evangelistic message" they originally believed for their eternal salvation and that they were now to continue in for their present sanctification-salvation.

Furthermore, to artificially separate the gospel of verses 1-2 from the gospel of verses 3-4 in order to maintain a crossless, resurrectionless gospel does not harmonize with the use of the word "gospel" in the rest of 1 Corinthians. Throughout this epistle, the gospel is never conceived of in a broader versus narrower sense. There are not two gospels spoken of by Paul, one without the cross and resurrection for the lost and one with Christ's work for the Christian's sanctification. There is only one gospel. In 1 Corinthians 1:17, we are told that this gospel that Paul preached to the lost included the message of the *"cross of Christ."* It was this same message that Paul preached to these Corinthians for their regeneration according to 1 Corinthians 4:15.

All of this harmonizes perfectly with 1 Corinthians 15:1-4. But if Paul was referring to a crossless, resurrectionless version of the gospel in

1 Corinthians 15:1-2, then where else in 1 Corinthians can we find such a narrower version of the gospel? There are no previous references to such a crossless, resurrectionless version of the gospel. Proponents of the new, aberrant form of the Free Grace gospel are at a loss here. They have not derived their meaning for "the gospel" from the context of 1 Corinthians 15, nor from the rest of the epistle, but they have imposed their own theologically-driven view of the gospel upon 1 Corinthians 15:1-4.

One final, important point must be made about the continuity between 1 Corinthians 15:1-2 and 15:3-4 with respect to the crossless gospel position. According to verses 3-4, the message of Christ's substitutionary death and bodily resurrection is no secondary matter when it comes to evangelizing the lost. It says in verse 3, *"For I delivered to you **first of all** (en prōtois) that which I also received: that Christ died for our sins."* When Paul states that the gospel that he received and delivered to the Corinthians is *"first of all,"* he means that the gospel is in first place when it comes to importance. And this gospel message that was to be first in importance is defined specifically as the message *"that Christ died for our sins...and that He rose again."*

This means that the message of Christ's substitutionary death and resurrection from the dead should not take a back seat to anything—including the message of guaranteed eternal life through faith in Jesus Christ, the last essential of the gospel. This certainly betrays the claims of crossless gospel proponents, who don't even include Christ's death and resurrection in the "THREE ESSENTIALS" or *sine qua non* of what must be believed for eternal life.[48] The fact that Christ's death and resurrection in the gospel are declared to be "first" in importance also flatly contradicts the crossless gospel claim that, "No one would ever accuse Paul of minimizing the cross and resurrection, but the bottom line of his gospel was that Jesus saves from eternal condemnation all who simply believe in Him."[49] The cross-work of Christ and His resurrection occupied first place in the preaching of the apostle Paul, and therefore they must never be removed from "the bottom line" in our "evangelistic message" either.

Interpretation #6: Belief in One Gospel for Both Justification & Sanctification

Having now surveyed five major interpretations on the meaning of *"saved"* in 1 Corinthians 15:2, along with the crossless gospel position on this passage, and having clarified what this passage is *not* saying, it is time to finally establish what *it is* saying. The biblical evidence best supports the interpretation that Paul is telling the Corinthians that there is only one gospel, which is necessary to believe initially for eternal life and to continue in, by

---

[48] Robert N. Wilkin, *Secure and Sure* (Irving, TX: Grace Evangelical Society, 2005), 74-75. See also, Myers, "The Gospel is More Than 'Faith Alone in Christ Alone'," 52.

[49] John H. Niemelä, "The Cross in John's Gospel," *JOTGES* 16 (Spring 2003): 26-27.

faith, for practical sanctification and spiritual growth. This interpretation of *"saved"* in verse 2 is espoused by Dennis Rokser in an extremely practical and edifying exposition of 1 Corinthians 15:1-4, entitled "Let's Preach the Gospel." There Rokser states:

> These Corinthians via the Gospel were being presently saved from the POWER OF SIN in their Christian lives as long as they remained steadfast to the Gospel, just like they had been saved from the PENALTY OF SIN (Hell) when they had trusted in Christ. In other words, the Gospel they had received would continue to have saving effects from spiritual damage upon their lives *"if you hold fast the word which I preached to you."*[50]

Interpretation #6 sees just one gospel being referred to in 1 Corinthians 15:1-4, which was necessary for the Corinthians to believe initially for justification and was also necessary for them to continue to believe for their practical sanctification. It must be clarified that though continual belief in the one, true gospel is absolutely necessary for continual spiritual growth and sanctification, *the gospel itself is not the message of how to live the Christian life*! This is a vital point since crossless gospel advocates are claiming that the gospel includes Christian life truths about how to be progressively sanctified. However, the content of the gospel does *not* include sanctification truths, though continuing to believe the gospel will have a sanctifying effect upon the Christian's life.

In this respect, interpretation #6 sees faith in Christ's death and resurrection as being essential to both one's justification and sanctification. It views the term *"saved"* in 1 Corinthians 15:2 as a direct reference to practical sanctification, with justification, regeneration, and eternal salvation assumed and implied by the various past tense verbs contained in verses 1-3. This interpretation harmonizes well with all the details of the passage, contextually, syntactically, lexically, and in terms of parallel Pauline passages and the biblical doctrines of justification and sanctification. Seven reasons will now be given in support of interpretation #6.

1) First, this view fits with the fact that Paul already regarded these Corinthians to be regenerated, justified, genuine believers in Christ (as explained in detail under interpretation #3). Paul was not seeking **proof** of genuine, saving faith from these Corinthians. In the larger context of 1 Corinthians we see that Paul was not questioning the legitimacy of their eternal salvation, but he definitely was questioning the present condition of their Christian lives and their spiritual walk (3:1-4). Therefore, it would

---

[50] Dennis Rokser, *Let's Preach the Gospel* (Duluth, MN: Duluth Bible Church, n.d.), 22. This interpretation is also held by David K. Lowery, "1 Corinthians," in *BKC*, ed. John F. Walvoord and Roy B. Zuck (Wheaton, IL: Victor Books, 1983), 542. It is also cited as a possibility by Johnson, "1 Corinthians," 1255, and by J. Hampton Keathley III, *ABCs for Christian Growth: Laying the Foundation*, 5th edition (n.p.: Biblical Studies Press, 1996-2002), 441-42.

be perfectly consistent in 1 Corinthians 15:2 for Paul to challenge these genuine believers regarding the sanctifying effects of continuing in the truth of the gospel.

2) Secondly, the one gospel for justification and progressive sanctification view fits with the larger context of 1 Corinthians and the doctrine of eternal security (as explained under interpretation #2). Since justification is eternal and cannot be lost, Paul must not have been exhorting the Corinthians to persevere in order to **keep** themselves in the saving grace of God. However, interpretation #6 also recognizes the biblical balance that goes with eternal security. This view recognizes that though justification is guaranteed, temporal sanctification and salvation from the power of sin is not. Interpretation #6 takes into account the spiritual condition of the Corinthians as stated in this epistle. Though they were saved from sin's penalty (hell) and eternally secure, they were also characteristically *"carnal"* (3:3) and not being sanctified and saved from sin's power as consistently as the Lord desired. In this larger context, Paul says to them in 1 Corinthians 15:2 that if they shifted on the gospel, the very foundation of their entire salvation, it would certainly have a damaging effect upon their Christian lives, yet without imperiling their eternal redemption.

3) A third reason why interpretation #6 is correct is because it best explains the tenses of the verbs used in the passage. If Paul was telling the Corinthians that in order to experience a present tense salvation they must continually hold fast to the one, true gospel that they originally believed, then we should expect to see a combination of past and present tense verbs indicating this in the passage—and we do. In verse 2, it says, *"by which also you are* ***saved*** (present tense, i.e., "being saved"), *if you* ***hold fast*** (present tense, i.e., "are holding fast") *that word which I* ***preached*** (past tense, i.e. when I first came to you with the gospel) *to you, unless you* ***believed*** (past tense, i.e. the hour you first believed and were born again) *in vain."* Appropriately, Paul's gospel preaching and the Corinthians' believing are both stated to be *past tense* events, while their being saved and their holding fast to the word are said to be *present tense* processes. This is exactly what we would expect if Paul is teaching that Christians are practically sanctified by holding to the very same gospel that we initially believe for our justification.

This point is further strengthened by noting the progression of verb tenses from verse 1 to verse 2. With the shift from the past to the present tense, we see again that Paul is primarily focusing on the Corinthians' present sanctification-salvation in verse 2. In 1 Corinthians 15:1-2, it says, *"Moreover, brethren, I declare to you the gospel which I preached to you, which also* ***you received*** *and in which* ***you stand,*** *2 by which also* ***you are saved,*** *if you* ***hold fast*** *that word which I preached to you—unless you believed in vain."*

According to verses 1-2, the Corinthians related to the gospel in three ways. First, they had *"received"* (aorist tense, active voice, indicative mood of *paralambanō*) it. Second, Paul says to them that the gospel was the message upon which, literally, *"you have stood"* (perfect tense, active voice, indicative mood of *histēmi*).[51] Third, it was the message by which they were also presently being *"saved"* (v. 2), as long as they would *"hold fast"* (v. 2) to it.

It is important to recognize the progression in verses 1-2 with the three verb tenses. With *"received"* (aorist tense, indicative mood) in verse 1, there is an emphasis upon how the Corinthians **initially** responded to the gospel. With *"stand"* or *"have stood"* (perfect tense, indicative mood) at the end of verse 1, there is a bridge between their initial **past** response and their **present** response, which is what the perfect tense indicates.[52] With *"saved"* and *"hold fast"* (both present tense, indicative mood) in verse 2, there is an emphasis upon their **present** response to the gospel and their present salvation. This progression from the aorist tense (*"received"*), to a perfect tense (*"have stood"*), to a present tense (*"are being saved...hold fast"*), underscores once again that the emphasis of *sōzō* in verse 2 is upon the present sanctification-salvation of the Corinthians.

Following the present tense of *"saved"* and *"hold fast"* in verse 2, Paul then switches back to the past tense of *"believed"* at the end of verse 2, followed by the past tense in verse 3. There Paul says, *"unless you **believed** in vain. 3 For I **delivered*** (both aorist tense, indicative mood, i.e. past tense) *to you first of all that which I also received: that Christ died."* By going back to a past tense for the message of Christ crucified and risen (vv. 3-4) as the message he first *"delivered"* and that they also *"believed"* (v. 2c), Paul is underscoring that the Corinthians must continue in this same gospel in order to be presently saved or sanctified. Interpretation #6 is perfectly consistent with this shifting of verb tenses in verses 1-3, something that the other five interpretations cannot adequately account for.

4) A fourth reason for interpretation #6 is that it fits with the intermediate context of 1 Corinthians 15 where the practical effects of either believing or not believing in the resurrection are spelled out. Paul explains this later in the chapter:

---

[51] The perfect tense of "stand" (*histēmi*) in verse 1 indicates an action in the past with the results continuing into the present, all from the standpoint of the writer. It indicates that from Paul's perspective, the Corinthians had stood upon the gospel after receiving it and this had continued up to the time of Paul's writing. Verse 1 does not necessarily need to be translated *"in which you have stood"* since the emphasis of the perfect tense is upon the abiding results in the present; and thus the translation, *"in which you stand"* (present tense emphasis) is perfectly valid in the KJV, NKJV, and NASB. It is only noted here because it could easily be assumed to be a simple present tense when reading our English texts with the past tense of the Greek text going unrecognized by the casual reader.

[52] The progression from an aorist, to a perfect, to a present tense verb should not be viewed as merely stylistic variation, or arbitrary and thus inconsequential. Paul's use of the perfect tense of "stand" in v. 1 is intentional. Regarding the perfect tense in Greek, one grammarian has written, "The perfect tense is used less frequently than the present, aorist, future, or imperfect; when it is used, there is usually a deliberate choice on the part of the writer" (Wallace, *Greek Grammar*, 573).

1 Corinthians 15:30-34

30 And why do we stand in jeopardy every hour?

31 I affirm, by the boasting in you which I have in Christ Jesus our Lord, I die daily.

32 If, in the manner of men, I have fought with beasts at Ephesus, what advantage is it to me? If the dead do not rise, "Let us eat and drink, for tomorrow we die"!

33 Do not be deceived: "Evil company corrupts good habits."

34 Awake to righteousness, and do not sin; for some do not have the knowledge of God. I speak this to your shame.

In verses 30-31, we see the positive effects in the Christian life of holding to the truth of the resurrection. This gospel truth had personally motivated the apostle Paul to be willing to stick his neck on the line for Jesus Christ on a daily basis! And in verse 32, Paul says that if there is no resurrection, instead of being willing to die for Christ, he may as well "live it up" hedonistically in this world. Then in verses 33-34, he admonishes the Corinthian Christians for letting the evil company of resurrection-deniers affect their own knowledge of God and their conduct. For the Corinthians to deny the gospel truth of the resurrection would certainly have had an adverse effect upon their Christian lives and their practical sanctification. This fact, as explained by Paul in vv. 30-34, is also consistent with the one gospel for justification and sanctification view.

5) A fifth reason why interpretation #6 is the most plausible is because it is most consistent with the meaning of the phrase *"in vain"* in the immediate context of 1 Corinthians 15:2, as well as with parallel Pauline usage. In 1 Corinthians 15:2, Paul tells the Corinthians that if they did not continue to hold fast to that word of the gospel that Paul previously preached to them, then that would mean that they had originally *"believed in vain."* As explained under interpretation #3, this does *not* mean that the Corinthians didn't genuinely believe the gospel in the first place.

The phrase *"in vain"* in Paul's writings and the rest of the New Testament carries the essential idea of not fulfilling an intended objective or purpose. Thus, it is possible to labor in vain (1 Cor. 15:58; Gal. 4:11; Phi. 2:16; 1 Thess. 3:5), boast in vain (2 Cor. 9:3), speak in vain (James 4:5), receive the grace of God in vain (1 Cor. 15:10; 2 Cor. 6:1), run in ministry in vain (Gal. 2:2; Phil. 2:16), suffer in vain (Gal. 3:4), die in vain (Gal. 2:21), and bear the sword in vain (Rom. 13:4). All of these activities would be *"in vain"* only if they somehow did not result in the fulfillment of their intended objective.

For the Corinthians to have *"believed in vain"* would simply mean that the God-intended purpose of sanctification and fruitfulness for their Christian lives would not be fulfilled if they did not continue holding to the gospel. That would mean that though they legitimately believed in Christ in the past and were justified, God's goal for the continuance and growth of their faith would tragically fall incomplete. Thus, the meaning and usage of *"in vain"* elsewhere in the New Testament corresponds perfectly with a continuous, sanctification-salvation in 1 Corinthians 15:2.

The phrase *"in vain"* also has this meaning right within the context of 1 Corinthians 15:2. In 1 Corinthians 15:10, Paul states, *"But by the grace of God I am what I am, and His grace toward me was not* ***in vain****; but I labored more abundantly than they all, yet not I, but the grace of God which was with me."* It is evident here that the grace of God would have been bestowed upon Paul *"in vain"* if it did not result in his fruitful labor for the Lord. In such an instance, the divinely intended purpose of grace would have gone unfulfilled. In the very same way, had the Corinthians not continued to be saved from sin's power in their Christian lives by continuing to hold fast to the one, true gospel, then even their initial, justifying faith would have been regarded as *"in vain."* What a sobering challenge from the Lord towards perseverance in the faith and the truth of the gospel! If the Lord is not satisfied with believers being merely justified for eternity but not practically sanctified, then neither should we be as Christians.

6) A sixth reason why present sanctification-salvation is in view in 1 Corinthians 15:2 is because of the use of *histēmi* ("stand") at the end of verse 1, *"Moreover, brethren, I declare to you the gospel which I preached to you, which also you received and in which you* ***stand****."* In 1 Corinthians 15:1-2, Paul is saying that the Corinthian believers had stood upon the gospel in the past and even up to the present. But this standing, like their sanctification-salvation, would only continue if they held fast to the gospel Paul initially preached to them. This usage of the verb *histēmi* in 1 Corinthians 15:1 is consistent with how the term is employed elsewhere in the Pauline Epistles, where it is used routinely of some *present* aspect of the Christian life. It is *never* a descriptive term for eternal salvation itself, nor as a term describing the condition for eternal salvation. These factors indicate that such a meaning in 1 Corinthians 15:1 would be anomalous, making it doubtful. However, this term is used quite frequently to describe the present Christian life. This usage of *histēmi* is demonstrated in the following passages:

- *"But if any man thinks he is behaving improperly toward his virgin, if she is past the flower of youth, and thus it must be, let him do what he wishes. He does not sin; let them marry. 37 Nevertheless he who* ***stands*** *(histēmi) steadfast in his heart, having no necessity, but has power over his own will, and has so determined in his heart that he will keep his virgin, does well"* (1 Corinthians 7:36-37). The standing referred to here is in reference to a Christian father's decision whether or not to let his daughter marry. In the context, *histēmi* is clearly used in reference to the Christian life, not eternal life.

- *Therefore let him who thinks he* ***stands*** *(histēmi) take heed lest he fall."* (1 Corinthians 10:12). This passage is often cited by Arminians to prove the possibility of losing one's eternal salvation. However, the context has nothing to do with either past tense salvation (justification, regeneration) or future tense salvation (glorification). The context is sanctification and living the Christian life. This is seen from verse 5, where the point is being *"well-pleasing"* to God, not obtaining or retaining eternal life. Likewise in verse 6, it says we should not lust after evil things, as the Israelites did. This too is a reference to sanctification and the Christian life, not eternal life. Then in verses 8-10, Paul warns against physical destruction due to disobedience, not eternal condemnation due to unbelief. The sense of verse 12 therefore is not, *"let him who thinks he is **saved** (eternally) take heed lest he fall (from eternal salvation)."* Rather, 1 Corinthians 10:12 is cautioning Christians that just because we may be standing for the Lord one moment, this is no guarantee that we'll be standing against temptation the next. We are to remain in yielded dependence upon the Lord at all times lest we fall into sin at any time.

- *Moreover I call God as witness against my soul, that to spare you I came no more to Corinth. 24 Not that we have dominion over your faith, but are fellow workers for your joy; for by faith you **stand** (histēmi)"* (2 Corinthians 1:23-24). The sense of *"stand"* here seems to be parallel to its use in Romans 14:4, coupled with Romans 14:22-23, where a Christian individually gives account to the Lord for the decisions he makes as he walks by faith throughout his Christian lifetime. So in 2 Corinthians 1:23-24, Paul is simply saying that he did not have dominion over their individual Christian lives, since the Corinthians each had their own individual faith in Christ for which they would each individually give an account to the Lord Jesus, not to Paul.

- *Therefore, having been justified by faith, we have peace with God through our Lord Jesus Christ, 2 through whom also we have access by faith into this grace in which we **stand** (histēmi), and rejoice in hope of the glory of God."* (Romans 5:1-2). The use of *"stand"* in verse 2 speaks of sanctification by faith. This is indicated by the use of the word *"also"* in verse 2, showing that Paul in verse 2 is going beyond the justification described in verse 1. In fact, all three tenses of salvation are referred to in the passage: *"justified by faith"* (v. 1, justification), *"this grace in which we stand"* (v. 2, sanctification), and *"in hope of the glory of God"* (v. 2, glorification). The fact that the reference to the present grace *"in which we stand"* is sandwiched between justification and glorification makes it a definite reference to present sanctification.

- *You will say then, "Branches were broken off that I might be grafted in." 20 Well said. Because of unbelief they were broken off, and you **stand** (histēmi) by faith. Do not be haughty, but fear"* (Romans 11:19-20). This passage is also commonly cited by Arminians as a proof-text for the possibility of losing one's eternal salvation. However, the context of the passage is not dealing with individual salvation. The context establishes that the Gentiles presently have a place of privilege, corporately, to be the primary channel of God's blessing to the world in this Church age, a position and privilege that Israel once possessed and will have yet again. The Gentiles are currently in the place of usefulness and service to God only because they have responded to God with faith in Christ to a greater degree than the Jews have. The context is corporate, not individual, dealing with the nation of Israel versus the Gentiles collectively. The context is not dealing with salvation but being in the privileged position of service to God and blessing to the world, a position Gentiles could forfeit by not continuing in faith, just as the nation of Israel had done. Thus, Romans 11:20 does not use the word *"stand"* in reference to eternal life.

- *Receive one who is weak in the faith, but not to disputes over doubtful things. 2 For one believes he may eat all things, but he who is weak eats only vegetables. 3 Let not him who eats despise him who does not eat, and let not him who does not eat judge him who eats; for God has received him. 4 Who are you to judge another's servant? To his own master he stands or falls. Indeed, he will be* ***made to stand*** *(histēmi), for God is able to make him* ***stand*** *(histēmi)"* (Romans 14:1-4). This refers to the believer's present, individual accountability to God in the use of his liberty as he walks with the Lord. This is also not a reference to eternal life.

- *"Finally, my brethren, be strong in the Lord and in the power of His might. 11 Put on the whole armor of God, that you may be able to* ***stand*** *(histēmi) against the wiles of the devil. 12 For we do not wrestle against flesh and blood, but against principalities, against powers, against the rulers of the darkness of this age, against spiritual hosts of wickedness in the heavenly places. 13 Therefore take up the whole armor of God, that you may be able to* ***withstand*** *(anthistēmi) in the evil day, and having done all, to* ***stand*** *(histēmi). 14* ***Stand*** *(histēmi) therefore, having girded your waist with truth, having put on the breastplate of righteousness, 15 and having shod your feet with the preparation of the gospel of peace; 16 above all, taking the shield of faith with which you will be able to quench all the fiery darts of the wicked one"* (Ephesians 6:10-16). This passage refers to the present Christian life as being one of spiritual warfare, in which we are to stand by faith in God's strength and provision for victory. It has nothing to do with eternal life.

- *"Epaphras, who is one of you, a bondservant of Christ, greets you, always laboring fervently for you in prayers, that you may* ***stand*** *(histēmi) perfect and complete in all the will of God"* (Colossians 4:12). Here too, *histēmi* is clearly used in reference to doing the will of God in the Christian life, not to eternal salvation.

What each of these usages of *"stand"* (*histēmi*) indicates is that the term is never used in the New Testament in reference to eternal salvation. The term is never used in contexts dealing with eternal salvation where it could be a synonym for saving faith.[53] The term is used predominantly of the Christian life and is therefore consistent with the one gospel for justification and sanctification view.

7) A seventh and final reason why interpretation #6 is correct is because it is perfectly consistent with other Pauline passages where continuing in the truth of the gospel is necessary for sanctification, growth, and a state of spiritual readiness in anticipation of Christ's imminent return for His Church. It is a constant theme in the Pauline Epistles that the cross and resurrection of Christ, along with the believer's identification with Christ in His work, form the foundation for the entire Christian life (Rom. 6:3-6; 1 Cor. 6:14, 19-20; 15:1-4; 2 Cor. 4:10-11; 5:14-16a; 13:4; Gal. 2:20; 6:12-16; Eph. 1:20; 5:25; Phil. 1:21; 2:5-8; 3:10-11; Col. 2:6, 20; 3:1-4; 2 Tim. 2:11). If the Corinthians did not continue to hold fast to that word about Christ's resurrection that Paul originally delivered to them in the gospel (1 Cor. 15:1-2), then an important plank upon which to live their Christian lives would be removed. The truth of the gospel directly affects the believer's practical sanctification.

This fact is corroborated by at least four parallel Pauline passages (Gal. 3:1-4; Phil. 2:12-16; Col. 1:22-28; 1 Thess. 2:1-3:13) where the Christian's continuance in God's Word, particularly the gospel, results in practical sanctification, spiritual growth, and a Christian life that is not *"in vain."*

---

[53] The term *histēmi* is used in a justification context in Romans 3:31, where it says, *"on the contrary, we* ***establish*** *(histēmi) the law."* Though this is a justification section of Romans, *histēmi* is applied to the law here, not justification itself. Likewise, *histēmi* is used in Romans 10:3, where it says, *"seeking to* ***establish*** *their own righteousness."* Though the context is justification again, *histēmi* is used here as a description of something unbelievers are presently doing, resulting in their NOT being saved. This reference also doesn't technically use the term as a synonym for either eternal salvation or the condition for it. In 2 Corinthians 13:1, it says, *"By the mouth of two or three witnesses shall every word be* ***established****."* Here too it is the "word" that is said to be established or standing, not eternal salvation. Finally, in the last remaining use of *histēmi* in the New Testament, in 2 Timothy 2:19 it says, *"the solid foundation of God* ***stands****, having this seal: "The Lord knows those who are His," and, "Let everyone who names the name of Christ depart from iniquity."* Even here, *"stands"* (*histēmi*) is not actually used in reference to eternal salvation according to the passage. It is not certain from the context whether the false teachers, Hymenaeus and Philetus, were saved or unsaved. In 2 Timothy 2:19, the quotations are from the Old Testament (Num. 16:5) and from an incident in which the question was not about the Lord knowing who was regenerated and who wasn't. Rather, as the context shows in Numbers 16 with rebellious Korah and here in 2 Timothy 2 with false teachers Hymenaeus and Philetus, the issue was God knowing who were His duly appointed leaders and spokesmen truly ministering on His behalf versus those who were not. The reference in 2 Timothy 2:25-26 to those (presumably Hymenaeus and Philetus) who needed repentance, being in the devil's *"snare,"* is most likely describing the condition of genuine but fallen saints since Paul had previously warned about this same possibility for a *"new convert"* when giving the qualifications for an overseer in 1 Timothy 3:6-7.

Only by holding fast to the gospel of God's grace will believers be growing in grace and be ready for the imminent coming of the Lord Jesus Christ (Phil. 2:16; 1 Thess. 2:19; 3:13).

- Galatians 3:1-4 is the first example of a Pauline passage parallel to 1 Corinthians 15:2:

1 *O foolish Galatians! Who has bewitched you that you should not obey the truth, before whose eyes Jesus Christ was clearly portrayed among you as crucified?*
2 *This only I want to learn from you: Did you receive the Spirit by the works of the law, or by the hearing of faith?*
3 *Are you so foolish? Having begun in the Spirit, are you* ***now being made perfect*** *by the flesh?*
4 *Have you suffered so many things* ***in vain****—if indeed it was* ***in vain****?*

Though this passage does not contain the word "gospel," clearly the problem in Galatia was a departure from the one, true gospel (Gal. 1:6-9). Here in Galatians 3:1-4, we see that the Galatian Christians had taken their eyes off the sufficiency of Christ's work on the cross and as a result were falling prey to legalistic false teachers who added works to God's grace as a means of both justification and sanctification (*"being made perfect"*). As a result of not continuing in the gospel truth of Christ's sufficient, substitutionary work on the cross and the grace of God that flows from that work, these Galatians were turning to a merit-based approach for acceptance with God in their Christian lives. The result of such a law-oriented approach is always a walk in the flesh, rather than a walk by means of the Holy Spirit's power (Gal. 5:16).

The Galatians had initially suffered at the hands of legalists shortly after they believed, and now to turn back to legalism would mean that their previous persecution for Christ would be *"in vain."* By following legalism instead of the gospel of grace, their Christian lives would be *"in vain."* They would not be fulfilling God's will, and their efforts in the flesh would ultimately be to no avail in His eyes (Gal. 4:11, 19). The very question of Galatians 3:3, *"are you now being made perfect by the flesh?"* speaks of sanctification rather than justification. According to Galatians 3:3, departing from the gospel directly affects the believer's sanctification and growth.

- Philippians 2:12-16 is also a passage that parallels the truth of 1 Corinthians 15:1-2. It says:

12 *Therefore, my beloved, as you have always obeyed, not as in my presence only, but now much more in my absence,* ***work out your own salvation*** *with fear and trembling;*

13 *for it is God who works in you both to will and to do for His good pleasure.*
14 *Do all things without complaining and disputing,*
15 *that you may become blameless and harmless, children of God without fault in the midst of a crooked and perverse generation, among whom you shine as lights in the world,*
16 ***holding fast the word** of life, so that I may rejoice in the day of Christ that I have not **run in vain** or **labored in vain.***

Clearly the context of verse 12 is also present tense salvation from sin's power in the Christian life, not eternal salvation. Philippians 2:12-16 is a sanctification passage. The eternal salvation of the Philippian believers was never in doubt, as they were partakers of God's grace (1:7), citizens of heaven (3:20), and their names were in the Book of Life (4:3). They could *"work out"* their salvation (2:12) only because it previously had been "worked in" by the Lord at the moment they were born again. Philippians 2:12 is not telling people to work *for* salvation, since a person cannot "work out" something they do not even possess! We can only "work out" that which has already been "worked in" by the Lord.

Within this clear sanctification context, there is a twofold reference to *"in vain"* in verse 16, as well as *"holding fast"* (*epechō*) the word of life. Though the word *epechō* could be translated either as *"holding forth"* (KJV, NIV) or *"holding fast"* (NKJV, NASB),[54] this passage should still be regarded as a present tense salvation passage paralleling the usage of *katechō* in 1 Corinthians 15:2. In this context, the believer is told in vv. 15-16 to be a light in a dark world, *"**holding fast** (epechō) the **word** (logos) of life."* This phrase parallels 1 Corinthians 15:2, *"by which you are (being) saved, if you **hold fast** (katechō) that **word** (logos) which I preached to you, unless you believed in vain."*

- Colossians 1:23 is also a parallel passage about continuing in the gospel as a matter of Christian growth or maturity. In Colossians 1:20-23, it says in reference to Jesus Christ:

20 *and by Him to reconcile all things to Himself, by Him, whether things on earth or things in heaven, having made peace through the blood of His cross.*
21 *And you, who once were alienated and enemies in your mind by wicked works, yet now He has reconciled*
22 *in the body of His flesh through death, to present you holy, and blameless, and above reproach in His sight—*
23 ***if indeed you continue in the faith**, grounded and steadfast, and are not moved away from the hope of the **gospel** which you heard, which was*

---

[54] Vern S. Poythress, "'Hold Fast' Versus 'Hold Out' in Philippians 2:16," *WTJ* 64 (Spring 2002), 45-53.

preached to every creature under heaven, of which I, Paul, became a minister.

Here the believer's once-for-all reconciliation to God through Christ's work on the cross is spoken of in the past tense as a settled, accomplished event (*"having made peace,"* v. 20; *"He has reconciled,"* v. 21). What was God's purpose for this reconciliation according to verse 22? It was, *"to* ***present*** *(paristēmi) you holy, and blameless, and above reproach in His sight."* But this presentation was contingent upon the Colossians' continuance in the faith and the gospel (v. 23). It is an undeniable truth of Scripture that God will *"present"* every child of God perfectly holy and blameless before Him in the future when we are glorified at the resurrection (2 Cor. 4:14; Eph. 5:27; Jude 24). This aspect of our salvation is guaranteed and is not contingent upon believers persevering in the faith. But is glorification itself the presentation that Paul has in mind in Colossians 1:22? Here, it is not glorification that is conditioned upon holding fast to the gospel; rather it is the Christian's present, continuous state of sanctification and spiritual preparedness in view of Christ's any moment appearing.

There are essentially two reasons why Colossians 1:22-23 is addressing practical sanctification and not glorification. First, the root word for *"present"* (*paristēmi*) in Colossians 1:22 and 28 is elsewhere used by Paul predominantly in reference to the present Christian life (Rom. 6:13, 16, 19; 12:1; 16:2; 1 Cor. 8:8; 2 Cor. 11:2; 2 Tim. 2:15; 4:17), rather than a future glorification (Rom. 14:10; 2 Cor. 4:14; Eph. 5:27). Though it is God's stated purpose for every reconciled believer to be presented holy before Him (Col. 1:22), the believer's volitional response of presenting himself to God is also necessary in order for actual sanctification to occur (Rom. 6:13, 16, 19; 12:1). Romans 6:13 is especially apropos to a study of 1 Corinthians 15:2, since it says believers should present themselves to God for practical righteousness *"as being alive from the dead."* Romans 6 teaches that believers have already been identified positionally with Christ in His death, burial, and resurrection. From that position of co-resurrection, we are to yield or present ourselves as servants of righteousness to God, resulting in holiness and sanctification (Rom. 6:19).

A second reason why Colossians 1:22 is addressing present sanctification and not glorification is found within the immediate context, where Paul continues in Colossians 1:27-29:

27 *To them (i.e., the "saints" [v. 26] of Christ's "church" [v. 24]) God willed to make known what are the riches of the glory of this mystery among the Gentiles: which is Christ in you, the hope of glory.*
28 *Him we preach, warning every man and teaching every man in all wisdom,*

that we may ***present*** *(paristēmi) every man* ***perfect*** *(teleios) in Christ Jesus.*
29 *To this end I also labor, striving according to His working which works in me mightily.*

When Paul says in verse 28, *"that we may* ***present*** *every man* ***perfect*** *in Christ Jesus,"* he is not speaking of final salvation at glorification, but of a state of spiritual growth and maturity in one's Christian life. This is how the term *"perfect"* (*teleios*) is used elsewhere by Paul (1 Cor. 2:6; 14:20; Eph. 4:13; Phil. 3:12, 15; Col. 4:12). Though God's stated objective is to *"present"* (*paristēmi*) every reconciled believer to Himself in a holy, sanctified condition (Col. 1:22-23), and Paul also labored in his teaching ministry to *"present"* (*paristēmi*) every Christian this way (Col. 1:28-29), the believer must still volitionally choose to *"present"* (*paristēmi*) himself to God in order for actual sanctification and growth to occur (Rom. 6:13-19). 1 Timothy 4:16 parallels this principle, where Paul says to Pastor Timothy, *"Take heed* (*epechō*, cf. Phi. 2:16, "holding fast"; cf. 1 Cor. 15:2, "hold fast") *to yourself and to the doctrine. Continue in them, for in doing this you will save both yourself and those who hear you."* Since Timothy was already born again and eternally saved, Paul here is obviously speaking of present tense salvation or sanctification. Though God is the principal agent in sanctification, the individual believer must still exercise his own volition to respond to sound doctrine in order to be presently saved from the power of sin in the Christian life. And the pastor's doctrine directly affects the sanctification of those who hear him. Thus all three parties are involved to some extent in the sanctification process: God, the individual believer, and the pastor. This parallels the thought of Colossians 1:28-29 and 1 Corinthians 15:2.

The apostle Paul had a shepherd's heart to see each and every believer not only justified before God but also sanctified, mature, and *"perfect"* in His sight. He labored (Col. 1:29), along with others (Col. 4:12), toward this end. The apostle Paul was not satisfied just to see sinners saved from hell; he shared the Lord's desire for every child of God to grow into Christ-likeness (Gal. 4:19). If this did not occur, he viewed his labors as being *"in vain"* (Gal. 4:11; Phi. 2:16). Since Paul lived with the eager expectation of Christ's return for the Church at any moment, he labored in ministry with the great objective of seeing every believer grow in Christ and be *"perfect"* (Col. 1:28), to be continuously ready for the Lord Jesus to appear at any moment. Thus the believer's presentation in holiness to God is not speaking of glorification itself, which is after this life, but of a present, continuous state of practical sanctification in anticipation of Christ's any moment coming.[55] Colossians 1:22-29 teaches that Christians must hold fast to the gospel in order to be spiritually sanctified and *"perfect."* This parallels 1 Corinthians 15:2.

- In 1 Thessalonians 2-3, there is yet another clear parallel to 1 Corinthians 15:2 and sanctification-salvation being contingent upon continuance in the faith. In 1 Thessalonians 2:1, Paul writes, *"For you yourselves know, brethren, that our coming to you was not in vain."* Then in verses 2-9, Paul mentions four times how he had brought them *"the gospel,"* and in verse 9 he mentions how he *labored* night and day in order to bring it to them. He then continues in 1 Thessalonians 2:10-13:

---

[55] Both Arminianism and Calvinism mistakenly assume that the presentation here is the believer's future glorification. Arminianism teaches that the believer must keep his or her salvation by holding fast to the gospel until the end of one's life; while Calvinism teaches that a person proves he or she is truly elect and destined for glory only by holding fast to the gospel until the end. In either case, making it to glory requires perseverance in faith. Some Free Grace advocates, who are neither Calvinist nor Arminian, also view the presentation of Colossians 1:22 as future, but not synonymous with glorification. Instead, they say, the presentation is synonymous with the judgment seat of Christ before which all believers will have their works evaluated. However, it is better to take the presentation as something in the present for several reasons. First, the phrase *"in His sight"* (*katenōpion*) in Colossians 1:22 is often assumed to be a reference to being in God's future, heavenly presence, but it is far more likely that the phrase simply refers to what God sees in men now, in the present. This term *katenōpion* occurs only 3 times in the N.T., with Jude 24 being a definite reference to the future in glory, but with Ephesians 1:4 being a debatable passage just like Colossians 1:22. However, the cognate root word, *enōpion*, occurs 17 times in Paul's epistles and in only one passage (1 Cor. 1:29) does it even *possibly* refer to the future, immediate presence of God in heaven. In all 16 remaining occurrences, it refers to being *presently* in the sight of either God (Rom. 3:20; 14:22; 2 Cor. 4:2; 7:12; 8:21; Gal. 1:20; 1 Tim. 2:3; 5:4, 20; 6:13; 2 Tim. 2:14; 4:1) or men (Rom. 12:17; 2 Cor. 8:21; 1 Tim. 5:20; 6:12). Secondly, when a study is done in both the Old and New Testaments of such general concepts and phrases as being *"in His sight,"* the *"sight of God,"* and the *"sight of the Lord,"* it is overwhelmingly evident that these phrases nearly always refer to what God sees right now in the present, not the future. Thirdly, to be presented *"holy, and blameless (amōmous), and above reproach (anegklētos)"* in God's sight does not necessarily refer to future glorification either. The believer is to be experientially holy now, in the present (1 Cor. 7:34; 2 Cor. 7:1; Titus 1:8; 1 Peter 1:15-16). Likewise, though Paul uses the term *amōmous* to refer to future glory (Eph. 5:27), he also uses it to refer to the present life of the believer *"in the midst of a crooked and perverse generation…in the world"* (Phil. 2:15). Similarly, though Paul also uses the term *anegklētos* to refer to future glorification (1 Cor. 1:8), more often he uses it of the present (1 Tim. 3:10; Titus 1:6, 7). Finally, some who condition final salvation and glorification on holding fast to the gospel until the end of one's life claim that Ephesians 5:27 must be a parallel passage to Colossians 1:22 because Ephesians and Colossians are parallel epistles. However, there is a significant difference in wording between Ephesians 5:27 and Colossians 1:22 that sets them apart. In Ephesians 5:27, there is the addition of the word *"glorious"* (*"to present to Himself a glorious church"*), which speaks of glorification. In addition, Ephesians 5:27 goes on to say, *"a glorious church, not having spot or wrinkle or any such thing."* This also indicates future glorification since no Christian can honestly say on this side of heaven that they are spiritually *"without spot or wrinkle or any such thing."* These significant additions are not found in Colossians 1:22. Since Ephesians 5:27 is speaking of glorification, a more appropriate Colossian parallel passage would be Colossians 3:4.

10 *You are witnesses, and God also, how devoutly and justly and blamelessly we behaved ourselves among you who believe;*
11 *as you know how we exhorted, and comforted, and charged every one of you, as a father does his own children,*
12 *that you would walk worthy of God who calls you into His own kingdom and glory.*
13 *For this reason we also thank God without ceasing, because when you received the* ***word*** *of God which you heard from us, you welcomed it not as the* ***word*** *of men, but as it is in truth, the* ***word*** *of God, which also effectively works in you who believe.*

The *"word"* that Paul labored to bring to the Thessalonians certainly included Christian life truths (1 Thess. 2:11-12; Col. 1:28), but that *"word"* was first of all *"the gospel"* (1 Thess. 2:2, 4, 8, 9). This again parallels 1 Corinthians 15:1-2, *"Moreover, brethren, I make known unto you the* ***gospel*** *. . . by which also you are saved, if you hold fast that* ***word*** *which I preached to you, unless you believed in vain."*

1 Thessalonians 3:1-10	1 Corinthians 15:1-11
3:2, *"concerning your* ***faith****"* 3:5, *"to know your* ***faith****"* 3:6, *"good news of your* ***faith****"* 3:7, *"by your* ***faith****"* 3:10, *"in your* ***faith****"*	15:2, *"unless you* ***believed*** *in vain"* 15:11, *"so you* ***believed****"*
3:8, *"if you* ***stand fast*** *(stēkō) in the Lord"*	15:1, *"in which you* ***have stood*** *(stēkō)"* 16:13, ***"stand fast*** *(stēkō) in the faith"*
3:2, *"fellow* ***laborer*** *in the gospel"* 3:5, *"our* ***labor*** *might be* ***in vain****"*	15:10, *"His grace toward me was not* ***in vain****, but I* ***labored****"* 15:58, *"your* ***labor*** *is not* ***in vain****"*

3:10, *"night and day praying exceedingly that we may see your face and **perfect** that which is lacking in your **faith**"*	15:1-2, *"I declare to you the **gospel**, which I preached to you, which also you received and in which you stand, 2 by which also you are saved, if you **hold fast** that word which I preached to you—unless you **believed** in vain."* Col. 1:28-29, *"that we may present every man **perfect** in Christ Jesus. To this end I also labor"* Col. 1:23, *"if indeed you **continue in the faith**, grounded and steadfast, and be not moved away from the hope of the **gospel**"*

All of these parallel Pauline passages indicate that continuing in the truth of the gospel is necessary for spiritual growth and sanctification, the very point of 1 Corinthians 15:1-2. In the case of the Thessalonians, if they did not persevere in faith through the persecution and opposition they were facing, then their faith would be *"lacking"* and not be *"perfect"* (1 Thess. 3:10), and Paul would have regarded his ministry efforts towards them as being *"in vain"* (1 Thess. 3:5). Likewise, whether it was the Colossians being presented holy before God by continuing in the gospel (Col. 1:22-23), or whether it was the Philippians working out their own salvation by holding fast the word of life in their generation (Phil. 2:12-16), or whether it was the Galatians standing fast in the liberty of a grace-gospel and not laboring in the flesh under legalism (Gal. 3:1-4)—all of these examples underscore the exact same truth that is taught in 1 Corinthians 15:1-2, that we as believers are sanctified before God by continuing to believe the very same gospel by which we were justified in His sight. The one, true gospel is the very foundation of our entire Christian life!

Conclusions on 1 Corinthians 15:1-2

1 Corinthians 15:1-2 is a passage of Scripture that is regrettably neglected by most Christians and consequently easily misunderstood, living as it does in the shadow of the great gospel verses that follow it in 1 Corinthians 15:3-4. Yet a thorough comprehension of 1 Corinthians 15:1-2 is foundational to

any study of the contents of the gospel and the question of what must be believed for eternal life, since it is inextricably linked to verses 3-4. The interpretation of verses 1-2 also has a significant bearing upon the soteriology of major theological systems such as Arminianism and Calvinism, which historically have buttressed their doctrinal positions with incorrect interpretations of this passage. When every detail of verses 1-2 is carefully considered, these verses reveal that Paul was urging the Corinthian saints to persevere in the gospel for their on-going spiritual growth and sanctification, not to *retain* eternal life (Arminianism) or *prove* that they possessed it in the first place (Calvinism).

In addition, an accurate understanding of 1 Corinthians 15:1-2 has significant implications for the crossless gospel and its doctrine. A thorough examination of this passage has revealed that verses 1-2 do not constitute a supposedly "narrower" gospel to the lost, which is merely a matter of "grasping the truth that Jesus Christ gives eternal life," while verses 3-4 contain a supposedly "broader" gospel to the regenerate for their practical sanctification. The message that the Corinthian saints needed to maintain was the exact same message they initially received for their justification and regeneration. 1 Corinthians 15:3-4 simply cannot be separated from 1 Corinthians 15:1-2.

Though the primary point of the term *"saved"* in verse 2 is the present sanctification-salvation of the Corinthian saints, this of necessity presupposes and assumes their eternal salvation. A person cannot be sanctified as a saint who has never been saved as a sinner. The initial salvation (justification and regeneration) of the Corinthians is clearly inferred in verses 1-2 by the very fact that their initial salvation experience is described with several past tense verbs (*"which I **preached** to you, which also you **received** and in which you **stand** [lit. "**have stood**"] . . . you **believed** . . . I **delivered** to you"*). The Corinthians could not be exhorted to *"hold fast"* to the gospel in order to be presently *"saved"* (v. 2) from sin's damaging power in their Christian lives if they had never previously been saved eternally at justification and regeneration. Their need to continue in the truth of the gospel for their sanctification-salvation presupposes that they were saved in the sense of justification-salvation by believing the very same gospel.

Having clarified the meaning of *"saved"* (v. 2) in this chapter, we now have a firm foundation established in order to examine 1 Corinthians 15:3-11 in the next chapter, where each element in the contents of saving faith, whether implied or explicit, will be observed in this classic gospel passage.

Chapter 14

What Is the Gospel According to 1 Corinthians 15:3-11?

OVERVIEW

Contrary to the denials of some Free Grace Christians in our day who have embraced the new crossless "saving message," 1 Corinthians 15 is still one of the most definitive passages in the entire New Testament on the contents of the gospel of our salvation. Certain elements of the gospel are explicitly stated in the passage such as the sole condition of believing, along with Christ's substitutionary death and His bodily resurrection. Other elements are only implicit, such as His humanity, deity, sinlessness, and even the satisfactory nature of His substitutionary death. 1 Corinthians 15:3ff is possibly an early Church confessional statement that contains elements of the gospel plus the corroborating, supporting evidences for the gospel. This traditional Free Grace distinction in 1 Corinthians 15:3-11 between the elements of the gospel and its evidences is not arbitrary. There are at least six scriptural reasons for identifying Christ's substitutionary death and bodily resurrection in verses 3-4 as elements of the saving message of the gospel rather than the burial and post-resurrection appearances in verses 4a and 5-8.

When you read or hear the word "gospel," what immediately comes to your mind? Some who are biblically illiterate might say rather humorously, "Matthew, Mark, Luther, and John"! Others, equally uninformed would say, "The Bible." Still others might think the gospel is just truth in general, as we often say, "That's the gospel truth!" But what does Scripture itself teach? Does the Word of God ever define this significant term? Or, does the Lord want us to remain in a state of spiritual limbo with just a vague, ambiguous, and semi-agnostic understanding of one of the most significant and frequently occurring terms in the entire New Testament?

When most evangelical and Bible-believing Christians think of the term "gospel," 1 Corinthians 15:1-11 invariably comes to mind. Here we have one of the clearest, succinct summations of the gospel in the entire Bible. In these eleven verses we learn the very content of "the gospel." It is the good news that by believing that Christ, the Son of God, died a satisfactory death for our sins and rose from the dead, we can have eternal salvation. Yet, as the last chapter began to explain, this classic understanding of "the gospel" is being rejected today by crossless gospel teachers who are radically redefining this key biblical term and reinterpreting this central, definitive passage. It is now held by some that, in 1 Corinthians 15:3-11, "Paul is not here explaining the saving message he shared with unbelievers."[1] Instead, we are told that Paul is explaining truths that are "Intended for Sanctification, Not Justification."[2] Jeremy Myers explains the rationale behind this novel view. Having just commented on the post-resurrection appearances of Christ in verses 5-8, Myers writes:

> Very few people in the history of evangelism have shared all these truths with unbelievers and required them to believe all these appearances in order to receive everlasting life. But, for the sake of argument, if somebody does start including all of this in their witnessing, including *faith alone in Christ alone* which they had to get from outside 1 Corinthians 15, they still have said nothing about the holiness of God, the deity of Christ, the virgin birth of Christ, or the sinless perfection of Christ. There are many who say that if a person believes that Jesus wasn't God, or wasn't sinless, then they are not born again. But these truths aren't here either.

---

[1] Bob Wilkin, "Another Look at 1 Corinthians 15:3-11," *Grace in Focus* 23 (January/February 2008): 1.

[2] Ibid., 2.

> Do you see where this leads? As soon as someone starts adding things to the list of what a person must believe in order to have everlasting life, there is no rational stopping place. It's all subjective to how much doctrine you want to throw into the mix. Some will have three essentials, another will have five, while someone else will have eight or ten. And of course, all of these truths can be shown to be essential to the *gospel* since all of them, in one place or another in the NT, are included in the *gospel*. But, as Appendix 1 reveals, there are at least fifty NT truths related to the *gospel* and nobody says you have to proclaim all fifty. . . . The conclusion then is that 1 Corinthians 15 does not contain the entire good news message. There are certainly elements of it there, but it is not all there. Therefore, it is not a definitive definition of the gospel. And it especially is not an explanation of what a person must believe in order to receive everlasting life. That is not in 1 Corinthians 15 at all.[3]

Though at first it may appear that the crossless position raises some valid objections, upon closer inspection their position is found to be laden with logical, exegetical, and doctrinal problems. These will be systematically explained and exposed throughout this chapter. At this point, it is sufficient to face head-on the main crossless contention that states that 1 Corinthians 15 was never intended to be a definitive passage on the gospel. Is this really true?

<u>1 Corinthians 15:1-11</u>

1 *Moreover, brethren, I declare to you the* ***gospel*** *which I preached to you, which also you* ***received*** *and in which you stand,*
2 *by which also you are* ***saved,*** *if you hold fast that word which I preached to you— unless you* ***believed*** *in vain.*
3 *For I delivered to you first of all that which I also received: that* ***Christ died for our sins*** *according to the Scriptures,*
4 *and that He was buried, and that* ***He rose again*** *the third day according to the Scriptures,*
5 *and that He was seen by Cephas, then by the twelve.*
6 *After that He was seen by over five hundred brethren at once, of whom the greater part remain to the present, but some have fallen asleep.*
7 *After that He was seen by James, then by all the apostles.*
8 *Then last of all He was seen by me also, as by one born out of due time.*
9 *For I am the least of the apostles, who am not worthy to be called an apostle, because I persecuted the church of God.*
10 *But by the* ***grace of God*** *I am what I am, and His* ***grace*** *toward me was not in*

---

[3] Jeremy D. Myers, "The Gospel is More Than 'Faith Alone in Christ Alone'," *JOTGES* 19 (Autumn 2006): 49 (ellipsis added).

*vain; but I labored more abundantly than they all, yet not I, but the **grace of God** which was with me.*
11 *Therefore, whether it was I or they, so we preach and so you **believed.***

As was demonstrated in the last chapter, Paul here in 1 Corinthians 15:1-11 is reiterating to the Corinthian believers the message that he initially evangelized them with for their eternal salvation. This gospel message was being subtly undermined by the inroads of worldly, Hellenistic, pagan philosophy with its false teaching that there is no resurrection from the dead.

In this context, Paul begins by stating explicitly, *"I declare to you the gospel (to euangelion) which I preached (euēngelisamēn) to you"* (1 Cor. 15:1a). The fact that Paul has in mind a particular and definitive message is indicated by the use of the definite article preceding "gospel." What Paul was about to specify did not just have the *character* of "good news," it contained the specific *content* and *identity* of "*the* gospel." This was the same message that Paul initially preached to them in the past for their justification and eternal life. This is evident from his use of the aorist tense, indicative mood verb in verse 1 for "preached" (*euēngelisamēn*), indicating a past tense for Paul's preaching of the gospel to them. In the following verses Paul then specifies the *content* contained in that good news starting with the conjunction "that" (*hoti*) in verse 3. Though it is true, as crossless proponents are quick to point out, that Paul also introduces Christ's burial and post-resurrection appearances in verses 4-8 with the term "that" (*hoti*), there are several substantial reasons why these are not included in "the gospel" but are rather supplemental to the gospel as its supporting evidences. These reasons will be covered later in the chapter.

Verse 11 also reveals that Paul was recollecting the specific content of his evangelistic message to the previously lost Corinthians. It states, *"Therefore, whether it was I or they, so (houtōs) we preach and so (houtōs) you believed (episteusate)."* By saying that the Corinthians had "believed" (*episteusate*—aorist tense, indicative mood) his evangelistic message in the past, Paul is connecting the thought of verse 11 with verse 1 and thereby establishing what he initially "preached" (v. 1, *euēngelisamēn*) to them as unbelievers for their eternal life. Verse 11 also serves as a summarizing statement for the content of his evangelistic good news from the preceding verses. This is evident from the double use of the adverb "so" (*houtōs*) in verse 11, where Paul is not indicating the communicative manner of his preaching but the resurrection-centered content of it. For these reasons verses 1-11 should be viewed as one literary unit in which the specific contents of the gospel and its supporting evidences are articulated. By doing so, Paul sets the stage to begin addressing the Corinthian problem of unbelief in the resurrection in the next major section of 1 Corinthians 15, namely verses 12-19.

Contrary to the claims of crossless gospel advocates, 1 Corinthians 15:1-4 is a clear and definitive statement of the saving gospel in summary form. Yet, today's new G.E.S. gospel will not allow for this conclusion. Even though the apostle Paul says very plainly under divine inspiration in verse 1, *"I declare to you the gospel"* that I evangelized you with, the crossless position must reinterpret Paul to say in effect, *"I do NOT declare to you the gospel* (that I originally evangelized you with)"! In their attempts to keep the cross and resurrection out of the essential message of eternal life, they must flatly deny that the gospel of our salvation has such specific and identifiable content. The crossless position leaves us with only paltry uncertainties about the contents of the "good news" that the lost must know and believe. The crossless gospel approach is little different from the social gospel of theological liberalism that denies the verities of Scripture and yet continues to speak in vague generalities with pseudo-sanctified agnosticism about "the good news of the gospel" when nobody really knows with certainty what it is.

By deconstructing and unspecifying the gospel, the crossless position amazingly arrives at the very opposite meaning of "the gospel" than the one intended by the Lord. In Myers's article, he actually includes in his list of all things labeled, "the gospel," the religious work of water baptism.[4] Yet, this is the very thing Paul says in 1 Corinthians 1:17 is NOT the gospel, *"For Christ sent me not to baptize, but to preach the gospel, not with wisdom of words lest the cross of Christ should be made of no effect."* This was the inevitable result of not properly recognizing that the Bible *contains* the gospel, but the Bible itself is *not* the gospel.

Not only have the teachers of the G.E.S. gospel left the door wide open for a works-gospel by their lexical mystification of *euangelion*, they have also muddied the waters by mixing the "bad news" with the "good news." They have done this by including such things as the baptism of fire in "the gospel."[5] Imagine, the fires of God's judgment are now part of "the good news"!? Surely, it is time for the Free Grace movement to speak out against these egregious errors and reclaim 1 Corinthians 15 as a definitive, Spirit-inspired articulation of the contents of the "saving message" of "the gospel."

It has been the thesis of this book that the Word of God consistently sets forth several specific and essential truths that form "the gospel" that Christians are to preach and that the lost are to believe today for their eternal salvation. These *sine qua non* of the gospel include Jesus Christ's person (deity & humanity) and finished work (satisfactory death for sin & bodily resurrection), along with salvation being solely by grace through faith in Christ. In this book, the *provision* and *condition* of salvation are normally kept together as one element of the gospel since this is the normal biblical pattern (Acts 10:43; 13:38-39; 16:31; Rom. 1:16; 1 Cor. 1:21; Eph. 1:13; 2:8-9; etc.). However, some may wish to divide this last element into

---

[4] Myers, "The Gospel is More Than 'Faith Alone in Christ Alone'," 53.

[5] Ibid.

two separate parts, as in the following diagram, so that the *provision* of salvation is separate from the *condition* of faith alone. The elements in the following diagram have not been subjectively and arbitrarily determined, as crossless gospel proponents often cynically claim. A careful and thorough study of this definitive text on the gospel will reveal that this passage harmonizes perfectly with the contents of the gospel of Christ set forth in the rest of the New Testament.

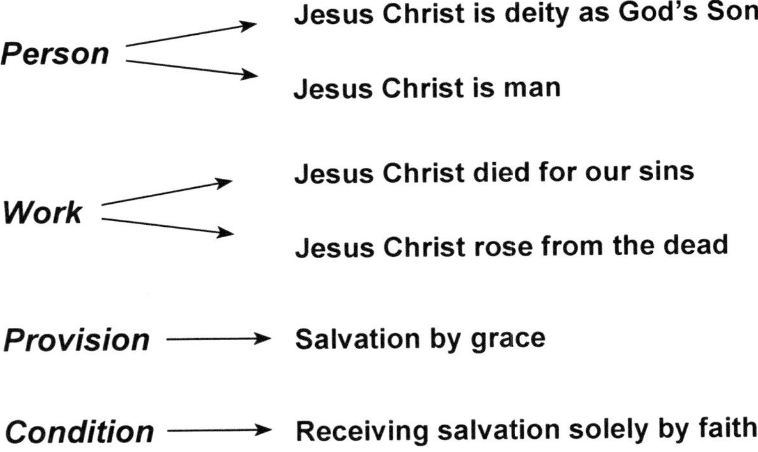
The Gospel Centers in a Specific . . .
Person
Jesus Christ is deity as God's Son
Jesus Christ is man
Work
Jesus Christ died for our sins
Jesus Christ rose from the dead
Provision
Salvation by grace
Condition
Receiving salvation solely by faith

The Provision of the Gospel: Salvation (15:1-2)

In 1 Corinthians 15:1-2, Paul begins, *"Moreover, brethren, I declare to you the gospel which I preached to you, which also you received and in which you stand, 2 by which also you are* ***saved****, if you hold fast that word which I preached to you—unless you believed in vain."* As explained in the previous chapter, Paul is referring here to the Corinthians' present, progressive sanctification-salvation in verse 2, rather than their justification. However, since only children of God who have already been justified are capable of being progressively sanctified, and since Paul is exhorting these believers to continue in the exact same gospel that they initially received at the new birth, the fact of their justification-salvation is clearly understood and implicit in the use of the term "saved" in verse 2.

An anticipated objection should be addressed at this point. Some might claim that nowhere in 1 Corinthians 15:1-11 does it say that the provision of salvation is included as *part of* the gospel message but that here it is only stated to be the *result* of believing. In response it should be noted that salvation is both an essential element of the gospel as well as the guaranteed result of believing it. For this reason, in some Scripture passages it is presented as the result of believing the gospel (Rom. 1:16; 1 Cor. 1:18, 21), while in other passages it is part of the message itself (Acts 13:23, 26, 38-39; Eph. 1:13).

In addition, it should be clarified that sometimes in Scripture the term "salvation" is not the exclusive term used for God's provision in the gospel. As was explained in chapters 9-10, the terms "salvation" and "saved" are often used broadly and inclusively of various aspects of divine deliverance through Christ. These would include such biblical concepts as forgiveness, justification, regeneration, and reconciliation. This explains why in some passages, Church age believers are instructed corporately to not only preach Christ's death and resurrection as part of the gospel but also to preach the forgiveness of sins promised through His name (Luke 24:47). As this relates to the provision of the gospel in 1 Corinthians 15, salvation *from sin* is also implicit by virtue of the fact that Christ died for "our sins" (v. 3). Whenever the good news of the Savior's substitutionary death for our sins is preached, it is inextricably tied to the gospel's provision of salvation from sin.[6] This point will be amplified later in connection with the substitutionary death of Christ.

The Sole Condition of the Gospel: Believe (15:2, 11)

It was shown previously in chapters 9-10 that the sole condition for eternal life, namely faith or believing, is also a necessary element of the gospel of our salvation. If lost people attempt to be saved by working for salvation rather than believing in Christ for their justification, they will surely remain lost (Rom. 4:4-5). The condition of faith or believing is not just the *response to* the gospel, it is itself an essential *element of* the gospel even as other Free Grace teachers maintain.[7] However, here in 1 Corinthians 15, we see the need for a proper response to Christ and His work. It is stated in verses 2 and 11 that the Corinthians "believed" (*episteusate*). Though Christ is not *explicitly* stated in the passage to be the Object of faith, it is clearly implied by the context that the Corinthians believed in Him by virtue of believing "the gospel." In verse 2, it says, *"if you hold fast that word (logō) which I preached (euēngelisamēn) to you—unless you believed (episteusate) in vain."* What the Corinthians "believed" in their past was clearly "the gospel" based

---

[6] J. B. Hixson, *Getting the Gospel Wrong: The Evangelical Crisis No One Is Talking About* (n.p.: Xulon Press, 2008), 148-49n6.

[7] Thomas R. Edgar, "What Is the Gospel?" in *Basic Theology: Applied*, ed. Wesley & Elaine Willis and John & Janet Master (Wheaton, IL: Victor Books, 1995), 158; J. B. Hixson, "Getting the Gospel Wrong: Case Studies in American Evangelical Soteriological Method in the Postmodern Era" (Ph.D. dissertation, Baptist Bible Seminary, 2007), 48n6, 52, 73-74; Charles C. Ryrie, *So Great Salvation: What It Means to Believe in Jesus Christ* (Wheaton, IL: Victor Books, 1989), 119.

on the reference to "that word" that Paul had evangelistically preached to them. This happened to be the same "word" mentioned previously in verse 1 where Paul wrote, *"Moreover, brethren, I declare to you the gospel (to euangelion) which I preached (euēngelisamēn) to you."* The terms "gospel" (*euangelion*), "preached" (*euangelizō*), "word" (*logos*), and "preached" (*kērussō*) are all used interchangeably throughout the passage for Paul's evangelistic saving message. What Paul preached to them was the gospel. What the Corinthians believed was the gospel. There should be no dispute concerning this fact. The problem, however, comes in the crossless contention that the passage says only that the Corinthians believed the gospel, not that they believed in Christ for eternal life. Again, Myers explains the G.E.S. perspective:

> But notice what is not mentioned here. How about one of the first things—faith alone in Christ alone. Yeah, there's this thing up there about believing, but it doesn't say anything about "believing in Christ." It's believing the gospel. And nothing here about works or lack of works, so people have to go to Romans or Galatians to get that.[8]

In Myers's statement, we see another false dichotomy created by the crossless position. It has created a contrast between "believing in Christ," which is necessary for eternal life, versus believing "the gospel," which is deemed to be unnecessary for eternal life. But does such a significant difference really exist in the passage? If Paul summarized the content of *"the gospel"* in verses 3-4 by saying, *"Christ died for our sins. . . . and that He rose again,"* then it seems obvious that the Corinthians believed in both Christ and the gospel. The gospel is the message specifically about Christ. Hence, Paul even writes to the Corinthians earlier, stating that it is the *"gospel of Christ"* (1 Cor. 9:12, 18) and that it is *"the message of the cross"* (1 Cor. 1:17-18). However, the reason crossless gospel proponents cannot see this point is because they have redefined both "the gospel" and the meaning of "the Christ." If believing in Jesus as "the Christ" now means believing in Him solely as the guarantor of eternal life, and if the Corinthians believed only that He died for their sins and rose again, then it can be concluded (falsely) that 1 Corinthians 15 doesn't contain sufficient information for saving faith. The crossless position has once again created a major theological contradiction where one does not exist in the Word of God.

There is a second claim made about this passage by crossless proponents that also needs to be refuted. As Myers stated, they believe this passage is deficient in leading a person to eternal life because it does not explicitly say "faith alone in Christ alone" or address the fact that justification is not by "works." Wilkin reiterates the same point in an article devoted to this passage, pronouncing:

---

[8] Jeremy Myers, "The Gospel is More Than 'Faith Alone in Christ Alone'," Grace Evangelical Society Grace Conference, Dallas, TX, March 2, 2006.

> Try hard but you'll not find a mention of justification by faith apart from works in this passage. You find that in Gal 2:15-16 and in Galatians 3 and Romans 3-4. But it just isn't here. Anywhere. While Paul does refer to the fact that his readers believed (vv 2, 11), he doesn't say that they believed that simply by faith in Jesus they were once and for all justified or given everlasting life that can never be lost. Surely if Paul were trying to show the believers in Corinth (and all believers of all time) how to share the saving message with people, he would have included this central feature he emphasized in Galatians and Romans.[9]

It is ironic that Wilkin repeatedly references Galatians and Romans but not the Gospel of John. In the same article, he concludes with an appeal to Free Grace people to use in evangelism the "saving message" that is found in passages such as John 3:16; 4:14; 5:24; 6:35, 47; and 11:26.[10] Yet none of these passages tell us that eternal life is by belief in Christ *and that it is not by works.* When the same hermeneutical standards are applied to the crossless position as are applied to the "traditional" Free Grace interpretation of 1 Corinthians 15, the inconsistency of the crossless position immediately becomes apparent. Ninety-nine times the Gospel of John states that the sole condition for eternal life is believing. Never once does it say explicitly that eternal life is not by "works." While this truth is clearly implied in John, just as it is in 1 Corinthians 15, it is never stated in so many words. So, should we conclude that the Gospel of John does not contain sufficient information for someone to have "faith alone in Christ alone"?

Obviously, when the word "believe" is given as the condition for eternal life, the sole condition is sufficiently stated. The same is true in 1 Corinthians 15, where believing is mentioned twice as the only requirement for salvation. Though the phrase used in other Pauline passages, "not of works," adds further clarification to this sole condition, and it is extremely helpful, the word "believe" is still a sufficient statement of the sole condition for eternal life. Otherwise, why doesn't God *always* add the phrase "not of works" *every* time the word "believe" appears in the Bible as the condition for eternal life? Furthermore, in 1 Corinthians 15 and the Gospel of John, the non-meritorious nature of salvation is clearly taught through implication by the fact of Christ's substitutionary and satisfactory work on behalf of sinners. When the Lord's substitutionary death for our sins and resurrection are proclaimed, the only thing left for the sinner to do is believe. This is exactly what the Corinthians had done according to 1 Corinthians 15:2, 11.

---

[9] Wilkin, "Another Look at 1 Corinthians 15:3-11," 1.

[10] Ibid., 2.

The Person of the Gospel: Christ, the Son of God (15:3)

If 1 Corinthians 15 is truly a definitive summary of the gospel, and it is, then we should expect to find each element of the gospel contained in it, at least implicitly, if not explicitly. J. B. Hixson affirms this historical, traditional position of the Free Grace movement on this passage, when he writes, "Indeed, all of the components of saving faith, which will be quantified in the next section, are contained in 1 Corinthians 15."[11] In this passage we find not only the provision and sole condition of the gospel but also the person of the gospel—the Object of our faith. He is prominently set forth by the title, "Christ." 1 Corinthians 15:3 declares: *"For I delivered to you first of all that which I also received: that **Christ** died for our sins according to the Scriptures."* We see from this verse that the gospel is first of all good news about a *person*, who is declared in verse 3 to be "Christ."

Christ

At this point, it should be recalled that the term "Christ" is not a generic religious label; rather it is pregnant with Old Testament revelational meaning, as the next chapter will explain in detail. God Himself set the definition of who the Messiah would be, and there is only one person in all of human history who is fit to bear the title of "Christ." For this reason the Lord Jesus spoke to His disciples on the road to Emmaus following His resurrection, saying: *"O foolish ones, and slow of heart to believe in all that the prophets have spoken! Ought not the Christ to have suffered these things and to enter His glory?"* (Luke 24:25-26). The next verse continues: *"And beginning at Moses and all the Prophets, He expounded to them in all the Scriptures the things concerning Himself"* (Luke 24:27). Likewise, Luke later records in 24:44-49 similar words spoken by the Lord to the eleven disciples where the risen Christ is giving them the Great Commission.

Luke 24:44-49

*44 Then He said to them, "These are the words which I spoke to you while I was still with you, that all things must be fulfilled which were written in the Law of Moses and the Prophets and the Psalms **concerning Me**."*

45 And He opened their understanding, that they might comprehend the Scriptures.

*46 Then He said to them, "Thus it is written, and thus it was necessary for **the Christ** to suffer and to rise from the dead the third day,*

47 and that repentance and remission of sins should be preached in His name to all nations, beginning at Jerusalem.

48 And you are witnesses of these things.

49 Behold, I send the Promise of My Father upon you; but tarry in the city of Jerusalem until you are endued with power from on high."

---

[11] Hixson, *Getting the Gospel Wrong: The Evangelical Crisis*, 149n6.

Do we not see here that the title "Christ" has an entire Old Testament context and meaning to it? What did the Law, the Prophets, and the Writings say about "the Christ"? They revealed that He would be the Son of God (Ps. 2:2, 7, 12; Prov. 30:4; Dan. 3:25) and Son of Man (Gen. 3:15; 12:3; 49:10; 2 Sam. 7; Ps. 80:17; Isa. 7:14; 11:1, 10), who would also suffer a satisfactory death for our sins (Ps. 22; Isa. 53; Dan. 9:26; Zech. 12:10; 13:7) and rise from the dead (Ps. 16:9-10; Isa. 53:10b, 12) to offer salvation to all who believe in Him. Is this not the gospel? Do we not see that the term "Christ" is a mirror reflection of the "gospel" in each of its elements? Surely this is not coincidental, but divinely designed. This also explains why at times the Scriptures speak of preaching "the gospel" (1 Cor. 1:17; 9:16, 18), while at other times they speak of just preaching "Christ" (Acts 8:5; 13:38; 2 Cor. 4:5; 11:4; Phi. 1:15, 16, 18). There is essentially no difference between the two when it comes to evangelism. To preach Christ-crucified and risen is to preach the gospel. This is also why the gospel at times is modified by the phrase, "gospel *of Christ*," in order to distinguish it from other forms of "good news" in the Bible that have different contents (the gospel of the kingdom; the everlasting gospel; the good news of the Thessalonians' faith and love; etc.).

All of this helps us to understand Paul's abbreviated description of the person of the Lord Jesus in 1 Corinthians 15:3 when he used the singular title, "Christ." Many crossless gospel proponents are quick to claim that the Lord's deity and humanity are absent from 1 Corinthians 15; and therefore, they say, these elements are not necessary to believe for eternal life. However, this is terribly naïve, for Scripture itself identifies exactly what Paul meant when he used the term "Christ," particularly in his initial evangelization of these Corinthians.

We have a record of this in the Book of Acts, which says regarding Paul's evangelistic mission in Corinth: *"And he reasoned in the synagogue every Sabbath, and persuaded both Jews and Greeks. When Silas and Timothy had come from Macedonia, Paul was compelled by the Spirit, and testified to the Jews that* ***Jesus is the Christ****"* (Acts 18:4-5). We see from this parallel passage that the Corinthians originally heard about the name of "Jesus" when the gospel of Christ was preached to them. Paul apparently spent considerable time and energy reasoning "in the synagogue *every Sabbath*" in order to persuade the Jews that Jesus fit the description of the Christ. How did Paul do this? It was through the same means employed by the Lord Himself with His disciples on the road to Emmaus (Luke 24:13-32). The apostle Paul used the Word of God to prove the distinguishable, identifying features of the Christ and how the Lord Jesus fulfilled the Scriptures, just as he had done on other occasions (Acts 13:14-49; 17:1-4; 28:23).

The Deity of Christ

Not surprisingly, promoters of the promise-only gospel summarily dismiss the idea that the Lord's deity is contained in the gospel in 1 Corinthians 15:1-11.[12] But this is also short-sighted. Though the Lord's deity is already inherent in the title "Christ" in 1 Corintians 15:3, we see from a parallel passage that Paul originally evangelized the Corinthians with the truth of Christ's deity. In 2 Corinthians, Paul also makes a passing reference to his initial evangelistic ministry to them, and in the process he reiterates the identity of the One whom he originally preached and in whom the Corinthians originally believed. In 2 Corinthians 1:19, it states, *"For **the Son of God, Jesus Christ**, who was preached among you by us—by me, Silvanus, and Timothy—was not Yes and No, but in Him was Yes."* The reference to Silas and Timothy marks the occasion of this evangelism as the very same historical instance as the one recorded in Acts 18:4-5. This also coincides with the time referred to in 1 Corinthians 15 by Paul's consistent use of the past tense in the terms "preached" (*euēngelisamēn*), "delivered" (*paredōka*), "received" (*parelabete/parelabon*), and "believed" (*episteusate*).

When the believers in Corinth originally received the letter of 1 Corinthians from Paul and read for the very first time these words: *"I delivered to you first of all that which I also received: that **Christ** died for our sins,"* the crucial term "Christ" had already been defined by Paul and consequently was so understood by the Corinthians. The question is not, "What do we think the term 'Christ' means in 1 Corinthians 15:3?" but "What did these Corinthians in this context originally think this term meant?" To 21st century Americans this term has lost its savor. It is little more than a last name or proper name. But to the original Corinthian audience, the term signified the "Son of God," the "Messiah," and the One who resolved their sin-problem by His substitutionary death and bodily resurrection.[13] The divinely revealed truth of the Old Testament must be allowed to inform us as to the meaning of the term "Christ" in 1 Corinthians 15:3, just as it did with Paul's original Corinthian audience.

We can be sure that the Corinthians didn't interpret the word "Christ" as a vacuous concept, whose meaning was individually determined by

---

[12] Wilkin, "Another Look at 1 Corinthians 15:3-11," 2.

[13] "Without doubt, however, '*Christos*' originally had titular significance in the confession of 1 Cor. 15:3ff. The intent was to say, 'that the *Messiah* died for our sins.' This declaration about the Messiah dying for us (*hyper hēmōn*) is for Paul the basis for numerous formulaic expressions." Martin Hengel, "Christological Titles in Early Christianity," in *The Messiah: Developments in Earliest Judaism and Christianity*, ed. James H. Charlesworth (Minneapolis: Fortress Press, 1992), 444-45. See also Gerhard Delling, "The Significance of the Resurrection of Jesus for Faith in Jesus Christ," in *The Significance of the Message of the Resurrection for Faith in Jesus Christ*, ed. C. F. D. Moule (London: SCM Press, 1968), 97; Martin Hengel, *Studies in Early Christology* (New York: T & T Clark International, 2004), 385; Larry W. Hurtado, "Christ" in *Dictionary of Jesus and the Gospels*, ed. Joel B. Green, Scot McKnight, and I. Howard Marshall (Downers Grove, IL: InterVarsity Press, 1992), 108.

each hearer or reader according to their own personal opinions of who this "Christ" was. A comparison of Acts 18:4-5 and 2 Corinthians 1:19 leads to the conclusion that Paul "reasoned" with them from the Scriptures while in their synagogue. Thus, the Corinthians knew that this *"Christ"* was also *"Jesus"*[14] and *"the Son of God"* (*ho tou theou huios Christos Iēsous*), which was a clear affirmation of His deity.[15] To deny this connection is to refuse to read this passage in light of its 1st century historical context and with the meaning intended by Paul for his original Corinthian audience. This would be a violation of sound hermeneutical principles. Who did Paul preach to the Corinthians? He preached the same person he preached everywhere else, as he states in 2 Corinthians 4:5, *"For we do not preach ourselves, but* ***Christ Jesus the Lord****, and ourselves your bondservants for Jesus' sake."* What this indicates is that Paul preached the person of *"Jesus"* (Acts 18:5) to the Corinthians as being no one less than *"the Lord"* in whom they believed (Acts 18:8), *"the Christ"* (Acts 18:5; 1 Cor. 15:3), and *"the Son of God"* (2 Cor. 1:19). This is in perfect harmony with the evangelistic message of the apostle John, who proclaimed that all who believe *"that Jesus is the Christ, the Son of God"* have *"life in His name"* (John 20:31). To preach Jesus as the Christ is to preach the gospel; and this necessarily involves the proclamation of His deity.[16] Thus, one New Testament scholar concludes "that for Paul, Jesus' identity as Son of God was integral to the gospel."[17] This is consistent with the conclusions of grace-oriented teachers and theologians. For instance, Charles Ryrie comments on 1 Corinthians 15:3 and the gospel, explaining that the issue of the gospel is the Lord Jesus as the God-man who took care of our sin-problem:

> Some of the confusion regarding the meaning of the Gospel today may arise from failing to clarify the issue involved. The issue is, How can my sins be forgiven? What is it that bars me from heaven? What is it that prevents my having eternal life? The answer is sin. Therefore, I need some way to resolve that problem. And God declares that the death of His Son provides forgiveness of my sin. "Christ died for our sins"—that's as plain as it

---

[14] Wilkin stresses the point that the name "Jesus" isn't even revealed in 1 Corinthians 15:3-11 in order to contend that this passage lacks sufficient content to be the saving message. He writes, "*In fact, the actual name of Jesus nowhere appears in this passage.* Except for one reference to *the Christ* in verse 3, all other references to the Lord Jesus in verses 3-11 use the third person singular pronoun, *He*." Wilkin, "Another Look at 1 Corinthians 15:3-11," 2 (italics original). This clearly fails to interpret this passage in its historical context and from the standpoint of original, authorial intent, which recognizes that the Corinthians had been informed from the very beginning that "Jesus" was "the Christ" (Acts 18:5).

[15] Ron Merryman, *Justification by Faith Alone & Its Historical Challenges*, revised edition (Colorado Springs, CO: Merryman Ministries, 2000), 116-17.

[16] Gordon D. Fee, *Pauline Christology: An Exegetical-Theological Study* (Peabody, MA: Hendrickson, 2007), 179-80.

[17] Douglas J. Moo, "The Christology of the Early Pauline Letters," in *Contours of Christology in the New Testament*, ed. Richard N. Longenecker (Grand Rapids: Eerdmans, 2005), 187.

> could possibly be. Sinners need a Savior. Christ is that Savior and the only valid one. Through faith I receive Him and His forgiveness. Then the sin problem is solved, and I can be fully assured of going to heaven. I do not need to believe in Christ's second coming in order to be saved. I do not need to receive Him as my present intercessor. But I do need to believe that He died for my sins and rose triumphant over sin and death. I do not need to settle issues that belong to Christian living in order to be saved. . . . Matters of carnality, spirituality, fruit-bearing, and backsliding relate to the Christian life, not to the issue of salvation. *Only the Lord Jesus, God who became man, could and did resolve that problem by dying for us. He had to be human in order to be able to die, and He had to be God in order for that death to be able to pay for the sins of the world. Keep the issue in the Gospel clear.*[18]

The Humanity of Christ

Besides Jesus' deity being conveyed by the term *"Christ"* in 1 Corinthians 15:3, and even corroborated by the expressions *"Son of God"* (2 Cor. 1:19) and *"Lord"* (Acts 18:8; 2 Cor. 4:5), there is also strong inferential support in the passage for His humanity. Once again, proponents of the promise-only gospel protest that "The perfect humanity of Jesus"[19] is not contained in this passage. Admittedly, this passage does not explicitly say, "Jesus Christ is fully human." But His genuine humanity is still clearly conveyed in this passage in at least three ways.

First, it says in verse 3 that He *"died."* Since neither angels nor God can die, and these are the only other categories of personal, intelligent beings in the entire universe, Christ had to be human (Heb. 2:5-8). In fact, the capacity to die for our sins was the very reason for His incarnation (John 12:23-27; Heb. 2:9, 14; 1 Peter 3:18). Christ's humanity cannot be divorced, either logically or biblically, from the cross.[20] Epistemologically, they are inseparable truths in a Christology that is truly biblical and saving (1 Tim. 2:4-6; 1 John 5:1-6).[21] Whether it is Christ's humanity or deity, both are essential not only for a correct Christology but also as the contents of saving faith.[22]

Secondly, Christ's death is specifically stated to be *"for our sins"* (1 Cor. 15:3). This is an unequivocal declaration of the Lord's substitutionary death. It is understood that the *"our"* in this passage is in reference to real human beings—the Corinthians and Paul. If Christ died for *"our"* sins,

---

[18] Ryrie, *So Great Salvation*, 40 (ellipsis & italics added).

[19] Wilkin, "Another Look at 1 Corinthians 15:3-11," 1.

[20] John T. Carroll and Joel B. Green, "'Nothing but Christ and Him Crucified': Paul's Theology of the Cross," in *The Death of Jesus in Early Christianity* (Peabody, MA: Hendrickson, 1995), 129; Leon Morris, *The Cross in the New Testament* (Grand Rapids: Eerdmans, 1965), 217-18, 287-89, 372-74.

[21] Martin Hengel, *The Son of God—The Origin of Christology and the History of the Jewish-Hellenistic Religion*, trans. John Bowden (Tübingen: J. C. B. Mohr, 1976), 88.

[22] A. C. Dixon, *The Glories of the Cross* (Grand Rapids: Eerdmans, 1962), 13-15.

then He had to be human in order to die in the place of the readers—real human beings. This passage is not teaching angelic substitution. Thus, if Christ died *"for our"* sins, He had to be human.

Thirdly, according to verse 4, He was *"buried"* and *"rose"* from the dead. These activities also necessitated His possessing a human body, since spirits cannot be buried. It is certainly true that "the incarnation is implied in His death and burial."[23] Therefore, the humanity of Christ is plainly revealed in this passage, even apart from an explicit statement saying, "Christ is human."

While His humanity is taught indirectly in 1 Corinthians 15 in several ways, and it is assumed knowledge on the part of the Corinthians, this does not negate the fact that it is still information that is essential to believe for everlasting life. Undergirding the truth of Christ's death and resurrection in this passage is the assumption that He is truly human. A person cannot believe in Christ's vicarious death and bodily resurrection (the "explicit" elements of 1 Cor. 15:3-4) without simultaneously believing in His humanity. This is why truth that is only implied in a passage can still be considered essential to saving faith. While the humanity of Christ is only implicit in 1 Corinthians 15, it is still required as the content of saving faith, which corresponds with other individual passages of Scripture where the requirement to believe in His humanity is stated unambiguously (John 6:51-53; 1 Tim. 2:4-6).[24] This does not mean, however, that the Corinthians had "implicit faith" in Christ's humanity versus "explicit faith" in the sense that these phrases are frequently employed.

Often the phrase "implicit faith" is set in contrast to "explicit faith" with the semantic connotation that "implicit faith" is a matter of believing something without being consciously aware of it. It can even refer to a merely blind trust or a faith without knowledge—an ignorant faith. Conversely, "explicit faith" often has the opposite sense of being a faith that involves conscious mental comprehension of particular information. But the Bible never speaks of such categories of "implicit faith" versus "explicit faith." Nor does it recognize such a dichotomy.[25] The faith that God recognizes and approves in His Word is always a volitional and cognitive response to some particular aspect of divine revelation, since a person can only believe what God has revealed and what he or she knows of that revelation.[26] There is no such thing biblically as someone believing

---

[23] Andrew J. Spallek, "The Origin and Meaning of *Εὐαγγέλιον* in the Pauline Corpus," *CTQ* 57.3 (July 1993): 186.

[24] Some theologians maintain that "explicit" belief in Christ's humanity is not necessary for eternal life but only "implicit" belief is required. For example, Geisler writes: "all who truly believe in Him unto salvation must have either explicit or implicit faith in Christ's humanity; none can explicitly deny it and be saved." Norman Geisler, *Systematic Theology* (Minneapolis: Bethany House, 2004), 3:538.

[25] Bruce A. Demarest, *The Cross and Salvation: The Doctrine of Salvation* (Wheaton, IL: Crossway Books, 1997), 261.

[26] Gordon H. Clark, *Faith and Saving Faith,* 2nd edition (Jefferson, MD: Trinity Foundation,

something without knowing they believe it. All saving faith is based on a certain amount of information or *"knowledge of the truth"* (1 Tim. 2:4); and even the humanity of Christ is *revealed* by God indirectly in 1 Corinthians 15 through His atoning death and bodily resurrection. Since it is part of God's revelation in the passage, even implicitly, it still must be believed. Thus, when the term "implicit" is used throughout this book in reference to an element of the gospel that is not spelled out in "explicit" terms in a given passage, this should not be misconstrued to mean that belief in such "implicit" truths is merely "implicit faith" in the sense that it does not involve conscious acknowledgement and acceptance of these truths.

The Sinlessness of Christ

One final point should be made about the person of Christ in 1 Corinthians 15. It is sometimes claimed by the proponents of a crossless gospel that in addition to our Lord's deity and humanity being absent from this passage, the text also says nothing about His sinlessness. Thus, Wilkin writes regarding 1 Corinthians 15:3-11, "Note that Paul didn't say here, as he did in 2 Cor 5:21, that Jesus never sinned. *A person could believe all of what Paul says here and yet believe that Jesus was a sinner just like us. Whether that is an essential truth that must be believed for one to be born again is open to question.* But, if it is, then clearly this passage isn't giving us all the essential truths that must be believed."[27]

Yet, Wilkin's doctrine seems to be a transparent rejection of what is clearly revealed in the passage as an implicit truth. A person CANNOT *"believe all of what Paul says here and yet believe that Jesus was a sinner just like us."* If the passage says that Christ *"died for our sins"* then He obviously did not die for His own sin. The implication of the passage is clear: if Christ had any personal sins of His own then He Himself would have needed a substitute. The fact that He died for *"our"* sins, according to the passage, clearly communicates to any objective reader without a preconceived theological agenda that He was a sinless substitute. While this is only implicit in the passage, it is nevertheless present by virtue of being inherent in the substitutionary death of Christ as expressed by the phrase, *"Christ died for our sins."* Furthermore, the passage cited by Wilkin in 2 Corinthians 5:21 clearly teaches the sinlessness of Christ, and it, like 2 Corinthians 4:5, is a representative summarization of Paul's evangelistic preaching to the lost, the kind of evangelism that these Corinthians would have already heard from Paul when he traveled to Corinth with the very same message (Acts 18:4-5; 1 Cor. 15:1). This means that in the historical context of 1 Corinthians 15 the Corinthian readers would have already understood and accepted this truth about Christ. In addition, if it is conceded that the term "Christ" inherently refers to the deity and

---

1990), 21, 107; J. Gresham Machen, *What is Faith?* (Grand Rapids: Eerdmans, 1946), 51-52.

[27] Wilkin, "Another Look at 1 Corinthians 15:3-11," 1 (italics added).

humanity of the incarnate Son of God then, of necessity, Christ would be sinless by virtue of being God. When someone believes that Jesus Christ is God-incarnate, it is assumed and implied that He is sinless and therefore able to be our satisfactory sacrificial substitute.

At this point we need to stop and consider the biblical implications if the preceding conclusions are incorrect. If Wilkin and those who are promoting the G.E.S. gospel are teaching that Christ's deity and sinlessness are *not* conveyed in this passage, then what are they really saying about Him? Regarding the sinlessness of Christ, are they actually teaching that someone can believe in "a sinful Savior" and still receive eternal life? While to date they have not yet explicitly affirmed this possibility in their public writing and speaking, they have come awfully close.[28] When someone believes that Christ is God-incarnate and believes every word of 1 Corinthians 15 and yet comes away believing *"that Jesus is a sinner just like us,"* isn't that really implying that someone can also be saved who believes that God is a sinner? The issue of Christ's potential sinfulness goes right to heart of theology proper, the attributes of God, and to the fundamental question of what it means to even believe in "God." It is likely that the next logical step in the tragic devolution of G.E.S. theology will be the denial that a person must even believe in "God" in order to be saved, for that too involves the recognition of His righteous nature or character.[29]

Believe vs. Deny

With respect to Christ's deity, humanity, and sinlessness, we need to address another relevant question at this point. Do these elements of the person of Christ have to be *known* and *affirmed* in order to receive eternal life? Or, do they simply not have to be *denied*? I have occasionally heard this distinction proposed in the midst of this controversy over the contents of saving faith, but it is an unhelpful and unbiblical distinction that only further obscures the issue rather than clarifies it. To claim, for instance, that "Some truths do not need to be known in order to be saved, they just cannot be denied" actually leads to serious doctrinal and practical error.

First, it leads to the unbiblical conclusion that God requires at least two different *conditions* for salvation and two different *contents* of saving faith in this dispensation. In one case, God would require a person to cognitively affirm some minimal information about Christ after being presented with it. (This would be true if a person heard the gospel through a missionary, for instance.) But the Lord would then require a second person (who was unreached with the gospel and ignorant of these truths) merely to not deny this additional information about Christ, such as His

---

[28] Bob Wilkin, "Essential Truths About Our Savior," *Grace in Focus* 23 (November/December 2008): 2n5.

[29] Ibid., 1.

deity, humanity, sinlessness, etc. The problem with this affirm vs. deny dichotomy is that it sets up two different *contents* of saving faith: content *with* Christ's deity, humanity, and sinlessness versus content *without* these elements. This would also result in two different *conditions* for salvation: the condition of a person having to agree with certain truths once they become known versus not denying these truths due to ignorance. In either case, whether it is due to ignorance or impudent denial, the result is the same—the person is still in a state of unbelief and therefore still condemned before God (John 3:18).

I have even heard the scenario proposed that a person could believe in Jesus for eternal life while still being undecided about the truths of His person and work and thus still be saved because that person has not out-rightly rejected such truths. It is claimed that such a person is "safe" because he or she is supposedly "neutral" on the matter of Christ's person and work. But this is patently unbiblical. If a person is not yet persuaded of the truth of the gospel of Christ, they are not "neutral" towards God; they are still in unbelief, and unregenerate, and under the wrath of God (John 3:36). Unbelief in Christ, whether due to ignorance or pride or some degree of both, does not result in the reception of everlasting life.

If God permitted two contrasting contents of saving faith and conditions for salvation, this would be neither biblical nor just. In fact, it would be, in essence, the same error as inclusivism. The false doctrine of inclusivism teaches that the unevangelized in foreign lands who have never heard about Jesus Christ do not need to hear and believe the gospel; but they can be saved merely by a sincere reception of whatever revelation they do have, which may only be the light of conscience and creation (Rom. 1:19-20). But, if that same person hears about Christ and then rejects Him, that person cannot be saved. The folly of such a doctrine is evident. It logically and practically leads to the absurd notion that less information is better because it leaves less truth to be rejected, thus increasing the likelihood that a person will not be in unbelief. But is minimal knowledge of Christ ever preferable to a saving knowledge of the truth (1 Tim. 2:4)? The false dichotomy between merely *not knowing* certain truths versus *not denying* them ultimately leads to the mortifying conclusion that it is better not to inform the lost of Christ's person and work lest we jeopardize their eternal destinies. Perish the thought!

To conclude this section on the person of "Christ" in 1 Corinthians 15, we see that the G.E.S. gospel allows for the possibility of a genuine saving belief in a non-divine, even sinful, "Christ." In the process of supporting their doctrinal position, they have not only redefined the gospel but also the key Christological titles of "Christ" and "Son of God." By their refusal to acknowledge the biblical meaning of "the Christ" and "the gospel," they have, with alarming alacrity, opened up a spiritual Pandora's Box of theological errors and unscriptural contradictions.

The Work of the Gospel: Christ's Substitutionary Death (15:3)

When most Bible-believing Christians think of "the gospel," it is the content of Christ's substitutionary death and bodily resurrection that immediately comes to mind based on 1 Corinthians 15:3-4. While this passage begins with "Christ" as the *person* of the gospel, verse 3 also sets forth the *work* of the gospel, specifically that *"Christ **died** for our sins."* It is undeniable that Christ's substitutionary death is an element of the gospel.[30] However, crossless gospel advocates have sought to diminish the necessity of believing in this truth for eternal life by acknowledging that though Christ's substitutionary death is truly part of the gospel, it is just one of at least 50 other items that are part of "the gospel."[31] Since it is absurd to require the lost to believe all fifty-plus items, then the mention of Christ's substitutionary death in this passage must also not be required.

A second approach to nullifying the substitutionary death clause in 1 Corinthians 15:3 that is sometimes employed is to downplay the significance of the phrase *"died for our sins."* They do this by insisting that this clause is far from an adequate explanation of vicarious atonement. They note that since many professing Christians who are actually unregenerate will say, "Christ died for my sins," then this clause must not be a sufficient explanation of the Savior's work to require the lost to believe it for their eternal salvation. But are these claims really true? Is the expression *"Christ died for our sins"* actually insufficient for the lost to believe and be born again?

Substitutionary Atonement

1 Corinthians 15:3 certainly teaches substitutionary atonement, even if it contains only a summary statement of this priceless truth.[32] This is evidenced by several factors in the passage, starting with the Greek preposition *huper* with the genitive case of "our sins" (*tōn hamartiōn hēmōn*). It says in verse 3 that Christ died "for" (*huper*) our sins. The Greek term *huper* is frequently used elsewhere in Scripture, along with another preposition, *anti*, to convey the substitutionary nature of Christ's death.[33] For example, 1 Timothy

[30] Hengel convincingly argues that underlying the clause about Christ's death "for our sins" in 1 Corinthians 15:3 was the doctrine of substitutionary atonement taken most likely from Isaiah 53. See Martin Hengel, *The Atonement: The Origins of the Doctrine in the New Testament* (London: S. C. M. Press, 1981), 33-75.

[31] Myers, "The Gospel is More Than 'Faith Alone in Christ Alone'," 52-56.

[32] Hixson, "Getting the Gospel Wrong: Case Studies," 48n6.

[33] BDAG, s.v. "ἀντί," 87-88; s.v. "ὑπέρ," 1030-31; Leon Morris, *The Apostolic Preaching of the Cross* (Grand Rapids: Eerdmans, 1956), 30-31, 59; John R. W. Stott, *The Cross of Christ* (Downers Grove, IL: InterVarsity Press, 1986), 147-48; J. H. Thayer, ed., *The New Thayer's Greek-English Lexicon of the New Testament* (Peabody, MA: Hendrickson Publishers, 1981), 49, 639; Richard C. Trench, *Synonyms of the New Testament* (Grand Rapids: Eerdmans, 1973), 310-13; Nigel Turner, *Grammatical Insights into the New Testament* (Edinburgh: T & T Clark, 1965), 172-73; idem, *Syntax*, Volume 3 of *A Grammar of New Testament Greek*, by J. H. Moulton, 4 vols.

2:6 says that Christ *"gave Himself a ransom (antilutron) for (huper) all."* The word "for" (*huper*) in this instance shows that He died "in the place of" all. Similarly, Romans 5:6 and 5:8 illustrate the same point saying, *"For when we were still without strength, in due time Christ died for (huper) the ungodly. . . . But God demonstrates His own love toward us, in that while we were still sinners, Christ died for (huper) us."* Christ's substitutionary death is also taught in Galatians 1:4 by the use of *huper* where it says, *"who gave Himself for (huper) our sins, that He might deliver us."*

One of the clearest uses of *huper* showing the substitutionary nature of Christ's death is in John 11:50-51. There Caiaphas, the unbelieving Jewish high priest, issues a prophetic prediction of Christ dying in the place of the whole Jewish nation. It says, *"nor do you consider that it is expedient for us that one man should die for (huper) the people, and not that the whole nation should perish. Now this he did not say on his own authority; but being high priest that year he prophesied that Jesus would die for (huper) the nation."* Many other passages demonstrate this substitutionary meaning of *huper* in contexts dealing specifically with Christ's death. It seems this was one of two primary prepositions of choice used by the 1st century writers of inspired Scripture to show the true nature and significance of Christ's death.

The substitutionary meaning of the preposition *huper* is so well established that most crossless gospel proponents will not argue against it. However, I have heard some deny that *huper* in the context of 1 Corinthians 15:3 necessarily indicates a substitutionary *atonement*. While it is obviously true that, by itself, the Greek preposition *"huper"* does not have the inherent meaning of "substitutionary atonement," it must be acknowledged that when it is combined with the other key words of *"death," "sins,"* and *"our"* in the context, it makes a semantic contribution that definitely conveys the truth of both *substitution* and *atonement*.

I have heard some crossless proponents refuse to acknowledge this, however, and then go on to claim that the reference to Christ dying for our sins in 1 Corinthians 15:3 is still not thorough or sufficient enough for someone to truly comprehend what Christ accomplished by His death. As a result of seeing this passage as soteriologically and epistemologically deficient, some crossless proponents now teach that this passage does not even contain the contents of saving faith. This conviction is explicitly taught, for example, by Bob Bryant. At one national conference of the Grace Evangelical Society, Bryant stated specifically regarding 1 Corinthians 15:3-4:

> Paul is writing to Christians to emphasize something about the big picture of the gospel, not trying to recap what someone must do to have eternal life. The gospel is a broad word in the New Testament. It can refer specifically to what someone must believe

---

(Edinburgh: T & T Clark, 1963), 270-71; John F. Walvoord, "The Person and Work of Christ, Part VIII: Christ in His Suffering and Death," *BSac* 118 (October 1961): 298.

> to have eternal life. It can refer to general truth about the good news; and part of that general truth is that Jesus died and rose again. So, I don't think Paul is trying to define what we tell people to believe for eternal life there at all.[34]

Similarly, at another point Bryant taught the insufficiency of 1 Corinthians 15:3:

> Never, never, does the Bible say, that someone will be saved by believing that Jesus died for our sins. In fact, there are millions of people who believe that Jesus died for our sins who are not saved. That's because they have never believed in Jesus for everlasting life, for which they will never thirst again. They have never believed that they are eternally secure, therefore they are not saved.[35]

While the effort of Bryant and others to emphasize the promise of eternal life in our evangelism is commendable, he and other teachers of a crossless saving faith have gone well beyond Scripture and have ended up creating a false dichotomy between believing that Christ died for our sins and believing in Him for eternal life. Scripturally, it is not an either/or proposition. It has been my experience that when people do not have the assurance that they possess everlasting life it is because they do not understand or accept the substitutionary, sufficient death of Christ for their sins.

Roman Catholics and the Death of Christ

In seeking to support their conclusions about the deficiency of 1 Corinthians 15:3, I have heard some crossless proponents use the example of unsaved Roman Catholics who profess, "Christ died for my sins," which supposedly shows that even unsaved Catholics believe 1 Corinthians 15:3. Thus, Bob Wilkin states:

> When I hear people point to 1 Corinthians 15:3-11 and boldly proclaim that is the precise evangelistic message Paul preached, I shutter [sic]. How could we get it so wrong? Yes, Paul did tell unbelievers about Jesus' death and resurrection. But *that was not the sum total of his evangelistic message.* Nor is Paul's evangelistic message the point of 1 Cor. 15:3-11. If 1 Cor. 15:3-11 is the evangelistic message we should preach, then Mormons are clear on the gospel. So are Roman Catholics, Eastern Orthodox, Arminians, Lordship Salvationists, and just about anyone in Christianity who says that Jesus died for our sins and rose again.[36]

---

[34] Bob Bryant, "Eternal Security: Do You Have to Believe It?" Grace Evangelical Society Grace Conference, Dallas, TX, February 28, 2006.

[35] Ibid.

[36] Bob Wilkin, "Justification by Faith Alone is an Essential Part of the Gospel," *JOTGES* 18 (Autumn 2005): 14. See also, Myers, "The Gospel is More Than 'Faith Alone in Christ Alone'," 48.

While some unsaved Roman Catholics might say, "Christ died for my sins," since they know His death had *something* to do with sin, the real question is, do they understand what this phrase means and do they personally believe it? Of course, merely saying it will not save anyone; but understanding and believing it will. No doubt it is true that when showing 1 Corinthians 15:3-4 to most professing but unsaved Christians, they will respond by claiming, "I believe that." Yet, they remain lost. It has also been my personal experience in evangelizing unsaved Roman Catholics that when I have shown them other verses, such as John 3:16 and even John 6:47, they immediately retort, "I believe that too." In fact, most Catholics claim to believe the entire Bible, including every verse in the Gospel of John, since it's all God's book! However, they do *not* believe what John 3:16 or John 6:47 are really saying, otherwise they would not be seeking to earn their way to heaven by their supposed human goodness.

As a former devout Roman Catholic seminarian, I can testify first-hand that I personally, as well as most of the practicing Catholics I knew, did not understand what it meant that *"Christ died for our sins."* Nor did we actually believe that Christ was our substitute for sin. We believed that our own good works were the substitute for our sins. Sunday after Sunday we would ritualistically recite the Nicene Creed and sometimes the Apostles' Creed, both of which referred to Christ's death but neither of which addressed substitutionary atonement. Weekly during each mass we would affirm, *"I believe in God the Father Almighty, Maker of heaven and earth, and in Jesus Christ His only begotten Son, our Lord, who was conceived by the Holy Spirit, born of the virgin Mary, and suffered under Pontius Pilate. He was crucified, died, and was buried. He descended into hell (hades), the third day He rose from the dead, ascended into heaven, and is seated at the right hand of God, the Father, etc."*[37] However, though both the Apostles' and Nicene Creeds state that Christ was *"crucified, died, and was buried,"* neither of them declares that He died *"for our sins."* Thus, *the two foundational creeds of Catholicism are not equivalent to 1 Corinthians 15:3.* Nor is this difference incidental and insignificant. This omission has devastating effects, for, in the practical thinking of most Roman Catholics, they must still pay for their own sins through penance and good works.[38] Consequently, the purpose of Christ's death is lost on them.

At this point, the Roman Church equivocates with theological legalese, explaining that Jesus Christ really did die for sin, but He didn't pay

---

[37] *The Catholic Encyclopedia*, ed. Robert C. Broderick (Nashville: Thomas Nelson, 1987), 423-24.

[38] "Sins must be expiated. This may be done on this earth through the sorrows, miseries and trials of this life and, above all, through death. Otherwise the expiations must be made in the next life through fire and torments or purifying punishments" (*Vatican II: The Conciliar and Post Conciliar Documents*, gen. ed. Austin Flannery [Northport, NY: Costello Publishing, 1992], 1:63); "The merit of man before God in the Christian life arises from the fact that

the temporal debt due for sin. In other words, He left us the balance to pay by our own good works.[39] Though most Roman Catholics are unaware of many of the fine points of their Church's teaching, in the practical thinking of most Catholics, they sincerely believe they have to pay for their own sins. What Christ accomplished by His death remains a mystery to them. This point was pressed home to me when I once asked a close Roman Catholic acquaintance, "How would your chances of getting to heaven be affected if Jesus Christ had *never* died for your sins 2,000 years ago?" After a long, awkward pause, he replied, "I honestly don't know. I must have forgotten the answer to that question from my childhood catechism days." The fact is, he had been Catholic for over fifty years and had *never* been taught the answer to that question, because Jesus Christ's death is practically a non-factor in the Roman Catholic approach to salvation. Jesus Christ is practically *persona non grata* in most religious people's efforts to acquire eternal life. It is simply naïve, therefore, to claim that even unsaved Roman Catholics believe *"Christ died for our sins"* and that they truly believe what 1 Corinthians 15:3 is teaching. Even though as an unsaved Roman Catholic I personally knew that Christ's death had something to do with "sin," I could not honestly say that Christ died as the substitute for my sins. Rather my own good works were the substitute that I believed in for my eternal salvation.

Substitution, Sufficiency, and Satisfaction

Another potential objection to all of this that some people might raise, including some crossless gospel proponents, is that the phrase *"Christ died for our sins"* is inadequate to believe in for eternal life because it speaks only of *substitution* but not necessarily of the *sufficiency* of Christ's work. But, this too would be an erroneous assumption and a serious misinterpretation of 1 Corinthians 15:3. For, the phrase *"Christ died for our sins"* not only teaches substitutionary atonement but it also implicitly teaches both sufficiency and satisfaction.[40] These can be seen from several factors in the passage.

God has freely chosen to associate man with the work of his grace. The fatherly action of God is first on his own initiative, and then follows man's free acting through his collaboration, so that the merit of good works is to be attributed in the first place to the grace of God, then to the faithful. Man's merit, moreover, itself is due to God, for his good actions proceed in Christ, from the predispositions and assistance given by the Holy Spirit. . . . Since the initiative belongs to God in the order of grace, *no one can merit the initial grace* of forgiveness and justification, at the beginning of conversion. Moved by the Holy Spirit and by charity, *we can then merit* for ourselves and for others the graces needed for our sanctification, for the increase of grace and charity, and for the attainment of eternal life." *Catechism of the Catholic Church*, English translation, Libreria Editrice Vaticana (Bloomingdale, OH: Apostolate for Family Consecration, 1994), 486-87 (ellipsis added; italics original).

[39] "The sinner must still recover his full spiritual health by doing something more to make amends for the sin: he must 'make satisfaction for' or 'expiate' his sins. This satisfaction is also called 'penance'" (*Catechism of the Catholic Church*, 366).

[40] Anthony C. Thiselton, *The First Epistle to the Corinthians*, NIGTC (Grand Rapids: Eerdmans, 2000), 1191.

First, it is stated that Christ "died" for our "sins." The very fact that Christ did something for our "sins," specifically that He "died," indicates that a debt was being paid. I am afraid most evangelical Christians have become so familiar with the language of 1 Corinthians 15:3 that we no longer pause to consider how peculiar it is to say that a man "died" for our "sins." What does death have to do with sin anyway? Why does 1 Corinthians 15:3 *not* say, for instance, that "Christ *prayed* for our sins" or that "Christ *lived* for our sins"? Praying and living would not be adequate substitutes for (*huper*) our sins. But why would they not be adequate? It is because these would not make satisfaction for sin. It is clearly implied by the passage that the sole means of substitution that adequately provided satisfaction for man's sin was the *death* of Christ. This is in keeping with the truth that *"the wages of sin is death"* (Rom. 6:23).

Secondly, the sufficiency of Christ's death for our sins is evident from the fact that His death is a single event in the passage. Notice that 1 Corinthians 15:3 does not say, "Christ is dying for our sins." Nor does it say, "Christ's deaths for our sins." Why not? How peculiar that it says only that "Christ died for our sins"! The verb "died" (*apethanen*) in verse 3 is in the aorist tense, active voice, and indicative mood in Greek. If Paul had wanted to say that Christ's death was a continuous, repeatable act, or even that He had to die more than once, he had other grammatical options available to him in the Greek language that he chose *not* to use in verse 3. The fact that Christ died once for our sins is the very argument used in the New Testament to show the sufficiency of His death in providing satisfaction for our sins. For example, Peter writes, *"For Christ also **suffered once for sins**, the just for the unjust, that He might bring us to God, being put to **death** in the flesh but made alive by the Spirit"* (1 Peter 3:18). Likewise, the writer of Hebrews states, *"By that will we have been sanctified through the **offering of the body** of Jesus Christ **once** for all. . . . But this Man, after He had **offered one sacrifice for sins forever**, sat down at the right hand of God. . . . For by **one offering** He has perfected forever those who are being sanctified"* (Heb. 10:10, 12, 14). What all of this demonstrates is that 1 Corinthians 15:3 sets forth not only the death of Christ on the sinner's behalf, but the *finished* work of Christ in paying for our sins! The gospel is the good news that God has already accomplished something on my behalf in order to settle my sin problem. That message must be believed for one's salvation. That is the message that is clearly taught in 1 Corinthians 15:3.

Thirdly, the sufficient, satisfactory death of Christ is at least implied in 1 Corinthians 15:3-4 by the fact that He was raised from the dead. The resurrection was evidence that the Father had favorably accepted the work of His Son and demonstrated it by raising Him from the dead (Rom. 4:24-25). It is noteworthy in 1 Corinthians 15:3-4 that Christ's death in verse 3 is in the active voice, "died" (*apethanen*), indicating an act done *by* Christ. However, by contrast, the verb in verse 4 for the fact that Christ "rose" (*egēgertai*) is in the passive voice, indicating an act done *to* Him by

God the Father (1 Cor. 15:15). Grammatically, this is consistent with the implied doctrinal truth that God the Father was satisfied with the work of His Son and proved it by raising Him from the dead (Isa. 53:10-12).

The critical phrase in 1 Corinthians 15:3 that *"Christ died for our sins,"* while not a thorough explanation of Christ's atoning work, is still a sufficient and succinct expression for the substitutionary and satisfactory aspect of Christ's death. All of this underscores how vitally important it is to tell people about the Savior's death for their sins, not just to believe in His promise of eternal life and trust in Him as the guarantor of eternal life. The primary reason that people *do not* believe in His promise of eternal life and lack assurance is because they do not realize or accept the fact that God has provided the substitutionary, sufficient, and satisfactory payment for our sins by the death of His Son.

The Work of the Gospel: Christ's Bodily Resurrection (15:4)

1 Corinthians 15:4 goes on to state, *"and that He was buried, and that He rose again the third day according to the Scriptures."* This passage reveals that the bodily resurrection of Christ is every bit as much a part of the gospel as His substitutionary death. In fact, what would the gospel be like without the resurrection? What would our Savior's death be without His glorious resurrection? A death without a resurrection would be like a bird with only one wing; like a train track with only one rail;[41] like nighttime without daybreak. It would be death without life or hope.

The resurrection of the Lord Jesus is so essential, in fact, that it forms the ground of our entire, eternal salvation (Rom. 5:10; 8:34). Like the Savior's death, without His resurrection, no man could be saved. Though the Lord's resurrection is often greatly neglected in our day, even in Bible-believing churches, 1 Corinthians 15 makes it plain that without it there would be no salvation possible. *"And if Christ is not risen, your faith is futile; you are still in your sins! Then also those who have fallen asleep in Christ have perished"* (1 Cor. 15:17-18). James Orr, the early 20th century theologian and defender of the fundamentals of the faith, summarized the resurrection's connection to our redemption:

> [The resurrection of Christ is] the natural and necessary *completion* of the work of Redemption itself. Accepting the above interpretation of Christ's death, it seems evident that, if Christ died for men—in Atonement for their sins—it could not be that He should remain permanently in the state of death. That, had it been possible, would have been the frustration of the very end of His dying, for if He remained Himself a prey to death, how could He redeem others?[42]

---

[41] G. Michael Cocoris, *Evangelism: A Biblical Approach* (Chicago: Moody Press, 1984), 61.

[42] James Orr, *The Resurrection of Jesus* (Cincinnati: Jennings & Graham, n.d.), 277 (brackets

Our salvation necessitates a living Savior, since a dead savior cannot save anyone.[43] Such a non-risen savior would not have fully overcome the last enemy caused by human sin, as he himself would still be subject to death (1 Cor. 15:26, 54-57). That is why 1 Corinthians 15 consistently portrays Christ as the One who not only rose once from the dead but who presently *stands* risen from the dead. This is evident from the fact that the word "rose" (*egēgertai*) in verse 4 is a perfect tense, indicative mood verb, indicating not only that Christ rose from the dead in the past but that the results of that glorious event remain to the present. He stands as a risen Savior![44] To be saved by believing in Jesus Christ for eternal life a person must believe that He is alive and not subject to death. Only then can a person be confident that He is the guarantor of everlasting life. This is what the gospel teaches. If someone believes that Christ died all over again after His initial death and resurrection, that person has placed their faith in another gospel and another Jesus (2 Cor. 11:4) that cannot save them. The Christ of 1 Corinthians 15:4, and thus the Christ of the gospel, is a living Savior who conquered sin and death and thus is able to bestow the free gift of eternal life to all who trust in Him as the Living One! The Bible consistently teaches that these truths about Christ, which form the very grounds of our redemption, are also the essential facts that we must believe to be saved, even the very same facts contained in the gospel. The Lord Jesus Christ, the gospel, and the grounds of our eternal salvation are all harmonious, mirror reflections of one another.

But what kind of resurrection did Christ experience? In personal correspondence with one proponent of the G.E.S. gospel, the objection was raised that 1 Corinthians 15 is not explicit enough in its contents to provide sufficient information for the unregenerate to believe in Christ and be born again. This included the mention of Christ's resurrection in verse 4. For example, this G.E.S. advocate objected that this passage isn't explicit as to whether Christ's resurrection was bodily or just spiritual, so the fact of Christ's resurrection obviously can't be part of the required content of saving faith. This objection, however, sounds eerily reminiscent of the claims of the cults and liberal neo-orthodoxy,[45] which purport to uphold belief in Christ's resurrection, but only a "spiritual" and non-corporeal

---

added).

[43] James Denney, *The Death of Christ*, ed. R. V. G. Tasker (London: Tyndale Press, 1960), 73; Stott, *The Cross of Christ*, 238-39.

[44] The perfect tense, passive voice, indicative mood (*egēgertai*) of the word "rise" (*egeirō*) is the form used almost exclusively of Christ's resurrection in this chapter (1 Cor. 15: 4, 12, 13, 14, 16, 17, 20). The aorist, active, indicative form (*ēgeiren*) is appropriately used twice by Paul in verse 15 to describe the past completed act of the Father in raising His Son.

[45] Norman L. Geisler, *The Battle for the Resurrection* (Nashville: Thomas Nelson, 1989), 80-107; Charles C. Ryrie, *Neoorthodoxy: An Evangelical Evaluation of Barthianism* (Chicago: Moody Press, 1956), 41.

resurrection. The objection to a physical resurrection in 1 Corinthians 15 is only the result of seeking to avoid the clear contextual meaning of "rose again" in verse 4. The words of resurrection scholar William Lane Craig are apropos here: "And really, even today were we to be told that a man who died and was buried rose from the dead and appeared to his friends, *only* a theologian would think to ask, 'But was his body still in the grave?' How much more is this true of first century Jews, who shared a much more physical conception of resurrection than we do!"[46]

While the explicit term "body" is not used in the immediate context of 1 Corinthians 15:1-11, it is strongly implied and just as clearly conveyed by the reference to Christ's burial in verse 4. Do people bury spirits or bodies? The resurrection of the "body" is also the clearly intended meaning based on the larger context of the chapter. Starting in verse 35, Paul specifically discusses the resurrection of the "body." In addition, the word "rose" (*egēgertai*) in verse 4 is a spatial-physical term indicating an upward motion that would be unnecessary if it was merely Christ's spirit that had resuscitated.[47] The substitutionary death and bodily resurrection of Christ are so evident in 1 Corinthians 15:3-4 that, in order for people to deny that these truths are present, they must make a conscious predetermination *not* to see them in this definitive gospel text.

Distinguishing the Elements vs. Evidences of the Gospel

So far it has been demonstrated that the person of Christ, His substitutionary death, bodily resurrection, and salvation solely through faith are all necessary components of the one, true gospel of Christ contained in 1 Corinthians 15:1-11. However, at this point some will raise the objection: "But you've conveniently skipped over the references to Christ's burial (v. 4) and post-resurrection appearances (vv. 5-8). Why aren't these also part of the gospel message that the lost must believe for eternal life?" The crossless gospel position must come up with some solid reasons for rejecting 1 Corinthians 15 as a definitive passage on the contents of saving faith in order to substantiate their doctrine. To this point in the development of the G.E.S. doctrine, they have yet to provide any substantive, exegetical basis for this rejection. Instead, they have merely pointed to an apparent inconsistency with the traditional evangelical approach to defining the gospel from this classic text. Jeremy Myers explains their new rationale:

> There is no reason to stop at verse 4, was there?! Remember I said, "that, that, that, that." Well if you read on there's other things Paul preached and Paul includes in his definition of the gospel.

---

[46] W. L. Craig, "The Historicity of the Empty Tomb of Jesus," *NTS* 31 (1985): 41.

[47] Craig, "The Historicity of the Empty Tomb of Jesus," 41, 61-62nn15-17; Kirk R. MacGregor, "1 Corinthians 15:3b-6a, 7 and the Bodily Resurrection of Jesus," *JETS* 49.2 (June 2006): 230.

> Look at verse 5, *"and that He was seen by Cephas, then by the twelve. And that He was seen by over five hundred brethren at once, of whom the greater part remain to the present but some have fallen asleep. And that He was seen by James, then by all the apostles, then last of all He was seen by me also, as by one born out of due time."* So why stop in verse 5 if you're looking for things to include as necessary to believe for eternal life? You can't stop at verse four. You have to include all of these appearances—His appearances to Cephas, and the twelve, and the five hundred brethren, and then James, and then the apostles, and then Paul. And if you're saying these are the things a person must believe to receive eternal life you have to tell them all that stuff too, and they have to believe all that stuff too. You can't stop in verse 4.[48]

> Most people who use 1 Corinthians 15 as a formal definition of the gospel arbitrarily stop at v 4. But Paul does not stop defining his gospel in v 4. He continues to define the gospel in vv 5-8. . . . So if 1 Corinthians 15 defines what a person must believe to receive everlasting life, not only must we include the death, burial, and resurrection of Jesus Christ, but also the appearances of Christ to Cephas, then the twelve, then to over 500 at once, then to James, then to the apostles, then last of all to Paul.[49]

Thus far, the crossless position's denial that 1 Corinthians 15 contains a definitive statement of the gospel for our eternal salvation seems to boil down to only one substantive argument. They insist that since Christ's burial and post-resurrection appearances are included in the passage, in addition to Christ's person and work, then the burial and appearances must also be included in any definition of "the gospel" as the saving message. They claim that it is purely "arbitrary" and inconsistent to differentiate between Christ's death and resurrection (vv. 3, 4b) as essential elements of the gospel versus His burial and post-resurrection appearances (vv. 4a, 5-8). However, it has been the standard Free Grace position even long before the advent of crossless doctrine that the burial and appearances are technically not the gospel but the proofs of it.[50] It has also been the interpretation of non-Free

---

[48] Jeremy Myers, "The Gospel is More Than 'Faith Alone in Christ Alone'," Grace Evangelical Society Grace Conference, Dallas, TX, March 2, 2006.

[49] Myers, "The Gospel is More Than 'Faith Alone in Christ Alone'," 48-49 (ellipsis added).

[50] Ronald B. Allen, *The Wonder of Worship: A New Understanding of the Worship Experience* (Nashville: Word Publishing, 2001), 65; Charles C. Bing, "How to Share the Gospel Clearly," *JOTGES* 7 (Spring 1994): 57; G. Michael Cocoris, *Evangelism: A Biblical Approach* (Chicago: Moody Press, 1984), 12; Thomas L. Constable, "The Gospel Message," in *Walvoord: A Tribute* (Chicago: Moody Press, 1982), 202-3; Edgar, "What Is the Gospel?" 158; Robert P. Lightner, *Sin, the Savior, and Salvation: The Theology of Everlasting Life* (Nashville: Thomas Nelson, 1991), 129-32, 160, 283; David K. Lowery, "1 Corinthians," in *BKC*, ed. John F. Walvoord and Roy B. Zuck (Wheaton, IL: Victor Books, 1983), 542; Alva J. McClain, *Romans: The Gospel of God's Grace* (Winona Lake, IN: BMH Books, 1973), 56; R. Larry Moyer, *Free and Clear: Understanding & Communicating God's Offer of Eternal Life* (Grand Rapids: Kregel, 1997), 16-17; Charles C.

Grace expositors and commentators that Christ's burial and appearances in 1 Corinthians 15 are semantically and theologically subordinate evidence for the two main points that form the gospel—Christ's atoning death and bodily resurrection.[51] It has been traditionally recognized that Christ's burial is simply the proof of the greater fact that He died a literal, rather than a merely metaphorical, death.[52] Likewise, His appearances following His resurrection are proof of the greater fact that He literally, physically rose from the dead with the same body in which He died.[53] This proper distinction is explained and diagrammed as follows by Charlie Bing, a proponent of the "traditional" Free Grace view of the gospel:

> Most of our readers should not need a review of the Gospel's content. It is laid out no more clearly than by Paul in 1 Corinthians 15. Paul reminds the Corinthians about the Gospel that he preached, that they received, and by which they were saved (vv 1-2). The message was the one Paul received personally from God (v 3; cf. Gal. 1:11-12). In vv 4-5 we find two great propositions of the Gospel and their supporting evidence. We could diagram the verses like this:

Ryrie, *Basic Theology* (Wheaton, IL: Victor Books, 1986), 267; idem, *So Great Salvation*, 39; Earl D. Radmacher, *Salvation* (Nashville: Word Publishing, 2000), 47.

[51] Gerald L. Borchert, "The Resurrection: 1 Corinthians 15," *RevExp* 80.3 (Summer 1983): 402-3; Denney, *The Death of Christ*, 73, 167; Gordon D. Fee, *The First Epistle to the Corinthians*, NICNT (Grand Rapids: Eerdmans, 1987), 725; David E. Garland, *1 Corinthians*, BECNT (Grand Rapids: Baker, 2003), 684; John Kloppenborg, "An Analysis of the Pre-Pauline Formula 1 Cor 15:3b5 in Light of Some Recent Literature," *CBQ* 40.3 (July 1978): 357; Jan Lambrecht, "Line of Thought in 1 Cor 15,1-11," *Gregorianum* 72.4 (1991): 662; Peter Stuhlmacher, *Das paulinische Evangelium: Vorgeschichte* (Göttingen: Vandenhoeck und Ruprecht, 1968), 274.

[52] Borchert, "The Resurrection," 402-3; Hans Conzelmann, "On the Analysis of the Confessional Formula in I Corinthians 15:3-5," *Int* 20.1 (January 1966): 21; Kloppenborg, "An Analysis of the Pre-Pauline Formula 1 Cor 15:3b5," 364n64; George Eldon Ladd, *I Believe in the Resurrection of Jesus* (Grand Rapids: Eerdmans, 1975), 106; Lambrecht, "Line of Thought in 1 Cor 15,1-11," 663. The reference to Christ's burial in 15:4a may not only point backwards to 15:3 in order to confirm the reality of the Lord's death but it may also point forwards to 15:4b to confirm the physical, bodily nature of His resurrection. See F. F. Bruce, *Paul: Apostle of the Heart Set Free* (Grand Rapids: Eerdmans, 1977), 91; William Lane Craig, "Did Jesus Rise from the Dead?" in *Jesus Under Fire: Modern Scholarship Reinvents the Historical Jesus*, ed. Michael J. Wilkins and J. P. Moreland (Grand Rapids: Zondervan, 1995), 147, 169n14; idem, "The Historicity of the Empty Tomb of Jesus," *NTS* 31 (1985): 40-41; G. G. Findley, "The First Epistle of Paul to the Corinthians," in *The Expositor's Greek Testament*, ed. W. Robertson Nicoll (Grand Rapids: Eerdmans, 1990), 919; Frederic Louis Godet, *Commentary on First Corinthians* (Grand Rapids: Kregel, 1977), 759; Ronald J. Sider, "St. Paul's Understanding of the Nature and Significance of the Resurrection in 1 Corinthians XV 1-19," *NovT* 19 (1977): 124-41; Thiselton, *The First Epistle to the Corinthians*, 1192-93; W. E. Vine, "1 Corinthians," in *The Collected Writings of W. E. Vine* (Nashville: Thomas Nelson Publishers, 1996), 106.

[53] Borchert, "The Resurrection: 1 Corinthians 15," 404. Just as Christ's burial may have pointed to the reality of both His death and resurrection, the post-resurrection appearances may have also served double-duty. Since the death-wounds of Christ were visible in His glorified, resurrected body, and this fact is emphasized in the accounts in the Gospel records (Luke 24:40; John 20:20-27), His appearances may have also confirmed the reality of His death. The death and resurrection are so intimately interconnected that even their proofs or evidences cannot be completely separated.

Christ died for our sins	1) First proposition
according to the Scriptures	1a) Scriptural proof
and was buried	1b) Physical proof
He arose	2) Second proposition
according to the Scriptures	2a) Scriptural proof
and was seen	2b) Physical proof[54]

Bing's distinction between the main clauses in verses 3-4 and the subordinate clauses is vital in any attempt to accurately interpret these verses and to determine the contents of saving faith. It has been the consistent Free Grace interpretation of this passage that the elements of Christ's death and resurrection are the essential contents while the burial and appearances are technically not part of the gospel but are the supporting proofs of it. Thus, Earl Radmacher states:

> Sometimes people refer to the gospel as "the death, burial, and resurrection of Jesus Christ." However, the burial of Jesus is not part of the gospel as such. Rather, it is the proof of the death of Christ.[55]

Likewise, Charles Ryrie writes:

> Paul gives us the precise definition of the Gospel we preach today in 1 Corinthians 15:3-8. The Gospel is the good news about the death and resurrection of Christ. *He died and lives—this is the content of the Gospel.* The fact of Christ's burial proves the reality of His death. He did not merely swoon only to be revived later. He actually died and died for our sins. The inclusion of a list of witnesses proves the reality of His resurrection. He died for our sins and was buried (the proof of His death); He rose and was seen by many witnesses, the majority of whom were still alive when Paul wrote 1 Corinthians (the proof of His resurrection). *This same twofold content of the good news appears again in Romans 4:25: He "was delivered up . . . and was raised."* Everyone who believes in that good news is saved, for that truth, and that alone, is the Gospel of the grace of God (1 Corinthians 15:2).[56]

Similarly, evangelical philosopher and theologian, Norman Geisler, sees only Christ's death and resurrection as forming the contents of saving faith in 1 Corinthians 15 rather than the burial and appearances. He states, "The *explicit* conditions of saving faith are Christ's deity, atoning death, and

---

[54] Charles C. Bing, "How to Share the Gospel Clearly," *JOTGES* 7 (Spring 1994): 57.

[55] Radmacher, *Salvation*, 47 (ellipsis added).

[56] Ryrie, *So Great Salvation*, 39 (italics added).

physical resurrection."[57] Geisler then continues addressing these elements of saving faith, saying: "As we have seen, Paul lists each as an inseparable part of the gospel message (1 Cor. 15:1-6; cf. Rom. 10:9), which alone is 'the power of God unto salvation' (Rom. 1:16 KJV). Those who disobey this one and only gospel are lost forever (2 Thess. 1:7-9), and 'if Christ has not been raised, your faith is futile; you are still in your sins' (1 Cor. 15:17)."[58]

Why have respected theologians such as Geisler, Ryrie, and Radmacher identified the death and resurrection of Christ in 1 Corinthians 15 as essential to the saving gospel rather than Christ's burial and appearances? Are they guilty of promoting a "groundless gospel" by not requiring the burial and appearances as some might claim who have rejected the traditional Free Grace position on 1 Corinthians 15?[59] I have even heard some Christians decry in response to the standard Free Grace interpretation of 1 Corinthians 15, "You've taken the burial out of the gospel. You've changed the gospel!" Several practical points of clarification are in order before answering these claims biblically and exegetically from 1 Corinthians 15:1-11.

First, it is quite common for Christians to reference 1 Corinthians 15:3-4 and then state that the gospel is the message that *"Christ died for our sins, was buried, and rose again."* This practice completely neglects any mention of Christ's post-resurrection appearances in verses 5-8. Why is the burial often included while the appearances are omitted? Is it because the burial is part of the gospel but the appearances are not? No, neither are technically elements of the gospel. Is it because the burial is more important than the Lord's post-resurrection appearances? No; of course not. The reason for this practice is undoubtedly due to the fact that verses 3-4 contain the two points that Christians deem essential to the gospel, namely Christ's substitutionary death and bodily resurrection; but since the burial happens to fall in-between these two pillars, it gets included each time this passage is quoted. While this practice is not wrong in itself, and I myself routinely quote it this way, we must also be fully cognizant of the Spirit-inspired syntax of the passage while quoting it. Otherwise, we may misinterpret the passage and draw wrong doctrinal conclusions from it. For instance, without an understanding of its syntax, we may

---

[57] Geisler, *Systematic Theology*, 3:518.

[58] Ibid., 519. Geisler never even *mentions* the burial or post-resurrection appearances in his entire chapter devoted solely to the contents of saving faith. Instead, he repeatedly states without variance Christ's atoning death and bodily resurrection as the explicit elements of saving faith for today (ibid., 527-29, 531-32, 538-39). The fact that Geisler cites 1 Cor. 15:1-6 instead of 1 Cor. 15:3-4 does not necessarily indicate that he believes the appearances in verses 5-6 are required content of saving faith. Charles Ryrie, in the previous quotation cited 1 Cor. 15:3-8, and yet he limits the gospel contained therein to the "twofold content of the good news" of Christ's substitutionary death and bodily resurrection.

[59] Bob Wilkin, "Essential Truths About Our Savior," 2n5; idem, "A Review of J. B. Hixson's *Getting the Gospel Wrong: The Evangelical Crisis No One Is Talking About*," *JOTGES* 21 (Spring 2008): 18n42.

leave the mistaken impression that the burial of Christ is somehow more important than the post-resurrection appearances and therefore verses 5ff can be separated from verses 3-4. The following outline of the passage demonstrates the Spirit-inspired structure of the passage and the grammatical relationship of the four key *hoti* clauses to one another:

15:3 For

I delivered to you first of all that which I also received

that (*hoti*) Christ died for our sins

- according to the Scriptures

15:4 and that (*kai hoti*) He was buried

and that (*kai hoti*) He rose again on the third day[60]

- according to the Scriptures

15:5 and that (*kai hoti*) He was seen

- by Cephas

- then by the twelve

From a purely grammatical perspective, Christ's burial, resurrection, and post-resurrection appearances in verses 5-8 all stand in parallel to the mention of His death in verse 3. To be consistent, Christians must recognize that

---

[60] Opinions among commentators are divided as to whether the phrase *"according to the Scriptures"* qualifies the entire statement, *"and that He rose again the third day"* (William L. Craig, "The Historicity of the Empty Tomb of Jesus," *NTS* 31 [1985]: 42-49; Gerhard Delling, "*τρεῖς, τρίς, τρίτος*," *TDNT*, 8:220; Fee, *The First Epistle to the Corinthians*, 726-28; Kenneth O. Gangel, "According to the Scriptures," *BSac* 125 [April 1968]: 123-28; Robert G. Gromacki, *Called to Be Saints: An Exposition of 1 Corinthians* [Grand Rapids: Baker Book House, 1977], 183; Charles Hodge, *Commentary on the First Epistle to the Corinthians* [Grand Rapids: Eerdmans, 1950], 314; H. K. McArthur, "On the Third Day," *NTS* 18 [1971]: 81-86; Michael Russell, "On the third day, according to the Scriptures," *RTR* 67 [April 2008]: 1-17; J. Wijngaards, "Death and Resurrection in Covenantal Context (Hos. VI 2)," *VT* 17 [1967]: 239), or whether it modifies only the statement about the resurrection, *"and that He rose again"* (Bruce, *Paul: Apostle of the Heart Set Free*, 91-93; Charles J. Ellicott, *St. Paul's First Epistle to the Corinthians: With a Critical and Grammatical Commentary* [Minneapolis: James Family, 1978], 228; Bruce M. Metzger, "A Suggestion Concerning the Meaning of I Cor. XV.4b," *JTS* 8 [1957]: 118-23; Leon Morris, *1 Corinthians*, TNTC [Grand Rapids: Eerdmans, 2000], 202; Sider, "St. Paul's Understanding," 138-39; Eduard Lohse, "*σάββατον, σαββατισμός, παρασκευή*," *TDNT*, 7:29n226; Thiselton, *The First Epistle to the Corinthians*, 1196-97).

the syntactical structure begins with the first "that" (*hoti*) in verse 3 and is then followed by three successive "and that" (*kai hoti*) statements in verses 4-5. This means that from a purely grammatical and syntactical standpoint, there is no reason why this passage should be artificially truncated at the end of verse 4. Even though it may be practical and convenient to include the burial of Christ when quoting the portions dealing with Christ's death and resurrection, it is quite unscriptural for some Christians to insist that the burial is part of the gospel while they simultaneously omit the list of post-resurrection appearances in verses 5-8.[61] Both the burial and appearances are parallel to Christ's death and resurrection according to the syntax of the passage, but this still does not make them elements of the saving gospel as we shall see.

Conceivable Cases of Inconsistent Belief

At this point some might object, "What difference does this make anyway? If people believe Christ rose from the dead, then of course they're going to believe He was seen by witnesses. And if people believe Christ died for their sins, then why wouldn't they also believe He was buried?" It is true that the odds of someone believing in Christ's death and resurrection while rejecting the facts of His burial and appearances are probably less than one in a thousand. The reason for this is obvious. If people are willing to accept the two propositions of greater theological magnitude (the substitutionary death and bodily resurrection of Christ), then why would they reject the two propositions of lesser import (the burial and appearances)? However, Christians can be inconsistent, and thankfully God doesn't require complete theological consistency on our parts in order to be saved.[62] Thus, when seeking to determine the contents of saving faith, we are not considering what is typical for most Christians, or even what is logical, but rather what is divinely required for eternal life according to the Word of God. And on this basis, it is *conceivable* that in rare cases a person could still believe in the essential truths revealed in the gospel, that Christ died for sin and rose again, while not believing in the supporting evidences for these two tenets of the gospel. Though such instances would be patently unbiblical and inconsistent, they must still be admitted as a possibility in rare situations.

Take, for example, the case of a seven year old boy named Billy. Billy believes that Christ died and rose from the dead. He also understands that only Christ's death made satisfaction for his sins and that he cannot

---

[61] Even Newell in his fine commentary on Romans (William R. Newell, *Romans Verse-By-Verse* [Grand Rapids: Kregel, 1994]) written from a grace perspective states variously that the gospel in 1 Corinthians 15 includes Christ's death, burial, resurrection, and appearances (ibid., 5-6, 21) but that the great facts of the gospel concern Christ's death, burial, and resurrection (ibid., 6, 19-20, 49).

[62] Norman Geisler, *Systematic Theology* (Minneapolis: Bethany House, 2004), 3:535.

earn eternal life. Consequently, Billy is resting his eternal destiny upon the finished work of Christ. And why does Billy believe these truths? Because his Christian parents have instructed him about these things, and he has come to have complete confidence in whatever his parents tell him. In other words, Billy has "child-like faith." But this is only true with respect to the word *of his parents* due to their authority and credibility in his life. So, on a particular Sunday at church, Billy hears his Sunday School teacher explain that Jesus was buried in a tomb for three days before He rose from the dead. He's also told that after Jesus rose from the dead He was seen by Peter, James, the 12 apostles, then five hundred disciples, and then by Paul. Yet, Billy doubts whether this is true, as he reasons, "My mom and dad have taught me many things about the Lord, but I've never heard them explain any of that before." Billy continues to reason, "And besides, my Sunday School teacher was wrong last week about the names of the twelve apostles." Is Billy saved or lost?

Take another example. This time it is an adult named Michael Smith. Mr. Smith is a hot-shot young lawyer who is used to arguing on just about any topic with his peers and usually winning the argument. He is very intelligent, but in his flesh, he can also be quite belligerent. At one point in his life, however, Michael is humbled and sees his need for the Lord. He hears about the person and work of Christ and the gift of eternal life promised to all who believe in Jesus Christ, and Michael believes in Jesus as his own personal Savior. As a new believer, Michael scans the Bible and finds the Book of Revelation to be quite captivating, and so he begins to read it with fervor. Not long after starting Revelation, Michael shares his new-found biblical wisdom gained from this fascinating book of the Bible while in the break room at his law firm. Another lawyer, Joe Johnson, has also just become a Christian and he happens to overhear the topic and decides to chime in. In the course of conversation, Joe mentions something about the burial of Christ in a tomb and how it was the custom for *all* Jews in that day to be buried, even for criminals. At this point, Michael's flesh rears its ugly head. Though he was never "churched" growing up and he has yet to read any of the four Gospels or 1 Corinthians, Michael is certain that Joe is wrong on this point. And so with pride in his new found biblical knowledge, Michael objects to Joe's claim that Christ was buried in a tomb before He rose from the dead. After all, everyone knows that burial was *not* the Jewish custom of the day, Michael reasons, as he then proceeds to cite the case of the two Jewish witnesses in Revelation 11:9-11 to prove his point. These two men are holy, and they are prophets, and they rise from the dead after 3.5 days, and yet they were never buried. Joe responds to all of this by reasoning and pleading with Michael, but to no avail. Michael Smith, while affirming the truth of Christ's substitutionary death and bodily resurrection, has just pridefully denied the burial of Christ. So, we must ask, has Michael truly been born again?

Regrettably, the same conversation has now degenerated into an argument. Joe is also functioning out of his fleshly, sinful nature; and with a bit of touché, he retaliates. He contests Michael's point about a 3.5 day interval before the two witnesses of Revelation 11 will rise from the dead. Joe has previously read the Gospel of John and so he is certain that it was the fourth day on which Christ rose from the dead (mixing this detail from Lazarus's resurrection account in John 11:39 with Christ's resurrection in John 20). But Joe is undeterred as he proceeds to reason that since the resurrection of the two witnesses must follow the same pattern and type of Christ's resurrection, and since Christ is the firstfruits of all that follow Him (don't you know!), then the two witnesses must therefore rise on the fourth day just like Christ. At this point, Michael picks up on Joe's chronological error and cannot pass up such a golden opportunity to get ahead in their argument. Michael knows that he has heard somewhere that Jesus rose on the third day, not the fourth day, and so he proceeds to correct Joe. By now, Joe's pride is wounded and he digs his heels just a little deeper and launches into a defense of the "fact" that Christ rose on the "fourth day" because the Gospel of John says so. For good measure, Joe also appeals to an argument from human physiology. He argues (wrongly again!) that it was precisely on the fourth day in which serious decomposition would have set in and that the miracle of the resurrection is magnified even more by a four day interval rather than a three day interval. Even though Joe believes wholeheartedly in Christ's substitutionary death and bodily resurrection and salvation solely by God's grace, he is vociferously denying the truth of 1 Corinthians 15:4 that Christ's resurrection occurred on *"the third day."* So, again we must ask, is Joe saved or lost?

As the preceding comedy of theological errors illustrates, whether it is Joe, Michael, or even the case of young Billy, *it is humanly possible* to believe in Christ's substitutionary death and bodily resurrection while rejecting the facts of His burial, three day interment, and post-resurrection appearances. This means that if the Scriptures reveal that a person is saved by believing the gospel (1 Cor. 4:15; 2 Thess. 1:8-10), and yet a person does not have to believe every detail of 1 Corinthians 15:1-11, then it is manifestly obvious that 1 Corinthians 15 contains more than the gospel.

Believing "Part of" the Gospel?

I have also heard some Christians insist rather indignantly that Christ's burial *must be* part of the gospel while also conceding that a lost person does not have to believe in it for salvation—the lost only have to trust in His atoning death and bodily resurrection. Perhaps without realizing it, these Christians are really saying in effect that a lost person can be saved by believing only *part of* the gospel. But Scripture nowhere endorses such a possibility. In the Bible, people are never said to be saved by believing "part of" the gospel but only by believing "the gospel." According to the New Testament, people either believe the gospel or they don't. To reject it in part is to reject it in whole. It is specious reasoning to insist that the gospel must include Christ's burial but a person doesn't ultimately have to believe it for his or her eternal salvation.

This can be demonstrated by assuming for a moment that the burial of Christ *actually is* part of the gospel. In such a case, this leads us to wonder, "What other parts of the gospel besides the burial can a person not believe and still be saved?" For instance, can a person believe in Christ's resurrection but not His substitutionary death and still be saved? Most evangelical Christians, besides those currently advocating a crossless gospel, would rightly recoil at this prospect. Let's ask ourselves another question. Can a person believe in the facts of Christ's deity, humanity, physical death and resurrection, but not the truth of substitutionary atonement and justification by faith alone, and yet still be born again? If this were true, the Protestant Reformation would have never occurred. Finally, there is a third scenario. Can a person believe in Jesus' humanity and bodily resurrection but not His deity and still be regenerated? The history of Protestant *and even Catholic* interpretation is against such a notion! When people reject these portions of the gospel, they are rightly regarded to be lost because they have not yet believed "the gospel."

The only reasonable, biblical conclusion to come to regarding 1 Corinthians 15 is to view it as containing not only the gospel but also *more than* the saving message of the gospel. As the former Executive Director of the Free Grace Alliance, J. B. Hixson, declares, "The problem with making 1 Corinthians 15 the definitive delimiting of the gospel is that it is too *broad*, not too *narrow*."[63] This conclusion is based not merely on deductive reasoning and hypothetical scenarios but on the biblical evidence from the passage itself. There are at least six biblical, exegetical reasons in support of the normal Free Grace position that 1 Corinthians 15:3-8 contains a definitive articulation of the saving message of the gospel (the person of Christ, His work, the provision and condition of salvation) *in addition to* the evidences for that gospel (burial, post-resurrection appearances). These six reasons will be provided as follows, but not necessarily in order of magnitude or importance.

Reason #1: The Gospel Is Not About Paul and the Other Apostles

The first reason why at least verses 5-10 are technically not part of the gospel is because this would make the gospel a message that revolves around the numerous disciples listed in verses 5-10 rather than a message centered upon the Lord Jesus Himself. Only a few evangelicals are willing

[63] Hixson, "Getting the Gospel Wrong: Case Studies," 48n6.

to press the point that 1 Corinthians 15:1-11 in its entirety is the gospel.[64] In addition, those propagating a crossless saving faith today frequently claim that if the death and resurrection in verses 3-4 are to be considered necessary elements of the gospel then consistency demands that we treat all of verses 3-11 (or at least vv. 3-8) as the gospel. However, as this section will explain, interpreting all of these verses to be the gospel is actually inconsistent and it leads to several strained and rather bizarre conclusions that render such an interpretation completely untenable.

For example, if all of verses 1-11 are the gospel, then this means that the gospel message contains substantial information about the apostle Paul himself, including the fact that he was *"born out of due time"* (v. 8, *ektrōmati*), that he was *"the least of the apostles"* (v. 9a), that he *"persecuted the church of God"* (v. 9b), and that he *"labored more abundantly than"* all the other apostles by God's grace (v. 10). If all of this information about Paul is considered to be part of the gospel, then it constitutes at least as much content, if not more, than about the Lord Jesus Himself in verses 3-4. In 1 Corinthians 15:1-11, Paul has obviously digressed into subpoints, and even sub-subpoints, in order to support the central facts of Christ's death for our sins and His bodily resurrection as the elements of his gospel. It is evident that there has been a digression on Paul's part throughout verses 1-11, so that not all of the content contained in these 11 verses is what he originally had in mind when he first mentioned "the gospel" in verse 1.[65]

Undoubtedly, most Christians will concede that including verses 9-11 in the content of the gospel is over-reaching; but some will still contend that all of verses 5-8 must be part of the gospel since these verses revolve around one theme—the post-resurrection appearances of Christ. It may be reasoned that if the burial in v. 4a supports the fact of Christ's death and this is part of the gospel, and all the witnesses of the resurrection in verses 5-8 form one collective testimony in support of Christ's resurrection, then these verses must also be part of the gospel. However, this would lead to another major interpretative dilemma. In verses 7-8 it says, *"After that He was seen by James, then by all the apostles. Then last of all He was seen by me also, as by one born out of due time."* We know from Galatians 1:11-12 that Paul received the gospel directly from the Lord Jesus Christ. We also know from 1 Corinthians 15:3 that Paul *"delivered"* to the Corinthians *"that which [he] also received."* If Paul delivered to the Corinthians the gospel that he received directly from Christ, and the post-resurrection appearances in verses 5-8 are truly part of the gospel that Paul received during his encounter with the risen Christ on the road to Damascus, then this leads to a gross historical anachronism. It would mean that even the sec-

[64] Harrison, for instance, writes concerning 1 Corinthians 15:1-11 that Paul "does not cease to state the gospel till he reaches the end of v. 11." Everett F. Harrison, "The Son of God Among the Sons of Men Part 15: Jesus and Mary Magdalene," *BSac* 105 (October 1948): 438.

[65] Lambrecht, "Line of Thought in 1 Cor 15,1-11," 665.

tion in verses 8-10 dealing with Paul must be included in the contents of the gospel that Paul received directly from Christ. Imagine the Lord telling Paul about His own appearing to Paul as part of the very gospel that He was currently delivering to Paul right there on the road to Damascus! Such a logical and chronological absurdity requires no refutation.

Furthermore, to insist that the Pauline-centered content of 1 Corinthians 15:8-10 is part of the gospel leads to another historical-theological predicament. If "the gospel" contains content about the apostle Paul, and if according to Acts 8:25 believers in Christ preached "the gospel" prior to Paul's conversion, then this would mean that these early Christians preached a message about Paul before he was even converted in Acts 9! Surely the early disciples did not go around announcing the "good news" that the Lord Jesus would one day appear to rabid, anti-Christian Saul and would make him an apostle who would labor more than all the other apostles of Christ! The traditional Free Grace interpretation of 1 Corinthians 15 that omits the contents of verses 5-8 from the saving gospel is seen to be eminently reasonable and hardly "arbitrary."

Finally, we must consider for a moment the implications if any portion of the witnesses mentioned in verses 5-8 comprise part of the saving gospel. What would this mean with respect to the contents of saving faith? Would this mean that the lost must not only know about the Savior who died for them and rose again (vv. 3-4) but also about each person listed as a witness in verses 5-8? And, as I have heard a few Christians contend, if only some portion of verses 5-8 is part of the gospel (usually just verse 5 in order to include *some* mention of the appearances in the gospel), then isn't this being arbitrary as well? The succession of "then" (*eita*) and "after that" (*epeita*) clauses in verses 5b-7b forms an unbroken, chronological structure just like the syntactically parallel "that" (*hoti*)/"and that" (*kai hoti*) clauses of verses 3b-5a.

If some Christians contend that every detail of verses 3b-5a must be included in the gospel, then it is purely arbitrary and special pleading to argue that only a portion of verses 5-8 is gospel-content. If only verse 5 constitutes the gospel, then why should a person's eternal destiny be dependent upon the reference to Cephas (v. 5) but not to the five hundred brethren (v. 6) or James (v. 7) or Paul (v. 8)? If a lost soul only heard the good news about Jesus Christ but never heard of Peter, Paul, James, the twelve, or the five hundred, would that person be lost for eternity due to lack of sufficient information? This would nullify the salvation of a vast percentage of God's children in the world today, many of whom cannot even identify the individual in verse 5 with the Aramaic name "Cephas." Likewise, many cannot specify which biblical "James" is being referred to in verse 7. For that matter, the reference to the "five hundred brethren" in verse 6 occurs only here in the entire Bible. If a person believed every word of the other 65 books of the Bible but didn't possess a copy of

1 Corinthians, would that person be lost for eternity? Perish the thought! It should be apparent to any unbiased student of Scripture that people are not saved by believing a message about Peter, Paul, James, or any other follower of Christ. They are saved by believing the truth about Jesus Christ Himself which is the gospel message. Once a person insists that the gospel extends through verse 5, presumably to have *some* post-resurrection appearances included in their gospel, then the gospel becomes a man-centered message, a saving message at least about Cephas and the twelve and possibly others.

Reason #2: Extra-Gospel Tradition ≠ Gospel Revelation

There is a second reason why the Lord's burial and appearances are technically not the gospel but are the corroborating evidences of the gospel. This reason is also a bit more complex than the other five, and consequently it will require a lengthier treatment. This reason essentially revolves around the interpretation of the term "received" in 1 Corinthians 15:3 and Galatians 1:12. If all of the information in 1 Corinthians 15:3-8 is "the gospel," then this means that Paul "received" this information directly from the Lord Jesus when He appeared to him on the Damascus Road, since Paul declares in Galatians 1:11-12 that he "received" the gospel directly from Christ without any human mediary. This would mean that all of the information in verses 5-8 about Peter, the twelve, the five hundred brethren, James, and even Paul himself(!) came directly from Jesus Christ. But none of the biographical sections of Scripture detailing Paul's conversion (Acts 9:1-8; 22:1-21; 26:1-8; Gal. 1:12-16; Phil. 3:4-9) mention or even imply anything about the burial of Christ or the many post-resurrection appearances. As other commentators have correctly noted,[66] it seems far-fetched to view Paul as receiving this additional information directly from the Lord Jesus on the Damascus Road. It would be simply untenable to view this additional information in 1 Corinthians 15:5-8 as either forming a second gospel or as being part of a broader, expanded form of the gospel,[67] for that would contradict the whole intent of Galatians 1:6-12.

It is more consistent with Scripture, therefore, to recognize that 1 Corinthians 15:1-11 is not part and parcel with the gospel but is a broader message than the gospel. It *contains* the gospel, but it also contains information *supplemental* to, and supportive of, the gospel. According to this interpretation, the *gospel* in 1 Corinthians 15 is the message that Paul received via *divine revelation* directly from the Lord Jesus on the road to Damascus, whereas the details in 1 Corinthians 15 that are *supplemental*

---

[66] F. F. Bruce, *Tradition Old and New* (Exeter, England: Paternoster Press, 1970), 31; Fee, *The First Epistle to the Corinthians*, 722; Ronald Y. K. Fung, "Revelation and Tradition: the Origins of Paul's Gospel," *EvQ* 57 (January 1985): 38n57.

[67] Knox Chamblin, "Revelation and Tradition in the Pauline *Euangelion*," *WTJ* 48.1 (Spring 1986): 2-3.

to the gospel were received by Paul via *human agency*, most likely passed down to him through word of mouth from the other apostles and eye-witnesses of Christ.

Most New Testament scholars and commentators[68] are now convinced that in verses 3-8, or some portion thereof, Paul is reciting what has been variously described as an early Christian creed, confession, kerygmatic formula or preaching outline, or tradition.[69] Or, it may be that Paul is simply summarizing the content of his previous preaching that contained the gospel but in the form of a series of propositional declarations.[70] If 1 Corinthians 15:3ff is in fact some sort of confessional, creedal statement, then it is impossible to determine with certainty whether it is pre-Pauline in origin and usage or whether Paul himself created it[71] on the occasion of writing this epistle in order to summarize his initial preaching to the Corinthians. Most interpreters opt for the first scenario—that the confessional statement of vv. 3ff is "pre-Pauline" and was devised extremely early in Church history, possibly within five years or less of Christ's death and resurrection.[72] Regardless, the interpretation that sees vv. 3ff as form-

---

[68] Henry Alford, *The Greek Testament* (Chicago: Moody Press, 1958), 2:603; Bruce, *Paul: Apostle of the Heart Set Free*, 84-94; Carroll and Green, "'Nothing but Christ and Him Crucified': Paul's Theology of the Cross," 119; Demarest, *The Cross and Salvation*, 174; Denney, *The Death of Christ*, 67; Fee, *The First Epistle to the Corinthians*, 721-22; idem, *Pauline Christology*, 533; Garland, *1 Corinthians*, 683-84; Godet, *Commentary on First Corinthians*, 758; George Eldon Ladd, "Revelation and Tradition in Paul," in *Apostolic History and the Gospel: Biblical and Historical Essays Presented to F. F. Bruce on His 60th Birthday*, ed. W. Ward Gasque and Ralph P. Martin (Grand Rapids: Eerdmans, 1970), 225; idem, *A Theology of the New Testament*, Revised edition, ed. Donald A. Hagner (Grand Rapids: Eerdmans, 1993), 427; J. Gresham Machen, *The Origin of Paul's Religion* (New York: Macmillan, 1936), 19; Spallek, "The Origin and Meaning of *Εὐαγγέλιον*," 184, 187; Gustav Stählin, "'On the Third Day': The Easter Tradition of the Primitive Church," *Int* 10 (July 1956): 294; Thiselton, *The First Epistle to the Corinthians*, 1186-88; Randall C. Webber, "A Note on 1 Corinthians 15:3-5," *JETS* 26 (September 1983): 265-69.

[69] I do not prefer the term "tradition" since it can be easily confused with the Roman Catholic notion of "Sacred Tradition" which is supposedly another source of divine revelation in addition to "Sacred Scripture." I have retained the term "tradition" here, however, due to the frequency with which it is employed even by evangelicals in the literature dealing with this passage and subject. It should be recognized that in the New Testament, the term "tradition" (*paradosis*) sometimes refers to religious beliefs that are of human origin and that are anti-scriptural (Matt. 15:3, 6; Mark 7:8-9, 13; Gal. 1:14; Col. 2:8), while sometimes it is used of doctrines or teaching that became part of the revelation of Scripture itself (1 Cor. 11:2, 23; 2 Thess. 2:15; 3:6), as here in 1 Corinthians 15 with the burial and appearances. It is in this latter sense that the term "tradition" is employed in this chapter.

[70] If this was Paul's own "confession" or even a "confession" shared by the other apostles, this would not necessitate it being used ritualistically among the early Christians. Though many churches historically have recited the Apostles' Creed or Nicene Creed as part of their liturgy, this is a very poor substitute for biblical exposition and instruction directly from God's Word.

[71] Garland, *1 Corinthians*, 684; Lambrecht, "Line of Thought in 1 Cor 15,1-11," 661.

[72] Craig, "The Historicity of the Empty Tomb of Jesus," 39; MacGregor, "1 Corinthians 15:3b-6a, 7," 226.

ing some sort of early creed or confessional statement certainly has some merit due to the terminology and structure of the passage.

The fact that the conjunction *hoti* ("that") in v. 3b is followed by three successive *kai hoti* ("and that") statements may point to a direct quotation or recitation here by Paul. Since Koine Greek had little if any punctuation, *hoti* occasionally served the purpose of introducing direct discourse and functioning as a virtual quotation mark.[73] The translation of certain passages in modern English Bibles reflects this fact (Luke 4:11; 7:16; Acts 14:22; 17:3).[74] The likelihood that Paul is providing a quotation or recitation in vv. 3ff is not based only on the occurrence of *hoti* in verse 3 but also on the scarcity with which similar *kai hoti* constructions are employed in the Greek literature of the same period. The repetition and coordinate syntactical structure of *three* successive *kai hoti* clauses is nearly unparalleled in the Koine literature.[75] Paul is doing something very unusual, therefore, in 1 Corinthians 15:3ff.

It is also worth noting that Paul's list of eyewitnesses for the resurrection in verses 5-8 is both structured and selective, which would be consistent with these verses forming a confessional statement or formal declaration of some kind. Verses 5-8 are built upon the sequence of appearances, as is evident from the repetition of "then" (*eita*) and "after that" (*epeita*).[76] The chronological ordering of appearances starts in verse 5 with Peter who saw Christ before the rest of the apostles (Luke 24:34-36). Next, verses 6-7 specify that the Lord appeared to the five hundred brethren and then to James, but these events are not mentioned elsewhere in Scripture. Then in verses 7b-8 the appearances to the apostles are mentioned again, followed by Christ's final appearance to Paul.

Besides the evident sequential structure of verses 5-8, the actual eyewitnesses in this list appear to be deliberately chosen as well. It is not a complete record of everyone who saw the risen Savior. For example, we know that several others who are documented in Scripture did not make the list, such as Mary Magdalene (Mark 16:9-11; John 20:11-18), the group of women (Matt. 28:9-10), and the two disciples on the road to Emmaus (Mark 16:12-13; Luke 24:13-33). It appears significant that only men are

---

[73] BDF, 246-47, §470; H. E. Dana and Julius R. Mantey, *A Manual Grammar of the Greek New Testament* (New York: Macmillan, 1955), 252, §222; Jerome Murphy-O'Connor, "Tradition and Redaction in 1 Cor 15:3-7," *CBQ* 43 (1981): 584; A. T. Robertson, *A Grammar of the Greek New Testament in the Light of Historical Research* (Nashville: Broadman Press, 1934), 1027-28; Thiselton, *The First Epistle to the Corinthians*, 1189; Turner, *Syntax*, 325-26; Daniel B. Wallace, *Greek Grammar Beyond the Basics: An Exegetical Syntax of the New Testament* (Grand Rapids: Zondervan, 1996), 454-55.

[74] See also 2 Clement 2:4; Ignatius, *Philadelphians*, 8:2.

[75] The only comparable example that I am aware of where a Koine writer uses three or more successive *kai hoti* clauses to set forth a series of propositions is Philo of Alexandria in his *On the Creation*, 172.

[76] Borchert, *The Resurrection*, 404.

included in the list of witnesses in 1 Corinthians 15:5-8. Paul certainly would have been aware of the fact that the testimony of women in 1st century Jewish culture was not deemed admissible as evidence,[77] and he may have written accordingly in order to suit this cultural situation without being sympathetic to it. This low regard for the testimony of women is even displayed by the eleven apostles towards the godly women who first testified to having witnessed the risen Lord, as Luke accurately reports their attitude of condescension, *"And their words seemed to them like idle tales, and they did not believe them"* (Luke 24:11). These facts fit with the conclusion that the male-only appearances in 1 Corinthians 15:5-8 constitute the supporting *evidence* for the gospel in verses 3-4 rather than forming part of the gospel itself. This would also be consistent with these verses being part of a formal creed or confessional statement that may have circulated among the early churches of a very patriarchal society.

If indeed Paul is reciting an early Church confession containing not only the gospel but also the corroborating evidence for the gospel that was passed down to him from the other apostles and disciples, then this would also fit the language in the passage about receiving and delivering. In verse 3, Paul writes, *"For I delivered (paredōka) to you that which I also received (parelabon)."* Lexical and philological research has confirmed that the root words for "deliver" (*paradidōmi*) and "receive" (*paralambanō*) sometimes refer to the transmission and reception of tradition, even with the sense of doctrinal instruction that is handed down either orally or in writing. *Paradidōmi* is sometimes used for the *transmitting* of tradition,[78] while *paralambanō* is sometimes used for the *receiving* of tradition.[79] There is a near consensus of opinion among New Testament scholarship that Paul is using these terms in 1 Corinthians 15:3 with the sense of receiving and passing on traditional material or doctrine, most likely in the form of a creed or confession.[80]

These terms are also used in 1 Corinthians 11 where Paul is receiving instruction about the Lord's Supper and transmitting it faithfully to the Corinthians. In language nearly identical to 1 Corinthians 15:3, Paul

---

[77] Craig, "The Historicity of the Empty Tomb of Jesus," 58, 66n83.

[78] BDAG, 762-63; LSJ, 1308.

[79] BDAG, 768; LSJ, 1315; J. H. Thayer, ed., *The New Thayer's Greek-English Lexicon of the New Testament* (Peabody, MA: Hendrickson Publishers, 1981), 484.

[80] William Baird, "What Is the Kerygma? A Study of 1 Cor 15:3-8 and Gal 1:11-17," *JBL* 76 (1957): 186-87; Borchert, "The Resurrection," 401; Conzelmann, "On the Analysis of the Confessional Formula," 18n18; Fee, *The First Epistle to the Corinthians*, 548, 721; Garland, *1 Corinthians*, 683; Joachim Jeremias, *The Eucharistic Words of Jesus*, trans. Norman Perrin (New York: Charles Scribner's Sons, 1966), 101-2; J. N. D. Kelly, *Early Christian Creeds*, 3rd Edition (New York: Continuum International, 2006), 17; Seyoon Kim, *The Origin of Paul's Gospel* (Tübingen: J. C. B. Mohr, 1981), 67-68; Kloppenborg, "An Analysis of the Pre-Pauline Formula 1 Cor 15:3b5," 351; Machen, *The Origin of Paul's Religion*, 144-45; MacGregor, "1 Corinthians 15:3b-6a, 7," 226; Sider, "St. Paul's Understanding," 133; Thiselton, *The First Epistle to the Corinthians*, 862, 1186-88; Webber, "A Note on 1 Corinthians 15:3-5," 266.

writes, *"For I (egō gar) received (parelabon) from the Lord that which I also delivered (paredōka) to you"* (1 Cor. 11:23). The use of these terms in this passage is consistent with the interpretation that in 15:3 Paul is combining in the term "received" (*parelabon*) two different *sources* of doctrine (Christ plus the other apostles/disciples) and two different doctrinal *contents* (the gospel plus the proofs of the gospel). This means that Paul is using the term "received" (*parelabon*) in 1 Corinthians 15:3 in a general, flexible sense, that encompasses both the evidences for the gospel passed on to him by other early Christians and the revelation of the gospel itself that he received directly from Christ.[81]

This encompassing usage of the word "received" (*parelabon*) can also be observed in 1 Corinthians 11:23 with respect to Paul's doctrine about the Lord's Supper. The source for Paul's instruction about the Lord's Supper may have been twofold. On the one hand, 1 Corinthians 11:24-25 repeats information that is shared by the Synoptic accounts in Matthew 26:26-29 and Mark 14:22-25.[82] Knowledge of these general details about the Lord's Supper was apparently the common property of all believers in the early Church even prior to the writing of Matthew and Mark, and Paul would have quickly acquired this traditional ("passed down") information as soon as he broke bread with the other apostles and disciples. On the other hand, 1 Corinthians 11:24-25 also contains precise revelatory content on the Lord's Supper that is uniquely Pauline. In 1 Corinthians 11:24b and 25b, the words of the Lord Jesus are quoted where He states, *"Do this in remembrance of Me."* Though the early Church certainly believed in the memorial view of the Lord's Supper before Paul ever became a Christian, these precise words attributed to the Lord Jesus are not found in either Matthew or Mark but conspicuously appear only in Luke's Gospel (Luke 22:19). We know that the third Gospel would have been heavily influenced by Paul since Luke accompanied him in their missionary travels (Acts 16:10-17; 20:5-15; 21:1-18; 27:1-28:16). The resulting question, therefore, is, "Where did Paul get this direct quotation of Christ that is found only in Luke 22:19 and 1 Corinthians 11:24b and 25b?" This leads us back to 1 Corinthians 11:23.

One interpretative problem in this verse that has long perplexed commentators is the matter of what Paul meant by receiving his doctrine about the Lord's Supper "from the Lord." Does this mean that Paul received it *directly* from the Lord via divine revelation without any human intermediary?[83] Or, does it mean that it was passed down to him by the other apostles and disciples and thus it came "from the Lord" in an *ulti-*

---

[81] Gangel, "According to the Scriptures," 124; Godet, *Commentary on First Corinthians*, 758.

[82] The Gospel of John does not address the Lord's Supper.

[83] Godet, *Commentary on First Corinthians*, 575-77; Gromacki, *Called to Be Saints*, 142; Hodge, *Commentary on the First Epistle to the Corinthians*, 221-23; Vine, "1 Corinthians," 2:79-80.

mate sense?[84] Or, is there a third option? It is possible that Paul uniquely "received" (*parelabon*) the Lord's *"Do this in remembrance of Me"* quotation *directly* "from the Lord" (1 Cor. 11:23) via an immediate revelation and then he passed it on to Luke, the Corinthians, and other Christians.[85] If this is the case, then Paul would have "received" (*parelabon*) the broader details about the Lord's Supper in 1 Corinthians 11:24-25, Matthew 26, and Mark 14 that were commonly known among early Christians "from the Lord" in an *ultimate* sense as they were passed down via word of mouth from the other apostles and disciples. One difficulty with this possible scenario, however, is that it seems unlikely that the other apostles did not also pass down to other Christians the exact words of the Lord Jesus that they heard at the Last Supper, *"Do this in remembrance of Me."*

It is possible that Paul uses *parelabon* in 1 Corinthians 11:23 in a broad, general sense to indicate the reception of divine truth that was passed down to him from other Christians but which ultimately came from the Lord. It is also possible that *parelabon* in 11:23 has a broad, general sense that encompasses two *sources* of doctrinal truth (the Lord Jesus and the apostles/other disciples) in addition to two *contents* of doctrinal truth (immediate divine revelation and early Church teaching/tradition). Either perspective of "received" (*parelabon*) in 1 Corinthians 11:23 would fit with the interpretation of 1 Corinthians 15:3ff that sees Paul receiving (*parelabon*) not only the gospel but also the evidences for the gospel. In 1 Corinthians 15, Paul would then be declaring both the gospel that he received via direct revelation from Christ plus the supporting evidences for that gospel which he would have received through the other apostles and eyewitnesses of the risen Savior. If this interpretation is correct, it harmonizes with the only other Pauline use of *parelabon*.

In Galatians 1:11-12, Paul states unequivocally that he received his gospel by revelation that came only from Jesus Christ and not from any other man. He writes, *"But I make known to you, brethren, that the gospel which was preached by me is not according to man (anthrōpon). For I neither received (parelabon) it from man (anthrōpou), nor was I taught it, but it came through the revelation (apokalupseōs) of Jesus Christ."* Before examining this verse in light of the contents of saving faith, we must first ask, "Is this passage referring to the source of Paul's gospel or to the object of his gospel?" Some interpreters insist that the revelation *"of Jesus Christ"* in verse 12 should be viewed as an objective genitive since Christ was clearly the

---

[84] Fee, *The First Epistle to the Corinthians*, 548; Garland, *1 Corinthians*, 545; S. Lewis Johnson, "The First Epistle to the Corinthians," in *The Wycliffe Bible Commentary*, ed. Everett F. Harrison (Chicago: Moody Press, 1962), 1248; Thiselton, *The First Epistle to the Corinthians*, 866-68.

[85] This is certainly possible since the Lord appeared to Paul several times after the Damascus Road experience in Acts 9 and gave him revelation on each of these occasions as well (Acts 18:9-10; 22:17-21; 23:11; 2 Cor. 12:1-9; Gal. 2:2).

object of revelation to Paul according to Galatians 1:16. There Paul states that it was God's sovereign plan *"to reveal His Son in me."*[86] While it is certainly true that the *object* of revelation given to Paul was the Son of God, the more immediate context of Galatians 1:11-12 contrasts the divine versus human *origin* of Paul's gospel. This would support more favorably a subjective genitive. But in the end, since Jesus Christ was both the source and content of Paul's gospel, we should not be forced to pick sides. The phrase "of Jesus Christ" in Galatians 1:12 is best interpreted as being both an objective and subjective genitive.[87]

It is clear from Galatians 1:11-12 that Paul received the gospel only from one source—Jesus Christ—not men. However, Paul is not so specific in 1 Corinthians 15:3 where he refers only to *"that which I received"* rather than "the gospel that I received." This allows for a broadened sense of *parelabon* in 15:3 that includes both the gospel and the extra-gospel evidences of the burial and post-resurrection appearances.

When comparing Galatians 1:11-12 with 1 Corinthians 15:3, there are essentially four interpretative possibilities: (1) every detail of 1 Corinthians 15:3ff is part and parcel with the gospel that Paul received from the Lord on the Damascus Road. Thus, in 15:3 Paul is reciting verbatim the gospel that he received directly from the Lord according to Galatians 1:12. This interpretation sees no distinction between the use of *parelabon* in 1 Corinthians 15:3 and Galatians 1:12.[88] The problem with this rather wooden interpretation is that, if it is true, we should expect to find *somewhere* in Paul's conversion accounts in Acts 9, 22, and 26 a verbatim recitation of the exact confession found in 1 Corinthians 15:3ff; but obviously we don't. (2) Paul knows all the details of 15:3ff before the Damascus Road encounter through his pre-conversion contacts with the Christians that he persecuted. In this case, Christ's appearance to Paul would have confirmed in an instant each bit of information that he previously knew but hadn't believed. According to this view, Paul would only be saying in Galatians 1:12 that he was not dependent upon any man to know whether the gospel is true. (3) Paul received the gospel itself directly from Jesus Christ (Gal. 1:12) but then learned all the supporting evidence for the gospel later from the other apostles and brethren and

---

[86] Bruce, *Paul: Apostle of the Heart Set Free*, 87n11; Ernest De Witt Burton, *A Critical and Exegetical Commentary on the Epistle to the Galatians*, ICC (Edinburgh: T & T Clark, reprinted 1988), 41-43; Chamblin, "Revelation and Tradition in the Pauline *Euangelion*," 6; Timothy J. Ralston, "The Theological Significance of Paul's Conversion," *BSac* 147 (April 1990): 203.

[87] Nigel Turner offers a balanced perspective on the objective vs. subjective genitive, explaining, "There is much ambiguity here in NT interpretation. Often a genitive might equally well be subjective or objective: it is moreover important not to sacrifice fullness of interpretation to an over precise analysis of syntax. There is no reason why a genitive in the author's mind may not have been both subjective and objective." Turner, *Syntax*, 210.

[88] Gromacki, *Called to Be Saints*, 182; Hodge, *Commentary on the First Epistle to the Corinthians*, 312; Vine, "1 Corinthians," 2:79, 105.

then recited it all together in the form of the confessional statement in 1 Corinthians 15:3ff.[89] (4) The fourth, and most likely, scenario combines elements of views #2 and #3. Paul probably knew the main claims of early Christians about the person and work of Christ even before his personal encounter with Christ. But he did not believe these elements of the gospel to be true, nor did he comprehend what these meant for his own salvation, until that great revelatory moment on the way to Damascus.

There can be no doubt that in his pre-conversion days as a Pharisee and persecutor of Christians, Saul of Tarsus was knowledgeable about the sect that he worked so feverishly to stamp-out and of the basic facts about Jesus of Nazareth.[90] Prior to his Damascus Road conversion, Paul's mind was no *tabula rasa* when it came to the general message (*kērugma*) being proclaimed by the early Christians.[91] He certainly would have known the claims of Jesus' followers that this Man had died a substitutionary death and risen from the dead and was Lord of all and the Son of God. This can be reasonably deduced from the fact that he participated in capital trials against believers in Christ (Acts 26:10) where he forced believers to renounce the faith that they confessed and thus to commit blasphemy (Acts 26:11).[92] Of course, Paul did not believe that Jesus was truly the risen Son of God until he had his life-transforming encounter with the Lord of glory (Acts 9). He surely did not grasp or believe the spiritual significance of Jesus' death and resurrection prior to this moment,[93] since he was spiritually proud and blind and trying to earn his justification before God by his meritorious law-keeping. But in a flash, Paul's prideful unbelief was shattered. His rejection of Christ turned to reception the instant he first believed. Seeing and hearing the risen Christ persuaded Paul of the truthfulness of the Lord's resurrection and all that it indicated, including the Lord's deity.[94] This would have immediately verified for Paul the witness of all the Christians he tortured and persecuted. It would have confirmed the witness of that great prophet and contemporary of Paul, namely John the Baptist, that Jesus was in fact the Lamb of God who took away the sin of the world. It would have confirmed the Lord Jesus' own claims to be the sacrificial sin-bearer for the salvation of all who believe in

---

[89] Baird, "What Is the Kerygma?" 191; Fung, "Revelation and Tradition," 38-40; Kim, *The Origin of Paul's Gospel*, 69-70.

[90] Baird, "What Is the Kerygma?" 189; Knox Chamblin, "Revelation and Tradition in the Pauline *Euangelion*," *WTJ* 48.1 (Spring 1986): 8; Kim, *The Origin of Paul's Gospel*, 51, 102-4; Machen, *The Origin of Paul's Religion*, 76, 145-46; Ralston, "The Theological Significance of Paul's Conversion," 214-15; Spallek, "The Origin and Meaning of *Εὐαγγέλιον*," 184.

[91] Kim, *The Origin of Paul's Gospel*, 103-4.

[92] Ralston, "The Theological Significance of Paul's Conversion," 209.

[93] Alford, *The Greek Testament*, 2:602; Chamblin, "Revelation and Tradition in the Pauline *Euangelion*," 9; Garland, *1 Corinthians*, 684.

[94] Ralston, "The Theological Significance of Paul's Conversion," 212.

Him.[95] And even the truth that justification is solely by God's grace would have been correctly inferred by Paul from the fact that the Lord commissioned him, a persecutor of the Church no less, to be His apostle and to proclaim to the Gentiles forgiveness of sins through faith in Him (Acts 26:18). Prior to this pivotal moment in Paul's life, the information he heard from Christians was nothing but a *skandalon* and foolishness (1 Cor. 1:23), but now in one defining moment, it personally became the power of God unto salvation for him.[96]

But how does all of this fit with 1 Corinthians 15:3ff and Galatians 1:11-12? Most commentators and theologians accept the theory that in 1 Corinthians 15:3-8 Paul is merely articulating an early form of an apostolic *kērugma*, creed, confession, or tradition that was handed down to him by Peter, James, and the other apostles.[97] If this is true, then this handing down or delivering of information (1 Cor. 15:3, "delivered," *paredōka*) would most likely have transpired during Paul's two-week visit to Jerusalem to meet the esteemed pillars, Peter and James the Lord's half-brother (Gal. 1:18-19).[98] On the occasion of such an important meeting

---

[95] Jacques Dupont, "The Conversion of Paul, and Its Influence on His Understanding of Salvation by Faith," in *Apostolic History and the Gospel: Biblical and Historical Essays Presented to F. F. Bruce on His 60th Birthday*, ed. W. Ward Gasque and Ralph P. Martin (Grand Rapids: Eerdmans, 1970), 194; Fung, "Revelation and Tradition," 26-30; Seyoon Kim, *Paul and the New Perspective: Second Thoughts on the Origin of Paul's Gospel* (Grand Rapids: Eerdmans, 2002), 45-52; Ralston, "The Theological Significance of Paul's Conversion," 207-12.

[96] Baird, "What Is the Kerygma?" 189.

[97] Alford, *The Greek Testament*, 2:603; Bruce, *Paul: Apostle of the Heart Set Free*, 84-94; Carroll and Green, "'Nothing but Christ and Him Crucified': Paul's Theology of the Cross," 119; Denney, *The Death of Christ*, 67; Fee, *The First Epistle to the Corinthians*, 721-722; idem, *Pauline Christology*, 533; Garland, *1 Corinthians*, 683-84; Godet, *Commentary on First Corinthians*, 758; Ladd, "Revelation and Tradition in Paul," 225; idem, *A Theology of the New Testament*, Revised edition, ed. Donald A. Hagner (Grand Rapids: Eerdmans, 1993), 427; Machen, *The Origin of Paul's Religion*, 19; Spallek, "The Origin and Meaning of Εὐαγγέλιον," 184, 187; Stählin, "'On the Third Day'," 294; Webber, "A Note on 1 Corinthians 15:3-5," 265-69.

[98] Baird, "What Is the Kerygma?" 190; William Lane Craig, "Did Jesus Rise from the Dead?" in *Jesus Under Fire: Modern Scholarship Reinvents the Historical Jesus*, ed. Michael J. Wilkins and J. P. Moreland (Grand Rapids: Zondervan, 1995), 147, 149, 153-56; Fung, "Revelation and Tradition," 40n64; Godet, *Commentary on First Corinthians*, 758; Gary R. Habermas, *The Historical Jesus: Ancient Evidence for the Life of Christ* (Joplin, MO: College Press, 1996), 155-56; Martin Hengel and Anna Maria Schwemer, *Paul Between Damascus and Antioch: The Unknown Years*, trans. John Bowden (Louisville: Westminster John Knox, 1997), 44, 290; MacGregor, "1 Corinthians 15:3b-6a, 7," 226-27; Sider, "St. Paul's Understanding," 133; Margaret E. Thrall, "The Origin of Pauline Christology," in *Apostolic History and the Gospel: Biblical and Historical Essays Presented to F. F. Bruce on His 60th Birthday*, ed. W. Ward Gasque and Ralph P. Martin (Grand Rapids: Eerdmans, 1970), 308. A few scholars believe that instead of Paul being handed this information during his visit to Jerusalem, he "received" (*parelabon*) it immediately following his conversion from the disciples in Damascus (Craig, "The Historicity of the Empty Tomb of Jesus," 39; William C. Robinson, *Christ the Hope of Glory* [Grand Rapids: Eerdmans, 1947], 146). But this view appears doubtful, especially for those who maintain that the entirety of 1 Corinthians 15:3ff is the precise gospel. If the confessional statement in 15:3ff was given to Paul within the first week of his conversion by believers in

between these great leaders, we can be sure that "they did not spend all the time talking about the weather."[99] Certainly they shared their testimonies of having seen the risen Christ, which in fact was a qualification to be an apostle (1 Cor. 9:1). It is not a coincidence, therefore, that Peter and James figure prominently in the list of post-resurrection witnesses in 1 Corinthians 15:5-7.

Beyond the mutually held belief that *"Christ died for our sins"* and *"rose again,"* this fifteen day meeting of early Church leaders would certainly have included the details of the post-resurrection appearances to Peter, James, the other apostles, and the five hundred brethren.[100] Though Paul may have known some of these details before his Damascus Road experience from the testimonies of persecuted Christians, it is doubtful that he knew all of these details or even the precise chronology laid out in 1 Corinthians 15. It is reasonable, therefore, to conclude from all of this historical background information that in 1 Corinthians 15:3ff Paul is going beyond an enunciation of the gospel itself to a fuller explanation of the gospel *plus* its supporting evidences.

This is hardly a novel interpretation among proponents of "traditional" Free Grace theology. In fact, it is the position commonly held by those conservative evangelical writers who address the connection between 1 Corinthians 15 and Galatians 1. For example, notice carefully what J. Gresham Machen states about this very subject in his classic defense of the divine origin of Paul's gospel:

> Bare detailed information about the words and deeds of Jesus did not in Paul's mind constitute a "gospel"; they constituted only the materials upon which the gospel was based. When he says, therefore, that he did not receive his gospel from men he does not mean that he received no information from Peter or Barnabas or Mark or James or the five hundred brethren who had seen the risen Lord. What he does mean is that he himself was convinced of the decisive fact—the fact of the resurrection—not by the testimony of these men, but by the divine interposition on the road to Damascus, and that none of these men told him how he himself was to be saved or what he was to say to the Gentiles about the way of salvation. *Materials for the proof of his gospel might come to*

Damascus, and everything in 15:3ff is truly the gospel, then this would conflict with Paul's statement in Galatians 1:16b where, after he received the gospel directly from Christ, he declares, *"I did not immediately (eutheōs) confer with flesh and blood."*

[99] C. H. Dodd, *The Apostolic Preaching and Its Developments* (London: Hodder & Stoughton, 1936), 16. It is also doubtful that Paul was handed this information by Barnabas and Silas/Silvanus, Paul's missionary partners (as proposed by Garland, *1 Corinthians*, 683n3), since this would have occurred several years after Paul's two-week meeting with Peter and James and it is inconceivable that either of these men would not have shared with Paul their testimonies of having seen the risen Savior.

[100] Bruce, *Paul*, 91-93.

> *him from ordinary sources of information, but his gospel itself was given to him directly by Christ.*[101]

Notice that when referring to the extra information in 1 Corinthians 15 that was passed down to Paul from other Christian men, Machen distinguishes between the *"proof of his gospel"* and *"his gospel itself."* This accords well with the fact that in 1 Corinthians 15:1, Paul specifically mentions "the gospel." But in verse 3, he does not say, "For I delivered to you the *gospel* that I also received." Rather, by saying, "I delivered to you *that which* I also received," Paul recites in confessional fashion a conflation of two different contents from two different sources—the gospel that he received directly from Christ (Gal. 1:12-16) and the supporting evidences that he received from other Christians including Peter and James (1 Cor. 15:5-7). Consistent with this distinction between the gospel itself and its evidences, the president of the Chafer Theological Seminary (a non-crossless Free Grace school) recently stated, "1 Corinthians 15 contains an adequate gospel message enabling one to be born again."[102] The operative word here is, of course, "contains." The gospel is contained within 1 Corinthians 15:1-11 but not all of 1 Corinthians 15:1-11 is the gospel.[103]

If this distinction between the gospel and its supporting evidences is denied, then this inescapably results in a gospel message that emphasizes Christ's post-resurrection appearances (vv. 5-8) more than His death and resurrection (vv. 3-4). This leads us to ask, when Paul originally preached the gospel to the Corinthians, was this really the emphasis of his evangelism? Is Paul in verses 5-8 really continuing to explain the gospel that these Corinthians originally "received" (v. 1) and "believed" (v. 2)? The reason so much emphasis is placed on the appearances is simple. It is because some of the Corinthians were currently denying the fact of resurrection itself when Paul wrote to them (v. 12). In anticipation of the following section in verses 12-19, Paul says in effect, "If you Corinthians want to deny the veracity of resurrection itself, then how do you escape the fact that I and so many others have actually seen One who has risen from the dead?"

After recounting the many witnesses to Christ's resurrection in verses 5-8, Paul concludes this literary unit of verses 1-11 by saying, *"Therefore, whether it was I or they, so (houtōs) we preach and so (houtōs) you believed"* (1 Cor. 15:11). The adverb "so" (*houtōs*) is used twice; and it is emphatic in the Greek sentence. *Houtōs* here does not indicate the communicative *manner* by which Paul and the other apostles preached but the *content*

[101] Machen, *The Origin of Paul's Religion*, 146-47 (italics added).

[102] George E. Meisinger, "The Gospel Paul Preached: A Church Age Model of Evangelistic Content," Chafer Theological Seminary Pastors Conference, Houston, TX, March 11, 2009.

[103] Thus Spallek even speaks of "the revealed gospel [being] contained in the traditional formula" of 1 Corinthians 15:3-8. See Spallek, "The Origin and Meaning of *Εὐαγγέλιον*," 186.

of their preaching, namely the resurrection of Christ.[104] The next verse, 1 Corinthians 15:12, confirms this, *"Now if Christ is preached that He has been raised from the dead, how do some among you say..."* What message had Peter, Paul, and James all uniformly[105] preached? One would think that if the post-resurrection appearances of verses 5-8 were really meant by Paul as being part of his "gospel," a summary statement about Christ being "seen" would be issued in verses 11-12. But Paul doesn't do this. Instead, he summarizes by saying in essence, "So we preach the resurrection." Verses 11-12 clearly delineate the resurrection as the main point of the apostles' preaching in the preceding 11 verses in distinction to the appearances which are subservient[106] to the resurrection and have "a confirmatory function" regarding its reality and validity.[107]

This is true even with respect to the burial and Christ's death in verses 3-4. The mention of the burial in verse 4 is subservient to Christ's death in verse 3 by proving the reality of His death. By including this, Paul added validity to his primary point in 1 Corinthians 15, namely, that Christ really did rise out from among *the dead,* and therefore bodily resurrection is true. The objective of corroborating evidences such as the burial and post-resurrection appearances is to convince the lost of the truth of the two primary propositions about Christ's substitutionary death and bodily resurrection.[108]

Reason #3: The Gospel Is "According to the Scriptures"

A third major reason why the burial and post-resurrection appearances of Christ are not technically part of the gospel, and therefore not part of the required content of saving faith, is the double occurrence of the phrase, *"according to the Scriptures"* in 1 Corinthians 15:3-4. This prepositional phrase provides symmetrical literary markers in the passage that distinguish the actual *content* of the gospel from the *evidences* for that gospel. The phrase *"according to the Scriptures"* conspicuously modifies only Christ's substitutionary death and bodily resurrection but not His burial or post-resurrection appearances. For this reason, other Free Grace writers are not hesitant to identify the cross and resurrection as the essential elements of saving faith in this passage, in distinction to the Lord's burial and appearances. Thus, Hixson writes:

---

[104] Alford, *The Greek Testament*, 2:605; Fee, *The First Epistle to the Corinthians*, 736; Garland, *1 Corinthians*, 695; Gromacki, *Called to Be Saints*, 185; Hodge, *Commentary on the First Epistle to the Corinthians*, 318; Lambrecht, "Line of Thought in 1 Cor 15,1-11," 664-65; Lowery, "1 Corinthians," 543; Thiselton, *The First Epistle to the Corinthians*, 1213.

[105] Chamblin, "Revelation and Tradition in the Pauline *Euangelion*," 3.

[106] If the appearances were passed down as part of an early Church confession or tradition, then we can agree that this "tradition stands in the service of the gospel, and not vice versa." Spallek, "The Origin and Meaning of *Εὐαγγέλιον*," 187.

[107] Lambrecht, "Line of Thought in 1 Cor 15,1-11," 670.

[108] Meisinger, "The Gospel Paul Preached."

> It also has been noted that the repeated phrase, "according to the Scriptures" (vv. 3, 4) may well mark out the core essence of the gospel, thus relegating the post-resurrection appearances to a place of supporting material as distinguished from the components that are a required part of the content of saving faith. That is, the death and resurrection of Christ are part of the explicit content of saving faith; whereas the burial and post-resurrection appearances of Christ are merely supporting evidences of His death and resurrection.[109]

The apostle Paul was selective and deliberate in his placement of the phrase, *"according to the Scriptures,"* making its usage in 1 Corinthians 15:3-4 quite significant. We know that when Paul came to Corinth with *"the gospel"* (1 Cor. 15:1) he reasoned with the unsaved Corinthian Jews in the synagogue *"every Sabbath"* (Acts 18:4). It is inconceivable that he would not have used the Scriptures week after week in an effort to persuade the Jews in Corinth that *"Jesus is the Christ"* (Acts 18:5), since this was his evangelistic pattern elsewhere (Acts 13:14-49; 17:1-4; 28:23). We also know from Romans 1:2 that each element of *"the gospel"* was revealed in the Old Testament (see chapter 7), and thus the gospel is in accordance with the Scriptures. We can deduce from this that since 1 Corinthians 15:3-4 only says that Christ's death and resurrection are *"according to the Scriptures,"* and yet Romans 1:2 explicitly states that *"the gospel"* is according to the Scriptures, that therefore Christ's burial and appearances must not be elements of the gospel. This also means that Paul did not consider the burial and appearances to be part of *"the gospel"* that he originally preached *to the Corinthians* (Acts 18:4-5) which he is restating in 1 Corinthians 15:1ff, though the burial and appearances certainly would have served a valuable corroborating role as he evangelized, especially his own eyewitness testimony of having seen Christ-crucified and risen.

Some Christians occasionally protest that Christ's burial and possibly His appearances in a general sense (Ps. 22:22) were also revealed in the Old Testament. Therefore, they say, the burial and appearances must also be regarded as being *"according to the Scriptures."* But this is a *non sequitur* since there are many New Testament truths about Christ that were also revealed in the Old Testament (see chapter 15) but which are never afforded the distinction in the New Testament of being said to be *"according to the Scriptures"* as Christ's death and resurrection are in 1 Corinthians 15. The indisputable fact that Christ's burial was also revealed in the Old Testament actually strengthens the claim that the cross and resurrection are elements of the gospel in distinction to the burial and appearances as its supporting evidences. For, if the burial is truly an element of the gospel, and every element of the gospel was foretold in the Old Testament

---

[109] Hixson, *Getting the Gospel Wrong: The Evangelical Crisis*, 149n6.

(Rom. 1:2), and yet Paul still chose to attach the phrase *"according to the Scriptures"* only to Christ's death and resurrection, then there must be some significant theological reason why this phrase was left off of the burial and post-resurrection appearances in 1 Corinthians 15:4-5. Why would Paul attach the phrase, *"according to the Scriptures,"* only to Christ's death and resurrection in 1 Corinthians 15:3-4 when in fact the death, *burial*, and resurrection are all *"according to the Scriptures"*? The reason is obvious: only Christ's substitutionary death and bodily resurrection are considered to be elements of the gospel.

This conclusion is also consistent with the other passages in the New Testament that specify the elements of the gospel as being in accordance with the Scriptures. Elsewhere in the New Testament, the evangelistic message that is specifically stated to be in fulfillment of the Old Testament Scriptures is said to consist of the cross and resurrection, but noticeably absent is any mention of the burial or appearances (Luke 24:44-46; Acts 3:18; 26:22-23). It should also be recalled from an earlier chapter on Paul's gospel to the Galatians that in his evangelism at Antioch of Pisidia in southern Galatia he speaks of the scriptural, prophetic "promise" (Acts 13:23) that God is said to have "fulfilled," and he applies this only to the Savior's death (Acts 13:27, 29a) and resurrection (Acts 13:32-33). It is highly significant that he does not apply the modifying terminology of promise and fulfillment to his preaching on the Lord's burial (Acts 13:29b) and post-resurrection appearances (Acts 13:31). When 1 Corinthians 15 is compared with this example of Paul's evangelism in Acts 13, the fact that the phrase *"according to the Scriptures"* modifies only the Lord's death and resurrection in verses 3-4 cannot be considered coincidental. It is deliberate and perfectly consistent with the rest of God's inspired Word. For these, and many other reasons, the vast majority of grace-oriented Bible teachers recognize that the contents of the saving gospel include Christ's death and resurrection in 1 Corinthians 15:3-4 but not the supporting evidences of His burial and post-resurrection appearances (see Appendix: Other Free Grace Voices).

Hypotaxis, Parataxis, and the Kai Hoti Clauses

Once it is recognized that the phrase *"according to the Scriptures"* in 1 Corinthians 15:3-5 distinguishes Christ's death and resurrection as elements of the gospel, then it becomes readily apparent that the burial and appearances are theologically *subordinate* to these two main points.[110]

---

[110] Conzelmann, "On the Analysis of the Confessional Formula," 21; Kloppenborg, "An Analysis of the Pre-Pauline Formula," 364n64; Lambrecht, "Line of Thought in 1 Cor 15:1-11," 661, 665n35. Even though Sider protests that this is "sheer speculation" on Conzelmann's part (Sider, "St. Paul's Understanding," 134-35), he doesn't even begin to consider the semantic, contextual, historical, or theological reasons in support of the subordination interpretation. Similarly, though Craig states, "The fourfold ὅτι serves to emphasize

The majority of New Testament scholars recognize this as well, such as Conzelmann, who states regarding verses 3-5, "The construction contains four elements but in reality the four verbs do not have equal weight. The two fundamental statements are: ἀπέθανεν and ἐγήγερται. Ετάφη and ὤφθη are attached. This has been normally recognized."[111] Among those scholars who are convinced that these verses were an early creed or confessional statement, some also believe that the most primitive form of this creed or confession contained only the clauses about Christ's death and resurrection.[112] This would mean that verses 3b-5a were "really a twofold confession: Christ died for our sins and He was raised."[113]

At this point, some proponents of the crossless gospel raise the objection that there are four independent clauses in verses 3-5. They claim that since these are syntactically parallel to one another as seen by the use of *hoti* for the first clause followed by three consecutive *kai hoti* clauses, this means that the contents of each clause must carry equal weight and be part of "the gospel" that Paul refers to in verse 1. But this is an erroneous conclusion that is based on a false assumption about Greek syntax. While it is an undeniable fact that from a strictly grammatical and syntactical standpoint these are "parallel clauses,"[114] this observation by itself establishes nothing semantically or theologically. Though these four clauses are syntactically coordinate, this does not override the significance of the *"according to the Scriptures"* phrase modifying only two of the four clauses. The proper interpretation of this passage must weigh more than sheer syntax, for syntax alone does not determine meaning. As one writer puts it rather pointedly, "Making an observation about the syntax of a Greek text does not magically provide the right interpretation."[115] Greek grammarian Daniel Wallace explains how this relates to coordinate and subordinate clauses:

> Although the two elements might be equal *syntactically*, there is often a *semantic* notion of subordination. For example, on the surface "I went to the store *and* I bought bread" involves two

---

equally each of the chronologically successive events, thus prohibiting the subordination of one event to another" (Craig, "The Historicity of the Empty Tomb of Jesus," 61n12), he also provides no explanation for why the phrase *"according to the Scriptures"* is appended only to Christ's sacrificial death and bodily resurrection.

[111] Conzelmann, "On the Analysis of the Confessional Formula," 20-21.

[112] Conzelmann, "On the Analysis of the Confessional Formula," 19; Kloppenborg, "An Analysis of the Pre-Pauline Formula," 359-65; Stuhlmacher, *Das paulinische Evangelium*, 274; Thiselton, *The First Epistle to the Corinthians*, 1187.

[113] Lowery, "1 Corinthians," 542. See also, Thiselton, *The First Epistle to the Corinthians*, 1187.

[114] Robertson, *Grammar of the Greek New Testament*, 1034.

[115] J. William Johnston, "Grammatical Analysis," in *Interpreting the New Testament Text: Introduction to the Art and Science of Exegesis*, ed. Darrell L. Bock and Buist M. Fanning (Wheaton, IL: Crossway Books, 2006), 61.

coordinate clauses joined by *and*. But on a "deep structure" level, it is evident that coordinate ideas are not involved: "I went to the store *in order that* I might buy bread."

Semitic languages are especially paratactic, as are the lower echelons of Hellenistic Greek. Narrative literature often reflects this, even among the more literary writers. Among NT books, Revelation (103 instances of καί per 1000 words) and Mark (84/1000) have the greatest frequencies of καί. Luke comes in a distant third with 66 per 1000.

Among other things, the abundance of parataxis illustrates the limited value of diagramming sentences, especially in narrative literature. **Paratactic structure (i.e., when whole clauses are joined) may or may not reflect the true semantic relationship.** Hypotactic structure, on the other hand, does reflect the deeper structure: One does not use hypotactic structure when parataxis is meant, because the more nuanced category reflects the true intention of the author more accurately.[116]

This means that if a particular clause is subordinate (hypotactic) with respect to grammar and syntax, it is not semantically coordinate (paratactic). However, the converse cannot be true. Therefore, a syntactically coordinate structure (such as the four clauses in 1 Cor. 15:3-5) may still possess a semantically subordinate relationship. Thus, it is possible to have "parataxis with subordination."[117] In other words, it is possible to have syntactical parataxis with semantical hypotaxis. The true semantic relationship between syntactically independent clauses is not determined by grammar and syntax alone but by a composite of all the linguistic features of a passage. In the case of 1 Corinthians 15:3-5, this includes the double use of the modifying phrase, *"according to the Scriptures,"* which points to the burial and appearance clauses being semantically subordinate to the death and resurrection clauses.

Other examples of consecutive *kai hoti* clauses from the Koine Period confirm that such clauses are not necessarily semantically paratactic. In the Greek New Testament there are 19 instances of the *kai hoti* construction aside from 1 Corinthians 15:4-5. In these 19 cases, *kai hoti* always occurs singularly; that is, it never occurs in succession with another *kai hoti* clause. In this respect, 1 Corinthians 15:3-5 is completely unique in the New Testament. In fact, the repetition of *three* successive *kai hoti* clauses is such a rare construction that a search of the literature from

[116] Wallace, *Greek Grammar*, 667n2 (bold added). See also, Johannes P. Louw, *Semantics of New Testament Greek* (Atlanta: Society of Biblical Literature, 1982), 73-89; Grant R. Osborne, *The Hermeneutical Spiral: A Comprehensive Introduction to Biblical Interpretation*, 2nd ed. (Downers Grove, IL: InterVarsity Press, 2006), 99-100.

[117] Robert L. Thomas, "The 'Comings' of Christ in Revelation 2-3," *MSJ* 7 (Fall 1996): 163.

the Koine Period[118] yields only one other comparable example.[119] In the Septuagint, *kai hoti* occurs a total of 41 times, and yet there are only two passages where two *kati hoti* clauses occur consecutively (Isa. 22:9-10; Ezek. 23:39-40). This means that there are no other instances of three *kai hoti* constructions occurring in succession in either the Septuagint or the Greek New Testament. This should make anyone pause before naïvely insisting that multiple *kai hoti* clauses *must be* semantically paratactic. We simply do not have a large enough sampling of comparable constructions from the same period to be so dogmatic and to draw such a sweeping conclusion. In fact, the existing evidence actually contradicts such a false assumption.

While some people may assume that the mere occurrence of successive *kai hoti* statements must indicate parataxis, this is not necessarily the case. A succeeding *kai hoti* clause may be hypotactic, as in Ezekiel 23:39-40 (LXX). There, two *kai hoti* constructions occur consecutively with the second *kai hoti* clause clearly being syntactically dependent and subordinate to the preceding independent *kai hoti* clause. This is evident from the imperfect, active, indicative verb, *epoioun*, in the first clause of verse 39, followed by the present participle, *erchomenois*, in the following clause of verse 40.

39 καὶ ὅτι οὕτως ἐποίουν ἐν μέσῳ τοῦ οἴκου μου
kai hoti houtōs epoioun en mesō tou oikou mou
and that they were doing thus in the midst of My house
40 καὶ ὅτι τοῖς ἀνδράσιν τοῖς ἐρχομένοις μακρόθεν
kai hoti tois andrasin tois erchomenois makrothen
and that to the men who were coming from afar

In addition, in the writings of the "Apostolic Fathers" in the Epistle of 2 Clement 7:1, a *hoti* clause precedes and introduces a *kai hoti* clause, similar to the clauses in 1 Corinthians 15:3b-4a, *"that (hoti) Christ died for our sins, and that (kai hoti) He was buried."* And yet we see that in 2 Clement 7:1, the *kai hoti* clause is clearly dependent and subordinate to the *hoti* clause and thus syntactically hypotactic. This is evident from the present participle, *katapleousin*, in the *kai hoti* clause.

1 So then, brothers, let us enter the contest, realizing (*eidotes*) that (*hoti*) the contest is at hand, and that while many come to enter the earthly

[118] This search included the complete Greek texts of the NT, LXX, Apostolic Fathers, Josephus, and Philo, but not the non-biblical papyri or the writings of the Atticist rhetoricians and grammarians (where parataxis is less likely to occur).

[119] Philo of Alexandria, *On the Creation*, 172. In this passage, Philo uses three successive and syntactically independent *kai hoti* clauses. This is followed by a fourth independent clause, a simple *kai* clause, and then a fifth independent clause, which is another *kai hoti* clause. Though this is quite similar to the syntax of 1 Corinthians 15:3-5, it is not exactly equivalent.

> contests (*kai hoti eis tous phthartous agōnas katapleousin polloi*), not all are crowned, but only those who have trained hard and competed well.[120]

This selection of examples is sufficient to demonstrate that the mere occurrence of a *hoti* + *kai hoti* construction, or the occurrence of successive *kai hoti* clauses, does not necessarily indicate that the two clauses are syntactically coordinate, to say nothing of semantic parataxis.[121] In the cases of Ezekiel 23:39-40 and 2 Clement 7:1, the *kai hoti* clauses are syntactically dependent and subordinate because they do not contain finite verbs. However, the grammar and syntax of Isaiah 22:9-10 (LXX) is different. Following the initial *hoti* clause in verse 9, both *kai hoti* clauses in verses 9-10 are syntactically independent clauses and yet they are still semantically dependent and subordinate to the preceding *hoti* clause.

> 9 And they shall uncover the secret places of the houses of the citadel of David: and they saw that (*hoti*) they were many, and that (*kai hoti*) one had turned (*apestrepse*) the water of the old pool into the city;
> 10 and that (*kai hoti*) they had pulled down (*katheilosan*) the houses of Jerusalem, to fortify the wall of the city.[122]

In the context of this passage, Isaiah prophesies that Judah will one day see a siege coming and the city of Jerusalem will make preparations for it. This includes protecting the water supply of Jerusalem by channeling the water into a pool inside the city. In addition, the inhabitants of Jerusalem will one day see their city walls having many breaches in need of repair, and consequently they will demolish homes in Jerusalem in order to use the materials to fill the breaches. In verse 9, there is an initial *hoti* clause about seeing that the breaches are great. This is followed in verses 9-10 by the two consecutive *kai hoti* clauses that, despite being syntactically parallel to the *hoti* clause of verse 9, are still semantically subordinate to it. The razing of the houses of Jerusalem to fortify the city wall (v. 10) is dependent upon first seeing the many breaches in its wall (v. 9). In this respect, though the two *kai hoti* clauses in Isaiah 22:9-10 are syntactically independent, they are still semantically dependent upon, and subordinate to, the *hoti* clause of verse 9.[123]

---

[120] English translation based on *The Apostolic Fathers: Greek Texts and English Translations*, updated edition, ed. Michael W. Holmes (Grand Rapids: Baker Books, 1999), 112-13. For a similar subordinate, dependent *kai hoti* clause, see *Shepherd of Hermas*, 23:4.

[121] For an example of two consecutive *kai hoti* clauses both functioning subordinately, see Josephus, *Antiquities of the Jews*, 10.20.

[122] English translation based on Lancelot C. L. Brenton, *The Septuagint with Apocrypha: Greek and English* (Peabody, MA: Hendrickson Publishers, 1986), 855-56.

[123] For New Testament examples of syntactical parataxis with a definite subordinate meaning, see Matthew 18:21; Luke 14:5; John 7:34; 10:12 (Thomas, "The 'Comings' of Christ in Revelation 2-3," 163). Though these references only use the conjunction *kai* rather than *kai hoti*, the point remains the same: a syntactically paratactic structure may still reflect semantic hypotaxis.

As this relates to 1 Corinthians 15:3-5, we could say that just as someone would not bury a living person, so the Lord's burial (v. 4a) was dependent upon Him dying first (v. 3b). And just as a person could not be seen by others unless he arose from the dead, so the Lord's post-resurrection appearances (v. 5a) were dependent upon Him rising from the dead first (v. 4b). In this respect, the burial and appearances are clearly seen to be semantically subordinate to the two main clauses in the passage. The claim that 1 Corinthians 15:3-5 contains a "golden chain"[124] of elements that *must be* of equal theological weight, and that *must* all be elements of the saving gospel, is clearly seen to be unfounded. Those who contend that all four clauses are of equal theological weight and are necessarily part of the gospel have yet to provide any plausible explanation for why the *"according to the Scriptures"* phrases are selectively applied only to the main clauses about Christ's substitutionary death and bodily resurrection.

Reason #4: The Person and Work of Christ

A fourth reason why only the substitutionary death and bodily resurrection of Christ are elements of the gospel in 1 Corinthians 15, in contrast to the burial and appearances, is because only the Lord's death and resurrection are part of the redemptive "work" of Christ.[125] When evangelical Christians employ the standard phraseology of the "person and work of Christ" they are normally referring to the redemptive work of Christ's death for our sins and His bodily resurrection. There are sound biblical reasons for such a conclusion.

In Scripture, only the Lord's death paid the wages of our sin, and only His resurrection overcame the deadly consequence of our sin. Therefore, of all the wonderful works performed by Christ during His earthly lifetime and even subsequently, only these two works provided the grounds of redemption for the entire human race. It is for this reason that Romans 4:25 states that Christ *"was delivered up because of our offenses, and was raised because of our justification."* Likewise, 1 Corinthians 15 declares that without the resurrection of Christ, *"your faith is futile; you are still in your sins"* (15:17) and those who have died *"have perished"* (15:18). Even regarding the Lord's death, 1 Corinthians 15:3 states that Christ *"died for our sins."* Yet, nowhere in 1 Corinthians 15, or anywhere else in Scripture for that matter, does it say that Christ was "buried for our sins" or that He was "seen for our sins" or "if Christ is not buried, your faith is futile; you are still in your sins," etc. Thus, by itself, it is not "good news" to state that a man was buried, for that is a sad, daily occurrence in our fallen world. But to know that the Man who was buried had previously died as a satisfactory

---

[124] Alan F. Johnson, *1 Corinthians*, InterVarsity Press New Testament Commentary (Downers Grove, IL: InterVarsity Press, 2004), 284.

[125] Lambrecht, "Line of Thought in 1 Cor 15,1-11," 662.

sacrifice for the sins of the world and that this Man is also now alive from the dead, that is truly *euangelion*—"good news"!

Occasionally, some Christians will object on the basis of 1 Corinthians 15:4a that our sin-problem and its consequences were not resolved entirely through Christ's work on the cross and resurrection but also required His burial. Strangely and inconsistently, though, appeal is never made to the post-resurrection appearances of 1 Corinthians 15:5-8 as having any additional part in procuring universal redemption from sin. In support of this claim for the redemptive role of Christ's burial, reference is sometimes made to John 12:23-24.

In this passage, the Lord Jesus speaks analogously about His death and resurrection, saying, *"The hour has come that the Son of Man should be glorified. 24 Most assuredly, I say to you, unless a grain of wheat falls into the ground and dies, it remains alone; but if it dies, it produces much grain."* It should be noted that the emphasis of this passage, in harmony with Christ's subsequent teaching in the immediate context (John 12:32-34), is clearly upon His death and resurrection rather than His burial. Thus, even in the second conditional clause of verse 34, the Lord says only, *"if it dies, it produces much grain."* He does *not* say, "if it dies *and is buried,* it produces much grain." The Lord leaves off the previous statement about a grain of wheat that *"falls into the ground"* while He retains the reference to the grain of wheat dying. As is true with the interpretation of all scriptural parables, not every detail in a biblical analogy must have a direct fulfillment or referent. But if this analogy is rigidly pressed in this manner, then it leads to the absurd conclusion that Christ was first buried and then He apparently died underground. For, verse 24 says, *"unless a grain of wheat falls into the ground and dies, it remains alone."* The point about the grain or seed being in the ground is not to depict that Christ had to be buried in order to procure eternal life but that He had to rise from the dead in order to be the firstfruits of a great harvest to follow (1 Cor. 15:23).

Besides John 12:23-24, appeal is also occasionally made to Leviticus 16 to support the doctrine of redemptive-burial. According to this view, the scapegoat on the Day of Atonement (Lev. 16:20-22) is supposedly a prophetic picture of Christ putting away the guilt of our sins by His burial.[126] However, the lifeless body of the Lord Jesus is hardly a suitable antitype for the living goat that escapes into the wilderness bearing the sins of the nation of Israel, never to return again. Christ's body *did* return and it was seen again after only three days! Therefore, the scapegoat must be interpreted differently. Walvoord, for instance, sees nothing of the Lord's burial in the scapegoat. He states that the "live goat of Leviticus 16 illus-

[126] Lewis Sperry Chafer, *Systematic Theology* (Dallas: Dallas Seminary Press, 1947-1948; Reprint, Grand Rapids: Kregel, 1993), 7:63-64. Though I have the utmost respect for Dr. Chafer coupled with a deep appreciation for his writings, I cannot agree with him on this point.

trates Christ bearing away our sins from before God—His present work as Advocate in contrast to His finished work on the cross."[127] Scofield also makes no connection to the burial but includes references to Christ's death and resurrection, saying, "The living goat typifies that aspect of Christ's work which puts away our sins from before God (Heb. 9:26; Rom. 8:33-34)."[128] Others interpret the live goat as simply typifying the permanent removal of our sins as a result of Christ's atoning work on the cross.[129] The latter interpretation has the most exegetical support in its favor.

There simply are no passages in the entire Bible that teach the redemptive-burial view, despite the fact that Bible-believing Christians have fondly sung for decades, "Buried, He carried my sins far away."[130] This is figurative and poetic language at best; and we must be careful not to let our hymnology determine our theology, but rather vice versa. In the final analysis, we must ask ourselves, had Christ never been buried would our sins still remain? No passage in all of God's Word teaches such a doctrine. Instead, the Bible is clear that our sin-problem was fully resolved by the finished work of Christ's death and resurrection, as His death on the cross paid for our sins and His resurrection overcame the hold that sin had on the human race in terms of its effects. Therefore, it is hardly "arbitrary" to insist that Christ's atoning death and bodily resurrection are the essential elements of saving faith in 1 Corinthians 15:3-4.

Reason #5: No Parallel Burial/Appearance Passages

A fifth reason why the traditional Free Grace position has not "arbitrarily" omitted Christ's burial and post-resurrection appearances from the gospel is because they are never presented anywhere else in Scripture as being either part of "the gospel" or as being essential saving truth. This is in sharp contrast to Christ's death for sin and resurrection from the dead, which abound in the New Testament. J. B. Hixson is biblically correct in affirming that "belief in Christ's burial and post-resurrection appearances, whether specifically or generally identified, are nowhere listed as components of

---

[127] John F. Walvoord, *Jesus Christ Our Lord* (Chicago: Moody Press, 1969), 72.

[128] *The Scofield Study Bible, New King James Version*, ed. C. I. Scofield, E. Schuyler English, et al. (Oxford: Oxford University Press, 2002), 173n.

[129] Charles L. Feinberg, "The Scapegoat of Leviticus Sixteen," *BSac* 115 (October 1958): 324, 333; William MacDonald, *Believer's Bible Commentary*, Old Testament, ed. Arthur Farstad (Nashville: Thomas Nelson, 1992), 153; C. H. Mackintosh, *Genesis to Deuteronomy: Notes on the Pentateuch* (Neptune, NJ: Loizeaux Bros., 1972), 386-87; J. Vernon McGee, *Thru the Bible with J. Vernon McGee* (Nashville: Thomas Nelson, 1981), 1:401; Allen P. Ross, *Holiness to the Lord: A Guide to the Exposition of the Book of Leviticus* (Grand Rapids: Baker Academic, 2002), 321, 324; Merrill F. Unger, *Unger's Commentary on the Old Testament* (Chattanooga, TN: AMG Publishers, 2002), 166.

[130] The words to the classic hymn, "One Day," written by J. Wilbur Chapman, state in the refrain, "Living, He loved me; dying, He saved me; Buried, He carried my sins far away; Rising, He justified freely forever: One day He's coming O glorious day!"

saving faith."[131] Thus, we never find, for example, something akin to this statement: *"The message of the burial is to those who are perishing foolishness"* (1 Cor. 1:18). Nor do we ever read something along this line: *"For I determined not to know anything among you except Jesus Christ and Him seen"* (1 Cor. 2:2). Nor do we read: *"If we confess with our mouth that Jesus is Lord and believe in our heart that He was buried, we shall be saved"* (Rom. 10:9). Likewise, we never see something even remotely approximating this: *"For if we believe that Jesus died and was buried, even so God will bring with Him those who sleep in Jesus"* (1 Thess. 4:14). In the New Testament, the substitutionary death and bodily resurrection of the Lord Jesus are the consistent theme of the gospel and the contents of saving faith.

Reason #6: The Frequency of Christ's Death & Resurrection

Sixthly, if Christ's burial and appearances are truly elements of the gospel of our salvation, and therefore essential to saving faith, then there is no adequate explanation to account for the fact that the death and resurrection most frequently appear together in the New Testament *without any mention of the burial and appearances.* This is a glaring oversight on the part of the writers of inspired Scripture, if indeed the burial and appearances are part of the required content of saving faith. Notice the regularity with which Christ's death and resurrection are emphasized in Scripture as an inseparable couplet without any reference to the Lord's burial or appearances: Matt. 16:20-21; 17:22-23; 20:17-19; Mark 8:29-31; 9:30-32; 10:32-34; Luke 18:31-34; 24:7, 26, 46; Acts 2:23-24; 3:15; 4:10; 5:30; 10:39-40; 17:3; 25:19; 26:23; Rom. 4:24-25; 5:9-10; 8:34; Gal. 1:1-4; 1 Thess. 4:14; 1 Peter 1:2-3, 11, 18-21; 3:18-21. The interpretation that views the four clauses of 1 Corinthians 15:3-5 as being semantically parallel, and therefore as all being necessary components of the gospel, is at odds with the entire pattern of the New Testament.

The Importance of Christ's Burial & Appearances

None of the preceding reasons should be misconstrued as teaching that the burial and post-resurrection appearances of Christ in 1 Corinthians 15:3-8 are somehow unimportant, inconsequential, or trivial. Nothing could be further from the truth. Though it has not been the purpose of this chapter to expound upon the tremendous value of the burial and appearances, an entire chapter in itself could be written about their role and significance in the Word of God. And even though the Lord's burial and appearances are not the required content of saving faith, they are part of the Bible; and God still expects them to be believed. No portion of God's Word can be rejected without some serious repercussions. But there is a crucial difference between

[131] Hixson, *Getting the Gospel Wrong: The Evangelical Crisis*, 148n6.

saying that Christ's burial and appearances are *important* versus saying that they are *essential* to be believed for everlasting life. Even though a person's eternal destiny does not rest upon whether they believe in Christ's burial and appearances but only in the finished work of His death and resurrection, the burial and appearances still have great significance in the Word of God. They demonstrate the omniscience of God and the veracity of His Word since they are the fulfillment of predictive prophecy (Isa. 53:9) and typology (Jonah 1:17; Matt. 12:40). They also effectively serve as the spiritual antidote to the insidious doctrine of Gnosticism with its denial of Christ's literal humanity, death, and bodily resurrection. Not coincidentally, the Lord's burial and appearances were even used apologetically in the early Church's battles with docetism.[132] Finally, at least with respect to Christ's burial, the believer's spiritual co-burial and identification with Christ via Holy Spirit baptism (Rom. 6:4; Col. 2:12) is a reality that is based upon Christ's burial. Thus, it constitutes growth-truth for every child of God. The factual and historical reality of Christ's burial and appearances, in conjunction with their value as being part of God's inspired revelation (2 Tim. 3:16-17), indicates that they have tremendous spiritual significance for every child of God, even if they are not technically part of the gospel or the contents of saving faith.

---

[132] Thiselton, *The First Epistle to the Corinthians*, 1192.

Part III

Clarifying the Christ of Saving Faith

Chapter 15

What Does "the Christ" Mean in the OT & Synoptic Gospels?

OVERVIEW

Since eternal life is conditioned upon believing that Jesus is "the Christ" (John 20:31), a question of paramount importance in determining the contents of saving faith then becomes, "What does it mean to be the Christ?" A consistent picture of the biblical Christ develops through a survey of the Old Testament prophecies about the Christ, combined with the teaching and preaching of the Lord Jesus in the Synoptic Gospels. This survey reveals that the biblical Christ of saving faith is none other than the One who is deity-incarnate, who died for our sins and rose again to provide salvation and forgiveness of sins. These essential elements form a common thread throughout the teaching of the Lord Jesus Himself on the subject of Him being "the Christ" and the "Son of God" and the "Son of Man." In contrast, the crossless gospel's emphasis upon everlasting life itself and the solitary fact that Jesus is the guarantor of such life simply cannot be found anywhere in the teaching of the Lord Jesus in the Synoptic Gospels.

What is a "Christian"? The question is simple enough, and even in our post-modern age the majority of Americans still claim this label for themselves. Most would agree that a "Christian" is anyone who believes that the historical Jesus of Nazareth is the Christ. However, when asked the next logical question, "What does 'the Christ' mean?" the majority of professing Christians honestly have no idea. In popular usage, the term "Christ" has devolved into little more than the last name of Jesus, the Savior of the world. This in itself is a terrible tragedy, considering that "Christ" is one of the most theologically freighted terms in the Bible and that a person's individual beliefs about "the Christ" carry the highest soteriological stakes. While a strict etymological meaning or lexical definition for the term "Christ" is certainly not necessary for a person to exercise saving faith, the *defining features of Jesus' person and work* as "the Christ" definitely *are* critical to know and believe. If, according to John 20:31, eternal life is given only to those who believe that Jesus is "the Christ, the Son of God," then a person's eternal destiny rests upon the proper comprehension of the biblical concept of the Christ.

The Crossless Interpretation of "the Christ, the Son of God"

It is imperative to understand that some Free Grace adherents associated with the Grace Evangelical Society are deriving a unique definition for the phrase, "the Christ, the Son of God," that is biblically distorted and crossless. They are doing so in a desire to frame assurance of eternal life as the definitive issue in salvation, rather than the person and work of the Savior. They believe the phrase "the Christ, the Son of God" in John 20:31 simply means that Jesus is the guarantor of eternal life, not that "Christ" inherently means One who is deity-incarnate who died for our sins and rose from the dead.

How do they arrive at this definition of "the Christ"? They correctly note that the precise phrase, "the Christ, the Son of God" (*ho Christos ho huios tou theou*), occurs only twice in John's Gospel, once in the purpose statement of John 20:31 and once in John 11:27. They reason that its usage in John 11:27 must therefore be identical to its meaning in John 20:31. Zane Hodges has explained the rationale behind this position, saying:

> It is precisely the ability of Jesus to guarantee eternal life that makes Him the Christ in the Johannine sense of that term. Our Lord's exchange with Martha in John 11:25-27 demonstrates this clearly. You remember it, don't you? "Jesus said to her, 'I am the resurrection and the life. He who believes in Me, though he may

> die, he shall live. And whoever lives and believes in Me shall never die. Do you believe this?'" (John 11:25-26). Her reply is a declaration that she believes Him to be the Christ. Martha said, "Yes, Lord, I believe that You are the Christ, the Son of God, who is to come into the world." (11:27). Notice here that to believe that Jesus is the Christ means to believe that He guarantees resurrection and eternal life to every believer.[1]

Hodges and other defenders of this new gospel are certainly correct about one thing regarding the "Christ." The term can be taken to mean that "the Christ" is inherently the guarantor of eternal salvation to all who place their faith in Him. However, it must also be admitted that this conclusion can only be reached through *deduction* and not through a direct, explicit declaration or definition in Scripture. There are many passages that directly and explicitly affirm the Christ to be One who is both God and man and who dies for sin and rises from the dead, and on *that* basis He is the guarantor of eternal life. Christ's being the guarantor of eternal life is derived from the fact that He is mankind's Savior as the perfect Divine-human mediator who gave His life in sacrifice for us and who thus assures eternal life to all who believe in Him. In this respect, it is true that John 11:27 can be taken deductively to mean that "the Christ" is inherently the guarantor of eternal life.

Of course, it is also true that many professing Christians who affirm Jesus' deity and the historical facts of His death and resurrection have never been born again. The promoters of the new G.E.S. gospel have a commendable desire to see such "Christians" believe in the "guarantor of eternal life" aspect of Jesus as "the Christ." This would require them to place their faith in Him *alone* for their eternal salvation, rather than their church, good works, human goodness, or whatever else is keeping them from new birth. I can testify firsthand that as a devout Roman Catholic prior to salvation, had I been asked if I believed Jesus was the Christ in the sense of Him being God-incarnate who died on the cross and rose from the dead, I would have affirmed all of these truths.

Yet, had I been asked if I knew that I had eternal life guaranteed by Christ, I would have said, "Absolutely not!" I believed in the fact of His death on Calvary as an historical event, but not the provision of eternal life issuing from His cross-work. I had a deficient view of Christ's death. I did not truly view His death as substitutionary or satisfactory on my behalf since I trusted that my good works were necessary to atone for my sins rather than the work of Christ. The fact that Christ guaranteed eternal life to anyone who believed in Him made absolutely no sense to me as long as I had to earn my salvation. However, once I understood that in order to be eternally saved I had to transfer my faith from myself and

---

[1] Zane C. Hodges, "How to Lead People to Christ, Part 1: The Content of Our Message," *JOTGES* (Autumn 2000): 4.

my works to Christ and His work, then and only then did Christ's guarantee of eternal life become comprehendible. Thus, for today's crossless gospel proponents to remove Jesus' cross-work from the very definition of "the Christ" in order to replace it with the guarantee of eternal life does not resolve the problem of an unregenerate professing populace within Christendom; it only compounds it.

In the process of clarifying one truth about Jesus being "the Christ," the teachers of the new crossless gospel have beclouded the content of saving faith by subtracting the other essential elements of His person and work that are inherent to being the Messiah. While Jesus is the guarantor of eternal life as "the Christ," is that all that the term means? Can someone truly believe in Jesus as "the Christ," the guarantor of eternal life, while not believing in His deity, death for sin, and resurrection from the dead? Simply because millions of professing Christians accept such historical facts about Jesus but have never trusted in Him alone for eternal life does not mean that we should change the definition of "Christ" to suit our doctrine. God's Word must define its own terms. When it is allowed to do so with respect to the term "Christ," it becomes apparent that "Christ" is a soteriologically loaded word, conveying much more than Jesus simply being the guarantor of eternal life.

While I certainly don't presume to cover in only four chapters the entire range of biblical Christology, a branch of theology that could fill multiple volumes, these next four chapters will seek to provide a broad survey of the term and concept of "the Christ." The intent of these chapters is not to provide a detailed exegesis of all the relevant Christological passages but merely to give a synopsis of how the term "Christ" is employed throughout the Old and New Testaments, thereby providing a basis for comparison with the way this term is understood by the crossless position.

The next three chapters in particular will demonstrate that the overwhelming emphasis of Jesus being "the Christ" in Scripture, especially in evangelistic contexts in the New Testament, is upon His deity, humanity, death for our sins, and resurrection from the dead. Scripture itself depicts these to be the essential defining features of "the Christ" that are necessary not only as the grounds of our salvation but also as the content of saving faith. It will be routinely demonstrated from the Gospels and Acts that when the Lord Jesus and the apostles address lost, unbelieving audiences, the explicit content of their preaching and teaching about "the Christ" centers in His person and work. Their emphasis is conspicuously *not* upon Jesus being merely the guarantor of eternal life. In this respect, the biblical concept of "the Christ" actually mirrors the biblical meaning of the "gospel" in Acts and the Epistles.

When Scripture itself is allowed to articulate the meaning of "the Christ," it will be observed that there is a perfect theological consistency between the Old Testament concept of the coming Christ, the Lord Jesus' own teaching about "the Christ" in the Gospels, and the use of the term in Acts and the Epistles by the apostles (including John). There is therefore no such thing, scripturally speaking, as a distinctively *"Johannine sense of that term,"* as crossless gospel advocates claim.[2]

"Christ" According to the Old Testament

If we are to determine what it means to believe in Jesus as "the Christ" for eternal life, we must determine what Scripture itself means by this key theological term. The English word "Christ" is simply the transliteration of the Greek word *Christos,* which means "Anointed One." The word *Christos* comes from the Greek word for "anoint" (*chriō*). The word *Christos* in Greek is itself a translation of the Hebrew/Aramaic word *Messias,* as we are told in John 1:41. *Messias,* of course, is where we get our English word "Messiah." Christ and Messiah are interchangeable terms therefore, one being the Greek form of the word and the other being the Hebrew form. The term *Messias* occurs only twice in the entire New Testament (John 1:41; 4:25), whereas the term *Christos* occurs over 500 times, most often as a proper name or title for the Lord Jesus.

When seeking to determine the Old Testament's conception of who "the Christ" would be, one must start by examining the Hebrew terms related to anointing. The verbal root, *māshaḥ* (מָשַׁח), is normally translated, "anoint"; and it occurs 70 times in the Hebrew Old Testament,[3] with nearly all occurrences being found in the Pentateuch and Historical books. Of the seven occurrences found in the Poetic and Prophetic books, two uses of the verb "anoint" (*māshaḥ*) have reference to Jesus as the Christ (Ps. 45:8; Isa. 61:1) according to the inspired interpretation given in the New Testament (Luke 4:18; Heb. 1:9). The nominal form, *mishḥāh* (מִשְׁחָה), occurs 26 times in the Old Testament. It is found only in Exodus-Deuteronomy and is normally translated "portion," "anointing," or "anointing oil." This term never has direct reference to the person of the coming Messiah. Finally, the adjectival form, *māshîaḥ* (מָשִׁיחַ), occurs 38 times in the Hebrew Old Testament and is normally translated "anointed." Though it is common for theological liberals to deny that this term is ever used in the Old Testament for the person of the coming Messiah, it nevertheless must be recognized that of the 38 occurrences of *māshîaḥ* there are at least 3 passages that refer unmistakably to the person of "the Christ" (Ps. 2:2; Dan. 9:25, 26).[4]

---

[2] Ibid., Hodges. See also Bob Wilkin, "Is the Evangelistic Message Jesus Preached a Sufficient Message Today?" Grace Evangelical Society Conference, Fort Worth, TX, March 5, 2008.

[3] These figures are based on the BHS 4th edition.

[4] The term *māshîaḥ* may also refer to Christ in five other passages (1 Sam. 2:35; 2 Chron. 6:42; Ps. 132:10, 17; Hab. 3:13), where the NKJV has actually capitalized the term, "Anointed."

Two of the three unmistakable references of *māshîaḥ* to the person of Christ are noteworthy for what they indicate theologically about the coming Messiah. In Psalm 2:2, we see from the context that the Lord's "Anointed" is actually called God's "Son" (2:7, 12), referring minimally to the deity of the coming Christ. Secondly, Daniel 9:26 predicts that the Messiah *"shall be cut off, but not for Himself"* (NKJV). This is a definite reference to the death of "the Christ" and even to a substitutionary death based on the surrounding context of this verse in Daniel 9:24-27. The Hebrew expression for the NKJV translation of Daniel 9:26, *"but not for Himself"* (*wĕʾên lô*), could also legitimately be rendered *"and have nothing,"* as in the NASB and NIV. This would mean that, at His death, the Lord Jesus would be left with nothing that was royally due Him in terms of His rightful dominion as Messiah the Prince. This is the translation and interpretation favored by most conservative commentators on Daniel.[5]

This interpretation is certainly correct doctrinally, and it may indeed be the more semantically precise rendering of verse 26. But it must also be acknowledged that the larger context[6] reveals that Messiah the Prince would be cut off as part of God's program *"for your people"* (Daniel's people Israel) and that the divine purpose of the Lord's Seventy Weeks program was *"to finish the transgression, to make an end of sins, to make reconciliation for iniquity"* and *"to bring in everlasting righteousness"* (Dan. 9:24). For this reason, Arnold Fruchtenbaum explains how Daniel 9:26 still indicates, at least contextually, the substitutionary atoning work of the Messiah:

> Stepping back in time and looking ahead from Daniel's perspective in verse 26, we see first, that *"the Messiah will be cut off and have nothing."* The Hebrew word translated *"cut off"* is the common word used in the Mosaic Law and simply means *"to be killed."* The implication of the term is that the Messiah would not only be killed, but also that He would die a penal death by execution. The Hebrew expression translated *"and have nothing"* has two possible meanings. It can also be translated *"but not for Himself,"*

---

[5] Harry Bultema, *Commentary on Daniel* (Grand Rapids: Kregel, 1988), 287; Charles Lee Feinberg, *Daniel: The Kingdom of the Lord* (Winona Lake, IN: BMH Books, 1981), 132; E. W. Hengstenberg, *Christology of the Old Testament* (Grand Rapids: Kregel, 1970), 435-36; C. F. Keil and F. Delitzsch, *Commentary on the Old Testament*, trans. by James Martin (Edinburgh: T & T Clark, 1866-1891; reprint ed., Peabody, MA: Hendrickson, 1996), 9:732-33; Stephen B. Miller, *Daniel*, New American Commentary, vol. 18 (Nashville: Broadman & Holman, 1994), 267-68; Renald E. Showers, *The Most High God: A Commentary on the Book of Daniel* (Bellmawr, NJ: The Friends of Israel, 1982), 125; Merrill F. Unger, *Unger's Commentary on the Old Testament* (Chattanooga, TN: AMG Publishers, 2002), 1667; John F. Walvoord, *Daniel: The Key to Prophetic Revelation* (Chicago: Moody Press, 1971), 229-30; Leon Wood, *A Commentary on Daniel* (Grand Rapids: Zondervan, 1973), 255; Edward J. Young, *The Prophecy of Daniel* (Grand Rapids: Eerdmans, 1949), 207.

[6] S. Jeff Heslop, "Content, Object, & Message of Saving Faith," in *Dispensationalism Tomorrow & Beyond: A Theological Collection in Honor of Charles C. Ryrie*, ed. Christopher Cone (Fort Worth, TX: Tyndale Seminary Press, 2008), 247.

> and the meaning would then be that *"He died for others rather than for Himself—a substitutionary death."* The latter meaning would be much more consistent with what the Prophets had to say about the reason for Messiah's death (e.g. Isaiah 53:1-12). The first three purposes of the Seventy Sevens—to finish the transgression; to make an end of sin; to make atonement for iniquity—have all to be accomplished by some means of atonement. The Law of Moses decreed that atonement is made by blood (Leviticus 17:11). It appears that Messiah's death, *"not for Himself"* but for others, would be the means by which Israel's transgression, sin and iniquity would be atoned for. The point of this phrase is that between the end of the second subdivision, the Sixty-ninth Seven, and before the start of the Seventieth Seven, Messiah would be killed and would die a penal, substitutionary death.[7]

This corresponds perfectly with the Old Testament's typological depiction of the Messiah being a substitutionary sacrifice for our sins. This also harmonizes completely with the New Testament teaching that Jesus is God-incarnate who died in our place as "the Christ."

Since the actual Hebrew term *māshîaḥ* only rarely refers to the person of the coming Christ, the Old Testament's concept of "the Christ" is based primarily on passages that do not use this particular word but which contextually describe the Messiah. A proper Old Testament Christology must be drawn more from a contextual and topical study, rather than a word study. This approach to defining "the Christ" is completely justifiable since it was the approach of the Lord Jesus and the apostles themselves according to the New Testament. In the Gospels and the Book of Acts, we see the Lord Jesus and the apostles consistently using the Old Testament Scriptures to prove that Jesus was "the Christ" (Luke 24:25-27, 45-47; John 2:22; 5:39, 46-47; 20:9; Acts 8:32, 35; 10:43; 17:2, 11; 18:4, 28; 26:22-23; 28:23; 1 Cor. 15:3-4). Surely they used more than just the three passages where the actual word *māshîaḥ* refers indisputably to the Messiah (Ps. 2:2; Dan. 9:25, 26).

The Old Testament painted a composite picture of the coming Christ that was amazingly descriptive, leaving no excuse for Israelites who possessed the Scriptures not to recognize Him in the person of Jesus of Nazareth. The Old Testament Scriptures revealed that "the Christ" would be:

1) *God's Son* (Ps. 2:2, 7, 12; Prov. 30:4; Dan. 3:25) *and therefore deity* (Ps. 45:6-7, cf. Heb.1:8-9; Ps. 80:17; 110:1; Isa. 7:13-14; 9:6-7; Jer. 23:5-6; Micah 5:2; Zech. 14:3-5; Mal. 3:1b-3)

[7] Arnold G. Fruchtenbaum, *Messianic Christology: A Study of Old Testament Prophecy Concerning the First Coming of the Messiah* (Tustin, CA: Ariel Ministries, 1998), 97.

2) *a biological descendant of Adam and therefore human* (Gen. 3:15; 12:3; 49:10; 2 Sam. 7; Ps. 80:17; Isa. 7:14; 11:1, 10; Micah 5:2 cf. Luke 3:38; Rom. 5:12-21; 1 Cor. 15:21-22; 1 Tim. 2:5)

3) *a biological descendant of Abraham* (Gen. 12:3 cf. Matt. 1:1)

4) *a biological descendant of the tribe of Judah* (Gen. 49:10 cf. Heb. 7:14; Rev. 5:5)

5) *a biological descendant of David* (2 Sam. 7; Isa. 11:1, 10 cf. Matt. 1:1, 22:43; John 7:4-42; Acts 2:30; 13:22-23; Rom. 1:3; 2 Tim. 2:8)

6) *a biological descendant of David not through Jeconiah* (Jer. 22:30 cf. Matt. 1:6-16, Luke 3:23-31)

7) *born in a certain city, Bethlehem of Judah* (Micah 5:2 cf. Matt. 2:4; Luke 2:11; John 7:41-42)

8) *born at a certain time* (Dan. 9:25)

9) *born of a miraculous virgin conception* (Gen. 3:15; Isa. 7:11-14 cf. Matt. 1:18-25; Luke 1:35)

10) *One who performs miracles demonstrating that the Kingdom of God is at hand* (Isa. 29:18-19; 35:4-6; 42:1-7; 61:1; Matt. 11:2-5)

11) *One who suffers death as an atoning sacrifice for sin* (Ps. 22; Isa. 53; Dan. 9:26; Zech. 12:10; 13:7)

12) *One who is buried with the rich* (Isa. 53:9)

13) *One who is raised from the dead* (Ps. 16:9-10; Isa. 53:10b, 12 cf. John 2:22; 20:9; 1 Cor. 15:4)

14) *One who provides salvation for the entire world* (Isa. 49:6; 52:15; 53:11; cf. Luke 2:30-32; 24:45-47; Acts 13:47; 26:23; 28:28)

15) *a Prophet* (Deut. 18:15-19 cf. Acts 3:22-23)

16) *a Priest* (Ps. 110:4 cf. Heb. 5:5-10; 7:1-8:1)

17) *One who provides physical, national deliverance to Israel* (Isa. 59:20 cf. Rom. 11:25-26; Zech. 12:1-10; 14:1-5)

18) *a King who reigns gloriously over Israel and the world* (Isa. 9:7; 11:1-10; Dan. 7:13-14, 26-27; Zech. 14:9)

With so much about "the Christ" revealed by God in the Old Testament, the question naturally arises, how many of these eighteen descriptions of the

Messiah are necessary to believe today in order to fulfill the condition for eternal life stated in John 20:31 of believing in Jesus as "the Christ, the Son of God"? Must lost sinners today explicitly know and believe all eighteen facts about Jesus in order to believe in Him as "the Christ"? Certainly not! We must distinguish between what is ontologically necessary for Jesus to be "the Christ" and what is epistemologically necessary for people to place their faith in "the Christ."

In order for Jesus to be divinely qualified as the Christ in an ontological sense, He had to fulfill every single Old Testament description of the coming Messiah; otherwise He would not be the true, promised Messiah in the eyes of God the Father. However, in an epistemological sense, God does not require the lost today to know Jesus' entire messianic résumé in order to truly believe in Him as "the Christ" for eternal life. This conclusion is supported by at least two lines of evidence, one more logically based and the other more explicitly stated in Scripture.

Logically speaking, certain revealed truths about the coming Christ are not directly related to His ability to provide eternal salvation to the world. Only those essential facts about Christ that are directly related to His ability to provide eternal salvation are necessary to know and believe today to receive eternal life. For example, the fact that Jesus was born in the particular town of Bethlehem in fulfillment of Micah 5:2 did not directly affect His ability to make propitiation for sin and provide eternal salvation to the entire world. But the fact that He was both God and man, as Micah 5:2 also indicates,[8] does have direct bearing upon Him providing eternal salvation to mankind. Being a man, Jesus could die in the place of mankind as our substitute; and by being God, He could also pay the infinite price of sin that only an omnipotent, eternal God could pay. Furthermore, only God can truly forgive sins (Mark 2:7). For Christ to provide true mediation and affect the reconciliation of mankind to God, He had to be both man and God. In addition to Christ being God-incarnate and dying for our sins, He had to rise from the dead in order to truly conquer sin and its wages—and because a dead Savior could save no one!

Thus logically, not all of the Old Testament qualifications of Jesus as "the Christ" were necessary for Him to provide the grounds of our salvation; and not coincidentally, neither are they essential to know and believe today in order to receive eternal life. It appears that the only Old

---

[8] The fact that the Messiah would be God is indicated in Micah 5:2 by the declaration that this *"Ruler"* is eternal, *"whose goings forth are from of old, from everlasting."* This cannot be said of any creature, including an angel. The humanity of the Messiah is indicated by the very fact that He would be *born* in that town of Bethlehem, of the lineage of Judah (Gen. 49:10), as only human beings can be *born*, not God in terms of His divine nature, nor even angels. For this reason, Fruchtenbaum concludes regarding Micah 5:2, "Again we have a passage that shows that Messiah is to be human—being born at some specific point in time and at some specific place—yet having existed since all eternity past, and therefore divine" (Fruchtenbaum, *Messianic Christology*, 64).

Testament qualifications of Jesus to be "the Christ" that must also be known and believed today for eternal life are His deity, humanity, death for sin, and resurrection from the dead. These foundational qualifications of Jesus to be "the Christ," which are also the essential contents of saving faith, are not arbitrarily chosen as crossless gospel advocates frequently claim in their efforts to deny this truth. These defining features of the Messiah's person and work correspond with the elements of the "gospel," as is discernable from a comprehensive study of the terms *euangelion* and *euangelizō* in the New Testament. In addition, these essential defining features of "the Christ" also correspond perfectly with passages that explicitly require belief in each component for eternal salvation (John 8:24; 1 Tim. 2:3-6; 1 Cor. 1:17-21; Rom. 10:9-10).

While it is certainly true that Jesus is the guarantor of eternal life as "the Christ," it is also evident from the New Testament that believing in Him as "the Christ" includes more content than the crossless gospel requires. Believing that Jesus is the Christ does not mean merely believing that one named "Jesus" can guarantee eternal life. The "Christ" is also God's Son, and therefore deity, who became incarnated and died for sin and rose again to provide everlasting life. This is the constant drumbeat of the New Testament as to the meaning of "Christ." At times, these essential Christological elements are stated in explicit terms, such as "Son of God," "Son of Man," "died," and "arose from the dead." At other times, these defining elements of the Christ are expressed implicitly through an array of New Testament imagery and terminology, such as the "Servant" (*pais*), "Prince of life," "Holy One," "Savior," "tree," and "right hand of God." But when the combined testimony of the Lord Jesus and His apostles is examined in the Gospels and Acts, it becomes abundantly clear what it means to believe that Jesus is "the Christ."

The Deity & Humanity of "Christ" According to the Lord Jesus

There are several critical passages in the New Testament bearing upon the proper understanding of "the Christ" which will now be considered. This chapter will focus upon the use of the term "Christ" in the Synoptic Gospels, while the next two chapters will cover its usage in the Book of Acts. The value of these passages from the Synoptic Gospels and Acts is threefold.

First, each of these passages in their respective contexts deals specifically with the identification and definition of Jesus as "the Christ" and "the Son of God." Since this terminology is identical to John's evangelistic purpose statement, these passages serve as legitimate parallels to John 20:31 in establishing the biblically correct meaning of Jesus as "the Christ."

Second, it will be observed that the meaning of "the Christ" and "Son of God" in each of these passages is provided by none other than the Lord

Jesus (in the Gospels) and His apostles (in Acts). In the context of each passage, it should be noted that it is not the unregenerate providing their fallible, human perspective on the identity and meaning of "the Christ"; it is Jesus' own self-revelation that is given, followed by the expositions of those specifically commissioned to preach Him as "the Christ" (Luke 24:46).

Third, in each of the following "Christ"/"Son of God" passages in the Synoptic Gospels and Acts, Jesus and the apostles are specifically defining "the Christ" *for unbelievers.* They are not presenting Christological truth for the sanctification of existing believers. In the Synoptic Gospels, Jesus is correcting national misconceptions about the mere humanity of the Messiah. In addition, His Great Commission to His disciples contains the evangelistic message about "the Christ" that is to be preached to the world for its salvation. In the next two chapters it will be seen from historical accounts recorded in Acts that the apostles are presenting Jesus as "the Christ" in evangelistic settings where they are calling their audiences to faith in Him for eternal salvation. The reason this is significant with respect to the crossless gospel is that in these episodes the deity, humanity, death, and resurrection of the Lord Jesus are routinely underscored for lost audiences to believe as the defining elements of Jesus being "the Christ." Before considering many passages that establish that the cross-work and resurrection of Jesus are inherent to Him being the Christ, the following passages will first demonstrate that the Lord's deity and humanity are integral to His Messiahship.

Matthew 26:59-66

59 *Now the chief priests, the elders, and all the council sought false testimony against Jesus to put Him to death,*

60 *but found none. Even though many false witnesses came forward, they found none. But at last two false witnesses came forward*

61 *and said, "This fellow said, 'I am able to destroy the temple of God and to build it in three days.'"*

62 *And the high priest arose and said to Him, "Do You answer nothing? What is it these men testify against You?"*

63 *But Jesus kept silent. And the high priest answered and said to Him, "I put You under oath by the living God: Tell us if You are* ***the Christ, the Son of God!****"*

64 *Jesus said to him, "It is as you said. Nevertheless, I say to you, hereafter you will see* ***the Son of Man sitting at the right hand of the Power,*** *and coming on the clouds of heaven."*

65 *Then the high priest tore his clothes, saying, "He has spoken blasphemy! What further need do we have of witnesses? Look, now you have heard His blasphemy!*

66 *"What do you think?" They answered and said, "He is deserving of death."*

Luke 22:66-71
66 *As soon as it was day, the elders of the people, both chief priests and scribes, came together and led Him into their council, saying,*
67 *"If You are* ***the Christ****, tell us." But He said to them, "If I tell you, you will by no means believe.*
68 *"And if I also ask you, you will by no means answer Me or let Me go.*
69 *"Hereafter* ***the Son of Man will sit on the right hand of the power of God."***
70 *Then they all said, "Are You then* ***the Son of God****?" So He said to them, "You rightly say that I am."*
71 *And they said, "What further testimony do we need? For we have heard it ourselves from His own mouth."*

The Son of Man

These passages, where the Lord Jesus is on trial before the Sanhedrin, are highly instructive as to the meaning of "the Christ." Here, the Lord is asked specifically if He is "the Christ, the Son of God" (*ho Christos ho huios tou theou*). This is the exact Greek construction found in John 11:27 and 20:31, and it is the only other such occurrence in all four of the Gospels with the exception of the Majority Text variant in Luke 4:41.

When adjured by Caiaphas the high priest to answer the question, the Lord Jesus breaks His silence but does not use the opportunity to divest the term "Christ" of any deistic import. Rather, the Lord unequivocally provides a conflation of the two concepts of humanity and deity in Himself as "the Christ." Though Jesus had previously and frequently referred to Himself by His phrase of choice, "the Son of Man," thereby linking Himself with mankind, here His use of the phrase has definite deistic connotations. It was for this reason, and due to their pronounced unbelief, that the Sanhedrin charged the Lord of glory with blasphemy.[9] These religious leaders who were well versed in the Scriptures immediately drew the connection between Christ's statement and the prophesied coming of the "Son of Man" in judgment in Daniel 7:13-14. In the Old Testament, clouds of heavenly glory often attended the appearing of God (Exod. 13:21-22; 19:9, 16; 1 Kings 8:10-11; Isa. 19:1; Jer. 4:13; Ezek. 10:4).[10] Since they refused to believe that Jesus was the Christ, the Son of God, there could be no other recourse. They must face Him one day as their glorious Judge,[11] which is the sole position and prerogative of deity.

In these passages, the Lord Jesus affirms in one fell swoop both His deity and humanity by inextricably connecting the terms "Christ," "Son

---

[9] Darrell L. Bock, *Luke 9:51-24:53*, BECNT (Grand Rapids: Baker Books, 1996), 1799-1801; Ron Merryman, *Justification by Faith Alone & Its Historical Challenges*, revised edition (Colorado Springs: CO: Merryman Ministries, 2000), 116.

[10] Seyoon Kim, *The "Son of Man" as the Son of God* (Tübingen: J. C. B. Mohr, 1983), 15; Walvoord, *Daniel: The Key to Prophetic Revelation*, 167.

[11] Thomas O. Figart, *The King of the Kingdom of Heaven: A Commentary of Matthew* (Lancaster, PA: Eden Press, 1999), 487.

of God," and "Son of Man."[12] Even though these terms are used appositionally at times in Scripture, as they are in Matthew 26:63-64 and Luke 22:67-70, this does not mean that they should be understood as completely synonymous.[13] They are used interchangeably, but there are shades of difference in meaning between them. It would also be a gross oversimplification to state that "Son of Man" means only that Jesus is human, while "Son of God" means that Jesus is God. There is certainly a great degree of truth in such a distinction, but it must also be recognized that there is a significant amount of semantic overlap between these two phrases. For this reason, many New Testament scholars and theologians rightly affirm that the title "Son of Man" is deistic and not merely a reference to Christ's humanity.[14] This is certainly the case here in Matthew 26:59-66 and Luke 22:66-71.[15]

The Right Hand of God

Besides the Lord Jesus establishing Himself messianically in these passages to be the divine-human person of the "Son of Man," He also states that these unbelieving religious leaders will see Him coming again from God's "right hand" on the clouds of glory. His position at God's "right hand" is taken by these unbelieving Jewish leaders to be a statement of blasphemy since the claim to be at God's "right hand" was evidently a profession of deity and equality with God. Following a comprehensive study on the subject of the "right hand" in biblical and ancient secular usage, one New Testament

---

[12] Mal Couch, gen. ed., *A Bible Handbook to the Acts of the Apostles* (Grand Rapids: Kregel Publications, 1999), 81.

[13] J. B. Hixson, "Getting the Gospel Wrong: Case Studies in American Evangelical Soteriological Method in the Postmodern Era" (Ph.D. dissertation, Baptist Bible Seminary, 2007), 59.

[14] W. Robert Cook, *The Theology of John* (Chicago: Moody Press, 1979), 45-46; Oscar Cullmann, *The Christology of the New Testament*, rev. ed., trans. Shirley G. Guthrie and Charles A. M. Hall (Philadelphia: Westminster Press, 1963), 162, 185, 270, passim; Millard J. Erickson, *The Word Became Flesh: A Contemporary Incarnational Christology* (Grand Rapids: Baker Book House, 1991), 19; W. Hall Harris, III, "A Theology of John's Writings," in *A Biblical Theology of the New Testament*, ed. Roy B. Zuck and Darrell L. Bock (Chicago: Moody Press, 1994), 187; Martin Hengel, *The Son of God—The Origin of Christology and the History of the Jewish-Hellenistic Religion*, trans. John Bowden (Tübingen: J. C. B. Mohr, 1976), 66; Kim, *The "Son of Man" as Son of God*, 5; I. Howard Marshall, *The Origins of New Testament Christology* (Downers Grove, IL: InterVarsity Press, 1976), 78; James Parker, "The Incarnational Christology of John," *CTR* 3.1 (1988): 41; David R. Potter, "The Substance and Scope of Johannine Christology," (Ph.D. dissertation, Bob Jones University, 1978), 118; Adele Reinhartz, "John 20:30-31 and the Purpose of the Fourth Gospel" (Ph.D. thesis, McMaster University, 1983), 216-34; Charles C. Ryrie, *Biblical Theology of the New Testament* (Chicago: Moody Press, 1959), 323-24; D. Moody Smith, *The Theology of the Gospel of John* (Cambridge: Cambridge University Press, 1995), 132; John A. Witmer, "Jesus Christ: Knowing Jesus as Man and God" in *Understanding Christian Theology*, ed. Charles R. Swindoll and Roy B. Zuck (Nashville: Thomas Nelson, 2003), 320-22.

[15] Couch, *A Bible Handbook to the Acts of the Apostles*, 81.

scholar has concluded that "he, with whom God shares his throne, must also be 'equal with God' (Phil. 2:6)."[16] This conclusion is confirmed by the astonishing fact that in Scripture no one other than Christ is ever said to be at God's right hand.[17] Though believers have a position of honor "in Christ," and it appears that believers may be at *Christ's* right hand (Matt. 20:21-23; Mark 10:37-40; Rev. 1:16, 20; 2:1), the special place of honor and privilege at *God's* right hand is exclusively reserved in Scripture for the one and only Son of God.[18] Thus, the Jewish leaders in Jesus' day were correct in interpreting the Lord's testimony before the Sanhedrin to be a profession of His deity, but they couldn't have been more incorrect that He spoke "blasphemy." This was certainly not the first time in the Lord's earthly ministry that He taught that He was the unique God-man as "the Christ." Consider the following "right hand" passages.

Matthew 22:41-45

41 *While the Pharisees were gathered together, Jesus asked them,*
42 *saying, "What do you think about* ***the Christ****? Whose* ***Son*** *is He"? They said to Him, "The Son of David."*
43 *He said to them, "How then does David in the Spirit call Him 'Lord,' saying:*
44 *'The LORD said to my Lord, "****Sit at My right hand,*** *Till I make Your enemies Your footstool"?'*
45 *"If David then calls Him 'Lord,' how is He his* ***Son****?"*
46 *And no one was able to answer Him a word, nor from that day on did anyone dare question Him anymore.*

Mark 12:35-37

35 *Then Jesus answered and said, while He taught in the temple, "How is it that* ***the scribes say that the Christ is the Son of David****?*
36 *"For David himself said by the Holy Spirit: 'The LORD said to my Lord, "****Sit at My right hand,*** *Till I make Your enemies Your footstool." '*
37 *"Therefore David himself calls Him 'Lord'; how is He then his* ***Son****?" And the common people heard Him gladly.*

The messianic title, "Son of David," seemed perfectly acceptable to the Jewish populace of Jesus' day, provided that he be only a human figure,

---

[16] Martin Hengel, "Sit at My Right Hand! The Enthronement of Christ at the Right Hand of God and Psalm 110:1," in *Studies in Early Christology* (New York: T & T Clark International, 2004), 225.

[17] In Ps. 45:9, it says that *"At Your right hand stands the queen in gold from Ophir."* While this may initially appear to teach that a human queen stands at the right hand of God (the Father), the Psalm is plainly messianic as evidenced from its quotation in Hebrews 1:8-9; and the reference to *"Your right hand"* is manifestly to the Messiah's right hand rather than God the Father's. The only other possible reference to mere mortals possessing a place at God the Father's right hand is Ps. 80:17, which is also clearly messianic and refers to the Messiah being at God's right hand. See Fruchtenbaum, *Messianic Christology*, 87.

[18] Harold H. Hoehner, *Ephesians: An Exegetical Commentary* (Grand Rapids: Baker Academic, 2002), 275.

albeit a glorious, reigning human messiah. The offense and perplexity of Jesus' Jewish audience arose, however, when considering that the Christ could be both human and divine. In these passages, the Lord Jesus took the initiative to establish from Psalm 110:1 that "the Christ" was more than "the Son of David." He would also be the Son of God and therefore deity and David's Lord.[19] For this reason, Bauer states:

> Matthew suggests that Jesus' Davidic sonship is secondary to another type of sonship (22:41-46; cf. Mk 12:35-37). No doubt Matthew has in mind that Jesus' divine sonship takes precedence over his Davidic sonship. In Matthew's Gospel Jesus is presented primarily as Son of God . . . and in only a secondary and supportive way as Son of David.[20]

Jesus' teaching in Matthew 22:41-46 and Mark 12:35-37 exposed the current scribal interpretation of "the Christ" as merely David's descendant (Mark 12:35) to be scripturally deficient. The popular Jewish assumption in Jesus' day that the Messiah would be a strictly human figure was utterly contrary to Old Testament revelation.[21] By explaining that "the Christ" would be at the Lord's (Yahweh's) "right hand," the Lord Jesus underscored again, in no uncertain terms, His deity as "the Christ."

Psalm 110:1 is not the only Old Testament passage attesting to the deity of the Messiah. Psalm 80:17 also indicates His deity by virtue of being at God's right hand, in addition to revealing His humanity. It says, *"Let Your hand be upon the man of Your right hand, upon the son of man whom You made strong for Yourself"* (NASB). Arnold Fruchtenbaum explains the Old Testament, messianic implications of being at God's "right hand":

---

[19] Herbert W. Bateman IV, "Psalm 110:1 and the New Testament," *BSac* 149 (October 1992): 453; James M. Gibbs, "Purpose and Pattern in Matthew's Use of the Title 'Son of David'," *NTS* 10 (1963-64): 460-64; Jack D. Kingsbury, "The Title 'Son of David' in Matthew's Gospel," *JBL* 95 (1976): 598-99, 601.

[20] D. R. Bauer, "Son of David," in *Dictionary of Jesus and the Gospels*, ed. Joel B. Green, Scot McKnight, and I. Howard Marshall (Downers Grove, IL: InterVarsity Press, 1992), 769 (ellipsis added). Concerning Mark 12:35-37, Bauer also writes, "Given Mark's accent on Jesus as Son of God (1:1, 11; 9:7; 15:39), he is probably contending here that Jesus should be viewed primarily as Son of God, and in only an ancillary way as Son of David" (ibid., 768).

[21] Shemaryahu Talmon, "The Concepts of *Māshîaḥ* and Messianism in Early Judaism," in *The Messiah: Developments in Earliest Judaism and Christianity*, ed. James H. Charlesworth (Minneapolis: Fortress Press, 1992), 113. It should be noted, however, that though this was the popular opinion, there is some evidence from the Qumran texts that the messiah figure was also expected to be "the Son of God," at least within the smaller, separated, Qumran community. For example, one Qumran text, 4Q 243, reads, "But your son shall be great upon the earth, O king . . . He shall be called son of the Great God . . . He shall be hailed as the Son of God and they shall call him Son of the Most High." Joseph A. Fitzmyer, "The Contribution of Qumran Aramaic to the Study of the New Testament," *NTS* 20 (1973-74): 394. See also John J. Collins, "A Pre-Christian 'Son of God' Among the Dead Sea Scrolls," *BR* 9 (June 1993): 34-38, 57; Kim, *"The 'Son of Man'" as Son of God*, 20-21.

> The whole of Psalm 80 deals with the national salvation of Israel just prior to the Second Coming. . . . Israel is now pleading for Messiah to return, but within their prayers there is one verse—verse 17—which is relevant to our study of Messiah's First Coming. Verse 17 is in fact a development of the teaching of Psalm 110:1, which should really be studied first. Israel is praying to God for deliverance and in verse 17 the One they ask to come and deliver them is the One seated at God's right hand. We are told in Psalm 110 that this is the Messiah who has ascended to the right hand of God following His rejection. Psalm 110 also states that Messiah will remain there until Israel repents and asks for His return. It is this repentance which is being described in Psalm 80. The title given to Messiah in verse 17 is "the Son of Man." This is a very common messianic title in the New Testament, particularly in the Gospel of Luke. To repeat the teaching of Psalm 110:1, since the "Son of Man" is sitting at the right hand of God, He must be equal with God; thus we have another verse which affirms that Messiah must be a God-Man.[22]

For the Messiah to be the "Son of Man" at God's "right hand" and to be David's "Lord" all indicates that He must be nothing short of deity-incarnate. It is imperative to observe, therefore, that *in the very passages in the Gospels where the Lord Jesus Himself defines the meaning of "the Christ," He takes the opportunity to emphasize both His deity and humanity*. If there was ever a time to teach that His existence as both God and man merely pointed to the greater Christological truth about Himself—that He is also the "guarantor of eternal life" in the crossless gospel sense—surely this was it. Apparently the Lord Jesus missed a golden opportunity to teach this key tenet of today's crossless, deityless gospel!

In the two separate instances observed thus far in the Synoptic Gospels where the Lord Jesus defines His Messiahship, He makes reference to being at God's "right hand." It is vital at this point to demonstrate that this position of honor is reserved solely for deity.[23] This can be seen in several additional New Testament passages that speak of Christ being at God's right hand.

<u>Hebrews 1:1-13</u>

1 *God, who at various times and in various ways spoke in time past to the fathers by the prophets,*

2 *has in these last days spoken to us by His Son, whom He has appointed heir of all things, through whom also He made the worlds;*

3 *who being the brightness of His glory and the express image of His person, and upholding all things by the word of His power, when He had by Himself*

[22] Fruchtenbaum, *Messianic Christology*, 87 (ellipsis added).

[23] Robert M. Bowman and J. Ed Komoszewski, *Putting Jesus in His Place: The Case for the Deity of Christ* (Grand Rapids: Kregel, 2007), 235-66.

purged our sins, ***sat down at the right hand of the Majesty on high,***
4 *having become so much better than the angels, as He has by inheritance obtained a more excellent name than they.*
5 *For to which of the angels did He ever say: "You are My Son, Today I have begotten You"? And again: "I will be to Him a Father, And He shall be to Me a Son"?*
6 *But when He again brings the firstborn into the world, He says: "Let all the angels of God worship Him."*
7 *And of the angels He says: "Who makes His angels spirits And His ministers a flame of fire."*
8 *But to the Son He says: "Your throne, O God, is forever and ever; A scepter of righteousness is the scepter of Your Kingdom.*
9 *You have loved righteousness and hated lawlessness; Therefore God, Your God, has anointed You With the oil of gladness more than Your companions."*
10 *And: "You, LORD, in the beginning laid the foundation of the earth, And the heavens are the work of Your hands.*
11 *They will perish, but You remain; And they will all grow old like a garment;*
12 *Like a cloak You will fold them up, And they will be changed. But You are the same, And Your years will not fail."*
13 *But to which of the angels has He ever said:* ***"Sit at My right hand,*** *Till I make Your enemies Your footstool"?*

This passage in Hebrews further confirms the interpretation of Jesus' teaching about "the Christ" being equal in deity with the Father by virtue of being at God's "right hand." Here in Hebrews 1, the deity of the Lord Jesus is seen by Him being the "Son" (1:2) of "God" (1:1).[24] The references to Christ being at the "right hand" of God in 1:3 and 1:13 serve as virtual book-ends, an *inclusio,* where His deity is declared (1:3),[25] then proven in various ways in the intervening verses (1:4-12), before finally being reaffirmed once again at the close of this section (1:13).[26] New Testament scholar Donald Hagner explains the significance of Hebrews 1 to the doctrine of Christology:

> In the opening chapter of Hebrews we have one of the strongest affirmations of the deity of Jesus Christ to be found in the New Testament. The passage stands with the prologue to the Fourth Gospel and the Christ hymns of Phil 2:6-11 and Col 1:15-20 as

[24] Benjamin B. Warfield, *The Person and Work of Christ*, ed. Samuel G. Craig (Phillipsburg, NJ: Presbyterian & Reformed, 1950), 75-77.

[25] John F. Walvoord, *Jesus Christ Our Lord* (Chicago: Moody Press, 1969), 50.

[26] Some commentators take either verses 3 or 4 through 14 as one section or paragraph. William L. Lane, *Hebrews 1-8*, WBC (Nashville: Thomas Nelson, 1991), 24; Ronald C. Merryman, *Verse-by-verse through HEBREWS: A Study Guide* (Colorado Springs: Merryman Ministries, 2005), 1:10. But verse 14 could also be viewed as a transitional statement leading into chapter 2. See Paul Ellingworth, *The Epistle to the Hebrews*, NIGTC (Grand Rapids: Eerdmans, 1993), 108.

> the high points of New Testament Christology. The stress on the deity of the Son at the beginning of Hebrews serves immediately to demonstrate the superiority of the Son over the angels. But as we proceed through Hebrews, it becomes evident that it serves other purposes that are even more significant. . . . More important for the writer of Hebrews than all of these, however, the deity of the Son finds its climax in the fully effective atoning work of the Son, who acts in the capacity of a unique high priest—which is something, as we will see, that becomes possible only because of his identity as the Son of God.[27]

Hagner's point about the interconnection of Jesus' deity with His "fully effective atoning work" in the Christology of Hebrews is absolutely critical to arriving at a truly biblical conception of "the Christ" of saving faith. Just as we see with Johannine Christology, in addition to the doctrine of "the gospel" throughout the New Testament, the deity and humanity of Christ's person cannot be extricated from the saving work of His death and resurrection. Christ's salvific work of mediation between two parties requires that He be both God and man (1 Tim. 2:3-6) so as to represent both parties to one another and to effectively accomplish reconciliation.

Acts 2:33-36

33 *Therefore being exalted to* ***the right hand of God,*** *and having received from the Father the promise of the Holy Spirit, He poured out this which you now see and hear.*

34 *For David did not ascend into the heavens, but he says himself: 'The LORD said to my Lord,* ***Sit at My right hand,***

35 *Till I make Your enemies Your footstool.'*

36 *Therefore let all the house of Israel know assuredly that God has made this* ***Jesus****, whom you crucified, both* ***Lord and Christ.***

In this portion of Peter's evangelistic preaching on the day of Pentecost, he twice makes reference to "Jesus of Nazareth" (2:22) being at God's "right hand." This clearly establishes Jesus' deity. The term "therefore" in verse 36a makes inseparable the idea of Jesus being at God's "right hand" (v. 34) with Him being "Lord and Christ" (v. 36b). It is an aphorism of Free Grace interpretation and theology that believing in Jesus as "Lord" (Acts 16:31; Rom. 10:9) means believing in His deity.[28]

---

[27] Donald A. Hagner, "The Son of God as Unique High Priest," in *Contours of Christology in the New Testament*, ed. Richard N. Longenecker (Grand Rapids: Eerdmans, 2005), 252 (ellipsis added).

[28] Charles C. Bing, *Lordship Salvation: A Biblical Evaluation and Response*, GraceLife Edition (Burleson, TX: GraceLife Ministries, 1992), 104; Robert P. Lightner, *Sin, the Savior, and Salvation: The Theology of Everlasting Life* (Nashville: Thomas Nelson, 1991), 204; Charles C. Ryrie, *So Great Salvation: What It Means to Believe In Jesus Christ* (Wheaton, IL: Victor Books, 1989), 69-70. Though Machen and Warfield were not proponents of the Free Grace position, on this particular point they were in hearty agreement with Free Grace theology. See J. Gresham

Acts 5:30-31

30 *The God of our fathers raised up* ***Jesus*** *whom you murdered by hanging on a tree.*

31 *"Him God has exalted to His* ***right hand*** *to be Prince and Savior, to give repentance to Israel and forgiveness of sins.*

In the context of this passage, Peter and the other apostles (5:29) are speaking to "the council" of the Sanhedrin (5:27), where they once again affirm that Jesus is at God's "right hand" and is the "Prince" and "Savior." The "right hand" reference establishes Jesus' deity as the Christ, as does the reference to Jesus being both "Prince" (*archēgos*[29]) and "Savior." The Sanhedrin would have been aware of Isaiah's teaching that besides the LORD (Yahweh) there is no Savior (Isa. 43:10-11). By such attributions to Christ, the apostles were clearly claiming deity for Jesus as the Christ.

Acts 7:52-58

52 *Which of the prophets did your fathers not persecute? And they killed those who foretold the coming of the Just One, of whom you now have become the betrayers and murderers,*

53 *"who have received the law by the direction of angels and have not kept it."*

54 *When they heard these things they were cut to the heart, and they gnashed at him with their teeth.*

55 *But he, being full of the Holy Spirit, gazed into heaven and saw the glory of God, and* ***Jesus standing at the right hand of God,***

56 *and said, "Look! I see the heavens opened and* ***the Son of Man standing at the right hand of God!"***

57 *Then they cried out with a loud voice, stopped their ears, and ran at him with one accord;*

58 *and they cast him out of the city and stoned him*

Machen, *Christianity and Liberalism* (Grand Rapids: Eerdmans, 1923), 97; Warfield, *The Person and Work of Christ*, 74-77.

[29] This term occurs only three other times in the New Testament (Acts 3:15, *"Prince of life"*; Heb. 2:10, *"the captain of their salvation"*; Heb. 12:2, *"the author . . . of our faith"*). The fundamental sense of this term in each instance is simply that of an originator or one who leads by beginning something (BDAG, 138-39); or as Louw and Nida define it, "an initiator" (L&N, s.v. "Begin, Start," 1:655, §68.2) or even "pioneer leader" (L&N, s.v. "Guide, Discipline, Follow," 1:466, §36.6). In this respect, its usage in Acts 5:31 most likely conveys the idea that Jesus is the originator and author of salvation (cf. Heb. 2:10) by virtue of His resurrection from the dead (cf. Acts 3:15). See R. C. H. Lenski, *The Interpretation of the Acts of the Apostles* (Minneapolis: Augsburg, 1946), 135. Since Christ has paid for sin on the cross, and has even overcome death by His resurrection, He has become the firstfruits of a great harvest (1 Cor. 15:22-23). As the life-giver, He leads a train of others in new life. In this sense, He is the "pioneer leader" and "initiator" of divine life among humanity. With respect to Acts 5:31, there is likely a significant amount of semantic overlap between the two terms "Prince" and "Savior," much like "Christ" and "Son of God" in John 20:31, while being shy of an actual hendiadys.

Here again, Jesus is declared to be deity through the testimony of Stephen as he sees the Lord Jesus *"standing at the right hand of God."* That the Jews in their unbelief considered this to be idolatrous blasphemy is evident from the fact that they assaulted Stephen and stoned him to death. They would not have done this if Stephen was proclaiming Jesus to be a mere man. In addition, this passage contains another use of the phrase "Son of Man" where it clearly goes beyond the humanity of the Lord Jesus to His inherent deity. Later in the passage, Stephen even prays directly to the Lord Jesus (7:58-59), an act which confirms the deistic import of his previous statements about Christ.

<u>Ephesians 1:20-21</u>
20 *which He worked in **Christ** when He raised Him from the dead and **seated Him at His right hand** in the heavenly places,*
21 *far above all principality and power and might and dominion, and every name that is named, not only in this age but also in that which is to come.*

<u>1 Peter 3:21c-22</u>
21 *through the resurrection of **Jesus Christ**,*
22 *who has gone into heaven and is **at the right hand of God**, angels and authorities and powers having been made subject to Him.*

Finally, both Paul and Peter refer to Jesus "Christ" being true deity by virtue of His position of special dignity and majesty at God's "right hand." As Walvoord states, "This position is obviously one of highest possible honor and involves possession of the throne without dispossession of the Father. The implication is that all glory, authority and power is shared by the Father with the Son."[30] As a result, in the context of both "right hand" passages in Ephesians 1:20 and 1 Peter 3:22, Christ's sovereign position as deity is demonstrated by the fact that even the angels must submit to Him.

The conclusion drawn from all of the preceding passages on the deity and humanity of Christ is that the Lord Jesus Himself, along with various believers (Peter, Stephen, the writer of Hebrews, Paul), consistently defined "the Christ" to be no One less than God-incarnate. This is the One whom they continually set forth to their lost audiences as the object of saving faith.

The Death & Resurrection of "Christ" According to the Lord Jesus

Besides the deity and humanity of "the Christ" being taught by the Lord Himself and His apostles, they also consistently define "the Christ" to be the One who died for man's sin and rose from the dead. In the following definitive New Testament passages on "the Christ," we observe once again the conspicuous, complete *absence* of any presentation of Jesus as merely

[30] Walvoord, *Jesus Christ Our Lord*, 224.

"the guarantor of eternal life." If, as the crossless position teaches, being the "guarantor of eternal life" is the very essence of Jesus' Messiahship and it is the only essential element about Him that the lost must believe in order to receive regeneration (besides knowing the name "Jesus"), then one would think that this solitary truth would be given special emphasis throughout the Gospels and Acts. But it is not—ever. Instead, we read repeatedly that Jesus is "the Christ" in the sense of being the crucified and risen Savior.

Matthew 16:13-23

13 *When Jesus came into the region of Caesarea Philippi, He asked His disciples, saying, "Who do men say that I, the Son of Man, am?"*

14 *So they said, "Some say John the Baptist, some Elijah, and others Jeremiah or one of the prophets."*

15 *He said to them, "But who do you say that I am?"*

16 *Simon Peter answered and said, "You are **the Christ, the Son of the living God.**"*

17 *Jesus answered and said to him, "Blessed are you, Simon Bar-Jonah, for flesh and blood has not revealed this to you, but My Father who is in heaven.*

18 *"And I also say to you that you are Peter, and on this rock I will build My church, and the gates of Hades shall not prevail against it.*

19 *"And I will give you the keys of the kingdom of heaven, and whatever you bind on earth will be bound in heaven, and whatever you loose on earth will be loosed in heaven."*

20 *Then He commanded His disciples that they should tell no one that He was Jesus **the Christ.***

21 *From that time Jesus began to show to His disciples that He must go to Jerusalem, and **suffer** many things from the elders and chief priests and scribes, and **be killed**, and **be raised** the third day.*

22 *Then Peter took Him aside and began to rebuke Him, saying, "Far be it from You, Lord; this shall not happen to You!"*

23 *But He turned and said to Peter, "Get behind Me, Satan! You are an offense to Me, for you are not mindful of the things of God, but the things of men."*

Here in Matthew 16:20-21, we see that Jesus as "the Christ" is going to be killed and raised from the dead. These two twin truths about "the Christ" are routinely presented by the Lord Jesus to His undiscerning disciples (Matt. 17:22-23; 20:17-19; Mark 8:29-31; 9:30-32; 10:32-34; Luke 9:43-45; 18:31-34). In the context of this passage, Peter has just made his great confession of faith in Jesus as *"the Christ, the Son of the living God"* (Matt. 16:16). And yet as great as Peter's confession is, the Lord Jesus tells the disciples *not* to proclaim Him to be *"the Christ"* from that point forward. Then, in a complete reversal of profession, Peter no longer expresses a divine perspective on Jesus (16:17) but a satanic viewpoint (16:23) as he actually rebukes the Lord Jesus (16:22) for teaching that He must go to the cross and rise again (16:21) as "the Christ" (16:20).

This episode raises an important question about Jesus being "the Christ." Why would Peter object to Jesus going to the cross if "the Christ" by definition was One who would die sacrificially and be raised from the dead and Peter by his own profession believed Him to be "the Christ"? The explanation is simple. Peter in his human viewpoint (16:23) didn't understand these essential Old Testament details about Jesus being the Christ until after the crucifixion and resurrection. From the divine perspective, Jesus still had to suffer and rise again as "the Christ" regardless of whether Peter and the disciples accurately comprehended Old Testament Christology at this juncture in the Lord's earthly ministry. Peter was corrected here by the Lord for having a deficient view of the identity of *"the Christ, the Son of the living God."* Peter was not alone in this erroneous conception of "the Christ." The rest of the nation of Israel shared this fatal misconception, as they looked for merely a glorious, reigning messiah who would rule the world as Israel's king. However, to continue to preach Jesus as "the Christ" without the essential content of His death and resurrection would only have perpetuated this erroneous understanding.

Even though Peter professed Jesus to be more than a prophet, even deity as God's Son (16:16), he still rejected the notion that "the Christ" should go to the cross, die, and rise from the dead. Make no mistake about it, at this point *Peter believed in a "crossless Christ"*; and he was severely censured by the Lord because of it. But after Calvary, Peter did not make the same mistake. From that point on, he always set forth for his lost, unbelieving audiences the only proper object of saving faith to believe in—the crucified, risen Christ. The lesson for us is patently obvious. We dare not retrieve Peter's partial, even satanic, notion of the "Christ" from Matthew 16 and allow such an un-crucified, un-resurrected "Christ" to be the object of faith for the lost today, since such a "Christ" doesn't even exist anywhere in the universe and is in reality "another Jesus" (2 Cor. 11:4).

A final, critical question for the crossless gospel position needs to be raised at this point regarding this passage. The crossless position maintains that the "saving message" of belief in "the Christ" as the guarantor of eternal life has never changed since the dawn of human history, even in spite of the evident progress of divine revelation.[31] The only change that now applies to the content of saving faith is that the unregenerate must believe that "Jesus" in particular is the promised Christ.[32] But the crossless position is left with an enormous dilemma regarding Matthew 16. Why would the Lord actually *"command"* his disciples *"to tell no one"* that He was *"Jesus the Christ"* (Matt. 16:20) if the saving message of faith in

---

[31] Bob Bryant, "How Were People Saved Before Jesus Came?" *JOTGES* 16 (Spring 2003): 64-65; John Niemelä, "The Message of Life in the Gospel of John," *CTSJ* 7 (July-Sept. 2001): 18; Robert N. Wilkin, "Salvation Before Calvary," *Grace in Focus* (January-February 1998).

[32] Robert N. Wilkin, "Is Ignorance Eternal Bliss?" *JOTGES* 16 (Spring 2003): 13.

Christ as the guarantor of eternal life is a timeless, unchanging message? Didn't the Lord Jesus want the unsaved to keep hearing the simple, minimum, crossless "saving message" that He, as the Christ, is the guarantor of eternal life to all who believe in Him as such? Didn't He want poor lost souls to continue hearing that He was "the Christ" and thereby continue receiving eternal life by believing this "saving message," with or without the additional knowledge of His death and resurrection? The crossless position simply cannot be reconciled with Matthew 16.

It is also significant by way of contrast with Matthew 16 that it is only *after* Jesus goes to the cross and rises from the dead that He commissions the disciples to preach Him as "the Christ" to the entire world for its salvation (Mark 16:15-16) and remission of sins (Luke 24:45-47). This is another clear indicator that believing in Jesus as "the Christ" for eternal life means believing in Him as the crucified, risen Savior.

Matthew 11:2-6, 11-12

2 *And when John had heard in prison about the works of Christ, he sent two of his disciples*
3 *and said to Him, "Are You the Coming One, or do we look for another?"*
4 *Jesus answered and said to them, "Go and tell John the things which you hear and see:*
5 *"The blind see and the lame walk; the lepers are cleansed and the deaf hear; the dead are raised up and the poor have the gospel preached to them.*
6 *"And blessed is he who is not offended because of Me."*
11 *"Assuredly, I say to you, among those born of women there has not risen one greater than John the Baptist; but he who is least in the kingdom of heaven is greater than he.*
12 *"And from the days of John the Baptist until now the kingdom of heaven suffers violence, and the violent take it by force.*

Matthew 11 is another passage that defines Jesus to be "the Christ." On the basis of this passage, however, a potential problem may be raised by some who hold to the crossless position. They may object that if the Lord Jesus points to His many miracles (Matt. 11:5) in order to prove to John the Baptist that He is the true Messiah, then shouldn't these miracles also be part of the content of saving faith today? We may also raise an additional question. We may ask, "Why didn't the Lord Jesus simply refer to His coming cross-work and resurrection as He did in Matthew 16:21 in order to validate Himself as the Messiah?" These vital questions need to be addressed for consistency's sake before proceeding on to other messianic passages in the Gospels that define "the Christ."

In answer to these potential objections being raised, it must be acknowledged first of all that, in Matthew 11, Jesus' messianic status is definitely being defined for John the Baptist. In verse 2, John hears of "the works of Christ (*tou Christou*)." In response in verse 3, John's messengers ask the Lord, *"Are you the Coming One, or do we look for another?"* The phrase, "Coming One" (*ho erchomenos*), is clearly a descriptive articular participle that functions as a messianic title, following as it does on the heels of the reference to "the Christ" in the previous verse and due to its use elsewhere in messianic contexts (Mark 11:9; Luke 13:35; 19:38; Heb. 10:37).[33] A nearly equivalent expression occurs in Martha's confession of faith in John 11:27 (*ho eis ton kosmon erchomenos*) where she associates the "Coming One" with "the Christ, the Son of God." The question is not whether Jesus' miraculous signs mentioned in Matthew 11:5 are legitimate distinguishing features of the Messiah since they do demonstrate that the Lord Jesus fulfilled Old Testament messianic prophecy (Isa. 29:18-19; 35:4-6; 42:1-7; 61:1). The real question is why Jesus here didn't refer to His approaching death and resurrection at this juncture in order to validate and define His Messiahship to John, especially since these are the essential defining elements of saving faith today. Is the interpretation of Matthew 16 given in the previous section at variance with this passage?

The solution to this apparent dilemma lies in understanding the dispensational, kingdom-oriented context of Matthew 11. John the Baptist had been preaching to the nation of Israel that the promised kingdom of heaven on earth was "at hand" (Matt. 3:2). Jesus and his disciples followed John's example by preaching the same message (Matt. 4:17, 23; 9:35; 10:7) and even performing miracles commensurate with the kingdom's appearance (Matt. 4:23-24; 8:3, 13, 15-16, 26, 32; 9:25, 30, 35; 10:8). But this caused John to become perplexed and to wonder whether Jesus was truly the Messiah. If the kingdom was about to appear and the Messiah had finally come to Israel, then why was the King's herald currently suffering unjustly in prison? Where was the promised kingdom of heaven on earth with its universal justice and righteousness?

In response to John's confusion, the Lord chose to simply re-affirm the many miraculous signs of His Messiahship (Matt. 11:5). These constituted indisputable and sufficient evidence to reassure John that Jesus was truly the Messiah, even if John could not foresee the imminent postponement of the kingdom. The reason that the Lord Jesus did not present His approaching death and resurrection to John at this time as evidence that He was truly "the Christ" was simply because John's dilemma was kingdom-oriented and at this juncture Jesus had not yet been officially rejected by the nation and its leadership as their Messiah.[34] At the time

---

[33] Stanley D. Toussaint, *Behold the King: A Study of Matthew* (Portland: Multnomah Press, 1980), 148.

[34] Though it is clear from Scripture that John the Baptist knew from the very beginning of the Lord Jesus' public ministry that Christ would die as "the Lamb of God" in order to take away the sin of the world (John 1:29), it is never revealed in Scripture just how much John understood about the Lord's death *as it related to the kingdom*. We know that the relationship of the cross to the kingdom was a major problem in the minds of others as well (Luke 24:19-21; Acts 1:3, 6-7; 1 Peter 1:10-11). It is entirely conceivable that John did not foresee the nation of Israel turning away from Jesus as their rightful Messiah with their subsequent rejec-

of Matthew 11, the kingdom was still presently being offered to Israel,[35] even though the rejection of the kingdom and its King were also suffering violence (Matt. 11:11-12) and would soon be officially and decisively rejected in Matthew 12:24-32.[36] This rejection of the kingdom and its King is followed by Christ's announcement of the mystery form of the kingdom in Matthew 13, which is then followed by John the Baptist's execution in Matthew 14:1-10. The Lord Jesus knew that John would not live to "see" or "hear" (Matt. 11:4) of the Lamb's (John 1:29) crucifixion and resurrection which were only announced by Christ starting in Matthew 16:21, where it says, *"From that time Jesus began to show to His disciples that He must . . . be killed, and be raised the third day."*

The empirical evidence that John the Baptist needed *at the time of Matthew 11* to verify that Jesus was "the Christ" consisted only of those signs which were contemporaneous with his own life and ministry as the herald of the King and His kingdom. John the Baptist was not an apostle commissioned to preach the gospel of Christ's death and resurrection. Though the miracles cited by Jesus in Matthew 11:5 did serve to identify Him as the Messiah, they were defining elements of His Messiahship specifically with respect to the offer and imminent appearing of the kingdom. They were *kingdom miracles* appropriate to John and his generation. Since the offer of the kingdom has subsequently been rescinded and the promised kingdom postponed, believers today are not to preach the gospel of the kingdom which can no longer legitimately be described as "at hand." The kingdom is at least seven years away, assuming the rapture occurred today. It is not coincidental that the preaching of this kingdom gospel was always attended by miracles authenticating the kingdom's appearance, such as healings, exorcisms, and raising the dead (Matt. 4:23; 9:35; 10:7-8).[37] In contrast, the gospel that the Church has been commissioned to preach to the world today for its salvation consists only of the miracle of Christ's substitutionary death and glorious resurrection (1 Cor. 15:3-4); and it does not need the accompaniment of authenticating miracles. Unfortunately, Charismatic and Pentecostal teaching today often mixes the gospel of the kingdom as found in the Synoptics with the gospel of Christ that we are to preach post-Pentecost. As a result, kingdom miracles are erroneously expected to attend the preaching of the gospel of grace in this Church age. For these reasons, Jesus' death and resurrection are

---

tion of Him in crucifixion. It is *possible* that John did *not* make the connection that Christ's rejection via crucifixion would be the very means by which He would become a sacrificial offering for the world.

[35] Toussaint, *Behold the King: A Study of Matthew*, 152. This is evidenced by the use of the term "now" (*arti*) in Matthew 11:12, *"from the days of John the Baptist until now (arti) the kingdom of heaven suffers violence."*

[36] Figart, *The King of the Kingdom of Heaven*, 217-22; Toussaint, *Behold the King*, 148-49.

[37] Mark R. Saucy, "Miracles and Jesus' Proclamation of the Kingdom of God," *BSac* 153 (July-September 1996): 282-83, 305.

the defining elements of Him being "the Christ" in the contents of saving faith today rather than the authenticating miracles mentioned by the Lord to John the Baptist in Matthew 11:5.

Luke 24:18-27

18 *Then the one whose name was Cleopas answered and said to Him, "Are You the only stranger in Jerusalem, and have You not known the things which happened there in these days?"*

19 *And He said to them, "What things?" So they said to Him, "The things concerning Jesus of Nazareth, who was a Prophet mighty in deed and word before God and all the people,*

20 *"and how the chief priests and our rulers delivered Him to be* ***condemned to death, and crucified Him****.*

21 *"But we were hoping that it was He who was going to* ***redeem*** *Israel. Indeed, besides all this, today is the third day since these things happened.*

22 *"Yes, and certain women of our company, who arrived at the tomb early, astonished us.*

23 *"When they did not find His body, they came saying that they had also seen a vision of angels who said* ***He was alive.***

24 *"And certain of those who were with us went to the tomb and found it just as the women had said; but Him they did not see."*

25 *"Then He said to them, "O foolish ones, and slow of heart to believe in all that the prophets have spoken!*

26 *"Ought not* ***the Christ*** *to have* ***suffered these things*** *and to enter into His glory"?*

27 *And beginning at Moses and all the Prophets, He expounded to them in all the Scriptures the things concerning Himself.*

Here is another vivid example of how the Lord Jesus Himself defined "the Christ" (24:26). According to the Lord, the disciples on the road to Emmaus should not have been surprised by His crucifixion and resurrection, since it was exactly how the Old Testament had defined "the Christ." They should have known "these things" about the Christ that were predicted in their Old Testament Scriptures.

It is also vital at this point to understand what it means in Luke 24:26 that *"the Christ . . . suffered these things."* Does Christ's suffering refer to something other than His death by crucifixion? In the context of Luke 24:26, the reference to *"these things"* in Jesus' statement (*"the Christ . . . suffered these things"*) points back to the two disciples' news report about Jesus being *"condemned to death, and crucified"* in verse 20. This connection is important to note, since later in Luke-Acts, Luke will repeatedly record the pairing of Christ's death and resurrection as the content of the apostles' evangelistic preaching, with Christ's death sometimes referred to simply as suffering (Luke 24:46; Acts 1:3; 3:18; 17:3; 26:23).

The Lord Jesus obviously suffered greatly leading up to the cross, and in this sense experienced "sufferings" (plural), but the incomparable agony of His physical *and spiritual* suffering on the cross constituted the chief means by which He suffered on our behalf. Thus the terms "suffer" and "suffering" in the New Testament are sometimes employed as synonyms of Christ's atoning death by crucifixion (Heb. 2:9-10; 13:12; 1 Peter 1:11; 3:18; 4:1).

Luke 24:45-47

45 *And He opened their understanding, that they might comprehend the Scriptures.*
46 *Then He said to them, "Thus it is written, and thus it was necessary for **the Christ** to **suffer** and to **rise from the dead** the third day,*
47 *and that **repentance** and remission of sins should be preached in His name to all nations, beginning at Jerusalem."*

Here is one final example from the Synoptic Gospels where the Lord Jesus Himself defines "the Christ" by the twin truths of His death and resurrection[38] in fulfillment of the Old Testament. From this point onward throughout Acts and the Epistles, we see that the condition for eternal salvation and forgiveness accompanies a description of Jesus as "the Christ." Here forgiveness is conditioned upon repentance, which is the change of mind inherent to faith in Jesus as the Christ. The next two chapters will examine the references to Jesus as He is presented to be "the Christ" in the Book of Acts. In such passages, it's as though the apostles can hardly mention the Lord's death and resurrection without also uttering in the same breath the offer of divine forgiveness and salvation, along with the condition for receiving it. By preaching the person and work of Christ, along with the provision and condition of salvation, the apostles were simply preaching the gospel of Christ for eternal salvation, just as they had been commissioned to do by Jesus Christ here in Luke 24:45-47. But this leads us to another significant consideration regarding the crossless gospel. Did the apostles carry out the commission of Luke 24:45-47 for the eternal salvation of the lost or was it merely for the sanctification of the saved?

The Gospel, "the Christ," and the Great Commission

One evidence that the content of faith required for eternal salvation includes belief in Jesus Christ's death and resurrection comes from a comparison of the Synoptic Gospels. In each, we have what is theologically and missiologically called "the Great Commission." The Great Commission of Mark's Gospel is the only one that contains the actual word "gospel."

---

[38] G. Michael Cocoris, *The Salvation Controversy* (Santa Monica, CA: Insights from the Word, 2008), 22; Joel B. Green, *The Gospel of Luke*, NICNT (Grand Rapids: Eerdmans, 1997), 856-57.

Correctly Interpreting Mark 16:15-16

In Mark 16:15-16, Christ says to the eleven disciples, *"Go into all the world and preach the gospel to every creature. He who believes and is baptized will be saved; but he who does not believe will be condemned."* Several key concepts in this passage relate to the question of the required contents of saving faith, as verses 15-16 declare that belief in the gospel is what will save a person from condemnation.

The use of "condemnation" in verse 16 is most likely a reference to eternal condemnation. In the New Testament, the word for "condemnation" (*katakrinō*) most often refers to the condemnation of the lost, i.e. eternal condemnation (Matt. 12:41-42; Rom. 8:1, 3, 34; 1 Cor. 11:32), though it is also used once of temporal judgment (Rom. 14:23).[39] The interpretation of *eternal* condemnation in Mark 16:16 would be most appropriate in this context since Christ is commissioning the disciples to preach the gospel to the lost world, not to those who are already believers in Christ. This preaching of the gospel would be necessary for the lost to be justified and to receive eternal life, not for the saved to become further saved or sanctified, as some crossless gospel teachers interpret this passage.

In Mark 16:16, the reference to *"and is baptized"* is merely a description of what normally follows *belief* in the gospel. This is consistent with the rest of Scripture, where the only requirement to avoid eternal condemnation is faith or belief. In Mark 16:16, the reference to water baptism serves merely as a *description* of those who receive salvation through faith; it is not a *prescription* for salvation. This is evidenced by the immediate context that describes those things that *"**will follow** those who believe"* (16:17-18). Baptism normally follows belief in the gospel. It is vital to note that Mark 16:17 says certain things will follow *"those who believe,"* NOT those who believe and are baptized. Just as those who believe *"**will** be saved"* (16:16a) and *"he who does not believe **will** be condemned"* (16:16b), so there will be certain confirmatory signs as fulfilled in the Book of Acts following those who believe. Believers *"**will** cast out demons"* and *"**will** speak with other tongues"* (16:17); and they *"**will** take up serpents"* and they *"**will** by no means hurt them,"* and they *"**will** lay hands on the sick,"* and they *"**will** recover"* (16:18). Each of these miraculous signs occurred in the days of the apostles (Acts 2:4-11; 16:18; 28:1-8) in order to establish the credibility of these disciples as Christ's apostolic ambassadors and to authenticate their message (Mark 16:20; 2 Cor. 12:12; Heb. 2:3-4). Though water baptism normally followed belief in the gospel according to Mark 16:15-16, the miraculous

---

[39] Romans 8:1 is included under "eternal condemnation" though it relates to the Christian life. Though Romans 8:1 does teach that we as Christians are no longer condemned to live a life of penal servitude to the flesh/sin nature, it is also true that this blessing is only for those "in Christ Jesus," and it is received at the moment of justification in God's sight. Furthermore, until someone is eternally saved they are still under such "condemnation."

signs described in Mark 16:17-20 were typical only for specific believers in Christ—those who also happened to be apostles of Christ. But since the authority of the apostles and their message was established as early as the 1st century, these authenticating signs served their purpose and ceased at that time as well, while baptism continues to follow those who have believed the gospel.

It appears that Mark 16:16 is simply teaching that the normal result of someone believing the gospel of Christ is that they get baptized, even though they do not *need* to get baptized to be saved. To use the common analogy of the bus, it is like saying, *"In order to get downtown* (i.e., heaven/saved), *you need to get on the bus* (i.e., believe the gospel). *So, he who gets on the bus and sits down* (i.e., gets baptized) *will make it to downtown."* But do you really need to "sit down" once you get on the bus in order to make it to downtown?! You could make it to downtown by standing up within the bus the whole way there! But the normal result of getting on the bus is that you sit down. And the normal result of believing the gospel is that you get baptized. Mark 16:16-18 is simply describing those who believe the gospel and are eternally saved, not prescribing multiple conditions for salvation.

The word "saved" (*sōzō*) in Mark 16:16 also needs clarification. Crossless gospel advocates claim that this term in Mark normally refers to physical, temporal deliverance and that it should be understood this way in Mark 16:16. They say that Mark 16:15-16 is teaching that faith *plus baptism* was required for certain Jewish, born again believers to be "saved" from the temporal wrath of God upon them due to disobedience. This is also how they interpret Acts 2:38,[40] which will be covered extensively in the next chapter. Regarding the use of the word "gospel" in the Gospel of Mark, Jeremy Myers writes, "There are occasional calls to *believe the gospel*, with the promised result not being everlasting life, but deliverance from coming wrath (Mark 1:15; 16:15-16)."[41] Myers also goes on to claim:

> Mark 1:15 may shed a lot of light on understanding Mark 16:15-16. If believing the gospel of the kingdom leads one to repentance (or the baptism of repentance) in order to escape temporal judgment, then the salvation of 16:16 is not everlasting life, but deliverance from judgment. If Mark is written to believers (as I believe it was), then 16:15-16 is a call to believers (cf. 16:14), not unbelievers. Mark records two conditions for believers to escape wrath: (1) repent and (2) believe the good news about the kingdom offer.[42]

---

[40] Zane Hodges and Bob Wilkin, "Short Discussions on Specific Passages" (Mark 16:16, Believe and Be Baptized?), Grace Evangelical Society website, www. faithalone.org/Audio/080905a.ram (accessed April 18, 2006).

[41] Jeremy D. Myers, "The Gospel is More Than "Faith Alone in Christ Alone"," *JOTGES* 19 (Autumn 2006): 43.

[42] Ibid., 43-44n.

While it is true that the word for "saved" (*sōzō*) in the Gospel of Mark is normally used in physical deliverance contexts, this is certainly not the correct interpretation of Mark 16:16. *Sōzō* is used at least one other time in Mark to refer to eternal life (10:17-26). It is also used this way many times throughout the four Gospels (Matt. 1:21; 18:11; 19:25; Luke 7:50; 8:12; 13:23; 18:26; 19:10; John 3:17; 5:34; 10:9; 12:47).

But there is a very simple reason why the word "save" (*sōzō*) in Mark's Gospel most often refers to deliverance of a person's physical life rather than eternal life. Throughout most of Mark, Christ's earthly ministry to Israel is described. The focus of His three year public ministry in Israel prior to Mark 16:15-16 was *not* upon spreading the gospel of eternal salvation to the whole world but upon announcing the gospel, or good news, of the coming earthly, physical kingdom. This is why at the beginning of Christ's public ministry He announced the fulfillment of Isaiah's prophecy describing His first coming, saying, *"The Spirit of the Lord is upon Me, because He has anointed Me [lit.] to preach good news to the poor; He has sent Me to heal the brokenhearted, to proclaim liberty to the captives and recovery of sight to the blind, to set at liberty those who are oppressed; to proclaim the acceptable year of the Lord"* (Luke 4:18-19). The introduction of the King and His kingdom would involve supernatural, benevolent miracles.

This is also consistent with the episode in Matthew 11 explained earlier. The miracles referred to in Matthew 11:4-5 served as proof or confirmation that the King of the literal, earthly, physical kingdom promised to Israel was present and that He was offering them the kingdom. However, this kingdom gospel program shifted with the rejection of Israel's King. From that point on, the Lord established a new program of proclaiming the gospel of the grace of God in Jesus Christ, on a universal scale, for the building of Christ's body the Church. With this dispensational shift in programs following Christ's death and resurrection came the necessary change in the form of the "gospel" to be preached, along with a change in emphasis towards eternal salvation for the entire world, rather than temporal, physical deliverance for the nation of Israel.

The vital question regarding Mark 16:15-16 is simply this: what is "the gospel" that men must believe to be saved from eternal condemnation? The gospel referred to in verse 15 is certainly the message of Christ's death and resurrection. This conclusion can be seen from the fact that Christ waits until *after* His death and resurrection before speaking of "the gospel" that is now to be preached to the entire world. Secondly, Mark 14:9 is the nearest antecedent reference to "the gospel" in Mark; and there "the gospel" that is predicted to spread throughout the whole world is in reference to Christ's death and resurrection, the very events anticipated in faith by the act of Mary of Bethany in anointing Christ's body prior to His death (Matt. 26:6-13; Mark 14:1-9; John 12:1-8).[43] Thirdly, the reference to "the gospel" in Mark 16:15 corresponds with the message the apostles were commissioned to preach in a parallel passage in Luke 24:46, which included Christ's death and resurrection, along with the condition of repentance for the remission of sins (24:47). What all of this indicates is that being saved from God's eternal condemnation is the result of believing that Christ died for one's sins and rose again. This is the gospel that must be believed according to Mark 16:15-16, not just a bare promise of eternal life for all who believe in the name "Jesus" without necessarily even knowing who He is or what He's done.

Crossless Interpretations of Great Commission Passages

But all of this leads to an insurmountable problem of enormous proportions for the crossless gospel position. Proponents of a crossless saving faith have painted themselves into a corner with respect to their interpretations of the Great Commission passages. They have interpreted these passages in such a way as to leave no Great Commission passages that tell us to preach the gospel to a lost world! They have effectively reinterpreted all the Great Commission passages as applying to those who are already saved, not the unsaved.

Advocates of the crossless view correctly recognize that the Matthew 28:16-20 version of the Great Commission does not contain an explicit reference to the *gospel for the lost.* It is the message of *discipleship* for those who are already saved and it presumes that the gospel of salvation has

---

[43] It seems Mary was the only one, or one of very few, who understood Christ's repeated prior warnings to His disciples that He was going to Jerusalem to die and rise again. The fact that *"this gospel"* in Mark 14:9 is not a reference to the Gospel of Mark itself, as some have interpreted the earlier reference to "gospel" in Mark 1:1, can be seen by the fact that this Marian episode is also recorded in the Gospels of Matthew and John. Second, Christ says this gospel will be *"preached"* and *"spoken of"*—not "written" per se. Nor is *"this gospel"* in Mark 14:9 referring to the gospel of the kingdom that the disciples previously preached *"only to the lost sheep of the house of Israel"* (Matt. 10:5-7). Rather, the content of *"this gospel"* is contextually determined and it concerns Christ's imminently approaching death and resurrection which Mary foresaw in faith. It was this message that was to be *"preached in the whole world"* (Matt. 26:13; Mark 14:9). It is also apparent that Mary's deed is not considered to be an element of the gospel itself as some, such as Wilkin have taught. Wilkin states, "This verse implies that the anointing of Jesus' head with costly oil by Mary (v 7ff) is part of the good news message" (Bob Wilkin, "The Gospel Is Good News about the Lord Jesus [Gal. 1:6-9; 2:14-21]," Grace Evangelical Society Conference, Fort Worth, TX, March 6, 2008). However, Christ promises Mary something beyond the gospel when He says, *"wherever this gospel is preached in the whole world, what this woman has done will also (kai) be told as a memorial to her."* Both Matthew 26:13 and Mark 14:9 have the adjunctive use of *kai* ("also") to show that Mary's deed is not properly an element of *"this gospel"* but is in addition to *"this gospel."* This account of Mary's great faith and deed would be told worldwide in conjunction with the gospel. Furthermore, in Mark 14:6 the Lord says, *"She has done a good work for Me."* Yet, the gospel is not about the good works we do for God but about the work of God's Son that He has done for us.

already been preached as a result of "going." For this reason, Wilkin affirms with respect to Matthew 28:18-20 that "in some expressions of the Great Commission the Lord only spoke of discipleship."[44] However, an important distinction must be recognized. Matthew's Great Commission to make *disciples* takes place in **Galilee** (Matt. 28:7, 10, 16-20; John 21:1ff) while the Great Commission to *preach the gospel* was given previously in **Jerusalem** and nearby Bethany (Mark 16:15; Luke 24:33, 47, 49, 50, 52; John 20:19-23; Acts 1:8).[45]

With this distinction in mind, crossless proponents are faced with a serious dilemma. They have reinterpreted the message of Christ's crucifixion, resurrection, and repentance for the remission of sins in Luke 24:46-47 as the message that is only directly applicable to those of us who are Christians for deliverance from the temporal wrath of God in our lives.[46] Thus, Wilkin teaches, "In the same way, the Great Commission in Luke concerns discipleship. Repentance is indeed a condition of fellowship with God and of the forgiveness associated with that fellowship (e.g., Luke 5:32; 15:4-32)."[47] Similarly, they do not believe that the forgiveness of sins referred to in John 20:19-23 is in reference to the lost receiving judicial forgiveness of sins and eternal life; but instead it is for those who are already saved in order to live a life of repentance and harmony with God as a Christian.[48] So, since Matthew's Great Commission is about making disciples of Christ following belief in the gospel, and since they have also reinterpreted Mark 16:15-16 to be about physical, temporal salvation from the wrath of God in the life of those who are already regenerate, what Great Commission passages do they have left that define the essential, saving message to the lost or even contain the command to evangelize the lost?! Matthew 28:18-20 is out. Mark 16:15-16 is out. Luke 24:46-47 is out. Even John 20:19-23 is out; if it is even to be properly considered a

---

[44] Robert N. Wilkin, "Does Your Mind Need Changing? Repentance Reconsidered," *JOTGES* 11 (Spring 1998): 43.

[45] The Galilean and Jerusalem commissions should be properly distinguished. While the Jerusalem and Galilean commissions are technically separate commissions, on the other hand, they cannot be separated in the sense that the Church today only accepts one but not the other. Nor should they both be dismissed as not being applicable for today, as hyper-dispensationalism teaches. Both commissions were given by the same Lord, Jesus Christ, to the same group of disciples, within the same general time frame, namely after Christ's death and resurrection but before His ascension. Therefore both are necessary for the establishment of Christ's Body, the universal Church, which began in Acts 2 on the day of Pentecost.

[46] Zane C. Hodges, *Harmony with God* (Dallas: Redención Viva, 2001), 8, 65. While they claim that God desires even the unregenerate to enter a life of repentance and harmony with God, this can only be done according to their view by believing in Jesus for eternal life. They do *not* claim that the message of Christ's death and resurrection and repentance for the remission of sins is the message that *directly* relates to the unregenerate world as the message they *must initially* hear and believe in order to receive eternal life.

[47] Wilkin, "Does Your Mind Need Changing? Repentance Reconsidered," 43.

[48] Hodges, *Harmony with God*, 66.

"Great Commission" passage. They've all become sanctification passages for those who are already justified in God's sight!

So what is the Church's Great Commission? While adherents of the G.E.S. gospel would certainly disavow this conclusion,[49] according to the logic of their own position, there is no longer a "Great Commission" given by Jesus Christ where the Church is obligated to preach the gospel of Christ's death and resurrection to a lost world as the message to be believed for eternal life and judicial forgiveness. The Church's commission based on these once universally recognized "Great Commission" passages has suddenly become a matter solely of sanctifying the saints, not saving the lost!

The Person and Work of "the Christ"

Based on the observations made thus far in this chapter we can now form a few preliminary conclusions about Jesus being "the Christ." First, as the immediately preceding section demonstrated, there is no material difference between the saving message of the gospel (Mark 16:15) and the saving message that Jesus is the Christ who died and rose again to provide remission of sins (Luke 24:45-47). Second, it has been observed from the Synoptic Gospels that on those occasions where the Lord Jesus specifically chose to provide some definitive explanation for the meaning of "the Christ," He Himself described the Christ to be no one less than true deity and true humanity. Thirdly, Jesus' death and resurrection are also stated to be essential aspects of His messianic identity as "the Christ" according to His own express teaching.

It is also highly significant that within the context of Luke 24 where the Lord Jesus defines Himself to be "the Christ" by virtue of His death and resurrection (Luke 24:26, 46), He also reveals to His apostles His sacrificial death wounds that have inhered to His eternal, glorified, resurrected body (Luke 24:39-40). The relevance of this fact for the content of saving faith cannot be overestimated. It means that the saving work of Christ's death and resurrection has now become inextricable with His very person (Rev. 5:6-12).[50] His deity, humanity, death, and resurrection form an indissoluble complex of attributes that comprise His very person, identity, and being.[51] This is the reason why belief in the person of Christ

---

[49] For example, Wilkin states, "However, we must remember the Great Commission was not merely a commission to evangelize. It was also a commission to disciple those who believe" (Wilkin, "Does Your Mind Need Changing? Repentance Reconsidered," 43). And yet, Wilkin offers no Scripture passages telling us which Great Commission passage is enjoining the evangelization of the lost.

[50] Herman N. Ridderbos, *The Gospel According to John: A Theological Commentary* (Grand Rapids: Eerdmans, 1997), 376; Gregory P. Sapaugh, "A Response to Hodges: How to Lead a Person to Christ, Parts 1 and 2," *JOTGES* 14 (Autumn 2001): 28.

[51] As Machen declared years ago, "The Christian doctrine of the atonement, therefore, is

for eternal life must now entail belief in Him as the once sacrificed but now risen Savior.[52]

This leads to another vital consideration. In contrast to the clear and repeated emphasis of the Synoptic Gospels upon the Lord's person and work as defining characteristics of Him as the Messiah, the crossless gospel's restricted meaning of "the Christ" as merely "the guarantor of eternal life" is *never found* in the Synoptics. Only two possibilities can account for this glaring omission. Either the crossless notion of "the Christ" is seriously amiss or else the Synoptic Gospels have a different meaning for "the Christ" than that of John's Gospel. Crossless advocates opt for the latter view and claim that there is a unique "Johannine sense" of the term "Christ." In addition, they insist that only the fourth Gospel is evangelistic in purpose. According to their view, this means that the Synoptics are merely edificational in purpose and designed primarily for those who are already believers in Christ. The end result of such reasoning is that crossless proponents are now able to view the defining elements of Jesus' Messiahship in the Synoptics—His deity, humanity, death, and resurrection—as only necessary to believe for one's edification and sanctification, not for eternal salvation. One major problem with this view, however, is that these defining characteristics of "the Christ" are proclaimed primarily to *unbelievers* in the Synoptic Gospels. Therefore, the person and work of Christ must be considered evangelistically necessary as the content of saving faith for *the lost* today. The same holds true not only with the Lord Jesus' own teaching about Himself as "the Christ" in the Gospels but also with the evangelistic preaching of the apostles in the Book of Acts, which will be the focus of the next two chapters.

---

altogether rooted in the Christian doctrine of the deity of Christ. The reality of an atonement for sin depends altogether upon the New Testament presentation of the Person of Christ." J. Gresham Machen, *Christianity and Liberalism* (Grand Rapids: Eerdmans, 1923), 126.

[52] This critical truth is also conveyed by the apostle John in his writings. Luke and John are in perfect doctrinal accord on the fact that belief in the person of Jesus Christ cannot be separated from His work.

Chapter 16

What Does "the Christ" Mean in Acts 2?

OVERVIEW

Acts 2 provides a test-case for the type of "saving message" preached by the apostles at the commencement of the Church age. In Peter's evangelism on the day of Pentecost, he presents Jesus as "the Christ" to a lost audience of unbelieving Jews in Jerusalem. The definitive elements of Peter's gospel—the defining elements of Jesus as "the Christ"—include Jesus' deity, humanity, and bodily resurrection. The crucifixion is also explicit in Peter's message, and even the substitutionary and satisfactory nature of that death is implicit. The forgiveness of sins offered in Acts 2:38 is also seen to be inherent to justification and is not merely offered in order to escape God's temporal, physical judgment as part of sanctification in the Christian life, as certain crossless adherents teach. This salvific forgiveness is conditioned upon repentance, which in the context involves a change of mind about the person and work of Jesus Christ. The requirement for eternal salvation in Acts 2:38 is not water baptism but a repentance or change of mind that rests upon (epi) "the name" of Jesus Christ. This interpretation is consistent with the Lord's previous Great Commission to Peter and the apostles, and it harmonizes with both the content of saving faith and the sole condition of faith/repentance found throughout the rest of Acts.

Our world is filled with various conceptions of "the Christ," largely due to the many cults and religions that vie for mankind's faith and devotion. For example, the messiah of Orthodox and Conservative Judaism is considered to be someone who is superhuman, who is able to bring in God's kingdom, and yet who is not divine. Nor is the "messiah" of Judaism someone who dies for mankind's sins.[1] There is also the "christ" of Islam. Its holy book, the Qur'an, hails Jesus as a great prophet[2] but not someone who is God-incarnate, since God has no equals.[3] In Islam, Jesus did not die on the cross nor rise from the dead.[4] Then there is the "christ" of the cults. According to Mormonism, Jesus is just a god, such as we may also become.[5] Nor did his death provide atonement for all of man's sins, since man himself must still provide atonement for the particularly heinous sins that he has committed.[6] Jehovah's Witnesses regard Jesus Christ to be a mighty god who is actually a spirit-being—Michael the archangel to be precise.[7] Nor did this "christ" rise from the dead in the same body that he died with, for Jehovah supposedly "disposed" of his earthly body.[8] Then there is the "christ" of Gnostic belief, who was never really material or human, who neither died upon the cross nor rose from the dead.[9] And finally, there is the "christ" of the New Age movement who, we are told, was a mere man who actualized the divinity inherent in every one of us and in the process achieved personal at-one-ment with the cosmic consciousness, leaving us a similar path to follow.[10] Nor did this "christ" truly die, for we are told that we must liberate our minds from the notion that God judged His own Son upon the cross for

---

[1] Louis Goldberg, *Our Jewish Friends* (Neptune, NJ: Loizeaux Brothers, 1983), 92-93.

[2] Sura 4:163.

[3] Sura 3:59; 4:171-72; 19:88-89.

[4] Sura 4:157-58.

[5] Brigham Young, *Journal of Discourses*, 9:286, www.journalofdiscourses.org (accessed September 21, 2008).

[6] Brigham Young, *Journal of Discourses*, 3:247, 4:220, www.journalofdiscourses.org (accessed September 21, 2008).

[7] *The Watchtower* (May 15, 1969): 307; idem, (December 15, 1984): 29.

[8] *The Kingdom Is at Hand* (Brooklyn, NY: Watchtower Bible and Tract Society, 1944), 259; *Things in Which It Is Impossible for God to Lie* (Brooklyn, NY: Watchtower Bible and Tract Society, 1965), 354; *The Watchtower* (September 1, 1953): 518; idem, (August 1, 1975): 479.

[9] "The Revelation of Peter," in *The Nag Hammadi Scriptures*, ed. Marvin Meyer (San Francisco: HarperCollins, 2007), 495-96; "The Letter of Peter to Philip," in *The Nag Hammadi Scriptures*, ed. Marvin Meyer (San Francisco: HarperCollins, 2007), 589.

[10] David Spangler, *Reflections on the Christ* (Forres, Scotland: Findhorn Publications, 1981), 14.

sin. At least this is what the channeled spirit of "Jesus" claimed in 1966 to the author of the now popular, *Course in Miracles*, when this so-called "Jesus" stated:

> You will not find peace until you have removed the nails from the hands of God's Son and taken the last thorn from his forehead. The Love of God surrounds His Son whom the god of the crucifixion condemns. Teach not that I died in vain. Teach rather that I did NOT die by demonstrating that I live IN YOU. For the UNDOING of the crucifixion of God's Son is the work of the redemption, in which everyone has a part of equal value. God does not judge His blameless Son.[11]

With so many different conceptions of "the Christ," how can anyone know with certainty which one, if any, is correct? Will any one of these "christs" suffice when it comes to believing in Jesus for eternal life? Satan has certainly foisted many false christs upon mankind in an effort to divert man's attention away from the true Christ (2 Cor. 4:3-7; 11:1-4). But there is only one proper object of saving faith—the Christ of the gospel. It is no coincidence, therefore, to observe that down through the centuries Satan has attacked with concentrated diabolical ferocity not only the truth of justification by grace through faith alone, but also the very pillars of Christ's person and work—His deity, humanity, substitutionary death, and bodily resurrection. If Satan cannot undo the miracle of the incarnation, or the work of Calvary and the empty tomb, then why does he bother trying to dissuade mankind from believing in these key Christological truths? It is precisely because he knows something that many Free Grace people have lost sight of, namely, that these are the essential, defining characteristics of Jesus as "the Christ" that are the very contents of the gospel that must be believed for eternal salvation—the very gospel that he actively resists (2 Cor. 4:3-4; 11:1-4).

In the Book of Acts, we have an inspired, infallible record of the evangelistic preaching of Christ's own apostles. There we see, starting with Peter's preaching at Pentecost, that the One in whom men are to intentionally place their faith is none other than the One who is both God and man, who died a substitutionary death on the cross and rose from the dead to guarantee forgiveness of sins to all who will repent by resting upon His "name"—by relying upon the person and work of the Lord Jesus Christ.

<u>Acts 2:22-41</u>

22 *Men of Israel, hear these words:* ***Jesus*** *of Nazareth, a* ***Man*** *attested by God to you by miracles, wonders, and signs which God did through Him in your midst, as you yourselves also know—*

---

[11] *Jesus' Course in Miracles*, ed. Helen Schucman and William Thetford (n.p.: Course in Miracles Society, 2000), 104 (capitalization original).

23 *"Him, being **delivered** by the determined purpose and foreknowledge of God, you have taken by lawless hands, have **crucified, and put to death;***
24 *"whom God **raised up**, having loosed the pains of death, because it was not possible that He should be held by it.*
25 *"For David says **concerning Him**: 'I foresaw the **LORD** always before my face, For He is at my right hand, that I may not be shaken.*
26 *Therefore my heart rejoiced, and my tongue was glad; Moreover my flesh also will rest in hope.*
27 *For You will not leave my soul in Hades, Nor will You allow Your **Holy One** to see corruption.*
28 *You have made known to me the ways of life; You will make me full of joy in Your presence.'*
29 *"Men and brethren, let me speak freely to you of the patriarch David, that he is both dead and buried, and his tomb is with us to this day.*
30 *"Therefore, being a prophet, and knowing that God had sworn with an oath to him that of the fruit of his body, **according to the flesh**, He would **raise up the Christ** to sit on his throne,*
31 *"he, foreseeing this, spoke concerning the **resurrection of the Christ**, that His soul was not left in Hades, nor did His flesh see corruption.*
32 *"This Jesus God has **raised up**, of which we are all witnesses.*
33 *"Therefore being exalted to the **right hand of God**, and having received from the Father the promise of the Holy Spirit, He poured out this which you now see and hear.*
34 *"For David did not ascend into the heavens, but he says himself: 'The LORD said to my Lord, "**Sit at My right hand**,*
35 *Till I make Your enemies Your footstool." '*
36 *"Therefore let all the house of Israel **know assuredly** that God has made this Jesus, whom you **crucified**, both **Lord** and **Christ**."*
37 *Now when they heard this, they were cut to the heart, and said to Peter and the rest of the apostles, "Men and brethren, what shall we do?"*
38 *Then Peter said to them, "**Repent**, and let every one of you be baptized in the **name of Jesus Christ** for the **remission of sins**; and you shall receive the gift of the Holy Spirit.*
39 *"For the promise is to you and to your children, and to all who are afar off, as many as the Lord our God will call."*
40 *And with many other words he testified and exhorted them, saying, "Be **saved** from this perverse generation."*
41 *Then those who gladly **received his word** were baptized; and that day about three thousand souls were added to them.*

Peter's preaching here on the day of Pentecost may be considered programmatic in the sense that it sets the direction for the evangelistic preaching recorded in the rest of Acts.[12] Its importance cannot be overstated as it is

---

[12] Stanley E. Porter, "The Messiah in Luke and Acts: Forgiveness for the Captives," in *The Messiah in the Old and New Testaments*, ed. Stanley E. Porter (Grand Rapids: Eerdmans,

utterly foundational to the rest of the book. It is the first example of apostolic evangelism in Church history. It is also by far the longest sermon in the Petrine portion of Acts in chapters 1-12. (Paul's preaching in Acts 13 is only slightly longer.) For these reasons, and due to the complexity of other interpretational factors in the passage, Acts 2 will be given its own separate treatment in this chapter.

In terms of the content of Peter's message in Acts 2 and the response called for from his audience, he simply follows the die cast by the Lord Jesus in His Great Commission to the apostles in Luke 24:45-47. The person and work of the Savior are preached, along with the condition and provision of salvation. This is nothing less than the gospel of Christ. Since Peter was addressing a Jewish audience in Jerusalem that had rejected Jesus as "the Christ" (Acts 2:36-37), the purpose of his preaching was plainly evangelization, not the sanctification of existing believers.

Eternal vs. Temporal Salvation

Another matter of paramount importance to correctly interpreting Acts 2 is determining if the salvation in view in Acts 2:38-40 is eternal or temporal. Were the Jews who were cut to the heart in verse 37 actually born again at that point, so that verses 38-40 address temporal salvation relative to sanctification rather than eternal life? In an attempt to explain Acts 2:38 in a manner consistent with God's grace, it has become somewhat vogue among Free Grace interpreters in recent years to see Peter's call for repentance and baptism as necessary for physical salvation from God's impending national destruction upon Israel due to its collective unbelief and rejection of the Messiah.[13] Though this interpretation admirably seeks to defend salvation by grace alone, it actually creates an entirely new set of doctrinal and hermeneutical problems. One major problem is the entire focus of Peter's message prior to Acts 2:37. If it is reasoned that Peter was only concerned with physical judgment in Acts 2:38-40, since the Jewish audience was supposedly born again by the time of Acts 2:37, then why wasn't the "focus"[14] of Peter's preaching in verses 22-37 on a "saving message" that centered upon the theme of eternal life instead of the death and resurrection of Christ?

While the destruction of Jerusalem in A.D. 70 was certainly a consequence of the nation's continued denial of Christ, a temporal salvation in

---

2007), 160.

[13] Zane C. Hodges, *The Gospel Under Siege*, 2nd ed. (Dallas: Kerugma, 1992), 117-18; idem, *Harmony with God: A Fresh Look at Repentance* (Dallas: Redención Viva, 2001), 89-107; Robert N. Wilkin, *Confident in Christ: Living by Faith Really Works* (Irving, TX: Grace Evangelical Society, 1999), 194-95; idem, "Does Your Mind Need Changing? Repentance Reconsidered," *JOTGES* 11 (Spring 1998): 43n13.

[14] Zane C. Hodges, "How to Lead People to Christ, Part 1: The Content of Our Message," *JOTGES* 13 (Autumn 2000): 8.

Acts 2 must be viewed as secondary to Peter's primary objective of judicial forgiveness for these unbelieving Israelites. When Peter implores his audience to *"be saved (sōthēte) from this perverse generation"* (2:40), this does not require a strictly temporal, physical deliverance envisaged by Peter. There is no reason why the use of *sōzō* in this context should be limited to temporal salvation. In the scope of Acts 2, Peter may simply be saying in essence, "Be saved out of this generation that is collectively characterized by unbelief and rejection of the Messiah and as a result is facing certain eternal condemnation and even possible physical destruction!" While a temporal judgment upon the nation due to its collective unbelief was certainly a consideration of Peter's in Acts 2, it appears that his primary concern was for the inception of a relationship between these Jews and God and thus for their eternal welfare.

Repentance as the Condition for Salvation in Acts 2

Before examining the all-important *content* of saving faith found in Peter's preaching, it is imperative that the sole *condition* for salvation (i.e., faith alone) be carefully considered. To do so we must squarely face Acts 2:38. If Peter is still addressing eternal, rather than temporal, salvation in Acts 2:38-40, then how do repentance and baptism fit with salvation by grace through faith alone? Acts 2:38 is a *crux interpretum*. It is a well-known "problem-passage" in the sense that it has left exegetes of various theological persuasions puzzled as to its proper meaning. Multiple interpretations exist for this one verse, but it is beyond the scope of this chapter to provide a comprehensive, exegetical analysis of each of these interpretations. Instead, an extensive portion of this chapter will be dedicated to clarifying the particular interpretation that I am convinced fits best with all the details of the passage and that harmonizes best with the rest of Acts and the New Testament. This view will also be contrasted with the interpretation of Acts 2:38 promulgated by the leading proponents of the crossless gospel, Zane Hodges and Bob Wilkin, since their unique views on repentance, wrath, forgiveness, and salvation all buttress their doctrine of a crossless content of saving faith. A detailed study of Acts 2:38 is also critical in laying the foundation for interpreting other related passages in Acts on the condition for salvation and the content of the saving message.

The Meaning of Acts 2:38

Though several interpretations of Acts 2:38 have been proposed that are doctrinally consistent with *sola gratia* and *sola fide*, I remain convinced of the interpretation that sees the remission of sins and gift of the Holy Spirit as referring to eternal salvation rather than some post-salvation, sanctification blessings. Moreover, I am persuaded that these are not conditioned upon water baptism but solely upon repentance and an implicit reliance upon the name of Jesus Christ.[15]

In verse 37, the Jews in Jerusalem who heard Peter's preaching were grieved over their sin of crucifying Jesus. They were *"cut to the heart"* as they began to understand the implications of Peter's message. However, they still needed to "repent" by being persuaded that salvation and forgiveness of sins were now provided on the basis of *"the name of Jesus Christ"* (2:38). As one grace-oriented expositor put it, they still needed to come "to an immediate and conclusive change of mind about Jesus of Nazareth, about who He is, and about what God has accomplished through Him."[16] Nothing in the text of Acts 2 indicates that they believed or were persuaded of these things by the time of verse 37, despite what some Free Grace proponents are now claiming about this verse. The interpretation of Zane Hodges on Acts 2:37-38 has steadily gained traction within Free Grace circles over the last two decades, accompanying in part the new redefinition of repentance that has taken place over that same span. Regarding Acts 2:37, Hodges's interpretation assumes that Peter's Jewish audience became born again believers in Christ by the time of verse 37. He claims:

> When the Pentecostal audience heard Jesus proclaimed as "both Lord and Christ" (Acts 2:36), they indicated their belief of this truth with the words, "Men and brethren, what shall we do?" (Acts 2:37). But to believe that Jesus is the Christ is to be born again and possess eternal life (Jn 20:30-31; 1 Jn 5:1). Thus at this point the hearers who asked this question had been eternally saved! What did they lack? They lacked *harmony with God,* whom they had so deeply offended. What did they need to do? Two things: "Repent, and let every one of you be baptized in the name of Jesus Christ" (Acts 2:38).[17]

But this is assuming too much in Acts 2:37. Were these Jews in Jerusalem already believers by the time of verse 37? According to this verse, they were convicted of their sin and were certainly on the cusp of salvation. But they had not yet come to that change of mind about the object of their trust that the Bible calls "repentance." They had not yet believed in Jesus as the Christ of the gospel. They had not yet fulfilled Peter's command in verse 36 to "know assuredly" (*asphalōs ginōsketō*) that the One they crucified was actually the Christ. To know this truth, and to know it with assurance, is

---

[15] Though I cannot agree with his final conclusion, Lanny Tanton has written a helpful survey of the various interpretations of Acts 2:38 weighing their relative strengths and weaknesses. See Lanny Thomas Tanton, "The Gospel and Water Baptism: A Study of Acts 2:38," *JOTGES* 3 (Spring 1990): 27-52. Unfortunately, Tanton's survey does not consider the interpretation proposed here.

[16] Ron Merryman, "Acts 2:38: An Exposition," *GFJ* (July 1998): 13.

[17] Hodges, *Harmony with God,* 98-99. See also Hodges, *The Gospel Under Siege,* 117-18.

simply another expression for saving faith.[18] But if the Jews had already come to believe in Jesus as the Christ by the time of verse 36, there would have been no need to issue the command, using the imperative mood of *ginōskō*, to "know assuredly." Although the truth began dawning on them while Peter was preaching that Jesus fit the biblical qualifications of the Messiah, they were not yet convinced about the fact that this crucified Jesus was the Lord and Christ upon whom they could confidently rest for their salvation and the forgiveness of their sins, though they were on the brink of this realization.

To be convicted of their sin, as verse 37 indicates, does not mean that faith, persuasion, or repentance upon Christ had already taken place. This agrees with the principle that sorrow for sin can lead to repentance but it is not the same as repentance (2 Cor. 7:9-10). It is even possible to be convicted about the sin of wrongly putting Jesus to death and yet still not have repented upon Him as the Christ for salvation. We see this from the account of the stoning of Stephen, where the Jewish religious leaders in Jerusalem are convicted by the Holy Spirit of the truthfulness of Stephen's message while simultaneously suppressing and rejecting this truth in unrighteousness (Rom. 1:18). It says in Acts 7:54, *"When they heard these things they were cut to the heart, and they gnashed at him with their teeth."* The severe reaction here to Stephen's preaching by the stiff-necked Jewish leaders demonstrates that it is possible to know the truth about Jesus being the Messiah without knowing it "assuredly" (*asphalōs*). To know it "assuredly" means to be persuaded of the truth in the sense of being in agreement with it and consenting to its truthfulness. To do this would be the exercise of saving faith. But to be convicted of sin does not mean someone has believed in Christ. The Holy Spirit presently *"convict[s] the world of sin, and of righteousness, and of judgment"* (John 16:8), but this does not mean that the whole world believes in Christ. The Jews in Acts 2 were convicted of the sin of crucifying Jesus Christ and yet by the end of Peter's preaching they were still just short of actual repentance upon Christ's name for salvation and the forgiveness of sins.[19] As a result of being under the intense conviction of the Holy Spirit (cf. Acts 7:51), they were *"cut to the*

---

[18] For further discussion of these terms according to Luke's usage, see Tom Stegall, "The Tragedy of the Crossless Gospel, Part 7," *GFJ* (Summer 2008): 8-9.

[19] Acts 7:54 and 2:37 should be viewed as parallel passages. In Acts 7:54 it says that the Jewish leaders in Jerusalem were *"cut to the heart"* (*dieprionto*). In Acts 2:37, it says that those gathered in Jerusalem at Pentecost were also *"cut to the heart"* (*katenugēsan*). The verb for "cut" in Acts 2:37, *katanussomai*, is a *hapax legomenon*. It is a compound word from the intensive preposition *kata* ("down," "through") and the verb *nussō* ("to pierce"). The verb for "cut" in Acts 7:54, *diapriomai*, occurs only one other time in the NT in Acts 5:33. It is also a compound word from the preposition *dia* ("through") and the verb *priō* ("to saw or cut"). While it *may be* possible that *diapriomai* carries the additional connotation of being angry, such anger would still be based on conviction or being "cut through" in one's heart and mind. Though the words for "cut" in Acts 2:37 and 7:54 are different, a person would be very hard pressed to see any substantive semantic or theological distinction between them.

heart" (Acts 2:37), and they asked Peter and the apostles, *"Men and brethren, what shall we do?"*

The Great Commission Interpretation

It is critical to note that in Peter's famous reply of Acts 2:38, he goes beyond providing an answer to the specific question, "What must we do *to be saved*?" Instead, he gives these already convicted sinners the comprehensive answer of (1) what they must do to be saved (i.e., "repent"/rely upon the name of Christ) as well as (2) what they must do as disciples of Christ after saving faith (i.e., "be baptized" to publicly identify with Christ as believers in Him versus identifying with that generation of unbelieving Israelites). The reason that Peter responded with his twofold answer of *"repent and be baptized"* in verse 38 is simply because they had asked him an open-ended question and because he was following the Great Commission's prescription received from Christ only days earlier. According to the Lord Jesus' own commission to Peter and the apostles, they were to (1) preach the gospel that people may believe and be saved, and (2) baptize believers as disciples of Christ.

In Acts 2:38, Peter simply provided the appropriate, fuller Great Commission response (Matt. 28:19-20; Mark 16:15-16; Luke 24:47) to their broad question of *"what shall we do?"* Peter was *not* answering the soteriologically specific question asked of Paul later in Acts 16:30 by the Philippian jailor, *"Sirs, what must I do to be saved?"* Had the Jews in Acts 2:37 asked the same question posed to Paul by the Philippian jailor, we can be sure that baptism would not have been part of Peter's answer in Acts 2:38. He would have responded only with the portion of his reply that states, *"Repent . . . upon the name of Jesus Christ"* (2:38), consistent with Paul's response in Acts 16:31, *"believe on the Lord Jesus Christ . . . and you shall be saved."* But since the question of the Jews in Acts 2:37 was broader as to the general divine will, Peter faithfully informed them of God's ultimate will which was twofold, including both repentance and public identification with Christ through baptism.[20]

---

[20] This interpretation of Acts 2:38 should not be confused with what is commonly called the "parenthetical" or "syntactical break" position. Though the Great Commission view espoused above and the parenthetical interpretation have similarities, they are technically distinct. Both interpretations see repentance in Acts 2, rather than baptism, as the sole condition for salvation. The parenthetical view has traditionally appealed primarily to the grammar of verse 38 for support. It is often noted that the command to "repent" is plural (*metanoēsate*), as are the recipients (*humōn*) of forgiveness who receive (*lēmpsesthe*) the gift of the Spirit. But the command to "be baptized" is singular (*baptisthētō*). This leads some to conclude that the reference to baptism must be parenthetical in this verse, with the soteriological blessings of forgiveness and the gift of the Holy Spirit conditioned upon the command to repent rather than the command to be baptized. Though the grammar allows for this conclusion (Daniel B. Wallace, *Greek Grammar Beyond the Basics: An Exegetical Syntax of the New Testament* [Grand Rapids: Zondervan, 1996], 370), the grammatical argument alone has never proven convincing or adequate to bear the weight of a syntactical break between

This "Great Commission interpretation" also has the advantage of allowing Peter to be commanding both repentance and baptism simultaneously, with the recognition that the command to be baptized is fulfilled externally only as one has already repented internally and is already relying upon (*epi*) the name of Christ for the remission of sins rather than the water baptism itself. The basic sense of *epi* as expressing *reliance* or *dependence upon* the name (i.e., person and work) of Jesus Christ also fits with this view and will be explained in greater detail later in the chapter. If this is the proper interpretation of *epi* + the "name" of Christ in Acts 2:38, then this also harmonizes with Luke's record of the Great Commission. In Luke 24:44-49, there is conspicuously no mention of water baptism as in the Great Commission accounts of Matthew 28 and Mark 16.[21] Luke 24:47 clearly conditions remission of sins solely upon repentance.[22] This parallel passage of Luke 24:47 confirms that Peter in Acts 2:38 was conditioning remission of sins solely on the repentance that rested upon (*epi*) the name of Jesus Christ rather than conditioning it on repentance plus baptism.[23]

But if baptism was not a condition for forgiveness, why then did Peter mention it at all in Acts 2:38? First, it was because the Lord Jesus had instructed all the apostles to do so on the occasion of the Galilean Great Commission in Matthew 28 and Mark 16, though not in the Judean Great Commission of Luke 24. Second, Peter included baptism because he was answering the question of the Jerusalem Jews from Acts 2:37, "What shall we do?" This was a broader question than asking, "What must we do to be saved?"

Since context reigns as king in proper hermeneutical methodology, the immediate context of Acts 2 (especially verse 37) coupled with the Great Commission impetus and background should be given primary weight when interpreting Acts 2:38.[24] In addition, other factors should be considered, such as the parallel usage of *epi* with *pisteuō* and *epistrephō* in Acts, the meaning of Christ's "name" throughout Acts, and the other parallel passages in Luke-Acts on forgiveness of sins.

---

repentance and baptism.

[21] Guy D. Nave, Jr., *The Role and Function of Repentance in Luke-Acts* (Atlanta: Society of Biblical Literature, 2002), 34n129.

[22] The textual variant of *kai* [MT] and *eis* [CT] does not materially affect the outcome of the passage. The weight of the external evidence between the two readings is approximately equal, though slightly favoring the Critical Text reading of "repentance upon His name *for* the remission of sins."

[23] Nave, *The Role and Function of Repentance*, 34n130.

[24] The strength of this interpretation comes primarily from its Great Commission context, rather than the implicit meaning of *epi* as expressing reliance upon the name of Christ. For this reason, I prefer to label this view the "Great Commission interpretation" rather the "*epi* view." The interpretation proposed above does not stand or fall upon *epi* meaning reliance, though this sense of the preposition provides further confirmation of the view's correctness.

This interpretation of Acts 2:38 also has the advantage of conforming to the pattern of Mark 16:15-16, a Great Commission passage which descriptively declares that all believers who are baptized will be saved while all unbelievers will be condemned. As explained in the previous chapter, the critical requirement in Mark 16:16 is *to believe the gospel, not to be baptized* (cf. 1 Cor. 1:14-21). In just the same way, Acts 2:38 is simply teaching that if these unbelieving Jews would repent and be baptized, they would receive the gift of the Holy Spirit and have their sins forgiven. But this verse *does not say* that if they would only repent but not be baptized, then God would withhold the remission of sins and gift of the Holy Spirit until a second condition (baptism) had been met. To read such a conclusion into the verse is forcing it to say what it does not. Just as the decisive condition in Mark 16:16b is to believe the gospel, not to be baptized (16:16a), so the critical command with respect to eternal salvation in Acts 2:38 is simply to repent/believe, not to be baptized.

This interpretation is much more consistent than the temporal, physical deliverance view that is being popularized within Free Grace circles today, for it has the further advantage of harmonizing with the teaching on repentance and forgiveness in the rest of Luke-Acts. In both the original prescription of the Great Commission by Christ in Luke 24:46-47 and in the subsequent description of the apostles fulfilling this commission throughout Acts, the remission of sins is always conditioned only upon repentance/faith (Acts 3:19; 5:31; 10:43; 13:38; 26:18) but never on water baptism.

Acts 3:19 and 5:31 are especially instructive as examples of Peter conditioning the remission of sins solely upon repentance. If baptism was truly necessary in Acts 2 for the remission of the sins for that "exceptional"[25] generation of "Palestinian"[26] Jews who crucified their Messiah, then why did Peter present only the condition of *repentance* to the *same* generation of Jews in Jerusalem in Acts 3:19 and 5:31? The answer is transparently obvious—because only repentance brings remission of sins; but baptism does not.[27]

But this raises a valid question. If baptism wasn't necessary for the forgiveness of sins even on the day of Pentecost but Peter presented it anyway in Acts 2:38 as part of God's broader will in the Great Commission, then why didn't Peter at least mention baptism in Acts 3:19 and 5:31? Shouldn't Peter still have presented both repentance and baptism in these passages

---

[25] Hodges, *The Gospel Under Siege*, 119; Wilkin, *Confident in Christ*, 195.

[26] Hodges, *Harmony with God*, 99-101.

[27] This same point was raised by Wilkin before changing his doctrine of repentance. Robert N. Wilkin, "Repentance and Salvation—Part 4: New Testament Repentance: Repentance in the Gospels and Acts," *JOTGES* 3 (Spring 1990): 17n11; idem, "Repentance as a Condition for Salvation in the New Testament" (Th.D. dissertation, Dallas Theological Seminary, 1985), 72.

to be consistent? It is likely that he dropped any reference to baptism on these two occasions because he wasn't answering the question of sincere seekers of God's general will as he was in Acts 2:37-38. In Acts 3 and 5, there is no conviction of heart or asking, *"What shall we do?"* Instead, in Acts 3 and 5, Peter must press the subject of the gospel with Jews who are still hardened and resistant in their unbelief and for whom believer-baptism isn't even a remote consideration until they are ready to repent. Why broach the subject of public identification with Christ through water baptism when they weren't even ready or willing to privately, internally believe in Him?

But this brings us back to the problem of the temporal, physical, national, "Palestinian" deliverance view advocated by Hodges and Wilkin. According to their view, repentance, which is a "turning from sin," is not a requirement for eternal salvation but is only for temporal deliverance from the wrath of God. But this presents a serious problem. If the divine requirement for that generation of Jerusalem Jews was twofold for deliverance from temporal, physical destruction—the type of deliverance supposedly conceived by Peter in Acts 2:38ff—then there appear to be no valid reasons why repentance and baptism should be omitted in Acts 3:19 and 5:31. Was that generation of Jews in Acts 3 and 5 still not facing physical destruction due to their special guilt? According to the Hodges-Wilkin view, were there not still the two preconditions of repentance and baptism to be met in order to avert this judgment regardless of whether their hearts were ready to repent about Jesus as the Christ like the Jewish crowd was in Acts 2:37-38? According to the Hodges-Wilkin view, one could argue that as the clock ticked and the plot advanced further into Acts 3 and 5, the need for Israel's remission of sins would be even more urgent. As a result, if both repentance and baptism were necessary for the remission of Israel's sins, shouldn't Peter's preaching on the necessity of baptism have become even more pronounced throughout Acts, rather than dropping out entirely, as in 3:19 and 5:31?

Forgiveness, Justification, and Regeneration

There is another major problem created by the Hodges-Wilkin interpretation of Acts 2:38 yet to be considered. According to their baptismal remission of sins view, the "Palestinian" Jews in Acts 2 bore special guilt before God (Matt. 27:25) and were under God's wrath *even after* they supposedly believed in Jesus for eternal life in Acts 2:37.[28] This would mean

[28] Wilkin, "Does Your Mind Need Changing? Repentance Reconsidered," 43n13. This is not to deny that this generation was truly guilty for crucifying their Messiah, and later for persecuting Christian leaders, just as Matthew 23:36 teaches. However, the guilt of sin that they bore was primarily a matter of eternal, rather than temporal, judgment before God (Matthew 23:32-33); nor would the prospect of such a temporal judgment remain following the new birth.

that from the very moment of their regeneration, these "Palestinian" Jews still had the temporal debt of their sins to pay. Because they were uniquely responsible for crucifying the Messiah, God purportedly prescribed the extra conditions of baptism and repentance for these "believers" before He would forgive their sins, grant His Spirit (2:38), and stay His wrath.[29] In this respect, this interpretation of Acts 2:38 bears a disturbing similarity to the Roman Catholic doctrine of temporal divine indebtedness.[30]

This interpretation of Acts 2:38 also ends up detaching God's forgiveness from His justification, which are inseparable soteriological blessings according to Scripture (Acts 13:38-39). However, biblically we know that at justification there is both an addition and a subtraction. According to Romans 4:6-8, justification involves the imputation of God's righteousness along with the forgiveness of our sins and lawless deeds. God does not declare believers righteous while simultaneously holding their sins against them (2 Cor. 5:19-21). The Hodges-Wilkin view also ends up separating forgiveness from regeneration for these "exceptional," "Palestinian," Jewish Christians; and yet divine forgiveness and regeneration are also simultaneous and inseparable (Col. 2:13; Titus 3:5). Something has gone fundamentally awry with our exegesis and systematic theology in the Free Grace camp when we are forced to conclude that these supposed new believers in Acts 2:37 were regenerated but still unforgiven in God's sight and under His fierce wrath at the very same instant that they became newborn babes in Christ and declared righteous in His sight.

The Meaning of Acts 22:16

At this point, some may raise the objection that Acts 22:16 contains a case of a "Palestinian" Jew of the crucifixion generation being required to be baptized for the remission of sins. There, Ananias says to Paul, *"And now,*

---

[29] Hodges, *The Gospel Under Siege*, 117-19; idem, *Harmony with God*, 89-107; Wilkin, *Confident in Christ*, 194-95.

[30] It is unbiblical to maintain that when God wipes away a person's sin with its eternal condemnation that a temporal divine judgment for sin remains to be paid toward God. Notice how the Roman Catholic Church justifies the need for purgatory and indulgences on this very same basis: "To understand this doctrine and practice of the Church, it is necessary to understand that sin has a *double consequence*. Grave sin deprives us of communion with God and therefore makes us incapable of eternal life, the privation of which is called the 'eternal punishment' of sin. On the other hand every sin, even venial, entails an unhealthy attachment to creatures, which must be purified either here on earth, or after death in the state called Purgatory. This purification frees one from what is called the 'temporal punishments' of sin. . . . The forgiveness of sin and restoration of communion with God entail the remission of the eternal punishment of sin, but temporal punishment of sin remains." *Catechism of the Catholic Church*, English translation, Libreria Editrice Vaticana (Bloomingdale, OH: Apostolate for Family Consecration, 1994), 370 (italics original; ellipsis added). See also "Apostolic Constitution on the Revision of Indulgences" in *Vatican Council II: The Conciliar and Post Conciliar Documents*, ed. Austin Flannery, O.P. (Northport, NY: Costello Publishing, 1992), 1:62-79; Ludwig Ott, *Fundamentals of Catholic Dogma*, trans. Patrick Lynch (Rockford, IL: Tan Books, 1960), 484-85.

why are you waiting? Arise and be baptized, and wash away your sins, calling upon the name of the Lord." Is this verse actually teaching that water baptism will remit sins, whether for regeneration or for subsequent fellowship with God? First, it must be conceded by all theological persuasions that this is a difficult verse to translate, to say nothing of proper interpretation. It is difficult to determine, for example, whether the aorist imperative *apolousai* ("*wash away* your sins") is grammatically connected to the previous aorist imperative *baptisai* ("be baptized") or to the following aorist participle *epikalesamenos* ("*calling upon* the name of the Lord"). If the "washing away" is connected to "calling upon" the name of the Lord, then there still exists the problem of determining whether the participle precedes the washing away ("*having called upon* the name of the Lord") or is simultaneous with the washing away (i.e., "wash away your sins [now] by calling upon the name of the Lord [now]").

It appears best to view Ananias' command to Paul to *"wash away your sins"* as figurative or symbolic of the judicial forgiveness that accompanies regeneration and Spirit-baptism. This is based upon the fact that Paul had already believed in Christ on the road to Damascus three days earlier. This would mean that he had already called upon the name of the Lord during the three day interval between his new birth and getting baptized. This would also mean that Paul was both forgiven and in fellowship with the Lord prior to Ananias' command. There are several weaknesses with the view of Hodges and Wilkin which teaches that, even though Paul was regenerated and justified on the Damascus road, he, as a "Palestinian" Jew of the crucifixion generation, remained unforgiven and guilty before God for three days until his baptism.[31] For example, Hodges claimed:

> If a man were converted, yet unforgiven, he would be a person possessing eternal life but unable to enjoy communion with God (Paul is for three days like this . . .). What is involved in Acts 2:38 is an experience of regeneration (at the point where faith occurs . . .) with real communion begun only when baptism is submitted to.[32]

Hodges's view has several weaknesses. First, Paul fasted (Acts 9:9) and prayed (Acts 9:11) during this three day interval; and in this respect, he was already *"call[ing] upon the name of the Lord."* Second, upon his new birth, Paul was immediately willing to do the Lord's will and to receive

[31] Hodges, *Harmony with God*, 100; Wilkin, *Confident in Christ*, 195.

[32] Zane C. Hodges, unpublished class notes for 227 Acts (Dallas Theological Seminary, Fall, 1984), 14, as quoted by Lanny Thomas Tanton, "The Gospel and Water Baptism: A Study of Acts 2:38," *JOTGES* 3 (Spring 1990), 50 (ellipses original). See also Hodges, *The Gospel Under Siege*, 119, where he writes, "If anyone thinks that Paul was not really converted on the Damascus road, this idea would be far-fetched in the extreme. Obviously, from that occasion onward, he was a believer in Jesus, whom he now calls Lord (Acts 22:10). But he was forgiven three days later!"

instruction from the Lord (Acts 9:6; 22:10), as he asked, *"Lord, what shall I do?"* Third, the profile of Paul conveyed by the text is that of a man who was immediately obedient (Acts 9:6-8; 22:10-11; 26:19) to the Lord, even from the first command to *"Arise and go into Damascus, and there you will be told all things which are appointed for you to do."* If the Hodges-Wilkin interpretation is correct, it is difficult to imagine Paul asking on the Damascus road, *"Lord, what shall I do?"* and Jesus responding in essence, "You must go to Damascus and wait three days before I will forgive you and have fellowship with you since I've decided to wait three days for Ananias to tell you to be baptized, even though you are ready to obey Me now and even though you will fast and pray to Me for the next three days."

The Hodges-Wilkin interpretation also suffers from the fact that the text *nowhere* states that Paul was unforgiven and out of fellowship with the Lord for those three days. That is merely an assumption that is needed to maintain the theological consistency of their new doctrines of repentance and forgiveness. Nor does the fact that Paul was blind for three days imply he was unforgiven by God, unless we are prepared to conclude from the similar example of Zacharias being muted in Luke 1:20-64 that this meant that he was unforgiven and out of fellowship with God for nine months. Even though in Zacharias' case, his inability to speak was the result of his initial sin of not believing the angel Gabriel (Luke 1:20), this does not mean he remained unforgiven and out of fellowship until his son John was born. That would be sheer assumption. It would be an even greater assumption in the case of Paul's blindness, since there is no mention in the text of any initial sin on Paul's part subsequent to his salvation that resulted in blindness for three days. Both Paul's blindness and Zacharias' muteness most likely served as tangible signs to each man and to others around them of the veracity of the message each received and of the solemnity of each occasion. And in the case of Paul's blindness, there may have been some intentional symbolism involved that corresponded with his mission of turning men from darkness to light by the preaching of the gospel (Acts 26:18, 23).

In addition, the fact that Ananias was sent to Paul after three days to restore his sight and that he might be *"filled (pimplēmi) with the Holy Spirit"* (Acts 9:17) does not prove that Paul had not yet received the remission of sins or been baptized by the Holy Spirit after the pattern of Acts 2:38.[33] It is *possible* that Paul may have been placed by the Holy Spirit into Christ the moment he first believed while he was on the Damascus road. It would be a mistake to equate the Holy Spirit's ministries of positional baptism into Christ with His filling for service. These are entirely distinct, though they may occur simultaneously in some instances (Acts 1:5, 8; 2:4). From the very beginning, with the infilling of John the Baptist in his mother's

---

[33] Ibid., Hodges.

womb (Luke 1:15), the ministry of the Spirit's filling in Luke-Acts is associated with the supernaturally imparted ability to be a verbal witness for Christ (Luke 1:15, 41, 67; Acts 1:8; 2:4; 4:8, 31; 9:17-20; 13:9).[34] It is significant that each of the three passages that recounts Paul's conversion experience emphasize his appointment as a specially chosen witness for the Lord (Acts 9:15-16, 18-22; 22:14-15; 26:16-18). It is far more likely, therefore, that the laying-on of hands by Ananias (Acts 9:17) was not intended for the forgiveness of Paul's sins or his restoration to fellowship with God. Rather, it was consistent with its practice elsewhere in Scripture as an act of public acceptance, approval, and appointment to service. The laying on of hands would have been especially poignant in Paul's case as a dreaded persecutor of the Church, of whom early Christians would have been naturally wary and reluctant to accept. This also fits with the fact that God chose Ananias, a man of great piety, character, and reputation (Acts 22:12) to be the one to actually lay hands on Paul. The effect of such a noted figure as Ananias laying his hands on this notorious former persecutor of Christians would have meant Paul's immediate public acceptance and approval among the disciples in Damascus (Acts 9:19).

The "Palestinian" Jewish Crucifixion Generation

At this point, we must address one more plaguing problem upon which the entire Hodges-Wilkin doctrine of repentance, remission of sins, and baptism rests. They interpret the repentance and baptism passages in Acts through a paradigm that views the generation of Jews living in "Palestine" as "exceptional" in their culpability for the crucifixion of Christ. As a result, we are told that this generation was given the unique and additional requirements of turning from sin and being baptized before they could receive the remission of sins and the gift of the Holy Spirit. This fundamental assumption of unique guilt for "Palestinian" Jews of the crucifixion generation was expressed by Hodges as follows:

> But the experience of people who lived in Palestine, where the great spiritual drama of salvation had its manifestation in history, was a unique experience. It can never be repeated. Thus too, as Acts discloses, those who lived in that land during these momentous times had some very special directions to follow along the pathway to membership in the Body of Christ, the Church.

---

[34] The root word for "filled" in Acts 9:17 is *pimplēmi*. Luke often uses this word to convey the idea of completion (Luke 1:23, 57; 2:6, 21, 22; 5:7; Acts 19:29). Thus, some lexicologists understand its meaning as "to cause something to be completely full—'to fill completely, to fill up'." L&N, s.v. "Full, Empty," 1:598, §59.38. Though Luke frequently uses the term *plēroō* in Luke-Acts to convey the idea of filling (as does Paul in Eph. 5:18), he does not employ *plēroō* in contexts of supernatural speaking ability. That is reserved strictly for the term *pimplēmi* by Luke. This may indicate that the filling (*pimplēmi*) of the Spirit referred to by Ananias in Acts 9:17 was for the commencement of Paul's special speaking ministry as an apostle, not for his fellowship with God.

> This special status as members of Christ's spiritual body, which was unknown even to the most godly saint in Old Testament times, could only be reached in the way specified by Acts 2:38. Those who have made Acts 2:38 a normative experience, applicable to all believers during the present age of the Church, have not studied their Bibles with sufficient care. Acts 2:38; 8:12-17; 19:1-7; and 22:16 belong to a transitional period in Christian history and, as all these texts show, they are aimed at Palestinians *and no one else!*
>
> Thus when Paul preaches to a Jewish audience *outside of Palestine* (in what was called the Diaspora [Dispersion]), he preaches the same message that he preached everywhere on the Gentile mission fields. As a result, in the synagogue at Antioch of Pisidia, we find him telling his Jewish hearers: "Therefore let it be known to you, brethren, that through this Man is preached to you the forgiveness of sins; and by Him everyone who believes is *justified* from all things from which you could not be justified by the law of Moses" (Acts 13:38-39).[35]

It is commendable that Hodges and Wilkin have attempted to account for the transitional nature of Acts while seeking a single unifying theme that will consistently interpret all the difficult baptism passages in Acts. However, their "exceptional," "Palestinian" Jewish believer interpretation is still built upon a flawed premise. Is it really true that only "Palestinian" Jews of the crucifixion generation had to repent and that this repentance was merely a post-regeneration/post-justification requirement in order to experience forgiveness of sins and receive the gift of the Holy Spirit? In the process of supporting their view that the Jewish "Palestinian" crucifixion generation bore unique guilt before God, both Hodges[36] and Wilkin[37] have cited Matthew 27:25. There the Jews who are gathered before Pilate's judgment seat declare regarding Christ, *"His blood be on us and on our children."* Whatever this statement may be teaching about actual culpability and its extent, it nevertheless appears to indicate that any special guilt born by Israel would have been bigenerational, not "exceptional" to only one generation, since it extends even to the "children" of that generation.

In addition, we must also consider that the Jews who were in Jerusalem who heard Peter's preaching on the day of Pentecost were from *"every nation under heaven"* (Acts 2:5). They were not strictly "Palestinian" Jews. They were in Jerusalem for the feast of Pentecost, and Peter addresses them corporately as *"Men of Israel"* (2:22). To this same group, Peter attri-

---

[35] Hodges, *Harmony with God*, 105-6.

[36] Ibid., 96.

[37] Wilkin, "Does Your Mind Need Changing? Repentance Reconsidered," 43n13.

butes some degree of collective responsibility for the Messiah's death, saying, *"you have taken by lawless hands, have crucified, and put to death"* (2:23). Peter did not put any distinction between "Palestinian" Jews and non-Palestinian Jews of the Diaspora, as Wilkin and Hodges require for the consistency of their doctrine of repentance.

Wilkin attempts to resolve this problem by claiming that the Jews who were present in Jerusalem for the feast of Pentecost in Acts 2 were also present over 50 days earlier at the feast of Passover, the time of Christ's crucifixion. He states, *"Peter was speaking to Jews who had been in Palestine during the Passover. They were thus responsible for participating in crucifying the Messiah whom they thought of as an imposter."*[38] But how do we know that Peter's audience in Acts 2 was in Jerusalem for the Passover? Isn't it just as possible that many of them did not stay in Jerusalem for a span of two entire months and that many of these diasporic Jews only came to the feast of Pentecost *after* Christ's crucifixion? We know from the example of Paul that 1st century Jews apparently did not feel constrained to attend *both* Passover and Pentecost, as Luke records the travels of Paul in the Book of Acts and informs us that *"he was hurrying to be at Jerusalem, if possible, on the Day of Pentecost"* (Acts 20:16). While making it for Pentecost, Paul would have missed Passover.[39] Furthermore, there are no passages in Acts or the rest of the New Testament that even hint that the multinational Jewish pilgrims stayed for both Passover and Pentecost.[40] Nor, for

---

[38] Wilkin, *Confident in Christ*, 194.

[39] It is questionable whether the injunction of Deuteronomy 16:16 for all male Israelites to travel to Jerusalem and offer sacrifice three times per year at the feasts of Unleavened Bread (and Passover by implication), Pentecost, and Tabernacles would have been viewed by 1st century Jews as binding upon those diasporic Jews living outside the land. Are we really to suppose, as Wilkin's view would require, that a Jewish man of the Diaspora living in Rome, for instance, would be required to travel to Jerusalem three separate times per year? Or, to travel to Jerusalem two times per year, with one extended stay for roughly two months from Passover to Pentecost? If we account for the additional travel time in the ancient world, this would mean that a Jewish man living in Rome would be gone for over 4 months out of each year, factoring in at least 3-4 weeks for a one way trip between Rome and Jerusalem.

[40] The mention of "Greeks" in John 12:20 being in Jerusalem for the Passover at the time of Christ's crucifixion is no exception. They are most likely God-fearing proselytes rather than Jews of the Diaspora (See C. K. Barrett, *The Gospel According to St. John*, 2nd edition [Philadelphia: Westminster Press, 1978], 421; D. A. Carson, *The Gospel According to John*, PNTC [Grand Rapids: Eerdmans, 1991], 435-36; Andreas J. Köstenberger, *John*, BECNT [Grand Rapids: Baker, 2004], 377; Stephen S. Smalley, *John: Evangelist and Interpreter* [Nashville: Thomas Nelson, 1984], 144n103, 154-55. Contra John A. T. Robinson, "The Destination and Purpose of St. John's Gospel," in *Twelve New Testament Studies* [London: SCM Press, 1962], 112n7). Even if these Greeks were Hellenistic Jews of the Diaspora, they are conspicuously not listed among the various nations and tongues of fellow Jews represented at Pentecost in Acts 2:9-11. But some may argue that this is because Hellenistic Jews represented diasporic Jews in general. In either case, even if the "Greeks" in John 12:20 were Jews rather than God-fearing Gentile proselytes, the specificity of the various nations and tongues in Acts 2:9-11 argues against viewing the "Greeks" in John 12:20 who were present at Passover as being

that matter, are there any passages that teach the actual premise of the Hodges-Wilkin theory, namely that repentance and baptism were additional requirements for that exceptional generation of Palestinian Jews. Such a conclusion is sheer assumption; and therefore it is a rather faulty foundation to build one's entire doctrine upon. This takes us back to the crucial passage of Acts 2:38 and to the question of what this verse is actually teaching about repentance, baptism, and the remission of sins.

The Gentile Pentecost

One additional support for interpreting Acts 2:38 from the Great Commission perspective explained earlier is the fact that this interpretation is also consistent with the manner in which *other Jewish Christians from Jerusalem* are said to have received the gift of the Holy Spirit. Acts 11 provides us with an inspired commentary on the events of Acts 2. In Acts 11, Peter was rehearsing for his Jewish brethren the "Pentecost of the Gentiles" that occurred in Acts 10 when Cornelius and the Gentiles received the remission of sins and the gift of the Holy Spirit.[41] In chapter 11, Peter is recounting to the Jewish Christians from Jerusalem how the gift of the Holy Spirit promised in Acts 2:38 was originally received *by these Jewish believers from Jerusalem.* In Acts 11, Peter does not say that the Holy Spirit was received on the basis of two conditions, namely faith *plus baptism*, but rather that it was *"when we believed on the Lord Jesus Christ"* (Acts 11:17). Why would Peter in Acts 11:17 describe only one condition to receive the gift of the Spirit for all Jews from Acts 2-11 as well as the Gentiles of Acts 10-11 (to believe on the Lord Jesus Christ), while Acts 2:38 presents two requirements (repentance/faith plus baptism)? If the Hodges-Wilkin Palestinian Jewish guilt theory is correct that fellowship and temporal salvation is conditioned upon both repentance and baptism, then why would Peter omit any reference to baptism in Acts 11:17 if it was a necessary condition for the remission of sins and the gift of the Spirit?

Those who advocate the Hodges-Wilkin baptismal remission of sins interpretation for Acts 2:38 (along with its new redefinition of repentance) might attempt to resolve this discrepancy in one of two ways. First, they might claim that Peter must be referring to *two distinct Jewish audiences* in Acts 11—an Acts 2 audience that met two conditions (repentance plus baptism) versus a non-Palestinian Jewish audience that needed only faith. Yet, in the context of Peter's "we believed" statement in Acts 11:17, Peter was specifically addressing and including his fellow "apostles and brethren" in "Judea" (11:1) and in "Jerusalem" (11:2). We know who these fellow Judean Jews included from the record of Acts to that point. We know, for

---

identical to the multinational contingent represented at Pentecost in Acts 2.

[41] Stewart Custer, *Witness to Christ: A Commentary on Acts* (Greenville, SC: Bob Jones University Press, 2000), 157; Everett F. Harrison, *Acts: The Expanding Church* (Chicago: Moody Press, 1975), 179.

instance, that initially on the day of Pentecost in Acts 2 those who received the Spirit numbered approximately 120 souls, including the apostles (Acts 1:15). But if the baptismal remission of sins view of Acts 2:37-38 is correct, are we seriously expected to believe that *none* of the 3,000 souls who repented and were baptized later on the same day (Acts 2:38-41) were also among these Jerusalem brethren whom Peter was addressing in Acts 11:17 who are said to have received the Holy Spirit by believing in the Lord Jesus Christ? Such a conclusion would be unwarranted and forced. It would be born only out of the necessity to maintain the consistency of one's theological system rather than to let the plain sense of Scripture speak for itself. It would be extremely unlikely if none of the original 3,000 "brethren" from Acts 2 were among "the circumcision" who "contended" with Peter in "Jerusalem" (11:2) when he spoke the words of Acts 11:17. This is especially true when considering that Peter says to this same group, *"the Holy Spirit fell upon them [Cornelius and the Gentiles], as upon us at the beginning"* (Acts 11:15). Who are the "us"? What was "the beginning"? It would be virtually impossible to deny that Peter's Acts 11 audience consisted of those Jews who had received the Holy Spirit on the same day as he and the rest of the apostles—on the day of Pentecost, the "beginning" of the Church.

Secondly, advocates of the Hodges-Wilkin view of Acts 2:38 might also be prone to appeal to the grammar of Acts 11:17 in order to discount the conclusion that the "Palestinian" Jews of Acts 2 didn't have to be baptized to receive the Holy Spirit and remission of sins but only had to believe. In Acts 11:17, the phrase, *"when we believed"* (NKJV) is admittedly only one possible translation of the aorist, dative, plural participle *pisteusasin*. The phrase in English, *"when we believed,"* is not based on the first person plural aorist indicative verb, *episteusamen*, as might initially be assumed from the NKJV translation. Since Greek participles do not have "person" as verbs do, it is grammatically possible that *pisteusasin* could be understood with either a first person sense, modifying "us" (*hēmin*), or with a third person sense, modifying "them" (*autois*). The NKJV reading reflects the former possibility. But if *pisteusasin* modifies "them" (*autois*), verse 17 would read, "If therefore God gave them (*autois*) the same gift as He also gave us *when they believed* (*pisteusasin*) on the Lord Jesus Christ, who was I that I could withstand God?" According to this translation, Acts 11:17 would then say nothing about the *means* by which Peter and his fellow Judean Jews received the gift of the Holy Spirit. Though the grammar and the flexibility of the Greek word order allows for such a translation, it is "less likely" due to the immediate proximity of *hēmin* with *pisteusasin* in the Greek sentence as opposed to the distance of *autois* from *pisteusasin* (*ei oun tēn isēn dōrean edōken autois ho theos hōs kai hēmin pisteusasin epi ton kurion Iēsoun Christon*).[42]

---

[42] The *NET Bible*, First Beta Edition (n.p.: Biblical Studies Press, 1996), 2048-49n30.

Perhaps the best rendering of this verse is the one that views *pisteusasin* as a temporal adverbial participle that retains some of the ambiguity of the Greek and allows it to be applied to both groups—that is, to both Jews and Gentiles, *"Therefore, if God gave them the same gift He gave us after believing upon the Lord Jesus Christ, who was I that I could withstand God?"* In such a case, Peter would then be "summarizing"[43] or combining the experience of the apostles and Jerusalem Christians from Acts 2 along with the experience of Gentile Christians from Acts 10. Peter would then be viewed as teaching that both groups received the *same* Spirit, the *same* way, and were now part of the *same* Body. This does seem to be Peter's point. This conclusion and the problem of identifying to which group the participle *pisteusasin* applies is fortunately resolved by the following verse, Acts 11:18. There "repentance" is stated as the sole condition common to both Jewish and Gentile Christians. In Acts 11:18, after hearing Peter's "when we believed" statement in the previous verse, the Jewish Christians of Jerusalem conclude, *"Then God has also granted to the Gentiles repentance to life."*

Repentance to Life

From Acts 11:18, the Jewish Christians in Jerusalem interpret Peter's account of the conversion of the Gentiles as *"repentance to life."* This is their summary expression used to describe the salvation of the Gentiles (11:14) through the baptism of the Spirit on the condition of believing in Christ (11:17). This interpretative statement by these Jewish Christians in verse 18 leads to a theological conclusion of great consequence. It reveals that the concepts of faith and repentance that occur throughout Acts 2, 3, 5, and 10 are used interchangeably.[44] This means that repentance in Acts is not something additional and subsequent to saving faith.

But those who subscribe to the baptismal remission of sins view in Acts 2:38 also sense what is theologically at stake with Acts 11:18, and thus they provide an alternative interpretation. Hodges, for instance, did not view *"repentance to life"* as referring to the Gentiles receiving *eternal* life but only that they "entered into the Christian life."[45] This means that, in Hodges's view, the Jerusalem Christians in Acts 11:18 were *not* equating repentance (v. 18) with believing (v. 17) but were drawing an inference that went beyond Peter's testimony in Acts 11. These Jewish Christians concluded that God had granted the Gentiles a repentant way of life that brings harmony and fellowship with Him subsequent to regeneration. Hodges defended this interpretation by raising an objection:

---

[43] Ibid.

[44] G. Michael Cocoris, *Repentance: The Most Misunderstood Word in the Bible* (Santa Monica, CA: Self-published, 2003), 27. This was also Wilkin's position originally, see his dissertation, "Repentance as a Condition for Salvation in the New Testament," 80n1.

[45] Hodges, *Harmony with God*, 118.

> If we thought that the reference in Acts 11:18 *was* a reference to *eternal* life, then we are left with a surprising and implausible idea in this context. We must infer in that case that the Jerusalem Christians just now realized that Gentiles could be eternally *saved!* But this is so unlikely as to be almost fantastic.[46]

Hodges goes on to support this contention by citing passages showing that the door of salvation was always open to the Gentiles, even before the Church age.[47] Hodges explains that if this has always been the case for the Gentiles (and it has), then why would Peter's fellow Jews be so surprised that Cornelius and the Gentiles are given eternal life in Acts 11? But we must ask, is it really that "implausible" and "almost fantastic" to view the "repentance to life" by the Gentiles as a reference to *eternal* life? Hodges's objection is, in fact, a *non sequitur.* For, if these Jewish Christians were not surprised that God had granted eternal life to the Gentiles since this was always available to them, then neither should the Jews have been surprised that God was granting Gentiles the opportunity to repent of their sins and have a harmonious way of life with God, since this was also true throughout the Old Testament. Was not Jethro a Gentile who had a relationship with God (Ex. 18:9-12) while standing outside of the covenant nation of Israel? Were not the Ninevites granted the opportunity first to believe the Lord (Jonah 3:5; Matt. 12:41; Luke 11:32) and then to turn from their evil ways (Jonah 3:10) and have a harmonious relationship with God, while still being uncircumcised Gentiles and not proselytes within the covenant people of Israel? Even Hodges admitted that "it is evident that by sparing the city God gave the Ninevites a renewed opportunity to come to know Him"[48] (i.e., "know Him" experientially). There is no evidence in the Old Testament that a saved Gentile living outside the chosen nation of Israel could not be forgiven in God's sight and in harmonious relationship with Him.

What is evident from the Book of Acts is that though God's divine economy had changed from Law to Grace, and the apostles had been commissioned by Christ to preach repentance and remission of sins to every nation (Luke 24:47) starting in Jerusalem (Acts 1:8), this does not mean that this seismic dispensational shift was actually comprehended by these early Jewish believers.[49] A Great Commission perspective was still lacking among the Jews in the early Church, which was probably due to their ethnic prejudice at the time which viewed Gentiles as unclean (Acts 10), coupled with an entrenched old covenant mindset that Israel

---

[46] Ibid., 117.

[47] Ibid., 117-18.

[48] Ibid., 79.

[49] Roy L. Aldrich, "The Transition Problem in Acts," *BSac* 114 (July 1957): 235-42; Ron Merryman, "The Transitional Nature of Acts, Part 1," *GFJ* (March 1999): 24-27; idem, "The Transitional Nature of Acts, Part 2," *GFJ* (May 1999): 15-17.

had been operating under for 1,500 years. For these reasons, the Jewish Christians in Jerusalem in Acts 11 were astonished that Gentiles were saved by God *as Gentiles,* without having to become Jewish converts first. The Scriptures themselves testify that this erroneous and unbiblical opinion was the deeply ingrained, traditional Jewish perspective of Peter's day (Matt. 23:15; Acts 15:1, 5, 11; Rom. 2:25-3:1; 3:30-4:12; Gal. 2:1-14; 5:2-12; 6:12-15). Though Cornelius was a devout Gentile who feared God, gave alms, prayed always, and was respected by the Jewish people (Acts 10:2, 22, 31), the Scriptures nowhere describe him as a circumcised convert. In fact, they teach just the opposite (Acts 11:3). The fact that Cornelius and his fellow Gentiles had not received the initiatory rite of Judaism, namely circumcision (Gen. 17:9-14), would have presented a major stumbling block for these Jewish Christians. This best explains why the cast of characters in Acts 10-11 are described as being either circumcised or uncircumcised (Acts 10:45; 11:2-3). The category of "uncircumcised believers" in the Lord Jesus Christ did not even register yet in the thinking of these early Jewish Christians.

Though it was evident to the Jewish Christians of Jerusalem in Acts 11:18 that the Gentiles had believed in Christ and received the Spirit and in this respect had repented unto life, the theological implications accompanying such an event were not yet fully realized or resolved among them. They lingered until Acts 15, where the question of whether uncircumcised believers were truly saved was directly and definitely dealt with (Acts 15:1). There, it was necessary for Peter to rehearse yet again the conversion of the Gentiles (Acts 15:7-11), saying that *"God, who knows the heart, acknowledged them by giving them the Holy Spirit, just as He did to us, and made no distinction between us and them, purifying their hearts by faith"* (Acts 15:8-9). Peter then concludes, significantly, that *"we [Jews] shall be saved in the same manner as they [Gentiles]"* (Acts 15:11).

By linking the Holy Spirit (15:8), purification (15:9), and salvation (15:11), Peter was reiterating several critical points found in Acts 10-11. There is a real parallelism between these two sections that should not be overlooked. In Acts 10:43, the Gentiles received the *"remission of sins,"* which corresponds to the statement about *"purifying their hearts"* in Acts 15:9. The baptism by the Holy Spirit is also referred to in Acts 15:8, *"giving them the Holy Spirit,"* which directly parallels Acts 10:44-47 and 11:15-17. Then Peter concludes in Acts 15:11 by saying that whether a person is a Jew or a Gentile, salvation is received *"in the same manner."* In what manner had the Jews and Gentiles both been "saved" (Acts 11:14)? According to Peter, it was "by faith" (Acts 15:9; cf. 11:17). This pattern of parallelism establishes conclusively that the real condition upon which the 3,000 Jews in Jerusalem on Pentecost received the remission of sins and the gift of the Holy Spirit in Acts 2:38 was repentance/faith, not baptism. It also establishes that being "saved" in Acts 2:40; 11:14; and 15:11 entailed *eternal* salvation and life, not merely the sanctification of "the Christian life."[50]

This leads us back to Acts 11:18 and the meaning of the expression, *"repentance unto life."* According to Hodges's view, this is not a summarizing statement made by the Jerusalem Christians that encapsulates the salvation experience of the Gentiles previously recounted by Peter. Instead, it is an expression for the repentant way of life, the Christian life of turning from sins, that these Gentiles were now privileged to embark upon subsequent to receiving eternal life. But if this interpretation is correct, then it presents another major problem for the Hodges-Wilkin view. How did the Jewish Christians in Acts 11 know that Cornelius and the Gentiles had actually "turned from their sins," assuming for the sake of argument that this is even the correct meaning of repentance? In the historical setting of Acts 11, Peter never mentions any sins being turned from by these Gentiles. So why would the Jews form such a conclusion in Acts 11:18? For that matter, turning from sins is not mentioned anywhere in Acts 10 either. There, the Gentiles simply believe the gospel message while Peter is preaching, and this constitutes the change of mind that is biblical repentance. Furthermore, wouldn't Cornelius and his fellow Gentiles have had to repent of some sins subsequent to their new birth in order for the Jerusalem Jews in Acts 11:18 to know that God had now granted to the Gentiles the "turning from sins for temporal life" (*"repentance unto life"*)? Wouldn't these new Gentile believers have to exhibit at least some repentance in "the Christian life" for the Jewish believers to know that they had turned from sin? If the Gentiles simply believed the gospel but had not yet repented of any sins, then how did these Jerusalem Jews determine that God had already—past tense—"granted" (*edōken*) the repentant way of life to the Gentiles?

Hodges attempted to address this problem by explaining that Cornelius was a "classic case" of a Gentile who had apparently already repented of his pagan idolatry based on the positive description of him provided earlier in Acts 10:2, 22.[51] However, this explanation presents at least two more problems. First, in the historical context of Acts 11, the Jerusalem Jews who interpret Peter's account of Cornelius' conversion are not told any of this background information about Cornelius and yet they still form the conclusion of Acts 11:18 that *"God has also granted to the Gentiles repentance to life."* The overall character of Cornelius is only supplied *to the reader of Acts* in chapter 10, not to Peter's *historical audience* in Jerusalem in chapter 11. Second, even if we may assume for the sake of argument that Cornelius's repentance is inferred in Acts 10 and Peter shared this with his Jewish audience, Acts 11:18 still refers to the "Gentiles" in the plural as being granted "repentance to life." Their sum-

[50] Hodges, *Harmony with God,* 118.

[51] Ibid., 83.

marizing statement, therefore, goes beyond just Cornelius. This leads us to ask, "How did these Jews in Jerusalem know the spiritual history of the many other 'Gentiles' assembled with Cornelius (Acts 10:24)?" Their spiritual backgrounds are never stated in either Acts 10 or 11.

It appears best, therefore, to interpret the expression in Acts 11:18, "repentance to life," as a summary expression for the condition and provision of salvation by faith experienced equally by the Jewish Christians of Judea and Jerusalem and by the Gentiles. The reception of the Holy Spirit via believing in the Lord Jesus Christ (Acts 11:16-17) was simply another way of expressing eternal salvation based on the nearness of the reference to the word "saved" in Acts 11:14. Even Hodges admitted that this salvation experience of the Gentiles in Acts 10 was a matter of receiving "eternal life."[52] Wilkin also acknowledges that Cornelius needed to be "born again"[53] at this point rather than sanctified as an already existing child of God. The Book of Acts is conclusive that Jews and Gentiles received the remission of sins and the gift of the Holy Spirit on the basis of faith/repentance, not baptism.

The Contents of Saving Faith/Repentance in Acts 2

Having carefully considered in Acts 2 the sole *condition* of repentance/faith for the remission of sins and gift of the Holy Spirit, we are now in a position to examine the *content* of salvific repentance in Acts 2:38. What was the content of saving faith presented by the apostle Peter in his preaching on the day of Pentecost? With respect to the crossless gospel, it is important to keep in mind that in Acts 2, Peter wasn't merely speaking for himself. According to Acts 2:14, John and the other apostles were also present consenting to Peter's preaching. This explains why at the conclusion of Peter's message, the Jews respond in Acts 2:37 by addressing *"Peter and the rest of the apostles,"* saying, *"Men and brethren, what shall we do?"* The apostles were unified in their saving message. There was not a "Johannine sense" of Jesus being the Christ versus a "Petrine sense." Peter and John did not have conflicting gospels. And what was the focus of Peter's evangelistic preaching to these unbelieving Jews? It was a presentation of the person and work of Jesus as the Messiah, coupled with an exhortation to change their minds about Him and be saved. Using diverse terminology to describe the Lord Jesus, Peter paints a portrait of Jesus as absolute deity, but also as man, who died and rose again to provide remission of sins for all who would repent concerning Him and be saved. Conspicuous by its absence,

---

[52] Hodges, *Harmony with God*, 81-83.

[53] Wilkin states, "First, we know from Acts 10:43-48 and 11:14 that Cornelius was not yet born again before Peter came to him. . . . Any view that suggests that Cornelius was already born again must thus be rejected." Bob Wilkin, "Can Unbelievers Seek God and Work Righteousness?" *Grace in Focus* 17 (November-December 2002): 1 (ellipsis added).

however, is any singular "focus" upon eternal life as would be required by the crossless gospel position.[54]

The Deity of Christ

Instead of the *gift* of eternal life itself being emphasized, we see throughout Peter's preaching that the *Giver* of life is emphasized in terms of His person and work as "the Christ." The personal identity of Jesus is stated beginning in 2:22, where His miraculous earthly ministry is recounted. The nation of Israel could not deny the miracles that Jesus had performed in their midst for the previous 3 years of His public ministry. These served as confirming evidence that Jesus was the rightful Messiah (Matt. 11:2-5), and yet Peter's Jewish audience had refused to recognize Him as such.

Peter goes on to unfold Jesus' true identity, character, and position as Messiah. He is identified as no One less than Yahweh in verse 25.[55] There Peter quotes David *"concerning Him"* (Jesus), saying, *"I foresaw the LORD always before my face"* (Ps. 16:8). The "LORD" in the Hebrew text of Psalm 16:8 is none other than God, Yahweh/Jehovah, and this name is attributed directly to Jesus by Peter in Acts 2:25. Next, in verse 27, Jesus is referred to as the "Holy One." Over 30 times in the Hebrew Old Testament the term *qādôsh* is applied as a title for God, such as in Isaiah 43:15, *"I am the LORD, your Holy One, the Creator of Israel, your King."* Peter then refers to Jesus being at the "right hand of God" (2:33-34), a position of highest honor alongside God Himself, a position reserved for deity alone.

In addition, Peter mentions all three members of the Triune Godhead in Acts 2:33, where Jesus receives the "Holy Spirit" from the "Father" in order to send Him on the day of Pentecost. Peter knew that it was the Lord Jesus who mediated the Spirit at Pentecost based on Christ's prior promise to do so before His ascension (Luke 24:49). This exercise of divine sovereignty in sending forth the very Spirit of God was not a right or capacity possessed by any mere man or angelic figure. By Peter pointing to Jesus as the source of the phenomenon of the Holy Spirit witnessed on Pentecost, he was clearly attesting to Jesus' deity. It was not Peter's intent to set forth the doctrine of the Trinity for his listeners at this point, as saving faith is not a matter of believing specifically in the Holy Spirit but in the Son of God (John 3:16; Acts 16:31). But by declaring that Jesus sent forth the Spirit of God, Peter was revealing to his audience another facet of the deity of Jesus the Christ.

Peter then concludes with the climactic designation of Jesus as "Lord and Christ" (2:36). The term "Lord" here is clearly deistic,[56] denoting the

---

[54] Zane C. Hodges, "How to Lead People to Christ, Part 1: The Content of Our Message," *JOTGES* 13 (Autumn 2000): 8.

[55] Larry W. Hurtado, *Lord Jesus Christ: Devotion to Jesus in Earliest Christianity* (Grand Rapids: Eerdmans, 2003), 181.

[56] Ibid., 182.

position and possession of absolute sovereignty. This again is the sole prerogative of deity. While some may interpret Acts 2:36 to be teaching that Jesus was not "Lord and Christ" until the resurrection (*"God has made this Jesus, whom you crucified, both Lord and Christ"*), it is better to view Jesus as being both Lord and Christ already during His earthly ministry.[57] Well before His resurrection, the Lord Jesus accepted the appellative of "Christ" applied to Himself, when Peter confessed, *"You are the Christ, the Son of the living God"* (Matt. 16:16). However, since Jesus was the Christ even before His death and resurrection, of necessity He still had to die and rise again in fulfillment of His messianic mission and identity in the plan of God. Furthermore, as we shall see this unfold in the next chapter dealing with the rest of Acts, it was particularly His crucifixion and resurrection that characterized Him as the Christ, with the resurrection serving as a powerful attestation that He is the Son of God (Rom. 1:4). The resurrection put His deity beyond dispute.[58]

From this first recorded evangelistic message in Church history, we see that the person of Jesus Christ was highly exalted in the evangelism of Peter through a diversity of terminology and imagery. Though there was no explicit statement declaring that "Jesus is God" or "Jesus is deity," Peter communicated this precise truth by describing Christ in terms of His name ("LORD" [*Yahweh*]) or title ("Lord" [*kurios*]); by His character and transcendence as "Holy One"; by His unique position of majesty and honor at the "right hand of God"; and by His functional sovereignty in sending the "Holy Spirit." Peter was calling upon his unsaved Jewish audience at Pentecost to believe that Jesus was more than a merely superhuman figure. They had to believe He was deity-incarnate. Theologian Charles Ryrie provides a summary of this conclusion, stating:

> This is what Peter asked the crowd to do on the day of Pentecost. They were to change their minds about Jesus of Nazareth. Formerly they had considered Him to be only a blasphemous human being claiming to be God; now they changed their minds and saw Him as the God-man Savior whom they would trust for salvation.[59]

The Humanity of Christ

Besides the deity of the Lord Jesus, His humanity is also proclaimed by Peter, though it is largely assumed on the part of Peter's audience and uncontested just as His miracles were in Acts 2:22. In verse 22, Jesus is

---

[57] C. Kavin Rowe, "Acts 2.36 and the Continuity of Lukan Christology," *NTS* 53 (2007): 37-56, esp. 54-55. The term "made" (*epoiēsen*) is an aorist, active, indicative verb and by itself simply does not indicate when this occurred exactly, only that from Peter's perspective in Acts 2:36 it was already true. Porter, "The Messiah in Luke and Acts," 160n66.

[58] Harrison, *Acts*, 61-62.

[59] Charles C. Ryrie, *A Survey of Bible Doctrine* (Chicago: Moody Bible Institute, 1972), 139.

referred to as a "Man." In Acts 2:30, Peter testifies that Jesus is a biological descendant of David, coming from *"his body, according to the flesh"* (2:30). In addition, the humanity of Jesus as the Christ is an implicit truth taught by the fact that He actually died physically, since spirits cannot die physically. Similarly, His humanity is taught implicitly through the fact of His bodily resurrection, as mere spirit beings do not rise from the dead in a body of flesh and bones such as Christ did (Luke 24:39). In connection with His resurrection, it is specifically stated in Acts 2:31 that it was His "flesh" that was raised. The genuine humanity of the Lord Jesus was an incontrovertible fact and an essential aspect of Him being "the Christ." Charles Ryrie concurs once again, stating:

> The humanity of Christ is mainly demonstrated in the book [of Acts] by references to the historic human Jesus of Nazareth and by identifying Jesus with the Christ. That Jesus was a real human being is assumed and accepted in Peter's Pentecostal message; that Jesus is the Christ is the point of his message (2:36). References to specific incidents in the earthly life of Christ are few, but those which are mentioned constitute proofs of His humanity (2:23; 8:32; 10:38).[60]

The Resurrection of Christ

In Acts 2, the thrust of Peter's preaching was undeniably the resurrection of Christ. This fact again exposes the imbalanced and erroneous conclusion of today's crossless, resurrectionless gospel that says we must make the guarantee of eternal life the focus of our evangelism. But Peter's emphasis on Christ's resurrection also raises a more serious question for the normative Free Grace position with respect to the contents of saving faith. If Peter's message was evangelistic (and it was), then why did he make the resurrection the concentration of his message and not the other elements of the gospel, such as Christ's deity or the substitutionary, satisfactory aspect of His death?

The answer to this question is relatively simple and obvious. It was Jesus' resurrection that validated each of the other Christological elements that make up the gospel and that define Him as the Christ of saving faith. For example, Jesus may have appeared to the natural eye to be an ordinary man prior to His resurrection, but in the resurrection He did something empirically verifiable that no man or angel had ever done in all of history to that point, nor since. He conquered death, which only God can do (John 1:1-4; Col. 1:15-19; Rev. 1:8, 17-18). Hence, Jesus is true deity.[61] Further, when Jesus died on the cross, what may have previously appeared to be just

---

[60] Charles C. Ryrie, *Biblical Theology of the New Testament* (Chicago: Moody Press, 1959), 109 (brackets added).

[61] Timothy J. Ralston, "The Theological Significance of Paul's Conversion," *BSac* 147 (April 1990): 212.

another death of a common criminal, a routine occurrence in Israel, now had to be radically reappraised. Craig aptly summarizes this point: "The resurrection turned catastrophe into victory. Because God raised Jesus from the dead, he could be proclaimed as Messiah after all (Acts 2:32, 36). Similarly for the significance of the cross—it was his resurrection that enabled Jesus' shameful death to be interpreted in salvific terms. Without it, Jesus' death would have meant only humiliation and accursedness by God; but in view of the resurrection it could be seen to be the event by which forgiveness of sins was obtained."[62] Since the Lord Jesus physically and spiritually overcame the wages of sin, namely death (Rom. 6:23), His own death must have actually been a spiritually divine and redemptive sacrifice rather than just another instance of a mere mortal succumbing to the bondage of corruption. Christ's resurrection tied together His person and work in a way that the other individual aspects of His deity, humanity, and atoning death could not have done by themselves. It changed everything, including the content of saving faith and the evangelistic message preached. This is why Peter made the resurrection the emphasis of his preaching at the beginning of the Church age.

Reliance upon Christ Implicitly Expressed with Epi

In Peter's message on the day of Pentecost, the work of Jesus Christ is also included as part of the content of saving faith. It is clearly conveyed by the fact that in Acts 2:38 Peter commanded repentance and baptism *"upon (epi) the name of Jesus Christ"* for the remission of sins and the gift of the Holy Spirit. Our understanding of this verse will be greatly enhanced by observing first what Peter does *not* say. He does not say, "Repent and be baptized every one of you and you shall receive the remission of sins." Rather, he says, *"Repent and be baptized every one of you UPON THE NAME OF JESUS CHRIST and you shall receive the remission of sins."* As chapter 6 explained, the *name* of Jesus Christ includes His redemptive work. In Acts 2:38, the use of the preposition *epi* ("upon") in combination with the "name" of Jesus Christ strongly implies reliance upon Christ's person and work. The Jews in Jerusalem in Acts 2 needed some basis upon which to repent and be baptized, and that was "the name" of Christ. Implicit within this twofold response was a reliance upon the person and work of Christ. They were to change their minds about the identity of Jesus and His finished work as the Christ, as well as be baptized to publicly proclaim their iden-

---

[62] William Lane Craig, "Did Jesus Rise from the Dead?" in *Jesus Under Fire: Modern Scholarship Reinvents the Historical Jesus*, ed. Michael J. Wilkins and J. P. Moreland (Grand Rapids: Zondervan, 1995), 159. See also, Jacques Dupont, "The Conversion of Paul, and Its Influence on His Understanding of Salvation by Faith," in *Apostolic History and the Gospel: Biblical and Historical Essays Presented to F. F. Bruce on His 60th Birthday*, ed. W. Ward Gasque and Ralph P. Martin (Grand Rapids: Eerdmans, 1970), 194; Ralston, "The Theological Significance of Paul's Conversion," 207-12.

tification with Him. Having believed in Christ, they were to be baptized while they continued to rest upon "the name" of the Savior. Consequently, the remission of sins and gift of the Holy Spirit were conditioned upon their repentance/faith rather than the act that symbolized their salvation in Christ—baptism.

It is noteworthy that in verse 38 Peter says to repent and be baptized literally "upon" (*epi*) the name of Jesus Christ. He does not say to do this "in" His name as most translations render it,[63] as if the underlying Greek preposition was either *en* or *eis*. In fact, this verse is the only instance in the entire New Testament where *epi* is used in connection with baptism. In every other occurrence of the verb form (*baptizō*) or the noun form (*baptisma, baptismos, baptistēs*), the prepositions that are employed are either *eis* or *en*, which are normally translated "in" or "into." Here in Acts 2:38, Peter was not prescribing a particular baptismal formula to be recited at the time of baptism, as if to say, "I baptize you *in* the name of Jesus Christ." Nor was *epi* depicting merely the believer's positional identification or association with Christ via Spirit baptism as other baptism passages do. Rather, Peter was commanding his Jerusalem audience to repent and be baptized while resting upon the name (person and work) of Jesus Christ.[64] This would not make the remission of sins and gift of the Holy Spirit contingent upon the fulfillment of two conditions, namely repentance plus baptism. That would make salvation the result of faith plus a work. Instead, the remission of sins and the gift of the Spirit were granted due to the very reason that these Jews were getting baptized, because they had changed their minds about the Savior and were resting upon His name!

According to this interpretation, the Greek preposition *epi* in Acts 2:38 when used adverbially implicitly conveys the idea of personal trust or reliance. We should not go so far as claiming that *epi* has its own verbal force, as if it functioned as a third verb in the sentence in addition to "repent" and "be baptized." There is no need to make *epi* stand on all fours and walk![65] Rather it functions adverbially here with *baptizō* and possibly even *metanoeō*. The term, *epi*, when used with the dative case (as

---

[63] Lewis Sperry Chafer, *Systematic Theology* (Dallas: Dallas Seminary Press, 1947-1948; reprint ed., Grand Rapids: Kregel, 1993), 3:383.

[64] Ron Merryman, "Acts 2:38: An Exposition," *GFJ* (July 1998): 14-15.

[65] This interpretation of *epi* should not be confused with the "causal *eis*" interpretation of Acts 2:38, which argues that the preposition *eis* in *"for (eis) the remission of sins"* should be interpreted according to its rare meaning of "because of." According to this interpretation, Acts 2:38 is really saying, "Repent and be baptized . . . *because of* the remission of sins," or in other words, "*because* your sins have already been forgiven." As others have observed, even though this interpretation has simplicity in its favor, it is too subtle and tendentious to be convincing. Instead, the Great Commission interpretation is based foremost upon context, while taking *epi* in its normal and most basic sense without special pleading.

in Acts 2:38), has the basic sense of "rest,"[66] and it helps to convey the basic idea of "resting upon" or "depending upon."[67] A. T. Robertson writes that the "Ground-Meaning" of *epi* "is upon as opposed to ὑπό. It differs from ὑπέρ in that ἐπί implies a real resting upon, not merely over."[68] Harris echoes this same sentiment, explaining its meaning as "Basically denoting position *on* something which forms a support or foundation, *epi* is the opposite of *hypo* ("under") and differs from *hyper* ("above") in implying actual rest upon some object."[69] Raymond Abba also concludes that with respect to a person's "name," the Greek preposition *en* normally connotes "participation in authority," whereas *epi* "has the sense of relying upon" or "resting upon" a person's name.[70] Thus Greek grammarian C. F. D. Moule can even speak of *epi* as indicating "reliance upon the Lord."[71] It is not surprising, therefore, that among Greek lexicons it is a well-recognized fact that *epi* with the dative can mean "depending on,"[72] "in dependence upon,"[73] and "of that upon which anything rests"[74] including "relying upon the name"[75] of someone. Thayer even cites the specific use of *epi* in Acts 2:38 and states that in this verse it means "to repose your hope and confidence in his Messianic authority."[76]

If we interpret *epi* in Acts 2:38 with this implicit sense of rest, repose, reliance, or dependence, then this is perfectly consistent with the fact that eternal salvation in this dispensation is conditioned upon personal trust in the Lord Jesus Christ. This interpretation also accords with the particular usage of *epi* in Luke-Acts. First, it should be recalled what was observed earlier in this chapter regarding Luke's Great Commission account. In Luke 24:47, there is no mention of baptism, only repentance. In addition, throughout Acts, remission of sins is conditioned upon repentance/faith rather than water baptism. This harmonizes with the conclusion that the remission of sins in Acts 2:38 is predicated on repentance or reliance upon the person and work of Christ, which is biblical saving faith.

---

[66] F. A. Adams, *The Greek Prepositions, Studied from Their Original Meanings as Designations of Space* (New York: D. Appleton & Co., 1885), 39, §55.

[67] Gessner Harrison, *A Treatise on the Greek Prepositions, and on the Cases of Nouns with which These Are Used* (Philadelphia: J. B. Lippincott & Co., 1858), 260, 285.

[68] A. T. Robertson, *A Grammar of the Greek New Testament in the Light of Historical Research* (Nashville: Broadman Press, 1934), 600.

[69] Murray J. Harris, Appendix on prepositions, *NIDNTT*, 3:1193.

[70] Raymond Abba, "Name," *IDB*, 3:507.

[71] C. F. D. Moule, *An Idiom Book of New Testament Greek* (Cambridge: Cambridge University Press, 1953), 50.

[72] BDAG, 364. See under §6, "marker of basis for a state of being, action, or result," where the sense in Luke 5:5 is "depending on Your word."

[73] LSJ, 622.

[74] J. H. Thayer, ed., *The New Thayer's Greek-English Lexicon of the New Testament* (Peabody, MA: Hendrickson Publishers, 1981), 232.

[75] Ibid.

[76] Ibid.

Secondly, in some non-soteriological passages in the Book of Acts, *epi* is used adverbially to imply or convey reliance or dependence (Acts 25:10, 12, 26 [2x]; 27:43-44). It is used in connection with other verbs, such as speaking or teaching to indicate that the speaking or teaching are being done with reliance or dependence upon the Lord (Acts 4:17-18; 5:28, 40). In one verse, Acts 14:3, the NASB has even opted to supply the words "with reliance" where the Greek text has *epi*, resulting in the translation, "speaking boldly *with reliance* upon the Lord."[77] The usage of *epi* with these verbs of speaking and teaching in Acts parallels its usage in Acts 2:38 with the verbs, *"repent"* and *"be baptized,"* showing that the Jerusalem Jews were to change their minds about Christ and be baptized with their dependence upon the name of Jesus Christ. Elsewhere in Acts, *epi* is also used specifically in connection with the "name" of Christ (Acts 3:16; 4:17-18; 5:28, 40).

When it comes to salvation contexts in the Book of Acts, *epi* is routinely used with this sense of reliance or trust, in combination with *pisteuō* (Acts 3:16; 9:35, 42; 11:17, 21; 13:12; 16:31; 22:19; 26:18, 20 [*metanoeō*]), in order to emphasize the idea of believing *upon* Christ as the object of one's spiritual rest.[78] Likewise, *epi* is also used in several verses with the verb *epistrephō* (Acts 9:35; 11:21; 14:15; 15:19; 26:18, 20) to intensify the concept of turning to Jesus Christ in reliance or dependence upon Him. Though the preposition *eis* is also used with *pisteuō* and *epistrephō* to indicate more of the *direction* of our faith, the use of *epi* expresses what or who our faith is ultimately *resting upon*. The basic idea of the *epi* + *epistrephō* construction in Acts is not merely that we turn "to" the Lord Jesus but that we turn in reliance and dependence upon Him as the saving object of our faith.

With the sole condition for salvation clarified in Acts 2:38, it becomes easier to apprehend the proper object and content of saving faith in this verse. Here Peter commands his Jewish audience in Jerusalem to repent and be baptized specifically *"upon the name of Jesus Christ."* It is demonstrable from Acts and the rest of Scripture that the "name" of Christ stands as a metonym for the person and work of the Savior (see chapter 6). Practically, this means that the unsaved person is to ground his or her confidence upon the only sure foundation for acceptance with God—the name of Jesus Christ. This truth was understood years ago by the writer of the classic hymn, "The Solid Rock," as he penned the following words: "My hope is built on nothing less than Jesus' blood and righteous-

---

[77] Similarly, Chafer went so far as to suggest that the word *believing* should be supplied in Acts 2:38 to complete the sense, *"Repent, and be baptized every one of you, [believing] upon the name of Jesus Christ."* Chafer, *Systematic Theology*, 3:383.

[78] For additional Lucan usage, see Luke 18:9 where *epi* appears with elision and *peithō* for those who "trusted upon themselves (*pepoithotas eph' heautois*) that they were righteous." Luke 24:25 also says, "slow of heart to believe upon (*epi*) all that the prophets have spoken." For Pauline uses of *epi* with *pisteuō* see Rom. 4:5; 9:33; 10:11; 1 Tim. 1:16. Titus 1:2 presents a case of *epi* used alone, without *peithō*, *pisteuō*, or *metanoeō*, where the sense is clearly resting in faith upon the hope/promise of eternal life.

ness; I dare not trust the sweetest frame, but wholly lean on Jesus' name. On Christ the solid Rock I stand—all other ground is sinking sand, all other ground is sinking sand." God has only provided one ground of redemption for mankind, and thus He requires us all to place our confidence upon that very same ground if we are to receive divine deliverance. Regarding Acts 2:38, this means that the unregenerate Jews in Jerusalem on the Day of Pentecost had to change their minds about Jesus Christ with their dependence upon His person and work in order to receive remission of sins—which is what the baptism upon His name signified. It is for this reason that Ron Merryman concludes concerning Acts 2:38:

> Involved in the "name of Jesus Christ" is the idea of his full identity. He is the Lord Jesus Christ, the unique Son of God. Subsumed in his name is his work at Calvary. As Jesus, the Messiah, "the Christ, the Anointed One," the one prophesied in the Old Testament, he died substitutionally for the sins of mankind, for your sins and for mine. Faith in that NAME, confidence in his full identity and mission as it is clarified in his cross and subsequent resurrection, brings immediate, absolute, and total judicial forgiveness of sins.[79]

The Death of Christ

In spite of the evident use of Christ's "name" throughout Acts standing for the person and work of the Lord Jesus Christ, some may still raise an objection at this point concerning the death of Christ. They may claim that the substitutionary, sacrificial aspect of Christ's death is not explicitly presented in Peter's Pentecostal sermon or even in the rest of Acts, and therefore it should not be viewed as a required element of saving faith. Such an objection, however, is hauntingly familiar. It is reminiscent of theological liberalism's spiritual blindness toward the Gospel of John, as exemplified in Rudolf Bultmann's claim that "the thought of Jesus' death as an atonement for sin has no place in John."[80] Others regard Luke-Acts in the same fashion, as Wilckens has stated, "The death of Jesus has no saving significance, and as a result Luke's christology completely lacks any soteriological content."[81] But this perspective reflects unbelief and willful

---

[79] Merryman, "Acts 2:38: An Exposition," 15. See also Ron Merryman, *Justification by Faith Alone & Its Historical Challenges*, revised edition (Colorado Springs, CO: Merryman Ministries, 2000), 117, 121nn2-3.

[80] Rudolf Bultmann, *Theology of the New Testament*, trans. Kendric Grobel (New York: Charles Scribner's Sons, 1951-1955), 2:54.

[81] Ulrich Wilckens, *Die Missionsreden der Apostelgeschichte: Form- und traditionsgeschichtliche Untersuchungen* (Neukirchen: Neukirchener Verlag, 1961), 216. See also Hans Conzelmann, *The Theology of St. Luke*, trans. Geoffrey Buswell (New York: Harper & Row, 1960), 201-2; Ernst Käsemann, "Ministry and Community in the New Testament," in *Essays on New Testament Themes*, trans. W. J. Montague (London: SCM Press, 1964), 92; D. A. S. Raven, "St. Luke and Atonement," *ExpT* 97 (July 1986): 291-94.

ignorance of Luke-Acts, for Luke's writings *do* present Christ's death as redemptive and substitutionary, rather than as a mere historical fact. Thus, John Stott writes, "It is often asserted that in the book of Acts the apostles' emphasis was on the resurrection rather than the death of Jesus, and that in any case they gave no doctrinal explanation of his death. Neither of these arguments is sustained by the evidence."[82]

While it is true that the substitutionary and satisfactory aspects of Christ's death are not stated in nearly as explicit terms in Luke-Acts as they are in the Epistles, this hardly means that these aspects are entirely absent.[83] For example, in Luke 24:20-21, the two disciples on the road to Emmaus recount to Christ how *"the chief priests and our rulers delivered Him to be condemned to death, and crucified Him. But we were hoping that it was He who was going to redeem Israel"* (Luke 24:20-21). This passage, just like the other passion scenes at the cross in the Synoptic Gospels, makes an obvious point through the rhetorical use of irony. The point to Luke's readers could not be missed. Though it appeared to the disciples on the road to Emmaus that all hope was lost when Jesus died, His resurrection changed everything. It demonstrated that Jesus *had* in fact provided *redemption* for Israel by that very crucifixion, and this redemption was proven by virtue of His resurrection.

The substitutionary, propitious, and redemptive nature of Christ's death is also clearly seen in Luke 22:19-20 and Acts 20:28.[84] In Luke 22:19-20, the context is the institution of the Lord's Supper. There the Lord Jesus stated that His coming sacrifice would be "for you" (*huper humōn*). This phrase occurs twice in verses 19-20. It is the only recorded account of the Lord's Supper in the Gospels that contains a *double* substitutionary reference, presumably for emphasis. In addition, Luke underscores the redemptive and propitious aspect of Christ's death in Acts 20:28, where Paul addresses the Ephesian elders and tells them *"to shepherd the church of God, which He purchased with His own blood."* The redemption price for

---

[82] John R. W. Stott, *The Cross of Christ* (Downers Grove, IL: InterVarsity Press, 1986), 32.

[83] Darrell L. Bock, "A Theology of Luke-Acts," in *A Biblical Theology of the New Testament*, ed. Roy B. Zuck and Darrell L. Bock (Chicago: Moody Press, 1994), 112; John T. Carroll and Joel B. Green, *The Death of Jesus in Early Christianity* (Peabody, MA: Hendrickson, 1995), 67; James Denney, *The Death of Christ*, ed. R. V. G. Tasker (London: Tyndale Press, 1960), 47-48; Joel B. Green, "The Death of Jesus, God's Servant," in *Reimaging the Death of the Lukan Jesus*, ed. Dennis D. Sylva (Frankfurt am Main: Anton Hain, 1990), 1-28, 170-73; Peter M. Head, "The Self-Offering and Death of Christ as a Sacrifice in the Gospels and the Acts of the Apostles," in *Sacrifice in the Bible*, ed. Roger T. Beckwith and Martin J. Selman (Grand Rapids: Baker, 1995), 111-29; Leon Morris, *The Cross in the New Testament* (Grand Rapids: Eerdmans, 1965), 108; Earl Richards, "Jesus' Passion and Death in Acts," in *Reimaging the Death of the Lukan Jesus*, ed. Dennis D. Sylva (Frankfurt am Main: Anton Hain, 1990), 125-52, 204-10.

[84] Head, "The Self-Offering and Death of Christ," 119-22; Douglas J. Moo, *The Old Testament in the Gospel Passion Narratives* (Sheffield: Almond Press, 1983), 132-38; C. F. D. Moule, "The Christology of Acts," in *Studies in Luke-Acts*, ed. Leander E. Keck and J. Louis Martyn (London: SPCK, 1968), 171.

every member of the Church was clearly the death of Christ, God-incarnate, not man's good works. In addition, the finality of Christ's death (and thus propitious nature of it) is observable from the fact that this purchase is already complete and spoken of in the past tense ("purchased") by the use of the aorist indicative (*periepoiēsato*) in Acts 20:28. While neither Luke 22:19-20 nor Acts 20:28 specifically reference "sin" or "sins" in connection with Christ's substitutionary, redemptive death, the resolution to the "sin" problem is clearly inferred from the fact that "remission of sins" is repeatedly promised as the benefit flowing from Christ to all believers in Him.[85] Since God never forgives sin out of sheer leniency but only through a sacrifice, Christ's death is the only possible sacrifice referred to in Acts by which God forgives sinners who believe in His Son.

Yet another evidence in the Book of Acts for Christ's death being substitutionary and truly efficacious toward sin is found in the various references to Jesus' death on a "tree" (Acts 5:30; 10:39; 13:29). The fact that Christ was hung on a "tree" (*xulon*) as opposed to the anticipated term, "cross" (*stauros*), shows that the early Church proclaimed Christ's death through the lens of Deuteronomy 21:22-23. There it is stated that whoever is hung on a tree is cursed by God. This clearly means that Christ bore the judgment that we justly deserved.

Finally, the vicarious and satisfactory nature of Christ's death is also taught implicitly in Acts by the suffering "Servant" (*pais*) motif contained in its earliest chapters (Acts 3:13, 26; 4:27, 30). This theme is undoubtedly taken from the Old Testament prophet and evangelist, Isaiah, particularly Isaiah chapter 53.[86] This connection is made explicit through Philip's witness to the Ethiopian eunuch in Acts 8 where he connects Jesus as the Lamb of God to Isaiah 53.[87] The topic of the suffering Servant will be explained more thoroughly in the next chapter which covers the use of *pais* in Acts 3:13, 26.

The gospel that Peter preached on the day of Pentecost did not merely include the historical fact of Jesus' death but it also implicitly contained the meaning and value of that death as sacrificial and substitutionary for

---

[85] Denney, *The Death of Christ*, 50; Louis Diana, "The Essential Elements of the Gospel Message in the Evangelistic Speeches in Acts" (M.A.B.S. thesis, Multnomah Graduate School of Ministry, 1992), 46-55.

[86] Bock, "A Theology of Luke-Acts," 127; Cullmann, *The Christology of the New Testament*, 73; Denney, *The Death of Christ*, 50; Joachim Jeremias, "παῖς θεοῦ," *TDNT*, 5:705-9; William J. Larkin, "Luke's Use of the Old Testament as a Key to His Soteriology," *JETS* 20.4 (December 1977): 325-35; Jacques Ménard, "*Pais Theou* as Messianic Title in the Book of Acts," *CBQ* 19 (1957): 83, 89; Otto Michel, "παῖς θεοῦ," *NIDNTT*, 3:610-12; Morris, *The Cross in the New Testament*, 141-42.

[87] In addition, since Luke-Acts is a unified two-part work, it may also be significant that the Lord Jesus in Luke 22:37 quotes from Isaiah 53 and interprets it as applying directly to Himself. The Lord Jesus was certainly conscious of the fact that He was fulfilling the prophecies of Isaiah and Luke brings this out (Luke 4:17-21). Larkin, "Luke's Use of the Old Testament as a Key to His Soteriology," 329-35.

the forgiveness of sins. In this respect, Peter's evangelistic "saving message" focused upon Christ-crucified and risen. Peter's gospel is found to be in perfect harmony with that of Paul, and John, and the rest of the New Testament. The contents of this gospel of grace preached by Peter at Pentecost are the very contents of saving faith required by God throughout the rest of the Church age, even today.

Chapter 17

What Does "the Christ" Mean in the Rest of Acts?

OVERVIEW

The Book of Acts provides the infallible historical record of what the apostles and earliest Christians believed about Jesus being "the Christ." In the evangelistic pericopes of Acts, we see the Lord Jesus' person and work presented to lost, unbelieving audiences as the necessary elements of the saving gospel. An emphasis upon eternal life itself or the solitary fact that Jesus is the guarantor of eternal life is completely absent from the teaching and preaching of the apostles and earliest Christians in Acts. Instead, we see the pervasive characterization of Jesus as "the Christ" via His deity, humanity, death for sin, and bodily resurrection. At times, this is explicit. At other times, it is only implied. But from beginning to end in the Book of Acts, the setting forth of Jesus as the Christ to lost audiences routinely consists of these elements of His person and work. In addition, the sole requirement for eternal salvation in Acts is also consistently declared to be repentance/faith, not works of any kind, such as baptism, circumcision, or keeping the law. The evangelistic, saving message of the apostle John is seen to be no different from that of Peter based on their partnership in preaching the gospel in Acts 2-5. Thus, there is no supposedly unique, crossless "Johannine sense" of Jesus being "the Christ."

It is axiomatic among believers who accept the inspiration and inerrancy of Scripture that when God's Word is correctly interpreted it never contradicts itself. The interpretation of "the Christ" in John's Gospel must be consistent with the interpretation of messianic passages found in the Book of Acts and throughout the rest of Scripture. If any apparent contradiction exists, the contradiction is only with our understanding of a particular passage, not with God's Word. But before considering in this chapter the litany of passages from Acts that repeat the Lord Jesus' death and resurrection as defining elements of Him being "the Christ," the question of how we should interpret John's Gospel must ever be kept in mind. As you read these various passages from Acts, ask yourself how Peter, John, Paul, and all the other evangelists in Acts understood the term "Christ." Did they interpret it in a manner consistent with the Old Testament and the Lord Jesus Himself? Did the apostles ever speak of "Christ" with the supposedly "Johannine sense" of Him being merely the "guarantor of eternal life," as is claimed by today's crossless adherents?

Fortunately, we do not have to speculate about the correct answers to these questions. God has provided for us in Acts the incontestable proof that the Lord Jesus' deity, humanity, death, and resurrection are essential to the very definition of Him as "the Christ." It is also worth noting from Acts that the settings for the proclamation of these essential characteristics of "the Christ" invariably occur in passages involving the evangelization of the lost rather than merely the sanctification of the saved. In this respect, we will discover from Acts that the apostles harmoniously testify to the contents of saving faith by consistently evangelizing the lost with the truth of Christ's person and work, along with the provision of salvation and the condition for it. In other words, the early Church preached the *gospel of Christ* with its marvelous message of salvation by grace through faith in Christ alone.

It has been the thesis of this book that the Word of God consistently sets forth several specific and essential truths that form "the gospel" that Christians are to preach and that the lost must believe for their eternal salvation. The contents of the gospel of Christ are equivalent to the contents of saving faith today. These elements of the gospel include Jesus Christ's deity, humanity, death for sin, bodily resurrection from the dead, and salvation solely by grace through faith in Him. In summaries of the gospel throughout this book, the *provision* and *condition* of salvation have normally been kept together as one element of the gospel since this is the normal biblical pattern (Acts 10:43; 13:38-39; 16:31; Rom. 1:16; 1 Cor. 1:21;

Eph. 1:13; 2:8-9; etc.). However, some may wish to divide this last element into two separate parts, as shown below, so that the *provision* of salvation is separate from the *condition* of faith alone.

The Gospel of Christ Centers in a Specific . . .

Person:	**Jesus Christ who is God and man**
Work:	**Christ died for our sins & rose from the dead**
Provision:	**Salvation by grace**
Condition:	**Through faith in Christ alone**

Each of these elements comprising the true gospel of salvation is amply attested throughout the Book of Acts. This is indicated from the categorization of passages for each element of the gospel found on the following page. A few observations should be noted regarding this categorization. First, each of these passages is taken from an evangelistic setting or context in Acts where souls are coming to faith in Jesus Christ for the very first time. This means that the following categorization of passages does not represent simply a doctrinal potpourri of all the passages in Acts that deal with Christ's deity, humanity, substitutionary death, and bodily resurrection. Each of these truths is specifically and evangelistically presented *to the lost* in the Book of Acts for their initial faith in Jesus Christ for salvation.

Second, the passages below have not been forced to fit together from various unrelated and disparate portions of Acts. The gospel, with its constituent parts as outlined above, has not been fabricated into a single, cohesive message. Rather, it must be observed that several of the key evangelistic pericopes of Acts contain all of these elements together within a single evangelistic presentation. This is true in Acts chapters 2, 3, 5, 10, and 13.

Finally, it is also necessary to clarify that several of the key terms that are used evangelistically in Acts encompass more than one category below. For example, the many references to the "Name" of Christ used throughout Acts speak of more than just His deity and humanity; they also include His redemptive work (see chapter 6). Likewise the theologically loaded phrases, "Son of God" and "Son of Man," have a significant amount of semantic overlap that goes beyond just signifying the Lord's deity and humanity respectively. Even the title "Savior" indicates more than the Lord's saving act of death and resurrection; it also reveals His deity (see chapter 10). Similarly, the key term now under consideration, "Christ," is intended to convey more than its strict etymological meaning of "Anointed One." It encompasses both His person and work.

Christ's deity: "Lord" (2:25, 36; 9:35, 42; 10:36; 11:21; 15:11; 16:31; 18:8); "Son" (7:56; 8:37 [TR]; 9:20; 13:33); "Savior" (5:31; 13:23 [CT/TR]); "Prince" (3:15; 5:31); "Right Hand" of God (2:25, 33-34; 5:31; 7:55-56); "Holy One" (2:27; 3:14; 13:35); "Judge" of all (10:42)

Christ's humanity: "Jesus of Nazareth" (2:22; 4:10; 10:38); "Man" (2:22; 7:56; 17:31); "flesh" (2:30-31); "seed" (3:25; 13:23)

Christ's death for sin: "Servant" (3:13, 26); "tree" (5:30; 10:39; 13:29); "Lamb" (8:32); "purchased with His own blood" (20:28)

Christ's resurrection: "concerning the resurrection of the Christ . . . nor did His flesh see corruption" (2:30-31; 3:15, 26; 4:10; 5:30; 10:40-41; 13:30, 34, 37; 17:31-32)

Provision: "remission/forgiveness of sins" (2:38; 5:31; 10:43; 13:38; 26:18); "justified" (13:39); "eternal life" (13:46, 48); "salvation" or "saved" (2:40; 4:12; 11:14; 13:26, 47; 15:11; 16:30-31)

Condition: "faith"/"believe" (4:4, 32; 8:12-13, 37 [TR]; 9:42; 10:43; 11:17, 21; 13:39, 41, 48; 14:1; 15:7, 9; 16:31, 34; 17:12, 34; 18:8); "repent/ance" (2:38; 3:19; 5:31; 11:18; 17:30; 20:21; 26:20); "persuaded" (17:4-5; 18:4; 19:8, 26; 26:28; 28:23-24); "turn" (3:19; 9:35; 11:21; 14:15; 15:3, 19; 26:18, 20; 28:27)

These essential elements of the gospel of Christ are contained in several of the evangelistic episodes in Acts, such as in Acts 3, which will be covered now. This chapter will resume its analysis of the preaching of the apostles in Acts and pick up where the last chapter left off with Peter's preaching on the day of Pentecost in Acts 2. Peter's evangelistic message in Acts 3 bears a remarkable similarity to his preaching on Pentecost.

Acts 3:12-26

12 *So when Peter saw it, he responded to the people: "Men of Israel, why do you marvel at this? Or why look so intently at us, as though by our own power or godliness we had made this man walk?*

13 *The God of Abraham, Isaac, and Jacob, the God of our fathers, glorified His* ***Servant Jesus,*** *whom you delivered up and denied in the presence of Pilate, when he was determined to let Him go.*

14 *"But you denied* ***the Holy One*** *and the* ***Just,*** *and asked for a murderer to be granted to you,*

15 *"and* ***killed*** *the* ***Prince of life,*** *whom God* ***raised from the dead,*** *of which we are witnesses.*

16 *"And His name, through faith in His name, has made this man strong, whom you see and know. Yes, the faith which comes through Him has given him this perfect soundness in the presence of you all.*

17 *"Yet now, brethren, I know that you did it in ignorance, as did also your rulers.*
18 *"But those things which God foretold by the mouth of all His prophets, that* ***the Christ*** *would* ***suffer,*** *He has thus fulfilled.*
19 *"****Repent*** *therefore and be converted, that your sins may be blotted out, so that times of refreshing may come from the presence of the Lord,*
20 *"and that He may send* ***Jesus Christ****, who was preached to you before,*
21 *"whom heaven must receive until the times of restoration of all things, which God has spoken by the mouth of all His holy prophets since the world began.*
22 *"For Moses truly said to the fathers, 'The LORD your God will raise up for you* ***a Prophet like me*** *from your brethren. Him you shall hear in all things, whatever He says to you.*
23 *'And it shall be that every soul who will not hear that Prophet shall be utterly destroyed from among the people.'*
24 *"Yes, and all the prophets, from Samuel and those who follow, as many as have spoken, have also foretold these days.*
25 *"You are sons of the prophets, and of the covenant which God made with our fathers, saying to Abraham, 'And in your seed all the families of the earth shall be blessed.'*
26 *"To you first, God, having raised up* ***His Servant Jesus****, sent Him to bless you, in turning away every one of you from your iniquities.*

This passage in Acts 3 will be covered more extensively than other passages in Acts due to its length and important foundational role as the complement to Peter's preaching on the day of Pentecost. Though Peter's preaching in Acts 2 is longer than here in Acts 3, this portion in Acts 3:12-26 should not be overlooked simply because it falls under the shadow of the epochal events of Pentecost. This record of Peter's preaching is even longer (15 verses) than his evangelization of Cornelius and the Gentiles in Acts 10:34-43 (10 verses) or Paul's preaching at the Areopagus in Athens in Acts 17:22-31 (10 verses). Acts 3 contains another Christologically rich and informative section of Scripture where Peter presents both the condition for eternal salvation and the contents of saving faith in an evangelistic setting in Jerusalem. But before focusing on the saving contents of Peter's preaching, the dispensational context of this passage must be considered first.

Dispensational Perspective

Diversity of opinion exists among dispensationalists on the proper interpretation of verses 19-21, where Peter is commanding repentance for the remission of sins, along with the coming of the times of refreshing, and the return of Jesus Christ. One dispensational view interprets Peter to be making a bona fide re-offer of the promised kingdom to that generation of Israelites contingent upon their collective, national repentance.[1] According to this view, Peter's re-offer of the kingdom is still considered legitimate, in spite of the fact that the Church age has barely begun, since Peter apparently did not fully grasp at this early juncture God's timetable and dispensational plan for the Church.[2] Other dispensationalists reject this view, insisting that only Jesus Christ Himself can make a full-fledged offer of the kingdom.[3]

A second dispensational view of Acts 3:19-21 sees Peter merely presenting to Israel "the conditions by which the nation will eventually enter into their covenanted blessings" when Christ returns and the millennial kingdom is established.[4] While this view also acknowledges that entrance into the eschatological kingdom is contingent upon repentance, it does not consider Peter to be offering an immediate reappearance of Christ coupled with the establishment of His kingdom once the condition of national repentance is met. With this view, Peter is simply stating the fact that repentance and forgiveness are required for entrance into the promised kingdom without necessarily addressing the timing of the King's return or the establishment of His kingdom.

A third interpretation of Acts 3:19-21 is held by some "progressive" dispensationalists. This view also recognizes that the blessings in verses 19-21 are contingent upon repentance but that they are separated into two different stages. According to this progressive dispensationalist view, the *"times of refreshing"* in verse 19 that *"come from the presence of the Lord"* occur in the present Church age. The sending of Jesus Christ and the *"restoration of all things"* in verses 20-21 refers to the future millennial kingdom. In order to maintain a chronological separation of these blessings, progressive dispensationalists apply a dual, *already/not yet* hermeneutic to this passage. They claim that the Davidic Covenant is "already" inaugurated and is being partially fulfilled as Christ is "already" reigning on David's throne today in heaven. Thus, with this view, the promised kingdom is "already" established in this present Church age, while the earthly millennial kingdom phase is "not yet" and awaits Christ's second coming.[5]

---

[1] Mal Couch, gen. ed., *A Bible Handbook to the Acts of the Apostles* (Grand Rapids: Kregel Publications, 1999), 55; Alva J. McClain, *The Greatness of the Kingdom* (Winona Lake, IN: BMH Books, 1959), 404-6; Stanley D. Toussaint, "The Contingency of the Coming of the Kingdom," in *Integrity of Heart, Skillfulness of Hands: Biblical and Leadership Studies in Honor of Donald K. Campbell*, ed. Charles H. Dyer and Roy B. Zuck (Grand Rapids: Baker Books, 1994), 230.

[2] Mal Couch, "The Church Dispensation and the 'Times of Refreshing'" in *Progressive Dispensationalism: An Analysis of the Movement and Defense of Traditional Dispensationalism*, ed. Ron J. Bigalke (Lanham, Maryland: University Press of America, 2005), 206-7.

[3] J. Dwight Pentecost, *Thy Kingdom Come* (Wheaton, IL: Victor Books, 1990), 274-76.

[4] Ibid., 276.

[5] Darrell L. Bock, "The Reign of the Lord Christ," in *Dispensationalism, Israel, and the Church*, ed. Craig A. Blaising and Darrell L. Bock (Grand Rapids: Zondervan, 1991), 55-61.

However, such a division of blessings in Acts 3:20-21 cannot be supported either grammatically or doctrinally.[6]

Repentance, Turning, and the Blotting Out of Sin

Regardless of which dispensational interpretation above is correct, all three are compatible with the view that the repentance and blotting out of sin in Acts 3:19 is salvific rather than merely sanctificational and temporal, as the crossless view holds. With the first dispensational view where Peter is literally reoffering the kingdom to Israel, the nation's repentance and remission of sins are viewed as contemporaneous with the return of Christ and the establishment of His kingdom. Thus, Peter views Israel's deliverance into the kingdom as soteriologically tied to its judicial forgiveness which is conditioned on repentance. With the second view, the repentance and forgiveness of Israel is also a prerequisite for entrance into the kingdom. However, this view sees Peter presenting repentance to Israel as necessary for judicial forgiveness regardless of whether the kingdom immediately follows. According to the third, "progressive" dispensational view, judicial forgiveness is still necessary for eternal salvation in the present Church age (the "times of refreshing") just as it will be in the future for entrance into the final phase of the kingdom on earth in the millennium.

The syntax and vocabulary of Acts 3:19-21 also support the conclusion that repentance is the condition for the remission of sins. In verse 19, the words "repent" (*metanoēsate*) and "be converted" (*epistrepsate*) are both aorist, active, imperative verbs. These two terms are used as virtual synonyms of one another in a manner similar to repentance being inherent to faith. When people repent (*metanoeō*) they simultaneously turn (*epistrephō*) to the Lord in faith. In the Greek text of verse 19 (*metanoēsate oun kai epistrepsate eis to exaleiphthēnai humōn tas hamartias*), the construction that combines the preposition *eis* + *to* with the infinitive of "blotted out" (*exaleiphthēnai*) can express either purpose or result.[7] This means that

---

[6] Charles Ryrie, *Dispensationalism* (Chicago: Moody Press, 1995), 170; Toussaint, "The Contingency of the Coming of the Kingdom," 230. The clause in verse 19c, *"times of refreshing from the presence of the Lord,"* is most likely syntactically and semantically coordinate with verses 20-21 based in part on the conjunction *kai* in verse 20 separating the two balanced, subjunctive mood verbs, *elthōsin* ("may come") and *aposteilē* ("may send"). Thus the times of refreshing that come from the presence of the Lord should not be separated chronologically from the sending of Jesus Christ. In verse 19, however, the purpose clause *eis to exaleiphthēnai humōn tas hamartias* (*"that your sins may be blotted out"*) is not necessarily coordinate with the clause which follows it, *hopōs an elthōsin kairoi anapsuxeōs apo prosōpou tou kuriou* (*"so that times of refreshing may come from the presence of the Lord"*), since the conjunction *hopōs* can function as either a subordinating conjunction or coordinating conjunction. The first dispensational interpretation would likely view *hopōs* as a coordinating conjunction, while the second and third dispensational interpretations above would more likely regard *hopōs* as a subordinating conjunction.

[7] BDF, 207, §369; C. F. D. Moule, *An Idiom Book of New Testament Greek* (Cambridge: Cambridge University Press, 1953), 138-39.

Peter commanded his fellow Jews to repent and turn to the Lord either (a) with the conscious intent and purpose of their sins being blotted out, or (b) resulting in their sins being blotted out. In either case, the remission of their sins is certainly conditioned upon repentance.

The second key term in Acts 3:19 is *epistrephō*, and it is used interchangeably with *metanoeō* as a condition for the blotting out of sins. It is unfortunate that *epistrephō* has become such a theologically freighted term in our day, having lost its simple, biblical meaning. Advocates of Lordship Salvation often import into this word the notions of commitment, obedience, service, and turning from the practice of sin in one's life—the full range of "conversion" conditions and what is properly the experience of daily discipleship in the Christian life. But biblically, and especially in Acts, *epistrephō* is used interchangeably with *believing* as the condition for an individual's salvation (John 12:40; Acts 9:35; 11:21; 14:15; 15:3, 19; 26:18, 20; 28:27; 2 Cor. 3:16; 1 Peter 2:25).[8] Bob Wilkin's original conclusions about this term were biblically correct when he wrote:

> The term ἐπιστρέφω was used by Peter in the sense of calling the people to turn their hearts to the Lord, to accept by faith God's free offer of forgiveness. Bruce rightly sees in this passage, "the heart of the gospel of grace."[9]

The idea of turning to the Lord in faith is clearly intended by the term *epistrephō* in Acts 3:19, since it is used in the context as the counterpart to repentance. But the associated term *apostrephō* ("turn away") also occurs later in the context in verse 26 and its meaning and usage must also be clarified.

In Acts 3:26, Peter declares to his fellow Jews in Jerusalem that God raised up His Servant Jesus and *"sent Him to bless you, in turning away (apostrephein) every one of you from your iniquities."* Unfortunately, many approach this verse with Lordship Salvation assumptions and think that God is requiring the lost here to amend their sinful pattern of behavior as proof of "genuine" faith in Christ for salvation. Without such a change, they say, a person has never really been born again. As a prime example of this doctrine, leading Lordship Salvation proponent, John MacArthur, states regarding Acts 3:19, *"Peter's meaning was unmistakable. He was calling for a radical, 180-degree turning from sin. That is repentance."*[10] We are told that this "kind" of repentance and turning to the Lord (*epistrephō*) necessarily *"results in behavioral change."*[11] Without such change, the repentance

[8] Robert N. Wilkin, "Repentance as a Condition for Salvation in the New Testament" (Th.D. dissertation, Dallas Theological Seminary, 1985), 215-31.

[9] Ibid., 218.

[10] John F. MacArthur, Jr., *Faith Works: The Gospel According to the Apostles* (Dallas: Word Publishing, 1993), 83.

[11] Ibid., 85.

is not genuine and a person is not truly saved. MacArthur goes on to reference Acts 3:26 in support of this conclusion, asserting, *"Clearly, from the beginning of the Book of Acts to the end, repentance was the central appeal of the apostolic message. The repentance they preached was not merely a change of mind about who Jesus was. It was a turning from sin (3:26; 8:22)."*[12]

With respect to the turning spoken of in Acts 3:26, someone may legitimately wonder whether this verse requires "a turning from sin" as the human requirement for salvation just as Lordship Salvationists claim. In response, it should be noted that if the blessing spoken of in Acts 3:26 is indeed referring to the blessing of judicial forgiveness, and thus eternal salvation, it may simply mean that God sent Christ to act as the agent of judicial forgiveness. The articular infinitive of verse 26, *en tō apostrephein*, is an infinitive of means.[13] This indicates that the very means by which God would bless the nation of Israel was by turning each one of them, in some sense, away from (*apostrephō*) their sins. The action of turning away in verse 26 is best interpreted in its context as a divine work, as something that is wrought by God for man, rather than as something man does in response to God. This is supported in the immediate context by the preceding verse, Acts 3:25, with its reference to the Abrahamic covenant. This covenant was based on God's promises to do something for Abraham, not what Abraham had to accomplish for God.[14] Secondly, in Acts 3:26, the emphasis is upon God's action of raising up His Servant Jesus to accomplish a specific divine purpose—turning us away from our iniquities.[15] This means that God's Servant Jesus is the One who blesses us by *His act* of turning us away from our sins.

But the critical question remains, in what sense does He turn us (*strephō*) away from (*apo*) our iniquities? Is the reference to being turned by the Lord away from our sins evidence for Lordship Salvation? Is it a proof-text for the doctrine that all who have truly repented (*metanoeō*) and turned to the Lord (*epistrephō*) for judicial forgiveness, as Acts 3:19 teaches, will also turn away from sinful deeds in their life because God will sovereignly cause it to happen and because this kind of repentance and turning to the Lord (*epistrephō*) necessarily *"results in behavioral change"*?[16]

In response, it must be stated that verse 26 may simply be teaching that Christ will separate all sinners who repent (i.e., change their minds) about Him from *the guilt* of their sins. This occurs when the lost receive

---

[12] Ibid.

[13] Daniel B. Wallace, *Greek Grammar Beyond the Basics: An Exegetical Syntax of the New Testament* (Grand Rapids: Zondervan, 1996), 598.

[14] Note the repetition of the divine "I will" in Genesis 12:1-3. In addition, in Genesis 15:7-21 when the covenant is ratified, it is God alone who passes through the middle of the offerings, not Abraham. This indicates that God was the sole agent binding Himself to uphold and fulfill the Abrahamic covenant promises.

[15] Darrell L. Bock, *Acts*, BECNT (Grand Rapids: Baker Academic, 2007), 181-82.

[16] MacArthur, *Faith Works*, 85.

the blessing of justification from God on the basis of faith in Christ. This is equivalent to what Romans 4:6-8 is teaching when it says: *"just as David also describes the blessedness of the man to whom God imputes righteousness apart from works: Blessed are those whose lawless deeds are forgiven, and whose sins are covered; blessed is the man to whom the Lord shall not impute sin."* In the context of Acts 3:26, the manner in which God sent His Servant Jesus "to bless" the nation of Israel was by turning them from their sins. If this blessing refers to the blessing of justification in which God judicially views a person as righteous, as separated from his or her sins, then this interpretation harmonizes with the immediate context of Acts 3:26. In Acts 3:25, Peter quotes from the unilateral covenant that God established with Israel through Abraham, promising that through his *"seed all the families of the earth shall be blessed."* This reference to Genesis 12:3 is used by the apostle Paul in two key chapters dealing specifically with the subject of justification—Romans 4 and Galatians 3. Both chapters not only refer to this promise of the Abrahamic covenant, but they specifically interpret it to mean that the "blessing" is justification by faith alone (Rom. 4:6-9; Gal. 3:8-9, 14), which includes God's imputed righteousness and judicial forgiveness of sins.

When people are justified in God's sight on the sole condition of repentance/faith, they not only receive God's own righteousness imputed to them as a gift, but they also simultaneously have their sins forgiven. As God promises in His Word, our *"iniquities"* He will remember *"no more"* (Heb. 10:17); and *"as far as the east is from the west, so far has He removed our transgressions from us"* (Ps. 103:12); and He *"will subdue our iniquities"* and *"will cast all our sins into the depths of the sea"* (Micah 7:19). It is in this sense that Christ Himself will perform the action of separating repentant sinners from their iniquities in Acts 3:26.

It is with good reason, therefore, that other sound Free Grace interpreters see the repentance preached by Peter in Acts 3 as referring to the eternal salvation[17] of the Jews in Jerusalem rather than as a turning from sin for sanctification or for temporal deliverance from impending physical judgment. In the context of Acts 3, Peter was addressing Jews in Jerusalem who had utterly and violently rejected Jesus as the Christ (Acts 3:13-15). Peter was not merely explaining "sanctification" truth to his audience when he reminded them of the Savior's death and resurrection. They were not already regenerated souls, justified in God's sight due to previous faith in some sort of crossless "saving message," as though they now only needed to escape God's temporal judgment due to their denial of Jesus. Such an interpretation, though it would be consistent

[17] Charles C. Bing, *Lordship Salvation: A Biblical Evaluation and Response*, GraceLife Edition (Burleson, TX: GraceLife Ministries, 1992), 74; J. B. Hixson, "Getting the Gospel Wrong: Case Studies in American Evangelical Soteriological Method in the Postmodern Era" (Ph.D. dissertation, Baptist Bible Seminary, 2007), 304.

with the crossless position, is completely at odds with Scripture. For later in the passage we are told that Peter's preaching is immediately interrupted after Acts 3:26 when the temple rulers arrest him and John (Acts 4:1-3). But what Peter shared to that point was sufficient enough for 5,000 people to "believe" (Acts 4:4).[18] Thus, this crowd of Jerusalem Jews who received "the word" (4:4) are described later in the context as being "those who believed" (Acts 4:32). Why is this so significant? Because the phrase, "those who believed," serves as Luke's inspired description of those Jews who had repented and turned to the Lord for judicial forgiveness (Acts 3:19, 26). This is another indication that repentance and faith are used interchangeably in Acts as the sole requirement for the remission of sins.

The view that repentance/faith in Acts 3 is the sole condition for the salvation of the Jerusalem Jews in the Book of Acts also harmonizes with Romans 9:30-33, where Paul explains that this generation of Jews *"stumbled at the stumbling stone"* of Jesus Christ (Rom. 9:32). Consequently, they did not obtain the gift of imputed righteousness by faith, which means that they were unbelievers who lacked justification before God. They were not believers in the "saving message" who now needed to hear about Christ's death and resurrection merely for their practical sanctification and temporal deliverance. Peter's command in Acts 3:19 to repent and turn to the Lord for the blotting out of their sins is clearly *evangelistic*. In this respect, Acts 3:19 and 2:38 should be considered parallel passages since they both present the same condition (faith/repentance) for judicial forgiveness, in addition to containing the same gospel message preached by Peter—the message of Christ's saving person and work.[19]

The Content of Salvific Repentance in Acts 3

Peter's preaching in Acts 3 is another example of an evangelistic setting in which "Jesus" is presented as the "Christ" (3:18, 20) whom the lost must believe in. Conspicuous by its absence, however, is any requirement to believe merely in the crossless gospel's *sine qua non* of saving faith, that Jesus is the guarantor of eternal life. Instead, we see the person and work of Christ set forth for the lost in similar fashion to Peter's preaching on the Day of Pentecost. Several key Christological terms and concepts are employed by Peter in the process, each depicting some aspect of the Savior. For instance, the Lord Jesus is presented as *"the Holy One and Just"* (3:14). The two adjectives here, "Holy One" and "Just," are used substantivally. They have the same case, gender, and number, and they are preceded by the article of the same case, gender, and number, and they are separated by the conjunction *kai*. For these reasons, they form a true Granville Sharp

---

[18] Wilkin, "Repentance as a Condition for Salvation in the New Testament," 73-74.

[19] G. Michael Cocoris, *Repentance: The Most Misunderstood Word in the Bible* (Santa Monica, CA: Self-published, 2003), 25.

construction in the Greek text.[20] Thus, they serve as descriptive metonyms for the Savior. The holy and righteous character of Christ is also highlighted in this passage in great relief against the backdrop of a "murderer" (3:14), namely Barabbas (Luke 23:18). But Peter's description here goes far beyond merely asserting innocence for the Lord Jesus. Once again we see an attestation of Christ's deity presented to this unregenerate and unbelieving audience. It is doubtful that these Jews could have misunderstood the Old Testament deistic terminology employed by Peter when he called Christ "the Holy One" and "the Just." Mal Couch explains:

> In both expressions, the deity of the Lord is clearly in view. For as God is called "the Holy One" in many Old Testament passages (e.g., Isa. 10:20; 30:12; 41:20), so He is referred to as "the Righteous One" (e.g., Deut. 32:4; Ps. 119:138; Jer. 12:1). . . . As God is described as morally righteous in character, likewise is Jesus, being God, so portrayed. New Testament prophets and personalities certainly refer to Christ's righteousness with His deity in mind.[21]

In addition, Peter applies to Jesus the title, *"the Prince (archegon) of life"* in verse 15. The immediate context supplies the meaning of this phrase. Peter was not referring primarily to regeneration or the endless duration of divine life. Rather, he was speaking of Christ's physical, bodily resurrection from the dead, as the next phrase in verse 15 indicates, where Peter says they *"killed the Prince of life, whom God raised from the dead, of which we are witnesses."* The nature or character of Christ is once again contrasted with Israel's depraved desire to have the Lord killed, and yet it is actually He who is the very ruler and author of life itself. This truth also establishes His deity, for though bodily resurrection will be the common experience of all humanity, whether saved or lost (Rev. 20:11-15), there is only One who is "the Prince," or Ruler, or Author of life itself—God. This is precisely John's point in his Gospel when he sets forth the deity of Christ for his readers to believe (John 1:4; 5:21-23; 14:6). Once again, we see from Acts that Christ's resurrection was proof of His deity (John 20:29; Rom. 1:3). Though the phrase *"Prince of life"* in Acts 3:15 *can be* used to support the truth that Jesus is also the *guarantor* of eternal life to others (i.e., believers), this phrase can only do so by implication and deduction based on the fact that Christ Himself rose from the dead and that He is God-incarnate.

Finally, one other portrait of Christ is presented by Peter to the Jews of Jerusalem in Acts 3. Peter cites the prediction from Deuteronomy 18:15-19 of the coming prophet who is like Moses, and he applies it directly to

[20] Wallace, *Greek Grammar*, 275.

[21] Couch, *A Bible Handbook to the Acts of the Apostles*, 76-77 (ellipsis added). Likewise, Stewart Custer states: "Here Peter applies divine titles to the Lord Jesus Christ. In the Old Testament God is the 'Holy One' (Ps. 103:1; Isa. 57:15) and the 'Just One' (Isa. 45:21; Zeph. 3:5)." Stewart Custer, *Witness to Christ: A Commentary on Acts* (Greenville, SC: Bob Jones University Press, 2000), 39.

the Lord Jesus in Acts 3:22-23.[22] The Lord Jesus' status as this Prophet is linked by Peter to Christ's second coming and the times of restoration of all things, when everyone must obey His voice or else face utter destruction (3:23).

It is important to realize that in the context of Acts 3, Peter uses this messianic portrait of Jesus in reference to Christ's second coming, not His first coming. This has significance for the content of saving faith in Acts 3. Someone may raise the objection that several messianic motifs are presented in Peter's preaching in Acts 3, so how do we know which portraits of Christ are essential to saving faith and which are not? Are we being "arbitrary" here and "cherry-picking" the contents of saving faith according to our own preferences, as crossless proponents claim?[23] Must a person believe that Jesus is "that Prophet" in order to possess eternal life?

In answer to these questions, it should be noted that when Peter issues the command for the Jews in Jerusalem to repent and turn to the Lord in Acts 3:19, he has only stated "first-coming" truth about the Lord Jesus up to that point. Peter has just exhorted them regarding Jesus' deity, death, and resurrection (3:13-18). The command to "repent" in 3:19 comes immediately upon the heels of Peter's claim that Jesus *"has thus fulfilled"* Old Testament prophecy specifically with respect to the fact *"that the Christ would suffer"* (3:18). Immediately following this statement, Acts 3:19 says, *"Repent therefore"* (*metanoēsate oun*). The conjunction "therefore" (*oun*) points backwards to the preceding verses (3:13-18),[24] thereby indicating the specific content of their salvific repentance. They were to change their minds about Jesus with respect to His righteous character/deity (3:14), His substitutionary death as Yahweh's "Servant" (3:13 15, 18), and His bodily resurrection (3:15). It is only *after* the call to repent in verse 19 that Peter goes on to inform his audience that Jesus is also "that Prophet" (3:22-23).

This interpretation of Acts 3 harmonizes perfectly with the rest of Scripture. There are only a few other places in the New Testament where "that Prophet" of Deuteronomy 18 is specifically referred to (John 1:21, 25; 6:14; 7:40; Acts 7:37), and yet in each instance eternal life is conspicuously

---

[22] Stephen does the same later in Acts 7:37. Even in the Church's infancy, Christians were quite conscious that Jesus was the fulfillment of Old Testament prophecy. Contrary to the claims of liberal theologians, this realization did not evolve within the early Church, as though the apostles fabricated the story about Christ's person and work and then later had to search the Scriptures for the evidence to support their mythical messiah.

[23] Zane C. Hodges, "The Hydra's Other Head: Theological Legalism," *Grace in Focus* 23 (September/October 2008): 3; Bob Wilkin, "Another Look at 1 Corinthians 15:3-11," *Grace in Focus* 23 (January/February 2008): 1-2.

[24] This is evident elsewhere in Acts where *oun* is used characteristically in direct discourse to refer to immediately preceding speech. See Acts 1:21; 2:30, 33, 36; 8:22; 10:29, 32-33; 11:17; 13:38, 40; 15:10; 16:36; 17:20, 23, 29, 30; 19:3, 36, 38; 21:22-23; 23:15, 21; 25:5, 11, 17; 26:4, 22; 28:20, 28.

never conditioned upon believing that Jesus is this Prophet. In addition, the Word of God nowhere requires belief in the truth of Christ's second coming to receive eternal life but only belief in what He accomplished at His first coming with respect to man's sin problem (Heb. 9:26-28).

The Suffering Servant of the Lord

There is one particular messianic motif in Acts 3 that is repeated twice for emphasis and which deserves special consideration due to its bearing on the contents of saving faith. In Acts 3:13 and 3:26, Peter refers to Christ as God's "Servant" (*pais*).[25] The description of Jesus as God's Servant should not in any way be viewed as a denial of His deity. While it may initially appear to our western minds that being God's "Servant" or "Son" indicates subservience, which in turn implies inferiority and therefore inequality, such reasoning would be completely foreign to a Jewish mindset that had been informed by Scripture. To the oriental and biblical mind, one could be a subservient "Son" in terms of function while still being equal to the "Father" in standing by virtue of sharing the same nature (John 5:17-30; 10:30-33; 14:28). For this reason, the fact that Christ is the "Servant" of God does not indicate a status of being less than fully God. Other passages of Scripture make this abundantly clear (Phil. 2:5-8). Peter's use of the "Servant" motif in early Acts (3:13, 26; 4:27, 30) simply served to identify Jesus as the *ebed Yahweh* of Isaiah 52:13-53:12.[26] This connection is relevant to the content of saving faith, for if Peter was actually alluding to Isaiah, then Acts 3 is implicitly teaching the substitutionary death of Christ and not merely the bare fact of His death.

Several factors from the immediate context lead to the conclusion that Peter was indeed referring to Isaiah's Servant who was predicted to suffer a substitutionary death for our sin. First, before Peter begins to expound upon Christ's rejection, suffering, and death in Acts 3, he starts his evangelism in verse 13 with the statement that God had "glorified" (*doxazō*) His "Servant" (*pais*) Jesus. Likewise, Acts 3:13-18 follows the same *pattern* and *terminology* as Isaiah 52-53.[27] Isaiah 52:13 is the prologue to Isaiah 53. It is the headline verse that precedes the description of Christ's substitu-

---

[25] Joel B. Green, "The Death of Jesus, God's Servant," in *Reimaging the Death of the Lukan Jesus*, ed. Dennis D. Sylva (Frankfurt am Main: Anton Hain, 1990), 1-28, 170-73.

[26] Couch, *A Bible Handbook to the Acts of the Apostles*, 79, 113; Oscar Cullmann, *The Christology of the New Testament*, rev. ed., trans. Shirley G. Guthrie and Charles A. M. Hall (Philadelphia: Westminster Press, 1963), 69-74; Joachim Jeremias, *The Eucharistic Words of Jesus*, trans. Norman Perrin (New York: Charles Scribner's Sons, 1966), 225-31; McClain, *The Greatness of the Kingdom*, 404; John R. W. Stott, *The Cross of Christ* (Downers Grove, IL: InterVarsity Press, 1986), 37, 145-46; Mark L. Strauss, *The Davidic Messiah in Luke-Acts: The Promise and its Fulfillment in Lukan Christology* (Sheffield: Sheffield Academic Press, 1995), 324-36.

[27] Cullmann, *Christology of the New Testament*, 73; Joachim Jeremias, "παῖς θεοῦ," *TDNT*, 5:704; Jacques Ménard, "*Pais Theou* as Messianic Title in the Book of Acts," *CBQ* 19 (1957): 89; Otto Michel, "παῖς θεοῦ," *NIDNTT*, 3:611.

tionary suffering in chapter 53, and it says, *"Behold, My Servant (pais,* LXX*) shall deal prudently; He shall be exalted and extolled (doxazō,* LXX*)."* This is the same terminology and order that occurs in Acts 3. The immediate context of Acts 3:13b-15 proceeds with a description of the Servant's rejection, death, and resurrection, which are also topics that feature prominently in Isaiah 53.

Secondly, Acts 3:18 specifically states that the suffering of "the Christ" as explained by Peter in Acts 3:13-15 was "foretold" by the "prophets." This means that though Peter had other Old Testament passages in mind dealing with the death of the Lamb, he certainly intended the greatest prediction of the Messiah's substitutionary suffering in the entire Old Testament—Isaiah 53.

Thirdly, the substitutionary, suffering Servant of Isaiah 53 is called *"My Righteous (dikaion,* LXX*) Servant"* (53:11), just like Peter's description of Him in Acts 3:14 as *"the Holy One and the Just (dikaion)."*

Fourthly, in the second reference to the "Servant" in Acts 3, Peter associates the Servant with the removal of Israel's sin (3:26). This is precisely what the Isaianic Servant accomplishes: *"By His knowledge My righteous Servant shall justify many, for He shall bear their iniquities"* (53:11); *"For He was cut off from the land of the living; for the transgression of My people He was stricken"* (53:8); *"We have turned, every one, to his own way; and the Lord has laid on Him the iniquity of us all"* (53:6).

Can there be any doubt that Peter was intentionally connecting Christ to the Suffering Servant of Isaiah 53, even without making an explicit reference to the prophet "Isaiah" in the passage? This conclusion is further supported by the fact that Peter himself in his first epistle draws heavily upon the Suffering Servant motif of Isaiah 53 (1 Peter 2:21-25).[28] Elsewhere, the New Testament also explicitly connects Isaiah 53 to the Lord Jesus (Mark 10:45 cf. Isa. 53:10, 12; Luke 22:37 cf. Isa. 53:12).[29] Paul also relates the Servant status of Christ specifically to the *kenosis* and crucifixion (Phil. 2:7-8). All of this shows that New Testament writers and apostles were conscious of the connection between Jesus Christ and Isaiah 53. This is even true of the Book of Acts in particular, where Philip in Acts 8:30-35 makes the explicit connection between the Lamb of Isaiah 53 and the Lord Jesus Christ.

Based on these observations we see that in the Book of Acts, Christ's death is not recorded as a mere historical, physical fact in order to advance solely the story of His resurrection, as some may be prone to claim. Rather, the work of His death and resurrection are both considered to be truly redemptive in purpose.[30] "From all this, we may fairly claim that the first

---

[28] F. W. Dillistone, *The Significance of the Cross* (Philadelphia: Westminster Press, 1944), 70.

[29] Craig L. Blomberg, *Jesus and the Gospels: An Introduction and Survey* (Nashville: Broadman & Holman, 1997), 312; Joachim Jeremias, "παῖς θεοῦ," *TDNT*, 5:704.

[30] John T. Carroll and Joel B. Green, *The Death of Jesus in Early Christianity* (Peabody, MA:

Christians thought of the death of Jesus as doing all that the death of the Servant does in Isaiah 53. This means that they thought of His death as substitutionary."[31] With Peter's extensive evangelistic preaching recorded in both Acts 2 and 3, we see both the person and work of Christ contained as essential evangelistic content, as well as the provision and condition of salvation. This pattern continues throughout Acts and the rest of the New Testament.

Acts 4:8-12

8 *Then Peter, filled with the Holy Spirit, said to them, "Rulers of the people and elders of Israel:*

9 *"If we this day are judged for a good deed done to a helpless man, by what means he has been made well,*

10 *"let it be known to you all, and to all the people of Israel, that by the name of* ***Jesus Christ of Nazareth****, whom you* ***crucified****, whom God* ***raised from the dead****, by Him this man stands here before you whole.*

11 *"This is the 'stone which was rejected by you builders, which has become the chief cornerstone.'*

12 *"Nor is there salvation in any other, for there is no other name under heaven given among men by which we must be saved."*

In Acts 4:10-12 we see again the defining elements of Jesus being "the Christ." Here, Jesus "Christ" of Nazareth is not presented by Peter as merely the guarantor of eternal life but as the One who was crucified and raised from the dead. In fact, the phrase "eternal life" is not even found here, as Peter's term of choice is "saved." Was Peter's preaching somehow "misfocused"? Up to this point in Acts, Peter has not even employed the phrase "eternal life." Certain crossless gospel proponents go so far as to claim that the New Testament rarely "if ever" uses the term "saved" (*sōzō*) in reference to "first tense" salvation,[32] that is, being delivered from the penalty of our sins which is the death of eternal separation from God. Yet, Acts 4:12 uses "saved" in just this sense, since the salvation in mind is the salvation needed by all men under heaven, not just in the process of Christian sanctification. This must include initial, eternal salvation.

Acts 5:28-32, 42

28 *Did we not strictly command you not to teach in this name? And look, you have filled Jerusalem with your doctrine, and intend to bring this* ***Man's blood*** *on us!"*

Hendrickson, 1995), 79; Louis Diana, "The Essential Elements of the Gospel Message in the Evangelistic Speeches in Acts" (M.A.B.S. thesis, Multnomah Graduate School of Ministry, 1992), 46-55; Earl Richards, "Jesus' Passion and Death in Acts," in *Reimaging the Death of the Lukan Jesus*, ed. Dennis D. Sylva (Frankfurt am Main: Anton Hain, 1990), 132-33.

[31] Leon Morris, *The Cross in the New Testament* (Grand Rapids: Eerdmans, 1965), 142.

[32] Robert N. Wilkin, "The Three Tenses of Salvation Reconsidered," audiotape, Grace Evangelical Society, 2003.

29 *But Peter and the other apostles answered and said: "We ought to obey God rather than men.*
30 *"The God of our fathers* ***raised up*** *Jesus whom you* ***murdered by hanging on a tree.***
31 *"Him God has* ***exalted*** *to His* ***right hand*** *to be* ***Prince*** *and* ***Savior,*** *to give* ***repentance*** *to Israel and* ***forgiveness of sins.***
32 *"And we are His witnesses to these things, and so also is the Holy Spirit whom God has given to those who obey Him."*
42 *And daily in the temple, and in every house, they did not cease teaching and preaching Jesus as* ***the Christ.***

Acts 5:42 is significant as it pertains to the contents of saving faith. If eternal life is dependent upon believing that Jesus is "the Christ" (John 20:31), then what does it mean in verse 42 that the "apostles" (Acts 5:40) did not cease from teaching and preaching Jesus as "the Christ"? The fact that they did "not cease" such evangelism casts the reader back in the context to see what they were preaching about Jesus *prior* to verse 42. Maximally, this may point all the way back to Acts 2. Minimally, it reaches back at least to the last recorded example of the apostles' teaching and preaching in the immediate context, which is Acts 5:29-32. There, all the elements of Jesus being "the Christ" of saving faith are clearly presented.

These elements run like a common thread throughout the Gospels and Acts. They include: Jesus' deity, humanity, death for sin, and resurrection. In addition, we see the condition and provision of the gospel contained here with the mention of "repentance" and "forgiveness of sins" (5:31).

It is noteworthy that this was also the apostle John's message concerning "the Christ," since verse 29 states that *"the other apostles"* joined Peter in preaching this message. And yet conspicuous by its absence once again is any distinctive "Johannine sense" of Jesus being "the Christ"—one who is merely the guarantor of eternal life irrespective of His sacrificial death and bodily resurrection.

Regarding the content of saving faith in Jesus as "the Christ," someone may raise the repeated mantra that only the historical fact of Christ's death is found in Acts 5:30, namely that He was *"murdered by hanging on a tree."* However, though the term "substitution" is not found here, it is still clearly taught by the reference to Christ's death on a "tree." Why would Peter use an expression that we westerners find so unusual? Why didn't he just say that Christ died on a cross for our sins?

There is nothing ambiguous about Peter's message of Christ's death and resurrection. Peter was trying to convey to his Jewish audience more than the mere fact that Jesus was unjustly struck dead through their act of murder, something which these religious leaders still refused to concede (Acts 5:28). Peter was referring directly to Deuteronomy 21:22-23 where it is taught that the person who is "hanged" on a "tree" is "accursed by

God."[33] We have every reason to believe that Peter expected his Jewish audience to know this passage from the Law. After all, if Peter previously assumed in Acts 3:22-23 that even the common citizens of Jerusalem (Acts 4:1-2) were aware of "that Prophet" described in Deuteronomy 18:15-19, then isn't another reference to Deuteronomy only fitting? Even before the death of Christ and the birth of Christianity, Judaism was already directly connecting Deuteronomy 21:22-23 to the Roman practice of crucifixion.[34] Similarly, even Seneca (4 B.C.—A.D. 65), the famous Gentile statesman of the era, expressed the Roman perspective on crucifixion by using both the terms "tree" and "accursed":

> Can anyone be found who would prefer wasting away in pain dying limb by limb, or letting out his life drop by drop, rather than expiring once for all? Can any man be found willing to be fastened to the accursed tree (*ad illud infelix lignum*), long sickly, already deformed, swelling with ugly weals on shoulders and chest, and drawing the breath of life amid long-drawn-out agony? He would have many excuses for dying even before mounting the cross.[35]

Certainly, Peter's particular audience in Acts 5 would have known that he was referring to Deuteronomy 21:22-23 by his *"hanging on a tree"* statement in Acts 5:30. Those whom Peter and the apostles were addressing in Acts 5:29-32 consisted of the "high priest" (5:17), the "Sadducees" (5:17), the "chief priests" (5:24), the "council" (5:21), and "all the elders of Israel" (5:21). Though these highly trained religious leaders would have immediately made the connection to Deuteronomy 21 when they heard Peter's "tree" statement in Acts 5:30, they would not have understood its correct spiritual application to Jesus until Peter expounded further in Acts 5:31.

By referring to *"hanging on a tree,"* Peter and the apostles were clearly teaching the substitutionary and satisfactory nature of the Messiah's death and not the mere fact of it.[36] These religious leaders were trying to evade guilt for Jesus' death when they exclaimed, *"you have filled Jerusalem with your doctrine, and intend to bring this Man's blood on us!"* (5:28). Though

---

[33] Stott, *The Cross of Christ*, 34.

[34] Joseph A. Fitzmyer, "Crucifixion in Ancient Palestine, Qumran Literature, and the New Testament," *CBQ* 40 (1978): 507; Josephus, *Antiquities of the Jews*, 11.266-68; C. Marvin Pate, *The Reverse of the Curse: Paul, Wisdom, and the Law* (Tübingen: Mohr Siebeck, 2000), 150-51.

[35] Cited in Martin Hengel, *Crucifixion in Antiquity* (Philadelphia: Fortress Press, 1977), 30-31.

[36] Ardel Caneday, "'Redeemed from the Curse of the Law' The Use of Deut. 21:22-23 in Gal. 3:13," *TrinJ* 10 (Fall 1989): 206-7; Diana, "The Essential Elements of the Gospel Message," 51; I. Howard Marshall, *Luke: Historian and Theologian* (Grand Rapids: Zondervan, 1970), 173; idem, "The Resurrection in the Acts of the Apostles," in *Apostolic History and the Gospel* (Grand Rapids: Eerdmans, 1970), 104-5; Morris, *The Cross in the New Testament*, 142-43; Stott, *The Cross of Christ*, 34.

they thought Jesus was guilty[37] and deserved to be hanged "on a tree" and that He was truly "accursed of God" (Deut. 21:23), Peter declared that God actually "raised" Jesus up (Acts 5:30) and "exalted" Him to God's "right hand" (5:31). Peter was teaching more than the fact that Christ was vindicated by God through the resurrection and exaltation. It is amazing that theological liberals only see in this passage the rectifying of a great miscarriage of justice done to Jesus. Peter was not denying in any way that the One who was hanged on Calvary's tree was truly *"accursed by God,"* in keeping with the literal truth of Deuteronomy 21:23 that *"he who is hanged is accursed of God."* Instead, he went beyond this fact. Peter was indicating that God's raising and exalting of Christ to be a Prince and a Savior was an indication of the value of that death on a tree, that it was substitutionary, and satisfactory, and that *"forgiveness of sins"* (5:31) was procured thereby.

Once again in Acts 5, we see that the content of the apostles' evangelistic preaching regarding "the Christ" did not center around "eternal life" per se but around the person and work of Jesus. If these details about the person and work of Christ in this setting are *not* the content of saving faith, then what are they? Why wouldn't Peter present these details of Christ's person and work here as the content of saving faith, especially considering that this was an unregenerate audience? Why do we not find the crossless gospel's three part *sine qua non* of saving faith anywhere in Acts: (1) to "believe" (2) in "Jesus" (3) for "everlasting life"? The audience of Jewish religious leaders in Acts 5 was clearly expected to change its mind (repent) about the true identity and accomplishment of Jesus of Nazareth. The content of saving faith/repentance in this passage once again consists of Christ's deity (*"Him God exalted to His right hand to be Prince and Savior"*), humanity (*"this Man's blood"*), substitutionary death (*"murdered by hanging on a tree"*), and resurrection (*"the God of our fathers raised up Jesus"*).

Acts 8:27-37

27 *So he arose and went. And behold, a man of Ethiopia, a eunuch of great authority under Candace the queen of the Ethiopians, who had charge of all her treasury, and had come to Jerusalem to worship,*
28 *was returning. And sitting in his chariot, he was reading* ***Isaiah the prophet****.*
29 *Then the Spirit said to Philip, "Go near and overtake this chariot."*
30 *So Philip ran to him, and heard him reading the* ***prophet Isaiah****, and said, "Do you understand what you are reading?"*
31 *And he said, "How can I, unless someone guides me?" And he asked Philip to come up and sit with him.*

[37] Frank J. Matera, "Responsibility for the Death of Jesus According to the Acts of the Apostles," *JSNT* 39 (1990): 83; Max Wilcox, "'Upon the Tree'—Deut 21:22-23 in the New Testament," *JBL* 96 (1977): 93.

32 *The place in the Scripture which he read was this: "He was led as a* ***sheep to the slaughter****; And as a* ***lamb*** *before its shearer is silent, So He opened not His mouth.*
33 *In His humiliation His justice was taken away, And who will declare His generation? For His life is taken from the earth."*
34 *So the eunuch answered Philip and said, "I ask you, of whom does the prophet say this, of himself or of some other man?"*
35 *Then Philip opened his mouth, and* ***beginning at this Scripture, preached Jesus*** *to him.*
36 *Now as they went down the road, they came to some water. And the eunuch said, "See, here is water. What hinders me from being baptized?"*
37 *Then Philip said, "If you believe with all your heart, you may." And he answered and said, "I believe that* ***Jesus Christ is the Son of God.****"*

Though the reading of Acts 8:37 is not found in either the Critical Greek Text or the Majority Text,[38] it still has tremendous value for us today by indicating what many in the early Church believed about personal faith in Jesus Christ being a prerequisite for water baptism. But with respect to the bearing of this passage upon the definition of "the Christ, the Son of God" (John 20:31), here is an example of Philip preaching Jesus to the eunuch out of Isaiah 53, which is undoubtedly the most thorough description of Christ's sacrificial, substitutionary death in the entire Bible.[39] Apparently many in the early Church believed that the Lord's death in Isaiah 53 defined what it meant to *"believe that Jesus Christ is the Son of God"* (v. 37 [TR]).

Acts 9:20

20 *Immediately he preached* ***the Christ*** *in the synagogues, that He is* ***the Son of God.***

Here the content of *Paul's* early evangelistic preaching reveals that preaching Jesus as "the Christ" means persuading people *"that He is the Son of God."* In this respect, the Pauline gospel and the Johannine gospel are completely harmonious (John 20:31). Within days of Paul's conversion and pivotal encounter with the risen, crucified Christ, he began preaching the

---

[38] The reading has an early pedigree within Christendom, being quoted by the Latin "fathers" Ireneaus and Cyprian in the late 2nd and mid 3rd centuries. For that reason it is also well attested in the Western branch of the early Church by several Italic manuscripts. However, the *omission* of this reading is overwhelmingly supported by two papyri (𝔓45,74), a host of uncials (א, A, B, C, Ψ, H, L, P), virtually all the lectionaries, and by the best representatives of the three principal language versions: the oldest mss. of the Latin Vulgate, the Syriac Peshitta, and the two principal Coptic dialects. The minuscules appear to be divided approximately equally. The omission of this verse is therefore justified.

[39] The resurrection is also referred to in Isaiah 53:10b, and though the passage does not record the full extent of Philip's exposition of this passage to the Ethiopian eunuch, it is difficult to imagine that Philip would omit any reference to Christ's resurrection, especially considering the overwhelming emphasis given to this great event in the evangelism of the early Church recorded in the rest of Acts.

gospel of Christ. The correspondence between preaching *"the gospel"* and preaching *"the Christ"* as *"the Son of God"* is confirmed by Paul himself in Galatians 1:11-12 and 1:16. In Galatians 1:11-12, Paul declares that he received his "gospel" directly from his personal encounter with the risen Christ, and yet he exclaims in the context that God was pleased *"to reveal His Son in me, that I might preach (euangelizōmai) Him among the Gentiles"* (Gal. 1:16).[40] The succeeding verses strongly imply that Paul did this "immediately" (Gal. 1:16b), which could be describing his evangelism of the Gentiles starting in Damascus according to Acts 9:20.[41] These passages demonstrate that Paul's "gospel" centered upon the truth of Jesus being the "Son of God." Acts 9:20 is therefore a summation of Paul's gospel.

With respect to Paul's preaching of Jesus as *"the Christ"* and *"the Son of God"* in Acts 9:20, the advocates of crossless saving faith should take no solace in the brevity of this reference to "the Christ," as though Paul's concept of "the Christ, the Son of God" was devoid of Jesus' deity, humanity, substitutionary death, and resurrection. The thesis of this book has been that these elements of the Savior's person and work are encapsulated in the key Christological titles, "Christ" and "Son of God." While it may be objected that these elements of the gospel are not explicitly stated in this passage, it must also be admitted that neither are any of the crossless gospel's *sine qua non* of (1) believing (2) in Jesus (3) for eternal life. Nor should we require Acts 9:20 to provide us with a full description of Paul's evangelistic content. Luke should be permitted to abbreviate and summarize at certain points in his narrative, as he is clearly doing in Acts 9:20. Narrative literature by its very nature does not require a full accounting of historical details within each pericope.[42] New Testament scholar F. F. Bruce clarifies this point, explaining:

> We need not suppose that the speeches in Acts are verbatim reports in the sense that they record every word used by the speakers on the occasions in question. Paul, we know, was given to long sermons (cf. Acts xx, 2, 7, 9; xxviii, 23); but any one of the speeches attributed to him in Acts may be read through aloud in a few minutes. But I suggest that reason has been shown to conclude that the speeches reported by Luke are at least faithful epitomes, giving the gist of the arguments used. Even in summarizing the speeches. Luke would naturally introduce more or less of his own style; but in point of fact it frequently seems to be less, not more. Taken all in all, each speech suits the speaker, the

---

[40] Margaret E. Thrall, "The Origin of Pauline Christology," in *Apostolic History and the Gospel: Biblical and Historical Essays Presented to F. F. Bruce on His 60th Birthday*, ed. W. Ward Gasque and Ralph P. Martin (Grand Rapids: Eerdmans, 1970), 307-8.

[41] Martin Hengel and Anna Maria Schwemer, *Paul Between Damascus and Antioch: The Unknown Years*, trans. John Bowden (Louisville: Westminster John Knox, 1997), 46, 82; Seyoon Kim, *The Origin of Paul's Gospel* (Tübingen: J. C. B. Mohr, 1981), 60.

[42] Hixson, "Getting the Gospel Wrong: Case Studies," 75.

> audience, and the circumstances of delivery; and this, along with the other points we have considered, gives good ground, in my judgment, for believing these speeches to be, not inventions of the historian, but condensed accounts of speeches actually made, and therefore valuable and independent sources for the history and theology of the primitive Church.[43]

Though Luke and Acts are certainly "theological" in nature and purpose, these books were not composed with the intention of being textbooks on systematic theology. Each book of Scripture has its own literary style and must be interpreted accordingly. The Gospels and Acts are not as direct and tightly argued as epistolary literature, for example, when it comes to conveying theological truth. Instead, they are of a literary genre known as "narrative" where doctrine is communicated through the development of a storyline and it is critical that the interpreter view single verses within this larger framework. At times, however, as with any modern storyline, a single sentence may be condensing or summarizing truth for the reader—truth that was developed elsewhere in the storyline. This is precisely what Luke is doing in Acts 9:20 by his use of the phrases "the Christ" and "the Son of God."

<u>Acts 10:34-48</u>

34 *Then Peter opened his mouth and said: "In truth I perceive that God shows no partiality.*
35 *"But in every nation whoever fears Him and works righteousness is accepted by Him.*
36 *"The word which God sent to the children of Israel, preaching peace through* ***Jesus Christ****—He is* ***Lord of all****—*
37 *"that word you know, which was proclaimed throughout all Judea, and began from Galilee after the baptism which John preached:*
38 *"how God anointed* ***Jesus of Nazareth*** *with the Holy Spirit and with power, who went about doing good and healing all who were oppressed by the devil, for God was with Him.*
39 *"And we are witnesses of all things which He did both in the land of the Jews and in Jerusalem, whom they* ***killed by hanging on a tree****.*
40 *"Him God* ***raised up*** *on the third day, and showed Him openly,*
41 *"not to all the people, but to witnesses chosen before by God, even to us who ate and drank with Him after* ***He arose from the dead****.*
42 *"And He commanded us to preach to the people, and to testify that it is He who was ordained by God to be Judge of the living and the dead.*
43 *"To Him all the prophets witness that,* ***through His name, whoever believes in Him will receive remission of sins****."*
44 *While Peter was still speaking these words, the Holy Spirit fell upon all those who heard the word.*

[43] F. F. Bruce, *The Speeches in the Acts of the Apostles* (London: Tyndale Press, 1942), 27.

45 *And those of the circumcision who believed were astonished, as many as came with Peter, because the gift of the Holy Spirit had been poured out on the Gentiles also.*
46 *For they heard them speak with tongues and magnify God. Then Peter answered,*
47 *"Can anyone forbid water, that these should not be baptized who have received the Holy Spirit just as we have?"*
48 *And he commanded them to be baptized in the name of the Lord. Then they asked him to stay a few days.*

Acts 15:7-11
7 *And when there had been much dispute, Peter rose up and said to them: "Men and brethren, you know that a good while ago God chose among us, that by my mouth the* ***Gentiles should hear the word of the gospel and believe.***
8 *"So God, who knows the heart, acknowledged them by giving them the Holy Spirit, just as He did to us,*
9 *"and made no distinction between us and them,* ***purifying their hearts by faith.***
10 *"Now therefore, why do you test God by putting a yoke on the neck of the disciples which neither our fathers nor we were able to bear?*
11 *"But we believe that through the* ***grace of the Lord Jesus Christ we shall be saved*** *in the same manner as they."*

Acts 10:34-43 establishes once again that Peter preached that "Jesus Christ" is deity (*"Lord of all"*), humanity (*"Jesus of Nazareth. . . . who ate and drank"*), and One who died a substitutionary death (*"whom they killed by hanging on a tree"*) and rose again (*"He arose from the dead"*) to procure forgiveness of sins through faith in Him (*"through His name, whoever believes in Him will receive remission of sins"*). In Peter's evangelism of these Gentiles, there is once again no "focus" upon a crossless, resurrectionless "saving message," as the new reductionist gospel requires. This passage is also significant in identifying for us what Peter considered to be his "gospel" (Acts 15:7) of salvation by grace through faith alone (15:8-11).

Crossless gospel advocates often demand of their grace brethren that we produce just one passage containing all the essentials that the unregenerate must believe for their eternal salvation, implying that no such passage can be found. However, Acts 10:34-43 certainly contains all the essentials, and it fits perfectly with the harmonious testimony of Scripture covered thus far regarding the contents of saving faith. Here, Peter is sent by God with the gospel of Christ to a group of unsaved Gentiles (Acts 11:14) assembled in the home of Cornelius, a devout, God-fearing Roman centurion (Acts 10:22, 24, 27) stationed in Caesarea. The priceless contents of Peter's soul-saving gospel are recorded here in Acts 10 and referred to later by Peter at the Jerusalem council in Acts 15:7-11. The significance of Peter's own connection of these two passages in Acts should not be missed since it deals another fatal blow to the crossless gospel. Peter indisputably identified his *"gospel"* (15:7) as a message of salvation by grace through faith alone (15:8-11). In the same passage (Acts 15:7-11), Peter also refers back specifically to the evangelistic episode in Acts 10 as the time when God used his *"mouth"* in order for *"the Gentiles [to] hear the word of the gospel and believe"* (15:7).

This has significance as it relates to the elements of Peter's gospel that he preached to Cornelius and the Gentiles for their salvation. If it can be demonstrated that "the gospel" (Acts 15:7) that Peter preached in Acts 10 contained the elements of Christ's deity, humanity, substitutionary death, and bodily resurrection, in addition to salvation by grace through faith, then the crossless gospel is refuted once again by the infallible testimony of God's Word. But are Acts 15 and Acts 10 really interrelated? Or, should these two chapters be viewed as isolated and unrelated to one another? The fact that Peter is connecting Acts 15:7-11 to Acts 10:34-43 can be observed in several ways. First, Peter states that God *"chose"* him in particular to go to these Gentiles (15:7). This also matches what is clearly taught earlier in Acts 10:9-22 and 11:4-12. Secondly, there is a reference to the Gentiles receiving the gift of the *"Holy Spirit"* (Acts 10:44-45; 11:15-17) in both sections (15:8). A third parallel to be observed is the means by which these Gentiles received the Spirit and were saved—that it was by simple *faith/believing* (Acts 10:43; 11:17; 15:7, 9). Lastly, in both sections it is stated that those who believe the gospel will be "saved" (Acts 11:14; 15:11), which is also described as receiving the forgiveness of sins (Acts 10:43; 15:9). Peter's evangelism of the Gentiles as documented in Acts 10 and 15 clearly establishes that the gospel itself is the saving message and that this is a message about the person and work of Christ, not just the bare promise of eternal life through believing in a non-descript entity named "Jesus."

The Gospel of the Kingdom & the Gospel of Christ

If chapters 10, 11, and 15 of the Book of Acts contain Peter's saving message, then it remains to be demonstrated what the contents of saving faith are in these passages. But before considering each of the elements in the gospel that Peter initially preached for the salvation of the Gentiles in Acts 10, it is critical to recognize that not all of Peter's message in verses 34-43 should technically be considered "the gospel of Christ" or the content of saving faith. Some proponents of a crossless saving faith may object that there is far more content shared with Cornelius and the Gentiles than just the Lord's deity, humanity, death for sin, and resurrection. They may even claim again that we are arbitrarily picking and choosing the ingredients of the gospel according to our own "orthodox" doctrinal "checklist."[44] This is hardly the case. Once again, we see that the inspired details of God's

---

[44] Hodges, "The Hydra's Other Head: Theological Legalism," 2.

Word placed right within the passage itself allow us to rightly divide the word of truth spoken by Peter.

Observe, first of all, that the Gentiles are informed of several things pertaining to the Lord's earthly ministry, including the word that He preached throughout all Judea after John the Baptist's ministry ended (10:37), His anointing with the power of the Holy Spirit (10:38), as well as the Lord's many miraculous healings and good deeds (10:38). If Peter preached all of this to Cornelius and company, then why isn't this additional information considered essential content for saving faith?

The answer is apparent from the passage. Within Peter's preaching, two forms of good news are to be distinguished—the gospel of the kingdom and the gospel of the grace of God. Peter leads into the saving gospel of Christ in 10:39-43 by first rehearsing the good news of the kingdom in 10:36-38, which was a message previously preached by Christ to Israel that was already familiar to Cornelius. However, it was the good news of Christ's person and work as spelled out in verses 39-43 that was necessary for Cornelius's salvation (11:14). The passage indicates that it was *"that word"* (10:37) that was *"proclaimed"* (past tense) *"to Israel"* which Cornelius already knew. What "word" was this? It was the gospel of the kingdom (Matt. 4:23; Mark 1:15-16; Luke 4:18, 43). The kingdom message pertained to the nation of Israel, not the Gentiles; but a God-fearing Gentile who was friendly towards the Jewish nation would have already known this good news. However, "the gospel" of the grace of God in Christ would have been a new message to Cornelius and his guests (Acts 15:7-11), and this is what Peter proclaims in Acts 10:39-43.

Several features in the passage support the conclusion that Peter is preaching to these Gentiles two consecutive forms of good news on the same occasion, one message already known (regarding the kingdom and Christ's earthly ministry) and one not yet known (regarding Christ's redemptive work). Peter states expressly in Acts 10:36-37 that there was a particular "word" or message that these Gentiles already knew. He says, *"36 The word (ton logon) which God sent to the children of Israel, preaching peace through Jesus Christ—He is Lord of all—37 that word (to rhēma) you know."* In verses 37-38, Peter clarifies what "word" or message they already knew with several descriptions. First, he states that it was a message that was already *"proclaimed throughout all Judea, and began from Galilee after the baptism which John preached"* (v. 37). Second, he says that they already knew *"how God anointed Jesus of Nazareth with the Holy Spirit and with power"* (10:38). Third, they already knew that this same Jesus *"went about doing good and healing all who were oppressed by the devil, for God was with Him"* (10:38).

These details follow a definite pattern outlined by each of the Synoptic Gospels (Matt. 4:12-24; Mark 1:9-16; Luke 4:14-18), as shown in the following chart. This particular "word" or message about Jesus of Nazareth had spread throughout the entire region *"surrounding"* Galilee (Luke 4:14) and even northward beyond Galilee *"throughout all Syria"* (Matt. 4:24). Since *"all Syria"* at that time included even the Mediterranean coastal cities of Tyre and Sidon far to the north of Caesarea where Cornelius was stationed, he was well within range of this amazing "news" of the day. That is why in verse 37, where it says *"that word you know,"* even the "you" is plural (*humeis*). This means that Peter assumed the other Gentiles accompanying Cornelius also knew this information about "Jesus of Nazareth." Even though the region or city of these Gentiles is not specified, as in the case of Cornelius, we may surmise that they were not too far from Caesarea since they are described as "relatives and close friends" (10:24) of Cornelius "who had come together" (10:27).

It is clear from the pattern of Acts 10:36-38, in comparison with parallel passages from the Synoptic Gospels, that the "word" (10:36-37) that Peter reviews with these Gentiles is the particular form of the *euangelion* specifically identified as *"the gospel of the kingdom"* (Matt. 4:23; Mark 1:14; Luke 4:18, 43). Liberal and non-dispensational theologians, who do not properly distinguish Israel and the Church or the gospel of the kingdom from the gospel of grace, are unlikely to acknowledge this fact. Instead, they are prone to view the entirety of Peter's preaching in Acts 10:34-43 as one seamless message. Thus, some interpret this passage as a kerygmatic formula or template used by the early Church in its evangelism.[45]

But isn't it far more fitting in light of the context of Acts 10 to view Peter as presenting a gospel that pertained specifically to *Israel* followed by a universal gospel applicable now to *Jews and Gentiles*? Would it not be appropriate at this juncture in the early Church's dispensational development for Peter to begin with Israel's kingdom gospel and then transition into the gospel for these Gentiles? This conclusion can also be supported from the larger context of Acts 10. When Peter refers to "the word" that these Gentiles already knew in Acts 10:36a (*ton logon*) and 10:37a (*to rhēma*), in each case he speaks of that "word" in the singular, preceded by the article in Greek. This means that in verses 36-38 he had a definitive message in mind that these Gentiles already knew. However, based on the larger context of Acts 10 it is clear that there was information necessary for their salvation that they did *not yet know*. That is why they needed to await the arrival of Peter (10:6, 33) to find out this saving message (11:14).

---

[45] C. H. Dodd, *The Apostolic Preaching and Its Developments* (London: Hodder & Stoughton, 1936), 54-56; Robert A. Guelich, *Mark 1-8:26*, WBC (Dallas: Word Books, 1989), 12; idem, "The Gospel Genre," in *Das Evangelium und die Evangelien: Vorträge vom Tübinger Symposium 1982*, ed. Peter Stuhlmacher (Tübingen: Mohr Siebeck, 1983), 204-17.

Matthew 3-4	Mark 1	Luke 3-4	Acts 10
"teaching in their synagogues, preaching the gospel (euangelion) of the kingdom" (4:23)	*"preaching the gospel (euangelion) of the kingdom of God, and saying, "The time is fulfilled, and the kingdom of God is at hand. Repent, and believe in the gospel (euangelion).* (1:14-15)	*"to preach the gospel (euangelizomai) to the poor"* (4:18) *"I must preach the kingdom of God to the other cities also...And He was preaching in the synagogues"* (4:43-44)	*"The word which God sent to the children of Israel, preaching (euangelizomai) peace through Jesus Christ..."* (10:36)
"Then His fame went throughout all Syria" (4:24)	*"His fame spread throughout all the region"* (1:28)	*"the report about Him went into every place in the surrounding region"* (4:14, 37)	*"...that word you know..."* (10:37)
"Jesus went about all Galilee" (4:12, 23)	*"Jesus came to Galilee"* (1:14)	*"Jesus returned . . . to Galilee"* (4:14)	*"...which...began from Galilee after..."* (10:37)
"In those days John the Baptist came preaching" (3:1)	*"John came baptizing . . . and preaching a baptism of repentance"* (1:3)	*"John the son of Zacharias...went . . . preaching a baptism of repentance"* (3:3)	*"... the baptism which John preached..."* (10:37)
"the heavens were opened . . . and He saw the Spirit of God descending...upon Him" (3:16)	*"He saw the heavens parting and the Spirit descending upon Him"* (1:9)	*"the heaven was opened . . . and the Holy Spirit descended . . . upon Him"* (3:21b-22)	*"...how God anointed Jesus of Nazareth with the Holy Spirit and with power..."* (10:38)
"those who were demon-possessed . . . and He healed them" (4:24)	*"He healed many . . . and cast out many demons"* (1:34)	*"He . . . healed them. And demons also came out of many"* (4:40-41)	*"...who went about doing good and healing all who were oppressed by the devil"* (10:38)

This means that within the collective preaching of Peter in Acts 10:34-43, he begins by first introducing in verses 34-38 the historical man whom they had already heard so much good news about, "Jesus of Nazareth." Peter utilizes this good news of the kingdom as a lead into the saving message of the gospel of Christ in verses 39-43. Peter begins to introduce the saving content of the gospel of Christ in verse 39 by explaining Jesus' substitutionary death "on a tree," followed by the Lord's bodily resurrection (vv. 40-41), and concluding with His sovereign position as deity (v. 42) and the promise of remission of sins through faith in Him (v. 43). This was the additional information that Cornelius and the Gentiles did not yet know that Peter was sent to convey as the saving message (11:14). If Cornelius and the Gentiles already knew all of these details about Christ's death, resurrection, and the forgiveness of sins through His name, then why would Peter even need to be divinely dispatched to Caesarea in the first place? It is apparent that there was crucial information needed by the Gentiles that would come only with Peter's arrival. Thus, before Peter begins preaching in Acts 10:34, Cornelius bids him to begin by saying, *"Now therefore, we are all present before God, to hear all the things commanded* (*protassō*) *you by God"* (10:33). The whole reason Cornelius implored Peter to begin speaking was because *"he had seen an angel standing in his house, who said to him, 'Send men to Joppa, and call for Simon whose surname is Peter, who will tell you words by which you and your household will be saved'"* (Acts 11:13-14).

One final observation is necessary in order to determine the portion of Peter's preaching that constitutes the gospel of Christ. If the saving gospel message to the Gentiles begins essentially in Acts 10:39, then where does it end? What more must be included in the contents of the gospel? The gift of the Holy Spirit (10:44-45)? Tongues-speaking (10:46)? Water baptism (10:47-48)? It is clear from the events recorded in the passage that the gospel of salvation ended in verse 43 with the promise of the remission of sins and the sole condition of believing in Christ! It is not coincidental that by the end of verse 43, the Holy Spirit fell upon these Gentiles (10:44). They had already heard and believed "the gospel" of their salvation (Acts 15:7-9). This means that the baptism by the Holy Spirit, and its historical evidence here of speaking in tongues, are not part of Peter's saving gospel; nor is water baptism.

Whatever was preached prior to 10:44 was sufficient information for Cornelius's household to be saved (11:14). The Book of Acts is abundantly clear that salvation is by faith in Christ (10:43; 11:17-18; 15:7-11), not by water baptism in the name of Christ (10:47-48). This is also perfectly consistent with Paul's testimony in 1 Corinthians 1:14-17. Peter, Paul, and all the apostles, preached the same gospel, though Paul was commissioned to go primarily to the Gentiles and Peter primarily to the Jews (Gal. 2:7-9). It is clear that in Acts 10, water baptism was not part of Peter's saving gospel. However, he "commanded" these Gentile believers to be baptized (10:48) for essentially two reasons. First, this was in keeping with Christ's previous instructions given in the Great Commission (Mark 16:15-16). In addition, Peter's apostolic authority was needed for the acceptance of these Gentile believers into the company of an exclusively Jewish-Samaritan Church at that point, which water baptism represented. Thus, even Peter's command (*protassō*) in Acts 10:48 to baptize the Gentiles was part of what the Lord previously "commanded" (*protassō*) Peter to say to Cornelius (10:33). Having established the parameters for Peter's gospel, we can now begin to examine the all-important content of that saving message.

Jesus Christ's Deity

In Peter's gospel to the Gentiles we see all of the essentials that the lost must believe in order to be born again. We will start by observing Jesus Christ's deity. First, Peter refers to Jesus' deity by describing Him as the *"Judge of the living and the dead"* (10:42), which is the sole prerogative of God. Second, we note that Peter preached "Jesus" as the "Christ" in Acts 10:36. In the context of this statement, Peter indicated the deity of Christ implicitly by his reference to Him as *"Lord of all."* In Acts 10:36-37, Peter declares, *"36 The word which God sent to the children of Israel, preaching peace through Jesus Christ—He is Lord of all—37 that word you know."* It should be noted that even though Peter's reference to Jesus as "Lord of all" falls within the portion of Peter's preaching where he is reviewing the gospel of the kingdom (10:36-38), it should still be viewed as vital content in the gospel of Christ, not in the gospel of the kingdom. Peter uses this critical deistic clause, *"He is (estin) Lord of all,"* as a parenthetical insertion in his review of the kingdom gospel. He even uses the present tense ("is") in verse 36 to set this clause apart in the midst of a series of past tense verbs in verses 36-38. By so doing, Peter is distinguishing Christ's current, post-resurrection position of absolute, sovereign authority, not something that was formerly true during the time of His earthly ministry to Israel.

It may be argued by some that to be called "Lord" (*kurios*) in that day did not necessarily convey absolute deity (John 4:11, 15, 19, 49; 5:7; 12:21; 20:15; 1 Peter 3:6). This is undoubtedly true since there were *"many gods and many lords"* (1 Cor. 8:5). Yet it must also be acknowledged that there can only be One who is called *"Lord **of all**"* (10:36). The fact that Jesus Christ is called the *"Lord of lords"* and *"King of kings"* in Scripture is an unequivocal declaration of His deity (1 Tim. 6:15-16). Cornelius was a "God-fearing" Gentile who was already devoted to the God of Israel (10:2, 22) and would have been well acquainted with Yahweh's claim to be Lord of all (Josh. 3:11, 13; Zech. 6:5) and the Judge of all (1 Sam. 2:10; 1 Chron. 16:33; Isa. 66:16). Therefore, despite the semantic latitude permitted by the singular term *kurios*, Cornelius could not have misconstrued Peter's claim for the "full" deity of Jesus Christ.

The proponents of the crossless gospel often speak derisively about the fact that Scripture nowhere uses the phrase "full deity" to express what someone must believe in order to receive eternal life. It should be clarified, however, that God's Word does not need to add the adjective "full" to either Christ's deity or humanity. Biblically and from God's perspective, an individual is either God/deity or no god/deity at all, regardless of what similar language may be employed by the polytheistic world. Scripture nowhere recognizes the legitimacy of a so-called "demi-god" or "semi-deity." Rather, the Bible actually testifies that *"an idol is nothing in the world, and that there is no other God but one. For even if there are so-called gods, whether in heaven or on earth (as there are many gods and many lords), yet for us there is one God, the Father, of whom are all things, and we for Him; and one Lord Jesus Christ, through whom are all things, and through whom we live"* (1 Cor. 8:4-6). Likewise, when it comes to the issue of humanity, the notion of someone being "almost human" or "half-human" versus "fully human" is totally foreign to Scripture. Such philosophical and theological distinctions have been employed by men in order to "aid" our understanding of difficult metaphysical concepts. Yet in this instance of the gospel's contents, such language can actually becloud the issue rather than clarify it.

Proponents of the crossless and deityless position may also raise the potential objection that Peter does not actually say in Acts 10 that "Jesus is God." Jehovah's Witnesses could, and sometimes do, make the similar point that no verse of Scripture uses this exact expression, including John 1:1. It should be realized, however, that biblical truths are often not stated in the precise theological terms we prefer. For instance, no passage of Scripture states that there are "three persons in One God," though that is still a biblical truth. Likewise, regarding eternal salvation, no passage of Scripture states that believers are "eternally secure." Yet eternal security is a wonderful and reassuring biblical truth that is often contextually determined and expressed through other phrases, such as eternal life (John 10:28), eternal salvation (Heb. 5:9), eternal redemption (Heb. 9:12), etc. The fact remains that Christ's deity is affirmed abundantly through a multiplicity of expressions in various contexts in Scripture, without ever having to use the exact statement, "Jesus is God."

One final qualification is necessary regarding Peter's declaration in Acts 10:36 that Jesus Christ is *"Lord of all."* Does Peter's use of this phrase establish what is popularly known today as "Lordship Salvation"? In other words, does Peter's use of the phrase *"Lord of all"* mean that the gospel requires submission to the Lordship of Christ in the lives of believers to either prove the genuineness of a person's initial salvation or to maintain that salvation? Or, does it simply mean that Jesus is the highest authority in the universe, namely God, and as such He is the one in whom we are to believe for our salvation? Normative Free Grace proponent Charlie Bing explains, "The acclamation of Jesus as Lord is an acclamation of His sovereign position as God over all and not a demand for individual submission."[46] To believe, therefore, that Jesus is *"Lord of all"* is simply to believe that He is God, the One who possesses final authority and the One to whom mankind is ultimately accountable as the *"Judge of the living and the dead"* (10:42). It does not require a committed, obedient life of service to Christ as Master in order to receive eternal life.

---

[46] Bing, *Lordship Salvation*, 104. See also Hixson, "Getting the Gospel Wrong," 77-78, and Robert P. Lightner, *Sin, the Savior, and Salvation: The Theology of Everlasting Life* (Nashville: Thomas Nelson, 1991), 204. Peter may also be using the expression *"Lord of all"* in this particular context of Acts 10-11 to emphasize that the way of salvation in Jesus Christ is open to "all" mankind, both Jews and Gentiles (Bing, *Lordship Salvation*, 104).

Lordship salvation proponents misconstrue Christ's *position* as "Lord of all" into a false, human *condition* for salvation. Submission to Christ as Lord over our lives is a matter of yielded obedience on the part of the person who is already eternally saved. It is an on-going sanctification requirement, not a justification requirement (Rom. 6:11-13). To claim that Christ's position as Lord necessitates that the condition for salvation be submission to the Lordship of Christ would be like saying that since Jesus Christ is God, then someone must be godly in order to get to heaven. Or, since Jesus Christ is love (1 John 4:8), then we must be loving in order to get to heaven. Or, since Jesus Christ is the truth (John 14:6), we must tell the truth in order to get to heaven. While all of these traits are commendable and desirable, they are not requirements to go to heaven. Otherwise, in very short order, we make eternal life legalistically unattainable by requiring an ethical pattern of life based on Christ's character. However, salvation is *not* a matter of emulating Christ's attributes and walk but of trusting in His person and finished work on our behalf.

Jesus Christ's Humanity

Besides Jesus' deity being included in Peter's gospel in Acts 10, His humanity is also indicated by several statements in Peter's preaching. Again, Peter did not say "Jesus is human," but he didn't have to. The Lord's humanity was expressed by Peter in other terms. For instance, it is at least implied by the fact that He was *"killed"* (10:39), as only a human can die (Heb. 2:9). His humanity is also affirmed by the fact that Jesus was from the town *"of Nazareth"* (10:38). Such terrestrial residency is never stated of any angel in the Bible. Also, from the time of John the Baptist (10:37) until His death, the Lord Jesus lived and ministered with His witnesses, the disciples, throughout *"the land of the Jews and Jerusalem"* (10:39). Additionally, Peter testified that the disciples *"ate and drank with Him"* (10:41). Some may object that even angels ate with men at times (Gen. 19:1-4), so this wouldn't necessarily establish Christ's humanity. While this is true, it must also be admitted that no angel ever walked among men ministering throughout all the land of Israel, day after day, for the length of time the Lord Jesus did. Peter indicates this time span to be from John the Baptist until Christ rose from the dead. Throughout Peter's preaching, the composite picture he presents of the Lord Jesus is that He is truly human. Christ's humanity is a gospel truth. Without the incarnation of Christ, there would be no substitutionary death for our sins or bodily resurrection from the dead.

Jesus Christ's Substitutionary Death

Jesus Christ's death is referred to by the fact that He was *"killed"* (10:39), and not only *"killed"* but *"by hanging on a tree"* (*kremasantes epi xulou*). This reference to Christ's death by *"hanging on a tree"* is undoubtedly a reference to the substitutionary aspect of Christ's death and not merely to the historical fact of His death. This statement in Acts 10:39 parallels Peter's exact expression in Acts 5:30 (*kremasantes epi xulou*) as well as Paul's similar declaration to the Galatians in Acts 13:29. In Acts 10:39, Peter is referring directly to Deuteronomy 21:22-23 where those who are hanged on a tree in Israel are said to be *"accursed by God."* The meaning to Cornelius and company is clear: Christ, the One anointed by God who went about Israel doing good because God was with Him, has also been accursed by God as a substitute for you, not for Himself. The fact that Peter is referring directly to Deuteronomy 21:22-23 is indicated not merely by the occurrence of the term *"tree"* but by the fuller expression *"hanging on a tree"* (*kremasantes epi xulou*). Peter not only tells Cornelius and company that Christ died on a *"tree"* (*xulon*) but he uses the same term for *"hanging"* (*kremannumi*) found twice in Deuteronomy 21:22-23 (LXX). The substitutionary significance of Christ's death in Acts 10:39 is further substantiated by Peter's "tree" reference in his first epistle. There he states in reference to Christ, *"who Himself bore our sins in His own body on the tree"* (1 Peter 2:24). If Peter's reference in Acts 10:39 to Christ being killed *"by hanging on a tree"* does not indicate substitution, then how else could *"the remission of sins"* be offered *"through His name"* to *"whoever believes in Him"* (10:43)? It is evident that Peter's gospel in Acts 10 included the substitutionary death of Christ for sin.

Jesus Christ's Bodily Resurrection

Besides the gospel elements of Christ's deity, humanity, and substitutionary death, His resurrection from the dead is also plainly attested in Peter's preaching as an indisputable element of the gospel (10:40-41). Peter states in verse 40 that Christ was *"raised up on the third day"* and again in verse 41 that *"He arose from the dead."* The fact that Peter is indicating a bodily resurrection and not merely a "spiritual" resurrection is apparent from the fact that Christ was genuinely human, even "after He arose from the dead" (10:41), as previously explained.

The Burial of Christ

Having covered the Lord's substitutionary death and bodily resurrection as elements of the gospel, some may question at this point why the burial of Christ is not included among these essential elements. Conspicuously absent from Peter's preaching in Acts 10 is any reference to the burial. Some crossless gospel proponents interpret 1 Corinthians 15:3-8 in such a way as to make Christ's death for sin, burial, resurrection, and post-resurrection appearances all theologically coordinate, of equal weight, and essential to their broader view of "the gospel." They often claim that traditional Free Grace adherents are being arbitrary and selective in the elements we believe are essential to the contents of saving faith.[47] But their reasoning is neither sound nor convincing.

In Acts 10, Peter's preaching includes the substitutionary death of Christ, the resurrection, and even the post-resurrection appearances to the apostles; but he never mentions Christ's burial *as he did with each of the elements of the gospel.* While Peter may have assumed that Cornelius and the Gentiles knew that the regular Jewish custom was to properly bury their dead out of respect for the human body, the fact remains that Peter chose to omit any reference to the Lord's burial *while referring to all the other elements of the saving gospel.* So, we must ask, was Peter negligent in carrying out his evangelistic duties? Did Peter fail to preach "the gospel" in Acts 10? Was he guilty of preaching a "groundless gospel"?

Some crossless proponents who charge their traditional Free Grace brethren with inconsistency for not also requiring the burial of Christ in the contents of saving faith may appeal to the mention of burial in Deuteronomy 21:22-23. This passage states, *"22 If a man has committed a sin deserving of death, and he is put to death, and you hang him on a tree, 23 his body shall not remain overnight on the tree, but you shall surely bury him that day, so that you do not defile the land which the LORD your God is giving you as an inheritance; for he who is hanged is accursed of God."* Crossless gospel advocates might be prone to reason that since Peter referred to this passage when he stated that Jesus was *"killed by hanging on a tree"* (Acts 10:39), then by implication Peter was also making the burial of Christ implicit in his preaching in Acts 10. They might continue to reason that if the substitutionary curse of God upon Christ was implied in Peter's preaching in Acts 10, then the burial must also be implied. However, the fact remains that Peter selected *only that portion* of Deuteronomy 21:22-23 dealing with Christ's death, not with His burial or the land of Israel. The reference to Christ's death *"by hanging on a tree"* pertains to Deuteronomy 21:22a and 23b. The intervening portions dealing with burial and defilement and inheritance of the land are completely passed over in Peter's use of this passage. The reason is apparent. These portions did not serve his purpose of illustrating the vicarious and punitive nature of Christ's death as the One who was accursed by God due to His death by hanging on a tree. According to Deuteronomy 21:22-23, God's curse is associated only with death by hanging on a tree, not with burial. The passage concludes, *"for he who is hanged is accursed of God."* It does not say, *"he who is buried is accursed by God."* It was the vicarious and satisfactory death of Christ that Peter sought to focus upon in his evangelization of the Gentiles, and this is why he was selective in his application of Old Testament Scripture.

---

[47] Zane C. Hodges, "The Hydra's Other Head: Theological Legalism," *Grace in Focus* 23 (September/October 2008): 3; Bob Wilkin, "Another Look at 1 Corinthians 15:3-11," *Grace in Focus* 23 (January/February 2008): 1-2; idem, "Essential Truths About Our Savior," *Grace in Focus* 23 (November/December 2008): 1-2; idem, "A Review of J. B. Hixson's *Getting the Gospel Wrong: The Evangelical Crisis No One is Talking About*," *JOTGES* 21 (Spring 2008): 18, 22.

It is also worth considering that in Peter's first epistle the couplet of Christ's redemptive death and resurrection occurs several times (1 Peter 1:2-3, 11, 18-21; 3:18-21). Yet conspicuously, the burial is never mentioned anywhere in 1 Peter (or 2 Peter for that matter). This raises a serious question and the same problem as the one posed previously in chapter 10 with respect to the burial being absent from Paul's Epistle of Galatians. Are we really to conclude that even though Peter preached the crucified, risen Savior, he didn't preach a saving gospel in either Acts 10, or in his two epistles, simply because the burial is not included? Something is seriously amiss with this reasoning and interpretation of 1 Corinthians 15:3-8 that underlies the accusations of arbitrariness made by crossless gospel proponents towards their traditional Free Grace brethren.

It must be affirmed once again that though the truths of Christ's burial and post-resurrection appearances are of inestimable worth as proofs of the Savior's actual death and bodily resurrection, which is what 1 Corinthians 15:3-8 teaches, neither of these were divine works that formed the grounds of our eternal redemption. Nor are they ever required elsewhere in Scripture to be believed for eternal life as are Christ's death and resurrection. For instance, nowhere does Scripture say, *"For if you confess with your mouth the Lord Jesus and believe in your heart that God buried Him, you shall be saved"* (Rom. 10:9). Even in an ontological sense the Bible does not teach that the burial inhered to Christ's very being and identity as His death and resurrection did (Luke 24:39-40; John 20:20-28). The burial is not part of Christ's person in the way that the death and resurrection now define Him as the crucified-living Lamb of God (Rev. 5:6). It is for this reason that neither Paul, nor Peter, or John ever professed anything approximating 1 Corinthians 2:2 with respect to the burial, such as, *"For I determined not to know anything among you except Jesus Christ and Him buried."* To believe in His person or very being—to believe "in Him" (John 3:15-18; 6:29, 40; Acts 10:43; Rom. 10:14; Phil. 1:29; 1 Tim. 1:16)—does not necessitate belief in His burial. For these, and many other reasons, belief in the person of Jesus Christ as the *object* of saving faith does not include His burial as part of the required *content* of saving faith.

Salvation by Grace through Faith

Lastly, having observed that Christ's deity, humanity, substitutionary death, and bodily resurrection are all contained in Peter's gospel to the Gentiles in Acts 10, we see that the provision and condition of the gospel are also included. Peter does not express the provision of the gospel in terms of "justification" or "eternal life" as the New Testament does elsewhere, but here he speaks of being *"saved"* (Acts 11:14; 15:11) and receiving the *"remission of sins"* (Acts 10:43; 15:9). Therefore, the basis of this salvation is simply *"the grace of the Lord Jesus Christ"* (Acts 15:11). The sole condition for this saving grace is simply to *"believe"* the message presented about Christ (Acts

10:43; 15:7, 9). Crossless gospel proponents may object that Peter never tells Cornelius that salvation is through faith "alone" or that it is "apart from works" or something similar. But this is implicit in the fact that the only condition stated is to believe (10:43) and that they are not saved through either "circumcision" (10:45) or water baptism (10:47-48). This is why in Acts 15:7-11, Peter himself interprets his message in Acts 10 to be nothing less than a message of salvation by grace through faith apart from works. Furthermore, for crossless advocates to argue on this basis would be inconsistent with their own position. They also maintain that salvation is by grace, and that works are not required, simply by virtue of the fact that John's Gospel routinely presents the sole condition for eternal life as strictly a matter of believing (John 1:12; 3:15-18; 5:24; 6:47; 20:31).

We may conclude that Peter's gospel in Acts 10 contains the very contents of saving faith. Christ's person and work are not merely presented as *sufficient* content for the Gentiles to believe but as the content *necessary* to believe to be saved (Acts 11:14; 15:1, 7-11). This harmonizes perfectly with Peter's first epistle where he states that *"the gospel of God"* (1 Peter 4:17) is not something merely sufficient for salvation and optional, but it must be *"obey[ed]"* (1 Peter 4:18) by believing it (1 Peter 2:6-8).

Acts 13:23-48

These verses are not printed here since they were treated previously in chapter 10. At this point, it is sufficient to summarize that the essential elements of the saving gospel are all contained in these verses. This includes Christ's deity (13:23, 33, 35), humanity (13:23, 38), death for sin (13:28-29), bodily resurrection (13:30-37), and provision of justification by grace through faith alone (13:38-43, 46, 48). While eternal life is definitely included in Paul's gospel to the lost here, two facts must be noted as it pertains to the matter of the crossless gospel. First, though Paul includes the message of eternal life twice in his evangelism (13:46, 48), it comes last in the order of presentation and is not even mentioned in Paul's initial gospel preaching at Antioch of Pisidia in Southern Galatia. By no stretch of the imagination can crossless gospel advocates rightfully claim that the "focus"[48] of Paul's evangelism here in Acts 13 is on the guarantee of eternal life instead of Christ's person and work. Second, the emphasis of Paul's preaching in this passage is on the deity of Christ, as well as His death and resurrection. Paul explicitly requires belief in Christ's "work" lest his audience "perish" (13:41). Once again, we see that the gospel of Christ is not just a *sufficient* message but the "saving message" that is *necessary* to believe in order to have eternal life.

---

[48] Zane C. Hodges, "How to Lead People to Christ, Part 1: The Content of Our Message," *JOTGES* 13 (Autumn 2000): 8.

Acts 17:1-4

1 *Now when they had passed through Amphipolis and Apollonia, they came to Thessalonica, where there was a synagogue of the Jews.*

2 *Then Paul, as his custom was, went in to them, and for three Sabbaths reasoned with them from the Scriptures,*

3 *explaining and demonstrating that* ***the Christ*** *had to* ***suffer*** *and* ***rise again from the dead,*** *and saying, "This Jesus whom I preach to you is* ***the Christ."***

4 *And some of them were* ***persuaded;*** *and a great multitude of the devout Greeks, and not a few of the leading women, joined Paul and Silas.*

This passage refers to "the Christ" two times, and how is He described? As the guarantor of eternal life? What "Christ" did Paul preach? We see once again that Paul preached the One whom the Old Testament described and predicted—the One who suffered (death) and rose from the dead. This meaning of "the Christ" is consistent with Paul's use of the term in his epistles. There, he "characteristically uses *Christos* (either alone or in connection with "Jesus") in passages that refer to Jesus' death and resurrection . . . and it is likely that these passages reflect Paul's familiarity with and emphasis on the early Christian conviction that Jesus' crucifixion was part of His mission as the 'Messiah'."[49]

In addition, we also see in this passage the sole response of the saving gospel. We read that *"some"* in Thessalonica who heard Paul's gospel *"were persuaded (peithō)"* (17:4) but some *"were not persuaded (apeithō)"* (17:5). This is the difference between belief and unbelief. 2 Thessalonians 1:8-10 interprets the response of those who were persuaded in 17:4 as being nothing less than belief in the gospel. And this was necessary in order to escape "everlasting destruction" (2 Thess. 1:9). The gospel presented to the Thessalonians in Acts 17 was not merely sufficient for eternal life, it was absolutely necessary to believe. Here is another clear example from Acts where saving faith involves a change of mind about Christ's person and work as contained in the gospel. In Acts, repentance is inseparable from faith in Christ.

Acts 17:18, 30-34

18 *Then certain Epicurean and Stoic philosophers encountered him. And some said, "What does this babbler want to say?" Others said, "He seems to be a proclaimer of* ***foreign gods,"*** *because he preached to them* ***Jesus*** *and* ***the resurrection. . .***

30 *Truly, these times of ignorance God overlooked, but now commands all men everywhere to* ***repent,***

31 *"because He has appointed a day on which He will judge the world in*

---

[49] Larry W. Hurtado, "Christ," in *Dictionary of Jesus and the Gospels*, ed. Joel B. Green, Scot McKnight, and I. Howard Marshall (Downers Grove, IL: InterVarsity Press, 1992), 108 (ellipsis added).

*righteousness by the **Man** whom He has ordained. He has given assurance of this to all by **raising Him from the dead.**"*

32 *And when they heard of the **resurrection of the dead,** some mocked, while others said, "We will hear you again on this matter."*

33 *So Paul departed from among them.*

34 *However, some men joined him and **believed,** among them Dionysius the Areopagite, a woman named Damaris, and others with them.*

While Paul's preaching to the "intelligentsia" at Athens was much longer than the portion printed above, the portion relevant for our consideration is shown above (Acts 17:18, 30-34). Here the Gentile, pagan audience seems to get seriously sidetracked by the subject of bodily resurrection. Why did Paul "focus" on Christ's resurrection here instead of the "saving message" of Jesus being the guarantor of eternal life? Didn't Paul know what some crossless advocates propose—that his audience might get turned off by the "unnecessary" doctrine of Christ's resurrection and never get to the *"three essentials"* of the "saving message"—the promise of *eternal life* to all who simply *believe* in *Jesus* for it? Why bring up non-essential subject matter that might stumble his hearers from listening later to the message of eternal life? Did Paul major in the minors here? Was his approach to evangelism *"flawed"*[50] since he focused so heavily on the resurrection and his audience never even heard the "message of life" that could save them? We must also ask, *"How could* [he] *get it so wrong?"*[51] Paul certainly would not have focused so heavily upon the fact of Christ's resurrection with his unsaved audience if he did not consider it content that was essential to saving faith.

<u>Acts 18:1-5</u>

1 *After these things Paul departed from Athens and went to Corinth.*

2 *And he found a certain Jew named Aquila, born in Pontus, who had recently come from Italy with his wife Priscilla (because Claudius had commanded all the Jews to depart from Rome); and he came to them.*

3 *So, because he was of the same trade, he stayed with them and worked; for by occupation they were tentmakers.*

4 *And he reasoned in the synagogue every Sabbath, and **persuaded** both Jews and Greeks.*

5 *When Silas and Timothy had come from Macedonia, Paul was compelled by the Spirit, and testified to the Jews that **Jesus is the Christ.***

<u>1 Corinthians 15:1-4, 11</u>

1 *Moreover, brethren, I declare to you the gospel which I preached to you, which also you **received** and in which you stand,*

2 *by which also you are saved, if you hold fast that word which I preached to*

---

[50] Hodges, "How to Lead People to Christ, Part 1: The Content of Our Message," 8.

[51] Robert N. Wilkin, "Justification by Faith Alone is an Essential Part of the Gospel," *JOTGES* 18 (Autumn 2005): 14 (brackets added).

you—unless you ***believed*** *in vain.*
3 *For I delivered to you first of all that which I also received: that* ***Christ died for our sins*** *according to the Scriptures,*
4 *and that He was buried, and that He* ***rose again*** *the third day according to the Scriptures.*
11 *Therefore, whether it was I or they, so we preach and so you* ***believed.***

2 Corinthians 1:19
19 *For* ***the Son of God, Jesus Christ,*** *who was preached among you by us—by me, Silvanus, and Timothy—was not Yes and No, but in Him was Yes.*

Here is the gospel Paul preached evangelistically to the Corinthians in order to bring them to eternal salvation during his second missionary journey. Notice that according to Acts 18:1-5, we are not told what the content of his evangelism was, except that he reasoned with them in the synagogue (presumably from the Old Testament) in order to "persuade" (18:4) them (i.e., lead them to "faith") *"that Jesus is the Christ"* (18:5). Once again, we see that in Acts, to be saved one must have a change of mind, which is biblical repentance. But what does it mean to be persuaded *"that Jesus is the Christ"* (18:5)? In the sovereign providence of God, the Holy Spirit recorded the contents of Paul's Corinthian preaching about Jesus being "the Christ" in Paul's two epistles to the Corinthians.

We are told in 1 Corinthians 15 that for these Corinthians to believe in Jesus as "the Christ" meant to believe He died for their sins and rose from the dead (1 Cor. 15:3-4). Here we see that the "focus" of Paul's evangelism was on the *work* of Jesus Christ. Later in 2 Corinthians 1:19 it is also revealed that on the same occasion referred to in Acts 18:1-5 and 1 Corinthians 15, Paul also preached the *person* of "Jesus Christ" as "the Son of God." This meant nothing less than to believe Jesus "Christ" was God the Son—deity. In fact, being the "Son of God" also entails His work, as the Savior's person and work cannot be separated. For the Corinthians to believe in Jesus as "the Christ" meant to believe in both the *person* and *work* of Jesus, not merely to believe that He is the guarantor of eternal life without requiring any knowledge of who He is or what He's done to guarantee that life.

Acts 24:24-25
24 *And after some days, when Felix came with his wife Drusilla, who was Jewish, he sent for Paul and heard him concerning* ***the faith in Christ.***
25 *Now as he reasoned about righteousness, self-control, and the judgment to come, Felix was afraid and answered, "Go away for now; when I have a convenient time I will call for you."*

This passage is also very revealing as to Paul's evangelistic approach. If the crossless gospel method is correct in which we are to focus on the message of eternal life rather than the solution to the sin problem, then why would

Paul be reasoning with Felix the governor about righteousness, self–control, and the judgment to come? Felix gets turned off (i.e., convicted) and tunes out—*before* Paul ever gets to the promise of eternal life in Jesus. Was Paul mis-focused in his evangelism here? Was he ignorant of the mold that John's Gospel had supposedly set for all evangelism? Didn't Paul know that *"Though the sin issue is important, John does not present it as the fundamental one facing the unbeliever"*?[52] Was Paul unaware that *"All forms of the gospel that require greater content to faith in Christ than the Gospel of John requires, are flawed"*[53] and that *"Instead we should be focusing on whether an individual believes that Jesus has given him eternal life"*?[54]

In Paul's attempt to lead Felix to *"the faith in Christ,"* he does not hesitate to establish certain pre-evangelistic essentials, such as belief that all men are sinners before a righteous God and in need of a Savior. When the message of eternal life is preached without respect to sin, then the cross of Christ becomes void. There is no *"offense of the cross"* (Gal. 5:11) in a crossless "saving message."

Acts 25:19

19 but had some questions against him about their own religion and about ***a certain Jesus****, who had* ***died****, whom Paul affirmed* ***to be alive.***

It is interesting to see how an unbeliever, Festus, summarizes Paul's evangelistic message. What did Festus recollect about Paul's saving message? Did it merely contain *"the three essentials"* of the name of Jesus, believing, and eternal life? No! It was the power of the gospel, which contains the twin truths of Christ's death and resurrection!

Acts 26:22-23

22 Therefore, having obtained help from God, to this day I stand, witnessing both to small and great, saying no other things than those which the prophets and Moses said would come—

23 "that ***the Christ*** *would* ***suffer****, that He would be the first to* ***rise from the dead****, and would proclaim light to the Jewish people and to the Gentiles."*

In this final passage from Acts for our consideration, we see again that Paul defines "the Christ" to be the One who would suffer death and rise again, consistent with the Old Testament depiction of "the Christ." We have found from the preaching of the apostles in the Book of Acts that it has repeatedly defined Jesus to be "the Christ" in the sense that He is God-incarnate who died for us and rose again in order to provide forgiveness of sins, justification, and eternal life through repentance/faith alone

[52] John Niemelä, "What About Believers Who Have Never Known Christ's Promise of Life?" *Chafer Theological Seminary Conference*, Houston, TX, March 13, 2006. See also Bob Wilkin, "The Way of the Master," *Grace in Focus* (July-August 2007): 1, 4.

[53] Hodges, "How to Lead People to Christ, Part 1: The Content of Our Message," 8.

[54] Ibid.

in Him. This analysis of the term "Christ" will end with Acts, since by the time of the Epistles, where this key term is used hundreds of times, "the Christ" had become a technical and established *title*[55] or virtual *name*[56] for the Lord Jesus, and its meaning is not defined or described to the same extent that it is in Acts.

Which "Christ" Did John Preach?

The acid test of what the apostle John himself required for saving faith is revealed in the Acts of the Apostles, where in chapters 2-5, through his association with Peter's leadership, John consents to the evangelistic preaching of a crucified, risen Savior as "the Christ." As the object of faith, Christ is never preached as being merely "the guarantor of eternal life." In Acts 2:14, John stands up with the rest of the apostles in support of Peter's evangelistic message on the day of Pentecost, where Jesus is presented to the unbelieving nation as Christ-crucified and risen. In Acts 3:1-11, John and Peter are both involved in the miraculous healing of a man in Christ's name, and according to Acts 4:1-2, 13, 17-20, John also *"spoke"* the same essential message as Peter, the message of Christ's death and resurrection as recorded in Acts 3:13-26. In Acts 4:33, John is again included among the apostles who *"gave witness to the resurrection of the Lord Jesus."* And in Acts 5:29-31, John is one of the other apostles who, again led by Peter, *"answered and said"* that Jesus was the Prince and Savior who had been crucified but now was risen. The composite picture of the apostles' preaching in Acts reveals that they consistently stayed "on message" with one another when they evangelized the lost. They harmoniously testified that Jesus is the Christ by virtue of His saving death and resurrection. These are the elements continually presented to the lost to define the Object of saving faith and the contents of the gospel.

But with respect to the fourth Gospel, we must ask, why would John have a different meaning for "the Christ" than the meaning he himself employs in his own evangelistic preaching as documented in the Book of Acts? The fact that the crossless gospel's interpretation of "the Christ" is at odds with the manner in which "the Christ" is presented in the Old Testament, by the Lord Jesus Himself, and by all the other apostles makes it dubious indeed.

---

[55] Douglas J. Moo, "The Christology of the Early Pauline Letters," in *Contours of Christology in the New Testament*, ed. Richard N. Longenecker (Grand Rapids: Eerdmans, 2005), 186-87; Stanley E. Porter, "The Messiah in Luke and Acts: Forgiveness for the Captives," in *The Messiah in the Old and New Testaments*, ed. Stanley E. Porter (Grand Rapids: Eerdmans, 2007), 159.

[56] Ferdinand Hahn, *"Χριστός," EDNT*, 3:479; John Kloppenborg, "An Analysis of the Pre-Pauline Formula 1 Cor 15:3b5 in Light of Some Recent Literature," *CBQ* 40.3 (July 1978): 357.

It is fair to say that the meaning of "the Christ" that crossless gospel advocates have imported into John's Gospel is not the Bible's own meaning, since they have stripped the term "Christ" of Jesus' deity, death for sin, and resurrection in order to perpetuate their unique *"Johannine sense of that term."*[57] In the process, they have created another christ and another gospel when it comes to salvation. Could it be that they have not only arrived at a "crossless gospel" by changing the meaning of "the gospel," but they have also now arrived at a "Christless gospel" by redefining and rejecting the biblical meaning of "the Christ"?!

In closing we can agree wholeheartedly with crossless gospel advocate, John Niemelä, about one thing when he writes, *"Specifically, John's Gospel expresses its purpose in terms of giving eternal life to those who lack it. He says to those who do not have eternal life: "You will have life, when you believe that Jesus is the Christ." John regarded this as a sufficient message for receiving eternal life."*[58] We can all shout a loud "AMEN" to the fact that believing Jesus is "the Christ" is sufficient to receive eternal life—provided we accept the meaning given to the term "Christ" by the composite testimony of the Old Testament, the Lord Jesus Himself, and all of the apostles. The Bible is perfectly consistent about the fact that being the "Christ" means that Jesus is the incarnate Son of God who died for our sins and rose from the dead to provide salvation for sinners on the basis of God's grace through faith alone in Him.

---

[57] Hodges, "How to Lead People to Christ, Part 1: The Content of Our Message," 4.

[58] John Niemelä, "The Message of Life in the Gospel of John," *CTSJ* 7 (July-Sept. 2001): 11.

Chapter 18

Is Belief in Christ's Virgin Birth Essential for Salvation?

OVERVIEW

The doctrine of the virgin birth is greatly misunderstood among genuine believers in our day. Scripturally, it is not essential to believe in this miracle in order to receive eternal life, though it must still be regarded as a fundamental doctrine of our Christian faith. Its purpose was technically not to protect the sinlessness of Christ but to serve as a "sign" of the incarnation and of the uniqueness of Christ's person—that He is "God with us." Though the virgin birth was the means of Christ's incarnation in the sovereign plan of God, it was not the necessary means, or grounds, of our salvation. Contrary to the assumptions of some crossless gospel proponents, it is never stated in Scripture that a virgin birth was essential in order to provide redemption for the world. Nor is the virgin birth ever said to be part of the gospel. With respect to the person of Christ, the necessary content that we must preach to the lost for their eternal salvation is the incarnation of the Son of God, not the means of the incarnation. Though denial of the virgin birth does not necessarily constitute denial of Christ's deity and incarnation, which would lead to eternal condemnation, it still must be considered a rejection of the authority of God's Word that has serious consequences.

No book dealing with the contents of saving faith would be complete without addressing the crucial and controversial subject of Christ's virgin birth. Apart from the necessity to believe in Jesus' deity, death for sin, and resurrection, the topic of His virgin birth surfaces more frequently than any other in evangelical discussions about the contents of saving faith. This often generates more heat than light. For this reason the virgin birth deserves special consideration among the many other Christological doctrines involved in the crossless gospel debate.

Even though most evangelical theologians correctly recognize that the lost do not need to be informed about Christ's virgin birth in order to believe in Him as their Savior, mass confusion and fuzzy thinking still persist on this fundamental doctrine of the faith. The proponents of the new crossless gospel have not helped matters either. They frequently deride the notion of having to believe in Christ's person and work, objecting that once specific doctrines about Christ start becoming prerequisites to eternal life there is no end to the list of doctrines that must also be believed. Invariably, the virgin birth is included as one of these unreasonable "extras."[1] On the other hand, a few over-zealous evangelicals (though very few in the Free Grace camp) have gone to the other extreme in their attempts to combat apostasy by mandating belief in the virgin birth for eternal life. In the process, they have actually exceeded the required content established by God Himself in the Bible.

In order to demonstrate why belief in Christ's virgin birth is *not* part of the essential content of saving faith, we must also address two other significant issues. First, what was the stated *purpose* of the virgin birth? Was it intended to be the necessary means of accomplishing Christ's sinless incarnation? Was a virgin conception and birth the only way the Son of God could have become the spotless Son of Man? Secondly, was a "virgin birth" historically necessary for Christ to be the Savior of mankind? In other words, was it part of the very *grounds* upon which our eternal salvation rests? For, if our redemption rests upon such an event, then con-

[1] Lon Gregg, "Alp upon Alp," *Grace in Focus* 24 (January/February 2009): 1, 4n4; Zane C. Hodges, "How to Lead People to Christ, Part 1: The Content of Our Message," *JOTGES* 13 (Autumn 2000): 4, 9; Jeremy D. Myers, "The Gospel is More Than "Faith Alone in Christ Alone"," *JOTGES* 19 (Autumn 2006): 49; Robert N. Wilkin, *Confident in Christ* (Irving, TX: Grace Evangelical Society, 1999), 10; idem, "Essential Truths About Our Savior," *Grace in Focus* 23 (November/December 2008): 2; idem, "Most Evangelicals Need Evangelizing," *Grace in Focus* 24 (March/April 2009): 2n1; idem, "Saving Faith in Focus," *JOTGES* 11 (Autumn 1998): 46; idem, "Should We Rethink the Idea of Degrees of Faith?," *JOTGES* 19 (Autumn 2006): 20; idem, "Tough Questions About Saving Faith," *The Grace Evangelical Society News* (June 1990): 4.

sistency demands that the virgin birth also be part of the essential contents of faith for eternal salvation. A final major problem to be addressed is the fate of one who actually *denies* the virgin birth. It is one thing to agree that a person can be uninformed and ignorant of Christ's virgin birth and yet still believe in Him as God-incarnate and thus be born again; but what about the person who after hearing of the virgin birth denies it? Has such a person necessarily denied the deity and incarnation of Christ, and are they automatically lost? In addressing these crucial questions related to the virgin birth, we must proceed with the utmost reverence, for we are treading upon theological holy ground with respect to the very person of our Lord Jesus Christ.

Though the virgin birth of Christ is easy to accept in childlike faith and appears simple at first glance, it is actually one of the most difficult doctrines in all of Scripture to grasp. Anyone who thinks otherwise has not peered into the biblical manger scene from Bethlehem 2,000 years ago and pondered deeply enough upon the Babe lying there. Though He once lay in such mean estate, any searching soul must come away paying due homage to this King whose glory was once veiled in His unresurrected flesh. This omnipotent and immaculate Sovereign wrapped in swaddling clothes has humbled the heart, bowed the head, and bent the knee of many a careful student of Scripture. How could such an event, so simple as a child's birth, be so staggering in its implications? Surely, this itself is evidence for the divine inspiration of the record of the Savior's birth now to be examined from Scripture. In contemplating this miraculous birth, we must attempt to synthesize some of the deepest truths and richest treasures ever revealed to man.

There are several complex, Christological issues that all intersect when seeking to determine whether the virgin birth of Christ is essential as the grounds of our salvation and thus as part of the contents of saving faith. We must resolve how Christ's deity, humanity, sinlessness, incarnation, and hypostatic union are related to the miracle of His virgin conception and birth. In the process, this creates many difficult questions to address. For instance, was the virgin birth necessary to prevent Christ from inheriting a sinful human nature? Was Joseph the only one who could transmit a sinful nature? What about Mary? Was Christ genetically related only to Mary? If Christ did not have an earthly father was He truly human and qualified to die as our substitute for sin? Was a virgin birth the only means by which God could bring Christ into the world without compromising His deity? Was a virgin birth necessary for Christ's humanity to be indissolubly joined with His deity in one person? In what way was Christ's virgin birth related to the miracle of His incarnation? The difficulty and confusion surrounding these questions is due in large measure to the abstract, metaphysical nature of the miracle that occurred. The entrance of the eternal, divine, sinless Son of God into the womb of a mere mortal in order to be united forever with a spotless human nature for the purpose of redeeming sinful humanity is something so extraordinary, supernatural, and complex that it can barely be comprehended even by a regenerate, spiritual mind.

In addition, we ourselves as fundamental, Bible-believing Christians have not helped matters by our failure to properly distinguish key terms and concepts. Our language on this subject, generally speaking, is far too loose; and we have contributed towards the confusion by obscuring several necessary distinctions. I include myself in this generalization, based on my own past teaching and assumptions. Permit me to explain.

Under the broad doctrinal label of "The Virgin Birth," Christians are often really referring to the sinless, immaculate conception of Christ whereby God Himself supernaturally and miraculously produced the conception and incarnation of His Son in Mary's womb. Without realizing it in most cases, we have equated events that are technically distinct. The sinless conception and incarnation of Christ are actually separate from (but related to) His "birth"; and they could have been accomplished by God whether or not Mary was a "virgin." As will be explained later, the critical issue with respect to Christ's incarnation and His qualification to be the Redeemer is the particular nature of His conception, not His "birth." The "virgin birth" itself served as the "sign" of His unique personhood, revealing that He was "God with us" and the royal, eternal Son of David.

This distinction between His conception and His birth will consistently be a factor in aiding our discernment on this difficult doctrine, and it should be kept firmly in mind throughout this chapter. This distinction must not be brushed off as "just a matter of semantics." Even James Orr, the great defender of the virgin birth in the classic *Fundamentals* of a century ago, was careful to note this distinction, saying:

> There was nothing, I grant, in the mere fact that Jesus was *born of a Virgin*—in that fact, I mean, considered by itself—to secure that Christ should be perfectly pure, or free from stain of sin. In conjunction, however, with the other factor in the miraculous birth—the *conception by the Holy Ghost*—we shall see afterwards that there was involved everything to secure it.[2]

The Sign of the Virgin Birth

Much of the fog surrounding this subject can be lifted by carefully distinguishing what the Word of God *does* say about the virgin birth from what it does *not* say. Nowhere, for instance, does the Bible actually say that the

---

[2] James Orr, *The Virgin Birth of Christ* (New York: Charles Scribner's Sons, 1907), 188-89 (italics added).

reason for Christ's virgin birth was to prevent His humanity from receiving a sinful nature, or to preserve His deity, or to produce the incarnation and hypostatic union of His deity and humanity in one theanthropic person. All of these could have been achieved through an immaculate conception with a divine, non-human paternity, in distinction to a "virgin birth." (This will be explained later in greater detail.) It is imperative that we note at the outset what the divinely stated purpose was for the virgin birth. The actual reason for the virgin birth given in Isaiah 7:14 is that it provided a "sign" indicating the Lord's preservation of the Davidic dynasty and the uniqueness of the One to be born who would guarantee such preservation. Isaiah 7:14 is the central passage on the virgin birth, which we will now consider.

<u>Isaiah 7:10-14</u>

10 *Moreover the LORD spoke again to Ahaz, saying,*
11 *"Ask a sign for yourself from the LORD your God; ask it either in the depth or in the height above."*
12 *But Ahaz said, "I will not ask, nor will I test the LORD!"*
13 *Then he said, "Hear now, O house of David! Is it a small thing for you to weary men, but will you weary my God also?*
14 *"Therefore the Lord Himself will give you a sign: Behold, the virgin shall conceive and bear a Son, and shall call His name Immanuel.*

In order to properly interpret this foundational text on the virgin birth and determine its relationship to our salvation, we must first understand the historical context in which it was given. The wicked king Ahaz (2 Kings 16:2-3) was reigning over Judah at the time Isaiah delivered this prophecy. In that day, Assyria was seeking to extend its control over greater portions of the Middle East, including the regions of Syria and the northern kingdom of Israel, referred to as "Ephraim" in the immediate context of Isaiah 7:2, 5, 8, and 9. The Syrian king, Rezin, and the unrighteous Israelite/Ephraimite king, Pekah, had banded together to form an alliance against the growing power of Assyria. They also desired the southern kingdom of Judah to join them, but king Ahaz was unwilling. As a result, they attacked Judah and its capital of Jerusalem (2 Kings 16:5-6) with the intent of installing their own puppet king in the place of Ahaz, the non-Davidic Aramean ben Tabel (Isa. 7:6). In the face of what constituted the greatest threat to the perpetuation of the Davidic dynasty since David's day, the Lord instructed Isaiah to deliver a message of hope to king Ahaz that Rezin and Pekah would not prevail (Isa. 7:3-9). However, Ahaz rejected it, along with the accompanying offer of a confirmatory "sign" (*'ôth*) from the Lord (Isa. 7:10-13). Ahaz trusted in the arm of flesh by allying himself with the king of Assyria, Tiglath-Pileser (2 Kings 16:7-20), instead of trusting the God of his father David.

A Sign to the House of David

It is in this context that Isaiah delivers one of the most significant prophecies of the Bible—the miraculous virgin birth of Immanuel. Several features of this prophecy must be noted before it can be correlated with the question of the necessary contents of saving faith. The first thing to observe from Isaiah's prophecy of the virgin birth is that this miracle was intended to serve as a great "sign" (*'ôth*) for the ages (Isa. 7:10-11).[3] When the Lord, through Isaiah, told king Ahaz to ask for a sign *"either in the depth or in the height above"* (Isa. 7:11), He was prepared to literally move heaven and earth in His providential protection of David's royal lineage. The Lord was prepared to offer Ahaz an amazing confirmatory sign that would have been literally unbounded in magnitude and scope. But because Ahaz rejected it in unbelief (Isa. 7:12), the Lord Himself determined what particular sign would be provided (Isa. 7:13-14). It is only reasonable to expect, based on this context, that God would do something truly unique and monumental in human affairs. The supernatural conception of "Immanuel" in a virgin's womb is certainly a fitting and proper interpretation of Isaiah 7:14!

Yet, many unbelieving commentators on Isaiah reject Jesus Christ as the fulfillment of this passage, claiming that the "sign" offered to Ahaz needed an immediate 8th century B.C. fulfillment. The assumption is that if Jesus Christ was the fulfillment of this prophecy, then this prophecy and "sign" would not have any contemporary relevance to king Ahaz as its original intended audience. However, since Ahaz refused God's offer of a sign in unbelief, the Lord Himself then determined the type of sign to be given (the virgin birth of Immanuel) and even to whom it would be given (the entire house of David, not merely Ahaz). The Lord, foreknowing Ahaz's unbelief, used this as the appropriate occasion to introduce new light on His divine plan for Israel and mankind. The sign, therefore, could be legitimately applied to future generations beyond Ahaz. One believing, conservative commentator on Isaiah explains how the Lord's sign could apply even to Ahaz, as well as future generations:

> The significance of a predicted virgin birth of the Messiah does have meaning to Ahaz. He will see Judah spared (however, by his alliances and not because of his trust in God), but he also, because of his lack of faith, will continue rolling Judah toward captivity, and he will not be established long as the ruler of Judah. Such graciousness of Yahweh to this ungodly ruler must be noted as

[3] Liberal, unbelieving critics of the virgin birth are quick to point out that the Hebrew word for "sign" (*'ôth*) may mean either something supernatural and miraculous (Num. 14:22; Deut. 11:3; 2 Kings 10:8; Isa. 38:7-8, 22) or merely something natural that is invested with significance (Gen. 4:15; Josh. 2:12; 4:6). While this may be true, the immediate context clearly indicates that the supernatural and miraculous meaning is intended here, since Isaiah predicts the virgin birth of Immanuel.

> a remarkable display of grace. This man, who brought a heathen altar into the temple, is privileged to receive a message of hope and a warning to turn from eventual destruction, and he rejects it. Therefore, the destruction must come, but yet there is hope for the house of David, for the virgin's son yet comes and He is God's "sign." There is, therefore, both a message for the age and a message for the ages.[4]

The extent and effect of this great sign's witness was therefore never intended by God to be confined strictly to king Ahaz (7:10-12). In the context, we learn that it was intended for the entire "house of David" (7:13). This conclusion is supported by noting the grammatical shift that occurs in Isaiah's address, from the singular form of "you" when addressing Ahaz in Isaiah 7:11, to the plural form of "you" when addressing the entire house of David in verse 14. Jeffrey Khoo explains the importance of this seemingly insignificant detail:

> Further, the plural לָכֶם of (Isa. 7:14) identifies who the recipients of this sign will be. The plural stands in marked contradistinction to the singular לְךָ of verse 11. No longer was God addressing Ahaz as an individual but the faithful remnant of the house of David. God was mindful of the Davidic covenant wherein He promised His servant a perpetual dynasty (2 Sam. 7:14-17). Disobedience within the Davidic clan will result in divine discipline, not covenant abrogation (Lev. 26:44). Since the sign was given to the community of faith, it behooves the reader to understand that the promised sign goes beyond an eighth century situation.[5]

The long-range fulfillment of this "sign" by Jesus Christ some 700 years later was a very strong affirmation from the Lord that the seed and royal lineage of David would last well beyond the impending 8th century B.C. threat from Syria and apostate Israel to the north—well beyond even the rising empire of Assyria, well beyond the coming Babylonian empire, and well beyond all human empires. This was an eternal sign. In it, the Lord affirmed, at the time of the Davidic dynasty's greatest threat, that David would indeed have an *eternal* seed, throne, and kingdom, just as He had promised (2 Sam. 7:16). It is conspicuous that in the New Testament birth narratives of Christ, the Davidic lineage of Christ (Matt. 1:1, 6, 17, 20; Luke 1:27, 32, 69; 2:4, 10), His perpetual reign (Luke 1:33), and His protection of Israel from its enemies (Matt. 2:6; Luke 1:51-52, 71, 74), are all mentioned. Surely it would take One whose goings forth had been from of old, from everlasting (Micah 5:2)—One who was the "mighty God" (Isa. 9:6)—to be such a great sign.

---

[4] Edward E. Hindson, *Isaiah's Immanuel: A Sign of His Times or the Sign of the Ages?* (Phillipsburg, NJ: Presbyterian & Reformed Publishing Co., 1979), 57.

[5] Jeffrey E. Khoo, "The Sign of the Virgin Birth: The Exegetical Validity of a Strictly Messianic Fulfillment of Isaiah 7:14" (M.Div. thesis, Grace Theological Seminary, 1991), 11.

Besides the fact that Immanuel's virgin birth was intended to serve as a great sign, a second vital conclusion to draw from Isaiah's prophecy is that His birth was to be *miraculous* and *supernatural*. This conclusion is only reasonable since it was physically impossible for any woman in Israel at that time to give birth and still be considered a "virgin."[6] In keeping with the purpose of this miracle to provide a great sign, we also learn from Isaiah that the human mother would still be a virgin at the time she bore a son, thus predicting a virgin *birth* and not merely a virgin *conception*. Based on the vocabulary and syntax of the Hebrew text of Isaiah 7:14, the prophecy literally states, *"Behold the pregnant virgin is bearing a son and she calls his name Immanuel."*[7] The prophecy does not explicitly refer

---

[6] Though there has been great debate in the last century surrounding the correct translation of the Hebrew word *'almâ* as meaning either "young woman" or "virgin," the matter is settled beyond dispute to all who believe that "all Scripture," including the New Testament, is the very inspired Word of God (2 Tim. 3:16). The Holy Spirit's choice of terms in the Greek New Testament quotation of this passage in Matthew 1:23 is *parthenos* for "virgin," a term that can only mean "virgin" and not merely "a young woman of marriageable age." Secondly, the Jewish scribes themselves who translated the Hebrew Old Testament into Greek in the Septuagint over two centuries before Christ also translated *'almâ* with the Greek word *parthenos*. Thirdly, if a young woman in Israel was to conceive and bear a son, in what sense would it be a great "sign" to the house of David since that occurred daily in Israel? Fourthly, Isaiah 9:6-7 makes clear that the son to be born called "Immanuel" was to be none less than the Son of God, the Mighty God, not the son of human parents, such as between Isaiah the prophet and his prophetess second wife (8:3), as has been conjectured by some. For an outstanding conservative defense of the traditional "virgin" interpretation of *'almâ* in Isaiah 7:14, see Edward E. Hindson, *Isaiah's Immanuel*, 25-63. See also George L. Lawlor, *Almah—virgin or young woman?* (Schaumburg, IL: Regular Baptist Press, 1973) and Richard Niessen, "The Virginity of the עַלְמָה in Isaiah 7:14," *BSac* 137 (April 1980): 133-47.

[7] The traditional translation of this passage with the future tense in most English versions, *"shall conceive and bear a son,"* is admittedly not the most literal rendering of the Hebrew text. In Hebrew, the feminine adjective for the "pregnant" (הָרָה) virgin, combined with the participle for "bearing" (יֹלֶדֶת), indicates that the scene is considered present in the prophetic foreview of Isaiah while he is prophesying. (Edward E. Hindson, *Isaiah's Immanuel*, 34; Robert G. Gromacki, *The Virgin Birth: Doctrine of Deity* [Grand Rapids: Baker Book House, 1974; reprinted 1981], 148). Some liberal critics have used this in an attempt to deny the long-range fulfillment of this prophecy in the virgin birth of Christ. They claim Isaiah must have been referring to a young woman in contemporary, 8th century B.C. Israel. However, in this same book, in the second half of Isaiah, the Babylonian invasion of Judah is some 150 years away, yet it is spoken of prophetically as something present and even past! One Old Testament scholar clarifies the matter of a present versus future sense of this prophecy: "It is incorrect to say that participles cannot be translated in future time, since it is always the context in Hebrew which determines the "time" of a participle. Compare, for example, Genesis 17:19 where the participle *yōledeth* ("shall bear") is identical with that of Isaiah 7:14 and is used to describe the birth of Sarah's son Isaac which, as the context shows, could only refer to the future. Moreover, the first term in question ("shall conceive") is not a participle, but a feminine adjective meaning "pregnant" ("woman with child"), and the adjective, just as the participle, is always in the same "time" as the context in which it is used. Nevertheless, the verse can be properly translated with the force of the present tense, namely, "the virgin is pregnant." In prophetic vision the Prophet Isaiah sees before him the virgin pregnant with the child who is to be called Immanuel. The emphasis in the vision is not upon time, but is concerned primarily with the fact that a virgin is with child. This is

to Immanuel's *conception* as many of our English translations imply ("a virgin shall conceive and bear") but to His *birth*. Of course His conception is implicit and assumed in the passage. How else could a "virgin" be "pregnant"? The passage literally prophesied that the virgin would retain her virginity until she gave birth to Immanuel, well beyond the time of the actual conception. A truly biblical doctrine of the virgin birth must include this aspect of Mary's virginity at the time of Christ's "birth."[8] Only by remaining a virgin until Messiah's birth could the birth itself fulfill its divinely intended purpose of being a supernatural "sign" to the house of David.[9] Perhaps it was for this very reason that Matthew included this information in his account of Christ's conception and birth, writing that Joseph *"did not know her till she had brought forth her firstborn Son"* (Matt. 1:25).

A Sign of Christ's Deity

A final important fact to consider from Isaiah 7:14 is that the *deity of Christ* was clearly associated in some way with His virgin birth. Not only did Isaiah 7:14 predict a virgin birth, but it also predicted that the Son who was to be virgin-born would be called "God with us" or "Immanuel." This does not mean that a "virgin birth," technically, was necessary to *preserve* the sinlessness and deity of Christ, or to *produce* the incarnation; but it definitely *proclaimed* His true identity and uniqueness as "God with us"—God in human flesh. For this reason, the deity of Christ was also declared by an angel to Joseph and Mary in both New Testament Gospel

---

what constituted it as a sign." Hobart E. Freeman, *An Introduction to the Old Testament Prophets* (Chicago: Moody Press, 1968), 205.

[8] Some have objected that the theological designation "virgin birth" is not quite as fitting or accurate as the phrase, "virgin conception." For example, regarding the "virgin birth," one otherwise sound evangelical theologian has written, "Technically not a birth at all, this expression refers to Mary's miraculous conception of Christ through the power of the Holy Spirit, without any male participation." Paul Enns, *The Moody Handbook of Theology* (Chicago: Moody Press, 1989), 649.

[9] Though admittedly the sign of the "virgin" birth was not as objectively verifiable as some other biblical signs, such as Christ's death and resurrection (Matt. 12:39-40), its truthfulness and significance are still expected by God to be believed. The divine conception of Christ perfectly accords with the Lord Jesus' uniquely sinless life, His unprecedented number of miracles, and His perfect character. In addition, the state of Mary's virginity could have been reasonably attested through corroborating circumstantial evidence and testimony in her day (Deut. 22:13-21). The case of Jonah being hidden in the belly of the great fish is similar to Christ's virginal conception in Mary's womb. Jonah's effectiveness as "a sign to the Ninevites" (Luke 11:30) was not mitigated by the fact that there were no recorded Ninevite eyewitnesses to his underwater organic submarine ride and dramatic expulsion (Jonah 2:10). Yet, the mariners who threw him into the sea could have vouched for his apparent drowning and original departure point had any in Jonah's day sought corroborating evidence. Jonah's preservation and transportation by the great fish reasonably accounted for the fact of his survival, for the significant change in his geographical location, and for the 180° change in his volition. It would have also reasonably accounted for Jonah's appearance possibly changing, being bleached by the gastric juices of the great fish.

accounts where the divine conception of Christ was announced (Matt. 1:23; Luke 1:32, 35).

The Sign of the Virgin Birth & the Grounds of Redemption

So how does all of this relate to the problem of the essential contents of saving faith? It must be recognized at the outset that the explicit reason given for the virgin birth in the foundational passage of Isaiah 7:14 is that it provided a great "sign." It does not go so far as to say that the virgin birth would provide the grounds of our eternal redemption. The sign of the virgin birth signified the preservation of the Davidic dynasty through One who would be "God with us." Though the deity of Christ and His incarnation were clearly signified by the virgin birth, nowhere in the original prophecy of Christ's virgin birth does it actually state that the purpose of this miraculous birth was to secure the very grounds of our eternal redemption, namely Christ's sinless incarnation and hypostatic union. While the divine, virginal conception of Christ was clearly the divinely ordained means and occasion of His incarnation, some Christians go too far by claiming that a virgin birth was the *only* way in which Christ could be deity-incarnate and completely sinless and thus qualified to be our Savior. To them, a denial of Christ's virgin birth is tantamount to a denial of His deity and sinless humanity; and if these are necessary to believe in for eternal life, then the lost must also believe in Christ's virgin birth to be saved. This is similar to the reasoning of crossless gospel teachers who say that the virgin birth was necessary for mankind's redemption, just like the cross and resurrection, and thus none of these truths form the required content of saving faith. Wilkin claims, for example, that "If the Lord Jesus had not been born of a virgin (Isa. 7:14), then He would have inherited a sin nature from his human father and He would have sinned. A sinful human being could not be the Savior (2 Cor. 5:21; Heb. 7:26-27)."[10] But is it necessarily true that a virgin birth was essential for Christ to be sinless and, therefore, capable of saving mankind? Does Scripture teach that a "virgin birth" was required for Jesus to be the sinless, incarnate Son of God? Or, are these just the conjectures of men?

Christ's Sinlessness & the Virgin Birth

With respect to the sinlessness of Christ, neither a *virgin* birth nor a *virgin* conception was actually required to prevent Christ's humanity from receiving any taint of sin[11]—but an *immaculate* conception was absolutely necessary! The phrase "immaculate conception" is unfortunately most often associated with Roman Catholicism's extra-biblical doctrine of

[10] Wilkin, "Essential Truths About Our Savior," 2.

[11] A. N. S. Lane, "The Rationale and Significance of the Virgin Birth," *VE* 10 (1977): 56.

Mary's own conception. Rome teaches that Mary was conceived without any taint of original sin, ostensibly to be a sanctified vessel or "ark" fit for the prenatal Christ.

It is most unfortunate that this theological phrase has been co-opted by religion and misapplied to Mary since, according to Scripture, Jesus Christ is the only human being worthy of the theological phrase "immaculate conception." Mary herself was a sinner who needed a "Savior" (Luke 1:47; Rom. 3:23), even her own Son! The Gospels emphasize that not only was Christ born of a virgin, He was also miraculously, supernaturally, and immaculately conceived without any sin in Mary's womb due to the Holy Spirit's overshadowing role (Luke 1:35).[12] All that was necessary for Christ to be born without inheriting any human sin was that He be perfectly, sinlessly conceived (i.e., "immaculately" conceived). This is technically distinct from being virgin-born.

Once married to Joseph, Mary theoretically could have first conceived Jesus' half brothers and sisters (Ps. 69:8; Matt. 12:46; 13:55; Mark 6:3; Luke 2:5; John 7:3; Gal. 1:19; Jude 1) through normal human paternity with Joseph (Matt. 1:18, 25). Then later, as a non-virgin, she could have received the sinless conception of Christ in her womb solely through the agency of God and completely apart from Joseph, and the Lord Jesus would still have been conceived without any human sin through a non-virgin. Of course, had this occurred, such a miraculously immaculate and divine conception would hardly be credible in the eyes of all who knew that Mary and Joseph were already married with several children. Though this hypothetical scenario would still have resulted in a truly supernatural miracle, it would not have provided the necessary "sign" to signify the utter uniqueness and magnificence of the One who was to be born. This is why conservative, grace-oriented theologian Charles Ryrie writes:

> What was the purpose of the Virgin Birth? It need not be the necessary means of preserving Christ sinless, since God could have overshadowed two parents so as to protect the baby's sinlessness had He so desired. It served as a sign of the uniqueness of the Person who was born.[13]

---

[12] The verb for "overshadow" in Luke 1:35, *episkiazō*, does not contain so much as a hint of sexual, carnal relations between God and Mary, as is sometimes blasphemously asserted by unbelieving critics of Christianity. This false caricature of Christianity's doctrine of the divine conception in Mary's womb is often held by Muslims, following the Qur'an's own misrepresentation that the Christian God consorted with Mary (Sura 6:100-102). *Episkiazō* is used only four other times in the New Testament to convey either the idea of God's glory-cloud enveloping Peter, James, and John on the Mount of Transfiguration (Matt. 17:5; Mark 9:7; Luke 9:34) or of Peter's shadow falling upon people for potential healing (Acts 5:15). *Episkiazō* is also used non-sensually in all four of its occurrences in the Septuagint (Ex. 40:35; Ps. 90:4, 139:8; Prov. 18:11).

[13] Charles C. Ryrie, *Basic Theology* (Wheaton, IL: Victor Books, 1986), 242.

Another conservative, evangelical theologian, Norman Geisler, clearly summarizes the matter, saying:

> God may have achieved our justification without Jesus being virgin-born . . . His sinlessness . . . soteriologically, is absolutely necessary, but virgin birth is not an absolute *condition* for His sinlessness. . . . God instead could have had Christ born through an immaculate conception, for example, but this would not have drawn the same attention to His supernatural origin, since a virgin birth is more empirically obvious than an immaculate conception. All that is absolutely necessary in this regard is for Christ not to have inherited Adam's sin nature; a virgin birth is one way (but not the only way) to accomplish this.[14]

The Transmission of Sin through Both Parents

Thus, Scripture itself indicates that the reason for Christ's virgin birth was not to preserve His sinlessness, but to serve as a great sign. In spite of the simplicity and perspicuity of Scripture on this point, some evangelicals have confused the matter by insisting that the sin nature is passed down from generation to generation only through males.[15] Consequently, they reason that a virginal conception was essential to protect Christ's humanity from receiving Joseph's sin nature. It must be noted, however, that this peculiar belief is merely assumed by its adherents, since Scripture nowhere indicates such a male-only transmission of the sin nature.

Romans 5:12 is sometimes enlisted to support this conclusion. It states, *"Therefore, just as through one man sin entered the world, and death through sin, and thus death spread to all men, because all sinned."* This passage, however, is not addressing the transmission of the sinful, fallen nature in a lineal fashion from one generation to the next. Rather, it is teaching that when Adam sinned in the garden, his individual act of sin, along with its guilt, was judicially *imputed* by God to every member of the human race, since we were all under Adam's federal headship with him positionally as the head of mankind. The old New England Primer put it well: "In Adam's fall, we sinned all." Romans 5:12 in its context is not referring to the *inheritance* of the sinful nature that gives man a propensity to commit individual acts of sin; rather it is teaching that Adam's sin and guilt were *imputed* to the entire human race, resulting in death for every man, woman, and child descended from Adam.[16]

In addition to Romans 5:12, sometimes Hebrews 7:9-10 is used to substantiate the view of male-only transmission of the sin nature. It says,

---

[14] Norman Geisler, *Systematic Theology* (Minneapolis: Bethany House, 2004), 3:535 (ellipsis added).

[15] M. R. DeHaan, *The Chemistry of the Blood* (Grand Rapids: Zondervan, 1943), 17-34.

[16] Lewis Sperry Chafer, *Systematic Theology* (Dallas: Dallas Seminary Press, 1947-1948; reprint ed., Grand Rapids: Kregel, 1993), 2:296-310; Ryrie, *Basic Theology*, 222-26.

"Even Levi, who receives tithes, paid tithes through Abraham, so to speak, for he was still in the loins of his father when Melchizedek met him." This passage clearly teaches that Levi was seminally in the loins of Abraham; but it says nothing about sin or the manner in which the sin nature is transmitted. It simply teaches that succeeding generations (Levi in this case) are genealogically and positionally identified with their predecessors (Abraham in this case, the progenitor of the nation of Israel).

Since Scripture nowhere specifically, or even inferentially, teaches that the sin nature is transmitted only through males, it is better to speak of it being passed down through our parents, rather than our parent (father-only). Thus, in regards to the *inheritance* of the sin nature, theologian Charles Ryrie can say, "Original sin is transmitted from one generation to the next and the next and the next. We inherit it from our parents as they did from theirs, and so on back to the first parents, Adam and Eve."[17]

The assumed doctrine of male-only transmission of the sin nature as held by some evangelical Christians apparently owes its origin to neo-orthodoxy rather than to careful and faithful exegesis of God's Word. Robert Gromacki explains:

> Karl Barth, the European existential theologian, in his *Credo* claimed that the "sin-inheritance" came through the male parent only. Some evangelicals have also accepted this position, but it doesn't really solve the problem of Mary's relationship to Jesus. Whatever Mary conceived, naturally or supernaturally, would bear her likeness. This would include not only her humanity but also her sinful nature. The relationship of physical characteristics and mental capacities between parent and child is reflected in the transmission of genes and chromosomes, both dominant and recessive. However, the sin nature is not contained within a gene or a chromosome. A child will not be a murderer just because his parents were. The sin nature involves a moral and spiritual transmission, not a material sequence. In such a transmission, only one parent is needed, but of course, apart from Christ's virgin conception, both parents have always been involved. It is too arbitrary to attribute His sinless humanity to the absence of human male fertilization.[18]

Christ's Genetic Connection to Mary

In addition to the erroneous assumption that a "virgin birth" (rather than an immaculate, divine "conception") was necessary to prevent Joseph's sin nature from being transmitted to Christ, some have held to a similar problematic perspective with respect to Mary. Some have gone so far as

---

[17] Ryrie, *Basic Theology*, 219.

[18] Gromacki, *The Virgin Birth*, 119.

to claim that Christ had to be genetically unrelated to Mary, in addition to Joseph, in order to remain untainted by human sin.[19] This view holds that Christ's body was actually a heavenly creation implanted into Mary's womb. It involved no egg, no genetic contribution from Mary, and thus no genetic connection to Mary, even though Christ's body was still physically dependent upon Mary for its nourishment and development. While this interpretation protects the truth of Christ's deity and sinlessness, it does so at too great an expense—sacrificing the truth of Christ's genuine humanity. If Mary was only a surrogate and did not contribute genetically in any way toward the humanity of Christ, then He was genealogically and genetically unrelated to the rest of humanity and unqualified to be our great Kinsman-Redeemer.

However, certain passages of Scripture testify that Jesus Christ was a biological descendant of David through Abraham, all the way back to Adam and Eve (Gen. 3:15; 12:3; Deut. 18:15-19; 2 Sam. 7:12; Acts 2:29-30; Gal. 3:8, 16). The Lord Jesus Christ, not merely Mary, was *"of the seed (spermatos) of David, according to the flesh"* (Rom. 1:3; 2 Tim. 2:8). He *"shared in the same"* humanity as us (Heb. 2:14), and *"in all things"* He was *"made like His brethren"* (Heb. 2:17a), with the exception of sin (Heb. 4:15), so *"that He might be a merciful and faithful High Priest in things pertaining to God, to make propitiation for the sins of the people"* (Heb. 2:17b). He is part of Adam's race as the Son of Man (Luke 3:23-38). Adam was called a "son of God" in Luke's genealogy (Luke 3:38) in order to show that he was preceded by no human parents. Adam was, in fact, the immediate creation of God. He was a man, but not a *"son of* man." In a similar vein, if Mary contributed nothing genetically to Christ and His humanity was also a distinct, immediate creation from God, then in what sense could Christ be properly called the *"Son of* Man"?

If Christ was genetically unrelated to Mary, and Adam, and the rest of the human race, He would have represented an entirely new line of human existence, being separate from us and unrelated to us, and thus unfit to die an atoning death in our place. He would, in fact, be an *alien* to the human race. But the wonder of the gospel is that He became one of us (except for sin), in order to die as our substitute and thereby redeem us and rescue us from our sin and its lethal consequences. As a result, the Lord Jesus is now the Head of the Church and the Head of a new redeemed humanity as *"the last Adam"* (1 Cor. 15:20-22, 45). Though the no-genetic-connection view of the virgin birth seeks to honor Christ's sinlessness and deity, it goes too far and ends up contradicting Scripture. It also errs by making the "virgin birth" the means of Christ's sinless incarnation.

---

[19] This view was held early in Church history by Gnostic leader Valentinus, and it resurfaced around the time of the Reformation, being held by some Dutch Anabaptists, as well as Menno Simons, founder of the Mennonites. See Chafer, *Systematic Theology*, 1:387-88; Timothy George, *Theology of the Reformers* (Nashville: Broadman Press, 1988), 281-85.

Christ's Incarnation, Deity, and the Virgin Birth

Having seen that a "virgin birth" was technically not necessary to secure the sinlessness of Christ, another critical question surrounding the doctrine of Christ's birth must be considered. Was a "virgin birth" the very means by which God united Christ's two natures in one person at the incarnation? Many evangelical and fundamental Christians assume so. However, the incarnation of the Son of God and the union of His deity with His humanity in one person actually took place as a result of His immaculate, divine conception, in distinction to a "virgin birth."[20]

Imagine for a moment there were two human parents (Joseph and Mary) for the humanity of Jesus but that God chose to supernaturally intervene in the process of conception in order to provide a sanctified, sinless conception and to prevent the transmission of a sin nature from either parent. If this is all that God did, the result would still be a *strictly human* (though sinless) child—a child with only a human nature, not two natures (one human and one divine).[21] The result of such a miraculous conception would only be a sinless human being, akin to Adam in his pre-Fall state. Though an immaculate conception was necessary for Christ's human nature to be conceived without inheriting a sin nature, the incarnation and hypostatic union of Christ required an additional simultaneous act by God. They required the miraculous overshadowing power and ministry of the Holy Spirit (Matt. 1:18, 20; Luke 1:35). By this, the human nature of Christ as the Son of Mary was miraculously and mysteriously joined to His deity as the Son of the Highest, so that He became one person with two natures from that point forever.

Strictly speaking, for Christ to have two natures in one person didn't require a "virgin birth." Mary theoretically could have had other children before the Lord Jesus and as a non-virgin later received from God both an *immaculate conception* and a *miraculous, paternal fertilization* completely apart from Joseph. The result would then have been a Son with both a sinless human nature and a divine nature—the unique, theanthropic person of our Savior and Redeemer. Mary did not need to be a *virgin*, technically and biblically speaking, in order for Christ's humanity to be produced by God and protected from sin at the time of conception. Her virginity, even up to the time of her delivery, served as a "sign" showing that Joseph had no part in the conception and that this magnificent miracle was wrought only by God. The "virgin birth" therefore was not the *means* of Christ's incarnation; it was the *sign* of it. The means of Christ's incarnation was the mysterious and miraculous overshadowing work of the Holy Spirit (Matt.

---

[20] Of course, semantically, most conservative theologians use the term "virgin birth" to speak of the virgin conception. This problem will be addressed later in the chapter.

[21] Gromacki, *The Virgin Birth*, 120.

1:18, 20; Luke 1:35) at the very moment of Christ's *conception* in the virgin's womb. Of course, this is what many evangelicals mean by "virgin birth," but this must be properly distinguished from a divine conception.

Not only did the sign of the virgin birth clearly reveal that a unique miracle had taken place, it also indicated the identity of the Child who was to be born. It signified that He was in fact "Immanuel"—none other than God-incarnate. The result of such a uniquely miraculous conception was a Child who was historically unique in the most magnificent way, being both fully God and fully human. This was also clearly predicted in the Old Testament passages relating to the Savior's birth (Gen. 3:15; Isa. 7:14; 9:6-7; Micah 5:2).

In Genesis 3:15, the humanity of the coming Redeemer is evident from the fact that He was to be of the "seed" of Eve. Yet, His deity is strongly implied by the magnitude of His redemptive task. Eve's future Son was to deal a crushing death-blow to Satan, who was originally the highest ranking angel and at that time the most powerful figure in the universe apart from God Himself. Surely, it would take more than a man or any other angel to defeat Satan and deliver fallen humanity from the bondage of sin—it would take the God-man. In Isaiah 7:14, the very fact that a virgin was to "bear a son" speaks of Christ's humanity, as women only give birth to humans. In addition, this Son was to be none other than Immanuel, "God with us"—"*with us* in the deeper sense of these words, which is, that He has become *one of us*."[22] The prophecy of Isaiah 9:6 also stated that a child would be born (referring to His humanity) and that a son would be given (an allusion to the incarnation? cf. John 3:16). Isaiah 9:6 continues to prophesy that this same child would be *"the mighty God, the everlasting Father, the Prince of peace."* Does this not set forth a divine-human Messiah? Finally, the prophecy of the Messiah's birth (Matt. 2:1-6) in Micah 5:2 depicts a divine-human Savior. Regarding this passage, Lewis Sperry Chafer observed, "One is seen to come to a geographical location on earth—Bethlehem—, which is a human identification, yet His goings forth are from everlasting."[23]

Based on the light of Old Testament revelation, the deity and humanity of the Messiah would have been a most reasonable expectation for any righteous person living in Israel at the time of Jesus Christ's birth. It is no coincidence therefore to see both the deity and humanity of Christ depicted in Luke 1:31-35, where the angel Gabriel announced to Mary the divine conception of Christ. There we see that the very person of Christ as God's incarnate Son was made manifest by the fact that He was conceived by the power of God alone.

---

[22] Chafer, *Systematic Theology,* 1:351.

[23] Ibid., 1:352.

<u>Luke 1:31-35</u>

31 *"And behold, you will conceive in your womb and bring forth a Son, and shall call His name JESUS.*
32 *"He will be great, and will be called the Son of the Highest; and the Lord God will give Him the throne of His father David.*
33 *"And He will reign over the house of Jacob forever, and of His kingdom there will be no end."*
34 *Then Mary said to the angel, "How can this be, since I do not know a man"?*
35 *And the angel answered and said to her, "The Holy Spirit will come upon you, and the power of the Highest will overshadow you; therefore, also, that Holy One who is to be born will be called the Son of God.*

In Luke 1:31, we see that the angel Gabriel announces to Mary that she is to conceive a Son named "Jesus." This was to be no ordinary son, for in verses 32-33, He was predicted to be Israel's king who would rule for eternity. But more than that, as to His very nature, He was to "be called the Son of the Highest" (v. 32). In verse 34, Mary does not doubt Gabriel's announcement but is thinking in physical terms and simply cannot comprehend *how* this is physically possible since she is a virgin. In response to her perplexity, Gabriel explains to her in verse 35 that this will be a supernatural, divine conception, with God "the Holy Spirit" and the power of "the Highest" overshadowing her, so that the result of this conception will be a "Holy" Child, who "will be called the Son of God." The angel reveals to Mary that *God* would provide the paternity for the conception of her Son, not a man. It is important in this regard to note that the angel Gabriel never refers to Mary's child as "the son of Joseph."

It seems evident from this passage that the existence of Christ as both God and man in one person occurred at this very moment, and that the miraculous, virgin conception of Christ was the divine means as well as moment of His incarnation. In this respect, the virgin birth truly signified Christ's deity. This is evidenced by several factors. First, in Gabriel's explanation in Luke 1:35 he connected the identity of the One overshadowing Mary with the One resulting from the conception. The inferential conjunction, "therefore" (*dio*), and the coordinating conjunction, "also" (*kai*), reveals this cause and effect relationship. The One who produces the conception is God Almighty, referred to unmistakably in verse 35 as *"the Highest"* (*hupsistos*). The offspring of such paternity is therefore "the Son of *the Highest* (*hupsistos*)" (v. 32), "the Son *of God*" (v. 35).

This does not mean that Christ's deity was created at this moment of conception, only that His humanity was conceived by God's supernatural power in an immaculate conception with Mary's ovum, resulting in the incarnation and the hypostatic union of His two natures in one person. Christ had only a divine nature as the eternal Son of God prior to this conception, so that His deity had no origin as His humanity did here. Therefore, His divine nature could not have been produced in this event.

Consistent with this is the testimony of Gabriel that Mary's Son was to "be called" the Son of God, not that He would "become" the Son of God as a result of the virgin conception.

A second reason why the existence of Christ as both God and man in one person is signified by this divine, miraculous conception is the fact that Christ was to "be called (*kaleō*) the Son of God" (v. 35). This directly corresponds with the original prophecy of Isaiah 7:14 where the Son of the virgin was to be called (LXX, *kaleō*) "Immanuel," meaning "God with us." This is an unmistakable reference to Christ's deity.[24] Some may object to this conclusion by claiming that when Joseph and Mary were instructed to name Christ (Matt. 1:25; Luke 2:21), they were not actually told to name Him "Immanuel" but "Jesus." Therefore, some would claim that we should interpret the "Immanuel" prediction of Isaiah 7:14 non-literally, as indicating only God's beneficent, providential visitation of His people through His general omnipresence all represented by a virgin-born child, not that the child himself would be literally "God with us." Such an interpretation is unfounded however, since Christ was called by Gabriel "the Son of God" and "the Son of the Highest," both clear references to His deity.[25]

---

[24] Joseph A. Alexander, *Commentary on Isaiah* (Grand Rapids: Kregel, 1992), 1:168, 173; F. Delitzsch, "*Isaiah*" in *Commentary on the Old Testament* by C. F. Keil and F. Delitzsch, trans. James Martin (Peabody, MA: Hendrickson, 1996), 7:142-43; Hindson, *Isaiah's Immanuel*, 62-63; S. Lewis Johnson, "The Genesis of Jesus," *BSac* 122 (October 1965): 338; Alfred Martin and John A. Martin, *Isaiah: The Glory of the Messiah* (Chicago: Moody Press, 1983), 57; J. Alec Motyer, *The Prophecy of Isaiah* (Downers Grove, IL: InterVarsity Press, 1993), 86; Peter A. Steveson, *A Commentary on Isaiah* (Greenville, SC: Bob Jones University Press, 2003), 66; Merrill F. Unger, *Unger's Commentary on the Old Testament* (Chattanooga, TN: AMG Publishers, 2002), 1162; Edward J. Young, *The Book of Isaiah* (Grand Rapids: Eerdmans, 1965; reprinted, 1981), 1:289-91.

[25] I must strenuously object to the opinions of some, such as Lucan commentator, Darrell Bock, who believes that the phrase "Son of God" in Luke 1:35 is merely in reference to Jesus' regal, Davidic role as the Messiah, not to His divine nature. See Darrell L. Bock, *Luke, Vol. 1: 1:1-9:50*, BECNT (Grand Rapids: Baker Book House, 1994), 123-25. Citing a parallel usage of "birth from God" terminology in the Qumran literature, Bock believes that this merely "describes a nondivine child who is born with a special kinship to God through an anointing by God's Spirit. Thus, in contemporary Judaism, the phrase could describe a person, without necessarily requiring ontological overtones" (ibid., 124). He continues, "The presence of a divine element in Jesus' birth does not require or focus upon an *explicit* statement of Jesus' metaphysical divinity" (ibid.). Bock concludes regarding Gabriel's "Son of God" explanation to Mary in Luke 1:35 that "she certainly is not portrayed as perceiving an announcement of a divine child here" (ibid., 125). In response to Bock's assertions, it should be observed that within Luke 1 there was indeed a true "birth from God" parallel to the Qumran citation. Luke 1:13-15 and 1:36-37 indicate that the conception of John the Baptist in Elizabeth's womb was definitely a "birth from God." This provides the more suitable parallel to the Qumran citation since John the Baptist, not the Lord Jesus, was "a nondivine child who is born with a special kinship to God through an anointing by God's Spirit." As great as John the Baptist was he is still set in stark contrast to the infinitely greater Son who is introduced in the very next section of Luke 1:26-35. According to Luke, we are told that John was to serve this "Son of the Highest" as His forerunner and prophet (Luke 1:76). Even

Even the name "Jesus," which means "Yahweh saves," was an indication of His true identity as "Yahweh" who "saves" (Matt. 1:21). This salvation was not the kind that a merely human, Old Testament deliverer or judge would provide for the nation of Israel, such as a physical, temporal deliverance from their enemies. It was to be a spiritual salvation *"from their sins"* (Matt. 1:21). To be identified as Israel's "Savior" in this sense was nothing short of an ascription of deity. Furthermore, the angelic pronouncement to Joseph in Matthew 1:21 declared that Jesus would save "His people" from their sins. This is most likely not saying that Israel was "His people" merely in the associational sense that Christ was part of them as a nation; rather it is teaching that Israel belonged to Jesus Christ in a possessive sense. The Lord (Yahweh) declared hundreds of times throughout the Old Testament that Israel was His possession and His people. No mere man, including the greatest man born of woman before Christ (i.e., John the Baptist, Matt. 11:11), could rightly say that Israel was "His people" in this sense. All of this points to the deity of the Lord Jesus at His birth.

These details of Matthew 1:21 also explain why Matthew 1:22-23 goes on to say, *"So all this was done that it might be fulfilled which was spoken by the Lord through the prophet, saying: 23 'Behold, the virgin shall be with child, and bear a Son, and they shall call His name Immanuel,' which is translated, 'God with us.'"* When Matthew writes that *"all this was done"* in fulfillment of Isaiah 7:14, the *"all"* of verse 22 refers back to the previous verse of Matthew 1:21 where the angel instructed Joseph to give Christ the name of "Jesus." The name of "Jesus" in Matthew 1:21 is thereby connected with the name "Immanuel" in Matthew 1:23. The "Yahweh who saves" is the "God who is with us."

All of this reveals that Christ's *virgin birth* demonstrated His deity and humanity in one unique person, while the *divine, miraculous conception*

---

though John's birth is also a "birth from God" in Luke 1, he is never described in Luke 1 in the superlative manner which Christ is, as "Son of God" and "Son of the Highest" and "Holy One" and "Lord." Though the Spirit of God was supernaturally involved in both John's birth and Christ's birth, the contrasting descriptions of the two point to the deity of the latter and the mere humanity of the former. As to Bock's claim that Mary did not perceive Gabriel to be announcing a divine child to her, this is also not supported by the context of Luke 1. In the immediately following section of Mary's visitation of Elizabeth, *both* women express belief that Jesus was "the Lord" (1:43-46). In Luke 1:43, Elizabeth calls the babe in Mary's womb "my Lord." Only two verses later, in Luke 1:45, when referring to the One who sent Gabriel, Elizabeth speaks unmistakably about God as "the Lord." Immediately in the next verse, Mary herself magnifies "the Lord" (1:46), whom she then describes as "God my Savior" (1:47). In Luke 1:43-46, there is no syntactical break that would indicate 2 different "Lords"—one a "nondivine child" and the other the "Lord" God Almighty. In addition, Mary exclaims in Luke 1:49, "holy is His name." This parallels the announcement to Mary by Gabriel that her child would be the "Holy One" (1:35). Though Mary probably did not comprehend the metaphysical complexities of the incarnation and hypostatic union at this time, she certainly does appear to have perceived the divine nature of the Son announced to her by Gabriel.

of Christ was the means by which God produced the sinless humanity, incarnation, and hypostatic union of His Son. Other grace-oriented theologians are in general agreement with this doctrinal conclusion. For example, Robert Lightner writes:

> The virgin birth settles the question of whether we have a natural or supernatural Christ. By means of the virgin birth God the Father united the divine nature with the human nature in one perfect, sinless, divine Person. Because of this Christ qualified to be the sinbearer.[26]

The late theologian John Walvoord also wrote:

> The whole tenor of Scripture as presented in both the Old Testament prophecies that He was to be God and Man and the New Testament fulfillment makes the virgin birth a divine explanation, insofar as it can be explained, of an otherwise insuperable problem. How could One who was both God and Man have perfectly human parents? The account of the virgin birth therefore, instead of being an unreasonable invention, becomes a fitting explanation of how in the supernatural power of God the incarnation was made a reality.[27]

Virtually all conservative theologians agree that Christ's divine conception in the Virgin Mary's womb was both the means and occasion of His incarnation.[28] This is the clear teaching of Scripture based strictly upon virgin conception/birth passages. It is a conspicuous fact that all biblical passages relating to Christ's conception and birth also emphasize His deity

---

[26] Robert P. Lightner, *Sin, the Savior, and Salvation: The Theology of Everlasting Life* (Nashville: Thomas Nelson Publishers, 1991), 59. By stating that the "virgin birth" was the means of Christ's incarnation, Lightner is speaking broadly and inclusively of Christ's conception as well, for he later adds, "The virgin birth encompasses both a virgin conception and Jesus' natural and normal delivery, like any other baby, but from his still virgin mother" (ibid., 62).

[27] John F. Walvoord, *Jesus Christ Our Lord* (Chicago: Moody Press, 1969), 104.

[28] This is not to say that virtually all conservative theologians claim that the virgin birth/conception of Christ was the *only possible* means, or even the *necessary* means, of Christ's incarnation. But virtually all conservatives will admit to the *prima facie* reading of Scripture that Christ's divine conception in the virgin's womb was the means God used historically to bring about the incarnation. See Louis Berkhof, *Systematic Theology* (Grand Rapids: Eerdmans, reprinted 1991), 334-35; James Montgomery Boice, *Foundations of the Christian Faith*, rev. ed. (Downers Grove, IL: InterVarsity Press, 1986), 556; James Oliver Buswell, *A Systematic Theology of the Christian Religion* (Grand Rapids: Zondervan, 1962), 2:40-41; Chafer, *Systematic Theology*, 1:354; Enns, *The Moody Handbook of Theology*, 222; Wayne Grudem, *Systematic Theology* (Grand Rapids: Zondervan, 1994), 530; Paul S. Karleen, *The Handbook to Bible Study: With a Guide to the Scofield Study System* (New York: Oxford University Press, 1987), 215; Robert P. Lightner, *Handbook of Evangelical Theology* (Grand Rapids: Kregel Publications, 1995), 78-79; Ryrie, *Basic Theology*, 242; Henry C. Thiessen, *Lectures in Systematic Theology*, revised by Vernon D. Doerksen (Grand Rapids: Eerdmans, 1979), 220; W. H. Griffith Thomas, *The Principles of Theology: An Introduction to the Thirty-Nine Articles* (London: Vine Books, 1978), 48.

in addition to His humanity (Isa. 7:14; 9:6-7; Micah 5:2; Matt. 1:18-25; Luke 1:31-35). What does this indicate if not that Christ's deity and humanity, united together at the incarnation, are revealed by the unique and miraculous manner of His conception and birth? This conclusion is supported further by the additional consideration that, throughout the Bible, there are several recorded examples of miraculous births wrought by God's supernatural intervention (Gen. 21:1-3; 25:21-23; 29:31; Judg. 13:6-8; 1 Sam. 1:1-20; Luke 1:13-17), but there is only one with an immaculate, virginal conception wrought solely by the agency of God. To this, we must pause for a moment to reflect and ask, why the distinct contrast? Clearly, God is trying to tell us that the type of conception experienced by the Lord Jesus was the sign of, as well as the means used to produce, the incarnation of His only beloved Son.

Divine Conception, Virgin Birth, & the Contents of Saving Faith

Though the means of Christ's incarnation was indeed the miraculous, divine conception in the womb of the Virgin Mary, does this fact, by itself, make belief in the virgin birth a requirement for eternal life? Does this necessarily require the lost to have knowledge of, comprehend, and believe in, Christ's virgin birth before they can believe in Him as God's sinless, incarnate Son who died as a substitute for their sins and rose again? While the biblical answer to this question is ultimately, "No," it will take some careful thinking to understand the reasons why.

The first reason why belief in the "virgin birth" of Christ is not a requirement for eternal life is because Mary's *virginity* at the time of Christ's conception and birth did not have a *direct* bearing upon His sinless incarnation. We must first clarify our terminology in order to distinguish what *is* essential from what is *not* essential. Technically, a *virgin birth* was not essential to provide the grounds of our eternal salvation. Nor was Mary's virginity at the time of Christ's conception necessary in order for God the Holy Spirit to supernaturally and miraculously produce the conception and incarnation of Christ in her womb. As was explained previously, Mary's virginity simply made it possible for Christ's birth to function as a "sign." What was essential in order for the incarnation and hypostatic union to occur at the moment of conception was the miraculous overshadowing ministry of the Holy Spirit. Somehow, God alone, supernaturally and miraculously, provided the paternity for Christ's humanity and then joined His humanity and deity together, inseparably in one person at the moment of conception and incarnation.

Therefore, the virgin birth itself, in distinction to Christ's conception, was a *sign* of the Savior's incarnation, not the actual means of procuring it. The means of procuring Christ's incarnation, however, was His miraculous, divine conception. A failure to recognize this distinction has led some evangelicals to speak of belief in the *virgin birth itself* as a requirement for eternal life, rather than belief in *Christ Himself* as the sinless, incarnate Savior, who is both the Son of God and Son of Man. This also leads, logically, to the fallacy that the virgin birth is an essential element of the gospel of our salvation, which Scripture nowhere teaches.

Much of this confusion in evangelical and fundamental circles is simply due to our imprecise terminology. Most often the label "virgin birth" serves as a doctrinal umbrella or theological shorthand for all the events involved in our Lord's earthly, human origin, from the Holy Spirit's overshadowing work at Christ's incarnation to the Savior's actual birth in Bethlehem. This is understandably convenient since it is less cumbersome to say "virgin birth" than to always provide the abstract qualification that Christ's sinlessness was not directly dependent upon Mary's status as a virgin either at the time of conception or birth. However, it is doubtful that the traditional phrase "virgin birth" will be replaced any time soon since it has become the established evangelical nomenclature for this doctrine. Furthermore, there is hardly a more precise, all-encompassing, yet concise expression on hand. To speak of the "divine conception" of Christ says nothing about His actual birth or the very important status of Mary's virginity. To speak of the "immaculate conception" still focuses solely on Christ's conception versus His birth; and it indicates nothing of Mary's virginity, to say nothing of its associations with Roman Catholic Mariolatry. For now, it seems easiest just to stick with the traditional phrase "virgin birth." But such convenience and custom will come at a price. We will continue to sacrifice scriptural accuracy, theological clarity, and practical comprehension, as confusion will persist about what is essential versus non-essential for eternal salvation, both for the grounds of redemption and for the necessary contents of faith.

The Means of the Virgin Birth & the Grounds of Salvation

A second reason why the virgin conception and birth of Christ are not essential to believe in order to receive eternal life is because they were not necessarily the grounds of Christ being the incarnate Savior of man, even though they were the means God employed. A critical distinction must be made at this juncture between divine *means* and divine *grounds* of redemption. Simply because something was the means God used to bring about salvation does not automatically make it the grounds of our salvation. While it is true that the virgin conception of Christ was the very means God employed to bring about the incarnation, can we really say that the virgin conception forms the necessary grounds of our salvation? For, if the virgin conception of Christ also formed the grounds of our redemption, then should it not also be included in the contents of saving faith? And should not the virgin conception also be included as an essential element of the gospel? There is much at stake by a failure to distinguish means from grounds.

Distinguishing Means from Grounds

All means are not grounds. This is demonstrable by considering Christ's death and resurrection. When it came to the means of Christ's substitutionary death for our sins, God the Father's plan entailed His Son undergoing a Roman crucifixion, at Calvary in Jerusalem, between 9 a.m. and 3 p.m., on the Passover, at the hands of both the Jews and the Romans (Acts 2:23). These were all the means God sovereignly ordained and employed to provide for our redemption, but were they *necessary* means? Could Christ have conceivably and theoretically died any other way and still provided the redemption price for our sins? Certainly! While it may have been absolutely necessary that He die through these means in order to fulfill many Old Testament prophecies and typology and for the very Word of God to be upheld, would the price of our sin not have been fully paid if He hung on the cross from 10 a.m. to 4 p.m.? Would there be no propitiation for our sins if Christ laid on the altar in the Temple and been voluntarily slain, instead of being nailed voluntarily (John 10:17-18) to a Roman crucifix at Golgotha? Would there be no redemption if He died on an upright stake or pole, instead of a cross, as Jehovah's Witnesses contend? Though all of the events that transpired in the death of Christ were divinely ordained according to the perfect will of God, and they were not merely the choices of men, what was necessary and essential in order to provide the grounds of our salvation was that He actually died for our sins, *"for the wages of sin is death"* (Rom. 6:23).

The same can also be said when it comes to the Lord's resurrection. Though God prophetically and typologically ordained that Christ should be in the tomb for *"three days and three nights"* (Jonah 1:17; Matt. 12:40; 26:61; 27:40, 63), would the grounds of our eternal redemption really be removed if Christ had risen on the fourth day, or the fifth, or the sixth, instead of the third day? Did it matter in providing the very basis for eternal salvation that He rose before sunrise on the first day of the week? Or could He have risen on the second day of the week? It mattered only that His once crucified body actually did rise gloriously from the dead. From the circumstantial details surrounding the crucifixion and resurrection of Christ, we see the crucial distinction that the divine *means* of eternal life are not necessarily the *grounds* for eternal life.

It is noteworthy that Christ's deity (Mark 2:5-12; Luke 7:48-49; John 5:18-29), humanity (Gal. 4:4-5; Heb. 2:9; 10:10), death for sin (Rom. 4:25; Heb. 9:22), and resurrection (Rom. 4:25; 1 Cor. 15:13-18) are all explicitly stated in Scripture to be essential as the very grounds of our salvation. Yet conspicuously by contrast, Scripture nowhere indicates the same for the virgin birth or conception, either explicitly or by implication and deduction. Why this difference? The virgin *birth* was surely God's means of providing the "sign" of Christ's uniqueness and greatness as the Son of

God and eternal Son of David. Likewise, the virgin *conception* was surely the means of Christ's incarnation; but does this necessarily make it the grounds of our redemption? What is essential as the basis of our entire salvation, and as the content of saving faith, is the *fact* of Christ's incarnation as the Son of God, not the particular *means* by which God chose to accomplish it.

At this point, I can already hear the objections of some. They will say, "But some means are also *necessary* means!" Is it really true that there was only one method or means by which God could have accomplished the incarnation? Some evangelicals and fundamentalists, like Robert Gromacki, affirm this to be so:

> If Jesus had been born through natural generation, He would have died like all mortals, but His death would not have had an infinite, eternal redemptive value. There *had to be* the incarnation of God the Son *through the virgin conception* to bring together into one person the two features necessary for redemption: human mortality and divine value.[29]

We should all agree with Gromacki on his initial point. Had Christ's conception and generation been merely "natural," the incarnation of the Son of God could not have taken place and Jesus would have died like all other men, and there would be no grounds for our salvation. But does it necessarily follow that the virgin conception and birth of Christ were the *only* conceivable means by which God could have achieved Christ's incarnation? Again, Gromacki believes so:

> To provide redemption for man from the penalty, power, and presence of sin, God the Son had to be virgin born to acquire a true humanity. *No other method* of incarnation would have secured the needed mediator and example.[30]

This affirmation seems to go one step too far; and it is a critical step that we should not take lest we cross the biblical line. We must be careful not to claim what Scripture doesn't claim regarding the virgin birth and conception. This is why J. Gresham Machen in the last century stated regarding the means that God *may have* chosen to accomplish the incarnation: "We may not, indeed, set limits to the power of God; we cannot say what God might or might not have done."[31] Machen's qualification holds true even if a virgin conception and birth is the only way in which *we* can conceive

---

[29] Gromacki, *The Virgin Birth,* 134 (italics added).

[30] Ibid., 135 (italics added). Besides using the terminology of "method," Gromacki also speaks of exclusive "means," saying, "There was only one means that could properly provide the channel for His incarnation: THE VIRGIN BIRTH" (ibid., 68, capitalization original).

[31] J. Gresham Machen, *The Virgin Birth of Christ* (New York: Harper & Brothers, 1930), 395.

of God accomplishing the incarnation. It is for this very reason that other evangelical theologians are careful not to overstate the implications of the virgin birth by dogmatizing about what God *had to do*.[32] For example, Wayne Grudem, after affirming that the virgin conception (and birth) of Christ was indeed the means God used to accomplish the incarnation, goes on to clarify:

> This is not to say that it would have been *impossible* for God to bring Christ into the world in any other way, but only to say that God, in his wisdom, decided that this would be the best way to bring it about, and part of that is evident in the fact that the virgin birth does help us understand how Jesus can be fully God and fully man. Whether any other means of bringing Christ into the world would have been "possible" in some absolute sense of "possible," Scripture does not tell us.[33]

This is scripturally sound and balanced. Certainly, the way God accomplished Christ's incarnation through the virgin conception and birth was the *best* way, for God can do no less; but was it the *only possible* way He could have done it? To answer this crucial question, it will be helpful for a moment to ponder several alternative possible means, not out of irreverence or doubt about God's Word but only due to the necessity and gravity of the question before us.

Conceivable Means That Do Not Alter Redemption

First, as to the *location* of Christ's birth, we should all readily agree that the fact of the incarnation would not have been jeopardized had Christ been born in some town other than Bethlehem. Inspired prophecy would have gone unfulfilled (Micah 5:2), God forbid; but this would have had no direct bearing on the fact of the incarnation. Nevertheless, a virgin birth in Bethlehem was one means God chose in bringing His Son into the world.

Secondly, as has been noted several times previously, the *virginity* of Mary did not have direct bearing on whether Christ would be sinlessly incarnate or not. It was the overshadowing ministry of the Holy Spirit that sanctified the humanity of Christ, not Mary's virgin status. Nevertheless, the means God chose to bring Christ into the world was through a virgin.

---

[32] Millard J. Erickson, *Christian Theology*, 1 vol. edit. (Grand Rapids: Baker Book House, 1983-85), 754-55; John M. Frame, "Virgin Birth of Jesus," in *The Evangelical Dictionary of Theology*, ed. Walter A. Elwell (Grand Rapids: Baker Book House, 1984), 1145; Lane, "The Rationale and Significance of the Virgin Birth," 52; Walter R. Martin, *Essential Christianity: A Handbook of Basic Christian Doctrines* (Santa Ana, CA: Vision House, Revised 1980), 46n; W. H. Griffith Thomas, *The Principles of Theology: An Introduction to the Thirty-Nine Articles* (London: Vine Books, 1978), 48-49.

[33] Wayne Grudem, *Systematic Theology* (Grand Rapids: Zondervan, 1994), 530n.

Thirdly, as to the *maternity* for Christ's humanity, did the Lord Jesus have to be born only through Mary in order to become incarnate and be the Savior of the world? Certainly, for Christ to be genetically related to a woman of Judah and of Davidic lineage in particular was necessary to prophetically and covenantally fulfill the Word of God; but were Mary's genes, in particular, absolutely necessary in order to provide the basis of redemption? For that matter, what if Mary had never been born? The existence of Mary was surely not the grounds of our eternal salvation, much to the chagrin of many Roman Catholics who hold her to be Co-Redemptrix and Co-Mediatrix of all graces.[34] Though Christ's conception through Mary in particular did not provide the basis of our eternal redemption, it was still the means God chose to employ in accomplishing the incarnation.

There is a fourth ontological possibility that must also be considered at this point; and as peculiar as it may initially seem, it is only proposed here to test the limits of the crucial distinction between divine means of redemption and the necessary grounds of our redemption. It is not proposed because I seriously regard it to be divinely probable or even acceptable, only that it was theoretically possible. We must ask the question regarding the *gestation* of Christ; did it have to occur inside Mary's womb in particular in order to provide the grounds of our redemption? In other words, could the Holy Spirit have overshadowed Mary and supernaturally extracted her ovum (thus linking Christ genetically to David, Abraham, and Adam) but then had the conception and development of the prenatal Christ occur in some other environment, such as heaven? After all, it might be reasoned by some that this would have been a much safer environment for His human growth and development; and He still would have been truly human; and the incarnation would have occurred just as surely. Furthering this line of thinking, some might even reason that if the Holy Spirit did a supernatural miracle at the moment of Christ's conception in order to produce His incarnation and sinless humanity, then why would a gestational miracle be impermissible, even though such a miracle would last a much longer period of time?

As absurd as this scenario may at first appear, it is still a theoretical possibility; and it is suggested only to test the limits of what is possible versus essential.[35] Of course, had the Lord chosen this as the means

---

[34] *Catechism of the Catholic Church*, English translation, Libreria Editrice Vaticana (Bloomingdale, OH: Apostolate for Family Consecration, 1994), 252-53.

[35] Galatians 4:4-5 does not necessarily contradict this possibility. Though our modern English versions say, *"God sent forth His Son, born of a woman, born under the law, to redeem those who were under the law,"* the KJV has *"made of a woman."* The Greek word for "made" or "born" here is the participle *genomenon*, from the verb *ginomai*. This term does not inherently mean the gestation and delivery of a baby. Other Greek phrases and terms convey specifically the state of being pregnant (Matt. 1:18, *heurethē en gastri*), childbearing (1 Tim. 2:15, *teknogonias*), and the actual birth or delivery of a baby (Gal. 4:24, *gennaō*; Rev. 12:2, 4,

of accomplishing the incarnation, how could we be sure Christ was truly human? If the incarnate Christ came into the world under such an arrangement—at 9 months or childhood or even adulthood—the world would have much greater difficulty accepting His genuine humanity, which would not have been as readily apparent. So, even though Christ's gestation in Mary's womb was not essential in providing the grounds of redemption, it was still the means God chose to accomplish Christ's incarnation.

Fifthly, as to the *paternity* for the Lord Jesus' humanity, it is not clearly revealed in Scripture what means God used. We know scientifically and genetically that humans and most mammals have their offspring's gender determined by the presence or absence of the male Y chromosome. In human reproduction, the presence of the SRY gene on the Y chromosome leads to a male gender, while its absence leads to a female gender. As a result, human males are heterogametic, having two distinct sex chromosomes (XY), while females are homogametic, having two of the same kind of sex chromosome (XX).

Theologically, this leads us to wonder where and how Christ received His male, Y chromosome. Did the Holy Spirit create an entirely new Y chromosome by divine fiat in order for the incarnation to occur? While we might believe this is inferred by Mary's question and Gabriel's answer in Luke 1:34-35, we must also admit that this passage does not reveal the method God used to create the humanity of Christ. Thus, theologian Charles Ryrie concludes regarding Gabriel's explanation to Mary in Luke 1:35, "The statement emphasizes more the fact of divine generation of the Child, than the method."[36]

---

tiktō). On the other hand, *ginomai* can refer to creation coming into existence or being (John 1:3), of various circumstances arising or occurring (Mt. 4:37; Luke 9:34), or of a change in nature, condition, or status (Rom. 2:25; Col. 1:23). In fact, *ginomai* is even used specifically of Christ's incarnation in John 1:14 where it says *"the Word became (geneto) flesh and dwelt among us."* It seems best to interpret *ginomai* in Galatians 4:4 to mean that God the Son came into a new state of existence (*genomenon*) being out from (*ek*) a woman, meaning that He partook of genuine humanity at the incarnation. Commenting on the phrase "born of a woman" (*genomenon ek gunaikos*) in Galatians 4:4, A. T. Robertson states: "As all men are and so true humanity, 'coming from a woman.' There is, of course, no direct reference here to the Virgin Birth of Jesus, but his deity had just been affirmed by the words 'his Son' (*ton huion autou*), so that both his deity and humanity are here stated as in Rom. 1:3....The fact of the Virgin Birth agrees perfectly with the language here." A. T. Robertson, *Word Pictures in the New Testament* (Grand Rapids: Baker Book House, n.d.), 4:301 (ellipsis added). Many other scholars are in agreement with Robertson. See Henry Alford, *The Greek Testament* (Chicago: Moody Press, 1958), 3:40; Ernest De Witt Burton, *A Critical and Exegetical Commentary on the Epistle to the Galatians*, ICC (Edinburgh: T & T Clark, reprinted 1988), 217; J. B. Lightfoot, *St. Paul's Epistle to the Galatians* (Peabody, MA: Hendrickson Publishers, 1993), 168; Frederic Rendall, "The Epistle to the Galatians" in *The Expositor's Greek Testament*, ed. Robertson Nicoll (Grand Rapids: Eerdmans, 1990), 3:176; Marvin R. Vincent, *Vincent's Word Studies in the New Testament* (Peabody, MA: Hendrickson, n.d.), 4:136.

[36] Ryrie, *Basic Theology*, 242.

Besides the possibility of creating an entirely new, male Y chromosome for Christ's humanity, we must also ask why, theoretically, the Holy Spirit could not have used a sanctified, pre-existing SRY gene and Y chromosome from some other male. If this was possible, was it also not possible that the Holy Spirit could have supernaturally overshadowed both Joseph and Mary in the process of conception and sanctified both of their genetic contributions? The result would have been a sinless human being. If God added the simultaneous, miraculous act of joining Christ's deity to His humanity in an incarnation, then why wouldn't this possible means have resulted in the sinless incarnation of Christ? This scenario must also be considered as one possible means for accomplishing the incarnation. Of course, had God done this, Christ's birth could not have served as a "sign" to anyone. It would have appeared to be a natural conception and birth, even though it still would have been truly supernatural. Charles Ryrie also addresses this possible scenario, explaining why the virgin birth was not the "necessary means" for Christ's sinless incarnation:

> What was the purpose of the Virgin Birth? It need not be the necessary means of preserving Christ sinless, since God could have overshadowed two parents so as to protect the baby's sinlessness had He so desired. It served as a sign of the uniqueness of the Person who was born.[37]

Putting aside the whole chromosomal discussion and the manner of Christ's divine paternity, we must admit that the exact means by which the Holy Spirit provided the sinless humanity of Christ is still shrouded in mystery.[38] Thus, Robert Gromacki concludes: "The virgin conception, pregnancy, and birth manifest a sacred, sanctified mystery. No man knows all that happened in that historic moment."[39]

---

[37] Ibid. Theologian Millard Erickson arrives at the same conclusion, explaining the entire matter rather concisely: "And accordingly, it should have been possible for Jesus to have two human parents and to have been fully the God-man nonetheless. To insist that having a human male parent would have excluded the possibility of deity smacks of Apollinarianism, according to which the divine Logos took the place of one of the normal components of human nature (the soul). But Jesus was fully human, including everything that both a male and a female parent would ordinarily contribute. In addition, there was the element of deity. What God did was to supply, by a special creation, both the human component ordinarily contributed by the male (and thus we have the virgin birth) and, in addition, a divine factor (and thus we have the incarnation). The virgin birth requires only that a normal human being was brought into existence without a human male parent. This could have occurred without an incarnation, and there could have been an incarnation without a virgin birth. Some have called the latter concept "instant adoptionism," since presumably the human involved would have existed on his own apart from the addition of the divine nature. The point here, however, is that, with the incarnation occurring at the moment of conception or birth, there would never have been a moment when Jesus was not both fully human and fully divine. In other words, his being both God and man did not depend on the virgin birth." (Erickson, *Christian Theology*, 755).

[38] Chafer, *Systematic Theology*, 1:354.

[39] Gromacki, *The Virgin Birth*, 120.

In fact, there are still *at least* three things unrevealed by Scripture that are a mystery concerning the miracle of Christ's conception and incarnation. First, as has just been discussed, we still do not know how exactly the Holy Spirit provided or supplied the paternity for Christ's humanity. Second, we still do not know *how* the ministry of the Holy Spirit protected Christ's humanity from receiving any taint of Mary's sin at the moment of conception. That it *did* happen we are sure; *how* it happened is a divine mystery. Thirdly, we still do not know how the Holy Spirit united the two natures of Christ into one theanthropic Person at the moment of conception and incarnation. Again, that it *did* happen is a fact; *how* it happened has never been revealed by God. Regarding these great mysteries of Christ's divine conception, we must heed the counsel of Deuteronomy 29:29 which teaches us that *"The secret things belong to the LORD our God, but those things which are revealed belong to us and to our children forever, that we may do all the words of this law."*

If God has not explicitly revealed these matters, how can we insist that the virgin birth was the only means of Christ's incarnation, or the very grounds of our salvation? And how can we then make the virgin birth a requirement to believe for someone's eternal salvation? It appears that what is essential epistemologically for saving faith is not *how* God accomplished the sinless incarnation of Christ but the fact that He *did* it. Though the virgin conception of Christ was certainly the means God chose to bring about the incarnation of His Son, Scripture itself never testifies that the virgin conception was the *necessary* means, or grounds, of the incarnation.

The Incarnation: A Miracle Itself

At this point, someone might still object that belief in the *miracle* of Christ's virgin conception is necessary for salvation since something supernatural must have occurred at Christ's conception in order to accomplish the incarnation. A miracle was required to protect His humanity from inheriting any sin and to unite His two natures in one person. This is true and no one should deny this; but it must also be recognized that this would not have required either a virgin conception or a virgin birth, only the miracle of the incarnation. Though it helps us logically to separate the sinlessness of Christ and His hypostatic union from the incarnation, these most likely entailed only one divine act by the Holy Spirit when the incarnation of Christ began at His conception (Luke 1:35). Since it was not even possible that the deity of the holy Son of God could have become incarnated with a sinful human nature, and since the hypostatic union entailed Christ's deity as the Son of God being joined ("in") to His human nature as the Son of man ("carnate"), we should not think of the incarnation as requiring three separate miracles. When all is said and done, are we not really requiring belief only in the miracle of Christ's incarnation, provided we agree that "incarnation" precludes a sinful Savior and two Christs—one divine and one human? Therefore, it is reasonable and scriptural to conclude that the incarnation of the Son of God is a miracle in itself that must be believed for one's salvation (John 3:13-16). Nor is it inconsistent to admit that belief in a "miracle" is necessary for salvation, since the substitutionary death of Christ for the sins of the world was a supernatural miracle as well, and yet God's Word requires belief in it. Additionally, the resurrection of Christ from the dead was also a stupendous miracle, and yet Scripture requires belief in it for eternal life.

As all of this pertains to the gospel, what is essential for the lost to believe is that Jesus Christ is both the Son of God and Son of Man and is therefore qualified to be our Mediator and Redeemer. It is the fact of the incarnation that we must preach and that the lost must believe, not the means of it. One great fundamentalist voice from the past and a true proponent of salvation by grace alone, W. H. Griffith Thomas, held this conviction as well:

> The preaching of the fact of the Incarnation rather than the mode is the true method of presenting the Gospel; first what Christ is and only then how He came to be what He is. In these considerations of the true perspective of Christian teaching we may rightly explain the silence of St. Paul and St. John. There was no need of the Virgin Birth for evangelistic purposes, but only for the intellectual instruction of Christian people.[40]

The Contents of Saving Faith, the Gospel, & the Virgin Birth

Besides the fact that Mary's virginity did not directly affect Christ's sinless incarnation and that the virgin birth and conception were not the grounds of our redemption, a third major reason why belief in the virgin birth is not essential for eternal life is because it is never stated in Scripture to be part of the gospel. Some crossless gospel proponents, who agree that belief in the virgin birth is not essential to receive eternal life, nevertheless hold that the virgin birth is part of the "gospel" in its "fullest form." For example, Bob Wilkin states:

> The term gospel may be used to describe the plan of salvation in its *fullest form*. We could in proclaiming the gospel mention Jesus' eternality, His leaving His heavenly throne, being born of a virgin, performing miracles which authenticated His message, living a sinless life, dying on the Cross, rising again, and our need to place our trust in Him alone. The term gospel may also be used to describe the plan of salvation in its *barest form*. It is possible to present only the core truth of the gospel: namely, that whoever believes in Jesus Christ has eternal life. That too is the

[40] Thomas, as cited in Orr, *The Virgin Birth of Christ*, 285.

> gospel—albeit the gospel in a nutshell. If, for example, in sharing the gospel we were to fail to mention Jesus' virgin birth, we would not necessarily be failing to explain it clearly. We would, however, necessarily be sharing it less fully.[41]

In spite of Wilkin's assertion that the virgin birth is part of the content of the biblical "gospel," at least in a fuller form, it is conspicuous that there is not even a single instance in Scripture where either the expression "gospel" (*euangelion*) or "preach the gospel" (*euangelizō*) includes the virgin birth. Yet, if the gospel must be believed for one's eternal salvation (Mark 16:15-16; Rom. 1:16; Eph. 1:13; 2 Thess. 1:6-10), and Christ's virgin birth is nowhere included in any of the 132 New Testament occurrences of *euangelion* and *euangelizō*, then we must conclude that it is not necessary to believe for one's eternal salvation. However, we should at least be willing to admit that Christ's virgin birth was "good news" in a general sense to Israel and mankind because of what it signified. But it must also be acknowledged just as readily that the virgin birth is never declared in the Bible to be part of "the gospel," the good news that we preach to the lost for their salvation.

Related to this observation is a fourth and final reason why belief in the virgin birth is not a requirement for eternal life. There simply are *no passages* in the Bible that require belief in the virgin birth for eternal life. It was observed in a previous section under *means versus grounds* that there are no references to Christ's virgin conception and birth being the *grounds* of our salvation. Here we note that there are also no individual passages in the Bible with the *specific requirement* to know about and believe in the virgin birth for eternal life.[42] This is again in marked distinction to the explicit requirements to believe in those doctrines that are part of the gospel and that also form the grounds of our salvation, namely Christ's deity (John 8:24), humanity (1 Tim. 2:4-5), death for sin (1 Cor. 1:17-21), and resurrection (Rom. 10:9-10). Those who would insist on requiring belief in Christ's virgin birth for eternal life cannot do so based on any explicit Scripture references. They must exceed Scripture and use only invalid inferential argumentation to prove their point.

Not only are there no verses in the Bible requiring belief in Christ's virgin birth for eternal salvation, there are surprisingly few passages in the New Testament that even refer to the virgin birth.[43] Even the Gospels

---

[41] Wilkin, "Tough Questions About Saving Faith," 4 (italics added). See also Jeremy D. Myers, "The Gospel is More Than 'Faith Alone in Christ Alone'," *JOTGES* 19 (Autumn 2006): 49, 53.

[42] Charles C. Ryrie, *So Great Salvation: What It Means to Believe in Jesus Christ* (Wheaton, IL: Victor Books, 1989), 119.

[43] This observation should not be misconstrued to imply what many unbelieving critics of the Bible have concluded from this, namely that the virgin birth is not important or even foundational to the Christian faith and can therefore be discarded. Some theological liberals even claim that Mark, John, Paul, and other first century Christians were ignorant of the doctrine of the virgin birth and that it must have evolved as an explanation for the

of Mark and John do not contain any direct references to it.[44] Must we conclude that a person could read the entire Gospel of John, or Mark, and not have adequate information upon which to place their faith in Christ? In fact, if someone reads the entire New Testament, all 260 chapters of it, with the exception of just 2 chapters (Matt. 1; Luke 1), do they still not have adequate information upon which to be saved? If the virgin birth was essential to believe for everlasting life, Scripture would clearly say so. Instead, what we find repeated in all four Gospels and the rest of the New Testament is the deity and humanity of the one person, Jesus Christ, as well as His vicarious death and bodily resurrection and the offer of eternal life by grace through faith in Him alone. If the Holy Scriptures are able and sufficient to lead a person to salvation through faith in Christ (2 Tim. 3:15-16), and yet they do not require belief in the virgin birth for regeneration, what right do we have to require more than God has in His Word? The great virgin birth defender of the last century, J. Gresham Machen, asked a similar question:

> What right have we to say that full knowledge and full conviction [of the virgin birth] are necessary before a man can put his trust in the crucified and risen Lord? What right have we to say that no man can be saved before he has come to full conviction

---

incarnation and deity of Christ. The implication, of course, is that it was a man-made doctrine. (See, for instance, neo-orthodox theologian, Emil Brunner, *Der Mittler: Zur Besinnung über den Christusglauben* [Tübingen: J. Mohr, 1927], 289.) In response to this, it must be firmly asserted that a rejection of the virgin birth is a direct rejection of the authority of God's Word, upon which our entire faith and practice rests.

[44] Some regard the objection of the Jews in John 8:41 to be John's way of indirectly documenting and affirming the virgin birth. There the unbelieving Jews say to Christ, *"We were not born of fornication; we have one Father—God."* By this, the Jews *might have been* insinuating that Mary was not a virgin at the time of Jesus' birth and that He was actually born out of fornication in contrast to a putative virgin birth. But this interpretation is far from clear and may be reading too much into the Jews' statement in John 8:41. Other evangelicals have sought to claim a variant reading of John 1:13 as evidence for a clear affirmation of the virgin birth in John's Gospel (J. Oswald Sanders, *The Incomparable Christ* [Chicago: Moody Press, 1971], 18-19). This variant reading, found in only one versional witness (a 5th century Old Latin ms.) along with a few Latin patristic quotations, contains the singular pronoun, "He." This makes the passage refer to a single person, namely Christ, as not being born of the will of man but of God. The verse then becomes an allusion to the virgin birth in anticipation of the great incarnation verse of John 1:14. However, as enticing as this possibility may seem, it must also be recognized that every extant Greek manuscript of John has the plural pronoun "who" (*hoi*), making the passage refer to those who are regenerated solely by God. While some evangelicals view this textual variant as plausible (Gromacki, *The Virgin Birth*, 185-86), others have considered it doubtful based on internal, contextual factors in John (Machen, *The Virgin Birth of Christ*, 255-58). The fact that it has extremely meager external, manuscript support (Bruce M. Metzger, *A Textual Commentary on the Greek New Testament*, 2nd edition [New York: United Bible Societies, 1994], 168-69) should make us quite reticent to regard it as a virgin birth passage.

> regarding the stupendous miracle narrated in the first chapters of Matthew and Luke?[45]

So, what must a person believe in order to be saved? In another volume on the virgin birth, author Robert Gromacki concludes his book by explaining how all of this relates to evangelism and the particular truths that we must share with the lost. He states:

> In dealing with drunks, collegians, or socialites, counselors probably never refer to the virgin birth. The latter must point out man's sinful condition, his inability to save himself, and his need to accept the redemptive provisions of Christ's death and resurrection. The invitation usually centers around the question: "Do you want to receive Jesus Christ as your personal Savior?" In essence, the evangelist is beseeching the sinner to put his trust in a person and in what that person had done. But this is the critical area. Who is this person? Faith in a mere human Jesus won't save anyone. Actually, faith in God only won't save either (James 2:19). Saving faith must rest in Him who is both divine and human. But how did He come to have two natures? The Scriptural explanation is through the virgin birth. In counseling, the evangelist must be sure that the sinner is asked to trust in Jesus Christ who was God but who also became man in order to die for the sins of men and to rise again for their justification.[46]

Denial of the Virgin Birth and Saving Faith

Sometimes in the course of conversation about the virgin birth the objection is raised, "If someone doesn't believe in Christ's virgin birth because they're ignorant of it, that's one thing. They can still believe in the deity of Christ and be saved. But if someone knows about the virgin birth and consciously rejects it, then they have denied the deity of Christ and they cannot be saved." Does a denial of the virgin birth really amount to a denial of Christ's deity? Is eternal life really dependent upon not rejecting the virgin birth? Many believe so. For example, after affirming that we must tell the lost about Christ's person and work in our evangelism, but not necessarily about the virgin birth, author Robert Gromacki goes on to conclude:

> After the believing sinner has been regenerated, he will automatically believe the record that Christ became incarnate through the virgin birth. If he rejects the truth of the virgin birth once it is shown to him, then that is evidence that he put his faith in a

[45] Machen, *The Virgin Birth of Christ*, 395 (brackets inserted).

[46] Gromacki, *The Virgin Birth*, 189-90.

> marred Jesus, one who was not God incarnate. Thus, he was not really saved in the first place.[47]

This line of reasoning about salvation and the virgin birth is held by a fair number of evangelicals and fundamentalists in our day, and it must also be addressed. Sometimes, as in the case of Gromacki's statement above, this conclusion is not reached through the plain teachings of Scripture but by the doctrinal presuppositions that one holds, which in Gromacki's case is the Calvinist doctrine of the perseverance of the saints. This doctrine teaches that one who has been genuinely born again will necessarily persevere in faith and good works until the end of his Christian life as evidence of his genuine faith. The doctrine of the perseverance of the saints therefore precludes the possibility of the believer apostatizing. If people completely cease to believe the gospel at any point or don't continue to believe it until their death, that proves they never genuinely believed and thus were never regenerated. This is quite different from the biblical doctrine of the preservation of the saints, or eternal security, which is not conditioned upon the Christian's abiding faithfulness but solely upon Christ's own faithfulness, finished work, and preserving grace.[48]

Scripturally, it is simply not true that people who are saved will automatically believe further truth about Christ after it is revealed to them, such as the virgin birth. Normally this is true, but it is not necessarily true. A prime example of this is the Galatians. There is no more serious error than to depart from the gospel of Christ; and yet that is exactly what the Galatian Christians were doing (Gal. 1:6-7) as genuine children of God (Gal. 4:6-7). Another example is the eleven disciples following the resurrection of Christ. Even the eleven apostles did not automatically believe that Christ had truly risen from the dead (Mark 16:11). In fact, when they were told about the resurrection from a second round of eyewitnesses, they still refused to believe it (Mark 16:12-13). Later, the Lord Jesus had to personally rebuke them all for their unbelief (Mark 16:14). Thomas was even adamant before his own personal encounter with the risen Lord, saying, *"Unless I see . . . I will not believe"* (John 20:25).

The faith of God's children is often feeble and failing. It is certainly not indefectible. If even the apostles could reject and deny such an essential truth as Christ's resurrection, at least initially, then surely some genuine but unfaithful Christians in our day could conceivably deny the virgin birth and still be saved.

In fact, if the doctrinal assumption is true that genuine believers will automatically accept cardinal doctrines about Christ when informed

---

[47] Ibid., 190.

[48] For a more extensive exposition of the Scriptural teaching on eternal security and the *preservation* of the saints which results from the *perseverance* of the Savior, see Tom Stegall, "Must Faith Endure for Salvation to be Sure? Parts 1-9," *GFJ* (March/April 2002—Fall 2003).

about them, then logically Christians should never embrace *any* false teaching. If a truly regenerate person will automatically believe the doctrine of the virgin birth after he is saved, then will he also automatically accept Christ's eternal Sonship if he's really saved? What about His impeccability? Many truly regenerated men have rejected these doctrines and in some cases later retracted their former beliefs and teachings.

The doctrinal position that says "Knowledge of the virgin birth isn't necessary to get saved, but a denial of it will negate salvation" is simply illogical and unscriptural. This line of thinking could be dangerous if carried to its logical conclusion. It would say, in effect, that it is better to remain ignorant about Jesus Christ than to gain greater knowledge of Him and so run the risk of jeopardizing one's eternal salvation. But is ignorance about Jesus Christ ever spiritual bliss? Or, is it always a serious blunder?

This line of reasoning also logically leads to two different contents of faith for salvation, a lesser content (the person and work of Christ *minus* the virgin birth) and a fuller content (the person and work of Christ *plus* the virgin birth). Yet nowhere in Scripture do we find two different standards required for salvation today, the larger gospel with more content and the streamlined version with less truth to be believed. What a person must believe up front is exactly what God requires afterwards, otherwise God would be guilty of changing the "rules" in the middle of the game, and He is not so unjust. God is always consistent, even if Christians aren't.

Though it would be terribly inconsistent to believe in the deity and incarnation of Christ and yet deny the miracle of the virgin birth, this would not necessarily seal a person's eternal doom. Admittedly, it is incongruous to affirm on the one hand that Jesus Christ is "the Son of the Highest" and "God with us," while on the other hand deny the very *sign* of that deity and incarnation. If someone can accept the greater fact of God's Son having become incarnate, why wouldn't he accept the lesser fact that it was accomplished through a virgin? It is similar to Christ's resurrection being *"the sign of the prophet Jonah"* (Matt. 12:39-40). Imagine a person believing that Jesus Christ rose from the dead after three days and three nights but then denying the miracle of Jonah being in the belly of a great fish for the same length of time. Why would someone accept the greater miracle of Christ's resurrection but reject the lesser miracle of Jonah's underwater preservation? Though this would be terribly illogical and inconsistent, it still would not jeopardize a person's eternal destiny, unless we are now prepared to claim that lost people today must also believe the story of Jonah to be saved! A denial of the virgin birth is not necessarily a denial of Christ's deity. Thankfully, the Lord does not require of us complete theological consistency in order to be saved. It is for this reason that Norman Geisler explains:

> Certain beliefs are necessary in order for our theological framework to be *consistent*, but this in itself doesn't make them necessary

> beliefs for our *salvation*. . . . For example, that it is inconsistent to deny the Virgin Birth does not thereby mean that the person who refuses to believe it cannot be saved. Illogical belief does not negate actual reality, and while some Christians argue that the rejection of such a fundamental doctrine makes salvation impossible, neither Jesus nor the New Testament authors affirmed this to be true.[49]

As Christians, we are not always consistent. Admittedly, one should not stand upon the very *grounds* of our salvation while at the same time fall down upon the *means* God used to provide that salvation. Is it possible for someone to believe in the incarnation of the Son of God and yet deny the miracle of the virgin birth? It is theoretically possible, but in actuality it is extremely rare. The great virgin birth apologist of the last century, James Orr, correctly noted that there is an "almost invariable concomitance of belief in the Incarnation with belief in the Virgin Birth."[50] He qualified that this pattern is "almost invariable" because "there are exceptions." One of these "exceptions" known to Orr in his day was a biblical commentator named Meyer who professed belief in the incarnation of Christ while also denying the miracle of the virgin birth.[51] However, the case of Meyer is exceptional. There is probably not one in a thousand among those who deny the virgin birth who actually believes in Christ's incarnation. The reason for this is simple: they are just being consistent with their own unbelief. When someone in unbelief rejects the proposition of greater import (Christ's incarnation), they are only being consistent by rejecting a proposition of lesser import (Christ's virgin birth).

Creation versus Evolution

One doctrinal area that relates to our salvation and in which Christians are often inconsistent is the whole matter of human origins. Is belief in a literal interpretation of Genesis 1-2 necessary for eternal salvation? Very few evangelical and fundamental Christians would contend that it is. Scripture nowhere indicates that it is necessary; nor is it ever said to be part of the gospel. But this also leads to the "denial" question. If an unbeliever doesn't have to believe in biblical creationism before he can become born again, then does that mean after he accepts Christ as his Savior he cannot *deny* creationism or else he was never truly saved in the first place?

There have been many unbelievers who were avowed, atheistic evolutionists before they came to faith in Christ. However, they then came to recognize their own personal sinfulness and lost condition; and they understood the gospel message and genuinely trusted Jesus Christ as

[49] Geisler, *Systematic Theology*, 3:529-30 (ellipsis added).

[50] Orr, *The Virgin Birth of Christ*, 18.

[51] Ibid.

their Savior. Yet after being born again, they still remained convinced evolutionists, usually seeking to accommodate evolution with their new beliefs by adopting the position of theistic evolution. When some believers do this, they end up denying the very *means* God used to bring the human race into existence. By choosing to believe that God used the mechanism of evolution to bring about the original man, Adam, and thus the entire human race including Christ, these theistic evolutionists fail to recognize how inconsistent this is with the gospel. For, if God used the mechanism of evolution to bring the entire human race into existence, then death was the mechanism that brought forth human life and existence, and death would even have preceded the original sin of Adam and Eve. Therefore, the theory of evolution ends up denying the biblical truth that death, which is the very wages of sin (Rom. 6:23), is a result of the fall. This is why Satan seeks to spread such an effective and damaging lie, for he knows that it will impinge upon belief in the gospel. However, just as with the virgin birth, a denial of the *means* that God used to bring the human race into existence does not necessarily constitute unbelief in the *grounds* of salvation. Theistic evolution is held by many regenerated souls, in spite of its many biblical and scientific inconsistencies.

In fact, in the last century there were quite a few fundamentalists who did not know how to reconcile the new, imposing theory of evolution with the Bible's own account of origins. They failed to see that the two cannot be reconciled; and so they capitulated to the new pseudoscientific dogma, accepting the theological position of theistic evolution. Among those early fundamentalists who accepted theistic evolution as being compatible with the Bible were men like Benjamin B. Warfield,[52] James Orr,[53] J. Gresham Machen,[54] and originally James Oliver Buswell.[55] Yet, what is amazing is that Warfield wrote the definitive work defending the doctrine of biblical inspiration;[56] while Machen and Orr wrote the two

---

[52] Mark A. Noll, "B. B. Warfield," in *Handbook of Evangelical Theologians*, ed. Walter A. Elwell (Grand Rapids: Baker Book House, 1993), 33. Warfield believed the doctrine of God's providence allowed for "not only evolutionism but pure evolutionism."

[53] Glen G. Scorgie, "James Orr," in *Handbook of Evangelical Theologians*, ed. Walter A. Elwell (Grand Rapids: Baker Book House, 1993), 19-20; James Orr, "Science and Christian Faith," in *The Fundamentals: The Famous Sourcebook of Foundational Biblical Truths*, ed. R. A. Torrey (Grand Rapids: Kregel Publications, reprinted 1990), 133-34.

[54] See D. G. Hart, "J. Gresham Machen," in *Handbook of Evangelical Theologians*, ed. Walter A. Elwell (Grand Rapids: Baker Book House, 1993), 135-36. Though it is true that Machen never publicly promoted evolution, he also would not deny it as being unbiblical when specifically called upon to do so in defense of biblical fundamentalism during the great Scopes Trial. At times, Machen even referred people to Warfield's views as the most sound, biblical position, thereby indirectly endorsing the theory of evolution.

[55] James Oliver Buswell, *A Systematic Theology of the Christian Religion* (Grand Rapids: Zondervan, 1962), 1:323-24.

[56] Benjamin B. Warfield, *The Inspiration and Authority of the Bible* (Phillipsburg, NJ: Presbyterian and Reformed, 1948).

most stalwart defenses of the Lord's virgin birth! So were these men not saved because of their inconsistency? Just as a lost sinner does not need to know or believe *how* Jesus Christ became incarnate in order to be born again (only that He *is* incarnate), so a person does not ultimately need to know or believe the scriptural truth of creation *ex nihilo* (Rom. 4:17; Heb. 11:3; 2 Peter 3:5; Rev. 4:11) in order to go to heaven.

Biblical Inspiration

The truth of the plenary, verbal inspiration of Scripture is another area, like the virgin birth, that is occasionally not understood or accepted by those who genuinely come to faith in Christ for salvation. If belief in the gospel of Christ is necessary for eternal life, and this gospel comes only from the Bible, then it would be quite inconsistent to believe the Bible's gospel message while at the same time denying the Bible's inspiration. Yet, Eta Linnemann is one such example of this inconsistency. She testifies that she "became a dyed-in-the-wool historical-critical theologian"[57] through the influence of liberal, unbelieving German critic, Rudolf Bultmann. Later in life, the Lord led her to the conviction that the Bible is truly the inspired Word of God.[58] She begins by declaring:

> I want to give you my testimony, beginning with a verse from God's word, 2 Timothy 3:16: "All Scripture is God-breathed and is useful for teaching, rebuking, correcting, and training in righteousness." This is very important. I was a theologian for decades but did not know about the inspiration of the Holy Scripture. I had to be born again to find this out.[59]

Later in Linnemann's testimony, she goes on to explain that when she came to faith in Jesus Christ and was born again, it was a process for her to eventually shed the liberal baggage of skepticism and unbelief that she had accumulated through years of historical-critical Bultmannian indoctrination. However, she eventually came to believe in such fundamental doctrines as Christ's virgin birth and second coming—but only after coming to believe that the "Jesus" of history was also the "Christ" of God, the true Son of God and Son of Man. It is important for our purposes to note that, for Linnemann, belief in the deity and humanity of Jesus Christ preceded belief in His virgin birth. She goes on to explain, saying:

> I noticed a struggle immediately within myself as I began to lecture on articles of the Christian faith. I had no problem saying I believed in Jesus, for I had all the material about the so-said his-

---

[57] Eta Linnemann, Personal Testimony, *Faith and Reason Series*, Grace Valley Christian Center, Davis, CA, November 7, 2001.

[58] Eta Linnemann, *Historical Criticism of the Bible: Methodology or Ideology?* trans. Robert W. Yarbrough (Grand Rapids: Baker Book House, 1990), 17-20.

[59] Linnemann, Personal Testimony.

> torical Jesus at my doorstep. But when it came to the next word, "Christ," it was a whole day fight. But finally I got it: he is Christ. Then it was another half-day fight each to find out that he is the Son of God and the Son of man. For historical critical theologians these are mere titles. They will say, "Yes, Jesus himself never said that he was Jesus or Christ or the Son of God. He merely connected himself in some way with the Son of Man, but only for the future, not for the present." They say that the early church pinned all those titles on the historical figure of Jesus to show those they wanted to lead to Christianity the importance of Jesus.
>
> But now I realized that these things were true. Jesus is the Christ, the Son of God and Son of man, God incarnate in human flesh. I began to teach these truths to my students, who had to that point only been getting historical critical teaching from me. Then I realized Jesus was born of the virgin and began to teach that. You must realize this was a Bultmannian saying these things! I had been taught that the virgin birth was just a legend, designed to show the importance of Jesus. But I realized that if Jesus was not born of a virgin, he would just have been an offspring of the first Adam. Then it could never be true that he was without sin, and if he was not without sin, he could not have died for our sins. In fact, he would have had to die for his own sin, and we would still be in our sins. I did not think all this out at once, but I did begin to tell my students, "Yes, Jesus is born of the virgin." Then my best student asked me, "Does this mean that you also believe that Jesus is coming again?" At that time, I could only say I did not yet believe it, but within two months, I could say that also was true, and after several years, the Lord gave me the task of criticizing the critical theology.[60]

The example of Eta Linnemann could be multiplied many times over. There will be scores of people in heaven who did not have complete confidence in the Bible as the inspired, inerrant Word of God, and yet they believed at least its gospel message of salvation in Jesus Christ and they were truly born again. We must conclude that, based on the testimony of Linnemann and the examples of theistic evolutionists, it is possible to inconsistently not believe certain biblical *means* that God uses, such as the virgin birth, while at the same time affirm the very essential *grounds* of our salvation in the person and work of the Lord Jesus Christ. Though we might wish that such cases did not really exist and that all who believe in Jesus Christ as Savior would immediately accept all Christological truths pertaining to Him, we cannot dismiss the fact that such cases do exist. As a result

---

[60] Ibid. Although I do not agree doctrinally with all aspects of Linnemann's testimony, the point in citing her is to provide an example of sincere belief in Christ's deity, humanity, incarnation, and apparently even His substitutionary death, all preceding her acceptance of the virgin birth.

of the real life examples of born again theistic evolutionists and biblical errantists, in addition to Scripture's silence about requiring belief in the virgin birth for eternal life, we must admit that God does not use either a positive affirmation of the virgin birth or a denial of it as His determining criteria for a person's eternal salvation.

The Importance of Belief in Christ's Virgin Birth

In closing, some biblical balance is needed. Simply because the virgin birth is not a doctrine that determines someone's eternal destiny doesn't mean it isn't critically important for the entire world to believe it. Christians, especially, must look upon the Savior's virgin birth as a fundamental doctrine of our faith, having major ramifications if it is denied. A refusal to believe in Christ's virgin birth is a direct assault upon the accuracy and authority of the Bible. To openly reject the virgin birth as it is set forth in Scripture is to obstinately and defiantly oppose God Himself. If Scripture can be dismissed as being in error on this point, then why should any of it be believed? Though the virgin birth may not be necessary to believe for one's eternal salvation, a rejection of it will most certainly stymie a Christian's sanctification and spiritual growth, as God cannot have fellowship with anyone who has a hardened, evil heart of unbelief (Heb. 3:7-14). This is why Reformed theologian John Frame summarizes the importance of the virgin birth in the following manner:

> Is belief in the virgin birth "necessary"? It is possible to be saved without believing it; saved people aren't perfect people. But to reject the virgin birth is to reject God's Word, and disobedience is always serious. Further, disbelief in the virgin birth may lead to compromise in those other areas of doctrine with which it is vitally connected.[61]

It is no coincidence that critics and infidels have persistently laid siege to the biblical account of Christ's supernatural birth. In the earliest days of Church history, the virgin birth was assailed by men such as Cerinthus, Trypho, and Celsus.[62] Even after 19 centuries the antagonism has not abated. The 20th century saw a renewed assault upon Christ's miraculous virgin birth, and leading the charge were men such as liberal American modernist, Harry Emerson Fosdick. He deceptively preached that the historical veracity of Christ's virgin birth could be either retained by more literal-minded Christians or it could just as easily be discarded "by equally loyal

---

[61] John M. Frame, "Virgin Birth of Jesus," in *The Evangelical Dictionary of Theology*, ed. Walter A. Elwell (Grand Rapids: Baker Book House, 1984), 1145.

[62] James P. Sweeney, "Modern and Ancient Controversies Over the Virgin Birth of Jesus," *BSac* 160 (April 2003): 151-58.

and reverent people."[63] Then came German historical-critical theologian Rudolf Bultmann, who sought to "demythologize" the Bible by purging it from any vestige of the miraculous and supernatural.[64] A host of contemporaries have followed Fosdick and Bultmann, including Episcopal bishop John Shelby Spong,[65] John Hick,[66] Gerd Lüdemann,[67] Robert Funk, John Dominic Crossan, and the entire Jesus Seminar.[68] These critics of the virgin birth invariably parrot the opinion of the modernist Fosdick that a sincere "Christian" may acceptably deny the virgin birth without any twinge of conscience, since it is just an inconsequential doctrine of the Christian faith. Isn't it peculiar, though, why after twenty centuries these men will not let such an inconsequential doctrine rest in peace!? Their claims of its irrelevance are betrayed by their desperate, relentless efforts to persuade the rest of us that the virgin birth is just pious fiction. If it is of no real consequence after all, then why so much wasted breath and spilt ink? Apparently there is more riding on this doctrine than the cynics care to admit.

The historical event of the virgin birth signified forever the utterly unique identity of the Lord Jesus. There has never been another human being who has ever had such a magnificent, regal entrance to our race; nor shall there ever be another. Such a miracle was reserved for the one and only Redeemer of mankind—Immanuel.

It is no marvel therefore to see that in the last 150 years especially, the ministers of Satan have been busy at work, introducing rationalism and destructive higher criticism, creating a climate of skepticism, cynicism, and stupefying disbelief. And to what end? To make the Lord of glory just an ordinary man, with an inglorious beginning and inglorious end. It is no coincidence, therefore, to observe that the resurrection of Jesus Christ has also been vociferously attacked. There has been a well orchestrated campaign underway by the god of this cosmos to *undeify* the Lord Jesus in the minds of the masses by making Him an ordinary man with an ordi-

---

[63] Harry Emerson Fosdick, "Shall the Fundamentalists Win?" A sermon given at First Presbyterian Church, New York City, May 21, 1922, published in the *Christian Century*, June 8, 1922.

[64] Rudolf Bultmann, *Jesus Christ and Mythology* (New York: Scribner's Sons, 1958), 15-16; idem, "The New Testament and Mythology," in *Kerygma and Myth*, ed. H. W. Bartsch (New York: Harper and Row, 1961), 5; idem, *The History of the Synoptic Tradition*, trans. J. Marsh (Oxford: Blackwell, 1963; reprint, Peabody, MA: Hendrickson, n.d.), 291-92.

[65] John Shelby Spong, *Born of a Woman: A Bishop Rethinks the Virgin Birth and the Treatment of Women by a Male-Dominated Church* (New York: HarperCollins, 1992).

[66] John Hick, ed., *The Myth of God Incarnate* (London: SCM, 1977).

[67] Gerd Lüdemann, *Virgin Birth? The Real Story of Mary and Her Son Jesus* (Harrisburg, PA: Trinity Press International, 1998); idem, *Jesus after 2000 Years: What Jesus Really Said and Did* (Amherst, MA: Prometheus, 2001).

[68] Robert W. Funk and Roy W. Hoover, eds., *The Five Gospels: The Search for the Authentic Words of Jesus* (New York: Macmillan, 1993); Robert W. Funk and the Jesus Seminar, *The Acts of Jesus: What Did Jesus Really Do?* (New York: HarperCollins, 1998).

nary beginning. The intended effect of this is to make the average citizen more reluctant to believe the gospel message of Him being God-incarnate who died for the sins of the world and rose gloriously from the dead.

Ever since the Garden, the goal of Satan has always been to cast doubt upon the origins and veracity of God's Word. It is not coincidental that Satan attempts this against both the inspired, *written* Word of God (especially with the foundational book of Genesis) and the *incarnate,* Living Word. The goal of the master deceiver has always been to strip the Lord Jesus Christ of His unique dignity and majesty—to dethrone Him and to deprive Him of the magnificent glory that is due His Name.

The faithful, discerning believer must surely recognize that even though God does not require belief in His Son's virgin birth for eternal life, He still requires it of every child of God as a matter of faithfulness to Him. The Lord also requires it of us in order to be faithful in the midst of the raging, spiritual conflagration taking place. The battle of the ages is pitched and the identity of Jesus Christ is under fierce assault. The Lord's virgin birth is a highly contested front on the spiritual battlefield; and we must not yield any of this prized ground to the enemy, for nothing less than the glory due to Immanuel is at stake.

Chapter 19

Why Does This Matter?

Everyone has a theology whether they admit it or not. Even those who believe that God doesn't exist still have a belief about Him and a life lived accordingly. What we believe about God shapes our entire existence—our present, our future, and even our eternal destinies. Theology does matter, regardless of many people's denials to the contrary. In fact, it is all that matters, since the whole purpose of our existence is to glorify God (1 Cor. 10:31; Rev. 4:11). All Christians, therefore, ought to esteem greatly the truth of the gospel and Christ's person and work contained in it. For Free Grace Christians in particular, the controversy over the contents of saving faith and the meaning of the gospel must not be dismissed as an insignificant, mere trifling matter. All ideas have consequences; and the crossless gospel is no exception. But what are these consequences? Why should we be concerned?

The Offense of the Cross Has Ceased

The apostle Paul wrote in Galatians 5:11, *"And I, brethren, if I still preach circumcision, why do I still suffer persecution? Then the offense of the cross has ceased."* According to this verse, allowing just one work (circumcision) to be added to God's grace for justification nullifies grace and cancels the offense of the cross (Gal. 2:21). When a lost sinner hears in the gospel that Christ died a satisfactory death for his sin, there are no works left for him to trust in except Christ's finished work alone. However, if the "saving message" of today's crossless gospel is true, then this means that the offense of the cross is removed altogether. For, we are told that the lost do not even need to know that they are sinners or that Christ died for their sins. They can simply believe in "Jesus" for everlasting life, regardless of any misconceptions they may have about the person and work of Christ. Such doctrine can only lead to a diminished recognition of man's sin-problem and the sinner's need to trust in Christ's work on the cross. This diminution is reflected in the teaching of John Niemelä, who states:

> When you look at Genesis 3, how many times do you see sin there? None. But you find death—and life . . . O.k. sin plunged us into the problem of death, but let's stop focusing so much on the solution of the sin-problem when the fundamental truth is the person is left without life. They need to hear the message of life. That's the fundamental problem that man is left with. Sin has been taken care of so completely at the cross that sin has ceased to be the big issue. The big issue becomes: people are separated from God for eternity and Christ has made a promise to give those who believe in Him for life—to give them life. Let's get means separated from ends and let's focus on the big things as the big things.[1]

When the crossless gospel subjugates sin as secondary to its result, namely death, the lost are effectively relieved of their need to acknowledge that they are sinners in God's sight (Gen. 2:17; Isa. 59:2; Rom. 3:23) and that Christ died in their stead. But in 1 Corinthians 15:3, we are told that the gospel that Paul preached actually majored on the fact *"that Christ died for our sins"* and that this was even a matter of *"first"* importance. In Scripture, Christ's death on the cross for sin is certainly a "big thing." It is the *"message of the cross"* that distinguishes believers from unbelievers (1 Cor. 1:17-21), not a sinless, crossless, "message of life."

The Potency of the Gospel

The preaching of a crossless "message of life" to the lost will also rob the gospel of its power and effectiveness to save souls (Rom. 1:16). In this seeker-sensitive generation of mega-Laodicean churches, a crossless "gospel" or "saving message" could potentially become quite popular due to its promise of guaranteed eternal life without any recognition of personal sin or guilt before God or the need for the cross. It is all promise and no cross. Yet, it will be impotent to save, since the Spirit of God only supports and energizes His own saving message—the gospel of Christ (Gal. 3:1-3; Eph. 1:13; 1 Thess. 1:5; 2 Thess. 2:13-14; 1 Peter 1:23, 25).

False Assurance

What will a crossless "message of life" result in, if not regeneration? No doubt it will lead to false professions. It is truly alarming to hear John Niemelä refer to a Mormon as "a believer" if that Mormon believes in "Jesus" for everlasting life but has not yet come to know or believe in the truth of Christ's person and work. He states regarding Mormons who believe the promise-only gospel, "if they believe *that* truth, now God could be dealing with them as a believer to bring them to the fuller explanation of *how* it

---

[1] John Niemelä, "What About Believers Who Have Never Known Christ's Promise of Life?" *Chafer Theological Seminary Conference*, Houston, TX, March 13, 2006.

is that Christ could be accepted as being able to give that."[2] According to Niemelä, this Mormon "believer" doesn't yet know the basis or grounds upon which Christ is able to guarantee everlasting life, but he doesn't have to know or believe this in order to be sure that he possesses eternal life. He can learn about Christ's substitutionary atonement for all his sins later, after he has become "a believer." But if this is really true, then maybe the Mormon is my brother after all;[3] and perhaps the divide really isn't so wide.[4] And maybe Mormon apologists have been correct all along that Mormonism doesn't have a different Jesus,[5] or at least it doesn't matter if He is a different Jesus with respect to receiving the gift of eternal life.

World Missions

The consequences of the crossless gospel extend beyond the cults to other world religions. If the Muslim is told that "Jesus" can guarantee him eternal life if he just believes in Him for it, the Muslim can go about his merry way rejoicing in his false assurance received from the promise-only evangelist that his eternal well-being is set. This is despite the fact that he is still believing the Qur'an's teaching that Jesus is not God's Son (since Allah has no equals), and that Jesus never died on the cross, and consequently that Jesus never rose from the dead. A similar situation with Hindus is not too difficult to foresee, since polytheists and pantheists do not have to believe that *"there is one God, and one Mediator between God and men, the Man Christ Jesus, who gave Himself a ransom for all"* (1 Tim. 2:4-6). In this respect, the emergence and proliferation of a crossless, promise-only gospel could have disastrous consequences for world evangelization if Zane Hodges's vision comes to fruition. He desired to see "missionaries and witnesses to the saving power of Jesus' name," because "Everyone who believes in that name for eternal salvation is saved, regardless of the blank spots or the flaws in their theology in other respects."[6]

This sentiment fits quite comfortably with the prevailing worldview where truth is deemed to be relative and the varying content of people's faith is esteemed equally. The value of one's faith now lies in "faith" itself, rather than the object or informational content of that faith. Consequently, the deconstructed "Jesus" of today's crossless, promise-only gospel plays right into this postmodern perspective and can only be counterproductive to world evangelism. No other generation like the present has witnessed

---

[2] John Niemelä, "Objects of Faith in John: A Matter of Person AND Content," Grace Evangelical Society Grace Conference, Dallas, TX, February 28, 2006.

[3] James R. White, *Is the Mormon My Brother? Discerning the Differences Between Mormonism and Evangelical Christianity* (Minneapolis: Bethany House, 1997).

[4] Craig L. Blomberg and Stephen E. Robinson, *How Wide the Divide? A Mormon & An Evangelical in Conversation* (Downers Grove, IL: InterVarsity Press, 1997).

[5] Robert L. Millet, *A Different Jesus? The Christ of the Latter-day Saints* (Grand Rapids: Eerdmans, 2005).

[6] Hodges, "How to Lead People to Christ, Part 1," 9.

such a marked rise in multiculturalism and syncretistic religious pluralism. But, unfortunately, this has not led to a proportionate increase in people's reception of gospel truth and the salvation of souls. For this reason, the need has never been greater for "Jesus" and "the Christ" and even the "gospel" to be biblically defined lest people believe in a "Christ" and a "gospel" that will not save—a "Jesus" and a "saving message" of their own devising and imagination.

The Basis for the Christian Life

The influence of the crossless, resurrectionless gospel will also profoundly impact the believer's entire basis for living the Christian life. In Romans 6:1-10, it is assumed that believers know that they have been identified with Christ in His death and resurrection. As believers, we are instructed by the very first command in the Epistle of Romans to reckon this to be true (Rom. 6:11). We are to yield or present ourselves to God for sanctification on the basis of our co-crucifixion and co-resurrection with Christ (Rom. 6:12-13). The believer's co-death and co-resurrection with Christ form the grounds for a walk according to the Spirit as described in Romans 8. But if Christ's cross-work and resurrection are now being downplayed as non-essential to know or believe for justification, will this not also lead to the downplaying of Christ's work as the basis for our sanctification? Indeed, I believe it already has. The New Testament's positional, identificational emphasis for living the Christian life has been sorely lacking in the literature of the Grace Evangelical Society over the last 20 years and even in the Free Grace movement as a whole.

Further Doctrinal Departure & Twisting of Scripture

It would be folly to dismiss the new G.E.S. theology as inchoate and aimless. In the last decade or so it has quickly crystallized into its own distinguishable belief system. Each component has already undergone sufficient theological development to begin buttressing its chief doctrine, the promise-only gospel. Such auxiliary components include: the doctrine of Johannine primacy; a single, transdispensational saving message despite progressive revelation; the strictly promissory meaning of the terms "Christ" and "Son of God" in Johannine literature; the expansive, non-soteriological meaning of the term "gospel"; the redefinition of the terms repentance, forgiveness, salvation, wrath, and the meaning of faith as merely passive persuasion. This large-scale renovation of Free Grace theology is justified by its supporters as simply a matter of fidelity to Scripture. For example, one proponent of the G.E.S. gospel, the president of Rocky Mountain Bible College and Seminary, Stephen R. Lewis, states:

> Free Grace people sometimes have our own traditions and these traditions sometimes blind us to the clear meaning of Scripture. Take the response of some in the FG camp to the writings of Zane

> Hodges as an example. Some rejected out of hand his view on assurance as being of the essence of saving faith. Others rejected, out of hand, his deserted island illustration and his suggestion that all who simply believe in Jesus have everlasting life that can never be lost. Still others in the FG movement rejected his explanation of the Gospel of John because it contradicted their tradition. These people did not carefully read and consider his Biblical arguments. If they had, their traditions would have given way to Scripture.[7]

It is unfortunate that this subject has been portrayed as a choice between Free Grace "tradition" versus "Scripture." It is precisely because Free Grace people did not yield to the innovative and novel views of Zane Hodges, but instead to Holy Scripture, that so many have stuck with "traditional" Free Grace theology. In fact, one tragic effect of the new gospel has been the twisting of Scripture on a massive scale in order to suit the new theological system. Passages that were once regarded as supportive of Christ's deity (John 8:24; 20:31), substitutionary death for sin (1 Cor. 1:17-23), resurrection (Rom. 10:9-10), the gospel and justification (Mark 16:15-16; Rom. 1:16; 1 Cor. 15:1-4), and final judgment or salvation (Rom. 2:4-5; 5:9-10) have all been re-interpreted in order make way for the new gospel. If there is no repentance on the part of these teachers and leaders, and this process is allowed to continue, the toll of exegetical casualties will only rise, as one classic gospel/salvation passage after another will be explained away as a "sanctification" passage.

It is also likely that other on-looking evangelical Christians will take note of this trend of exegetical fallacies, and the end result will be a further discrediting of the Free Grace position as it is perceived to be built upon special pleading rather than sound exegesis. Some observers who are not Free Grace may even be reasoning already, "See, we told you the so-called Free Grace view was radical and unscriptural." They may even consider the crossless gospel to be just the logical and eventual conclusion of the whole Free Grace position. But they will be wrong in doing so, for this is not the case whatsoever. The majority of Free Grace people view the crossless gospel as an unacceptable aberration of our position, not just a novel yet tolerable expression of it. In the words of one spokesman for the movement, "The current iteration of the GES gospel means that they have left the tradition of all that can properly be called Free Grace."[8]

The Unity of the Faith

Let's face the facts. In what is called the "Free Grace Movement" today, we have two different gospels. One doesn't require the knowledge of sin or

---

[7] Stephen R. Lewis, "Consensus Theology Stinks," *Grace in Focus* 24 (May/June 2009): 4.

[8] Fred R. Lybrand, "GES Gospel: Lybrand Open Letter" (April 14, 2009), p. 14. Lybrand is the current president of the Free Grace Alliance.

that Christ is the unique God-man or that He died for man's sins and rose from the dead. The other requires all of these to be born again. These two messages are completely incompatible and irreconcilable. This is more than a slight nuance of difference. There is a gaping chasm between these two positions—a chasm that seems to grow wider with each passing year. This difference is reflected in the contrasting doctrinal statements or articles of faith between the Free Grace Alliance and the Grace Evangelical Society. The former maintains that a person must be persuaded of the finished work of Christ to receive eternal life, whereas the latter repudiates this position as "theological legalism" that "seeks to co-opt Free Grace theology"[9] and "subvert the biblical gospel."[10] As a result, the F.G.A. leadership in 2009 felt constrained to publish the following:

> After much discussion and reflection, the FGA Executive Council has concluded that in the light of misunderstandings in our broader Christian community, it is important for us to issue the following statement:
>
> *The Free Grace Alliance is not associated with the Grace Evangelical Society and does not endorse the GES Gospel (also referred to as "crossless" or "promise only" by some). We invite those who share our heart for the Gospel's clarity and declaration, of both the Person and Work of Christ, to join hands with us.*[11]

I am sure that virtually all Grace people sincerely desire unity with one another. That is certainly true with me. But a real unity that is produced by the Holy Spirit (Eph. 4:3) will only come as a result of speaking the truth in love (Eph. 4:15), not by compromising the truth. The current breach desperately needs to be healed for the good of the Body of Christ, the furtherance of the gospel, and the glory of Jesus Christ. It is my plea that those who have been advocating the crossless, promise-only gospel will reconsider their doctrines in light of Scripture, repent before the Lord, and even publicly retract their published teachings on the subject. The division among us is tragic, but it can be healed by returning to the truth of Scripture and holding fast to the gospel of Christ.

The Glory of the Lord Jesus Christ

The glory of Jesus Christ is the final and most significant consequence in the current controversy over the contents of saving faith and the meaning of the gospel. Ultimately, this is not a G.E.S. versus F.G.A. issue. Nor is this about the views of any single Free Grace teacher, such as Zane Hodges or

---

[9] Zane C. Hodges, "The Hydra's Other Head: Theological Legalism," *Grace in Focus* 23 (September/October 2008): 2.

[10] Ibid., 3.

[11] http://www.freegracealliance.com/about-fga/ges-gospel-statement/ (accessed June 22, 2009).

Charles Ryrie. It is about our common Lord and Savior, Jesus Christ. It is without dispute by all parties that the Lord Jesus is worthy of all glory; and therefore, we must seek to glorify Him in everything that we do (1 Cor. 10:31). But only when the gospel is handled and preached accurately (2 Cor. 4:2) does it glorify its principal subject, the Lord Jesus Christ (2 Cor. 4:4, 6). And this is only accomplished by gospel preaching and teaching that uplifts the cross of Christ, as the apostle Paul wrote to the Galatians, *"But God forbid that I should glory, save in the cross of our Lord Jesus Christ"* (Gal. 6:14, KJV). When the necessity of the saving death of Christ is preached and believed, not only do sinners gain the proper assurance of everlasting life, but most importantly, the very *"Lord of glory"* (1 Cor. 2:8) receives the honor that is rightly due to Him. This must be our chief concern, for it is the issue of greatest consequence when it comes to *"the gospel of the Christ."*

Appendix: Other Free Grace Voices

The following quotations from other grace-oriented believers of the past and present provide a point of comparison with the conclusions of this book. These quotations reveal the degree of departure from the faith once for all delivered unto the saints (Jude 3) that has now taken place with the advent of the new crossless gospel. The contrast is evident.

Harry Ironside

> No man preaches the Gospel, no matter what nice things he may say about Jesus, if he leaves out His vicarious death on Calvary's Cross.[1]

W. H. Griffith Thomas

> And just as the result of Abraham's faith was righteousness in the sight of God, so the outcome of faith in our Lord as having died and risen again is forgiveness and righteousness for us. . . . There is also a point of very great importance here in the association of faith with our Lord Jesus Christ. In [Romans] ch. iii. 25 our faith is exercised "in His blood," that is, in His atoning death. But in [Romans] ch. iv. 24 our faith is exercised in God Who raised Him from the dead, that is, in connection with the resurrection. So faith is concentrated on Him Who was dead and is now alive for evermore.[2]

M. R. DeHaan

> The gospel means "good news." According to Paul it is the good news concerning the death and the resurrection of Jesus Christ. This indeed is good news for the sinner. Man by nature is lost, depraved, helpless and hopeless. But God sent His Son to bear our sins on the Cross, and declared His complete satisfaction with the work of the Son of God by raising Him from the dead on the third day. And

---

[1] H. A. Ironside, "What is the Gospel?" in *God's Unspeakable Gift: Twelve Select Addresses on Evangelical Themes* (Adrian, MI: Lifeline Philippines, n.d.), 35.

[2] W. H. Griffith Thomas, *Commentary on Romans* (Grand Rapids: Kregel, 1974), 143-44 (ellipsis and brackets added).

now the poor, hopeless, helpless sinner can be saved, simply by receiving in faith the finished work of the Lord Jesus Christ.[3]

Lance Latham

Saving faith is, first of all, faith in the work of Christ on the Cross! It is impossible for us to understand the delivering nature of the gospel and the assurance that He is ours in Christ because of His grace, without also considering the significance of His glorious Resurrection. When the Apostle Paul explains the gospel in 1 Corinthians 15:3-4 he reminds us that: Christ died for our sins according to the scriptures; and that he was buried, and that he rose again the third day according to the scriptures. Forgiveness comes to us because of the death of Christ on the cross. But we must remember, however, that this forgiveness could not be assuredly ours apart from the testimony of the Resurrection. The Resurrection of Christ is linked inseparably with His death on Calvary. Our destiny for eternity depends upon our knowing who He is, and having put our faith in what He accomplished on the Cross. . . . The Resurrection of Jesus Christ is the great proof that Jesus is truly God and the Son of God. How majestically God speaks in Romans 1:4, telling us that Christ was . . . declared to be the Son of God with power, according to the spirit of holiness, by the resurrection from the dead. Believing this truth is absolutely necessary for our salvation. Jesus told the unbelieving Jews: I said, therefore unto you, that ye shall die in your sins: for if ye believe not that I am he, ye shall die in your sins (John 8:24).[4]

Many may well believe that we encourage others to just believe the facts of Christianity, that Christ is the Son of God and that He died for the sins of the world. We do have this as our basis. However, when we tell them to put their faith in Christ as the Son of God who bears our sins, we mean they are to place their reliance for eternity

---

[3] M. R. DeHaan, *Studies in First Corinthians* (Grand Rapids: Zondervan, 1956), 167.

[4] Lance B. Latham, *The Two Gospels* (Streamwood, IL: Awana Clubs International, 1984), 31-32 (ellipses added). It should be noted that though Doc Latham's book is entitled, *The Two Gospels, nowhere* in his book does he advocate that Christ's death for sin and resurrection are a second, larger gospel for the Christian's sanctification and therefore not necessary for the unsaved to believe, as today's crossless gospel advocates are teaching. Latham taught that the unsaved must believe those specific, precious truths of the gospel for their justification. He then went on to teach that God has "good news" for Christians—that our sanctification is also wholly by God's grace and based on the very same death and resurrection of Christ that was proclaimed in the gospel for our justification. In spite of Latham's title, not once in his entire book does he cite a verse of Scripture containing the word "gospel" to teach that the sanctification truths of the Christian life are part of what the Bible calls "the gospel."

upon what was done for them and to individually rest their hope there.[5]

Adding any condition to Christ's being crucified and risen would destroy *the truth of the gospel*. The great center of the truth of the gospel is that God accepts us just as we are once we believe that JESUS IS THE SON OF GOD, and rest our hope in the fact that God paid the price in full for *our* sins when Jesus paid the full price at Calvary. God will allow nothing added to Calvary as our hope![6]

C. I. Scofield (and editors)

The word "gospel" means *good news*. As used in the NT, the word deals with different aspects of divine revelation. Absolutely essential to man's salvation is the Gospel of the grace of God (Rom. 2:16, refs.). This is the good news that Jesus Christ died on the cross for the sins of the world, that He was raised from the dead on account of our justification, and that by Him all who believe are justified from all things. . . . The word "gospel," therefore, includes various aspects of the good news of divine revelation. But the fact that God has proclaimed the good news of the Gospel of grace, the Gospel of the coming kingdom, and the everlasting Gospel of divine judgment upon the wicked and deliverance of believers does not mean that there is more than one Gospel of salvation. Grace is the basis for salvation in all dispensations, and is under all circumstances the only way of salvation from sin.[7]

And what is the Gospel? Is it the Gospel that One came from the glory up yonder, the uncreated Son of God, the Word which was in the beginning with God and was God, and that He was made flesh and tabernacled among us? Yes, that is part of it. That makes the Gospel possible, but that is not the Gospel. The Gospel is that One who was in the beginning with God and was God, was made flesh and tabernacled among us, and then went upon the cross and bore our sins in His own body on the tree, and died for us, and there faith begins. And there our faith, all faith must begin. The belief in the incarnation is essential, because only the Incarnate One could be the sin-bearer, but the incarnation was unto the cross, and in itself had no saving merit whatever. Therefore we might occupy ourselves forever with the excellencies of character, with the beauty of the words and the marvelous works of our adorable Lord during His

---

[5] Ibid., 61.

[6] Ibid., 99 (capitalization & italics original).

[7] *The Scofield Study Bible, New King James Version*, ed. C. I. Scofield, E. Schuyler English, et al. (Oxford: Oxford University Press, 2002), 1735 (ellipsis added).

earthly life. We cannot dwell upon these things too much for our edification, we who are Christians. Remember that. But there is in that no Gospel for the sinner—no word for the Gentile out of Christ. On the cross, there is all acquaintanceship on our part with Christ to begin; all real faith begins there.[8]

Charles Ryrie

The very first statement in the Gospel concerning the new birth makes it dependent upon faith (John 1:12). The verse also mentions the object of faith, Christ. Thus it is throughout the Gospel—the Son as the bearer of salvation must be the object of faith (3:15-16, 18, 36; 4:29, 39, 39; 7:38; 8:24; 20:29, 31; 1 John 3:23; 5:1, 12). Faith involves the most thorough kind of appropriation of the person and work of Christ as the basis for the believer's confident persuasion for salvation. The figure of eating His flesh and drinking His blood attests to that thoroughness (6:53-56). Faith in His person involves belief in His deity (John 3:13; 8:24; 9:22; 12:42; 1 John 2:23; 4:15), and faith in His work involves belief in the efficacy of His death to effect deliverance from sin (John 1:29; 3:14-17; 13:19). In John's thought faith that saves is joined directly to the person and work of Jesus Christ.[9]

John does not use the word *gospel* at all. In Acts, Luke records the dissemination of the good news, but it is Paul who gives us the technical definition of the word as it relates to us today. The classic passage is 1 Corinthians 15:3-8. Christ's death and resurrection are, literally, "of first importance." The good news is based on two facts: a Savior died and He lives. The mention of Christ's burial proves the reality of His death. He did not merely swoon only to be revived later. He actually died. The list of witnesses (vv. 5-8) proves the reality of His resurrection. He *died* and was buried (the proof); He *rose* and was seen (the proof). Christ's death and resurrection are the foundations of the gospel of the grace of God. Notice the same twofold emphasis in Romans 4:25: He "was delivered up . . . and raised . . ." Everyone who believes that good news is saved (1 Corinthians 15:2). That, and that alone, is the whole gospel of the grace of God.[10]

---

[8] C. I. Scofield, *Where Faith Sees Christ* (Grand Rapids: Baker Book House, Reprinted 1967), 14-15.

[9] Charles Ryrie, *Biblical Theology of the New Testament* (Chicago: Moody Press, 1959), 340.

[10] Charles Ryrie, *What You Should Know About Social Responsibility* (Chicago: Moody Press, 1982), 22-23.

In the classic passage, 1 Corinthians 15:3-8, Christ's death and resurrection are said to be "of first importance." The Gospel is based on two essential facts: a Savior died and He lives. The burial proves the reality of His death. He did not merely faint only to be revived later. He died. The list of witnesses proves the reality of His resurrection. He died and was buried; He rose and was seen. Paul wrote of that same twofold emphasis in Romans 4:25: He was delivered for our offenses and raised for our justification. Without the Resurrection there is no Gospel.[11]

Paul gives us the precise definition of the Gospel we preach today in 1 Corinthians 15:3-8. The Gospel is the good news about the death and resurrection of Christ. He died and lives—this is the content of the Gospel. The fact of Christ's burial proves the reality of His death. He did not merely swoon only to be revived later. He actually died and died for our sins. The inclusion of a list of witnesses proves the reality of His resurrection. He died for our sins and was buried (the proof of His death); He rose and was seen by many witnesses, the majority of whom were still alive when Paul wrote 1 Corinthians (the proof of His resurrection). This same twofold content of the good news appears again in Romans 4:25: He "was delivered up... and was raised." Everyone who believes in that good news is saved, for that truth, and that alone, is the Gospel of the grace of God (1 Corinthians 15:2).

In days past (and even today) we heard much about the "full Gospel" which included experiencing certain ministries of the Holy Spirit. To be saved one not only had to believe but also, for example, receive the baptism of the Holy Spirit. Churches which taught this doctrine were sometimes called "full Gospel" churches.

Today we hear about the "whole Gospel," which includes the redemption of society along with the redemption of individuals. But Paul wrote clearly that the Gospel that saves is believing that Christ died for our sins and rose from the dead. This is the *complete* Gospel, and if so, then it is also the true full Gospel and the true whole Gospel. Nothing else is needed for the forgiveness of sins and the gift of eternal life.[12]

Earl Radmacher

Some churches offer what they call the "full gospel," which supposedly includes tongues-speaking. Others plead for a "whole gospel," which envisions not just the redemption of individuals but the redemption of society. Others claim that a gospel that does not

---

[11] Charles C. Ryrie, *Basic Theology* (Wheaton, IL: Victor Books, 1986), 267.

[12] Charles C. Ryrie, *So Great Salvation* (Wheaton, IL: Victor Books, 1989), 39-40.

include discipleship is not good news. Surely, the church must take more seriously the need to disciple its members, but discipleship differs from the gospel that saves from eternal damnation. . . . How readily some fall into the trap of adding requirements to the gospel beyond simply believing that Christ died for our sins and rose from the dead.[13]

Robert Lightner

To be sure, there are essentials the sinner must know before he can be saved—he is a guilty sinner (Rom. 3:23), sin's wages is death (Rom. 6:23), Christ died in the sinner's place (Rom. 5:8; 1 Cor. 15:3), the sinner must trust Christ alone as his sin bearer (John 3:16; Acts 16:31). These are the essentials of the Gospel.[14]

Christ's work alone saves, but unless His Person and work are received by faith, no benefit comes to the individual sinner. Man's faith must have the proper object before salvation results. God does not simply demand belief in the ultimate triumph of good, or faith in the evangelical church, or even faith in His own existence and power, as that which brings salvation. It is always faith in God's Son as the divine substitute for sin which brings life to the spiritually dead sinner.[15]

Thomas Constable

The unregenerate man does not need to understand the atonement in all of its aspects to be saved. But he must understand enough of it to turn from his self-effort, to cling in intelligent faith to Christ, and to believe that what Christ has done is sufficient for his need.[16]

A person becomes a Christian when he transfers his trust from whatever he may have been relying on for salvation to Jesus Christ and what He did on the cross.[17]

The most important of those gospels in the present study is the so-called Christian gospel. Many texts clearly explain what the Christian gospel is (cf. John 1:12; 3:16, 36; 5:24; 6:47). Basically it is the good news that God loves man and has sent His Son, Jesus Christ, to pay the penalty for man's sins. Christ did that when He

---

[13] Earl D. Radmacher, *Salvation* (Nashville: Word Publishing, 2000), 117 (ellipsis added).

[14] Robert Lightner, *Sin, the Savior, and Salvation* (Nashville, TN: Thomas Nelson, 1991), 160.

[15] Ibid., 160-61.

[16] Thomas L. Constable, "The Gospel Message," in *Walvoord: A Tribute* (Chicago: Moody Press, 1982), 211.

[17] Ibid., 206.

died on the cross of Calvary as man's substitute. God raised Him from the dead to demonstrate the acceptability of His sacrifice. The benefit of Christ's work must be appropriated individually by faith. One of the texts that summarizes the gospel is 1 Corinthians 15:3-4. "For I delivered to you as of first importance what I also received, that Christ died for our sins according to the Scriptures, and that He was buried, and that He was raised on the third day according to the Scriptures. . . ." This is the essential message of good news that must be believed for salvation. It contains these facts: (1) man is a sinner, (2) Christ is the Savior, (3) Christ died as man's substitute, and (4) Christ rose from the dead[18]

Thomas Edgar

The biblical message of the Gospel is stated in many passages (such as John 20:31; Acts 10:43; 13:39; Rom. 1:16-17; 3:22-24; 4:3-5; 10:4; 1 Cor. 15:3-7), but is summed up well in Acts 16:31. In answer to the Philippian jailer's question, "What must I do to be saved?" Paul and Silas answered, "Believe on the Lord Jesus Christ and you will be saved." People must hear that Jesus is the Son of God; that is, His deity, He is Lord. They must also hear that He died for our sins; thus, we can be forgiven. They must hear that He rose from the dead and is living now. The Gospel includes this content to specify that Jesus Christ is the object of our belief. The Gospel also includes what we must do in order to receive this salvation: we must believe on Jesus Christ, the Living Lord.[19]

R. Larry Moyer

The Gospel as found and preached in the Bible concerns the objective, finished, proven, never-changing fact: Christ died and arose! Often, what we share with the lost is the entire Bible—everything from Genesis to Revelation. Yet we leave out the message God most wants the non-Christian to hear. The Bible *contains* the Gospel, but the Bible is not the Gospel. The Bible includes everything from God's creation of the earth in Genesis to His creation of a new earth in Revelation. The Gospel, however, is the message of the death of Jesus Christ for our sins and His resurrection.[20]

G. Michael Cocoris

The Great Commission demanded and the apostles practiced

---

[18] Ibid., 202-3.

[19] Thomas R. Edgar, "What Is the Gospel?" in *Basic Theology: Applied*, ed. Wesley and Elaine Willis & John and Janet Master (Wheaton, IL: Victor Books, 1995), 158.

[20] R. Larry Moyer, *Free and Clear* (Grand Rapids: Kregel, 1997), 19.

> preaching the gospel of the grace of God, that is, that Christ died for sins and arose from the dead. When we evangelize we must tell people exactly that. Like the two wings of a bird or the two rails of a track, both the death and resurrection of Christ are necessary and important.[21]
>
> If faith presupposes knowledge, what does a person need to know? The object of faith in the New Testament is Jesus Christ. If you were to look up all the occurrences of "believe" and "faith" in the New Testament to see what a person must know about Christ, you would discover that a person must believe four things: (1) that Christ is God (John 20:31) and yet (2) a real man (1 John 4:2); (3) that He is the one who died for sins (Rom. 3:25) and (4) rose from the dead (Rom. 10:9). In the New Testament those last two facts are called the gospel (1 Cor. 15:3-5). Mark says to preach the gospel, and the one who believes it will be saved. Peter says that the Gentiles heard of the gospel and believed (Acts 15:7). Paul says he is not ashamed of the gospel, for it is the power of God to salvation to everyone that believes (Rom. 1:16). The object of faith is Jesus Christ, the God-Man, who died and arose. It is not just any "Christ." The object of faith must be the Christ who is offered in the gospel, the one revealed in Scripture.[22]

Charlie Bing

> To emphasize the quality of one's faith necessarily means that the object of faith is de-emphasized. The proper object of faith is the person and work of Jesus Christ as declared in the gospel (1 Cor 15:1-11, 14, 17). Genuine faith in an improper object cannot save (Jas 2:19).[23]
>
> What makes saving faith different from any other faith is its object. Therefore, saving faith is defined as trust or confidence in the Lord Jesus Christ as the Savior from sin. It is a personal acceptance of the work of the Lord Jesus Christ on the cross for the sinner.[24]

Steven J. Lewis

> While it is true that all of the work of salvation is accomplished by God on behalf of the helpless sinner, the unsaved individual must understand some of the details of this work, agree that it is necessary,

---

[21] G. Michael Cocoris, *Evangelism: A Biblical Approach* (Chicago: Moody Press, 1984), 61.

[22] Ibid., 74.

[23] Charles C. Bing, *Lordship Salvation: A Biblical Evaluation and Response* (Burleson, TX: GraceLife Ministries, 1997), 57.

[24] Ibid., 58.

and rely on the completed work of the Lord Jesus Christ—the One Who has done all the work required to accomplish salvation.[25]

On the other hand, the completeness with which salvation depends on the work of Christ alone must be balanced against the biblical call for the unsaved to exercise saving faith in that finished work of Christ on their behalf. This cannot mean that God does most of the work, leaving man to complete the final act. A proper definition of saving faith views it as a passive reception of the completed work of Christ. This involves a conscious awareness of the truths of the gospel, an agreement with those truths, and a trusting acceptance or acquiescence.[26]

Jonathan Smith

What greater issue exists than one's eternal salvation? Of all subjects before us personally and the church corporately, we must be clear on this one. This is a life-or-death issue from which there is no escape, and we ought to lay down our lives and everything else for a clear statement that says salvation is a gift of God's grace received by faith in Christ's work on the cross. None of us can afford to be in the grandstands on this issue. We all need to be vitally involved against the powers of evil in the cause of a clear Gospel.[27]

This is the Gospel. This is the good news—that Jesus is my righteous Substitute and offered to God His work. When I trust in that, I have salvation.[28]

Dennis Rokser

According to these verses, an integral part of the Gospel Paul preached was the recognition of the person of Jesus Christ—God in human flesh. . . . You are heralding first of all, a PERSON—the unique and eternal Son of God, the Lord Jesus Christ, the one and only Savior of the World. . . . So when Paul came to Corinth to evangelize these lost pagans, he not only heralded the person of Christ but also His finished work as part of the Gospel.[29]

John Cross

If someone was to ask you, "How can I get to Heaven?" you should be able to answer: To live in Heaven we need to be pure and perfect,

---

[25] Steven J. Lewis, "What is the Nature of Saving Faith?" *CTJ* 9 (August 2005): 187.

[26] Ibid., 190.

[27] Jonathan Smith, *True Grace* (n.p.: J & M Books, 2005), 7.

[28] Ibid., 60.

[29] Dennis Rokser, *Let's Preach the Gospel* (Duluth, MN: Duluth Bible Church, n.d.), 31-32 (ellipses added).

just as God is pure and perfect. If we put our faith in God, believing that when Jesus was dying on the cross, he was dying in our place for our sin, then God will clothe us in his righteousness and we will be accepted completely.[30]

This brings us to the question, *"To know forgiveness of sin and gain this righteousness offered by God, just what must one believe?"*. . . . As we have seen, the Bible clearly reveals a unique God—the Lord *YAHWEH*—who is the Supreme Being, Creator, and Owner of all. It is this God who came to earth in the person of the Lord Jesus Christ. It is in him we must trust to the exclusion of all other gods, goddesses, spirits, ancestors, or idols. Only he is worthy of our trust, no others. . . . At a point in time in history, Jesus died on a cross for our sin. Three days later he was resurrected. We must believe both. . . . To believe on the Lord Jesus Christ is to believe in *who he is* and *what he has done.*[31]

Andy Stanley

"For God so loved the world that he gave his one and only Son, that whoever believes in him shall not perish but have eternal life." "Whoever" includes everyone who is willing. Believing in him is the only requirement. Believing means placing one's trust in the fact that Jesus is who he claimed to be and that his death accomplished what he claimed it accomplished.[32]

J. B. Hixson

But in essence, the gospel is the good news that God loves man and has sent His only Son, Jesus Christ, to pay the penalty for man's sins. Christ accomplished this when He died on the cross at Calvary as man's substitute. The benefit of Christ's work must be appropriated individually by faith. What is the essential message of the gospel that must be believed for salvation? One of the best passages which summarizes the gospel is 1 Corinthians 15:3-4. . . . This summary contains everything that is essential to saving faith: man is a sinner; Christ is the only Savior; Christ died as man's substitute; Christ arose from the dead.[33]

---

[30] John R. Cross, *The Stranger on the Road to Emmaus* (Olds, Alberta: GoodSeed International, 2004), 273.

[31] John R. Cross, *by this Name* (Olds, Alberta: GoodSeed International, 2007), 338-39 (ellipses added).

[32] Andy Stanley, *How Good is Good Enough?* (Sisters, OR: Multnomah Publishers, 2003), 91.

[33] J. B. Hixson, "What is the Gospel?" http://www.hixson.org/docs/Soteriology/What%20is%20the%20Gospel.pdf (accessed October 26, 2007), 2-3 (ellipsis added).

Bibliography of Works Cited

Books, Commentaries, Reference Works

Abba, Raymond. "Name." In *Interpreter's Dictionary of the Bible*. Edited by George A. Buttrick. 4 vols. Nashville: Abingdon Press, 1962. 3:500-8.

Adams, F. A. *The Greek Prepositions, Studied from Their Original Meanings as Designations of Space*. New York: D. Appleton & Co., 1885.

Aland, Kurt, and Barbara Aland. *The Text of the New Testament: An Introduction to the Critical Editions and to the Theory and Practice of Modern Textual Criticism*. Translated by Erroll F. Rhodes. 2nd ed. Grand Rapids: Eerdmans, 1989.

Alexander, Joseph A. *Commentary on Isaiah*. Grand Rapids: Kregel, 1992. Reprint.

Alford, Henry. *The Greek Testament*. 4 vols. Revised by Everett F. Harrison. Chicago: Moody Press, 1958.

Allis, Oswald T. *Prophecy and the Church*. Phillipsburg, NJ: Presbyterian & Reformed Publishing, 1947.

Andersen, Francis I. *Job: An Introduction and Commentary*. Downers Grove, IL: InterVarsity Press, 1976.

The Apostolic Fathers: Greek Texts and English Translations. Updated Edition. Edited by Michael W. Holmes. Grand Rapids: Baker Books, 1999.

Aune, David E. *The New Testament in Its Literary Environment*. Philadelphia: Westminster Press, 1987.

Baker, Charles F. *A Dispensational Theology*. Grand Rapids: Grace Bible College Publications, 1971.

__________. *Studies in Dispensational Relationships*. Grand Rapids: Grace Publications, 1989.

Barnhouse, Donald Grey. *God's Wrath: Romans 2—3:1-20*. Grand Rapids: Eerdmans, 1953.

__________. *Man's Ruin: Romans 1:1-32*. Grand Rapids: Eerdmans, 1952.

Barr, James. *The Semantics of Biblical Language*. London: Oxford University Press, 1961.

__________. "The Synchronic, the Diachronic and the Historical: A Triangular Relationship." In *Synchronic or Diachronic? A Debate on Method in Old Testament Exegesis*. Edited by Johannes C. de Moor. Leiden: E. J. Brill, 1995.

Barrett, C. K. *A Commentary on the Epistle to the Romans*. New York: Harper & Row, 1957.

__________. *The Gospel According to St. John*. Philadelphia: Westminster Press, 1978.

Bauer, D. R. "Son of David." In *Dictionary of Jesus and the Gospels*. Edited by Joel B. Green, Scot McKnight, and I. Howard Marshall. Downers Grove, IL: InterVarsity Press, 1992.

Bauer, Walter. *A Greek-English Lexicon of the New Testament and Other Early Christian Literature*. Translated by W. F. Arndt and F. W. Gingrich. Revised and augmented by F. W. Danker. Chicago: University of Chicago Press, 1979.

_________. *A Greek-English Lexicon of the New Testament and Other Early Christian Literature*. Revised and edited by Frederick Danker. 3rd ed. Chicago: University of Chicago Press, 2000.

Becker, Ulrich. "*εὐαγγέλιον*." In *The New International Dictionary of New Testament Theology*. Edited by Colin Brown. 4 vols. Grand Rapids: Zondervan, 1986. 2:107-15.

Behm, Johannes. "*αἷμα, αἱματεκχυσία*." In *Theological Dictionary of the New Testament*. Edited by Gerhard Kittel, Gerhard Friedrich, and Geoffrey W. Bromiley. Translated by Geoffrey W. Bromiley. Index compiled by Ronald E. Pitkin. 10 vols. Grand Rapids: Eerdmans, 1964-76. 1:172-77.

Bensley, R. L., J. R. Harris, and F. C. Burkitt. *The Four Gospels in Syriac: Transcribed from the Sinaitic Palimpsest*. Piscataway, NJ: Georgias Press, 2005.

Berkhof, Louis. *Systematic Theology*. Grand Rapids: Eerdmans, Reprinted 1991.

Bernard, J. H. *A Critical and Exegetical Commentary on the Gospel of St. John*. International Critical Commentary. 2 vols. Edinburgh: T & T Clark, 1929.

Best, Ernest. *A Commentary on the First and Second Epistles to the Thessalonians*. New York: Harper & Row, 1972.

Bietenhard, Hans. "*ὄνομα*." In *Theological Dictionary of the New Testament*. Edited by Gerhard Kittel, Gerhard Friedrich, and Geoffrey W. Bromiley. Translated by Geoffrey W. Bromiley. Index compiled by Ronald E. Pitkin. 10 vols. Grand Rapids: Eerdmans, 1964-76. 5:242-81.

Bing, Charles C. *Lordship Salvation: A Biblical Evaluation and Response*. GraceLife Edition. Burleson, TX: GraceLife Ministries, 1992.

Bird, Michael F. *The Saving Righteousness of God: Studies on Paul, Justification and the New Perspective*. Carlisle, England: Paternoster Press, 2007.

Black, David Alan. *New Testament Textual Criticism: A Concise Guide*. Grand Rapids: Baker, 1994.

Blass, Friedrich, and Albert Debrunner. *A Greek Grammar of the New Testament and Other Early Christian Literature*. Translated by Robert W. Funk. Chicago: University of Chicago Press, 1961.

Blomberg, Craig L. *Jesus and the Gospels: An Introduction and Survey*. Nashville: Broadman & Holman, 1997.

_________, and Stephen E. Robinson. *How Wide the Divide? A Mormon and an Evangelical in Conversation*. Downers Grove, IL: InterVarsity Press, 1997.

Bock, Darrell L. *Acts*. Baker Exegetical Commentary on the New Testament. Grand Rapids: Baker Academic, 2008.

_________. "Hermeneutics of Progressive Dispensationalism." In *Three Central Issues in Contemporary Dispensationalism: A Comparison of Traditional and Progressive Views*. Edited by Herbert W. Bateman IV. Grand Rapids: Kregel Publications, 1999.

_________. *Luke 1:1-9:50*. Baker Exegetical Commentary on the New Testament. Grand Rapids: Baker Books, 1994.

_________. *Luke 9:51-24:53*. Baker Exegetical Commentary on the New Testament. Grand Rapids: Baker Books, 1996.

_________. "The Reign of the Lord Christ." In *Dispensationalism, Israel, and the Church*. Edited by Craig A. Blaising and Darrell L. Bock. Grand Rapids: Zondervan, 1991.

__________. "A Theology of Luke-Acts." In *A Biblical Theology of the New Testament*. Edited by Roy B. Zuck and Darrell L. Bock. Chicago: Moody Press, 1994.

Boettner, Loraine. *The Reformed Doctrine of Predestination*. Phillipsburg, NJ: Presbyterian & Reformed Publishing, 1932.

Boice, James Montgomery. *Foundations of the Christian Faith*. Rev. ed. Downers Grove, IL: InterVarsity Press, 1986.

Bowman, Robert M., Jr., and J. Ed Komoszewski. *Putting Jesus in His Place: The Case for the Deity of Christ*. Grand Rapids: Kregel Publications, 2007.

Boylan, Patrick. *St. Paul's Epistle to the Romans*. Dublin: M. H. Gill & Son, 1947.

Brenton, Lancelot C. L. *The Septuagint with Apocrypha: Greek and English*. Peabody, MA: Hendrickson Publishers, 1992.

Broyles, C. C. "Gospel (Good News)." In *Dictionary of Jesus and the Gospels*. Edited by Joel B. Green, Scot McKnight, and I. Howard Marshall. Downers Grove, IL: InterVarsity Press, 1992.

Bruce, A. B. "The Synoptic Gospels." In *The Expositor's Greek Testament*. 4 vols. Edited by W. Robertson Nicoll. Grand Rapids: Eerdmans, Reprinted 1990.

Bruce, F. F. *1 & 2 Thessalonians*. Word Biblical Commentary. Waco, TX: Word Books, 1982.

__________. *The Book of the Acts*. Rev. ed. New International Commentary on the New Testament. Grand Rapids: Eerdmans, 1988.

__________. *Commentary on Galatians*. New International Greek Testament Commentary. Grand Rapids: Eerdmans, 1982.

__________. *The Gospel of John*. Grand Rapids: Eerdmans, 1983.

__________. *The Speeches in the Acts of the Apostles*. London: Tyndale Press, 1942.

Brunner, Emil. *Der Mittler: Zur Besinnung über den Christusglauben*. Tübingen: J. Mohr, 1927.

Bullinger, E. W. *Figures of Speech Used in the Bible*. Grand Rapids: Baker Book House, 1968.

Bultema, Harry. *Commentary on Daniel*. Grand Rapids: Kregel, 1988.

Bultmann, Rudolf. *The Gospel of John: A Commentary*. Translated by G. Beasley-Murray, et al. Philadelphia: Westminster, 1971.

__________. *"Historie; Geschichte/geschichtlich; historisch."* In *Handbook of Biblical Criticism*. Edited by Richard N. Soulen. Atlanta: John Knox Press, 1981.

__________. *The History of the Synoptic Tradition*. Translated by J. Marsh. Oxford: Blackwell, 1963; Reprint, Peabody, MA: Hendrickson, n.d.

__________. *Jesus Christ and Mythology*. New York: Scribner's Sons, 1958.

__________. "The New Testament and Mythology." In *Kerygma and Myth*. Edited by H. W. Bartsch. New York: Harper and Row, 1961.

__________. *The Theology of the New Testament*. 2 vols. Translated by Kendrick Grobel. New York: Charles Scribner's Sons, 1951-1955.

Burdick, Donald W. "Gospel of Mark." In *The Wycliffe Bible Commentary*. Edited by Everett F. Harrison. Chicago: Moody Press, 1962.

__________. *The Letters of John the Apostle*. Chicago: Moody Press, 1985.

Burridge, Richard A. *What Are the Gospels? A Comparison with Graeco-Roman Biography*. 2nd ed. Grand Rapids: Eerdmans, 2004.

Burton, Ernest De Witt. *A Critical and Exegetical Commentary on the Epistle to the Galatians*. International Critical Commentary. Edinburgh: T & T Clark, Reprinted 1988.

__________. *Syntax of the Moods and Tenses in New Testament Greek*. Chicago: University of Chicago Press, 1900; Reprint, Grand Rapids: Kregel, 1976.

Burton, Philip. *The Old Latin Gospels: A Study of their Texts and Language*. Oxford: Oxford University Press, 2000.

Buswell, James Oliver. *A Systematic Theology of the Christian Religion*. Grand Rapids: Zondervan, 1962.

Carroll, John T., and Joel B. Green. "'Nothing but Christ and Him Crucified': Paul's Theology of the Cross." In *The Death of Jesus in Early Christianity*. Peabody, MA: Hendrickson, 1995.

Carson, Donald A. "Atonement in Romans 3:21-26." In *The Glory of the Atonement: Biblical, Historical & Practical Perspectives: Essays in Honor of Roger Nicole*. Edited by Charles E. Hill and Frank A. James III. Downers Grove, IL: InterVarsity Press, 2004.

__________. *Exegetical Fallacies*. Grand Rapids: Baker Books, 1984.

__________. *The Gospel According to John*. Pillar New Testament Commentary. Grand Rapids: Eerdmans, 1991.

__________, and Douglas J. Moo. *An Introduction to the New Testament*. 2nd ed. Grand Rapids: Zondervan, 2005.

Catechism of the Catholic Church. English translation. Libreria Editrice Vaticana. Bloomingdale, OH: Apostolate for Family Consecration, 1994.

The Catholic Encyclopedia. Revised and Updated Edition. Edited by Robert C. Broderick. Nashville: Thomas Nelson, 1987.

Chae, Daniel Jong-Sang. *Paul as Apostle to the Gentiles: His Apostolic Self-Awareness and its Influence on the Soteriological Argument in Romans*. Carlisle, England: Paternoster Press, 1997.

Chafer, Lewis Sperry. *The Kingdom in History and Prophecy*. Chicago: Moody Press, 1915.

__________, and John F. Walvoord. *Major Bible Themes*. Rev. ed. Grand Rapids: Eerdmans, 1974.

__________. *Systematic Theology*. 8 vols. Dallas: Dallas Seminary Press, 1947-1948. Reprint, 8 vols. in 4, Grand Rapids: Kregel, 1993.

Chay, Fred, and John P. Correia. *The Faith that Saves: The Nature of Faith in the New Testament*. N.p.: Schoettle Publishing, 2008.

Clark, Gordon H. *Faith and Saving Faith*. 2nd ed. Jefferson, MD: Trinity Foundation, 1990.

Clines, David J. A. *Job 1-20*. Word Biblical Commentary. Dallas, TX: Word Books, 1989.

Cocoris, G. Michael. *Evangelism: A Biblical Approach*. Chicago: Moody Press, 1984.

__________. *Repentance: The Most Misunderstood Word in the Bible*. Santa Monica, CA: Self-published, 2003.

__________. *The Salvation Controversy*. Santa Monica, CA: Insights from the Word, 2008.

Coenen, Lothar. "κηρύσσω." In *The New International Dictionary of New Testament Theology*. Edited by Colin Brown. 4 vols. Grand Rapids: Zondervan, 1986. 3:48-57.

Collins, Adela Yarbro. *Mark: A Commentary*. Hermenia. Minneapolis: Fortress Press, 2007.

Collins, Raymond F. *Studies on the First Letter to the Thessalonians*. Bibliotheca Ephemeridum Theologicarum Lovaniensium, LXVI. Leuven: Leuven University Press, 1984.

Constable, Thomas L. *Expository Notes on John*. Garland, TX: Sonic Light, 2005.

_________. "The Gospel Message." In *Walvoord: A Tribute*. Edited by Donald K. Campbell. Chicago: Moody Press, 1982.

Conzelmann, Hans. *The Theology of St. Luke*. Translated by Geoffrey Buswell. New York: Harper & Row, 1960.

Cook, W. Robert. *The Theology of John*. Chicago: Moody Press, 1979.

Corner, Daniel D. *The Believer's Conditional Security: Eternal Security Refuted*. Washington, PA: Evangelical Outreach, 2000.

Couch, Mal, gen. ed. *A Bible Handbook to the Acts of the Apostles*. Grand Rapids: Kregel Publications, 1999.

_________. *An Introduction to Classical Evangelical Hermeneutics*. Grand Rapids: Kregel Publications, 2000.

_________. "The Church Dispensation and the 'Times of Refreshing'." In *Progressive Dispensationalism: An Analysis of the Movement and Defense of Traditional Dispensationalism*. Edited by Ron J. Bigalke. Lanham, Maryland: University Press of America, 2005.

Cox, William E. *Amillennialism Today*. Phillipsburg, NJ: Presbyterian and Reformed Publishing Co., 1966.

Craig, William Lane. "Did Jesus Rise from the Dead?" In *Jesus Under Fire: Modern Scholarship Reinvents the Historical Jesus*. Edited by Michael J. Wilkins and J. P. Moreland. Grand Rapids: Zondervan, 1995.

Cranfield, C. E. B. *The Gospel According to Saint Mark*. Cambridge Greek Testament Commentary. Cambridge: Cambridge University Press, 1959.

_________. *A Critical and Exegetical Commentary on the Epistle to the Romans*. International Critical Commentary. 2 vols. Edinburgh: T & T Clark, 1975.

Crenshaw, Curtis I., and Grover E. Gunn, III. *Dispensationalism Today, Yesterday, and Tomorrow*. 3rd ed. Memphis, TN: Footstool Publications, 1994.

Cross, John R. *by this Name*. Olds, Alberta: GoodSeed International, 2007.

_________. *The Stranger on the Road to Emmaus*. Olds, Alberta: GoodSeed International, 2004.

Cullmann, Oscar. *The Christology of the New Testament*. Rev. ed. Translated by Shirley G. Guthrie and Charles A. M. Hall. Philadelphia: Westminster, 1963.

_________. *Salvation in History*. Translated by Sidney Sowers. London: SCM, 1967.

Custance, Arthur C. *The Sovereignty of Grace*. Phillipsburg, NJ: Presbyterian & Reformed Publishing, 1979.

Custer, Stewart. *Witness to Christ: A Commentary on Acts*. Greenville, SC: Bob Jones University Press, 2000.

Dana, H. E., and Julius R. Mantey. *A Manual Grammar of the Greek New Testament*. New York: Macmillan Publishing Co., 1927.

Daniel, Curt. *The History and Theology of Calvinism*. Dallas: Scholarly Reprints, 1993.

Davis, John J. *Paradise to Prison: Studies in Genesis*. Grand Rapids: Baker Book House, 1975.

Deffinbaugh, Robert L. *That You Might Believe: A Study of the Gospel of John*. N.p.: Biblical Studies Press, 1998.

DeHaan, M. R. *The Chemistry of the Blood*. Grand Rapids: Zondervan, 1943.

Delling, Gerhard. "The Significance of the Resurrection of Jesus for Faith in Jesus Christ." In *The Significance of the Message of the Resurrection for Faith in Jesus Christ*. Edited by C. F. D. Moule. London: SCM Press, 1968.

Demarest, Bruce A. *The Cross and Salvation: The Doctrine of Salvation*. Wheaton, IL: Crossway Books, 1997.

Denney, James. *The Death of Christ*. Edited by R. V. G. Tasker. London: Tyndale Press, 1960.

Dibelius, Martin, and Hans Conzelmann. *The Pastoral Epistles: A Commentary on the Pastoral Epistles*. Hermeneia. Philadelphia: Fortress Press, 1972.

Dillistone, F. W. *The Significance of the Cross*. Philadelphia: Westminster Press, 1944.

Dillow, Joseph C. *The Reign of the Servant Kings: A Study of Eternal Security and the Final Significance of Man*. Miami Springs, FL: Schoettle Publishing, 1992.

Dixon, A. C. *The Glories of the Cross*. Grand Rapids: Eerdmans, 1962.

Dodd, C. H. *The Apostolic Preaching and Its Developments*. London: Hodder & Stoughton, 1936.

__________. *The Interpretation of the Fourth Gospel*. Cambridge: Cambridge University Press, 1955.

Donahue, John R., and Daniel J. Harrington. *The Gospel of Mark*. Sacra Pagina Series. Vol. 2. Collegeville, MN: Liturgical Press, 2002.

Dunn, James D. G. *Romans 1-8*. Word Biblical Commentary. Dallas: Word Books, 1988.

Dupont, Jacques. "The Conversion of Paul, and Its Influence on His Understanding of Salvation by Faith." In *Apostolic History and the Gospel: Biblical and Historical Essays Presented to F. F. Bruce on His 60th Birthday*. Edited by W. Ward Gasque and Ralph P. Martin. Grand Rapids: Eerdmans, 1970.

Duty, Guy. *If Ye Continue: A Study of the Conditional Aspects of Salvation*. Minneapolis: Bethany House, 1966.

Dyer, Charles H. "Biblical Meaning of 'Fulfillment'." In *Issues in Dispensationalism*. Edited by Wesley R. Willis and John R. Master. Chicago: Moody Press, 1994.

Edgar, Thomas R. "What Is the Gospel?" In *Basic Theology: Applied*. Edited by Wesley and Elaine Willis & John and Janet Master. Wheaton, IL: Victor Books, 1995.

Edwards, James R. *The Gospel according to Mark*. The Pillar New Testament Commentary. Grand Rapids: Eerdmans, 2002.

Ellicott, Charles J. *St. Paul's First Epistle to the Corinthians: With a Critical and Grammatical Commentary*. Minneapolis: James Family, 1978.

Ellingworth, Paul. *The Epistle to the Hebrews*. New International Greek Testament Commentary. Grand Rapids: Eerdmans, 1993.

Ellis, E. Earle. "The Role of the Christian Prophet in Acts." In *Apostolic History and the Gospel: Biblical and Historical Essays Presented to F. F. Bruce on his 60th Birthday*. Edited by W. Ward Gasque and Ralph P. Martin. Grand Rapids: Eerdmans, 1970.

Elwell, Walter A., ed., *Handbook of Evangelical Theologians*. Grand Rapids: Baker Book House, 1993.

English, E. Schuyler. *The Rapture*. Neptune, NJ: Loizeaux Brothers, 1954.

Enns, Paul. *The Moody Handbook of Theology*. Chicago: Moody Press, 1989.

Erickson, Millard J. *Christian Theology*. One-volume Edition. Grand Rapids: Baker Book House, 1983-85.

__________. *The Word Became Flesh: A Contemporary Incarnational Christology*. Grand Rapids: Baker, 1991.

Fanning, Buist M. "A Theology of Hebrews." In *A Biblical Theology of the New Testament*. Edited by Roy B. Zuck and Darrell L. Bock. Chicago: Moody Press, 1994.

__________. *Verbal Aspect in New Testament Greek*. New York: Oxford University Press, 1990.

Fee, Gordon D. *1 and 2 Timothy, Titus*. New International Biblical Commentary. Peabody, MA: Hendrickson, 1984.

__________. *The First Epistle to the Corinthians*. New International Commentary on the New Testament. Grand Rapids: Eerdmans, 1987.

__________. *Pauline Christology: An Exegetical-Theological Study*. Peabody, MA: Hendrickson Publishers, 2007.

Feinberg, Charles Lee. *Daniel: The Kingdom of the Lord*. Winona Lake, IN: BMH Books, 1981.

__________. *Millennialism: The Two Major Views*. 3rd edition. Winona Lake, IN: BMH Books, 1985.

Feinberg, Paul. "The Case for the Pretribulation Rapture Position." In *The Rapture: Pre-, Mid-, or Post-Tribulational?* Grand Rapids: Zondervan, 1984.

Figart, Thomas O. *The King of the Kingdom of Heaven: A Commentary of Matthew*. Lancaster, PA: Eden Press, 1999.

Finley, Thomas J. *Joel, Amos, Obadiah*. Wycliffe Exegetical Commentary. Edited by Kenneth L. Barker. Chicago: Moody Press, 1990.

Fitzmyer, Jospeh A. "Romans." In *The New Jerome Biblical Commentary*. Edited by Raymond E. Brown, Joseph A. Fitzmyer, and Roland E. Murphy. Englewood Cliffs, NJ: Prentice Hall, 1990.

__________. *Romans: A New Translation with Introduction and Commentary*. Anchor Bible. New York: Doubleday, 1993.

Foerster, Werner. "Ἰησοῦς." In *Theological Dictionary of the New Testament*. Edited by Gerhard Kittel, Gerhard Friedrich, and Geoffrey W. Bromiley. Translated by Geoffrey W. Bromiley. Index compiled by Ronald E. Pitkin. 10 vols. Grand Rapids: Eerdmans, 1964-76. 3:284-93.

__________. "κύριος, κυρία, κυριακός, κυριότης, κυριεύω, κατακυριεύω." In *Theological Dictionary of the New Testament*. Edited by Gerhard Kittel, Gerhard Friedrich, and Geoffrey W. Bromiley. Translated by Geoffrey W. Bromiley. Index compiled by Ronald E. Pitkin. 10 vols. Grand Rapids: Eerdmans, 1964-76. 3:1039-98.

__________, and Georg Fohrer. "σῴζω, σωτηρία, σωτήρ, σωτήριος." In *Theological Dictionary of the New Testament*. Edited by Gerhard Kittel, Gerhard Friedrich, and Geoffrey W. Bromiley. Translated by Geoffrey W. Bromiley. Index compiled by Ronald E. Pitkin. 10 vols. Grand Rapids: Eerdmans, 1964-76. 7:965-1024.

Forsyth, P. T. *The Cruciality of the Cross*. Carlisle, England: Paternoster Press, 1997.

Frame, John M. "Virgin Birth of Jesus." In *The Evangelical Dictionary of Theology*. Edited by Walter A. Elwell. Grand Rapids: Baker Book House, 1984.

France, R. T. *The Gospel of Mark: A Commentary on the Greek Text*. The New International Greek Testament Commentary. Grand Rapids: Eerdmans, 2002.

Freeman, Hobart E. *An Introduction to the Old Testament Prophets*. Chicago: Moody Press, 1968.

Friedrich, Gerhard. "εὐαγγελίζομαί, εὐαγγέλιον, προευαγγελίζομαί, εὐαγγελιστής." In *Theological Dictionary of the New Testament*. Edited by Gerhard Kittel, Gerhard Friedrich, and Geoffrey W. Bromiley. Translated by Geoffrey W. Bromiley. Index compiled by Ronald E. Pitkin. 10 vols. Grand Rapids: Eerdmans, 1964-76. 2:707-37.

Friedrichsen, G. W. S. *The Gothic Version of the Gospels: A Study of Its Style and Textual History*. London: Oxford University Press, 1939.

Fruchtenbaum, Arnold G. *Ariel's Bible Commentary: The Messianic Jewish Epistles*. Tustin, CA: Ariel Ministries, 2005.

__________. *Messianic Christology: A Study of Old Testament Prophecy Concerning the First Coming of the Messiah*. Tustin, CA: Ariel Ministries, 1998.

Fudge, Edward W. *The Fire That Consumes: The Biblical Case for Conditional Immortality*. Revised Edition. Carlisle, England: Paternoster Press, 1994.

Fuller, Daniel P. *Gospel & Law: Contrast or Continuum? The Hermeneutics of Dispensationalism and Covenant Theology*. Pasadena, CA: Fuller Seminary Press, reprinted 1991.

Funk, Robert W. and Roy W. Hoover, eds. *The Five Gospels: The Search for the Authentic Words of Jesus*. New York: Macmillan, 1993.

Gaffin, Richard B. "Atonement in the Pauline Corpus." In *The Glory of the Atonement: Biblical, Historical & Practical Perspectives: Essays in Honor of Roger Nicole*. Edited by Charles E. Hill and Frank A. James III. Downers Grove, IL: InterVarsity Press, 2004.

__________. *Resurrection and Redemption: A Study in Paul's Soteriology*. 2nd ed. Phillipsburg, NJ: Presbyterian & Reformed Publishing, 1987.

Garland, David E. *1 Corinthians*. Baker Exegetical Commentary on the New Testament. Grand Rapids: Baker, 2003.

Geisler, Norman L. and William E. Nix. *A General Introduction to the Bible*. Rev. ed. Chicago: Moody Press, 1986.

__________. *Systematic Theology*. 4 vols. Minneapolis: Bethany House, 2002-2005.

George, Timothy. *Theology of the Reformers*. Nashville: Broadman Press, 1988.

Gerstner, John H. *Wrongly Dividing the Word of Truth: A Critique of Dispensationalism*. Brentwood, TN: Wolgemuth & Hyatt, 1991.

Glasswell, Mark E. "The Beginning of the Gospel: A Study of St. Mark's Gospel with Regard to Its First Verse." In *New Testament Christianity for Africa and the World: Essays in Honour of Harry Sawyerr*. Edited by Mark E. Glasswell and Edward W. Fasholé-Luke. London: SPCK, 1974.

Godet, Frederic Louis. *Commentary on First Corinthians*. Edinburgh: T & T Clark, 1889. Reprint, Grand Rapids: Kregel, 1977.

Goldberg, Louis. *Our Jewish Friends*. Neptune, NJ: Loizeaux Bros., 1983.

Gould, Ezra P. *The Gospel According to St. Mark*. International Critical Commentary. New York: Charles Scribner's Sons, 1913.

Grassmick, John D. "Gospel of Mark." In *The Bible Knowledge Commentary*. Edited by John F. Walvoord and Roy B. Zuck. 2 vols. Wheaton, IL: Victor Books, 1983.

Green, Joel B. "The Death of Jesus, God's Servant." In *Reimaging the Death of the Lukan Jesus*. Edited by Dennis D. Sylva. Frankfurt am Main: Anton Hain, 1990.

__________. *The Gospel of Luke*. New International Commentary on the New Testament. Grand Rapids: Eerdmans, 1997.

Gromacki, Robert G. *Called to Be Saints: An Exposition of 1 Corinthians*. Grand Rapids: Baker Book House, 1977.

__________. *New Testament Survey*. Grand Rapids: Baker Book House, 1974.

__________. *Stand True to the Charge: An Exposition of 1 Timothy*. Grand Rapids: Baker Book House, 1982.

__________. *The Virgin Birth: Doctrine of Deity*. Grand Rapids: Baker Book House, 1974. Reprinted 1981.

Grudem, Wayne. *Systematic Theology*. Grand Rapids: Zondervan, 1994.

Grundmann, Walter. "*χρίω, χριστός, ἀντίχριστος, χρῖσμα, χριστιανός*." In *Theological Dictionary of the New Testament*. Edited by Gerhard Kittel, Gerhard Friedrich, and Geoffrey W. Bromiley. Translated by Geoffrey W. Bromiley. Index compiled by Ronald E. Pitkin. 10 vols. Grand Rapids: Eerdmans, 1964-76. 9:493-580.

Guelich, Robert A. "The Gospel Genre." In *Das Evangelium und die Evangelien: Vorträge vom Tübinger Symposium 1982*. Edited by Peter Stuhlmacher. Tübingen: Mohr Siebeck, 1983.

__________. *Mark 1-8:26*. Word Biblical Commentary. Dallas: Word Books, 1989.

Guthrie, Donald. *New Testament Introduction*. 4th ed. Downers Grove, IL: InterVarsity Press, 1990.

Gundry, Robert H. *Mark: A Commentary on His Apology for the Cross*. Grand Rapids: Eerdmans, 1993.

_________. "Recent Investigations into the Literary Genre 'Gospel'." In *New Dimensions in New Testament Study*. Edited by Richard N. Longenecker and Merrill C. Tenney. Grand Rapids: Zondervan, 1974.

Habermas, Gary R. *The Historical Jesus: Ancient Evidence for the Life of Christ*. Joplin, MO: College Press, 1996.

Hagner, Donald A. "The Son of God as Unique High Priest." In *Contours of Christology in the New Testament*. Edited by Richard N. Longenecker. Grand Rapids: Eerdmans, 2005.

Hahn, Ferdinand. "Χριστός." In *Exegetical Dictionary of the New Testament*. 3 vols. Edited by Horst Balz and Gerhard Schneider. Grand Rapids: Eerdmans, 1990-93. 3:478-86.

Hahneman, Geoffrey Mark. *The Muratorian Fragment and the Development of the Canon*. Oxford: Oxford University Press, 1992.

Hamilton, Victor P. *The Book of Genesis*, Chapters 1-17. New International Commentary on the Old Testament. Grand Rapids: Eerdmans, 1990.

Hanson, A. T. *The Pastoral Epistles*. The New Century Bible Commentary. Grand Rapids: Eerdmans, 1982.

Harris, Murray J. "Appendix." In *The New International Dictionary of New Testament Theology*. Edited by Colin Brown. 4 vols. Grand Rapids: Zondervan, 1986. 3:1171-1215.

_________. *Jesus as God: The New Testament Use of Theos in Reference to Jesus*. Grand Rapids: Baker, 1992.

Harris, III, W. Hall. *1, 2, 3 John: Comfort and Counsel for a Church in Crisis*. N.p.: Biblical Studies Press, 2003.

_________. *The Gospel of John: Introduction and Commentary*. N.p.: Biblical Studies Press, 2001.

_________. "A Theology of John's Writings." In *A Biblical Theology of the New Testament*. Edited by Roy B. Zuck and Darrell L. Bock. Chicago: Moody Press, 1994.

Harrison, Everett F. *Acts: The Expanding Church*. Chicago: Moody Press, 1975.

Harrison, Gessner. *A Treatise on the Greek Prepositions, and on the Cases of Nouns with which These Are Used*. Philadelphia: J. B. Lippincott & Co., 1858.

Hawkins, John C. *Hore Synopticae: Contributions to the Study of the Synoptic Problem*. Oxford: Clarendon Press, 1909.

Hawthorne, Gerald F. "Name." In *The International Standard Bible Encyclopdia*. Rev. ed. Edited by Geoffrey W. Bromily, 4 vols. Grand Rapids: Eerdmans, 1980-88. 3:480-83.

Head, Peter M. "The Self-Offering and Death of Christ as a Sacrifice in the Gospels and the Acts of the Apostles." In *Sacrifice in the Bible*. Edited by Roger T. Beckwith and Martin J. Selman. Grand Rapids: Baker, 1995.

Hemer, Colin. *The Book of Acts in the Setting of Hellenistic History*. Winona Lake, IN: Eisenbrauns, 1990.

Hengel, Martin. *Acts and the History of Earliest Christianity*. London: SCM Press, 1979.

_________. *The Atonement: The Origins of the Doctrine in the New Testament*. London: S. C. M. Press, 1981.

_________. "Christological Titles in Early Christianity." In *The Messiah: Developments in Earliest Judaism and Christianity*. Edited by James H. Charlesworth.

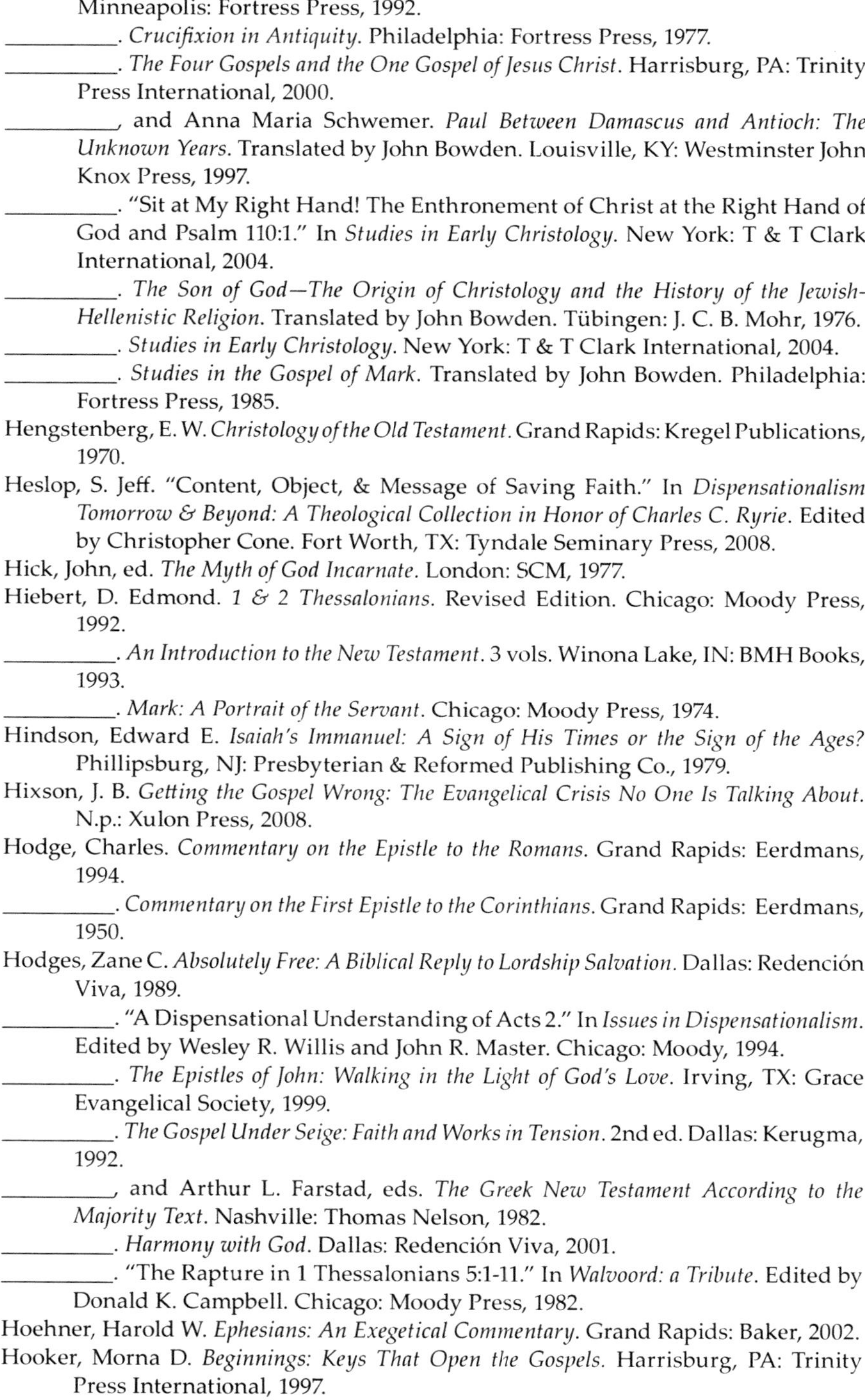

Minneapolis: Fortress Press, 1992.

__________. *Crucifixion in Antiquity*. Philadelphia: Fortress Press, 1977.

__________. *The Four Gospels and the One Gospel of Jesus Christ*. Harrisburg, PA: Trinity Press International, 2000.

__________, and Anna Maria Schwemer. *Paul Between Damascus and Antioch: The Unknown Years*. Translated by John Bowden. Louisville, KY: Westminster John Knox Press, 1997.

__________. "Sit at My Right Hand! The Enthronement of Christ at the Right Hand of God and Psalm 110:1." In *Studies in Early Christology*. New York: T & T Clark International, 2004.

__________. *The Son of God—The Origin of Christology and the History of the Jewish-Hellenistic Religion*. Translated by John Bowden. Tübingen: J. C. B. Mohr, 1976.

__________. *Studies in Early Christology*. New York: T & T Clark International, 2004.

__________. *Studies in the Gospel of Mark*. Translated by John Bowden. Philadelphia: Fortress Press, 1985.

Hengstenberg, E. W. *Christology of the Old Testament*. Grand Rapids: Kregel Publications, 1970.

Heslop, S. Jeff. "Content, Object, & Message of Saving Faith." In *Dispensationalism Tomorrow & Beyond: A Theological Collection in Honor of Charles C. Ryrie*. Edited by Christopher Cone. Fort Worth, TX: Tyndale Seminary Press, 2008.

Hick, John, ed. *The Myth of God Incarnate*. London: SCM, 1977.

Hiebert, D. Edmond. *1 & 2 Thessalonians*. Revised Edition. Chicago: Moody Press, 1992.

__________. *An Introduction to the New Testament*. 3 vols. Winona Lake, IN: BMH Books, 1993.

__________. *Mark: A Portrait of the Servant*. Chicago: Moody Press, 1974.

Hindson, Edward E. *Isaiah's Immanuel: A Sign of His Times or the Sign of the Ages?* Phillipsburg, NJ: Presbyterian & Reformed Publishing Co., 1979.

Hixson, J. B. *Getting the Gospel Wrong: The Evangelical Crisis No One Is Talking About*. N.p.: Xulon Press, 2008.

Hodge, Charles. *Commentary on the Epistle to the Romans*. Grand Rapids: Eerdmans, 1994.

__________. *Commentary on the First Epistle to the Corinthians*. Grand Rapids: Eerdmans, 1950.

Hodges, Zane C. *Absolutely Free: A Biblical Reply to Lordship Salvation*. Dallas: Redención Viva, 1989.

__________. "A Dispensational Understanding of Acts 2." In *Issues in Dispensationalism*. Edited by Wesley R. Willis and John R. Master. Chicago: Moody, 1994.

__________. *The Epistles of John: Walking in the Light of God's Love*. Irving, TX: Grace Evangelical Society, 1999.

__________. *The Gospel Under Seige: Faith and Works in Tension*. 2nd ed. Dallas: Kerugma, 1992.

__________, and Arthur L. Farstad, eds. *The Greek New Testament According to the Majority Text*. Nashville: Thomas Nelson, 1982.

__________. *Harmony with God*. Dallas: Redención Viva, 2001.

__________. "The Rapture in 1 Thessalonians 5:1-11." In *Walvoord: a Tribute*. Edited by Donald K. Campbell. Chicago: Moody Press, 1982.

Hoehner, Harold W. *Ephesians: An Exegetical Commentary*. Grand Rapids: Baker, 2002.

Hooker, Morna D. *Beginnings: Keys That Open the Gospels*. Harrisburg, PA: Trinity Press International, 1997.

Horner, George W. *The Coptic Version of the New Testament in the Northern Dialect*, *otherwise called Memphitic and Bohairic.* 4 vols. Oxford: Clarendon Press, 1898-1905.

__________. *The Coptic Version of the New Testament in the Southern Dialect, otherwise called Sahidic and Thebaic.* 7 vols. Oxford: Clarendon Press, 1911-24.

Hubbard, David A. "1 Thessalonians." In *The Wycliffe bible Commentary.* Chicago: Moody Press, 1962.

Hughes, Philip E. *The Second Epistle to the Corinthians.* New International Commentary on the New Testament. Grand Rapids: Eerdmans, 1962.

Hurtado, Larry W. "Christ." In *Dictionary of Jesus and the Gospels.* Edited by Joel B. Green, Scot McKnight, and I. Howard Marshall. Downers Grove, IL: InterVarsity Press, 1992.

__________. "The Doxology at the End of Romans." In *New Testament Textual Criticism: Its Significance for Exegesis. Essays in Honor of Bruce M. Metzger.* Edited by Eldon J. Epp and Gordon D. Fee. Grand Rapids: Eerdmans, 1981.

__________. "Gospel (Genre)." In *Dictionary of Jesus and the Gospels.* Edited by Joel B. Green, Scot McKnight, and I. Howard Marshall. Downers Grove, IL: InterVarsity Press, 1992.

__________. *Lord Jesus Christ: Devotion to Jesus in Earliest Christianity.* Grand Rapids: Eerdmans, 2005.

Ice, Thomas D. "Dispensational Hermeneutics." In *Issues in Dispensationalism.* Edited by Wesley R. Willis and John R. Master. Chicago: Moody Press, 1994.

Ironside, H. A. "What is the Gospel?" In *God's Unspeakable Gift: Twelve Select Addresses on Evangelical Themes.* Adrian, MI: Lifeline Philippines, n.d.

Jeffery, Steve, Michael Ovey, and Andrew Sach. *Pierced for Our Transgressions: Rediscovering the Glory of Penal Substitution.* Wheaton, IL: Crossway Books, 2007.

Jeremias, Joachim. *The Eucharistic Words of Jesus.* Translated by Norman Perrin. New York: Charles Scribner's Sons, 1966.

__________. "παῖς θεοῦ." In *Theological Dictionary of the New Testament.* Edited by Gerhard Kittel, Gerhard Friedrich, and Geoffrey W. Bromiley. Translated by Geoffrey W. Bromiley. Index compiled by Ronald E. Pitkin. 10 vols. Grand Rapids: Eerdmans, 1964-76. 5:654-717.

Jervis, L. Ann, and Peter Richardson, eds. *Gospel in Paul: Studies on Corinthians, Galatians and Romans in Honour of Richard N. Longenecker.* Sheffield: JSOT Press, 1994.

Johnson, Elliott E. *Expository Hermeneutics: An Introduction.* Grand Rapids: Zondervan, 1990.

Johnson, S. Lewis. "1 Corinthians." In *The Wycliffe Bible Commentary.* Edited by Charles F. Pfeiffer and Everett F. Harrison. Chicago: Moody Press, 1962.

Johnston, J. William. "Grammatical Analysis." In *Interpreting the New Testament Text: Introduction to the Art and Science of Exegesis.* Edited by Darrell L. Bock and Buist M. Fanning. Wheaton, IL: Crossway Books, 2006.

Kaiser, Walter C., Jr. "An Epangelical Response." In *Dispensationalism, Israel and the Church: The Search for Definition.* Edited by Craig A. Blaising and Darrell L. Bock. Grand Rapids: Zondervan, 1992.

__________. "The Old Testament as the Plan of Salvation." In *Toward Rediscovering the Old Testament.* Grand Rapids: Zonvervan, 1987.

Karleen, Paul S. *The Handbook to Bible Study: With a Guide to the Scofield Study System.* New York: Oxford University Press, 1987.

Käsemann, Ernst. "Ministry and Community in the New Testament." In *Essays on*

New Testament Themes. Translated by W. J. Montague. London: SCM Press, 1964.

Keathley, III., J. Hampton. *ABCs for Christian Growth: Laying the Foundation*. 5th edition. N.p.: Biblical Studies Press, 1996-2002.

Keck, Leander E. *Romans*. Nashville: Abingdon Press, 2005.

Keil, C. F. and F. Delitzsch. *Commentary on the Old Testament*. Translated by James Martin. 10 vols. Edinburgh: T & T Clark, 1866-1891. Reprint, Peabody, MA: Hendrickson, 1996.

Kelly, J. N. D. *Early Christian Creeds*, 3rd ed. New York: Continuum International, 2006.

__________. *The Pastoral Epistles*. Black's New Testament Commentary. Peabody, MA: Hendrickson, 1960.

Kent, Homer A. *The Pastoral Epistles*. Revised Edition. Winona Lake, IN: BMH Books, 1982.

Kim, Seyoon. *The Origin of Paul's Gospel*. Tubingen: J. C. B. Mohr, 1981.

__________. *Paul and the New Perspective: Second Thoughts on the Origin of Paul's Gospel*. Grand Rapids: Eerdmans, 2002.

__________. *The "Son of Man" as the Son of God*. Tübingen: J. C. B. Mohr, 1983.

Kistemaker, Simon J. "Atonement in Hebrews." In *The Glory of the Atonement: Biblical, Historical & Practical Perspectives: Essays in Honor of Roger Nicole*. Edited by Charles E. Hill and Frank A. James III. Downers Grove, IL: InterVarsity Press, 2004.

Knight, George W. *The Pastoral Epistles: A Commentary on the Greek Text*. New International Greek Testament Commentary. Grand Rapids: Eerdmans, 1992.

Knowling, R. J. "The Acts of the Apostles." In *The Expositor's Greek Testament*. Volume II. Grand Rapids: Eerdmans, Reprinted 1990.

Koester, Helmut. *Ancient Christian Gospels: Their History and Development*. Philadelphia: Trinity Press International, 1990.

Köstenberger, Andreas J. *John*. Baker Exegetical Commentary on the New Testament. Grand Rapids: Baker Academic, 2004.

Ladd, George Eldon. *The Gospel of the Kingdom: Scriptural Studies in the Kingdom of God*. Grand Rapids: Eerdmans, 1959.

__________. "Revelation and Tradition in Paul." In *Apostolic History and the Gospel: Biblical and Historical Essays Presented to F. F. Bruce on His 60th Birthday*. Edited by W. Ward Gasque and Ralph P. Martin. Grand Rapids: Eerdmans, 1970.

Lagrange, M.-J. *Évangile selon Saint Marc*, 4th ed. Paris: J. Gabalda et Fils, 1929.

Lane, William L. *The Gospel According to Mark: The English Text with Introduction, Exposition and Notes*. Grand Rapids: Eerdmans, 1974.

__________. *Hebrews 1-8*. Word Biblical Commentary. Nashville: Thomas Nelson, 1991.

__________. *Hebrews 9-13*. Word Biblical Commentary. Nashville: Thomas Nelson, 1991.

Latham, Lance B. *The Two Gospels*. Streamwood, IL: Awana Clubs International, 1984.

LaVerdiere, Eugene. *The Beginning of the Gospel: Introducing the Gospel According to Mark*. 2 vols. Collegeville, MN: Liturgical Press, 1999.

Lawlor, George L. *Almah—virgin or young woman?* Schaumburg, IL: Regular Baptist Press, 1973.

Lenski, R. C. H. *The Interpretation of the Acts of the Apostles*. Minneapolis: Augsburg Press, 1946.

Levinsohn, Stephen H. *Discourse Features of New Testament Greek: A Coursebook on the*

Information Structure of New Testament Greek. 2nd ed. Dallas: SIL International, 2000.

Lewis, Stephen R. "The New Covenant." In *Progressive Dispensationalism: An Analysis of the Movement and Defense of Traditional Dispensationalism*. Edited by Ron J. Bigalke, Jr. Lanham, MD: University Press of America, 2005.

Liftin, A. Duane. "1 Timothy." In *The Bible Knowledge Commentary*. Edited by John F. Walvoord and Roy B. Zuck. Wheaton, IL: Victor Books, 1983.

Lightfoot, J. B. *St. Paul's Epistle to the Galatians*. Peabody, MA: Hendrickson Publishers, 1993.

Lightner, Robert P. *Handbook of Evangelical Theology*. Grand Rapids: Kregel Publications, 1995.

__________. *Portraits of Jesus in the Gospel of John*. Eugene, OR: Resource Publications, 2007.

__________. *Sin, the Savior, and Salvation: The Theology of Everlasting Life*. Nashville: Thomas Nelson, 1991.

Linnemann, Eta. *Historical Criticism of the Bible: Methodology or Ideology?* Translated by Robert W. Yarbrough. Grand Rapids: Baker Book House, 1990.

Lock, Walter. *A Critical and Exegetical Commentary on the Pastoral Epistles*. International Critical Commentary. New York: Charles Scribner's Sons, 1924.

Longenecker, Richard N. *Contours of Christology in the New Testament*. Grand Rapids: Eerdmans, 2005.

__________. *Galatians*. Word Biblical Commentary. Dallas: Word Publishing, 1990.

López, René A. *The Jesus Family Tomb Examined: Did Jesus Rise Physically?* Springfield, MO: 21st Century Press, 2008.

__________. *Romans Unlocked: Power to Deliver*. Springfield, MO: 21st Century Press, 2005.

Louw, Johannes P., Eugene A. Nida, et al. *Greek-English Lexicon of the New Testament Based on Semantic Domains*. 2 vols. New York: United Bible Societies, 1988.

__________. *Semantics of New Testament Greek*. Atlanta: Society of Biblical Literature, 1982.

Lowery, David K. "1 Corinthians." In *The Bible Knowledge Commentary*. Edited by John F. Walvoord and Roy B. Zuck. Wheaton, IL: Victor Books, 1983.

Lüdemann, Gerd. *Jesus after 2000 Years: What Jesus Really Said and Did*. Amherst, MA: Prometheus, 2001.

__________. *Virgin Birth? The Real Story of Mary and Her Son Jesus*. Harrisburg, PA: Trinity Press International, 1998.

MacArthur, John F., Jr. *1 Corinthians*. MacArthur New Testament Commentary. Chicago: Moody Press, 1984.

__________. *Faith Works: The Gospel According to the Apostles*. Dallas: Word Publishing, 1993.

__________. *The Gospel According to Jesus*. Grand Rapids: Zondervan, 1988.

__________. *Kingdom Living Here and Now*. Chicago: Moody Press, 1980.

MacDonald, William. *Believer's Bible Commentary*. 2 vols. Edited by Arthur Farstad. Nashville: Thomas Nelson Publishers, 1990-1992.

Machen, J. Gresham. *Christianity and Liberalism*. Grand Rapids: Eerdmans, 1923.

__________. *The Origin of Paul's Religion*. New York: Macmillan, 1936.

__________. *The Virgin Birth of Christ*. New York: Harper & Brothers, 1930.

__________. *What is Faith?* Grand Rapids: Eerdmans, 1946.

Mackintosh, C. H. *Genesis to Deuteronomy: Notes on the Pentateuch*. Neptune, NJ: Loizeaux Brothers, 1972.

Marcus, Joel. *Mark 1-8: A New Translation with Introduction and Commentary*. Anchor Bible. New York: Doubleday, 2000.

Marshall, I. Howard. *Aspects of the Atonement: Cross and Resurrection in the Reconciling of God and Humanity*. Carlisle, England: Paternoster Press, 2007.

_________. *Commentary on Luke*. New International Greek Testament Commentary. Grand Rapids: Eerdmans, 1978.

_________. *A Critical and Exegetical Commentary on the Pastoral Epistles*. International Critical Commentary. Edinburgh: T & T Clark, 1999.

_________. *Kept by the Power of God: A Study of Perseverance and Falling Away*. Minneapolis: Bethany House, 1969.

_________. *Luke: Historian and Theologian*. Grand Rapids: Zondervan, 1970.

_________. *The Origins of New Testament Christology*. Downers Grove, IL: InterVarsity Press, 1990.

_________. "The Resurrection in the Acts of the Apostles." In *Apostolic History and the Gospel*. Edited by W. Ward Gasque and Ralph P. Martin. Grand Rapids: Eerdmans, 1970.

_________. "Romans 16:25-27—An Apt Conclusion." In *Romans and the People of God: Essays in Honor of Gordon D. Fee on the Occasion of His 65th Birthday*. Edited by Sven K. Soderlund and N. T. Wright. Grand Rapids: Eerdmans, 1999.

_________. *The Work of Christ*. Exeter: Paternoster Press, 1969.

Martin, Alfred, and John A. Martin. *Isaiah: The Glory of the Messiah*. Chicago: Moody Press, 1983.

Martin, Ralph P. *2 Corinthians*. Word Biblical Commentary. Dallas: Word Publishing, 1986.

_________. "Gospel." In *The International Standard Bible Encyclopedia*. Edited by Geoffrey W. Bromiley. 4 vols. Grand Rapids: Eerdmans, 1982. 2:529-32.

Martin, Walter R. *Essential Christianity: A Handbook of Basic Christian Doctrines*. Santa Ana, CA: Vision House, Revised 1980.

Martuneac, Lou. *In Defense of the Gospel: Biblical Answers to Lordship Salvation*. N.p.: Xulon Press, 2006.

Marxsen, Willi. *Mark the Evangelist: Studies on the Redaction History of the Gospel*. Translated by James Boyce, Donald Juel, William Poehlmann with Roy A. Harrisville. Nashville: Abingdon, 1969.

McClain, Alva J. *The Greatness of the Kingdom*. Winona Lake, IN: BMH Books, 1959.

McGee, J. Vernon. *Thru the Bible with J. Vernon McGee*. 6 vols. Nashville: Thomas Nelson, 1981.

McGrath, Alister E. *Iustitia Dei: A History of the Christian Doctrine of Justification from 1500 to the Present*. Cambridge: Cambridge University Press, 1986.

McIlwain, Trevor. *Firm Foundations: Creation to Christ*. 2nd ed. Sanford, FL: New Tribes Mission, 2009.

Meisinger, George E. "Salvation by Faith Alone." In *The Fundamentals for the Twenty-First Century: Examining the Crucial Issues of the Christian Faith*. Edited by Mal Couch. Grand Rapids: Kregel, 2000.

Merryman, Ronald C. *Galatians: God's Antidote to Legalism*. Rev. ed. Casa Grande, AZ: Merryman Ministries, 1999.

_________. *Justification by Faith Alone & Its Historical Challenges*. Rev. ed. Colorado Springs, CO: Merryman Ministries, 2000.

_________. *Verse-by-verse through HEBREWS: A Study Guide*. 2 vols. Colorado Springs: Merryman Ministries, 2005.

Metzger, Bruce M. *The Canon of the New Testament: Its Origin, Development, and Significance*. Oxford: Oxford University Press, 1987.

__________. *The Text of the New Testament: Its Transmission, Corruption, and Restoration*. 3rd ed. Oxford: Oxford University Press, 1992.

__________. *A Textual Commentary on the Greek New Testament*. 2nd ed. New York: United Bible Societies, 1994.

Meyer, Marvin, ed. *The Nag Hammadi Scriptures: The International Edition*. San Francisco: HarperCollins, 2007.

Michel, Otto. "*παῖς θεοῦ*." In *The New International Dictionary of New Testament Theology*. Edited by Colin Brown. 4 vols. Grand Rapids: Zondervan, 1986. 3:607-13.

Michel, Walter L. "Confidence and Despair: Job 19, 25-27 in the Light of Northwest Semitic Studies." In *The Book of Job*. Edited by W. A. M. Beuken. Bibliotheca Ephemeridum Theologicarum Lovaniensium, CXIV. Leuven, Belgium: Leuven University Press, 1994.

Miller, Stephen B. *Daniel*. New American Commentary. Nashville: Broadman & Holman, 1994.

Milne, H. J. M., and T. C. Skeat. *Scribes and Correctors of the Codex Sinaiticus*. London: British Museum, 1938.

Minear, Paul S. *The Obedience of Faith: The Purposes of Paul in the Epistle to the Romans*. Naperville, IL: Alec R. Allenson, 1971.

Moloney, Francis J. *The Johannine Son of Man*. Rome: Libreria Ateneo Salesiano, 1976.

Moo, Douglas J. "The Christology of the Early Pauline Letters." In *Contours of Christology in the New Testament*. Edited by Richard N. Longenecker. Grand Rapids: Eerdmans, 2005.

__________. *The Epistle to the Romans*. New International Critical Commentary. Grand Rapids: Eerdmans, 1996.

__________. *The Old Testament in the Gospel Passion Narratives*. Sheffield: Almond Press, 1983.

Morris, Henry M. *Miracles: Do They Still Happen? Why We Believe in Them*. Green Forest, AZ: Master Books, 2004.

Morris, Leon. *1 Corinthians*. Tyndale New Testament Commentary. Grand Rapids: Eerdmans, 2000.

__________. *The Apostolic Preaching of the Cross*. Grand Rapids: Eerdmans, 1956.

__________. "Blood." In *Evangelical Dictionary of Theology*. Edited by Walter A. Elwell. Grand Rapids: Baker Book House, 1984.

__________. *Commentary on the Gospel of John*. New International Commentary on the New Testament. Edited by F. F. Bruce. Grand Rapids: Eerdmans, 1971.

__________. *The Cross in the New Testament*. Grand Rapids: Eerdmans, 1965.

__________. *The Epistle to the Romans*. Pillar New Testament Commentary. Grand Rapids: Eerdmans, 1988.

__________. *The First and Second Epistles to the Thessalonians*. Grand Rapids: Eerdmans, 1959.

__________. *Jesus is the Christ: Studies in the Theology of John*. Grand Rapids: Eerdmans, 1989.

__________. *Studies in the Fourth Gospel*. Grand Rapids: Eerdmans, 1969.

__________. "The Theme of Romans." In *Apostolic History and the Gospel*, ed. W. Ward Gasque and Ralph P. Martin. Grand Rapids: Eerdmans, 1970.

Motyer, J. Alec. "Blood, Sacrificial Aspects of." In *Evangelical Dictionary of Theology*. Edited by Walter A. Elwell. Grand Rapids: Baker Book House, 1984.

__________. *The Prophecy of Isaiah*. Downers Grove, IL: InterVarsity Press, 1993.

Moule, C. F. D. "The Christology of Acts." In *Studies in Luke-Acts*. Edited by Leander E. Keck and J. Louis Martyn. London: SPCK, 1968.

__________. *An Idiom Book of New Testament Greek*. Cambridge: Cambridge University Press, 1953.

__________, ed. *The Significance of the Message of the Resurrection for Faith in Jesus Christ*. London: SCM Press, 1968.

Moulton, James Hope. *A Grammar of the New Testament Greek*. 4 vols. Edinburgh: T & T Clark, 1976.

__________, and George Milligan. *Vocabulary of the Greek Testament*. London: Hodder & Stoughton, 1930. Reprint, Peabody, MA: Hendrickson, 1997.

Mounce, William D. *Pastoral Epistles*. Word Biblical Commentary. Nashville, TN: Thomas Nelson, 2000.

Navas, Patrick. *Divine Truth or Human Tradition? A Reconsideration of the Roman Catholic-Protestant Doctrine of the Trinity in Light of the Hebrew and Christian Scriptures*. Bloomington, IN: AuthorHouse, 2006.

Nave, Guy D., Jr. *The Role and Function of Repentance in Luke-Acts*. Atlanta: Society of Biblical Literature, 2002.

NET Bible. First Beta Edition. N.p.: Biblical Studies Press, 1996.

The New Testament in the Original Greek: Byzantine Textform 2005. Compiled and Arranged by Maurice A. Robinson and William G. Pierpont. Southborough, MA: Chilton Book Publishing, 2005.

Newell, William R. *Romans Verse-By-Verse*. Grand Rapids: Kregel, 1994.

Niehaus, Jeffrey. "Obadiah." In *The Minor Prophets: An Exegetical & Expository Commentary*. Edited by Thomas Edward McComiskey. Grand Rapids: Baker Book House, 1993.

Novum Testamentum Graece. Edited by Barbara and Kurt Aland, Johannes Karavidopoulos, Carlo M. Martini, and Bruce M. Metzger. 27th rev. ed. Stuttgart: Deutsche Bibelgesellschaft, 1993.

Nygren, Anders. *Commentary on Romans*. Translated by Carl C. Rasmussen. Philadelphia: Fortress Press, 1949.

O'Hair, J. C. *Did Peter and Paul Preach Different Gospels? How Many Gospels in the Bible?* Comstock Park, MI: Bible Doctrines Publications, 2001.

__________. *The Unsearchable Riches of Christ*. Chicago: Self-published, 1941.

Orr, James. *The Progess of Dogma*. London: Hodder & Stoughton, 1901.

__________. "Science and Christian Faith." In *The Fundamentals: The Famous Sourcebook of Foundational Biblical Truths*. Edited by R. A. Torrey. Grand Rapids: Kregel Publications, Reprinted 1990.

__________. *The Virgin Birth of Christ*. New York: Charles Scribner's Sons, 1907.

Osborne, Grant R. *The Hermeneutical Spiral: A Comprehensive Introduction to Biblical Interpretation*. 2nd Edition. Downers Grove, IL: InterVarsity Press, 2006.

__________. *Romans*. InterVarsity Press New Testament Commentary. Downers Grove, IL: InterVarsity Press, 2004.

Ott, Ludwig. *Fundamentals of Catholic Dogma*. Translated by Patrick Lynch. Rockford, IL: Tan Books, 1960.

Pate, C. Marvin. *The Reverse of the Curse: Paul, Wisdom, and the Law*. Tübingen: Mohr Siebeck, 2000.

Pawson, David. *Once Saved, Always Saved? A Study in Perseverance and Inheritance*. London: Hodder & Stoughton, 1996.

Payne, J. Barton. " הָוָה." In *Theological Wordbook of the Old Testament*. Edited by R. Laird Harris, Gleason L. Archer, and Bruce K. Waltke. 2 vols. Chicago: Moody

Press, 1980. 1:210-12.

Pentecost, J. Dwight. *Things to Come: A Study in Biblical Eschatology*. Findlay, OH: Dunham Publishing, 1958.

__________. *Thy Kingdom Come*. Wheaton, IL: Victor Books, 1990.

__________. *The Words and Works of Jesus Christ*. Grand Rapids: Zondervan, 1981.

Pettingill, William L. *The Gospel of God: Simple Studies in Romans*. Findlay, Ohio: Fundamental Truth Publishers, n.d.

Pinnock, Clark H. "An Inclusivist View." In *Four Views on Salvation in a Pluralistic World*. Edited by Dennis L. Okholm and Timothy R. Phillips. Grand Rapids: Zondervan, 1995.

__________. *A Wideness in God's Mercy: The Finality of Jesus Christ in a World of Religions*. Grand Rapids: Zondervan, 1992.

Plummer, Alfred. *The Gospel According to St. Mark*. Cambridge Greek Testament. Cambridge: Cambridge University Press, 1914.

Porter, Stanley E. "The Messiah in Luke and Acts: Forgiveness for the Captives," in *The Messiah in the Old and New Testaments*. Edited by Stanley E. Porter. Grand Rapids: Eerdmans, 2007.

Pusey, P. E. and G. H. Gwilliam, *Tetraeuangelium Sanctum: juxta simplicem Syrorum versionem*. Oxford: Clarendon Press, 1901.

Ramsay, William M. *The Church in the Roman Empire before A.D. 170*. New York: G. P. Putnam's Sons, 1919.

__________. *A Historical Commentary on St. Paul's Epistle to the Galatians*. New York: G.P. Putnam's Sons, 1900; Reprint edition, Grand Rapids: Baker Book House, 1965.

Rawlinson, A. E. J. *The Gospel according to St. Mark*. Westminster Commentaries. London: Methuen, 1949.

Rendall, Frederic. "The Epistle to the Galatians." In *The Expositor's Greek Testament*. Edited by Robertson Nicoll. Vol. 3. Grand Rapids: Eerdmans, 1990.

Rengstorf, K. H. "Ἰησοῦς." In *The New International Dictionary of New Testament Theology*. Edited by Colin Brown. 4 vols. Grand Rapids: Zondervan, 1986. 2:330-48.

Richard, Earl. "Jesus' Passion and Death in Acts." In *Reimaging the Death of the Lukan Jesus*. Edited by Dennis D. Sylva. Frankfurt am Main: Anton Hain, 1990.

Richard, Ramesh. *The Population of Heaven: A Biblical Response to the Inclusivist Position on Who will be Saved*. Chicago: Moody Press, 1994.

Richards, Jeffrey J. *The Promise of Dawn: The Eschatology of Lewis Sperry Chafer*. Lanham, MD: University Press of America, 1991.

Ridderbos, Herman N. *The Gospel of John: A Theological Commentary*. Translated by John Vriend. Grand Rapids: Eerdmans, 1997.

Roberts, C. H. and T. C. Skeat. *The Birth of the Codex*. London: British Academy, 1983.

Robertson, A. T. *A Grammar of the Greek New Testament in the Light of Historical Research*. Nashville: Broadman Press, 1934.

__________. *Word Pictures in the New Testament*. 6 vols. Grand Rapids: Baker Book House, n.d.

Robinson, John A. T. "The Destination and Purpose of St. John's Gospel." In *Twelve New Testament Studies*. London: SCM Press, 1962.

__________. *Redating the New Testament*. London: SCM Press, 1976.

Ross, Allen P. "The Biblical Method of Salvation: A Case for Discontinuity." In *Continuity and Discontinuity: Perspectives on the Relationship Between the Old and New Testaments*. Edited by John S. Feinberg. Wheaton, IL: Crossway Books, 1988.

__________. *Creation & Blessing: A Guide to the Study and Exposition of Genesis*. Grand Rapids: Baker Books, 1996.

__________. *Holiness to the Lord: A Guide to the Exposition of the Book of Leviticus*. Grand Rapids: Baker Academic, 2002.

Ryrie, Charles C. *Basic Theology*. Wheaton, IL: Victor Books, 1986.

__________. *The Basis of the Premillennial Faith*. Neptune, NJ: Loizeaux Bros., 1953.

__________. *Biblical Theology of the New Testament*. Chicago: Moody Press, 1959.

__________. *Come Quickly, Lord Jesus: What You Need to Know About the Rapture*. Eugene, OR: Harvest House, 1996.

__________. *Dispensationalism*. Chicago: Moody Press, 1995.

__________. *First and Second Thessalonians*. Chicago: Moody Press, 1962.

__________. *The Miracles of Our Lord*. Neptune, NJ: Loizeaux Brothers, 1984.

__________. *So Great Salvation: What It Means to Believe In Jesus Christ*. Wheaton, IL: Victor Books, 1989.

__________. *A Survey of Bible Doctrine*. Chicago: Moody Bible Institute, 1972.

Sailhamer, John H. *The Pentateuch as Narrative: A Biblical-Theological Commentary*. Grand Rapids: Zondervan, 1992.

Sanders, J. Oswald. *The Incomparable Christ*. Chicago: Moody Press, 1971.

Saucy, Robert L. *The Case for Progressive Dispensationalism: The Interface Between Dispensational & Non-Dispensational Theology*. Grand Rapids: Zondervan, 1993.

__________. "The Church as the Mystery of God." In *Dispensationalism, Israel and the Church: The Search for Definition*. Edited by Craig A. Blaising and Darrell L. Bock. Grand Rapids: Zondervan, 1992.

Schnackenburg, Rudolf. "'Das Evangelium' im Verständnis des ältesten Evangelisten." In *Orientierung an Jesus*. Edited by Paul Hoffmann. Freiburg: Herder, 1973.

Schneider, Johannes, and Colin Brown. "*σωτήρ*." In *New International Dictionary of New Testament Theology*. Edited by Colin Brown. 4 vols. Grand Rapids: Zondervan, 1975-78. 3:216-17.

Schreiner, Thomas R. *Romans*. Baker Exegetical Commentary on the New Testament. Grand Rapids: Baker Academic, 1998.

Scofield, C. I. *Where Faith Sees Christ*. Grand Rapids: Baker Book House, Reprint 1967.

__________. Gen. Ed. *The Scofield Reference Bible*. Oxford: Oxford University Press, 1909.

Scott, Jack B. "אָמַן," In *Theological Wordbook of the Old Testament*. Edited by R. Laird Harris, Gleason L. Archer, and Bruce K. Waltke. 2 vols. Chicago: Moody Press, 1980. 1:51.

Scrivener, Frederick H. *Bezae Codex Cantabrigiensis*. Reprint; Eugene, OR: Wipf and Stock Publishers, n.d.

Shank, Robert. *Life in the Son*. Springfield, MO: Westcott Publishers, 1961.

Showers, Renald E. *Maranatha: Our Lord, Come!* Bellmawr, NJ: The Friends of Israel Gospel Ministry, 1995.

__________. *The Most High God: A Commentary on the Book of Daniel*. Bellmawr, NJ: The Friends of Israel, 1982.

__________. "The Meaning of Psalm 2:7." In *The Eternal Sonship of Christ*. Neptune, NJ: Loizeaux Bros., 1993.

Schucman, Helen, and William Thetford, eds. *Jesus' Course in Miracles*. N.p.: Course in Miracles Society, 2000.

Shuler, Philip L. *A Genre for the Gospels: The Biographical Character of Matthew*. Philadelphia: Fortress Press, 1982.

Silva, Moisés. *Biblical Words and their Meaning: An Introduction to Lexical Semantics*. Rev. Ed. Grand Rapids: Zondervan, 1994.

Smalley, Stephen S. *1, 2, 3 John*. Word Biblical Commentary. Dallas: Word Publishers, 1984.

Smeaton, George. *The Doctrine of the Atonement According to the Apostles*. Peabody, MA: Hendrickson Publishers, 1988.

_________. *John: Evangelist and Interpreter*. Nashville: Thomas Nelson, 1984.

Smith, D. Moody. "HO ΔE ΔIKAIOΣ EK ΠIΣTEΩΣ ZHΣETAI." In *Studies in the History and Text of the New Testament in Honor of K. W. Clark*. Edited by B. L. Daniels and M. J. Suggs. Salt Lake City: University of Utah, 1967.

_________. *The Theology of the Gospel of John*. Cambridge: Cambridge University Press, 1995.

Smith, James E. *The Promised Messiah*. Nashville: Thomas Nelson, 1993.

Smith, Jonathan S. *True Grace*. N.p.: J & M Books, 2005.

Spangler, David. *Reflections on the Christ*. Forres, Scotland: Findhorn Publications, 1981.

Stam, Cornelius R. *Our Great Commission: What Is It?* Germantown, WI: Berean Bible Society, 1984.

_________. *Things That Differ: The Fundamentals of Dispensationalism*. Chicago: Berean Bible Society, 1951.

Stanton, Gerald B. *Kept from the Hour: Biblical Evidence for the Pretribulational Return of Christ*. Miami Springs, FL: Schoettle Publishing, 1991.

Steveson, Peter A. *A Commentary on Isaiah*. Greenville, SC: Bob Jones University Press, 2003.

Stifler, James M. *The Epistle to the Romans*. Chicago: Moody Press, 1960.

Stott, John R. W. *The Cross of Christ*. Downers Grove, IL: InterVarsity Press, 1986.

_________. *The Message of Romans*. Bible Speaks Today Series. Downers Grove, IL: InterVarsity Press, 1994.

Strauss, Mark L. *The Davidic Messiah in Luke-Acts: The Promise and its Fulfillment in Lukan Christology*. Sheffield: Sheffield Academic Press, 1995.

Strombeck, J. F. *First the Rapture: The Church's Blessed Hope*. Grand Rapids: Kregel Publications, 1992.

Sungenis, Robert A. *Not By Faith Alone: The Biblical Evidence for the Catholic Doctrine of Justification*. Santa Barbara, CA: Queenship Publishing, 1997.

Talbert, Charles H. *What Is a Gospel? The Genre of the Canonical Gospels*. Philadelphia: Fortress Press, 1977.

Talbot, Louis T. *Bible Questions Explained*. Grand Rapids: Eerdmans, 1952.

Talmon, Shemaryahu. "The Concepts of *Māshîaḥ* and Messianism in Early Judaism." In *The Messiah: Developments in Earliest Judaism and Christianity*. Edited by James H. Charlesworth. Minneapolis: Fortress Press, 1992.

Tasker, R. V. G. *The Biblical Doctrine of the Wrath of God*. London: Tyndale Press, 1951.

Taylor, Vincent. *The Gospel According to St. Mark: The Greek Text with Introduction, Notes, and Indexes*. New York: St. Martin's Press, 1966.

Tenney, Merrill C. *John: The Gospel of Belief*. Grand Rapids: Eerdmans, 1976.

_________. *New Testament Survey*. Rev. ed. Downers Grove, IL: InterVarsity Press, 1992.

_________. *The Reality of the Resurrection*. Chicago: Moody Press, 1972.

The Text of the Earliest New Testament Greek Manuscripts. Edited by Philip W. Comfort and David P. Barrett. Wheaton, IL: Tyndale House Publishers, 2001.

Thayer, J. H., ed. *The New Thayer's Greek-English Lexicon*. Peabody, MA: Hendrickson, 1981.

Thiessen, Henry C. *Introductory Lectures in Systematic Theology*. Grand Rapids: Eerdmans, 1949.

_________. *Lectures in Systematic Theology*. Revised by Vernon D. Doerksen. Grand Rapids: Eerdmans, 1979.

Thiselton, Anthony C. *The First Epistle to the Corinthians*. New International Greek Testament Commentary. Grand Rapids: Eerdmans, 2000.

Thomas, Robert L. *Evangelical Hermeneutics: The New Versus the Old*. Grand Rapids: Kregel Publications, 2002.

_________. *Exegetical Digest of First Timothy*. N.p.: Self-published, 1985.

_________. "The Hermeneutics of Progressive Dispensationalism." In *Progressive Dispensationalism: An Analysis of the Movement and Defense of Traditional Dispensationalism*. Edited by Ron J. Bigalke, Jr. Lanham, MD: University Press of America, 2005.

Thomas, W. H. Griffith. *Christianity Is Christ*. New York: Longmans, Green, and Co., 1911.

_________. *Genesis: A Devotional Commentary*. Grand Rapids: Kregel Publications, 1988.

_________. *The Principles of Theology: An Introduction to the Thirty-Nine Articles*. 6th rev. ed. London: Vine Books, 1978.

Thrall, Margaret E. "The Origin of Pauline Christology." In *Apostolic History and the Gospel: Biblical and Historical Essays Presented to F. F. Bruce on His 60th Birthday*. Edited by W. Ward Gasque and Ralph P. Martin. Grand Rapids: Eerdmans, 1970.

Tischendorf, Constantin. *Novum Testamentum Graece, ad antiquissimos testes denuo recensuit apparatum criticum omni studio perfectum apposuit commentationem isagogicam praetexuit Constantinus Tischendorf, editio octava critica maior*. 2 vols. Leipzig: J. C. Hinrichs, 1869-1872.

_________. *Novum Testamentum Sinaiticum*. Leipsig: F. A. Brockhaus, 1863.

_________. *Novum Testamentum Vaticanum, post Angeli Maii aliorumque imperfectos labores ex ipso codice*. Leipsig: Giesecke and Devrient, 1867.

Toussaint, Stanley D. *Behold the King: A Study of Matthew*. Portland: Multnomah Press, 1980.

_________. "The Contingency of the Coming of the Kingdom." In *Integrity of Heart, Skillfulness of Hands: Biblical and Leadership Studies in Honor of Donald K. Campbell*. Edited by Charles H. Dyer and Roy B. Zuck. Grand Rapids: Baker Books, 1994.

Tov, Emanuel. "Scribal Practices and Physical Aspects of the Dead Sea Scrolls." In *The Bible as Book: The Manuscript Tradition*. Edited by John L. Sharpe III and Kimberly Van Kampen. New Castle, DE: Oak Knoll Press, 1998.

Towns, Elmer. *The Gospel of John: Believe and Live*. Old Tappan, NJ: Fleming H. Revell, 1990.

Trobisch, David. *The First Edition of the New Testament*. Oxford: Oxford University Press, 2000.

Tregelles, Samuel P. *An Introduction to the Textual Criticism of the New Testament*. London: Longmans, Green, and Co., 1856.

Trench, Richard C. *Synonyms of the New Testament*. Grand Rapids: Eerdmans, 1973.

Turner, E. G. *Greek Manuscripts of the Ancient World*, 2nd ed. London: Institute of Classical Studies, 1987.

Turner, Nigel. *Grammatical Insights into the New Testament*. Edinburgh: T & T Clark, 1965.

_________. *Prolegomena*. 3rd ed. Volume 1 of *A Grammar of New Testament Greek*, by J. H. Moulton. 4 vols. Edinburgh: T & T Clark, 1908.

_________. *Syntax*. Volume 3 of *A Grammar of New Testament Greek*, by J. H. Moulton. 4 vols. Edinburgh: T & T Clark, 1963.

Unger, Merrill F. *Unger's Commentary on the Old Testament*. Chattanooga, TN: AMG Publishers, 2002.

Vaganay, Leon, and Bernard Amphoux. *An Introduction to New Testament Textual Criticism*. New York: Cambridge University Press, 1991.

Vatican Council II: The Conciliar and Post Conciliar Documents. Edited by Austin Flannery, O.P. 2 vols. Northport, NY: Costello Publishing, 1992.

Vincent, Marvin R. *Vincent's Word Studies in the New Testament*. Peabody, MA: Hendrickson, n.d.

Vine, W. E. *The Collected Writings of W. E. Vine*. 5 vols. Nashville: Thomas Nelson Publishers, 1996.

_________. *Vine's Expository Dictionary of Old and New Testament Words*. 4 vols. in 1. Old Tappan, NJ: Fleming H. Revell Company, 1981.

Wallace, Daniel B. *Greek Grammar Beyond the Basics: An Exegetical Syntax of the New Testament*. Grand Rapids: Zondervan, 1996.

Waltke, Bruce K. "Joshua." In *The International Standard Bible Encyclopedia*. Edited by Geoffrey W. Bromiley. 4 vols. Grand Rapids: Eerdmans, 1982. 2:1133-34.

Walvoord, John F. *Daniel: The Key to Prophetic Revelation*. Chicago: Moody Press, 1971.

_________. *Jesus Christ Our Lord*. Chicago: Moody Press, 1969.

_________. *The Rapture Question*. Revised and Enlarged Edition. Grand Rapids: Zondervan, 1979.

_________. *The Thessalonian Epistles*. Findlay, OH: Dunham Publishing, 1955.

Wanamaker, Charles A. *The Epistles to the Thessalonians: A Commentary on the Greek Text*. The New International Greek Testament Commentary. Grand Rapids: Eerdmans, 1990.

Warfield, Benjamin B. *The Person and Work of Christ*. Edited by Samuel G. Craig. Phillipsburg, NJ: Presbyterian & Reformed, 1950.

Watts, Rikki E. "'For I Am Not Ashamed of the Gospel': Romans 1:16-17 and Habakkuk 2:4." In *Romans and the People of God: Essays in Honor of Gordon D. Fee on the Occasion of His 65th Birthday*. Edited by Sven K. Soderlund and N. T. Wright. Grand Rapids: Eerdmans, 1999.

Wenham, John. *Redating Matthew, Mark, and Luke: A Fresh Assault on the Synoptic Problem*. Downers Grove, IL: InterVarsity Press, 1992.

Westcott, B. F. *The Epistle to the Hebrews*. Grand Rapids: Eerdmans, n.d.

_________. *The Gospel According to St. John*. Grand Rapids: Eerdmans, 1967.

White, James R. *The Potter's Freedom: A Defense of the Reformation and a Rebuttal of Norman Geisler's* Chosen But Free. Amityville, NY: Calvary Press Publishing, 2000.

White, Newport J. D. "First and Second Epistles to Timothy and the Epistle to Titus." In *The Expositor's Greek Testament*. Volume IV. Edited by Robertson Nicoll. Grand Rapids: Eerdmans, 1990.

Wilckens, Ulrich. *Die Missionsreden der Apostelgeschichte: Form- und traditionsgeschichtliche Untersuchungen*. Neukirchen: Neukirchener Verlag, 1961.

Wilkin, Robert N. *Confident in Christ*. Irving, TX: Grace Evangelical Society, 1999.

_________. *The Road to Reward*. Irving, TX: Grace Evangelical Society, 2003.

_________. *Secure and Sure*. Irving, TX: Grace Evangelical Society, 2005.

Witherington, Ben. *The Acts of the Apostles: A Socio-Rhetorical Commentary*. Grand Rapids: Eerdmans, 1998.

__________. *The Many Faces of the Christ: The Christologies of the New Testament*. New York: Herder & Herder, 1998.

Witmer, John A. "Jesus Christ: Knowing Jesus as Man and God." In *Understanding Christian Theology*. Edited by Charles R. Swindoll and Roy B. Zuck. Nashville: Thomas Nelson, 2003.

Wood, Leon. *A Commentary on Daniel*. Grand Rapids: Zondervan, 1973.

Young, Edward J. *The Book of Isaiah*. 3 vols. Grand Rapids: Eerdmans, 1972.

__________. *The Prophecy of Daniel*. Grand Rapids: Eerdmans, 1949.

Zahn, Theodor. *Introduction to the New Testament*. 3 vols. Translated from the 3rd German edition. Edinburgh: T & T Clark, 1909.

Zeller, George W. "Development or Departure?" In *Progressive Dispensationalism: An Analysis of the Movement and Defense of Traditional Dispensationalism*. Edited by Ron J. Bigalke. Lanham, Maryland: University Press of America, 2005.

__________, and Renald E. Showers. *The Eternal Sonship of Christ*. Neptune, NJ: Loizeaux Brothers, 1993.

Zerwick, Maximilian. *Biblical Greek Illustrated by Examples*. Adapted from the 4th Latin edition. Rome: Editrice Pontificio Instituto Biblico, 1963.

__________, and Mary Grosvenor. *A Grammatical Analysis of the Greek New Testament*. Rome: Editrice Pontificio Instituto Biblico, 1996.

Zuck, Roy B. *Basic Bible Interpretation*. Wheaton, IL: Victor Books, 1991.

Booklets, Tracts

Bryant, Bob, and Zane Hodges. *You Can Be Eternally Secure*. Irving, TX: Grace Evangelical Society, 2006.

Hodges, Zane C. *Did Paul Preach Eternal Life? Should We?* Mesquite, TX: Kerugma, 2007.

Rokser, Dennis M. *Bad News for Good People and Good News for Bad People*. Duluth, MN: Duluth Bible Church, 2007.

__________. *Let's Preach the Gospel*. Duluth, MN: Duluth Bible Church, n.d.

Wilkin, Robert N. *Saving Faith in Focus*. Irving, TX: Grace Evangelical Society, 2001.

Periodical Articles

Aldrich, Roy L. "The Transition Problem in Acts." *Bibliotheca Sacra* 114 (July 1957): 235-42.

Anderson, Chip. "Romans 1:1-5 and the Occasion of the Letter: The Solution to the Two-Congregation Problem in Rome." *Trinity Journal* 14.1 (Spring 1993): 25-40.

Arnold, Gerhard. "Mk 1.1 und die Eröffnungswendungen in griechischen und lateinischen Schriften." *Zeitschrift für die neutestamentliche Wissenschaft und die Kunde der älteren Kirche* 68 (1977): 123-27.

Ashmon, Scott A. "The Wrath of God: A Biblical Overview." *Concordia Journal* 31.4 (2005): 348-58.

Baird, William. "What Is the Kerygma? A Study of 1 Cor. 15:3-8 and Gal. 1:11-17." *Journal of Biblical Literature* 76 (1957): 181-91.

Bateman, Herbert W. "Psalm 110:1 and the New Testament." *Bibliotheca Sacra* 149 (October 1992): 438-53.

Bergmeier, Roland. "Die Bedeutung der Synoptiker für das johanneische Zeugnisthema. Mit einem Anhang zum Perfekt-Gebrauch im vierten Evangelium." *New Testament Studies* 52 (2006): 458-83.

__________. "ΤΕΤΕΛΕΣΤΑΙ Joh 19:30." *Zeitschrift für die neutesamentliche Wissenschaft und die Kunde der älteren Kirche* 79 (1988): 282-90.

Bird, Michael F. "'Raised for Our Justification': A Fresh Look at Romans 4:25." *Colloquium* 35.1 (May 2003): 31-46.

Black, David Alan. "The Text of John 3:13." *Grace Theological Journal* 6 (Spring 1985): 49-66.

Borchert, Gerald L. "The Resurrection: 1 Corinthians 15." *Review & Expositor* 80.3 (Summer 1983): 401-13.

Boring, M. Eugene. "Mark 1:1-5 and the Beginning of the Gospel." *Semeia* 52 (1990): 43-81.

Boyer, J. L. "The Classification of Infinitives: A Statistical Study." *Grace Theological Journal* 6 (Spring 1985): 3-27.

__________. "The Classification of Participles: A Statistical Study." *Grace Theological Journal* 5 (Fall 1984): 163-79.

Brindle, Wayne A. "'To the Jew First:' Rhetoric, Strategy, History, or Theology?" *Bibliotheca Sacra* 159 (April 2002): 221-33.

Bruce, F. F. "The Romans Debate—Continued." *Bulletin of the John Rylands Library* 64 (1982): 334-59.

__________. "When Is a Gospel Not a Gospel?" *Bulletin of the John Rylands Library* 45.2 (March 1963): 319-39.

Bryant, Bob. "How Were People Saved Before Jesus Came?" *Journal of the Grace Evangelical Society* 16 (Spring 2003): 63-70.

Campbell, Douglas A. "Romans 1:17—A *Crux Interpretum* for the ΠΙΣΤΙΣ ΧΡΙΣΤΟΥ Debate." *Journal of Biblical Literature* 113.2 (1994): 265-85.

Campbell, W. S. "Why Did Paul Write Romans?" *Expository Times* 85 (1974): 264-69.

Caneday, Ardel. "'Redeemed from the Curse of the Law' The Use of Deut. 21:22-23 in Gal. 3:13." *Trinity Journal* 10 (Fall 1989): 185-210.

Carson, Donald A. "Why Trust a Cross? Reflections on Romans 3:21-26." *Evangelical Theological Review* 28.4 (2004): 345-62.

Cavallin, Hans C. C. "'The Righteous Shall Live by Faith': A Decisive Argument for the Traditional Interpretation." *Studia Theologica* 32.1 (1978): 33-43.

Chamblin, Knox. "*EUANGELION* in Mark: Willi Marxsen Revisited." *Westminster Theological Journal* 59 (1997): 31-40.

__________. "Revelation and Tradition in the Pauline *Euangelion*." *Westminster Theological Journal* 48.1 (Spring 1986): 1-16.

Charlesworth, S. D. "T. C. Skeat, $\mathfrak{P}^{64+67}$ and $\mathfrak{P}^{4}$, and the Problem of Fibre Orientation in Codicological Reconstruction." *New Testament Studies* 53 (2007): 582-604.

Collins, John J. "A Pre-Christian 'Son of God' among the Dead Sea Scrolls." *Bible Review* 9 (June 1993): 34-38, 57.

__________. "The Suffering Servant at Qumran?" *Bible Review* 9 (December 1993): 25-27, 63.

Conzelmann, Hans. "On the Analysis of the Confessional Formula in I Corinthians 15:3-5." *Interpretation* 20.1 (January 1966): 15-25.

Craig, William L. "The Historicity of the Empty Tomb of Jesus." *New Testament Studies* 31 (1985): 39-67.

Cranfield, C. E. B. "Romans 1.18." *Scottish Journal of Theology* 21 (1968): 330-35.

Crockett, William V. "Wrath That Endures Forever." *Journal of the Evangelical Theological Society* 34 (June 1991): 195-202.

Croy, N. Clayton. "Where the Gospel Text Begins: A Non-theological Interpretation of Mark 1:1." *Novum Testamentum* 43.2 (2001): 105-27.

Davey, Daniel K. "The Intrinsic Nature of the Gospel." *Detroit Baptist Seminary Journal* 9 (2004): 145-60.

Davies, Rupert E. "Christ in Our Place—The Contribution of the Prepositions." *Tyndale Bulletin* 21 (1970): 71-91.

deSilva, David A. "Paul's Sermon in Antioch of Pisidia." *Bibliotheca Sacra* 151 (January 1994): 32-49.

Dockery, David S. "Romans 1:16-17." *Review & Expositor* 86.1 (Winter 1989): 87-89.

Dodd, Brian. "Romans 1:17—A Crux Interpretum for the ΠΙΣΤΙΣ ΧΡΙΣΤΟΥ Debate?" *Journal of Biblical Literature* 114 (1995): 470-73.

Domeris, William R. "The Confession of Peter according to John 6:69." *Tyndale Bulletin* 44 (1993): 155-67.

Dunn, James D. G. "Jesus—Flesh and Spirit: An Exposition of Romans I.3-4." *Journal of Theological Studies* 24 (1973): 40-68.

Dyer, Sydney D. "The Salvation of Believing Israelites Prior to the Incarnation of Christ." *Journal of the Grace Evangelical Society* 14 (Spring 2001): 43-55.

Ekem, John D. K. "A Dialogical Exegesis of Romans 3:25a." *Journal for the Study of the New Testament* 30.1 (2007): 75-93.

Elgvin, Torleif. "The Messiah Who Was Cursed on the Tree." *Themelios* 22 (April 1997): 14-21.

Elliott, J. K. "ΚΑΘΩΣ and ΩΣΠΕΡ in the New Testament." *Filologia Neotestamentaria* 7.4 (1991): 55-58.

Fahy, T. "Epistle to the Romans 16:25-27." *Irish Theological Quarterly* 28 (1961): 238-41.

Farstad, Arthur L. "An Introduction to Grace Evangelical Society and Its Journal." *Journal of the Grace Evangelical Society* 1 (Autumn 1988): 3-10.

Feinberg, Charles L. "The Scapegoat of Leviticus Sixteen." *Bibliotheca Sacra* 115 (October 1958): 320-33.

Feinberg, Paul D. "The Christian and Civil Authorities." *Master's Seminary Journal* 10 (Spring 1999): 87-99.

Fitzmyer, Joseph A. "The Contribution of Qumran Aramaic to the Study of the New Testament." *New Testament Studies* 20 (1973-74): 382-407.

__________. "Crucifixion in Ancient Palestine, Qumran Literature, and the New Testament." *Catholic Biblical Quarterly* 40 (1978): 493-513.

Fosdick, Harry Emerson. "Shall the Fundamentalists Win?" A sermon given at First Presbyterian Church, New York City, May 21, 1922, published in the *Christian Century*, June 8, 1922.

France, R. T. "The Beginning of Mark." *Reformed Theological Review* 49 (1990): 11-19.

Fung, Ronald Y. K. "Revelation and Tradition: The Origins of Paul's Gospel." *Evangelical Quarterly* 57 (January 1985): 23-41.

Gangel, Kenneth O. "According to the Scriptures." *Bibliotheca Sacra* 125 (April 1968): 123-28.

Gibbs, James M. "Purpose and Pattern in Matthew's Use of the Title 'Son of David'." *New Testament Studies* 10 (1963/64): 446-64.

Gibson, David. "Eating Is Believing? On Midrash and the Mixing of Metaphors in John 6." *Themelios* 27.7 (Spring 2002): 5-15.

Grant, Ralph. "Doesn't God Save Everybody the Same Way?" *Grace in Focus* 13 (January/February 1998): 1, 4.

Gregg, Lon. "Alp upon Alp." *Grace in Focus* 24 (January/February 2009): 1, 4.

Grogan, Geoffrey W. "The Experience of Salvation in the Old and New Testaments." *Vox Evangelica* 5 (1967): 4-26.

Grossman, Philip W. "Jewish Anticipation of the Cross, Part 1." *Bibliotheca Sacra* 106 (April 1949): 239-49.

Guelich, Robert A. "The Beginning of the Gospel." *Papers of the Chicago Society of Biblical Research* 27 (1982): 5-15.

Gundry, Robert H. "ΕΥΑΓΓΕΛΙΟΝ: How Soon a Book?" *Journal of Biblical Literature* 115 (1996): 321-25.

_________, and Russell W. Howell. "The Sense and Syntax of John 3:14-17 with Special Reference to the Use of οὕτως . . . ὥστε in John 3:16." *Novum Testamentum* 41 (1999): 24-39.

Harris, III, W. Hall. "The Ascent and Descent of Christ in Ephesians 4:9-10." *Bibliotheca Sacra* 151 (April 1994): 198-214.

Hart, John F. "Why Confess Christ? The Use and Abuse of Romans 10:9-10." *Journal of the Grace Evangelical Society* 12 (Autumn 1999): 3-35.

Hemer, Colin J. "Acts and Galatians reconsidered." *Themelios* 2.3 (May 1977): 81-88.

Hodges, Zane C. "Assurance: Of the Essence of Saving Faith." *Journal of the Grace Evangelical Society* 10 (Spring 1997): 3-17.

_________. "Eternal Salvation in the Old Testament: The Salvation of Saul." *The Grace Evangelical Society News* 9 (July-August 1994): 1, 3.

_________. "God Wishes None Should Perish 2 Peter 3:9." *Grace in Focus* 24 (July/August 2009): 4.

_________. "How to Lead People to Christ, Part 1: The Content of Our Message." *Journal of the Grace Evangelical Society* 13 (Autumn 2000): 3-12.

_________. "How to Lead People to Christ, Part 2: Our Invitation to Respond." *Journal of the Grace Evangelical Society* 14 (Spring 2001): 9-18.

_________. "The Hydra's Other Head: Theological Legalism." *Grace in Focus* 23 (September/October 2008): 2-3.

_________. "Jesus Is the Propitiation for All, But Only the Mercy Seat for Believers: Romans 3:25 and 1 John 2:2." *Grace in Focus* 21 (July/August 2006): 1, 3-4.

_________. "The Message of Romans." *The Kerugma Message* 6 (February 1997).

_________. "The Moralistic Wrath-Dodger: Romans 2:1-5." *Journal of the Grace Evangelical Society* 18 (Spring 2005): 15-21.

_________. "Repentance and the Day of the Lord." *Grace in Focus* 14 (September-October 1999): 1, 3-4.

_________. "The Women and the Empty Tomb." *Bibliotheca Sacra* 123 (October 1966): 301-9.

Hoerber, Robert G. "Galatians 2:1-10 and the Acts of the Apostles." *Concordia Theological Monthly* 31 (August 1960): 482-91.

Hooker, Morna D. "ΠΙΣΤΙΣ ΧΡΙΣΤΟΥ." *New Testament Studies* 35 (1989): 321-42.

Hughes, Philip E. "The Blood of Jesus and His Heavenly Priesthood in Hebrews, Part 1: The Significance of the Blood of Jesus." *Bibliotheca Sacra* 130 (April 1973): 99-109.

Ironside, H. A. "A Voice from the Past: What is the Gospel?" *Journal of the Grace Evangelical Society* 11 (Spring 1998): 47-58.

Jewett, Robert. "Romans as an Ambassadorial Letter." *Interpretation* 36.1 (January 1982): 5-20.

Johnson, S. Lewis. "The Genesis of Jesus." *Bibliotheca Sacra* 122 (October 1965): 331-42.

_________. "The Gospel That Paul Preached." *Bibliotheca Sacra* 128 (October 1971): 327-40.

Joubert, H. L. N. "The Holy One of God (John 6:69)." *Neotestamentica* 2 (1968): 57-69.

Kaiser, Walter C., Jr. "Salvation in the Old Testament: With Special Emphasis on the

Object and Content of Personal Belief." *Jian Dao* 2 (1994): 1-18.

Keck, Leander E. "The Introduction to Mark's Gospel." *New Testament Studies* 12 (1966): 352-70.

Kelhoffer, James A. "'How Soon a Book' Revisited: *Euangelion* as a Reference to 'Gospel' Materials in the First Half of the Second Century." *Zeitschrift für die neutestamentliche Wissenschaft und die Kunde der älteren Kirche* 95.1-2 (2004): 1-34.

Kingsbury, Jack D. "The Title 'Son of David' in Matthew's Gospel." *Journal of Biblical Literature* 95.4 (1976): 591-602.

Kloppenborg, John. "An Analysis of the Pre-Pauline Formula 1 Cor 15:3b5 in Light of Some Recent Literature." *Catholic Biblical Quarterly* 40.3 (July 1978): 351-67.

Koester, Craig R. "'The Savior of the World' (John 4:42)." *Journal of Biblical Literature* 109 (1990): 665-80.

Koester, Helmut. "From the Kerygma-Gospel to Written Gospels." *New Testament Studies* 35 (1989): 361-81.

Lambrecht, Jan. "Line of Thought in 1 Cor 15,1-11." *Gregorianum* 72.4 (1991): 655-70.

Lamp, Jeffrey S. "Paul, the Law, Jews, and Gentiles: A Contextual and Exegetical Reading of Romans 2:12-16." *Journal of the Evangelical Theological Society* 42 (March 1999): 37-51.

Lane, A. N. S. "The Rationale and Significance of the Virgin Birth." *Vox Evangelica* 10 (1977): 48-64.

Larkin, William J. "Luke's Use of the Old Testament as a Key to His Soteriology." *Journal of the Evangelical Theological Society* 20.4 (December 1977): 325-35.

Lewis, Stephen R. "Consensus Theology Stinks." *Grace in Focus* 24 (May/June 2009): 3-4.

Lewis, Steven J. "What is the Nature of Saving Faith?" *Conservative Theological Journal* 9 (August 2005): 170-91.

Leyrer, Daniel P. "Exegetical Brief: Romans 3:25: 'Through Faith in His Blood'." *Wisconsin Lutheran Quarterly* 104.3 (Summer 2007): 207-9.

Lopez, René A. "Do Believers Experience the Wrath of God?" *Journal of the Grace Evangelical Society* 15 (Autumn 2002): 45-66.

Lowe, Bruce A. "Oh διά! How Is Romans 4:25 to be Understood?" *Journal of Theological Studies* 57.1 (April 2006): 149-57.

MacGregor, G. H. C. "The Concept of the Wrath of God in the New Testament." *New Testament Studies* 7.1 (1961): 101-9.

MacGregor, Kirk R. "1 Corinthians 15:3b-6a, 7 and the Bodily Resurrection of Jesus." *Journal of the Evangelical Theological Society* 49.2 (June 2006): 225-34.

MacLeod, David J. "Eternal Son, Davidic Son, Messianic Son: An Exposition of Romans 1:1-7." *Bibliotheca Sacra* 162 (January 2005): 76-94.

Makidon, Michael D. "Soteriological Concerns with Bauer's Greek Lexicon." *Journal of the Grace Evangelical Society* 17 (Autumn 2004): 11-18.

Martin, Robert P. "The Just Shall Live By Faith" Habakkuk 2:4 in Romans 1:16-17." *Reformed Baptist Theological Review* 3.2 (Fall 2006): 3-26.

Matera, Frank J. "The Prologue as the Interpretative Key to Mark's Gospel." *Journal for the Study of the New Testament* 34 (1988): 3-20.

__________. "Responsibility for the Death of Jesus According to the Acts of the Apostles." *Journal for the Study of the New Testament* 39 (1990): 77-93.

McArthur, H. K. "On the Third Day." *New Testament Studies* 18 (1971): 81-86.

McCoy, Brad. "Secure Yet Scrutinized 2 Timothy 2:11-13." *Journal of the Grace Evangelical Society* 1 (Autumn 1988): 21-33.

Ménard, Jacques. "*Pais Theou* as Messianic Title in the Book of Acts." *Catholic Biblical Quarterly* 19 (1957): 83-92.

Merryman, Ron. "Acts 2:38: An Exposition." *Grace Family Journal* (July 1998): 13-15.

_________. "The Transitional Nature of Acts, Part 1." *Grace Family Journal* (March 1999): 24-27.

_________. "The Transitional Nature of Acts, Part 2." *Grace Family Journal* (May 1999): 15-17.

Metzger, Bruce M. "A Suggestion Concerning the Meaning of 1 Cor. XV.4b." *Journal of Theological Studies* 8 (April 1957): 118-23.

Mitchell, Curtis. "Praying 'In My Name'." *Chafer Theological Seminary Journal* 4:3 (July 1998): 21-30.

Morgardo, Joe. "Paul in Jerusalem: A Comparison of His Visits in Acts and Galatians." *Journal of the Evangelical Theological Society* 37.1 (March 1994): 55-68.

Morris, Leon. "The Biblical Use of the Term 'Blood.'" *Journal of Theological Studies* 3 (1952): 216-27.

Munck, Johannes. "*Evangelium Veritatis* and Greek Usage as to Book Titles." *Studia Theologica* 17.2 (1963): 133-38.

Murphy-O'Connor, Jerome. "Tradition and Redaction in 1 Cor 15:3-7." *Catholic Biblical Quarterly* 43 (1981): 582-89.

Myers, Jeremy D. "The Gospel is More than 'Faith Alone in Christ Alone'." *Journal of the Grace Evangelical Society* 19 (Autumn 2006): 33-56.

Neff, Ken. "What Is the Free Grace Gospel?" *Grace in Focus* 24 (March/April 2009): 3-4.

Newell, William R. "Paul's Gospel." *Journal of the Grace Evangelical Society* 7 (Spring 1994): 45-50.

Niemelä, John. "The Cross in John's Gospel." *Journal of the Grace Evangelical Society* 16 (Spring 2003): 17-28.

_________. "Faith Without Works: A Definition." *Chafer Theological Seminary Journal* 6 (April-June 2000): 2-18.

_________. "Finding True North in 1 John." *Chafer Theological Seminary Journal* 6 (July-September 2000): 25-48.

_________. "James 2:24: Retranslation Required, Part 1." *Chafer Theological Seminary Journal* 7 (January-March 2001): 13-24.

_________. "James 2:24: Retranslation Required, Part 2." *Chafer Theological Seminary Journal* 7 (April-June 2001): 2-15.

_________. "The Message of Life in the Gospel of John." *Chafer Theological Seminary Journal* 7 (July-September 2001): 2-20.

Niessen, Richard. "The Virginity of the עַלְמָה in Isaiah 7:14." *Bibliotheca Sacra* 137 (April 1980): 133-47.

Overstreet, R. Larry. "John 3:13 and the Omnipresence of Jesus Christ." *Journal for Baptist Theology and Ministry* 2.2 (Fall 2004): 135-53.

Parker, James. "The Incarnational Christology of John." *Criswell Theological Review* 3.1 (1988): 31-48.

Poythress, Vern S. "'Hold Fast' Versus 'Hold Out' in Philippians 2:16." *Westminster Theological Journal* 64 (Spring 2002): 45-53.

Quarles, Charles L. "From Faith to Faith: A Fresh Examination of the Prepositional Series in Romans 1:17." *Novum Testamentum* 45.1 (2003): 1-21.

Ralston, Timothy J. "The Theological Significance of Paul's Conversion." *Bibliotheca Sacra* 147 (April 1990): 198-215.

Raven, D. A. S. "St. Luke and Atonement." *Expository Times* 97 (July 1986): 291-94.

Reed, Annette Yoshiko. "ΕΥΑΓΓΕΛΙΟΝ: Orality, Textuality, and the Christian Truth in Irenaeus' *Adversus Haereses*." *Vigiliae Christianae* 56 (2002): 11-46.

Rowe, C. Kavin. "Acts 2.36 and the Continuity of Lukan Christology." *New Testament Studies* 53 (2007): 37-56.

Russell, Michael. "On the third day, according to the Scriptures." *Reformed Theological Review* 67 (April 2008): 1-17.

Russell, III, Walter B. "An Alternative Suggestion for the Purpose of Romans." *Bibliotheca Sacra* 145 (April 1988): 174-84.

Ryrie, Charles C. "The Mystery in Ephesians 3." *Bibliotheca Sacra* 123 (January 1966): 24-31.

Saucy, Mark R. "Miracles and Jesus' Proclamation of the Kingdom of God." *Bibliotheca Sacra* 153 (July-September 1996): 281-307.

Sapaugh, Gregory P. "A Response to Hodges: How to Lead a Person to Christ, Parts 1 and 2." *Journal of the Grace Evangelical Society* 14 (Autumn 2001): 21-29.

Sider, Ronald J. "St. Paul's Understanding of the Nature and Significance of the Resurrection in 1 Corinthians XV 1-19." *Novum Testamentum* 19 (1977): 124-41.

Skeat, T. C. "Irenaeus and the Four-Fold Gospel Canon." *Novum Testamentum* 34.2 (1992): 194-99.

__________. "The Oldest Manuscript of the Four Gospels?" *New Testament Studies* 43 (1997): 1-34.

Smith, D. Moody. "When Did the Gospels Become Scripture?" *Journal of Biblical Studies* 119.1 (2000): 3-20.

Spallek, Andrew J. "The Origin and Meaning of *Εὐαγγέλιον* in the Pauline Corpus." *Concordia Theological Quarterly* 57.3 (July 1993): 177-90.

Stagg, Frank. "Gospel in Biblical Usage." *Review & Expositor* 63.1 (1966): 5-13.

Stählin, Gustav. "'On the Third Day': The Easter Tradition of the Primitive Church." *Interpretation* 10 (July 1956): 282-99.

Stanton, Graham N. "The Fourfold Gospel." *New Testament Studies* 43 (1997): 317-46.

Stegall, Thomas L. "Does Water Baptism Picture Spirit Baptism into Christ?" *Grace Family Journal* (Winter 2005): 12-18.

__________. "Must Faith Endure for Salvation to be Sure? Parts 1-9." *Grace Family Journal* (March/April 2002–Fall 2003).

__________. "The Tragedy of the Crossless Gospel, Parts 1-9." *Grace Family Journal* (Spring 2007-Fall 2008).

Stein, Robert H. "The Relationship of Galatians 2:1-10 and Acts 15:1-35: Two Neglected Arguments." *Journal of the Evangelical Theological Society* 17 (Fall 1974): 239-42.

Sweeney, James P. "Modern and Ancient Controversies Over the Virgin Birth of Jesus." *Bibliotheca Sacra* 160 (April 2003): 151-58.

Talbert, Charles H. "Again: Paul's Visits to Jerusalem." *Novum Testamentum* 9 (January 1967): 26-40.

Tanton, Lanny Thomas. "The Gospel and Water Baptism: A Study of Acts 2:38." *Journal of the Grace Evangelical Society* 3 (Spring 1990): 27-52.

Taylor, John W. "From Faith to Faith: Romans 1.17 in the Light of Greek Idiom." *New Testament Studies* 50 (2004): 337-48.

Thomas, Jeremy M. "The 'Mystery' of Progressive Dispensationalism." *Conservative Theological Journal* 9 (December 2005): 297-313.

Thomas, Robert L. "The 'Comings' of Christ in Revelation 2-3." *Master's Seminary Journal* 7.2 (Fall 1996): 153-82.

Toussaint, Stanley D. "The Chronological Problem of Galatians 2:1-10." *Bibliotheca Sacra* 120 (October 1963): 334-40.

Turner, C. H. "Text of Mark 1." *Journal of Theological Studies* 28 (1926): 145-58.

Waetjen, Herman C. "The Trust of Abraham and the Trust of Jesus Christ: Romans 1:17." *Currents in Theology and Mission* 30.6 (December 2003): 446-54.

Wallis, Wilber B. "The Translation of Romans 1:17—A Basic Motif in Paulinism." *Journal of the Evangelical Theological Society* 16.1 (Winter 1973): 17-23.

Walvoord, John F. "The Person and Work of Christ, Part VIII: Christ in His Suffering and Death." *Bibliotheca Sacra* 118 (October 1961): 291-303.

_________. "Prayer in the Name of the Lord Jesus Christ." *Bibliotheca Sacra* 91:364 (October 1934): 463-72.

Webber, Randall C. "A Note on 1 Corinthians 15:3-5." *Journal of the Evangelical Theological Society* 26.3 (September 1983): 265-69.

Wedderburn, A. J. M. "The Purpose and Occasion of Romans Again." *Expository Times* 90 (1979): 137-41.

Wijngaards, J. "Death and Resurrection in Covenantal Context (Hos. VI 2)." *Vetus Testamentum* 17 (1967): 226-39.

Wikgren, Allen. "ΑΡΧΗ ΤΟΥ ΕΥΑΓΓΕΛΙΟΥ." *Journal of Biblical Literature* 61 (1942): 11-20.

Wilcox, Max. "The Promise of the 'Seed' in the New Testament and the Targumim." *Journal for the Study of the New Testament* 5 (1979): 2-20.

_________. "'Upon the Tree'—Deut 21:22-23 in the New Testament." *Journal of Biblical Literature* 96 (1977): 85-99.

Wiley, Galen W. "A Study of 'Mystery' in the New Testament." *Grace Theological Journal* 6.2 (1985): 349-60.

Wilkin, Robert N. "Another Look at 1 Corinthians 15:3-11." *Grace in Focus* 23 (January/February 2008): 1-2.

_________. "Can Unbelievers Seek God and Work Righteousness?" *Grace in Focus* 17 (November-December 2002): 1, 4.

_________. "Does Your Mind Need Changing? Repentance Reconsidered." *Journal of the Grace Evangelical Society* 11 (Spring 1998): 35-46.

_________. "Essential Truths About Our Savior." *Grace in Focus* 23 (November/December 2008): 1-2.

_________. "Four Free Grace Views Related to Two Issues: Assurance and the Five Essentials." *Grace in Focus* 24 (July/August 2009): 1-2.

_________. "Is Ignorance Eternal Bliss?" *Journal of the Grace Evangelical Society* 16 (Spring 2003): 3-15.

_________. "Justification by Faith Alone is an Essential Part of the Gospel." *Journal of the Grace Evangelical Society* 18 (Autumn 2005): 3-14.

_________. "Lordship Salvation for Dummies." *Grace in Focus* 21 (September-October 2006): 2-3.

_________. "A Review of J. B. Hixson's *Getting the Gospel Wrong: The Evangelical Crisis No One is Talking About*." *Journal of the Grace Evangelical Society* 21 (Spring 2008): 3-28.

_________. "Salvation Before Calvary." *Grace in Focus* 13 (January/February 1998): 2-3.

_________. "Should We Rethink the Idea of Degrees of Faith?" *Journal of the Grace Evangelical Society* 19 (Autumn 2006): 3-21.

_________. "Tough Questions About Saving Faith." *The Grace Evangelical Society News* (June 1990).

_________. "The Way of the Master." *Grace in Focus* 22 (July/August 2007): 1, 4.

_________. "We Believe Jesus Is Lord." *Grace in Focus* 23 (March/April 2008): 1-2.

_________. "Zane Hodges: The New Testament Scholar Who Actually Studied the New Testament." *Journal of the Grace Evangelical Society* 21 (Autumn 2008): 3-14.

Williams, Philip R. "Paul's Purpose in Writing Romans." *Bibliotheca Sacra* 128 (January 1971): 62-67.

Witherington, III, Ben. "The Waters of Birth: John 3.5 and 1 John 5.6-8." *New Testament Studies* 35 (1989): 155-60.

Ziesler, J. A. "The Name of Jesus in the Acts of the Apostles." *Journal for the Study of the New Testament* 4 (1979): 28-41.

Unpublished Materials

Christianson, Richard W. "The Soteriological Significance of ΠΙΣΤΕΥΩ in the Gospel of John." Th.M. thesis, Grace Theological Seminary, 1987.

Diana, Louis. "The Essential Elements of the Gospel Message in the Evangelistic Speeches in Acts." M.A.B.S. thesis, Multnomah Graduate School of Ministry, 1992.

Giamba, Bruno R. "The Essential Content of Saving Faith in Response to Inclusivism." Th.M. thesis, Dallas Theological Seminary, 2004.

Gillogly, Shawn. "Romans 1:16-17: An Apologetic for the Gospel." Paper presented at the Evangelical Theological Society Southeastern Regional, March 16-17, 2001.

Hebron, J. Dean. "A Study of ΠΙΣΤΕΥΩ in the Gospel of John with Reference to the Content of Saving Faith." Th.M. thesis, Capital Bible Seminary, 1980.

Hixson, J. B. "Getting the Gospel Wrong: Case Studies in American Evangelical Soteriological Method in the Postmodern Era." Ph.D. dissertation, Baptist Bible Seminary, 2007.

Johnston, Wendall Graham. "The Soteriology of the Book of Acts." Th.D. dissertation, Dallas Theological Seminary, 1961.

Khoo, Jeffrey E. "The Sign of the Virgin Birth: The Exegetical Validity of a Strictly Messianic Fulfillment of Isaiah 7:14." M.Div. thesis, Grace Theological Seminary, 1991.

Linnemann, Eta. Personal Testimony in *Faith and Reason Series*, Grace Valley Christian Center, Davis, CA, November 7, 2001.

Lopez, René A. "An Exposition of 'Soteria' and 'Sozo' in the Epistle to the Romans." Th.M. thesis, Dallas Theological Seminary, 2002.

Lybrand, Fred R. "GES Gospel: Lybrand Open Letter." April 14, 2009.

Makidon, Michael. "The Strengthening Constraint of *Gar* in 1 and 2 Timothy." Th.M. thesis, Dallas Theological Seminary, 2003.

Niemelä, John H. "The Infrequency of Twin Departures: An End to Synoptic Reversibility?" Ph.D. dissertation, Dallas Theological Seminary, 2000.

__________. "Objects of Faith in John: A Matter of Person AND Content." Paper prepared for the Chafer Theological Seminary Bible Conference, Houston, TX, March 2006.

Potter, David R. "The Substance and Scope of Johannine Christology." Ph.D. dissertation, Bob Jones University, 1978.

Reinhartz, Adele. "John 20:30-31 and the Purpose of the Fourth Gospel." Ph.D. thesis, McMaster University, 1983.

Schultz, Thomas. "Saving Faith in the Old Testament." Th.M. thesis, Dallas Theological Seminary, 1959.

Spallek, Andrew John. "St. Paul's Use of ΕΚ ΠΙΣΤΕΩΣ in Romans and Galatians: The Significance of Paul's Choice of Prepositions with ΠΙΣΤΙΣ as Object and

Its Bearing Upon Justification by Faith." S.T.M. thesis, Concordia Seminary, 1996.

Waltke, Bruce K. "The Theological Significations of Ἀντί and Ὑπέρ in the New Testament." Th.D. dissertation, Dallas Theological Seminary, 1958.

Wilkin, Robert N. "Gospel Means Good News." Paper presented at the Grace Evangelical Society National Conference, March 6, 2008, Fort Worth, TX.

__________. "Repentance as a Condition for Salvation in the New Testament." Th.D. dissertation, Dallas Theological Seminary, 1985.

Wilson, Jr., H. Graham. "The Importance of the Incarnation to Resurrection." Paper presented at Grace Evangelical Society Conference, Fort Worth, TX, March 31, 2009.

Zeller, George W. "The Mystery of Godliness: Its Application to the Local Assembly (1 Timothy 3:14-16)." M.Div. thesis, Grace Theological Seminary, 1975.

Internet Sources

da Rosa, Antonio. "Believe Christ's Promise and You are Saved, No Matter What Misconceptions You Hold." May 25, 2006. http://freegrace.blogspot.com/2006_05_01_archive.html (accessed August 20, 2007).

__________. "How Much Information is Really Needed?" May 6, 2006. http://unashamedofgrace.blogspot.com/2006/05/how-much-information-is-really-needed.html (accessed August 20, 2007).

Lopez, René A. "Basics of Free Grace Theology, Part 1." http://www.scripture unlocked.com/papers/basicsfgprt1.pdf (accessed August 6, 2007).

__________. "Basics of Free Grace Theology, Part 2." http://www.scriptureunlocked.com/papers/basicsfgprt2.pdf (accessed August 6, 2007).

Myers, Jeremy. "Just the Gospel Facts P's Misc. Texts." http://www. tillhecomes.org/ Other%20Writings/Just%20the%20Gospel%20Facts%20Ps.htm (accessed March 6, 2007).

Wilkin, Bob. "God Has Always Revealed the Saving Message." November 20, 2008. http://unashamedofgrace.blogspot.com/2008_11_01_archive.html (accessed November 30, 2008).

Wright, N. T. "The Cross and the Caricatures: a response to Robert Jenson, Jeffrey John, and a new volume entitled *Pierced for Our Transgressions*." http://www.fulcrum-anglican.org.uk/news/2007/20070423wright.cfm?doc=205 (accessed October 18, 2008).

Zeller, George W. "The Epistle to the Romans: A Verse By Verse Study." http://www.middletownbiblechurch.org/romans/romans.htm (accessed May 14, 2009).

Audio Recordings

Bryant, Bob. "Eternal Security: Do You Have to Believe It?" Grace Evangelical Society Conference, Dallas, TX, February 28, 2006.

__________. "The Search for the Saving Message Outside of the Gospel of John." Grace Evangelical Society Conference, Fort Worth, TX, March 6, 2008.

da Rosa, Antonio. "Checklist Evangelism and the Dangers of It." Grace Evangelical Society Southern California Regional Conference, August 25, 2007.

Hodges, Zane C. "In the Upper Room (John 13-17) with Jesus the Christ." Grace Evangelical Society Conference, Fort Worth, TX, March 4, 2008.

__________. "Miraculous Signs and Literary Structure in the Fourth Gospel." Grace Evangelical Society Conference, Fort Worth, TX, March 5, 2008.

López, René A. "The Use and Abuse of 1 Corinthians 15:1-11." Grace Evangelical Society Conference, Fort Worth, TX, March 31, 2009.

Meisinger, George E. "The Gospel Paul Preached: A Church Age Model of Evangelistic Content." Chafer Theological Seminary Pastors Conference, Houston, TX, March 11, 2009.

Myers, Jeremy. "The Gospel Is More Than 'Faith Alone in Christ Alone'." Grace Evangelical Society Conference, Dallas, TX, March 2, 2006.

Neff, Ken. "What Is the Free-Grace Gospel?" Grace Evangelical Society Conference, Fort Worth, TX, March 31, 2009.

Niemelä, John. "The Bible Answer Men." Panel Discussion at the Grace Evangelical Society Seattle Regional Conference, September 29, 2007.

__________. "Is Evangelism Merely a Life and Death Matter?" Grace Evangelical Society Conference, Dallas, TX, March 7, 2007.

__________. "Objects of Faith in John: A Matter of Person AND Content," Grace Evangelical Society Conference, Dallas, TX, February 28, 2006.

__________. "The Sign of the Cross—What Does It Signify?" Grace Evangelical Society Omaha Regional Conference, July 28, 2007.

__________. "What About Believers Who Have Never Known Christ's Promise of Life?" *Chafer Theological Seminary Conference*, Houston, TX, March 13, 2006.

Wallace, Brandon. "Free Grace Theology for Beginners." Grace Evangelical Society Conference, Dallas, TX, February 27, 2006.

Wilkin, Bob. "The Current State of Grace." Grace Evangelical Society Conference, Dallas, TX, February 27, 2006.

__________. "The Gospel Is Good News about the Lord Jesus (Gal. 1:6-9; 2:14-21)." Grace Evangelical Society Conference, Fort Worth, TX, March 6, 2008.

__________. "Gospel Means Good News." Grace Evangelical Society Southern California Regional Conference, August 24, 2007.

__________. "Is the Evangelistic Message Jesus Preached a Sufficient Message Today?" Grace Evangelical Society Conference, Fort Worth, TX, March 5, 2008.

__________. "The Three Tenses of Salvation Aren't about Justification, Sanctification, and Glorification." Grace Evangelical Society Georgia Regional Conference, Hampton, GA, September 23, 2006.

__________. "The Three Tenses of Salvation Reconsidered." Audiotape EDW 211, Grace Evangelical Society, 2003.

__________. "Trusting in Christ is Not Quite the Same as Believing in Him." Grace Evangelical Society Conference, Dallas, TX, March 1, 2006.

__________. "What Was Paul's Message of Christ and Him Crucified? 1 Corinthians 2:2 Reconsidered." Grace Evangelical Society Conference, Fort Worth, TX, March 30, 2009.

__________. "Why the Romans Road Ends in a Cul de Sac." Grace Evangelical Society Conference, Dallas, TX, March 1, 2006.

Author & Person Index

Subject Index

Scripture Index

Breinigsville, PA USA
06 December 2009
228695BV00004B/1/P

9 780979 963742